HINTERLANDS & INLANDS

McDONALD INSTITUTE MONOGRAPHS

HINTERLANDS & INLANDS

The Archaeology of West Cambridge and *Roman Cambridge* Revisited

By Christopher Evans and Gavin Lucas

With contributions by
Katie Anderson, Grahame Appleby, Nick Armour, Sarah Austin, Rachel Ballantyne, Lawrence Billington, Steve Boreham, Marcus Brittain, Matthew Brudenell, Craig Cessford, Andy Clarke, Chantal Conneller, H.E.M. Cool, Jane Cowgill, Brendan Coyle, Nina Crummy, Alison Dickens, Natasha Dodwell, Charles French, Val Fryer, Kasia Gdaniec, Chris Going, Andrew Hall, Kevin Hayward, J.D. Hill, Ruoyun Hui, Jacqui Hutton, Sarah Inskip, Toomas Kivisild, Duncan Mackay, Ian Marsden, Francesca Mazzilli, Paul Middleton, Gwladys Monteil, Richard Mortimer, Bram Mulder, Peter Murphy, Benjamin Neil, Richard Newman, Josh Pollard, Vida Rajkovača, Richard Reece, Rob Scaife, Christiana Scheib, Ellen Simmons, Adam Slater, Chris Stevens, Letty Ten Harkel, Simon Timberlake, Anne de Vareilles, Dave Webb, Justin Wiles, Steve Williams, Jennifer Wills, Patricia Wiltshire and Eftychia Yannouli, and the late Anthony Baggs

Graphics by Crane Begg, Andrew Hall, Vicki Herring and Paul White

CAU Landscape Archives
New Archaeologies of the Cambridge Region Series (3)

Published by:

McDonald Institute for Archaeological Research
University of Cambridge
Downing Street
Cambridge, UK
CB2 3ER
(0)(1223) 333538
(0)(1223) 339336 (Production Office)
(0)(1223) 333536 (FAX)
eaj31@cam.ac.uk
www.mcdonald.cam.ac.uk

Distributed by Oxbow Books
United Kingdom: Oxbow Books, 10 Hythe Bridge Street, Oxford, OX1 2EW, UK.
Tel: (0)(1865) 241249; Fax: (0)(1865) 794449; www.oxbowbooks.com
USA: Casemate Academic, P.O. Box 511, Oakville, CT 06779, USA.
Tel: 860-945-9329; Fax: 860-945-9468

ISBN: 978-1-902937-89-2

On the cover: *Fox's* Archaeology of the Cambridge Region*'s Roman Map (1923) juxtaposed with Loggan's 'Cambridge from the West' engraving (1690; front) and, on the back, with the Darwin Family's Huntingdon Road Estate (1888 OS Map).*

Cover design by Christopher Evans, Andrew Hall and Ben Plumridge.
Typesetting and layout by Ben Plumridge.

Edited for the Institute by James Barrett (*Series Editor*).

Printed and bound by Short Run Press, Bittern Rd, Sowton Industrial Estate, Exeter, EX2 7LW, UK.

Contents

Figures

Tables

Acknowledgements and Amassed Context

With so many sites presented here, there are many to acknowledge. New Hall's excavations were greatly facilitated at the College by Patricia Ackhurst and Christopher Stevenson, and we are grateful that Phillip Walker of English Heritage arranged for an additional grant to complete the fieldwork. The excavations were directed by Christopher Evans, with Gerry Wait and Bob Butler its site supervisors. During the subsequent phases of excavations at what is now Murray Edwards College, we remain grateful to the then Bursar, Paola Morris. For neighbouring excavations, we duly thank the Fellows, ground-staff and Bursars of Trinity Hall and Fitzwilliam College; particularly, at the latter, Christopher Pratt, who promoted both its Library Site excavation and that at Marion Close.

The Vicar's Farm excavation, after over a decade of developer-funded fieldwork (with much, though happily not all, determined by baseline economics), enabled us to engage in a more academic approach. The results represent a unique level of collaboration. Under the auspices of Michael Bienias and Stephen Fallon (and subsequently Peter Taylor), the University of Cambridge's Estates Management and Building Services (EMBS) acted in a most responsible manner throughout and, from the outset, gracefully shouldered the burden of the site's significant archaeology. They went on to voluntarily adopt an exemplary archaeological master plan for the West Cambridge development as a whole. In this regard, thanks must also go to the project's archaeological consultant, John Walker. As one of the development's major tenants, Microsoft Research Ltd generously made available an additional grant allowing us to fully computerize the site's record and the analytical 'fruits' of this have been born out many times over (benefiting from the advice of Dominic Powlesland). The support here of Prof. D. McAuley, then Assistant Director of Microsoft Research Ltd. in Cambridge, is gratefully acknowledged. We also owe a great debt to the University's Office of the Vice-Chancellor for making available a special grant towards a schools' visits week and site open day. Each attracted almost a thousand participants, and it was inspiring to – with adequate preparation and appropriate infrastructure – be able to host these varied guests. Not only did this draw schoolchildren, families and many academics to the site, but also much of the 'old guard' of Cambridge's archaeology. It is indeed a rare pleasure when a site can become *an event*. We therefore thank John Carman, then of the Dept. of Archaeology, for co-ordinating these ventures and organizing the display materials, and also the University's Press and Publications Office – particularly, Alison McFarquhar and the graphic skills of Mark Mniszko – whose assistance proved crucial.

At the CAU, we are deeply grateful to the role played by Paula Whittaker, who admirably served as the site's co-director. Post-excavation GIS analyses were undertaken by Marc Berger and, then, Jon Moller.

The High Cross excavations were facilitated by Brian Lees and Andrew Merrick of EMBS, with Heather Topel responsible for the 2015 evaluation work (which Sam Stevens of the Dept of Veterinary Medicine greatly helped with). At EMBS, Ron Kay – together with Steve Clarke of SDC – organized the Kettle's Yard work, where the enthusiasm of Andrew Nairne and his gallery staff were crucial for the project's success. The Wilberforce Road fieldwork was also commissioned by the University of Cambridge and, in particular, we are grateful to David Berry and Hilary Glegg for their assistance throughout.

It would be unfeasible for us to separately list the individuals involved in the many other projects summarised here; nonetheless, we are grateful that St Edmund's, Jesus, St John's, Newnham and Trinity Colleges have supported the excavations on their respective grounds.

None of this work would have occurred without the active co-operation of the County Council's archaeological development control officers/curators, being variously over the years Bob Sydes, Simon Kaner, Gemma Stewart, Andy Thomas and Kasia Gdaniec.

Crane Begg was primarily responsible for the Unit's graphics relating to the New Hall and Vicar's Farm excavations up to around 2005; this role was therafter taken up by Andrew Hall and who – as with the series' other volumes – can only be acknowledged as close collaborator (i.e. you simply 'realise' more working with him). The book's artefact illustrations were variously done by the two of them, as well as Paul White and Vicki Herring. Until the middle of the last decade, photography was largely undertaken by site directors (Evans at New Hall and Lucas at Vicar's Farm); for subsequent sites, the much greater skills of the Unit's photographer, Dave Webb, are only all too apparent here and he, in addition, has also been responsible for this book's studio photography.

The finds of the many projects presented here have been processed with great efficiency and skill, under the successive supervision of Julie Boast, Norma Challands, Jason Hawkes and, now, Justin Wiles.

Obviously, compiling a volume like this draws on the work of many site directors and, hopefully, they feel appropriately acknowledged in the text that follows. Here, though, the input of our colleagues, Craig Cessford and Richard Newman must be highlighted, as well as, in their time, Duncan Mackay, Letty Ten Harkel, Gwladys Monteil, Katie Anderson, Matt Brudenell, JD Hill, Chris Going and Leo Webley… the list could go on. Yet, to be singled out in this capacity is Alison Dickens. Almost with the Unit from the first (and, here, providing some New Hall's finds' studies), amongst the many other projects she has managed are most of Cambridge's urban sites and, of those summarized in this volume, she oversaw the WYNG Gardens, Jesus College West and the School of Pythagoras investigations.

Over the last decade, first tackling Colne Fen's Roman settlements and, then, that at Mucking, the Unit's encounters with Roman archaeology have benefited immensely from the insights of, and discussions with, Colin Haselgrove, Martin Millett, Richard Reece and Jeremy Taylor. They greatly aided our 'becoming Roman' as it were and, in particular, Martin's advice has proven invaluable for the western Cambridge sites; he has also been this book's 'official' reader. In additional, for last four years or so, Evans has been a participant in the University of Reading's Roman Rural Settlement Project, which has only been a source of inspiration; thanks, therefore, go to Mike Fulford, Neil Holbrook and Alex Smith.

At Oxford Archaeology East, we would like to sincerely thank Alice Lyons, Steve Macaulay and Elizabeth Popescu for being generous in the provision of information.

Marta Lahr is to be thanked for allowing access to the University's Duckworth Collection's New Hall skulls. The Murray Edwards College archivist, Elizabeth Ennion-Smith, helped us by providing the photograph of *The Orchard* (Horace Darwin's house) that features in Chapter Three. Taken just prior to its demolition in the 1960s by Jane Renfrew, it was kind of her to allow us to use it (and it is a pleasure to be able to include the handiwork of a long-standing friend and colleague).

As much as we have been able to, at least, 'problematize' Alexander and Pullinger's early-era Roman Cambridge results (see Chap. 2), we have been grateful for insights provided by Paul Craddock, Greg Gregory and Dave Haigh. Craig Cessford's assistance in this is also appreciated and, too, for facilitating Vicar's Farm's aDNA study in connection with Cambridge's Wellcome Trust-funded, After the Plague Project. With the latter very much an 'late-in-the-day' addition to the book, Sarah Inskip, John Robb and, now at Estonia's University of Tartu, Christiana Scheib and Toomas Kivisild must certainly also be thanked in this capacity.

At Lucy Cavendish College, Alison Vinnicombe kindly consulted the archives for any Macalister material and references; the results, alas, proved negative. We have been grateful for comments from Richard Cushing, Martin Henig, Catherine Hills, John Mack, John Pickles and Christopher Walker as regards the Bullard Laboratory's relief sculpture panels, though without any clear resolution as to their source. Equally, as regards 'the science' of West Cambridge, as always, conversational flights with Simon Schaffer have only been stimulating.

Maurice Hooper of Mott MacDonald kindly allowed us to use WYAS's high quality Wilberforce Road (West) geophysical surveys (Chap. 7).

Aside for thanking Sam Lucy for her well-honed text-proofing skills, it is only a privilege to be able to publish thorough site-based accounts such as these, though one fears that their future production in this manner is not assured. Accordingly, we are only all the more grateful that the McDonald Institute agreed to include this Cambridge-regional series in its Monograph Series. We thank its Research Committee and, in particularly, its Deputy Director, James Barrett and, too, the post's sometime acting Deputy, Simon Stoddart. The end-game production of this book was generously facilitated by special grants from Historic England, the Cambridge Antiquarian Society and Murray Edwards College. In this capacity, Kath Buxton,

Paola Filippucci, Catherine Hills, Rob Hopwood and Barney Sloane must each be variously thanked.

Finally, for all the reason noted above – and many more – on the eve of what is sadly her retirement from the Unit after decades, and in acknowledgement to her contribution to Cambridge's archaeology generally, it is entirely appropriate that the volume's dedication is to Alison (Dickens).

Mapping the past is complicated by the way in which *the past endlessly amasses new territories.* (C. Drazin 2016, *Mapping the Past: A Search for Five Brothers at the Edge of Empire,* 11; emphasis added)

Only the best art can order the chaotic tumble of events … Only the best can realign chaos to suggest both the chaos and order it will become.

Within two years of 1066, work began on the Bayeux Tapestry, Constantin the African brought Greek medicine to the western world. The chaos and tumble of events. The first sentence of every novel should be: 'Trust me, this will take time but there is order here, very faint, very human.' *Meander if you want to get to town.* (M. Ondaatje 1987, *In the Skin of a Lion,* 146; emphasis added)

Chapter 1

Introduction – *Mapping and Sociable Knowledges*

Echoing the image of south Cambridge that introduced the first volume in this series, *Borderlands* (Evans *et al.* 2008; hereafter *BLS*), and rendered by the same artist, David Loggan, with both engravings appearing in his 1690 portfolio, Figure 1.1 shows his view of Cambridge from the west. With the town's silhouette in the background, its landmark buildings have seen a degree of vertical exaggeration: King's College Chapel far right, then the tower of Great St. Mary's and Trinity's recently built Wren Library, continuing in this manner to Cambridge's Castle on the left side.

We have attempted to identify Loggan's perspective; he probably drew it from somewhere near the later junction of Clarkson and Grange Roads, looking across the later area of St. John's Playing Fields – in other words, the (near-)West Cambridge lands. It is the picture's foreground that holds the greatest interest. Almost reminiscent of Bruegel's *The Harvesters* (1565), with the harvest well under way, it is an active scene with the landscape full of labourers. The geometry of the fields' furrows appears emphasized for the purposes of artistic 'framing'. The engraving certainly conveys a sense of the area's intense arable land-use and its 'busy-ness' goes far to explain why so much Late/Post-Medieval material is found in the area's fieldwalking and metal-detecting surveys (see Chap. 4; see also Hall & Ravensdale 1976 concerning the lands' earlier agricultural organization).

Suburban Archaeology and Subtle Topographies

Until recently, farmland has been the abiding image of the western Cambridge lands, at least beyond the city's 'bicycle suburb' that developed with the off-College housing of dons during the later nineteenth century (Fig. 1.2; Guillebaud 2007). As available open space bordering a world-status University town it also saw diverse use and, as we will see, it is somewhere that 'interesting things' happened. Take, for example, its 1888 Ordnance Survey mapping. By that time, College sporting facilities – playing fields and cricket grounds – had come to dominate the swathe just west of Queen's Road. A close look at the map's bottom third reveals the circle of the University bicycle path, as well as the long strip of its rifle range (Figs. 1.2.3–4 & 1.3.3–4); in the mid field there are the grounds of the University's Observatory (est. 1822) and, to the northeast, a park-like rectangle alongside Huntingdon Road that was the Darwin Family Estate (Fig. 1.2.8; see Chap. 3, *Inset*).

Over the course of the last century various University-allied research facilities came to be sited there, ranging from a meteorological station to the National Poultry Institute Farm and the headquarters of the British Antarctic Survey. To this can be added experimental crop-trials, large-scale quarrying and further College colonization (Girton from 1869 and, in 1962, Churchill). Housed in what were the buildings of the Rockefeller Plant-breeding Station, the Cambridge Archaeological Unit's (CAU) current offices lie on its eastern edge (Figs. 1.2 & 1.3.E). To reach them, going along Storey's Way – where the philosopher, Wittgenstein, lived his last days at No. 76 – you pass a series of fine Baillie Scott Arts & Crafts Movement houses (Haigh 1995).[1] Just along the hedge-line from the Unit is the Ascension Parish Burial Ground (Figs. 1.2.7 & 1.3.7), where among those laid to rest are, along with Wittgenstein and the Darwin family, the anthropologist, James Frazer, the archaeologist, R.A. Stewart Macalister, and the philosopher, George Moore. Exploring this landscape's unique dynamics, all of these – and more – will have their place here.

These books invariably run the risk of digression. What is outlined here is a very specific kind of *suburban archaeology*, one that could only occur in the hinterland of a world-rank University town/city. It has generated a landscape of tangential associations. While the lands of western Cambridge can by no means be seen as any kind of 'universal', the arbitrary nature of specific

Figure 1.1. *Loggan's* c. *1690* Cambridge West View, *with a reworking of Bruegel's* The Harvesters *of 1565 inset (by V. Herring; see Evans & Hodder 2006b, fig. 6.1).*

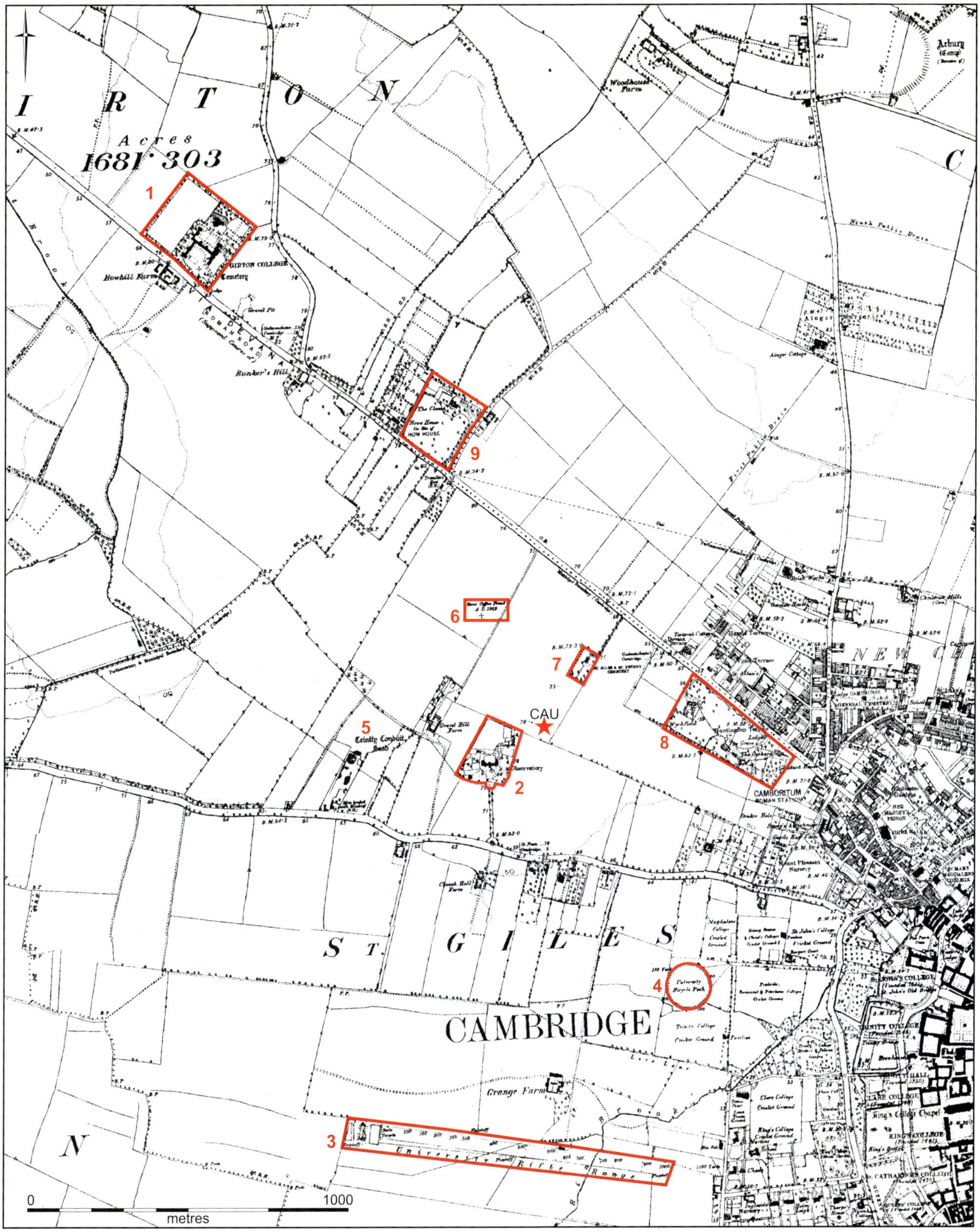

Figure 1.2. *Highlighted western Cambridge map, with CAU offices indicated by the star (OS 1888; see Fig. 1.3 for detail of Nos. 1–7): 8) Darwin Family Estate (see Fig. 3.41); 9) Howe's House.*

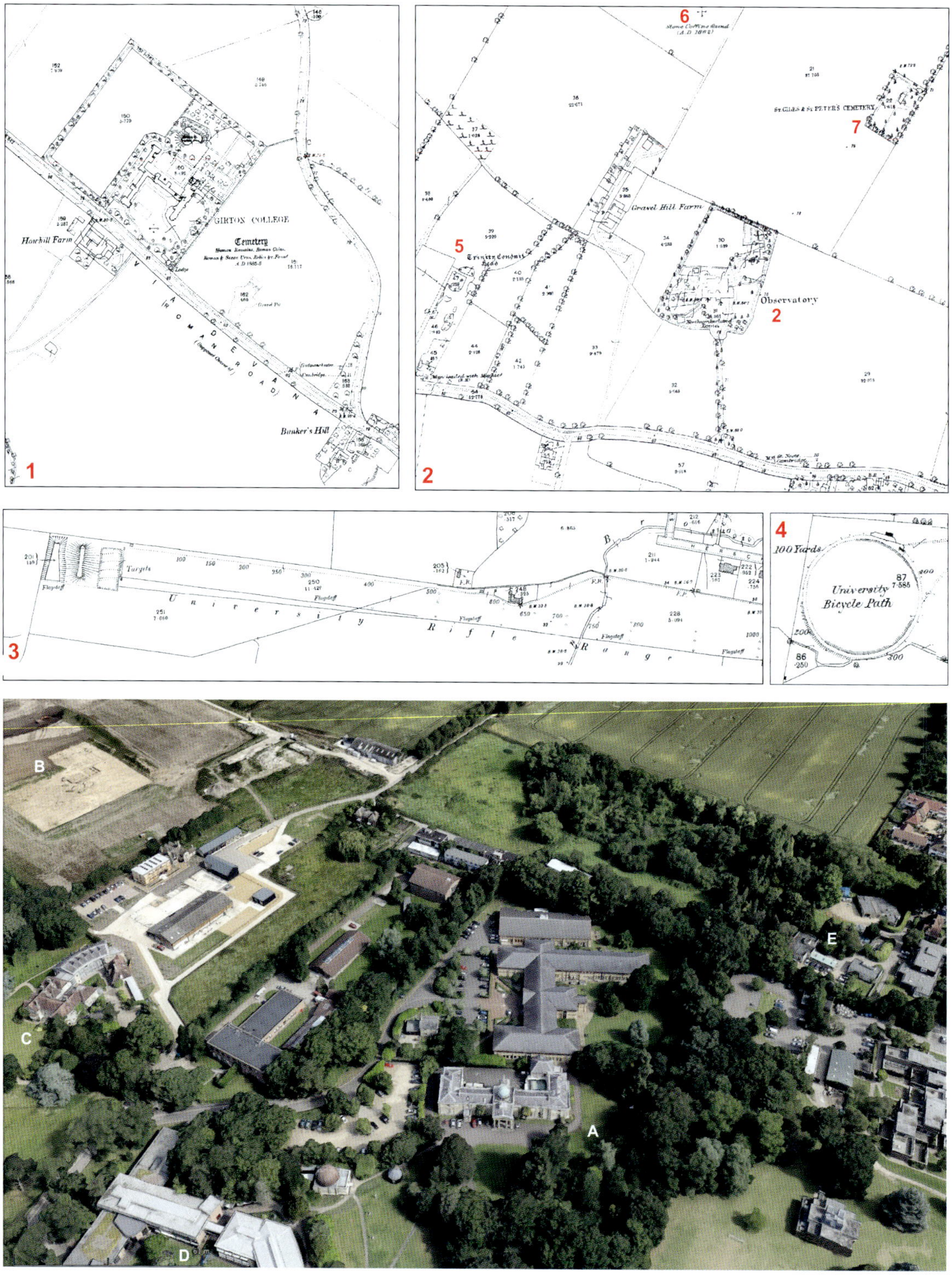

Figure 1.3. *Map highlights (see Fig 1.2): 1) Girton College and Huntingdon Road's* Via Devana *naming (note roadside gravel pit); 2) the Observatory (2), Trinity Conduit Head (5), find-spot of Traveller's Rest Pit Roman stone coffins (6; see Fig. 1.5), St Giles & St. Peter's Cemetery and Mortuary Chapel (later named Ascension Parish Burial Ground; 7); 3) University Rifle Range (see Fig. 7.36); 4) University Cycle Path; below, aerial image showing the Observatory (A), Guthrie and Pope's cob model (B), the former University Astronomer's* Madingley Rise *residence (C; see Chap. 7), the Kavli Institute (D; see Chap. 4) and, far right, the CAU offices (E; Google Earth, 2017).*

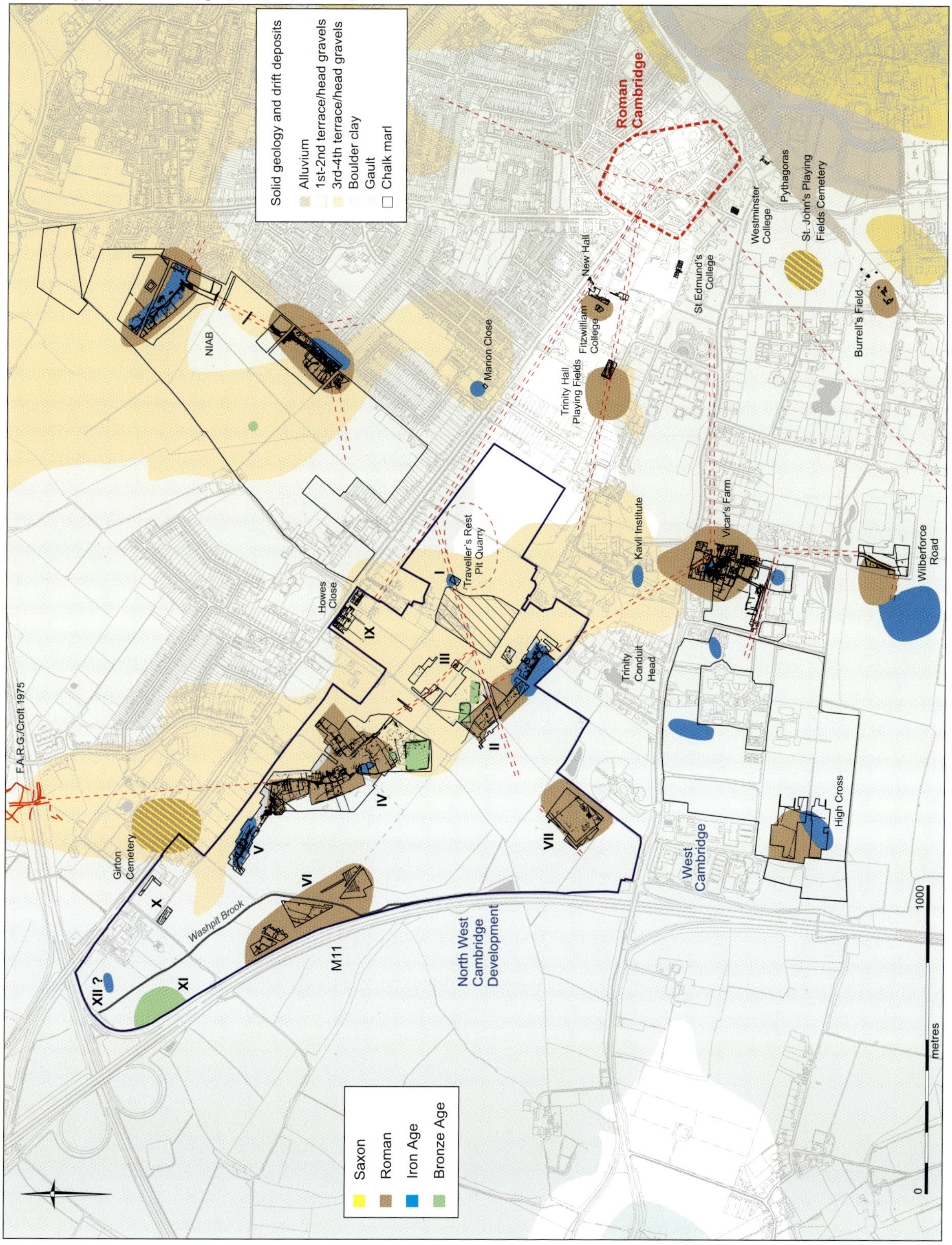

Figure 1.4. *West and North West Cambridge sites, with geology indicated (see Fig. 1.10).*

locales – and all that has occurred there – serves as a counterpoint to the overly simplistic 'landscape narratives' that are now so widely espoused in archaeology. In truth, many of these often amount to no more than chronology masquerading as storyline (see Evans 2013).

As explored in the second volume of this series, *Riversides…* (Evans *et al*. 2018; hereafter *RVS*), our main interests lie in the dynamics of *landscape and social change*, as opposed to the over-emphasis seen in much regional archaeology on long-term settlement continuities. While retaining a fundamental concern with *the local*, we also need to admit far-flung connections, distant linkages and unexpected possibilities. Representative of this 'no-terrace-is-an-island' ethos is, for example, the finding of a finely moulded Roman furniture piece at North West Cambridge, rendered in Holm oak from the Mediterranean, that had clearly been imported; this resonates with the earlier recovery of what was apparently a seed from oriental plane tree in one of Castle Hill's Roman contexts (Alexander & Pullinger 2000, 44; hereafter *RCAM*).[2]

Envisaged as a single volume, together the two *Hinterlands/Inlands* books are concerned with a 3.3 sq. km triangular sector of land along Cambridge's western fringes (see Figs. 1.4 & 1.10). Extending from Castle Hill west to the M11, a distance of *c*. 2.2–3.1 km, the nature of their coverage varies on a number of counts. There has only been comprehensive 'total-site' recovery across the westernmost sector: the *c*. 47 ha extent of the University's West Cambridge and its North West Cambridge developments (*c*. 140 ha). The focus of this book is on the intervening findings/sites between Castle Hill's Roman town and those two areas, as well as the West Cambridge (development) Lands' sites. The North West Cambridge investigations feature in the second book (hereafter *NWC*).

The northern, more elevated third of the area consists of chalk marl; from northwest of the Traveller's Rest Pit this is overlain by 3rd–4th terrace/head gravels (i.e. Observatory Beds; Fig. 1.4). From this ridge, the land falls away to the south and the geology changes to heavy Gault clays; though, as will become clear (see Chap. 7), these also display considerable variation. Obviously, as much of the area consists of heavy clay and a great deal of it has been built over (with large portions also seeing intense nineteenth-century quarrying), aerial photography has contributed little to the detection of sites; generally, they have only been discovered through evaluation trial-trenching.

A theme of these books, and the region's 'inland' archaeology generally (i.e. off-main river valleys; see Evans & Patten 2011), is the achievement of regular water supplies. The location of main spring-line sources becomes critical, as does that of the one watercourse in the immediate area, Washpit Brook; this runs along the western margin of the area, and then follows a minor valley running northwards out beyond Girton. Its route is best appreciated in reference to Fox's maps (e.g. see Fig. 1.7); with its headwaters up by Madingley (fed from spring sources off the Coton/Hardwick Ridge), from there it flows out through a gap in a northwestward continuation of western Cambridge's gravel ridgeway at Oakington/Westwick and joins with the Old West River by Smithey Fen. This – and the area's other minor waterways – would have served as communication corridors through these heavy claylands. Indeed, it is along a similarly minor stream-line at Longstanton that Mesolithic scatters have been found (*BLS*, 176, fig. 3.21); certainly, during that period, and probably also the Neolithic, their courses would have provided routeways through densely wooded lands.

It is essential that, from the outset, the main axes of the clay plain north of Cambridge are appreciated. In the past, it has been mistakenly characterized – and, effectively, dismissed – as the 'fen hinterland', but it is a swathe of highly fertile countryside and one with its own distinct topographical dynamics. Today, it is largely dominated by the axis of the A14/ Cambridge-to-Huntingdon/Godmanchester Road, but 'behind' it and through the clay, our 'inland' gravel ridge runs northwest up through Longstanton to the fens at Willingham and Over; cross-cutting this is the north–south drainage of the area's streams. Admittedly, the area lacks the drama of the region's chalk downs or a major river, and it is not the kind of landscape that has attracted antiquarians or, now, 'cultured walkers' (e.g. MacFarlane 2012; see also *RVS*, chaps. 2 & 6). Its *subtle topography* has, nevertheless, determined much of its land-use history. Indeed, as related in the course of this book, it has taken considerable time (and exposure) for us to appreciate the lingering impact of the area's clayland slight rises and troughs.

Background Framing

Leaving aside Alexander *et al*.'s excavations within the walled town-area itself (see Chap. 2), the western Cambridge lands have seen considerable early fieldwork. At either end the area is framed by renowned early cemeteries: to the east, on St John's College Playing Fields and, at its west end, that at Girton (Fig. 1.3.1). Both dug by von Hugel and Jenkinson, these featured prominently in Fox's 1923 study (242–3 & 246–9), with neither properly published in their time (Girton's cemetery eventually being published by Hollingworth and O'Reilly in 1925; see also Liversidge 1977, 15–16).

The other significant focus of fieldwork has been in the Traveller's Rest Pit Quarry, north of the Observatory and bordering Huntingdon Road. Burkitt and Marr recovered quantities of Palaeolithic finds (plus later flintwork) there in the early decades of the last century, as well as some Roman material. The latter harks back to still earlier quarry findings. As indicated on the Ordnance Survey map (see Figs. 1.2 & 1.3.3), in 1861 Roman cremations were found there, as were two stone coffins in the following year. The larger of these had apparently been repaired and only had a disturbed skeleton within it; the other contained a female with rich grave-goods: several glass vessels, a pot and a jet amulet and, also in jet, two pins (Fig. 1.5; Babington 1864 and 1883, 35–6;

Figure 1.5. *Roadway Findings:* Via Devana *milestones (upper left) and Roman glass vessels from the coffined burial found at the Traveller's Rest Pit (upper right; from Babington 1883); bottom, Huntingdon Road's nineteenth-century* Devana *Terrace (Nos. 118–24).*

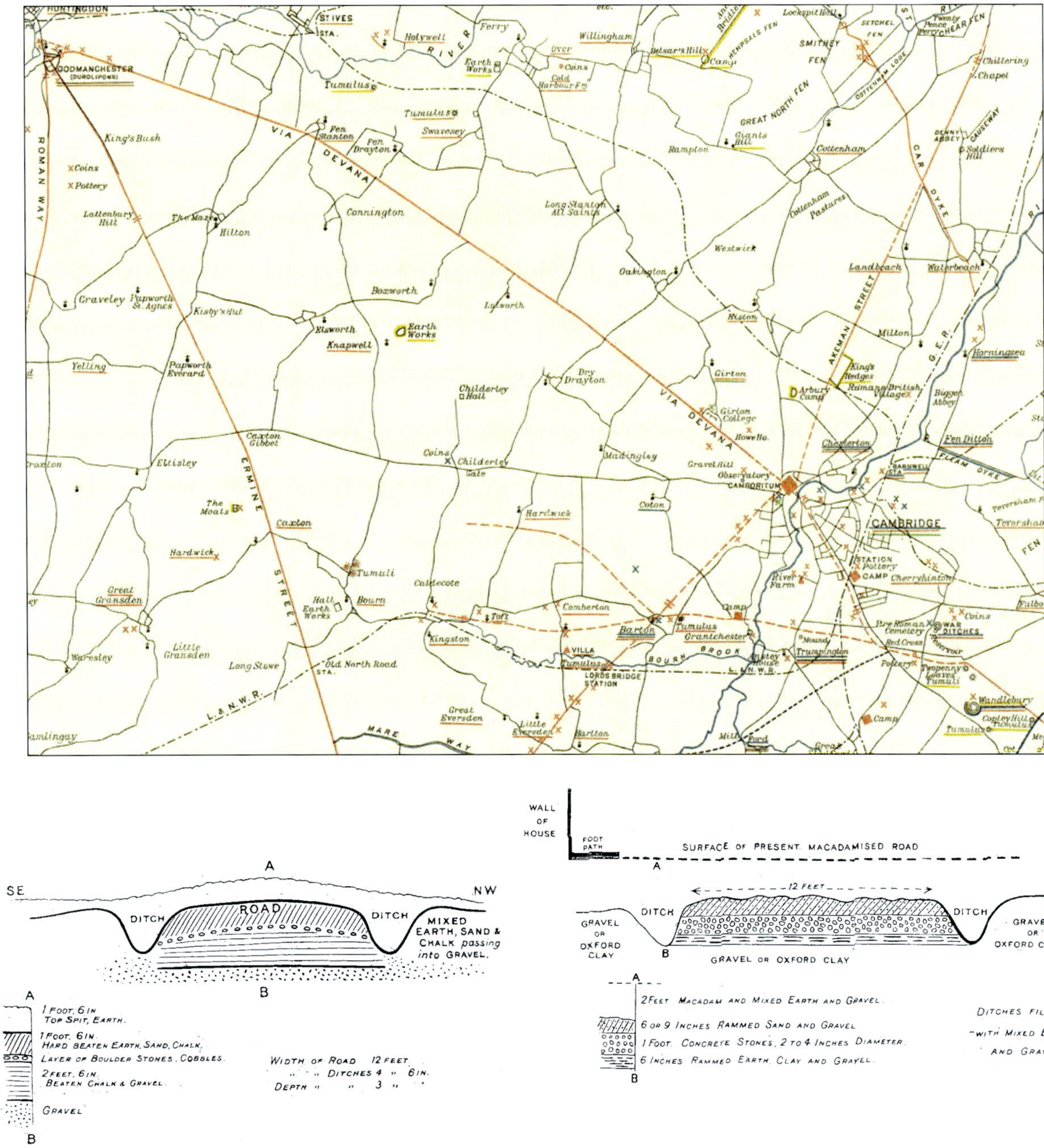

Figure 1.6. *Detail from Walker's 1910 'Roman Roads into Cambridge' map (top) and, below, section of* Akeman Street *by Bull's Close, Barton (left; 1910, fig. 2) and the* Via Devana *at Godmanchester (right; ibid., fig. 3).*

see RCHM[E] 1959, pl. I). Having vague affinities with Girton's richly accompanied Roman cremations (and the sculptural fragments coming from that cemetery; see Fig. 1.12), this tells of a degree of local wealth. Admittedly, in the course of our excavations no more burials of this quality were recovered; however, other markers of elevated status certainly were.

Bookending the length of the North West Cambridge investigations and effectively describing 'time's arrow' – from the Palaeolithic to Anglo-Saxon – both the Traveller's Rest Pit and Girton cemetery findings will feature in the next book (including relevant notebook extracts; see *NWC*, chap. 1). At this time, the only other findings that need concern us relate to the Roman route to Godmanchester (Figs. 1.3 & 1.6). This was identified as the *Via Devana*, and as corresponding with the Roman route from Colchester to Chester (i.e. *Deva*), in *c.* 1750 by one Charles Mason, a Cambridge

Professor of Geology. Referring to the Lysons' *Magna Britannia* of 1808 (II, pt. I, 44), Babington wrote of it:

> ... the *Via Devana* passed out at the north-western gate of the station [Cambridge], just west of the present junction of the Huntingdon and Histon roads, and *kept to the left of the line of the existing road* {i.e. south], but "passed though the fields of the ancient hamlet called How's House, where a barrow containing several Roman coins was removed in making the present road" (1883, 35; emphasis added; in his 1864 version of this text Babington stated that the road passed through the grounds of *The Grove*; see Chap. 3).

Not only is this passage noteworthy for its reference to a possible Roman barrow at How's/Howe's – that 'ancient' hamlet' excavated, in part, at North West Cambridge's Site IX (Fig. 1.2.9) – but also for how firmly it locates that route 'left' of the Huntingdon Road-line (i.e. south). In recent years, within the area of the Roman town itself, its line has come to be established with some confidence (Evans & Ten Harkel 2010). Yet, its precise westward route has been a source of much speculation and, as outlined in Chapter Three, its eventual 'fixing' has taken considerable effort.

Said to come from about three miles (*c.* 4.8 km) from Cambridge (locating them near Catch Hall and some 2.5 km beyond Girton), two Roman milestones were apparently found close to the Godmanchester/Huntingdon Road-line in 1812 (these were later acquired by the Fitzwilliam Museum and are now held by the University Museum). Thought to date to the first half of the fourth century AD, not only are they significant for their marking of the road but also for their inscriptions (Fig. 1.5; RIB 2236 & 2237). Babington thought the one likely to have been erected 'in honour of Constantinus Pius by the Fifth Legion (?) in the reign of his father Constantine the Great' (1883, 42). If an accurate reading, this would imply that some part of the Legion was then stationed in the vicinity. As it is not, though, otherwise known that the Fifth had ever been in Britain (*ibid.*, 40–2), this casts doubt upon its translation. Subsequent readings of the stones' inscriptions indicate two texts and their 'overwriting': a prime one dating to the time of Antoninus Pius in the mid second century AD, with a secondary commemorating Constantine I (AD 305–6); the latter reworking probably relates to the local community's saluting of the new emperor (see e.g. Sauer 2014).

To all this can also be added various finds recovered through College construction and 'incidental' activities. Accumulated on an *ad hoc* basis, there is no point in attempting now any kind of over-arching review of the surrounding landscape; instead, these will be drawn upon where relevant in the text that follows.

Mapping Knowledge

Roman roads feature highly in these books. In his 1910 paper, 'Roman Roads into Cambridge', Walker listed their defining traits:

> How can we be positive that a road bearing the name Roman is really a Roman one?
> There are several characteristics which help us to determine this.
> Wherever a section can be made, we know by its structures whether a road is Roman or not.
> By its *straightness*.
> By the milestones (*milliaria*) found along its line. ... (150; emphasis added).

Yet, tracing their routeways rarely prove as straightforward a matter as either Walker or Fox would have it:

> The situation of the writer, passing from the Early Iron to the Roman Age, may be likened to that of a traveller who, traversing a countryside inadequately surveyed and utilizing in his journey such boggy paths and rutted droveways as appear to lead in the direction he wishes to go, suddenly reaches *a broad metalled highway with guide-posts and milestones ... before us stretches the exact alignment of the Roman Road* (Fox 1923, 159; emphasis added).

In contrast, we have employed as a motto a passage from Ondaatje's novel, *In the Skin of a Lion* (1987), 'Meander if you want to get to town'.

As in the first two volumes of this series, Fox's *The Archaeology of the Cambridge Region* of 1923 still informs this study. But look closely at his maps of our immediate study-area. Apart from marking the Girton Cemetery Site, the Traveller's Rest Pit coffins and Howe's barrow findings (Fig. 1.7), there are few indications within the western Cambridge lands (which reflects his dismal view of the region's 'cold claylands': 1923, 62). While, therefore, always a useful guide to Cambridge's early research history, in this specific case his direct relevance is limited. That said, the 'core story' of these two books is arguably the construction of Figure 1.4's distribution map of settlements and this, of course, is something of which Fox – if standing over our shoulders as it were – would have entirely approved.

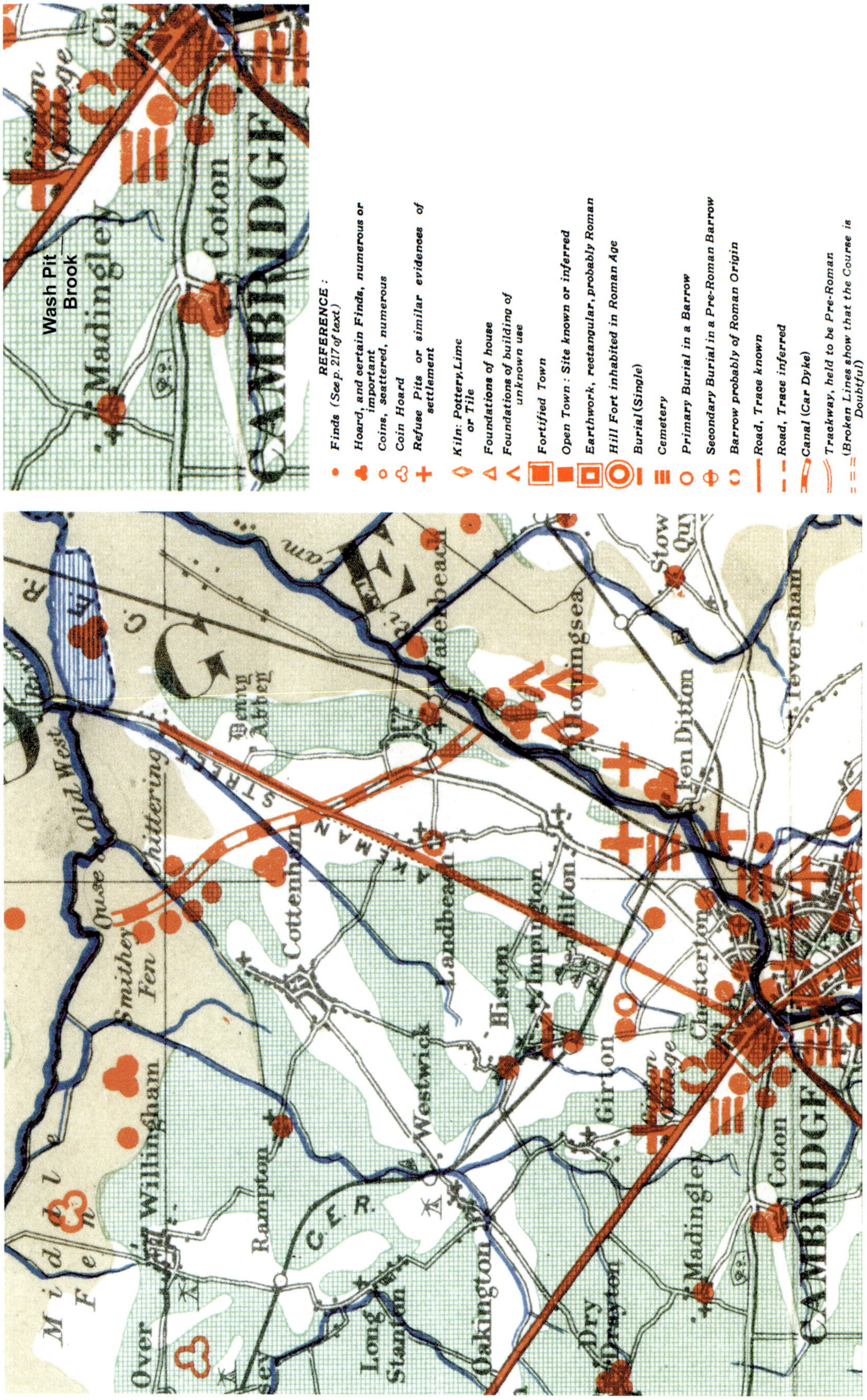

Figure 1.7. *Details from Fox's 1923* Archaeology of the Cambridge Region *Roman Age map.*

With that map having taken us more than 20 years to amass,[3] the nature of '*topographical learning*' is central here. In exploring just what kind of knowledge-basis this involves, these books have been informed by other 'companions'. One has been Schlögel's *In Space We Read Time* (2016). Among its many space-time vignettes is one concerned with the British in India; the argument is that 'Cartesian' mapping was a necessary adjunct of empire. But is this really true, at least in the case of Roman Britain? While the great *Forma Urbis* map-relief-sculpture demonstrates that in the empire's core accurate mapping could be achieved (see Fig. 1.8 and *Inset*), there is little, if any, indication of this in provincial Britain. Certainly, individual grand buildings and constructions reflect high levels of surveying skills (e.g. Castor's palace or Hadrian's Wall). Locally we see this in the straightness of their roads and, on occasion, the exact right-angle layout of some enclosures. But did they actually ever map the western Cambridge lands and its settlements in a manner in any way comparable to ours?

Here the thirteenth-century Medieval copy of the Roman-period *Tabula Peutingeriana* map may be insightful (Gautier-Dalché 2003). The elongated portrayal of the 6.75 m long scroll, with major forests, rivers and mountains indicated, basically depicts the length of the empire's long-distance roads. Is this how they 'officially' envisaged landscape: primarily in a linear-itinerary manner as described by main road networks, marked with milestones and knowing the distance from destination stops (i.e. towns and cities)? If so, the situation might have been akin to how things were, for example, until recently in parts of Nepal (prior to the wide availability of satellite imagery). Without accurate maps showing every village and hamlet, step off of the main highways and get into the web of their linking trails and trackways, then local knowledge was required (Evans 1999; see also e.g. Gell 1985 on 'practical navigation' and way-finding). Given the straightness of western Cambridge's many Roman routes, this parallel cannot be pushed too far. Nevertheless, the lattice-like pattern they describe – although reflecting some degree of organized land-blocking – would not indicate any sense of 'master planning' (i.e. centuriation; see e.g. Nicolet 1991).

(In)Visible Cities – *Forma Urbis Romae*

Our title here references Calvino's short story collection, *Invisible Cities* (1974), and its exposition of intertextuality and the impossibility of ever adequately mapping/knowing the many facets of urban space. In a similar vein, we could also cite Borges' 'Museum, of the Exactitude in Science', concerned with a guild of cartographers and their desire to construct 'the Perfect Map':

> In time, … the Cartographers Guilds struck a Map of the Empire whose size was that of the Empire, and which coincided point for point with it. The following Generations, who were not so fond of the Study of Cartography as their Forebears had been, saw that the vast Map was Useless, and not without some Pitilessness was it, that they delivered it up to the Inclemencies of Sun and Winter (1998, 325; see also Vrbančic 2012).

Our specific concern at this point is with Piranesi's 1762 engraving of the *Forma Urbis Romae* (Fig. 1.8). Not only is it of relevance for issues of ancient mapping abilities and 'portrayal', but also because it is simply an extraordinary image of 'the fragments of the past' and one that we will use for our own purposes in the next book in collaboration with our artist-colleague, Issam Kourbaj.

Covering *c.* 13 × 18 m, the enormous *Forma Urbis* marble-slab map had apparently been constructed between AD 203–11 and was displayed on a wall of the Temple of Peace in the Imperial Fora (Koller *et al.* 2005). It was rendered at a scale of 1:240 and showed the ground-level plans of all the city's principal architectural features and streets. Yet, with its some 1200 surviving pieces now the subject of a major digital reconstruction project (*ibid.*), this is estimated to amount to only some 10 per cent of the original; it having been broken up and used as building material in Medieval times and only rediscovered in the sixteenth century.

To a singular degree, cities require visualization to understand, 'command' and negotiate their dense, multi-tiered components. They are complex places — albeit to a lesser degree, as we will see, so also are their hinterlands — and their reading requires various aids (Fig. 1.9). By the same token, the latter-day comprehension of antique cities has also involved innovative modes of rendering; particularly three-dimension modelling, with renowned examples including eighteenth- and nineteenth-century 'realizations' of Jerusalem and Pompeii (e.g. Evans 2004).

Figure 1.8. *Depicting Cities (I): Piranesi's 1762 engraving of* Forma Urbis Romae *fragments (top) and, below, Pierino Di Carlo with part of his model of ancient Rome (c. 1935; from Packer 2008, fig. 3).*

Figure 1.9. *Depicting Cities (II): Bronze-cast rendering of Cambridge's central town-core erected in front of Great St. Mary's Church in 2000 (with braille legend; top); middle, Pope and Guthrie's master plan cob model,* Tomorrow, Today *and, below, as rendered in Kettle's Yard Gallery.*

In the case of Rome, Mussolini commissioned a great model of the city for a 1937 exhibition in the Museo della Civilta Romna to commemorate the birth of Augustus, (see e.g. Packer 2008). Drawing on Lanciani's *Forma Urbis Romae* of 1893–1901 and other early attempts to reconstruct Rome's plan, the model showed the city at the time of Constantine in the earlier fourth century AD. Under the supervision of Italo Gismondi, it was built by one Pierino Di Carlo and, at more than 16.75 m across, its scale was comparable to the Severan-era marble-slab setting (Fig. 1.8; see Verstegen & Ceen 2013). Its construction apparently involved a degree of exaggeration of its major buildings (15–20% larger) to promote their impact and, up until 1973, the model continued to be revised in the light of new discoveries.

Model-rendering is something of an underlying theme within these books. Such tactile modes of depiction have, in fact, a long pedigree in both archaeology and the sciences (Evans 2004) and, apparently at one time, the western Cambridge lands were rendered in that manner. Accounts of the International Geographical Congress, held in Cambridge in 1928, relate that John Marr – for years recording the geology and archaeology of the Traveller's Rest Pit (see *NWC*, chap. 2) – displayed a model illustrating Cambridge's terrace-strata based on the quarry's exposures (J.H.R. & A.J.P. 1928). Unfortunately, attempts to now locate either this model or any photographs of it have come to naught.

In conjunction with our Traveller's Rest Site at North West Cambridge, the project's artists-in-residence – Nina Pope and Karen Guthrie – made a vast, 'field-size' cob model of the development's master plan (Fig. 1.9). They have a long-standing interest in utopian schemes and the work is appropriately entitled *Tomorrow, Today*. Its cob-rendered buildings stand up to 1.5 m high and it is somewhat akin to a more pronounced *Forma Urbis*. If rather playfully, its construction in 2014 amounted to a comment on the building programme's idealistic intentions. (Pope and Guthrie have since conducted their own *Prospection* survey project, annually recording the development's 'inhabitation'.)

Today, some four years on and with the initial stages of the 'real' development all but completed, their now much-weathered cob-version effectively shows it as a ruin (Fig. 1.3.A). Although unanticipated at the time of its conception, the model-form operates as if a millennium or more in advance of the 'real' building programme. Speaking of time and transience, there is a distinct resonance here with the architect, John Soane and his neo-classical Bank of England in London. Soane had his artist-collaborator, Joseph Gandy, paint the then newly completed bank as if a Piranesi-esque Roman ruin (1830; Lukacher 2006, 161–3, fig. 175; Evans 2000, fig. 1). As further detailed in the next book, we have since hosted public excavation events – *Digging the Future* – having them reduce portions of the model and collect its topsoil-derived artefacts. Moreover, a still further reduced-scale portion of the model featured in a Kettle's Yard Gallery art exhibition of Pope and Guthrie's work (2014; Fig. 1.9, bottom).

Another 'book-companion' has been Yale's 2016 study, *Sociable Knowledge: Natural History and the Nation in Early Modern Britain*. This concerns the construction of Britain's natural history during the seventeenth century, as well as its antiquarian studies. It details how crucial 'travelling to knowledge' was, and the role played by its practioners' networks of correspondence by letter: figures such as John Aubrey and Edward Lhuyd amassed vast paper archives (in addition to their collection-cabinets of curiosity). Yale convincingly argues that their open-ended and collective archives became an end in themselves and that, in effect, their eventual single-author publications amounted to an arbitrary 'truncation' of researches. As we will see, with these two *Hinterlands/Inlands* books now reflecting the efforts of so many participants for so long – and that many of our conclusions must invariably have an 'interim' status given that the current intense pace of fieldwork will continue in the near-future – parallels can be drawn between these seventeenth century and today's 'sociable knowledge' practices.

This book's other quote inspiration, Drazin's on 'mapping the past' and its expanding territories (2016, 11), also clearly complements the theme of 'topographical knowledges'. That volume traced five of his Irish family's brothers who, all serving in the Royal Engineers, mapped various far-flung corners of Britain's empire during the late nineteenth century and first decades of the twentieth. This has relevance for issues of empire raised in these books, as well as, more pragmatically, for the simple appreciation of military surveying skills. The latter's relevance for the development of archaeology has long been recognized (e.g. Wheeler 1954; Evans 2014; see e.g. Stone 1988). The lack thereof in the case of Cambridge's early-era archaeology unfortunately runs as something of a leitmotif through these books. This is in some contrast to Oxford's fieldwork history and there is no obvious explanation for why so much of Cambridge's fieldwork has been so poorly 'fixed'. This ranges from any kind of proper planning of either the Girton or St John's Playing Fields cemeteries to Macalister's Bandy-Leg Walk findings (see Chap. 2; Fig. 1.12). Indeed, we will also see that John Alexander and his colleagues' *Roman Cambridge* campaigns are ill-served by the cartoon-like location and phase maps that accompany that volume (see Fig. 2.3). The enduring legacy of so much imprecision only makes it all the harder to appraise and attempt to work with Cambridge's earlier findings.

This Book – Text and Context

At its root this book outlines three major excavations (Fig. 1.10) and, over the years, each has amassed their own considerable archival 'grey literature':

New Hall (Chap. 3)

Evans, C., 1993. *Archaeological Investigations at New Hall, Cambridge, 1993*. Cambridge Archaeological Unit Report No. 86

Evans, C., 1996. *New Hall, Cambridge. Prehistoric Land-use and Roman Hinterland Investigations: The 1994 Excavations*. Cambridge Archaeological Unit Report No. 190

Figure 1.10 *(opposite). Western Cambridge plan, with sites and gazetteered Roman roads indicated; also shows, within area framed by M11 and Histon Road, large-scale fieldwork evaluations that have not produced significant site-find results (for MPH see Fig. 2.23; for MAG see Barlow 2018 and, for Star, Ladocha & Muldowney 2014).*

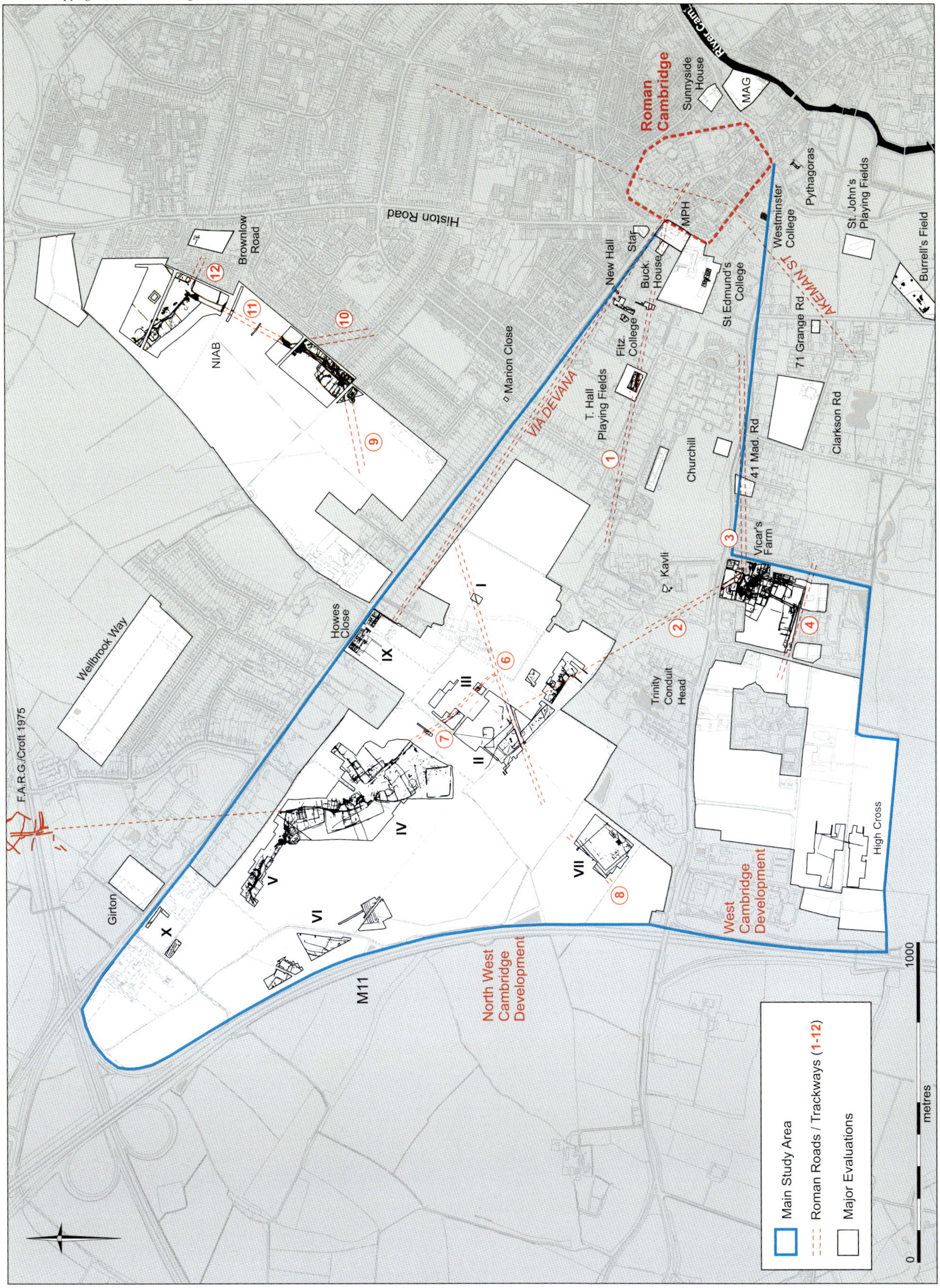
Roman Cambridge
River Cam
Sunnyside House
MAG
Histon Road
Brownlow Road
NIAB
Marion Close
New Hall
Star
MPH
Buck. House
Fitz. College
T. Hall Playing Fields
VIA DEVANA
St Edmund's College
Westminster College
Pythagoras
St. John's Playing Fields
Burrell's Field
AKEMAN ST
71 Grange Rd
Clarkson Rd
41 Mad. Rd
Churchill
Vicar's Farm
Kavli
Trinity Conduit Head
Howes Close
Wellbrook Way
F.A.R.G./Croft 1975
Girton
M11
North West Cambridge Development
West Cambridge Development
High Cross
Main Study Area
Roman Roads / Trackways (1-12)
Major Evaluations
0
1000
metres

Vicar's Farm *(Chaps. 4–6)*

Whittaker, P. and C. Evans, 1999. *Vicar's Farm, West Cambridge: An Archaeological Evaluation*. Cambridge Archaeological Report No. 336

Lucas, G. and P. Whittaker, 2001. *Vicar's Farm, Cambridge Post-Excavation Assessment Report. Volumes 1 and 2*. Cambridge Archaeological Unit Report No. 425

High Cross *(Chap. 7)*

Whittaker, P., 2001. *The Archaeology of West Cambridge: The High Cross Field Evaluation*. Cambridge Archaeological Report No. 422

Timberlake, S., 2010. *Excavations at High Cross, West Cambridge, University of Cambridge*. Cambridge Archaeological Report No. 942

Brittain, M. and C. Evans, 2015. *West Cambridge Archaeology, Department of Veterinary Medicine Paddocks: An Archaeological Evaluation*. Cambridge Archaeological Unit Report 1292

Newman, R., 2017. *Merton Hall Farm, West Cambridge: An Archaeological Evaluation*. Cambridge Archaeological Unit Report No. 1384.

Beyond this, the first two sites also have 'allied excavations': immediately adjacent fieldwork whose direct relevance is such that their results must be incorporated alongside those of the original sites. At New Hall, this involves further work within the College's grounds (now renamed Murray Edwards), as well as in the neighbouring Fitzwilliam College:

Gdaniec, K., 1991. *Archaeological Investigations at The Grove, Fitzwilliam College, Cambridge*. Cambridge Archaeological Unit Report No. 5

Lucas, G,. 1999b. *Archaeological Investigations at Buckingham House, New Hall, Cambridge*. Cambridge Archaeological Unit Report No. 305

Webley, L. and C. Evans, 2003. *New Hall, Cambridge: An Archaeological Evaluation at 67 Storey's Way, with an Assessment of the Extent of Post-medieval Quarrying*. Cambridge Archaeological Unit Report No. 579

Cooper, A., 2003b. *Fitzwilliam College Library, Cambridge: An Archaeological Evaluation*. Cambridge Archaeological Unit Report No. 539

Slater, A., 2008a. *Fitzwilliam College Library, Cambridge: An Archaeological Excavation*. Cambridge Archaeological Unit Report No. 817

Hutton, J., 2009a. *Orchard Court, Murray Edwards College, Cambridge: An Archaeological Evaluation*. Cambridge Archaeological Unit Report No. 901

Webb, D. and R. Newman, 2011. *Orchard Court, Murray Edwards College, Cambridge: An Archaeological Excavation*. Cambridge Archaeological Unit Report No. 1054.

In the case of Vicar's Farm, this involves four further exposures:

Lucas, G., 2001. *An Archaeological Evaluation along the Marconi Access Route and Future Nano Fabrication Building*. Cambridge Archaeological Unit Report No. 440

Armour, N., 2001. *An Archaeological Investigation on the site of the Future Nano Fabrication Building, West Cambridge*. Cambridge Archaeological Unit Report No. 453

Timberlake, S. and R. Patten, 2006. *An Archaeological Evaluation on the site of the New Physics for Medicine Building, University of Cambridge, West Cambridge*. Cambridge Archaeological Unit Report No. 726

Slater, A., 2011. *Whittle Jet Propulsion Laboratories, West Cambridge: Archaeological Trenching and Excavation*. Cambridge Archaeological Unit Report No. 983.

'Late in the day', and only after this book had largely been completed, yet another site was dug and required incorporation here:

Tabor, J., 2017. *University of Cambridge Sports Pitches and Athletics Track, Wilberforce Road, Cambridge: An Archaeological Evaluation*. Cambridge: Cambridge Archaeological Unit Report No. 1381

Brittain, M. and C. Evans, 2018. *University of Cambridge Sports Ground, Wilberforce Road, Cambridge: An Archaeological Excavation*. Cambridge Archaeological Unit Report No. 1402.

While a Roman settlement had been predicted in that general location (see Chap. 2, *Cambridge Southwest-Sector Sites*), this only received confirmation when the plot of the University's Wilberforce Road Sports Grounds was trench-evaluated in the autumn of 2017 (Tabor 2017). It was subject to full excavation in the late winter of the following year, when the eastern side of another Romano-British farmstead with a bordering road/trackway was exposed. Although this represents a major excavation in its own right, restrictions of space and its 'aftermath' incorporation dictates that its presentation here is somewhat more summary than might otherwise have been (see Chap. 7).

Other 'landscape-ancillary' investigations will also be included; primarily those at St Edmund's College and Trinity Hall's Playing Fields (see Chap. 2), with this book also encompassing other minor sites. A truly vast amount of archaeology is, therefore, presented here. With its archives spanning many hundreds of page and thousands of features, generally this precludes close reportage. There is just too much data at hand for that, but the background archival texts are all readily available for further reference.

In many respects the pivotal excavation of the Unit's western Cambridge hinterland investigations was actually the 2008 Kavli Institute Site within the grounds of the University's Observatory (Evans & Newman 2011). Primarily directed towards the exposure of the foundations of a great nineteenth-century telescope – truncating late Medieval quarries backfilled with Iron Age and Roman material (see Chap. 4) – and with familial connections relating to the basis of the University's West Cambridge development, it encapsulates much of what makes the study-landscape so distinct. Moreover, as outlined in this book's last chapter, our tracking of this site's inter-connections highlights something of a local mystery: the origins of the Bullard Laboratory sculpture fragments (see Fig. 7.39).

The New Hall and Vicar's Farm Sites have seen considerable interim reporting (Evans in *RCAM*, 255–8 and Evans & Ten Harkel 2010; see also *BLS*, fig. 2.56), with both Vicar's Farm and the North West Cambridge's main Roman settlements featuring in a regional case-study within the recent *The Rural Settlement of Roman Britain* volume (Smith *et al.* 2016, 193–206, figs. 5.56 & 5.63; see also Perring & Pitts 2013, 72).[4] Reflective of Lucas' theoretical leanings, facets of the Vicar's Farm sequence have featured in his subsequent publications. Including a paper in *The Journal of Material Culture*, 'Disposability and dispossession in the twentieth century' (2002), it has a prominent role in his 2005 book, *The Archaeology of Time* (104–13; see Chap. 6, *Inset*); its data has also featured in Evans' 'comparative settlement' studies (2013; Evans *et al.* 2013b, table 2.54).

As alluded to here, there is no escaping differences in the approaches of the book's main authors and vestiges of this linger here. In the portions that Lucas first drafted (Chaps. 4–6), there is a deep concern with fine-grained depositional context and less strictly functional interpretation, whereas Evans is more given to formal structural-sequence emphasis. There has been a degree of reworking of the original Vicar's Farm text, but this 'mixed' quality remains. Hopefully, though, seeing past sequences through diverse perspectives can only be considered a virtue.

Also relevant to this book's 'style' and content is the duration of the fieldwork. With the addition of latest phase of excavation at West Cambridge's Wilberforce Road Sports Ground Site (see Chap. 7), it spans a quarter of a century – from 1991 to 2018[5] – a period which saw major changes in the nature of site reporting and, especially, computing applications. In many cases we are dealing with three or four 'generations' of contributing specialists, reflecting the changing nexus of fieldwork units (and their associative alliances). These years also marked the uptake of computer graphics in archaeology. As a consequence, while New Hall's illustrations were largely hand-drawn, those from Vicar's Farm now have an 'early (computing) days' style and almost cartoon-like qualities. It was only with the High Cross Site in the later 2000s that the Unit established its hallmark red-on-black graphics style. Though the latter site, therefore, links relatively seamlessly with the subsequent North West Cambridge reporting, uniform modes of site presentation could not be attempted in this book given available resourcing. Budgets will simply not stretch to an entire reworking all of New Hall's figures and tables (nor can its analyses be undertaken again to produce standard formats). The upshot of this is that this book, at points, has near-scrapbook-like qualities. In this manner it shares attributes with the Unit's two Mucking Excavation volumes (Evans *et al.* 2016a; Lucy & Evans 2016). Indeed, with the latter appearing in the CAU's *Historiography and Fieldwork* Series, this book similarly involves the Unit's own historiography.[6]

In terms of further scene-setting, it is intended that this is a more straightforward account than the subsequent companion volume. It will still have its *Insets*, highlighting tangential issues (for example, Chap. 3's Darwin Family Estate section and the Sebro Shorts bomber factory in the final chapter's 'Cambridge at War' entry). In the series' second volume, *Riversides...*, the activities and influence of other key 'players' were expanded to include both Neville and Haddon. Here yet others, including local collectors, will be added to the 'historiographic cast' (see Fig. 1.11; see also Fig. 7.40), with John Alexander and his enormous impact on the archaeology of Roman Cambridge and its environs having the leading role.[7] Other figures will take the stage in the next book, where many of the landscape's broader themes will be explored in depth.

While making a virtue out of necessity and embracing diverse approaches, there is no escaping the 'big data' that underpins these books and the challenge posed by its daunting numbers must be acknowledged. Eventually, they will have to include fifteen moderate- to major-scale sites and seven cemeteries (excluding NIAB Lands), with many others summarized. If their comparative potential is to be realized, a degree of systematic nomenclature is required. Generally, specific place-name reference will suffice for the sites proper and it is only at North West Cambridge that they will need some enumeration. However, Romano-British cemeteries to the west of Cambridge will require specific reference to facilitate their detailed analysis and tabulation; accordingly, they will be consecutively numbered in a gazetteer, with the same approach taken for the area's Roman roads and trackways (Fig. 1.10). Also, in an effort to further site-type depositional comparison, we will continue in the use of artefact-density 'league tables' (Table 7.10; see Evans 2013) and selectively employ volumetric analysis (see Chaps. 2 & 4; Fig. 4.32); the

latter having first featured in the 2018 *Riversides …* volume (*RVS*, table 4.57 & 5.25; fig. 6.3).

With sites and fieldwork invariably a product of their immediate time, in many ways it has to be regretted that both the New Hall and Vicar's Farm excavations were not fully published earlier.[8] That said, allowing them to 'mature' now has the advantage of far greater contextual understanding of their sequences, respective roles and landscape situation.

The acquisition of such context clearly takes sustained local landscape commitment. Indeed, in hindsight, it is now difficult to appreciate just how little relevant background there was during the fieldwork of those two sites. There really was no idea of what settlement densities could be expected; any true sense of this was only first achieved with the huge-scale evaluation surveys in the Trumpington/Addenbrooke's and Longstanton lands (see *BLS*, chap. 3), and, further afield, at Stansted and Camborne (respectively, Cooke *et al.* 2008 and Wright *et al.* 2009).[9]

Explored in greater detail in their respective chapters, the circumstances of the three main sites varied greatly. Fieldwork at High Cross was undertaken as part of the much larger programme and its coverage and funding was entirely adequate. Conversely, marking the first large-scale developer-funded site within Cambridge, New Hall was dug on what would now have to be thought of as a 'shoestring' budget. In many respects, New Hall's contrast with Vicar's Farm could not have been greater. As the first West Cambridge site and, in part, excavated in anticipation of Microsoft's new European Research Centre, Vicar's Farm amounted to something of a flagship exercise, albeit a modest one. Not only did it have a dedicated public-outreach component, but the 'host-company' made an additional grant available towards its computerization and, accordingly, it represents one of the earliest excavations in the region to have full computer graphics and the subsequent potential for finds distribution. In consequence, and reflective of Lucas and Evans' shared interests, from the outset the site aspired to be 'different'. Admittedly, it may not now seem as

Figure 1.11. *'Local archaeological players': Horace Darwin (1851–1928), engineer and, as shown here, sometime Mayor of Cambridge (top; see Chap. 3,* Inset*); middle, Robert Alexander Macalister (1871–1950), archaeologist (shown here, centre, at Nablus in 1907; Wolff 2015b, fig. 2; see Fig. 2.28); bottom, John Alexander, archaeologist (1922–2010; see Evans* et al. *2011 for Alexander's obituaries and appreciation).*

such a radical departure, but hopefully something of this ethos is still apparent in the text's close-grained depositional analyses and the contextual emphasis paid to its artefact assemblages.

It has proven salient to look back on – effectively revisit – these early Unit excavations and appreciate the changes that have arisen as the area's excavation-context has built up. A number of traits become apparent on rereading their texts. Given the paucity of excavations in the immediate area, there was a tendency to exaggerate interpretation. By way of example, the recovery of a single military-type belt buckle at New Hall led to the suggestion of a Roman army presence in the vicinity. In the light of so many Roman-site results, it would now take far more to sustain such a claim.

Equally, with the location of so few contemporary sites then known, those that were found were approached in a somewhat more 'precious' manner than would be the case today. An obvious instance of this relates to the effort expended explaining a site's location, with Vicar's Farm being a prime exemplar. Seen in relative isolation, the reasons for the settlement's location became the source of much speculation. Now having a much firmer grasp of the region's/neighbourhood's contemporary settlement densities, this no longer seems quite so pressing an issue. One of the main reasons why any single settlement was sited where it was is because so many other locations were then occupied; from at least the later first millennium BC, the landscape was far from being a blank slate (see Fig. 1.4). This is not to say that specific locational conditions did not influence what any one settlement became, variously curtailing and offering possibilities. Nonetheless, in the light of these settlement densities, landscape 'choice' must now play a more limited role than it once did in the interpretation of sites.

Further concerning the impact of accrued context, issues of 'naming' are common to both this and the next North West Cambridge book. Featuring in Chapter Six's discussion, amongst our concerns is just 'what is/was a (Roman) farm'? In the next volume, what distinguished higher status settlements, particularly roadside and estate centres, and the attributes of villas as such, will feature. Here, the question of the role of the period's aisled buildings looms large; this is despite the fact that Vicar's Farm was the only one of this book's sites to produce such a structure. Some 14 m long and 6 m wide, with its walled footprint probably spanning *c.* 18 × 9 m, it would certainly have been an impressive structure. Drafting this text, the structure was first entitled an 'Aisled Hall', largely on the grounds that it arguably would have been multi-purpose, incorporating living-/working-/storage-space functions and would not just have been an agricultural barn (see e.g. Taylor 2013, 178–9). Yet, in the final months of preparing things for publication, as part of North West Cambridge's Site VII 'villa complex' we excavated what was truly an aisled *hall*. With enormous postholes – upwards of 1 m deep and 1.2 m across – and having masonry wall footings surviving, it had been tile-roofed with tessellated floors. At *c.* 26 m length and 13 m wide, with an additional porch on one of its long sides, this clearly was a building of some architectural pretentions, against which the aisled example at Vicar's Farm pales. Other building parallels will be explored in Chapter Six below, but in this case – rather than 'aisled barn' or 'hall' – the more neutral term, 'building', will here be employed in order to keep matters open.

With hindsight, the shortcomings of many of the early-era developer-funded sites included here now seem obvious and, today, larger areas would generally be exposed. This reflects the more limited strength of archaeological planning constraints during the first half of the 1990s. Indeed, developers then often had to be cajoled to undertake – let alone adequately fund – development-related fieldwork. Here, one New Hall-related example will suffice. When first approached, the College naturally baulked at the work's expense and disruption on the grounds that 'so many famous archaeologists had been fellows both there and in the neighbouring Fitzwilliam College, and that if there was any archaeology present then surely they would have known of it'. While we explained just how hard it can be to see such cut-feature-based archaeology in the course of ongoing construction programmes, this was only fully brought home to them when it was realized that their earlier constructed parking lot had actually cut through a Roman cemetery (see Chap. 3).

Further to the limitations of our early-day excavations and 'science', more environmental bulk sampling would now generally be implemented. That said, reflective of the Unit's involvement in English Heritage's Fenland Management Project of the early 1990s (e.g. Evans 2003), and drawing on many of its specialist participants (e.g. French, Murray, Scaife and Wiltshire), the scope of the main site's environmental programmes were, for their time, thorough. Indeed, in the case of the work at New Hall, the possible distinction of 'pollution' is an issue that only now – 25 years on – is beginning to receive attention (see, e.g., Gilgen *et al.* 2019).

The aDNA analysis of Vicar's Farm's inhumations was very much an 'eleventh-hour' addition and one made possible as part of the background studies for the Department of Archaeology's 'After the Plague' project concerned with Cambridge's Medieval populace.

Featuring in Chapter Five, the arising results are of tremendous importance. So much so that they could lead us to question the 'familiarity' of single-settlement inhabitation, to reconsider their 'elemental structures of kinship' (Lévi-Strauss 1969) and the composition of the 'ancient family' (e.g. Martin 1996). Yet, there is no getting over the fact that the aDNA results were only received after this volume had been written and on the verge of going to print. Their potential implications nonetheless makes you realize just how deeply ingrained the concept of 'closed' familial-based settlements is to site interpretation. Once challenging this, the ramifications could be wide-ranging; for example, the degree to which precepts of 'landed-ness' and accumulative inheritance underpins individual site material culture assemblages. While in the light of Vicar's Farm's aDNA there has been some due tempering of this book's text, this can only go so far until further comparative Roman-period community-composition data-sets are forthcoming from Cambridge's environs and a greater sense of patterning is achieved.

Thinking Hinterlands (1), Ritual and 'Rule-bound Behaviours'

The aim in this book is to thoroughly discuss the 'specifics' of the immediate sites; any overarching discussion of, for example, settlement types and period-densities must largely await the next volume. To this extent, the ultimate aim of these books is two-fold: first, to model and address the area's 'inland' land-use sequence and its prehistoric colonization; second, to explore the dynamics of Roman Cambridge's hinterland.

In order to do justice to these themes, the actual processes and trajectories of 'Romanization' will need to be considered (e.g. Millett 1990; see also e.g. Fincham 2002 and Gardner 2013). This is not just a matter of trying to elucidate later Iron Age to Early Roman settlement sequences and Conquest Period interrelationships, but also trying to comprehend what 'being Roman' implied on different levels (Woolf 2000; Trow *et al.* 2009): not just by any set criteria of its urban or villa 'lifeways', but also what it was to be a Roman farmer and peasant (Taylor 2001 and 2013; McCarthy 2013). More fundamentally, in these books we will try to gauge the status and function of Cambridge's surrounding settlements: which were producers and which consumers? Were there rural markets and fairs? At an even more basic level, we will need to establish just what a 'typical' farm of the period involved, as they certainly varied greatly from more recent and 'familiar' historic-era versions of the same (see Chap. 6).

The only realistic way to address the latter point will be *comparatively* (see e.g. Evans 2013). This will be a matter of statistical density-gauging and in relationship to both more recent, Post-Medieval farmyard layouts (see *Vicar's Farm* proper in Chap. 4) and other Roman examples. For the latter we will draw on published sources as far as possible and, here, Langdale Hale's layout and data will be widely cited (Evans *et al.* 2013b, chap. 2). However, in order to thoroughly explore this theme, this will be the one case where one of North West Cambridge's sites is widely referenced (No. II) and, in effect, 'forwarded' (see Chap. 6), as it is particularly informative in this regard.

There were, of course, other types of site and monuments within the area, not just farms. The top right corner of Figure 1.2's map shows the arc of Arbury Camp's Iron Age ringwork, south of which was the Arbury's King's Hedges Roman villa (Fig. 1.12). Another probable villa is known to the east at Teversham (Pullinger & White 1991) and, near the city's airport, an enormous Iron Age and Conquest Period complex has long been investigated (see Gibson & Lucas 2002 and *RVS*, fig. 6.22). Leaving aside the probable cemetery/mausoleum complexes at Girton and Arbury (see above and Fell 1956) – both of which will feature in the next book – there is a final element to acknowledge here: Horningsea's mass-scale pottery industries, located alongside the River Cam at the southern end of the Roman Car Dyke canal system. First seriously investigated in the early years of the last century (Hughes 1903b; Walker 1913), they had an enormous impact on the region's Roman pottery trade and have recently been the subject of a major review (see J. Evans *et al.* 2017).[10]

While Roman Cambridge's hinterland clearly saw much settlement variability, its fabric was evidently underpinned by farmsteads, by far the most frequent site-type of the period in the region (see Smith *et al.* 2016, 192–212). The implications of this cannot be ignored and, as outlined in Chapter Two, are highlighted in the discussion of Green's 1975 modelling of Roman Godmanchester. Given the recovery patterns of the day, it was almost entirely focussed on the town and its surrounding villa production, with no real acknowledgement of any lower status farmstead infrastructure. In this capacity, issues of off-site/'distant' ownership (*vs.* various forms of immediate tenancy) will need to be addressed, particularly as regards Vicar's Farm's Roman farm, as well as the potential role of North West Cambridge's ridge-top settlements. As outlined in Chapter Seven, Vicar's Farm's Post-Medieval usage – with its owner living at Madingley Rise up on the high ground overlooking the farm – may provide a parallel for what occurred in Roman times.

Attempting any kind of overview of so much amassed data, as we must here, is a daunting task.

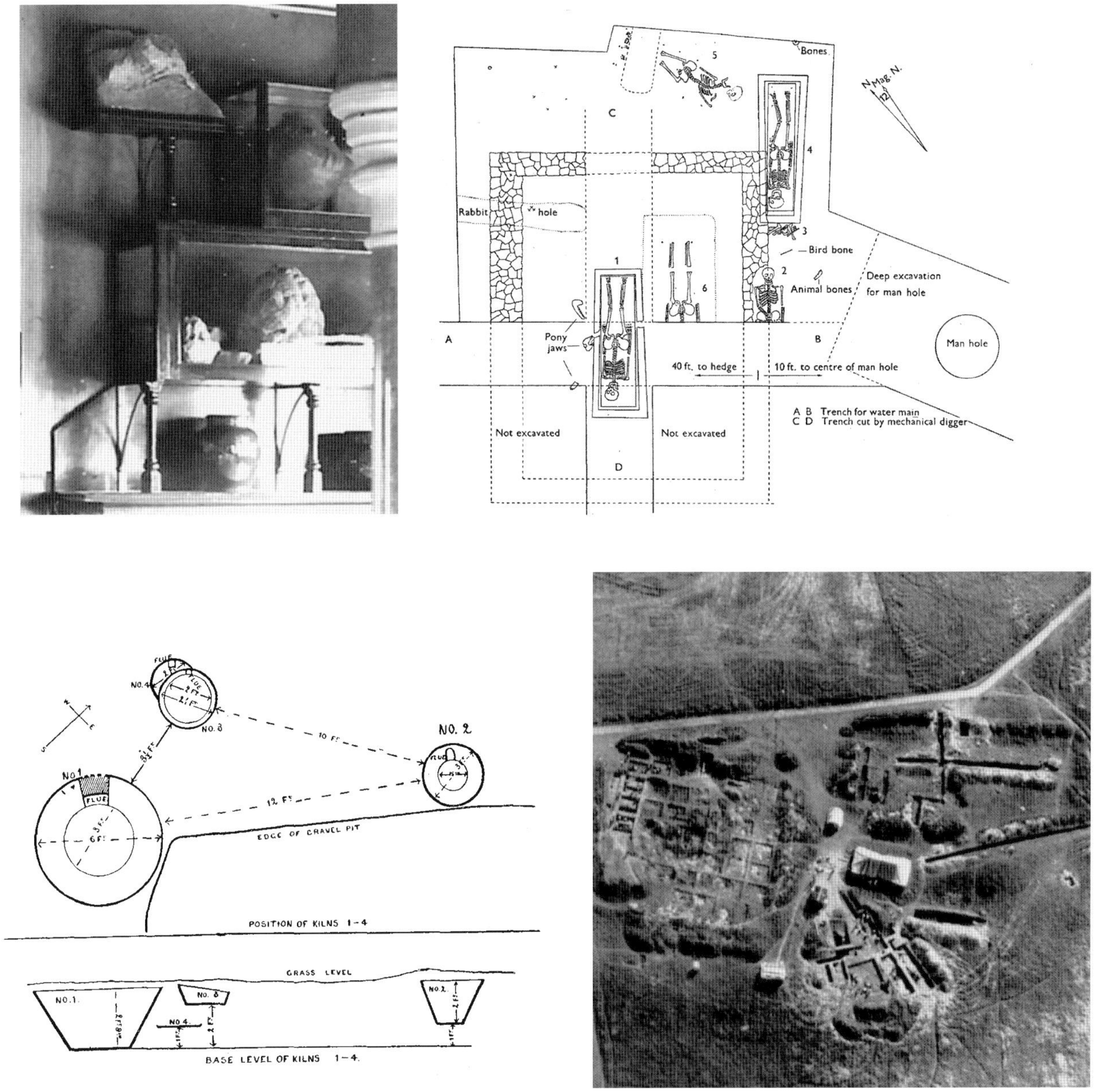

Figure 1.12. *Early Findings and Excavations: Roman lion head sculpture found in the Girton College cemetery (early twentieth century, College's Old Wing-entrance display; top left); Clare Fell's Arbury Road mausoleum plan (1956, fig. 1; upper right); Walker's Horningsea kiln plan (1913, fig. 4; lower left); aerial photograph of John Alexander's 1960s Arbury Villa excavations (notice use of Wheeler Box-technique; Alexander 1970, frontispiece; lower right).*

We are now greatly aided by having available not just the findings of the University of Reading's Rural Settlement of Roman Britain Project (Smith *et al.* 2016 and 2018; Allen *et al.* 2017), but also Taylor's *Atlas …* (2007), Medlycott's … *Great Chesterford* (2011), Perring and Pitts' *Alien Cities: Consumption and the Origins of Urbanism in Roman Britain* (2013), and various other Iron Age/Roman landscape and hinterland studies (e.g. Gaffney *et al.* 2007; Halkon *et al.* 2015; Rippon 2018).

This will require review of Roman Cambridge's data; in the first place, in an attempt to determine whether it was, in fact, a 'town' and, then, what yardsticks might be available to gauge its relationship with its hinterland settlements (see Chap. 2). Just as crucial will be the determination of Roman Cambridge's limits: where did they actually stop in the Early Roman period (its walled-defences plan being 'Late') and the countryside begin? As will become all too apparent, we are hampered in this as little modern-standard excavation has been undertaken in Cambridge's Roman Castle Hill area since Alexander *et al.*'s 'early-day' efforts. This is unfortunate, as the questions raised here would only benefit from the further application of archaeological environmental science and stricter site-excavation procedures. In many respects this will have to be a matter of Cambridge's hinterland informing the interpretation of its 'core'. That said, notice that we have here qualified the Hinterland's portion of our sub-title with '1'. This is simply to acknowledge that the nature of hinterland relationships is something that will have to be thought about again (and again) in these books.

Finally, another theme underlies this study: the degree to which Romano-British society was rule-bound in its behaviours. This issue features, for example, in the discussion of Roman Cambridge's status, as there is evidence both of some industrial activity and a few burials within its bounds. Does this preclude it potentially being small town? In the same way that at Vicar's Farm a cemetery occurred within its primary phase layout (see Chaps. 5 & 6), so is evidence of industry – especially metalworking – commonly found within Roman small towns (Burnham & Wacher 1990, 5, 46–7) and occasionally burials also. This 'breaking of set rules' is not held to be particularly problematic in Roman studies.[11] It is with no small irony that, through the influence of post-processualism (e.g. Scott 1989, Hill 1996, Fulford 2001 and Gosden 2005), the identification of ritual activity – particularly 'special' animal deposits – has itself become increasingly 'rule-bound' and prescriptive (see e.g. Atkinson & Preston 2015, table 6.5).

The question of how a specific period or community's 'ritual code/logic' is identified and analysed – as opposed to the mechanical application of 'ritual rules' – was a theme of our *Riversides* ... volume (chap. 4) and also requires airing here. Does, for example, as Jeremy Evans (*et al.*) has recently argued of New Hall's great F.1/2 pottery assemblage (2017, vol. 2, chap. 10, 26; see Chap. 3), the recovery of complete or nearly so pottery vessels necessarily imply ritual deposition or simply reflect large-scale domestic-source clearance? Equally, must the occurrence of a few articulated remains amid dumps of faunal remains denote intentional placement, as opposed to inefficient butchery? By the same token, what of complete animal burials? Are these *de facto* a matter of sacrifice or could some have been discarded due to disease-tainted meat? To deny out of hand the latter possibility is to dismiss questions of differential stock-management practices in Roman times and, too, what might have been new concepts of hygiene. Accordingly, we will not here naively or mechanically apply 'rules' to such bone groups and will instead explore their depositional context.

Notes

1 The 'in-field' situation of the Unit's offices has contributed to our appreciation of the local landscape and its resonances. It has been a singular experience to have been based in the same landscape where we have worked for so long. For five years in the late 1990s, we were housed in 16 linked portacabins bordering the western side of West Cambridge and, then (following some years in the city centre at the University's Old Music Rooms) where we remain today, at the end of Storey's Way behind the Observatory.

2 See Evans *et al.* 2016a (524–6) on how archaeology has since the 1990s – largely through the impact of science – been willing to allow more dynamic and distantly connected pasts. In *Riversides* ... we outlined how the source of some of the region's more exotic reportedly local findings might have been through personal or 'grand tour' collection, with the provenance of many considered suspect (i.e. sold to museums by collectors claiming to come from local quarries; *RVS*, chap. 1). That said, in the name of 'possibilities', a 1909 account such as 'Greek Coins and Syrian Arrowhead dug up in a Roman Cemetery at Godmanchester' by the Rev. Walker (certainly a 'respectable' researcher) should now, for example, perhaps be granted greater credence than it would have received a few decades ago. As outlined in the next book (chap. 1), to this can be added the possible Egyptian-source of some of Girton's glass vessels or the use of mastic resin from the Mediterranean in the Arrington infant's lead-lined oak coffin burial (Taylor 1993; Brettell *et al.* 2014). Equally, a stone-coffined burial at Kate's Cabin near Durobrivae, found in 1754, is said to have included a piece of 'white wood' inscribed with VTERE FELIX and some illegible Greek words (Noble 1911, 80; see also, e.g., Cool 2010 on 'finding foreigners' in Roman Britain).

3 On Figure 1.4, the only substantive fieldwork not undertaken by the CAU has been Albion Archaeology's 2012–13 excavations across the former NIAB lands north of Huntingdon Road (Fig. 1.4; Barker & Meckseper 2015). Of direct relevance to North West Cambridge's findings, we are grateful that they have provided a summary of their work, which duly features in the next book.

4 It tells of the pace of the region's Roman archaeology that five relevant volumes appeared during the production of this book. This not only included, in 2017, the second Reading University review volume (Allen *et al.*) and J. Evans' (and colleagues) Horningsea pottery study, but also, early in following year, Green's *Roman Godmanchester*, Upex's *Lynch Farm* and Reading's third volume (Smith *et al.* 2018) In much the same way, it is impossible to incorporate the results of the huge-scale excavation programmes that were subsequently conducted within the county. While limited citation will be made to findings at Northstowe/Longstanton, the number of settlements dug for the A14 improvement – and awaiting their reportage – simply makes their integration unfeasible.

5 As outlined above, during the course of producing this book, still other relevant West Cambridge investigations

occurred during 2017–18 that require some inclusion here and these are duly 'postscripted' within Chapter Seven.

6 We were tempted to include this book in that series. As presented in Chapter Two, there is also a major historiographic dimension to this volume's discussion of *Roman Cambridge*'s earlier fieldwork. In terms of any appraisal of that book's results, it is unfortunately not a 'good news' story.

7 Other connections could be highlighted here, including William St John Hope (1854–1919; see Fig. 2.1) for his links with the Macalister Family (see Chap. 2) and his co-direction of the Society of Antiquaries' Silchester excavations (see e.g. Fulford *et al.* 2011). The Darwin Family's earlier earthworm researches at that site could also be cited (see e.g. Evans 2009); space, though, precludes this.

8 With New Hall's text first drafted in the mid 1990s and Vicar's Farm's a decade later, both have obviously now required updating. So as to not unduly impede the immediate context of their formulation (and 'flow'), in the body of their texts this will largely be confined to footnoted references; in their main discussion-sections, though, updates have been more directly integrated.

9 See also, for example, Mills 2007 and Clay 2002 on clayland site densities generally.

10 Other significant local Roman sites – variously at War Ditches and Dam Hill – were variously précised in the *Borderlands…* and *Riversides…* volumes.

11 This burial prohibition – the *pomerium*/sacred ground boundary – only really applied to settlements with a chartered legal status as a town, and this could well have excluded Roman Cambridge.

Chapter 2

Roman Cambridge (Revisited) and its Immediate Environs

Walled Roman Cambridge could, at best, have only been a very small town. Its main east–west axis was just 400 m long and can be walked in three to four minutes. Based on the evidence to date (lack of civic buildings, *etc.*), we even have to doubt whether it amounted to a town as such, as opposed to a major settlement that, in Late Roman times, had a fort sited upon it; determining this is not helped by the standard of its excavation and reporting.

There are facets of the *Roman Cambridge* volume (*RCAM*) that are not particularly convincing. This is not helped by the cartoon-like quality of its phase maps, in which major liberties of 'reconstruction' have clearly been taken. One very obvious instance is the projection of the line of town defences within the northeastern sector (see below). Another is the portrayal of a regular street grid south of the *Via Devana* (Streets 1–3). These are not minor points. On them hang much of the argument that the settlement might actually have been a town, as – along with its defences – they would have been the features to distinguish it from the period's rural settlements.

This chapter begins by reviewing facets of Roman Cambridge's Castle Hill-top archaeology and the findings presented in the 2000 volume. Its aim is to determine whether the settlement deserves to be designated a town. There will also be a précis of the recent work at Kettle's Yard, as it is argued that the findings there reflected distinctly 'urban behaviours'. It then reviews both recent and historical findings within Roman Cambridge's lower east-bankside, as well as those within Castle Hill's immediate surroundings; the intention is to establish the actual size of Cambridge's overall Roman settlement. There will finally be a summary of findings from Cambridge's southwestern sector (i.e. south of the main West/North West Cambridge study-area) for the purposes of comparison, and particularly to appraise the extent of the adjacent western riverside settlement.

Prior Observations and Source Criticism – *Things Missing*

Babington only referred to Roman Cambridge as a 'station' (1883, 3), whereas St John Hope certainly considered it something more: "From its area, 28 acres, the Roman work must have been something more important than a mere fort or camp, and nearer akin to a small town like Caerwent" (1907, 344). As published, *Roman Cambridge* offers limited discussion of the settlement's status (Taylor in *RCAM*, 75–7). In compensation, though, there is Alexander's 1975 conference paper, 'The development of urban communities: the evidence from Cambridge and Great Chesterford'. Typically, he brought a global perspective – particularly African – to this issue. In it he listed seven characteristics of 'imposed' urbanism: regularity of street plan, planned roads between towns, monumental public buildings, public services (water and drainage), commercial and industrial zones, a range of house-types and, finally, imported goods (1975, 103).

His review only included excavation results up to 1975 and concentrated on the southwestern Mount Pleasant/Ridgeons Garden's findings; it did not therefore extend to the later, Shire Hall-area investigations (particularly the *mansio*). Of Roman Cambridge's second- and third-century AD evidence, while noting its two parallel streets and that '*Durolipons* seems the most likely name of the settlement' – *duro*, a fort, and *yliponti*, a specific river's name (i.e. 'fort by a marshy place') – on the whole, Alexander was dismissive of Cambridge's town status:

> No masonry constructions and no public buildings, with the possible exception of a shrine, have been found. Rubbish pits and buildings have been found over some 40 acres (16 ha) north of the river, and ribbon development along the main road on

> the gravel spur south of the river covered another 40 acres; hence the settlement was a considerable one. *This fact is supported by its cemeteries which stretch for over a mile along the north-east road*. It might be that two nuclei of settlement existed, one on both sides of the bridge and one at the crossroads. Remnants of a larger sepulchral monument and of a stone religious diptich or triptich suggest some considerable constructions, but give little hint of the status of the settlement (*ibid.*, 106; emphasis added).

He took much the same attitude to its walled fourth-century AD expression:

> This settlement cannot be said to offer much evidence of urban development and it is best seen as *a fortified, and probably garrisoned, village* blocking the route along the river from the sea, and thus an ancillary fort of the Saxon Shore system (*ibid.*, 108; emphasis added).

Weighing the evidence, he concluded that,

> Cambridge has two periods when slightly differing forms of urban life are possible; in the second-to-third centuries; and in the fourth century when it was constricted by walls and intensive settlement is found inside. *In both periods it lacks almost all the phenomena listed at the beginning of this paper* (*ibid.*, 109; emphasis added).

Aside from his own Castle Hill excavations, most of the evidence that Alexander could then draw upon were casual spot-find observations. This underpinned, for example, his statement that its cemeteries stretch for over a mile along the north–east road (i.e. *Via Devana*); we will see that, rather than large-scale cemeteries, this instead must reflect the density of smaller cemeteries within the landscape. At the time of his writing, with so few large open-area excavations then undertaken, he had very little basis against which to compare Roman Cambridge's findings. In our brief review of Roman Cambridge's status and findings we will not be overly concerned with any 'check-list' definitions of urbanism, but will instead focus on issues of scale and whether it constituted a self-sufficient settlement as regards its potential settlement provisioning from its hinterland.

Burnham and Wacher (1990, 246–9) in their summary outline of Roman Cambridge only accredit it the status of 'minor defended settlement'. While noting that Alexander's identification of its first-century AD fort (*RCAM*, 30–2) is inconclusive, Jeremy Evans and his colleagues in their recent review emphatically state – based largely on the samian and coin supply – that there is no evidence that the enclosure was a fort (2017, vol. 2, 31).

At this time there is still no definitive plan of Roman Cambridge's 'Late' walled perimeter and it can only be said to be firmly 'fixed' along its southwestern, Mount Pleasant sector and along its northern length. Both Babington and St John Hope posited rectangular plans (Fig. 2.1; 1883 and 1907), tying its southeastern side to the embankment along the upslope-side of Magdalene College's grounds (and trenched by Walker; 1911). In *Roman Cambridge* this has been moved north by some 40 m, following the finding of the wall at Kettle's Yard (see below).

In the plan accompanying his 1975 paper Alexander proposed the perimeter of its northeastern sector (along the eastern side of the Castle mound; Fig. 2.2) as an 'alternative town wall conjuncture'. The distinctly polygonal plan in which this results – with a very short southeastern riverside front (having some affinities with Great Casterton's plan; see Medleycott 2011, fig. 3.28) – has, in *Roman Cambridge's* phase plans become the definitive version (Fig. 2.3); however, this seems far from certain. Depending on which version is considered accurate, Roman Cambridge's walled defences would have either extended over *c.* 9 ha (polygonal plan) or *c.* 11.4 ha (rectangular). By way of comparison with its nearest walled town neighbours, Great Chesterford's angular-oval perimeter enclosed *c.* 14.7 ha and Godmanchester 9.9 ha with a more rectangular-polygonal layout (*ibid.*, 51, figs. 3.4 & 3.28).

Another issue to contend with is the 'uncomfortable' kinking of Roman Cambridge's main north–south road axis: Alexander's Street 1 and the northward line of Akeman Street in relationship to the latter's much more southwesterly route south of Castle Hill (see Figs. 1.10 & 2.23). This is something that will be considered on more than one occasion below (see ... *Roman Town Fringe* and Chap. 3). Given the nature of Castle Hill's excavation, it is a problem without ready resolution, but at least it now can now be explored in the light of new evidence.[1]

Roman Cambridge is both an inconsistently, and severely under-illustrated account. The manner of its presentation format, with any one site's phase plans scattered throughout the volume and appearing at different scales (and portions), can make it difficult to achieve any real sense of the intensity of its settlement.[2] In an attempt to address this, here we have appropriately 'reassembled' the published plans of its most thoroughly excavated site: Ridgeons Garden (Figs. 2.4 & 2.8). What is particularly striking in these

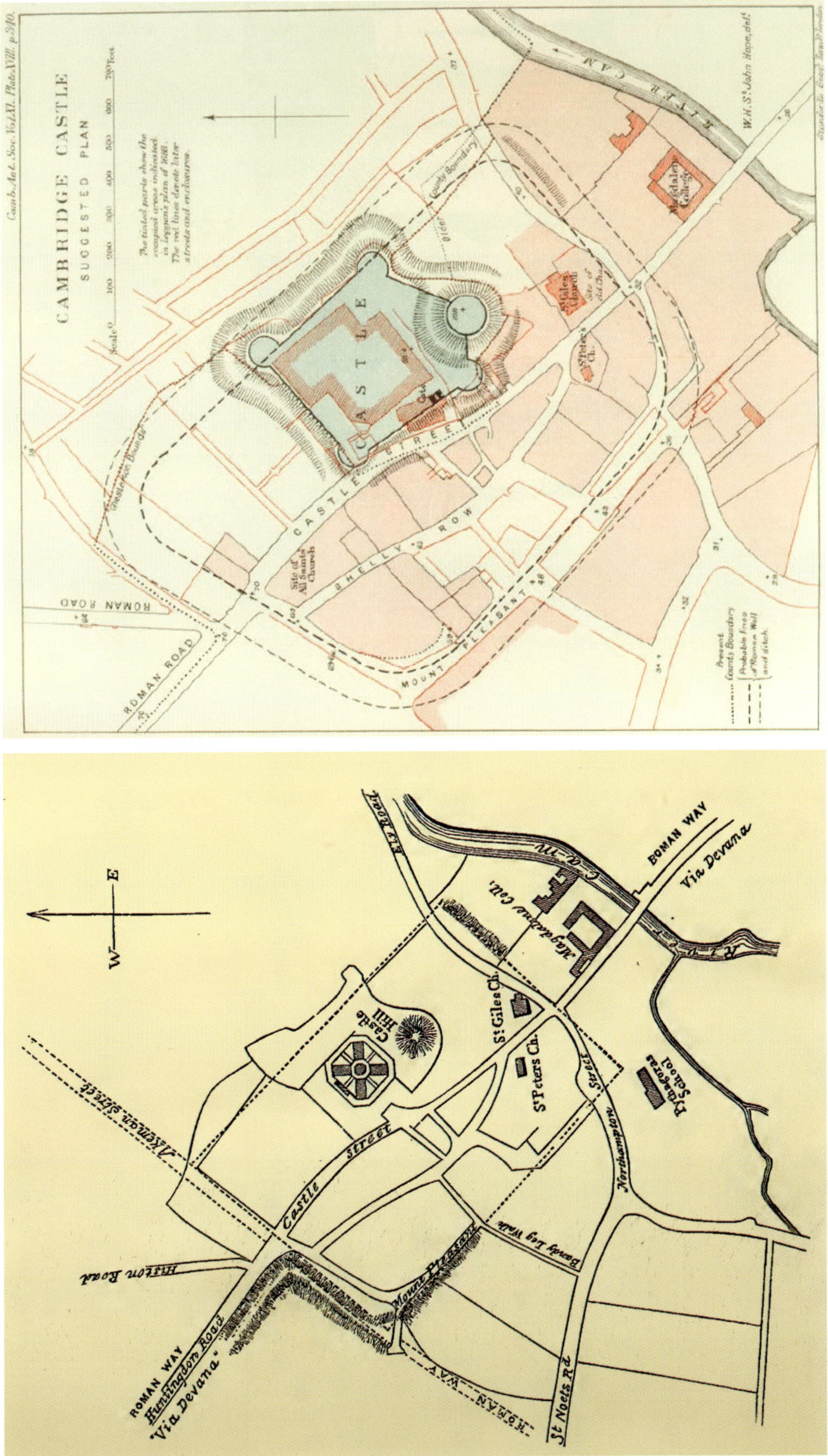

Figure 2.1. *Roman Cambridge, early renderings (1): Babington's* Ancient Cambridgeshire *mapping (1883; left) and, right, St John Hope's of 1907.*

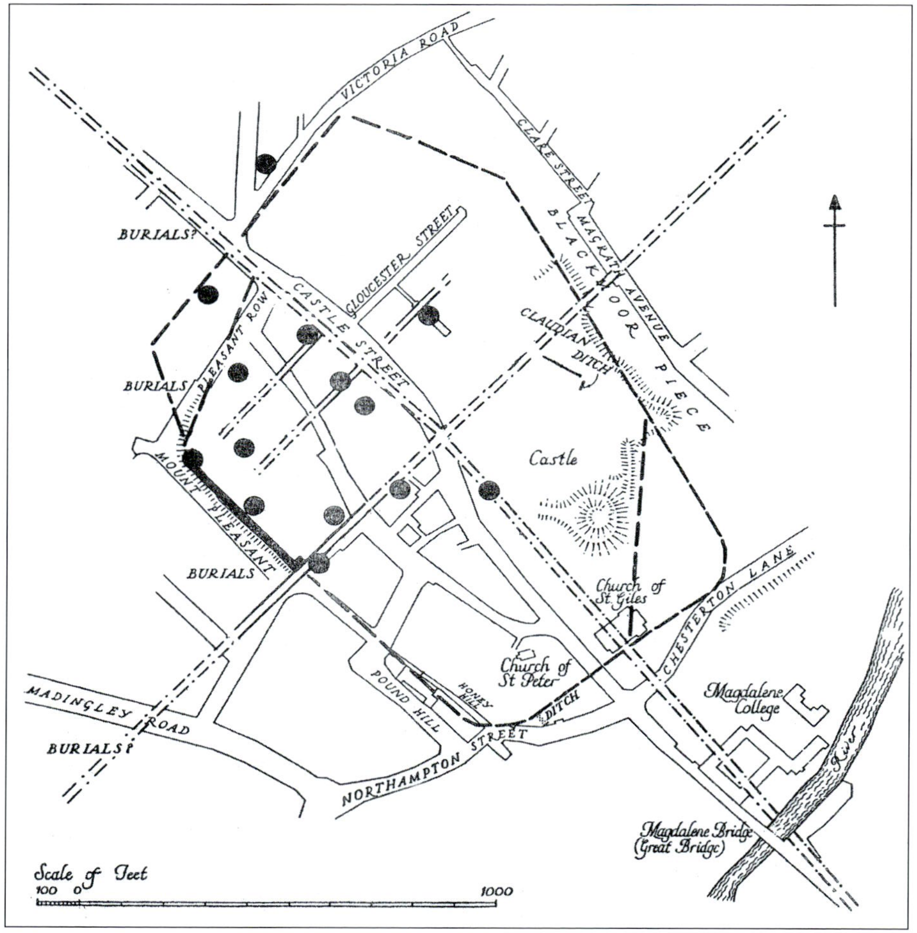

Figure 2.2. *Roman Cambridge, early renderings (2): left, Browne's 1974* Gazetteer *mapping (Map 1; showing find-spots in southern 'settlement fringe', see Fig. 2.28) and, right, Alexander's 1975 plan.*

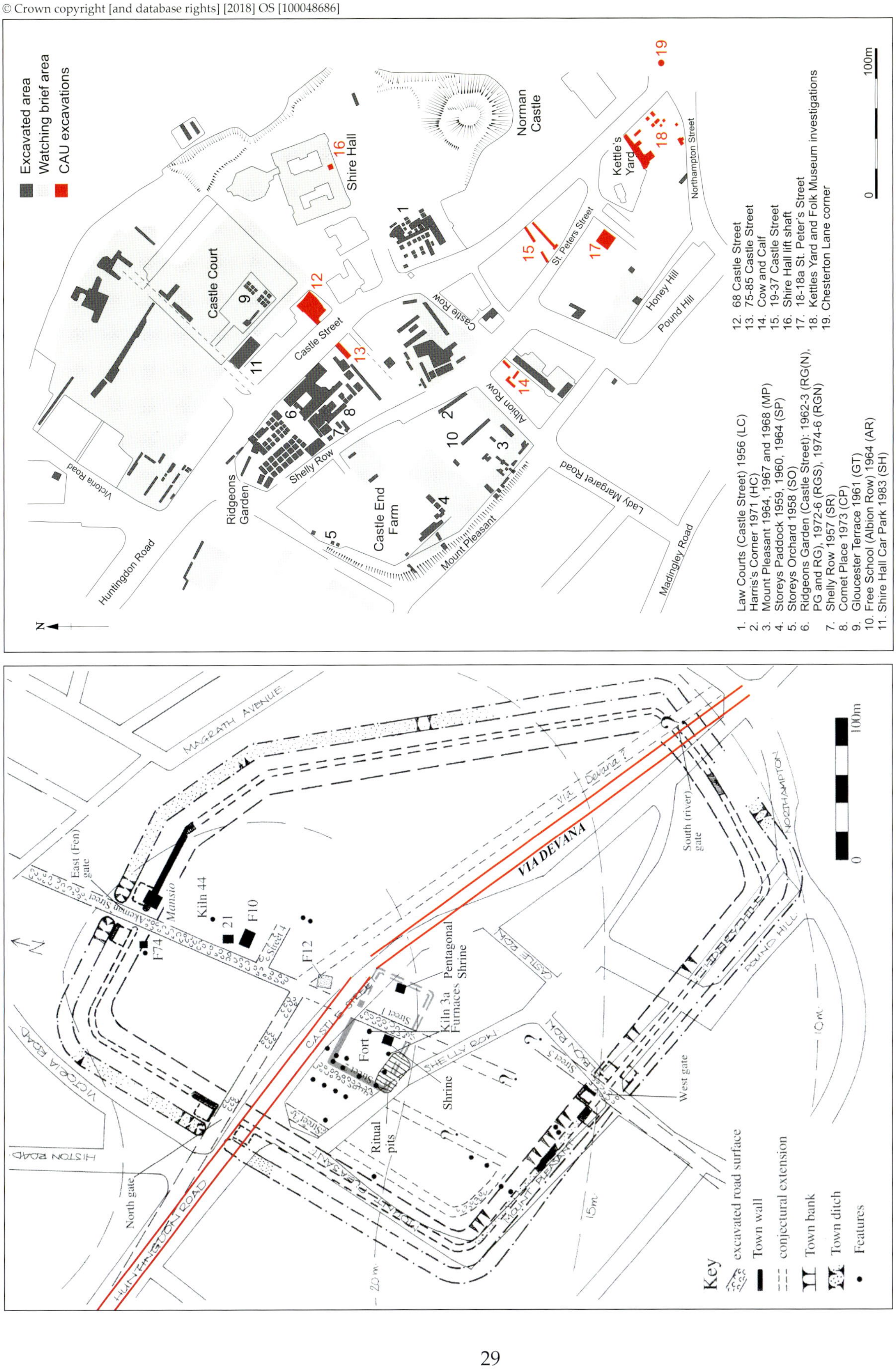

Figure 2.3. *Late* Roman Cambridge *phase plan, with revised route of* Via Devana *(left; after* RCAM, *fig. 7.2 and Evans & Ten Harkel, 2010, fig. 1) and, right, Urban Archaeological Data-base mapping of pre-1990 excavations with main later investigations added.*

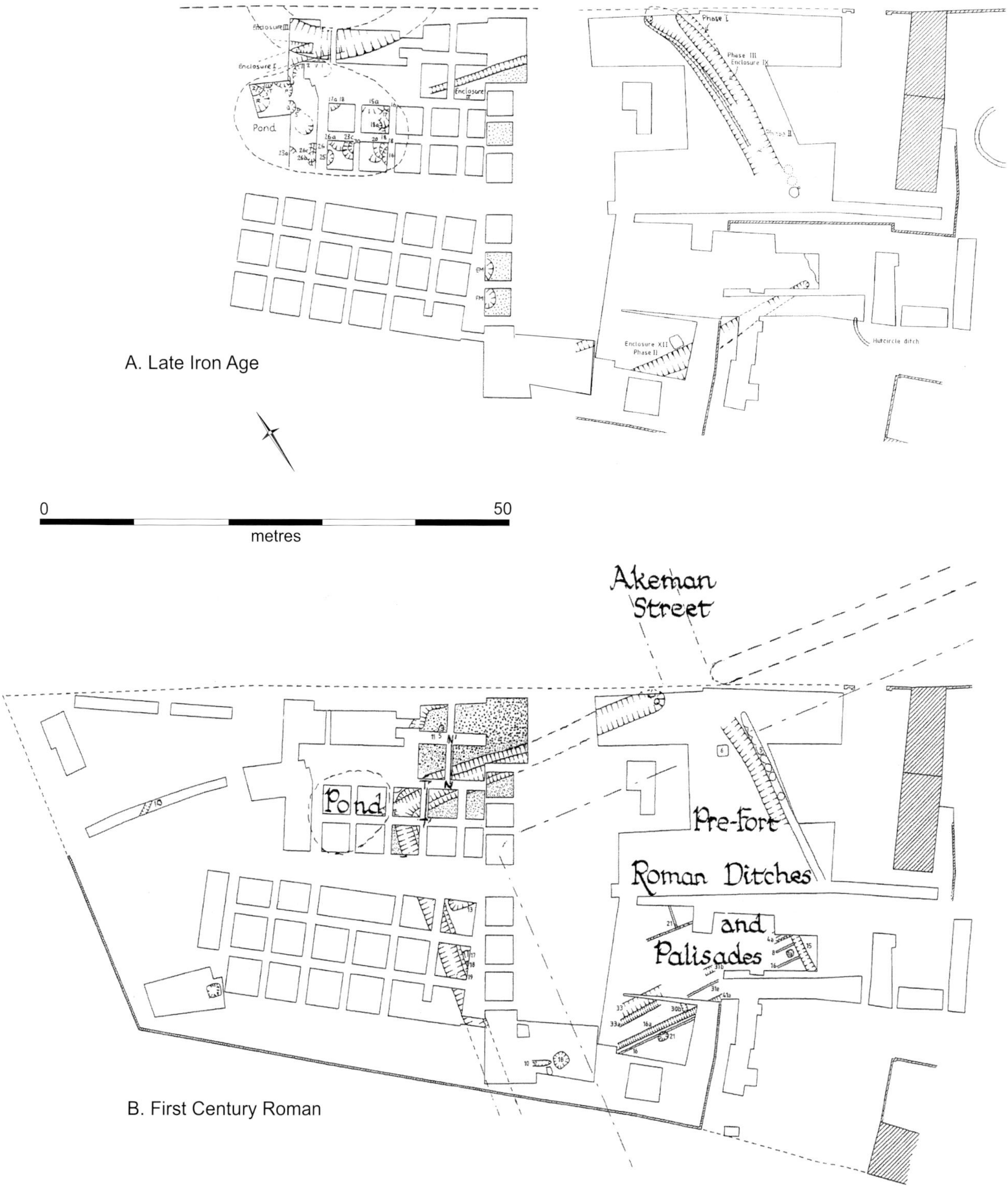

Figure 2.4 *(above and opposite). Ridgeons Garden, phase plans* (RCAM, *figs. 2.2, 2.7, 3.5, 4.3, 5.3 & 6.25).*

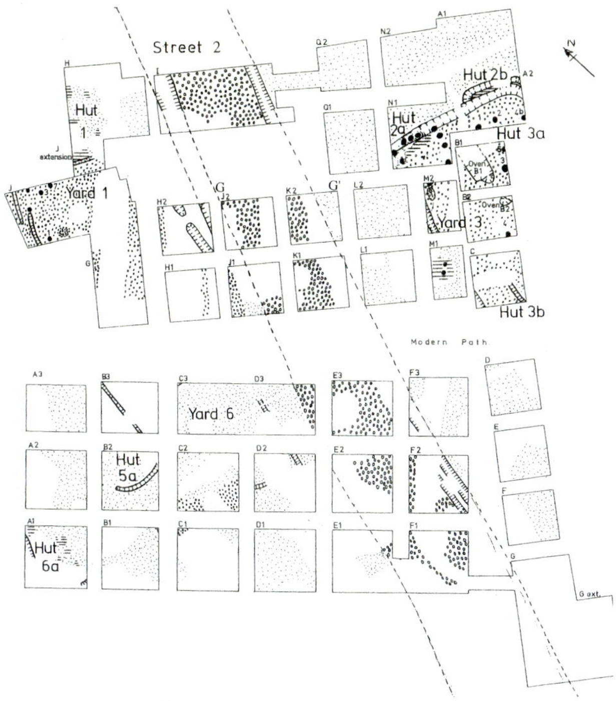

C. Second Century

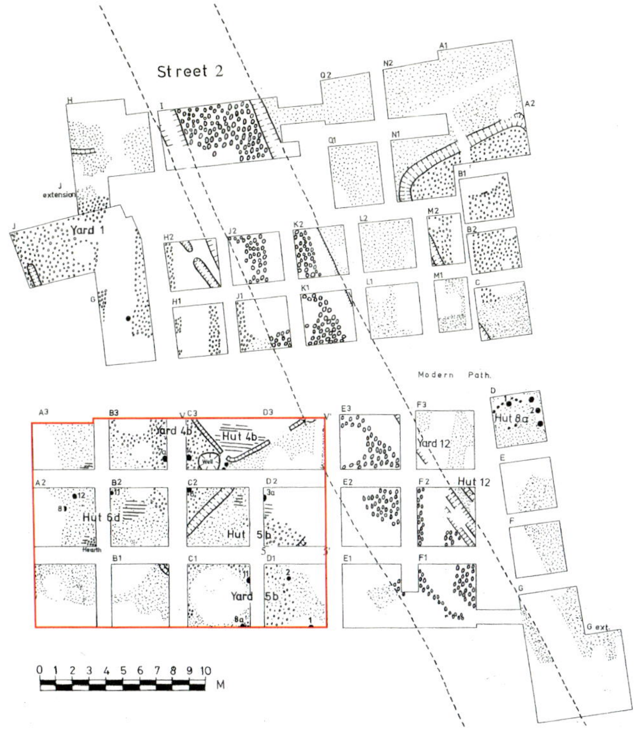

D. Fourth Century

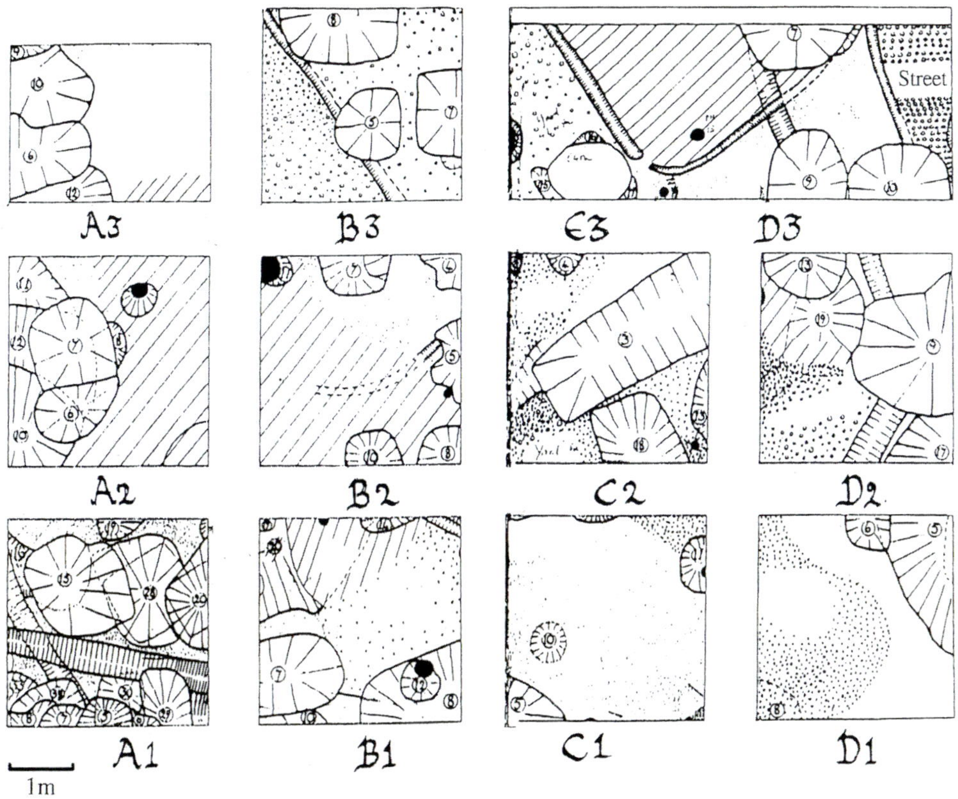

E. Late Third - early Fourth Century

plans is the density of its Late Roman occupation, which is also shown in a larger scale (Fig. 2.4.E; see also *RCAM*, 69–73, fig. 5.3). The later-phase plans of the subsequently dug eastern Ridgeons Garden simply do not feature in the book, despite the fact that its sections suggest *c.* 0.3–1 m depth of strata there (e.g. *ibid.*, figs. 4.13, 4.15, 5.8 & 5.10).

While there is almost no discussion of their respective methodologies, *Roman Cambridge* includes outline histories of the Alexander (*et al.*)-era excavations (*ibid.*, 12–15). Most of the fieldwork was undertaken on shoestring budgets, involving some 80 volunteers for a month *per annum* under the auspices of various training schools (W.E.A and the local Antiquarian Society Research Group, plus both Cambridge and London University's Extra-Mural Archaeological Summer Schools; see Fig. 2.5). Until the 1960s the main Ridgeons Garden, Shelley Row and Comet Place 'site block' had lain as nurseries and was dug as the land became free prior to any immediate threat of development. Although their Wheeler Box-technique can be difficult to fathom, from the published material it would seem that there had been had been greater control in Alexander's early 1960s sites – the main Ridgeons Garden 'box-grid' portion and Gloucester Terrace (see *RCAM*, fig. 2.3) – and this is apparent in the effort that went into the phasing matrix shown in Figure 2.6 (reproduced and explained in Alexander 1970, fig. 11, 71–4). For the most part, the later-dug portions do not seem to have seen such in-depth post-excavation analyses. That said, there is a 'cartoon' quality to even the plans of the Wheeler Box-areas. While the cut features change between Figure 2.4's second and fourth century AD versions (C & D), their horizontal spreads (road metalling and yards, *etc.*) remain constant.

In *Roman Cambridge* there are, in fact, no accurate location plans for a number of its key elements, such as the cellared shrine and 'ritual shafts' (see below; *RCAM*, figs. 4.14 & 5.7).[3] These are now plotted in Figure 2.7 using fixed-point information provided in a 1978 *Current Archaeology* interim (Selkirk & Selkirk 1978; archive plans have subsequently been located on which their plotting is confirmed). Notice, though, just how few features are shown within the west half of that area. Unfortunately, very little of Roman Cambridge's Akeman Street frontage seems to have been thoroughly excavated, with the 1983 Shire Hall Site providing the most convincing exposure (see Fig. 2.8 and *RCAM*, 23–4 & 40–2). Between what was exposed at Ridgeons Garden South and the minimal excavation accompanying the massive expansion of Shire Hall in the 1980s (*ibid.*, figs. 1.1, 2.12 & 2.13), within Roman Cambridge's walls approximately two-thirds of the street's length has gone.[4] This has enormous implications for any appraisal of the density of the settlement's buildings and greatly limits what can be said of the character of its occupation as a whole.

The manner in which the sites' second- and fourth-centuries AD sequence is portrayed in Figures 2.4.C and D begs, of course, the question of the third century AD. This phase plan has now been located within the archives and is reproduced here in its 'raw state' (Fig. 2.9). Inscribed '?Late C2nd/C3rd features', it basically represents an amalgam of all the minor features on the plans that date before and after. It is a crucial source on two counts. First, for what it tells of the post-excavation methodology: this is essentially a working base plan of all the post first-century AD Roman cut features, from which some have then been assigned to their respective centuries. Second, is the manner in which its buildings/'huts' and their plots are depicted. As shown here, Huts 2a/b appear somewhat larger and far more 'complete' as timber buildings than in the published plans. Indeed, this is the most convincing plan there is of the settlement's layout. It documents a series of rectilinear timber buildings, aligned northwest–southeast, on either side of the street (and parallel with it) that appear to be set within larger sub-rectangular/-ovoid ditched plots. Suggesting a much denser and regular settlement layout than any of the published phase plans (especially if Fig. 2.7's 'extra' buildings are added), here the problem is one of 'archival authority' and which version to trust. Issues relating to 'versions' also plagued our work with Mucking's archives (Evans *et al.* 2016a), but those were generally in a much better state than Cambridge's. This is further compounded here by the Wheeler Box-technique; few of the intervening baulks were evidently reduced and, accordingly, there is invariably ambiguity as to projection/connection of linear features between its squares.[5]

Taken as a whole, sadly there is a sense of far too many 'things missing' in Roman Cambridge/*Roman Cambridge*. As outlined below, this is not just a matter of its lack of public buildings but its archaeology generally. Where are the many minor features that one would have expected across the eastern half of the Ridgeons Garden (*et al.*) 'block'? Even the feature-sequence depicted in the 'assembled' base plan of the Shire Hall 1983/Trench VI exposure just to the north (Fig. 2.8) is no greater than would be expected on a dense rural settlement of the period. Yet, an illustrated Akeman Street section from the Shire Hall/Castle Court development swathe (edge-of-excavation?; Fig. 2.8) indicates that, at least locally, there were horizontal strata but which is largely unreported in *Roman Cambridge*. The unease of 'the missing' is only compounded by the

Figure 2.5. *Ridgeons Garden excavations: top, the 1960s hand-dug Wheeler Boxes and, below, one of the 1970s trench-areas (unspecified; notice the age of some of the training school participants). The photographs would suggest that these areas were generally machine-stripped to within 10–20 cm of the top of the natural. While the archives include plans of cut features and some surface deposits from those portions, most of these never appeared in the publication (nor do they seem to have ever been seriously worked through).*

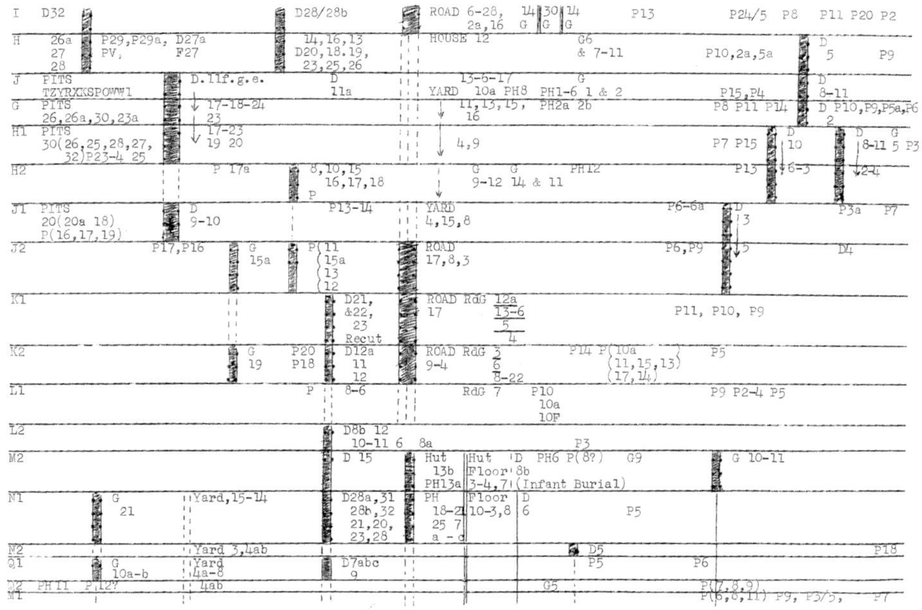

CAMBRIDGE EVENING NEWS, Tuesday, January [illegible], 1972

Roman Cambridge: Will the prize be lost?

by Rodney Tibbs

SHELLEY ROW, Mount Pleasant and Albion Row are all in an area which is steadily becoming more and more derelict. Usually dereliction in Cambridge signifies the meeting point of a past which is finished and a future which has not yet begun. But the Shelley Row area could be different. Beneath lies the largest exposed Roman site currently available for excavation in Britain.

A number of archaeologists I have spoken to are keen that work should get started. They point to one or two of the derelict buildings which remain and suggest that they would make excellent headquarters for such a dig. The prize, they say, would be a far greater knowledge of Roman Cambridge, for it is underneath this area on the side of Castle Hill that the Roman city was established.

SAXON

But digs cost money and money is something which can take a considerable amount of time to organise. Getting the priorities right for a further investigation of Roman Cambridge is not as easy as one might imagine. Dr. John Alexander, who has already carried out digs on the site, estimates that something like 28 digs have already been carried out there at various times in the past. If they were costed in full—in fact much time was devoted free—the figure would work out in the region of £[illegible].

He is far more concerned about Saxon Cambridge and those parts of early Cambridge which lie on the other side of the river. Here the problem is the reverse. Sites suitable for archaeological work do not become available all that often, and when they do the almost total disinterest on the part of Civic authorities and private owners makes satisfactory investigation extremely difficult. In the Lion Yard Market Hill area the opportunities of going underground are very restricted, consequently less is known about early occupation of the area.

On Castle Hill, however, it looks as though the area is likely to remain accessible for some time. Talks are still in progress between the city council and such majority of landowners as St. John's College and managements of such remaining items as the Storey's Charity. According to Mr. Maynard Brookes, of the City Planning Department, such talks are in an early stage. Cambridge could look forward to another characteristic period of desolation.

DILEMMA

In spite of the number of digs which have already been carried out at Castle Hill, relatively little is known about the general disposition of streets in the Roman town. The Roman defences are known to be responsible for the revetment or high bank which still exists on one side of Mount Pleasant. The upper part of Castle Street is believed to follow exactly the line of the Via Devana, now the Huntingdon Road, which clearly passed through the centre of the Roman town.

As far back as 1934 excavators considered that they had found one of the main gates of the Roman town while various walls and defences have come to light at various times.

Over the past ten years the work by Dr. John Alexander and his pupils has enabled a line to be drawn over a modern map with a fair degree of accuracy, although in the Magrath Avenue area it is conjectural. Roman defences, a bank and traces of a wall have now also been established and even traces of the west gate have been located at the junction of Mount Pleasant and Albion Row.

DEFENCES

But there are problems of pre-Roman occupation. Traces of habitation from an earlier period have been located in Gloucester Street behind the Shire Hall an area which, if current ideas are correct, lay within the later Roman wall.

If sufficient details of Roman occupation are not known, then this is certainly the case of later occupation. A curious gap appears in many places for that period when the Romans left and subsequent patterns of occupation had yet to be established and Cambridge is no exception.

The dilemma, therefore, is an acute one. To learn more of Anglo-Saxon Cambridge by endeavouring to gain access to those sites which come within council and individual jurisdiction, or to learn even more about a period which is a little better understood.

Money and resources are always the problem. However if, when Roman Cambridge is subsequently built over and its secrets remain out of reach for good, the 1970s will not be blessed by future investigators for ignoring such an opportunity.

Above: Dereliction and decay marks the site of the original Roman town, but the streets and houses still wait beneath the surface.

Figure 2.6. *Archive sources: top, portion of Alexander's Ridgeons Garden (1962/63) phasing matrix that, in total, extends over three A3 sheets; below 1972* Cambridge Evening News *account of Roman Cambridge's prospects. Aside from highlighting the lack of rescue excavations within the city's lower Medieval core, the article emphasizes the opportunity to excavate those portions of Castle Hill that still lay derelict, particularly the Shelley Row-area:*

> *"Money and recourses are always the problem" and "Dr. John Alexander, who has already carried out digs on the site, estimates that something like 28 digs have already been carried out there at various times in the past. If they were costed in full – in fact much time was devoted free – the figure would work out in the region of £26,000."*

Starting that year, the area was dug over four annual seasons (as Comet Place, and Ridgeons Garden South & North; RCAM, *13).*

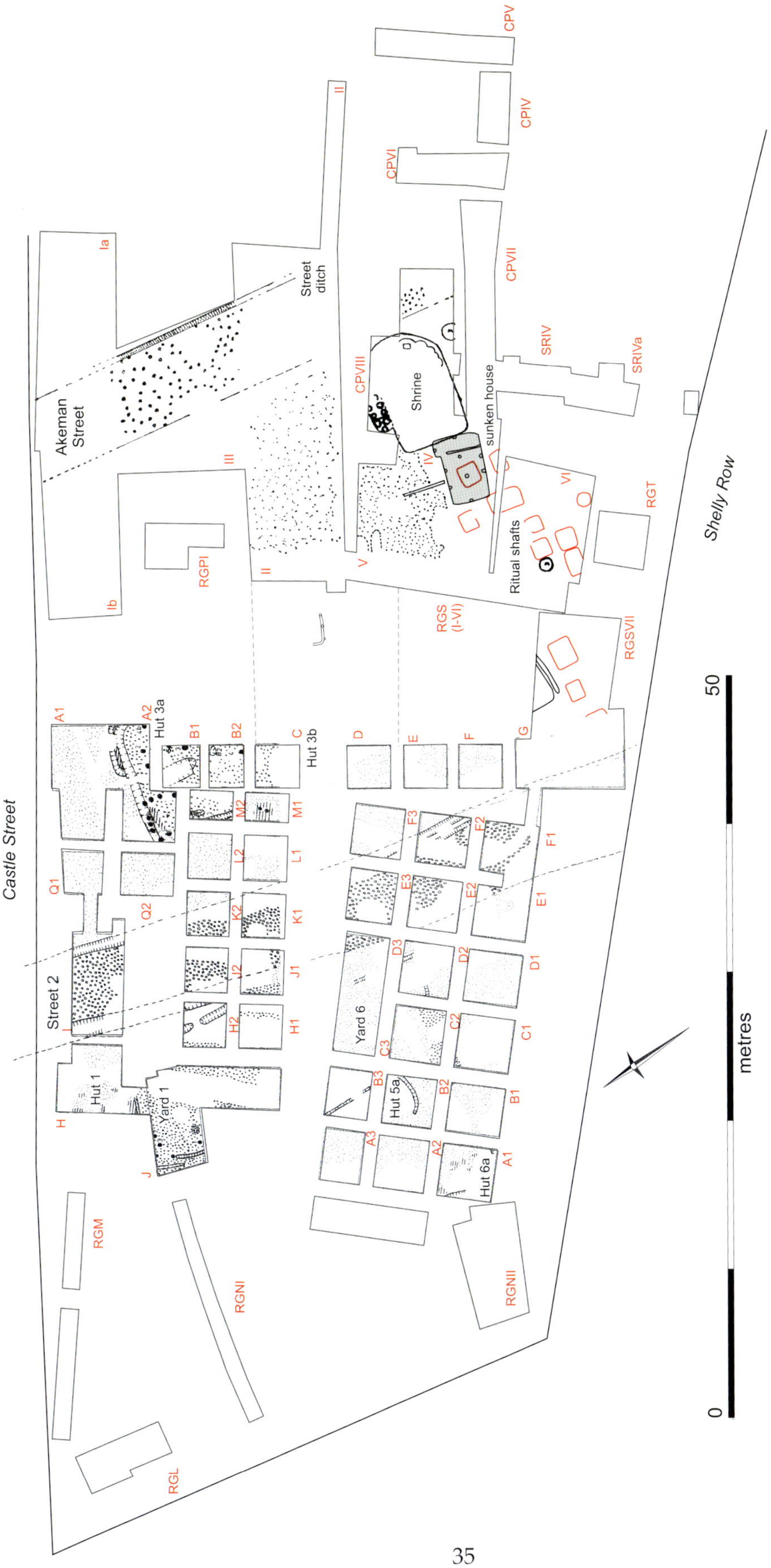

Figure 2.7. *The 'assembled' greater Ridgeons Garden* (et al.) *plan, showing second-century* AD *features (see Fig. 2.4.C) and incorporating* Current Archaeology*'s 1978 'fixed-pointed' shrine and ritual shaft plans (note their spatial interrelationship and alignment); shown here are two Romano-British buildings occurring on archival plans and, in grey-tone, the 'Late Sunken House' cellar (see Fig. 2.22). Probably relating to the cellared apsidal shrine's superstructure, also added from archival sources is 'timber slot 23' (ibid., 45).*

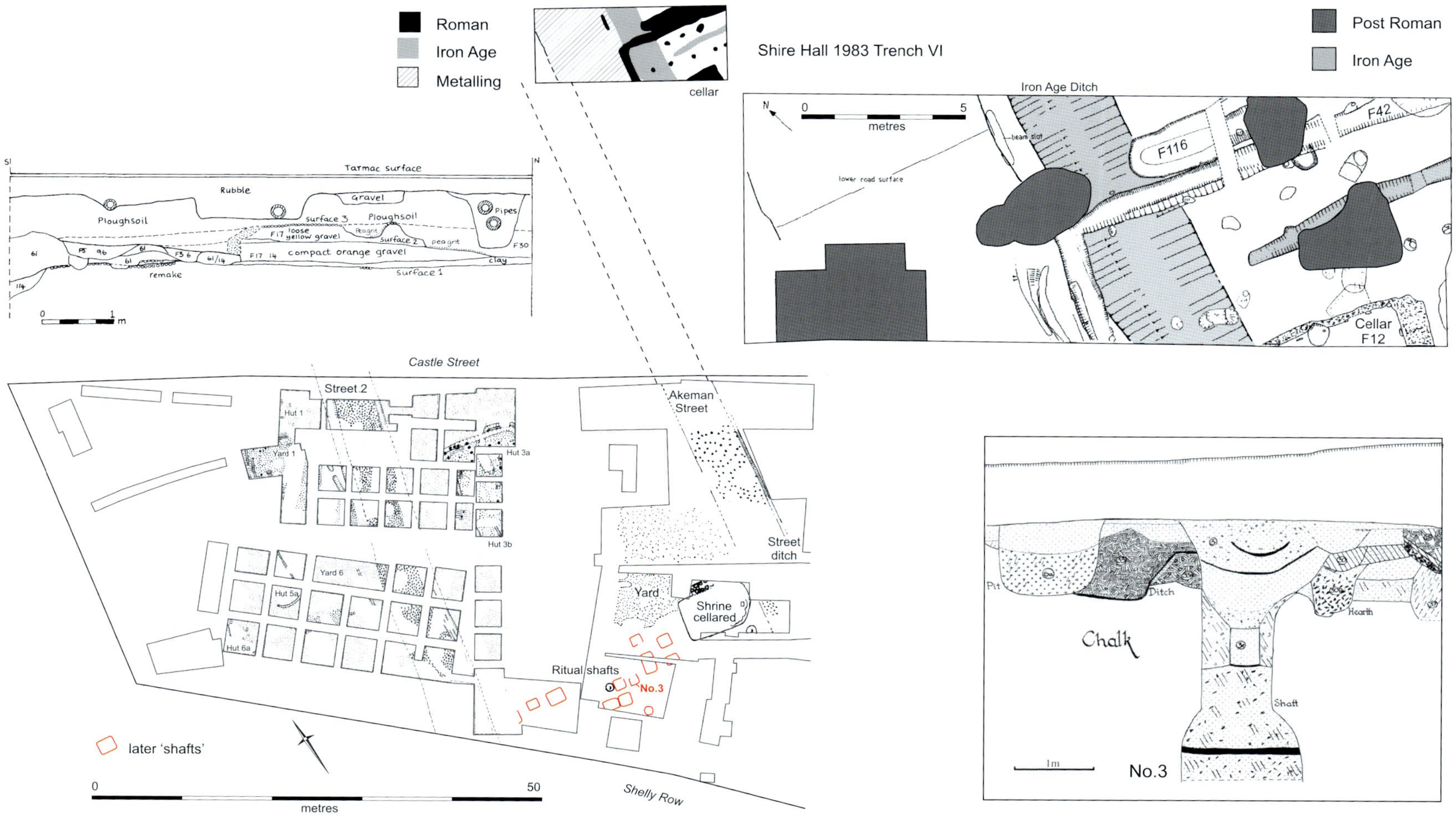

Figure 2.8. *Akeman Street archaeology. The line of Akeman Street is here projected from Ridgeons Garden to the Shire Hall 1983 Trench VI exposure. Inset upper right is the Shire Hall 1983/Tr. VI site's base plan as 're-assembled' (from* RCAM, *figs. 2.13 & 4.9). With Akeman Street's surface labeled,* Roman Cambridge *provides no information concerning the other features, aside from detailing Cellar F12 and the underlying 'Iron Age Ditch'* (ibid., *23–4 & 40–2). Presuming that ditches F42/116 mark the limits of the plot in which the cellared structure lay, their layout in relationship to the illustrated postholes could even suggest that the cellar was part of an elaborate courtyard-/atrium-type building. Note that the offset line of Akeman Street between the two sites may well reflect its staggering in relationship to the* Via Devana *which, based on Figure 2.3's plotting, would have fallen between them; inset lower right is Well/Shaft 3's section* (ibid., *fig. 5.8) and, upper left, the Akeman Street section from Castle Court (trench-location unspecified;* ibid., *fig. 3.10).*

Figure 2.9. *Late second-/third-century* AD *'raw' archive phase plan.*

total quantity of pottery estimated to have been recovered. In that volume said to be some 250,0000 sherds (*c.* 158,500 stratified; *RCAM*, 141), Jeremy Evans (*et al.*) suggest in a recent reappraisal that this is a considerable underestimate (2017, vol. 2, chap. 10, 2). Even taking into account the quantities that would have been generated from the 100% feature-excavation practices of the day (*vs.* sample-digging of linear features; Evans *et al.* 2016a, 2–5), this seems a huge amount and completely disproportionate to the archaeology outlined and illustrated in *Roman Cambridge*.[6]

Castle Hill-top Investigations – *Water Supply and Buildings* (with Marcus Brittain and Craig Cessford)

Since the time of the No. 68 Castle Street excavations and its published review of Early Roman Cambridge's sequence (Evans & Ten Harkel 2010), there have been few excavations within the area of the (walled) town proper of any consequence. One was undertaken in 2015 by Oxford Archaeology East within Shire Hall itself (Fig. 2.3) and related to the construction of a lift shaft (*c.* 2.5 × 3.10 m; Rees 2016). All seemingly of early to mid first-century AD date – the Late Iron Age/Roman transition – an intense three-phase sequence was revealed involving successive ditch and occupation horizons. Aside from more 620 sherds of pottery (all pre-Flavian), including both imported Terra Nigra and Terra Rubra (but not samian; see *Inset*, below), a Colchester brooch (along with fragments of probably another copper alloy brooch) and a simple iron bow brooch were recovered. Its animal bone assemblage (375 pieces) was dominated by sheep/goat; also found were 31 fish bones and a small quantity of marine shellfish, and, taken as a whole, the evidence could suggest a relatively high-status settlement.

Another recent excavation of note related to an extension to the Kettle's Yard Gallery, initially in 2011 and then, again, in 2015 (Cessford 2011; Brittain & Evans 2016), and its findings warrant reporting in some detail. The first of these investigations occurred within the cellars of Numbers 4–5 Castle Street (with a 3.3 m deep Medieval and later stratigraphic sequence dug in the yard behind; Fig. 2.10). With the buildings still standing and space restricted, this only permitted 'keyhole' work; nevertheless, it revealed first- to fourth-century AD Romano-British deposits.

The hillside's natural topography proved steep (*c.* 1 in 4) and over the length of the trenches the character of geological gravel strata varied: downslope, to the southeast, they were loose and, subject to collapse, contained perched groundwater, which in the past had evidently created boggy conditions (see Fig. 2.15). Until the early/mid third century AD the area seems to have seen midden-like make-up deposition and an unusual clay deposit had locally been inserted, perhaps in order to plug a loose seam in the gravels from which groundwater flowed freely. Probably relating to the establishment of town's fourth-century AD defences, there then had been a major act of terracing to create a flat expanse: where firm natural gravels were exposed these were utilized and, otherwise, a robust cobble surface had been laid. This only appears to have been used briefly, perhaps for just a few decades and, thereafter, further wet 'sticky' deposits occurred (dated by a mid fourth-century AD coin).

Only a relatively small pottery assemblage was recovered from this fieldwork phase (136 sherds). Spanning the Roman period (peaking in the mid first–second centuries AD), it generally comprised medium- and large-sized sherds as reflected in its high mean sherd weight (MSW) of 28.3 g. Although the animal bone was not particularly distinguished, both charred and waterlogged plant remains occurred in the environmental bulk samples. The cereals consist of spelt (*Triticum spelta*) and rye (*Secale cereale*), while herbs possibly used in cooking included watercress (*Apium* sp.), linseed (*Linum usitatissimum*) and black mustard (*Brassica nigra*); opium poppy (*Papaver somniferum*) was also recovered. Probably incidentally harvested alongside the cereals, the wild seeds suggest that damp, fertile, clay-rich soils were being cultivated. With the latter observations having obvious implications for western Cambridge's Roman *clayland* settlements as regards the town's food supply, evidence of this had also been identified in the Castle Street Site's samples (Evans & Ten Harkel 2010, 51).

The subsequent, 2015 investigations occurred within the area of the Gallery proper (Brittain & Evans 2016) which, in part, represented an extension to the 1994 excavations along the Gallery's eastern side (see below and summary in *RCAM*, 255–6).[7] Aside from excavating a deep sequence within its western entrance patio, in 2015 two areas were dug within the building's footprint: B and C (Fig. 2.10). The latter involved a 4 m long trench within the cellar of the then still standing Gallery. When its floor was removed only truncated geological clay natural was exposed (lying at *c.* 7.35 m OD) and, despite the use of deep test pits, *no evidence whatsoever was found there of the town's Late Roman defensive ditch* (see Fig. 2.15). This finding is of significance as it relates to Hogg's 1949 Northampton Street exposure of its line, whose 'spatial fixing' is somewhat ambiguous (Fig. 2.11; RCHME 1959, no. 15). Apparently dug on behalf of the University Archaeological Field Club, the ditch section he exposed was *c.* 12 m wide and 2.6 m deep, with a flat base 3.6 m across. As 'officially plotted', the ditch should have been present within our basement-area trenches; the berm between its line and the wall elsewhere being 4–10 m (see Fig. 2.3 and below; *RCAM*, 58–68).[8]

Some 2.5 m wide and surviving 0.5 m high, the wall itself was exposed by Woudhuysen and Pullinger in 1984 during the Gallery's construction (Fig. 2.11; *RCAM*, 15).[9] Unfortunately their trenches were also not plotted with any precision (*ibid.*, 65, fig. 6.17) and they have simply been 'fixed' as best we can in Figure 2.10. This does seem to work, as in our Area A patio-exposure the wall's deep Medieval robbing cut was present (its profile thereafter being subject to intense pitting).

The question then is why the ditch was not present within our trenches. As shown on Figure 2.14's section, the upper edge of a cut-line was visible along the eastern lower side of our patio-area trench (F.117) and was sealed by rubble deriving from the wall. As exposed in the south section, the cut was *c.* 0.7 m deep with a flat base lying at *c.* 7.8 m OD and just *c.* 0.5 m above the depth of the truncation level in our Area C section. While other interpretations are conceivable (e.g. some manner of settlement boundary-marking), this probably represents the western side of the terracing cut observed in the section at Numbers 4–5 Castle Street. Probably pre-dating the construction of the wall itself, based on this the terrace would have been some 14.5 m wide. In relationship to it – and the top of the (truncated) marl geology exposed in the 1994 pathway-side section (*c.* 11.5 m OD; Figs. 2.13 & 2.15) – it is estimated that the eastern wall-face would then have stood 'proud' to a height of some 3 m below the level of the upslope natural ground-slope. Although it is possible that the defensive ditch ran in the 8.75 m gap between our Area C and 4–5 Castle Street exposures, based on its projected line (we could not dig there due

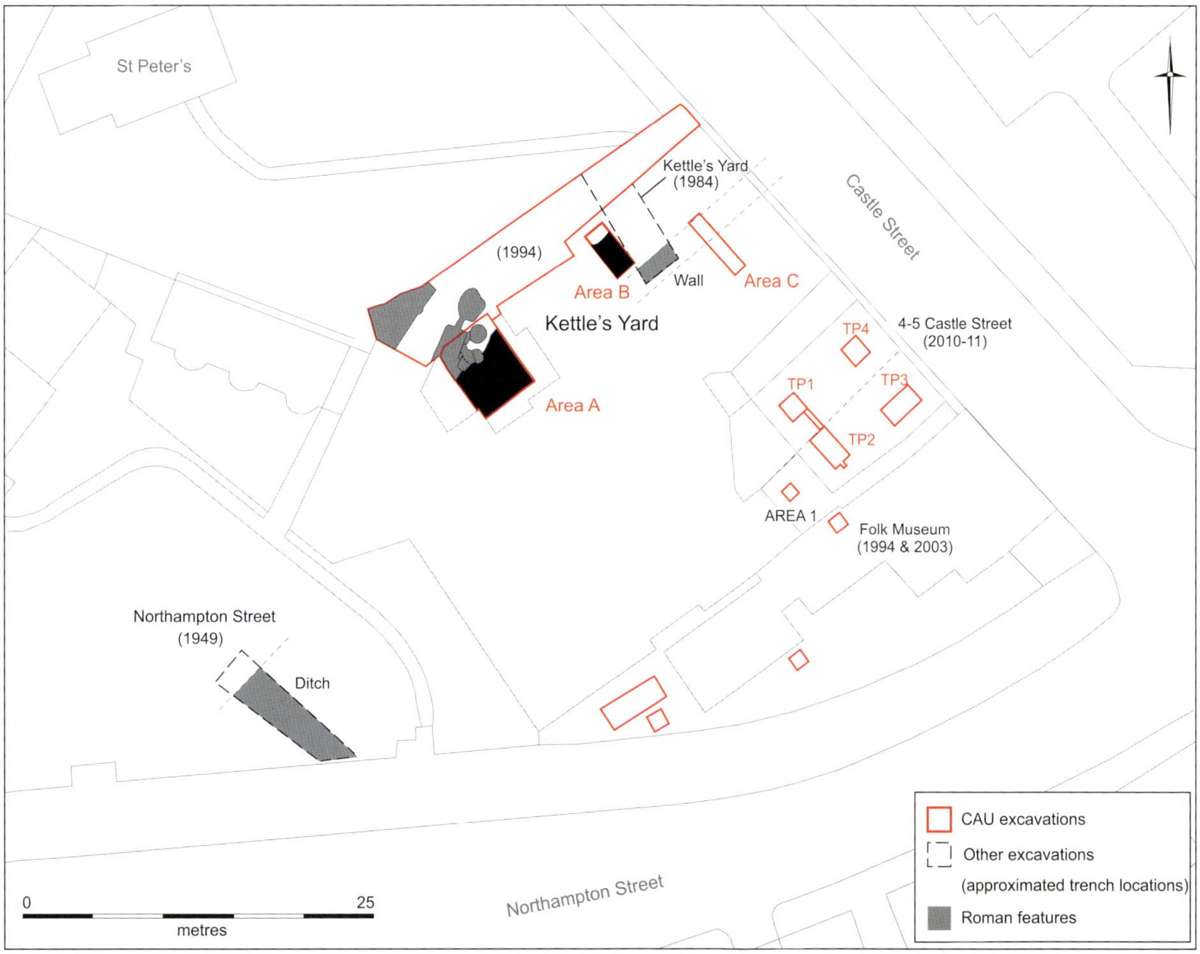

Figure 2.10. *Kettle's Yard: Top, photograph looking up Castle Hill from Chesterton Lane corner, with Folk Museum/ Museum of Cambridge at far left and the rebuilt Kettle's Yard Gallery behind (note the pillar centre-right, which is Michael Fairfax's sculpture representing 'Layers of Cambridge History' and marks the 2000 Chesterton Lane Corner excavations); below, Kettle's Yard, plan showing the CAU's three excavation areas, with Woudhuysen and Pullinger's 1984 trench indicated (*RCAM, *fig. 6.17).*

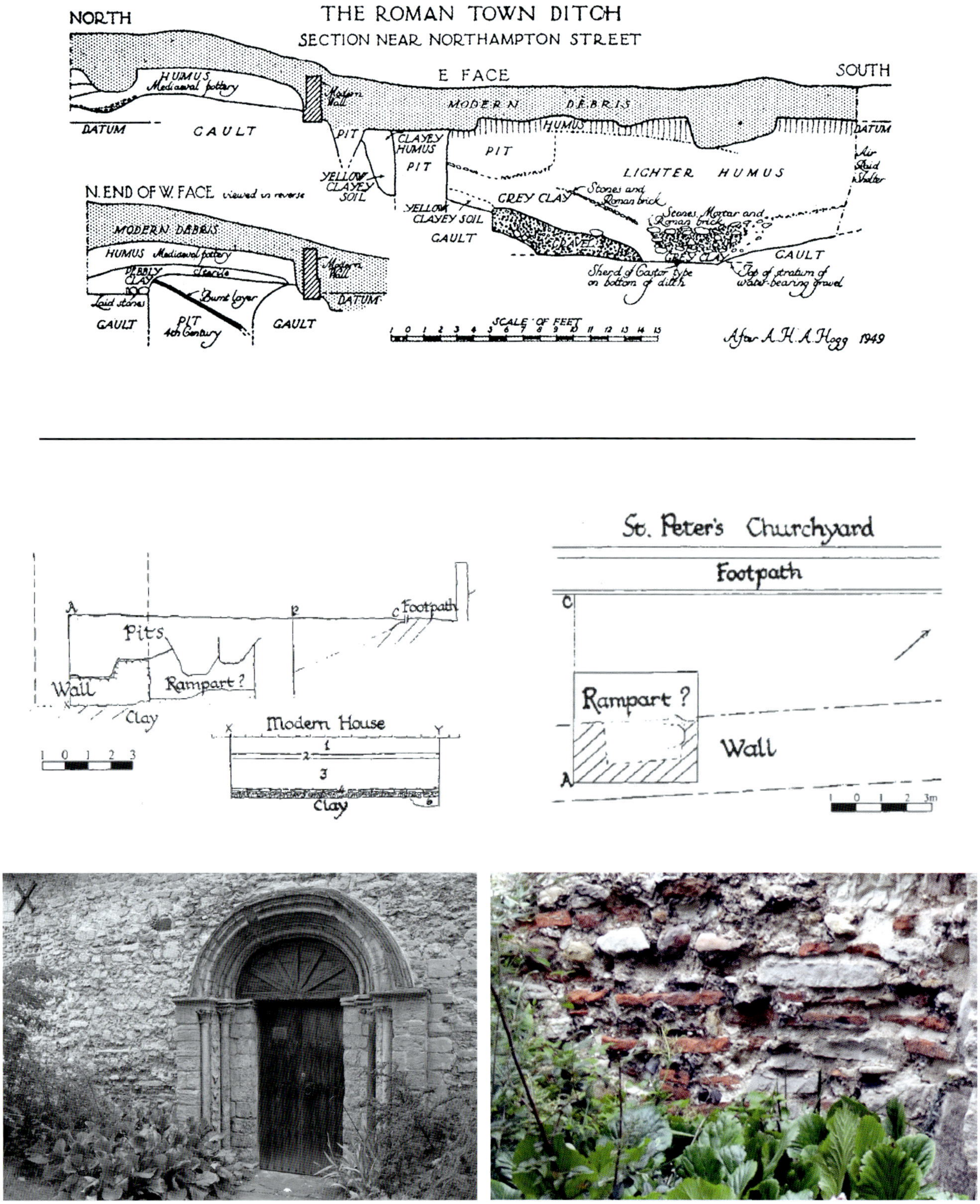

Figure 2.11. *Earlier investigations and church fabric: Hogg's 1949 Northampton Street trench across the Roman defensive ditch (top); plan and section of 1984 Kettle's Yard exposure of the Roman Wall* (RCAM, *fig. 6.17; middle); bottom, St Peter's Church. Thought to originally date to the twelfth century, the church has been extensively rebuilt; notice the re-used Roman tiles within the lower fabric on the left-side of doorway (left), with detail of such, right.*

Figure 2.12. *Site photographs: the patio-area (Area A), top right, looking northwest with St Peter's Church in background and, below, looking southwest; top right, the 1994 trench with rammed footing.*

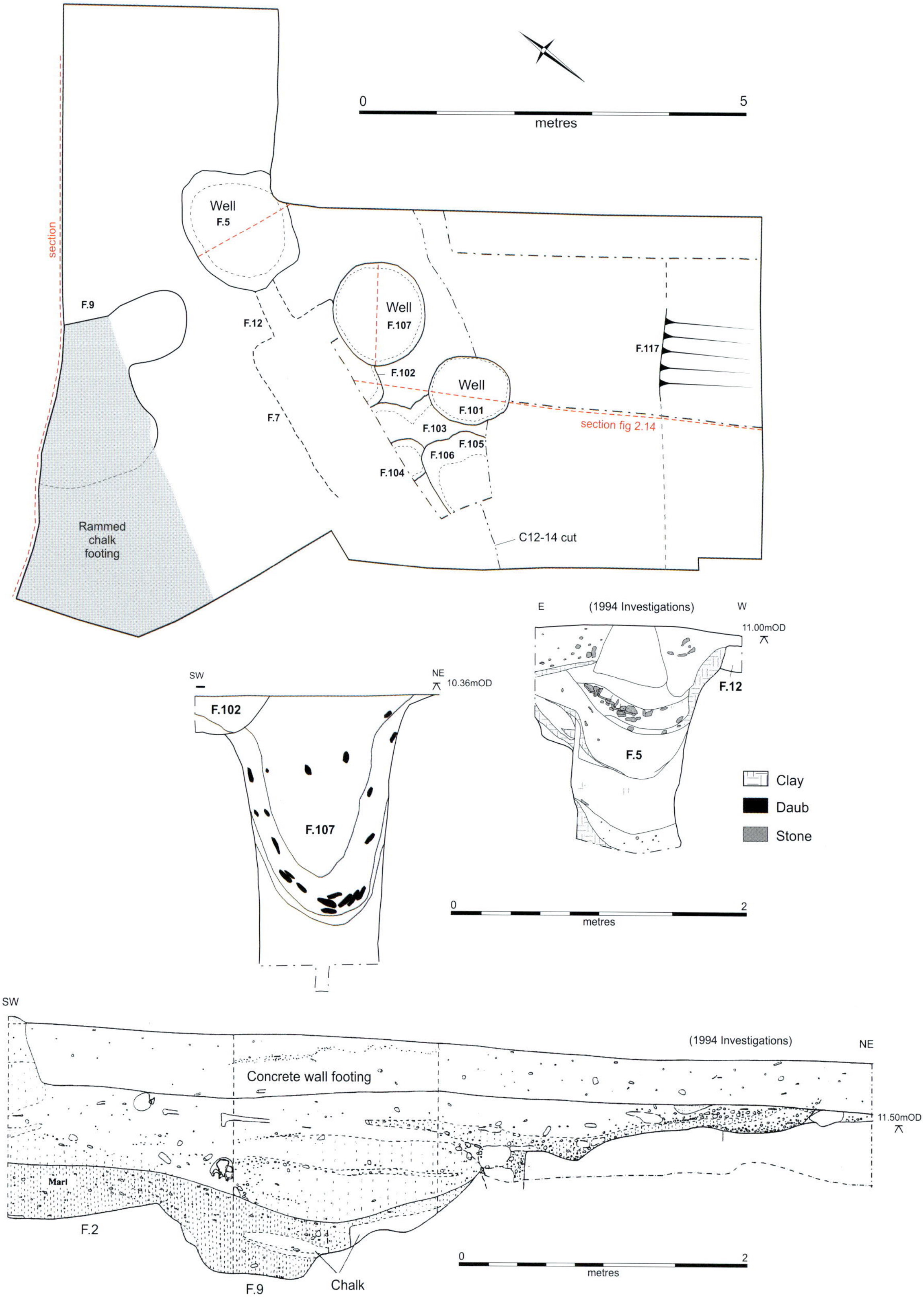

Figure 2.13. *Combined 1994 and 2015 patio-area site plans, with 1994 pathway-side section indicated and including, above right, wells F.5 and F.107's sections.*

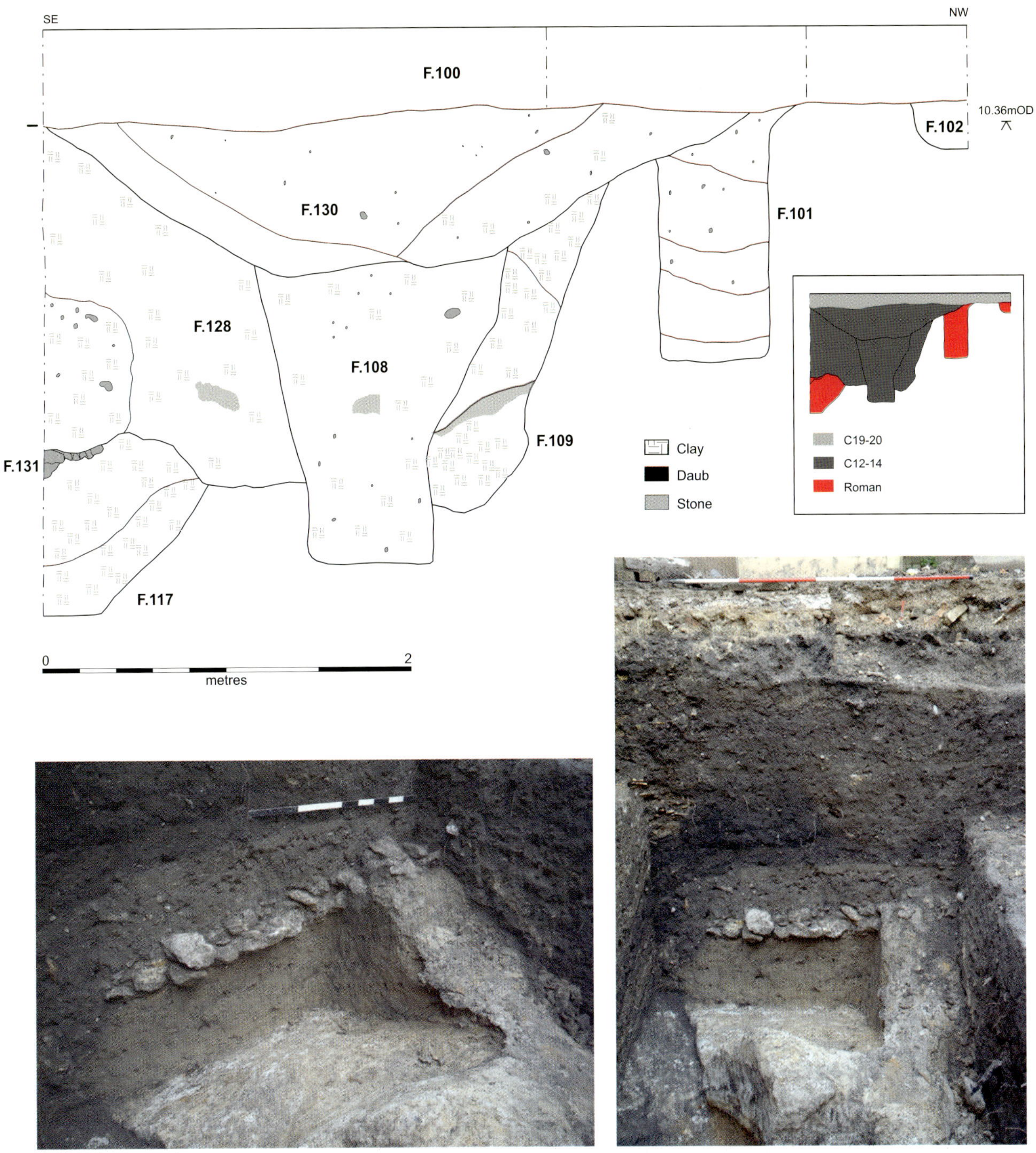

Figure 2.14. *Area A, the patio-area south section and, below, photographs showing wall-related rubble sealing F.117's terrace-truncation cut.*

to a passageway and load-bearing walls; there was no evidence of any building subsidence), the downcut face of the wall may itself have been sufficient defensive barrier. Accordingly, the ditch there may not have been considered necessary, especially as the terracing could have supplied enough upcast for its rampart. Also, because of the very active groundwater flow in this area, a ditch at this point would probably have been subject to rapid collapse and could even have threatened to undermine the wall.

Of pressing importance is the evidence of the immediate area's earlier Roman occupation. This

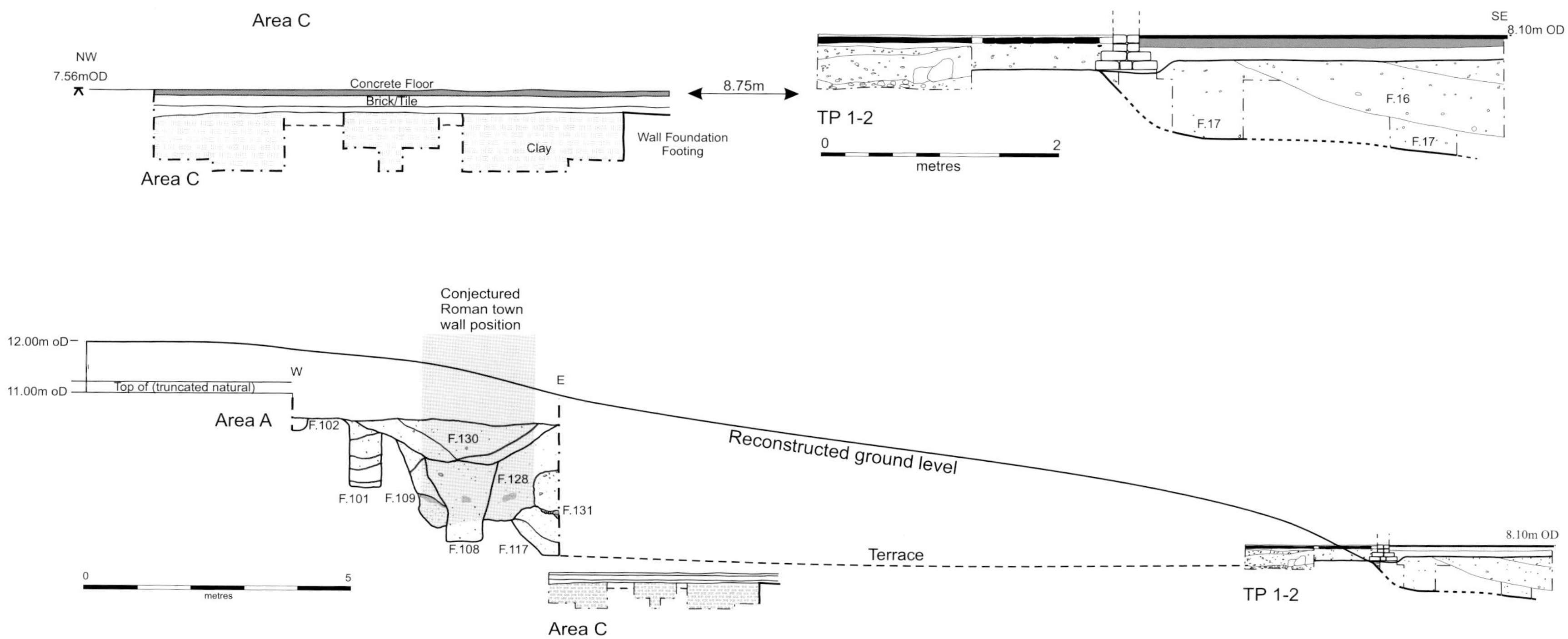

Figure 2.15. *Hill-slope sections: top, Area C section shown relative to 2011 TP1–2 section; below, combined cross-site section/elevation depicting the terrace truncation and wall reconstruction. As shown, based on the cut's stratigraphic sequence, it seems likely that the wall here could only have been c. 2.20 m wide. Even given this, it is difficult to understand the nature of F.117's fill below the eastern foot of the wall. It suggests that either the terracing had nothing to do with the wall's construction or, if related, then this fill might have occurred behind a masonry kerb along/below the wall's foot; this then would probably have lain some 1 m or more beyond the wall-face (and our edge-of-excavation). Lower section shows projection of Area C's and TP1–2's sections.*

amounted to an extension of what had been exposed by the CAU in 1994 within the pathway west of the building (Evans 1994; *RCAM*, 255–6). The main feature then present was a robust rammed masonry foundation (F.2); due to its limited exposure there was some question of whether this might relate to the defences or a high status building (Figs. 2.12–13). Directly south of it were features that were then thought to be associated with a 'water-based processing facility', with one (F.5) a 1.5 m+ deep, circular 'shaft' (1.4 m across) and, clearly, a well.

Two comparable shaft-wells were found nearby in the 2015-area (Fig. 2.13). The smaller, F.101, was 0.7 m in diameter and 1.3 m deep; the other, F.107, was 1.4 m across and 1.9 m deep (*c.* 0.7 m+ should be added to the original depths of these features as a result of the 1994 path-level truncation). While in themselves significant features, equally important was the manner of their infilling and assemblages. F.107 had been backfilled with over 105 kg of substantial slabs of applied clay wall-rendering (Fig. 2.17) and they contained five semi-complete pottery vessels between them (four in F.101; Fig. 2.16).

With this walling material constituting the majority of the fill's matrix, lesser quantities occurred in other features within this cluster (including well F.101). A 'pargeting' form of render, in most instances the clay had been applied against reed-lathes (others involved wattle) and then rolled in keyed chevron/herringbone patterns (Fig. 2.18). (A copper alloy finger-ring found

Figure 2.16. *Site finds (from top): Nene Valley colour-coat hunt-cup; samian vessel stamp, Africanus II (*AD *155–180); semi-complete pots from wells F.101 and F.107; finger-ring embedded within clay-render. As reported by Mazzilli, including the material from the 1994 excavations, 682 Roman sherds were recovered (16,018 g), with the majority dating to the late first–second centuries* AD *(63.5%), with* c. *22 and 14 per cent respectively assigned to the second–third and mid/late third–fourth centuries* AD*. Non-local Late Roman finewares are rare (three sherds each of Hadham red-slipped ware and Nene Valley colour-coated, plus two parchment ware sherds); Central Gaulish Samian formed four per cent of the total assemblage (27 sherds), with a second such vessel also being stamped (Felicio IV:* AD *110–150).*

Of note within the site's Roman-feature animal bone studied by Vida Rajkovača was the occurrence of a Mallard bone and another from an unidentified wader bird, with well F.107 having the remains of a partial dog skeleton (juvenile).

Figure 2.17. *Pargeting wall-render within well F.107.*

Figure 2.18. *Pargeting-render, showing reed-lathe and rolled chevron impressions; notice below the impression of twine that had evidently been used to bind the reeds to the wall's timber frame.*

embedded within the clay of one of the pieces had probably slipped off during the material's preparation; Fig. 2.16.) With the faced wall-rendering evidently having been carried on a timber framework, this type of application is variously found in villas and first–second-century AD urban contexts, such as Colchester, Verulamium and London (Perring 1999, 94; see also Wallace 2015, 86) and would certainly indicate that a high-status building stood nearby. A single fragment of lime-based wall plaster was also present in the fill of F.107 (as was an imported rotary lava quernstone). Although just one fragment of tile was found (a *pila*), amongst the other building materials recovered was mortar (1.5 kg; including *opus caementicum*), large iron nails (up to *c.* 90 mm length) and a lead flashing. There were also fragments of largely unworked Lincolnshire ragstone, but these mainly occurred in Medieval features and must have derived from the robbing of the defensive wall.[10] That said, the upper profile of the earlier excavated well (F.5) had horizons of ragstone fragments dumped into it (plus eroded sandy mortar and large pottery sherds).

A number of salient points arise from the recent Kettle's Yard investigations. First, with the rammed footing and the site's quantity of patterned wall-render slabs, there can be no doubt that we are seeing the remains of a very impressive high-status building.[11] This is given further credence by the large Roman bricks/tiles visible within the lower fabric of St Peter's Church immediately 'above' the courtyard-area exposure. Although clearly reset within the church's fabric and not *in situ*, it is the only location within the city where, as it were, Roman Cambridge can actually be seen (see Fig. 2.11). Second, the manner of that structure's demolition – especially the 'purity' of the mass-dumped building materials – seems a distinctly 'urban-type behaviour'. It is the kind of thing widely encountered, for example, in Roman London, but nothing like it has been found in all the Unit's years of digging major Roman rural settlements.

There is another issue to address: *water supply*. A very basic need, this is highlighted through the clustering of the site's wells and, as evinced in the flow of groundwater within the cellars of Numbers 4–5 Castle Street, it is surely not coincidental that these are found on this 'mid-slope' location at the spring-line interface of marl and clay.

Siting a town on a hill-top, although defensively sensible, can make the obtaining of water difficult. Unless otherwise somehow 'introducing' water (e.g. via aqueducts), deep wells are the only realistic option; something it is known that the Romans were entirely capable of (for example, one at Mucking was more than 15 m deep: Lucy & Evans 2016, 40–6). Though some were sub-square, as at Kettle's Yard, Castle Hill's earlier excavated wells generally consisted of vertical-sided circular shafts (0.95–1.35 m diam.), some having evidence of timber linings. With recorded depths ranging from 0.7 m to 6.40 m, but with none of the deeper ones actually bottomed – they would probably have needed to go down 8–9 m to reach the permanent watertable (see Fig. 2.19) – in two instances their lower profiles 'belled' outwards and foot-/hand-holes had been cut into the chalk marl sides to facilitate access (Fig. 2.20; *RCAM*, 29, 32, 44–5, 53–3 & 72, figs. 4.13 & 5.5). In one, an infant had been set into its backfill and, from another, a human femur was recovered (respectively, RGS VI, Wells 16 & 25). Dug to 3.5 m depth (but not bottomed), the deepest *shaft* at Ridgeons Garden South – Number 3 – also had a lower 'belling' profile (see Fig. 2.8). Admittedly, this may have originally functioned as a well; its final assignation as a 'ritual shaft' was based on the fact that within its fills had been placed a small wooden coffin/casket wherein an infant's mandible survived, with the rest of the body apparently recorded as a stain (*ibid.*, 53–4, fig. 5.8).

This latter well occurred amidst a series of 'ritual shafts', dating to the third–fourth century AD and up to 3.5 m deep, at the same site (see Fig. 2.8 and *RCAM*, fig. 5.7). Each that was fully excavated apparently included both the burial of a mature dog and a human infant, in some instances two children. In total, thirteen such infant burials were recorded, with five accompanied by studded shoe fragments said to have fitted five- to six-year-olds (*ibid.*, 53–6, figs. 5.9–14). It is difficult to fully evaluate these findings.[12] In most cases the children were only represented by a few bones, mainly mandible fragments, which itself is surprising as bone survival should have been good in Castle Hill's marls. In any case, this certainly attests to cult activity and suggests an interrelationship between the wells and the 'shafts'. It may have been that some of the latter could even perhaps have started as wells and when they failed to achieve year-round water at such shallow depths, ritual appeasement may have been made to gods to ensure/return the water supply. Apart from the very deep Shaft/Well 3, the shafts were all much shallower than the main wells; of sub-square/rectangular plan (*vs.* the circular form of the wells) and seemingly aligned behind the apsidal shrine (Fig. 2.8), they do seem to have been dug as a distinct ritual expression.

Directly connecting the second-century AD apsidal shrine (see below and Fig. 2.8) and the later shafts, in discussing *Roman Cambridge* Taylor fore-fronted cult activity as amongst the settlement's main functions (*ibid.*, 78–80). While ritual was undoubtedly a significant component – as it is now known to be on many Roman-period sites (see e.g. Chap. 6 below) – there

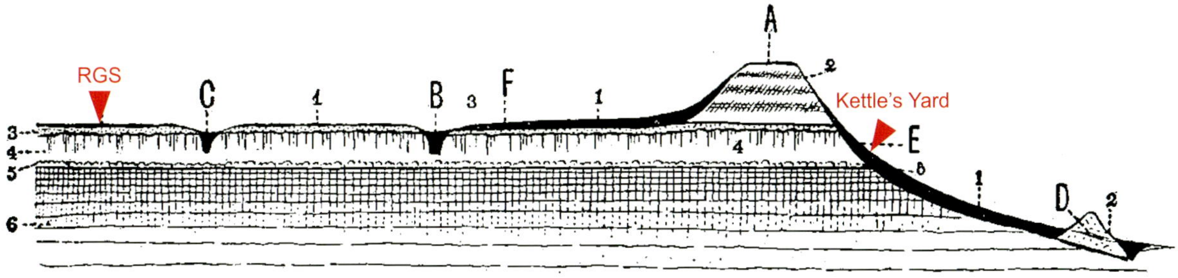

Fig. 2. Section N.E. and S.W. through the Burh. Length of section, 380 yards.

1. Talus and later made earth.
2. Earlier made earth of mound and rampart.
3. Pleistocene gravel.
4. Chalk.
5. Phosphate bed at base of Chalk.
6. Gault.
A. The mound.
B First fosse of Burh.
C. Second fosse of Burh.
D. Bank in Magdalene College grounds.
E. Position of tunnel where solid chalk was pierced after passing through made earth.
F. Position of excavation for new house, see p. 175.

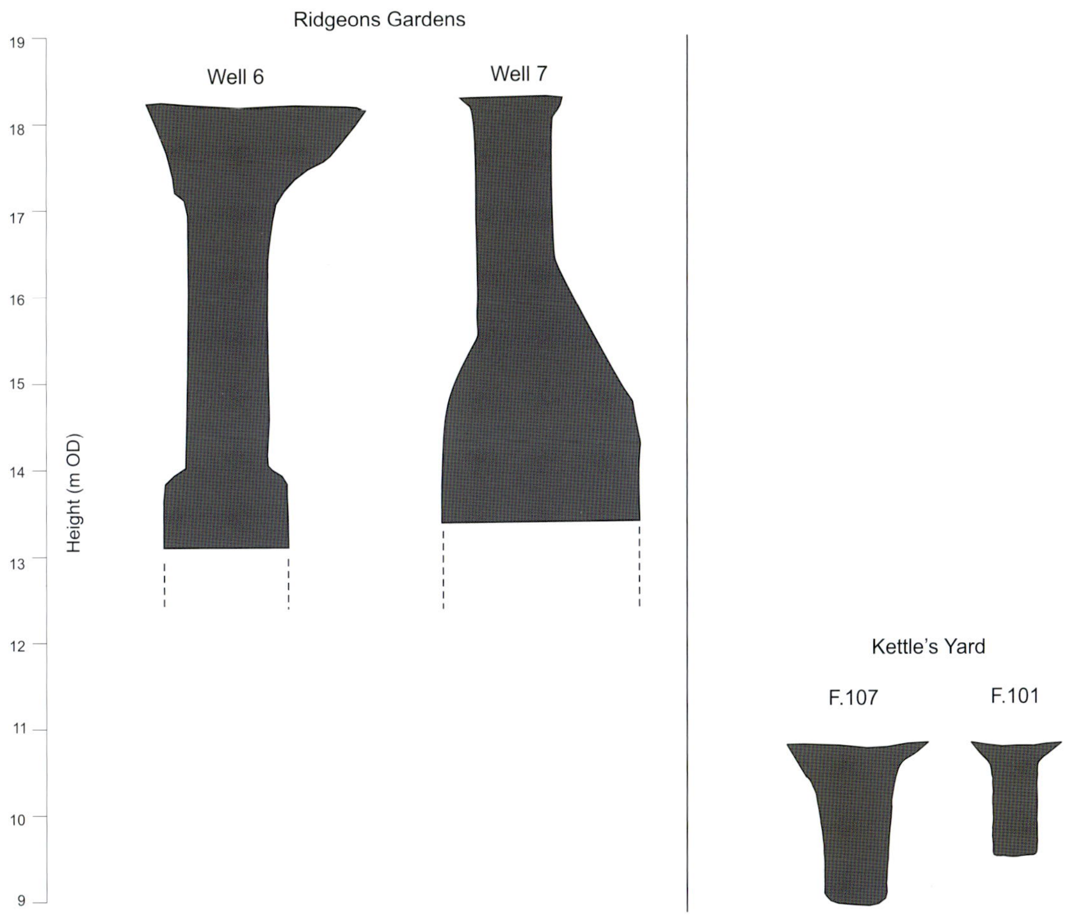

Figure 2.19. *Hughes' schematic geological section through Castle Hill and its mound (top; 1904, fig. 2); below, relative elevation depths of Kettle's Yard and Ridgeons Garden wells (see Fig. 2.20).*

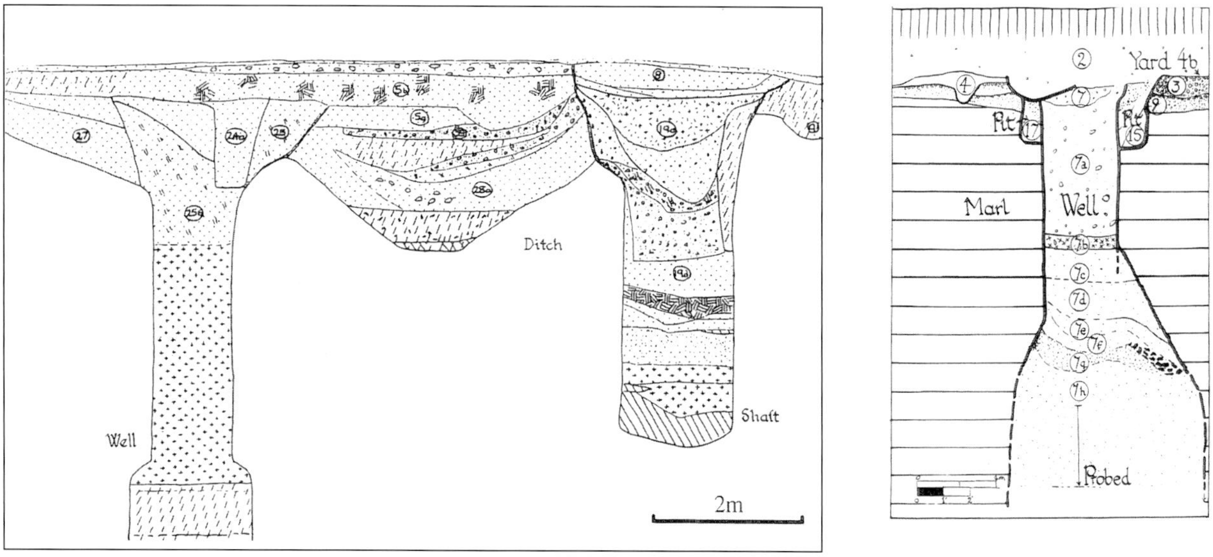

Figure 2.20. Roman Cambridge, *well sections: Well VI (25) and Pit VI (19; left) and, right, Well 7 (top;* RCAM, *figs. 4.13 & 5.5).*

seems no convincing basis to accredit it as Roman Cambridge's prime function.[13]

Evidence of recent Cambridge early settlement findings beyond its walls will be presented below. Here, though, it is worth briefly reviewing the structural evidence recovered within the earlier excavations. It is difficult to present any meaningful overview of the town's earlier excavated buildings. In *Roman Cambridge* no attempt was made to either illustrate or gazetteer them all and although 24 'Houses' are enumerated, the usage of that appellation – along with 'Structure' and 'Hut' – is inconsistent.[14] Apparently largely of second–third-century AD date, most buildings excavated within the hill-top-area seem modest. Defined by gravel and/or marl surfaces with shallow beam-slot trenches and postholes, they generally seem to have been sub-rectangular/-square. At *c.* 2–4.9 m wide and 3.5–6.1 m long, these though seem small by comparison to other contemporary timber buildings at, for example, War Ditches or Godmanchester (White 1964; Green 1975). One suspects that this, in part, related to Alexander's use of a Wheeler Box-technique and that in a number of cases their full plans were simply not recovered; of the sites dug after the early 1960s, the lack of attention seemingly paid to horizontal stratigraphy (and any shallow-footed structures therein) would also have contributed.[15]

It is not Roman Cambridge's 'standard' timber buildings that need particularly concern us, as most of the structures of this type and quality would not be out of place on rural settlements. Instead, foremost would have to be the second-century AD *mansio* (Fig. 2.21; *RCAM*, 39–49, fig. 4.5), both in relation to the Kettle's Yard's evidence and Roman Cambridge's status generally. Of masonry build, with a hypocausted room, there must be some doubt that it was actually a *mansio* as opposed to a high-quality private residence. Also of second-century AD date was the corner of what was evidently a tiled-roofed building with a cellar and painted plaster walls recovered close to the *Via Devana* and Akeman Street crossroads (Fig. 2.8; F.12; *ibid.*, 40–2, figs. 4.7–9).[16] Located alongside the Akeman Street/Street 1 projection, was another cellared building, one with a staircase along one side (Fig. 2.21). This was considered a shrine on account of it being apsidal-ended and its extraordinary three-dog carcass setting, as well as other animal remains (including a horse burial surrounded by complete pottery vessels; *RCAM*, 45–7, figs. 4.14–19).[17] Indeed, as shown in Figure 2.22, another cellared building – following the alignment of the apsidal shrine (see Fig. 2.7) – also lay in this area; however, there must be some doubt concerning its dating. Such structures are hardly ever found in (non-villa) rural settlements. While not common, they are more widely encountered in strictly urban and major villa contexts (Perring 2002, 183–5).[18] Certainly, to have two (if not three) recovered within 60 m of each other along the same street is unusual and further highlights just what a loss the paucity of excavation along Cambridge's Akeman Street entailed. Although no distinctly civic buildings have been distinguished within Roman Cambridge (aside from the putative *mansio*), taken together – and now with the Kettle's Yard evidence – it clearly certainly had a number of 'quality' buildings.

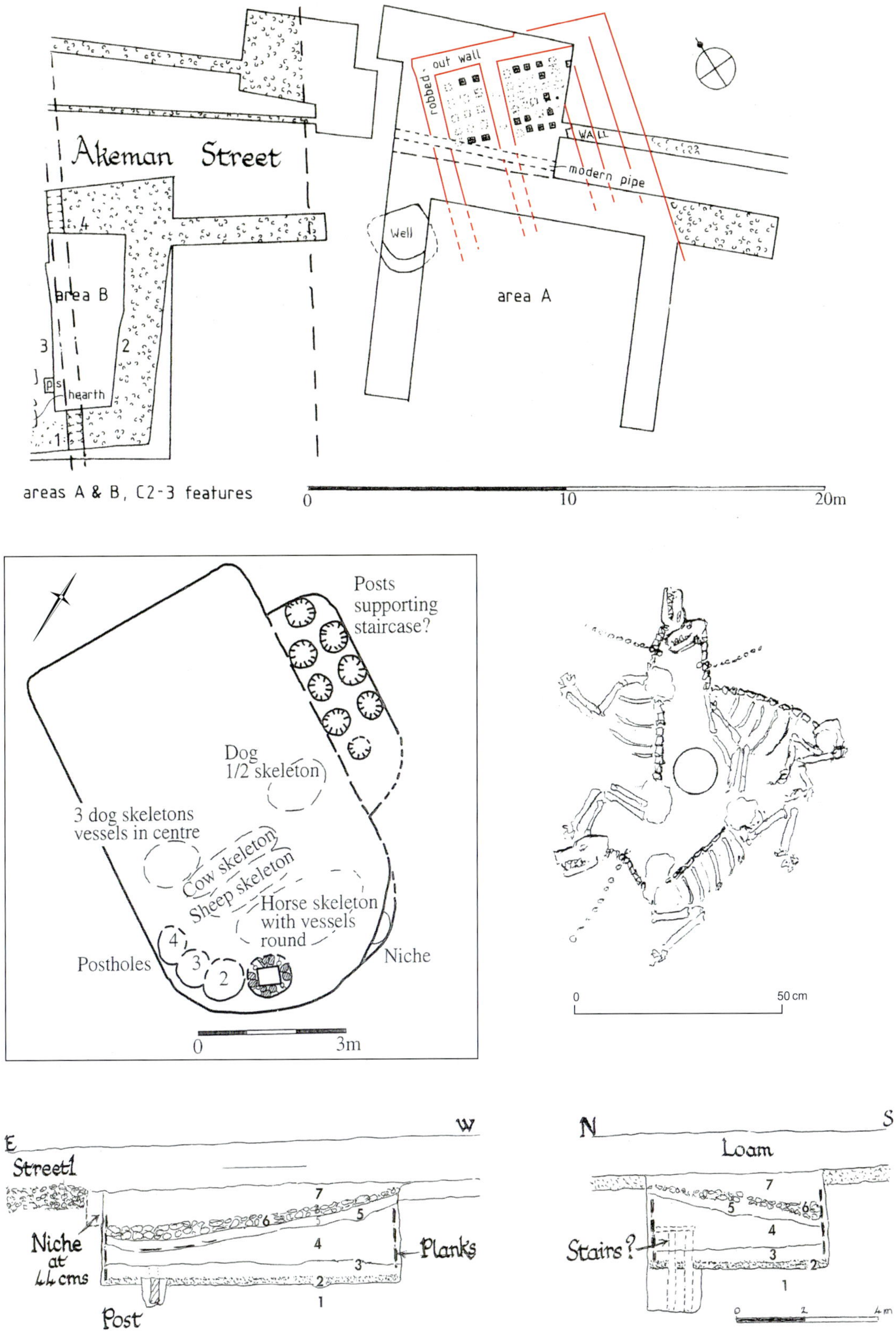

Figure 2.21. Roman Cambridge *buildings:* Mansio *(top;* RCAM, *fig. 4.6); below, the cellared shrine with sections and sketch plan of its three-dog setting* (ibid., *figs. 4.14, 4.15 & 4.17).*

Figure 2.22. *Ridgeons Garden, 'Late Sunken House' cellar: There must be some doubt concerning this structure's Roman* vs. *Saxon attribution. Extending over 2.80 × 4.70 m, with vertical sides 1.18 m deep, there were postholes in its base (including ones centrally set at either end of its long axis); its short sides curved slightly, there was evidence of plank-lining and said to be an small entrance 'annexe' on its southeast side corresponding with the line of the stain of an interior timber partition within its upper fill. Its fills were described in the 1994 Alexander (*et al.*) manuscript:*

> The infilling of loam, chalk marl lumps and clay contained many Romano-British sherds, mainly of fourth century, bone fragments, three late third century coins and two fifth century ones (House of Honorius, Appendix). A few small 'Saxon' sherds (Appendix) were found in the layer of earth lying on the floor. A number of square-headed nails, and badly corroded iron hinges and brackets were also found in the fill around the edge. The upper fills of the features were cut by a large eleventh to twelfth century pit, IV (17), and by a small oval pit of the twelfth to thirteenth century, IV (12).

This was assigned to the fifth–sixth century, but its form would better suit a Late Saxon date and be comparable to other such large cellared buildings at, for example, Flaxengate (Perring 1981). Yet, pending review of its finds, there must be some suspicion of it being Late Roman; as indicated on Figure 2.7, it apparently lay immediately behind/west of the apsidal shrine and close to its alignment.

Quarry Imprint and Roman Town 'Fringe' (with Duncan Mackay, Richard Newman and Letty Ten Harkel)

Evidence of coprolite quarrying was found across much of the northern half of St Edmund's College when, in 1996, its grounds were trench-evaluated (Dickens 1996a). The impact of this mining produced an intriguing stratigraphic reversal across what proved to be the College's undisturbed southwestern quarter. There, upcast, pure chalk-marl deposits had been spread to infill the intervening furrows of an upstanding ridge-and-furrow agricultural system. With the crowns of its ridge subsequently levelled, this initially led us to think that their dark-striped imprints were actually cut features; upon realizing this pattern for what it was, these trenches had to be machine-stripped again.

Early in 1999 evaluation fieldwork took place in the grounds of Buckingham House adjoining the east side of New Hall (Lucas 1999b). Falling only *c.* 100 m outside the line of the Roman defensive wall and along the projected route of the (southern) New Hall Roman road (see Chap. 3; Figs. 2.23 & 3.2), this was considered a promising site. Unfortunately, the two trenches cut across the plot showed that it had been entirely quarried away in recent times. However, the recovery of first-/second-century AD pottery sherds and a human femur attest to Romano-British activity – probably including burials – in the vicinity. The Buckingham House quarrying presumably related to the extraction of coprolites occurring in the chalk-marl geology, as is also true of the southern end of the main New Hall Site (and further confirmed in later test pitting there: Webley & Evans 2003; see Fig. 2.23 concerning the recent Mount Pleasant House investigations).

As shown on Figure 2.23, plotting of this quarrying shows that the coprolite workings actually surround the grounds of The Grove/Orchard and the boundaries of what was to become, in effect, the Darwin Family Estate (see *Inset*, Chap. 3). Indeed, in the case of New Hall's main southern-area exposure, the quarry-zone was observed to fall hard along the line of the property's brick-wall limits. While this means that we actually have the Darwin family to thank for the fact that there is any archaeological survival at all within the area, this recognition led to a need to reappraise the 1991 evaluation trench results within the southern part of Fitzwilliam College's grounds (Gdaniec 1991). Occurring just south of the Darwin Estate limits (but along what should have been the line of New Hall's Roman road), no 'early' remains were present. Instead, there was only evidence of nineteenth-century landscaping on marl natural/geology and, in hindsight, the immediate area had also clearly been quarried away. After starting in the 1850s in the Cambridge Region, coprolite mining peaked in the 1870s/80s, and there are references to the workings west of Castle Hill (O'Connor 1998, 41), including that St Edmund's College was reportedly built on a quarry field (Pennings & Jukes-Brown 1881, 8). A major source of employment, coprolite quarrying involved extraction up to some 6.5 m depth and, experience shows, nearly totally destroyed any archaeological evidence (Fig. 2.24; see Grove 1976).

At the time of the fieldwork we had not appreciated the scale of this mining and, directly bordering the southwestern quarter of the Roman town and lying just beyond its Late Roman defences, there were high expectations for the St Edmund's College investigations. These, moreover, were furthered by the fact that the RCHME map of the Roman town indicated that burials of that period had been recovered from the College (1959, lxi, though this finding is otherwise unreferenced in that volume). This may relate to Babington's mention that, when digging coprolites in 1871, interments and Roman pottery were found in "the field opposite to Storey's Almshouses. ... This spot lay in the angle between *Akeman Street* and the *Via Devana*" (1883, 29; see also Browne 1974, map 1, no. 23). The County Sites and Monuments Record also attributes findings there to 'JB 1936' and notes that 'skeletons with Roman rubbish pits' were found, citing as its source the University Museum of Archaeology and Anthropology (CUMAA). Accordingly, an extensive search was made of the Museum's records, though to little avail. It holds two large bags of pottery recovered during the 1936–7 extension to the College but has no associated records; nor can any be found in the College's archives. Given these indications, it does seem safe assume that 'JB' was John Bromwich (see Smith in Evans & Hodder 2006b, 13 for biographical outline) and that these findings were made within the area of College's chapel, which was constructed in those years.

Lucas assessed the Museum's 100+ sherds from the site:

CUMAA Z25205 - A large bag of variously-sized and abraded pottery, including some very large fragments. The majority of the sherds are locally made coarse grey wares. The vessels include a rilled jar, a 'Belgic' carinated bowl, a flat-rimmed bowl, a lid, a narrow-mouthed jar, and a handmade storage jar with thumb strokes on the lower body (?Horningsea). Other wares include a mortarium (Colchester?), a cornice-rimmed bag-shaped beaker (Nene Valley?) and some South Gaulish Samian (Dragendorff – hereafter 'Dr.' – 18 dish and a Dr.27 cup). The overall date range of this mixed assemblage is later first–early second-century (*c.* AD 70–120).

CUMAA Z23187 - A small collection of locally made Gallo-Belgic-type vessels, including a platter and a segmental bowl; probably Flavian (*c.* AD 70–90).

Carrying a date of 1859, also included within the same Museum box is a near-complete vessel, save the rim, of a small globular flask and which also probably dates to the later first century AD (Z23186).

Before proceeding, another local early finding warrants mention. Occupying Ayerst's Hostel (founded 1884), St Edmund's House was established as a Roman Catholic lodging in 1896 (only joining the University's collegiate system in 1965; Sweeney 1980). Its main buildings stand upon the site of *Drake's Hole*, a large pond that apparently supplied the upper town's Castle-End district with water. Presumably fed by Drake's Spring – a minor stream assigned considerable antiquity by Bowtell (nd.) – it was only infilled in 1893 and the plot still carried that name on the 1888 OS map. In describing his findings from nearby Bandy-Leg Walk (now Lady Margaret Road; see below), Macalister related that a skeleton had been recovered from the grounds of Ayerst's Hostel. Referring to Drake's Pond, he speculated that its interment there

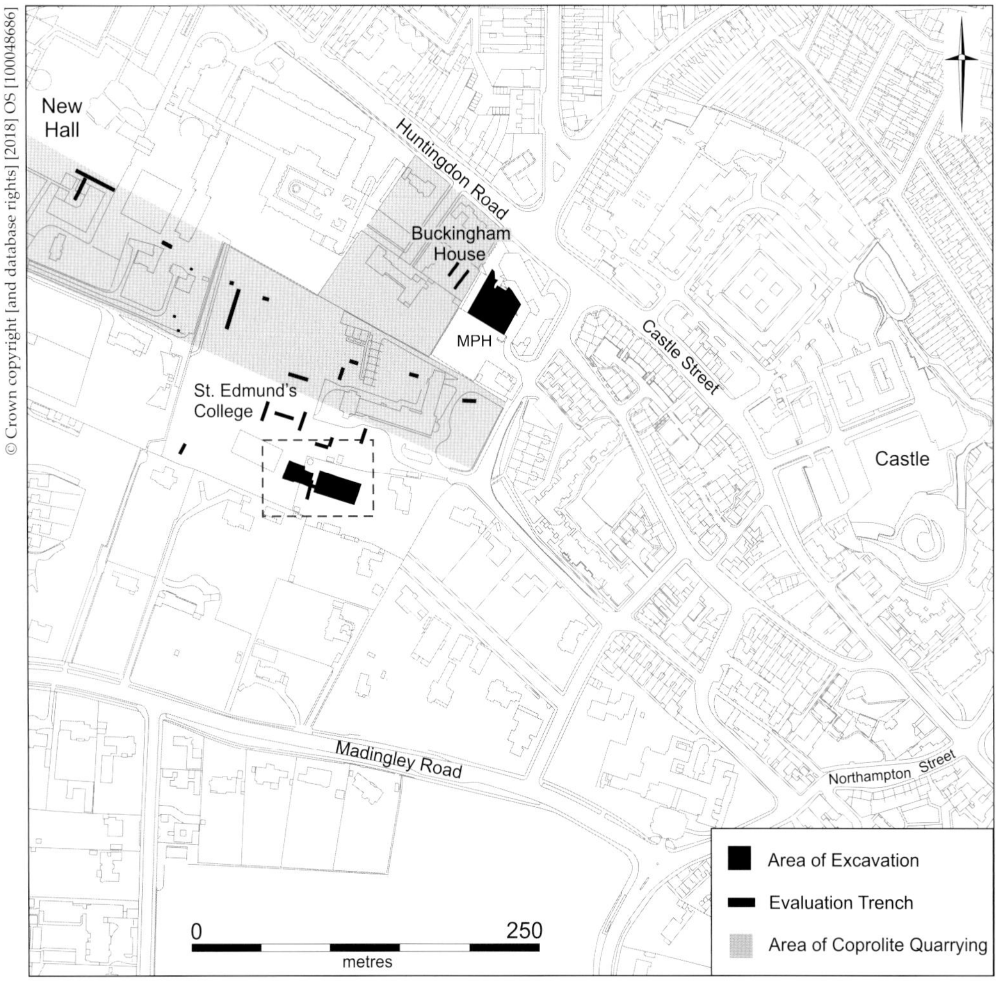
© Crown copyright [and database rights] [2018] OS [100048686]
New Hall
Huntingdon Road
Buckingham House
MPH
Castle Street
St. Edmund's College
Castle
Madingley Road
Northampton Street
0
250
metres
Area of Excavation
Evaluation Trench
Area of Coprolite Quarrying

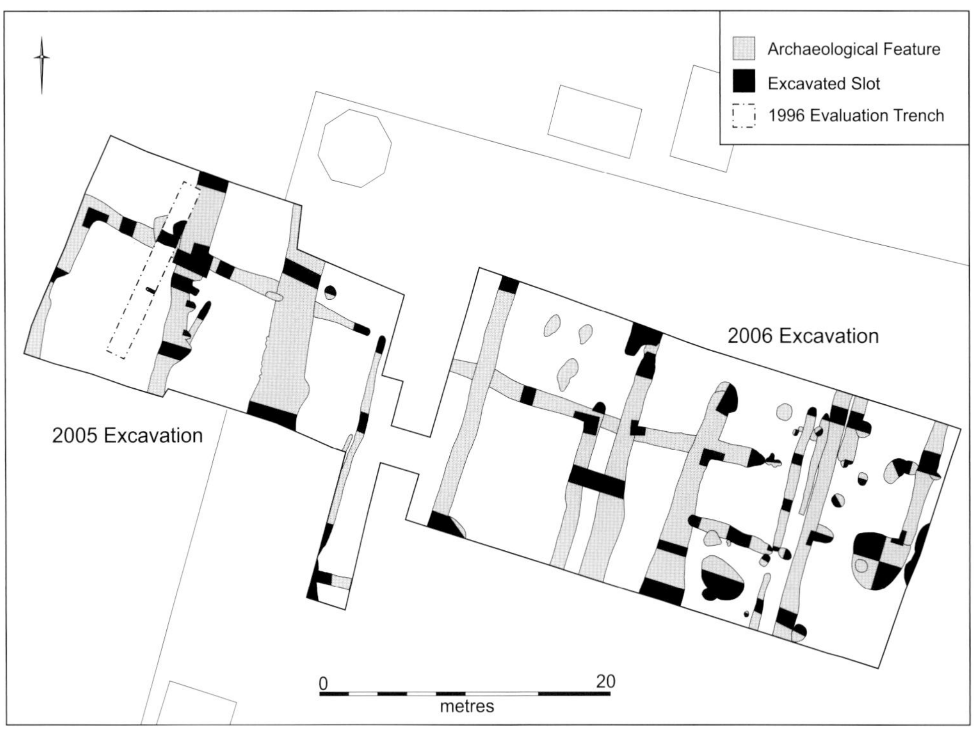
Archaeological Feature
Excavated Slot
1996 Evaluation Trench
2006 Excavation
2005 Excavation
0
20
metres

Figure 2.24 *(above). Cambridgeshire coprolite working (top): Orwell, 1860–70s (right) and, left, Abington Pigotts, 1883 (from O'Connor 1998, 37); below, site photograph from St Edmund's College, looking east.*

Figure 2.23 *(opposite). St Edmund's College excavations: location map (showing wider extent of coprolite quarrying) and base plan below. MPH indicates the 2017 excavations by Archaeological Solutions at Mount Pleasant House (Barlow & Newton 2018; see also* RCAM*, 13). Portions of the plot had variously been truncated through post-War construction and, earlier, coprolite extraction. As a consequence, only a handful of Roman-period pits – some likely quarry-related – survived (two short lengths of ditch were also thought to be of that date). Of mid/later second to third century* AD *date, all told 560 Roman-period sherds were recovered. While no evidence was retrieved relating to the area's roads, resonating with the Buckingham House findings, the recovery of four (+) loose human bone fragments from two pits (plus one unstratified) are of some significance and are further discussed in Chapter Three.*

may have either been the result of a drowning accident or foul play (1896, 28–9). While a seductively emotive interpretation, in the light of the 'JB' findings, in all likelihood these human remains derive from disturbed Roman burials.

Although a few late and Post-Medieval ditches were found to be present within the 16 trenches dug across the College in 1996, only 11 Romano-British sherds were then recovered. Widespread in their distribution, many were little more than chips and all but one heavily abraded, thereby suggesting a manuring source. Otherwise, there were only two findings of note. In the only trench excavated in the lawn east of the College's front (Trench 14), make-up dumps were observed to continue below a depth of 1.90 m. Probably relating to the infilling of Drake's Pond, a fragment of human skull was recovered from these deposits. Moreover, the unaccompanied skeleton of a three- to five-year-old child was exposed in a trench along the southern margin of the grounds. Although poorly preserved, the latter was left *in situ* awaiting the outcome of the College's planning application. It was to feature again when, in 2005/2006, further investigations occurred within the area and, in this case, the work extended into the neighbouring southeastern plot. There, initial trenching led to the recovery of a series of near-parallel ditches (Ten Harkel 2006). While the three Romano-British sherds recovered were also abraded and considered possibly residual, it was thought that these ditches might still prove to be of Roman date. Accordingly, it was decided that an area of some 830 sq. m would be targeted for excavation, albeit successively dug over two years (Figs. 2.23–4).

The child's burial (F.23), found nearly a decade before, was included within the western area (Mackay 2006), and was then lifted (Fig. 2.25.B). Another grave was found nearby, this time an adult (the bones being too poorly preserved to determine its sex; F.24). While both were without accompanying grave-goods, that both bodies lay in an extended supine position with their heads to the west, suggested they were, in fact, Roman. In addition, a series of ditch boundaries extended throughout this area. One (F.15) truncated the adult burial and, together with ditch F.25, would seem to relate to a Post-Medieval droveway. Aside from a few small pits, the remaining features all seemed of Roman attribution, though as only 18 pottery sherds of that date were recovered, there was still much ambiguity concerning the site's sequence.

Our understanding of the area's archaeology only became firm when the eastern area was exposed in the following year (Ten Harkel 2006), and the fieldwork there generated more than 265 sherds of Late Iron Age and Romano-British pottery. Amounting to 208 pieces (1849 g), the latter material was predominately of first–second-century AD date and only very few later Roman sherds were present. The vast majority consisted of locally made coarsewares and little of it could be sourced: just two Southern Gaulish Samian sherds, with one each of Central Gaulish Samian, Nene Valley colour-coated and Verulamium whiteware. Almost entirely wheelmade in coarse sandy fabrics, the Iron Age pottery dated to AD 0–50, with sherds from several storage jars and at least one carinated bowl present (see Anderson & Brudenell in *ibid.*).

Iron Age occupation was represented by three, substantial pits along the site's eastern margin (with the attribution of one only being tentative; Fig. 2.25.A). Located in the lowest (and wettest) corner of the site, and variously *c.* 0.4–0.75 m deep, these were all interpreted as small wells or watering-holes.

The area's Roman usage clearly began in the mid/later first century AD, and also included a pit-well/watering-hole (F.110) in the vicinity of the Late Iron Age features of the same function. Otherwise, apart from a few minor pits scattered throughout the site's eastern third (though some of the unphased pits/postholes there might also be related), its Roman phases were marked by a network of ditches. Of first-/second-century AD date, these boundaries were generally small, 0.6–1.2 m wide and 0.2–0.3 m deep. As is clear on Figures 2.25.B and 2.25.C, their density and layout would suggest more than just 'open' agricultural fieldsystems. Given this, and corresponding to the quantity of pottery recovered (as well as the human burials; see below), they were probably part of a paddock system falling along the margins of settlement *per se*. In fact, as shown on Figure 2.25.C, the rectilinear configuration of two of its ditch settings could suggest that they marked the location of beam-constructed buildings, perhaps sheds, *etc.*

Cut into the top of one of Iron Age pits, the site also included one other significant feature, pit F.132. This contained the remains of an adult cremation with 807 g of blue/grey to white burnt bone. Also recovered from this deposit were 13 iron fragments/objects, including a large ferrous conglomeration (95 g) that had fragments of burnt bone embedded within it (Fig. 2.26). Andrew Hall has reported of this group:

> The individual fragments include two complete nails and two further incomplete examples. The former are both 40 mm in length and all have square-section shanks. Cremated bone adheres to three nails and traces of organic material are visible within the corrosion products on at least one example. In addition, there are six fragments (two refitting) of narrow plates or strips of either 10 or 14 mm wide. These are of varied length due to fragmentation, with two examples pierced at one end with a short nail or rivet. The intact terminals of these strips appear to be slightly rounded. One displays a 90-degree

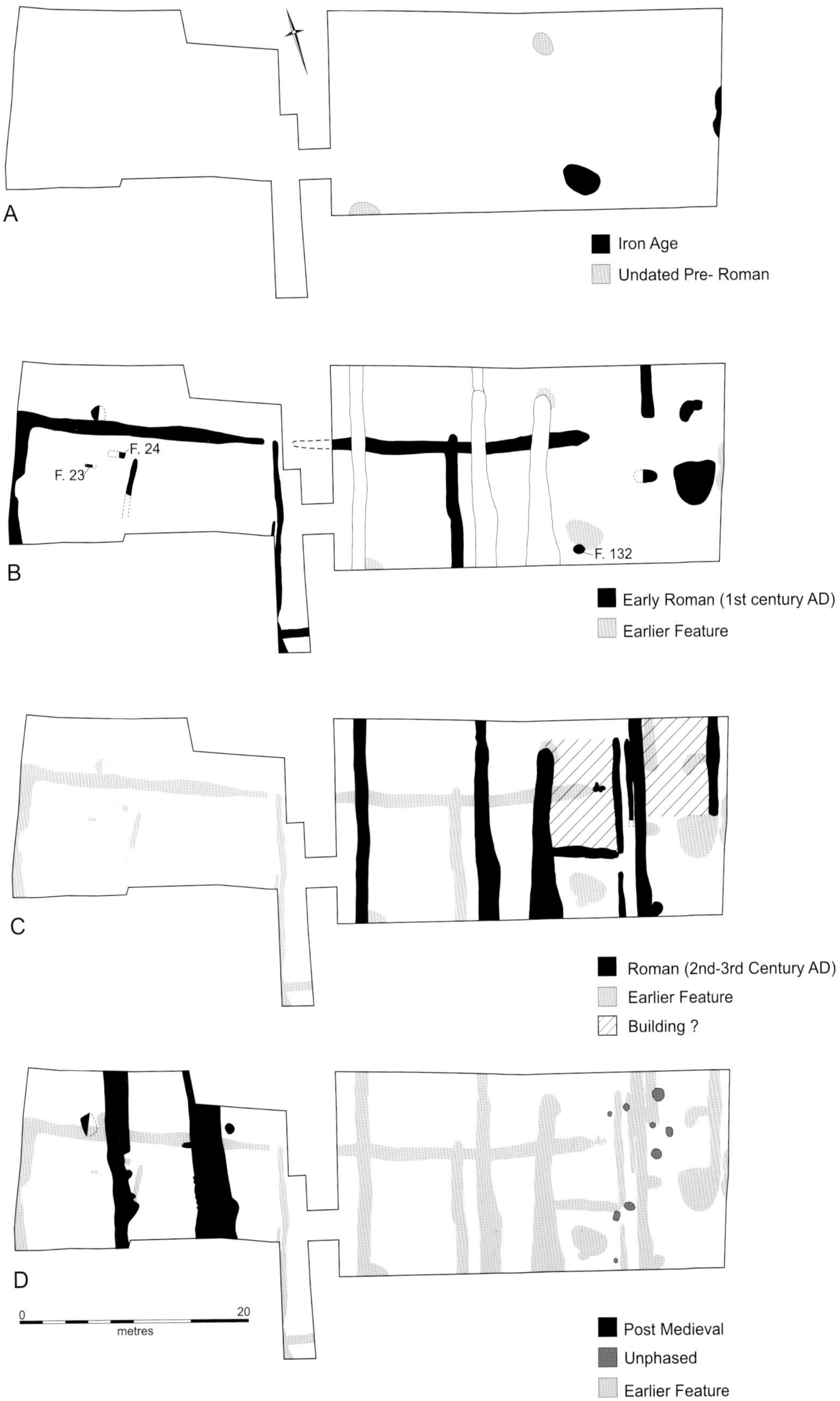

Figure 2.25. *Phasing sequence.*

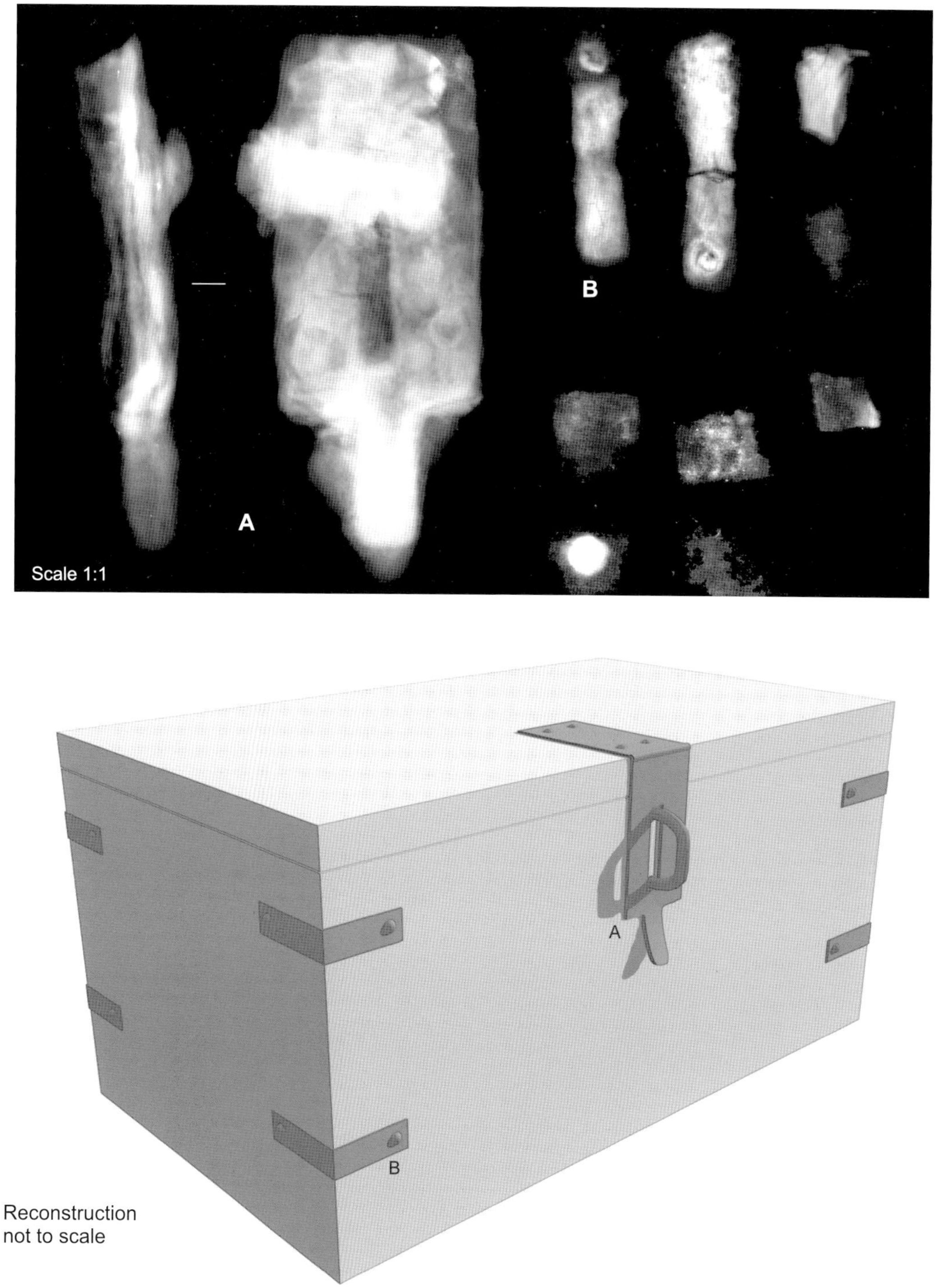

Figure 2.26. *Cremation casket fittings and reconstruction.*

bend, suggesting that it was attached around the corner of a larger object, perhaps for reinforcement. The minimum length of each strip along each side is 34 mm. Three more such strips adhere to the corroded mass that was subject to X-ray (Fig. 2.26.B). The main identifiable form within the corrosion group is a rectangular iron plate, 55 × 32 mm of approximately 2 mm thickness (Fig. 2.26.A). The X-ray reveals a centrally positioned rectangular projection at one end, and a rectangular aperture of 20 mm length and 5 mm width within the main body of the plate. Traces of a possible hinged back-plate are visible within the side view, although it is difficult to ascertain from which end it is hinged. Further organic traces are clear within the corrosion.

The right-angled strips with nails at the terminals (Fig. 2.26.B) are likely to be corner brackets from an Early Roman casket, and possible parallels occurred at Skeleton Green within Burials 30, 35 and 59 (Partridge 1981). The rectangular plate may well be a hinged hasp. This would be attached to the upper surface of the lid and fold down over the front of the casket. A projecting loop would then pass through the hasp aperture, allowing the box to be locked with a padlock. A tentative reconstruction is provided with Figure 2.26.

While this interpretation is by no means definitive, a casket attribution does provide the most plausible explanation for these numerous fittings with close association to cremated human bone. Casket burials involve the placing of the cremated remains within a small box prior to burial. They are recorded at several sites within the South-East and East Anglia, including King Harry Lane, St Pancras and Skeleton Green. They date, in the main, to the first century AD (*ibid.*). It is interesting that no further pottery or other artefacts were retrieved from the excavated context, as this type of burial often contains glass or pottery vessels, brooches or coins.

The other iron pieces recovered from the site's various Roman contexts within the 2006 area were all nails (or parts thereof), apart from a folded or layered iron sheet from [1103] (a patch of sub-soil; only metalwork of Post-Medieval attribution was recovered from the 2005 area).

Otherwise, as reported upon by Chris Swaysland, almost 700 animal bones were recovered (both areas), though only six identifiable pieces were from Iron Age contexts: four of cattle; two, sheep/goat. As shown in Table 2.1, cattle similarly dominated the 40 identifiable bones from its Roman features.

Very little charred plant material was present within the eight bulk soil samples processed and studied by Ann de Vareilles. However, the mollusc remains from all were indicative of damp and shady environments, with the snails from pits F.108 and F.109 demonstrating that they were seasonally waterlogged. Similarly, the soils within the latter feature, as well as F.110 and F.134, were evidently sufficiently damp to preserve waterlogged seeds of elder. In fact, their numbers within pit F.110 were such to suggest that elder shrub must have occurred nearby.

In summary, although the College excavation was too limited to detail the character of the area's Iron Age and Early Roman usage, its importance lies in the demonstration that settlement of these dates extended beyond the immediate Castle Hill/Mount Pleasant core of the *later* Roman town. There is no particular reason to consider this as any kind of extra-mural occupation (i.e. industrially related or 'town-ancillary'), but rather that *Cambridge's later Roman walling reflected a significant reduction in the area of the settlement.*

Table 2.1. *Romano-British faunal remains (NISP).*

Species	Romano-British
Cattle	16
Sheep/goat	10
Pig	3
Horse	10
Dog	1

From the available evidence, there is, moreover, no reason to suspect that the Roman remains from the earlier, 1936 investigations were anything markedly different; again, they simply demonstrate that first-/second-century AD settlement occurred well beyond what was to later become the town's limits. The distribution of graves was not sufficiently dense to denote a formal cemetery. Instead, they are the type of dispersed interments typically found within the margins of many settlements of the period.

In 2015, Oxford Archaeology East excavated a comparable Late(st) Iron Age to mid Roman sequence at Westminster College (*c.* 450 sq. m; Graham 2016 and Graham & Lyons 2018). It was located on Gault Clay, *c.* 500 m southwest of the St Edmund's Site and, like it, also lay some 100 m beyond the line of the Late Roman defences (Fig. 2.27). With ditched paddocks and successive northeast–southwest oriented ditches – plus pitting and evidence of a possible timber building – of the some 1850 Roman sherds recovered, the vast majority predated the mid third century AD. Two Late Roman inhumations were present (one truncated by the site's only Anglo-Saxon feature, a pit), and five coins and a Colchester brooch were recovered.[19]

The recovery of Roman inhumation burials at these two sites is not particularly unexpected. Such scattered interments are commonly found on the margins of the period's settlements and here it essentially reflects the extra-mural status of this area in relation to the *Late Roman* town. Far more noteworthy is the St Edmund's *Early Roman* casket cremation. Its recovery highlights just how few such burials are known from Roman Cambridge, especially given the town's known inhumation cemeteries and, also, the frequency of 'Early' cremation cemeteries on the hinterland settlements (one occurring at Vicar's Farm and three within the main North West Cambridge ridge-top settlements). Within the immediate southern fringe-area, the best candidate for their location would have to be the St John's Playing Fields cemetery, dug in 1888 by von Hügel and Jenkinson.[20]

At this point, the findings made between these two sites require review. Indicative of the 'gentlemanly archaeology of Cambridge's bicycle suburb', these were related in R.A.S. Macalister's utterly charming – and confusing – account, 'On some antiquities discovered near Bandy-Leg Walk' of 1896 (see also Macalister 1893). This outlines recent findings, largely retrieved by workmen, made in the newly developed house plots (acre-sized) around Lady Margaret Road. The 'site' locations are given by their names, variously *Torrisdale*

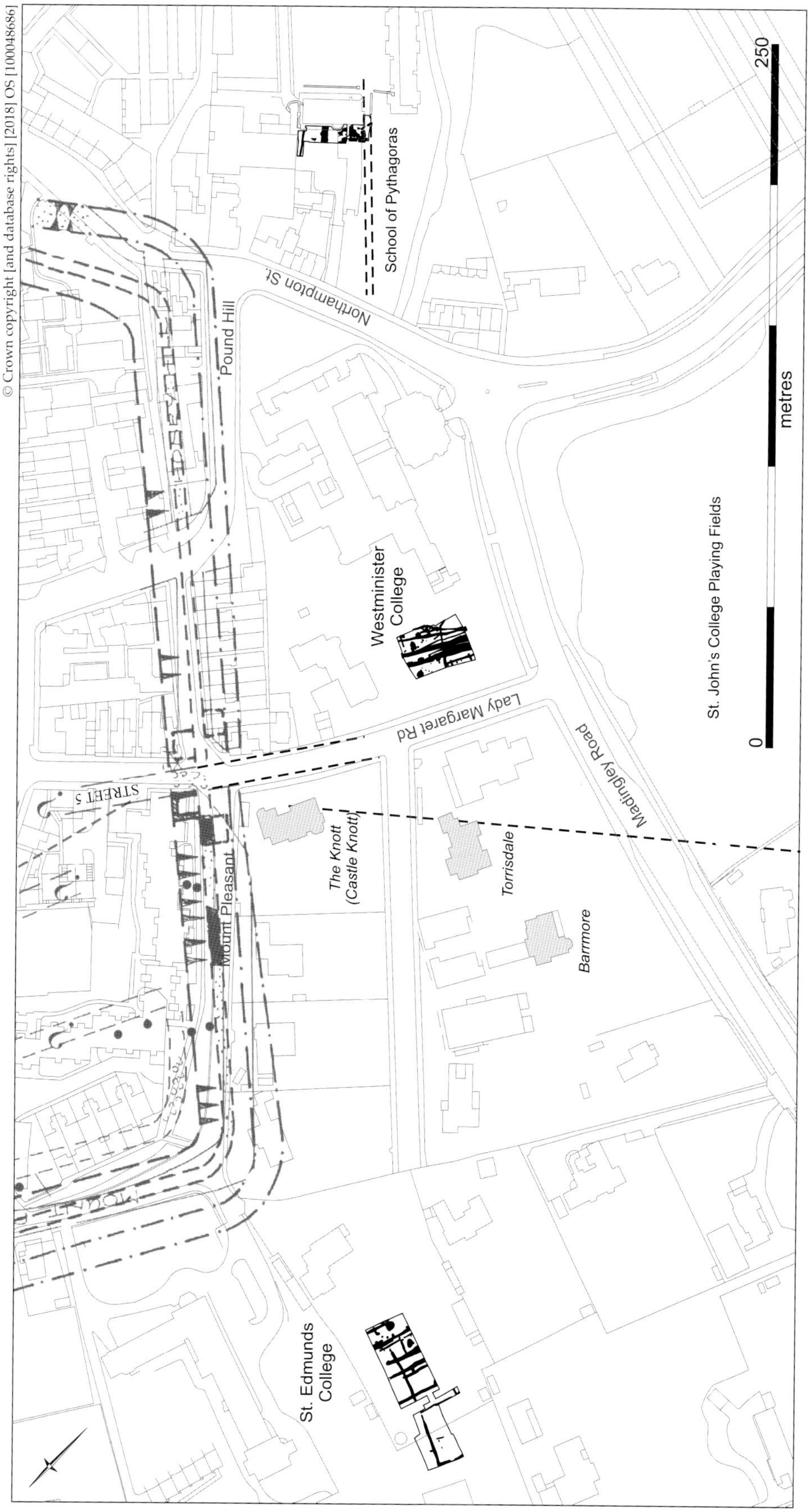

Figure 2.27. *Roman Cambridge's lower south side 'settlement fringe' sites.*

Figure 2.28. *Bandy-Leg Walk houses. Now incorporated within Lucy Cavendish College, this shows* Barrmore *(left) and, right,* Torrisdale, *the Macalister Family home (now renamed College House). In the early years of the last century, concerning his Grange Road investigations when the house,* Saxmeadham, *was built and – reflective of the scale of Cambridge's construction at that time (and the ensuing archaeological loss) – the Rev. Walker remarked:*

> *This incident emphasizes the need of some one person in Cambridge being officially deputed to care for all antiquities occurring in the neighbourhood and being in touch with the College and Town authorities, so that information of any disturbances of the soil might be reported to him (1912, 124).*

*The son of Alexander Macalister (1844–1919), University Professor of Anatomy, as well as a recognized Egyptologist and, serving as President of the Cambridge Antiquarian Society (1887–8) – achieving national attention when, with St John Hope (see Fig. 2.1), in 1910 he studied the exhumed remains of Henry VI in Windsor (*The Times *12/11/1910) – in the last years of the nineteenth century, Robert Alexander Macalister (see Fig. 1.11) undertook a series of excavations in Palestine, most notably at Tel Gezer. Although they are not held to have been particularly successful (see Wolff's 2015a volume,* Villain or Visionary? R.A.S. Macalister and the Archaeology of Palestine*; see also Wolff 2015b), between 1901 and 1909 he was appointed director of excavations for the Palestine Exploration Fund. Having a highly varied career, thereafter he became Professor of Celtic Archaeology in University College, Dublin and worked at Tara.*

Macalister Senior was active in the foundation of the neighbouring Westminster College and, as outlined in Note 19, collected Roman finds during its construction. The College's records note that, in 1921, the family then donated further material collected by the then 'Late Professor', including a bracelet from the arm of a skeleton.

or *Elterholm, etc.* (his paper is entirely un-illustrated; see Figs. 2.27–8 and, also, Guillebaud 2007, fig. 2 on the expansion of 'gentry' housing in western Cambridge, with the Bandy-Leg plots actually developed by Macalister's father: *ibid.*, 206). With this area of former meadowland largely falling just beyond the scope of Hammond's map, by way of example, this is amongst the paper's most intriguing and frustrating mentions:

> Had the field been inhabited in Hammond's time, he might possibly have extended his map to include houses built upon it; as he has not done so, we may perhaps infer that it contained no dwelling places in 1592. But I am informed by Prof. Marshall, that on the site of his house, which occupies the S.W. corner of the field, *the foundations of two buildings, one over the other, were unearthed. It does not appear that any record has been preserved of their plan or approximate size. If our inference from Hammond's silence be justifiable, the fact that one of these houses superseded the other indicates that the latter must have been of considerable antiquity* (Macalister 1896, 27; emphasis added).

Leaving aside the various Medieval and later material listed, what is of interest is sheer quantity of the Roman finds. He notes the recovery of human remains – two men, a woman and a child – at *Castle Knott* ('Mr Ainslie's house'), plus samian and traces of a ditch at *Torrisdale* (Prof. Macalister's house, the author's father). Most of the Roman finds, though, were made at *Barrmore*, where from its foundation trenches over 1000 sherds were retrieved and ".... it is believed that had the digging operations been watched at the other places with the same care which the latest excavations have been superintended, each would have yielded a similar number" (*ibid.*, 29).

With coins also recovered there, apparently 'a kind of terrace ... formed of rather large stones' was encountered 18 inches below ground surface in one of the trenches; he also related:

> From this I would infer that the field was at one time pitted over its surface with small hollows, varying from two to three feet in depth.
>
> At the bottom of one of these depressions a singular and partly inexplicable discovery was made. The workmen struck a small hollow, which they unfortunately enlarged by hunting for 'treasure'. When I saw it it was a pocket about a foot or eighteen inches every way, with a dome-shaped roof. No "treasure" was found in it, but a stone which shewed evident marks of firing, and a small cup, in fragments, but complete: the walls of the opening were blackened with wood ash. That some cooking operation on a small scale had taken place at this spot is plain: but why any one should cook on this site, which in Roman times must have been very unsavoury; and how and why the pit was filled in without filling the hollow at the bottom, are questions which I cannot solve (*ibid.*, 31).

Whether this was a kiln, oven or even a cremation, we will simply never know, but certainly there were major Roman remains in the area.[21]

As shown on Figure 2.27, *Barrmore* and *Torrisdale* are two of the large houses that were taken over by Lucy Cavendish College in the 1970s; *Castle Knott* being 'The Knot' located just to the northeast and, just outside the Roman defences, at the junction of Mount Pleasant and Lady Margaret Roads. Given their locations, these findings therefore directly correlate with the results of the recent excavations to either side of this area. When considered together, all this raises questions concerning of the scale of the Early Roman town's margins. At the St Edmund's Site there was no sense that either the town's western or southern limits had there been exposed and, certainly, Westminster College's Roman settlement features continued south of their recent exposure. This would imply that early settlement originally extended for upwards of 150–200 m beyond its Late Roman defences.[22]

Finally, there are issues of alignment. In this regard, the St Edmund's findings pose no problem as the orientation of its ditch axes seem to reflect that of the southern New Hall road (see Chap. 3). The same, though, is not true of the Westminster College layout. With its ditches generally oriented further east-over-north, they would seem to complement the alignment of the road passing through the Mount Pleasant South Gate, Street 5 (Fig. 2.27; *RCAM*, figs. 6.1 & 6.7).[23] Yet, what of the projected southern route of Akeman Street, which also appears to have run towards that gate and whose line, at least southwest of Grange Road, is firmly plotted? At the Westminster College Site only the possible posthole structure would seem to match its alignment and, otherwise, that site's main features diverged from the road. Did the southern length of Akeman Street kink to join with 'Street 5' or was it a matter of a 'Y'-shaped street configuration meeting at the gate? If the latter, which seems most likely, then for whatever reason the Akeman Street route would seem to have had almost no influence on the early settlement's immediate layout. Be this as it may, the number of burials so 'casually' found at *Castle Knott* /'The Knott' could well suggest the location of yet another Late Roman inhumation cemetery immediately outside the town's South Gate.

There is another Roman cemetery that requires attention, in the area of the School of Pythagoras in St John's College, lying outside the wall and near the river, *c.* 180 m east of the Westminster College Site (Fig. 2.27). With its publication expectedly shortly (Newman in prep and see 2013), here only a brief outline will be presented (and that omitting any of the programme's Medieval building-related findings). The area lay just northwest of a palaeochannel of the River Cam and what was probably the historic course of the Bin Brook (Figs. 2.29–30). Augering unfortunately failed to produce any dateable samples, but it is presumed that it would have been flowing and open in Roman times. Indeed, apparently navigable until the early thirteenth century, its earthwork had been identified as 'the ditch of the Roman Granta' by Stukeley (1746, 36).

Within the site-area proper, a surprisingly intense Roman-period sequence was found by the CAU in 2011 (Fig. 2.29; Newman 2013). While a first-century AD presence was demonstrated by several quarry pits and through redeposited ceramics – plus the recovery of two Colchester Derivative brooches (a third having been found previously; see below) – its main occupation dated from the early–mid second century AD until the mid third century AD. Marked by a series of pits and ditches, these lay alongside a metalled trackway running northwest back from the river. Altogether, some 1650 sherds of Roman pottery were recovered, with ironworking debris indicating

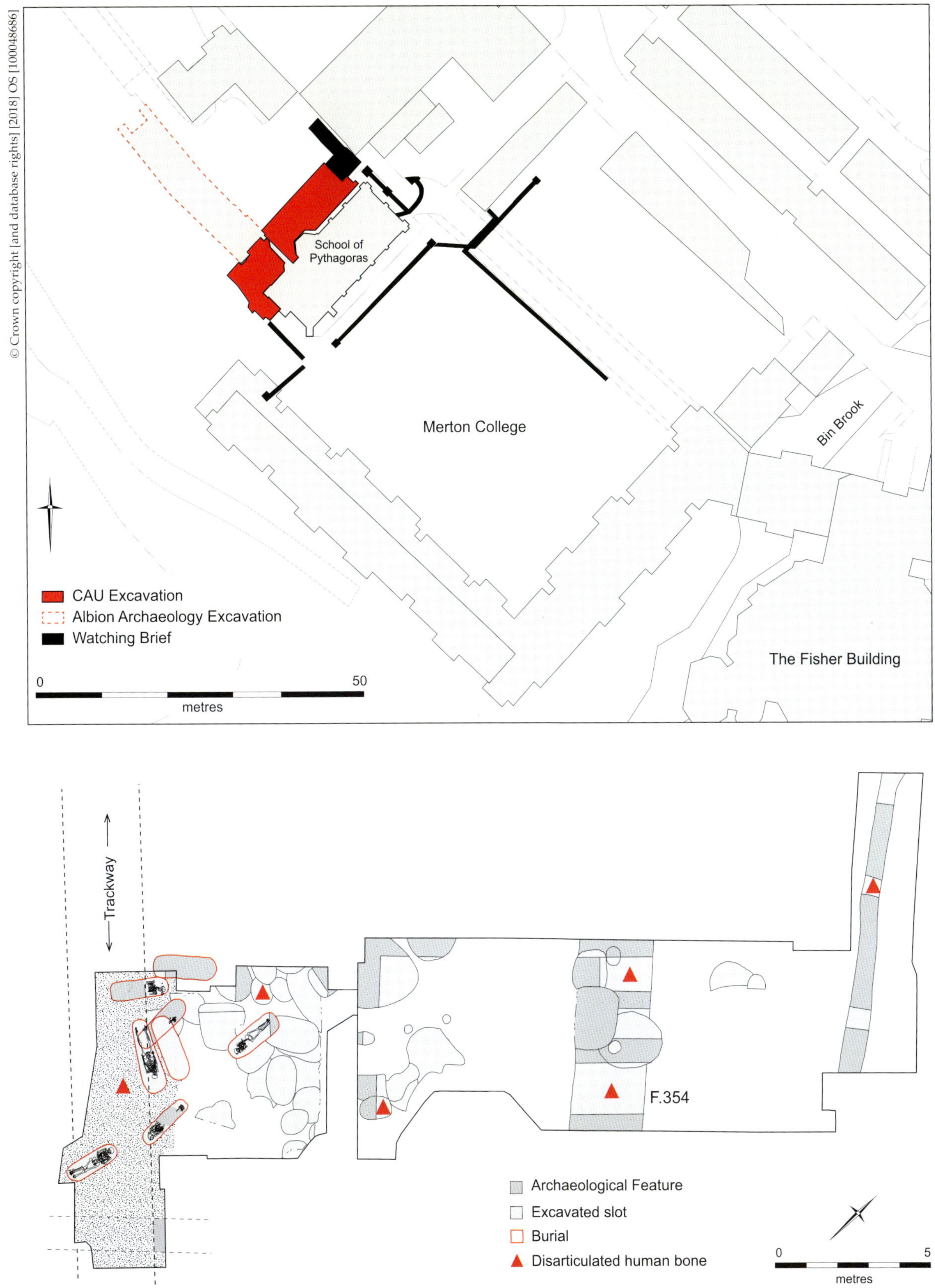

Figure 2.29. *School of Pythagoras investigations, location map and base plan.*

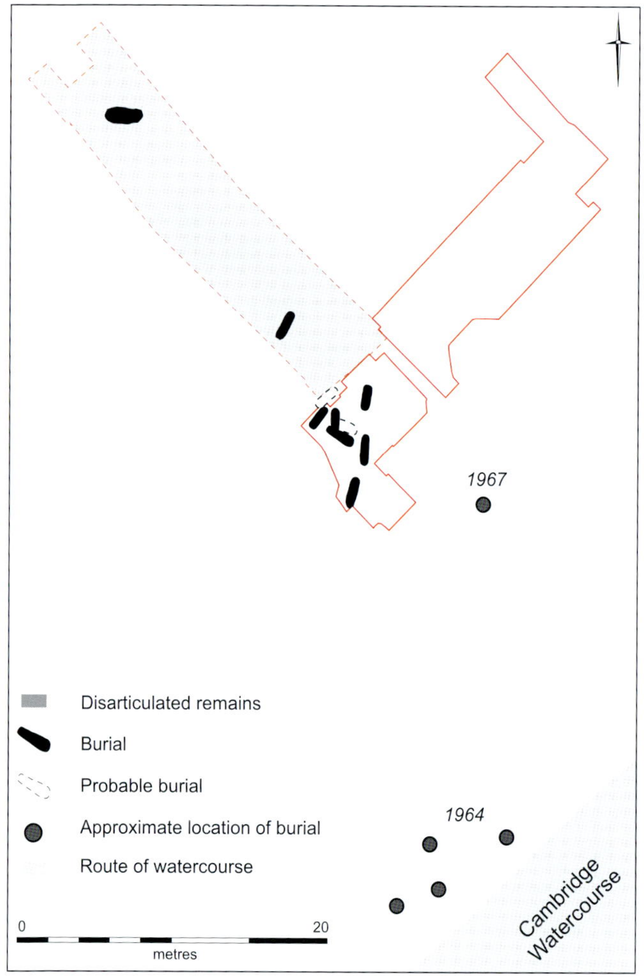

Figure 2.30. *Photograph, looking south, showing Roman-phase ditch F.354 passing beneath the School's Medieval fabric (top right) and, left, plan of Roman burial locations; below, Colchester Derivative brooch and, right, the shale bracelet that accompanied one of the inhumations.*

some industrial activity. In the later third century AD, the area was turned over to cemetery usage. Aside from quantities of disarticulated human bone (subject to radiocarbon dating and found to date to the third to fourth century AD), six adult inhumations were present – two males and three females (one only probable and another unsexed) – with one of the women accompanied by hob-nail shoes, a shale bracelet and an iron finger-ring. To this can be added seven other inhumations from this immediate area found in the course of earlier investigations,[24] which takes the total to 13 burials (plus loose/disturbed bone representing at least 12 further individuals) now found across an area of some 4800 sq. m (Fig. 2.30).

Aside from further demonstrating town-fringe settlement – again, some 150 m (+) beyond the later walls – plus documenting yet another trackway/road route and a further cemetery, what is of singular importance is that a cemetery would occur so close to the riverside. This is most unusual, but not entirely without precedent; parallels could be found, for example in the burials alongside the headwaters of the Walbrook in London, beyond the walls (Harward *et al.* 2015). Yet, there they occurred beside a tributary stream and not close to the Thames. Here in Cambridge, interment evidently took place alongside the main river course (counting also the WYNG Gardens burials; see below). Effectively occurring in 'front-space', this can only suggest that – in Late Roman times at least – this area of its waterfront was not a hub of commercial activity; presumably any barge-docking and transhipment facilities would have lain downstream of the bridge/ford and probably within what is Magdalene College's grounds.

If this 'beyond-the-walls' spread had been uniform on all sides, then – combined with the evidence of findings on the western bank of the Cam (but not the eastern riverside's lower 'town' evidence) – Early Roman Cambridge could have been as large as 33 ha. This can only be tentatively suggested, as comparable evidence of a settlement fringe has yet to be found along its northern perimeter.[25] Yet, even if we lower this figure by, say, a quarter, it markedly demonstrates just what a reduction occurred in the scale of Late Roman Cambridge as defined by its defences (i.e. by *c.* two-thirds).

Obviously, given how limited the 'fringe-area' investigations have been, there are many outstanding issues here. If the Castle Hill 'core' had a regular/parallel street grid, did this extend down into the early settlement's margins or was – prior to its 'Late' walling – the hilltop-area always distinct? There is no reason to think that the extent of Roman Cambridge's 'early fringe' need have been concentric to the later layout of its walls. As we will see in relationship to New Hall's findings (see Chap. 3), the early settlement/town may well have continued further out along its main road axes; this could add a *c.* 3 ha to its overall extent on its western side.

Another issue arising is the occurrence of the palaeochannel found by the School of Pythagoras Site and whether it marked what would have been the western side of a mid-stream island within the Cam's floodplain. If so, what activities, if any, did it see in Roman times? Unfortunately, with no excavation having occurred there – nor likely to in the near-future – this will have to remain a question. In contrast, though, there have been a number of sites within the river's east-bank area and 'lower town' Cambridge, and it is these that we will now consider.

East Cam-Bank Investigations

Despite many minor scale 'interventions', during the 1990s there was only one really significant finding of Roman occupation within the area of lower, eastern Cambridge, on the site the new library at St John's College. This is outlined below. At the time when the publication of Alexander's (*et al.*) *Roman Cambridge* (2000) meant that the potential status of Roman Cambridge was being reappraised by some, important discoveries were made within the southeastern quarter of lower Cambridge; these led us to reconsider its scale once again. This began in 2001, when a cemetery was found during house refurbishment at Numbers 35–37 Jesus Lane; later that same year further Roman features and inhumations were recovered during building work at Number 11 Park Street (Fig. 2.31). The results of these two sites have been fully published in the *Proceedings of the Cambridge Antiquarian Society* (M. Alexander *et al.* 2004) and, therefore, need only brief outline here.

The burials at Jesus Lane were found when replacing the basement floors in three conjoining terrace houses (these were cut into the truncated top of Terrace gravels, 1.9 m below modern pavement level). As indicated on Figure 2.32, it made for a macabre spectacle to have the floor-areas of poster-bedecked student rooms packed with the dead. A total of 32 skeletons were revealed, six being accompanied by modest grave-goods; three were decapitated (with their heads placed lower down beside the body). Seventeen males, nine females and two juveniles were identified. Most lay supine with their heads to the southwest and appeared to have been buried in shrouds, although there were possible coffin nails in some graves. The copper alloy grave-goods included two copper alloy rings with one woman, and a bracelet with another; iron hob-nails from boots had

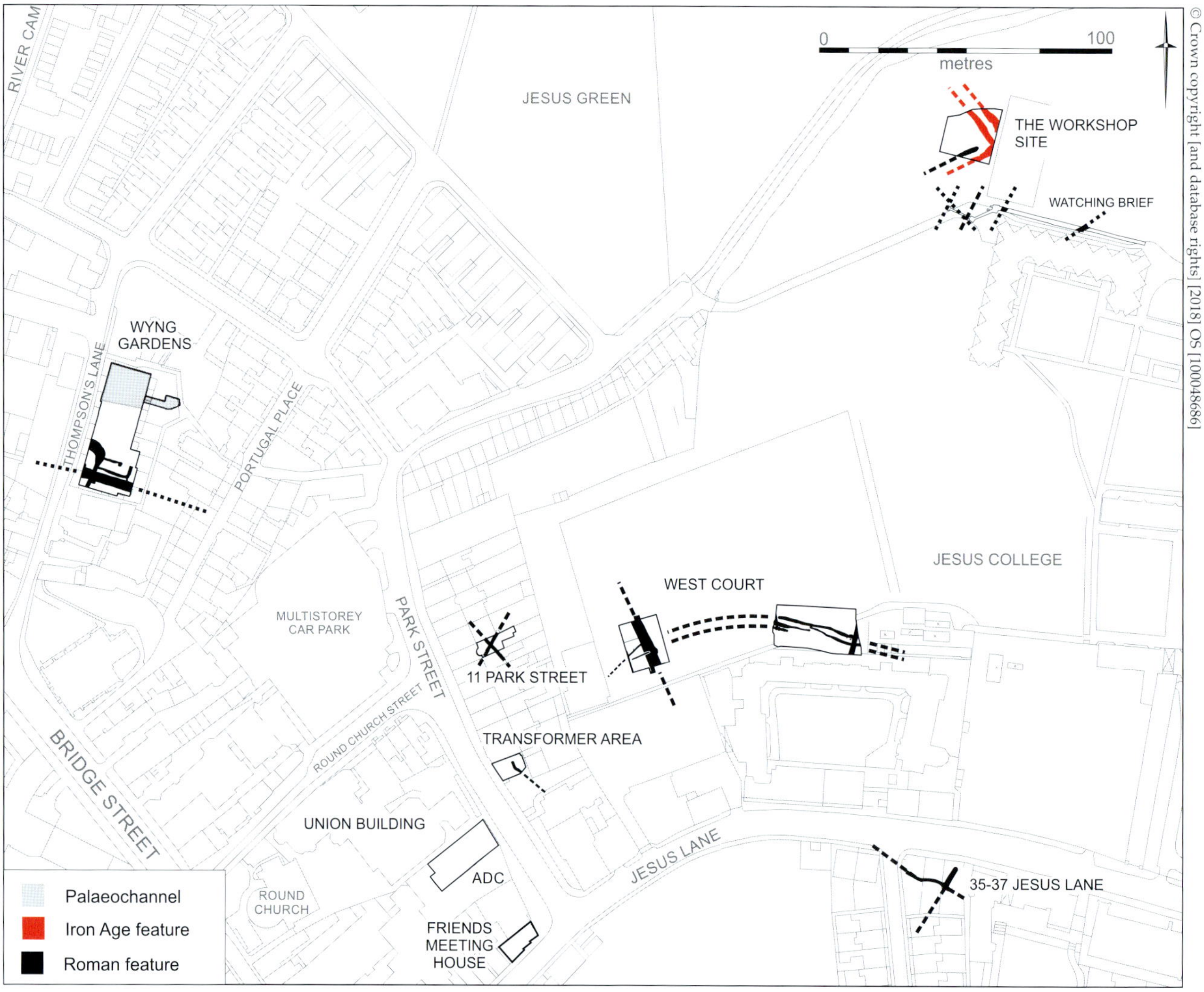

Figure 2.31. *Lower East Cam-side Roman Cambridge, showing site locations and main Roman-period features.*

been placed alongside three bodies, and there was a small Nene Valley pot with one juvenile and a pottery flask with an older woman. Analysed by Dodwell, it was a predominantly mature population exhibiting pathologies associated with heavy work and old age, and the cut marks on the vertebrae of the decapitated males were consistent with heavy-blade blows.

At two points the graves were seen to truncate earlier ditches, F.1 and F.2 (1–1.5 m wide and up to 0.5 m deep; Fig. 2.32).[26] A substantial body of finds were recovered from these, suggesting they were settlement-related. This included some 160 animal bones attributable to Roman contexts (62% cattle, 32% sheep, with pig and horse also present). Apart from the grave-good vessels and a sherd of first-century AD Terra Nigra, the 657 sherds of pottery mainly dated to the mid–later second to third centuries AD. Studied by Monteil, the assemblage is jar-dominated and suggests a rural-type pattern, whereas the diversity of the pottery in terms of its supply could reflect a more urbanized way of 'Roman living'. Attesting to local industry and relating to earlier evidence of Roman pottery production within the immediate area (Hughes 1903a), two possible wasters were also recovered.

The evidence as whole – the date of the earlier settlement features, the paucity of accompanying grave-goods (one burial having a later fourth-century AD Nene Valley vessel; another, a much used late second–third-century AD flask), the exclusive use of inhumation, the occurrence of hob-nails and the practice of decapitation – suggests that the cemetery dates from the later third–fourth centuries AD. As will later be highlighted in an overview of Roman Cambridge's many cemeteries, this one remains distinctive both on

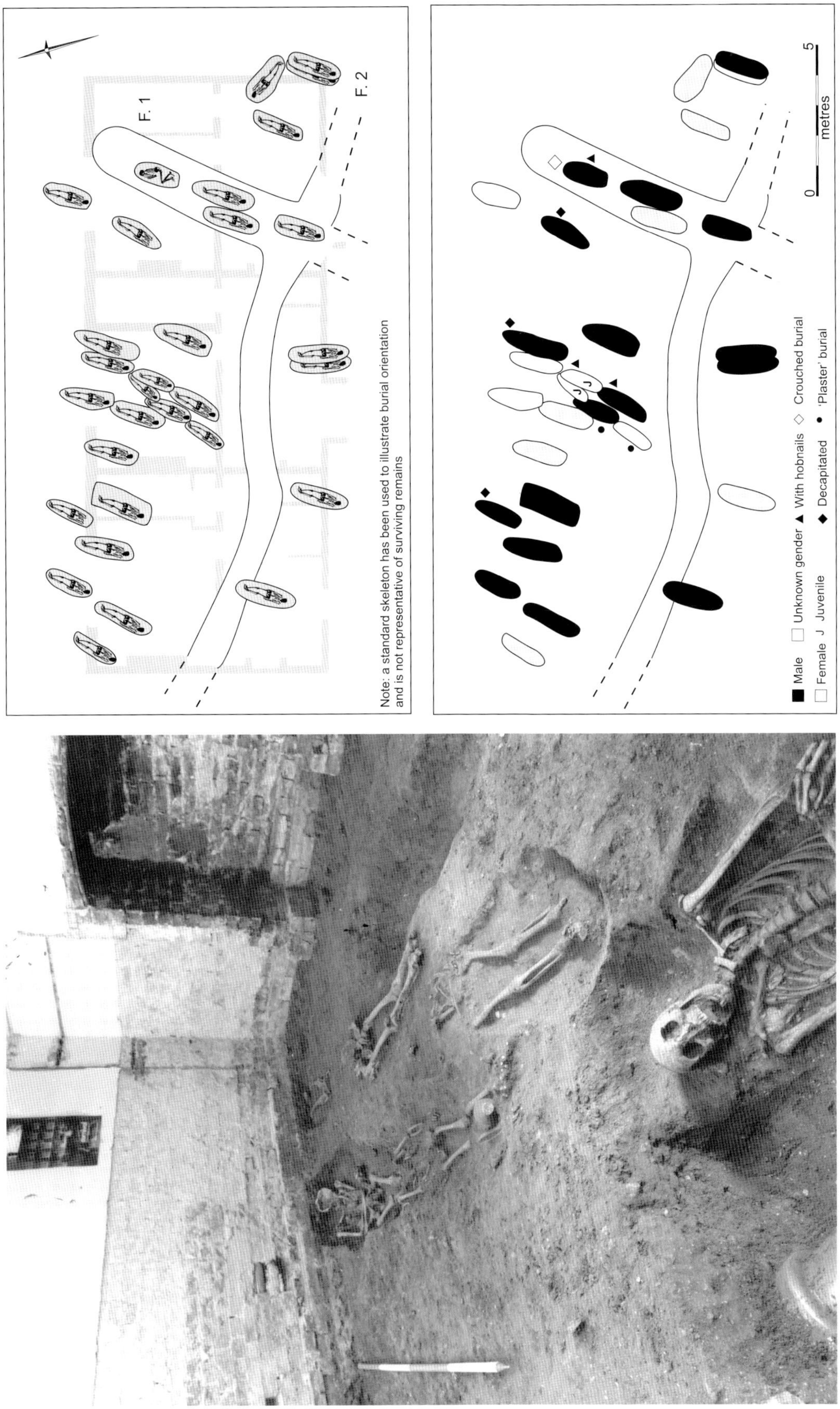

Figure 2.32. *Jesus Lane Cemetery, 2000 excavations: photograph (by Gwill Owen), base plan and burial-type distribution.*

account of its decapitation burials and its predominantly male population (see Chap. 7).

Following almost immediately, work at Number 11 Park Street in 2001, *c.* 170 m to the northwest, also unearthed cemetery remains, with the graves of two adults (one buried with a neonate) and the disarticulated remains of a sub-adult and five neonates being identified (Fig. 2.31; M. Alexander *et al.* 2004). A total of 54 sherds (2375 g) of pottery was recovered, mostly dating to the late second and third centuries AD, with some fourth-century AD material also present.

Whilst it is conceivable that, together with the Jesus Lane plot, this reflects one large cemetery, the Park Street portion is quite distinct given its frequency of neonates. The orientation of its graves differed from the Jesus Lane burials, suggesting that they were, in fact, separate burial grounds. However, other finds in the immediate area could argue against this. Although not recorded in the County's Sites and Monuments record, human remains excavated over a century ago at the Union Building, Friends' Meeting House and along Jesus Lane are catalogued in the both the Duckworth Collection and the Cambridge University Museum of Archaeology and Anthropology (see Fig. 2.31; see Alexander *et al.* 2004, 92). Unfortunately, the human bone in the Duckworth Collection consists only of disarticulated material (mainly skulls and leg bones) and in most cases it is poorly provenanced (e.g. '0409A, Cambridge Jesus Lane Drainage works, 1896, Baron Von Hugel' or '0597A, Cambridge behind Round Church [Union], Prof. Hughes'). In addition, dating this material is difficult. Both Roman and Anglo-Saxon material has been found in the area and those human remains recovered from behind the Round Church may be later and derive from the church graveyard. With these reservations, a total of 24 skulls are held in the Duckworth Collection having some reference to either Jesus Lane, the Friends' Meeting House or the Union Building (see below). The long bones held in the Duckworth Collection, all collected during drainage works, have been briefly examined and derive from a minimum of 15 individuals: 12 adults and three sub-adults.[27]

Jesus College Investigations

There have been other more recent excavations in College grounds that are of relevance here and warrant summary presentation (Fig. 2.31).

West Court (with Simon Timberlake and Dave Webb)
In 2015 the CAU undertook watching brief monitoring of building works at Jesus College's West Court (the Webb & Rank Buildings and Wesley House), with reduction occurring in four separate areas and archaeological remains present in three (Fig. 2.33; Timberlake & Webb 2016). In the largest, Basement Area (280 sq. m), behind/north of Wesley House, a series of shallow east–west oriented ditches were exposed, with there being another on a more southwest–northeast axis. While all seemed to be of Roman date, a more substantial ditch (NNE–SSW) along its eastern side could well have been Medieval (F.411). The Roman boundaries truncated a dense 'quarry field', involving intercutting hollows, 0.8–5 m across/long and 0.15–1 m deep. Although only summarily investigated, Roman pottery was recovered from a number. Moreover, in one ditch the upper half of a middle-aged female adult (human) was found, whose arms had been arranged in an unusually splayed manner.

Within the western Soakaway Area (207 sq. m) comparably minor ditches associated with a few minor pits might represent the southwestern continuation of the same boundary-perimeter as in the Basement Area. There, these also truncated a densely intercut quarry swathe (0.15–0.3 m deep). In this case, though, these were observed to post-date a much more major NNW–SSE oriented ditch-line (F.17), whose broad 'V'-shaped profile was some 4 m across and at least 1 m deep. (Amongst the Roman-attributed finds from this exposure was a single piece of iron smithing slag.)

Within the very small, westernmost area ('Park Street Transformer'; 20 sq. m) were exposed three oval pits, a posthole and a curvilinear ditch-length (Fig. 2.31). The conditions only allowed for one pit to be sectioned, but pottery recovered both from it and as surface finds dated to the late first–early second to third–early fourth centuries AD. These features were sealed by an occupation surface of Roman date and, all told, more than 460 sherds were recovered from this small area (8813 g), with most dating to the late third–fourth century AD (46%; 36% being late first–second-century AD); whereas just 97 (1656 g) and 34 sherds (519 g) were recovered from the Soakaway and Basements Areas respectively.

Aside from the scale of the exposed Roman quarrying (especially as no Roman road other than the *Via Devana* is known in the area; see Chap. 3) and the size of the pre-quarry boundary ditch within the Soakaway Area, of major importance is whether the double-ditch line within the Basement Area (arguably continuing east across the Soakaway Area) might actually mark the north limits of the lower Early Roman settlement (Fig. 2.33). If so, it then becomes relevant that the Jesus Lane cemetery – whose interments truncated 'Early' boundaries – lay some 150 m 'inside' and south of this line. Equally noteworthy is the scale of the assemblage recovered from the very small Park Street exposure.

The Maintenance Workshop Site (with Steve Williams)
In 2004 the CAU undertook excavations across a *c.* 260 sq. m plot in the northwest quarter of Jesus College's grounds in advance of the construction of a new Workshop and Gardener's Compound. This was well away from any of its known early buildings or that of the preceding nunnery (Fig. 2.31; Evans *et al.* 1998; Evans & Williams 2004).[28] The site was situated on Second Terrace gravels at *c.* 5.75–6 m OD and lay just above the floodplain of the River Cam. The scarp down to the Jesus Ditch at the edge of the College grounds, just to the north and west of the site, probably marks the floodplain-edge. The Jesus Ditch itself is an artificial channel, although it has been argued by Hughes (1907a, 413) that it follows an ancient river course.

Against a background of dispersed Neolithic/Bronze Age activity, the excavations revealed evidence of Iron Age settlement and a Roman boundary (and later features; Fig. 2.34). Accordingly, when shortly thereafter a major service trench was cut just south of the site, monitoring over a 120 m length provided further insights into the scale of this area's early land-use; its results are also outlined below (with Medieval and later features omitted).

A sparse scatter of unstratified and residual worked flint across the site (11 pieces) evinces 'background' activity from the Late Mesolithic/Early Neolithic and the later Neolithic. However, the only unequivocal early prehistoric feature was an irregular hollow F.114 containing two later Neolithic worked flints and four sherds of Beaker pottery. As identified by Mark Knight, the latter including refitting sherds from a Rusticated Beaker (Fig. 2.35); in addition,

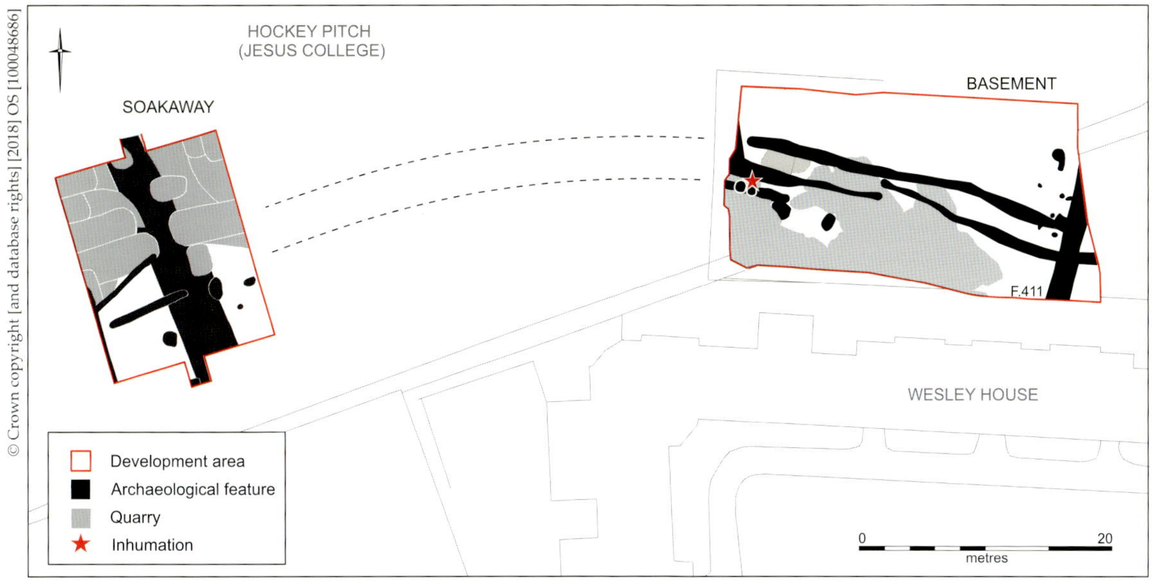

Figure 2.33. *Jesus College West Court: main area Roman-feature base plan and, below, photograph of Basement Area looking east.*

two small sherds of thin-walled Beaker were recovered from the evaluation phase, with one having all-over comb-type decoration.

A series of features excavated in the eastern half of the site are of definite Middle/later Iron Age attribution (Fig. 2.34). Across its northeastern half, four ditches ran parallel on a northwest–southeast alignment; three appeared to successively intercut: F.124 (0.6 m wide; 0.48 m deep), F.101 (1.4 m wide; 0.8 m deep) and F.102 (0.9 m wide; 0.28 m deep). Just south of these and the line of F.122 (a gully tentatively assigned to the Bronze Age), ditch F.107 ran parallel (*c.* 1.9 m wide; 0.7 m deep). Along the eastern edge of excavation the

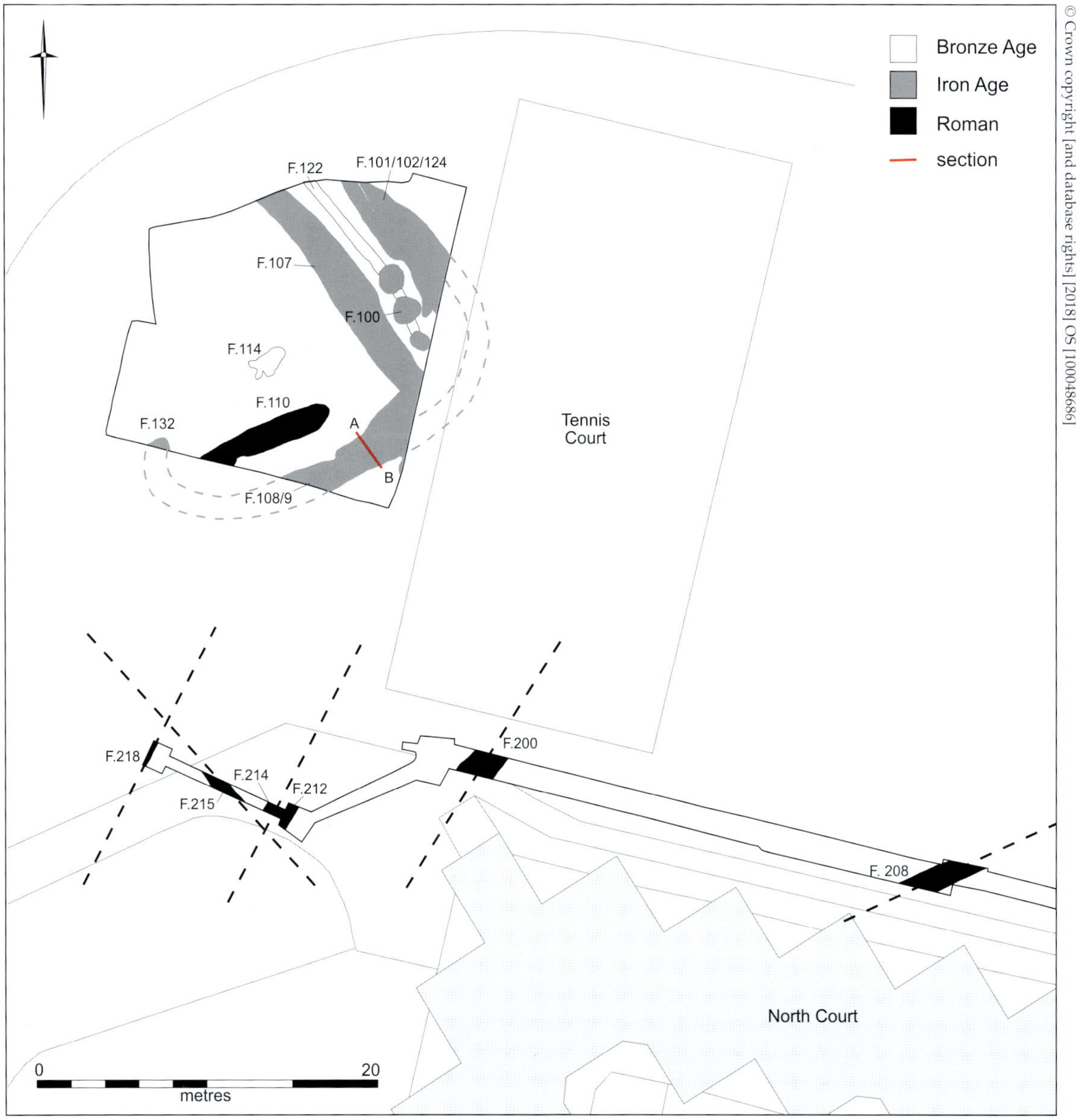

Figure 2.34. *Jesus College, Maintenance Workshop Site, prehistoric- and Roman-phase base plan.*

latter both terminated and also truncated ditch F.109, that was aligned on the return, northeast–southwest axis (2 m wide; 0.6 m deep). It, in turn, recut a somewhat more curvilinear ditch, F.108 (1.7 m wide; 0.6 m deep), but which essentially followed the same line.

Three pits can also be attributed to this phase, each truncating the F.122 gully (and set along its alignment). Of these, only F.100 was excavated (*c.* 1.4 m diam.; 0.5 m deep) and it yielded a small quantity of Iron Age pottery.

Only one feature was definitely of Romano-British attribution: F.110, a northeast–southwest-aligned ditch (*c.* 0.7 m wide; 0.35 m deep). This had second- to fourth-century AD pottery and a later Roman coin; three further later Roman coins, including a Barbarous Radiate, were found in residual contexts.

Amidst what were obviously Post-Medieval quarries and 'late' linear features, five probable Romano-British ditches were identified along the length of the adjacent service trench (F.200, F.208, F.212, F.215 & F.218; Fig. 2.34). Their dating was based on the character of their fills and associated finds, and all produced second- to third-century AD pottery. While only one sherd of Iron Age ware was recovered (residual within F.215), it is possible that some of the undated 'linears' might well have been of that period.

Artefact Assemblages

Some 105 sherds of Iron Age pottery were recovered from the excavation (Fig. 2.35), making a total of 116 sherds (1933 g) when the material from the earlier evaluation-phase is also considered. Fully reported upon by Leo Webley (in Evans & Williams 2004) and, on the grounds of form and fabric, virtually the whole assemblage can be dated to the Middle/later Iron Age, after *c.* 400/300 BC. It is typical for southern Cambridgeshire in this period in that dense quartz-tempered fabrics dominate, and that most vessels are Plain Wares with only occasional Scored Ware sherds.

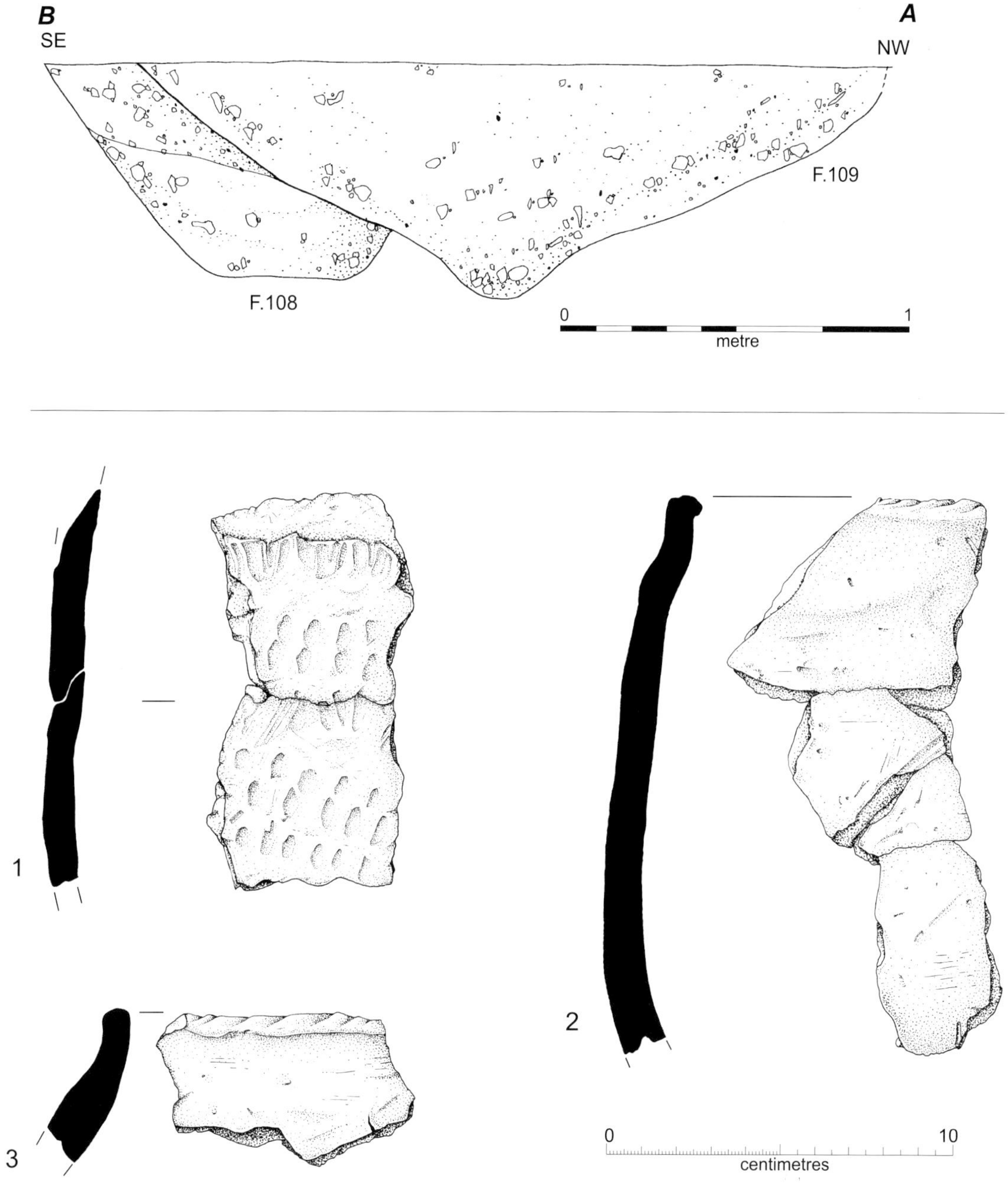

Figure 2.35. *Section across Iron Age ditch (above) and, below, prehistoric pottery: 1) Rusticated Beaker (F.114); 2) Middle Iron Age jar with rim-top fingernail decoration (quartz-tempered; F.2, from evaluation equating with F.108/109); 3) Middle Iron Age bowl with rim-top fingernail decoration (quartz-tempered; F.109).*

Studied by Anderson (*ibid.*), 35 sherds of Roman pottery were recovered (422 g). For the most part, these were small and abraded. With the exception of five unstratified pieces, all came from ditch F.110. They included a Central Gaulish Samian Dr.18/31 dish dated to the mid second century AD, sherds from Hadham oxidized ware vessels (mid third–fourth-century AD), a black-slipped dog dish (second–fourth century AD), sherds of Oxfordshire oxidized ware and sandy greywares, and also Nene Valley colour-coated wares; one of the latter being decorated with white painted swirls and berries, dating it to the third century AD. Comparable to the other assemblages from this part of the lower town, this material is firmly dated to the mid second to fourth century AD.

Faunal and Plant Remains

Only a small assemblage of animal bone was recovered (169 fragments). Of these, as studied by Swaysland, 74 fragments were identified to species and a further 21 were attributable to broad size-categories.

Table 2.2. *Withers heights of F.110 species.*

Species and Element	Length (cm)	Factor	Withers (cm)
Horse radius 1	34.7 (lateral length)	4.34	150.6
Horse radius 2	33.5 (lateral length)	4.34	145.4
Cow humerus	25.2 (length from caput)	4.77	120.2

Of the species-composition of the Iron Age animal bone, cattle and sheep/goat are dominant (*c.* 27% & 20% NISP respectively), and for both species a mixture of meat and non-meat bearing elements are present. Dog is represented by 13 bones (22%), which seem to have come from one partially articulated individual; there were three horse bones (5%).

Whilst the Roman assemblage from F.110 is too small to be in any way meaningful, it did yield three complete long bones: two left horse radii and a cattle humerus. These were measured and a withers (shoulder) height calculated using Kiesewalter and Matolcsi's factors (in von den Dreisch & Boessneck 1974; Table 2.2). The occurrence of two complete horse bones of the same element and side in such a small assemblage is uncommon. Moreover, the measurement indicates that, by the standards of the preceding Iron Age, these are larger animals and are likely to represent stock improvements, either by local improvements of husbandry or introductions of new varieties (Dobney 2001; see also Bower *et al.* in Evans *et al.* 2013b, 140–3).

Twelve bulk samples, from mostly ditch contexts, were analysed for their plant and mollusc remains and reported on by Rachel Ballantyne. Burial conditions appear to have been slightly dynamic; low to moderate amounts of untransformed rootlets, and two Elder seeds (*Sambucus nigra* L.) from ditch sample F.110 probably represent intrusive modern material (further evidence for intrusive ecofacts was provided by the mollusc shells).

The representation of plant remains within the samples is generally poor. The five samples taken from Iron Age ditch contexts only contain few remains. The majority of items were cereal grains; there was a mixture of wheat and barley, with neither clearly more abundant. There was no indication of the type of barley cultivated, and the wheat appears to have been a hulled variety: probably emmer or spelt wheat. One hulled wheat glume base (chaff fragment) was recovered from F.107, but is too heavily fragmented to identify further.

Charred seeds were rare, but occurred in pit F.100 and ditch F.108. The taxa, particularly stinking mayweed (*Anthemis cotula*) and scentless mayweed (*Tripleurospermum inodorum*), are types often found in association with Iron Age and Roman period cereal crops in southern Britain (cf. Jones 1981).

Discussion

The evidence of pre-Iron Age activity at this site does little more than further hint of the utilization of the local stretch of the terraces of the River Cam during the Neolithic and Bronze Ages.

Of the subsequent, Middle/later Iron Age phase, given the quantity of associated artefacts, there can be little doubt that we seeing occupation *per se* and that its ditches relate to some manner of settlement compound. Those of its early layout – F.101/F.102/F.124 in the case of its northwest–southeast axis, and F.108 for the southwest-northeast return – are rather more curvilinear and irregular than the boundaries that apparently superseded them (respectively F.107 & F.109; Fig. 2.34). This allows us to postulate an original, sub-rectangular rounded-corner settlement compound, with F.132 (an undated feature in the southwest corner) representing the terminal of a return to the F.108 axis. Of course, given the limited excavation exposure any reconstruction of its layout can only ever be an approximation; nevertheless, such an enclosure-plan would be typical of the period.

Thereafter, the two succeeding Iron Age boundaries (F.107/F.109) are straighter and seem to repeat the alignment of the initial F.122 gully, at least on the northwest–southeast axis. This orientation, moreover, then goes on to be 'echoed' in the layout of the Romano-British boundary, F.110 and also those ditches of the period exposed within the watching brief trench.[29]

Although only one definite Romano-British feature was identified within the excavation proper, the number of ditches attributable to this period within the adjacent service trench (and the quantity of associated artefacts) could well suggest the occurrence of settlement and not just a fieldsystem. If so, it may be relevant that only one Roman 'linear' seemed to be present over the easternmost 50 m of the watching brief trench.

The importance of this site lies in its provision of the first clear indication of what is probably a discrete Iron Age/Roman farmstead on Roman Cambridge's East-Cam bankside. Lying some 250 m north of what seems to be the northern edge of the main lower town settlement as exposed at Wesley House, this would seem to be a separate settlement (i.e. comparable to that of Burwell's Field south of Castle Hill; see below).

Other Investigations

An account of the 2014 excavations at WYNG Gardens on Thompson's Lane and other adjacent sites recently appeared in the *Proceedings of the Cambridge Antiquarian Society* (Cessford 2016a and 2017) and, accordingly, these will only be briefly summarized. The WYNG Gardens Site lay close to the river's eastern floodplain and there was a large east–west palaeochannel – apparently of Bronze Age origin – along the site's northern third (Figs. 2.31 & 2.36). The Roman sequence there was initiated in the first century AD when a major east–west ditch (3.4 m wide and 1.1 m deep), probably with an external bank on its northern side, crossed the southern side of the site-area; broadly contemporary alluvial deposits at its northern end indicate that the area was then subject to seasonal flooding.[30] In the mid second century AD, the bank was levelled and the ditch partially infilled. This created a platform-like area on which was constructed a post-in-trench timber building (4.6 × 9 m+). Accompanied by a few pits, on the building's demolition in the mid third century AD a new ditch-line, evidently relating to a west-lying enclosure, was established. A pathway was also created running down to the site's northern wetter margin and, at the edge of alluvium there, were two adult male graves. The upper portion of one had been scoured away and from the later deposits was recovered disarticulated human bone representing at least five adults. A coin occurred in one of the graves (AD 268–70) and, in total, there were 34 coins dating from the first to the later fourth centuries AD. A substantial quantity of pottery was recovered (*c.* 1940 sherds), including a high percentage of finewares, and a samian sherd that had graffiti on it – something rare in Cambridge's assemblages.

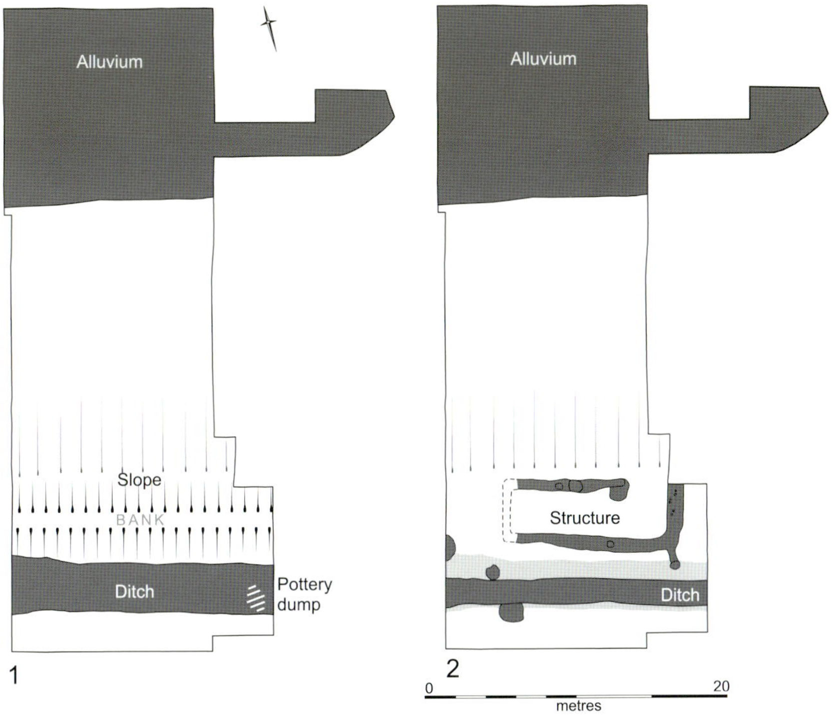

Figure 2.36. *WYNG Gardens: Roman-phase plans (above) and, below, photograph of southern end Roman-phase features (looking east).*

Aside from the occurrence of burial activity close to the river (and, thereby, seemingly comparable to the burials at the School of Pythagoras), the size of the first-century AD ditch along the site's southern side is important. Like Jesus College's West Court boundaries, this also may have marked the lower town's northern limits.

Roman archaeology was also encountered in the 2007–8 work on the so-called St John's Triangle Site north of All Saints Garden, between Trinity and Bridge Streets (see Fig. 2.41.10). The main excavation there occurred within the Old Divinity School and was directed towards its Medieval cemetery (Cessford 2015); however, pre-dating this was a dense Roman quarry field (possibly supplying metalling for the *Via Devana*; see Chap. 3) and a Late Roman burial was also recovered. Otherwise, the exposures consisted of scattered small trench-excavations and watching brief areas and, together, amounted to just under 200 sq. m of cover (Newman 2008a). Because of the depth of the stratigraphic sequence there (up to 4.5 m+) in a number of these, Roman levels were not actually achieved.

Of greatest relevance were the exposures in the vicinity of Number 68 Bridge Street and close to the *Via Devana's* frontage (the Corfield Court Site; see Fig. 2.41). There, again, probable first-century AD quarry pits were present. These were overlain by a series of refuse pits and Roman plot boundaries (a fence-line superseded by ditched gullies). These boundaries were found to extend for some 20 m back from the road and, given the areas of 'pit avoidance' within them, are likely to have marked a house plot. (To the rear, *c*. 0.5 m depth of 'dark earth-type' horticultural soil was observed in section.) In addition to both second- and third-century AD coins, over 500 sherds of pottery were recovered and, locally, the finds densities were

Acculturation and Illiterate Stamping – *Terra Nigra*

Analogies with historic European 'folk-culture' house symbols and their equipment- and stock-marking variants were highlighted in the second Haddenham Project volume (Evans & Hodder 2006b, 247) in relation to issues of later prehistoric household goods and inventories. No such evidence of 'marking' has yet to be found in our prehistoric assemblages, even those from waterlogged sites.[32] Yet, come the Romano-British era, 'signing' suddenly abounds in, for example, pottery graffiti, owner's marks and stamps (see e.g. J. Evans 1987). This raises issues of how widespread literacy was; items such as styli and wooden message tablets are obviously significant markers here (see e.g. Evans *et al*. 2013b, 161–2).

In this context, a marker that seems to be particularly telling is 'illiterate', or at least 'non-named', Terra Nigra and Terra Rubra stamps. These distinct latest Iron Age/earliest Roman finewares were imported from Gaul, but were also imitated locally. Based on a very small regional data-set, these wares are not common when compared to samian; there do, though, seem to have been two types of 'illiterate' stamping.[33] Both forms featured in the *Borderlands* volume and other local examples have since come to light. One occurred in the rich Conquest Period cremation burial at Clay Farm, Addenbrooke's (F.566; *BLS*, 157–66). Along with its patera fittings, a triangular knife, two worked bone dice, silver plaques, a samian platter, an amphora and a flagon, were three Terra Nigra vessels. The latter included two plates stamped with conventional makers' names (i.e. 'readable'; as was also the samian plate); but there was also a Terra Nigra cup stamped with a swirling linear pattern (*BLS*, fig. 3.12.3).[34] In the 2005 Newnham College Kitchen excavations a platter base-sherd with what appears to be half of the same pattern (or a near-match) was recovered (Fig. 2.37). Effectively amounting to a cartouche, almost as if it had been impressed by a signet ring, although not a name as such, there is nothing unsophisticated in such die-makers. Indeed, they seem akin to modern-day 'logos'.

The other form of marker seems, in effect, to imitate written script-names. The example illustrated in *Borderlands* (fig. 1.10; see also fig. 2.30.4), from the Cambridge Airport investigations (Cooper 2003a), occurred on a locally made imitation of a Terra Nigra-type platter. Set in in a long rectangle, directly like a 'named' stamp (as opposed to the squarer shape of the cartouche types), it consists of three circles impressed into triangles. This is similar to a locally made stamped Gallo-Belgic platter from Duxford (Lucas in Price *et al*. 1997, 65, fig. 30). This cruder form of stamped marker would still have distinguished a potter or workshop, but this 'script-suggestive' form seems to tell more directly of acculturation in the Conquest Period and, effectively, the *mimicking of writing*.

While two of the vessels within the Snailwell burial – a Terra Rubra plate and a Terra Nigra cup – had 'signature stamps', another Terra Nigra cup had an unnamed stamp (Lethbridge 1954, 33–5, fig. 3). That 'warrior' burial's assemblage thus tells of the juxtapositions arising from 'contact acculturalization'. The quality of its imported pottery and metalwork jars against its decorated check-pieces/snaffle-bits (*ibid.*, 31–2, fig. 2), whose crude circle-and-dot and chevron-motif decoration – with vague affinities to the repertoire of local Gallo-Belgic illiterate stamps – could happily sit in the Early Iron Age, if not the Late Bronze Age (referencing the *Iliad*, Lethbridge drew parallels with such bits from All Cannings Cross: *ibid.*, 32).[35] Clearly, these reflect an underlying tradition of 'basic' decoration that had been current for upwards of a 1000 years.

Nine Gallo-Belgic stamped pottery vessels were recovered from Cambridge itself (plus other apparently 'literate' stamps; *RCAM*, 118, pl. XX; see also *Gallo-Belgic pottery database: internet edition* at http://www.ox.ac.uk). As is evident from Rigby's distribution map of such vessels (1973, fig. 8), there is a high frequency of such wares in the greater Cambridge Region (see also Fox 1923, 201–2 & pl. XX) and, together with Cambridge's brooches (see below), this also indicates the status and scale of its Late Iron Age/Conquest Period settlement.

Of further interest are the linkages of our Cambridge examples with sites to the south such as those at Duxford and Addenbrooke's. This, in itself, tells of the axis of Cambridge's Late Iron Age/Conquest Period northern Aylesford-Swarling-border connections (see Hill *et al.* 1999).

Figure 2.37. *Cambridge stamping Gallo-Belgic pottery: the Newnham College Kitchen platter (top) and, below, Roman Cambridge vessel stamps* (RCAM, *pl. XXXV).*

high (up to 38 sherds per metre-square). The pottery was of second- to fourth-century AD date, with most attributable to the second and third centuries AD.

At this point we could continue to review a series of early antiquarian findings within the area and other investigations of the last 25 years. The first category would include Hughes' observations of great quantities of Roman finds during the construction of the Student Union Building (1898 and 1907a), and within the latter category would be the 2002 evaluation trenching within the yard of the ADC Theatre on Park Street where, in one of its two small trenches, dense Roman archaeology was encountered (again, largely of second–third-century AD date, but with some fourth-century AD activity; Whittaker 2002). There could also be enlisted the excavations in 1992 at St John's College New Library Site (see Fig. 2.41; Dickens 1996b). Predominantly of fourth-century AD date, it would seem that a series of quarry pits in one area there had contributed to a gravel surface in another. This was sealed by a dark humic silty clay in which an east–west pathway was established and, lying close to the river, by then the area had clearly reverted to wetland (overlying alluvial deposits attesting to inundation in the Anglo-Saxon period). In total, some 315 Roman sherds were recovered.

There is little point in continuing in this manner, as clearly the East Cam-bank findings now warrant a much more comprehensive review. Hopefully, though, this summary has been sufficient to indicate that Roman Cambridge did indeed have a significant 'lower' settlement on either side of the river crossing (and which now corresponds with evidence from the School of Pythagoras). While the WYNG Gardens-area might well mark its northern riverside limits, all that can be said based on fieldwork to date is that it may not have extended as far south as Trinity College.[31] What is particularly relevant is the evidence of Late Roman activity. It seems to have been both extensive and dense, and occurring well outside the area of the defences – and along the *Via Devana* for, at least, *c.* 400 m, south of the river-crossing – this would certainly suggest that Late Roman Cambridge was more than just a 'fortified village'.

Extending over some 5.7 ha, as depicted in Cessford's 2017 paper, the lower town-area's 'Late' imprint has largely been defined/confined by its contemporary cemetery evidence. In the same way that Castle Hill's 'Early' settlement (first to early–mid third century AD) was much more extensive than the area that was eventually walled, this is also true of its lower East Bank settlement. The Jesus College-area findings are most significant here. Leaving aside the evidence of the Maintenance Workshop farmstead to the north and what seems to be the main settlement's northern limits in the two West Court exposures, the scale of the second- to third-century AD occupation evidence at Numbers 35–37 Jesus Lane is crucial and definitely pre-dates its 'Late' inhumation cemetery. Accepting that this was fully a part of the lower town, this would add, as a minimum, a further 2.8 ha to its area and take the lower settlement's total to at least 8.5 ha. Two other observations are warranted concerning the East Bank settlement. First, despite the recovery of a sherd of Terra Nigra from the cemetery site's preceding phase, the area apparently lacks the Late Iron Age occupation of the Castle Hill-area (and its immediate 'fringe'; see, though, below concerning the Union Building-area findings). The second point will only really be appreciated when the area's other cemeteries are presented in this and the next book: with Park Street's number of neonates and Jesus Lane's high proportion of males and decapitated burials, just how very different the lower settlement's burial populace seems.

Cambridge Southwest-Sector Sites

There is not the scope here to outline the results of the many small-scale interventions that have taken place along the city's southwestern perimeter, and from the West Cambridge lands south towards Barton Road. We will present here a summary of the more major findings, particularly those early settlements running along the western side of the river. However, given the *ad hoc* character of fieldwork-recovery across this swathe, settlement densities are not something that can be established from its findings to date.

Burrell's Field (with Kasia Gdaniec)

In 1992 six 5 × 5 m test squares were dug in advance of the construction of student hostel pavilions in Trinity College's Burrell's Field grounds south of St John's Playing Fields and immediately northwest of the Bin Brook (Fig. 2.38; Gdaniec 1992). Three with archaeological features were then expanded and augmented by trenching. Apart from one in the northeast (enlarged to investigate a series of intercutting Medieval ditches), this was restricted to the two southwestern areas containing pre-Medieval features.

In Area 1, a prehistoric ditch-line ran across the northwestern side of the exposure coming to a southern butt-end just before the western edge of excavation. In the east, it arced to the north and its line was again exposed in an additional trench dug along its projected alignment. This was 0.75 m wide and 0.35–0.4 m deep, and 38 fragments of bone, four worked flints (Late Neolithic/Early Bronze Age) and 32 burnt stones were recovered from the three metre-long segments excavated along it. While it cannot be dated with absolute certainty, in all likelihood it relates to the scraps of Iron Age pottery found elsewhere in this area (and in Area 2).

A series of Roman features were also present there. These include two parallel ditches, 4.5–5 m apart, which may represent a droveway. The western of these was generally more minor, being *c.* 0.3–0.5 m wide and 0.05–0.2 m deep, whereas the eastern showed a more complicated sequence of recutting. Given the quantity of Romano-British sherds found in their fills (and the complete lack

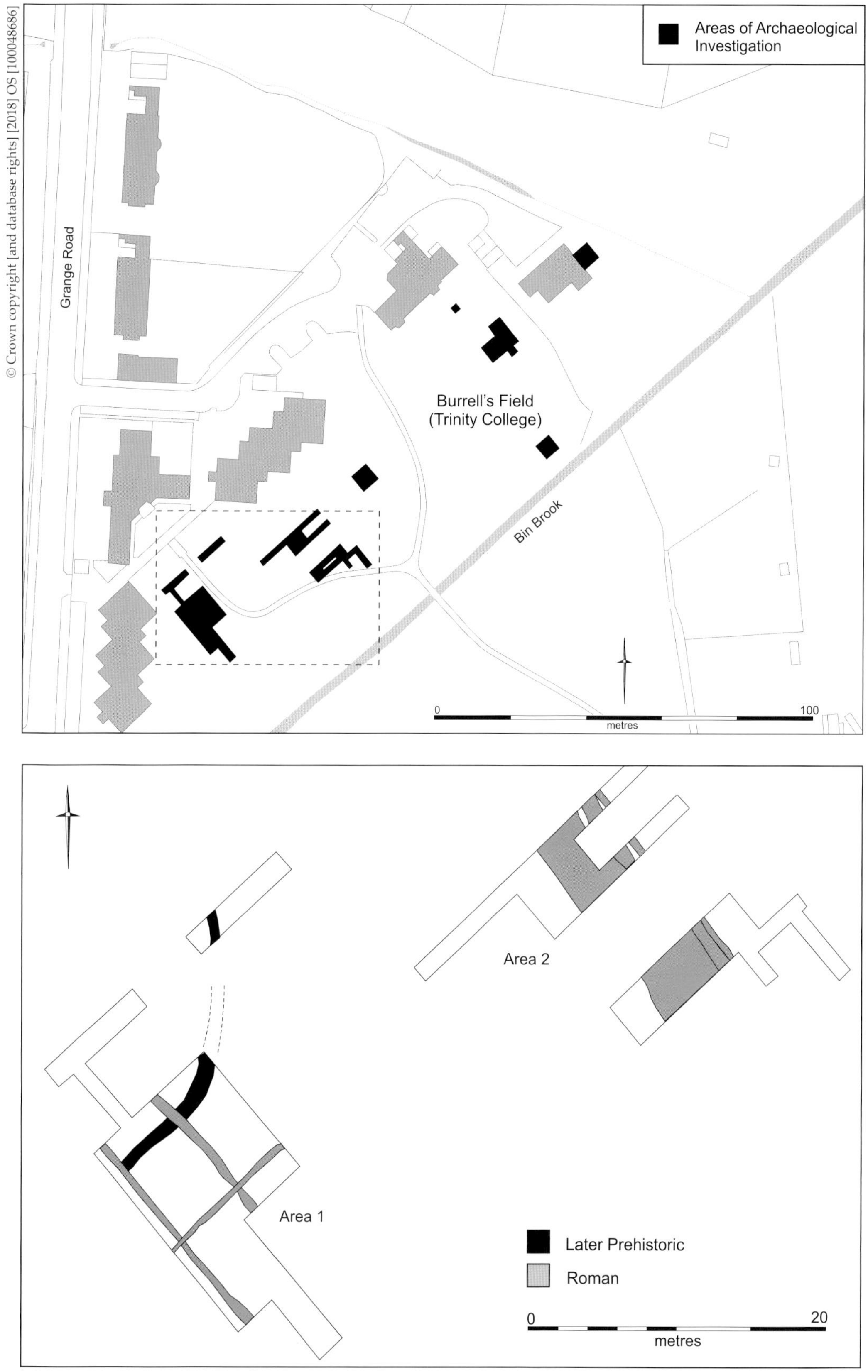

Figure 2.38. *Burrell's Field excavation, location map and prehistoric and Roman-phase base plan.*

of later material), there can be little doubt of the Roman date of these features. The same cannot be said of the northeast–southwest-oriented ditch (F.6) that cut across them. With a 'beam-slot-like' profile, although assigned to the same period based on its finds (a flint flake and three Roman sherds), it could conceivably have been later (e.g. Medieval or Post-Medieval).

Within Area 2, a small east–west-oriented palaeochannel – presumably an early meander of the Bin Brook – was found to be cut by a succession of parallel, intercutting Roman ditches. Collectively 6 m across and 0.5–0.7 m deep, the quantity of Roman pottery recovered from them (with no later material present) left no doubt of their attribution.

In keeping with the limited scale of the excavations, the resultant finds assemblages were modest. Just eight later Iron Age sherds were recovered (though it included one that was wheelmade from clearly non-local oolitic limestone-derived clays). Three of the sherds are decorated with incised lines (including the wheelmade one), with two having incised horizontal lines and, the third, a curved line on a burnished surface.

The Romano-British pottery assemblage of 59 sherds broadly dates to the later first/very early second century (i.e. *c.* AD 70–120). The material is abraded and there are few diagnostic sherds, but there is an element of the Flavian 'Gallo-Belgic' type vessels characteristic of the region (e.g. beakers and flasks/flagons), with a lack of the more typical second-century AD Roman forms and fabrics. There was one noteworthy sherd: a lead-glazed piece from an open form that may be a Roman lead-glazed ware bowl of the Southeast English group.

Although the few animal bones recovered were not very informative the bulk sampling for plant remains, as studied by Chris Stevens, provided some interest. Two samples were analysed from the prehistoric ditch in Area 1, from which only a single seed of Chenopodiaceae, a possible seed of plantain (*Plantago major*) and a single grain of barley (*Hordeum* sp.) were recovered. A lump of possible dung or bread was also identified.

Seven samples were examined from Romano-British contexts. Few of these were particularly rich in remains, with the exception of ditch [020] in Area 2. There is evidence for the cultivation of both barley and glume wheats, probably spelt. The [020] sample indicated the cultivation of at least wet, and perhaps also drier sandy soils from the presence of charlock (*Raphanus raphanistrum*), prickly sedge (*Carex muricata* (group)) and sheep's sorrel (*Rumex acetosella*). There was no indication of the farming of floodplain grasslands, usually shown by the presence of seeds of spikerush (*Eleocharis* sp.), nor of heavy clay soils by the absence of seeds of *Anthemis cotula* that are present upon similarly dated sites in the region.

Prior to the stripping of the areas, metre-squares were hand-dug though the soil horizons to gauge their finds densities. With single pieces of worked flint found in just two of the eight test pits, this density can only be considered very low when compared to other riverside terrace-contexts (e.g. Over: Evans *et al.* 2016). That said, a respectable quantity of 23 pieces of worked flint was recovered as a whole. Though generally of Late Neolithic/earlier Bronze Age attribution – and including a barbed-and-tanged arrowhead – there was at least one diagnostically earlier Neolithic item, a blade. The residues from one of Area 2's bulk samples (residual in a Roman-phase ditch) had 10 small flint flakes, which could well attest to local flintworking.

The Burrell's Field Site seems to represent the eastern margin of an Early Roman settlement that was preceded by a degree of Iron Age occupation (and, before that, Neolithic and Bronze Age usage). It is noteworthy that the Roman ditch-lines all lay at a right-angle to the unusual alignment of the Bin Brook stream over this length – from the area of Robinson College northeast to the Cam in the grounds of St John's College – which is parallel with Roman Akeman Street. The stream appears 'regularized' at this point, and this raises the possibility that its straightening occurred in Roman times.

In 1996 trenching behind the University Library in advance of a new Western Bookstack Range (Gibson 1996) identified a northwest–southeast-oriented ditch. With no direct dating evidence, it appeared 'pre-Medieval' and, given its shared alignment with the Roman ditches at Burrell's Field, probably related to that settlement's fieldsystem.[36]

Newnham College/Sidgwick Site Area (with Nick Armour, Simon Timberlake and Dave Webb)

The Newnham-area has long been archaeologically renowned, primarily for the extraordinary Late Iron Age burial excavated, at the turn of the last century, by Von Hugel at Newnham Croft south of Barton Road (Fox 1923, 81, pl. XV; Lethbridge 1954; Cra'ster 1973; see also Parfitt 1995). Nearby, in the vicinity of Croft Lodge, Anglo-Saxon burials have been unearthed since the late nineteenth century (Meaney 1964) and the College grounds would appear to be bracketed by settlements of that date. To the north, a small seventh-century inhumation cemetery was excavated in 2000 during an expansion to King's College Garden Hostel and, two years later, a settlement of comparable date was dug on the site of the University's new Criminology Institute, some 300 m to the south (Fig. 2.39). As the Anglo-Saxon phases of these two sites have been fully published (Dodwell *et al.* 2004) they need not concern us here, and rather it is their traces of earlier occupation that require outlining.

The only 'early' feature at the Garden Hostel excavation was a single pit. This yielded some 50 sherds of Post-Deverel Rimbury pottery, representing at least 10 vessels, and these were associated with animal bone (Dodwell 2001). In total, 20 worked flints were recovered, the majority of Late Bronze Age/Early Iron Age date. Only nine small and abraded Roman sherds were recovered, probably derived from manuring (second century AD; a Roman coin re-used as a brooch was included in one of the Anglo-Saxon graves).

At the Criminology Site, 34 sherds of mid second- to fourth-century AD pottery were recovered, along with eight worked flints (one an earlier Neolithic core; Armour *et al.* 2003). Although the Roman material was abraded and probably represents a manuring spread, it led us to suspect that the site lay closer to the core of a nearby Roman settlement.[37] This, indeed, proved to be the case when work commenced at Newnham College proper during the 2005 development of its former Kitchen and Buttery along Sidgwick Avenue (Fig. 2.39; Webb *et al.* 2006). A network of substantial Roman-period ditches was present, with an associated pottery dump; some 160 sherds of first- to fourth-century AD date were recovered (including a stamped Terra Nigra platter; see *Inset*, above), along with a fourth-century AD coin.

The University Museum holds some Roman-period pottery (plus some metalwork) that has, over the years, been recovered from the College. This includes material found during the construction of air raid shelters in 1939, when a group of five inhumations was excavated by Dorothy Garrod (Hills 2010). These are now known to be Anglo-Saxon in date (S. Leggett pers. comm.). Unfortunately, their exact location was undocumented and, in 2010, Access Archaeology (ACA) dug two trenches within the central College grounds to determine where the 1939 fieldwork had taken place (Ranson 2016). Although neither evidence of the air raid shelters or further inhumations were found, Roman ditch-features were, with some 300 sherds of second- to fourth-century AD date recovered.

The limited fieldwork undertaken at Ridley Hall (both CAU and ACA), to the west, has demonstrated a long span of usage (Brittain 2009; Lewis *et al.* 2013). As well as a high density of flintwork (140 pieces) dating from the Mesolithic to the Bronze Age, a handful of Late Iron Age sherds were present and at least one feature was suspected to be of that date. In the main, though, the ditch systems there are of first- and second-century AD date, with some 50 Roman-period sherds recovered; that there were also tiles – some with mortar adhering – could attest to an impressive building nearby. Also present were Early Anglo-Saxon occupation spreads, with 12 sherds of that date.[38]

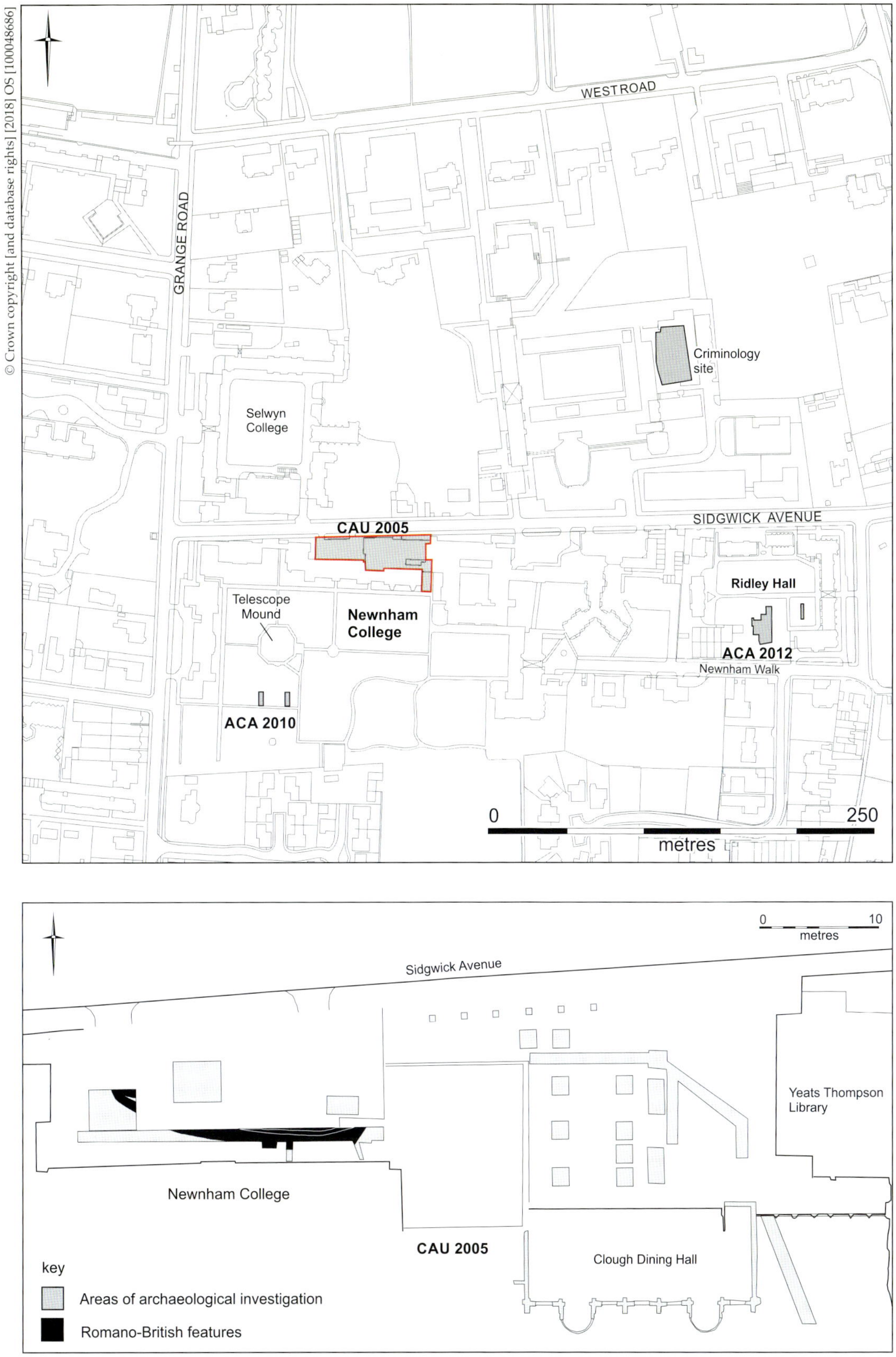

Figure 2.39. *Newnham College, location map and plan of 2005 Kitchen investigations.*

Barton Road (with Duncan Mackay)
A 31.5 ha plot bordering the southern side of Barton Road near its junction with the M11, and just south of the line of Roman Akeman Street, was trench-evaluated in 2001 (Fig. 2.40; Mackay 2002). With predominantly Gault Clay geology, the soil survey records a local outcropping of Lower Chalk across its southwest quarter, which may relate to the fact that the west-central part of the area had been truncated through coprolite quarrying. Iron Age ditches, pits and gullies extended throughout some 2.8 ha of the area's central swathe (the settlement being truncated by the quarries and extending into the road corridor in the north). Of the some 325 prehistoric pottery sherds recovered (4.9 kg), there was a minor Early Iron Age/Late Bronze Age component, which appeared to focus in the south of the settlement core. The vast majority of the pottery was, however, grog-tempered wheelmade wares of Late Iron Age date and probably of the first century BC. A quantity of animal bone was also found in association, and there can be no doubt of this being a substantial Iron Age settlement. Only one definite Early Roman sherd was recovered and there seems no question of settlement continuity into the Roman period.

Lying on a distinct rise some 700 m south of this settlement is an extensive (and dense) cropmark site, located on Lower Chalk deposits (Fig. 2.40). In the main, it consists of a ladder-like series of sub-square/-rectilinear compounds, which are linked by more minor field- and, possibly, droveway-related boundaries. Plotted across 5.6 ha, this complex clearly extends further southwards and is probably at least 6.75 ha in area, if not greater. What seems to be the northern arc of a circular configuration lies outside the main complex (Fig. 2.40.A). Some 40 m across, this surely is prehistoric and may either mark a barrow or a large ring-ditch (alternatively it could relate to one side of an 'organic' Iron Age settlement compound).

At first glance the layout of the main cropmark settlement seems very different to, for example, that of Vicar's Farm (see Chap. 4): seemingly more extensive and of a general east–west orientation. Yet its core compounds (Fig. 2.40 inset) are basically laid out on the same 'generic' northwest–southeast axis as Vicar's Farm; it is only the westernmost rectangle (Fig. 2.40.B) and some of the interlinking boundaries that follow the east–west orientation. Informal fieldwalking has occurred across this area, with Early Roman material collected.[39]

The recovery of evidence for both earlier prehistoric (e.g. Neolithic and Bronze Age), as well as both Iron Age and Roman-period settlement, at Burrell's Field was held at the time to be something quite 'special'; it was, after all, a first within Cambridge's immediate environs. Now, though, with a much greater appreciation of actual early settlement densities across much of the county, particularly in its main river valleys (*BLS*, chap. 3), it can no longer be counted as anything extraordinary. Even the occurrence of a Roman settlement just some 500 m south of the Roman town and another *c.* 600 m south of it at Newnham's riverside will be seen to be nothing out of the ordinary, reflecting the same general settlement intervals as across most of West/North West Cambridge's lands. Indeed, as is discussed in the *Riversides...* volume (chap. 6), in some areas – for example alongside the Cam at Trumpington or the Ivel near Biggleswade in Bedfordshire – the period's riverside settlement interval reduces to 200–300 m. It is in fact likely that other such settlements still await discovery along this Cambridge South–Newnham swathe. Candidates would include Tyndale House in Selwyn Gardens (Wills 2003a). Dispersed Roman features have been encountered there and in other locations. However, it can be difficult to even detect Roman settlements, given the often low internal density of their features, making their extent and even their existence far from certain.

Walker's recovery of six skeletons during house construction at 71 Grange Road is salient for discussions of Roman Cambridge's neighbouring farmsteads, and also the scale of its associated cemeteries (1912). Variously of Roman and Anglo-Saxon date (there also being a few Anglo-Saxon cremations), one of the Roman-attributed males was buried with a pot, an iron spearhead and a piece of *lorica segmentata* armour plate (*ibid.*, 123–5, pl. xii). Although no early remains were recovered during more recent evaluation trenching in the back of that property (Mortimer 1995; Fig. 1.10), Walker reported that during the house's construction 'a good deal of Roman pottery was turned out' (*ibid.*, 123), which suggests settlement of that date in the immediate area. Bordering the west side of Akeman Street and Roman Cambridge's southern approach, how are we to account for this? Lying some 450 m southwest of the Roman defences (and 300 m beyond Madingley Road in that direction; see Fig. 1.10), do the graves represent an extension of the St John's Playing Fields cemetery (of which von Hugel provided no accurate mapping)? If so, Grange Road's evidently domestic remains could attest to continuous 'suburban' roadside settlement, equivalent perhaps to that at New Hall (see Chap. 3), or similar to what Green proposed for Godmanchester (Fig. 2.42; see below). Alternatively, these – and not the Burrell's Field Site – could relate to the first 'independent' farmstead south of Roman Cambridge. Unfortunately, at this time there is simply not adequate information to determine this.

Are the area's Anglo-Saxon densities – especially now with cemeteries known in St John's Playing Fields, at King's College Garden Hostel and Croft Lodge in Newnham – something that was distinct to Cambridge? While this interval of cemeteries may seem high, recent recovery rates of contemporary settlements within the Cam Valley south of Cambridge are also very high (see *RVS*, chap. 6). Accordingly, one suspects that here, in Cambridge's 'shadow' as it were, this just evinces basic landscape-wide distributions and was not somehow town-specific or necessarily 'ancestral' (cf. Taylor 1999, 39–50).

Yet Newnham has clearly been something 'special' and a long-term place in its own right. Starting with its extraordinary Iron Age burial, its subsequent Roman settlement was thereafter flanked by Anglo-Saxon cemeteries – at King's Garden Hostel and Croft

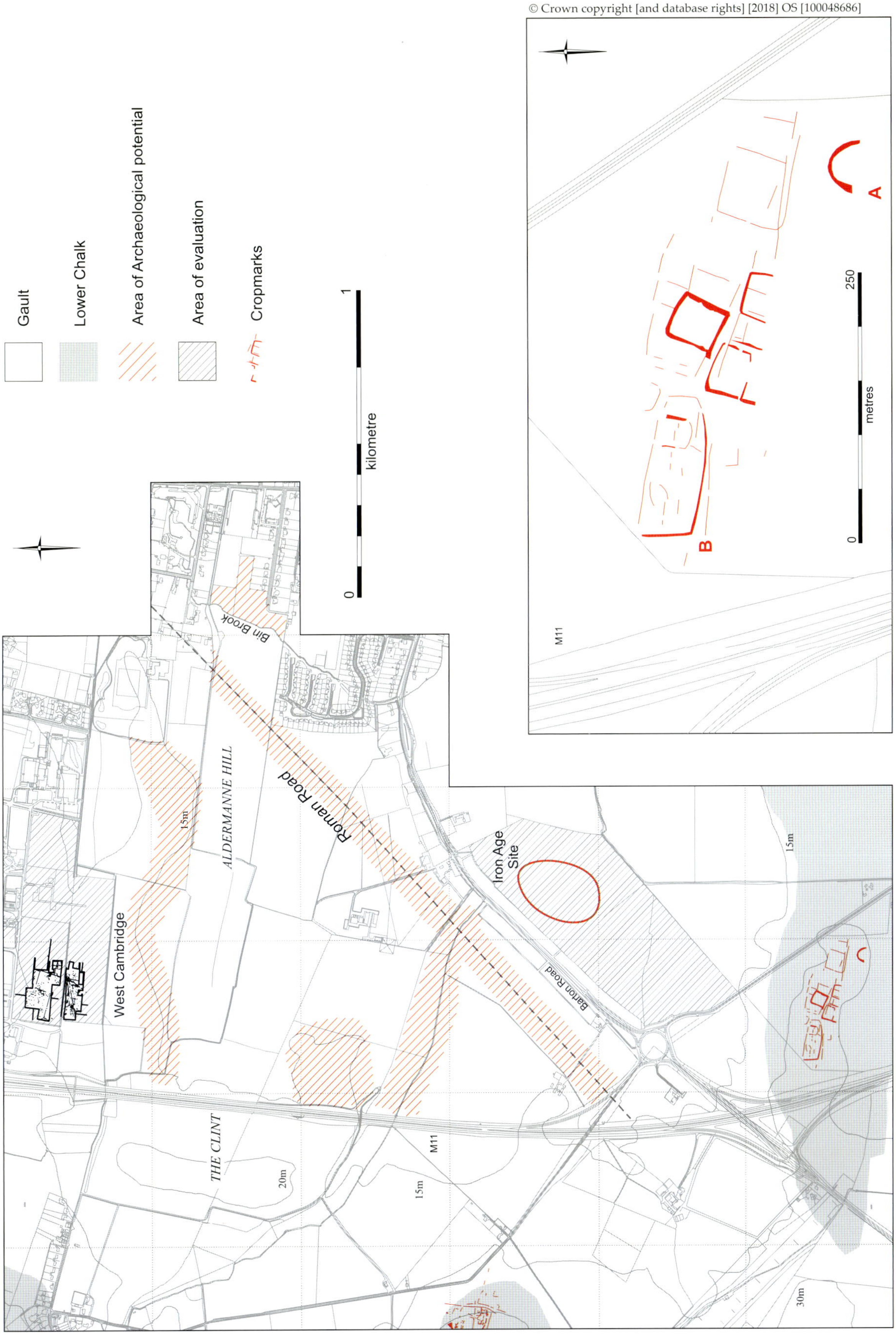

Figure 2.40. *West Cambridge, southwest-sector map, showing Barton Road Iron Age settlement, cropmark sites and postulated critical site-location swathes (only within the line of the M11).*

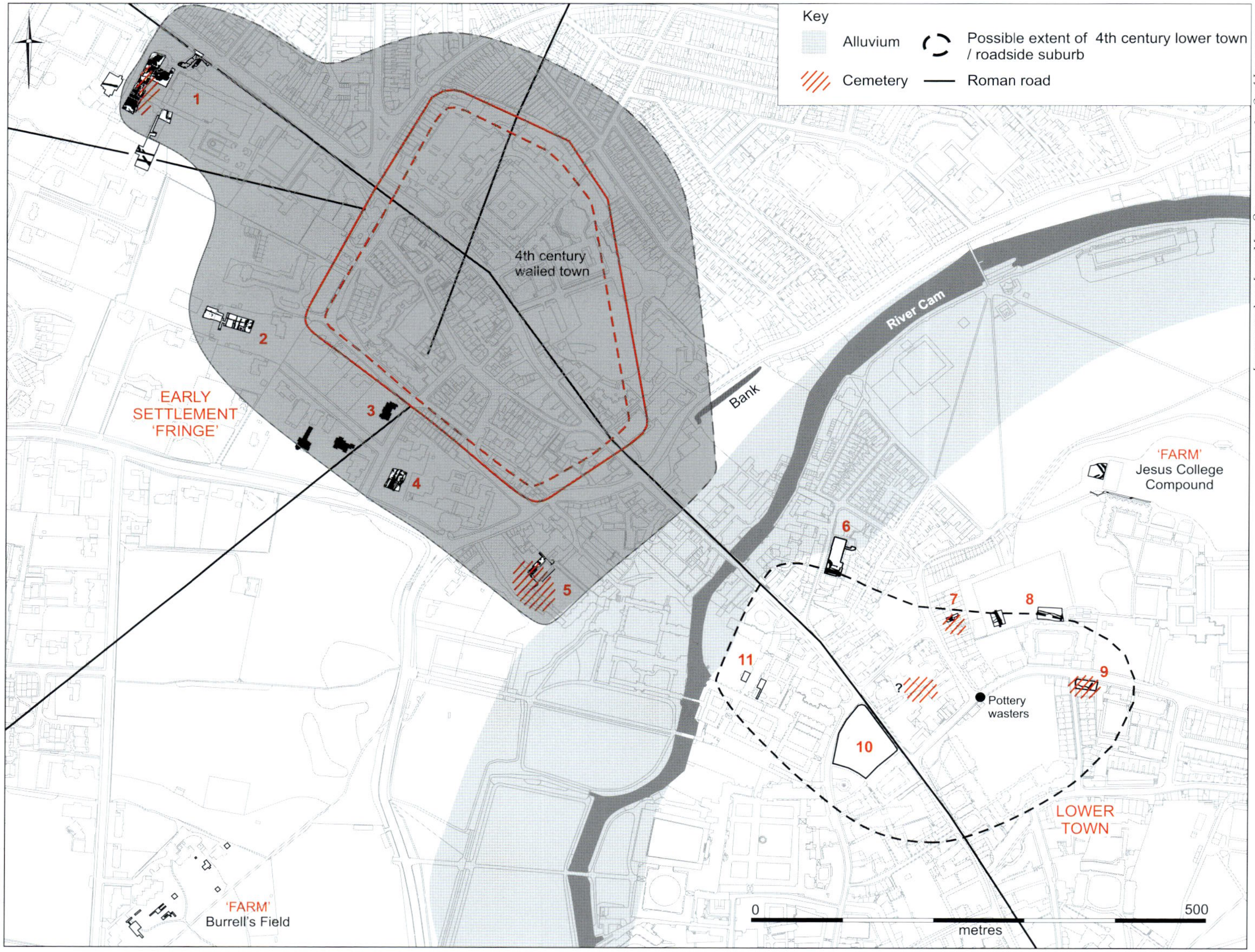

Figure 2.41. *Greater Roman Cambridge: 1) New Hall/Fitzwilliam Colleges; 2) St Edmund's College; 3) Macalister's 'house' investigations (see Fig. 2.27); 4) Westminster College; 5) School of Pythagoras; 6) WYNG Gardens; 7) 11 Park Street; 8) Jesus College West Court; 9) 35–37 Jesus Lane; 10) St John's 'Triangle'/Corfield Court; 11) St John's College Library.*

Lodge (and now in the College grounds themselves) – and, also, settlements of that date (Institute of Criminology and Ridley Hall). Undoubtedly significant on a number of counts, it seem unlikely that this complex will ever be adequately understood, given the degree to which it has already been built on and, otherwise, the restrictions of working in well-kept college grounds.

It is difficult to appreciate the significance of the Barton Road Site pending further fieldwork, although its Iron Age date and size is clearly significant. Indeed, this is one of the problems of now having worked at such a landscape-wide scale as in West/North West Cambridge. One realizes just how many settlements existed within *networks* and it becomes difficult to talk with any confidence about the 'meaning' of isolated individual sites.

Certainly, Cambridge's southwestern-sector appears as a 'desert' when compared to the northern-area focus of these books. The Unit has outlined its archaeological potential in a number of commissioned studies (e.g. Evans & Dickens 2002). It has heavy clay-land throughout, and it is only on the lower chalk that outcrops just south and west of the area that cropmarks register. The few finds that have been incidentally recovered there are not particularly insightful or necessarily representative.[40] We have nevertheless been able to suggest some crucial locales, based on 'heavy-land' fieldwork to date – for example, at Longstanton and Cambourne (*BLS*, 174–81, fig. 3.21 and Wright *et al.* 2009) and, now, West/North West Cambridge. These include the length of its Roman road, the course of the Bin Brook (which might have attracted settlement of all periods but, particularly, during the Mesolithic/Neolithic) and along the southern slopes of the area's higher ground: the length of the *Aldermann Hill* ridge and, in the west, the sides of *The Clint* (Fig. 2.40). It is likely that three or four Roman settlements still lie undetected within the area, along with a comparable number of Iron Age sites.[41]

Discussion – *A Betwixt Place* – Settlement Status, Parallels and Densities

So much of the core of Roman Cambridge was destroyed, with only minimal excavation during the County Council's building programmes – first in the 1930s and, then again, in the 1980s – that there are many pressing issues relating to its settlement that can no longer be resolved. This is only compounded by the fact that future developments within the area of its walled perimeter are likely to be small-scale and undertaken on a piecemeal basis; these will probably be inadequate to address the major questions raised here.

At this point we need to appraise the status of Roman Cambridge and try to judge whether it was actually a small town. In its 'Early', first–second-century AD form it would certainly have extended over 28 ha and could have been as large as *c.* 40 ha or more, based on the evidence of recent investigations within its immediate 'fringe' and the Lower East-bank settlement (Fig. 2.42). Size alone, though, is not necessarily *the* defining criteria. Very large rural centres are known within the region. This would include Colne Fen's Camp Ground port-village complex (to judge by its 7.4 ha full cropmark-register); similarly, the ongoing excavations at Longstanton's Site 18 roadside settlement extend over more than 20 ha (*BLS*, figs. 3.21–2). Nearer at hand, North West Cambridge's Site IV complex – lying along the south side of the *Via Devana* opposite Girton College – must have been as large as *c.* 10 ha.

To this, though, can be added the evidence of Roman Cambridge's buildings. Admittedly Girton/North West Cambridge's Site IV and Longstanton's Site 18 settlements both apparently had 'quality' masonry structures, and in this capacity the Arbury and Teversham villas can also be cited (see *NWC*, chap. 1), but only at Cambridge have Roman cellared buildings been recovered. There is also the evidence of Cambridge's walling, with the scale of the Late Roman lower town settlement and its inhumation cemeteries (Jesus Lane, Park Street and School of Pythagoras, plus possibly WYNG Gardens) showing that it still remained a significant centre at that point. There is also the nature of its overall layout: situated at the river-crossing and at a major long-distance crossroads, with a walled, upper hill-top-core and a lower riverside settlement. It would, in principle, be broadly comparable to other Roman small towns, particularly Lincoln (e.g. Jones *et al.* 2003); although with an entirely different geology and with a *colonia*, Lincoln certainly does not provide a close parallel. The evidence that Cambridge had any kind of distinct lower suburban settlement specializing in industrial activity is not clear-cut: there are just hints of such in the Jesus Lane-area's pottery wasters and from the ironworking debris from the School of Pythagoras.[42]

Roman Cambridge's potential street grid is also relevant here. Look again at Figure 2.8; with Akeman Street (No. 1) and Street 2 lying parallel some 30 m apart, you do not find this kind of layout in contemporary rural settlements. It is true that the existence of its other claimed streets (Nos. 3 and 4; *RCAM*, 36, fig. 4.1) seems far more tenuous and they – and any 'grid' – are not substantiated in *Roman Cambridge*.[43] This does not, though, detract from the arrangement of Streets 1 and 2 and this raises crucial issues. Did they continue in this manner beyond the later line of the walls and into the settlement's 'fringe', or were its later

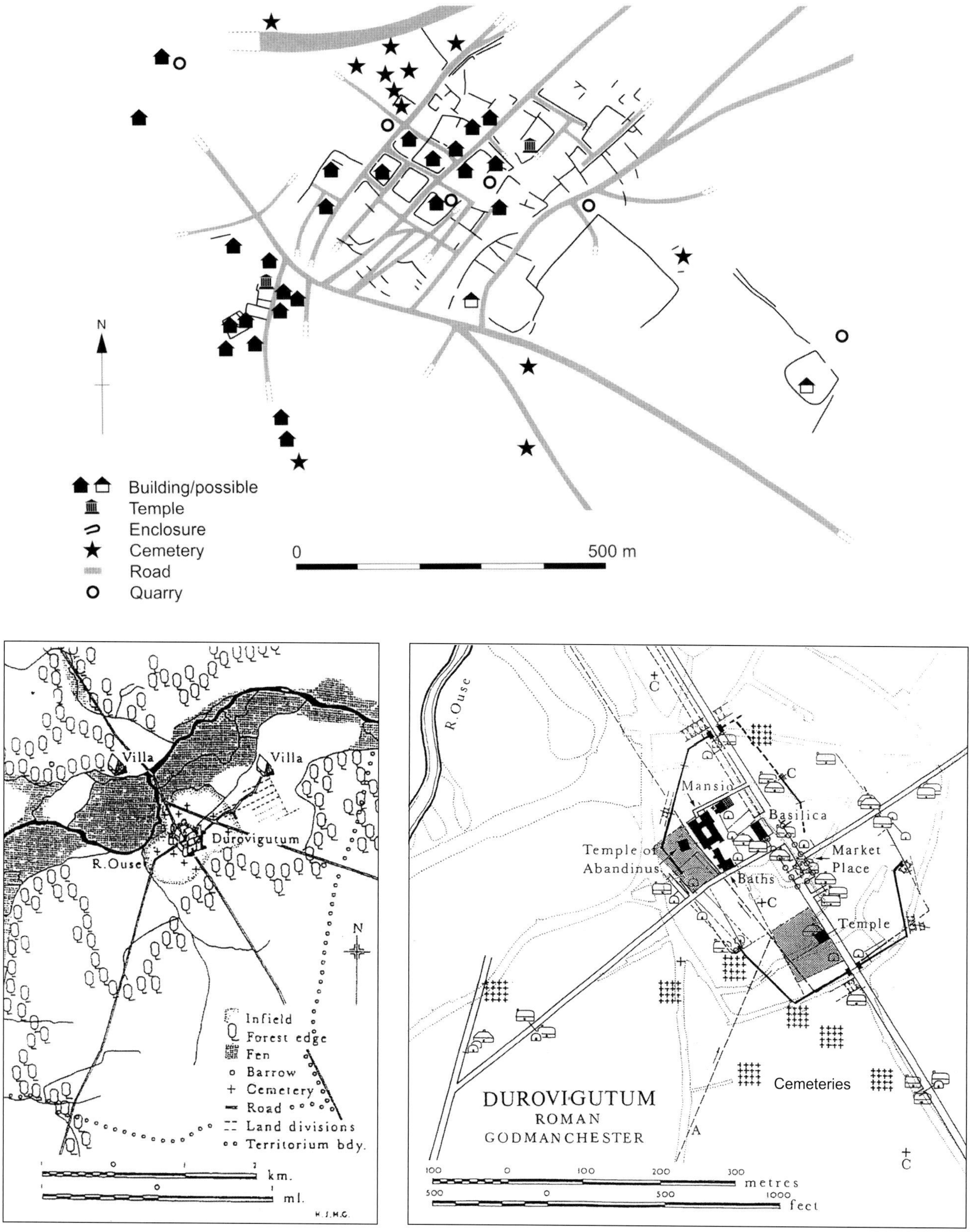

Figure 2.42. *Comparative Roman Small Town plans: Baldock (top; after Smith* et al. *2016, fig. 6.19) and, below, Godmanchester plans (after Green 2018, fig. 2.5).*

limits also somehow demarcated at an earlier date? If the latter, then this could explain what seems to have been the 'Y'-junctions of early roads at Cambridge's later South and West Gates (see Fig. 2.27).

Any declaration that Roman Cambridge amounted to a small town would have to be severely caveated. Despite the recovery of the paraphernalia of administration (e.g. a stylus, a scale and part of a seal-box; *RCAM*, 89) – as well as any above-cited claims of 'urban behaviours' – only its would-be *mansio* aspired to architectural pretensions (see Fig. 2.21) and no distinctly public buildings/civic facilities have otherwise been recovered. Certainly, any potential administrative function seems limited and, perhaps, just comparable to that of some of the 'higher level' rural settlements (e.g. Vicar's Farm, see Chaps. 4–6, or the Colne Fen Sites: Evans *et al.* 2013b). Jeremy Evans has recently pronounced that the character of Roman Cambridge's pottery assemblage would not be of typical 'urban-type' (J. Evans *et al.* 2017, 122–3).[44] This, though, is qualified, largely in light of its amphorae: "Overall the site [Castle Hill] has some urban characteristics and some rural ones and perhaps ought to be regarded as something between a village and a small town" (*ibid.*, 123).

Comparison for Roman Cambridge could be sought at Baldock, which 'officially' only has the status of an 'Undefended [Roadside] Settlement' (Stead & Rigby 1986; see Burnham & Wacher 1990, 281–8 and Smith *et al.* 2016, 223 for summaries). With settlement remains extending over at least 30 ha, its core also appears to have had a quasi-regular street grid (Fig. 2.42). Like Cambridge, it developed out of a Late Iron Age centre, with its floruit in Early Roman times, but it equally seems to have seen little in the way of specialized buildings or public amenities.

There seems no justification for Alexander's claim that Cambridge had a Claudian-period fort (*RCAM*, 30–2; cf. J. Evans *et al.* 2017, vol. 2, chap. 10, 31), but this need not diminish its importance as a Late Iron Age/Early Roman centre. Although difficult to gauge fully from *Roman Cambridge*'s reportage, this has might be reflected in the eight Iron Age coins from the earlier excavations (*RCAM*, 109), as well as the frequency of stamped Gallo-Belgic wares (see *Inset* above) and the 33 first-century BC/AD brooches that were recovered (see Chap. 7; *RCAM*, 85–6). The rate of recovery of Colchester-type brooches since, plus the findings from the recent Shire Hall Lift Shaft Site (see above; Rees 2016) would add to this. Yet, in marked contrast to Baldock, is Cambridge's lack of contemporary cemeteries. In light of the St Edmund's casket cremation, it must be suspected that other early cremations may have gone unnoticed amidst the St John's College Playing Field burials; there were also reports of 'cinerary urns' from the western portion of Jesus Lane and the Union Building (see Alexander *et al.* 2004, 92). Indeed, Fox identified the latter as having Iron Age settlement pre-dating the Castle Hill occupation:

> In the town itself the Castle Hill area yields evidence of prolonged occupation. Here a few pre-Flavian coins (of Germanicus, Claudius and Nero) have been recorded ... Romano-British pottery which certainly dates from the I century, has been obtained from this area, but it is important to notice that no terra sigillata of pre-Flavian date is preserved or recorded. On the right bank of the river (where the La Tène Celts lived) Flavian terra sigillata and a coin of Claudius have been found, and evidence suggesting continuity of occupation is provided by the rubbish pits at Trinity Hall, which yielded Roman wares mixed with La Tène sherds. Similar material (now in Cambridge Museum) was found under the Union Society's buildings at the tip of the gravel spur from which the causeway to Castle Hill originated and, as we have seen, pottery kilns must have been established at or near Jesus Lane at an early date. It is fairly certain, then, that the town on Castle Hill is of I century foundation; and the Romanization of the La Tène folk on the east side of the river may date from pre-Flavian times (1923, 227–8).

Be this as it may, given what is now known to be the extent of Cambridge's first century AD occupation, its currently 'missing' cremation cemeteries are certainly noteworthy.

While, as mentioned, Godmanchester's polygonal-walled plan would bear comparison to Cambridge's, thus far little evidence of a regular street grid has there been found (see Burnham & Wacher 1990, 122–9 and Casa-Hatton in Lyons forthcoming for summaries). That said, with its central basilica, huge mansio complex, formal temple and developed road-ribbon suburbs, there seems little doubt of Godmanchester's town status.[45] In light of this, and as noted in the previous chapter, the manner in which Green modelled its hinterland in his 1975 overview is most relevant for our purposes. Given the available evidence, it is a remarkable study, drawing widely on classical world sources. In it he postulated the scale of its in- and outfields based on surface pottery/manuring distributions (108 & 144 ha respectively; Fig. 2.42; Green 1975, 202) and, allowing for corn tax and annual seed corn allocation, estimated that Roman Godmanchester would have had a total resident population of some 200 persons or 40–50 households. Yet, all this was founded on an over-riding supposition:

> The nature of the social and tenurial framework of the community would, even with total excavation, be an intractable problem. There were clearly substantial landowners in the area, as evidenced by villa sites at Huntingdon, Great Staughton and outside Godmanchester, but within the town housing is more appropriate to small holders, tenants or even landless labourers.
>
> Whatever the exact tenurial arrangements it may reasonably be assumed that *the community was self-supporting* (*ibid.*; emphasis added).

The crucial point here is that Green essentially based this on a strict town-to-hinterland-*villa* model (see also Green's 1978 villa paper) and without knowledge of the extent of its more lowly hinterland farmsteads. As outlined in Chapter One, the recognized extent of these are one of the most singular outcomes of the last 25 years of developer-funded archaeology (Smith *et al.* 2016, 21–33) and, in recent years, these have been forthcoming in Godmanchester's environs (e.g. Wait 1992, Evans & Standring 2012 and Patten 2016). It is their existence and density that radically transforms our understanding of the layout and carrying capacity of the Roman countryside and its towns and other centres.

The density of Roman Cambridge's hinterland settlements may thus reflect its status. The key point relates to Figure 2.41 and the full *c.* 30 ha+ scale of 'Early' Roman Cambridge. Put simply, if this was not a town then we would expect that much of its populace to have been engaged in agricultural production. Accordingly, it would be reasonable to suppose that there should have been a wide stand-off between it and its neighbouring settlements, wherein farming occurred to support and employ its many residents. But that figure's distributions show the opposite. The distance of the Trinity Hall Playing Fields (see Chap. 3) and Burrell's Field settlements to Roman Cambridge – plus, relative to the lower town, the Jesus College Maintenance Workshop settlement – was at the same interval as across the western Cambridge lands as a whole (see Fig. 1.4 and above concerning Walker's even closer Grange Road findings). It is these and other settlements that surely would have supplied Cambridge with its foodstuffs.[46] Their very occurrence and proximity marks Roman Cambridge out as something quite different: undoubtedly a major local centre and, thereby, perhaps more likely to have been a town. This is an argument that will receive much greater nuancing as the North West Cambridge sites are presented, as clearly *not all hinterland settlements were the same.*

Having then, if not established, at least rehearsed Roman Cambridge's small town credentials (a designation we will cautiously use on occasion, while still suspecting that it is likely destined to retain its 'betwixt' status), the remainder of this section will be given to a consideration of its overall artefact densities.

Gauging Roman Cambridge

Following now-established CAU analytical procedures (e.g. Evans 2012), an attempt was made in the Castle Street paper to quantify Roman Cambridge's earlier excavation finds densities on a per-hectare basis (see Evans & Ten Harkel 2010, table 8). That cannot be taken as any kind of absolute measure, as it is difficult to get a sense of accurate quantification from fieldwork of Alexander *et al.* Katie Anderson and Francesca Mazzilli have, though, variously analysed some 6670 Roman sherds recovered from the main 'subsequent' Castle Hill investigations (see *RCAM*, 255 and Evans & Ten Harkel 2010, 35–8 for site summaries). Unfortunately there is not the scope for any detailed presentation of their findings and, instead, Figure 2.44's plots of their overall frequencies/characteristics will have to suffice (see also Fig. 2.43 and Chap. 7).

Figure 2.43. *Castle Hill, pottery from CAU sites (from Cow & Calf unless otherwise indicated): 1) Sandy greyware jar, second/third century* AD, *Chesterton Lane Corner; 2) Greyware jar, Romano-British; 3) Shell-tempered jar, Romano-British; 4) Verulamium white ware flagon, first century* AD; *5) Sandy greyware rilled jar,* AD *240–410, Chesterton Lane Corner; 6) Greyware dish/bowl, Romano-British; 7) Imitation Black Burnished ware jar or bowl, first/second century* AD; *8) Red slipped greyware jar, first/second century* AD; *9) Imitation Black Burnished ware jar, second/third century* AD; *10) Sandy greyware jar with everted rim, second/third century* AD, *Chesterton Lane Corner; 11) Large greyware jar, Romano-British; 12) Buff coloured sandy fineware with red painted lattice and feather decoration, Pre-Flavian, 19–37 Castle Street; 13) Large greyware jar, Romano-British; 14) Sandy greyware carinated bowl with small beaded rim, Roman-British; 15) Oxidized sandy greyware with black slip lid with small beaded rim, Roman-British; 16) Sandy greyware lid, first/second century* AD, *Folk Museum; 17) Central Gaulish Samian Dr.37 with ovolo decoration,* AD *120–50; 18) Central Gaulish Samian Dr.18R with makers stamp 'SOUIMNI',* AD *120–70; 19) Central Gaulish Samian Dr.37 decorated with goat and stag,* AD *120–50.*

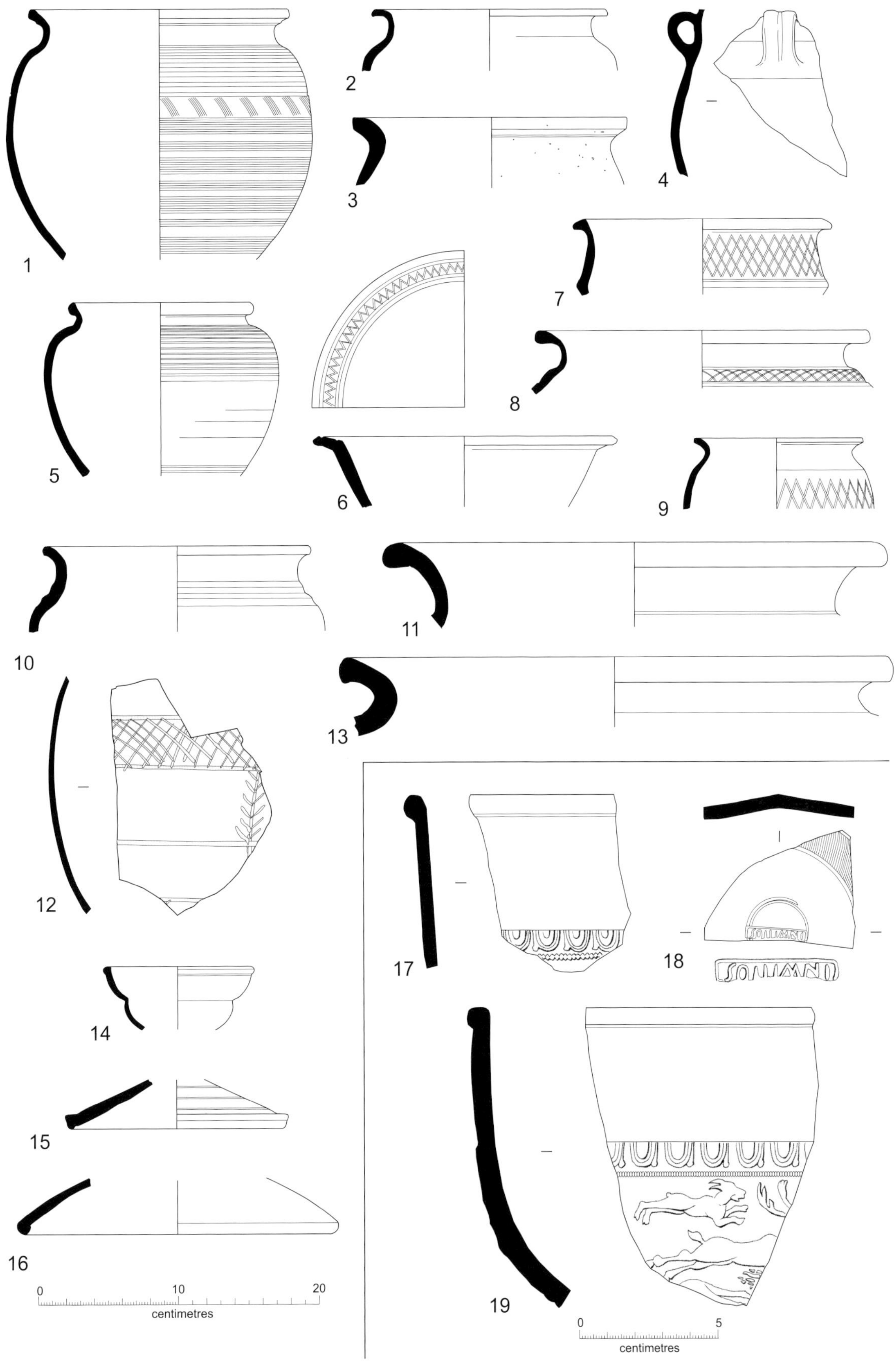
1
2
3
4
5
6
7
8
9
10
11
12
13
14
15
16
17
18
19
0
10
20
centimetres
0
5
centimetres

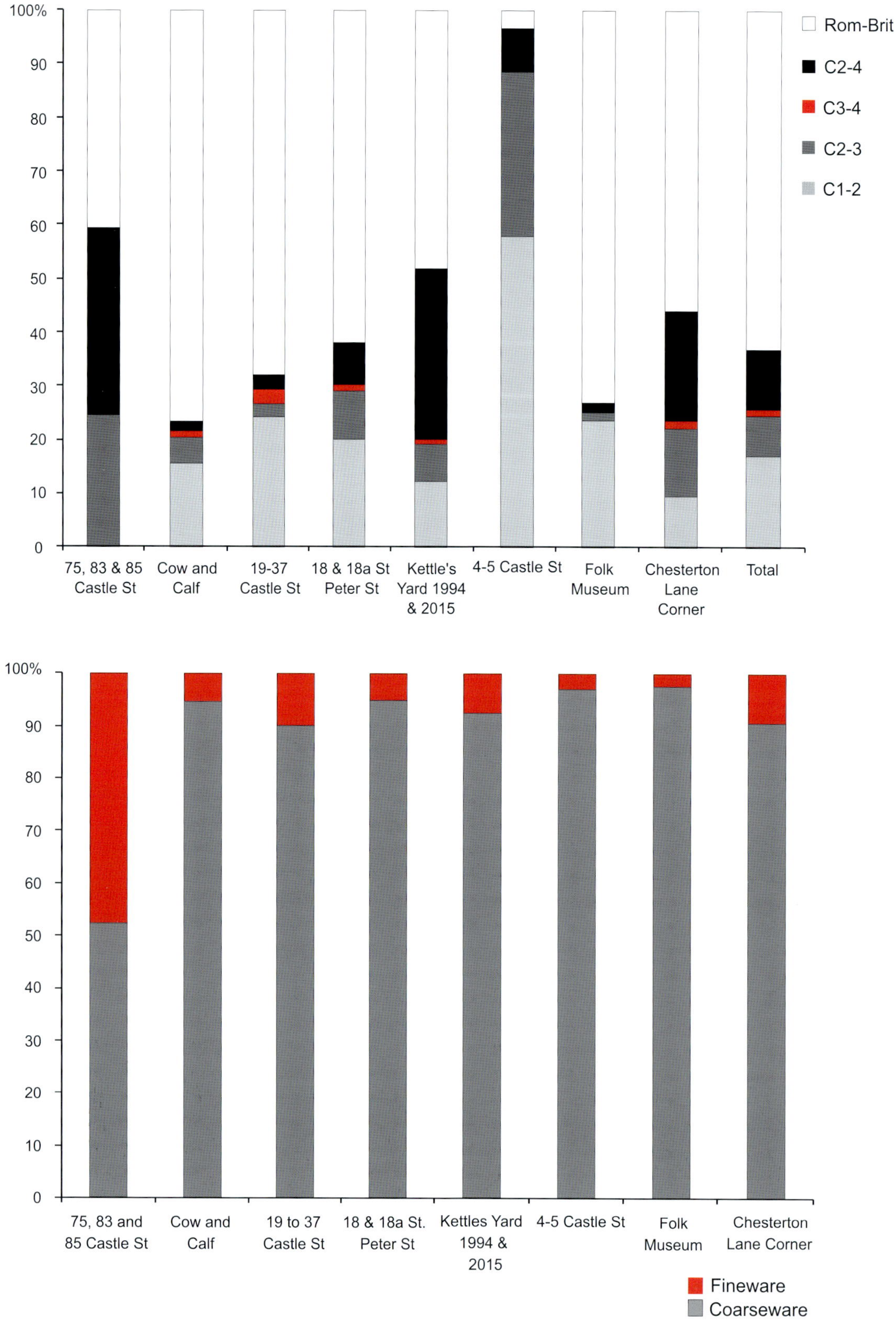

Figure 2.44. *Castle Hill, pottery from CAU sites: dating and coarse/fineware frequencies.*

Over the years, the Unit has attempted to quantify the recovered pottery densities from these investigations on a square-metre basis. Due largely to differential horizontal preservation (and varying excavation-sample intensity), these have not resulted in any kind of convincing patterning, and it has not proven possible to find any ready means to compensate for this. In, for example, Kettle's Yard's patio-area the groundsurface had been laterally truncated, whereas at the eastern foot of Castle Hill at Chesterton Lane Corner the depth of Roman-period strata was *c.* 1 m. Lying in a hollow at the foot of the slope, the latter does seem atypical of its core-area and, generally, the maximum depth of Castle Hill's stratigraphy is in the region of *c.* 0.5–0.8 m (see above concerning the depth of strata in the Ridgeons Garden-area).

Acknowledging the limitations of the data, as shown in Table 2.3, the Chesterton Lane Corner Site had the highest pottery density: *c.* 147 per sq. m. Based on this criterion – by which *Roman Cambridge*'s densities (i.e. pre-1990s excavations) would equate to approximated 20 sherds per sq. m – six post-Alexander investigations would have higher values. As well as the Chesterton Lane Site, this would include the neighbouring Folk Museum (82 sherds per sq. m), the Shire Hall Lift Shaft outlined above (71 sherds; but which is extraordinary as it only had pre-Flavian deposits/finds) and, respectively, at 23 and 15 sherds per sq. m, the Park Street Transformer and Corfield Court Sites in the lower town.

Setting aside the Chesterton Lane Corner and Folk Museum values in an effort to avoid potential issues of slope-accumulation, in many respects it is the Shire Hall Lift Shaft and Cow & Calf densities that are most relevant. With an average of 82.5 sherds per sq. m, this would equate to 825,000 sherds per hectare. These are certainly high values (see e.g. Taylor 2013, fig. 1) and, in theory, could provide a gauge by which to consider

Table 2.3. *Roman pottery densities (see Figs. 2.3, 2.31 & 2.41 for site locations).*

Location	Site	Count	Weight (g)	Area (sq. m)	Count per sq. m	Weight per sq. m
Walled Town	Cow & Calf	3125	36,791	30	104.2	1226.4
	Shire Hall lift shaft	622*	9417	8.7	71.4	1082.4
	Cambridge urban core (*RCAM*)	252,200	-	12,000	20.0	-
	68 Castle Street	879*	16,040	60	14.6	267.3
	Kettle's Yard (combined CAU phases)	818	19,868	73.2	11.2	271.4
	19–37 Castle Street	594	7973	100	5.9	79.7
	18/18a St Peter's Street	382	4669	250	1.5	18.7
	75–85 Castle Street	63	1352	c. 70	0.9	19.3
'Fringe'	Chesterton Lane Corner	1028	15,160	7	146.9	2165.7
	Folk Museum	659	6327	8	82.4	790.9
	School of Pythagoras	1623	18,346	135	12.0	135.9
	New Hall (1994)	10,500	168,000	2077	5.0	80.8
	Murray Edwards (combined phases)	532	4977	74.2	7.2	67.1
	Westminster College	1851	27,404	790	2.3	34.7
	St Edmund's College	226	-	830	0.3	-
Lower Town	Park Street Transformer	462	8813	20	23.1	440.6
	ADC Theatre	132	1436	8	16.5	179.5
	Corfield Court	510	6154	33.5	15.2	183.7
	35–37 Jesus Lane	657	9357	142.8	4.6	65.5
	WYNG/St Clement's Gardens	1942	37,448	640	3.0	58.5
	Old Divinity School	625	8219	272	2.3	30.2
	11 Park Street	54	2375	42.5	1.3	55.9
	West Court, Jesus College Soakaway	97	1656	208	0.5	8.0
	St John's College Library	316	-	175	0.2	-
	West Court, Jesus College Basement	34	519	280	0.1	1.8

Figure 2.45. *Visualizing Volumetrics: Further to calls to employ more standard measures in the analysis of site finds-densities (Evans 2013; Fulford & Holbrook 2018), until they are more widely used it can be difficult to appreciate volumetric expressions. To this end, while excavating North West Cambridge's Site VII in the autumn of 2018, we took the opportunity of having a mini-digger on-site to explore this. The results amount to no more than an exercise in visualization (i.e. not a formal 'experiment'). A cubic metre of soil was generated by cutting 1 m wide, 2 m long and 0.5 m deep flat-bottomed trench (left). The spoil was then reintroduced to it; first with 100 'sherds' added and, then, sequentially, further hundreds up to 500. Our 'sherds' variously consisted of broken flowerpot pieces (up to* c. *10–15 cm length) and, to make up numbers, red spray-painted poker chips (2 cm across). 'Sherd'-size clearly proved a significant factor and we attempted to keep the same approximate 90:10 small/large ratio in each hundred.*

This was all done on a fairly ad hoc *basis and would have certainly benefitted from greater control (e.g. further breaking up soil lumps and more even 'sherd'/spoil mixing). What was, nonetheless, evident is that you only really appreciate that the 'sherds' constitute an obvious component of the fill matrix – in other words, the arising deposit seemed 'midden-like' – when densities of 400–500 were achieved and, for example, densities of 200 per cubic metre made little visual impact. The central and right-side images here display the 500 density; duly red-highlighted in the right-hand image, the 'sherds' visually amount to just 3.2 per cent of the area.*

the hinterland settlement figures. It is entirely inappropriate, though, to directly equate the artefact values of 'layered' sites with the hinterlands' plough-truncated settlements on the basis of area-densities. Accordingly, for these six sites their pottery densities have been calculated relative to the approximate volume/depth of their Roman-period strata, as *cubic values* (see Figs. 2.45 & 4.32):

Shire Hall Lift Shaft (4.5 cu. m), 138 sherds per cu. m
Cow & Calf (1.93 cu. m), 115 sherds per cu. m
Park Street Transformer (3.7 cu. m), 113 sherds per cu. m
Chesterton Lane Corner (7.9 cu. m), 48 sherds per cu. m
Corfield Court (16.75 cu. m), 30 sherds per cu. m
Folk Museum (3.5 cu. m), 3 sherds per cu. m.

With these figures only reflecting *in situ* Roman finds densities, the Folk Museum's low value (relatively to its sq. m register) attests to the high level of residual material in its overlying Medieval deposits. Given this, the 'town-threshold' figure could, therefore, perhaps be pegged at a level of *c.* 110+ sherds per cu. m.

Within the remainder of this book (and the next), those discrete features with the highest pottery densities in the respective hinterland sites will also be calculated and plotted on this basis (see Fig. 4.32).[47] Not only should this provide a means by which to compare their 'highs' against those of Roman Cambridge's 'core', but this is also a way of exploring the middening dynamics of the hinterland settlements and how they tally on a cross-site basis.

Notes

1 As further discussed in the next book, the plotted northward route of Akeman Street appears to have an 'uncomfortable' relationship with the layout of the Arbury Villa complex cropmarks (see Timberlake 2006 for summary). That said, just to the north – at the so-called Gypsy Ditches Site – its line was detected in that plot's perimeter ditches (see Evans & Knight 2002, 44, figs. 16 & 17).

2 Nor is comprehension aided by the fact that there are no plans of the sites' Anglo-Saxon and Medieval phases, so that truncation of earlier features cannot be appreciated.

3 In compiling this account, we had access to a copy of Alexander, Pullinger and Woudhuysen's original, largely complete 1994 manuscript of Castle Hill's excavations. The text includes the Anglo-Saxon and Medieval phases, but unfortunately is entirely unillustrated. While lacking final specialist reports and having undeveloped discussions – the term 'the Roman Town' is, though, employed in the text – its Roman-period text runs to some 70,000 words. Its essentially 'descriptive-list' format was adhered to in the published version; the presentation of specific pit features is, though, detailed in the original. Taken as a whole, it is a usable, if 'workman-like', account. The root problem is that, with so little illustrated (apart from labelling on *RCAM*'s 'sketch' phase plans), much of *Roman Cambridge*'s archaeology is simply unintelligible.

While we have also consulted the many interim pamphlet-notices issued relating to the earlier sites, and appraised portions of their archives, a comprehensive review has yet to be undertaken (Evans has, though, previously worked with records from others of Alexander's sites and is well aware of their shortcomings: see *BLS*, 166–70 and Evans & Knight 2002). It is hoped that in the future a major review can be made of this material, as well as also the Arbury and Teversham villa excavation archives.

4 In recent years the CAU have monitored the length of a service trench dug across the north side of the 1980s Shire Hall development swathe. As exposed, the ground surface had been truncated and no Roman-period features were observed, suggesting that the degree of construction-related destruction was severe (Robinson 2013).

5 Notice that this plan shows what must be a later-dug trench (with a major cut feature) west of the southern three excavation squares. Coinciding with the western edge of the 1970s Ridgeons Garden South Area/Trench V, its machined-cutting would explain why the plans that do exist show an 'empty swathe' devoid of surface deposits along the later exposed and expanded areas to the west (RGS II & V; Fig. 2.7); the cut feature in that trench does not appear on any of the published phase plans. There is another archive plan which indicates that the area immediately west of and bordering RGS II had, at one time, also been exposed and has traces of another timber building and other Roman-phase features depicted (and labelled thus; see Fig. 2.7). This does not appear on any of the finished plans, nor is the area shown on *Roman Cambridge*'s master plan (*RCAM*, fig. 1.6).

6 Evans and John Alexander were quite close (see Evans *et al.* 2011), and the harshness of *Roman Cambridge*'s appraisal here only saddens him. Given, though, matters of 'reflexivity' and intellectual honesty, it is nonetheless necessary. Indeed, one can only regret that this was left for so long, and that John and Joyce are no longer with us to discuss their site work.

7 Impinging upon the side of St Peter's Church-yard, many inhumations were then recovered and subsequently reburied in its grounds.

8 Nearby, a watching brief recording of an Anglia Water sewer shaft in 2000–1, at the corner of Pound Hill, revealed what was probably the edge of the Roman defensive ditch (M6 in Cessford 2008).

9 Not reproduced here, while considerably more detailed, in its essentials our Area B east–west section (Brittain & Evans 2016, fig. 10) would broadly match that recorded in 1984.

10 Two of these pieces had been roughly dressed/squared and two others had mortar adhering to them.

11 Kettle's Yard's wells are, for example, reminiscent of a well excavated at Castle Hill's Fulbourn Manor Nursery Site in 1984–5. Partially overlain by the fourth-century AD town wall, and lying just west of the *mansio*, it had

been backfilled with ashy loam deposits and building materials, including painted wall plaster evidently derived from that building (*RCAM*, 44, fig. 4.11). In addition, the infill of Ridgeons Garden South's Well 25 apparently had 'much daub with timber laths attached' (*ibid.*, 52); unfortunately, the earlier recovered daub was not reported in any detail (*ibid.*, 251).

12 When excavating at Arbury's King's Hedges villa, it was claimed that one of Alexander (*et al.*)'s sub-sites – AR III – also had lines of 'ritual pits'. Much shallower than those at Castle Hill, and without human bone, these have since been reinterpreted as the aisled postholes of a large timber barn/hall (see *NWC*, chap. 1).

13 Another 'shrine' has been excavated nearby at the 1988 Castle Street Site (*RCAM*, 57). Designated as such on account of its *pentagonal* plan, with no directly associated votive deposits, there seems a marked discrepancy between the structure's photograph and plan, with the latter just indicating a *circular* eavesgully (*ibid.*, figs. 5.16–17).

With its emphasis on the later Roman shafts, Taylor's *Roman Cambridge* Discussion was clearly influenced by the then recent publication of the Folly Lane, Verulamium complex (Niblett 1999; see also Pearce 2013, 121). In terms of formal 'town behaviours', no adult inhumations occurred within the excavated portions of Stonea, but it did have infant burials (Jackson & Potter 1996); whereas the Colne Fen's great Camp Ground port-village complex had, in addition to 12 infants, cremation and inhumation burials (plus disarticulated human remains; Evans *et al.* 2013b, 230–6 & 440–4; see, though, Chap. 1 above on burial 'behaviours'). Note that J. Evans *et al.* essentially accept Taylor's interpretation of Cambridge as a ritual centre, at least during the second and third centuries AD, though they admit that there is very little evidence of such deposition before that date (2017, 125–6, table 5.4). Medlycott (2011, 91–3) discusses Great Chesterford's ritual pits and other votive deposits (see also *ibid.*, 89–91, figs. 5.9–10 on its apsidal building and its regional parallels); see also Burnham and Wacher 1990, 286 on Baldock's possible third-century AD ritual shaft/pit deposits, with Clarke 1997 and Grimm 2010 providing further discussion of 'shafts' elsewhere.

14 The 1994 manuscript refers to all of the timber structures as 'huts'.

15 One of *Roman Cambridge*'s more convincing building plans (but which was not designated as such) was apparently of first-century AD date – F10 – a 13 × 6.3 m rectangular ditch 'enclosure' (ditches *c.* 1 m wide; *RCAM* 32, fig. 3.9), which would have parallels on other settlements excavated since (*BLS*, 87, fig. 2.37). Again, arguing against Cambridge's urban credentials, J. Evans *et al.* emphasised its lack of strip buildings (2017, 122); given, however, the nature of most of Castle Hill's excavations it seems unlikely that they would have been recovered and/or recognized.

16 See Evans and Ten Harkel 2010 on the location of Roman Cambridge's crossroads; based, for example, on *Roman Cambridge*'s figure 2.12 – combined with the evidence of the Shire Hall 1983 exposure (Fig. 2.8) – its plotting of the area north of Castle Street seems unsubstantiated.

17 The shrine's extraordinary placed deposits and finds assemblages are detailed in *Roman Cambridge* (45–7). Dating to the later second century AD (augmented by later infill-dumping) and including the burnt remains of the building's evidently elaborate superstructure, a remarkable range of material was recovered from it. Apart, for example, from 45 hinges/brackets, glass vessels, gaming pieces, jet items, an intaglio and a bone flute, were some 6500 oyster shells and, as detailed by Hull and Pullinger (in *ibid.*, 144), some 21,840 sherds from a minimum of 1966 vessels (170 samian and more than 250 flagons; see J. Evans *et al.*'s appraisal of the building's pottery: 2017, vol. 2, chap. 10, 4–5 & 25–6). Bearing broad comparison with New Hall's enormous F.1/2 pottery deposits (see Going, Chap. 3 and Fig. 4.32), the cellar's sherd cubic-density would be 245 per cu. m.

18 See also Smith *et al.* 2016, 65-6, fig. 3.17 for cellared buildings, though this also seems to include shallow 'sunken floor' structures.

19 In addition to a single Anglo-Saxon cremation urn, apparently a quantity of Roman pottery was recovered by Macalister ('the Senior'; see Fig. 2.28) during College construction in 1897–8, which he subsequently presented to their library. Having a considerable samian component, in the course of the recent excavations there this material has now been reviewed and reported upon (see Wadeson in Graham 2016, 58–60); unfortunately, we have been unable to locate the finds from the nearby Bandy-Leg Walk houses.

20 While largely of Anglo-Saxon date, involving hundreds of both cremations and inhumations, Fox noted its quantity of Roman findings in his review of its otherwise unpublished material; he concluded, though, that all of that period's brooches probably occurred in later, post-Roman graves (1923, 242–3). It, nevertheless, seems likely that – like the Girton cemetery – it too may have had Roman origins. Restricted to the south-centre of the Playing Fields, what little trench investigation has since occurred has yet to definitely locate the cemetery site (Fig. 1.10; see Evans 1991a & b and Cessford 2009). Aside from evidence of Post-Medieval quarrying, it has only revealed dispersed/occasional Roman-period ditches and indications of no more than agricultural usage (i.e. fieldsystems).

21 Aside from the intrinsic value of Macalister's findings, equally interesting is the manner of their reporting and what it tells about how the built fabric and 'change' was understood. Comparable to the casual non-mapped spatial reference of many nineteenth-century excavation accounts (Evans 2007) – of 'they occurred in the bottom corner of the lower field by the road'-type – the way in which Macalister 'fixes' the findings by just their house-names is almost as if he expected them to stand the test of time and last, and that significant change was not anticipated. As will be explored in the final chapter here, the experience of West Cambridge's lands over the last quarter of a century has certainly taught us otherwise.

22 Apparently a substantial quantity of first-century AD pottery was also recovered from this area by a Mrs Baker in 1952 (Browne 1974, 1/15; CUMAA 1952.434; see Fig. 2.2).

23 For some unknown reason, in the published plans (see Fig. 2.3) the gates have not been labelled in accordance with their true cardinal locations (i.e. the indicated 'West Gate' is actually in the south, the 'North' [Huntingdon Road/*Via Devana*] Gate is actually in the west, *etc.*); here the reference will be according to their true cardinal positions.

24 Four skeletons were found nearby during the construction of the Cripps Building in 1962–4. Subsequently, in 1967, under the aegis of Glyn Daniel, Alan Carter and James Graham-Campbell excavated within the School itself; Roman features and a further burial were then recovered. (Unfortunately, neither of these campaigns were ever written up apart from brief notes in the College's magazine, *The Eagle*: Boys Smith 1964 and Graham-Campbell 1968.) In 2008 Albion Archaeology undertook limited investigations within Merton Hall, when two more skeletons – one a female and the other a juvenile – and much disarticulated human bone was recovered (Meckseper 2014).

25 Much of Roman Cambridge's north-side 'fringe' archaeology was lost through nineteenth-century brick pits. Unfortunately, evaluation fieldwork at Sunnyside House – a large plot immediate exterior to Castle Hill's walled northeastern perimeter – showed that it had been severely truncated and, therefore, no such evidence was forthcoming (Fig. 1.10; Wills 2003b). The same was also true when the site of the former Star Service Station, at the corner of Huntingdon and Histon Roads, was recently trench-investigated (see Fig. 1.10; Ladocha & Muldowney 2014).

26 The only other definite pre-cemetery feature was a large pit, 1.8 m across, that lay along the west side of the central house. Truncated by two graves, it was dug to a depth of 1 m but could not be bottomed due to safety concerns.

27 It is possible that any larger cemetery may have also included earlier cremation burials as Roman 'cinerary urns' found in Jesus Lane and under the Union Building are held in the Museum of Archaeology and Anthropology (1901.43 and 1893.125 respectively); any cremated bone was not kept.

28 In 2016, Archaeological Solutions excavated a minor extension to the site (Mustchin 2016). Essentially just confirming our earlier findings, their Trench 1-area results indicated that early features continue to the west there.

29 Samples of charred seeds were submitted for absolute dating from two Iron Age features: F.107 ([055]), 1000±40 BP; cal. AD 980–1060 and cal. AD 1080–1150 (2 sigma; Beta-195165); F.108 ([121]), 900±40 BP; cal. AD 1020–1210 (2 sigma; Beta-195166). Unfortunately, both are *c.* 1200–1400 years younger than anticipated and could, instead, suggest a Late Saxon/Early Medieval attribution. Given, however, their stratigraphic context and finds assemblages, these cannot be accurate; as demonstrated for the site's plant and mollusc remains, this material must have been introduced through intrusive action (i.e. a 'dynamic' burial environment).

30 Deep alluvial deposits were also encountered during a summer school hand-dug test pitting programme conducted in the back of the yards of Jesus College's Lower Park Street houses. While a few Romano-British sherds were present, the vast majority of the recovered pottery was of eighteenth- to twentieth-century date. Evidently relating to the area's development for College servants (including a major household clearance horizon of *c.* 1870–1900), of the more than 1860 such sherds only two were College ceramics (Cessford 2016c). Nearby, watching brief monitoring of the stripping of topsoil at the Jesus Green tennis courts revealed no significant archaeology (Cessford 2012).

31 Babington, though, records that Roman material was found nearby during building works in 1880 at Trinity Hall (1883, 9; see also Fox 1923, 228). Equally, a few Roman-period features were encountered during small-scale excavations within Gonville and Caius College's Bateman Building in 1995 and, four years earlier, residual Roman pottery had been recovered from investigations at King's College (Alexander 1995; Evans in *RCAM*, 259). While this might evince the southward continuation of the lower town's riverside occupation, alternatively it might attest to the first Roman farmstead on the Cam's east bank south of the lower town proper; as such, it could be the equivalent of the Burrell Field settlement opposite (see below). South of this area, albeit at a low density, Roman-period features have been encountered during expansion of the Chemistry Department off Union Road (Dickens 1999) and, further southwest at Dam Hill, by the river at Latham Road, there clearly was yet another settlement (see Fox 1923, 103, 205; Mackay 2004; *BLS*, fig. 2.55; *RVS*, 18–19).

32 What seem to be individual owner's marks are found on arrow finds from the Danish Iron Age (see Jorgensen *et al.* 2003). See, for example, Hartley and Standen 1959 for a series of ten vessels recovered from the same ditch at Horsey Toll, Stanground, Peterborough, all of which shared the same owner's mark.

33 In her 1973 review Rigby noted that the total number of Terra Nigra and Terra Rubra stamps in Britain was then 751, of which 560 were names as such.

34 Another contemporary cremation (10909) subsequently excavated nearby by Oxford Archaeology East (Phillips & Mortimer 2012), contained 13 accessory vessels, of which five were stamped Gaulish imports (Rigby with Lyons forthcoming).

35 See, for example, Creighton 1995 for the possible implications of 'circle imagery' on Late Iron Age coins.

36 Nine years later, College-related development led to an evaluation at 3 Sylvester Road located immediately west of Robinson College's grounds (Brudenell 2005). Lying on Gault Clays and falling immediately east of the projected line of Akeman Street, it was hoped that further Roman settlement evidence might be recovered. This, however, proved not to be the case and no archaeology whatsoever was present.

37 For our purposes here, there is no need to detail or even list the many small-scale evaluations that have occurred in the West Road-area. Despite the recovery of (occasional) prehistoric, Roman and Saxon material, only very few discrete features have been found.

38 Much further to the west, in 2011 small-scale excavations (180 sq. m) occurred on an Early/Middle Anglo-Saxon settlement at Leckhampton House in the grounds of Number 25 Cranmer Road (Timberlake 2011).

39 Rog Palmer has plotted another cropmark complex on the western margin of this area, on the lower eastern flank of the major Lower Chalk spur (TL 41055740; Fig. 2.40). With a rectilinear layout and the same approximate orientation as the Vicar's Farm settlement (and seemingly of comparable arrangement), this is also presumed to be of Romano-British date.

40 The fieldwalking that occurred prior to the construction of the M11 cannot be considered successful, as demonstrated by the non-recovery of North West Cambridge's Site VI (Haigh 1975).

41 After having written, this there was some satisfaction that yet another Roman settlement – the next one south of that at Vicar's Farm – was discovered at one of the locales predicted here east end of Aldermann Hill. This followed unexpected fieldwork at the Wilberforce Road Sports Ground from late in 2017, as presented in Chapter Seven.

42 That kilns and furnaces also apparently occurred within the walled town itself (*RCAM*, 73), would not be enough to disqualify Cambridge as a town but would instead imply that formal 'urban rules' were either not strictly adhered to or did not apply in this case.

43 Further to arguments that 'many things' seem missing in *Roman Cambridge*, nowhere in that volume are any features illustrated in the trenches west and east of the main Ridgeons Garden 'block-area', aside from three minor features shown on Figure 2.4.B's plan (the Comet Place trenches were aimed at excavating a dense Medieval cemetery, as well as underlying Roman features; Craddock & Gregory 1973 and nd; Cessford with Dickens 2005, 95 and Cessford & Dickens forthcoming). Based on the feature density of the 'southern fringe' sites (see Fig. 2.27) – or, indeed, almost any other Roman rural settlement in the region – this does not amount to negative evidence; rather, something seems seriously amiss in the volume's presentation of basic data (i.e. records have either gone missing or simply were never fully worked through for publication).

44 The relative frequency of Cambridge's pottery graffiti – only seven– is low (*RCAM*, 157; see also J. Evans 1987).

45 Appearing early in 2018, there is now also Green's long-anticipated *Roman Godmanchester* volume. Complied by Tim Malim, this rather scrapbook-like collection of text fragments and previous issued papers includes a number of 'raw' archival plans. It provides insights into the working procedures of an earlier era and, as such, bears comparison to Alexander and Pullinger's *Roman Cambridge* (see also Jones 2003). See Millett's forthcoming review of the Godmanchester volume, in which he casts doubts on a number of Green's public building attributions.

46 Although difficult to quantify (and not fully enumerated in *RCAM*, 90), a very basic measure of this is the much lower density of quernstone on Roman Cambridge's sites when compared to those in its hinterland, and with most of those consisting of small stones (see Table 7.10 and Evans *et al.* 2013b, table 2.54). That said, there was a high number of quernstones, evidently employed as road metalling, within the *Via Devana's* surface in the Murray Edwards Sites (see Chap. 3). Equally, no corn-driers have been found at Roman Cambridge, in contrast to Baldock (Burnham & Wacher 1990, 285).

47 In both the presentation of these and the area-values, it is imperative that absolute sherd numbers are also included. As will become apparent in the tabulation of New Hall's densities (see Chap. 3), it is one thing to have dumped one or two basket-loads of refuse into a small feature (involving upwards of a few hundred pottery sherds) and, thereby, generate a high cubic density (e.g. its F.221). Yet, though it had a lower overall density, the mass-infilling of that site's huge F.1/2 feature-group – involving almost 5000 sherds – represents middening or dumping on an entirely different scale.

Chapter 3

Roads West – New Hall and Fitzwilliam College Excavations

At the time, the four month-long excavation along the western side of New Hall in the winter of 1993/94 was one of the largest sites within Cambridge (Evans 1996). Extending over 1.5 ha, more than 2000 sq. m were excavated in three areas:

I) Main Area (1242.5 sq. m)
II) Back-College Zone (690 sq. m)
III) The Huntingdon Road-side (145 sq. m)

Confined to the development's building footprint, the area had been evaluated the year before, with archaeology found in five out of the nine trenches then excavated (Evans 1993). Indicated on Figure 3.1, no features were present in Trenches A and I; in hindsight, given its location, there must now be doubts concerning the former (as outlined in the previous chapter, Trench I simply exposed coprolite quarrying).

The fieldwork took place prior to the main publication of Alexander *et al.*'s excavations (*RCAM*; in which a summary of its results was included: 257–9) and the recovery of such dense archaeology – 290 features and *c.* 16,000 artefacts – on a site lying only 250 m west of the *walled* Roman town's Huntingdon Road gate came as something of a surprise. So much so, in fact, that English Heritage made available an additional grant to allow two further weeks of excavation to augment the College's sponsorship of the basic work.

The results proved significant. Not only was there evidence of extensive prehistoric activity and dense Roman settlement, but a Roman road was found running east towards the town (Road 1). The latter amounted to a major discovery, adding an important dimension to the study of Cambridge's hinterland, as hitherto its western side had been dominated by the Cambridge to Godmanchester road (i.e. *Via Devana*).

The site's geology consisted of 4th Terrace gravels pocketed with chalk-marl, and a deep section cut in the course of construction revealed that the gravel lay as a *c.* 0.4 m thick band upon the underlying Castle Hill-side chalk. As exposed across the areas of excavation, the site's topography was unremarkable, varying from 18.5–20 m OD. Generally, the ground surface sloped down from east to west, and was highest within Area II (19.7–20 m OD).

For the most part, an intense excavation-sample was implemented; indeed, much more so than would be commonplace today. Against this, though, where ground-levels had been reduced through early quarrying, portions of the Roman settlement could only be sondage-investigated and this greatly affects our grasp of its sequence there. It needs also to be mentioned that, in the light of the site's low metalwork numbers, feature fills were metal-detected and, therefore, this negative recovery is 'real'.

While the basic layout of this site's presentation is close to how it was first drafted more than 20 years ago (see Chap. 1), given the much greater landscape-context that has accrued since, key aspects of its interpretations have been modified. Gone, for example, is any kind of Roman military emphasis; conversely, we now know that the scale of site's quarry-field was something quite distinct and must essentially have been (Roman) road-related and not settlement-associated. Also, as will be explored at length below, there is a far stronger grasp of both Roman Cambridge's actual hinterland settlements, as well as the scale of the early town's 'surround'. Moreover, as already outlined in Chapter Two, adding to this is a much firmer knowledge of the impact of nineteenth-century coprolite quarrying immediately east of New Hall (now Murray Edwards), as this implies that we are probably here rather dealing with a 'suburban settlement' (as opposed to a separate hinterland one).

The time and place of the fieldwork is, nevertheless, a significant factor here. In order to do justice to this, a degree of reflexivity will be introduced (but subject to footnoted updating where necessary). New

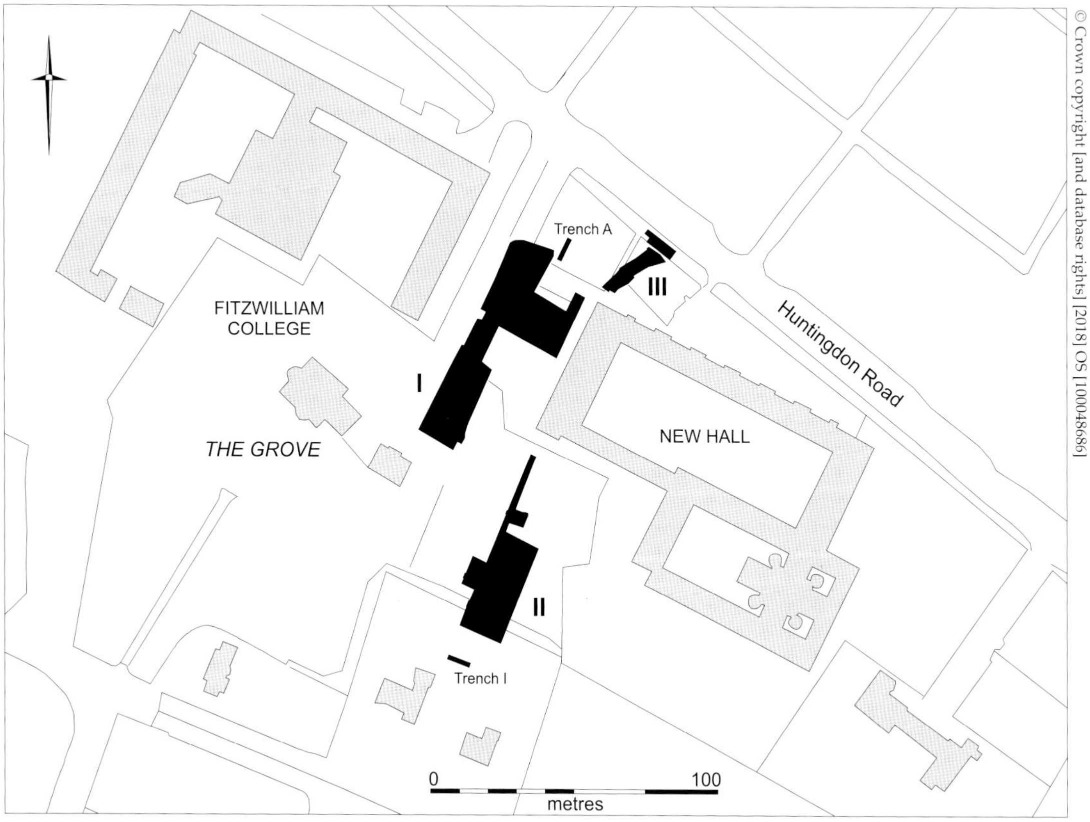

Figure 3.1. *New Hall, 1993–4, site location plan.*

Hall's results will first be presented in what is close to their original format, including the plan of how the site's enclosure system was then – in the 1990s – envisaged (see Fig. 3.30). This will subsequently be revised following the presentation of the results from later adjacent excavations (cf. Fig. 3.57); after all, *it is only appropriate that greater context leads us to revise our thinking and that is something that should not be glossed over.*[1]

Finally, the site's phasing merits notice. The basic tripartite periodization of the original text will be followed here – Prehistoric (I), Roman (II) and Post-Medieval (III) – with the latter, though, only receiving summary mention. For reasons outlined in the Period II introductory text below, the overly rigid text-section phasing structure originally employed has since been simplified. This has been done both to ease presentation and to reflect more honestly the 'fluid' or open-ended nature of much the sequence's phasing.

Prehistoric Activity (Period I)

The site's prehistoric remains contribute an important dimension to the area's sequence. This will become more apparent when compared to the adjacent findings from Fitzwilliam College (see below) and, especially, when North West Cambridge's prehistory is outlined in the next book. The scale/extent of the wider area's later Bronze Age activity has only become apparent since the 1994 excavations. Accordingly, there is considerable ambiguity concerning the actual date of Area II's pre-Roman features.

Bronze Age

In total, 275 pieces of struck flint were recovered (plus a further 290 fragments of burnt flint), although the majority were not associated with features. As analysed by Dickens (see below), approximately 10–15 per cent of the site's lithic assemblage was of Neolithic date; some flints were definitely Early Neolithic and the assemblage may even include a Mesolithic component. There was also evidence of a minor Late Neolithic/Early Bronze Age presence. However, the majority of the assemblage is of Middle–later Bronze Age date. The site's pre-Iron Age ceramics have a similar profile. As discussed by Pollard below, 64 sherds from a minimum of eight vessels were identified. The bulk of the material could be accommodated within Barrett's post-Deverel Rimbury 'plain-ware' tradition dating to the centuries around 1000 cal. BC (1980).

Figure 3.2. *Excavation photographs, Area I; looking south, with the* The Grove's *coach house in the background (top); below, looking east to New Hall's buildings.*

All the features of pre-Iron Age attribution were within the middle swathe of Area I aside, possibly, from a single pit and the original cutting of an Iron Age ditch in Area II (F.92 & F.20/F.211; see below). An evidently 'early' east–west oriented ditch with distinctive fills was excavated there, F.163, although so truncated that it was at first difficult to define (Figs. 3.3 & 3.13). As reconstructed, it would be some 2.50 m wide and 0.55–0.85 m deep (deepening to west), with broadly splaying sides and a concave base. It terminated in a sub-circular butt, which turned slightly southward.

The ditch fill consisted of pale leached mid brown sandy silt and fine–medium gravel with occasional larger cobbles. There was limited evidence of primary weathering and it appeared backfilled. Quantities of bone were recovered throughout and within its base was what seemed to be a 'placed' deposit: a cattle skull aligned along the ditch length with a pair of pig mandibles upon on its forehead; two (cattle) leg bones and a stone pebble-hammer/macehead lay on its northern side (Fig. 3.3; see Dickens below).

A sub-circular pit, possibly a large posthole, F.175, was equally severely truncated (Fig. 3.3). At *c.* 0.7 m across and 0.45 m deep, its sides sloped down to a concave base, and it was filled with mid brown sandy silt with gravel. It was clearly associated with F.163, and much bone was also recovered from its upper fill. Although the precise relationship between F.175 and F.163 was not established, in all likelihood the pit was either truncated by the ditch or had been dug through its base.

Midway along the length of the ditch, on its southern side, another pit – F.254 – was definitely cut by F.163 (Fig. 3.3). This was so truncated by this and other later features that it is difficult to say much concerning its form, apart from that it seemed to be sub-circular (est. diam. 0.8–1 m) and some 0.3 m deep. It was filled with a fine mid/dark grey-brown loam, with no finds recovered.

Aside from a handful of worked and some burnt flint, no other direct dating evidence was recovered from ditch F.163. Despite sharing the same rough alignment as the later, Roman ditches in this immediate area, it must be considerably earlier to judge by its distinctly leached fills and the character of the placed deposit (and finds generally). This is not to deny that such obviously ritual practices could occur in Roman times, but the combination of factors, and the density of residual prehistoric material (largely of Bronze Age date) from across that area, would suggest its earlier attribution.

It is difficult to ascertain if any other discrete features within the area were contemporary. The best candidate, a 0.6 m deep elongated ovoid pit within the northeastern area – F.232 – was entirely devoid of finds (see Figs. 3.16 & .18). After long deliberation it has been assigned a later date (as a Roman quarry) due to the 'respect' given to it in the layout of later features. Beyond the five pieces from F.163, some 173 struck flints were recovered in residual contexts from later features within the area (seven from Area III). Similarly, 118 burnt flints and 39 sherds of 'pre-(Middle) Iron Age' prehistoric pottery were also retrieved from Area I.

Pollard identified 19 such sherds as coming from Area II. Within that area were only a few features of identifiably Bronze Age date (Fig. 3.4). One was F.211, the sub-square butt-end of a 1.5–1.6 m wide ditch, that was only *c.* 0.25 m deep and had a broad concave profile with a flat base (Fig. 3.5). (It could only be exposed over a length of 1.50 m, being truncated to the north by a Post-Medieval cellar.) Its lower profile was filled with mid grey sandy clay silt streaked with orange sandy (weathered) 'natural' silty clay; the upper portion contained dark grey clay silt loam. Throughout were charcoal flecks, scorched cobbles (the latter constituting 10–20% of the fill matrix by volume), much burnt and struck flint (30 and 40 pieces respectively) and bone (27 pieces; a large piece of wattle-impressed daub was also found). As noted by Hill below, four shelly ware sherds (of ambiguous assignation) were recovered from it. This is significant, for Dickens stresses the distinct character and 'coherence' of that feature's flintwork, which would certainly point to a pre-Iron Age date (i.e. Bronze Age).

The other relatively unequivocal later Bronze Age feature in that area was F.63, from which 10 small sherds of flint-tempered pottery were recovered (Fig. 3.4). This was a northwest–southeast-oriented linear cut, 1.95 m+ long, whose trapezoidal plan was actually suggestive of a grave. Near-vertically sided, its width tapered (from 0.5–0.9 m; Fig. 3.5) and its base sloped down from the northwest to the southeast. Over its southeast half it was 0.25–0.3 m deep. Lying 1.15 m to the south, and sharing the same alignment, was the northwestern end of a similar/matching feature, F.85. Also steep-sided (*c.* 0.3 m deep), it only survived over a length of 0.65 m. What seems, however, to have been its eastern end appeared to survive in the side of a later, Roman ditch. These two 'box-like' cuts were filled with homogeneous dark brown/grey clay silt loam. A few pieces of bone and scraps of pottery were recovered from F.63, while a struck flint flake came from F.85. Cutting through the northern end of F.63 was an ovoid posthole, F.65, and F.85 appeared to truncate a shallow pit F.92 (*c.* 0.5 m deep and 1.2 m across) in which one 'early' sherd was present (plus

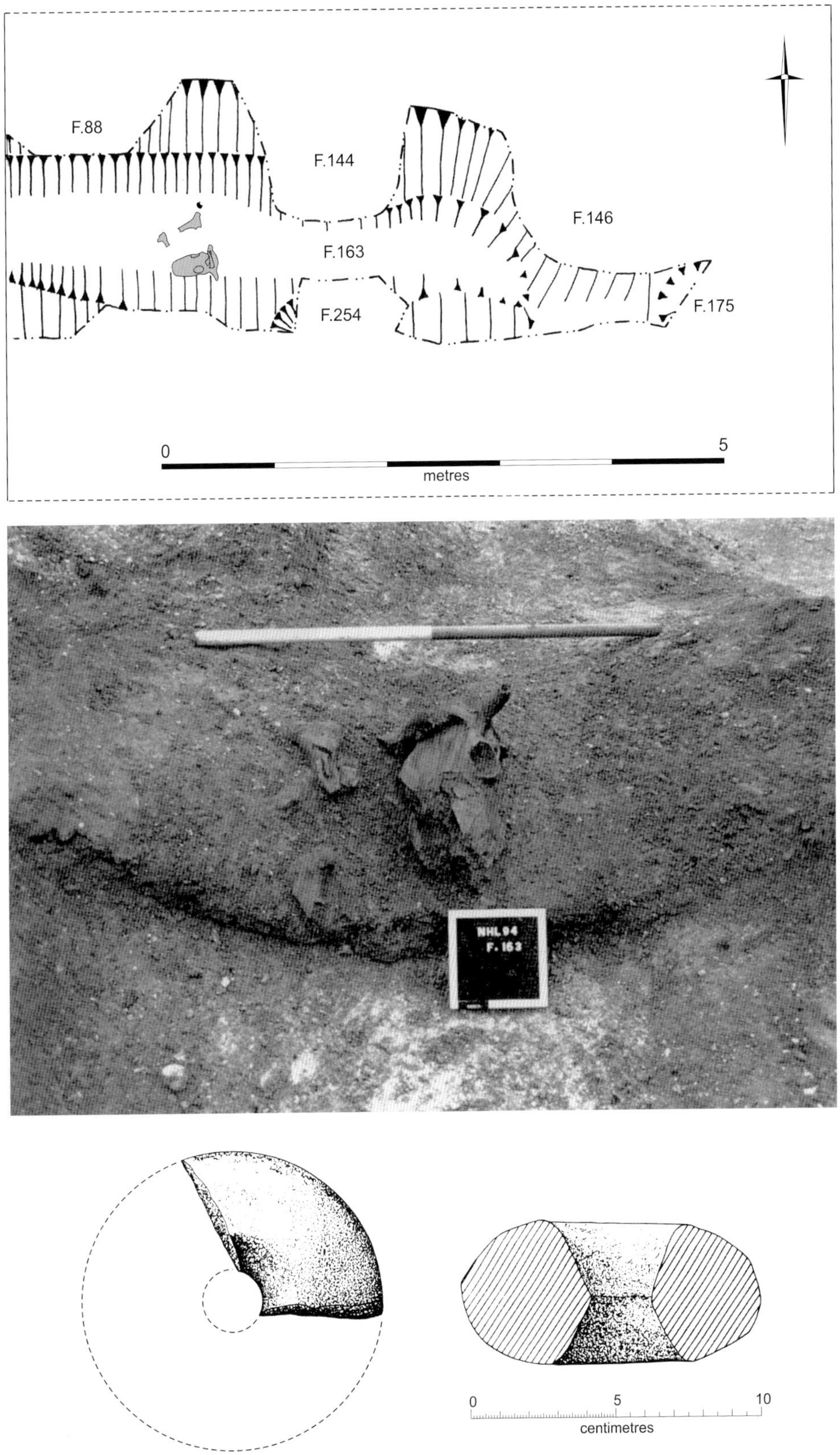

Figure 3.3. *Bronze Age feature, F.163 (plan and photograph), with the pebble-hammer/macehead (below; see Figs. 3.13 & 3.24 for location).*

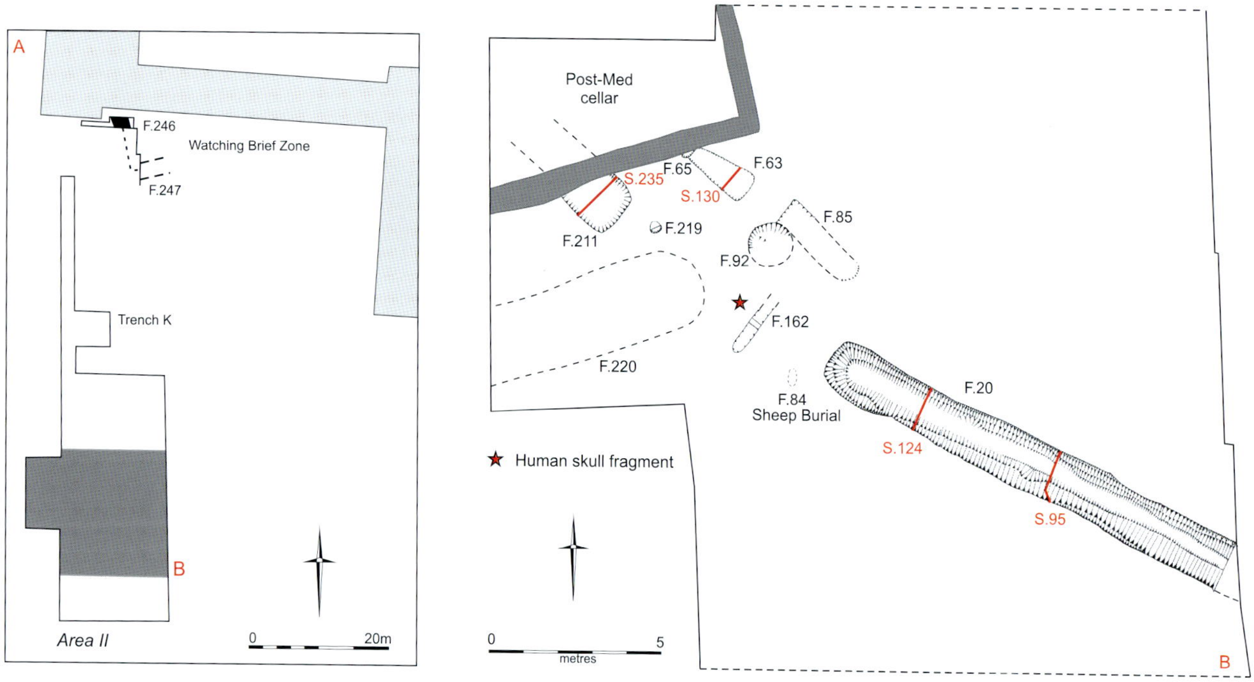

Figure 3.4. *Area II, prehistoric features, base plan.*

bone and worked and burnt flint). A number of other potentially early features also occurred in that area (Fig. 3.4); for reasons outlined above, these will be most appropriately considered in the next section.

Iron Age (?)

The question-mark in the title above essentially relates to the fact that the only definite later Iron Age wares from Area II all came from Roman-phase features (see Hill below). While we suspected that all of the main features within that area and outlined here were Bronze Age, based on their plans and similar excavated features, the two radiocarbon dates achieved indicate a later date (see *Overview* below).

The Bronze Age ditch alignment of F.211 was continued as F.20, with a gap of 7 m, though markedly deeper (*c.* 1 m; Fig. 3.4). Generally 1.3–1.35 m across, the latter's sides sloped steeply in a 'V'-shaped profile down to a slightly concave base (Fig. 3.5), with a splaying upper profile; it terminated in the northwest in a sub-square butt. Its basal fill generally consisted of dark grey clayish silt with occasional charcoal flecks, above which were deposits of redeposited natural (marl and brown sandy clay silts) locally streaked with grey silts; the ditch had clearly been backfilled. A distinct shelf, 0.1–0.15 m wide, survived in places along its upper northern side. This distortion in the ditch's profile was evidently produced through a major recutting following its backfilling, the concave-profiled recut being 0.65–0.7 m deep. Filled with mid grey silt loam, it was slightly darker (loamier) towards the top. Lenses of gravel were present, especially towards the base, and, locally, a distinct charcoal lens was observed.

While a few struck flint flakes were recovered, the artefact-dating evidence for this ditch is provided by a handful of small sherds of shell-tempered pottery recovered from its butt-end (see Hill, below). Due to the density of domestic refuse found within this feature (bone and hearth stones), following initial sampling, it was more intensively excavated and eventually all of its available length was dug by metre-long segments. The vast majority of artefacts recovered from this feature came from the recut fill, and most of those from its uppermost 0.1–0.20 m.

A sheep burial was found lying adjacent to the terminal of F.20 (Figs. 3.4 & 3.5). It lay within a slight 'scoop', F.84, within the surface of the sub-soil and must have been deposited within the buried soil (a large fragment of human skull was recovered nearby from one of the Roman ditch-lines). Another potentially early feature was F.162, a trough/gully running at a right-angle to F.85 (Fig. 3.4). Approximately 0.3 m wide, its concave profile was just *c.* 0.05–0.07 m deep and it petered out at its northern end. Filled with mid grey clay silt loam, the only find recovered from it was a large fragment of burnt stone. Although possibly structural, the status of this slight, 'stain-like' feature

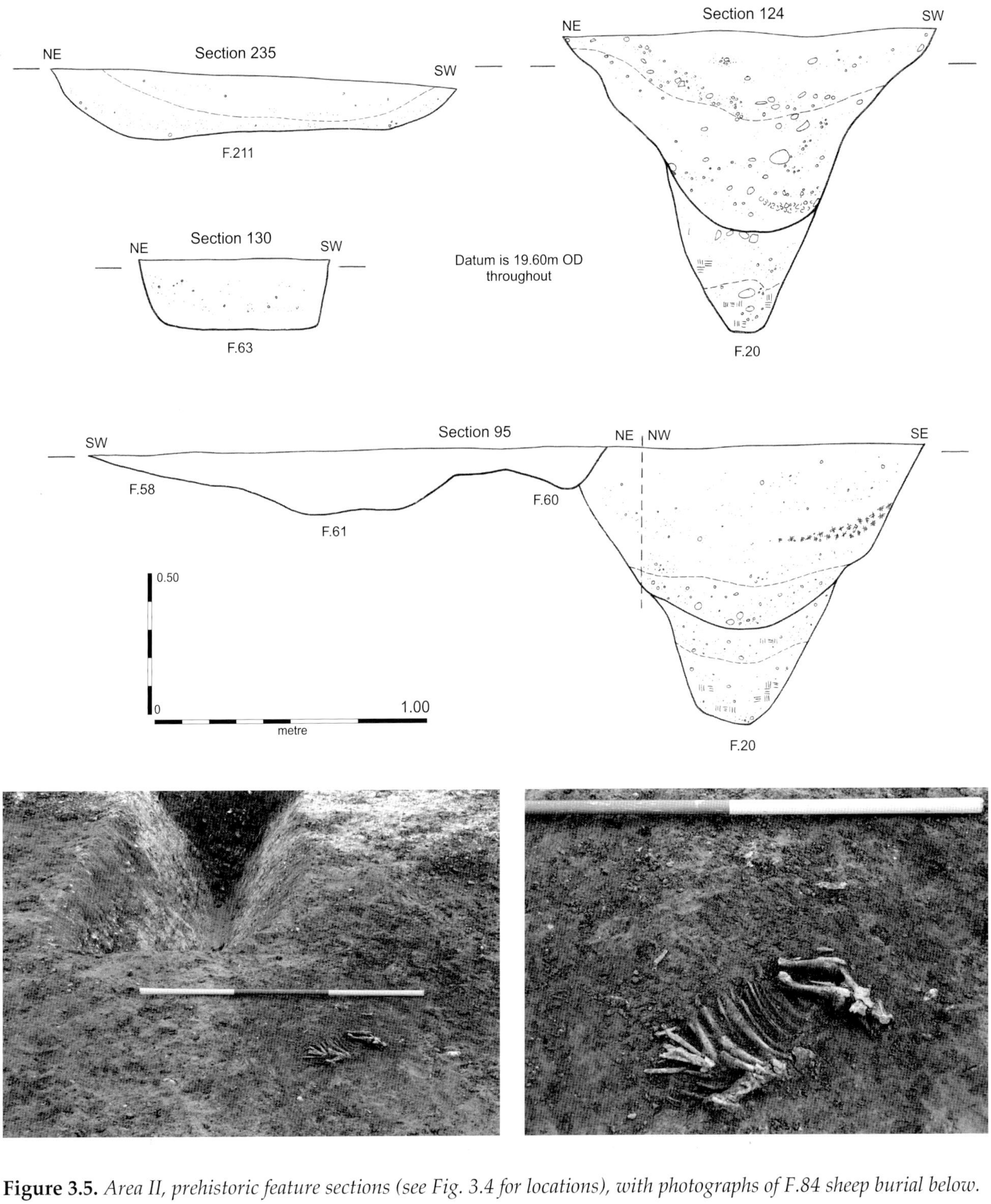

Figure 3.5. *Area II, prehistoric feature sections (see Fig. 3.4 for locations), with photographs of F.84 sheep burial below.*

was difficult to determine. A sub-circular posthole, F.219, also lay close to the butt-end of F.211.

Aside from F.20 being deeper than F.211, the early features here demonstrate a formal symmetry, with the trapezoidal 'box-like' cuts of F.63/85 blocking/controlling the ditch-line's entranceway; these all appear to have been interrelated. There is, though, a complication. Described in the Roman section below, roadway-flanking ditch F.220 deepened markedly close to the terminal of F.211; only prehistoric material was recovered from its preserved basal profile (Fig. 3.4). It is conceivable that this length related to the F.20 boundary and had subsequently been recut.

Only one feature of probable Iron Age date was exposed within Area I: a shallow gully, F.73, that arced across its southern end (Fig. 3.19). Only some 0.04 m deep at its sub-circular butt-end, with a broad concave profile (0.25–0.35 m wide), it was 0.1 m deep where it was truncated by a later ditch along the eastern side of the area. Filled with mid brown sandy clay silt, no finds were recovered from its limited excavation. Whilst generally aligned northwest–southeast, it curved northwards over its eastern length. Although its status was ambiguous, it is assigned to this phase based on the fact that its western length was close to the alignment of the primary features in Area II and it was cut by a Roman ditch.

Artefact Studies

Relevant artefact assemblages will be presented here, with the prehistoric faunal remains and environmental data examined later in this chapter.

The Lithic Assemblage (Alison Dickens)

Of the 275 pieces of struck flint were recovered, the majority (248) deriving from later features. The overall impression from the assemblage is one of crudity and a lack of skilful hands at work, which suggests a late date for the bulk of the material. However, a small number of pieces (*c.* 10–15% of the total), identified on the basis of their heavy patination and technology, attest to possible Mesolithic–Neolithic activity. While showing a slight concentration in the North Field quarries, that probably simply reflects the intensity of excavation there (see below); the material occurred in all three areas of the site and suggests no more than dispersed low-density activity. These pieces, nonetheless, include a number of utilized and edge-trimmed narrow flakes and blades: a knife on a large trimming flake (surface find) and a core tablet reworked as an end scraper (from Roman ditch, F.33, in Area III). Although none of this material would be out of place in an earlier Neolithic assemblage, a blade segment from a South Field-area quarry pit possesses Mesolithic 'style' abrupt unilateral retouch, and could imply that the material is more chronologically mixed than first appears. A minor Late Neolithic/Early Bronze Age component is suggested by a few pieces, such as a broken scraper with fine semi-invasive retouch from one of the North Field quarry hollows.

The assemblage is dominated by debitage – waste flakes, cores and shatter pieces – which constitutes 76 per cent of the whole. Implements and retouched pieces are scarce (6.5%) and only 11 other pieces showed obvious signs of utilization. The only traditional implement types identified were scrapers, of which seven (2.5%) were recovered. The scrapers do not conform to a single type and vary considerably, both in the extent of retouch and the steepness of the retouch angle. Three were formed on primary cortexed flakes and four on tertiary flakes. Two were complete and were two broken end-scrapers; one complete and a broken three-quarter round scraper, while two were opportunistic steep retouch on irregular flake edges, one retouched on opposing edges. As a group they are not clearly diagnostic, suggesting a combination of curation and opportunistic retouch.

The largest debitage category is 'flake', making up 60 per cent of the total assemblage. Of these 43.6 per cent were 'squat' (i.e. with a breadth:length ratio of 5:5 or greater; Fig. 3.6), whilst only 5.4 per cent were narrow (breadth:length ratio of 2:5 or less). (Only two pieces were identified as true blades, having straight edges and parallel scars on the dorsal face, indicating that they were struck from a prepared core.) The occurrence of hinge and snap fractures at the distal end of flakes was also high (28.4%), which together with the frequent occurrence of 'bashed' bulbar ends, exaggerated conchoidal features and incipient impact cones on cores, suggest

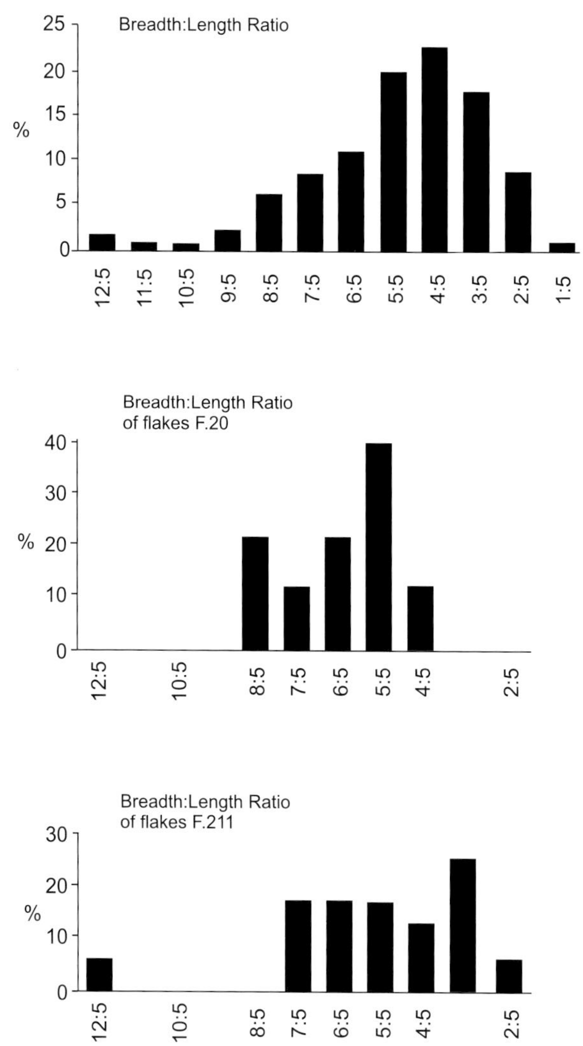

Figure 3.6. *Histograms of worked flint breadth-to-length ratios.*

the unskilled application of a hard hammer. These factors all tend to support the initial impression of a lack of technological sophistication in the flintworking.

Thirteen cores and 12 possible cores (flaked pieces) were recovered. Of the certain examples, 10 had a single platform, two had two platforms and one had three. Both groups together only made up 9.1 per cent of the total. None of the cores showed evidence of deliberate preparation for the production of standardized flakes. The reduction techniques appear to be opportunistic and not directed towards the creation of specific tool types. The average discard length of the cores was 35–54 mm. This is 7 mm longer than the average flake length, indicating that the cores were generally discarded before the point of exhaustion. There is some evidence for informal core rejuvenation, but again this does not appear systematic. No examples of re-fitting were observed and no obvious knapping clusters were recovered. The incidence of 'chips' (< 15 mm long), was very low, with only 11 pieces identified (4%). Sieving was not conducted systematically across the site, but the samples that were did not add significantly to the chip numbers. Chips are a useful indicator of *in situ* knapping, tending not to move from their area of origin. The lack of these smaller pieces in this assemblage tends to suggest that the incidence of knapping activity in the area of the site was minimal.

Following the arguments in Ford *et al.*, a common element in later lithic technologies is the progressive loss of technical competence (1984, 162). In general, this indicates less control over the raw material, as demonstrated by the increased incidence of irregular, i.e. hinge and snap, end fractures. These features are commonplace amongst the New Hall assemblage, which suggests a Middle–Late Bronze Age date for the bulk of the material.

Some 291 pieces of burnt flint were also recovered. Of this, *c.* 10–15 per cent appeared previously worked. Whilst undiagnostic, including squat flakes and core fragments, all of these could be of Bronze Age attribution.

Feature 211 /20

The largest single group came from F.211 in Area II (see Fig. 3.6), 30 pieces of burnt and 42 pieces of struck flint (the latter comprising 23 flakes, three definite and eight possible cores, six shatter pieces and two scrapers). Seventeen (40%) of the struck pieces were 'squat', and 65% were cortexed. The eight possible cores are all similar, being crudely struck cobble ends that could have served as cores or primary preparation, but upon which the same action has been carried out. There is no evidence of *in situ* knapping, either into the feature or in the material that was dumped into it. The nature of the assemblage – so much larger than that in any other feature – suggests the dumping of material resulting from a specific action.

In contrast, ditch F.20, which was on the same rough alignment as F.211, had only 14 pieces of flint (10 struck and four burnt) recovered from the 15 metre-segments excavated along its length. The struck pieces were all flakes, slightly more 'squat' than those from F.211, 50 per cent of which were cortexed. The number of primary flakes may represent primary reduction but, given the distribution along the ditch length, probably does not relate to a single incident. The dissimilarity between the material in F.211 and its nearest contemporary neighbour serves to highlight further the unusual nature of that deposit.

The Pebble-hammer/Macehead

A segment of a quartzite 'pebble-hammer' was recovered from the F.163 Bronze Age ditch (Fig. 3.3). The fragment, representing approximately a quarter of the original, was 47 mm deep with an external diameter of about 100 mm. The piece, formed from a quartzite cobble with a brown surface, was pierced with an hourglass-shaped hole, the diameter of which was *c.* 19 mm at the narrowest point. There were 'battering' marks around the external circumference.

The New Hall piece is typical of pebble-hammers from across the country as described and defined principally by Roe (1968; 1979). They differ from other categories of shaft-hole implements in being made from unmodified pebbles or cobbles, commonly quartzite, often with a rich brown surface; they usually have a central hourglass-shaped hole, formed by pecking and grinding, and show signs of use. The selection of the pebbles conforms to a fairly restricted shape and size-range, with the hole tending to be centred in both planes. This, rather usefully, allows reconstruction of the many broken examples. The New Hall piece presents a little difficulty in this regard, however, as it is not clear from the surviving fragment whether the original was truly round or more irregular in shape. Approximations of the original shape place it within the size-range of Roe and Radley's main group (1971, 170)

Dating for this group of artefacts is ambiguous. While Rankine believed them to be Mesolithic (1949), Roe and Radley point out that all his finds from or near Mesolithic sites were either loose or 'dated tenuously by pollen analysis' (*ibid.*, 169). They feel that whilst Rankine's Mesolithic link is not disproved, there is ample evidence to suggest that pebble-hammers were in use in the Neolithic and probably lasted into the Bronze Age (*ibid.*, 175). As a tool type, the lack of sophistication in manufacture has led to an assumption that pebble-hammers are more primitive than other shaft-hole implements such as 'battle-axes' and 'mace-heads'. With such a long period of use, however, the pebble-hammer would seem to have had an exclusive function that meant its continued utilization (*ibid.*, 175).

Roe and Radley discuss possible functions for pebble-hammers in some detail. Of the characteristic features noted for the artefact, two – both apparent on the New Hall piece – certainly seem to indicate that they were functional rather than ceremonial or symbolic. Many pebble-hammers show signs of battering on the ends or around the edges. In many, the central 'ridge' of the hourglass-shaped perforation is polished. The combination of polish and battering may suggest that the pieces were hafted and used as a hammer, possibly associated with flint knapping (*ibid.*, 173). As Roe and Radley discuss, the hourglass-shape of the hole would, though, tend to make the head of such a tool unstable and difficult to haft securely. Whilst some may well have been used as hammers, others may have been suspended, the polish resulting from friction from a cord or thong, and served as weights, perhaps as part of a loom (*ibid.*).

Pebble-hammers have a wide distribution across the country and are certainly as common in the north as in the south. Their distribution, in Yorkshire at least, reflects well that of other Neolithic and Bronze Age material (*ibid.*, 172). Several examples of pebble-hammers are known from the Cambridgeshire area, including half a small pebble from Hurst Fen (*ibid.*, 174) and a larger complete head from Fen Ditton (Clough & Green 1972, fig. 9).[2]

Late Bronze Age and Early Iron Age Pottery (Josh Pollard)

Amongst the ceramic assemblage are 64 sherds/crumbs of pottery (382 g) from a minimum of eight vessels that are identified as Bronze Age –predominantly 'Late' – or Early Iron Age on the basis of fabric and vessel form (Fig. 3.7).

Five fabric groups have been defined, of which the flinty Fabrics 1, 2 and 4 account for 92.3 per cent of the sherds by weight (Table. 3.1). Both coarse- and finewares in Fabrics 1 and 2, categorized largely on the basis of surface finish, are present.

1) Hard fabric with common fine SAND and common to very common small FLINT. Orange-brown to black exterior and interior.

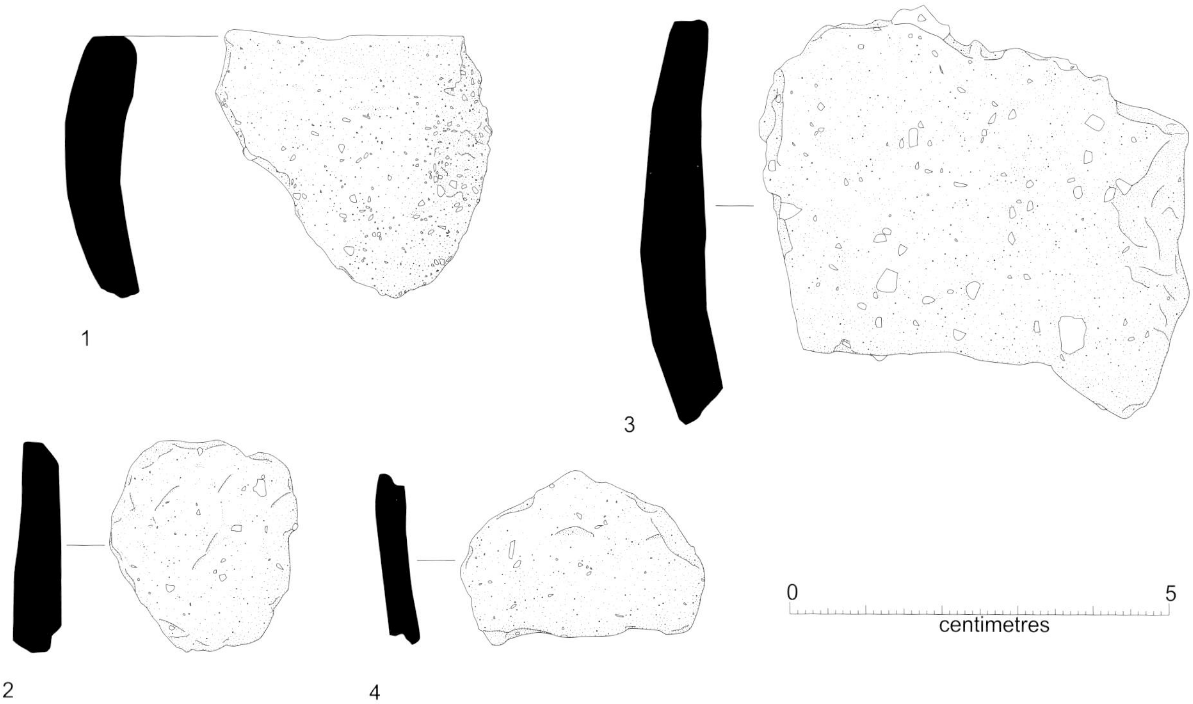

Figure 3.7. *Earlier prehistoric pottery: 1 & 2) Area I, Western Quarry sondage; 3) Area I, F.74; 4) Area II, roadway ditch (F.58/60/61).*

2) Hard fabric with common small to medium FLINT, moderate to common fine SAND and sparse small GROG. Black to pale grey-brown exterior and interior.
3) Hard fabric with common small GROG and very sparse fine SAND. Pale grey-brown exterior and grey core and interior. Possibly Early Bronze Age.
4) Hard fabric with common small to medium FLINT, patchilly distributed, common small GROG and sparse to moderate SAND. Pale orange-brown exterior and interior and pale grey core.
5) Soft fabric with common fine SAND and rare small FLINT. Brown exterior (with reduced slip?) and dark grey core and interior. Possibly not Late Bronze Age.

The bulk of the assemblage can be accommodated within Barrett's post-Deverel Rimbury 'plain-ware' tradition, dating to the centuries around 1000 cal. BC (Barrett 1980). Vessel forms are difficult to reconstruct given the limited nature of the assemblage and the small size of the majority of the sherds (most being 40 mm or less in maximum dimension). However, enough feature sherds are present to enable the identification of Class I and II jars, bowls and possibly one cup (*ibid.*, 302–3). There is one shoulder from an angular jar or bowl, three sherds from vessels with unpronounced shoulders and one from a slack-profiled jar. Of two rims, both are simple, one being externally expanded along part of its length, the other (from a bowl or jar of closed form) flattened. A single, uninformative, base-angle is also present.

Table 3.1. *Late Bronze Age and Early Iron Age pottery fabrics.*

Fabric	No. of Sherds	Wt. (g)
1	28	174
2	27	101
3	1	4
4	3	78
5	5	25
Total	*64*	*381*

Four sherds in Fabric 1 possess traces of simple decoration and three have single fingernail impressions, and the fourth two fine horizontal incised lines. One of the fingernail-impressed sherds was perforated prior to firing, a feature more common on Deverel Rimbury bucket urns (cf. Longworth *et al.* 1988, fig. 27, 129–44) than on vessels of the post-Deverel Rimbury tradition (though cf. Bradley *et al.* 1980, 234 & 268).

A comparable local assemblage is that recovered from a similar Cam terrace location at Green End Road, Chesterton (Barrett 1980, fig. 5, 13–16). Even accepting post-depositional attrition, the excavations at New Hall produced few sherds. The material may have been generated by limited duration occupation or could mark the periphery of a larger settlement area.

There were five sherds in Fabric 5, a fine flint-tempered fabric paralleled in other Late Bronze Age and Early Iron Age assemblages across the region.

Later Iron Age Pottery (JD. Hill)

The excavations produced a small quantity of definitely or probably Later Pre-Roman Iron Age pottery (*c.* 300 BC–AD 40/60). The majority of this material consists of shelly wares that probably date to the early and middle first century AD, spanning the Conquest Period. One feature, F.17 – of Early Roman date – produced definitely Later Pre-Roman Iron Age pottery. Three other features, F.88, F.20 and F.211, also contained some probable material of that attribution. While the small quantity and sherd size of this material provides evidence of activity of this period, but not necessarily domestic occupation *per se* across the excavated area.

The assemblage consisted of only a small collection of just 20 sherds, weighing 156 g. This mainly comprises small and very small sherds (Mean Sherd Weight 7.8 g) recovered either from the few features which pre-date the main Roman phases of activity on the site or residually from Roman contexts. There were no complete or partial profiles recovered and just two small-/medium-sized rim sherds. This small collection was analysed using the pottery recording system recommended by the *Prehistoric Ceramics Research Group*. All sherds were assigned a fabric type, after macroscopic examination and the use of a hand lens (x10 magnification). The two diagnostic sherds were examined and assigned a form type as appropriate with further variables recorded as detailed in *The Study of Later Prehistoric Pottery: Guidelines for analysis and publication* (*PCRG* 1997).

The recovered material displayed two broad fabric types: those with quartz sand inclusions (Q1) and those with white shell inclusions (S1, S2 & S3). Feature 17 produced small quantities of typical handmade Later Pre-Roman Iron Age sandy (Q1) pottery that dates to *c*. 300 BC–AD 40/60. This is a hard, dense, unoxidized black fabric with common rounded medium-sized quartz sand grains. The two larger sherds have burnished exteriors, and the single upright tapered rim comes from a thin-walled, rounded-bodied bowl (internal rim diam. *c*. 140 mm). Both this fabric and vessel form are common features of 'Middle Pre-Roman Iron Age' handmade vessels in the region. Although such fabrics and forms start as early as *c*. 300 BC, and are usually described as 'Middle Iron Age', it would appear that such handmade forms continue to be made and used on at least some sites in the region into the 'Late Iron Age' of the first centuries BC/AD. As such the label 'Later Iron Age' for such material might be preferable.

The shelly fabrics are less easy to place. Two variants of shelly fabrics – S1 and S2 – can be distinguished in this collection through the quantities of shell inclusion present and the colour of the fabric. The former is characterized by a hard, dense, smooth feeling fabric containing very common well-sorted shell fragments (1–3 mm in length). This material has a brick-red oxidized exterior and black unoxidized interior and is similar to a fabric used at the first centuries BC/AD ringwork site at Wardy Hill, Ely to make large 'storage' jars (Hill & Horne 2003). The other fabric, S2, is similar, but has only moderate quantities of the shell inclusions, and has a grey brown exterior and grey interior colour. These shelly fabrics were not recovered from the same features as the sandy material and came from F.20 and F.211. Dating these shelly wares on the basis of a handful of sherds and a single non-diagnostic rim sherd is difficult, as shelly fabrics were used from the later Bronze Age to the Roman period in the region in small quantities. This pottery is probably not Late Bronze Age or Early Iron Age in date, as many of the shelly fabrics of this date are characterized by large grey pieces of fossil shell. Similar fine white shell fabrics occur in some quantities at the first centuries BC/AD at Wardy Hill (*ibid*.) and are also here probably later Pre-Roman Iron Age. The one rim sherd came from a very wide mouthed (internal rim diam. *c*. 320–360 mm), thick-walled and flat-rimmed vessel. There are no obvious parallels for this small sherd, but it could possibly be from a handmade, local copy of a first-century AD high-walled platter or 'dog bowl', or from a large, simple rimmed bowl/jar. The one sherd in Fabric S3 supports the Late Iron Age/immediately post-Conquest dating of these shelly fabrics on the site. This was recovered from the surface of F.88 and is in an orange buff very hard and dense fabric with moderate quantities of white shell fragments 0.5–2 mm in size. This appears to be wheelmade and from a Late Iron Age/Early Roman form with two narrow cordons running horizontally across the sherd's body. It probably dates to the early/middle first century AD.

Overview

Despite differences in their depth/profile, given their shared alignment and matching terminals there can be little doubt that ditches F.20 and F.211 within Area II were directly related (Fig. 3.4). Lying parallel to, and bridging the gap between them, the two symmetrical trapezoidal cuts 1.5 m to the northeast – F.63 and F.85 – would seem to have formed some manner of gateway structure. Two aspects cast some doubt on this grouping, however. First is the discrepancy of profile/depth between the two main ditches (F.20 & F.211). Second is the fact that, while shell-tempered wares were recovered from F.20, generally only earlier, Bronze Age pottery/finds were associated with the more northwesterly features (F.63, F.85, F.211 & F.219; a single shell-tempered sherd was found in F.211). The key point is that when New Hall's prehistoric pottery was analysed it was generally understood such tempering was largely an attribute of the region's Middle Iron Age assemblages, though Hill admitted the broad potential duration of shell-tempering at the time. Only in the next decade – with excavations at Fitzwilliam College (see below) and other sites – did the realization develop of how widely this temper was also employed in local Middle Bronze Age wares.

There can be no doubt that there was a major prehistoric enclosure system within Area II; hereafter, this will be referred to as Enclosure A. In an effort to try to resolve its dating, two animal bone samples from ditch F.20 were submitted to the Godwin Laboratory for radiocarbon dating:

1) From primary fill ([399] <535>) 2005±100 bp/205 cal. BC–245 cal. AD (Q-3260)
2) From recut ([399] <601>) 1920±100 bp/125 cal. BC–340 cal. AD (Q-3261).

The results indicate the later Iron Age of that feature. Although not entirely satisfactory as an explanation, it can only be presumed that, while probably originating in a Bronze Age layout, the F.20 ditch-length had later been recut.

Pollen samples taken from two features associated with this enclosure indicate that – as was also the case in the Roman period – the area supported 'open, weedy, grassland' (see Wiltshire, below). Perhaps indicative of adjacent occupation and/or later 'introduced', relatively large amounts of microscopic charcoal detected in the basal fill of F.85 has prompted the interpretation of nearby fires.

With limited exposure, little can be said concerning the F.163 ditch and the few associated features within Area I. Unfortunately, when a sample from its cow skull was submitted for dating it failed due to insufficient carbon. The ditch was probably settlement-related and contemporary with the residual Bronze Age material found in Roman contexts. The settlement may have either fallen to the north and/or south, and it need not necessarily have been entirely (ditch-) enclosed; any associated discrete features were probably lost through later quarrying (see, though, the Fitzwilliam College findings below). Relative concentrations of early material (struck/burnt flint and Bronze Age pottery) were found, redeposited within later features, in both ends of Area I.

The prehistoric attribution of the curvilinear ditch in the southern end of Area I is indirect, based on its plan and that it pre-dated other features there.

As outlined by Yannouli below, although a sheep burial was recovered (F.84), throughout later prehistory the local economy would seem to have been predominantly cattle-based (this, though, is in some contrast to the frequencies seen at the nearby Marion Close enclosure; see below). No cereal remains were forthcoming from the prehistoric contexts, although one must acknowledge the site's low intensity of bulk environmental sampling. Charred seeds of elderberry were present in one of the samples from F.20 (No. 8; see Fryer & Murphy, below) and a small fragment of saddle quern found in a later feature probably reflects some degree of prehistoric arable activity.

Roman Land-use and Settlement (Period II)

Presentation of the Roman period remains will largely be grouped 'thematically' by area to facilitate a more coherent presentation. Although this ordering has chronological implications, these are not absolute; for example, while at some points ditches were recorded as truncating quarry pits (and in no instance did a quarry cut a ditch), this does not imply that the earliest ditches were not contemporary with the quarries.

A Roman-period phasing structure is outlined below (see *Overviewing Settlement Structures*). This is based on broad principles; not all features will necessarily be assigned to a distinct phase. This reflects the 'organic character' of much of the archaeological evidence, especially its quarries, and the fact that portions of the site could only be sondage-investigated (i.e. the south half of Area I) because of this heavy disturbance.

Road, Ditch Systems and Enclosure B (Area II)

This section concerns the excavation's most singular discovery: Area II's entirely unexpected Roman road-line (Road 1). A series of related ditched boundaries are also outlined here, along with a major enclosure that was observed (during watching brief recording) to extend under the Nuffield Building.

Aligned northeast–southwest, a straight ditch crossed Area II, F.17 (Fig. 3.8). Its width varied from 1.4–1.80 m, but generally it had a regular broad 'U'-shaped profile and was 0.6–0.7 m deep (Fig. 3.9). The survival of a slight shelf along its northwestern side suggested recutting. It was filled throughout with quite homogeneous, fine mid grey brown silty loam, with only very limited evidence of any primary weathering (darker and loamier in the upper profile). Generally, the ditch was excavated through a series of metre-long sample-segments (four, at 3 m intervals). Due to the low density of artefacts, and in order to elucidate cut relationships with prehistoric features, the intervening segments between two were also subsequently dug.

Apart from the recut maintenance of F.17 itself, an earlier ditch (or version thereof) – F.59 – was found to run along the northern side of the western three-quarters of F.17 (Fig. 3.8). Its existence was first apparent on the surface, as a strip of white marl was visible along that side. Attesting to its backfilling, this redeposited natural filled the upper profile of F.59; otherwise, it fills consisted of mid grey brown silty loam. This earlier ditch was 0.6–0.75 m+ wide (estimated total width *c.* 1.30 m) and 0.45–0.5 m deep, with a broad 'U'-shaped profile. Although backfilled, this earlier ditch had clearly dictated the line of F.17.

A distinct sub-circular butt was apparent on the northern side of F.17 – three-quarters of the way along its eastern extent – the later length extending its line eastwards. This ditch-line was further exposed when the area was locally expanded to the west, where four additional metre-segments were dug. Although the basic ditch sequence found in the main area continued (i.e. F.17 recutting F.59), a further element/complication arose as the ditch deepened (to 0.8–0.90 m) and the basal profile became much steeper. In fact, a distinct sub-square butt-end was apparent 5.4 m beyond the western edge-of-excavation, from where the base dropped markedly. This would seem to denote the original ditch along this line, which had largely been truncated away by F.17; it was designated F.220 (Fig. 3.8). The primary fill of the deeper ditch (surviving to a depth of 0.1–0.2 m within the base) consisted of quite sticky, sandy dark grey silty clay with streaks of white marl and orange-brown clay natural. This would seem to represent primary weathering and there was no evidence of backfilling. Burnt and worked flint occurred in each of the four western fill segments (1–10 and 2–5 pieces per metre-segment, respectively). No Roman pottery was recovered from F.220's fills and it might well have been of prehistoric date, even though it appeared to dictate the recut line of F.17/59, as discussed above.

Beside the western edge-of-excavation, a flat-based 'depression' of sub-square plan (0.55 × 1 m+; 0.08 m deep), F.212, conjoined the top of F.17. It was filled with dirty mid orange-brown sticky sandy clay with medium–large gravel. Corresponding with a clay 'plug' in the sub-soil, its gravelly 'fill' surely derived from road metalling, though this hollow was probably a geological occurrence.

Within the main area, a series of more minor intercutting ditches ran roughly parallel with F.17, 6.6–7.2 m to the south. Collectively 2.1–2.3 m wide, three main ditches were identified (from south to north; Figs. 3.8–9):

1) *F.61* – 0.65–0.7 m wide and 0.13–0.18 m deep; generally with a concave profile
2) *F.58* – 0.7–1.3 m wide and 0.18–0.24 m deep; profile varies from a flat base (0.5 m wide in east) to regularly concave, with local evidence of re-/double-ditch cutting
3) *F.60* – 0.65–0.7 m wide and 0.13–0.18 m deep; regular concave profile.

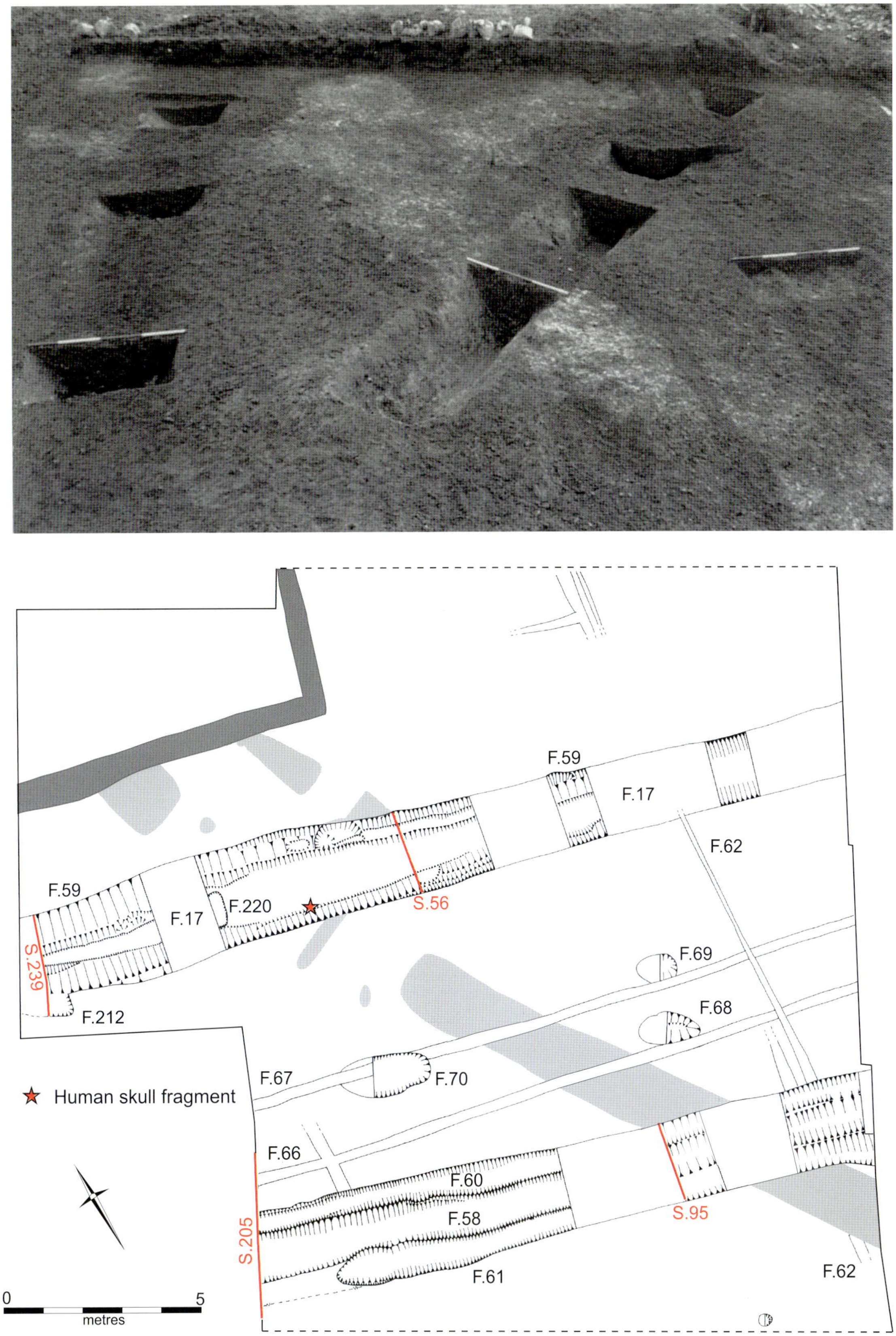

Figure 3.8. *Area II, Roman features, base plan and photograph.*

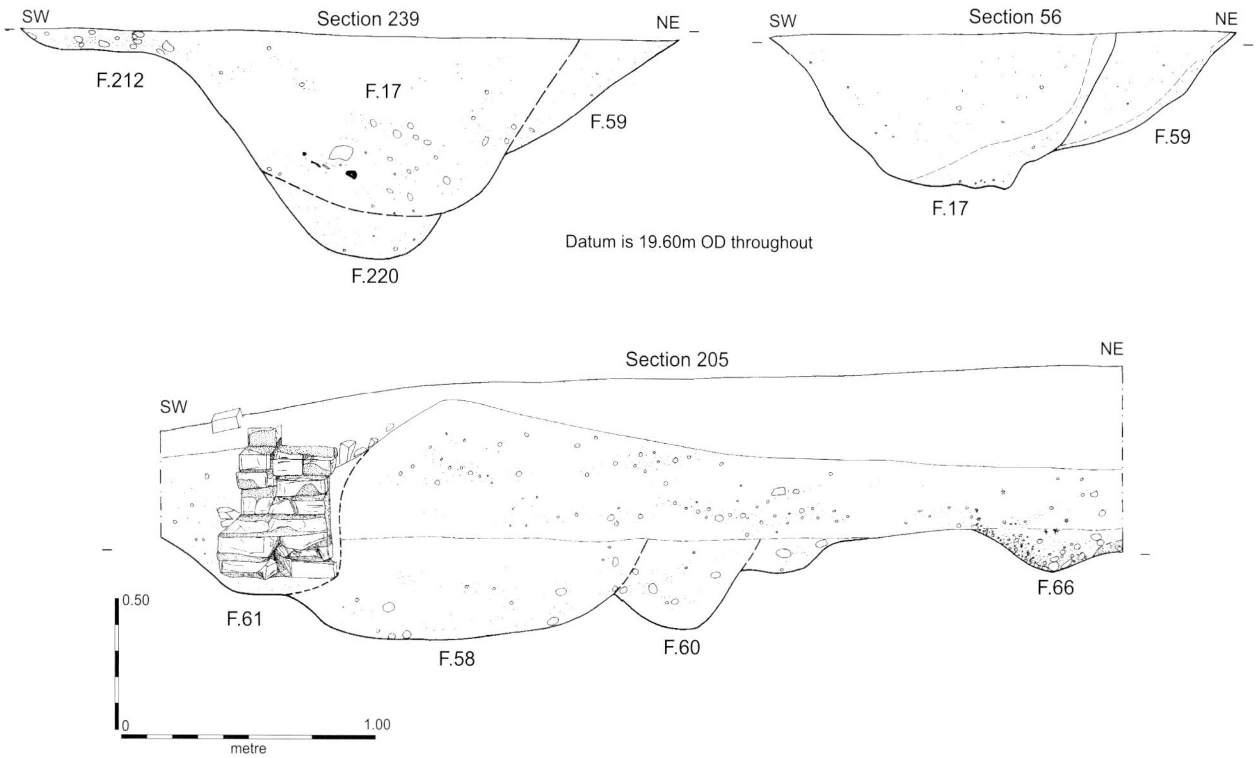

Figure 3.9. *Area II, Roman feature sections (see Fig. 3.8 for location).*

Apart from the southernmost (which butt-ended shy of the western edge-of-excavation), these ditches seemed to cross the site parallel with each other. Given their shallowness and homogeneous mid grey-brown silt loam fills (F.61 & F.60 both had frequent local gravel inclusions), it was difficult to establish their sequence. As far as could be ascertained, they were (re-)dug from south to north: F.61, earliest; F.60, latest. That said, considerable variability was apparent along their lengths (especially of F.58) and identification of further ditch recuts probably eluded their segmented sample-excavation. Given the distance between, and the parallel relationship of, ditches F.20 and F.58/60/61, from the outset they were interpreted as bounding a road some 7 m wide.

Within Trench K, extending north from Area II, only one group of potentially 'early' features – a series of northeast–southwest-oriented troughs – was present, and a 5 × 5 m area of excavation was subsequently opened up on the eastern side of the trench. These linears continued across this area and two proved to be relatively robust, both filled with mid grey-brown slightly sandy silt loam:

F.81 - 0.25–0.4 m wide and 0.2 m deep with a 'U'-shaped concave profile.

F.82 - *c.* 0.3 m wide and 0.2 m deep with a concave profile; recut on southern side: 0.3 m wide and 0.12 m deep.

A similarly wide, but shallow 'strip' (*c.* 0.05 m deep) and four narrow troughs (0.08–0.12 m wide; 0.09–0.1 m deep) were also present. All ran roughly parallel with F.81/82 and were filled with mid grey silt loam.

Whilst F.81 and 82 seem to have been 'dug' ditches as such, given their size and profiles, the 'troughs' may have just been parallel plough-lines. Although only one struck flint flake was recovered from their collective excavation, from the character of their fill and their shared alignment with features within Area II, they would appear to be of Roman date.[3]

During the monitoring of basement-reduction, further north along the southern side of the College's Nuffield Building, two very substantial ditches were exposed in section (Figs. 3.4 & 3.10):

F.246 (north section) – 2.4 m wide, with a 'V'-shaped profile, 1.2 m deep. The basal third appeared backfilled with deposits of pure brown clays and marls streaked with lenses of sand and silt. A deposit of quite homogeneous mid yellow-brown sandy clay silt extending down the western edge of the cut could attest to bank-slip. In the main, it was filled with mid grey-brown clay silt loam with localized lenses of charcoal. Whereas quantities of large bone and burnt cobbles were present within the upper tertiary fill, only a single burnt cobble was found in the basal deposits.

F.247 (eastern section) – 2.35 m wide, with a steep 'U'-shaped profile, 1.05 m deep. The fill sequence was essentially as F.246, although its basal backfill included a higher gravel component; great quantities of large bones were recovered from the upper fill.

Time permitted only limited excavation back into the two sections to establish the alignment of these ditches. Both ran obliquely to the sections: F.246, northwest–southeast; F.247, northeast–southwest. 'Matching' and lying at right-angles to each other, there can be little doubt that these two ditches represent two sides of a deeply ditched compound: the southwest corner of a sub-rectangular/square enclosure that extends north beneath the Nuffield Building. (F.246 was observed not to extend beyond the projected junction of the two ditches, as it was not present within a section 5 m south of that point.)

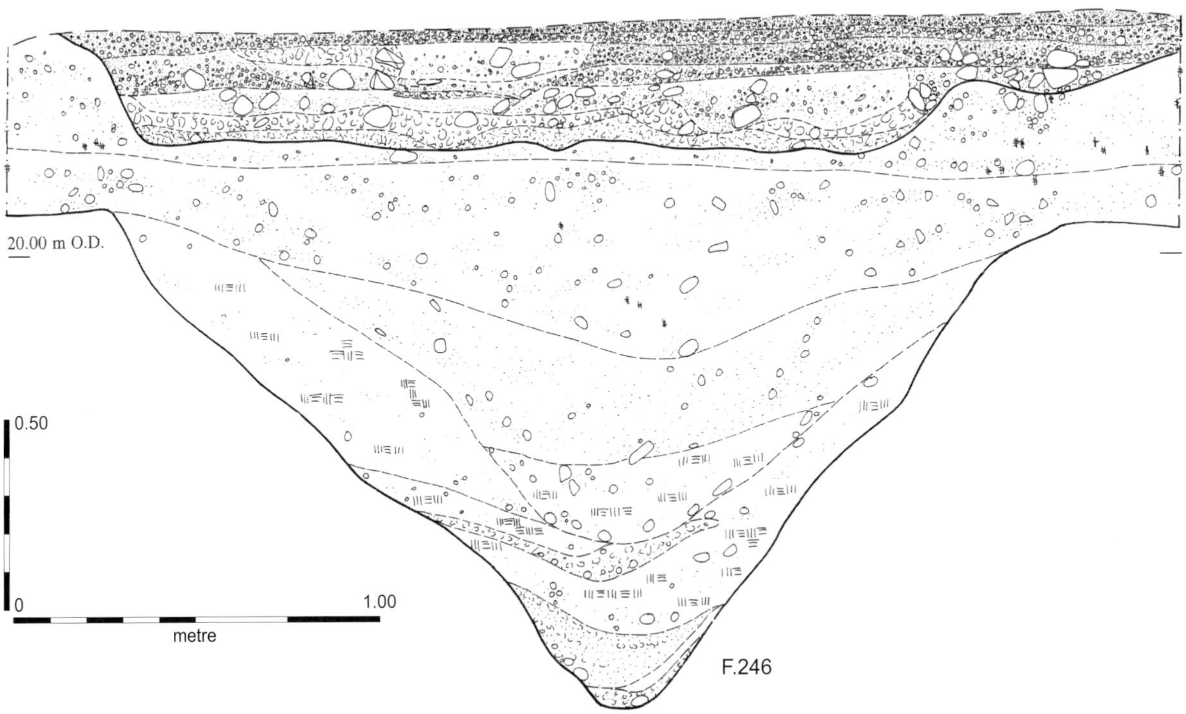

Figure 3.10. *Watching brief zone, photograph, looking north with F.246 (left) and F.247 ditches (right, with section of former below; see Fig. 3.4 for location).*

The alignment of F.246 and F.247 closely followed that of Area II's roadway. Although the character of the ditches, especially F.246 (profile and bone frequency) was similar to that of the main later prehistoric boundary in the area (F.20), they did not share its alignment (the profile of F.246 is also close to that of the northern Roman roadside ditch over its western end). This enclosure will hereafter be referred to as 'Enclosure B'.

Within Area III a northwest–southeast-oriented ditch, F.33, was exposed across the northern third of the area (Fig. 3.11). Generally 0.7–0.85 m wide and 0.28–0.38 m deep, it had a 'U'-shaped profile with a flat base 0.2–0.4 m across. Along the southernmost 1.5 m of its extent the profile was more 'V'-shaped with a narrow concave base. Although certainty is not possible given the 'awkwardness' of its exposure adjacent to the northern section of the trench, over its northernmost 0.5 m its alignment appeared to veer slightly eastwards.

Over its entire length, the ditch had two distinct fills. The basal half of its profile consisted of mid orange-brown clay silt with marl flecks/streaks and medium to large flint pebbles/cobbles. The frequency of charcoal within this apparently backfilled deposit varied from occasional to frequent, and many large bone fragments were recovered from it. The upper profile was filled with quite homogeneous mid grey silty clay loam (secondary weathering).

Feature 33 did not extend north into the pavement/road-verge trenches and must, therefore, have terminated immediately beneath the trench-edge kerb (hence its northeastern kinking). However, after an interval of *c.* 1.8 m a near-matching ditch, F.174 (Fig. 3.11), continued its line northwards. Ending in a sub-circular southern butt-end, in the main it was 0.6–0.7 m wide. As excavated, it was *c.* 0.3 m deep (*c.* 0.38 m deep in the edge-of-excavation section). The western side sloped down steeply to a concave base; the eastern edge sloped much more broadly with a distinct shelf suggestive of off-centre recutting. It was filled with mid brown/orange-brown clay silt loam; the basal profile and lower western side included a major lens of charcoal in siltier grey-brown loam.

Within the immediate Huntingdon Road-side trenches a minor ditch/trough, F.179, ran parallel to F.33. With a sub-circular northern butt-end, it was 1.65 m+ long; the configuration of its edges suggested a total length not greater than *c.* 1.8 m (0.3–0.4 m wide and *c.* 0.15 m deep, with a steep 'U'-shaped profile). Feature 179 was filled with mid grey-brown silt loam; bone was recovered.

Between these two linear features, the southern side (?third) of a shallow, 0.08 m deep concave-profiled sub-circular 'hollow' – F.182 – *c.* 1.5 m in diameter, extended 0.4 m into the trench. Filled with dark orange-brown silty clay loam, just one pottery sherd and a bone were recovered from this amorphous feature (possibly the southern 'cone' of a much larger pit).

East of the southern butt-end of F.174 was an extremely truncated, sub-circular posthole/scoop, 0.3 m in diameter with a 0.1 m deep concave base, F.189. It was filled with dark orange-grey/brown sandy clay.

The association of the discrete and apparently settlement-related features (F.182 & F.189) with the linear features is inferential. However, the major charcoal lens/horizon within ditch F.174 and the quantity of bone and cobbles in F.33 would suggest adjacent occupation (as could also the entranceway gap between ditches F.33 & F.174). The three ditches – F.33, F.174 and F.179 – all shared the same alignment, which matched that of the Area II road to the south. The key importance of this is the unequivocal evidence that this ditch system continues beneath the present line of Huntingdon Road and its postulated precursor of the route to Godmanchester (i.e. *Via Devana*).

Running parallel and *c.* 7.5 m apart, ditches F.17 and F.58/60/61 must have flanked a substantial thoroughfare. Whether it deserved the title of 'road', as opposed to droveway, depends on defining criteria and is probably irresolvable, given the available evidence. If the presence of metalling is taken as the sole factor, then it must be considered a droveway. Yet, whilst little was apparent within its flanking ditches and none visible in the buried soil/edge-of-excavation sections, this could well have been dispersed through later ploughing. Two Post-Medieval garden bedding trenches (originally thought to be Roman cart ruts) crossing the area of the thoroughfare were filled with 'churned' gravels, which could have derived from its eradicated surface. With these caveats in mind, given its size and the broader context of its alignment, it will hereafter be termed *a road* (No. 1).

The southern roadside ditches (F.58/60/61) were quite minor and are comparable to the Area III and Trench K field boundaries/gullies. More important, perhaps, is that F.17/59 seems to represent a major boundary, as suggested both by its size and the frequency of artefacts within the fills. The distribution of finds across the roadside ditches suggests that any settlement would lie to the north, not south of it; the low finds density within the southern ditches suggest that the land was 'open' on that side (i.e. fields only).

That the succession of recutting/extension of the northern roadside ditch was apparently from west to east (F.220 > F.59 > F.17), and not from Roman Cambridge 'outwards', is intriguing. Although certainty in this matter is difficult, this could suggest the existence of an immediately west-of-site 'place' from where the road was extended towards Roman Cambridge.

Apparently of an agricultural function, there can be little doubt that the Trench K ditches running parallel with the Area II road were essentially contemporary with it. In Area III, the F.33/174 and F.179 ditches seem to have had a similar function and suggest the existence of an extensive system of landscape enclosures coming off the road. Much more substantial, the F.246 and F.247 ditches (Enclosure B) exposed during the watching brief seemed of quite different character and could relate to a distinct settlement compound. Whilst their profile and the character/quality of finds within them (burnt stone and bone but a general lack of pottery apart from a sherd of prehistoric pottery recovered from the buried ground surface beside the ditch in the eastern section) could suggest a relationship with the prehistoric enclosure system in Area II (cf. F.20), the alignment of these ditches definitely followed that of the Roman road. Indeed, their deep 'V'-shaped profile has affinities with the western length of the northern roadside ditch (F.220).

Quarries, Ditches and Postholes (Area III)

This section will be concerned with developments at the opposite end of the site: Area III's possible 'early-phase' features (Fig. 3.11). It begins with the few

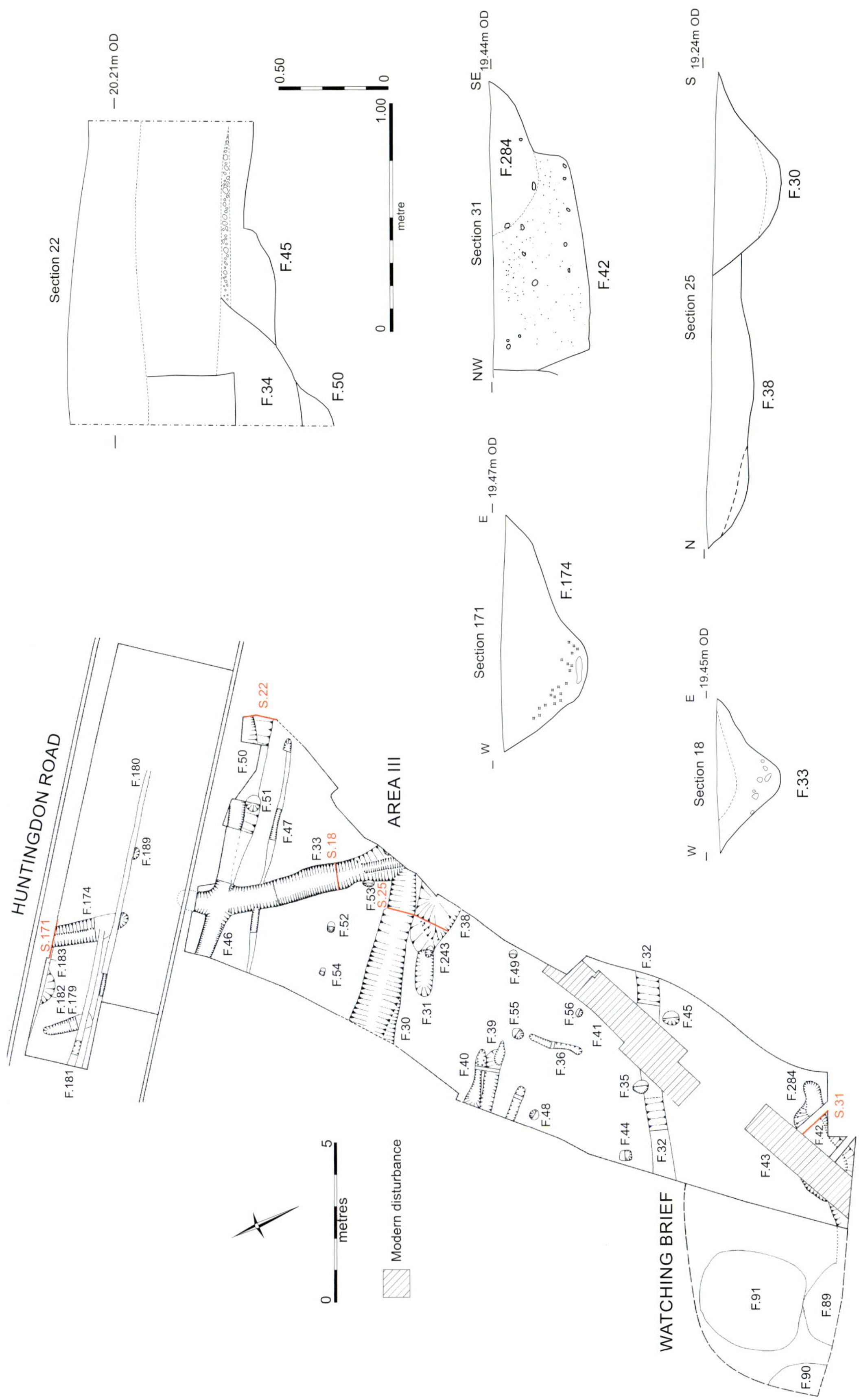

Figure 3.11. *Area III (Huntingdon Road-side) base plan.*

quarrying pits/hollows there; the dynamics of the site's quarrying is explored in much greater detail below in relationship to Area I's 'fields'.

An irregular pit, F.42, whose 'pear-shaped' plan was probably the product of intercutting, was excavated along the southern edge-of-excavation in Area III. In total 3.3 m long, it was 1–1.8 m wide with steep sides and a sloping flat base, 0.4–0.5 m deep. It was filled with mid–dark brown slightly sandy silt loam with pockets/lenses of redeposited (natural) sandy gravel. Given its irregular/intercutting plan, the character of its fills (and proximity to Area I's dense quarrying; see below), this must have been a quarry.

When the contractors laid the approach road to the site, the southwestern corner of the trench was extended by 4 m (due to the pressure of the construction timetable, this had to be treated as a watching brief, rather than excavation). Three large cut features were then exposed, F.89–91. Upwards of 2.6–3.4 m across, Romano-British pottery was recovered from the surface of one (F.91) and it is likely that these were all quarry pits.

Within the main trench-area, a large ovoid feature extended east into the edge-of-excavation, F.38. More than 2 m long, with a maximum surviving width/diameter of 1.40 m, along the east edge it had a concave profile, *c.* 0.45 m deep. In the main, this was filled with dark brown loamy clay silt, but in its basal profile this was mixed with lenses of marl; the latter probably attested to weathering, but possibly reflected some redeposition. Though considerable quantities of pottery were recovered from this feature, it too was likely to have been a quarry pit.

There is no direct evidence that these pitting-*cum*-quarry clusters were directly contemporary. The dark loamy fill of the northernmost (F.38) was much like that of ditch F.30, which truncated its northern edge. It could be the case that the date of this quarry pit is slightly later than those in the south of that area, attesting to long-term activity. One such pit there (F.42) was cut by a ditch (F.284), and the latter may well have been contemporary with the main Back-College Road ditch system (Road 1). If so, this could support an Early Roman date in the site's sequence for this quarrying activity.

Having outlined its quarries, we will now progress to the area's other features (Fig. 3.11).

A northeast–southwest-oriented ditch, F.284, appeared to truncate the easternmost southern quarry (F.42). Not discretely excavated, its 'reconstruction' is based upon its overall plan configuration and sections. It would seem to have had a broad concave profile, 0.5–0.7 m wide and 0.25–0.3 m deep; its fill was mid brown slightly sandy silt loam.

A very slight, 0.6–0.8 m wide ditch, F.32, crossed the southern third of the trench. Running east–west, its alignment diverged slightly southwestwards over the western half of its length. With a broad concave profile, it was only 0.05–0.06 m deep. Although laterally truncated, it must have been shallow (*c.* 0.1–0.25 m max. depth). It was sample-excavated in two metre-long segments and proved to be filled with quite homogeneous mid grey-brown clay silt loam; a single piece of bone and pot were the only finds recovered (see below concerning the western extent of this feature).

Although the basis of any argued relationship between the two ditches – F.32 and F.284 – has to be inferential, it seems a reasonable proposition based upon their similar (minor) scale. The alignment of the northern of the two (F.32) also diverged southwards at roughly the point of the butt-end of the southern ditch (F.284) and from there they ran parallel. Lying *c.* 4.5 m apart, they may have flanked a drove- or minor trackway. With no evidence of recutting, it is unlikely that this route was maintained for any substantial length of time. How far to the west do the ditches run? Although Trench A was said to contain no features, in the field it was noted that a third of the way north along its length the natural sub-stratum changed from gravel to chalky marl. At the boundary between the strata a possible east–west-oriented 'trough' was investigated. Deemed at that time to be a geological feature, in hindsight it may have corresponded to the western continuation of ditch F.32.

A series of postholes, F.52–4 and F.57, were found across the northern third of the area. Variously of ovoid and sub-square plan (0.18–0.31 m across), their depths ranged from 0.07–0.15 m. Other postholes were present throughout the middle portion of the trench (F.48, F.49, F.55, F.56 & F.243), which were generally larger than those to the north (0.2–0.4 m across and 0.18–0.4 m deep). Apart from one, F.55, all were relatively 'clean' and otherwise lacked the obvious attributes of the site's Post-Medieval features. In the north, the line of postholes F.48, F.55 and F.49 ran parallel with the F.284 and F.32 ditches, with posthole F.243 falling at a right-angle from F.49 (F.56, which could be a root-hole, had no obvious associations). Whereas the two westernmost postholes of the southern group are both parallel with the Huntingdon Road-side ditches (see below), the relations of the eastern pair seem to have been with the F.17 ditch.

The dating of the postholes is uncertain and they could attest to a number of minor structures. Whilst suggestive, in part, of house-plans, no buildings were obvious from their arrangement. Nevertheless, these post-settings could have been contemporary with the ditch system-activity, probably reflecting some degree of settlement *per se*.

As presented thus far, the site's Roman sequence has been relatively straightforward: a Back-College road (No. 1), with aligned ditch systems and a probable settlement compound obviously laid out in relation to it. The key point is that these lay well off any Huntingdon/Godmanchester Road alignment. Given that ditch F.30 in Area III (which was different in character and ran far closer to the Godmanchester Road-line, see below) definitely cut the F.33 field boundary, it appears to indicate a major change in landscape organization. A simple, but nevertheless crucial relationship, it suggests that *the Back-College Road system pre-dated any Godmanchester Road/Via Devana-line*. This is the predominant 'fact' of the sequence in the two areas, compared to which other factors are of only minor significance.

The alignment of ditches F.32 and F.284 was close enough to that of F.17 and F.58/60/61 to suggest their general contemporaneity, and their southwestern orientation could indicate that they gave access to 'something' in Area I. As its possible existence was only extrapolated through post-excavation analysis, there is considerable ambiguity concerning the status of the southern ditch, F.284. The key point is that it apparently truncated a quarry and, thereby, indicates how early in the site's Roman sequence such extraction-pitting occurred.

Huntingdon Road-side Features (Area III)

The focus here is with those features within Area III that seemed potentially to have a relationship with the

Godmanchester/*Via Devana* roadway (Fig. 3.11). At the time, all this was highly speculative and it was only with the investigations at the later renamed Murray Edwards College that any firm resolution of the road's location was achieved (see *Accruing Context*... below).

Continuing right the way across the trench and cutting the line of ditch F.33 (and pit F.38) was a 0.9–1.4 m wide ditch, F.30 (Figs. 3.11 & 3.12). Some 0.35–0.5 m deep, the feature broadened and deepened towards the west, and its profile changed from a concave 'U'-shape to a splaying 'V'. A slight shelf along its southern side would suggest recutting and indicate a slightly different orientation

Figure 3.12. *Area III, photograph with ditch F.30 crossing the centre; below, detail of the same showing pottery* in situ.

(northeast–southwest). Two distinct fills were evident: an upper dark brown clay silt loam and, a lower, that included lenses of sandy gravel and sandy silt. A considerable quantity of artefacts was recovered from its excavation (including large pot sherds, 256 in total and 112 bones); the majority came from its secondary fills and suggests backfilling with midden-derived deposits.

Lying on the southern side of F.30 was a short linear hollow with rounded butt-ends, F.31; this just 'overlapped' the western end of pit F.38 (it was not possible to establish their interrelationship) and truncated posthole F.243. It was 1.35 m(+) long and 0.5–0.58 m wide; it had a flat/slightly concave base, only 0.05–0.08 m deep, and was filled with dark brown loamy silty clay.

Dug in poor winter conditions, it is difficult to make much sense of the interrelationship and status of F.31/38 at this point. Their overall plan configuration is suggestive of that of F.42/284 in the southern end of the trench. Feature 38 may have been a quarry pit, while F.31 was probably the butt-end of a minor ditch that continued east, presumably cutting the pit. As the backfill of a recent construction trench protruded through the face of the edge-of-excavation, F.38 could not be fully distinguished in section and only its profile could be recorded.

Running roughly parallel with the ditch, and cutting over the top of the F.33 ditch, was a narrow linear trough, F.47, that terminated just shy of the eastern edge-of-excavation. Some 0.2 m wide, it was 0.15–0.25 m deep with steep sides and a slightly concave base. Its fill consisted of mid–dark brown slightly sandy clay loam with fine–medium gravel. It appeared to be a 'real' cut feature (as opposed to an impressed rut or a service trench); it may have held some manner of fence-line.

A *c.* 0.5 m wide ditch, F.50, extended along the southern side of the Huntingdon Road pavement-verge. It was steep-sided (0.4 m deep) with a flat base, 0.25 m across, and was filled with homogeneous brown-grey sandy loam with gravel. Over its eastern length this ditch veered to the northeast. It appeared to have been recut by another ditch, F.46, whose alignment was more directly southeast–northwest; 0.50 m+ wide, its flat base was 0.15–0.25 m deep and its fills consisted of mid brown sandy loam.

A sub-circular hollow, F.51, 0.45 m across and 0.15 m deep, cut F.46. Though its function is unknown, it possibly related to the postholes immediately to the south.

While relatively few finds were recovered from the pavement-side ditches, most of those that were suggest a Roman date. The recovery of one or two Post-Medieval sherds could point to a later attribution, but these were probably intrusive from a later ditch on this line that was observed in the upper section.

Finally, bedding upon 0.07–0.1 m of buried soil in the eastern section, ditch F.46 was sealed by a 0.03–0.04 m thick layer of gravel mixed with off-white marl ([048]). Probably a yard surface, or possibly even locally surviving road metalling (extending only 0.4 m south from F.46), it may have been bordered by the F.47 'slot'.

The arrangement and interrelationships of Area III's features at this time have major ramifications for the understanding of the site's sequence as a whole. Directly superseding the Back-College Road's ditch-alignment, most crucial is that their orientation followed the line of the Huntingdon/Godmanchester Road.

The two ditches – F.30 and F.46/50 – were of very different character and, lying only 4.5 m apart, it is unlikely that they *together* bounded a road. Of course, their relationship may have been successive. Each could have marked its southern side at different times, in which case the routes respectively must have been greater than 10 m and 4.5 m wide. It may be that neither ditch was directly associated with the Roman road (both appear to veer slightly northwards over their eastern ends) and, instead, they may have simply been a ditch-system laid out in relationship to the off-site (more northerly) road, the *Via Devana*. That no gravel was found subsided into the upper profile of ditch F.33 within this immediate area, and that very little metalling was visible in section, could support this. However, these features were interpreted as 'probably' marking the southern side of the Godmanchester Road. Regardless of their precise status, the key point is the change in ditch orientation from the earlier period, as represented by ditch F.33, and that the Godmanchester route-alignment was clearly secondary in relationship to the Back-College Road.

Finally, attention should be drawn to the midden-like backfill of ditch F.30, as it was similar to that of a major feature cluster within Area I (see *Northwest Enclosure Complex*, below). While F.30's pottery was largely of Hadrianic–Antonine date like the latter grouping, much of it was abraded and its assemblage also included later Roman wares (*c.* AD 250+).

Quarrying (Area I)

Any appreciation of the site's myriad Roman quarrying pits/hollows is best achieved from the area beside the car park – *The North Field* – where these features were relatively discrete and most intensively excavated (Fig. 3.13). Their exposure within the south (*The South Field*) was largely by sondage-cuttings. Accordingly, this outline will focus on the former area, with the South Field results being more summarily presented.

A wide array of pits/quarry hollows were densely distributed across the North Field-area. Rather than describe each individually, the following types have been identified:

1) Small sub-circular pits
2) Irregular/bulbous configurations produced through the intercutting of 'Type 1' features
3) Small ovoid hollows (*c.* < 3 m length)
4) Elongated 'sausage-like' hollows
5) Large sub-circular/ovoid features (often collectively a part of irregularly intercut configurations; see '7' below)
6) Large elongated hollows (often through the compounding of 'Type 4' features)
7) Large irregular configurations (as compounded).

Of course, the division between these categories is much blurred and typological absolutism is not the goal of this analysis.

The vast majority of the 61 such features individually distinguished were less than 0.5 m deep (Fig. 3.14). Just 13 were deeper than this (*c.* 21%), with only six greater than 0.7 m (*c.* 10%); the deepest pit being 0.90 m. As a rough gauge, it is estimated that, in total, these features would have generated some 122 cubic metres of gravel. The majority were of the smaller types, 1–4 (40; *c.* 66%), whereas by volume most of the gravel would have been produced from the larger configurations (Types 5–7; *c.* 78%).

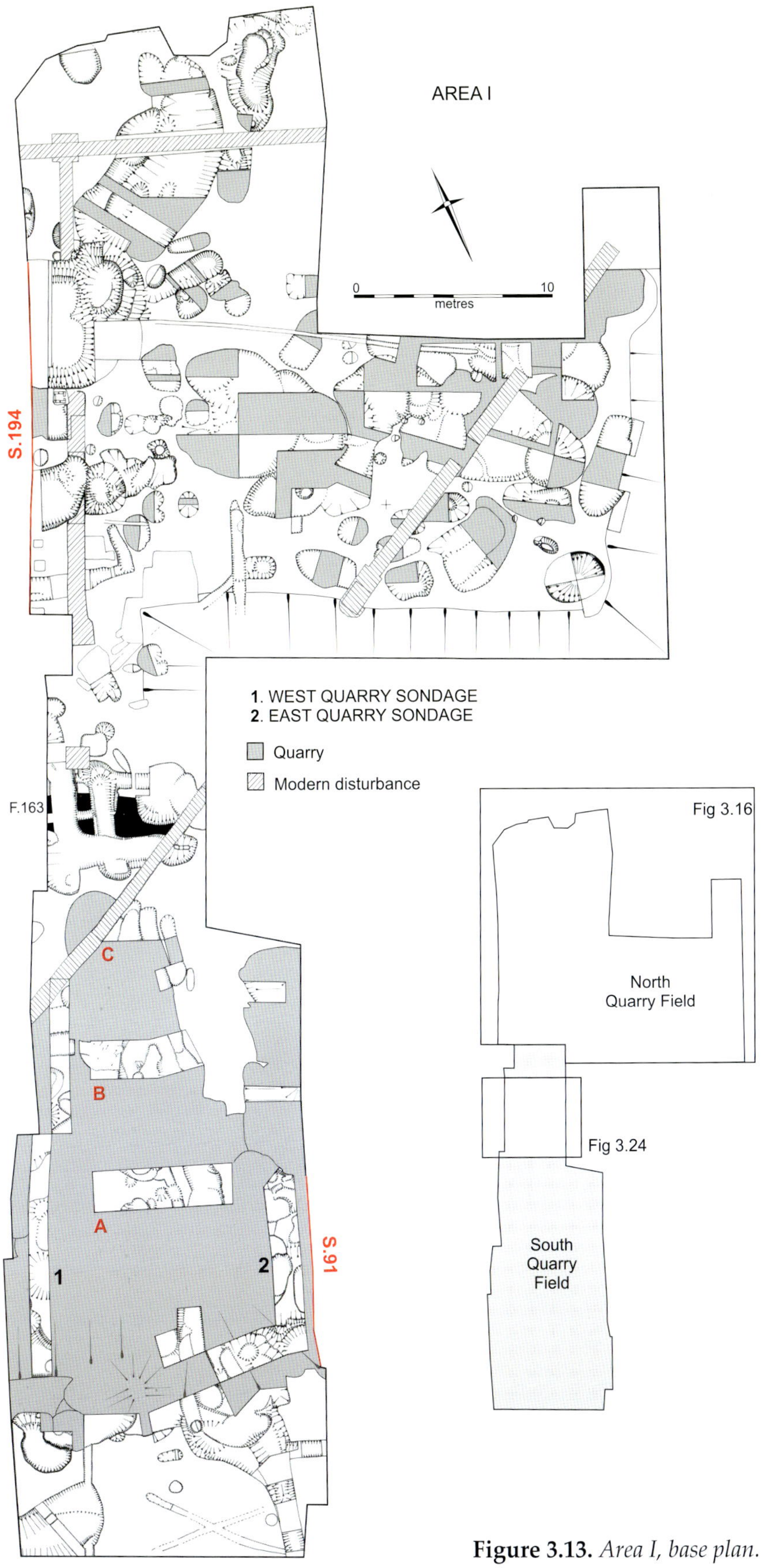

Figure 3.13. *Area I, base plan.*

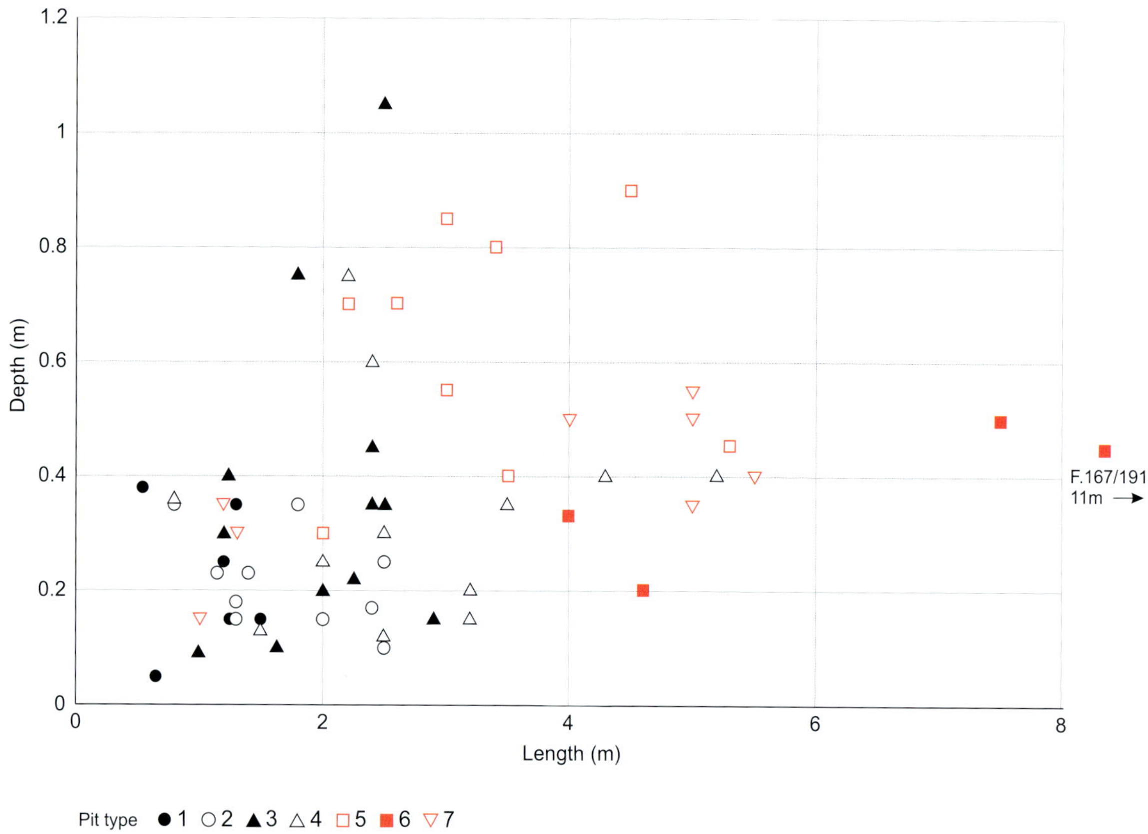

Figure 3.14. *Plot showing depth/length of site's Roman quarrying pits (by type).*

Although detailed presentation will not be made of each pit, the logic of their layout and expansion warrant consideration. The most readily apparent pattern is the 'ripple-like' configuration across the eastern half of the area's northern quarter (Fig. 3.17). There, F.4, a large ovoid hollow, seems to have been the first substantial feature dug. Even within its generally flattish base (0.45 m deep) was a raised spine, suggesting that it actually consisted of two intercutting sub-circular hollows (each 2.4–2.7 m diam.). Cut through that feature's collective backfill, F.195 extended off its southern side. A large sub-circular hollow (*c.* 4.5 × 5 m), undulations within the *c.* 0.5 m deep base of F.195 also suggested that its size was a product of collective intercutting. The ground surface down to its western edge had been broadly truncated to create a ramp-like slope, possibly relating to the approach into the quarry workings (in a number of instances broad reduction zones surrounded major quarry clusters).

Large 'sausage-like' pits were extended off the eastern circumference of the F.4/195 sub-circular core. First (innermost), was F.16/196, beyond which lay F.233/225. Themselves displaying evidence of sequential intercutting expansion, these pits were also 0.5–0.6 m deep (F.196, 0.9 m deep). The ripple-like pattern of these crescent-shaped hollows confirms the section evidence that the extraction pits were generally not backfilled to the surface level (only a half to two-thirds of their profile); therefore, the locations of quarries would have been obvious when digging subsequent hollows.

To the east, beyond the arc of F.233/225, the quasi-circular pattern fragmented and the area was peppered with large circular pits and irregular interconnecting hollows. Nevertheless, vestiges of the concentric expansion principle can be seen in F.249/267 and in the arrangement of F.210, F.248 and F.237. The latter is much more obvious when it is recognized that they were linked by a 'reduction zone'. This latter configuration would seem to mark the eastern extent of the circular pattern, whose border was picked out by a series of large circular pits (F.158, F.234 & F.235) that continued north into the southwest corner of Area III; this alignment was repeated in F.151, an elongated hollow situated on the eastern edge of Area I.

The pattern of concentric expansion also extended to the arrangement of individual features, with F.237 and F.166/167 being the most obvious examples. The former was collectively a sub-rectangular/ovoid (3 × 4 m), whose long axis curved slightly northward. Yet, in section it could be seen to be formed from three elongated, parallel, almost ditch-like troughs. Apparently sequentially recut from east–west, individually they were 1.2–1.75 m wide and 0.28–0.35 m deep.

Arcing over a distance of 11 m in the northern quarter of the area, F.166/167 was a much more extreme example of this type of curvilinear quarry. So much so, in fact, that when first excavated it was thought to be an 'early' ditch (i.e. pre-Roman) The main cut, F.167, was *c.* 3.5 m wide (0.35–0.45 m deep) and it was generally regular/uninterrupted along this distance, though localized troughs were apparent along its base (F.155 & F.193). However, a definite elongated 'sausage-like' trough – F.166 – was cut along its western edge (1.5–1.8 m wide; *c.* 0.5 m deep), mirroring the arc of the original feature for a distance of 7.50 m; its bulbous ends might suggest recut enlargement. Whilst similar to curvilinear quarries elsewhere on the site, the scale and regularity of this feature could reflect other factors. In particular, the Northwest Enclosure Complex's main features (see below), with the quarry hollow terminating in relationship to the F.1/2's northeastern end and that its northward arc occurred in relationship to the western interior of the enclosure, with the quarrying possibly to provide bank-upcast. The fills of the

Figure 3.15. *Area I, photograph of Quarry North Field (from southeast), with well F.121/122 in foreground.*

Figure 3.16. *Area I, North Field, detailed base plan with section locations indicated.*

semi-circular quarry hollow were, though, generally quite clean. They included few artefacts apart from those of prehistoric date, which could suggest that it was rather an earlier Roman 'action'.

Generally, the distribution of pit-types is a matter of 'trend' rather than exclusivity. The most obvious example of this is the concentration of small scoop-type features within the northwest quarter of this area. Given their broad patterning, it is tempting to relate them to the occupation features which bordered the western edge-of-excavation. Yet similar features also occurred within the main northern quarry field (e.g. F.224 & F.259; other such minor hollows surely went unrecorded amid recut larger features and broader reduction zones), and nothing was recovered from their fills to suggest a direct settlement association. Having said that, locally the immediate configuration of these minor features indicated their interrelationship with enclosure-system features. A clear instance was the linear configuration of pits at the western end of ditch F.6 (see below). Truncated by 'special pit', F.7, the ditch alignment was directly continued westwards in the arrangement of F.134, F.136 and F.137. This was repeated in an alignment of five 'scoops' extending over 5.5 m in a line *c.* 1 m to the north (F.152–4 & F.268). The western end of this group appeared to stop in relation to a putative east–west bank (F.301, see below) and, in the east, the core of the main concentric quarry configuration, F.4/195.

South of the ditch F.6 'scoop alignment' a similar, though less intense, linear pattern was apparent: pit F.198 appeared to be dug in relation to ditch F.187 (bounding the F.300 bank; see below), with F.148 and F.274 continuing eastwards. (The arrangement of quarry hollows in the extreme northeast corner of this area will be discussed in the context of their demarcation of a north–south oriented trackway; see below).

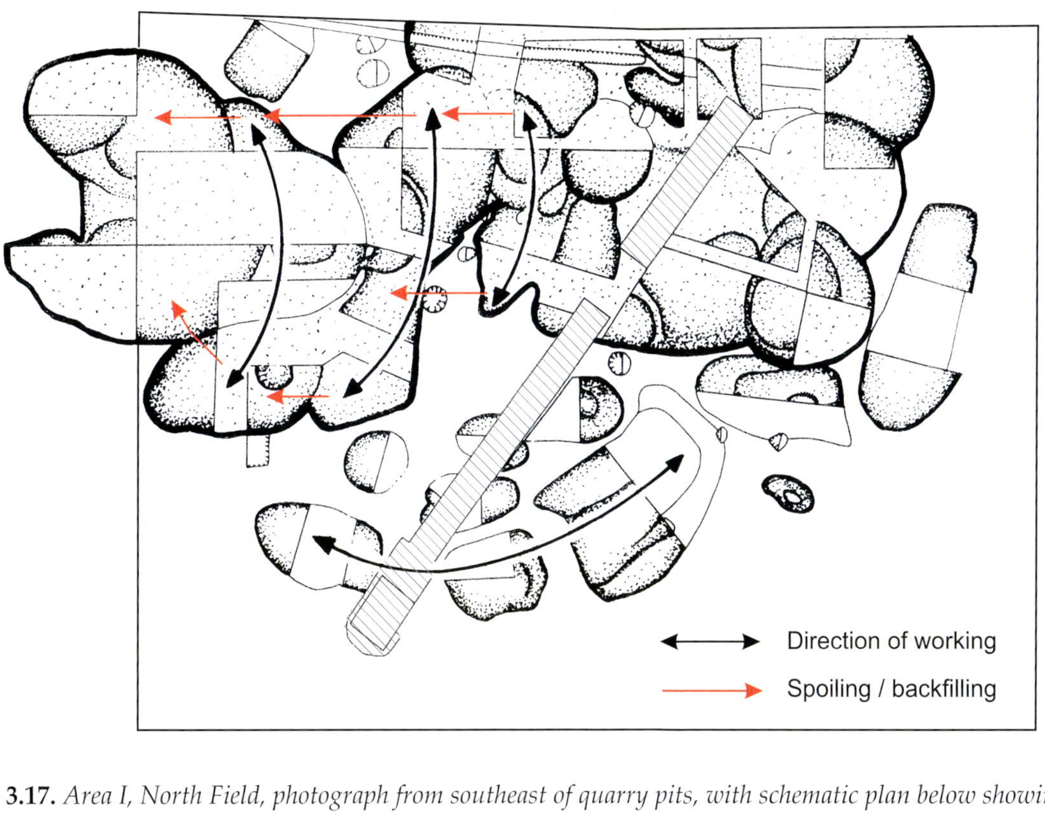

Figure 3.17. *Area I, North Field, photograph from southeast of quarry pits, with schematic plan below showing sequence of their digging/working.*

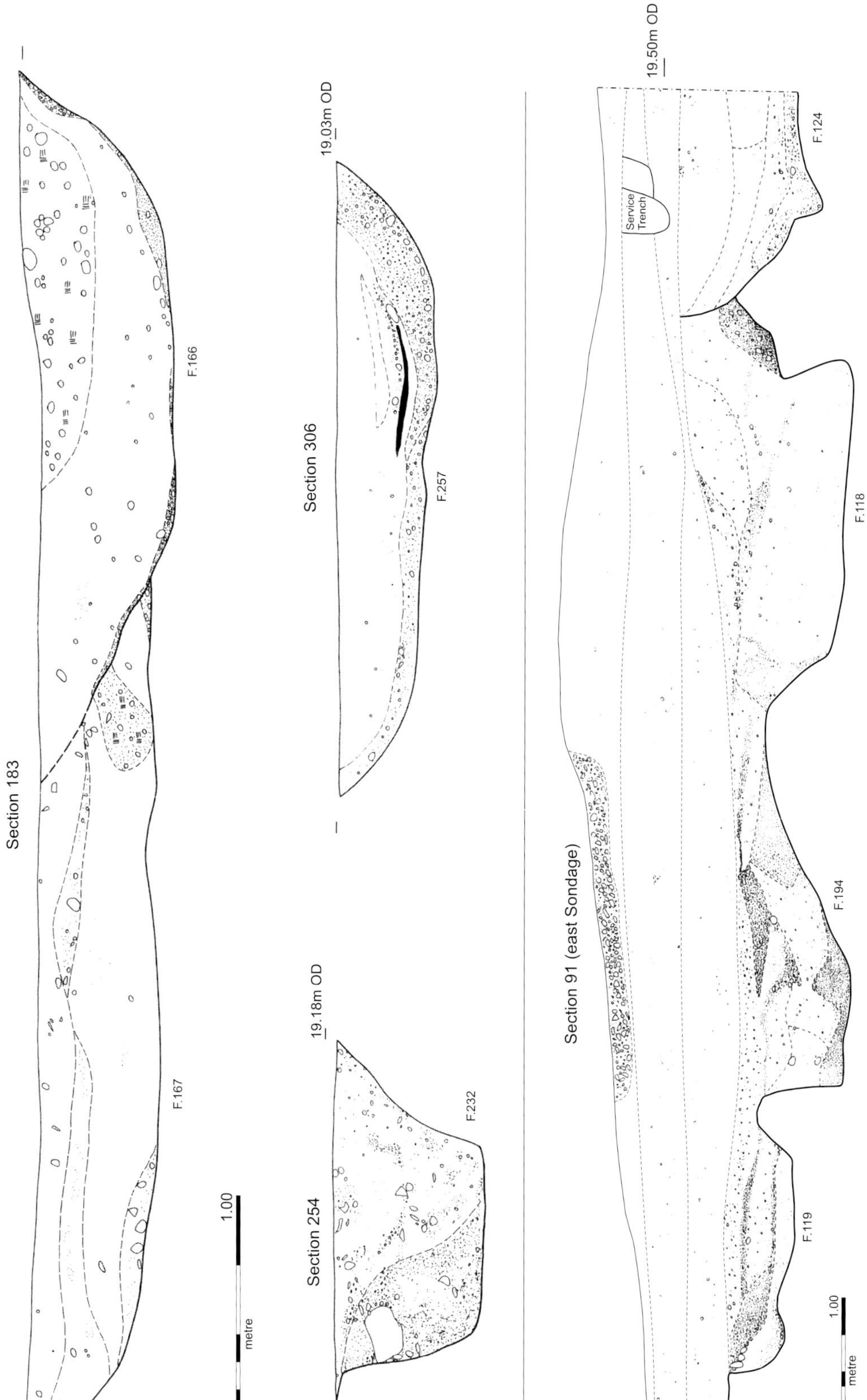

Figure 3.18. *Area I sections (see Figs. 3.13, 3.16 & 3.19 for location).*

Within the South Field-area, a swathe 14.5–27 m across/long (north–south) had been entirely quarried out; the backfilled surface-level there had been reduced by approximately 0.5 m (Figs. 3.13 & 3.18). Faced with this 'challenge', and given budgetary restrictions, an expedient excavation strategy was adopted. While individual features were sectioned in the 'field's' northern and southern ends, their excavation was otherwise limited to a series of trench-sondages: these were located along the eastern and western sides of the area, with three more taken east–west across its central part. Each revealed lunar-like configurations and were densely pockmarked by quarry hollows. No spines of gravel natural were left upstanding to their full height and, for the most part, individual features could only be distinguished in the lower *c.* 0.3 m of their profiles.

Nothing would be gained by attempting to individually described the hollows and here the eastern edge-of-excavation exposure will have to suffice. While there was variability (e.g. recut broadening), these largely consisted of elongated 'slug-shape' cuts, 2–3 m long and *c.* 1 m wide, with flat bases 0.5–0.75 m deep.

Two basic fill-types were identified:

1) Lower, redeposited natural sands and gravels (no/few finds)
2) A continuous/inter-feature upper fill horizon of very dark grey-brown sand silt with gravels, from which occupation material was recovered (including moderate charcoal fragments).

In a few instances, especially within upper fills of the hollows along the area's northern limits, higher finds densities were more widely encountered. In the 'Mid-Zone' (see Fig. 3.24), two features proved to be surprisingly deep: F.147 (0.75–0.80 m) and F.146 (0.8–0.90 m). Kidney-shaped, the former was obviously the product of cumulative quarry-intercutting, whereas the latter was sub-rectangular/ovoid, and just possibly something different (a well?).

Whilst generally the quarrying was intense across the North Field-area, and there is also evidence of zoning by 'type' (crescent-pattern core; a large circular pit alignment in the east; the westward small 'scoop-zone'), there was nothing necessarily to suggest the hand of a co-ordinating authority. Given the 'collective configuration' of even the largest individual pits, each could have probably been dug out by a person in a day. The scale and form of the features themselves, and the irregular layout of the quarry field as a whole, would imply that maximization of returns for minimum expenditure of labour governed the extraction. The most distinct method of quarrying here – concentric 'ripple-like' expansion – simply related to the successive 'daily' backfilling of spoil into open hollows that had previously been dug.

Generally, there seems little evidence of overall planning. In this regard, there may, however, have been a marked difference between the northern and southern 'fields' within Area I. Extraction across the latter was far more intense: hardly a spine of gravel was left upstanding and there was evidence of *en masse* backfilling (though the latter may, in part, relate to subsequent occupation; see below). Moreover, there was a clear sense that this activity was zoned and delineated, suggesting some degree of 'planning', at least along its southern limits. Indeed, there was even a hint of 'staged' successive working, with those east–west-oriented hollows seeming to truncate those on a more north–south axis. Be this as it may, the quarrying lacked the sense of clear patterning of, for example, nineteenth-century hand-dug strip-quarries (see e.g. Evans & Hodder 2006b, 300, fig. 6.17).

Northwestern Enclosure Complex

Presented here is the evidence for the eastern margins of a complicated settlement layout, whose bulk must lie west under Fitzwilliam College. This involve major ditch features, horizontal elements in the form of a bank and trackway system, as well as some truly enormous finds assemblages (Figs. 3.19–23).

The Ditch Systems

Of the many features within the northern quarry field, two along the western edge were quite distinct, although their status is somewhat ambiguous. Seemingly of east–west orientation, F.6 was some 2.9 m wide and extended for 3 m into the area of excavation (Figs. 3.20 & 3.23). After running parallel, it 'turned' to the northeast to terminate in a sub-circular butt (possibly a recut, see F.123, below); the base was flattish, *c.* 1.5 m across at 0.9 m depth. Its fill consisted of:

1) *Primary* – mid grey-brown sandy silt
2) *Secondary* – as 1, but distinguished by major lenses of sandy gravel
3) *Tertiary* – dark grey-black loam (Figs. 3.22–3).

These included great quantities of settlement material (839 sherds; 335 bones), among which were four near-complete pots. The terminal of this feature appears to have consisted of a recut (F.123); its fill sequence differed little from the main feature.

A truly massive feature configuration lying immediately to the north – F.1/2 – was first seen in the evaluation, and it was the quantity of material recovered from it that alerted us to the density and potential of the site. Some 6 m across, it extended for 5.5 m into the area of excavation (Figs. 3.20–1). Along most of its length its northern and southern edges ran straight (east–west), before turning to the northeast and a sub-circular end. In the main 2 m deep, with its basal deposits below the watertable, the excavation of this feature proved difficult (it was dug in quadrants, with all but the southeast quarter excavated to provide maximum section control).

Originally having a 'U'-shaped profile, *c.* 1.7 m deep and 3.5 m wide (seen in the northern side of its western section: F.2), there was definite evidence of two major phases of recutting in F.1/2. First, a 1.7 m deep pit-like feature (3.5–4 m across) was cut in its northern end; thereafter, the southern side of the original profile was recut (*c.* 4 m wide; 2 m deep; broad 'U'-shaped profile: F.1). This cut sequence left this feature with a sub-square basal eastern edge with a pit-like recut in its northeast terminal. It was difficult to ascertain whether this grouping represented an intercutting series of large deep pits/wells or was a massive ditch terminal, much recut. The latter is considered to be the most likely from its plan and broader context. Whatever the case, the recutting of this 'feature-complex' obviously resulted in the mixed date of its pottery assemblage (see Going below); unfortunately, its fills were not separately distinguished and dug in the detail that, in hindsight, they evidently deserved.

There is little point in describing in detail the many contexts assigned to the fills of F.1/2; its basic sequence will suffice. The basal deposits (up to 0.5 m thick) consisted of primary edge-collapsed fine gravels and sands interspersed with lenses of black organic-reduced clay that were partially waterlogged. (The remains of a compressed plank, 0.09 × 0.3 × 0.56 m, lay in the base; poorly preserved, it was

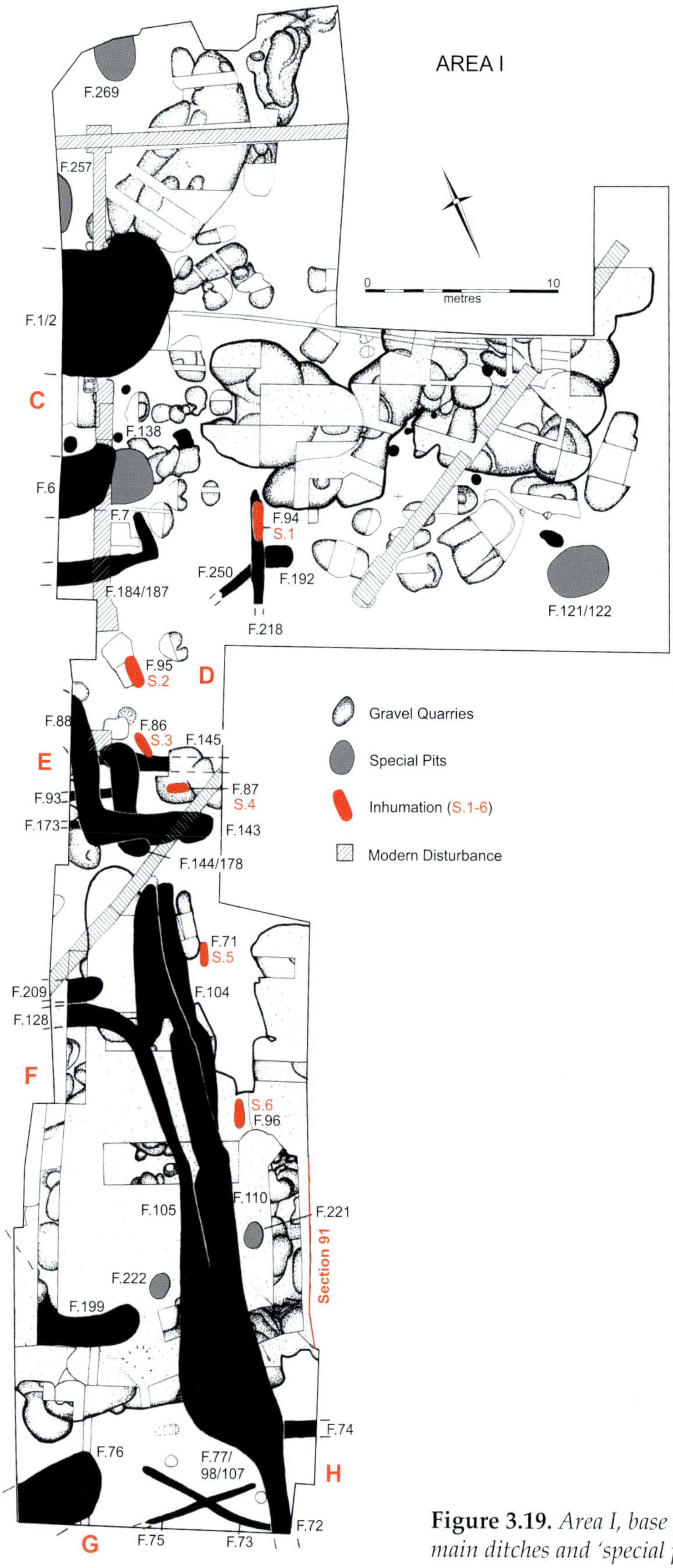

Figure 3.19. *Area I, base plan with enclosures, main ditches and 'special pits' indicated.*

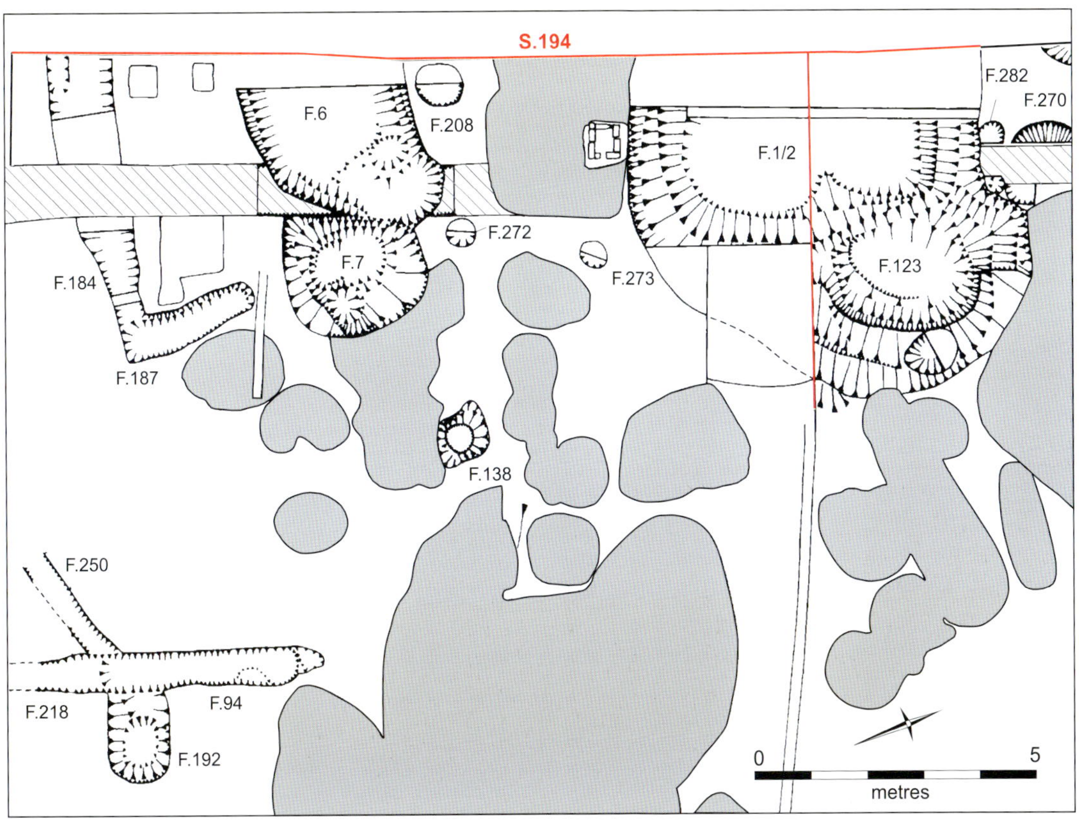

Figure 3.20. *Area I, detailed plan of features associated with Enclosure C (with quarries grey-toned); above, photograph of F.1/2 (from northeast).*

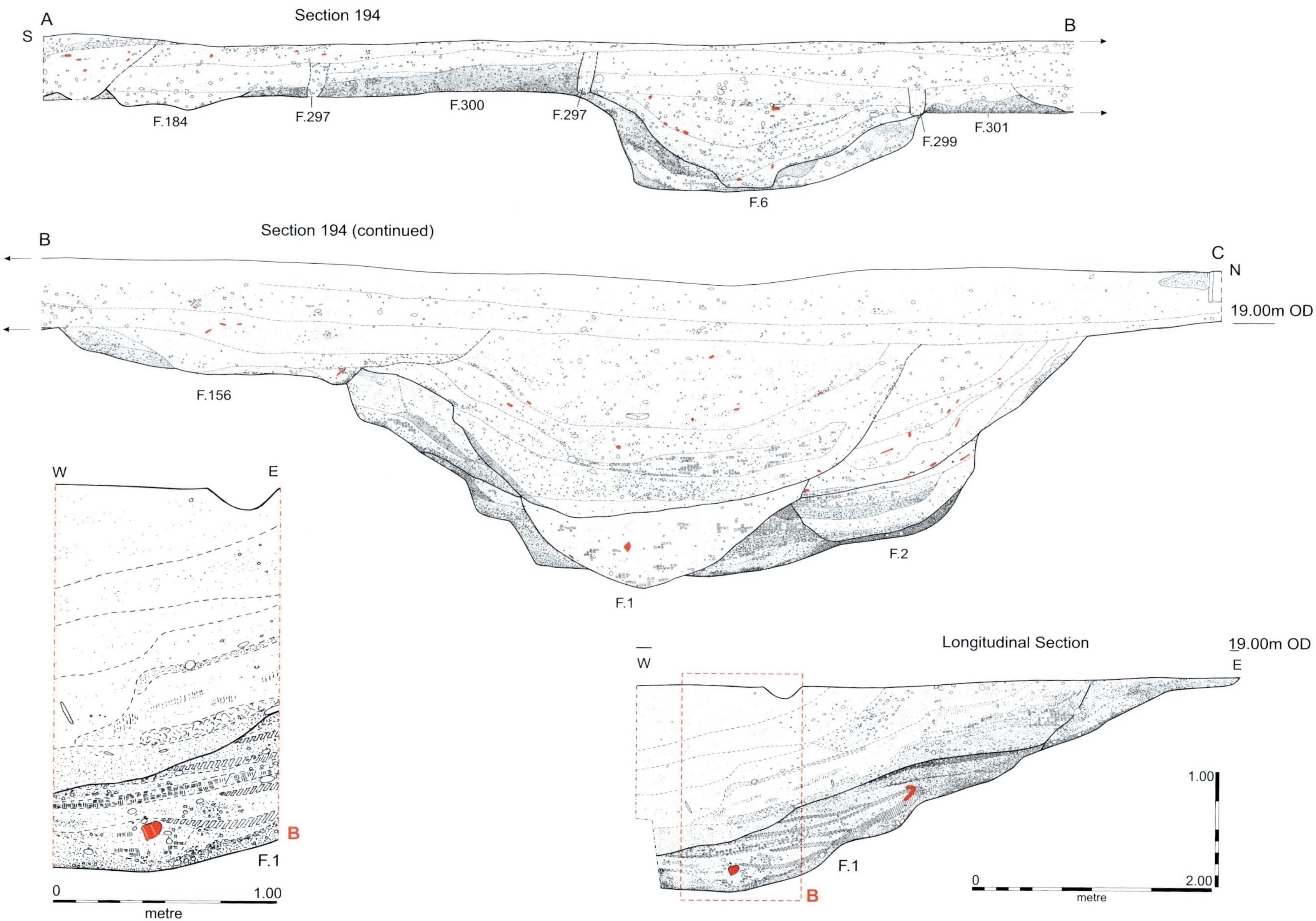

Figure 3.21. *Area I, Enclosure C feature sections, with pottery red-highlighted (F.1/2, F.6, F.184 & F.300/301; see Figs. 3.16 & 3.20 for location).*

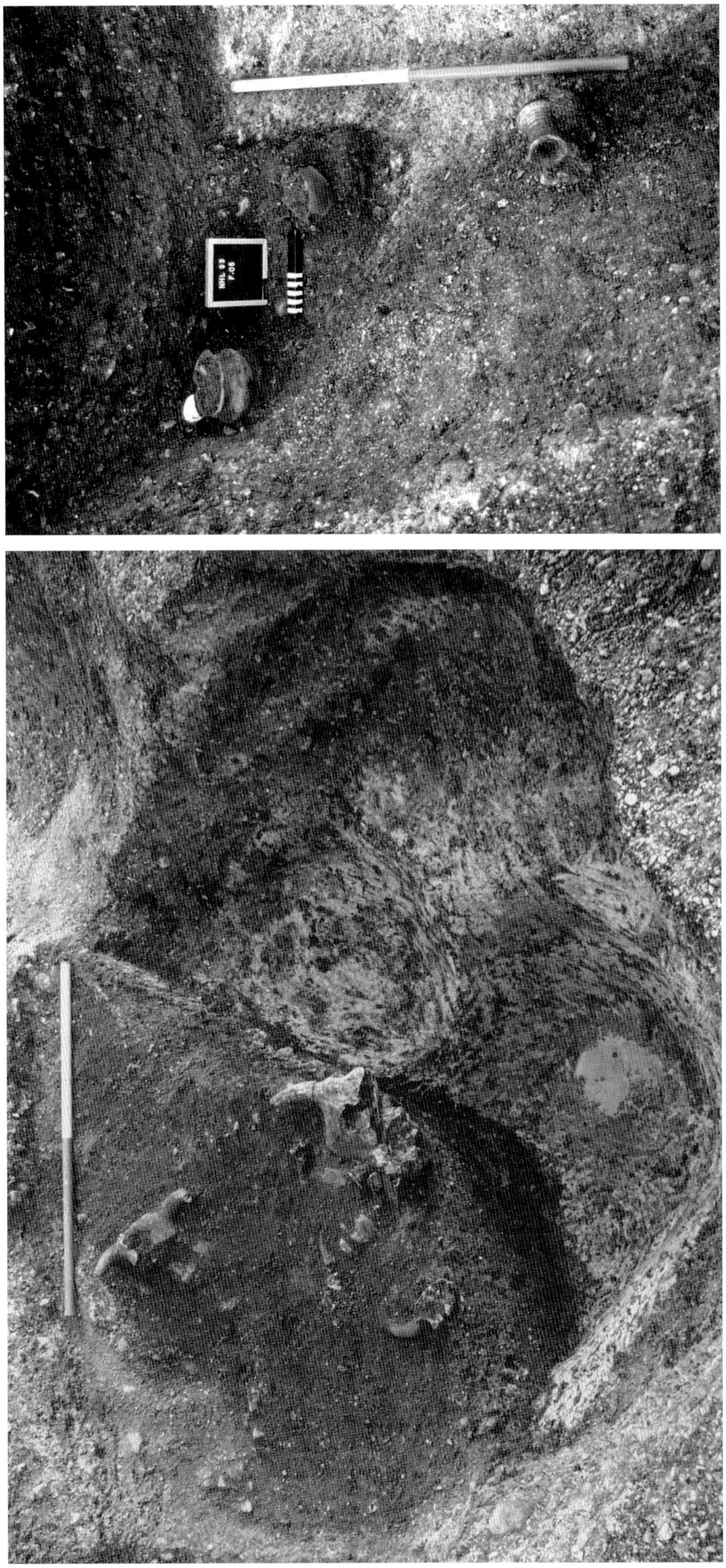

Figure 3.22. *Photographs showing pottery* in situ *within F.6 (right) and, left, cattle skulls in F.7 (see Fig. 3.23).*

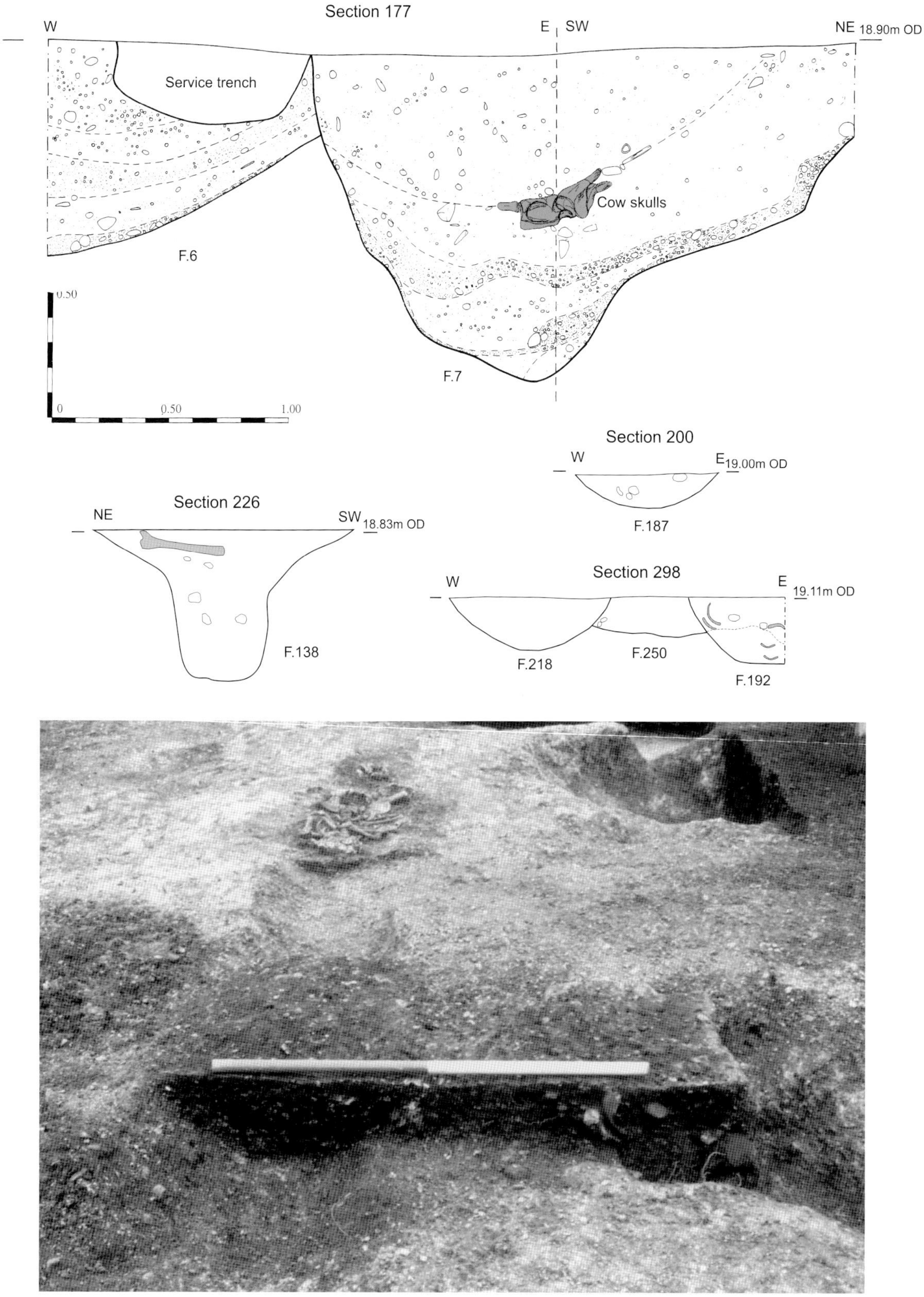

Figure 3.23. *Enclosure C feature sections (see Fig. 3.16 for location) and, below, photograph looking north down F.218 ditch-line with Skeleton 1/F.94 in background.*

identified as probably oak by Maisie Taylor.) Above this was a series of backfilled deposits, generally dark grey-brown/black silty clay loam intermixed with major lenses of pure clays and ash/charcoal (the latter displayed some evidence of deposition while still smouldering). A compressed organic horizon was identified within a monolith taken through the fills. Although humified, laminae of straw/hay litter were detected, possibly deriving from stable sweepings (see Murphy, below). Occurring consistently throughout the feature were extraordinary quantities of pottery, including a number of near-complete vessels. Involving, in total, some 5,800 sherds of pottery (80 kg), it constitutes a major closed-group assemblage and accounts for almost half of the sherds from the excavation as a whole (see Note 7 below concerning the feature's sieve-column results). In marked contrast, only *c.* 650 bones and a little building material were recovered.

Within the northern third of Area I, F.250, a *c.* 0.4 m wide gully (0.1–0.15 m deep) had a slightly concave profile filled with dark grey-brown loam with gravel and chalk flecks (Fig. 3.20). This was either conjoined or was cut by a pit (F.192) at its northwestern end. Of ovoid plan (1.1 × 1.20 m), the steep sides of F.192 stepped to a basal profile, 0.1–0.2 × 0.40 m. Some 0.5 m deep in total, its base had been lined with cobbles. Above this, in the centre of the pit, was a deposit ('lump') of burnt clay, pottery sherds and lenses of unburnt clay; otherwise, its fill was as F.250. Whilst the clay sheets/lumps could suggest that the feature held an oven, there was no evidence of *in situ* burning. Instead, given its profile and form, these were thought more likely to have been re-deposited within a post-pipe.

An east–west-oriented ditch, F.184, projected for 5 m from the edge-of-excavation south of F.6, where it was met by a short northern return-length (F.187; Fig. 3.20). As visible in the westernmost section, F.184 was 1.15 m wide and 0.15 m deep. This, though, was a 'collective width' as it had evidently been recut, its profile included two conjoining concave bases (the southern only 0.12 m deep). The southernmost apparently petered out/butt-ended shortly beyond the western section; thereafter, only the northern ditch continued (0.45–0.5 m wide, 0.07 m deep). It was filled with a mid grey-brown clayish loam containing gravels and chalk flecks. With a maximum width of 0.70 m, the ditch's northwesterly return, F.187, tapered towards its sub-circular butt; its fill was basically as the east–west length (dark grey-brown clay silt with gravel and chalk flecks; Fig. 3.23).

Northwest of the line of F.184/187 was a definite posthole, F.138 (Fig. 3.23). Some 0.6 m deep, from an ovoid top (0.85 × 1.10 m), *c.* 0.2 m down it sloped into a 0.4 m diameter post-impression. It was filled with stiff dark grey-brown clay loam with gravel and chalk flecks; the post-impression was marked out by a bedding of large horse bones.

Another possible posthole, F.155, lay just to the north amid a series of quarry scoops. This 0.14 m deep sub-circular cut (*c.* 0.3 m diam.) was filled with stiff dark grey-brown clay loam with chalk flecks and gravel.

A 0.35–0.65 m wide gully, F.218, was excavated east of F.184/187 for a total length of 4.70 m. Ending in an angular tapered butt, it survived 0.07–0.2 m deep and its profile varied from a broad 'V' to concave. It was filled with dark grey-brown silty loam with gravel. This ditch clearly truncated F.250's obliquely aligned gully and a Late Roman burial had been cut into F.218's northern butt-end, indicative of its lingering influence as an earthwork (see below).

The Bank System

A spread of redeposited gravel natural was apparent in the western edge-of-excavation section between ditch F.184 and the southern ditch, F.6 (Figs. 3.21–2). Approximately 0.25 m high at its northern end (beside F.6), its top surface was roughly flat for 0.9 m from where it sloped down to feather-out beside F.184. Although not distinguished during machine-stripping, this had the appearance of a substantial upcast bank (F.300). That no buried soil was apparent beneath it indicates that the area had been de-turfed down to the sub-stratum previous to its deposition. (That no discrete features were found within the area between these two ditches would support the proposition that it was sealed, presumably by a bank.)

The northern edge of the bank was vertical and a 0.12 m wide posthole, F.297, situated at upper southern edge of ditch F.6, might reflect its revetment. A similar posthole, F.298, was seen cutting through the southern end of the bank and yet another, F.299, on the northern side of ditch F.6. The latter was within the southern tail of another upcast horizon that extended north from F.6. With a maximum height of 0.15 m, it was truncated by a quarrying pit 1.25 m to the north (F.156). It is presumed that this gravel layer, F.301, was also a bank and that it would have continued north to F.1/2. During the course of the initial evaluation, traces of a 0.3 m high upcast bank were identified in the trench section along the southern side of F.1/2.

Given the section information, there seems little doubt that F.300 and F.301 were east–west-oriented banks relating to ditches F.1/2, F.6 and F.184; their profile would not suggest a road, and a thoroughfare in this location would make little obvious sense. Ambiguity surrounds the status of the postholes observed in section, whose posts had presumably rotted *in situ*. Their tops extended well above the level of the banks into a horizon of buried soil-like mid grey-brown silty loam that sealed these upcast features (and the top of the ditches), which presumably formed following the abandonment of the site. The evidence has been fully weighed as to whether these could have been Post-Medieval features, and that they were not excavated as such makes determination difficult. A series of obviously more recent, square post-settings (backfilled with pure clay marl with their rotted post-bases still in place) were found along the foot of the edge-of-excavation south of ditch F.184. In section these were of entirely different character and, apparently lacked packing pits, were probably driven.

Between ditches F.1/2 and F.6, three possible postholes were distinguished in plan (F.157, F.272 & F.273; Fig. 3.20); they were *c.* 0.3 m in diameter and 0.04–0.1 m deep. Again, their interpretation is not without ambiguity; by their configuration they suggest the plan-continuation of the postholes visible in section (a fourth such feature, north of F.157 and west in line with F.273, was probably eradicated by a modern service feature). Most telling is the fact that the two eastern postholes – F.272 and F.273 – stopped in line with, and complemented the orientation of, the terminals of F.6, F.1/2 and F.184/187.

The Trackway

Up to 0.1 m thick, a continuous horizon of compact brown/orange sandy clay and 'heavy' gravels lay in the upper profile of the large curvilinear quarry cluster in the northern end of the area (F.166/167; Fig. 3.18). Beyond the line of a concrete drain, the central zone of this immediate area had been laterally truncated by modern intrusions (cable trenches and a stanchion); therefore, there is little certainty concerning the form/existence of any features in the vicinity. Nevertheless, on the projected line of the gravel-capped quarry, in section along the northern edge-of-excavation, the natural strata was sealed by a 0.05–0.08 m thick layer of grey-brown silty loam with gravel. This bedded down to fill a 0.20 m deep north–south oriented cut, F.280. Although possibly reflecting no more than a quarry-related reduction, given the area's broader feature configuration, this gravel-filled cut (and the gravel horizon sealing the quarry to the south) probably related to a north–south trackway, some 4.5–5 m wide; projected southwards, its line would have run within the 5 m wide gap between gullies F.187 and F.218.

Further attesting to this trackway's existence/influence, is the pattern of intercut quarry hollows in the extreme northeast corner of this area (Fig. 3.16). Collectively these formed a 'L'-shaped configuration in a sinuous quasi-linear pattern that continued along the line of the northern edge-of-excavation before turning south to run beside the line of the F.166/167 quarry and the postulated trackway for *c.* 5.5 m (2–3 m wide; F.164, F.165, F.170–172 & F.275). Thought in the field to include a ditch-line, this feature-group was intensively excavated. Although a ditch could not be definitely identified amid the intense quarry intercutting, its existence remains a nagging possibility (the eastern line of this configuration would correspond with the projected alignment of the southern F.46/50 boundary in Area III). Yet, regardless of whether this was a ditch-and-quarry configuration or just a line of intercut quarries, the layout of these much-recut features could well have been in relation to/bordered the eastern edge of the postulated trackway. Certainly, given the 'chaos' of the quarries in this area, it would otherwise be a remarkable coincidence that the southward line of this configuration corresponded with the projected northward alignment of the gully, F.218.

North Field Postholes

Scattered amid the quarry hollows in the northeastern arm of the area were a number of possible postholes (F.161 & F.259–266; Fig. 3.16). Suffering truncation, and despite lacking definite structural attributes (e.g. post-pipes), at 0.2–0.8 m across and 0.05–0.45 m deep they were too small to be considered quarrying 'scoops'.

As they lay 'isolated' beside the northern edge-of-excavation, little can be said concerning F.259 and 260, or, indeed, whether they were postholes at all. Features 261–4 and F.266, on the other hand, seemed much more convincing and to constitute a northwest–southeast-oriented line extending over a distance of 6 m, which in the south was aligned on the large posthole, F.192, at the end of ditch F.250.

Although complicated by recutting, F.1/2 and F.6 would certainly seem to be something more than just quarry pits. The first of these was truly massive and the deepest feature on the site. This, of course, need not rule out the possibility that it could have consisted of a series of intercutting processing pits and/or wells, but its formality of plan – mirrored by F.6 to the south – suggests otherwise. Both of these features seem to be (quasi-) linear: their butt-ends terminated on the same easterly line (the same as the F.184 ditch-return: a divide) and elongated/turned slightly to the northeast. (While the argument could be made that the 'terminal' of F.1/2 originally turned northeastwards following the orientation of the F.167 quarry, this would not account for the matching alignment of F.6.) Although some degree of uncertainty must remain, F.1/2 and F.6 are interpreted as the eastern terminals of a double-ditch enclosure system[4]; hereafter, it will be referred to as Enclosure C.

Another significant factor that relates F.1/2 and F.6 is that they had been backfilled with extraordinary quantities of occupation debris, especially pottery (see Going, below). This would, again, distinguish them from the site's other pit features and suggest that the postulated enclosure was settlement-related. Taken as a whole, the relationship of the major ditch terminals (F.1/2 & F.6) and their associated post-revetted upcast banks (the southern of which was clearly bounded by the F.184/187 gully-line) suggests that a major double-ditched enclosure system extended across the western side of the northern end of the area. What was its configuration? If of rectangular layout, that the banks lay to the south of the two main ditches would suggest that the enclosure's interior also lay in that direction. However, over the 50 m exposure of Area I, no obviously matching southern ditch-line was evident. Of course, if mirroring F.1/2 and F.6 (and without an eastern ditch-line), the terminals of any southern ditch may have stopped shy of the western edge-of-excavation. If they lay within the enclosure's interior, it is impossible to imagine what function the southward-lying ditches (see below) would have had, unless the system was vast and these were only related to intra-enclosure division. An alternative interpretation suggested by the northeastern 'pull' of the terminals of the main ditches is that the enclosure's interior lay to the northwest. This would make the exterior placing of the banks unusual, but it could be more logical given the evidence of the site as a whole. Unfortunately, the site-area's exposure was simply too limited for definite resolution. The fact that the F.184/187 gully so closely complemented the layout of F.1/2 and F.6 would, however, confirm that these were also 'formal' ditches (i.e. not pits).

It is impossible to be certain whether the east–west ditch, F.184/187, was directly contemporary with either the 'diagonal' gully F.250 or the north–south ditch that superseded it (F.218). On the one hand, the east–west length of F.184 lay at a right-angle to the latter; on the other hand, its northwesterly return, F.187, was closer to the alignment of gully F.250. The F.187 return and ditch F.218 both terminated on the same northward line (at the end of bank F.300) and, in all likelihood, the western ditch-line (F.184/187) was contemporary with both eastern ditches (F.250 & F.218).

Collectively, these features denote a western access running south of Enclosure C. If projected southwestwards, the line of the 'diagonal' gully (F.250) would run to the northern end of ditch F.88/143 in the 'Mid-Zone' (see below). The distance between the northern end of that ditch and F.184 is the same as the gap between F.184/187 and F.250. Given this, the succession of the diagonal gully (F.250) by the north–south ditch F.218 possibly marks the replacement of a northeast–southwest track by the north–south metalled way. Running along the eastern side of the embanked double-ditch enclosure, while providing access to the more southerly paddocks (see below), nevertheless, the western portion of this thoroughfare would have probably continued in use south of Enclosure C.

The Mid-Zone Ditches

All of the linear features within the Mid-Zone followed the same alignment (Figs. 3.13, 3.19 & 3.24). The frequency of their replacement at this point suggests a

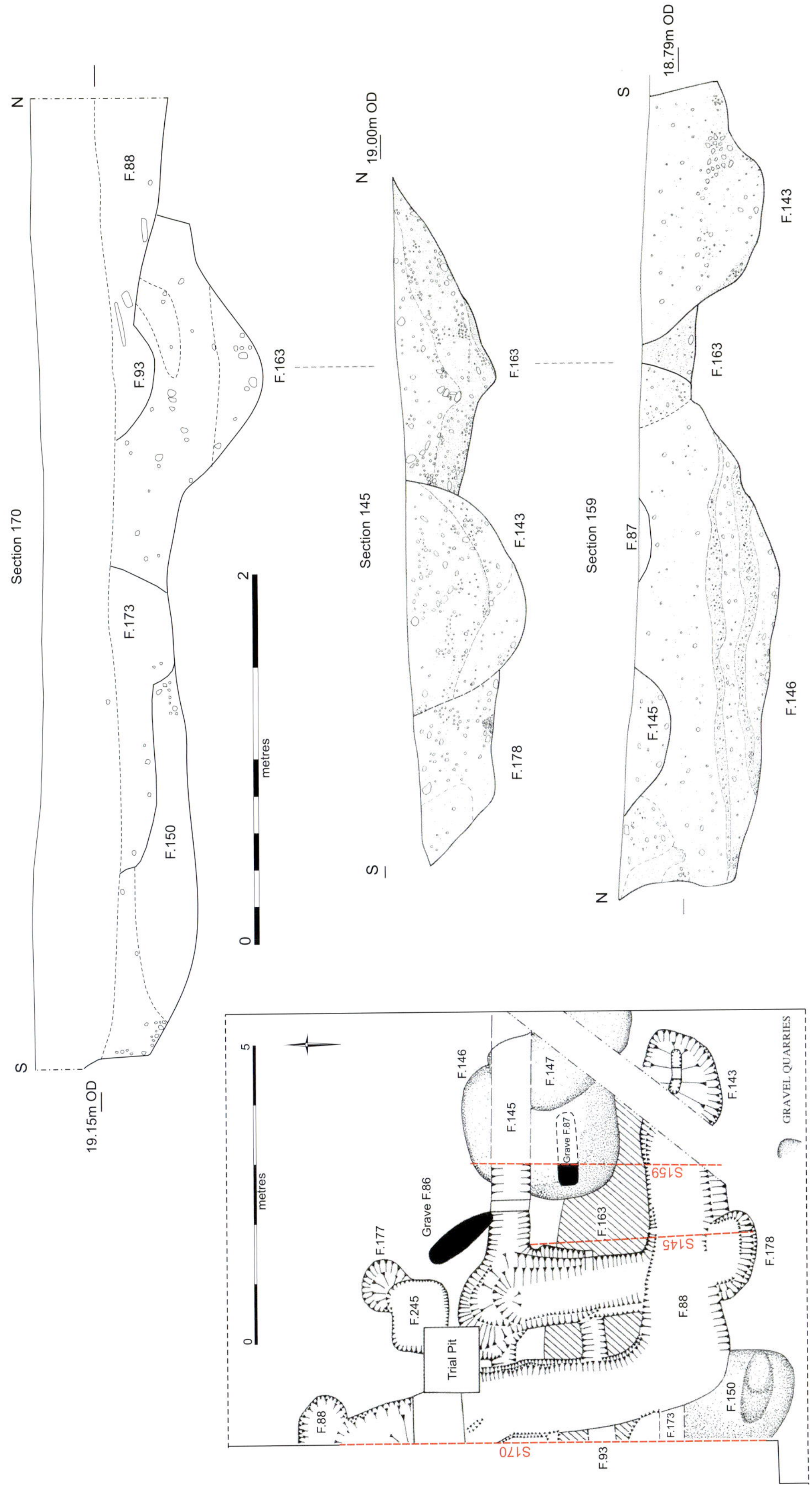

Figure 3.24. *Mid-zone ditches plan and sections.*

major boundary division. Evidently a much-defined nodal point, a key stratigraphic relationship was that the earliest of the three-fold series of ditches truncated a quarry pit.

An east–west oriented ditch, F.145, cut over the top of quarry pit F.146. This concave-profiled boundary was 0.5–0.8 m wide, had a maximum depth of *c.* 0.3 m and was filled with dark grey-brown clayish sandy silt with gravel. Excavated over a distance of 3.70 m, it was truncated at either end.

A similar ditch, F.93, also extensively truncated, lay parallel 1.1 m to the south. Some 0.6 m wide, its concave profile survived to a depth of 0.2 m and was filled with dark brown clayish silts. Although truncated to the east, it probable continued for more than 1 m in that direction before returning northward to conjoin F.145. Similarly, while cut away to the west by F.88, it continued into the edge-of-excavation section.

Again lying parallel, ditch F.173 was 0.5 m wide. With a concave profile, 0.15–0.3 m deep, it was filled with dark grey silt loam.

A north–south-oriented ditch, F.144/178, 1.1–1.3 m wide and *c.* 0.5 m deep, truncated both of the two northernmost 'linears' (F.145 & F.93). Its northern and southern extremes kinked slightly and broadened to create a somewhat 'S'-shaped plan; it was filled with green stained, dark greyish brown silty loam with gravel.

Appearing aligned with the northern end of ditch F.144/178 was a square pit, F.245, 1.2 × 1.5 m and 0.75 m deep. Its sides were vertical (locally undercut) and the base flat. It was filled with pale–mid grey-brown sandy silt, and deposits of orange-brown clay silt could suggest an element of backfilling; much Roman pottery was recovered from its base.

Another ditch, F.88/143, 1.3–1.7 m wide and 0.45–0.6 m deep (cutting across the western side of F.145, F.93 & F.173), extended for *c.* 6 m (north–south) from the western edge-of-excavation before returning eastwards (where it truncated the northern end of F.144/178). Concave-profiled, it was filled with dark grey-brown silt loam.

These boundaries all essentially followed the same east–west alignment as the Enclosure C ditches (F.1/2, F.6 & F.184; see above). Moreover, both the line of the F.144/178 length and the F.143 terminal corresponded with the eastern extent of the Enclosure C features. The F.88/143 ditch must relate to the projected south-western line of the F.250 ditch and mark the southern side of the western return of the postulated trackway route. Having said that, by its character, the unusual secondary ditch (F.144/178) had its closest parallel to the immediate south: the eastern ditch-line, F.104/105 (see below).

The Southern Ditches

Apart from in the extreme end of the area (I), the recovery of ditches south of the car park proved difficult. Whilst at points 'linears' could be distinguished, they were hard to trace (Fig. 3.19). Their recognition was not aided by the fact that some of the quarry pits seemed to be of elongated form and respected ditch-lines; thus, although there can be confidence that the basic enclosure pattern was recovered, there is no certainty that all ditches there were identified.

At the southern junction of the ditch system and quarries, a quadranted excavation technique was adopted to ensure maximum retrieval of section evidence (Fig. 3.13). North of that point they were further traced through the excavation of three hand-excavated east–west sondages (A–C). Other ditches were discovered within the western edge-of-excavation sondages and further traced through both machine- and hand-stripped reduction.

Crossing the line of later prehistoric gully, F.73, at the southern end of the area (it was not possible to establish the relationship of their intercutting) was a 0.25–0.3 m wide linear 'stripe', F.75 (Fig. 3.19), oriented northeast–southwest. Consisting of little more than a stain of grey-brown sandy loam, it could not be formally excavated given its insubstantial nature. However, following the ditch alignment in Area II, it seemed similar to the F.81 and F.82 ditches in Trench K (and like them there must be some ambiguity of its attribution; it is possibly comparable to the Post-Medieval troughs from Area III).

Within the extreme southeast corner of the area, a north–south oriented ditch, F.72, was excavated over a length of 6 m. Between 1–1.85 m wide and 0.4–0.6 m deep, its concave profile deepened and broadened northwards. It was generally filled with mid–dark brownish grey sandy clay silts and had an upper fill of dark grey-brown silty clay loam. Graded with fine–medium gravels throughout, relatively few finds were recovered.

On its eastern side, F.72 'conjoined' a 0.8 m wide and 0.25–0.3 m deep concave-profiled ditch (F.74); it was filled with brown grey sandy silt loam. Running east–west, and lying at approximate right-angles to ditch F.72, it appeared to be cut by the north–south ditch. At the point of their junction, the western edge of F.72 curved westwards. This configuration would seem to be the result of the occurrence of a previous iteration of ditch F.72, F.107. This earlier ditch 'ghosted' along the southern length of F.72 and was only apparent as a concave shelf on its western side. However, beside its junction with F.74, F.107 became distinct as a ditch in its own right (concave-profiled, 0.3 m deep and 1.1 m wide; it must originally have been *c.* 1.25 m across).

Lying just west of this intercut ditch configuration was an elongated feature, F.98. Roughly 1.1 m long, 0.6 m wide and 0.1 m deep, filled with mid brown clayish sandy loam, this may have been a fragment of a locally surviving terminal of either ditch F.74 or F.107.

On reaching the quarry zone the north–south ditch-line became largely indistinguishable from the extraction pits (hence the adoption of a quadranted excavation technique: though to little avail). Encountering the quarries, the base of ditch F.72 dropped (by 0.6 m into F.77/110) to the level of the base of the quarries (1.1 m total depth). Both the quarries and ditches seemed to share the same fills and recutting was not visible. Certainty in this matter is not possible, but it may be the case that the quarries were dug out either to form a deeper western arcing ditch/enclosure or to incorporate a well along the continuing ditch. Although fragmentary ditch lengths were distinguished within the quadranted segments, the key point was that on leaving this zone along the northern side at least two north–south ditches were apparent: F.105 (west), F.110 (east).

Whilst clearly continuing north of this point, the ditch-lines braided. Excavated in three 2 m wide hand-excavated sondages, north–south-oriented ditches certainly ran along this line, though their braided configuration made their distinction difficult. Basically, they seemed to constitute a parallel double-ditch-line. Though there was evidence locally that the western (F.105) was truncated by the eastern (F.104) at its northern end, they seemed to have been laid out in relation to each other. While there was considerable variability in their profiles (from broad 'V'-shape to concave), they generally matched each other, with a *c.* 1.5 m width and 0.5–0.65 m depth being the 'model' form. The western ditch, F.105, was recorded as recut at its northern sub-circular terminal (F.104's northern terminal was more rectangular); similar recutting probably occurred elsewhere along their lengths.

Though confused by its intercutting with the quarries, the massive enlargement and westward turning of the F.77 (*et al.*) eastern ditch in the southern quarter of the area would seem to relate to an enclosure entrance, whose interior lay to the west. Given that this seems the only feasible explanation for the ditch's locally bulbous configuration, the northwest side of the enclosure would be formed by F.76. During excavation it was difficult to ascertain whether this northeast–southwest-oriented linear feature was actually a quarry or a ditch. However, its form certainly contrasted with the extraction pits in the southern field and, given its layout and quasi-symmetrical relationship to the eastern ditch, it must also have been an enclosure ditch: the western side of an enclosure entrance 5 m across.

With a sub-circular terminal, F.76 was *c.* 3.1–3.3 m wide. A basal shelf would suggest an episode of recutting of the terminal. Otherwise, the butt-end was flat (0.45 m deep), with the feature deepening by 0.3 m over its length and its profile changing to a 'V'-shape. Its fill sequence indicates that it had been left open: above basal weathering, in the main it was filled with grey-brown sandy loam.

A flat-based ditch, F.199, 1.4–1.8 m wide, was observed to truncate the southern quarries along the western side of the area, north of ditch F.76. Its southern side sloped down near-vertically, whereas its northern edge was concave, gradually sloping down to meet the base. Its fill consisted of mid brown-grey silty sand with lenses of sandy gravel; there was evidence of recutting along the upper northern side (*c.* 0.4 m deep with a concave base).

Some 13 m further to the north, another east–west oriented ditch – F.128 – 'emerged' from the myriad quarries. In the western edge-of-excavation section this concave-profiled feature (truncating quarry backfill) was 0.8 m wide and 0.4–0.45 m deep. Along the eastern side of the sondage, its upper northern edge sloped broadly to narrow the main profile to only 0.6 m in width (*c.* 0.3 m deep); although it was difficult to distinguish with certainty, within Sondage B its base could be traced arcing off to the southeast to conjoin the western of the eastern double-ditches (F.105).

Within the main western section, F.128 could be seen recutting an earlier, parallel ditch, F.209. Generally 0.2–0.25 m deep, its side gently sloped down to a flat base; the fill was of mixed mid grey-brown/orange sandy silt with gravel. While there cannot be absolute certainty about the existence of this feature as an earlier, parallel ditch-line, just beyond the edge of the western sondage its eastern end could be seen (in plan) to form a semi-circular butt-end.

As discussed, only in the extreme southeastern corner of the southern half of Area I can the existence and form of the ditches be considered unambiguous. Even there, the status of the F.75 'stripe' is questionable, as it may have been a Post-Medieval bedding trench. Otherwise, although linear features were clearly present at points, it was extremely difficult to trace them. Troublesome definition discouraged excavation subtlety, meaning that while basic configurations were recovered, not all ditches may have been distinguished (some could have been overlooked within the eastern quarry sondage); the layout of the ditch system will be fully considered within the discussion of the Western Enclosure System below.

Discrete Settlement Features

A number of 'pit-type' features were excavated, which by either their form and/or finds assemblages seemed distinct from the quarries (Fig. 3.19).

Few features were present in the corner north of Ditch F.1/2 and west of the quarry pit F.166/167: the Northwestern Enclosure's interior. Two were distinct by the quantity of occupation debris within them:

F.269 – A sub-circular pit, 1.75–2 m across and 0.4 m deep with a flat base. Above a basal fill of dark brown-black silty clay loam was a discontinuous lens of chalk-marl and sands/gravels; the upper profile was backfilled with dark grey-brown clay loam and gravels mixed with occupation debris including oyster shell, bone (28 pieces) and pottery (280 sherds).

Given its form, it is just possible that this feature was actually the southern terminal of a north–south oriented ditch. If so, by its alignment and the character of its fills (e.g. dark loam with high finds density), it could be comparable to ditch F.30 in Area III. However, its flat base could equally suggest that it related to gravel extraction and had simply been backfilled with occupation material.

F.257 – This was the eastern end of a 2.4 m wide pit that only extended 0.5 m beyond the western edge-of-excavation. Also 0.4 m deep, it had a flattish base that sloped down from south to north. It may have been recut along the northern end. There was evidence that it had remained open for a period (primary basal silting/weathering), but it was largely filled with mid brown silty loam. Distinct lenses of dark grey/black ashy silt and reddish brown (scorched) silty loam were present within the lower profile. Similar to the burnt deposits within F.1/2 immediately to the south, moderate quantities of occupation materials were recovered relative to the proportion of the feature available for excavation (e.g. 20 sherds of pottery).

Largely due to their depth and from the character of the deposition within them, a number of features were distinguished from the quarry 'background' in the northern half of the area (Fig. 3.19):

F.121/122 – A 1.6 m deep sub-circular pit (2.4 × 3.10 m; Fig. 3.25). To a depth of 0.50 m its edges were near-vertical; below this it sloped down to a steep/near-pointed concave base. The lower third of its profile consisted of edge-collapsed/weathered fine sandy gravels with orange-brown clayish sands. Above this, it had been backfilled with deposits of orange-brown clayish sands, gravels and grey-brown sandy loam.

At a depth of *c.* 0.20 m, a complete calf burial was exposed within the northwestern quarter of F.121/122. It had been placed with its legs tucked under its body and its head to the south. Otherwise, considerable quantities of artefacts were recovered from this feature, including oyster shell, nails, bones (33) and pottery sherds (227).

Located in the extreme southeast corner of the northeast arm of the area, this feature seemed distinct from the line of large circular pits that extended north from this point (F.158, F.234 & F.235; see Fig. 3.16). While it was of similar size to them (3–3.5 m diam.), it was considerably deeper (F.158: 0.85 m; F.234: 0.8 m and F.235: 0.40 m). Even excluding the recovery of the animal burial, considerably greater quantities of finds were recovered from F.121/122 (e.g. F.158: 69 sherds of pottery and 15 bones; F.234: 31 pieces of pot and 13 bones). Given this, and that its base penetrated some 0.7 m below the level of the gravel sub-stratum into the underlying chalk-marl, F.121/122 may have been something other than just a quarry and it probably functioned as a well.

F.7 – This unusually deep pit, and one rich in finds, was situated beside the eastern terminal of the southernmost of a pair of major ditches along the northwestern edge of the area, and fell at the western end of a series of interconnecting minor hollows which continued the western line of ditch (F.134, F.136 & F.137; Figs. 3.22, 3.23 & 3.29). Recorded as possibly 'clipping' the western ditch (F.6), given the configuration between the respective edges, their relationship was probably more one of 'bordering' (i.e. F.7's cut respecting the ditch; the apparent truncation of F.6 by F.7 derives from a later recut of the pit).

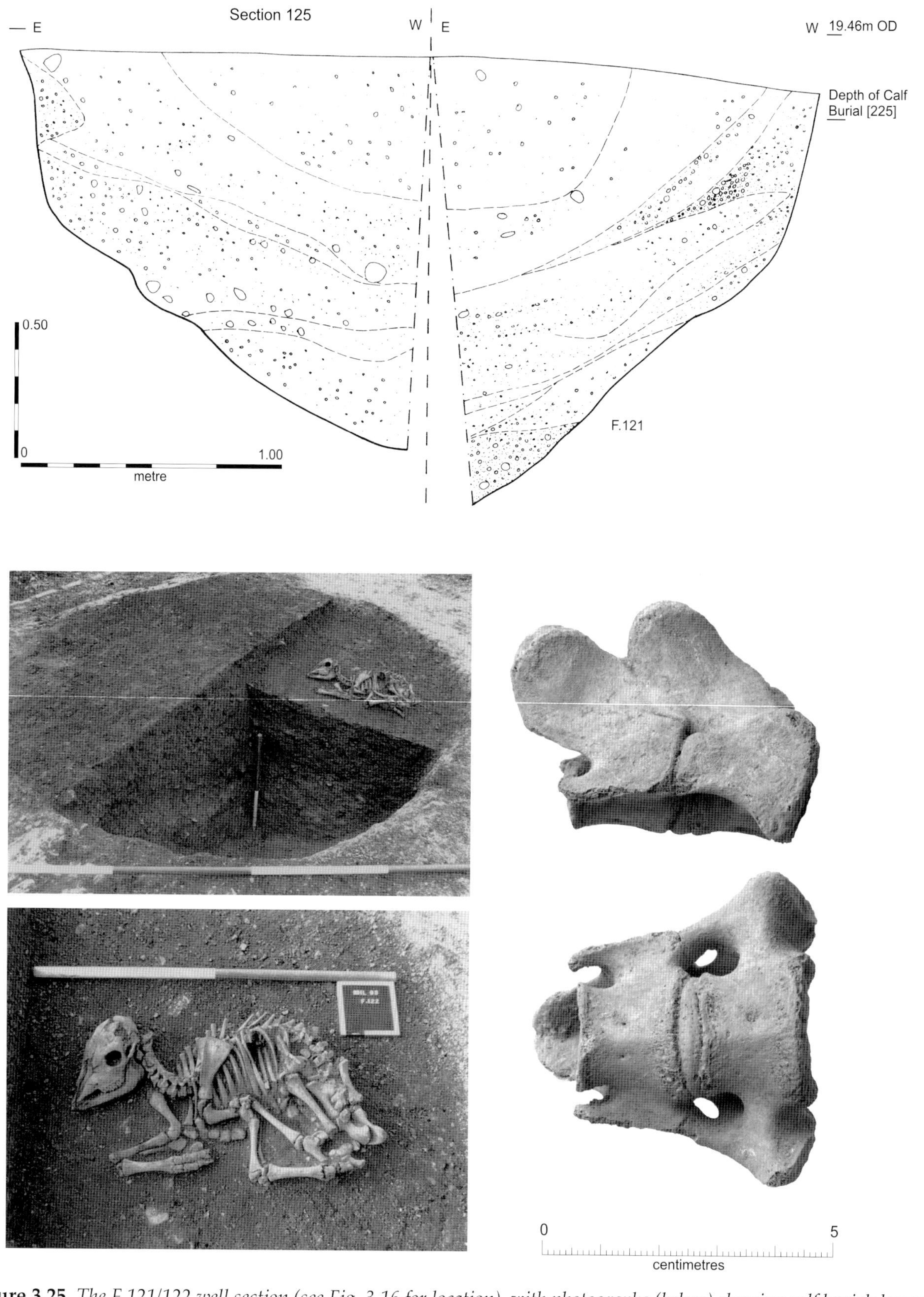

Figure 3.25. *The F.121/122 well section (see Fig. 3.16 for location), with photographs (below) showing calf burial; lower left, detail of its fused vertebrae.*

Feature 7 was 2–2.5 m across and 1.3 m deep. Its western edge sloped down steeply to a concave base (0.7 m across); the eastern side shelved 0.65 m down; its basal profile was ovoid (1 × 1.6 m) and 0.4 m deep. The lower stepped profile displayed evidence of 'open' weathering. Above this, the pit appeared to have been backfilled with light–mid grey clay silt loam and, then, possibly recut (recut *c.* 1.9 m diam.; 0.6 m deep with a concave profile). A number of cattle skulls lay in the base of this secondary cutting; above this, it was filled with mid grey-brown silty loam. Due to the quantity of cattle skulls and horncores recovered, it was initially thought that this feature and F.1/2 to the north (and other interconnecting pits in the vicinity) could have related to tanning. Consequentially, monoliths were taken from it and F.1/2; no indication was forthcoming of such processing and the interpretation was subsequently dismissed (see Murphy, below). Reflective of the area's 'organic' character, this feature is now thought to have been settlement-related. In support of this, while much primary bone refuse was recovered from it (251 pieces in total), so too was much pottery (554 sherds).

Flanking the eastern F.72 ditch-line, discrete pits were excavated cutting through the quarry backfills (Fig. 3.19):

F.221 – Ovoid (1.05 × 1.6–1.90 m), *c.* 0.45 m deep with flattish base. Filled with loose mid–dark grey clay silt with distinct lenses of pure clay and scorched 'soil'/daub (possibly a clay-lined hearth), much occupation debris was recovered (103 pieces of pottery, 14 bones and oyster shells).

F.222 – Ovoid (*c.* 1.1 × 1.25 m) with concave base, 0.38 m deep, this was filled with mid–dark grey sandy clay silt loam (only one piece of Roman pot, a bone and seven worked flints were recovered).

Although these were the only discrete occupation-type pits excavated with the southern portion of Area I, due to the contingent nature of the excavations there, others surely went unrecognized.

The interpretation of these pits represents something of an 'umbrella' grouping, largely based upon the quantity of occupation material within them and their form, which suggests that they were not quarries. From the character of their assemblages and their spatial proximity, three appear to have been associated with the Northwestern Enclosure Complex: F.7, F.257 and F.269. Although lying at a remove, the deep pit/well, F.121/122, otherwise shared characteristics with F.7 and could have had a similar (settlement-related) function. The southern pits are simply unusual, with one, F.221, certainly having a high density of occupation material relative to its size.

The Western Enclosure System – A Development Model

The Mid-Zone ditches appear to mark a major division within the western enclosure complex (Fig. 3.19). While north and south of this point there was only limited evidence of recutting (the various paddocks were relatively pristine), the 'mid-zone' seems to have been a point of enclosure overlap or interface, with at least three episodes of boundary recutting. In terms of dating evidence, this area marks the divide between the earlier (northern) and later (southern) Roman distributions, indicating that not all the components within this system were necessarily contemporary. Given these factors, the following growth model can be presented (letter allocation continues previous series):

Enclosure C - The northwestern double-ditch enclosure (F.1/2 & F.6) was constructed with a 'thoroughfare' on its eastern side that may have turned to the southwest between ditches F.184/187 and F.250 (*c.* 5 m wide).

Enclosure D - Defining an enclosure, 10 m+ × 9 m, the eastern thoroughfare ditch (F.250) was replaced by F.218 that turned to the south as F.145 (a 'multiple' ditch-line, F.145 was probably bordered by F.93 and F.173). Given the relationship of ditch F.218 to F.184/187, there is every reason to think that Enclosure C and its surrounding thoroughfare system were still extant at this point.

As indicated by the compact gravel horizon surviving in the top of F.166/167 and the northern edge-of-excavation, a metalled surface seems to have run north–south along the eastern side of the Enclosure C double-ditches between F.187 and F.218 to provide access into Enclosure D and, originally, the southern F.184-flanked 'thoroughfare'.

Enclosure E - The southern ditch-line of Enclosure D was superseded by F.88/143, and F.209 may represent a western entrance terminal on its southern side. If this was the case, F.143 and F.209 could have delineated a paddock approximately 8.50 m+ × 7 m in area. The manner in which the northern end of ditch F.88 returned to the west, 5 m south of F.184 – the 'thoroughfare interval' – indicates that the Enclosure C was still probably extant.

Enclosure F - The laying-out of the eastern double-ditch line, F.104/105, extended across and along the eastern side of Enclosure E. Possibly originally corresponding to F.144/178, F.143 appears to have defined its northern limits; ditch F.209 was replaced by F.128, with F.199 representing its southern side. These, thereby, defined a paddock, 8.50 m+ × 14 m; the eastern double-ditch boundary F.72/107 extended south, delineating Enclosures G and H.

Enclosure G - The eastern and northeastern sides were formed by ditches F.72 and F.107, and the southwestern by F.76, leaving a 5 m wide northwestern entrance. The paddock extended over 5 m+ × 9 m+.

Enclosure H - The west side was formed by ditches F.72/107 and the north side by F.74 (2 m+ × 4 m+).

An example of lateral settlement shift, the major division in this sequence seems to come between C/D and E, with Enclosure E–G's paddocks all potentially contemporary. Yet, while the dating sequence could indicate a north-to-south succession, there is nothing in terms of stratigraphic succession that necessitates this. Enclosure C, in the northwest, could have overlapped with Enclosure-paddocks G/H, with the stratigraphic 'build-up' in the mid-zone simply marking the zone of enclosure overlap and/or alignment compromise.

The organic development of the complex is obvious. Yet, set against this are elements of formality; specifically, the consistent thoroughfare distance of 5 m, which repeats in the interval between the southwest ditch of Enclosure F and the northwestern ditch of G, and also in the northwestern entranceway gap into G. Two alignments are, nevertheless, apparent within this system. The main alignment (having its immediate origins in Enclosure C/D) does not relate to the orientation of any contemporary road system in the vicinity.

Only one linear feature is largely unaccounted for in this development model: the somewhat bulbous north–south ditch segment in the mid-zone, F.144/178. Truncating the primary series of east–west-oriented gullies/minor ditches, it was itself cut by the 'L'-shaped ditch-line, F.88/143. Although its closest spatial relationships therefore lie with F.88/143, in terms of its 'character' (i.e. its irregular form), its greatest affinities were with the eastern double-ditch line, F.104/105. The arrangement of the southern terminal of F.144/178 and the northern end of F.105 could suggest an entranceway. If this was the case, it would disrupt the relationship of Enclosure E ditches and the establishment of the eastern double-ditch boundary. The details of these interrelationships must lie buried in the sinuous, often recut character of the eastern ditch-line.

Apart from the fact that it did not continue into Area II, how far Enclosure H extended to the east is unknown. Similarly, because of the already noted difficulty of recognizing linear features within the southern quarry zone, it is conceivable that another such enclosure-paddock lay east of the F.104/105 ditches north of H. All that can be said with certainty concerning the extent of this enclosure system is that C and the northern end of D did not continue into the northeast arm of the area, and that they appeared to be bounded by the north–south metalled track.

Extending over *c.* 15 m+ × 75 m+, when considered as a whole there is little that distinguishes the pattern of interlinked sub-rectangular paddocks of the western enclosure complex from other typical rural settlements of the time. That said, the apparent double-ditch arrangement of Enclosure C seems unusual in its formality. What also makes it seem distinct is the very fact that the complex as a whole occurred in such proximity to Roman Cambridge. (The distinction of this enclosure from the southern paddocks is further emphasized by the postulated trackway that returns along its southern side, separating it from Enclosure D and E.)

Given the layout of the overall system and the quantity of finds recovered, there is every reason to think that it was settlement-related. The absence of buildings *per se* probably related to the relative situation of the area of excavation: not in the middle of any paddock, but along the eastern seam of the system. Previous caveats relating to the compromised character and conditions of excavation throughout the southern quarry field are also relevant here, as buildings could have gone unrecognized in that densely pitted zone. Yet, belying the amount of pottery and animal bone recovered, only very limited quantities of any building material were present (tile, mortar, stone and daub; see Building Materials, below). The character of the assemblage as a whole could attest to midden-derived deposition of pottery and bone, with the paucity of constructional materials suggesting that any contemporary structures lay at some remove. However, 'everything' was represented within F.1/2: great quantities of pottery, bone, and a wide variety of 'special finds'. Indeed, it appears as if a 'household' had been backfilled into that feature group. Although the evidence of burning from F.1/2 could possibly be indicative of a building's demise, it may instead represent the dumping of spent fuel.

The evidence of pottery production identified within the F.1/2 assemblage (wasters and also a possible kiln bar) is worthy of note; this could suggest specialization of the household. The distribution of slag and bloomery waste throughout the two northern areas would also suggest ironworking in the vicinity (see Industrial Waste, below).

The Cemetery (No. 1)

Six inhumations were uncovered within Area I, although they were badly disturbed by the contractor's machining (Fig. 3.19). With the exception of Skeleton 4 (east–west; head to west), all were generally oriented north–south (head to south). Skeletons 3 and 4 (F.86 & F.87) both lay face-down and Skeleton 1 (F.94) was partially crouched (on its back) with its hands crossed on its chest; the other three burials lay on their backs and were extended.

The only accompanying grave-good was a bone comb with Skeleton 2 (female; Fig. 3.27); only it and Skeleton 1 had associated nails, suggesting possible coffin burials.

Collectively, the distribution of these burials – echoing ditched boundaries – might suggest a landscape 'seam' within Area I (Fig. 3.19). While only Skeleton 1 was actually interred within a ditch *per se*, the others all followed adjacent boundary alignments:

1) Skeleton 4 – Parallel to the eastern return of the northern Enclosure E ditch
2) Skeletons 5 & 6 – On the west side of the F.72/104 boundary
3) Skeletons 2 & 3 – Roughly following the projected northern continuation of western Enclosure E/F boundary (F.104).

While it might be attractive to relate the prone burial position of Skeleton 4 to its east–west orientation,

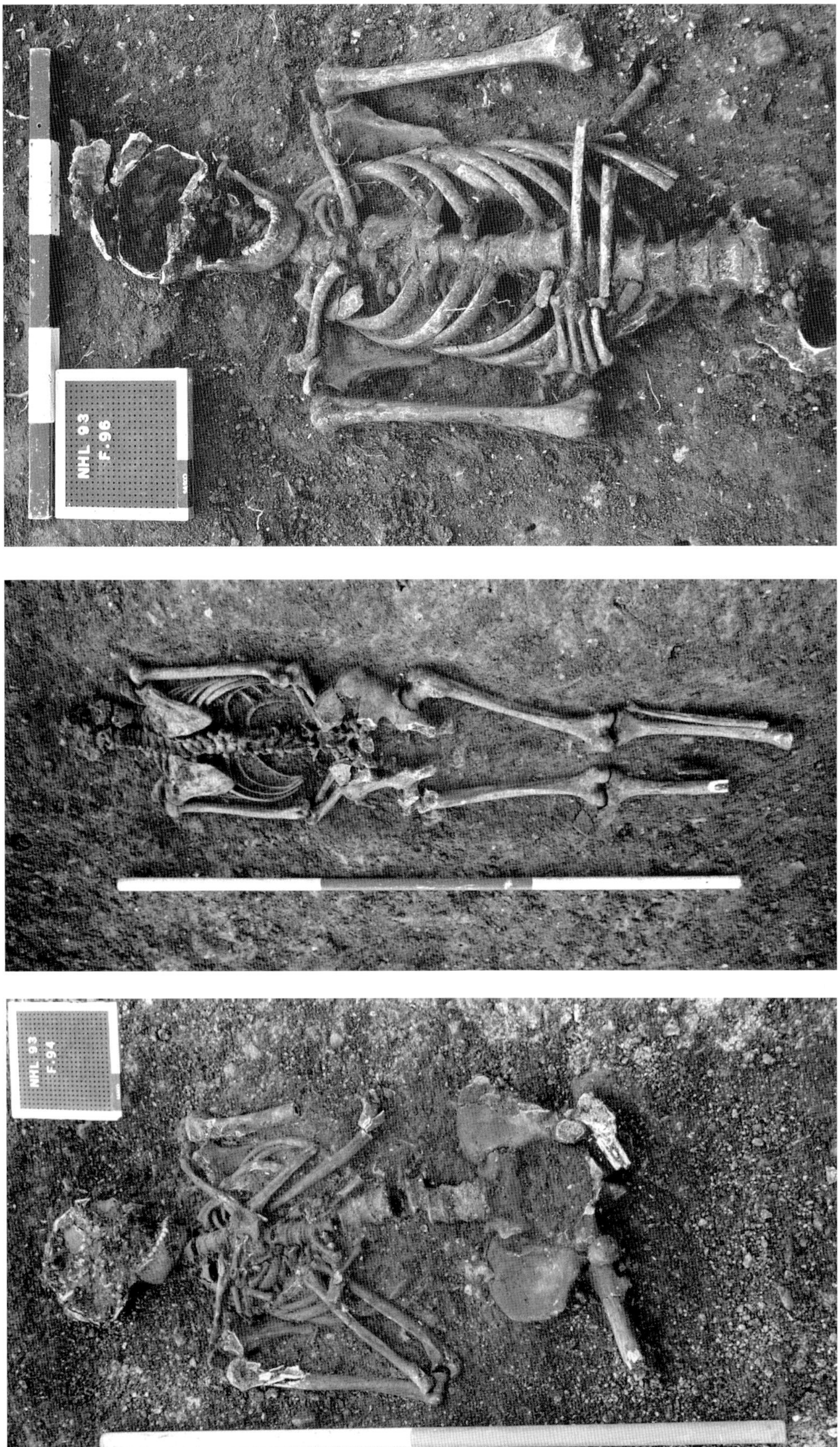

Figure 3.26. *Inhumations (I): Skeleton 1/F.94 (left); middle, Skeleton 3/F.86; Skeleton 6/F.96 (right; see Fig. 3.19 for location).*

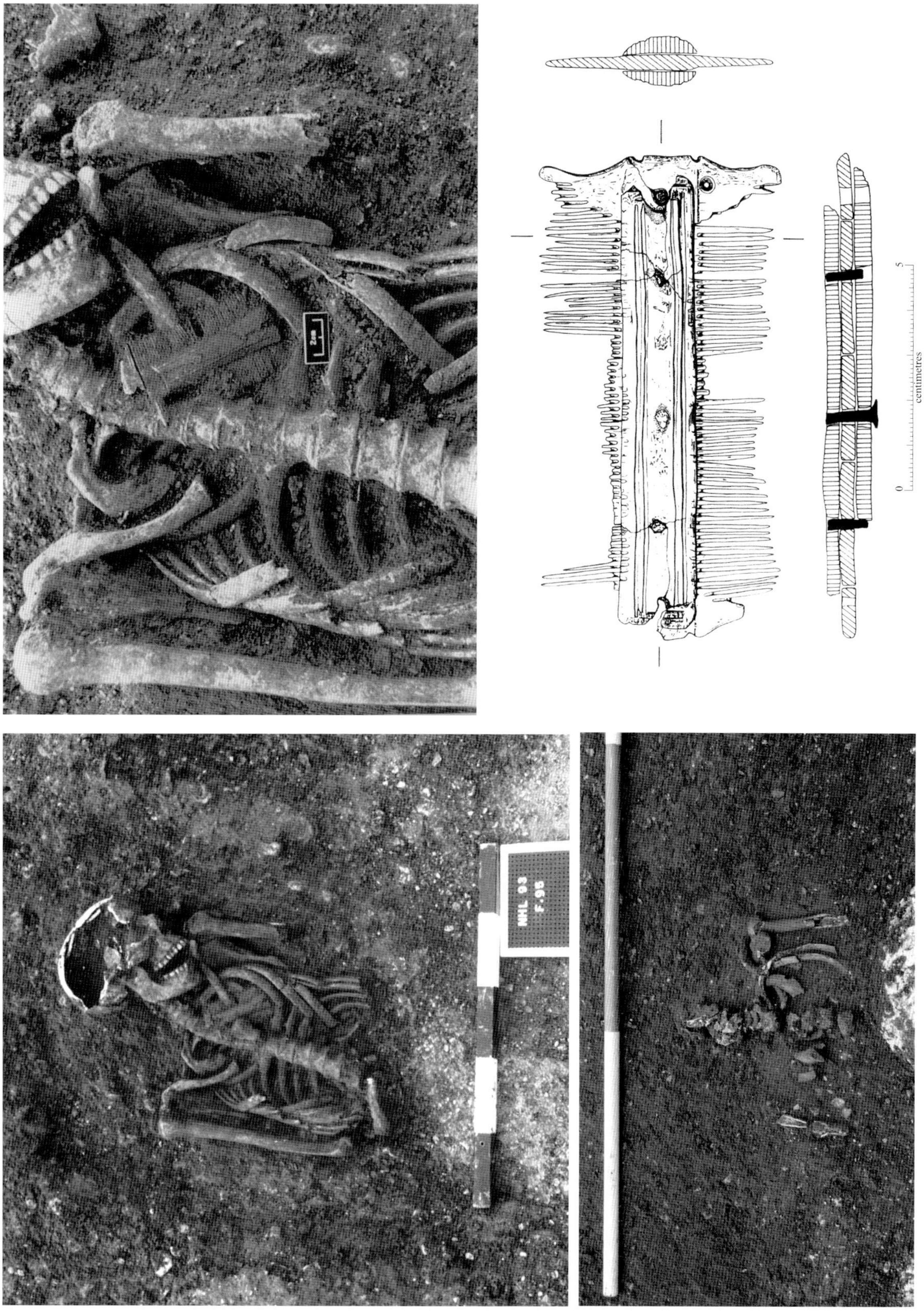

Figure 3.27. *Inhumations (II): Skeleton 2/F.95, with detail upper right of comb on chest and drawing of same below; lower left, Skeleton 4/F.87 (see Fig. 3.19 for location).*

Skeleton 3 was also buried in this manner and this could suggest that the burials in the ditch system corners adhered to this position.

The interval between the three burials within the area of the Mid-Zone Ditches (*c.* 2 m) was closer than in the extremes of the cemetery (where it was 8–9 m); this could suggest that burials continued eastwards on the line of these ditches. The generally wide spacing between the inhumations would, nevertheless, seem to indicate a short history of interment and the absence of intercutting suggests that their locations were known/marked. The only direct dating evidence of these inhumations was provided by the Late Roman antler comb, of probable fourth-century AD date, with Skeleton 2.

With four females and two males recovered, the interred population seems a fairly typical representation by sex. Whilst, given Roman burial customs, it is not surprising that no infant burials were present (cf. the child burials associated with Alexander's Ridgeons Gardens shrine complex; see Chap. 2), the absence of juveniles (< 17 years) is noteworthy.

Grave Catalogue (Ian Marsden; with a contribution by Sarah Austin)

The cemetery's population is summarized in Table 3.2 below. The condition of the surviving bones was, in all cases, excellent. Little damage due to weathering, soil conditions, animal or insect activities could be recognized. It is unfortunate that the circumstances of the discovery of the assemblage accounted for the major losses. In particular, removal of overburden using a mechanical excavator had resulted in damage to skull and pelvic fragments (these being the parts that are highest in the grave once the corpse has skeletonized and collapsed into itself).

Skeleton 1 (F.94; Figs. 3.23 & 3.26)

Age – 18–19 years; determined by the state of fusion of various skeletal elements.

Sex – Probable male; determination based on robusticity characteristics of skull (mastoids and mandible).

Stature – Ulna 26.7 cm indicates individual 172 cm tall.

Palaeopathology

1) Deposits of striated and porous lamellar bone noted on the anterior cortical surface of the right femur, stretching from proximal end to mid shaft. This suggests a non-specific infection of the periosteum; a similar case is discussed with respect to Skeleton 5.
2) Slight deposits of calculus on lingual surfaces of all surviving dentition.

Skeleton 2 (F.95; Fig. 3.27)

Age – 20–28 years; determination based on sternal rib end method described by Iscan *et al.* (1984; see Bass 1987, 97). Probably at older end of this range since clavicles completely fused.

Sex – Possible female; determination based on measurement of the length of the clavicle and the heads of the femora.

Table 3.2. *Cemetery population (*determinations not possible).*

Skeleton	Age	Sex	Stature
1/F.94	18–19	Male	172 cm
2/F.95	20–28	Female	-
3/F.86	40+	Male	171–172 cm
4/F.87	old	Female	- *
5/F.71	- *	Female	157–158 cm
6/F.96	17	Female	-

Stature – No determination possible.

Palaeopathology

Minor degeneration in the body joints of three mid thoracic vertebrae. This consists of a roughening of the joint surface, a degree of mild porosity and the development of small osteophytes projecting horizontally from the upper, anterior bodies. These fall in the size-range 2.5–2.7 mm. This disease process is identical to the vertebral osteophytosis noted in Skeleton 4 (see below), though at a much earlier stage in its expression.

Grave Good: The Bone Comb (S. Austin) – There was just one artefact originating from the burials, a composite, double-sided comb found on the chest of this skeleton. Although fragile, it is fairly well-preserved and reasonably complete (Fig. 3.27). It has features characteristic of Roman provincial double-sided combs, dating principally to the last third of the fourth century AD: a stepped connecting plate which serves both a functional and stylistic purpose, the decorative shaping of the end tooth plates, and a rectangular shape with the proportions 2:1 (Crummy 1983, 56; Galloway 1979, 247). Whilst this comb is a typical example, it is unlikely that an identical form can be found due to the fact that uniqueness in the shaping of the tooth end segments is in itself a definitive characteristic (*ibid*). However a close parallel is that from Grave 258, the Butt Road cemetery, Colchester (Crummy 1983). It has been suggested that similar modestly decorated combs from Poundbury were locally made under the influence of traditional styles originating from Roman outposts of the Rhineland and Belgium (Farwell & Molleson 1993), and this may also be the case with respect to the New Hall comb. The skeleton from Grave F.95 has been sexed as possibly female based upon the clavicle length and femoral head diameter. The presence of the comb cannot be taken to provide confirmation of this tentative sexing, as comparative examples show that combs are not exclusively found in female graves (Grave 258, Butt Road and Graves 5 & 413, Lankhills: Crummy *et al.* 1993).

Both the connecting plates and the eight tooth plates are manufactured from antler and are joined together by five iron rivets. The rivets are positioned strategically along the comb's length between the tooth plates in all but the third and fifth gaps; the resulting pattern is, thus, symmetrical on either side of the central rivet. Both connecting plates have two-stepped bevelling and the edges are marked where the teeth have later been cut, a feature that could also serve a decorative purpose. The comb's total length is 105 mm and its width 56 mm, although the teeth lengths may be somewhat reduced over time through use and burial. One of the end tooth segments has a perforation for the means of suspension, 2 mm in diameter. As mentioned earlier, these segments are shaped and, as with some of the Butt Road examples, are possibly zoomorphic in design (horse head).[5]

Skeleton 3 (F.86; Fig. 3.26)

Age – 40+; determination based on analysis of pubic bone using method described by Brooks and Suchey 1990 (see also Chamberlain 1994, 16) and, for analysis of tooth attrition, Brothwell (1972, 67).

Sex – Male; determination based upon robust characteristics of the skull (mastoids and mandible), and structural differences in the pelvic area (narrow sciatic notch).
Stature – Tibia 36.8 cm indicates individual 171–2 cm tall.
Palaeopathology

1) *Osteoarthritic* changes are widespread throughout the skeleton as follows:
   i) Severe porosity on joint surface at articular facet of tubercle of left and right ribs, being slightly more severe in upper portion of the thorax. This is accompanied by large, wide-based outgrowths of bone, known as osteophytes (8 × 3 mm), flowing inferiorally from the lower joint margins. Osteophytes are a response to mechanical stress being placed on the joints; in this case they are a functional response, designed to spread the load by increasing the surface area available for stress-bearing (Manchester 1983, 66).
   ii) Porosity is common on all vertebral body surfaces, ranging from mild on the cervical and lumbar spine to medium on the fifth to seventh thoracic vertebrae. These latter three also have developing osteophytes projecting 6.1 mm from their upper bodies. The third lumbar vertebra has similar osseous developments; in this case the osteophyte projects horizontally 8 mm and is beginning to turn down vertically.
   iii) The sterno-clavicular joint exhibits a pitted, porous aspect on the surfaces of the joint. This indicates the development of subchondral cysts.
   iv) Small lytic (bone destructive) lesion present on trochlea of distal left humerus. This is an oval cavity 5.5 × 4.5 mm eroded through the articular surface. Correspondingly the trochlea notch of the left ulna has developed a smooth nodule of new bone. These features may relate to a wearing out of the protective cartilaginous material present in the elbow joint at the point in question.
   v) Similar lytic, erosive changes may be seen at the distal radio-ulna joint of the right wrist. Here, the main effect is on the ulna where the joint surface exhibits a cavity 30 mm in diameter situated on the articular surface of the head. The anterior lip of the head of the ulna has, furthermore, become down-turned and roughened by the growth of nodules of new bone.
   vi) Right hip joint also exhibits an erosive lesion situated on the posterior lip of the acetabulum. This is 2.8 mm in diameter and is accompanied by an osteoblastic response in the form of the growth of an area of well-remodelled new bone, 8 mm in diameter, adjacent to the cyst.
   vii) The head of the right femur has a single osteophyte, projecting 12 mm above the joint surface originating from the lip of the fovea. This was a porous and still active lesion at the time of death.

   Such widespread arthritic changes would no doubt have affected the daily life of the individual concerned; we may envisage stiffness and pain in the joints, as well as some limitation of movement. However, it should not be thought that these changes are in any way unusual since they are readily explained as the normal consequence of ageing. They result directly from the progressive wearing out of the cartilaginous tissue from between the joint surfaces due to the constant stresses of weight-bearing and daily physical activity.
2) Skeleton 3 also appears to have suffered a crushing injury to the chest. The result of this was at least three broken ribs down the right side of the thorax, and one on the left. The fractures were, however, very well-healed, since only lumps of smooth, remodelled bone remained visible at the point of fracture. This indicates that the fractures occurred a considerable time before death (Chamberlain 1994, 28). Furthermore, due to the smooth way in which the bones have knitted, it may have been that the individual was able to afford a period of immobilization in order to recover from his injury.
3) A widespread resorption of the alveolar bone had occurred throughout the mandible and maxilla. On average, this meant that 6.5 mm of tooth root was exposed below the crowns. This was not accompanied by the carious destruction of teeth. The alveolar margin itself is rounded and remodelled. Taken together these are classic symptoms of periodontal disease (Brothwell 1972, 147), an infection of the gums which in its advanced stage leads to the loss of teeth. The infection being experienced by Skeleton 3 was still very active at the time of death and most of the teeth are loose in their sockets.
4) A single groove was visible on the canines and premolars of the mandible. This suggests that enamel hypoplasia was experienced by this individual.
5) Medium–severe deposits of calculus were present on all teeth, being especially thick on the lingual surfaces.

Skeleton 4 (F.87; Fig. 3.27)
Age – No definite determination possible, but tooth attrition may suggest an individual in the middle/old age category.
Sex – Possible female; determination based on measurement of clavicle length.
Palaeopathology

1) Six concurrent thoracic vertebrae affected by vertebral osteophytosis. This consists of small and medium osteophytes (3 mm wide). Some of these project horizontally only (max. 2.3 mm, min. 2 mm), but at least two others run vertically down the anterior surface of the vertebral body and would have been in the process of becoming fused together. This would have resulted in the fixing of the two adjacent vertebrae at this point in the spine. Some limitation of movement would have been experienced by the individual.

   All of these developments in the spine of Skeleton 4 can be linked to the body's attempts to deal with stress being placed on the joints of the spine. The bio-mechanical advantages of osteophytes have been discussed above with respect to Skeleton 3. The same kind of process of degeneration in the cartilaginous tissues may be suggested for Skeleton 4. The near-'fixing' of adjacent vertebrae is simply another aspect of this, suggesting that the degeneration has gone so far as to lead to the near-total failure of the cartilaginous disc between these two vertebral bodies.
2) Degenerative changes associated with osteoarthritis are also present in both shoulder joints, in particular in the joints between the acromial and clavicular bones. This was more marked on the left side where the clavicle had an acromial end on which the joint surface had been obliterated by the development of roughened and porous bone. Also, at the posterior margin of the joint an osteophyte measuring 8.3 mm projects superiorly.

   The acromial end of the right clavicle had fine porosity on the articular surface (corresponding to sub-chondral cysts) and a small osteophyte projecting 2.3 mm from the border of the joint.

   Further minor arthritic changes were noted on the glenoid cavity of the right scapula. These consisted of a slightly depressed joint surface and the development of small para-articular osteophytes.
3) Carious cavities were noted on the right second molar and the left third molar of the mandible. Both were located on the lingual side of the tooth and consisted of small, shallow blackened pits approximately 2.5 mm in diameter. These are areas in which the mineral of the enamel surface of the tooth has been eroded away by dietary acids (Hillson 1979, 150). If allowed to continue the tooth concerned will be invaded by bacteria and eventually be lost due to the resulting infection.

Table 3.3. *Skeletal pathologies and trauma. Abbreviations: Arth = osteoarthritis/vertebral osteophytosis; NSI = non-specific infection; ENHP = enamel hypoplasia (*data absent; i.e. no teeth); Calcul = calculus; Perio = periodontal disease; Fract = fracture/trauma.*

Skeleton (sex)	**5/F.71** (F)	**3/F.86** (M)	**4/F.87** (F)	**1/F.94** (M)	**2/F.95** (F)	**6/F.96** (F)
Arth	ribs	general	spine	no	spine	no
NSI	femur	no	no	femur	no	no
ENHP	yes	yes	yes	no	- *	yes
Caries	no	no	yes	no	-	no
Calcul	yes	yes	yes	yes	-	yes
Perio	no	yes	no	no	-	no
Fract	no	yes	no	no	no	no

4) Medium to severe deposits of calculus were present on the buccal surfaces of all teeth.
5) Irregular pitting can also be seen on the enamel surfaces of both lateral mandibular incisors. This does not appear to be post-mortem damage since the edges of the pits are smooth and rounded. It may, therefore, be a hypoplastic defect or enamel hypoplasia, different in expression, but similar in aetiology to the grooves noted in Skeletons 5 (see below) and 3.

Skeleton 5 (F.71)
Age – Unknown
Sex – Probable female[6]; determination based on small mastoid, shape of mandible and measurement of humeral head.
Stature – Humerus of 29.6 cm suggests individual 157–8 cm tall.
Palaeopathology
1) Mild pitting and porosity on articular facets of the tubercle of three left, most probably mid thorax, ribs. These consist of areas approximately 2 mm in diameter located centrally on the joint surface. Such features are usually associated with abnormal stress being placed on the joints in question, either through occupational factors, or simply due to the normal wear and tear of the ageing process. The pressure caused by such stress leads to the development of sub-chondral cysts that erupt through the bone of the articular surface, hence the porous appearance of the bone (Manchester 1983, 67). This is a disease process which may be categorized as degenerative joint disease or osteoarthritis.
2) Deposits of well-remodelled, lamellar bone seen on the mid shaft of the left femur. This bone was striated and slightly porous, indicating a still active disease process. These are characteristic features of infection, in this case restricted to the periosteum (the membrane surrounding the outer bone surface). At the stage being experienced by this individual, such non-specific infections need not be especially debilitating.
3) Faint groove noted on the left canine and first premolars of the mandibular dentition. This was horizontal and located 5 mm above the alveolar bone. Such grooving is a characteristic expression of enamel hypoplasia and occurs due to a hiatus in the formation of the tooth crowns during the growth period (i.e. childhood).
4) Small flecks of a dense, gritty material adhering to the lingual surfaces of the teeth. This is mineralized plaque, known as calculus: a common finding on the dentition of archaeological specimens. In the case of Skeleton 5, this condition can be classified as mild.

Skeleton 6 (F.96; Fig. 3.26)
Age – 17 years; determination based on state of fusion of various skeletal elements.
Sex – Probable female; determination based upon wide sciatic notch and shape of the mandible.
Stature – No determination possible (long bones not fused).
Palaeopathology
1) Horizontal groove noted on the mandibular dentition, visible from left first molar to right first molar. This is identical to the condition noted on Skeletons 5 and 3 and is also an incidence of enamel hypoplasia.
2) Slight, isolated flecks of calculus on lingual surfaces of all dentition.

The palaeopathology of the cemetery's population is summarized in Table 3.3. In general, the incidence of disease on the skeletons of this small sample is relatively low. As noted above, preservational conditions are not a factor and, therefore, we may exclude taphonomic influences in the derivation of this overall view. The one factor running contrary to this pattern was the high rate of enamel hypoplasia seen on the teeth of the population. Four out of five individuals with teeth surviving showed signs of this condition. Although the specific causes of these marks upon teeth have yet to be identified, it is generally accepted that the majority of cases are related to health or nutritional stresses experienced by individuals during the period of enamel formation (Huss-Ashmore *et al.* 1982, 441). Such stresses may relate to failure of harvests, chronic diarrhoeal and other infections, or simply to an inadequate diet. Given the very minor evidence for infections discussed below, we may tend towards a dietary explanation as most appropriate in this context. In any case, it is clear that stresses of the kind referred to above were a fact of life for the New Hall population, or at least for that portion of the population available for study.

More evidence for the diet of the individuals can be seen in the incidence of caries and calculus. To an extent these conditions are mutually exclusive, in that they are linked to opposing patterns of dietary behaviour. Caries are localized areas of infection caused by the destruction of tooth enamel due to the consumption of foods high in carbohydrates. Calculus, on the other hand, is the build-up of mineralized plaque deposits around the tooth crowns and is associated with diets high in protein (Hillson 1979, 150). In the site's

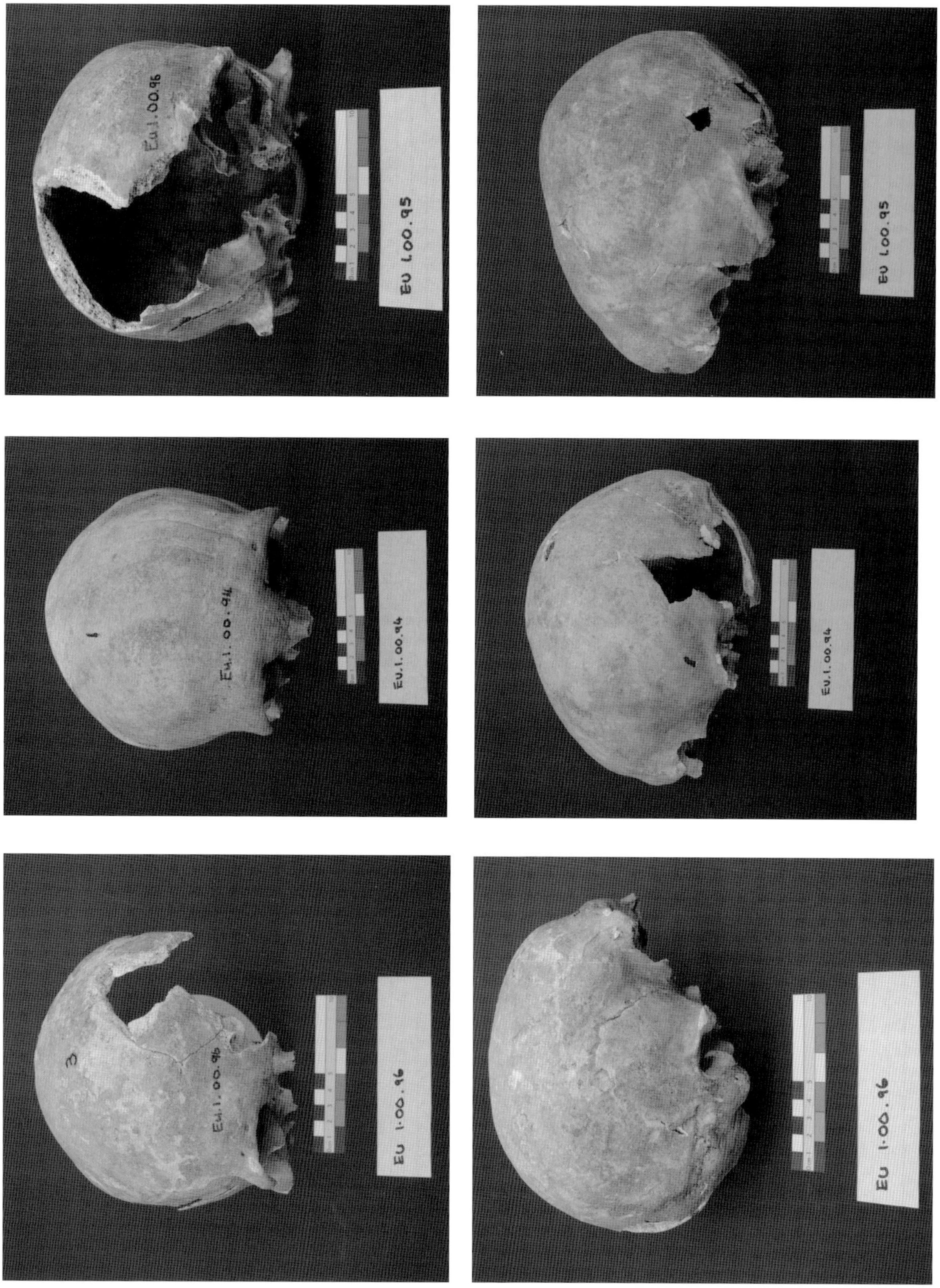

Figure 3.28. *Inhumations (III): the Duckworth Collection skulls, from left, Skeletons III, I and II.*

skeletons calculus occurred on all surviving dentition and in some case was quite thick (Skeletons 3 & 4), but dental caries was only seen in the case of Skeleton 4. As in most cases caries only occurs due to the regular consumption of sugary foods, we can assume that such substances (which were available in the Roman world as luxury items) were not a regular part of the diet of the New Hall individuals. Given the ubiquitous nature of the calculus deposits, we may also assume that dental hygiene was not a priority amongst this group of people.

As mentioned, apart from two cases of very minor periosteal infection (Skeletons 1 & 3), evidence of infective lesions was entirely absent. This is not to say that they did not occur, since many infective processes do not impact on the bones of individuals, or may become obliterated due to the constant reparative processes of normal bone development. However, the least we may conclude is that levels of disease were unlikely to have been endemic.

Arthritic changes did occur; the pattern that they follow, though, is the expected one since the more severe incidence of joint degeneration can be seen in the older aged individuals. This suggests that the main factors involved in the development of arthritic disease in this population are linked to the normal processes of ageing.

In general, the patterns of arthritis, infection, dental pathology and trauma are unexceptional amongst the cemetery's population. Only the level of enamel hypoplasia is unusual and this may suggest that relatively high levels of health or nutritional stress had been experienced by these individuals.

Figure 3.29. *Inhumations (IV): detail of thickened, Duckworth Collection skull, Skeleton V.*

The Duckworth Collection Skulls (Benjamin Neil)

The skulls were found during the construction of New Hall in 1964–5. The exact circumstances of recovery are unknown, but it is understood that they came from the area of its western parking lot. Given the time of their finding, it was fortunate the material was recognized and kept at all. It is presumed that the skulls were excavated in a fragmented state and at some point were refitted, where possible, using an epoxy resin. The collection is curated at the Duckworth Laboratory, Cambridge University.

Sex estimation was accomplished by identifying the dimorphic dimensions of the skull using methods outlined by Buikstra *et al.* (1994). Age at death estimation was based on ectocranial suture closure (Meindl & Lovejoy 1985).

Skeleton I (EU 1.94; Fig. 3.28) Female? young adult - Refitted fragments of calvaria represent this individual. Moderate expression with slight spiculation of the left and right temporal lines on the frontal bone was noted; it marks the origin of the temporalis muscle, which is a major elevator of the mandible thus inferring a strong bite force. The frontal bone has asymmetrical grooves, (an epigenetic variant) running upwards in the lateral portion, medial to the temporal line: the left groove has greater expression and originates from the supraorbital foramen.

Skeleton II (EU 1.95; Fig. 3.28) Male, mature adult - Refitted fragments of calvaria represent this individual. No pathology, trauma or activity markers were noted.

Skeleton III (EU 1.96; Fig. 3.28) Male, mature adult - Refitted fragments of calvaria represent this individual. Slight marginal lipping and surface irregularity of the left mandibular fossa was noted on the left side and much less so on the right side, denoting osteoarthritis of the tempomandibular joint. Symptoms may have manifested as unilateral pain in the muscles of mastication, radiating to the ear and jaw.

Skeleton IV (EU 1.97) Female? adult - Fragments of calvaria and right mandible (some refitted) represent this individual. A small irregular button lesion was observed on the inner table, relative to the right eminence of the frontal bone; it is not likely to be an osteoma, but rather a hamartoma represented by spontaneous growth disturbances wherein cells of a circumscribed area outstrip those of the surrounding tissue (Eshed *et al.* 2002). Peri-mortem loss of RM_1 (30) with complete alveolar resorption was observed. Also lost peri-mortem was RM_2 (31) though there was incomplete alveolar resorption, together with a distal root remnant, rounded in occlusal plane. A fragment of occipital bone includes the left condyle, which showed signs of minor lipping and microporosity, suggesting initial stages of osteoarthritis in the atlantooccipital joint.

Skeleton V (EU 1.98) Sex indeterminate, adult - A single fragment of frontal bone was noted for hyperostosis; a near doubling in thickness was observed, evidenced by a remnant horizontal margin through the diploe (Fig. 3.29); it does not resemble the 'cottonwool' appearance of Paget's disease, though there is some loss of definition between the dipole and inner and outer tables. Because this is a fragment, it was not possible to determine the condition as diffuse or focal; however, differentially this may be hyperostosis frontalis interna, a condition characterized by a benign overgrowth of the inner table. The condition has been associated with diabetes (Andrews 1942) and obesity and is seen most commonly in older females (Western & Bekvalac 2017).

Overviewing Settlement Structures

Before progressing to outline the site's environmental/economic data and Roman-phase finds, it is worth first taking stock and considering facets of its layout/phasing and distributional patterning.

Inter-Area Correspondence and Phasing

Bracketing the northern and southern ends of the site, the existence of the two roads – the Godmanchester/*Via Devana* and Back-College Roads – goes far to explain the irregular plan of the western Area I enclosure system. Whereas the southern enclosure-paddocks (E–H), like Enclosure B, roughly followed the orientation of the southern roadway, in the northwest, Enclosure C, its access track and Enclosure D were more closely aligned with the northern Godmanchester route. Their inter-road (spanning) situation accounts for the north-to-south 'twisting' of the enclosures and, perhaps, also explains why the point at which the two alignments met – the Mid-Zone Ditches – saw such intense recutting/definition.

It is at this point that a phasing structure needs to be attempted. For the purposes of demonstration, we will here employ the site's original plan (Fig. 3.30), which was published in *Roman Cambridge*'s updated summary-section (Evans in *RCAM*, fig. XII.4). The projection of its main enclosures (and the Godmanchester Roadway) will later be modified in the light of subsequent findings (see Fig. 3.57); nevertheless, it suffices for our immediate needs here, while providing a degree of 'reflexive honesty' (i.e. showing how our interpretations have changed).

In many respects, the most crucial relationship is that, in Area III, the F.33/174 ditch-line clearly predated any Godmanchester Road-related features. With that ditch lying on the same alignment as Enclosure B, along with ditches F.81/82 in Trench K and F.75 in the southern end of Area I, these all followed the orientation of the Back-College Road and, thereby, define the primary *Phase 1* system.

Phase 2.1 is then initiated with the establishment of the Godmanchester Road and its two quarry fields (though, see below concerning the question of the latter's direct contemporaneity). *Phase 2.2* covers the foundation and usage of the Northwest Enclosure Complex (Enclosures C & D) and its trackway-access. Similarly, possibly relating to a secondary routeway, Area III's ditches, F.32 and F.284, are thought to have been associated, as was also the usage of the F.121 well. While questions of dating-attribution will largely be kept until this Chapter's *General Discussion*, what is important here is that this complex had clearly gone out of use by the third quarter of the second century AD. It is in relation to this that the southern enclosures, E–H – and also the inhumation cemetery – are designated as *Phase 3*. The layout of these enclosures surely overlapped with that of the Enclosure C/D arrangement, but unlike it they evidently continued in use until the later Roman period (later third–fourth centuries AD).

Quarrying

Whilst found throughout most of Area I, across the site as a whole the distribution of quarries was limited: they were only present in the southwestern corner of Area III and absent from Area II. Given that the development of gravel extraction across the northern end of Area I has been shown to have been in a quasi-circular pattern, these offer little direct insight as to their relationship with the Enclosure C/trackway ditches. That said, the Enclosure F/G ditches both cut quarries and had extraction hollows that respect them within the southern half of the area. This suggests that quarrying activity continued for a considerable period and that it was initiated relatively early in the site's (Roman) sequence.

When this section was first drafted it was posited that much of the site's quarrying actually related to its settlement and not the period's road. Now, with the advantage of hindsight and much more context, this is no longer valid. The last decades of Roman settlement excavation within the region have shown that quarrying at this scale was not a feature of the period's settlements. As will be further outlined elsewhere in this chapter (see *General Discussion* below), other comparable quarry-'fields' have since been encountered – though New Hall's still seems the largest – but these were, arguably, primarily road-related.

The intensity to which the North Field quarries were excavated allows us to gauge the scale of the site's gravel provisioning. As outlined above, that area's extraction hollows/pits would represent a capacity of *c.* 97 cu. m. Combining this with the distribution of Area III's quarry-features, it is estimated that, as a *minimum*, the North Field quarrying could have extended over *c.* 117 sq. m and have yielded some 239 cu. m of gravel. The total (minimum) estimated area of the South Field quarry-zone is 479 sq. m and, thus, it could have generated *c.* 287 cu. m of mineral. Together amounting to a capacity of 336 cu. m, in theory, this would have been sufficient to have metalled a 9 m-wide road to a thickness/depth of 5 cm – in other words, the *Via Devana*/Godmanchester route (see below) – over a distance of some 750 m.

This is only the roughest of measures. The site's very small, Type 1–3 pits/hollows may have largely been for immediate domestic consumption and not road construction at all. Conversely, the overall estimates of the two quarried areas are entirely minimal 'guesstimates' and both could have been much more extensive. Time and sequence may, of course, also have been factors here. The site's quarry-pattern was a cumulative product. Roads, too, would have required repair and resurfacing; therefore, the actual road-length that New Hall's quarries could have covered may been much more restricted. As we will see, nevertheless, these figures still provide a useful datum with which to think.

In terms of the arguments presented here, it is possible that the two quarry fields were not directly contemporary. The South Field alone might have related to the Godmanchester route's initial construction, while the north-area's more piecemeal extraction rather reflects its patching and resurfacing. If this was the case, then – based on the above-figures – the South Field would have only generated sufficient gravel to cover a *c.* 635 m length of the road.

Finally, note that we have here presumed that all of the quarry's gravels went towards the northern, Godmanchester route. This is largely determined by that routeway's lack of any obvious main flanking ditches. This contrasts with that of the south-lying road. There, the delineating ditches would, in effect, have served as quarries; it is estimated that each metre-length of its F.17 ditch

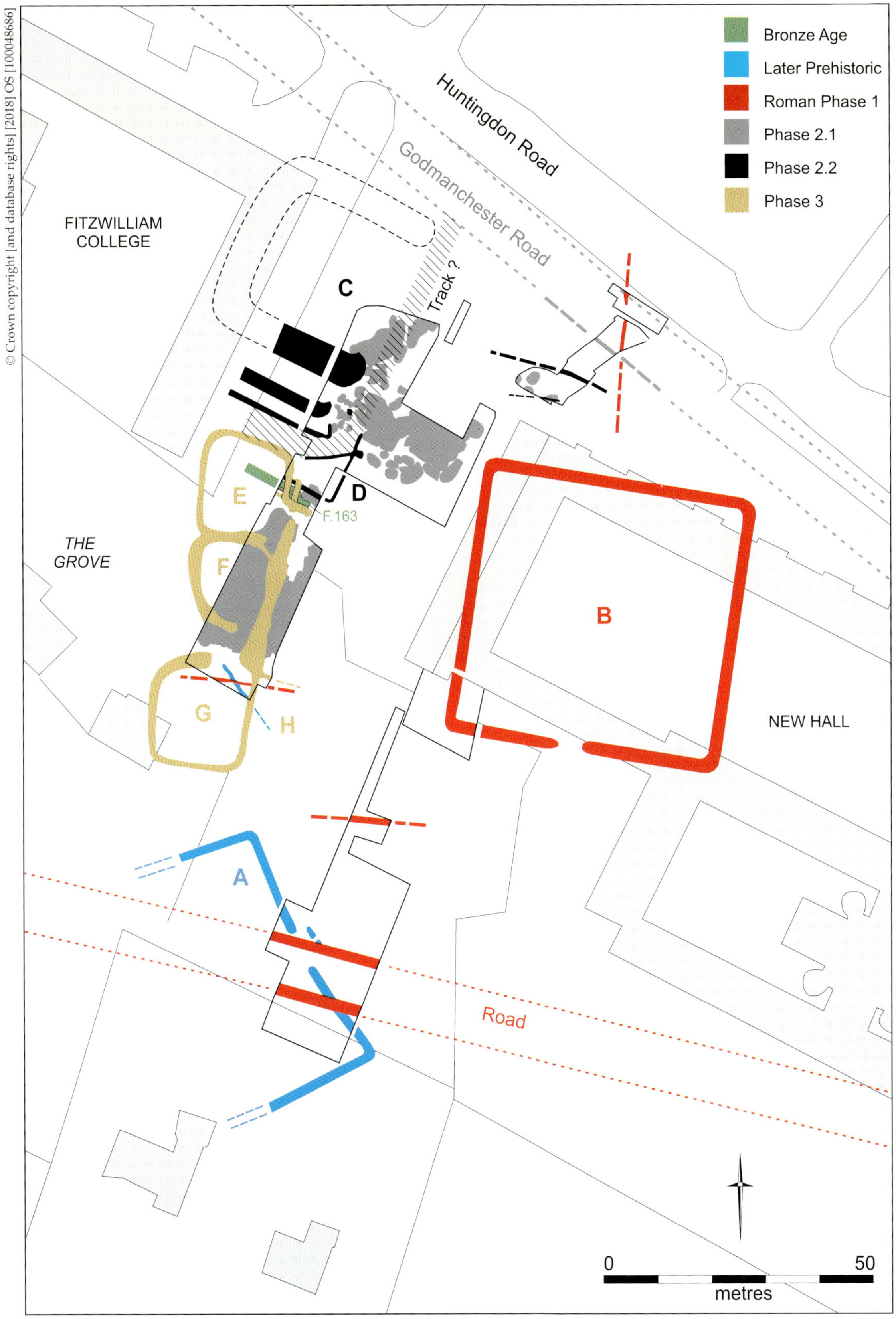

Figure 3.30. *Phase plan (see Fig. 3.57 for later revised version).*

could, in theory, have generated *c*. 0.70 cubic metres of gravel and more than enough to metal the corresponding width/length of the road. Whatever might be implied by whether or not a roadway was ditched is an issue best left for this Chapter's final *General Discussion*.

Artefact Densities and Distributions

Although there are grounds for thinking that within Area I the functional usage of the quarries and enclosure-occupation overlapped, generally the quarry pits were quite 'clean' and produced relatively few finds. Such inference risks circular argument as discrete features producing quantities of occupation material have been designated as settlement features. However, whilst this possibility must be acknowledged, the settlement pits were few in number and most displayed other 'non-quarry' characteristics (depth, evidence of burning and/or discretely 'lensed' backfilling). In the southern half of the area, a much higher proportion of occupation debris was retrieved from the reduced quarry zone and, for example, 200 pieces of pottery and 85 bones were recovered from the upper fill of the eastern sondage alone (plus much oyster/mussel shell; two flints and a whetstone). The fact that it is confined to the upper profile of the extraction hollows means that this material has been interpreted as representing settlement 'colonization' of the quarry zone (i.e. dumping) and/or subsided later occupation horizons.

In contrast to other finds categories, an extraordinarily low density of prehistoric artefacts was present within the backfills of the main linear features of Enclosure C – F.1/2, F.6 and F.7 – just three, one and three flints respectively (with only one Bronze Age sherd occurring in the latter). This could either suggest that the fills derive from a source distant from the immediate area of the Neolithic/Bronze Age settlement or, more probably, that the main area of Roman occupation, Enclosure C, had been previously stripped of its buried soils (and any early finds therein). The latter interpretation would be consistent with the fact that in many cases prehistoric finds were the predominant artefacts recovered from Roman quarry hollows.

A major issue of concern is the source of the Roman material deposited on-site. Adopting a minimalist approach, the site could be characterized as no more than a series of roadside agricultural paddocks/fieldsystems and a quarry, with its rich artefactual assemblage deriving from the town. This would presume carting refuse over a distance of some 0.25 km; the uniformity of the material within F.1/2 and 6 could, admittedly, be consistent with town-midden sources, with the similarity of their matrices speaking of *en masse*, rather than piecemeal, deposition. A maximal reading of the site's record would have these major groups redeposited from a settlement-source in the immediate area, with Area I lying along its eastern periphery. Lacking associated occupation horizons against which to compare this dumped material, resolution of this issue is impossible. However, it is here that the site's hinterland context is relevant, inasmuch as the ('big feature') redeposited assemblages included evidence of industrial activities not usually permitted within Roman towns (pottery production and ironworking). Whilst obviously falling short of absolute confirmation of its more local origin, this could further support such an interpretation (although this presupposes that small Roman towns actually followed 'rules'; see Chap. 1).

The distribution of artefacts along the three major ditch-lines within Area II is clearly complicated (Figs. 3.4 & 3.8), not least due to the influence of intercutting features belonging to different phases of the site. For example, along the length of the F.20 boundary there is a rough correspondence between the 'highs' in the distribution of bone and those in the distribution of prehistoric pottery and lithic finds (Figs. 3.31 & 3.32). Given the quantities of bone in the northern terminal of the prehistoric ditch system (F.211; 36 pieces), it would be logical to presume that the similarly large numbers of animal bones which occurred in the Roman ditch that was later cut across the area (through the enclosure's entranceway; F.17/59: 24, 38 and 60 pieces per segment) were residual and derived from prehistoric usage. However, whilst equally high values were not found elsewhere (10–16 pieces per segment being the next highest values), significant quantities of bone occurred along the entire Roman ditch-line, possibly indicating that the high values in the area of the Iron Age entranceway do, in fact, represent Roman deposition. Relatively large quantities of Roman pottery were also recovered along the length of F.17/59 (highs of 15/21 and 37 respectively at its western and eastern ends). In the area of the highest bone deposition (corresponding to Enclosure A's entrance), nine and 12 sherds of pottery occurred within neighbouring segments.

All this indicates that the finds distributions are not straightforward and that the site's multi-period usage complicates patterning. However, that the northern Roman roadside ditch saw much higher levels of deposition than the southern is readily apparent in the distribution plots. This would suggest that settlement either lay directly to the north (towards or in Enclosure B) or the northwest (in the southern extent of the Area I enclosures).

Apart from the fact that the highest quantities of bone were in the F.20/211 terminals, it is difficult to see much obvious depositional patterning of the prehistoric material in Area II. That said, the percentage of residual prehistoric material within the Roman roadside ditches was generally greater west of the F.20/211 ditch-line, suggesting that the interior of the postulated enclosure system lay to the southeast. Indeed, as has been discussed, from this comes the possibility that the Roman ditch-line might even have been cut along an earlier boundary (F.220).

The ratio between artefact categories within the Iron Age ditch (F.20) also warrants comment. Bone was found in consistently high values (range: 5–35 per segment; 19.5 ave.), whereas the pottery occurred in low and inconsistent numbers (range: 0–4 per segment; 0.85 ave.). The pottery was, moreover, 'scrappy', suggesting that it had been ploughed in. Given this and that most of the F.20 finds occurred in the ditch's upper profile, it could be suggested that the bone was introduced from another source. Throughout, there has been a nagging suspicion that the bone present within the Area II's F.20 boundary had a relationship with that observed within Enclosure B to the north. From its parallel orientation to the southern road there can be little doubt of Enclosure B's Roman attribution. If this was the case, two depositional alternatives are possible:

1) The bone within the Enclosure B ditches was residual and derives from previous prehistoric usage, or
2) The bone in the upper profile of the F.20 ditch derived from the earliest Roman usage of the site relating to Enclosure B and pre-dates the layout of the road (prehistoric features backfilled with Enclosure B-generated refuse prior to road construction).

Certainly, very different depositional factors are evident in the character of the Enclosure A assemblage and that of the northwestern Roman enclosure complex. Within ditch F.20, for example, bone predominated over what little pottery was recovered, with a ratio of 1:0.04. Conversely, in the Roman features, pottery was far more frequent than faunal remains. It varied, for example, from 1:2.2 and 1:2.5 in F.7 and F.6 respectively, rising to 1:6.9 and 1:7.4 in F.121 and F.1/2. These ratios suggest contrasting depositional practices. Whereas bone waste appears to have been directly backfilled into the prehistoric ditches, the Roman assemblages suggest redeposition from a 'structured' midden source and that much of the bone went elsewhere (probably to dogs and pigs, see below). Certainly, the favoured 'hoarding' or deposition of so much pottery presumes a well-organized community.

This patterning is most marked across the northern half of Area I and across Area III. Five features in Area I (F.1/2, F.6, F.7, F.121 & F.269) and three 'secondary' features in Area III (F.30, F.31 & F.38) account for nearly three-quarters of the site's entire Roman assemblage – 7650 sherds (73%) – whereas their animal bone remains represent only 44 per cent (1585 pieces) of the period's faunal

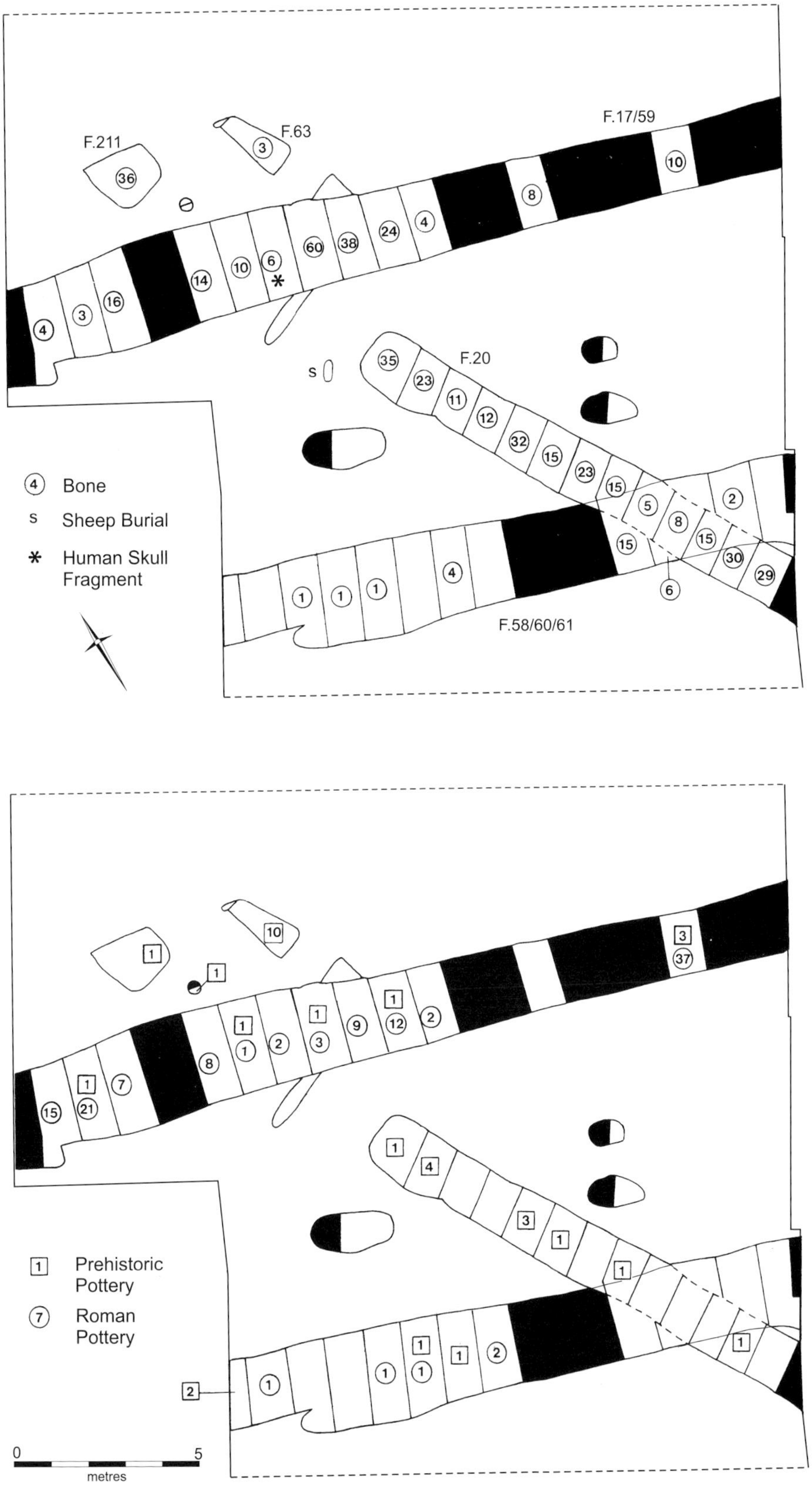

Figure 3.31. *Area II artefact distributions (I): animal bone (top) and, below, pottery.*

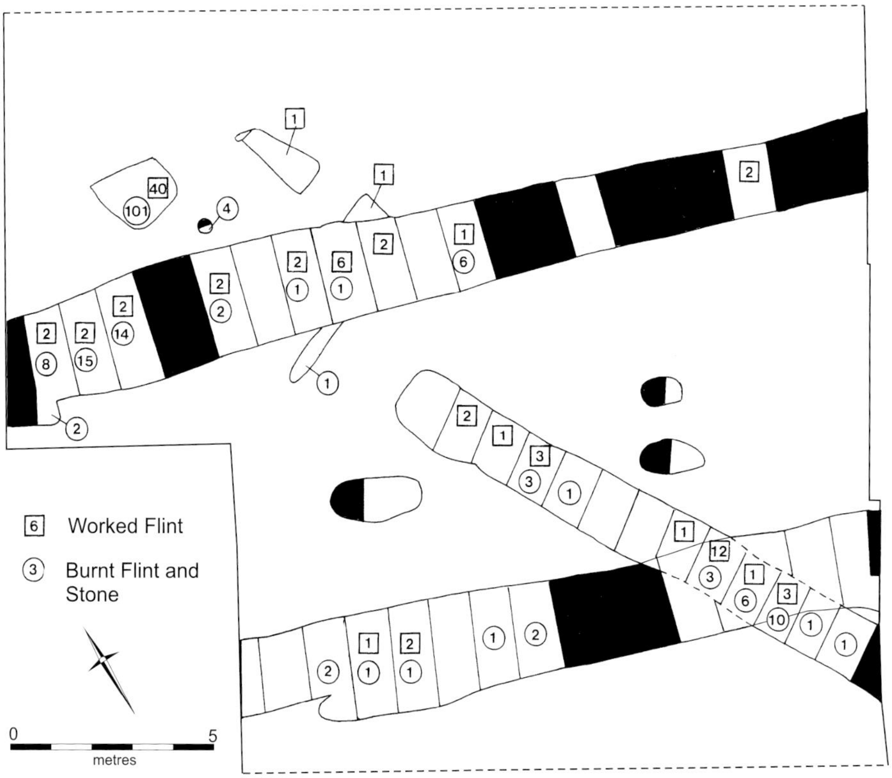

Figure 3.32. *Area II artefact distributions (II): worked and burnt flint.*

assemblage.[7] This indicates that the pattern of pottery-dominated midden-derived deposition was largely confined to the northwestern portion of Area I and to Area III, and that the bone was more evenly distributed across the site. It would, moreover, firmly demonstrate that this was a 'secondary' Roman distributional pattern, for the ratio of bone-to-pottery in ditches F.33 and F.174 within Area III was markedly different: 1:0.04. Given that the Roman attribution of F.33 and F.174 is indisputable, this evidence would go far to confirm the suggestion that the depositional patterning within F.20 was largely the result of (Early) Roman infilling (and this might account for what seems to be its unduly late radiocarbon assays).

The distributional dynamics of the site's Roman settlement are certainly complex. It will be a topic that we will return to in this Chapter's concluding *General Discussion* after the results of other adjacent excavations have been considered.

Burial, Ritual and Hygiene

The recognition of the northwestern high-density zone discussed above may reflect on the nature of Roman usage, as it seems distinct from the area of the cemetery. The midden-type deposition was evidently associated with Enclosure C and the Godmanchester Road-side features. No inhumations were present within this northern swathe; instead, they began and continued south from the terminal of ditch F.250, the entranceway into Enclosure D. Falling roughly along the same north–south line at the extreme eastern margin of the area, confirmation of this as a 'cognitive divide' might also be offered by the F.122 calf burial in the top of well F.121.

Caution must, though, be exercized in the assumption that the distribution of inhumations was purely linear. Though this would be a plausible burial pattern, based on precedent, the burials could have extended much further east and have been lost in the car park's construction. Indeed, this is the likely source of the Duckworth Collection's five skulls recovered during the College's construction in the 1960s. Apparently retrieved without any formal archaeological monitoring, other inhumations may well have gone unnoticed there; a total burial populace of between 15–25 can therefore be suggested. Given this, it is clearly the phasing/duration of the separate enclosure that determined the location of the cemetery: it lay to the east of the Late-phase settlement (Enclosures E–G; also, north of H).

That two of the site's burials – Skeletons 3 and 4 – are 'aberrant' and lay face down is significant. This, however, is an issue best left until there is further comparable context and will be returned to in this book's final chapter.

Finally, the status of the F.122 animal burial is intriguing. Given its careful deposition, there can be no doubt that it was 'placed' (Fig. 3.25). Was it actually, though, a ritual offering? It would now be commonly classed as such and, indeed, that is how it was originally interpreted by us. Increasingly, though, we have begun to see a number of such Roman-period animal burials as relating to the disposal of sick/diseased animals, thereby potentially reflecting on broader issues of hygiene (see e.g. Phillips & Grassam 2006 concerning the mass interment of horse and cattle carcasses at West End, Haddenham). We will return to this theme in relation to the Vicar's Farm findings (see Chap. 6). The status of F.122's calf is, nonetheless, interesting. While certainly not just haphazardly slung into a feature, the animal was clearly suffering from a significant pathological condition (see Yannouli below), leading it to have fused vertebrae. It would probably have eventually died from this; if it was a ritual offering, then it was a very convenient one. The knife cuts identified on the animal's ribs only add to this ambiguity, as these do not indicate skinning cuts. They suggest, instead, that meat had been taken from it prior to burial, making its careful arrangement within the top of the well even more noteworthy.

Material Culture

As will be further discussed below, variations in the scale of the site's individual finds assemblages raise significant questions about the character of its usage. What does the paucity of its tile and metalwork mean relative to its pottery (*c.* 10,500 sherds)? As has already been observed, there were major differences in the depositional patterns across its areas; when the results of the other adjacent excavations are brought to bear (e.g. the Fitzwilliam and Murray Edwards College investigations; see *Accruing Context...* below), this becomes even more marked.

Romano-British Pottery (Chris Going, with a contribution by Francesca Mazzilli)

The site produced an unexpectedly substantial assemblage of Romano-British pottery (*c.* 168 kg). This spanned the later first to the mid third centuries AD and after. The entire assemblage was spot-dated (see below and Archive), and the largest and most important features analysed in some depth, making it possible to attempt an overview of the ceramic supply to second-century Roman Cambridge. At times spot-dating was difficult, as over 90 per cent of the contexts produced less than 1 kg of material; the condition of much was also generally rather poor. As the bone from the site was fairly well-preserved, it is unlikely that soil conditions were responsible for the state of the ceramics and it seems probable that much of it was redeposited. These factors work against close dating. The most notable exception was F.1/2, from which *c.* 80 kg of pottery was forthcoming (*c.* 5800 sherds). This was probably dumped in the early Antonine period. The dating indicates that the bulk of the site assemblage – whatever the date of its final deposition – was mainly manufactured in the later first or second centuries AD. While some pottery dating until to the end of the Roman period was noted, pottery manufactured after AD 200 was remarkably rare. This suggests that, although site activity continued into the later Roman period, after the second century AD it was not intense.

During the spot-dating a watch was kept for groups that merited quantification. The basic criteria for selection were two-fold. The contexts needed to be fairly closely dated, and to contain, in aggregate, more than 5 kg of pottery. Contexts which fell into this category included F.1/2 and F.6; however, only F.1/2 was examined more fully, with the southern roadway feature assemblages also separately examined and commented on. Subsequently, in order to provide a measure of statistical cross-site comparison, Mazzilli undertook full analysis of a representative sample of F.1/2's assemblage (*c.* 20%; 1084 sherds) and of all of the pottery from F.6, F.7, F.30, F.121, F.245 and F.269 (Table 3.4).[8]

Feature 1/2

The pottery from this feature is discussed by fabric below and, then, as a whole. Although not representing a lengthy accumulation of material, the overwhelming majority was abraded and none of the breaks recorded were very fresh.

Gaulish Imported Colour-coat (Greene 1978) – Colour-coated wares were not at all common in the group, which suggests that the feature was closed before the development of the principal production centres in the middle decades of the Antonine era (see, though, below).

Figure 3.33.1: Base of a small bag-shaped beaker, probably rough-cast (for the shape see Greene 1978, fig. 21.16); slightly abraded.

Nene Valley Colour-coat (Going 1987: Fabric 2) – No certain Nene Valley colour-coated products were noted in the feature, although there were two sherds of a later form in the related F.6. This lack is of some interest. M.G. Wilson identified colour-coated vessels in Antonine levels at Verulamium as Nene Valley products, which suggests that they ought to occur here. The St Albans identifications now, however, seem doubtful. There is probable production in the Hadrianic period, but the major impetus behind colour-coat production seems to come after *c.* AD 150. The lack of Nene Valley vessels in this large group would support a later, rather than an earlier expansion.

Miscellaneous Oxidized Wares (Going 1987: Fabric 27) – Oxidized wares comprised a small fraction of the assemblage. For the most part, vessels in the fabric were open forms (e.g. bowls). Among them were three unusual bossed-footring bowls, sherds of which were found in several contexts. Their origin is a matter of some uncertainty. J. Evans' 1990 study of the Cherry Hinton production centre reveals nothing like them there; no obvious local parallels have been found elsewhere.

Figure 3.33.2: Footring bowl with an angular bead rim decorated with pushed out bosses.
Figure 3.33.3: As above, but with corrugated zone below the rim; base probably as No. 2.
Figure 3.33.4: Larger example of above type, with grooving above a bossed zone; base probably as No. 2.

White-slipped Oxidized Fabric – A single vessel was identified in this fabric. This was a restricted-foot beaker (the upper part is missing), decorated with upright painted stripes with applied flanking dots (cf. Green 1960, fig. 4, no. 19).

Figure 3.33.5: As above; decorated in cream-coloured paint, now abraded.

Upper Nene Valley Cream Mortaria – Wares resembling Upper Nene Valley white or cream wares were restricted to mortaria, of which there were two well-preserved specimens. While Lower Nene Valley mortaria production is attested in the Hadrianic–Antonine periods (Perrin & Webster 1990, 40), the trituration grits of these vessels are a mixture of brownish and blackish ironstone characteristic of the Upper Nene Region rather than the more consistent ironstone grits of the Caster–Stibbington Region products (cf. Hartley in Brown 1994, 49). Both vessels were stamped; the date-range of the forms would seem to be Hadrianic–Antonine.

Figure 3.33.6: Large single sherd including half of spout; for the form, cf. Cam 297; lightly impressed, illiterate stamp.
Figure 3.33.7: Large single sherd comprising much of vessel (cf. Cam 297) save spout; double retrograde stamp reads MINOM.

Lead Glazed Ware (Arthur 1978) – One large rim/body sherd of a bowl form was found. This was from a vessel loosely resembling and clearly modelled on, the Dr.37 (cf. Arthur 1978, Type 7, fig. 7.6). The fabric is the 'South East English Group', whose probable origin is Staines (*ibid.*, 298–301 and figs. 8.2–3). Another local find of this ware consists of a beaker from the cemetery at Girton (*ibid.*, Type 2, fig. 8.2). A sherd from what is possibly the same vessel as was also found in F.151.

Verulamium Region Wares (Going 1987: Fabric 26) – This fabric is generally well-represented at Cambridge, and this deposit has the three principal products of the industry: the segmented, reeded-rimmed bowl (Fig. 3.33.8), the ring-necked flagon (Fig. 3.33.10–11), and the 'figure 7'-rimmed jar (Fig. 3.33.9). Interestingly, there are no certain mortaria represented.

Figure 3.33.8: Rim of a segmental bowl.
Figure 3.33.9: 'Figure 7'-rimmed necked jar in creamy brown fabric; abraded.
Figure 3.33.10: Rim sherd of a ring-necked flagon; abraded; pinkish fabric.
Figure 3.33.11: Sherd of a similar, but smaller flagon.
Figure 3.33.12: Tall flagon neck with moulding on mid section; handle scar only.
Figure 3.33.13: Lower body and base of a flagon, possibly from same vessel as No. 12.

Miscellaneous Buff Wares – This fabric group is usually restricted to sherds of open forms, such as bowls, or else closed forms such as flagons. It is of uncertain origin. There were no definite Colchester products. Figure 3.33.15 resembles a Verulamium Region form, but the fabric does not and, rather, a Mancetter Hartshill source seems possible.

Figure 3.33.14: Neckless, ledge-rimmed jar; abraded.
Figure 3.33.15: Ledge-rimmed bowl; the body shape is generally similar to the Verulamium Region segmental bowl type.

Shell-tempered Wares (Going 1987: Fabric 50) – Extremely rare in this assemblage (probably <1%). The forms represented comprise ledge-rimmed, or (rarely) necked jars. The origins of shell-tempered wares are not entirely certain. Forms are not exclusive and sourcing sub-fossil shell inclusions remains difficult (cf. Woods 1994, 99–104). However, it seems probable that the pottery originated either in the kilns at Harrold, Beds., some 50 km to the west (Brown 1994), or perhaps from a more northern source – either in the kilns at Bourne or Greetham (Bolton 1968; see also Perrin & Webster 1990, 41 for a comment on their provenance) – or from a variety of centres both west and north of Cambridge. An Essex origin is unlikely as shell-tempered production there was in decline by the end of the first century AD (see Going 1987; Lucy & Evans 2016).

Fine Reduced Wares – These are characterized by a well-levigated fabric, fired to a dark slate/grey black, which changes on wetting to a dense 'night black' and usually dries to a dark grey. Vessels are usually finely burnished overall. The fabric is generally similar to 'London Ware' and may have been manufactured at one of the centres producing this style of pottery, which include West Stow, Suffolk (Rigby 1989, 80–4), and an undiscovered location in the Nene Valley (Perrin 1980; for a distribution, see Marsh 1978, fig. 6.6). The forms encountered are almost exclusively open: plate and platter types, with the occasional beaker (e.g. No. 20) and, here, a lid (No. 21). The vessels occur in the Flavian–Trajanic periods and shortly after, and are presumably an attempt to manufacture a ware that copied, somewhat loosely, a variety of plain samian open forms (e.g. the Dr.36). Possible sources of production include the Nene Valley (and the occurrence of these wares in some quantities at Godmanchester supports the idea of a supply route via that town). The manufacture of the forms seems to have been comparatively short-lived, and no attempt at ornamentation was made. They are competently made and highly fired.

Figure 3.33.16: Fine grey; dish (Class C; cf. Marsh 1978, Type 34).
Figure 3.33.17: Fine grey ware bowl (C10; cf. *ibid.*).
Figure 3.33.18: Fine grey ware bowl, type (C6; cf. *ibid.*).
Figure 3.33.19: Slightly micaceous grey fine (C).
Figure 3.33.20: Fine grey closed form, possibly a beaker.
Figure 3.33.21: Fine grey open form, possibly a lid (Type J).

Horningsea Wares (J. Evans 1991) – Products of the Horningsea kilns were in evidence in the feature. Many of the rim forms presented in Jeremy Evans' 'production' typology (1991; see also J. Evans *et al.* 2017) are represented on the site and the form repertoire seems to be fairly wide, but here in this context definite Horningsea products seem to be restricted to storage jar types. The rim shapes are not very closely paralleled, but Number 23 resembles Evans' Number 2 (1991, 39). The jars almost all appear to have the characteristic decorative styles, such as vertical combing, either overall (No. 22) or in vertical zones (No. 24).

Figure 3.33.22: Everted, small rounded rim, short neck; the body is lightly decorated with vertically combed zones.
Figure 3.33.23: Grey core, reddish surfaces; widely splayed, rounded rim with prominent finger-marks on the interior; vertical combing on body overall.
Figure 3.33.24: Neck sherd, rim missing; decorated with vertical combed zones.

Romanizing Wares (Going 1987: Fabrics 39 & 45) – Not a strict fabric group, more a description of a firing process, but a useful classification nevertheless. Numbers 25–8 are unusual and probable local products, possibly from the putative kiln invoked to account for the wares below (Nos. 29–55). The other vessels are possibly also local products. Sherds of other vessels in Romanizing fabric were noted, but their origins are more varied.

Figure 3.33.25: Bowl (rim missing) with corrugated upper body (for the form cf. below, Fig. 3.33.26).
Figure 3.33.26: Squat, sharply carinated jar form, similar to the possible kiln products noted below and possibly from the same source.
Figure 3.33.27: Bowl with flat reeded-rim, corrugated upper body and wide base; probably a kiln product.
Figure 3.33.28: Closed form, probably a drinking vessel, decorated with deep grooving separating zones decorated impressions from a small object, such as a straw.

Reduced Local Kiln Fabric – One of the most common fabrics in the assemblage was a soft, coarseware, usually-coloured mid-grey but merging to (rarely) black–grey. The bulk of the vessels are fairly hard, but a substantial fraction is under-fired and there are some distorted sherds. The forms are very stereotyped and several are clearly from the same hand. It is suggested that this sub-standard pottery emanated from a close by, but undiscovered, kiln. There is only one 'second' in the group, but it is so distorted that it might more properly be termed a 'waster'. The most commonly encountered form is a squat-necked jar with a piriform-shaped body (cf. Figs. 3.33.30–44). It is more usually left undecorated but may be ornamented with a light linear burnish on the upper part. An uncommon variant with a taller neck and a narrower mouth, decorated with rilling, was also noted. Other forms in the fabric include a globular-bodied jar, decorated similarly, or left plain (Figs. 3.33.46–7). Other vessel classes represented included Number 52, a strap-handled flagon, possibly with a trefoil rim.

There were also some lids (Figs. 3.33.53–5); these ended in a plain rim and may have had terminal grips.

This pottery, although not unequivocal waste, is in its general appearance remarkably uniform and was certainly made by the same hand. It constitutes so well-defined a portion of the assemblage that it is hard to resist the idea that it is a deliberate dump. Feature 1/2 produced charcoal and burnt ash apparently deposited 'still smouldering', which raises the possibility that this sub-assemblage was a cache of pottery damaged in an accidental fire, possibly in a building. Alternatively, the ash and burnt debris could represent only the rakings of a kiln firing which produced a sub-standard batch of pottery. The presence of a near-waster from the feature's [340] fill-deposit (not illustrated) supports this view. Evidence of ceramic manufacture has been found elsewhere in Cambridge, most notably at Jesus Lane, where pottery datable stylistically to the third century AD was found in 1901 (Hartley 1960). The date of the New Hall material is substantially earlier. The forms and fabrics are very similar to Horningsea products (although there were no definite waste versions of storage jars). On balance, it seems likely that we have here evidence of a kiln producing wares in the same or a very similar tradition at New Hall, to the west of the town.[9]

Figure 3.33.29–39: Jars with everted, rounded rims, small cordons at the base of the neck and mid body carinations; the lower body is almost invariably lightly fettled. They are usually burnished overall externally but are, otherwise, left undecorated; surfaces mostly friable and abraded.
Figure 3.33.40–4: As Numbers 29–39, but with a light linear burnish, applied to the upper body either as a lattice or single lines; fabric, and other finish detailing as above.
Figure 3.33.45: Neckless, rilled jar.
Figure 3.33.46: Underfired, necked jar, with a fine everted, bifid rim; the upper body is rilled.
Figure 3.33.47: Necked jar with slightly bifid rim; undecorated.
Figure 3.33.48: Small globular-bodied, necked jar; smoothed exterior.
Figure 3.33.49: Small storage jar with everted rounded rim; oblique comb stabbing on the upper body.
Figure 3.33.50: Everted-rimmed beaker with overall decoration.
Figure 3.33.51: Beaker, as Number 50, but with panelled dots applied *en barbotine*.
Figure 3.33.52: Neck of a flagon, with strap handle scar evident; probably a trefoil-rimmed type.
Figure 3.33.53–55: Three lids; exteriors smoothed, but otherwise left undecorated.

Grey Ware – In this category have been allocated all of the unassignable wares that appear not to be products of the local pottery industry noted above. The origins of this fabric group are likely to be diverse, but there are few recognizable vessels from known Essex industries. Among the open forms are bead-rimmed dishes of Cam f. 37, but there are no signs of the later, Antonine variant (the Cam f. 38), which suggests that the group largely predates *c.* AD 150.

Figure 3.33.56: Trifid-rimmed, deep bowl, exterior wiped, otherwise left undecorated.
Figure 3.33.57: Ledge-rimmed bowl form, similar to Number 15.
Figure 3.33.58: Neckless ledge-rimmed jar.
Figure 3.33.59: Necked jar with oval rounded rim.
Figure 3.33.60: Narrow necked jar in grey ware. Slightly dunted rim, possibly a second.
Figure 3.33.61: Neckless cordoned jar.

Samian (Figs. 3.33.63–69 & 3.33.76; Fig. 3.34) – Samian from this feature comprised mostly plain wares of various forms, mainly platters of Dr.18, 18/31 and 31, cups of Dr.27, and a few sherds of Dr.37 (including D6; see below). The overwhelming majority of the wares were from Central Gaulish potteries, although some South Gallic wares were noted; this suggests a Hadrianic–Antonine date. Many of the vessels had been lead-bracket/-staple repaired (see below and Fig. 3.34).

Feature 1/2 and Antonine Pottery Supply

At *c.* 80 kg, the assemblage from this massive feature complex is sufficiently large for a number of generalizations to be made from it about the ceramic supply to Cambridge in the early–mid second century AD (Fig. 3.36). This period is of some interest for it is at this time that many ceramic industries were emerging from the early second-century *caesura* that ended the Flavian boom (for this period, see Going 1992). We will first consider Continental imports, then wares from more distant provincial manufacturers, and finally local wares, which constitute the bulk of the total.

Continental imports are notable for their absence and it is samian, almost inevitably, which is the most common imported ware, providing dishes and the occasional bowl, as well as the majority of the fine drinking vessel class. Comparatively little of it was South Gaulish material, the bulk being provided by the major Central Gaulish production centres. While the most common import, samian comprised less than 5 per cent (by either weight or EVEs) of the total assemblage, and plain wares far outnumber decorated wares: the usual situation in the small towns and rural settlements of Roman Britain (Millett 1980, 66). Other imported tablewares were virtually absent, with the exception of the small cup (Fig. 3.33.1) that is possibly an import from Gaul or Germania. No certain wine amphorae were found in F.1/2 and, from the site as a whole, there was very little imported material of this kind; sherds of the ubiquitous (at least on urban sites) olive-oil bearing Dressel 20 coming from only a very few contexts.

While products of the provincial insular industries are not strongly in evidence, the fabrics represented are of considerable interest. Most commonly found in the 'fineware' category are a series of open forms in 'London Ware' (one source is probable but not certain). The distribution of these products is given in Marsh 1978. With the exception of a few sherds, the number of bowl forms noted in the style of the Dr.29–30 and 37 – staple 'London Ware' products – is very small, but the bowls noted as Figure 3.33.16–18 are in a fabric in the same tradition and it seems probable that they are from the same production centre or centres.

Colour-coated wares are generally lacking. This is largely because the assemblage predates the full re-emergence of the major provincial production sites, such as Colchester and the Nene Valley, and the few sherds noted are likely to be from Continental imports (such as Fig. 3.33.1). The assemblage is a useful benchmark for the appearance of Nene Valley colour-coated wares: there are no products which match those seen by Hayes, for example, at Fengate (1978, 12–13), and it is only during the Antonine period that Nene Valley colour-coats are first claimed at even such sites as St Albans (Wilson 1972), so their absence at Cambridge some years before this date is unsurprising. Of more immediate interest is the absence from F.1/2 of wares from the Cherry Hinton potteries (J. Evans 1990). During the Flavian period this remarkable production site, which lay only *c.* 4 km to the east of the Roman town, produced a range of beakers (of Gallic influence) with barbotine *appliqué* decoration in a striking biscuit fabric. This industry might have been expected to re-emerge strongly in the Hadrianic period and after, but it is not in evidence here – or in other features on the site for that matter – which strongly indicates that the kilns themselves had gone out of production. Its collapse (or more strictly its failure to revive) is of some surprise and a strong indication that even during the Antonine period the town had insufficient

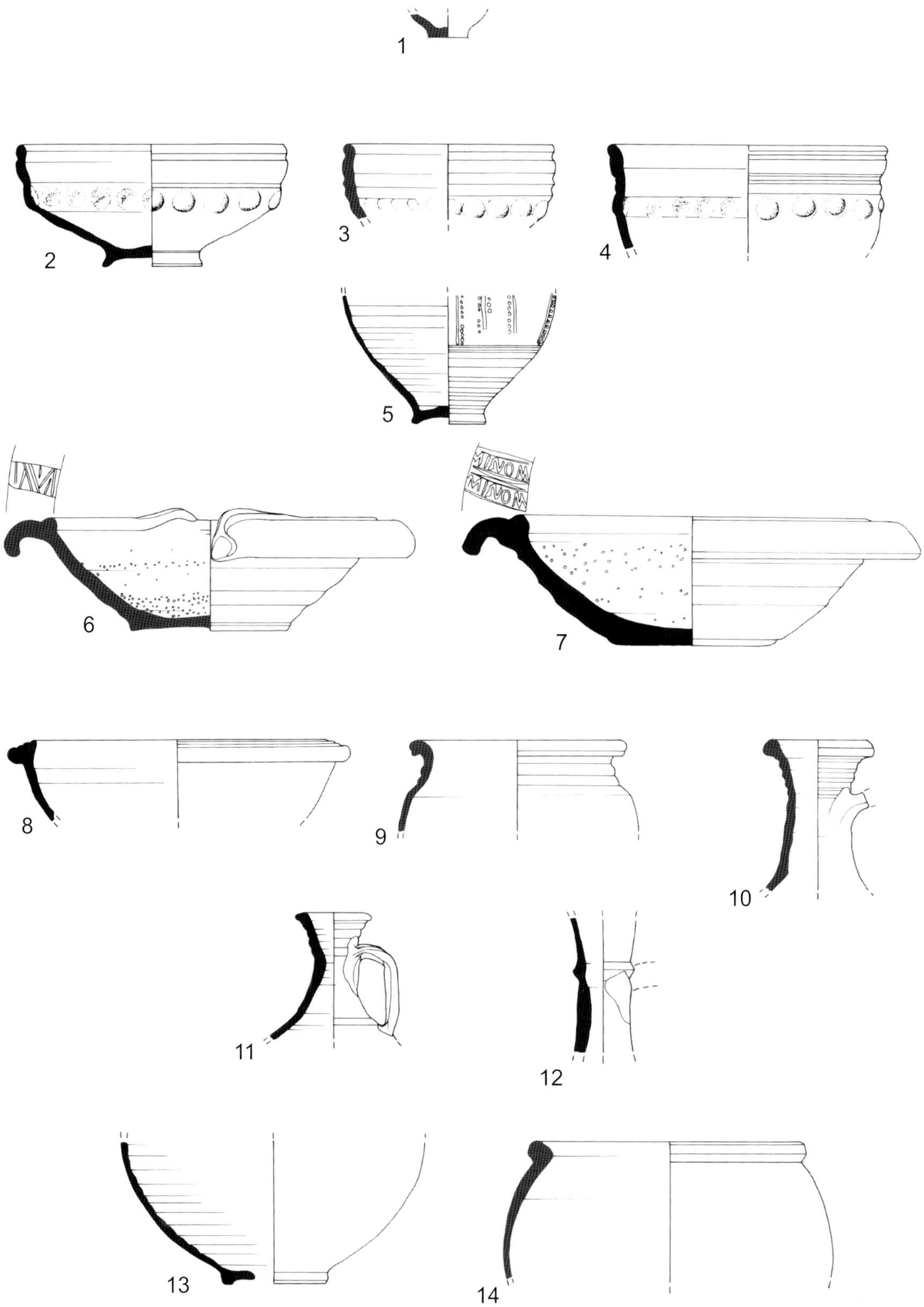

Figure 3.33. *Roman pottery illustrations (see text).*

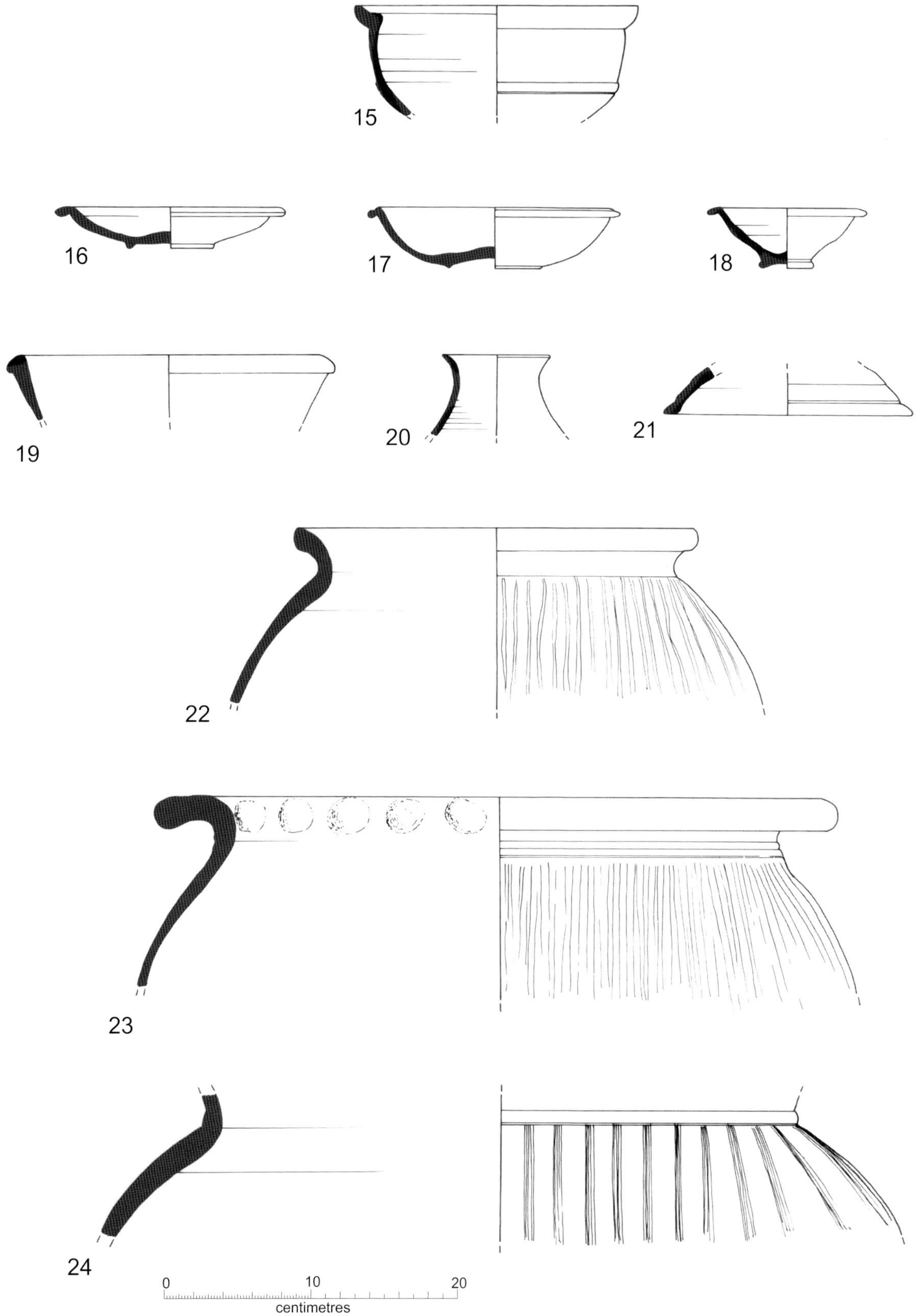

Figure 3.33 *(cont.).*

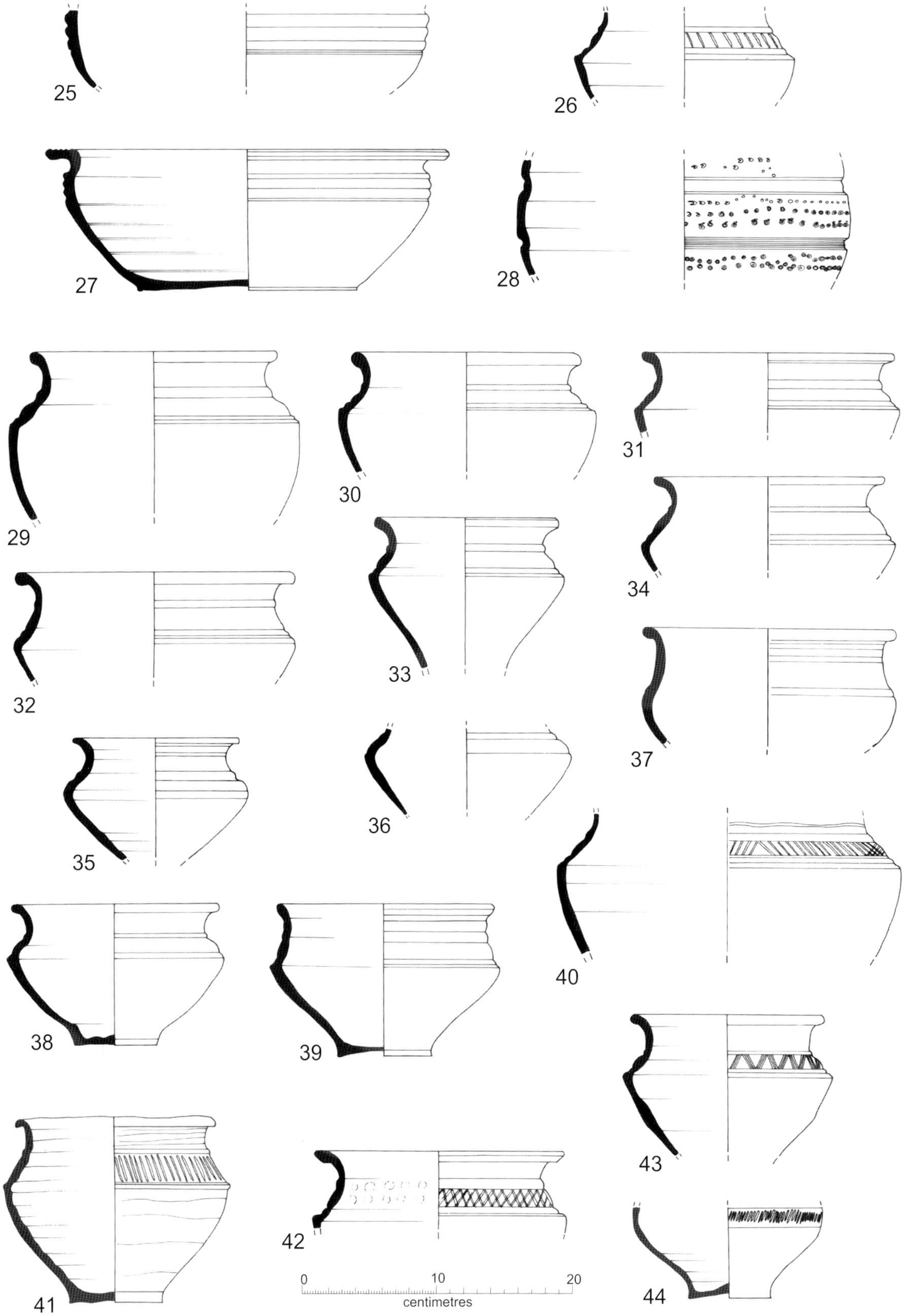

Figure 3.33 *(cont.).*

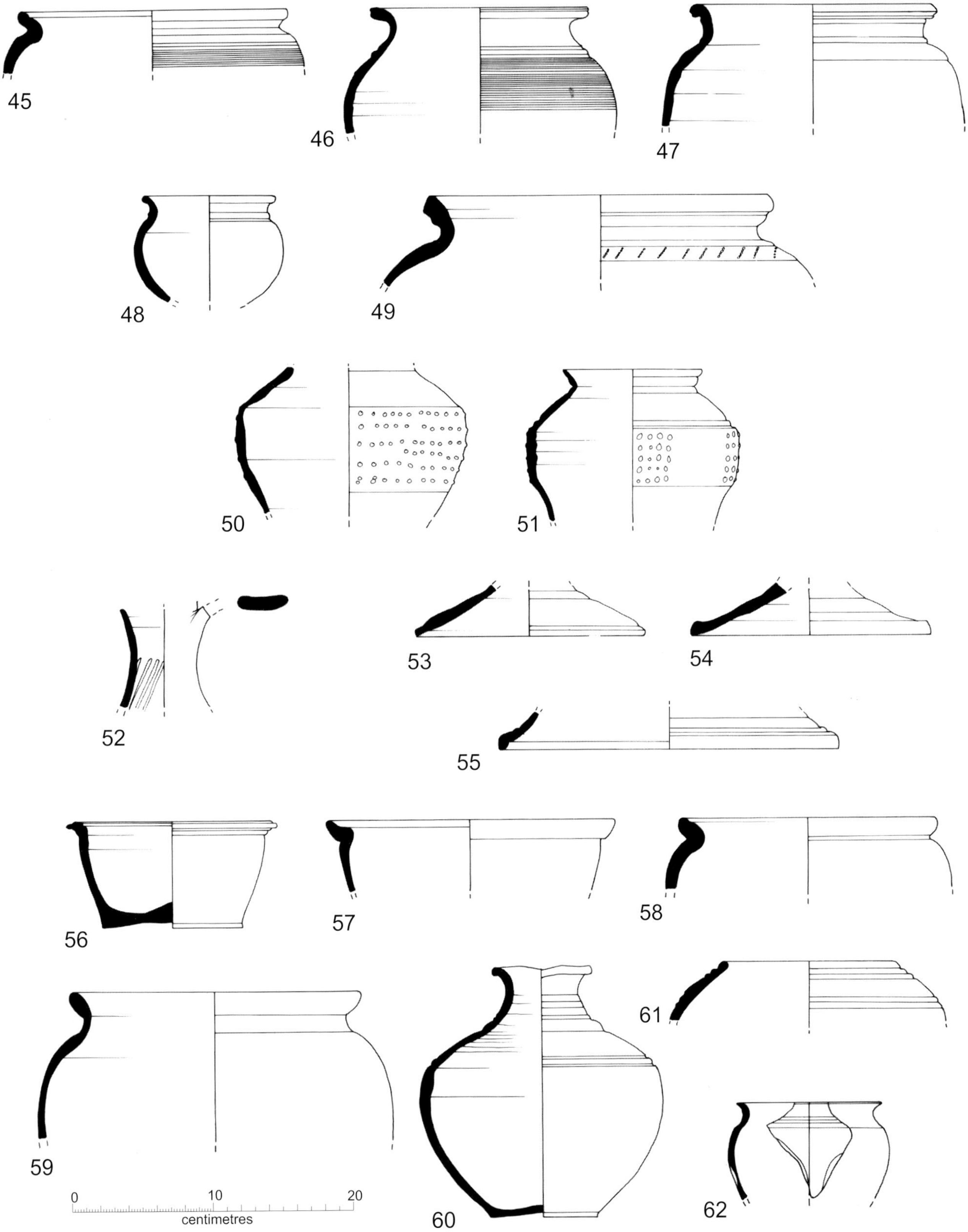

Figure 3.33 *(cont.).*

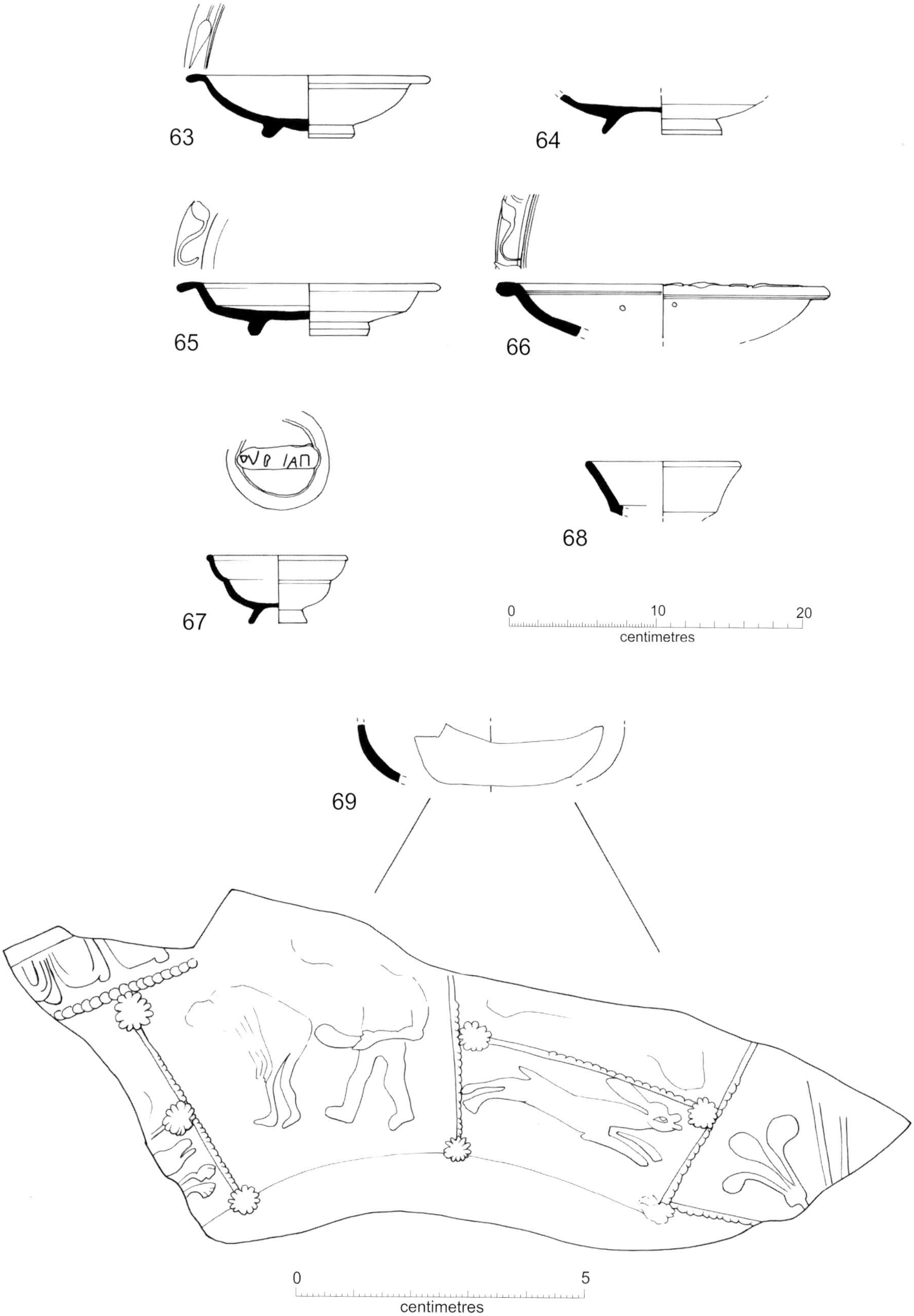

Figure 3.33 *(cont.).*

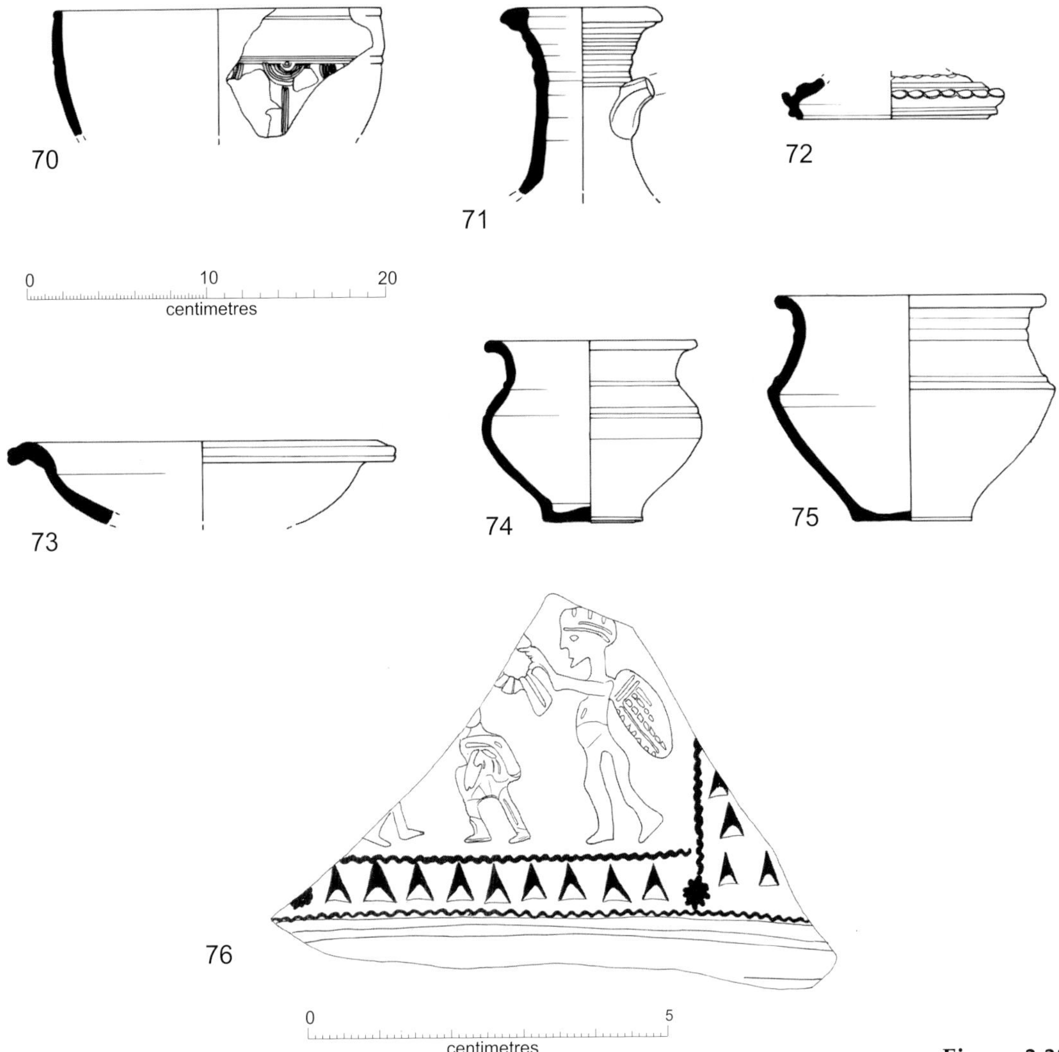

Figure 3.33 *(cont.).*

resources to sustain its own fineware industry. From that time onwards, Roman Cambridge would be almost wholly reliant for its finewares on the Nene Valley and other production sites, such as Oxfordshire and Much Hadham. Almost to underscore the point, the only unequivocal Nene Valley colour-coated product, a scale-decorated folded beaker sherd, came from a slumping level at the top of the related F.6.

Regionally traded coarse and 'specialist' wares include products of the Verulamium Region potteries south of St Albans. These potteries appear to have supplied Roman Cambridge with flagons (principally ring-necked types), and also with reeded-rimmed bowls, and 'figure 7'-rimmed jars. It was certainly a supplier of mortaria as well, although the vessels from F.1/2 are not from here but rather from an Upper Nene Valley source, and possibly also the Mancetter Hartshill area, to which there was emigration from Brockley Hill by the turn of the second century AD.

Other wares and production sites are largely unrepresented. Essex products, for example, make an unexpectedly poor showing, with Colchester unrepresented (either mortaria, colour-coats or products that might be assigned there on stylistic grounds), and there was a general lack (but not a complete absence) in this feature of shell-tempered products. During this period the Harrold (Beds.) production centre and those of the Nene Valley were certainly manufacturing shell-gritted pottery and the products of the former industry, at least, are found elsewhere in Cambridge. This lack may be because of the unusual preponderance of locally manufactured reduced wares. These are much in evidence, forming the majority of the pottery types and forms present in F.1/2. These are difficult to differentiate on fabric grounds and are perhaps best left unclassified for the present time. The forms are all paralleled in the typology of the Horningsea kilns recently examined by Jeremy Evans, and there is evidence as well of more local production. These indicate that the principal stylistic influence is in the southeastern wheel-thrown tradition current in Essex and Kent.[10]

Specialist Wares and Material of Intrinsic Interest

During the spot-dating, pottery of intrinsic interest from contexts that did not themselves merit further attention was found; this material is presented by fabric below.

London Wares (Going 1987: Fabric 30) – Flavian–Trajanic or later. Found in various sites at Cambridge, also more commonly at Godmanchester (cf. discussion of these wares in F.1/2).

Figure 3.33.70: Bowl in a fine, slightly micaceous reduced ware with combed ovolos from which vertical-combed zones descend.

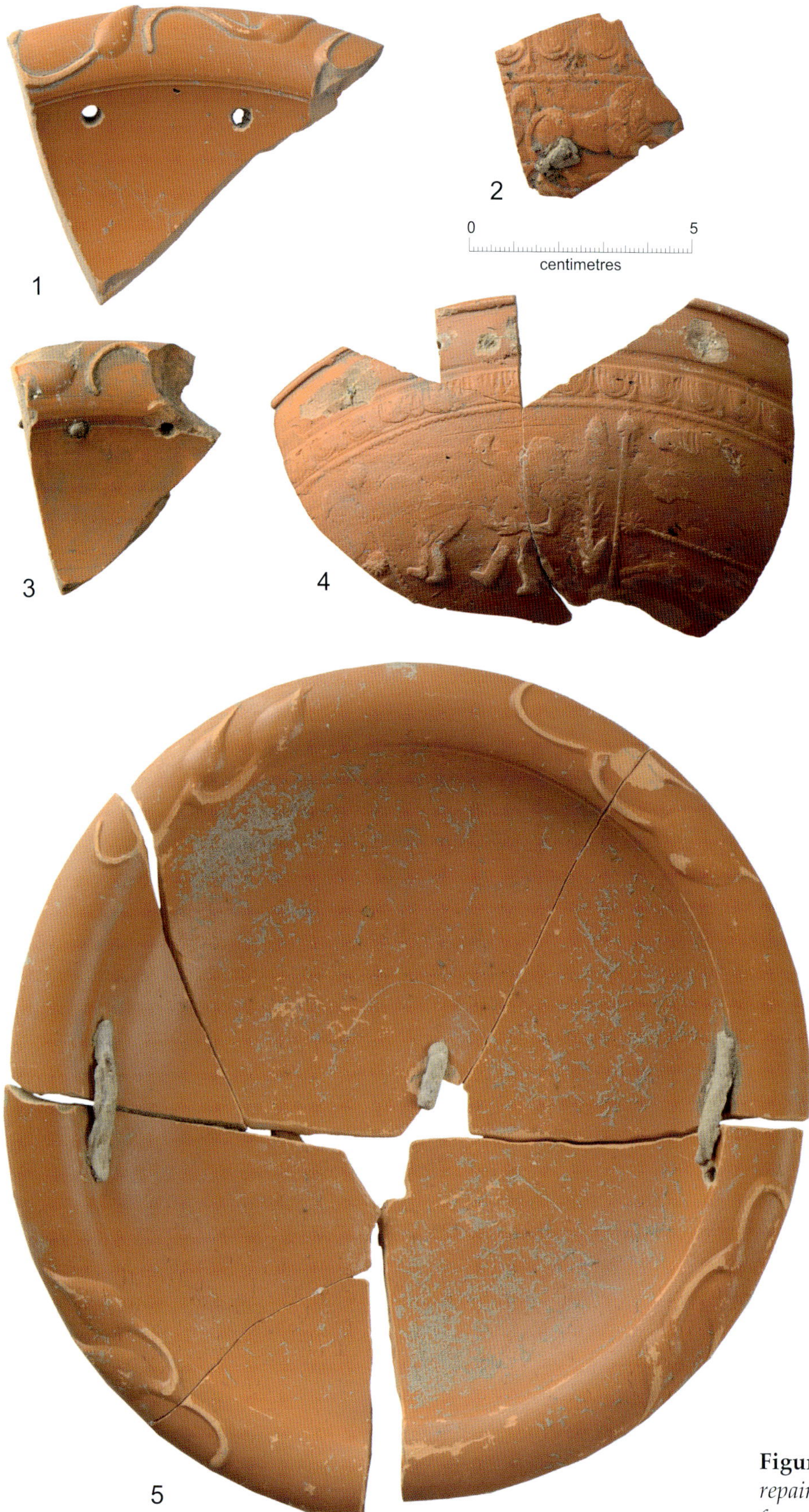

Figure 3.34. *Staple-repaired samian from F.1/2.*

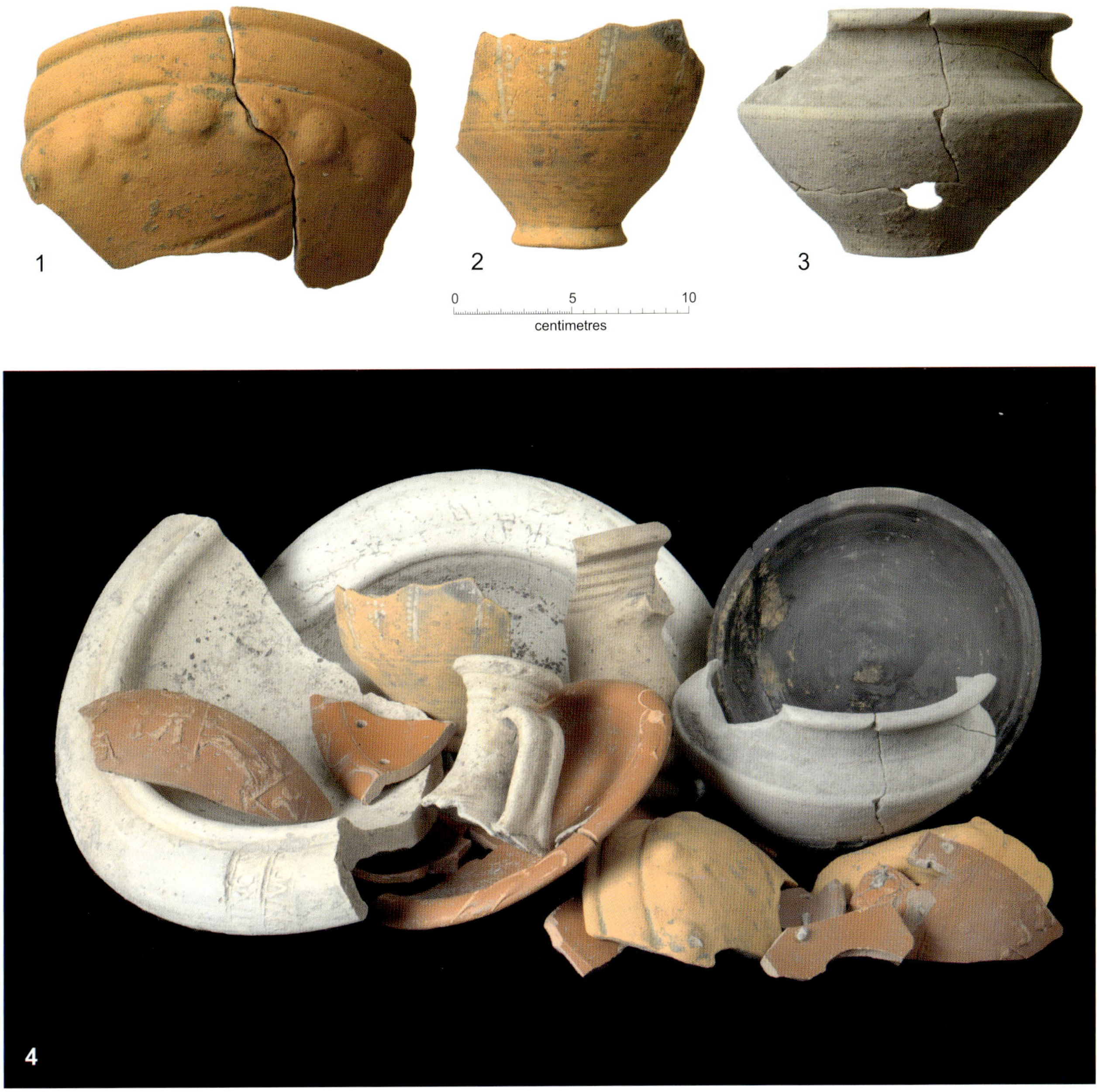

Figure 3.35. *The Feature 1/2 pottery assemblage, individual vessel and 'ensemble' photographs.*

Verulamium Region Wares (Going 1987: Fabric 27) – Products of this production centre are present in Cambridge, though in small quantities, from the Flavian period to the later Antonine era (for a discussion of the fabric, see under F.1/2, above).

Figure 3.33.71: Large ring-necked flagon, later Hadrianic or Antonine in date.

Romanizing Grey Wares (Going 1987: Fabrics 39 & 45) – This fabric grouping comprises a basic style consisting of jars and open forms fired in a predominantly reducing atmosphere. Surfaces are grey black to black, margins pinkish grey to brownish grey, and the core may be greyish brown. The fabric is basically in vogue in the first to early second centuries AD, before giving way for the most part to grey wares. The majority of coarsewares from Cambridge during the first to early second centuries AD are in fabrics of this group.

Nene Valley Mortaria (Going 1987: Fabric 27) – Mortaria are present on the site from probably the later first to early second century AD, when products appear to have been traded from the Nene Valley. Later products from sources in the Lower Nene are rare, like other later Roman wares, but the fabric is present.

Late Nene Valley Colour-coats – Rare on the site, but a definite presence in some later Roman contexts (e.g. F.88, fourth century AD). Forms encountered are mainly either dishes and bowls, or flagons or drinking vessels.

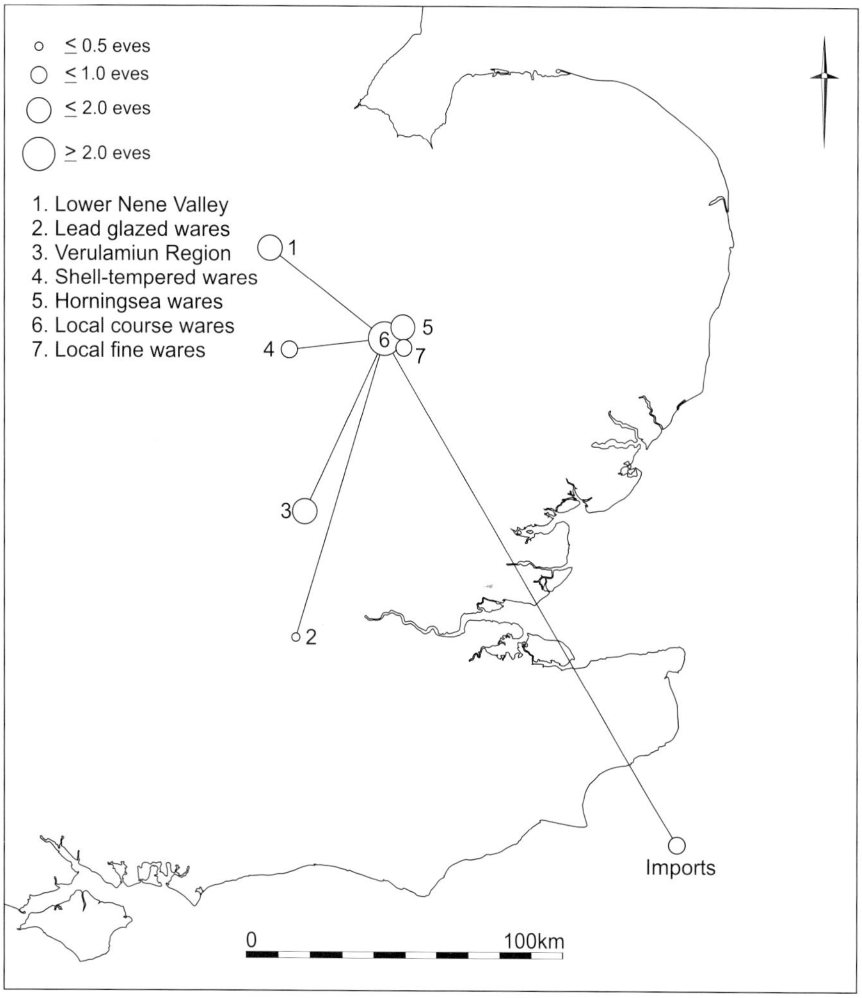

Figure 3.36. *Roman Cambridge, Antonine-period pottery supply based upon F.1/2 assemblage.*

Horningsea Ware (J. Evans 1991) – Products of the Horningsea potteries were certainly present in some quantities on the site, but the bulk of the products, being of reduced wares, are largely inseparable from the mass of the recovered reduced wares. The most obvious products stylistically are the storage jars, which are distinctively decorated and were traded over some distance from the site. Storage jars were noted from F.22, F.7 (later third century AD); F.91 (first/second centuries AD); Trench J ([052]) and F.176.

Amphorae (Peacock & Williams 1986) – Amphorae were not well-represented on the site as a whole, and the entire amphora assemblage totals much less than 10 per cent by weight. This is very much in keeping with the general pattern seen away from the more important settlements and route centres, such as London and Colchester, where the range found is comparatively wide. The bulk of the sherds found at New Hall were fragments of Dressel 20, the classic olive oil-bearing amphora from the Guadalquivir region of Baetica in Southern Spain (Peacock & Williams 1986, 136–41). There were some sherds of wine amphorae – probably Gallic vessels such as Gauloise 5 – but the quantities present were negligible. No *dipinti* or other marks were observed, and none of the sherds warranted illustration.

Buff Ware – Sherds from an unusual stamped bowl form. The stamp resembles an 'ovolo' employed on its side. The fabric is similar to a vessel from Sandy, Bedfordshire (unpublished), which was also stamped, and with an ovolo motif seen at Brixworth (Woods 1972). There are also passing similarities with 'Parisian' stamped wares (see Elsdon 1982; cf. a stamped bowl parallel from Great Dunmow: Going & Ford 1988, fig. 55.20). Rodwell's 1978 survey of Early Roman stamped wares does not deal with these products.

Lead Glazed Ware (Arthur 1978) – Not common in Cambridge and, when recovered, often employed as grave goods (e.g. Girton: Hollingworth & O'Reilly 1925). Lead glazed wares are characteristically later first-century AD in date. Occurring in F.151, possibly same vessel as in F.1/2.

Provincial Colour-coats (Howe *et al.* 1980) – Not common here for chronological reasons, it includes:

1) Base of a restricted foot beaker, probably folded (cf. Howe *et al.* 1980, fig. 4.42); F.77, *c.* AD 235+.
2) Two body sherds of a ?single folded-scale decorated beaker (cf. *ibid.*, figs. 4.38–9); F.6.
3) Rim of either a plain-rimmed bag-shaped beaker (cf. *ibid.*, fig. 4.34) or a folded beaker (e.g. fig. 4.43); F.86, *c.* AD 200+.

Grey Ware (Going 1987: Fabric 47) – Reduced wares constitute the majority of coarsewares from Roman Cambridge with the exception of the Romanizing types in the first century AD. Most of the forms represented in the fabric are entirely characteristic of the region and are well-represented; for example, in F.1/2 (forms noted there are not discussed here).

Figure 3.33.72: Frilled rim of a narrow-necked jar (cf. Teversham; Pullinger & White 1991, 74–5, no. 86); F.143, *c.* AD 200+.

Hadham Red Wares (Going 1987: Fabric 4) – Hadham wares were supplied to the town in some quantities from the middle of the third century AD onwards, occurring at Arbury, at Teversham (Pullinger & White 1991) and elsewhere. Both fabrics (the oxidized and the reduced) were found. Vessels in each are usually slipped when exported over any distance. They are prolifically common at Wimpole Lodge (Lucas 1995), which lies on the principal northern trade route of the industry. The forms represented are typical products of the industry; the most common vessel class seems to be the flagon.

1) Closed form, probably a flagon; later third century AD (F.248, North Field quarry pit).
2) Neck of a flagon (F.17); third century AD onwards.
3) Base of a flagon (F.7); later fourth century AD.

Rhenish Ware – Bowl sherd (for the form, see Greene 1978, fig. 2.3.7) from F.88; fourth century AD in date.

Harston Obelisk Kilns Wares (Pullinger & Young 1981) – The Harston kilns are enigmatic, as they were clearly more extensive than realized at the time of their excavation (see *addendum* to Pullinger & Young 1981). Harston products are clearly found at Cambridge and, perhaps, Great Chesterford as well.

Figure 3.33.73: Rim and part of the bowl of a large carinated bowl (cf. Pullinger & Young 1981, fig. 13.17–19); F.248, North Field quarry pit.

Samian – The assemblage contained a minimum of 150 sherds. These were for the most part plain forms, with the decorated sherds coming from a total of less than 10 vessels. The percentage of samian wares as a total of the fabric assemblage was under 5 per cent, which puts the assemblage at the lower end of the scale (Millett 1980, 66). The bulk of the material was Central Gaulish and derived from one or more of the major production centres. There was little first-century AD material save for a couple of sherds of Dr.29 (D1–2):

Decorated Sherds

D1: SG Dr.29, Late Flavian (F.6).
D2: SG Dr.29, chip (F.123).
D3: EG Dr.37, three sherds; later second century AD? (F.218/250).
D4: CG Dr.37, small, battered sherd of an uncertain vessel form (Area I).
D5: CG Dr.37, four joining sherds; ?Hercules standing left, *etc.* (Area I, F.133, South Quarry Field sondage).
D6: x2 Dr.37, Flavian (F.1/2).
D7: Dr.37 (F.77).
D8: SG Dr.37, a body sherd, with a winged figure holding a garland (Victory) in a rectangular panel bordered by wavy lines AD 90–110 (F.30; Fig. 3.33.76).
D9: CG, a body sherd, most likely of a bowl, with a lion and ovolo as upper border of the design AD 100–120 (F.1/2; Fig. 3.34.2).
D10: SG, Dr.37, two joining body sherds, showing a phallic scene and an animal in two separate rectangular panels divided by wavy lines; ovolo as upper border of the design AD 90–110 (F.1/2; Fig. 3.33.69 & 3.34.4).

Stamped Sherds

S1: CG Dr.31R stamped DOMID[...]; Hadrianic? (F.1/2; Fig. 3.33.67).
S2: CG Dr.31, stamped CITVA'FEC; Hadrianic–Antonine? (F.1/2).
S3: CG Dr.31, terminus of illegible stamp; second century AD? (Evaluation Trench B).

The Southern 'Back-College' Road

The primary version of the road's northern ditch-line, F.220, contained only one fragment of undateable pottery. Superseded by ditch F.59, its pottery – including the rim of a Horningsea storage jar of an early type – was almost all abraded coarsewares datable to the first and second centuries AD. The ceramics from the boundary's main version, F.17, were generally abraded and worn, and mostly also date in the first and second centuries AD. There was, though, some later material: a Hadham ware flagon-top that is unlikely to pre-date the middle decades of the third century AD; no fourth-century material whatsoever occurred in these features.

The southern ditches, F.58, F.60 and F.61, yielded comparatively little useful material. From F.58 came some sherds assigned a later second-century AD date; the material from F.59 was datable, without exception, to the first to second centuries AD, as was also that from F.60. The general condition of the material was rather worn and abraded, suggesting that the features may have been filled at a rather later date; the lack of later material is, nonetheless, noteworthy.

Other Features

Of the other feature assemblages that were subsequently analysed (Table 3.4), an early date can be assigned to F.6 (from the mid first to the second century AD), whereas the other features seem to be somewhat later (roughly from the second to the third century AD); only F.7 has finewares from the mid third to the fourth century AD. The quality and quantity of samian in F.6, F.7, F.30 and F.121 is relatively poor, with none present in F.269. The high percentage of Horningsea Ware within F.1/2 also characterizes F.6, F.30 and F.269, suggesting that Horningsea pottery was the settlement's main local pottery-supply source.

The date-range of the pottery is restricted. With the bulk attributable to the first and second centuries AD, it does not allow us to compile an overview of any changes in the supply pattern to Roman Cambridge over time.[11] There was not a very substantial quantity of material of the middle first century AD, and the pottery from the site dates, for the most part, to the Flavian period or later. By way of compensation, however, F.1/2 provides us with the first substantial assemblage of Romano-British ceramics (*c.* 80 kg) to be recovered from Cambridge in over a decade. While there is some later second- or third-century AD material in that feature's uppermost levels (e.g. a folded-scale decorated beaker), this is likely to represent slumping and the deposit as a whole appears to have been dumped in some time towards the end of the second quarter of the second century AD. It gives us an overview of pottery supply to the town during the Hadrianic–Antonine period, a time when – after protracted difficulties – many ceramic industries were once more expanding production (for the background, see Going 1992).

The assemblage largely consists of reduced coarsewares. Dominating this fabric-class, which

Table 3.4. *Selected feature Roman pottery fabric frequencies.*

Fabric	Total			F.1/2			F.6			F.7			F.30			F.121			F.269		
	No.	Wt. (g)	%	No.	Wt. (g)	%	No.	Wt. (g)	%	No.	Wt. (g)	%	No.	Wt. (g)	%	No.	Wt. (g)	%	No.	Wt. (g)	%
Black burnished 2	*27*	*733*	*0.8*	6	546	0.5										21	187	6.2			
Black slipped ware	*13*	*247*	*0.4*	1	40	<0.1				1	17	0.1				11	190	3.2			
Buff ware	*3*	*8*	*0.1*	3	8	0.3															
Coarse sandy greyware	*1188*	*12,454*	*35*	279	3784	25.7	321	3152	45.2	311	2865	52	117	910	25.1	141	1637	41.5	19	106	9.6
Coarse sandy greyware (white slip)	*1*	*2*	*<0.1*							1	2	0.1									
Coarse sandy oxidized	*68*	*542*	*2*	15	128	1.4	5	53	0.7	23	111	3.8	5	67	1	20	183	5.8			
Coarse sandy oxidized (white slip)	*6*	*28*	*0.2*							2	9	0.3				4	19	1.1			
Early Roman shelly	*39*	*1037*	*1.1*							37	993	6.2	1	33	<0.1	1	11	0.3			
Fine reduced ware	*40*	*353*	*1.1*	8	142	0.7	19	122	2.7	2	6	0.3	11	83	2.3						
Fine sandy greyware	*125*	*956*	*3.7*	37	241	3.4	7	69	1	19	205	3.2	47	327	10	15	114	4.4			
Fine sandy greyware (white slip)	*3*	*23*	*0.1*							3	23	0.5									
Fine sandy oxidized	*30*	*178*	*0.9*	7	44	0.6	7	36	1	7	24	1.2	3	34	0.6	1	29	0.3	5	11	2.5
Unsourced colour-coated ware	*1*	*8*	*<0.1*				1	8	0.1												
Flinty greyware	*158*	*3263*	*4.6*	67	1392	6.2	53	1197	7.5	14	327	2.3	22	162	4.7	2	185	0.6			
Hadham red-slipped	*2*	*29*	*<0.1*							2	29	0.3									
Horningsea ware	*1236*	*26,465*	*36.4*	447	12,135	41.3	218	4150	30.6	121	2637	20.2	211	4933	45.3	85	1592	25	154	1018	78.2
Nene Valley coloured coated ware	*10*	*32*	*0.3*	1	2	<0.1	3	3	0.4	4	23	0.7				2	4	0.6			
Nene Valley greyware	*3*	*41*	*0.1*							2	26	0.3				1	15	0.3			
Nene Valley whiteware	*12*	*243*	*0.3*							7	176	1.1				5	67	1.4			
Oxford red-slipped	*1*	*5*	*<0.1*							1	5	0.1									
Reduced local kiln ware	*256*	*2562*	*7.5*	144	1521	13.3	50	576	7	8	66	1.4	34	230	7.3	4	59	1.2	16	110	8.1
Samian ware	*67*	*1033*	*2*	36	722	3.3	8	168	1.1	12	63	2	9	48	1.9	2	32	0.6			
Late Roman	*1*	*10*	*0.03*							1	10	0.1									
South-east glazed ware	*2*	*63*	*<0.1*	2	63	0.2															
Whiteware	*106*	*1595*	*3.2*	31	465	2.9	19	392	2.7	20	124	3.3	6	89	1.3	27	496	7.9	3	29	1.5
Total	*3398*	*51,910*	*100*	*1084*	*21,233*	*99.8*	*711*	*9926*	*100*	*598*	*7741*	*99.5*	*466*	*6916*	*99.5*	*340*	*4745*	*100.4*	*197*	*1274*	*99.9*

is ubiquitous in southeastern Britain, are products of local industries, with the Horningsea potteries strongly represented: an unsurprising showing in view of their proximity. As mentioned, the site also produced evidence of more local manufacture, for a quantity of reduced wares was found in F.1/2 which, if not plainly 'seconds', clearly represents some kind of production-waste from a kiln very close by.

The remainder of the assemblage was, for the most part, quite unexceptional and its supply pattern is unsurprising considering its geographical position. That said, there were some unexpected elements: for example, in the first or early second centuries AD there was a general lack of wares from the kilns at Cherry Hinton (J. Evans 1990). Generally, there was an impression that supply to Cambridge was met locally, with wares emanating from more distant centres, such as Colchester, being all but absent. This is not the case at Chelmsford, for example (Going 1987, Ceramic Periods 2–3), where a substantially wider range of fabrics was found. But this town lay on the principal road linking Colchester – Britain's premier Roman town – and the Province's emerging capital at London, so a wide range of fabrics is hardly surprising. Pottery from Hertfordshire was more evident at New Hall, with the presence of flagons, bowls and mortaria from the Verulamium Region potteries. There appeared to be fewer mortaria in the latter wares than other vessel classes, perhaps reflecting the site's chronology and the emerging production sites at Mancetter Hartshill and the Nene Valley that appear to have been manufacturing mortaria from the very early second century AD.

As noted, there is very little evidence of Roman pottery that could be dated to after *c.* AD 200. The flange-rimmed bowl (the Cam f. 305), for example, which appears to have originated after *c.* AD 225 and indicates later Roman activity, is barely present on the site, either in reduced wares or in Nene Valley colour-coat.

What later Roman pottery there is has been dated largely on fabric grounds. Fabrics include Hadham oxidized red wares, evident throughout East Anglia from the later third century AD onwards (and in particular during the fourth century AD), as well as late shell-tempered pottery. Nene Valley thick white wares are also evident in the latter part of the third and fourth centuries AD. Shell-tempered pottery of late type (Sanders 1973; Brown 1994) came from F.104/5 and F.64; no sherds of Oxfordshire wares were noted.

Metalwork (Alison Dickens)

Eleven copper alloy objects were recovered, all probably dating to the Roman period:

<955> F.34 – Small copper sheet, 19 × 14 × 1 mm.

<094> F.38 – Two pieces:
(i) broken doubled over? piece, almost like thick wire; end twisted into a 'knot' and probably the head of a pin; ?Roman.
(ii) small piece of a flat sheet with a slight lip, 12 × 9 × 1 mm.

<1066> F.38 – Three pieces of a pin/needle (total length, 52 mm); date unknown.

<174> F.30 – Segment of broken pin, 25 × 2 mm; date unknown.

<158> F.1/2 – Decorated object, 36 × 2.5 mm, probably a hair pin (cf. Crummy 1983, fig. 27); Roman.

<152> F.1/2 – Narrow strip (38 mm long, 2 mm wide broadening to 4 mm at one end; 1 mm thick), with a longitudinal groove up the centre; possibly the handle of a toiletry item; Roman.

<159> F.1/2 – Small 'tear-shaped' piece, 18 × 7 mm; possibly a small spatula end or the head of a pin (see Crummy 1983, fig. 31.503 for decorated example); Roman.

<156> F.1/2 – Pierced piece, 54 × 16 × 1.5 mm (Fig. 3.37.1); probably a fragment of an open-work mount, which served as part of a belt buckle. These are generally considered to have a military association, although civilian versions have been recorded in this country (cf. Hinchcliffe & Sparey Green 1985, 209). A late second–early third century AD date is suggested by the Oldenstein corpus (1976); similar pieces are shown in Oldenstein, Tafel 64, 816–20.

<177> F.229 – Finger-ring, having a broad top with a recess possibly for a glass or enamel setting, although no traces survive. The piece is decorated with engraved lines running from the top almost to the base, and around the top itself. The ring appears to have either been mended or reduced in size, as there is a small overlap towards the base which has been soldered. Roman.

<180> F.1/2 – Section, probably of a hair pin, 56 mm long; Roman.

Only three Roman coins were recovered:

<099> F.202 – NUMMUS (Æ4), House of Constantine, AD 318–24
Obverse: bust facing to left, legend includes CONSTAN…, rest illegible.
Reverse: Garland or laurel wreath, CAESARVMN O STROR-XXI

Top of F.104 – Allectus, AD 293–6
Obverse: IMP.C.ALLECTUS P.F AVG
Reverse: VIRTVS AVE. (galley) IN EX QC
RIC 128/SEAR 3596

Spoil F.112 – Antonius Pius, AD 138–61
Obverse: ANTONINIVS AVG.PIUS…
Reverse: Possibly Equity holding scales.

Most of the ironwork fragments recovered from the excavation were nails (91 of 99); otherwise, just various pin/wire lengths and small rings were recovered. The nails were assessed against the head-shape groupings used by Mills at Poundbury (1993, 115–17). Most were flat-headed and just three of these were large, having diameters greater than 20 mm; five diamond-head examples were present and there were 11 of 'T'-shape-type.

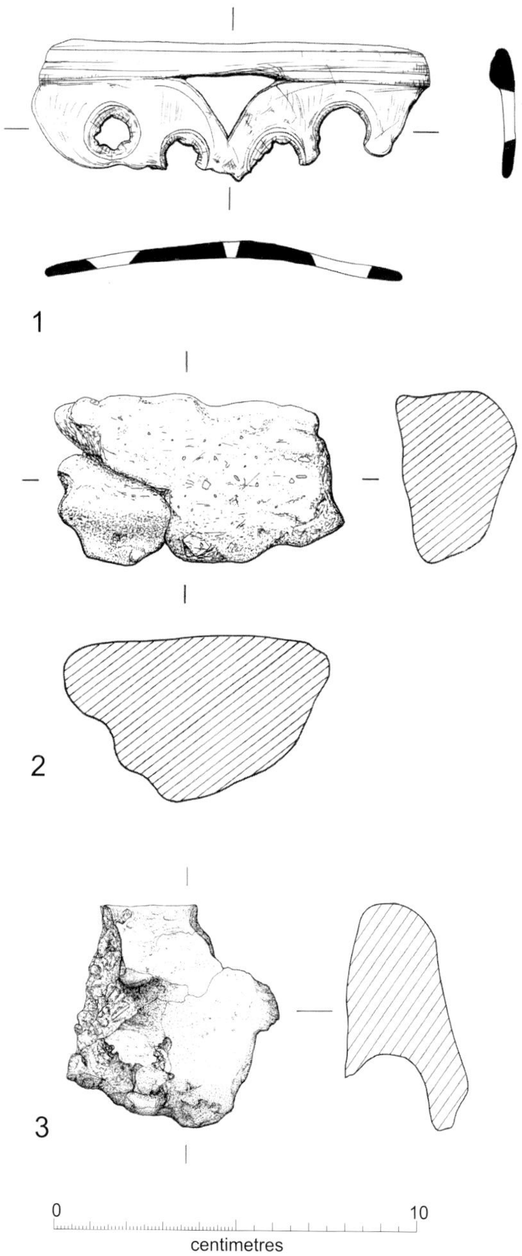

Figure 3.37. *Selected small finds (all F.1/2): 1) copper alloy belt buckle; 2) fired clay kiln furniture; 3) hearth- or furnace-lining fragment.*

Glass (Alison Dickens)
Sixteen pieces of glass were recovered from the excavation. Of these, seven were Post-Medieval and nine probably Roman. All the latter pieces, with one exception – F.1 (<2004>) – are from mould-blown vessels which tend to be the most common glass finds on sites of Roman date (Vose 1980, 46). The <2004> handle was also most probably attached to a mould-blown vessel, from which it has broken. The fragments would have been part of jars, jugs and short-necked bottles. Vose (*ibid.*) suggests a first and second century AD date for vessels of this type.

<2001> *F.1/2* – 40 × 30 × 2 mm. Clear pale blue from vessel; mould-blown, shiny interior surface, matt outer. Part of strap handle and small part of body at point of join. Bubbles in both, but more in the handle.

<2004> *F.1/2* – 25 × 18 × 7 mm. Mid green translucent, strap handle formed as two ribs. Bubbles within elongated by process of pulling-out handle.

<157> *F.1/2* – 20 × 15 × 3 mm. Clear pale green with occasional bubbles; edge folded to form rim. Part of vessel, possibly a bowl; possibly of Post-Medieval attribution (?intrusive).

<2002> *F.6* – 21 × 17 × 1 mm. Clear pale greeny blue, occasional bubbles, from vessel; mould-blown, shiny interior surface, matt outer. Slight decorative swelling, not as pronounced as in <2000i>.

<2005> *F.6* – 25 × 20 × 3 mm. Clear amber from vessel, no bubbles; mould-blown, shiny interior surface, matt outer. Fine striations visible on outer surface.

<1099> *F.7* – 22 × 20 × 1.5 mm. Clear pale greeny blue, from vessel; mould-blown, shiny interior surface, matt outer. Series of fine undulating lines on outer surface may be integral pattern or post-depositional damage.

<2003> *F.7* – 14 × 7 × 1 mm. Clear deep amber, fine bubbles, from vessel; mould-blown, shiny interior surface, slightly matt outer.

<2000> *F.168*
(i) 21 × 20 × 1 mm. Clear pale green, occasional bubbles, from vessel; mould-blown, shiny interior surface, matt outer, small decorative ridge.
(ii) 19 × 10 × 2 mm. Clear pale green, slightly curved from vessel; mould-blown, shiny interior surface, matt outer.

Building Materials – Tile, Fired Clay and Building Stone
Given the overall quantity of Roman finds recovered, the paucity of the site's associated building materials is remarkable. Only seven pieces of unequivocal Roman ceramic building material were recovered, including three fragments of *pedalis* brick (F.1, F.17 & F.110) and two *tegulae* fragments (F.1/2 & F.287 *et al.*), as well as individual *imbrex* and box-tile pieces (both from F.1/2). Beyond this, a handful of 'probable' Roman fragments were found in features of that date (e.g. F.1/2 & F.110) and, residually, in later contexts (e.g. F.101 & F.11). Similarly, only two pieces of mortar were recovered, one having evidence of moulding (F.221) and the other with a rectangular impression in one face (F.7); a single piece of tessera occurred in the fill of F.269.

Although there were great quantities of small to medium river cobbles (many scorched and most probably deriving from later prehistoric contexts), no obvious building stone was present, aside from a rough-dressed rectangular sandstone block (10+ × 10.3 × 6 cm) in F.137.

Some 50 fragments of burnt/fired clay were recovered from Roman contexts (see Austin in Evans 1996, App. 17). Having variously grog, quartz and organic temper, the vast majority of these are likely to have been daub. Two carried traces of mortar/plaster (both F.1/2) and another two had wattle impressions (F.1/2 & F.211). Otherwise, intensively burnt pieces may derive from hearth surfaces (F.1/2 [× 3], F.31 & F.50) and another two may have been from loomweights (F.1/2 & F.40). In addition, a moulded and flattened piece from F.1/2, rendered in a buff orange grog-tempered fabric, appears to have been a piece of kiln furniture (Fig. 3.37.2).

Worked Stone

As reported by Austin (Evans 1996, App. 18; with stone identifications by S. Laurie of the Sedgwick Museum, Cambridge), two worked stone fragments were recovered from the F.20 Iron Age ditch. Both Derbyshire sandstones, one is a possible whetstone (<082>) and, the other, smoothed and chamfered with rounded corners, appears to have been for polishing (<101>).

Four worked pieces were derived from Roman contexts. Three are sandstones, of which one is a definite whetstone (F.1/2, <576>) and another possibly served the same function (from the Eastern Quarry Sondage, <395>). The third sandstone piece, a smoothed oval handle-pebble, appears to have been used as a rubber (F.221, <728>). Worked from Derbyshire Millstone Grit, only one rotary quern fragment was recovered, which has an estimated original diameter of *c.* 40 cm (F.1/2, <1149>). Also, presumably of residual status and probably prehistoric, a small fragment of saddle quern was recovered from F.1/2.

Industrial Waste

As identified by Dr C.A. Shell, four pieces of iron slag were recovered from Roman features (F.30 [× 2], F.46 & F.235), and a piece of fused forging clinker from F.1/2. In addition, three variously fused and/or vitrified hearth- or furnace-lining fragments were also found (F.1/2, F.50 & F.196; Fig. 3.37.3). All this material probably related to iron production/working; rendered in a fine sandy grey fabric, a small piece from either a mould or crucible was also recovered from F.1/2.

Environmental and Economic Data

Although, due to financial constraints, none of the specialist reports within this section were taken to the level of full analysis, the inclusion of these detailed assessment studies is warranted on the grounds that little archaeological science was ever undertaken for Alexander's (*et al.*) Cambridge sites (*RCAM*). These reports thus have intrinsic site-specific value (and clearly resonate in relationship to the Vicar's Farm and Marion Close results; see below), and also go some way to reflect on the area's broader economy and environment. While the faunal assemblage is certainly substantial, the site's bulk environmental sampling would now be seen as insufficient; in some compensation, though, the breadth of its environmental programme was considerable.

Animal Bone (Eftychia Yannouli)

The faunal material consisted of more than 4100 fragments. Of these, 2959 animal bones were identified to species or size-class and these constitute the 'recordable' sample (skeletal parts which were broken into two or more fragments during excavation were treated as one specimen). An additional 1212 specimens were counted, but were too small to be analytically useful; these are mostly slivers and splinters and constitute the non-identifiable material (NONID).

The bones were identified in the Archaeozoology Laboratory of the Department of Archaeology in Cambridge. No detailed analysis was undertaken, but the material was recorded in sufficient detail to enable comparisons at a general level. Quantification was carried out by the NISP (Number of Identified Specimens) and MNI (Minimum Number of Individuals) method; 'diagnostic zones' were also recorded, allowing greater precision in quantification.

Bone preservation was generally good and marks – made by humans or animals – were fairly easy to distinguish. Dog gnawing has been recorded on some specimens but is rather uncommon in the pre-Roman specimens.

The range of species present on the site is modest (Table 3.5). Domestic animals are most in evidence and cattle have contributed more than half of the specimens recorded by species. Horse occurs in Roman deposits only, as does frog and bird (?fowl). Wild animals appear in Bronze Age contexts only and are represented by the probable wolf and Roe deer. The Roman assemblage contains an unusually small number of domestic fowl or bird bones.

Bronze Age

Two features, F.175 (pit/posthole cut) and F.163 (ditch), are definitely dated to the Bronze Age. They contained a total of 96 specimens, only two of which were found in F.175.

Cattle are more common than any other domestic mammal, both by NISP and MNI. They account for *c.* 76 per cent of the specimens identified by species and are represented by the greatest variety of skeletal parts. In the ditch there was found the skull of a mature beast (>4 years), probably male, including the horncores and maxillae. Several other specimens from the same context (the axis vertebra, right mandible, scapula-humerus-radius, pelvis-femur, and a few vertebrae) indicated a similar age group and were probably part of the same carcass. Apart from this animal, four other individuals have been identified in the sample: 1–4 months, 6–7 months, <11 months/2 years and >11 months/2 years.

Sheep/goats, pigs and dogs are represented by sporadic finds. Dental evidence suggests the presence of two ovicaprids (6–12 mths and 3–4 yrs of age; the youngest one was positively identified as sheep), a male pig (11–19 mths) and a young dog (6–7 mths). Both the pig and dog are represented by mandibles only.

Apart from the bones of domestic food mammals, two more species have been identified: Roe deer and the right scapula from

Table 3.5. *Distribution of the faunal material by species and phase (bone identified by size alone is excluded; *incl. sheep skeleton, F.84).*

Species	Bronze Age		Iron Age		Roman		Total	
	NISP	MNI	NISP	MNI	NISP	MNI	NISP	MNI
Cow	47	6	57	8	391	37	495	51
Horse	-	-	-	-	88	16	88	16
Sheep/Goat	5	2	12 (84)*	4	252	46	269 (353)*	52
Pig	3	1	6	3	34	14	43	18
Dog	2	1	2	1	38	13	42	15
Fowl	-	-	1	1	2	2	3	3
Bird	-	-	-	-	6	5	6	5
Wolf(?)	1	1	-	-	-	-	1	1
Roe deer	1	1	-	-	-	-	1	1
Frog	-	-	-	-	2	1	2	1
Total NISP	*59*	*12*	*78 (150)**	*17*	*813*	*134*	*950 (1034)**	*163*

what is probably a wolf. These are the only wild species recovered from the total sample. The Roe deer bone is a proximal metatarsal (fused) and it came from the same context as the wolf scapula.

Iron Age
The 'Iron Age' assemblage is derived from six features from Area II and totals 194 animal bones.[12] Most of the material (*c.* 55%) was excavated from a *c.* 12.5 m section of a ditch, F.20, at the southern end of the site. Feature 84, a pit just off of the ditch's butt-end, contained the skeleton of a 4–6-year-old sheep comprising the rib case, most vertebrae, the scapulae, humeri and left mandible. One of the ribs had been fractured at an earlier stage of the animal's life but was subsequently healed. Other ovicaprid bones were found in F.20 and F.211. These probably belonged to three individuals, of which two could be aged (1–2 and >3 years).

As in the Bronze Age, cattle remains predominate. Feature 20 contained more than half of the cattle bones from this period (MNI=6), a significant proportion of which were mandibles at various stages of dental eruption and wear. One mandible showed erupting d_2 and was probably foetal; the remaining individuals were all older than 2–2½ years. Skeletal parts from younger animals were found only in other contexts (F.63 & F.211). It is not possible to ascertain whether this segregation of cattle bones by age was deliberate. The oldest animal in the collection (>5 months) showed pathology. The tooth row was obliquely placed in relation to the dental axis and both the P_4 and P_2 were missing (ante-mortem tooth-loss).

The other species represented in the Iron Age are pig, dog and fowl. The first two are represented in F.20 only by one (adult) and three (11–19 months, 23–31 months and >30–34 months) individuals respectively. The chicken bone, from F.211, is the distal part of the metatarsal.

Roman
The overwhelming majority of the faunal specimens were excavated from features of Roman date. Ditches and pits of various sizes, shapes and functions were recovered in all three areas and these are considered according to six sub-groups/distinct activity loci (Table 3.6).

In general, the Roman remains comprise the usual range of domestic species, including horse, and sporadic finds of domestic fowl, unidentified birds, and two frog bones. There is no osteological evidence for exploitation of wild species. Cattle and ovicaprids are by far the most frequent species, with 80 per cent and 65 per cent of the NISP and MNI of the domestic sample respectively (Table 3.6). Horse is the third most important species with 88 specimens from 16 individuals (from the northern ditch of Area II, the Northwest Enclosure Complex and general features). Pigs (NISP=34; MNI=14) and dogs (NISP=38; MNI=13) are the least frequent domestic mammals.

Sub-groups 1 and 2 - The first sub-group corresponds to a system of road-related ditches in the north and south of the site. The northern Area III ditches contained more bone, although the size of the sample involved is in both cases small (Table 3.7). Most of the identified individuals were adult or mature animals and none of the bones from this sub-group showed unfused epiphyses or deciduous dentition. Moreover, many of the specimens were articulated joints, probably dumped into the ditches as meal leftovers. Horse was only present in the north area (III). The horse finds belong to one individual and it seems that they represent a single disposal episode. Comparison of the species distribution between the northern and southern ditches shows a clear association of the former with horse and of the latter with cattle. Sub-group 2 yielded a very modest collection of cattle and pig bones. One cattle horncore from F.33 had cut marks near the base and was possibly chopped off the skull.

Sub-group 3 - This sub-group is represented by Enclosure B's ditches F.246 and F.247, the former containing twice as many specimens as the latter. Both ditches present the same (limited) range of species: cattle 78 per cent, sheep/goat 9 per cent and 13 per cent pig (NISP; N = 45). With the exception of a newborn calf and two juvenile pigs, all the animals identified were killed when mature or old. The calf is represented by the left mandible containing the complete deciduous dentition; the second premolar was half erupted while the other

Table 3.6. *Size of faunal sample for each Roman sub-group.*

Sub-group	Description	NISP	%
1	Southern Roadway Ditches (Area II)	85	5.83
2	Area III Ditch-system	19	1.31
3	Enclosure B (Areas I)	45	3.09
4	F.30 (Area III)	58	3.98
5	Northwest Enclosure Complex (C; Area I)	658	45.16
6	General Features	592	40.63
	Total	*1457*	*100*

Table 3.7. *Quantification of faunal remains by NISP and MNI in Roman features from Areas II and III (Sub-groups 1 & 2). KEY Bt=Cattle* (Bos taurus)*; Ec=Horse* (Equus caballus)*; OC=Sheep/goat* (Ovis/Capra)*; Su=Pig* (Sus scrofa)*; Cf=Dog* (Canis familiaris)*; Ml=Mammal large (cow size); Mm=Mammal medium (sheep size); Ms=Mammal small (dog size;* F.179 & F.182 contain only NONID material).*

	Area II Sub-group 1											**Area III Sub-group 2**		
	Road-side ditches (north)							**Road-side ditches** (south)				**Group 1 Features**		
	F.17						**F.59**	**Fs 58, 60 & 61**				**Fs 33, 174,** (179, 182)*		
	Bt	**Ec**	**OC**	**Cf**	**Ml**	**Mm**	**Bt**	**Bt**	**OC**	**Ml**	**Ms**	**Bt**	**Su**	**Ml**
Skull														
Skull frag.	-	-	1	-	1	-	-	-	-	-	-	-	-	-
Horncore	-	-	-	-	-	-	-	-	-	-	-	1	-	-
Maxilla	-	-	-	2	-	-	-	-	-	-	-	-	-	-
Mandible	-	-	2	2	-	-	-	-	-	-	-	-	-	-
Sub-total 1	-	-	*3*	*4*	*1*	-	-	-	-	-	-	*1*	-	-
Fore Limb														
Humerus sh.	-	-	-	-	-	-	-	-	-	-	-	1	-	-
Humerus d.	-	2	-	-	-	-	-	-	1	-	-	-	-	-
Radius wh.	-	-	-	-	-	-	-	1	-			-	-	-
Radius p.	-	-	-	-	-	-	-	1	-	-	-	1	-	-
Radius sh.	-	-	1	-	-	-	-	-	-	-	-	-	-	-
Radius d.	-	1	-	-	-	-	-	-	-	-	-	-	-	-
Ulna	-	-	-	-	-	-	-	1	-	-	-	-	-	-
Metacarpal wh.	-	-	-	1	-	-	-	-	-	-	-	-	-	-
Metacarpal p.	1	-	-	-	-	-	-	-	-	-	-	-	-	-
Metacarpal sh.	-	-	1	-	-	-	-	-	-	-	-	-	-	-
Metacarpal d.	-	-	-	-	-	-	1	-	-	-	-	-	-	-
Sub-total 2	*1*	*3*	*2*	*1*	-	-	*1*	*3*	*1*	-	-	*2*	-	-
Hind Limb														
Pelvis	-	-	1	1	-	-	-	-	-	-	-	-	-	-
Femur p.	-	1	-	-	-	-	-	-	-	-	-	-	-	-
Tibia p.	-	-	-	-	-	-	-	1	-	-	-	-	-	-
Tibia shaft	1	-	-	-	1	-	-	-	-	-	-	-	-	-
Metatarsal wh.	-	1	1	-	-	-	-	-	-	-	-	-	-	-
Metatarsal sh.	-	-	1	-	-	-	-	-	-	-	-	-	-	-
Sub-total 3	*1*	*2*	*3*	*1*	*1*	-	-	*1*	-	-	-	-	-	-
Tooth/upper	1	1	-	-	-	-	-	-	-	-	-	-	-	-
Tooth/lower	-	5	-	-	-	-	1	-	-	-	-	1	2	-
Rib	-	-	-	-	14	3	1	-	-	-	1	-	-	9
Vertebra	-	6	-	1	17	-	1	-	-	-	-	-	-	4
Long bone	-	-	-	-	1	-	-	-	-	1	-	-	-	-
Phalanx 1st	-	2	-	-	-	-		-	-	-	-	-	-	-
Sub-total 4	*1*	*14*	-	*1*	*32*	*3*	*3*	-	-	*1*	*1*	*1*	*2*	*13*
Total	*3*	*19*	*8*	*7*	*34*	*3*	*4*	*4*	*1*	*1*	*1*	*4*	*2*	*13*
MNI	1	1	1	1	-	-	1	1	1	-	-	1	1	-
NONID	126						-	7				25		

two teeth were unworn. It is likely that the animal in question was between birth and three weeks old. The older pig (>3 years) was a sow, presumably kept for reproduction. Most of the bones are skeletally associated or form articulated joints. One cow and one pig skull were also found, hacked open to obtain the brain.

Sub-group 4 - Animal bone from this sub-group has been retrieved from one context, F.30, a ditch in Area III. Although the size of the sample is too small for comparison, this assemblage differs from any other examined at least in three ways (Table 3.8). Firstly, this is the first instance of ovicaprids outnumbering their larger relatives. Secondly, pigs are relatively more numerous here than in other contexts. Lastly, the animals identified in the ditch are generally younger than those identified elsewhere.

Sub-group 5 - This is a feature complex in the northwest part of Area I containing the remains of at least 58 animals (Tables 3.9 & .10). One of the main distinguishing characteristics of the faunal sample from this context is the number of broken skulls and horncores of cattle. Sheep/goats also appear with increased cranial material. The main features of this sub-group are a large recut ditch butt (F.1/2) that contained *c.* 56 per cent of the recovery from this sub-group, and a ditch terminal (F.6) with *c.* 25 per cent. The posthole F.138 had only horse bones, the remains of two young individuals. Comparison of species proportions in the different contexts of the complex reveals an unequal distribution. Cattle, for example, are proportionately more common in pit F.7 than in any other context (Fig. 3.38). It was this feature that contained the high numbers of cattle horncores and skull fragments (Figs. 3.22–3). The horncores are usually broken at the top and attached to the frontal part of the skull. Occasionally, the orbital and occipital parts were also preserved. Cut marks at the points of attachment make it evident that the horns had been loosened with a knife to remove them. The low number of mandibles indicates that these were disarticulated from the cranium at an earlier stage, which was then dumped elsewhere; both F.6 and F.1/2 contain more mandibles than other skull bones and a spatial segregation of waste is suggested. None of the cattle bones belonged to young beasts and, although the ageable sample is not substantial, it can be safely predicted that both the skulls and postcranial material are derived from mature animals.

Table 3.8. *Quantification of faunal remains by NISP and MNI in the ditch of Sub-group 4.*

	F.30						
	Bt	OC	Su	Cf	Ml	Mm	Total
Skull							
Skull frag.	1	-	-	-	-	-	*1*
Maxilla	1	-	1	-	-	-	*2*
Mandible	1	3	1	-	-	-	*5*
Hyoid	-	1	-	-	-	-	*1*
Sub-total 1	*3*	*4*	*2*	-	-	-	*9*
Fore Limb							
Scapula	-	-	1	-	-	-	*1*
Humerus sh.	-	1	-	-	-	-	*1*
Radius sh.	-	2	-	-	-	-	*2*
Metacarpal d.	1	-	-	-	-	-	*1*
Sub-total 2	*1*	*3*	*1*	-	-	-	*5*
Hind Limb							
Femur d.	-	-	-	1	-	-	*1*
Tibia shaft	1	1	-	-	-	-	*2*
Metatarsal wh.	-	-	1	-	-	-	*1*
Metatarsal d.	1	-	-	-	-	-	*1*
Sub-total 3	*2*	*1*	*1*	*1*	-	-	*5*
Tooth/upper	-	2	-	-	-	-	*2*
Tooth/lower	-	-	2	-	-	-	*2*
Rib	-	-	-	-	4	22	*26*
Vertebra	-	-	-	-	1	1	*2*
Long bone	1	-	-	-	4	-	*5*
Metapodial d.	1	-	-	-	-	-	*1*
Phalanx 1st	-	1	-	-	-	-	*1*
Sub-total 4	*2*	*3*	*2*	-	*9*	*23*	*39*
Total	*8*	*11*	*6*	*1*	*9*	*23*	*58*
MNI	1	2	2	1	-	-	*6*
NONID	38						*38*

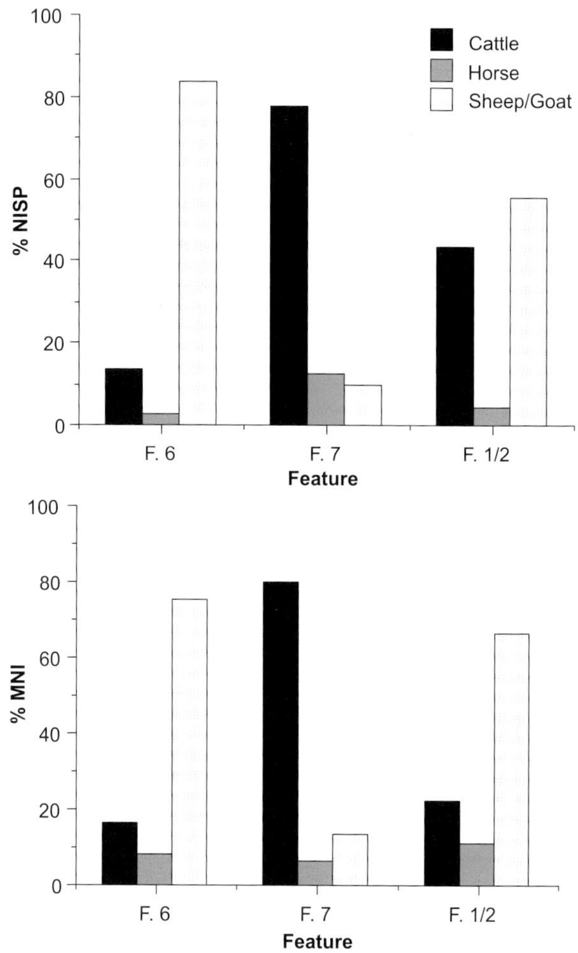

Figure 3.38. *NISP-based distribution of the main domesticates in the main features of Sub-group 5 (top); below, MNI-based distribution of the main domesticates in the main features of Sub-group 5.*

Table 3.9. *Quantification of faunal remains by NISP and MNI in the Northwestern Enclosure complex (Sub-group 5; pt. 1).*

	F.6 Ditch butt							F.7 Pit								F.134 Pit					F.138 PH
	Bt	**Ec**	**OC**	**Su**	**Cf**	**Ml**	**Mm**	**Bt**	**Ec**	**OC**	**Su**	**Cf**	**Brd**	**Ml**	**Mm**	**Bt**	**Ec**	**OC**	**Ml**	**Mm**	**Ec**
Skull																					
Skull frag.	-	-	2	-	-	-	1	16	-	-	-	-	-	2	-	-	-	-	-	-	-
Horncore	-	-	-	-	-	-	-	23	-	-	-	-	-	-	-	-	-	-	-	-	-
Maxilla	-	-	1	1	-	-	-	5	-	-	-	-	-	-	-	-	-	-	-	-	-
Mandible	4	1	16	1	-	-	-	3	-	2	1	3	-	-	-	-	-	1	-	-	-
Hyoid	-	-	1	-	-	-	-	-	-	-	-	-	-	-	-	-	-	-	-	-	-
Sub-total 1	*4*	*1*	*20*	*2*	-	-	*1*	*47*	-	*2*	*1*	*3*	-	*2*	-	-	-	*1*	-	-	-
Fore Limb																					
Scapula	1	-	2	-	1	-	-	-	1	-	-	-	-	-	-	-	-	-	-	-	-
Sternum	-	-	-	-	-	-	-	-	-	-	-	-	-	-	-	-	-	-	-	-	-
Coracoid	-	-	-	-	-	-	-	-	-	-	-	-	-	-	-	-	-	-	-	-	-
Humerus p.	-	-	-	-	-	-	-	-	1	-	-	-	-	-	-	-	-	-	-	-	-
Humerus sh.	-	-	2	-	-	-	-	-	-	-	-	-	-	-	-	-	-	-	-	-	-
Humerus d.	-	-	-	-	-	-	-	-	-	1	-	-	-	-	-	-	-	-	-	-	-
Radius p.	-	-	1	-	-	-	-	-	-	-	-	-	-	-	-	-	-	-	-	-	-
Radius sh.	-	-	5	-	-	-	-	-	-	-	-	1	-	-	-	-	-	-	-	-	-
Radius d.	1	-	-	-	-	-	-	-	-	-	-	-	-	-	-	-	-	-	-	-	-
Ulna	-	-	-	-	-	-	-	-	-	-	1	-	-	-	-	-	-	-	-	-	-
Metacarpal wh.	-	-	-	-	-	-	-	1	3	-	-	-	-	-	-	-	-	-	-	-	-
Metacarpal p.	-	-	2	-	-	-	-	-	-	1	-	-	-	-	-	-	-	-	-	-	-
Metacarpal sh.	-	-	3	-	-	-	-	-	-	-	-	-	-	-	-	-	-	-	-	-	-
Metacarpal d.	-	-	-	-	-	-	-	-	-	-	-	-	-	-	-	-	-	-	-	-	-
Carpal	-	-	-	-	-	-	-	-	-	-	-	-	-	-	-	1	-	-	-	-	-
Sub-total 2	*2*	-	*15*	-	*1*	-	-	*1*	*5*	*2*	*1*	*1*	-	-	-	*1*	-	-	-	-	-
Hind Limb																					
Pelvis	1	-	3	-	-	-	-	2	-	-	-	-	-	1	-	-	-	-	-	-	-
Femur wh.	-	-	1	-	-	-	-	-	-	-	-	-	-	-	-	-	-	-	-	-	-
Femur p.	2	-	-	-	-	-	-	-	-	-	-	-	-	-	-	-	-	-	-	-	-
Femur d.	-	-	-	-	-	-	-	-	-	-	-	-	-	-	-	-	-	-	-	-	-
Tibia wh.	-	-	2	-	-	-	-	-	-	-	-	-	-	-	-	-	-	-	-	-	1
Tibia p.	-	-	3	-	-	-	-	-	-	-	-	-	-	-	-	-	-	-	-	-	-
Tibia sh.	-	-	2	1	-	-	-	-	-	-	-	2	-	-	-	-	-	-	-	-	1
Tibia d.	-	-	2	-	-	-	-	1	-	-	-	-	-	-	-	-	-	-	-	-	1
Metatarsal wh.	-	-	2	-	-	-	-	-	-	-	-	-	-	-	-	-	-	-	-	-	-
Metatarsal p.	1	-	2	-	-	-	-	-	-	-	-	-	-	-	-	-	-	-	-	-	-
Metatarsal sh.	-	-	2	-	-	-	-	-	-	-	-	-	-	-	-	-	-	-	-	-	-
Metatarsal d.	-	-	2	-	-	-	-	-	-	-	-	-	-	-	-	-	-	-	-	-	-
Calcaneum	-	-	-	-	-	-	-	2	-	-	-	-	-	-	-	-	-	-	-	-	-
Astragalus	-	-	-	-	-	-	-	1	-	-	-	-	-	-	-	-	-	-	-	-	-
Sub-total 3	*4*	-	*21*	*1*	-	-	-	*6*	-	-	-	*2*	-	*1*	-	-	-	-	-	-	*3*
Tooth/upper	1	-	2	-	-	-	-	1	-	2	-	2	-	-	-	-	1	-	-	-	1
Tooth/lower	-	-	-	-	-	-	-	-	-	1	1	-	-	-	-	-	-	-	-	-	-
Rib	-	-	-	-	-	28	27	-	-	-	-	-	-	8	-	-	-	-	1	-	-

Table 3.9 *(cont.).*

	F.6 Ditch butt							F.7 Pit								F.134 Pit					F.138 PH
	Bt	**Ec**	**OC**	**Su**	**Cf**	**Ml**	**Mm**	**Bt**	**Ec**	**OC**	**Su**	**Cf**	**Brd**	**Ml**	**Mm**	**Bt**	**Ec**	**OC**	**Ml**	**Mm**	**Ec**
Vertebra	-	-	1	-	-	-	2	-	1	-	-	-	-	3	-	1	-	-	1	-	1
Long bone	-	-	8	-	-	3	19	-	-	-	-	-	1	5	6	-	-	-	-	4	-
Metapodial sh.	-	-	-	-	-	-	-	-	-	-	-	-	-	-	-	-	-	-	-	-	-
Phalanx 1st	-	-	-	-	-	-	-	-	1	-	-	-	-	-	-	-	-	-	-	-	-
Phalanx 2nd	-	1	-	-	-	-	-	-	1	-	-	-	-	-	-	-	-	-	-	-	-
Phalanx 3rd	-	-	-	-	-	-	-	-	1	-	-	-	-	-	-	-	-	-	-	-	-
Sub-total 4	*1*	*1*	*11*	-	-	*31*	*48*	*1*	*4*	*3*	*1*	*2*	*1*	*16*	*6*	*1*	*1*	-	*2*	*4*	*2*
Total	*11*	*2*	*67*	*3*	*1*	*31*	*49*	*55*	*9*	*7*	*3*	*8*	*1*	*19*	*6*	*2*	*1*	*1*	*2*	*4*	*5*
MNI	2	1	9	2	1	-	-	12	1	2	1	1	1	-	-	1	1	1	-	-	2
NONID	82							165								17					40

Table 3.10. *Quantification of faunal remains by NISP and MNI in the Northwestern Enclosure complex (Sub-group 5; pt. 2).*

	F.1/2									Total									Grand total
	Bt	**Ec**	**OC**	**Su**	**Cf**	**Brd**	**Frg**	**Ml**	**Mm**	**Bt**	**Ec**	**OC**	**Su**	**Cf**	**Brd**	**Frg**	**Ml**	**Mm**	
Skull																			
Skull frag.	2	-	-	1	-	-	-	4	-	18	-	2	1	-	-	-	6	1	*28*
Horncore	-	-	-	-	-	-	-	-	-	23	-	-	-	-	-	-	-	-	*23*
Maxilla	4	-	1	-	-	-	-	-	-	9	-	2	1	-	-	-	-	-	*12*
Mandible	11	-	21	-	2	-	-	-	-	18	1	40	2	5	-	-	-	-	*66*
Hyoid	-	-	1	-	-	-	-	-	-	-	-	2	-	-	-	-	-	-	*2*
Sub-total 1	*17*	-	*23*	*1*	*2*	-	-	*4*	-	*68*	*1*	*46*	*4*	*5*	-	-	*6*	*1*	*131*
Fore Limb																			
Scapula	1	-	4	-	-	-	-	1	-	2	1	6	-	1	-	-	1	-	*11*
Sternum	-	-	-	-	-	1	-	-	-	-	-	-	-	-	1	-	-	-	*1*
Coracoid	-	-	-	-	-	1	-	-	-	-	-	-	-	-	1	-	-	-	*1*
Humerus p.	-	-	-	-	-	-	-	-	-	-	1	-	-	-	-	-	-	-	*1*
Humerus sh.	1	-	1	-	-	-	-	-	-	1	-	3	-	-	-	-	-	-	*4*
Humerus d.	-	-	-	-	-	-	-	-	-	-	-	1	-	-	-	-	-	-	*1*
Radius p.	2	-	4	-	-	-	-	-	-	2	-	5	-	-	-	-	-	-	*7*
Radius sh.	1	-	13	-	-	-	-	-	-	1	-	18	-	1	-	-	-	-	*20*
Radius d.	1	1	-	-	-	-	-	-	-	2	1	-	-	-	-	-	-	-	*3*
Ulna	4	-	1	-	1	-	-	-	-	4	-	1	1	1	-	-	-	-	*7*
Metacarpal wh.	-	-	2	-	-	-	-	-	-	1	3	2	-	-	-	-	-	-	*6*
Metacarpal p.	1	-	1	-	-	-	-	-	-	1	-	4	-	-	-	-	-	-	*5*
Metacarpal sh.	1	1	-	-	-	-	-	-	-	1	1	3	-	-	-	-	-	-	*5*
Metacarpal d.	1	-	1	-	-	-	-	-	-	1	-	1	-	-	-	-	-	-	*2*
Carpal		-	-	-	-	-	-	-	-	1	-	-	-	-	-	-	-	-	*1*
Sub-total 2	*13*	*2*	*27*	-	*1*	*2*	-	*1*	-	*17*	*7*	*44*	*1*	*3*	*2*	-	*1*	-	*75*
Hind Limb																			
Pelvis	8	-	2	-	-	-	-	-	-	11	-	5	-	-	-	-	1	-	*17*
Femur wh.	-	-	1	-	-	-	-	-	-	-	-	2	-	-	-	-	-	-	*2*
Femur p.	7	-	-	-	-	-	-	-	-	9	-	-	-	-	-	-	-	-	*9*
Femur d.	-	-	1	-	-	-	-	-	-	-	-	1	-	-	-	-	-	-	*1*

Table 3.10 *(cont.).*

	F.1/2									Total									Grand total
	Bt	Ec	OC	Su	Cf	Brd	Frg	Ml	Mm	Bt	Ec	OC	Su	Cf	Brd	Frg	Ml	Mm	
Tibia wh.	-	-	-	-	-	-	1	-	-	-	1	2	-	-	-	1	-	-	*4*
Tibia p.	1	-	-	-	-	-	-	-	-	1	-	3	-	-	-	-	-	-	*4*
Tibia sh.	-	-	2	-	-	-	-	1	-	-	1	4	1	2	-	-	1	-	*9*
Tibia d.	-	-	2	-	-	-	-	-	-	1	1	4	-	-	-	-	-	-	*6*
Metatarsal wh.	1	-	-	-	-	-	-	-	-	1	-	2	-	-	-	-	-	-	*3*
Metatarsal p.	1	-	1	-	-	-	-	-	-	2	-	3	-	-	-	-	-	-	*5*
Metatarsal sh.	1	1	6	-	-	-	-	-	-	1	1	8	-	-	-	-	-	-	*10*
Metatarsal d.	1	-	1	-	-	-	1	-	-	1	-	3	-	-	-	1	-	-	*5*
Calcaneum	2	-	-	-	-	-	-	-	-	4	-	-	-	-	-	-	-	-	*4*
Astragalus	1	-	-	-	-	-	-	-	-	2	-	-	-	-	-	-	-	-	*2*
Sub-total 3	*23*	*1*	*16*	-	-	-	*2*	*1*	-	*33*	*4*	*37*	*1*	*2*	-	*2*	*2*	-	*81*
Tooth/upper	3	-	-	-	-	-	-	-	-	5	2	4	-	2	-	-	-	-	*13*
Tooth/lower	1	1	3	-	-	-	-	-	-	1	1	4	1	-	-	-	-	-	*7*
Rib	-	-	-	-	-	-	-	66	76	-	-	-	-	-	-	-	103	103	*206*
Vertebra	-	-	-	-	-	-	-	5	5	1	2	1	-	-	-	-	9	7	*20*
Long bone	2	-	5	-	-	-	-	33	27	2	-	13	-	-	1	-	41	56	*113*
Metapodial sh.	-	-	-	2	-	-	-	-	-	-	-	-	2	-	-	-	-	-	*2*
Phalanx 1st	-	2	1	-	-	-	-	-	-	-	3	1	-	-	-	-	-	-	*4*
Phalanx 2nd	1	-	-	-	-	-	-	-	-	1	2	-	-	-	-	-	-	-	*3*
Phalanx 3rd	2	-	-	-	-	-	-	-	-	2	1	-	-	-	-	-	-	-	*3*
Sub-total 4	*9*	*3*	*9*	*2*	-	-	-	*104*	*108*	*12*	*11*	*23*	*3*	*2*	*1*	-	*153*	*166*	*371*
Total	*62*	*6*	*75*	*3*	*3*	*2*	*2*	*110*	*108*	*130*	*23*	*150*	*9*	*12*	*3*	*2*	*162*	*167*	*658*
MNI	4	2	12	1	2	1	1	-	-	19	7	24	4	4	2	1	-	-	*61*
NONID	206									510									

The scarcity of young animals is not only applicable to cattle. Mortality patterns for sheep/goats suggest that *c.* 46 per cent of the flock was killed as yearlings. No spatial segregation of the remains of ovicaprids by age was observed (see Fig. 3.39); nor were sheep horncores identified, but radius shafts are very common.

Horse did not contribute a substantial percentage of bone finds, but at least seven individuals have been identified in the sample. They represent various age groups and their bones seem to have been dumped on several occasions. The pig is represented by very few individuals, and two out of the four animals were identified as female; one of the sows was over 35 months old. Dog is represented by four individuals, whose age could not be assessed.

The sample as a whole contained several pathological specimens. One sheep/goat mandible (F.6) had the P_2 missing and the alveolus filled with bone before the age of slaughter (2–3 years). An ovicaprid maxilla from the same feature and context showed displaced M_1 and abnormal form of P_4. Premolar displacement (P_3) was also observed in another ovicaprid mandible (4–6 years) from the same feature. Pathological examples from F.7 include two mandibles showing oligodonty: a sheep/goat mandible (4–6 years) with P_2 missing and dog jaw with P_3 missing.

General Features

The last assemblage to be examined is not associated with a particular grouping and is derived from diverse/remaining pits and ditches of Roman attribution. These contained a considerable number of bones, with cattle accounting for the majority. In general, cattle were slaughtered as young adults and mature individuals, while horse showed a more varied age distribution. A substantial proportion of sheep/goats (*c.* 85%) were dead by the age of three years and almost one-third of the flock was killed before one year. Pigs tend to be rather old and dogs relatively young.

An important feature of this group is pit F.121/122, in the northeast part of Area I (Fig. 3.25). It contained a complete calf burial, the animal concerned being 5–6 months old (D_2 half erupted/ M_1 just erupting through bone). The animal was suffering from a pathological condition (ankylosis spondylosis), which caused two of the lumbar vertebrae to fuse together. No osseous formation was observed around the affected vertebrae, probably because of the young age of the calf. Knife cuts were most commonly seen on ribs.

Also, pit F.186 contained a cattle skull with broken horncores; the frontal part of the skull was preserved whole (both sides). Feature 186 contained one more pathological specimen: a lower M_3 from a cattle jaw was missing its third cusp (<026>).

The pre-Roman fauna identified at New Hall is dominated by ruminants. Cattle are particularly common in the Bronze Age, where both juvenile and older beasts are present. An important aspect of the Bronze Age material is the identification of the Roe deer and the probable wolf, the only wild animals in the sample as a whole. Pigs and dogs are relatively uncommon in

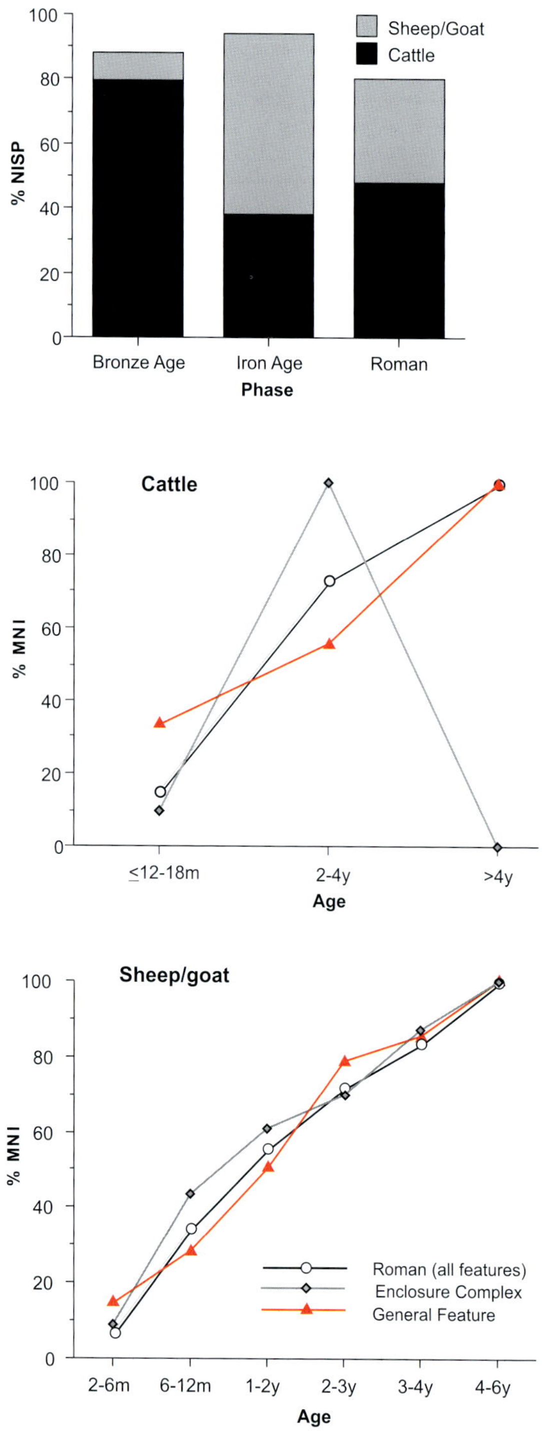

Figure 3.39. *Relative proportions of cattle and sheep in the Bronze Age, Iron Age and Roman periods (based on the sample identified to species; top); middle, cattle mortality in Roman features, based on known-age individuals; bottom, sheep/goat mortality in Roman contexts and comparison of Enclosure Complex with general features.*

both periods, and the single fowl bone from the Iron Age deposits, if not intrusive, proves little more than the mere presence of this animal on the site.

The pre-Roman material is quantitatively inadequate to sustain propositions about animal use, but it does provide some basic information for comparisons on a superficial level. Fragment counts suggest an increase in ovicaprid remains in the Iron Age, although cattle continued to be an important source of meat and raw material (Fig. 3.39, top). In Roman times, a more balanced distribution is suggested.

The scarcity of fowl bones in the Roman assemblage is not typical of the period and could reflect a non-subsistence focus of the activities represented at the site. Another characteristic aspect of the sample is the low proportion of very young animals. Cattle are generally young adult or mature animals; the greatest kill took place in the 'meat' years and only 15 per cent were killed young. Most of the 2–4-year-olds seem to have ended up in the Northwest Enclosure Complex features, while older animals were more common in the general features (Fig. 3.39, middle).

Sheep/goats are more uniformly distributed with regard to age than cattle, although the Northwest Enclosure Complex has more young sheep (≤2 years) in its fills compared to the general features (Fig. 3.39, bottom). The pig sample is too small for assessing age distribution. A small number of individuals are represented at the site and a substantial number of them were kept over the optimal age for meat. In some cases it was possible to confirm that these old animals were sows. No piglets were found and a small number were slaughtered at 11–19 months. This seems to support the proposition that pig slaughter at the site concerned animals at the end of their useful life; these were probably killed for on-site consumption as opposed to younger individuals, whose absence suggests that they were kept (and probably consumed) elsewhere.

Macrofossils (Val Fryer and Peter Murphy)
Amounting to 495 litres, 23 samples from features of Bronze Age (Nos. 14 & 20), Iron Age (Nos. 7 & 8) and Roman date were submitted for assessment; the latter included well, pit and ditch fills and a burnt pit lining.

The flots were collected in a stack of 0.5 mm, 1 mm and 2 mm mesh sieves. The dried flots were scanned under a binocular microscope at low power and the macrobotanical and other remains noted are listed in Table 3.11. Samples 1, 2, 3 and 11 were from wet/waterlogged contexts and all material was identified where possible. Only carbonized remains and mollusc shells were identified from the remaining samples. All tabulated material is carbonized unless otherwise stated. Modern contaminants, including fibrous roots, seeds/fruits, straw, wood fragments and invertebrates were present in most samples.

Table 3.11. *Macrobotanical and other material. KEY + = present, ++ = common, +++ = abundant, nc = not carbonized, pmc = possible modern contaminant.*

	BA	IA			Roman																	
SAMPLE No.	**14**	**7**	**8**	**20**	**1**	**2**	**3**	**4**	**5**	**6**	**9**	**10**	**11**	**12**	**13**	**15**	**17**	**18**	**19**	**21**	**22**	**23**
CONTEXT No.	**556**	**115**	**117**	**475**	**463**	**340**	**642**	**212**		**109**	**059**	**155**	**152**	**195**	**195**	**354**	**360**	**557**	**441**	**559**	**596**	**619**
FEATURE No	**163**	**20**	**20**	**211**	**1/2**	**1/2**	**1/2**	**6**	**7**	**17**	**30**	**72**	**72**	**104**	**104**	**166**	**174**	**144/178**	**192**	**246**	**257**	**269**
Cereal indet. (caryopses)	-	-	-	-	-	+	+	-	+	-	-	-	-	+	-	-	-	-	+	-	+	-
Triticum sp.(caryopses)	-	-	-	-	-	-	+	-	+cf	-	-	-	-	+	-	-	-	-	+	-	-	-
(spikelet bases)	-	-	-	-	-	+	-	-	-		-	-	-	-	-	-	-	-		-	-	-
Ranunculus acris/ repens/bulbous	-	-	-	-	+nc	-	-	-	-	-	-	-	-	-	-	-	-	-	-	-	-	-
R. parviflorus L.	-	-	-	-	-	+	-	-	-	-	-	-	-	-	-	-	-	-	-	-	-	-
Cruciferae indet.	-	-	+cf	-	-	-	-	-	-	-	-	-	-	-	-	-	-	-	-	-	-	-
Sinapis sp.	-	-	-	-	-	+cf	-	-	-	-	-	-	-	-	-	-	-	-	-	-	-	-
Raphanus raphanistrum L.	-	-	+cf	-	+nc	-	-	-	-	-	-	-	-	-	-	-	-	-	-	-	-	-
Stellaria sp.	-	-	-	-	+nc	-	-	-	-	-	-	-	-	-	-	-	-	-	-	-	-	-
Arenaria sp.	-	-	-	-	-	+cf	-	-	-	-	-	-	-	-	-	-	-	-	-	-	-	-
Chenopodium album L.	-	-	-	-	++ nc	-	-	-	-	-	-	-	-	-	-	-	-	+	-	-	-	-
C. ficifolium Sm.	-	-	-	-	-	+	-	-	-	-	-	-	-	-	-	-	-	-	-	-	-	-
Atriplex sp.	-	-	-	-	+nc	+	-	-	-	-	-	-	-		-	-	-	-	-	-	-	-
Malva sp.	-	-	-	-	-	+	-	-	-	-	-	-	-	-	-	-	-	-	-	-	-	-
Leguminosae indet.	-	-	-	-	-	+	-	-	-	-	-	-	-	-	-	-	-	-	-	-	-	-
Vicia/Lathyrus sp.	-	-	-	-	-	+	-	-	-	+	-	-	-	-	-	-	-	-	-	-	-	-
Epilobium sp.	-	-	-	-	-	-	-	-	-	+cf	-	-	-	-	-	-	-	-	-	-	-	-
Conium maculatum L.	-	-	-	-	+nc	-	-	-	-	-	-	-	-	-	-	-	-	-	-	-	-	-
Polygonaceae indet.	-	-	-	-	+nc	-	-	-	-	-	-	-	-	-	-	-	-	-	-	-	-	-
Polygonum aviculare L.	-	-	-	-	+ cfnc	-	-	-	-	-	-	-	-	-	-	-	-	-	-	-	-	-
Rumex sp.	-	-	-	-	++ nc	+cf	+	-	+	-	-	-	-	-	-	-	-	-	-	+	+	-
Rumex acetosella L.	-	-	-	-	++ nc	+	-	-	-	-	-	-	-	-	-	-	-	-	-	-	-	-
Urtica dioica L.	-	-	-	-	+nc	-	-	-	-	-	-	-	-	-	-	-	-	-	-	-	-	-
Hyoscyamus niger L.	-	-	-	-	+nc	-	-	-	-	-	-	-	-	-	-	-	-	-	-	-	-	-

Table 3.11 *(cont.).*

	BA	IA			Roman																	
SAMPLE No.	**14**	**7**	**8**	**20**	**1**	**2**	**3**	**4**	**5**	**6**	**9**	**10**	**11**	**12**	**13**	**15**	**17**	**18**	**19**	**21**	**22**	**23**
CONTEXT No.	**556**	**115**	**117**	**475**	**463**	**340**	**642**	**212**		**109**	**059**	**155**	**152**	**195**	**195**	**354**	**360**	**557**	**441**	**559**	**596**	**619**
FEATURE No	**163**	**20**	**20**	**211**	**1/2**	**1/2**	**1/2**	**6**	**7**	**17**	**30**	**72**	**72**	**104**	**104**	**166**	**174**	**144/178**	**192**	**246**	**257**	**269**
Labiatae indet.	-	-	+cf	-	-	-	-	-	-	-	-	-	-	-	-	-	-	-	-	-	-	-
Plantago lanceolata L.	-	-	-	-	-	+	-	-	-	-	-	-	-	-	-	-	-	-	-	-	-	-
Galium sp.	-	-	-	-	-	-	-	-	+	-	-	-	-	-	-	-	-		-	-	-	-
Sambucus nigra L.	-	-	-	-	+nc	+	-	-	-	-	-	-	-	-	-	-	-	-	-	-	-	-
Eleocharis sp.	-	-	-	-	-	+cf	-	-	-	-	-	-	-	-	-	-	-	-	-	-	-	-
Cladium mariscus (L.) Pohl	-	-	-	-	-	+cf	-	-	-	-	-	-	-	-	-	-	-	-	-	-	-	-
Carex sp.	-	-	-	-	+nc	+	-	-	-	-	-	-	-	-	-	-	-	-	-	-	-	+
Gramineaea indet.	-	-	+	-	-	+	-	+	-	-	-	-	-	+cf	-	-	+	-	-	-	-	-
Bromus sp.	-	-	-	-	-	+	+	-	-	-	-	-	-	-	-	-	-	-	-	-	-	-
Charcoal <5 mm	+	+	++	+	++	++	++	++	+	-	++	+	-	-	-	-	+	++	++	+	++	++
Carbonized root/ rhizome/stem	+	-	+	-	-	+	-	-	-	-	-	-	-	-	-	-	-	-	+	-	-	-
Fibrous roots	-	-	-	-	++ nc	-	-	-	-	-	-	-	+++ pmc	-	-	-	-	-	-	-	-	-
Indet. stemfrags.	-	-	-	-	++ nc	++ nc	+nc	-	-	-	-	-	-	-	-	-	-	-	-	-	-	-
Indet. thorn	-	-	-	-	-	+nc	-	-	-	-	-	-	-	-	-	-	-	-	-	-	-	-
Bone	-	-	-	-	-	-	+	+	-	-	-	-	-	-	-	-	-	-	-	-	-	-
Fish bone	-	-	-	-	+	+	-	-	-	-	-	-	-	-	-	-	-	-	-	-	-	-
Small animal/ amphibian bone	-	-	-	-	-	+	+	+	+	-	-	+ pmc	-	-	-	-	-	-	-	-	-	+ pmc
Eggshell	-	-	-	-	-	-	-	-	-	-	-	-	-	-	-	-	-	+	-	-	-	-
Invertebrates	-	-	-	-	+	-	-	-	-	-	-	-	-	-	-	-	-	-	-	-	-	-
Small coal frags.	+	-	+	-	-	+	-	++	-	-	++	+	-	+	-	-	-	+	+	-	+	++
Silicieous globules	-	-	-	+	+	-	-	-	-	-	-	-	-	-	-	-	-	-	-	-	-	-
Black tarry droplets	-	-	+	++	-	-	-	-	-	-	+	++	+	-	+	+	+	++	++	+	+	+
Black porous 'cokey' material	+	+	+	++	-	+	-	++	-	++	+	+	+	-	+	-	-	++	-	+	++	-
Sample volume (lit.)	**22.5**	**22.5**	**22.5**	**30**	**15**	**22.5**	**22.5**	**7.5**	**15**	**30**	**22.5**	**22.5**	**30**	**22.5**	**15**	**22.5**	**30**	**22.5**	**30**	**22.5**	**15**	**30**
% flot sorted	100	100	100	100	25	50	100	100	100	50	100	50	100	100	100	100	100	100	100	100	100	100

Table 3.12. *Molluscs. KEY + = present, ++ = common, +++ = abundant, b = burnt, o = operculum, p = presence.*

	BA	IA			Roman																	
SAMPLE No.	**14**	**7**	**8**	**20**	**2**	**3**	**4**	**5**	**6**	**9**	**10**	**11**	**12**	**13**	**15**	**16**	**17**	**18**	**19**	**21**	**22**	**23**
CONTEXT No.	**556**	**115**	**117**	**475**	**340**	**642**	**212**		**109**	**059**	**155**	**152**	**195**	**195**	**354**	**440**	**360**	**557**	**441**	**559**	**596**	**619**
FEATURE No.	**163**	**20**	**20**	**211**	**1/2**	**1/2**	**6**	**7**	**17**	**30**	**72**	**72**	**104**	**104**	**166**	**171**	**174**	**144/178**	**193**	**246**	**257**	**269**
Woodland/ shade loving species																						
Carychium sp.	-	-	+	-	+nc	+	-	-	+	+	-	+	-	-	+	-	-	+nc	-	+	+nc	-
					++b													+b			+b	
Vertigo sp.	-	-	+	-	+	+	-	-	+	+	-	+	+	-	-	-	-	-	-	-	+b	+
Lauria cylindrica (da costa)	-	-	-	-	+cf	-	-	-	-	-	-	+cf	-	-	-	-	+cf	-	-	-	-	-
Ena sp.	-	-	-	-	-	-	-	-	+cf	-	-	-	-	-	-	-	-	-	-	-	-	-
E. Obscura (Muller)	-	-	-	-	-	-	-	-	-	-	-	-		-	-	-	-	-	-	+	-	-
Punctum pygmaeum (Draparnaud)	-	-	-	-	-	-	-	-	++	-	-	++	+	-	-	-	-	++	+	-	-	-
Discus rotundatus (Ferussac)	-	-	-	-	-	+b	-	-	-	-	-	-	-	-	-	-	-	-	-	-	-	-
Vitrea sp.	-	-	-	-	+	-	-	-	-	-	-	-	-	-	-	-	-	-	-	-	-	-
V. crystallina (Muller)	-	-	-	-	-	-	-	-	-	-	-	-	-	-	-	-	-	-	-	-	+	-
Aeqopinella nitidula (Draparnaud)	-	-	-	-	-	-	-	-	-	-	-	-	-	-	-	-	-	-	-	+	-	-
Oxychillus sp.	-	-	+cf	+cf	-	-	-	-	+cf	-	-	-	-	+	-	-	-	+	-	-	+	+cf
Clausilia bidenata (Strom)	-	-	-	-	-	-	-	-	-	-	-	-	-	-	-	-	-	-	-	+	-	-
Open Country Species																						
Truncatellina cylindrica (Ferussac)	-	-	-	-	-	-	-	-	+	-	-	+	-	-	-	-	-	+	-	-	-	-
Pupillidae indet.	-	-	-	-	-	-	-	-	-	+	-	-	-	-	-	-	-	-	-	-	-	-
Pupilla muscorum (Linne)	+cf	-	+cf	-	-	-	+cf	-	++	+cf	-	++	+	++cf	-	+cf	+	+	+	-	+	+cf
Vallonia sp.	-	+	-	+	+nc	+	++	+	+++	+	-	++	++	+	+	+	+	+	++	-	+	++
					+b																	
V. costata (Muller)	-	-	-	-	+	+b	+	+	+++	+	-	++	++	+	+	-	-	++	+	+	+	-
V. exentrica (Sterki)	-	-	-	-	+cf	-	+cf	-	-	+cf	+	++cf	+	++cf	-	-	-	+	++	+cf	+cf	+cf

Table 3.12 *(cont.).*

	BA	IA			Roman																	
SAMPLE No.	**14**	**7**	**8**	**20**	**2**	**3**	**4**	**5**	**6**	**9**	**10**	**11**	**12**	**13**	**15**	**16**	**17**	**18**	**19**	**21**	**22**	**23**
CONTEXT No.	**556**	**115**	**117**	**475**	**340**	**642**	**212**		**109**	**059**	**155**	**152**	**195**	**195**	**354**	**440**	**360**	**557**	**441**	**559**	**596**	**619**
FEATURE No.	**163**	**20**	**20**	**211**	**1/2**	**1/2**	**6**	**7**	**17**	**30**	**72**	**72**	**104**	**104**	**166**	**171**	**174**	**144/178**	**193**	**246**	**257**	**269**
V. pulchella (Muller)	-	-	-	-	-	-	-	-	+cf	+cf	-	++cf	+cf	+cf	+cf	-	-	++	++	+	+cf	+
Heliciidae indet.	-	-	+cf	-	+b	-	-	-	-	-	-	+	+	+	-	-	-	+	-	+	-	-
Hellicella itala (Linne)	-	-	-	-	-	-	-	-	+cf	+	-	+	+	+	+	+cf	+cf	+cf	+	+cf	-	+cf
Catholic Species																						
Cochlicopa sp.	-	-	-	-	-	-	+	+	++	-	-	+	+	-	-	-	-	+	+	-	+	-
Tricia hispida group	+	-	-	-	+b	+	++	+	+++	+	+	++	++	++	-	+	+	++	++	+	++	+
Marsh/ freshwater slum species																						
Lymnaea sp.	-	-	-	-	+b	+cf	-	-	-	-	-	+	+	++	-	-	-	+	-	-	+	-
Vertigo antivertigo (Draparnaud)	-	-	+	-	+	-	+b	+cf	+	-	-	+	+	+	-	-	-	+	+	+	+	-
							+nc															
Vertigo anquisitor (Jeffreys)	-	-	-	-	+	-	-	-	-	-	-	-	-	-	-	-	-	-	-	-	-	-
Succinea sp.	-	-	-	-	+b	-	-	-	-	-	-	-	-	-	-	-	-	-	-	-	-	-
Fresh water species																						
Valvata cristata	-	-	-	-	+b	+cf	-	-	-	-	-	-	-	-	-	-	-	-	-	-	+b	-
Bithynia sp.	-	-	-	-	+ob	+cfb	-	-	-	-	-	-	-	-	-	-	-	-	-	-	-	-
					+																	
Armiger crista	-	-	-	-	+b	-	-	-	-	-	-	-	-	-	-	-	-	-	-	-	-	-
Gyraulus albus	-	-	-	-	+b	-	-	-	-	-	-	-		-	-	-	-	-	-	-	-	-
Anisus leucostoma	-	-	-	-	+cf	+	+cf	-	-	-	-	-	-	-	-	-	-	-	-	-	+cfb	-
Planorbis sp.	-	-	-	-	+b	-	-	-	-	-	-	-	-	-	-	-	-	-	-	-	-	-
P. planorbis sp.	-	-	-	-	+	-	-	-	-	-	-	-	-	-	-	-	-	-	-	-	-	-
Cecilioides acicula	p	p	p	p	p	p	p	p	p	p	p	p	p	p	p	p	p	p	p	p	p	p
Sample volume (lit.)	**22.5**	**22.5**	**22.5**	**30**	**22.5**	**22.5**	**7.5**	**15**	**30**	**22.5**	**22.5**	**30**	**22.5**	**15**	**22.5**	**22.5**	**30**	**22.5**	**30**	**22.5**	**15**	**30**
% flot sorted	100	100	100	100	50	100	100	100	50	100	50	100	100	100	100	100	100	100	100	100	100	100

Cereal grains and/or chaff were present at a very low density in six samples (2, 3, 5, 12, 19 & 22). Preservation was poor, with all grains having become puffed and distorted during carbonization and subsequently abraded and fragmented. *Triticum* sp. (wheat) was the only cereal identified.

Seeds/fruits were noted in 13 samples. Common segetal and ruderal species were predominant and included *Raphanus raphanistrum* (wild radish), Sinapis sp. (mustard), *Atriplex* sp. (Orache), *Chenopodium album* (fat hen), *C. ficifolium* (fig-leaved goosefoot), *Stellaria* sp. (chickweed), *Arenaria sp.* (sandwort), *Malva* sp. (mallow), *Vicia/Lathyrus* sp. (vetch/vetchling), *Conium maculatum* (hemlock), *Epilobium* sp. (willow herb), *Urtica dioica* (stinging nettle), *Rumex* sp. (dock), *R. acetosella* (sheep's sorrel), *Polygonum aviculare* (knotgrass), *Hyoscyamus niger* (henbane), *Plantago lanceolata* (ribwort plantain), *Galium* sp. (goosegrass), *Bromus* sp. (brome) and intermediate grasses. Damp grassland and wetland species were also present and included *Ranunculus acris/repens/bulbosus* (meadow/creeping/bulbous buttercup), *R. parviflorus* (small flowered buttercup), *Carex* sp. (sedge), *Eleocharis* sp. (spike-rush), and Cladium *mariscus* (saw-sedge). Carbonized seeds of *Sambucus nigra* (elderberry) were noted in Sample 8 (F.20). Small/medium charcoal fragments were present at a low to moderate density in all but seven samples (6, 11, 12, 13, 15, 16 & 20). Other macrobotanical material included fibrous roots, carbonized and waterlogged stem fragments and an indeterminate thorn.

Other material present included bone fragments, fish and small mammal/amphibian bone, eggshell, invertebrates, and small coal fragments. Siliceous globules, black tarry droplets and fragments of black porous 'cokey' material were all probably derived from the over-combustion of organic material.

Mollusc shells, some of which were burnt, were noted in all but Sample 1 (F.1/2), at low to moderate densities (Table 3.12). The shells recovered fall into all four of John Evans' (1972) ecological groups, namely woodland/shade-loving species (*Lauria cylindrica, Carychium* sp., *Vertigo* sp., *Vitrea* sp., *V. crystallina, Discus rotundatus, Punctum pygmaeum, Oxychillus* sp., *Ena obscura, Clausilia bidentata, Aegoplinella nitidula)*, open country species (*Vallonia* sp., *V. costata, V. pulchella, V. excentrica, Pupilla muscorum, Truncatellina cylindrica, Helicella itala,* Pupillidae indet.) and marsh/freshwater slum species (*Lymnaea* sp., *Vertigo antivertigo, V. augustior, Succinea* sp.). Freshwater species were also present and included *Valvata cristata, Bithynia* sp., *Armiger crista, Gyraulus, Anisus leucostoma, Planorbis planorbis* and *Planorbis sp.* Shells of *Cecilioides acicula* occurred in all samples except Number 1, but as this is a burrowing species, these are probably modern contaminants. The shells in Sample 19 (F.192), the burnt lining of a pit, may also be intrusive as they are unburnt.

The macrobotanical and other material present is probably principally derived from a low-density scatter of general and/or domestic refuse with elements of the local flora occurring in the waterlogged deposits. The composition of the molluscan assemblage suggests that the ditches were semi-shaded and occasionally damp and the lack of macrobotanical material within the fills may suggest that they were kept clear of vegetation. Some of the pits (see Samples 4 & 22; respectively, F.6 & F.257) appear to have been semi-permanently water-filled, while others (Samples 5 & 16; respectively, F.7 & F.171) only intermittently held standing water. None of the macrofossils present give any indication of the function of these features.

Feature-Monolith Samples (Peter Murphy)
Two deep Roman-phase features with wet basal fills cut through sands and gravels into chalky marl were sampled:

- *F.1/2* – Two 50 cm monoliths were taken from the dark organic basal fill for pollen and macrofossil analysis (tops of monoliths at 135 cm from top of section).
- *F.7* – A Kubiena box was taken for pollen analysis from the basal chalky deposits, across the boundary with the natural marl (top at 65 cm from top of section); a single bag of deposit from the lowest 10 cm of fill was collected for macrofossils.

Bone waste including cattle skulls had led the excavator to suggest that these features may have been associated with tanning. The main purpose of the samples collected was to check whether the features might have related to any other industrial process involving plant material (e.g. retting).

The large monolith from F.1/2 for macrofossil assessment included the following deposits:

- 0–17 cm – Dark greyish-brown loam; very stony with flints and fragments of ?mortar/plaster; sharp boundary
- 17–22 cm – Black firm peaty deposit: merging boundary
- 22–50 cm – Very dark greyish-brown organic loam; wood fragments; becoming more sandy towards base.

The basal fill of F.7 was a highly calcareous clay/silt loam with chalk fragments.

Macrofossils
Sub-samples of 100 g each were removed from the monolith from F.1/2 at 0–10, 17–22 and 40–50 cm, and a similarly sized sample from the basal fill of F.7 was assessed for macrofossil remains. The samples were disaggregated in hot water, with manual agitation, then wet-sieved in 2 mm and 0.5 mm meshes prior to scanning under a binocular microscope at low power. The following macrofossils were noted:

- *F.1/2* (0–10 cm) – Fruits/seeds of Chenopodiaceae, *Sambucus nigra* and *Rumex*; degraded wood scraps; rare charcoal fragments; rare *T. spelta* glume bases and Poaceae culm nodes; a few shells of *Vallonia* and *Carychium*.
- *F.1/2* (17–22 cm) – Fruits/seeds of *Ranunculus acris/repens/bulbosus, Brassica* sp., *Reseda luteola, Raphanus raphanistrum, Rumex acetosella, Urtica urens, Potamogeton* sp., *Eleocharis palustris/uniglumis, Carex* spp. (all very compressed); small laminated masses of monocotyledonous stems; woody and fibrous roots; rare charcoal; occasional poorly preserved insect remains; hard humified peaty aggregates.
- *F.1/2* (40–50 cm) – Fruits/seeds of *Stellaria media*-type, *Montia fontana* subsp. *chondrosperma, Polygonum aviculare, Rumex* sp., *Urtica dioica, Urtica urens, Aethusa cynapium, Carex* spp.;

rare charcoal; twigs, woody and fibrous roots; charred *T. spelta* glume bases and Poaceae culm nodes; mollusc shell fragments; fish-scales.
F.7 (60–70 cm) – Rare charcoal fragments.

The samples examined provided no evidence from plant macrofossils for the function of these features. The taxa identified from F.1/2 are indicative of local weed and wet grassland vegetation, entirely typical of settlement sites. The peaty deposit at 17–22 cm in the monolith from F.1 appears to represent a very compressed layer of organic material. Although it is largely humified, there seem to be laminae of straw/hay litter within it. A fruit of *Potamogeton* sp. suggests deposition under standing water. The basal fill of F.7 has evidently been subject to intermittent desiccation, with consequent humification of plant material.

Pollen (Patricia Wiltshire)
Inspection visits were made to assess the potential for pollen analysis of excavated features. None then excavated were waterlogged and it was considered that pollen preservation would be poor. However, in view of the paucity of sediments suitable for palynological analysis, it was decided to undertake a pollen assessment. Accordingly, a total of eight samples were analysed from Bronze/Iron Age and Roman features.

In view of the possibility of low pollen concentrations, 2 g of sediment was processed for each sample. Samples were subjected to standard concentration techniques, except that hydrofluoric acid treatment was extended to two weeks because of high silt content.

Palynomorphs proved to be exceedingly sparse; it is obvious that there was differential preservation and that most palynomorphs had been lost through decomposition. This is emphasized by the prevalence of Lactuceae, a pollen type which is resistant to decay. Nevertheless, some of the taxa recorded are among those considered to be more vulnerable to corrosion. It is thus reasonable to suppose that the pollen assemblage presented here might give some indication of the vegetation prevailing during deposition of the sediments. The results must be viewed with caution, but a very crude picture of the local vegetation of the area is given.

Bronze/Iron Age
F.85 [168] – Microscopic charcoal was found in both the upper and lower fills, but there was a particularly high concentration in the lower deposits. Pollen of only Poaceae (grasses) and Lactuceae (ligulate Compositae e.g. *Taraxacum* [dandelion] or *Sonchus* [sow thistle]) was found. Fungal spores were abundant and fungal hyphae were very much in evidence in the lower fill.

The paucity of palynomorphs makes detailed environmental reconstruction impossible, but it would seem that open, weedy grassland prevailed at the site. The abundance of fungal remains would also indicate that the original deposit had been derived from plant material falling into the ditch as the sediment accumulated. The relatively large amounts of microscopic charcoal in the basal fill are difficult to explain, but it might have been derived from fires nearby. The sparser charcoal in the upper fill might suggest that soot was being derived from fires slightly further away.

F.20 – Again, the most abundant pollen taxa were those of Lactueae and Poaceae, but a single cereal-type grain was found along with a single grain of Coryloid (c.f *Corylus*, hazel). Fungal spores were relatively abundant throughout, and the hyphae were abundant in the sample at 30 cm. Vesicles of a vesicular-arbuscular myccorhizal fungus (c.f *Glomus*) were found at 30 cm and 90 cm, whilst microscopic charcoal was found in every sample.

In spite of the very poor pollen results, it would appear that the area was exceedingly open. The presence of hazel pollen cannot be taken to indicate close proximity of the shrub, since this wind pollinated plant produces large amounts of pollen, which can be disseminated relatively long distances. There might have been cereal-growing and/or processing being carried out locally, but it must be remembered that cereal pollen could be derived from faeces, or even from harvested cereals transported throughout the site.

The abundant fungal remains indicate that the deposit had contained organic material (even plant debris) and was probably derived from aerated, bioactive soil. This conclusion is strengthened by the presence of *Glomus*-type. Mutualistic fungi of this type are ubiquitous where soils support herbaceous vegetation and where phosphate levels are somewhat low. Indeed, all myccorhizal fungi tend to be suppressed by high levels of phosphorus.

The comparatively small amount of microscopic charcoal might represent soot from fires some distance away from the ditch.

Roman
F.17– The only pollen grains found were those of Lactuceae, Poaceae, *Plantago* sp. (c.f. ribwort plantain), and *Sinapis*-type (e.g. *Cardamine hirsute*, hairy bitter cress). A single grain of *Pteridum* (bracken fen) was present at 20 cm. Fungal hyphae and spores were relatively abundant. *Glomus*-type and urediniospores of Uredinales (c.f. *Puccinia*, fungal rust) were also abundant; microscopic charcoal was found in all samples.

The palynomorph assemblage suggests a very open, weedy grassland with some well-drained, acid soil in the area (as evidenced by the calcifuge bracken). The relatively large amounts of fungal hyphae and spores could have been derived from plant debris deposited in the accumulating sediment, or possibly from bioactive, organic-rich soil being washed into the feature. Soil inwash is certainly indicated by the abundance of *Glomus*-type vesicules and, as already stated, this might indicate that the accumulating deposits were derived from rather nutrient-deficient soils.

The presence of *Puccinia*-type soils urediniospores is interesting, particularly as several were seen within intact tetrads. Fungal rusts are obligate parasites of plants, attacking a wide range of taxa and *Puccinia graminis is* one of the most economically important rust pathogens of cereals and grasses. The fact that the spores were in tetrads suggests either that they were dropped into the ditch from cereals or grasses overhanging the feature or that they were growing on the leaves which had fallen into the ditch. It is unlikely that they had been disseminated very far, since the tetrads break up very easily into individual spores. The relatively sparse microscopic charcoal suggests that it represented soot from fires some distance from the ditch.

Interpretation of these very sparse data should be viewed with extreme caution, but the evidence suggests that over the two phases the site supported open, weedy grassland and bioactive, organic-rich soils. The abundance of myccorhizal vesicules suggests that the humified ashy aspect of the later prehistoric and Roman soils were somewhat nutrient poor, particularly in terms of available phosphorus. The comparatively large amounts of microscopic charcoal in the basal fill of F.85 suggest fires close to the feature. The charcoal from later fills might represent sooty deposits from fires further away than the immediate locality.

Soil Micromorphology (Brendan Coyle and Charles French)

Eight soil blocks were taken for micromorphological analysis from three ditches representing the main phases of use at New Hall. This included two contiguous samples taken from the upper, tertiary brown silt loam fill of an earlier Romano-British ditch (Profile 1; F.35, [45]), three spot samples taken from the three major fill horizons – tertiary, upper secondary, lower secondary/primary – of a later Romano-British ditch (Profile 2; F.30, [59]), and three contiguous samples taken from the upper very dark brown loam fill of an Iron Age ditch (Profile 3; F.20). The purpose of the investigation was to establish whether the fills represented 'Dark Earths' or were the result of subsequent ploughing in the area.

The soil samples were prepared according to the methods outlined by Murphy (1986) and were described following the conventions of Bullock *et al.* (1985). The micromorphological description of the profiles is summarized in tabular form in Evans 1996, Appendix 1.

Essentially the same basic fabric was present in each ditch fill examined, with similar inclusions and only slight variations between samples in terms of fabric density and proportions, and the frequency of inclusions. All the fills were homogeneous sandy loams with a 2:1 coarse/fine ratio, minor amounts of illuvial clay coatings of grains and voids as well as within the groundmass, and spongy, rather porous microstructures that were essentially similar (Fig. 3.40, top). There was a varied and occasionally quite high, fine gravel content present that was most likely derived from slippage of subsoil material from the sides of the ditches and/or adjacent bank material.

There were a number of inclusions observed in most of the samples. Fine fragments of burnt clay, shell and bone were among the archaeological materials identified in thin-section (Fig. 3.40, middle and bottom), although these were rare at best. There seemed to be no connection between the presence or absence of these materials and the profile/ditch from which a particular sample came.

Fragments of charcoal, as well as sesquioxide impregnated pseudomorphs of plant tissue, were observed in all the samples, although in each case they were a rarity. Fine punctuations of amorphous organic matter were much more common, generally constituting somewhere between a fifth and a third of the fine groundmass. Profile 3 varied slightly from this in consistently showing a fine organic content not exceeding a quarter of the fine groundmass. Excremental pedofeatures resulting from earthworms were occasionally observed in various samples. Microsparite calcium carbonate or wood ash (Fig. 3.40, bottom) was found throughout the groundmass in each of the samples. Amorphous sesquioxide impregnation of the groundmass, though present in all samples (barely in Profile 3B) was invariably rather weak in character. Sesquioxide nodules and manganese concretions were also present, though infrequent.

Interpretation

Micromorphological analyses highlighted the similarity in the fills from the three ditches, thereby hinting at comparable origins for these deposits. This result in itself is of significance as it may imply continuity of anthropogenic practice over a long period of time, spanning from the Middle/later Iron Age to later Romano-British times. Furthermore, initial speculation that the sampled fills represented 'Dark Earths' (after Macphail 1983; Macphail & Courty 1985; Dockrill & Simpson 1994) does, indeed, seem warranted on the strength of the micro-fabric analyses.

The term 'Dark Earth' is a rather loose description for anthropogenic deposits that could form from a number of processes including soil dumping, refuse dumping and the reworking of collapse/destruction debris from insubstantial structures. The fact that much of the fabric consisted of the mineral component of a soil does not in itself have much significance as this would be expected whether or not the fills were 'Dark Earths'. More informative are the consistently low percentages of illuvial clay. This points towards a freely draining soil system, and probably also suggests there was not much post-depositional disturbance in the layers overlying the sampled fills. Specifically, if the fills themselves or the layers above them had been ploughed, a much greater proportion of dusty/dirty clay coatings would be expected, especially in the lower fills, even in a relatively freely draining soil system (Jongerius 1983; Macphail

Table 3.13. *Basic porosity and mineral component associated with thin sections (coarse/fine ratio: 100 um; *consisting of vughs and channels in about equal proportion; **consisting mainly of flint with some ironstone; wrs stands for 'weakly reticulate striated').*

Thin section	Porosity*	Gravel**	Coarse Min.	Fine Min.	Silt Fraction	Clay Fraction	Illuvial Clay	Bire-fringence***
Profile 1								
1/1	10–25%	<5%	35%	65%	15%	30%	<5%	wrs in places
1/2	5–20%	<5%	35%	65%	15%	30%	<5%	wrs in places
Profile 2								
2/1	5–20%	10–15%	35%	65%	15%	35%	none	speckled
2/2	10–40%	10%	35%	65%	15%	35%	<2%	speckled
2/3	5–30%	15%	27%	73%	18%	40%	<2%	speckled
Profile 3								
3A	15–40%	20%	45%	55%	15%	25%	<2%	speckled
3B	10–40%	5%	45%	55%	15%	25%	<2%	speckled
3C	10–40%	5%	37%	63%	18%	30%	<5%	wrs in places

Figure 3.40. *Soil Photomicrographs (frame width = 4.5 mm; cross-polarized light): top, sandy loam fabric with dusty clay void coatings (Sample 1/1); middle, a degraded, burnt bone fragment with partial iron oxide stained dusty clay replacement (Sample 3C); bottom, pottery fragment (lower left) and pale grey micritic ash (Sample 2.2).*

et al. 1990). Hence, it seems unlikely that the fills represent deposits dragged into the ditches by ploughing.

The organic component present in the fills was substantial, although not particularly abundant. The amount of charcoal present was rather low throughout and was probably mainly due to prevailing oxidizing conditions that encouraged the breakdown of the organic fraction. Such conditions were indicated by the porous nature of the deposits, as well as by the omnipresent amorphous sesquioxide impregnation, which suggested the oxidation of a damp soil matrix. Furthermore, the nature of some of the voids, as well as the excremental pedofeatures observed, hinted at the presence of earthworms in the fills, which would also explain the homogeneity of the fabric and the comminution of the uncarbonized organic component.

The high levels of microsparite calcium carbonate observed in the fill samples are believed to represent wood ash (Wattez & Courty 1987). As it generally occurs as punctuations throughout the entire groundmass, rather than as discrete or even relatively well-integrated aggregates of ash, this indicates that ash and soil were subjected to rigorous mixing processes by soil faunal activity. The absence of any quantities of burnt soil rules out a hearth or fire on an earthen floor as the origin of the ash. Yet, if the ash was removed from the place of burning without soil contamination then the question arises as to where the dominating soil component of the fills came from. The most likely explanation for the origin of the soil component in the ditch fills is that it was introduced into the ditches at the same time as the ash.

This scenario envisages an intermediate stage between the clearing out of the place of burning and the introduction of the ash into the ditches. The ash was probably initially scattered or dumped as refuse into a 'backyard'-type environment where it became mixed in with the soil, as well as archaeological materials such as pottery, bone and oyster shell. Subsequently this anthropogenic debris, along with substantial amounts of soil, was redeposited in a nearby, unused ditch. The thorough intermixing of the ash and soil could then have resulted from earthworm activity, either before or after the redeposition, as well as the act of redeposition itself. The slight surface degradation of some of the land snails seems to support the idea that the fills were lying exposed for a certain period.

As a final note, it should be pointed out that the similarity of fabric observed among the various fill samples suggests that similar activities were going on in their formation. This is quite remarkable as it perhaps implies continuity of practice going from the Iron Age period right through Roman times.

In conclusion, following on from the work of Macphail and Courty (1983; 1985), it seems appropriate to describe the ditch fills from New Hall as 'Dark Earths', with the main anthropogenic component of these deposits being wood ash.[13] The following sequence is envisaged for the formation of the 'Dark Earth' as found in the Iron Age/Romano-British ditch deposits:

1) Rake out of wood ash from an area of intense burning not in contact with soil.
2) Dumping or scattering of the ash into an environment where it became mixed with soil as well as other anthropogenic materials such as pottery, oyster shells, bone and other organics.
3) After a period of exposure, the ash, soil, and other materials were redeposited into a disused ditch in the vicinity, perhaps in connection with a cleaning up operation.
4) Over time, earthworm activity thoroughly mixed the ash into the soil and the oxidizing conditions in the fill led to a humification of the organic content.

Table 3.14. *Inclusions within groundmass of soil thin-sections (*sub-angular in shape, generally <2 mm, additionally in Thin Section 2/1 has a large fragment 5–15 mm across: **shells belong to landsnails, addition Thin Section 2/3 had two large fragments of oyster shells; ***including amorphous sesquioxide-impregnated pseudomorphs of organic material; r = rare; vr = very rare).*

Thin Section	Archaeological Materials			Organics		Microsparite CaCO3 (wood ash)			Am. Sesquioxide	
	Burnt Clay*	Shell**	Bone	Charcoal***	Fine <100um	Discrete	Integrated	Punctuations	Present?	Strength
Profile 1										
1/1	vr	none	none	r	25–35%	<2%	<2%	≥20%	yes	weak
1/2	vr	vr	none	vr	10–30%	none	<5%	≥30%	yes	weak
Profile 2										
2/1	r	vr	vr	r	25–35%	<2%	5%	≥30%	yes	weak–mod.
2/2	vr	vr	none	vr	20–30%	<5%	5%	40%	yes	weak
2/3	r	vr	vr	r	25–35%	<2%	<5%	40%	yes	weak
Profile 3										
3A	vr	vr	vr	r	15–25%	<2%	<2%	≥30%	yes	weak
3B	vr	vr	none	r	15-25%	<2%	<2%	40%	v. little	weak
3C	none	vr	none	r	10-25%	<2%	<2%	40%	yes	weak

The 'Archaeology' of the Darwin Family Estate

There is something wonderfully absurd about Figure 3.46's photograph of Fitzwilliam College's New Library Site excavations and the fact that Bronze Age ditches clearly extend beneath *The Grove*, the house of Darwin's widow. Apparently feeling lonely in the emptiness of Kent's Down House, following the great man's death in 1882, Emma (*nee* Wedgwood) bought *The Grove* in the following year, living there with her daughter, Bessy, during winters, with two of her sons also then resident in Cambridge. On acquiring the landholding of Jacob Smith (shown on the 1805 Enclosure map), in 1814 the architect and surveyor, William Custance, designed and had built his Regency-style house there (Fig 3.41), along with its various outbuildings and Huntingdon Road-side lodge (Fig. 3.52; still extant, as is its rear coach house, see Fig. 3.2).

With Emma Darwin's move to Cambridge, during the 1880s her two sons built their own houses within the mature park-like plot, turning it effectively into a *c.* 6 ha family estate. At the northwestern end, Francis/Frank Darwin (the third son and University Reader in Botany; Berra 2013, 112–30) had *Wychfield* built, the house later being acquired by Trinity Hall (Fig. 3.41).[14] Horace, the fifth son, had *The Orchard* built in the ground's eastern end, which stood until it was demolished to make way for New Hall (the University buying the plot in 1957 and dividing it between that College and Fitzwilliam). Studying at Cambridge, Horace was a civil engineer/inventor and, eventually, served as the town's mayor (1896–7; Fig. 1.11); he is best known as the founder of the Cambridge Scientific Instrument Company (1881; see Cattermole & Wolfe 1987; Berra 2013, 153–71). As part of the Grand Arcade investigations, in 2007 the Company's second, Tibb's Row offices were excavated (see Fig. 3.42 and Cessford & Dickens forthcoming). As shown in Figure 3.42, Horace himself donated Roman pottery from *The Grove's* grounds (presumably found during the construction of his house) to the University Museum of Archaeology and Anthropology.[15]

There are other Darwin family connections in the local landscape. George (the second son and father of the artist, Gwen Raverat) was the University Plumian Professor of Astronomy (Berra 2013, 81–104) and, succeeded in the post by Eddington, will appear again in the next book's Observatory Site studies.[16] In 1910 Frank Darwin had the Arts & Crafts-style *Conduit Head House* built as a wedding present for his daughter, the poet, Frances Cornford, and it features in discussions of North West Cambridge's water supply. Frances, along with the brothers, Frank and Horace, was buried – amongst other Cambridge academic luminaries – in the Ascension Burial Grounds, located just west of Storey's Way (see Chap. 1).[17]

It is not our intention here to further fuel Darwin hagiography, but with a long-standing interest

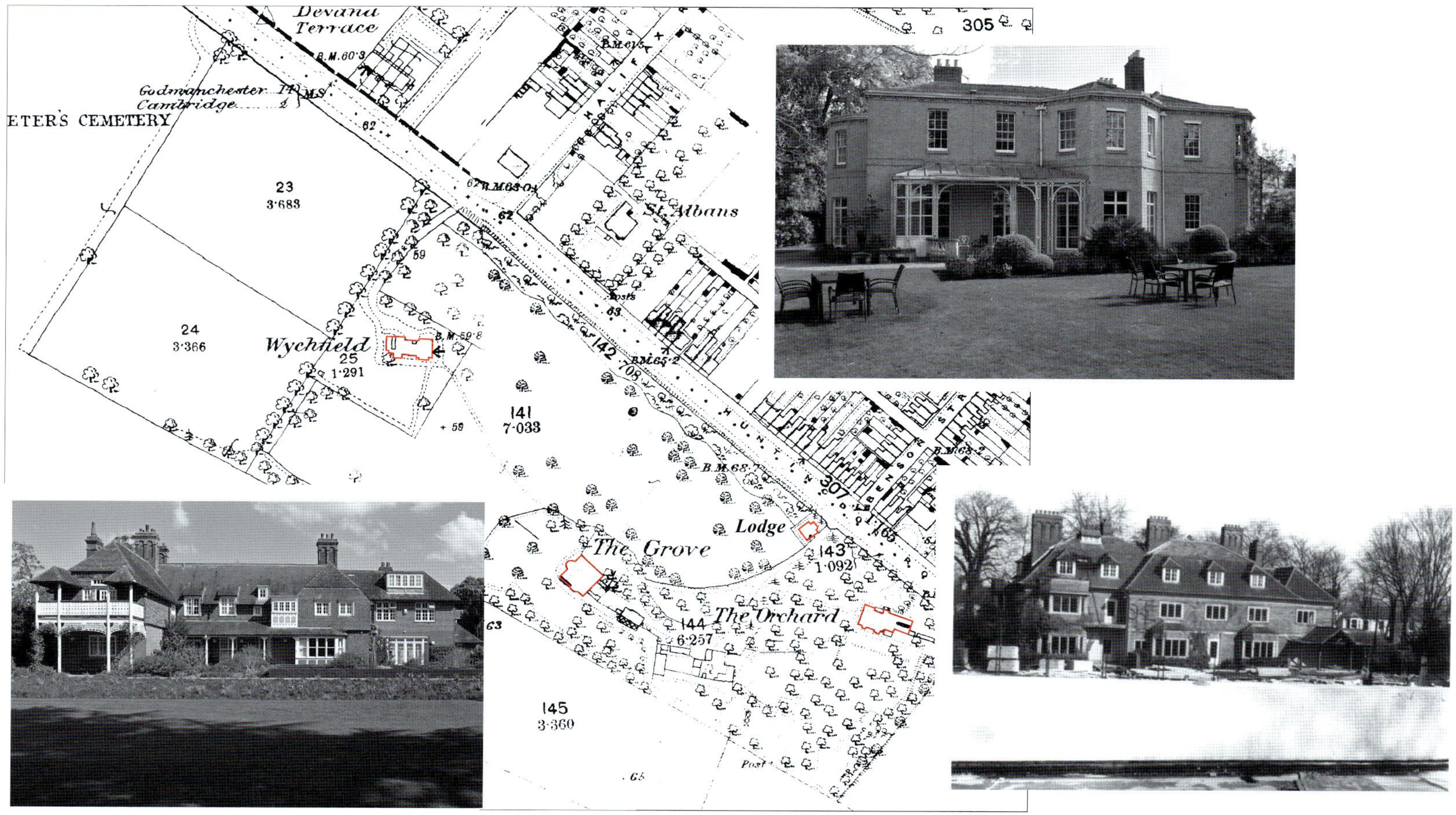

Figure 3.41. *The Darwin Family Estate (1888 OS map; see Fig. 1.2.8), with photographs of* Wychfield *(lower left) and, right,* The Grove *(top) and* The Orchard *(bottom).*

Figure 3.42. *Darwin Family archaeology: Grand Arcade excavations, 2005, showing the lower walls of the Cambridge Scientific Instrument Company, established in 1881 and moving to this, their Tibb's Row location, the following year (upper left); logo-symbol of Cambridge Scientific Instrument Company combining an electrical 'cam' and a 'bridge' (i.e. 'Cam+bridge'; upper right); below, Roman pottery recovered from* The Grove *and* The Orchard *given by Horace Darwin to the Cambridge University Museum of Archaeology and Anthropology.*

in his influence on archaeology (e.g. Evans 2009), it is fair to say that most Cambridge residents are today unfamiliar with the extent of the family's West Cambridge connections (see, though, Raverat's 1952 memoir, *Period Piece*, 194). Indeed, had we been more aware of this at the time, greater attention might have been given to the traces of *The Grove's* outbuildings that occurred across the southern portion of the 1994 New Hall Site.

Finally, it also warrants mention that the 'shadow' of John Henslow's looms over the family estate lands. Best known as Darwin's mentor and a close friend, Henslow (1796–1861) held the chair of the Regius Professor of Botany at the University of Cambridge and was responsible for the remodelling of its Bateman Street botanical gardens (Walters & Stow 2001). Publishing many books, one of his many claims to fame is that, in 1860, he chaired the famous debate on Darwinian evolution held between Huxley and Hooker (Henslow's son-in-law) on the one side and, on the other, the Bishop of Oxford, Samuel Wilberforce. Earlier ordained into the clergy, on his retirement in 1837 Henslow was appointed Rector of Hitcham parish in Suffolk. Aside from championing numerous philanthropic causes (including the founding of Ipswich Museum), his departure from Cambridge allowed him to further his own archaeological interests, these having been outlined in *Riversides*... (chap. 2, note 6).

After discovering coprolite beds at Felixstowe in 1842, Henslow actively promoted the local fertilizer industry and, patenting a means for the extraction of phosphate from the 'bone-soil' nodules, apparently even helped to set up a processing works at Hauxton (O'Connor 1998, 3–4; Walters & Stowe 2001, 211–13). There is no small irony in that, though something of an antiquarian himself, if indirectly, his involvement in the coprolite industry significantly contributed to the destruction of so much of South Cambridgeshire's past. Its impact in the West Cambridge lands was certainly dramatic and, arguably, had it not been for the Darwin Family Estate-holding, it is likely that all the immediate area's archaeology would have been quarried away (Fig. 2.23). As at the Observatory (see Evans & Newman 2011), the land's dense tree-planting would have served to screen the unsightly scars of the surrounding works, almost like an oasis.

Accruing Context – Allied Investigations

It is little more than conceit to imagine that sites and archaeology are self-explanatory; they are not and our thinking is only refined by the acquisition of context and through comparative sources. As outlined in this chapter's introduction, this has clearly happened here. Digging New Hall in relative isolation, we thought of its findings in certain ways and in long-established frameworks. Over the some 20 years since, far more knowledge of sites in the immediate area has been gained. Generally of a fairly small-scale and, together, something of a hodgepodge ensemble, each reflects on different facets of New Hall's findings and, in effect, they only help us to 'think better'.

The Marion Close Enclosure (with Richard Mortimer)
Straight after the New Hall excavations, in December 1996 a watching brief was called in mitigation of the development for Fitzwilliam College to the rear of 138 Huntingdon Road at the corner with Marion Close (Fig. 3.43; Mortimer & Evans 1997). Lying along what was then thought to be the projected line of the Godmanchester Road, this was a stroke of remarkable good fortune and it offered a chance to directly test the location of this Roman route. Negotiations were immediately instigated with the College's Bursar, who appreciated the unique research opportunity and promptly gave permission to change the recording coverage to a positive trenching programme (extending beyond the footprint of the new building).

In the first instance, a northeast–southwest-oriented trench was cut over a distance of nearly 30 m; no evidence of the Godmanchester Road, nor any Roman finds or features whatsoever were recovered (as outlined below, firm evidence of the route of the former to the south of Huntingdon Road only came to light some years later). In the course of this limited trenching programme a major Middle/later Iron Age enclosure was, however, found. An entirely unanticipated discovery, it was again only through the goodwill of the College that further funding was made available, enabling its full exposure and permitting test excavation throughout the area of the building's footprint. The main area of excavation was approximately 9 × 13 m (117 sq. m; Fig. 3.44).

The Enclosure
The enclosure had an intercutting double-ditch circuit (Figs. 3.44–5). While no features were exposed within its interior, a number of more minor features related to its ditches were identified. Two, deep post-pit 'slots'

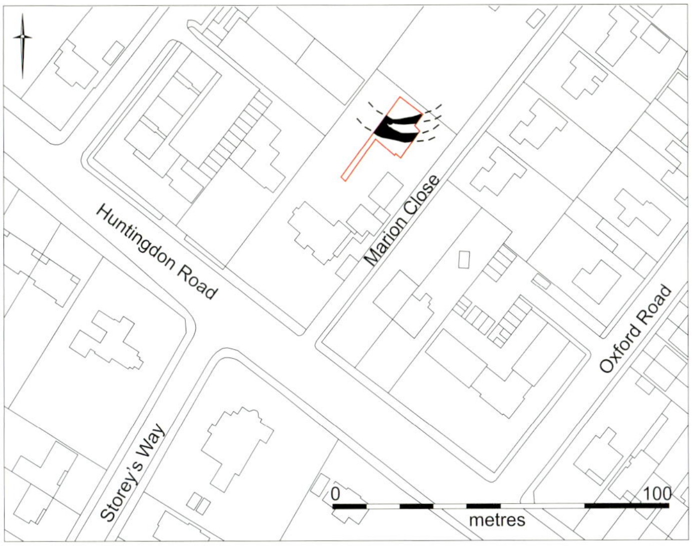

Figure 3.43. *The Marion Close Enclosure, site location plan and excavation photographs.*

(F.4 & F.12) and a driven posthole, F.13 (0.3 m diameter and 0.5 m deep), were possibly associated with some manner of gateway structure.

The Outer Circuit

In the east of its length, the original outer ditch, F.6, was *c.* 1.4 m wide by 0.9 m deep. This expanded to being *c.* 2 m across and 1.35 m deep at its butt-end. The profile changed from a broad 'U'-shape in the east to a near-vertical sided, flat-bottomed terminal. The fill sequence differed considerably in the two excavated sections. In the east (Fig. 3.45, Section 5), the primary and secondary fills – respectively a light brown sandy silt/gravel and a mid to dark brown silty sand – were both central to the ditch. A band of slumping and weathering covered these on the northern edge; the accumulated tertiary fill was a mid brown silty sand with gravel inclusions. At the butt-end, all the fills lay steeply against the almost vertical northern edge. The primary fills consisted of weathered and slumped bands of light orange-brown silty clays, the main fill above being a mid grey-brown silty clay with charcoal and pottery. The surviving upper fill (truncated by ditch F.3) was a thick dump of redeposited sandy clay natural.

For much of its length, the southern side of ditch F.6 was recut by F.3. Like the earlier ditch, its size dramatically increased over its westward length. It widened from *c.* 1.9 m to 6 m and deepened from 0.75 m to 2.25 m, and the impression gained from the bedding of the fills was that the ditch continued to deepen beyond the edge-of-excavation. Its profile, however, remained fairly constant throughout: a broad 'U'-shape with a rounded, slightly stepped base. In the east the fill sequence had a primary fill of mid brown silt, secondary fills of mid to dark brown and yellow/brown sandy clays, with darker brown loamy tertiary deposits. There was a thick band of slumped redeposited natural sandy clay at the northern edge. At the broader western length (Fig. 3.45, Section 3), the deep basal fill was a clean blue/grey silty clay overlain by a secondary fill of slightly gritty, marl-specked yellow/brown clay. The tertiary fill was a compact, light brown clay with occasional gravel inclusions and diffused iron staining. All the fills were evidently accumulations, with very little, if any, deliberate dumping. There was a stabilization level at the surface of the tertiary fill: a dark brown clay silt turf-line. This was sealed by a depth of grey-brown clay loam subsoil and dark brown/black loamy garden soil.

The Inner Circuit

Truncated by the final form of the outer circuit (and subsequently recut as ditch F.5; see below), the upper part of one or both edges of ditch F.8 had been removed. In the east, it was *c.* 1.7 m wide by 0.85 m deep; the central length narrowed to *c.* 1 m wide and deepened to 1.15 m with a steep 'V'-shaped profile. Against the western section, the ditch again widened to *c.* 2 m, deepened further to 1.35 m and, judging by the angle of the fills, it continued to deepen beyond the edge-of-excavation.

The fill sequence varied with the depth and shape of the feature. In the east (Fig. 3.45, Section 2), only the primary fill and part of the secondary survived: a light grey gravelly, sandy silt (with occasional charcoal inclusions) and a light brown sandy silt. In the narrow central section (Fig. 3.45, Section 4), the basal deposits were a fine silver-white sand and an orange clay sand; the surviving secondary fill, a light brown clay with charcoal inclusions. Slumped orange sand lay above this at the

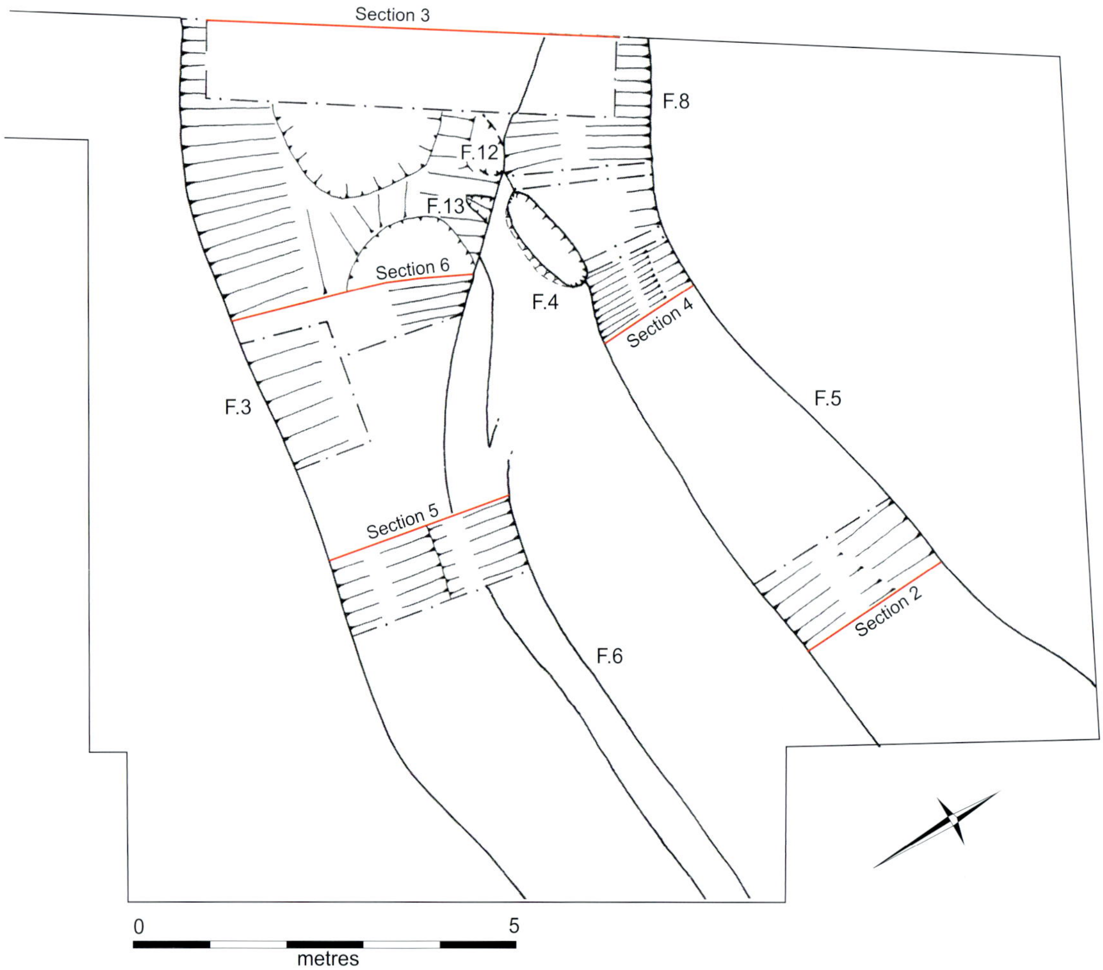

Figure 3.44. *The Marion Close Enclosure, site plan.*

northern edge. In the west (Fig. 3.45, Section 3), the primary fills were yellow/orange and grey/yellow sandy clays; the secondary fill, a yellow/brown clay with occasional marl flecks. The two tertiary fills were both derived from episodes of dumping: the lower, a dark yellow/brown silty clay with frequent charcoal fragments, occupation debris and natural clay pieces; the upper, a light brown to yellow-brown natural clay.

Feature 8 was recut by ditch F.6, beginning at the point where the earlier ditch turned to the northwest (corresponding to both the turn in F.3 and the butt-end of F.6) and from where it continued eastwards. At its butt-end the ditch was 1.2 m wide and 0.55 m deep, increasing to 1.8 × 0.75 m in the east. The fill sequence at the deeper eastern end showed a primary fill of dark grey humic sandy silt with moderate charcoal inclusions, with a secondary fill of light brown, mottled yellow, coarse sandy silt with small pebbles and occasional charcoal fragments. The tertiary fill, a dumped infilling, was a dark brown sandy silt with bone, daub, charcoal, burnt stone and pottery inclusions.

The stratigraphic sequence indicates that ditch F.3 post-dates all of the other features, with the exception of the recut ditch, F.5. The upper part of the latter had been infilled with occupation debris, whereas the deeper part of F.3 had been left to fill gradually. The finds recovered from F.3 (apart from one localized area along its southern edge) had entered the ditch through weathering; there was no evidence that it had been maintained and it had evidently been left to silt up.

None of the ditch features had a constant width or depth. Those of the outer circuit increased in size to the west (F.3 & F.6); F.5, of the northern interior, to the east; and F.8, to both the northwest and east. While the variation in their profiles may have been a recurrent feature around the enclosure's (presumed) circuit, it could also relate to the provision of an entrance: F.6 terminated in a deep butt-end and it is possible that F.8 and F.3 may also, as both deepened adjacent to the edge-of-excavation. Feature 4 and F.12 appear to have been post-pits and may have continued the line of the butt-end of F.6, perhaps as part of a gateway structure (with the large posthole, F.13, possibly related). They were superseded by F.3,

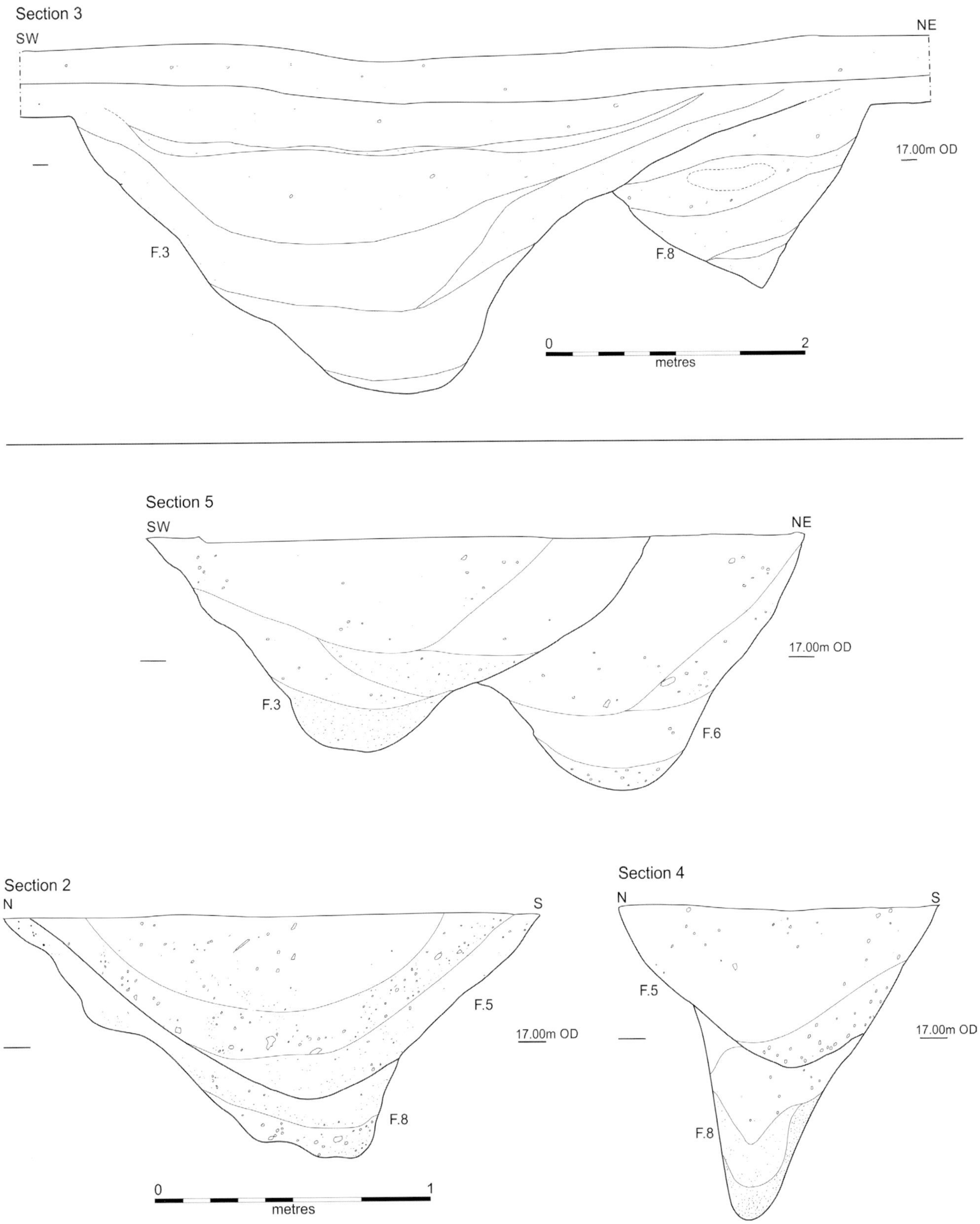

Figure 3.45. *The Marion Close Enclosure, sections (see Fig. 3.44 for location).*

whose upcast sealed them. Alternatively, rather than relating to an entranceway as such, the 'complication' of these ditches (i.e. multiple terminals) could reflect the larger plan of the enclosure as a whole. Essentially, this was a double/bi-vallate circuit converging beside the western edge-of-excavation and this pattern could possibly suggest a complicated outworks/antennae-ditch system (see e.g. the Wardy Hill Ringwork; Evans 2003).

No direct evidence was found to indicate the position of ditch-associated banks. Within all their profiles there was, however, evidence for the re-deposition of sub-soils and occupation debris/soils entering from their northern sides, clearly marking this as the enclosure interior. The plan and curvature of the ditches would point to the same conclusion and that the secondary ditches recut to the south of the original circuit provides further confirmation: the ditch's banks must have lain to the north. Therefore, it can only be assumed that the ditches had accompanying banks and, in the case of the final ditch – F.3 – this may have been of considerable size. That F.3 has been left to infill, with none of its fill deposits deriving from bank material, could suggest that it remained as a substantial earthwork feature long after the enclosure's abandonment.

Across the small area exposed within the interior ditch circuit there was no direct evidence of occupation *per se* (house gullies, *etc.*). However, with attendant banks thought to occupy the larger part of this area, there would be little immediate space for settlement features. The quantity of occupation-derived material recovered, particularly within the inner ditch F.5, would itself attest to settlement within the interior of the enclosure.

Given the limited scale of the fieldwork, the excavations proved quite prolific in finds. Aside from the pottery and faunal assemblages that are detailed below, five worked flints and 260 pieces of fired clay (2.80 kg) were recovered. Most of the latter appear to be daub, with many having smoothed faces and some wattle impressions. No distinct loomweight or spindlewhorl fragments were, however, present.

Pottery (JD. Hill)

Amounting to 316 sherds (1438 g), the density of the pottery suggests that this material derived from activities in the immediate vicinity, although the sherd size in general is small, with few medium-sized sherds (*c.* 10-20 g) and no large sherds or substantial portions of vessels typical of 'fresh' dumps of rubbish or 'special' deposition. All of the pottery is handmade in predominantly sandy or coarse sandy fabrics with a significant presence of plant-tempered pottery. Rims and bases (13 & 5 respectively) are typical of Middle/later Iron Age handmade forms. The four base sherds are either those simply with steep-sided walls coming straight from the bottom of the base or with the distinct step between the base and wall common on vessels of this date. There are almost no burnished or decorated sherds in this collection and only one lightly scored sherd. This one decorated sherd is in a possibly non-local 'rock'-tempered fabric. Rims are generally variants of simple upright and flat-topped undecorated forms, again common across the region. The only different rim comes from a crudely 'S'-profiled bowl/jar; at West Stow, northeast Suffolk, the later Iron Age pottery showed an increasing trend towards 'S'-profiles through time (West 1989). The example from Marion Close (F.5, upper fill) is roughly paralleled at Haddenham V and the early phase at Wardy Hill, Coveney (Hill & Horne 2003 and Hill & Braddock 2006).

Animal Bone (Eftychia Yannouli)

Faunal remains were recovered from a total of five features, and these are presented in Table 3.15. The ditches differed in profile and depth, and *c.* 84 per cent of the animal bone comes from F.3 and F.5, the latest in the sequence. In general, there is considerable evidence for residuality, which together with the small size of the faunal sample makes any observable patterns impossible to confirm. There is some evidence that F.5 contained domestic debris from inside the enclosure and that F.3 remained open for some time after its abandonment, with its deeper part representing natural infilling.

The animal bone sample consists entirely of the remains of domestic mammals and no bone of dog, bird or wild animals was identified (Table 3.15). The material shows moderate to poor preservation, and there are many abraded and gnawed specimens. The bone had lost most of its organic content and was, therefore, friable and prone to damage during excavation and handling. Most of the non-identified specimens were fragments produced during excavation and storage. The identifiable/non-identifiable bone ratio is 1:0.8, precisely the ratio recorded for the New Hall sample. Burrowing animals accounted for most of the marks observed on the bone surface. Dogs, although not osteologically present, have chewed several of the softer epiphyses away and left distinctive tooth-marks on shaft bones. Cut marks have been recorded on a Bos first phalanx (F.3) only, but it is possible that many other marks have been obliterated by abrasion. Among the burnt specimens were the proximal broken epiphysis of a Bos radius (>12–18 months) in F.5, and the first maxillary molar of an adult horse in F.8. Other aspects of the sample include a sheep mandible (6–12 months) with the M_1 root penetrating the ventral portion of the ramus (upper fill of F.6).

Taken as a whole, the Marion Close ditches contained the remains of at least three bovines, four ovicaprids, a pig and one horse. This calculation is based on the assumption of maximal bone interdependence and is quoted only by way of indication. No bones were present that allowed sexing of the finds. Anatomical

Table 3.15. *Number of identified specimens (NISP) by species and feature (* includes original feature numbers F.1, 2, 7, 9 & 10).*

	Sheep (Oa)/ **Goat**	**Cattle**	**Horse**	**Pig**	**Mammal** (large)	**Mammal** (medium)	**Identified Total**	**Non-identified**
F.6	3 (1 Oa)	-	-	-	2	1	6	-
F.8	1	-	1	-	-	-	2	1
F.4	1	1	-	-	-	1	3	8
F.5	12 (2 Oa)	19	1	4	6	6	48	18
F.3*	10 (2 Oa)	7	6	-	10	1	34	50
Unstrat.	1	-	-	-	1	3	5	-
Total	*28*	*27*	*8*	*4*	*19*	*12*	*98*	*77*

Table 3.16. *Distribution of anatomical elements with MNI (cr=cranial; l=lumbar; th=thoracic; p=proximal; sh=shaft; d=distal; * plus 2 long bones).*

	Sheep/Goat	**Cattle**	**Horse**	**Pig**	**Total**
Skull					
Mandible	5	4	-	-	9
Loose tooth (upper)	2	-	4	-	6
Horncore	1	1	-	-	2
Sub-total 1	8	5	4	-	17
Axial Skeleton					
Vertebra	-	1 (cr), 4 (l), 1 (th)	-	-	6
Pelvis	1	4	-	-	5
Sub-total 2	1	10	-	-	11
Fore Quarters					
Scapula	1	-	-	-	1
Humerus	1 (sh), 1 (d)	-	-	1 (d)	3
Radius	2 (sh), 1 (d)	1 (p), 1 (d)	-	-	5
Ulna	-	-	-	1	1
Metacarpal	1 (p), 1 (sh)	-	1 (p), 1 (d)	1 (p)	5
Sub-total 3	8	2	2	3	15
Hind Quarters					
Femur	-	1 (sh)	-	-	1
Tibia	2 (p), 1 (sh), 1 (d)	1 (p), 1 (sh), 1 (d)	-	1 (d)	8
Metatarsal shaft	1 (p), 1 (sh), 1 (d)	1 (p), 1 (d)	1 (p), 1 (d)	-	7
Calcaneum	1	1	-	-	2
Phalanx I	1	2	-	-	3
Phalanx II	-	1	-	-	1
Sub-total 4	9	10	2	1	22
Total	*26**	*27*	*8*	4	65
MNI	4	3	1	1	9

element distribution shows differential representation for different species (Table 3.16). Ovicaprids and cattle predictably display the greatest variety of skeletal parts. In both species, bones from the skull and hind quarters constitute a high proportion of the sample. However, the axial skeleton is better preserved in cattle (10 specimens, 37% of the cattle sample) than in sheep (one specimen, *c.* 4%), and the opposite is true for the fore quarters: two cattle specimens (7%) and eight sheep bones (*c.* 31%). If this skeletal distribution is representative, then it seems that a good number of meaty joints were consumed and/or disposed of elsewhere. However, several aspects of the sample composition are suggestive of canid interference; these include the total absence of sheep (or generally small-size) vertebrae, the paucity of ribs, the absence of softer parts that are usually preferred by chewing dogs (e.g. the proximal humerus), and the predominance of the hardest skeletal components that are generally avoided by these species.

Plant Remains (Chris Stevens)
Eight samples were analysed for charred plant material. Most of the samples were relatively rich in charred plant macro-fossils, and all produced evidence for cereals, especially in the form of glume bases from which the cultivation of spelt wheat, *Triticum spelta*, could be identified, as well as having several grains of glume wheats *Triticum dicoccum/spelta*. In addition, the cultivation of barley *Hordeum* sp. could also be identified from rachis fragments and grains, although the preservation of these was not sufficient enough to determine whether they represent the six-row or hulled forms.

The samples were floated for the extraction of charred plant remains, using a 500 mm mesh to catch the flot and a 1 mm mesh to retain the residue. The flots were sorted using a low-powered stereo-binocular microscope and the extracted plant remains were then identified and quantified.

Of the seeds of wild species, many probably represent weed species brought in with crop. Represented in the samples are many seeds of fat hen (*Chenopodium album*), clover (*Trifolium* sp.) and oats (*Avena* sp.). In addition were seeds of blinks (*Montia fontanum* subsp. *minor*); redshank (*Persicaria maculosa*); knotgrass (*Polygonum aviculare*); black bindweed (*Fallopia convolvulus*); marsh bedstraw (*Galium palustre*); vetch/tare (*Vicia* sp.); brome grass (*Bromus* sp.), meadow grass (*Poa* sp.); nettle (*Urtica dioca*); fig-leaved goosefoot (*Chenopodium ficifolium*); red goosefoot (*Chenopodium rubrum*); orache (*Atriplex* sp.); stitchwort (*Stellaria media*.); ribwort plantain (*Plantago lanceolate*); dock (*Rumex* sp.); woodrush (*Luzula* sp.), scentless mayweed (*Tripleurospermum inodorum*); spikerush (*Eleocharis palustris*); prickly sedge (*Carex muricate*); timothy (*Phleum pratense*); henbane (*Hyoscyamus niger*); field speedwell (*Viola arvensis*); white charlock (*Raphanus raphanistrum*); hedge parsley (*Torilis* sp.); red bartsia (*Odontites verna*); creeping buttercup (*Ranunculus repens*), and self-heal (*Prunella vulgaris*).

The high ratio of glume bases to glume wheat grains suggest that the samples are derived from the fine-sieving waste from final processing, particularly pounding, of glume wheats taken from storage. Of interest is the predominance of small weed seeds, such as those of clover and fat-hen, which suggests that the crop was stored prior to these weed seeds being removed by fine-sieving. Such a pattern has not been observed at other Iron Age sites in the region, such as Little Thetford, West Fen Road, Wandlebury, and also to the northwest at Broom Quarry, Bedfordshire, where crops appear almost always fine-sieved before storage (see e.g. Stevens in Evans *et al.* 2013a, 197–201). Such differences have been linked to the levels of both household and inter-household co-operation, as well as possibly increased emphasis on pastoral activities upon those sites displaying little processing prior to storage.

The large number of barley rachis fragments (which are usually removed by threshing) in the sample from F.3 would also indicate that fine-sieving would not appear to have been carried out prior to storage for this crop either.

In terms of the weed seeds, large numbers of seeds of the Chenopodiaceae, as well as other species associated with nitrogen-rich soils such as stitchwort and nettle, are a common feature of Middle Iron Age sites, often in conjunction with low numbers of seeds of vetch/tare (*Vicia/Lathyrus* sp.; Stevens 1996). Such an assemblage would probably suggest a greater predominance of spring, as opposed to autumn, sowing, and little nitrogen loss through either over-cropping or leaching of nitrogen via flooding. In general, wetland species are fairly poorly represented in most of the samples, although the sample from F.3 contains seeds of both blinks, marsh bedstraw, white charlock and spikerush, all species associated with wet soils.

Several species are present which are associated with drier acidic soils, such as sheep's sorrel (*Rumex acetosella*) and prickly sedge (*Carex muricate*), as well as those of wetter soils, white charlock and blinks. Both self-heal and ribwort plantain, which are more characteristic of alkaline soils, are found in the same samples and possibly suggest some mixing of crops grown on differing soil types.

Discussion
The discovery of the previously unknown Middle/later Iron Age Marion Close enclosure is of significance. Aside from its intrinsic value, especially its economic evidence, we will see that there seems to have been a relative paucity of Middle Iron Age occupation within the investigated West Cambridge lands. Leaving aside at this time issues of the period's land-use densities (see *BLS*, chap. 3), the key question is the enclosure's scale and character. While there is a slight and regular curvature to its circuit, it is impossible to estimate its size given the limited exposure.[18] If taking the maximum profile of the outer ditch (F.3) as being typical of the whole – 6 m wide and 2.25 m deep – it could be compared to the area's 'great' enclosures of the period (i.e. Wandlebury and Arbury; see *RVS*, Chap. 6). This, however, seems unlikely and that ditch's scale most probably relates to a local phenomenon, such as in-ditch 'welling' and/or entrance-related deepening. While its layout may well have been complicated (i.e. multi-circuited) and possibly even defended (see e.g. the Wardy Hill Ringwork; Evans 2003), it is far more likely that this was a 'domestic-type' enclosure; this interpretation gains further credence by the quantity of occupation material associated with it.

Fitzwilliam College (with Adam Slater)
Anticipating the construction of a new library, in 2008 excavations occurred over 500 sq. m within the grounds

Figure 3.46. *Fitzwilliam College, New Library Site: excavation photograph looking south with* The Grove *behind (top) and, below, diverse pottery (note Medieval strap-handled lower centre and, bottom right, Deverel Rimbury ware).*

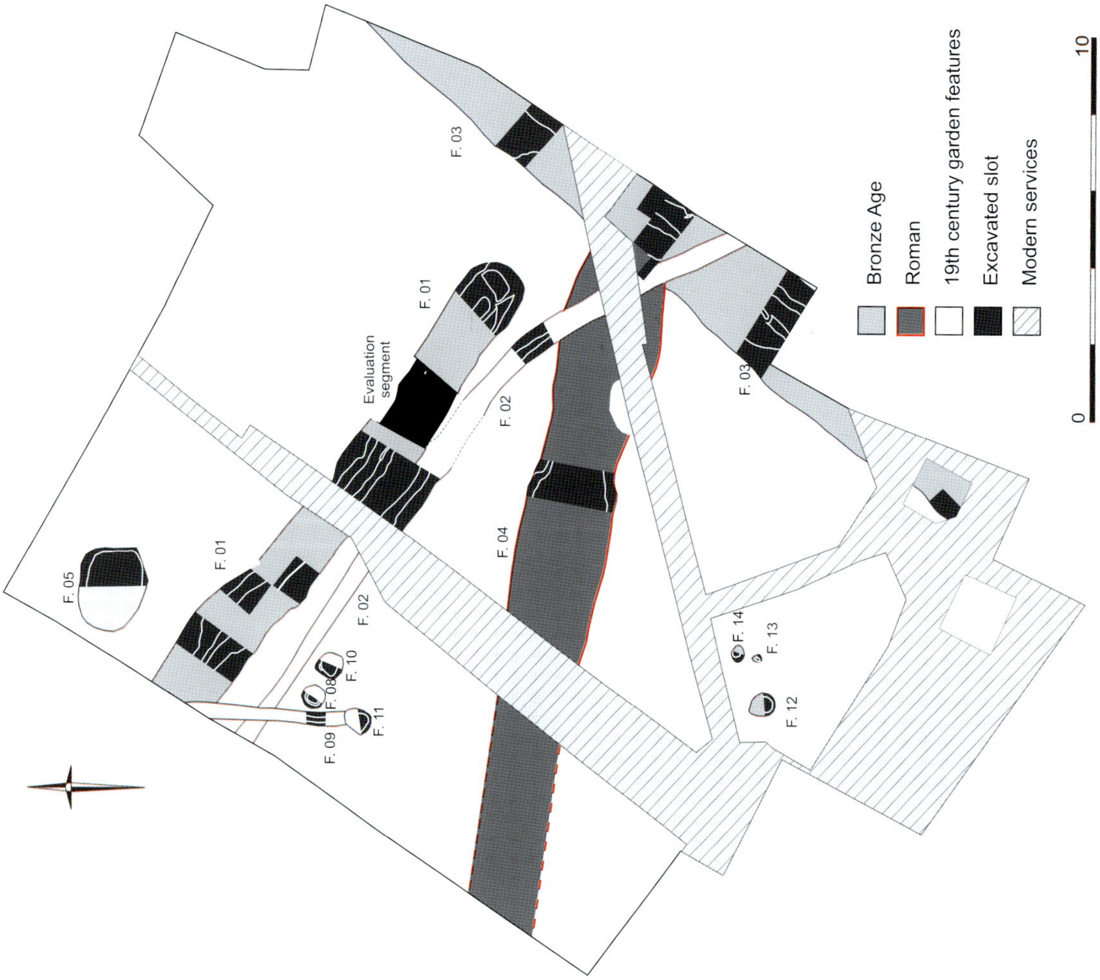

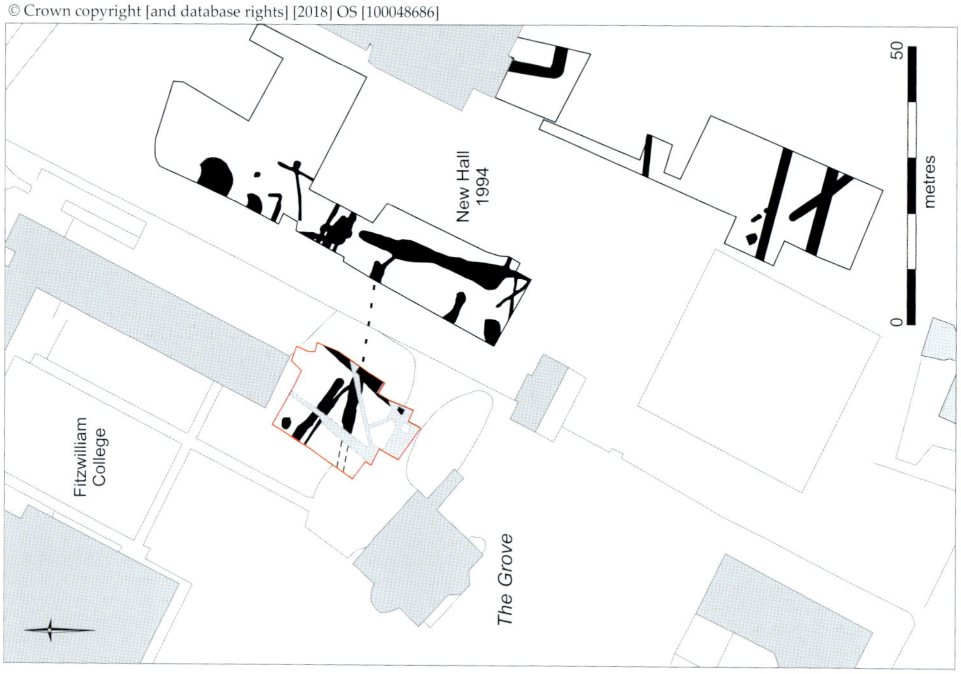

Figure 3.47. *Fitzwilliam College, New Library Site, plans.*

of Fitzwilliam College (Fig. 3.47; Slater 2008a). The site-area lay just 15 m west of New Hall's main area (I) and it certainly proved a useful further exposure of the area's archaeology; not least, as its sequence was more readily intelligible, not having seen Roman quarrying activity.

With the site situated immediately in front of *The Grove*, there was evidence of intensive landscaping and that various probably nineteenth-century planting beds and shallow ditches/troughs were present was not at all surprising (see Fig. 3.46 and *Inset* for the Darwin Family Estate findings). Leaving aside any possible implications of a large Medieval strap-handle sherd recovered from a tree-bowl (F.5), there was only one definite Roman-period feature (F.4). Just a few second–third-century AD sherds and a small number of animal bones (a cattle skull, mandible and a red deer antler) were recovered from the two sections dug across this 2.1 m wide ditch (*c.* 0.25 m deep); with the same alignment as New Hall's 'back-road', it appeared to lie on the projected line of one of the earlier site's ditches (F.209).

Somewhat unexpected was the size and extent of the Fitzwilliam Library Site's Middle Bronze Age features (Fig. 3.47). Oriented northeast–southwest, the one such ditch, F.3, was up to 2.85 m across and 1.2 m deep. Lying on the return-axis to it (with a *c.* 2.2 m wide entrance-gap between), another – F.1 – was *c.* 1.9 m wide, 0.7 m deep and 'V'-shaped (its terminal end, F.7, had been recut and was shallower: *c.* 0.45 m deep). As reported on by Mark Knight, 37 sherds of shell-tempered Deverel Rimbury pottery (70 g) were recovered from these two features and included one with a fingertip-impressed raised cordon (Fig. 3.46, front centre). Samples processed from these ditches yielded seeds of elder, two cereal grains and a culm node. Some quantity of animal bone was, moreover, present in their fills (286 pieces), particularly within their uppermost levels. Characteristic of the period's assemblages, this was dominated by cow (64% NISP), followed by pig (18%) and sheep/goat (10%; there were also three Red deer bones).

A Late Bronze/Early Iron Age sherd occurred in one of a cluster of three postholes in the site's southern end and it is conceivable that they all related to 'early' settlement.[19]

Trinity Hall Playing Fields (with Jennifer Wills)

Prior to the New Hall excavations, a limited trial trenching programme had been undertaken in 1991 along the southeastern side of Fitzwilliam College for the new Wilson Building. Situated south of *The Grove* and beside New Hall, this fell close to the (later) projected line of the Roman road (Gdaniec 1991). Yet, apart from a few small scraps of Roman pottery, no early features or material were recovered, and it would seem that nineteenth-century landscaping and quarrying had greatly disturbed the area (see *Quarrying Imprint*... Chap. 2 above). There were similarly negative results when, a decade later, the Norfolk Archaeological Unit cut trial trenches across the southwestern quarter of that College's grounds in advance of yet further building (Adams & Penn 2001). Though recovering three Medieval sherds, the absence of the road-line came as a surprise given the location of their trenches and, to be frank, it almost made one doubt the validity of the New Hall results.

It was for this reason that the CAU subsequently welcomed the opportunity to undertake trial investigations in the neighbouring plot of Trinity Hall's Playing Fields to the west in January 2004. The results this time were immediately positive. Not only was the New Hall southern Roman road obviously present (Road 1), but there was also a density of accompanying Roman archaeology (Figs. 3.48–9) Accordingly, over four weeks in May and June of that same year a *c.* 0.2 ha area was excavated (Wills 2004a & b).

The Roadway and Settlement

The road was generally defined by its flanking ditches, which lay parallel 6–8 m apart (Fig. 3.49). These, in the main, were 0.8–2.5 m wide and 0.3–1.2 m deep (e.g. F.1036/1037 & F.1021). Across the western half of its exposed length they had, however, been 'ropily' recut in more minor gullies (e.g. F.1009, 1.3 m wide and 0.4–0.5 m deep). For the most part their fills were unremarkable, being largely orange/brown silty clays. They generated few finds: a low density of first–second-century AD sherds and animal bones; a first-century Nauhiem Derivative brooch was, though, recovered from the surface of F.1021 (Fig. 3.51.2). This only really varied in the case of F.1091, along the road's northwestern length. Of rather larger irregular form (2.85–3.25 m wide), this produced a higher density of material. Including second to third century AD pottery, plus fragments of tile and bone, this may attest to immediate settlement (or, alternatively, quarry-related disturbance/deposition; see below). It is also noteworthy that a complete horse skeleton (i.e. a carcass) had been deposited in the northern roadside ditch midway along its length (F.1037; Fig. 3.50).

Along its length, swathes of the road surface were found to have been locally reduced and, at one point (F.1085), its metalled surface survived. This makes its attribution as a routeway unequivocal.

The southern roadside ditches were observed to truncate a ditch corner (F.1038 & F.1040/1041), whose boundaries were 0.9–1.3 m wide and *c.* 0.5 m deep. This would seem to correlate with similar ditch-lines north of the road: running parallel, F.1001 and, on a north–south return axis, F.1002/1003, whose southern terminal was just truncated by the roadway. These ditches had homogeneous, grey-orange/brown clay/sandy silt fills and produced few finds (only a handful of sherds of first-/second-century AD pottery and fragments of bone).

Given their layout it is difficult to know whether these features should best be termed 'paddocks' or considered part of a fieldsystem. Regardless, their complementary layout and the fact that the shared axis of their eastern boundaries coincided would indicate that the road here passed through – or, better, 'arrived at' – a distinct settlement. Whilst the road's ditches did

Figure 3.48. *Trinity Hall Playing Fields excavation, photograph looking east along Roman road-line towards Fitzwilliam College.*

indeed truncate these boundaries, thereby implying that at least theoretically the settlement may have predated it, it is clear from their interrelationship that they co-existed. This is also apparent in the pattern of 'ropey' recutting of the roadway's ditches upon entering the area of the paddocks/fieldsystem. It is, in fact, possible that the southwesterly kinking in the line of the southern roadway boundary reflects that an arm or spur of this route turned into the settlement proper at that point.

Later Roman Activity

Extensive evidence of Roman quarrying was found south of the northern paddock/fieldsystem boundary, which extended throughout the area of the road (Fig. 3.49). Generally these consisted of discrete sub-circular/ovoid pits, 0.9–2.2 m across and 0.15–0.7 m deep, though in some instances these had been compounded into larger irregular hollows. However, within the area of the road proper more linear configurations were present (e.g. F.1094), the largest being F.1083. This was 2.2–4 m across and 0.6–0.8 m deep; extending for some 18.50 m, it definitely truncated the roadway's metalling. A considerable quantity of domestic refuse was recovered from the three excavated segments of that feature. As well as animal bone, oyster shell and a fragment of glass and a worked limestone block, 52 sherds were recovered from it, including a half-complete samian dish and a Nene Valley greyware dish; a coin of Allectus (AD 293–5) was also found in its upper fills.

A grave, F.1088, cut the western terminal of long quarry hollow (Fig. 3.50). This contained the poorly preserved skeleton of a gracile female in a supine position (without accompanying grave-goods). The very disturbed and fragmented remains of another adult, F.1112, whose lower legs only appeared to survive *in situ*, was found in the southeast corner of the site. There was evidence of other disturbed graves in the vicinity, with fragments of skull (adult, parietal bone) recovered from pit F.1089 and, nearby, a radius midshaft from the northern road-side ditch (F.1036).

Figure 3.49. *Trinity Hall Playing Fields excavation, site plans.*

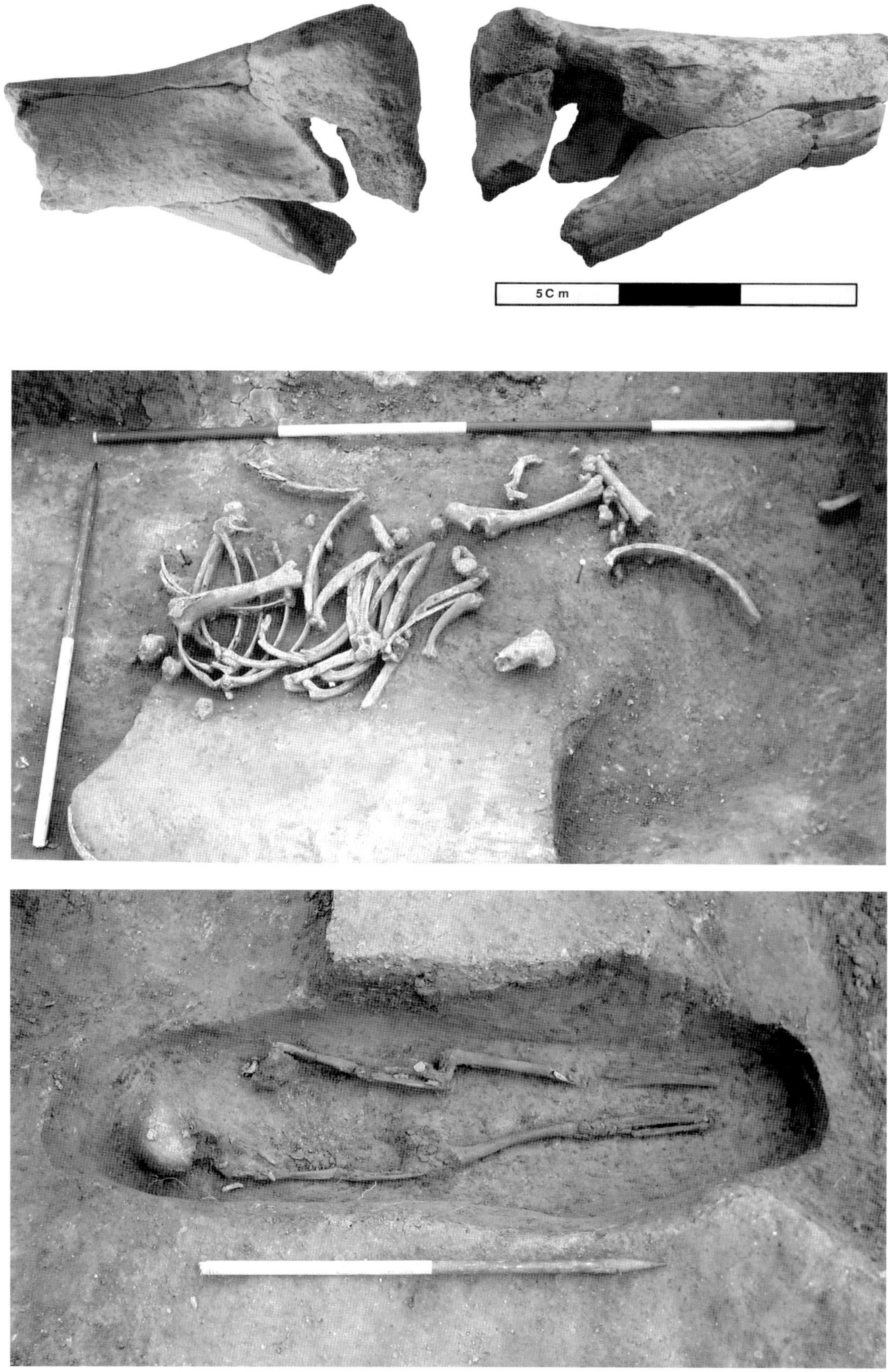

Figure 3.50. *Trinity Hall Playing Fields excavation, photographs of aurochs humerus midshaft (F.1038; top), horse carcass (F.1037; middle) and, bottom, Skeleton F.1088.*

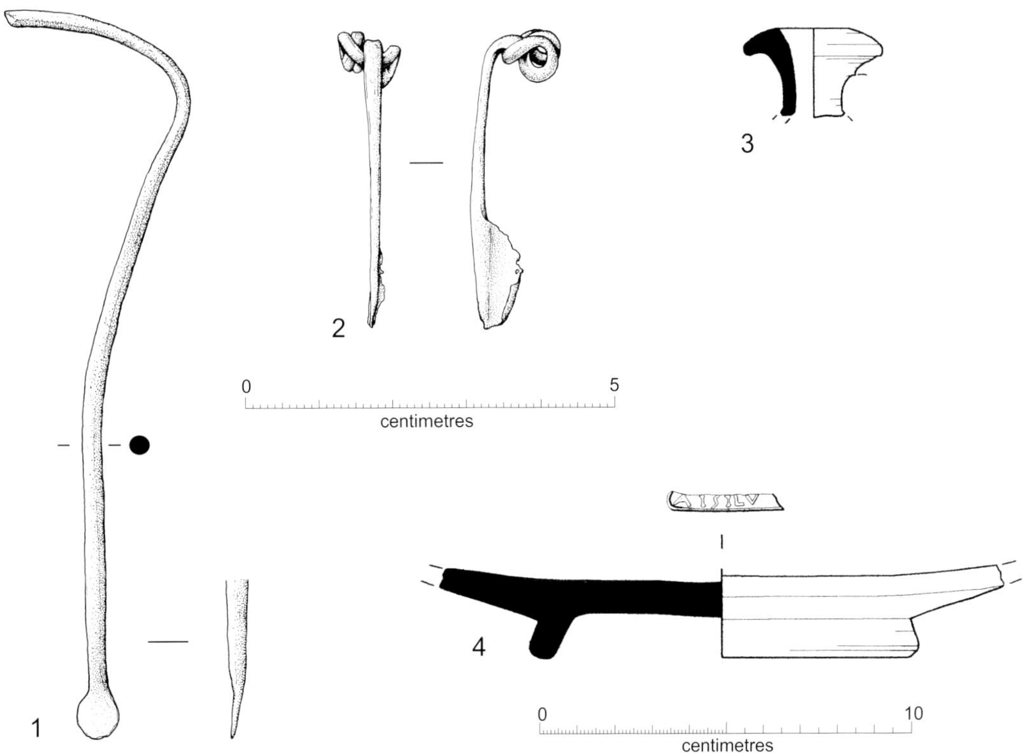

Figure 3.51. *Trinity Hall Playing Fields excavation finds: 1) copper alloy* Ligula; *2) Nauheim Derivative brooch (copper alloy); 3 & 4) Roman pottery (see text).*

Roman Pottery (Katie Anderson)
Weighing 1458 g, 214 sherds of Roman pottery were recovered from excavations, with a further 30 sherds (676 g) forthcoming from the earlier evaluation phase (Table 3.17).

From the first, evaluation phase, several sherds are of interest. This includes two from Rhodian pink amphora, dated second century AD, and apparently from different vessels. These were recovered from F.18, one of the roadway ditches, and [013]; the latter, a Post-Medieval context. Feature 8, the southern roadway boundary, yielded a large body sherd with handle-stump from an early Baetican amphora dated mid first to mid second century AD.

Three of the features produced sherds of Central Gaulish Samian, dated *c.* AD 120–150 (F.13 & F.14), including a base from a small cup (Dr.33) in F.8. The base was stamped, however, due to the level of abrasion it was illegible and thus can only be dated AD 120–150 (Fig. 3.51.4). Otherwise, with few exceptions (including the amphorae), the pottery was small and very abraded. All the material that could be accurately dated was of the first and second century AD.

The pottery from the excavation proper consisted of both local and non-local wares and represents 3.73 EVEs. The most common fabric types are grey sandy wares, which accounted for 37 per cent of the total assemblage and oxidized sandy wares that represent 34 per cent. Black slipped wares are also common, some of which are burnished and may have been local imitations of Dorset Black Burnished ware. All of these wares are likely to have been locally made, although their exact origin is unclear.

Non-local wares represent *c.* 12 per cent of the total assemblage and consist of three different types of finewares. The most common is Central Gaulish Samian, of which there are 20 sherds (191 g). However, this figure may be slightly misleading, as 15 of the sherds are from a single vessel, a Dr.18/31 with a stamped base in F.1083. This, too, is heavily abraded and thus illegible; it dates to approximately AD 120–150. Central Gaulish Samian was also found in four other features (including another vessel from F.1083). All of these are very small and abraded, and no further vessel forms can be identified.

Table 3.17. *Showing all fabric types from excavation and evaluation.*

Fabric	No.	Wt. (g)
Baetican amphora	1	429
Black slipped wares	29	191
Central Gaulish samian	23	201
Colchester samian	1	15
Nene Valley greyware	5	102
Oxford red slipped ware	1	20
Oxidized sandy ware	83	641
Rhodian amphora	2	51
Sandy greyware	94	477
Southern Gaulish samian	5	7
Total	*244*	*2134*

Five sherds of Southern Gaulish Samian were recovered from two different contexts. Feature 1021 had two sherds from a Dr.42, a small handled bowl, dating to AD 69–100, and from F.1093 there were three sherds, all of which are non-diagnostic and, therefore, can only be dated to AD 40–100.

There are two British finewares in the assemblage, consisting of a single sherd from a Colchester Samian flagon, dated AD 155–180, and a sherd from an Oxfordshire or Hadham red-slipped bowl dating to the third–fourth century AD. Other sherds of known origin consist of five sherds from a Nene Valley greyware dog dish of mid–late second-century AD attribution, although no colour-coated sherds were found.

The pottery was generally small and abraded, and therefore only a small number of sherds are diagnostic. Of these, the most common vessel forms are beaded rim jars; these represent 44 per cent of all the diagnostic sherds but only 11 per cent of the total assemblage. Other vessel forms include two beaded bowls, two flanged bowls and a flagon.

The Roman pottery from each of the site's main feature-/'component'-allocations will be discussed separately:

Enclosure Ditches - Four of the enclosure ditches contained Roman pottery: F.1001, F.1003 and F.1100. All had single sandy greyware sherds, while F.1099 had seven such sherds. All of are non-diagnostic and, therefore, can only be generically dated as 'Romano-British'.

The Roadway - A total of 34 sherds of Roman pottery (133 g) were recovered from six segments excavated along the length of the southern roadside ditch, F.1021. Dated to the mid first–second century AD and including two Southern Gaulish Samian sherds, the remaining sherds are locally produced coarseware vessels. Only four vessel forms can be identified: a beaded-rim jar, a flanged bowl, a lid/dish and the samian Dr.42. The sherds were generally small and abraded, with a mean weight of only 4 g. While suggesting that they may have been redeposited, this feature is unlikely to date beyond the mid second century AD.

Feature 1036, the northern roadway ditch, contained 15 sherds of pottery (187 g), with a mean weight of 12.5 g. This is significantly higher than that of F.1021. This result may be slightly deceptive due to the presence of four large sherds weighing between 34 and 42 g. However, this does imply that they are less likely to have been redeposited. The fabrics are similar to those found in F.1021, consisting of sandy wares and black-slipped wares. Vessel forms that can be identified include two beaded-rim jars and two flat bases, which are probably from jars/beakers. This pottery is also dated mid first to second century AD, confirming this as the date of the roadway.

The Quarries - The bulk of the Roman pottery was recovered from features related to quarrying, with 119 sherds (918 g), with a mean weight of 8 g. These features appear to have been the latest evidence of Roman activity on the site. The pottery from them had, however, a more varied date range and includes sherds dating from the mid first century AD to the third century AD. This is somewhat expected, since the pottery is unlikely to have purposefully deposited in the quarry pits and those sherds that were found are likely to have either come from earlier features or may have been on the surface for a period of time before being deposited within the quarry pits.

The pottery from these features had a range of fabrics and forms, including 18 sherds of Central Gaulish Samian, three Southern Gaulish Samian pieces and five Nene Valley greyware sherds. The remaining sherds consisted of grey and oxidized sandy wares and black slipped wares. Several different vessel forms could be identified, including necked jars, a beaded bowl and a shallow dish, as well as the Dr.18/31 mentioned above. Most of the sherds are however, non-diagnostic and abraded.

Perhaps unsurprising since it was one of the largest pits on the site, F.1083 contained the largest quantity of pottery with 52 sherds. This includes some large, unabraded sherds, such as the half-complete samian dish and the Nene Valley greyware shallow dish. Vessels of an earlier date were, though, also found in this feature.

In general, all of the Roman pottery is small and abraded, which suggests that it may have been redeposited from elsewhere, or perhaps that sherds were on the surface for a period of time before being deposited. This seems a likely explanation, given the nature of the site's features, as pottery may have been on the surface of the Roman roadway for a period of time. The quarry pits had pottery of various dates, which supports the view that many of the sherds were redeposited. The nature of the pottery, in terms of forms and their functions, suggests that this was primarily a domestic assemblage and that there was a settlement site in the vicinity.

The numbers of fineware and imported vessels, however, can be considered significant, accounting for 18 per cent of the total assemblage (including material from the evaluation) by count and 57 per cent by weight. The higher percentage by weight is, in part, due to the presence of a large amphora sherd found during the evaluation. However, for such a small assemblage the quantity of finewares and imported wares is intriguing. It suggests that there may have been a somewhat wealthier than average site within the vicinity that had good access to trade networks, even in the Early Roman period.

The bulk of the pottery dates to the first to second century AD. There were also some vessels from the mid–late second century AD, consisting of the Central Gaulish Samian and the Nene Valley greyware dish. There is also the Oxfordshire/Hadham red-slipped bowl dating to third–fourth century AD. This vessel is, therefore, very unusual since it is the only one to date to the later Roman period. There were however, three coins recovered dating to the third and fourth centuries AD, which suggests that there may have been some activity taking place at this time, though on a much reduced scale than previously.

Metalwork (Matt Brudenell and Andrew Hall)

The site, both its features and topsoil, was subject to a comprehensive metal-detector survey. Aside from the coin of Allectus (AD 293–5) found in the fill of the 'long' quarry hollow (F.1083), two other Roman coins were recovered. These are an issue of Victorinus (AD 265–70) from F.15 – a quarry pit exposed during the evaluation – and a coin of Theodosian II dating to AD 388–402 from a Post-Medieval pit (F.1011).

A Nauheim Derivative brooch from the northern roadside ditch (F.1021) is plain with a narrow flat-sectioned and a tapering bow; its pin and catch-plate return are missing (Fig. 3.51.2). It is similar to a brooch recovered from Skeleton Green (No. 32; Partridge 1981, 138) and Brooch 11 from Alexander's Ridgeon's Garden excavations in Cambridge (*RCAM*, 85).

A *ligula* toilet spoon, 11.5 cm long with a flattened end-scoop (Fig. 3.51.1), was found in F.19 during the evaluation. Used for extracting and mixing cosmetics (though in this style possibly also for pushing back cuticles; Crummy 1983, 59), such items were in use throughout Roman times.

Apart from a lead casting droplet (undated), the other metalwork recovered through the surveys comprised Medieval and Post-Medieval items, and ranged from a musket ball to buckles, jettons/seals and a fifteenth-century silver penny of Edward IV.

Environmental Remains and Economic Data

As reported by Ellen Simmons, 14 bulk environmental samples were analysed from a variety of Roman feature/context types. In contrast to the molluscan assemblage, which was generally abundant and well-preserved, there was a marked paucity of charred plant remains. In this case surely indicative of poor preservation conditions, items of culm material (straw) were, nevertheless, recovered from both the north paddock/fieldsystem boundary (F.1001) and also a roadside ditch on that side (F.1109). These are significant as they attest that crop-processing occurred within the vicinity and, as such, are another signature of settlement *per se*.

All the samples contained land snails that were either catholic in their habit requirements or characteristic of damp grassy vegetation (e.g. F.1009). Some of the deeper roadside ditches produced assemblages of aquatic molluscan taxa representing a waterlogged environmental niche. The occurrence, for example, of *Planorbis planorbis*, *Valvata cristata* and *Planorbis crista* in F.1109 and F.1091 suggest seasonal standing water in their lower profiles (see Simmons and table 5 in Wills 2004b for full analysis).

First studied by Chris Swaysland (using a modified version of the POSAC methodology; Davis 1992), and subsequently by Vida Rajkovača, the animal bone assemblage consisted of 1184 fragments (7683 g). The most common represented species was horse (15; 38.4%). Although only counting as one find, this includes the disturbed, partially articulated horse skeleton recovered from F.1036 (Fig. 3.50, middle). The left radius, ulna, carpals and metacarpal were found in close association, as well as a number of ribs and vertebrae. The bones were mature, but there was no further evidence for a more precise age or sex. It is estimated that the horse had a withers height of *c*. 1.39 m, equating to 13.7 hands.

Cattle was the second-most frequent species (13; 33.3%), with a mixture of meat- and non-meat-bearing bones present; sheep/goat was represented by eight bones, with pig and dog by just one bone each (as was also the aurochs; see Note 19).

Discussion

Although the quantity of Roman finds recovered from the excavations was somewhat less than prolific, it is certainly sufficient to suggest the existence of a settlement within the local environs. This presumably lay within the axes of its flanking paddock boundaries and, based on the evidence of ditch F.1091, its focus must lie just west of the site's limits. While most of this material is of second–third-century AD date, there are indications, for example, the samian, brooch and amphorae, to suggest that it had its origins in earlier Roman times. Indeed, the quality of some of the material, including the *ligula* – as well as the prominence of finewares and imported vessels within the pottery assemblage – suggest that this was a settlement of some status.

The late history of the road, at least over this immediate length, would seem to be one of, essentially, waste ground. The evidence of the quarrying, as well as the two inhumations, would indicate that by the third–fourth century AD it had gone out of use. The horse carcass deposited within in its northern flanking ditch (F.1037), likely attesting to the convenient disposal of a sick animal, would equally indicate that its boundaries were no longer being maintained. That being said, as indicated on Hall and Ravendale's West Fields sketch-map (1976) and shown on Figure 7.10, the route of the Medieval *Grithow Weye* track – leading from Cambridge to the 'quarry hamlet' of its namesake (see Chap. 4, *Allied Investigations*) – would appear to roughly coincide with the route of the Roman road. Perhaps a matter of lingering earthwork survival, a similar instance occurred in relationship to the Roman road linking North West Cambridge's Sites II and IV, which is detailed in the next book.

Murray Edwards (with Jacqui Hutton, Richard Newman and Dave Webb)

A summary of the 2009 fieldwork along New Hall's Huntingdon Road-side (the College, by then, having changed its name to Murray Edwards) featured in a previous paper concerned with Roman Cambridge's early settlement (Evans & Ten Harkel 2010, fig. 4; see Hutton 2009). Given, however, the importance of its findings for the town's *Via Devana* approach road – as

Figure 3.52. *Murray Edwards excavation, photograph showing Area 1 trench beside* The Grove's *Huntingdon Roadside gatehouse.*

well as the need to incorporate yet another phase of investigation there – their further inclusion here is warranted.

In the course of the 2009 programme two areas of investigation were targeted: a *c.* 12 m long trench immediately west of Grove Lodge (Area 1) and a smaller sondage at the eastern end of the College (Area 2; Figs. 3.52–3). Although disturbed by nineteenth-century features, Roman road metalling was exposed in both and, in Area 1, layers of gravel and cobbling extended to at least a width of 6.6 m (Fig. 3.54). Given the limited scale of these exposures, a substantial pottery assemblage was recovered: 322 sherds (3487 g). Dating from the late first to earlier third centuries AD, this included both a Colchester whiteware sherd and London Wares, with the bulk of this material coming from the larger Area 1. While possibly deriving from the adjacent New Hall/Fitzwilliam College settlement (though a north-of-road source is equally possible; see below), this generally consisted of small and abraded pieces incorporated within the road metallings. In contrast, the some 70 sherds recovered from the surface in Area 2 were larger and fresher, and suggested yet another, more easterly, settlement-source.

A small fragment of an adult human parietal bone and three fragments from a lower Niedermendig lava quernstone were also recovered, both from the road's metalling. Even greater quantities of broken-up quernstones were present when, in 2011, Area 1 was extended to the north and east alongside Huntingdon Road (Webb & Newman 2011). With the road's metalling then exposed to its full width of 9 m, a series of intercutting quarry pits (containing second-century AD material) occurred along the route's northern edge. In addition, four further features were recovered, including pits and a shallow gully, which all appeared settlement-related (Fig. 3.53).

As reported on by Simon Timberlake, in addition to two unworked building stones (one limestone; the other, a small glacial erratic boulder with mortar adhering), four further fragments of rotary quern were then recovered. One was in 'standard' Millstone Grit,

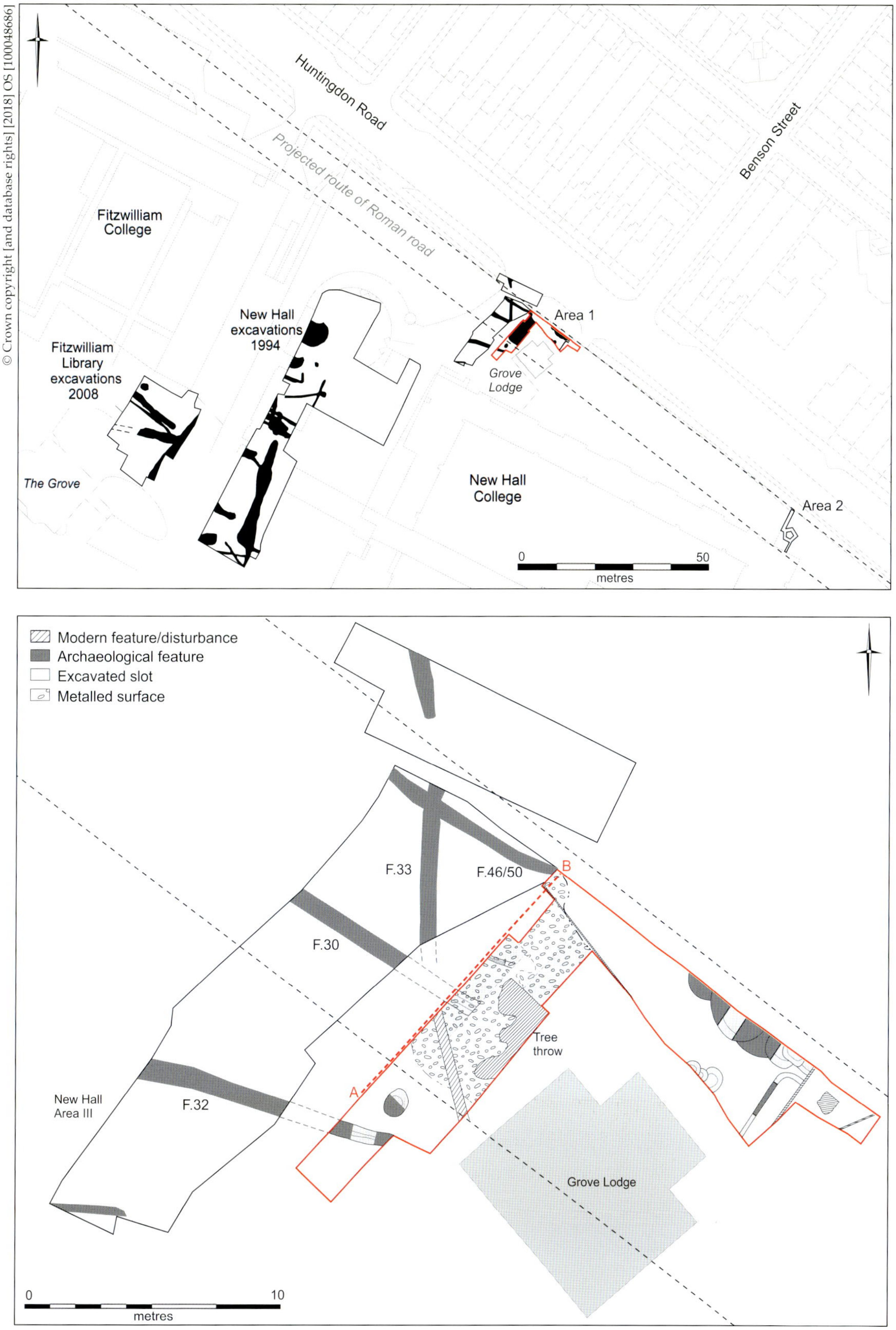

Figure 3.53. *Murray Edwards excavation, location map and Area 1 feature plan.*

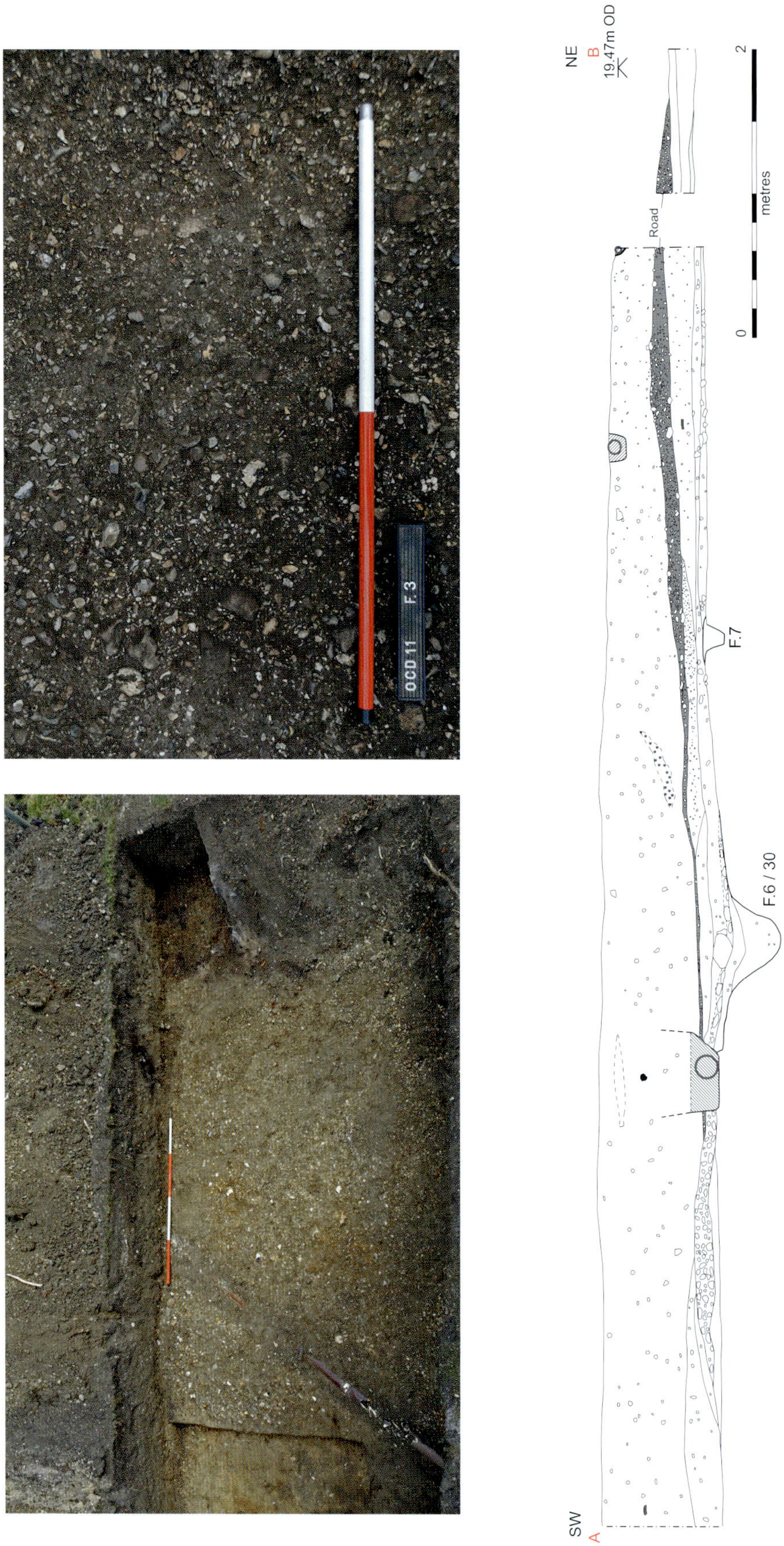

Figure 3.54. *Murray Edwards excavation, Area 1, main section (below) and photographs of road metalling.*

Table 3.18. *Pottery fabrics and sources.*

Fabric	2009		2011		Combined total	
	No.	Wt. (g)	No.	Wt. (g)	No.	Wt. (g)
Black-slipped ware	5	42	1	19	6	61
Buff sandy ware	68	327	4	23	72	350
Coarse sandy greyware	171	1454	152	950	323	2404
Colchester whiteware	1	315	-	-	1	315
Fine sandy greyware	2	4	3	16	5	20
Horningsea greyware	21	687	-	-	21	687
London Ware	3	67	-	-	3	67
Nene Valley colour-coat	2	3	-	-	2	3
Oxidized sandy ware	16	117	3	21	19	138
Reduced sandy ware	11	236	9	75	20	311
Samian (Central Gaulish)	7	16	31	134	38	150
Samian (East Gaulish)	2	14	-	-	2	14
Samian (South Gaulish)	1	1	-	-	1	1
Shell-tempered ware	-	-	1	4	1	4
Slipped	8	126	-	-	8	126
White-slipped	1	12	1	2	2	14
Whiteware	3	66	4	41	7	107
Amphora	-	-	1	205	1	205
Total	*322*	*3487*	*210*	*1490*	*532*	*4977*

another fashioned from quartzitic sandstone, while two are in Old Red Sandstone and were probably imported from the southwest of the country (e.g. Mendips, Wye Valley or Forest of Dean). Also present was small quantity of burnt clay and mortar, with the two pieces of the latter having a coating of lime plaster.[20]

Finally, in the course of this work (and as also studied by Katie Anderson), a further 210 sherds of Roman pottery were recovered. Including sherds from at least four samian vessels, further whitewares and a sherd from a second–third-century AD amphora base (probably a Dressel 20-type), this takes the combined 'Murray Edwards-phase' total to over 500 sherds (4977 g). As indicated in Table 3.18, together finewares account for 8.4 per cent, with samian represented at 7.7 per cent (and higher than its <5% frequency in most Cambridgeshire assemblages). This could suggest a relatively high-status settlement-source for this material, as might also the building stones, plastered mortar and quernstone imported from afar.

It is difficult to be certain of the date of route's foundation. Respecting the road's northwest–southeast alignment, a ditch sealed by its surfaces included a few mid to later first-century AD sherds. While it is possible that this attests to an earlier phase of an unmetalled 'way', its surfaces – which were not evidently ditch-flanked – would appear to be of late first- to early second-century AD date; it could, therefore, still be the case that the more southerly 'New Hall'/Margery 231 route was earlier. For the first time, however, these excavations indubitably 'fix' the line of the Godmanchester Road west of Roman Cambridge proper: falling on a more northwest–southeast axis than projected in Alexander and Pullinger's *Roman Cambridge* mapping (*RCAM*; see Fig. 2.3).

East of *The Lodge*, a slight linear rise is apparent in the grounds beside the road. While possibly relating to later landscaping and/or recent road construction, it might also mark the Roman road-line. It may also be relevant that in the later nineteenth century, in his plan of Roman Cambridge, Babington (1883, 5) indicated an upstanding earthwork embankment along the southern side of Huntingdon Road west of the *Via Devana*'s gate. His plan is, admittedly, only a sketch and its orientation can only be considered approximate; nevertheless, it could well correspond with our plotting of the road's route.

General Discussion

Given the partial exposure of portions of New Hall's Roman settlement, the excavations contribute relatively little to the understanding of the period's settlements; the site's main contribution relates to shedding light on the organization of Roman Cambridge's road system. Certainly, the entirely unexpected discovery of the Back-College Road is itself significant and adds an important dimension to the landscape of Roman Cambridge.

Roads West

As projected northeastward, the alignment of the Back-College Road (No. 1) would correspond with the observation of a western Roman gate at Morley's Garage by St Joseph (*RCAM*, 67, fig. 6.18). This is a 'neat' interrelationship, inasmuch as a gate at this point would bisect the line of the later western defences. This coincidence, and the fact that the gate siting also roughly matches the converging alignment of (the south-of-Huntingdon Road) Godmanchester route, encourages this interpretation of the axes of the western Roman town. That said, by the time that Roman Cambridge was walled New Hall's road may no longer have been operational; this will be further discussed below. The 'Y'-shaped configuration of these routes could have earlier been a significant point, one possibly marked by a shrine and/or market-place; in other words, a configuration not unlike that now postulated for the town's South Gate and where a cemetery was possibly situated (see Chap. 2). The same might, in fact, true of the West Gate-area in the light of the area's human remains. As outlined in the preceding chapter, perhaps relating to St Edmund's College's findings, the recovery of loose human bone from the limited investigations at both the Buckingham and Mount Pleasant House Sites (see Fig. 2.23) – each variously seeing historical and latter-day large-scale extraction/construction – could also suggest the location of a Roman-period cemetery adjacent to the roads' 'apex'. Unfortunately, though, due to the area's extreme disturbance, this matter will never now be resolved with certainty.

Within the Roman town itself, New Hall's road would have run perpendicular to Akeman Street and Alexander's Street 1. The 2006 Castle Street excavations established the route of *Via Devana* within the town – it ran further south than Alexander *et al.* would have had it (see Evans & Ten Harkel 2010, fig. 1, 55 & 56). The central crossroads identified by Alexander may have actually been where Akeman Street and the Back-College Road met. Their axial alignment would appear to complement that of both Cambridge's central Late Iron Age enclosures and its main earliest Roman feature: the would-be Claudian fort (*RCAM*, figs. 2.1, 3.1 & 7.2)

West of Cambridge, the New Hall southern roadway could generally correspond with the route to St Neots and possibly Bolnhurst, crossing Ermine Street at Caxton Gibbet: Margary Route no. 231 (Margary 1955, 26; see also Wilkes & Elrington 1978, 16 & 26).[21] At many points, its precise route is uncertain (Bagshawe & Johnston actually had it leave the town through the southwest gate, sharing it with the Cambridge-Wimpole Road: 1964, 264–7, 491–3). During the mid 1960s Liller inspected a service trench dug from Madingley Road to the University Observatory Buildings, directly across its inferred line (1966, 136). Obviously expecting the road to be of robust construction, careful search was apparently made for "metalling, mortar, and other signs of Roman road construction", but to no avail.

Now, however, that we know the route lies further to the southwest at the Trinity Hall Playing Fields, it would clearly have run north of the Observatory.[22] There can be no doubt whatsoever that the road there was the direct continuation of New Hall's. There are two points that arise from the Trinity Hall excavation. First, the road was evidently entering a separate settlement to the west, arguably one of some status. Lying at a distance of just *c.* 200 m from New Hall/Fitzwilliam College, the Trinity Hall Site was obviously the next settlement in that direction. While this might seem a very close interval, this is in keeping with the period's known settlement densities within the region, as discussed at length in both the *Borderlands...* and *Riversides...* volumes. Second, Trinity Hall's Roman road had clearly gone out of use by the third century AD. While there could be some question of the route's actual duration based on the New Hall findings, the quarrying hollows cut across the route leave no doubt that it had ceased to function by that time and had, in effect, been turned to 'waste ground', seeing both the disposal of animal carcasses and human burials.

While ditch F.30 in New Hall's Area III may have first marked out the southern side of the *Via Devana*/ Godmanchester Road (with the F.46/50 boundary perhaps being another version of the same; see Fig. 3.53), these cannot have been road-flanking ditches as such. The lack of 'robust' ditches flanking that route goes far to explain why it has previously proven so difficult to locate. Indeed, Hughes records that he observed the sections of a deep trench cut from Huntingdon Road across *The Grove*, but found no trace of it (1893, 203). While now, in the light of the Murray Edwards College results, we can be assured that it ran south of Huntingdon Road, those two exposures are insufficient to project its alignment over any great distance to the west.

As will be more fully discussed in the next book, no clear evidence of that road's route was found at North West Cambridge. Most important in this regard was that programme's Howe's Close Medieval hamlet excavations (Site IX; Fig. 1.4). Occurring over 0.47 ha and for a distance of 50 m back from the Huntingdon Road frontage (immediately west of the Traveller's Rest pub) – with evaluation trench-exposure from a further 75 m back from that – the Godmanchester Roman road should certainly have crossed that area. Yet, very little Roman material was recovered at all; what was present was entirely residual and there were no Roman-phase features as such. This surely indicates that the Godmanchester route could not have been ditched there and, as at New Hall/Murray Edwards, its metalling must have come from a separate quarry-source.

Two, possibly three, previously unknown Roman roads were, though, discovered in the course of North West Cambridge's fieldwork. Their detailing is best left to the next book; what is of relevance here is that for its background studies Rog Palmer plotted what appeared to be a quasi-circular quarry-pit configuration. Located *c.* 125 m south of the Huntingdon and Girton Road junction (and 1.75 km west of New Hall), this fell within a swathe of Post-Medieval gravel quarrying and was not excavated as such (i.e. trenched only); there can be no certainty about its attribution. Nonetheless, appearing almost barrow-like in its circularity, and evocative of New Hall's North Field quarry, it might well mark another Roman Godmanchester Road-side quarry.

What was the duration of the *Via Devana*/Godmanchester Road? Based on the quantity and date of the material found deposited across its surfaces in the Huntingdon Road-side trenches, the argument could be mounted that it had also ceased by the mid third century AD. Yet, this would probably be misleading, as most of the pottery was small and very abraded. Accordingly, it seems to have been dumped as an *ad hoc* metalling or, at least, a levelling layer deriving from a relatively high-status settlement-source. Correlating with the fourth-century AD re-inscription of the roadway's westward milestones (see Chap. 1), it seems likely that it continued in operation after this date, even if 'fresh' gravel supplies may no longer have been available. The quantity of material found across/in the road's surface in the eastern roadway-exposure (Area 2) at Murray Edwards College need not necessarily imply that it coincided with further Roman settlement at that immediate point, although this seems likely given the pottery recovered from *The Orchard* (see *Inset*).

Among the most striking of New Hall's findings was the relative insignificance of the Roman Huntingdon/Godmanchester Road alignment. While over its northern third (Enclosure C) the layout of the Area I enclosure system and its eastern track skewed to be closer to that road's alignment, only two ditches within Area III definitely followed it. If not for them, and prior to the Murray Edwards' trenches, the road's position relative to the site (if not its very existence) could have been considered suspect. Certainly, there can be no doubt that the Back-College Road preceded the establishment of any Godmanchester route, as the northwest–southeast running ditches that extended across the northern third of the area were definitely cut by the Huntingdon Road-side ditches and those running parallel. This sequence of road construction would support Green's assertion that the road from Cambridge may have post-dated the later first century AD (1975, 196). From this and the site's dating evidence, it is reasonable to see the Back-College Road as a 'primary Roman phenomenon'. Probably dating to the third quarter of the first century AD, the Godmanchester route, and the site's Phase 2 developments, would then have dated some decades after. Indeed, based on the Antoninus Pius reference of the primary inscription of the *Via Devana's* milestones, a second-century AD date could even be postulated for that road.

Something should be said on the fact that New Hall's southern road was *a ditched route*, whereas metalling for the Godmanchester Road derived from separate quarries. Although an expedient means of achieving gravels, robust flanking ditches would have restricted access to the road: wheeled transport would only be able to get on and off it at set points. In contrast, routes such as the *Via Devana*/Godmanchester Road would have been fully accessible.[23]

While both types of road are likely to have demanded the participation of surveyors, the organizational needs of non-ditched ones would have been considerably more complex; if nothing else, they would require the acquisition of gravels. The hand of a higher-level co-ordinating authority can perhaps be inferred by the intensity of extraction-pitting within New Hall's South Field quarry.

Roman Quarrying

In its time it was difficult to appreciate the scale of the New Hall excavation's quarry field, particularly the degree to which it was road- or settlement-specific, or a combination of both. The realization that it was primarily road-related only came when the actual metalled route of the Godmanchester Road was found alongside Huntingdon Road and when comparably dense quarries had been found on other sites. Exposures of these within the lower town have already been outlined in Chapter Two. While that at St. John's Divinity School and its related 'Triangle' investigations was presumably associated with the construction of the *Via Devana* (Newman 2008a; Cessford 2015), no such association with a known roadway is identified for the quarries at Jesus College's West Court development (see Chap. 2). Located behind Wesley House on Jesus Lane, and at a distance from the line of the *Via Devana*'s, given its size it must either have provided gravels for some other civic function or for an as yet unidentified roadway.

Other directly road-related quarrying has, however, been encountered in the south of the city. In 2010, as part of the CB1 development alongside Hills Road adjacent to the southeasterly route of the *Via Devana* (Figs. 3.55 & 3.56; Slater 2010; see also Cessford & Dickens forthcoming, fig. 6.1), in an area of 390 sq. m clusters of intercut quarry pits were found to extend right the way along the site's southern frontage and continued both east and west of the excavation-area. Not surprisingly, there were traces of both modern and Post-Medieval activity. There were a number of pits of broadly Medieval date cutting through the agricultural soil horizon that otherwise sealed the hollows.[24]

Nearly 90 Roman quarrying pits were identified, and three main episodes of their cutting were distinguished (Fig. 3.55). They were of sub-circular to ovoid plan, 1.2–3.35 m across/along and *c.* 0.5–0.8 m deep. Evidently left open to weather, these largely had homogeneous brown-grey silty clay fills; there was, though, some slumping from exposed gravel edges and backfilling of deposits into their still-open profiles from later cut features.[25]

The site's finds were not prolific. Aside from some Early Bronze Age sherds and a single piece of Late Bronze/Early Iron Age flint-tempered ware (and 15 Late Neolithic-Bronze Age worked flints), altogether only 12 Early Roman sherds were forthcoming (these possibly including a few Late Iron Age wares).

Evaluation fieldwork in 2011 in the area of the Old Cattle Market exposed another dense quarry which, in total, must have extended over *c.* 1800 sq. m (Mackay 2001; see Cessford & Dickens forthcoming, fig. 6.1). There was some ambiguity as to its precise date (the area did not proceed to excavation as such); nevertheless, given its location and lack of related material, this must also have been of Early Roman date and roadway-related.

Still further south, the route of the *Via Devana* was evidently ditch-flanked within the area of the Perse School villa and was *c.* 15 m wide at that point (Walker 1910, 166–7; RCHM[E] 1959, 5–6). Yet, for much of its length the road apparently lacked side-ditches and its metalling must, instead, have been quarry-generated. This could account for the negative results where its postulated route has been trenched within, for example, the grounds of Homerton College and in the vicinity of the Botanical Gardens.

One of the most instructive recent quarrying-related excavations has been that at Kings' Dyke/Bradley Fen (Knight & Brudenell forthcoming). Its main Roman settlement lay on the crest of Whittlesey's island and was arranged around the 11–14 m wide ditch-flanked portion of the Fen Causeway route, which from there continued northwestwards across the fen marshes towards Peterborough's terrace-landfall. A major quarry cluster extending over more than *c.* 4600 sq. m lay adjacent to the settlement, at a distance of some 220 m and on the island's western flanks. It was itself accessed by a separate, minor trackway (ditch-flanked). Given its scale, this quarry must surely have related to the carting out of gravels for where the Fen Causeway extended onto the embayment's marshes. It demonstrates that, however tempting, we must avoid any simple equation of 'formal' separate quarry-source roads as reflecting a civic responsibility, with ditched routes as private initiatives. This may sometimes have been the case, and surely the construction of the Fen Causeway across the marshes would have been the responsibility of a higher authority. Yet, major routes probably had their metalling generated by flanking ditches at points, though ditching might have related as much to property delineation. Again, there was evidently much variability in the Roman countryside; things rarely seem strictly 'rule-bound' and, instead, 'make-do' convenience and immediate availability appear to have played a significant role.

Settlement and Waste Land

The main significance of the 2008 Fitzwilliam College Library Site excavations primarily related to its prehistory. Although not on the same alignment as the features in New Hall's Enclosure A – but respecting its F.163 boundary (Area I) – it confirmed that there had been a major Middle Bronze Age presence. It seems to have consisted of robustly ditched rectilinear paddocks, akin to those found at, for example, the Addenbrooke's landscape (see *RVS*, chap. 6). These are comparable to those since recovered along the gravel ridge at North West Cambridge; there the Middle Bronze Age clearly marked the first colonization-horizon of that inland locale despite seeing earlier visitations. Whether or not this was a matter of year-round permanent settlement or largely seasonal usage is an issue best addressed in the next book.

The Library Site's Roman-phase remains add little to the earlier excavation's findings (Fig. 3.57). That the ditch-line clearly lay on the same projected alignment as one of New Hall's has caused us to reconsider how the earlier site's enclosures were portrayed. As opposed to Figure 3.30's small interlinked-paddock system, the settlement's layout was evidently on much larger scale than was first envisaged. Also noteworthy is simply the fact that New Hall's South Field quarry did not extend west into the 2008 excavation-area.

The manner in which New Hall's Enclosures B and C were originally depicted, and their features projected (see Fig. 3.30 and Evans in *RCAM*, fig. XII.4), clearly

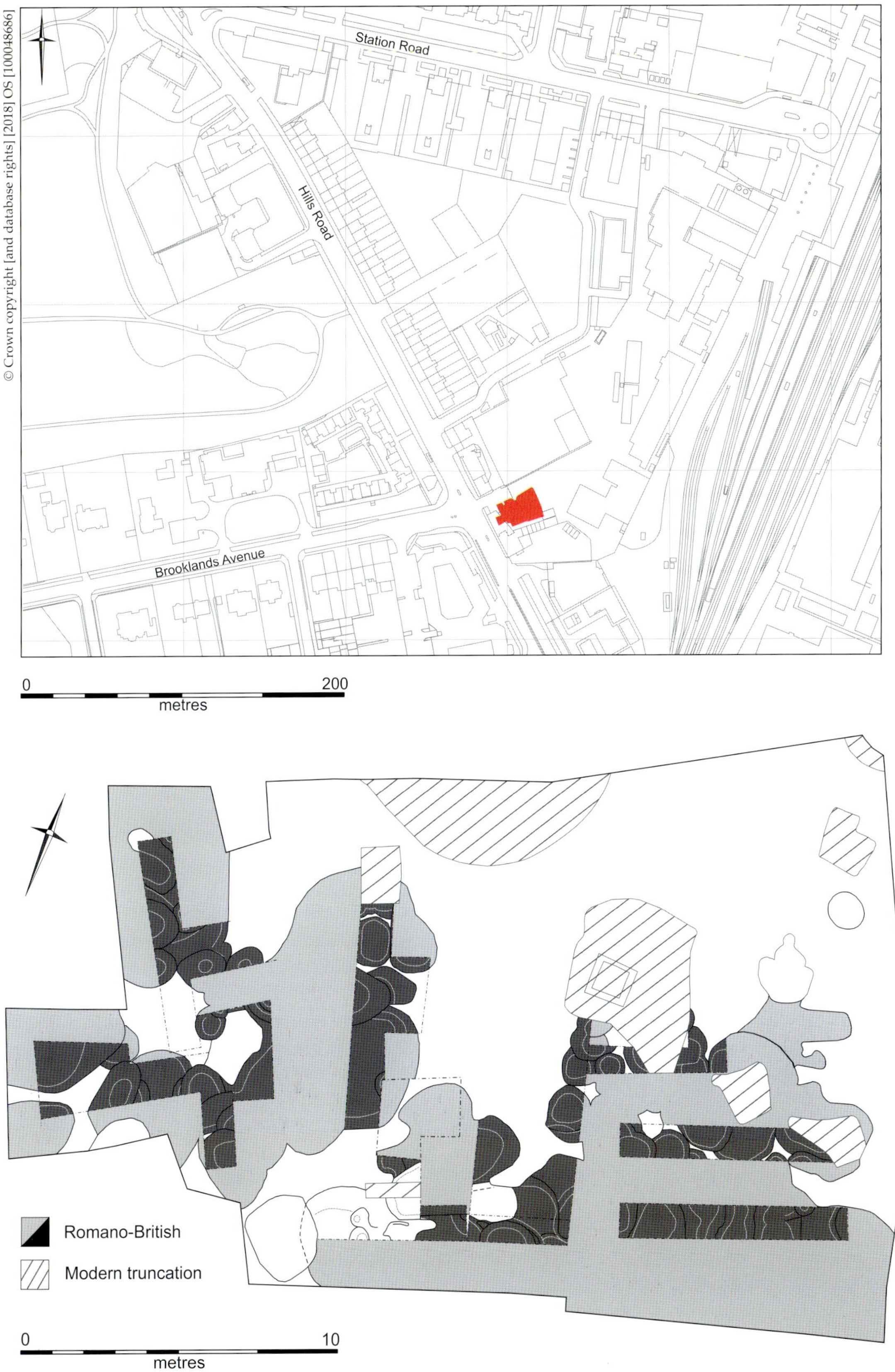

Figure 3.55. *CB1 investigations, location map and Roman quarrying-area site plan.*

Figure 3.56. *CB1 investigations, excavation photograph of quarry pit-area.*

related to how aspects of the New Hall Site's Roman presence were then conceived. Then over-emphasizing the recovery of its possible military-origin belt buckle (<156>; Fig. 3.37.1), phrases were used such as 'Enclosure C's *commanding* of the western route into the town'. Indeed, to be honest, reconstructing it in the manner we did made it evocative of a mile fort.

While we would no longer advocate a military interpretation, there is nevertheless no escaping the fact that these enclosures seem markedly 'different': both from each other and the period's other enclosures on the site. The latter (E–H) were more organic in their layout and their ditch boundaries were of much smaller 'standard domestic'-scale (Fig. 3.57). In contrast, the plans of both Enclosures B and C seem far more regular and formal, and their ditching was on an entirely different scale. Enclosure B's large 'V'-profile boundaries could (normatively) suggest a short-lived military function, but no finds were recovered to suggest its purpose (but which, of course, may itself have been a telling attribute).

Enclosure C's seemingly three-circuit concentric layout also certainly seems 'special'. The manner in which eastern terminals of its ditches turned slightly northward suggests that its interior lay in that direction and, if so, its eastern side would then have been open. If a ditch (and its symmetry with the F.6 and F.184/187 boundaries makes that likely), then F.1/2 would have been enormous. It is this that also prompted the earlier suggestion that Enclosure C 'commanded' the road. While one would no longer be quite so emphatic in this regard, the idea that it might have been some kind of 'station' or the like might still be reasonable. This interpretation would, moreover, be consistent with Murphy's identification of possible straw/hay litter – perhaps from stables – in F.1/2.

With the establishment of the Godmanchester Road and its attendant quarries, for a period much of the site-area may well, in effect, have been waste ground, with its quarry hollows a place of convenient refuse dumping. The potential scale and duration of this depositional activity conspires to undermine the settlement's interpretation. Apparently generated on-site, this seems not too great a problem for their assemblages given the coherence and extent of the prehistoric material occurring in the North Field's quarries.

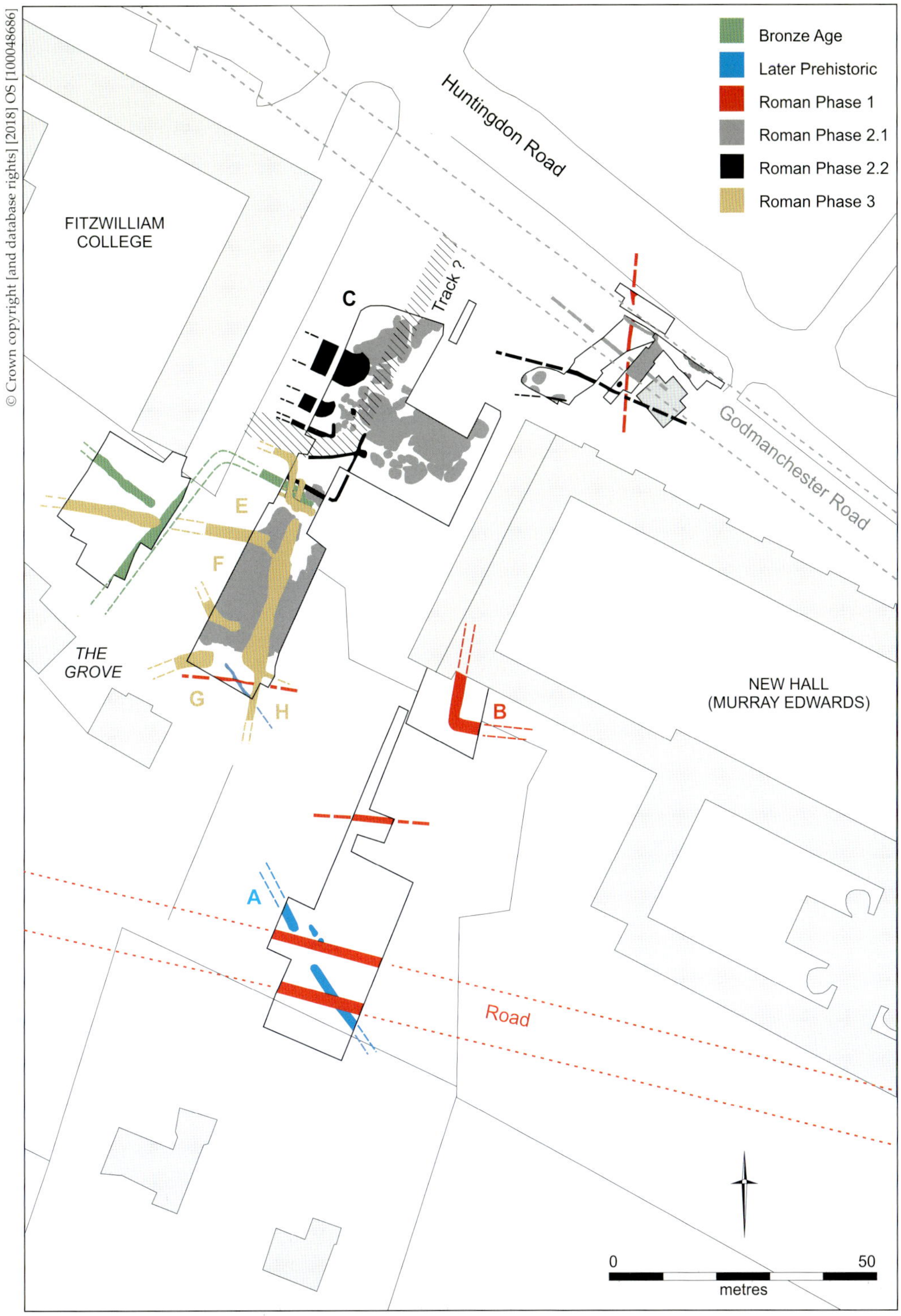

Figure 3.57. *New Hall* (et al.), *revised phase plan (compare to Fig. 3.30).*

The same, though, is not true of the backfills of Enclosure C's main features, nor the dumped spreads that sealed the South Field's quarry. As further discussed below, the latter had distinct urban 'Dark Earth-type' qualities, leading to the question of whether the site's Roman occupation was sufficiently intense to generate such deposits. Similar issues arise in relation to the scale of Enclosure C's feature assemblages, especially the vast ones from F.1/2. We are fully aware of just how intense Roman settlement middening practices can be and how they can generate great, highly localized artefact concentrations. On the other hand, if the finds densities from F.1/2 are compared to the Fitzwilliam College settlement ditches – just one and three sherds per metre segment from these 'pristine' samples – it does become difficult to see F.1/2's assemblage as deriving from an immediate on-site source.

As in the preceding chapter, the cubic finds-densities of the site's main Roman high-value features warrant listing for the purposes of comparison:

F.30 (0.82 cu. m), 382 sherds per cu. m (466 sherds)
F.269 (0.95 cu. m), 187 sherds per cu. m (197 sherds)
F.6 (3.30 cu. m), 215 sherds per cu. m (711 sherds)
F.221 (0.44 cu. m), 234 sherds per cu. m (103 sherds)
F.1/2 (31.10 cu. m), 186 sherds per cu. m (5,800 sherds)
F.7 (9.76 cu. m), 61 sherds per cu. m (598 sherds)
F.121/122 (4.90 cu. m), 169 sherds per cu. m (340 sherds)

Murray Edwards
Area 1 (9.84 cu. m), 48 sherds per cu. m (463 sherds)
Area 2 (0.25 cu. m), 276 sherds per cu. m (69 sherds).

With the exception of the small F.221 pit at the far end of Area I, these all fell along the site's northern quarter, adjacent to the Huntingdon/Godmanchester Road. Indeed, the second-highest density – 276 sherds per cu. m – was actually from the road surface deposits towards the eastern end of the College's roadside grounds and in Murray Edwards' Area 2. While possibly also reflecting yet another settlement-source within that immediate vicinity, this would correlate with the fact that the highest-value feature, ditch F.30, was associated with the roadway in New Hall's Area III. (That the other roadway-area exposure values in Murray Edwards' Area 1 were five times less than those within Area 2 must reflect how much more underlying 'soil strata' was excavated there, as opposed to just the road's surface; see Fig. 3.53.)

The fifth-highest densities occurred within pit F.269 at the northern end of Area I (Fig. 3.19). In that area, while the value of 169 sherds per cu. m from well F.121/122 is itself relatively high (and certainly contrasts with the low levels within the quarry hollows there), it pales in comparison to ditch F.6: 215 sherds per cu. m.

As we will see, these levels of 50 to 400 sherds per cu. m are far higher than are found on most settlements, and densities at Vicar's Farm were well below this (see Chap. 4). Indeed, these figures are considerably higher than even Roman Cambridge's core-area feature values (see Fig. 4.32) and, as outlined in Chapter Two, are even greater than its backfilled apsidal shrine (see Chap. 2, Note 17); arguably, they reflect town-related levels as opposed to those of an 'average' rural settlement.[26] Given the densities that occurred within the fills of New Hall's Enclosure C features – plus the high roadway values – it is likely that the settlement there was probably not itself the source of this material. Instead, it surely attests to the transport of town-generated, with material from similar sources also being used to 'metal' the road itself. These kind of mass-dumping practices are documented in Medieval times ('dunghills': Cooper 1843, 332 & 335; R. Jones 2004, 184) and major public dumps were a feature of Roman towns (see e.g. Furlan 2017). All this again makes it likely that this settlement actually lay at the western 'fringe-edge' of the main Roman town, rather than being a separate hinterland settlement.

If a number of the settlement features had been backfilled with town-source material, then some of their assemblage characteristics (e.g. the frequency of F.1/2's samian and the evidence of its repair) and the activities represented therein – such as local pottery manufacture – are not otherwise evident in the site's deposits. We could argue that this manufacturing occurred in other uninvestigated portions of the settlement; nonetheless, it certainly adds to the suspicion that much of the Enclosure C assemblage might have been 'imported' from an off-site source.

In his recent appraisal of New Hall's F.1/2's pottery assemblage Jeremy Evans commented that (*contra* the 1990s interpretation) the material would not indicate any military connection; based on the numbers involved, he further suggested that it might have been of a ritual character (J. Evans *et al.* 2017, vol. 2, chap. 10, 26–9). While fully recognizing the validity of the first point, there seems no basis for the second whatsoever; instead, it probably represents an 'introduced' clearance horizon brought to the site from the town. Its mid–later second-century AD date range would essentially match that of Roman Cambridge's two cellared buildings (see Chap. 2, figs. 2.5 & 2.18), both of which were evidently destroyed by fire (*RCAM*, 40–2, 45–7 & 144). This could tell of some large-scale 'disaster event', in whose wake the New Hall material could have been carted out to the edge of town. To convincingly argue this will require more in-depth analyses of the finds than is currently possible. Here we will restrict ourselves to a single observation, whose basis will be outlined in greater detail in the next book. The manner of lead-bracket/staple repair applied to F.1/2's samian also occurred on a bowl of that type in Castle Hill's Shire Hall Car Park Site (Form 37, Trajanic or Hadrianic; Dickerson in *RCAM*, 134, pl. xxxviii, D29). In contrast, at North West Cambridge's Site IV, and also at one of Longstanton/Northstowe's Roman settlements – where no such bracket/staple repairs were recovered – samian was repaired using birch tar. While the evidence is slight, does this imply distinctly different town-*vs*-countryside methods of pottery repair?

The dating evidence for the Roman settlement needs review (acknowledging the caveats this argument of imported material raises concerning the overall interpretation of the site, which will be turned to below). The vast majority of its pottery dates to the later first to early–mid second century AD. Largely deriving from 'open', often recut features, there were no *in situ* occupation horizons at the New Hall Site. The date of the pottery relates to disuse of features and the paucity of (closed) later first-century AD groups need not imply that the settlement's origins post-dated that time. While there is little or no material of pre-Flavian attribution, for reasons outlined above it reasonable to assign its primary developments (Phase 1) – including the southern roadway and Enclosure B – to the third quarter of the first century AD, with the first use of the Godmanchester Road and its quarries dating to either the end of that century or the early decades of the next (Phase 2.1).

Evocative of 'dark earth' deposits, a number of the features had been backfilled with near-black loamy midden soils, including quantities of first/second-century AD material and with only limited third-century AD or later elements (e.g. F.1/2, 7 & 30; the probable military-associated belt buckle recovered from Ditch F.1/2 has a suggested late second- to early third-century AD date; see Dickens, above). If the site's ceramic frequency directly represents the intensity of settlement usage, then its floruit was clearly during the early–mid second century AD. It is likely that Enclosure C (Phase 2.2) had probably been established shortly after the Godmanchester Road, either late in the first century AD or in the first decades of the second, and was abandoned by later second century AD. Clearly laid out in relationship to it, the usage of the southern enclosures (E–H; Phase 3) overlapped with Enclosure C, but their operation evidently continued later, until the earlier third century AD. Ceramic usage on the site had evidently all but stopped after the mid third century AD. The evidence is sufficient to indicate that the area was not entirely abandoned thereafter; its inhumation cemetery is likely to have continued in use until the fourth century AD and F.7's assemblage included some probable fourth-century AD vessels, the sherds being very abraded.

Despite metal-detector scanning of feature spoil, only three Roman coins were recovered and, of these, two are identifiable to a specific date. One of Allectus (AD 293–6), from the upper fill of the eastern double-ditch system in south of Area I, would confirm its 'late' attribution. The other two, an issue of Antonius Pius (AD 138–61) and a House of Constantine (AD 318–24), both came from the fills of South Field quarry pits. Generally, however, the paucity of the site's later Roman coinage would attest to just how little third–fourth-century AD activity had occurred there.

Activities, Environment and Economic Evidence

New Hall's palynological evidence would indicate that during later prehistory and the Roman period the site supported open weedy grassland (see Wiltshire, above). While the pollen was generally not particularly well-preserved or informative, the presence of *Puccinia graminis* in one of the Back-College Road ditches (F.17) would suggest either grasses or cereals within the immediate vicinity – i.e. arable fields or pasture – an observation borne out by the lack of settlement features within 40 m of its northern side.

Analyses of macrofossil and monolith samples from Roman features were also relatively unrewarding (see Fryer & Murphy, and Murphy, above). There was a fairly wide representation of fruits/seeds present within 13 out of 23 bulk-samples assessed, whereas cereal grains and/or chaff were only present in six. Apart from Sample 12 from the eastern double-ditches, all of the deposits producing carbonized cereals were associated with northwestern Enclosure C (Area I; Samples 2, 3, 7, 19 & 22). The mollusc shells would attest to diverse ecological groups: shade-loving woodland species, open-country species and marsh/freshwater slum and freshwater types. In short, a variety of site conditions, both tree-shaded and open, and deep wet features.

Inferences drawn from the animal bone provide a fuller picture of site usage (see Yannouli, above). Not surprisingly, wild species – wolf and Roe deer – were present only during the Bronze Age. Cattle appear predominant during that period and the Iron Age: 50 & 47% respectively (MNI), decreasing to 27.6% in the Roman period. Using the same criteria (MNI), over the three periods the percentage of ovicaprids increased from 16.6 to 23.5 and 34.3 per cent respectively. Horse bone is only present in the Roman assemblage (11.9%), when bird/fowl are also represented (5.2%; 7 MNI; one chicken bone in an Iron Age context was probably intrusive).[27] Dogs constitute 9.7 per cent of the Roman assemblage (38 bones, 13 MNI; cf. two bones from each in Bronze and Iron Age assemblages), and their gnawing, uncommon on the pre-Roman samples, is recorded on a number of the Roman specimens. The presence of dogs, and their characteristic dietary habits, might help account for the generally low proportion of bone compared to pottery within the site's Roman 'midden-type' backfills. Also present within the Roman assemblage, pigs (34 bones, 14 MNI, 10.4%; cf. three bones in Iron Age) are another potential agency of bone-loss and their churning of soils might also have contributed to the creation of 'Dark Earth-type' deposits.

Despite the relatively greater range of species represented in the Roman assemblage, Yannouli remarks on the paucity of fowl/bird and pig bones (all animals kept close to the house whereas ruminants demand greater space). She suggests that sheep/goats and cattle may have been kept near or just beyond the town boundaries and slaughtered/processed in extra-mural loci; the high frequency of cattle cranial fragments and horncores in the faunal assemblage from the Area I quarry pits could attest to this potential supply basis.[28] Yet, the New Hall settlement was certainly not just a 'supply' community and meal leftovers have been identified.[29] The problem throughout is that, at least for the western settlement complex, what was effectively excavated was only the (eastern) margin of a 'town-fringe' community (i.e. 'peri-urban'). It is, therefore, difficult to distinguish the immediate settlement-edge deposition of bone waste from any wider pattern of town-related supply/slaughter (e.g. the high number of articulated joints in the Area II & III assemblages suggests meal left-overs/on-site consumption).

While the evidence from the western Area I settlement may be ambiguous, the relatively high number of animal bones recovered from Enclosure B may tell of patterns in the broader area. Rapidly excavated during the watching brief, a number of animal bones were recovered (45; MNI: three cattle, three pigs and two ovicaprids, although no pottery). Articulated joints were identified and the assemblage suggests slaughter, processing and consumption for specific on-site needs, rather than town supply (see Yannouli, above).[30]

Also potentially telling of community specialization is the site's evidence of pottery production, but as these only derived from Enclosure C's features in the northwest of Area I (F.1/2's wasters and kiln bar) this raises the spectre of the potential importation of this material into the settlement. Although not occurring in great numbers, iron slag and furnace-/hearth-lining pieces were frequent enough and sufficiently dispersed throughout Area I and II's Roman features to suggest ironworking (i.e. they did not result from an isolated dumping episode; see 'Industrial Waste', above). Such evidence of industrial activity could have contributed to the "siliceous globules, black tarry droplets and fragments of black porous 'cokey' material" identified by Fryer and Murphy in many of the bulk macrofossil samples (which they, above, interpret as "probably derived from over-combustion of organic material"). What is remarkable is that this material was present within samples from both the prehistoric and Roman phases.

Similarly, in all three soil micromorphological profiles Coyle and French observed high quantities of wood ash, postulated to derive from intense burning of material subsequently dumped and/or scattered so as to become mixed with soil; degeneration of the organic content resulted from oxidation and earthworm activity. Again, this occurred in both the later prehistoric and Roman samples. Finally, the pollen from Bronze and Iron Age features suggests similar processes as significant amounts of microscopic charcoal and 'sooting' of pollen grains was identified (and to a lesser degree in the Roman sample; see Wiltshire, above). Collectively, the correspondence of environmental analyses could point to both intense and extensive burning. Again, the remarkable thing is that it appears to have been present in both prehistoric and Roman horizons.

This phenomenon seems largely to have been evident at the micro-scale. No charcoal was originally observed, for example, in F.85, which apparently contained large quantities of palynologically-identified fine charcoal. Similarly, the fills of ditches F.33 and F.20 appeared relatively sterile, seemingly contradicting the micromorphological analysis of Profiles 1 and 3 (the upper deposit of the latter only locally including a substantial charcoal lens). Only in F.1/2 was any quantity of burnt debris encountered. There was no evidence of widespread scorching on-site to indicate the occurrence of a major fire and, instead, this seems to have been a by-product of industrial activity. Theoretically, this could have occurred as a result of Post-Medieval activity. However, whilst some small fragments of clinker/coal occurred within 'late' features and the topsoils (i.e. Period III), this was not widespread and within the context of *The Grove's* grounds – a highly unlikely site of industry – can be considered incidental. The source of the site-wide microscopic burnt residues/ash is likely to have been *Roman* industrial activity; somehow soil processes had occurred which incorporated this comminuted microscopic material into earlier features. Given that no great concentrations of charcoal were superficially apparent (apart from within F.1/2), this begs the question of whether these contaminants effectively amount to *pollution*.

Many of the immediate site findings reflect on broader themes and raise questions: for example, the disposal of diseased animals as opposed to ritual sacrifice. Equally, how representative were its burials and what might be implied by its 'aberrant' prone burials? These, like many other issues – ranging from the dynamics of prehistoric landscape colonization, pottery supply and role of markets/exchange to the character of roads – will best be addressed when considered comparatively and in the light of other local-site data. It is then appropriate that, progressing outwards to the town's hinterland, we now consider the results from West Cambridge, starting with the Vicar's Farm excavations.

Notes

1 The inclusion of this later-era fieldwork – with their fully computer-generated graphics – can seem somewhat jarring when set against New Hall's hand-drawn illustrations (especially when 'jumping' the intermediate stage of early computer-rendering as seen in the Vicar's Farm chapters that follow). Reflecting changes in practice, this cannot now be realistically altered, and nor should we pretend that 'time' is not a major factor here.

2 Since the time of this study's writing other comparable examples have been recovered from earlier/Middle Bronze Age contexts at Over (Evans *et al.* 2016b) and also feature in the next, North West Cambridge book.

3 Note, however, that despite the 'cleanliness' of their fills, their alignment and scale were close to that of a series of 'late' garden bedding trenches in the south of the area and a Post-Medieval attribution must, therefore, remain a possibility.

4 Given the general regularity of F.1/2's edges, apart from its interpretation as a reworked ditch terminal, the only other explanation that would seem feasible is for it to be comparable to the great waterlogged quarry hollow at Stonea Grange (Jackson & Potter 1996).

5 Also likely to date to the later fourth century AD, the <710> double-sided composite comb found in the 1994 Duxford pipeline investigations (Boothroyd in Price *et al.* 1997, 119, fig. 66.18) is very similar to New Hall's (see also *RCAM*, pl. XII.197, 88).

6 Note that the categories possible male/female, probable male/female or simply male/female have been used as an ascending scale of the reliability of the sexing data available.

7 Employing a 5 mm mesh, 0.5 × 0.5 m sieve-columns were excavated within the lower fills of F.1/2 and F.6. Taken down through the full depth of its profile, that in the latter yielded, in total, 15 sherds and 20 animal bones, which equates to a cubic density of 85.5 sherds and 114 pieces. This can be compared, for example, to the average cubic densities calculated for either Trumpington Meadows' Anglo-Saxon SFBs (*c.* 11 sherds and 349 bones) or that site's Early Iron Age upper pit-profile midden fills (129 and 211 respectively; max. 261 sherds and 826 bone per cu. m; see *RVS*, tables 4.3 & 5.25). While the sieve-column densities of the animal bone in the basal 0.4 m of F.1/2 were also in that range (210 pieces per cu. m), at 1380 sherds per cubic metre its pottery density was of an altogether different order.

8 The assemblages were analysed following the guidelines set out by the Study Group for Roman Pottery (Darling 1994) and the National Roman Fabric Reference Collection (Tomber & Dore 1998); all the percentage figures arising from Mazzilli's study are based on sherd counts (Table 3.4).

9 Since the time of this study's writing a number of first-century AD kiln pottery-production sites have been found within the region. Within the immediate Cambridge environs, this includes those at Greenhouse Farm, by the airport off of Newmarket Road (Gibson & Lucas 2002), and at Addenbrooke's Hutchinson Site (*BLS*, 57–62). Further afield would be the kilns recently dug at Duxford (Anderson & Woolhouse 2016) and Brampton (Lyons & Blackbourn 2017); see also Chapter Seven concerning the recovery of a kiln at the Wilberforce Road Pitches Site in 2018.

10 Overall, the representative sample of F.1/2's pottery that was systematically analysed by Mazzilli; complements Going's discussion regarding the mid first-century to second-century AD date of that feature and its pottery supply (especially its wide variety of unsourced local wares). Of the samian ware – mostly first- to second-century AD date – of particular interest are the semi-complete riveted decorated bowl (Dr.37) and dish (Dr.36). These are common forms of riveted samian vessels found in settlements in Britain (Willis 2004). In the case of Cambridgeshire, they seem to be recovered mostly at Castle Hill, including in its apsidal shrine (see Chap. 2 and J. Evans *et al.* 2017, 19).

A significant result of the analysis of this assemblage is detailing of the pottery from two of the major local pottery production centres: Horningsea and Godmanchester. This has been possible in light of recent publications on Horningsea production by J. Evans (*et al.* 2017) and on Roman Godmanchester by Alex Jones (2003). Not surprisingly, here Horningsea pottery (41.2%) – including a significant quantity from the mid first to the second century AD – greatly outnumbers Godmanchester pottery (2.9%). This dominance of Horningsea-source pottery also occurred in other features on the site (F.6, F.30 & F.269; see Table 3.4).

11 There is no point in reproducing here Going's actual spot-dating list. With his statement concerning the Back-College Road's assemblage included in the main text above, the only features that had Late Roman wares (post-*c.* AD 250) were F.7, F.30, F.77, F.88, F.143, F.145, F.248, F.104/5 and F.110; including some late shell-tempered wares, later Roman pottery also occurred in the vicinity of ditches F.104/5, suggesting activity there in that period.

12 The period's assemblage may involve a degree of 'mixing' depending upon the Bronze *vs.* Iron Age assignation of specific features (see Period I text above). Given, however, that the bulk of the material derived from F.20, which is likely to reflect an Iron Age recutting, Yannouli's analysis still has a validity (see, though, *Artefact Densities and Distributions* above concerning that feature's possible Roman bone-source).

13 Whilst this contribution raises many interesting issues concerning the nature of 'Dark Earth-type' deposits, only Profile 2 was from a black loam finds-rich fill (at the macro-scale) normatively considered an urban 'Dark Earth'; '1' was quite leached/indistinct and, '3', an agricultural loam. Nevertheless, all were organic-rich loams with occupation debris. Spanning three of horizons of use, the

lack of micromorphological distinction between them suggests that what is being 'read' are generic settlement traces, perhaps equivalent to the microscopic charcoals remains/sooting present throughout the palynological samples (see Wiltshire, above).

14 Wychfield House was eventually taken over by John Chivers of the Chivers & Sons' fruit and vegetable company. A major local employer, having more than a 1000 staff at the turn of the last century, they were renowned for their jams, marmalade and canned produce. Given this, there is some small irony that, as shown in Figure 3.46, it was a later nineteenth century stoneware jar of their chief rival's marmalade, James Keiller & Sons, that was recovered from the Fitzwilliam Collage Library Site; arguably, it related to the Darwins' occupancy. Also, a glass Lea & Perrins sauce bottle was recovered from *The Lodge*-area trenches (Murray Edwards works; see below) and was presumably also of Darwin Family 'vintage'; a number of the other wares recovered are of earlier nineteenth-century date and probably relate to the time of Custance's ownership.

15 He also contributed a paper to the *Proceedings of the Cambridge Antiquarian Society*, 'On Monuments to Cambridge Men at the University of Padua' (1895).

16 George set up residence further afield and acquired Newnham Grange in 1885. Located beside the River Cam on the south side of Cambridge, it became Darwin College shortly after the death of his son, Charles Galton Darwin, in 1962.

17 Apparently on Emma Darwin's death the house was sold to the Armstrong family, Charles Armstrong owning Cambridge's Star Brewery.

18 To this end, aerial photographs have been consulted, but to negative result: the area of the site had been almost completely built over by the beginning of the 1960s and any earlier photographs of the immediate surroundings are distant oblique shots.

19 Just one worked flint was recovered from the site proper, with five from its evaluation-phase (see Cooper 2003b). The right midshaft of an aurochs humerus was recovered from one of the Roman paddock ditches (F.1038; see Fig. 3.50). Almost certainly residual (see e.g. Evans 2015), the attempt to date it failed due to insufficient carbon.

20 Further resonating with New Hall's earlier findings, also recovered were worked flints; of later prehistoric attribution (e.g. with evidence of hard hammer-usage), they occurred residually in later features. Just 71 animal bones were retrieved. Of the 19 identified to species, nine were ovicaprid, followed by cow (seven), pig (two), and there was also a single dog specimen. Despite metal-detecting all the 2009 strata, and hand-digging throughout, no metalwork was recovered.

21 The route was excluded from Walker's 1910 and Fox's 1923 discussions of Roman Cambridge's roads. Although undemonstrated, the sway held by the Godmanchester Road as *the de facto* dominant western route has remained; Fox's 'twinning' of Roman Cambridge and Godmanchester has obviously had a lingering interpretative influence.

Much further west at Cambourne, the A428 is thought to follow the route of Road 231; interestingly, there it does not appear to have attracted much roadside settlement, with the majority of the period's sites lying some distance south of it (Wright *et al.* 2009, 87–8, fig. 33; see Abrams & Ingham 2008, 37–9 & fig. 3.1 for an alternative 231 Route).

22 Despite its ditch-flanking (and that it was 'targeted'), the route of the Back-College Road was not itself actually distinguished within North West Cambridge's evaluation fieldwork, nor was its alignment reflected in the settlement layout of that immediate landscape.

23 One of the ditched roads at North West Cambridge (that bisecting Site II's farm) was found to run out where it left the gravel ridge and crossed down onto the clays; no quarries were found at its end and, therefore, no attempt seemed to have been made to cart gravel out to extend its route. The road may have continued (as a 'track'), but if so it would have been unsurfaced. Telling of expediency, this would also indicate that the main function of the flanking ditches were as quarries and not drainage, as the need for latter would have there have been far greater across the downslope clays than on the gravels.

24 There were also two suspected prehistoric features, both cut by Roman-phase hollows. One was just a tree-throw, whereas the other seemed a pit proper (sub-circular: 2. × 2.7 m and *c.* 0.8 m deep). Its dating was largely based on the presence of three worked flints and four small sherds of grog-tempered Early Bronze Age pottery.

Subsequently, in 2012, as part of CB1/Railway Station-area development, watching brief monitoring occurred within the vicinity of Fosters Mill, which led to the discovery of a Neolithic pit cluster (Brittain & Billington 2012). This involved controlled exposure over *c.* 835 sq. m. There, aside from a series of Post-Medieval features, 10 small pits and three possible postholes were present across an area of 4 × 8 m. Each was half-sectioned and, in total, 13 pieces of Early Neolithic flintwork were recovered from six of them (plus two as residual/surface finds), with a couple of very small sherds of contemporary flint-tempered pottery present in one. A maximum of four flints occurred in any one; that included a large core (1352 g) likely to derive from flint-bearing upper chalk beds (i.e. a non-local source; see Atkins 2012 concerning recent evidence of Neolithic activity along Cambridge's riverside).

25 A relatively small quarry pit-cluster was excavated at Vicar's Farm (see Chap. 4, below). Only extending, in total, over *c.* 270 sq. m, it was thought that it related to the construction of a small barrow sealing the settlement's cremation cemetery. With many of its quarry hollows comparable to those at New Hall, it is relevant that they too were all fairly shallow and, generally, just *c.* 0.2–0.4 m deep.

26 Based on actual excavated soil-volume figures (*vs.* our approximated plan/section calculation method), see Millett and Woodhouse's much more systematic cubic artefact-density analyses from the Hayton Project (2015): the volume of pottery within its pits/wells was

on average 60 sherds per cu. m and the highest recorded ditch-density was 111.5 sherds per cu. m (*ibid.*, illus. 19.2 & table 19.2). Amongst wells' values at Colne Fen's The Camp Ground and Langdale Hale settlements were, respectively, F.532's 90 sherds per cu. m (1423 sherds from half-section with 467 separate vessels represented) and F.871's 19 sherds per cu. m (1599 sherds/123 vessels; Evans *et al.* 2013b, 94, 169 & 222 and figs. 2.16 & 2.18 and 3.8 & 3.29).

27 As outlined by Yannouli above, horse also occurred in Marion Close's Iron Age faunal assemblage and, there, ovicaprid was actually the dominant species (*c.* 42% NISP/four MNI *vs.* cattle, *c.* 40%/three respectively).

28 As further discussed in the final chapter (see *Economic Matters ...*), while overall the site's main Roman-period animal domesticate frequencies broadly reflect the regional pattern (see Smith *et al.* 2016, 204), with cattle dominant at *c.* 51 per cent, there was significant variability between individual features. Within its northern sector, three of its major features had higher sheep/goat percentages: F.1/2, F.30 and F.6. At almost 81 per cent, the latter's frequency is particularly marked; while at 44 per cent that of F.30 may seem relatively low, this reflects its enhanced pig bone-value: 25 per cent (at just 25 NISP the size of its assemblage is, though, small and it may not be widely representative).

As outlined in Chapter Seven, a higher frequency of sheep/goat would actually seem to be characteristic of Roman Cambridge's 'town-core' figures and this might then further reflect upon the source of these specific features' assemblages. In contrast, at *c.* 74 per cent, F.7's cattle remains were very high – with sheep/goat at just *c.* 12 per cent – possibly the result of its somewhat later attribution.

29 Shellfish evidently also contributed to the Roman diet (they were not present in prehistoric contexts). Of the 500 recovered, the vast majority were oyster; a few mussels were also present. Fish bones were also present in the bulk samples from F.1/2 and fish scales were identified within that feature's monolith sample.

30 Yannouli's relating of articulated joints to meal leftovers would now be at odds with the predominant ritual attribution of such remains; see Chapter Six for further discussion of this issue.

Chapter 4

Vicar's Farm – *Baseline Matters*

The excavations at Vicar's Farm were initiated as part of the University's West Cambridge development. The project was commissioned by the University's Estates Management and Buildings Service in advance of the construction of a new Department of Computing (The William Gates Building) and Microsoft's European Research Centre. The excavation's framing was extraordinary as regards issues raised in this book's first and last chapters concerning the 'landscape of science': situated below the University's Observatory, to the south was the (new) Cavendish Laboratory and, to the west, the Whittle Laboratory (see Fig. 4.4 and Chap. 7).

Covering some 6 ha, the site-area had originally been divided into two fields: a smaller northern one, previously used as pasture and, to the south, a larger wheat field (Fig. 4.1). The potential of the site was first revealed during a programme of geological test pitting in 1998 undertaken across much of the University's West Cambridge lands, which was subject to archaeological monitoring. Archaeological features were identified within three of the 12 test pits situated within the vicinity of the Vicar's Farm Site, although no dating evidence was found. Background research and previous fieldwork in the immediate area did not suggest anything earlier than Medieval land-use (see below).[1] Given the ambiguity of the evidence, it was decided to undertake a field evaluation of the area in September 1999, consisting of 13 trenches spaced across the two fields and comprising a total length of *c.* 650 m (Whittaker & Evans 1999). Archaeological features, variously of later prehistoric, Roman and Post-Medieval date, were found in every trench across the site, while Mesolithic, Neolithic and Medieval artefacts were also retrieved. The vast majority of the site's finds and features related to the Roman period, and suggested the presence of a dense settlement, with its core clearly within the proposed development area. It was clear that a major excavation would be required if the development was to proceed and so, between December 1999 and May 2000, the whole area was stripped of topsoil and all archaeological features recorded and sample-excavated. In June and early July 2000, this was followed by an intensive watching brief of the area under the modern farmyard and the northern part of the east-side bund.

Methodologies

Prior to machining, four 50 × 50 m sample squares were fieldwalked (A–D), each sub-divided into 10 × 10 m grid-squares. The conditions were not optimal for surface collection given the clayey nature of the soil, but sufficient finds were recovered to enable a basic appraisal. A range of artefacts were retrieved, a great many of which were modern or Post-Medieval. Figure 4.2 shows the plots of prehistoric worked flint and Roman pottery, both revealing greatest densities in Square A. This confirmed the findings of the evaluation trenches, which indicated that the core of activity lay in that general area. Beyond this, the fieldwalking data might provide a useful comparative measure in terms of core-periphery densities on clay soils. For the Roman pottery, Squares A and B were selected and their basic statistics compared (Table 4.1); the figures are small but indicate that towards the core of a settlement an average of two sherds per 10 m square might be expected, against one sherd every five squares in peripheral areas. The numbers in the actual core, which lay just to the north of A, may even have been higher, although this area was

Table 4.1. *Comparison of fieldwalking Squares A and B for Roman pottery.*

Square	Total	Ave. no. sherds per 10 sq. m
Core (A)	54	2.16
Periphery (B)	5	0.2

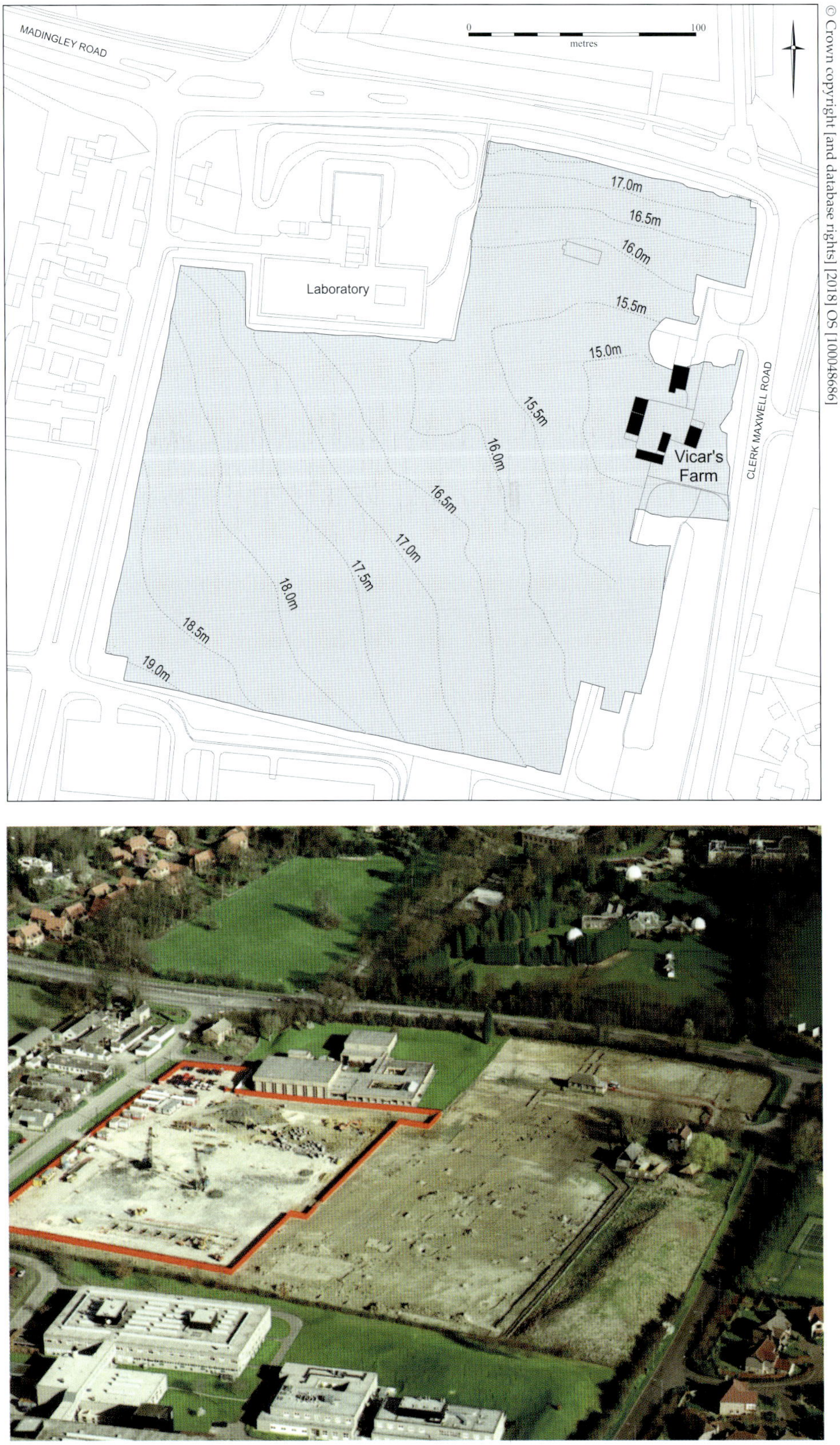

Figure 4.1. *Vicar's Farm, surface topography (with extant farm buildings) and, below, aerial photograph looking north to excavations in progress (note University Observatory in top right corner).*

Figure 4.2. *Fieldwalking distributions: prehistoric flint (left) and, right, Romano-British pottery.*

not fieldwalked. All in all, however, these numbers seem remarkably low for what was subsequently encountered beneath the topsoil in terms of the density of features, a fact explained, perhaps, by the poor conditions and clay soil.

Excavation began in December 1999 with a small area opened up in the core of the site, which was expanded to cover the whole field in late January and February the following year (Fig. 4.3). Machining of the topsoil took place under archaeological supervision, with two to three tracked 360° mechanical excavators working together at any one time, loading spoil into dumper trucks. The ground conditions were, at times, very wet and, consequently, deep rutting obscured and disturbed the archaeology along their access route, although nothing major was lost. Base-planning and intensive metal-detector surveys were conducted in the wake of machining, and over selected areas, geophysical (magnetic susceptibility) and geochemical (phosphate) surveys were conducted. During the main excavation, all pre-modern features were either fully, or sample excavated: 50 per cent of each discrete feature was excavated through half-sectioning and, as far as possible, standard metre-long slots were cut through linear features at regular intervals (Fig 4.4). This procedure was compromised to the extent that slots at intersections between features were also required to resolve stratigraphic relationships. During the watching brief phase (June–July 2000), excavation was more strategic and focused where possible on resolving major elements in this part of the site.

All retrieved finds were retained, although in the case of large pieces of unworked stone only a sample was kept, with a record of the discarded material made. Bulk environmental samples were taken from all major features and, additionally, column samples for pollen and micromorphology were taken from selected contexts. A three-tiered recording hierarchy of context, feature and group was employed in the excavation and post-excavation process. Contexts represented the basic unit of excavation (e.g. deposit, cut), their numbers indicated by square brackets (e.g. [001]). Features comprise the broader entity of which contexts were a part (e.g. ditch, posthole), and numbers were prefixed with an 'F'. Finally, groups represent a collection of interrelated features (e.g. enclosure, structure, cemetery), their numbers being prefixed with a 'G'. While groups were frequently identified in the course of excavation, their full ascription and designation was applied in the post-excavation stage.

All finds were catalogued by generic material by context and indicated by 'arrow' brackets (e.g. <001>); small finds were also assigned a separate number and located either by context position or x/y co-ordinates within the site grid. In total, over 3450 units were excavated and recorded, over 300 samples collected and over 39,000 finds retrieved.

A major goal of this project was to integrate the recording system with a GIS package (ArcView) in order to facilitate the analysis and interpretation of the site, and most of the spatial analysis was conducted in this manner. To this end, all the excavation slots were

Figure 4.3 *(above and opposite). Excavation photographs (top): left, looking east towards standing Vicar's Farmyard buildings and, right, south towards the new Cavendish Laboratory; below, as built, the development's park-and-cycle lot (left) and, right, the William Gates Building.*

Figure 4.4. *Site plan showing all features and excavated segments.*

assigned a number in the post-excavation programme and, apart from the finds recovered through metal-detector survey (plotted EDM), all finds are located by their excavation slot.

Public and Computing Initiatives

The scale of the excavations provided scope for a series of initiatives allowing us to explore different facets of fieldwork and presentation. The most prominent was a 'School Visits' week. Funded through a special grant from the Office of the University's Vice-Chancellor, this allowed us to, in effect, halt the fieldwork for a week and give the time to school tours. Under the co-ordination of Dr John Carman, accompanying brochures were distributed to all visitors and throughout the neighbourhood, and educational/finds displays were mounted in the Old GPO building that then still stood on the site (see Fig. 4.5).

The timing of this programme coincided with the University's National Science Week events and on its first Saturday the site was opened to the public at large, with live video relays to the McDonald Institute in the centre of town where there were also related displays. Each event – the open-day and school visits – attracted upwards of 1000 visitors, and both proved gratifying experiences. Further commemorating the excavations, a large permanent signboard outlining their findings has since been erected on the site: a first for the University.

The computing aspect of the programme is worthy of note. Knowing that distributional analysis was

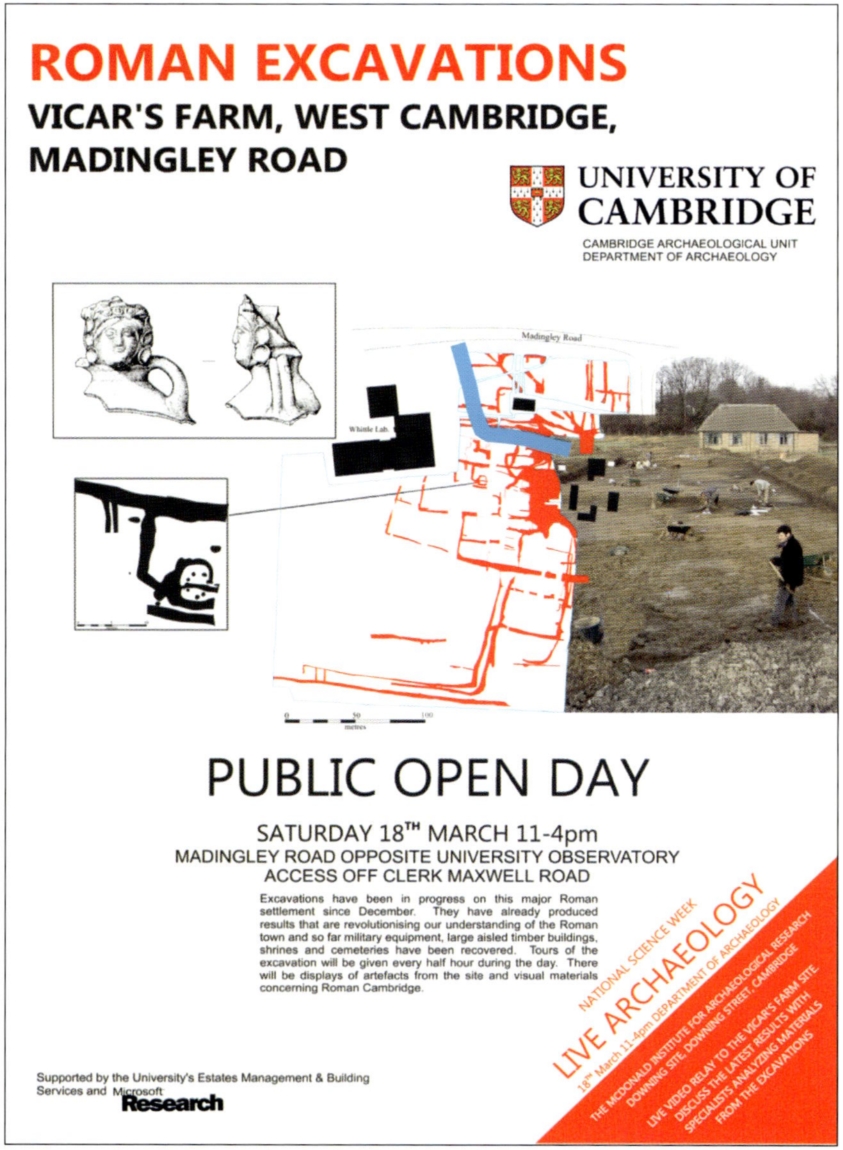

Figure 4.5. *Public initiatives: open-day poster, Roman settlement reconstruction illustration (by A. Hall) and, bottom right, John Carman conducting a school class visit to the site (in old GPO Building).*

one of the main components of the site we wished to explore, and given the computing context of the construction programme, we approached Microsoft to support the excavations' full computerization. This proved successful and, after first exploring other options, the site plans were digitized into AUTOCAD MAP. Primary data was attached to the graphical objects created in CAD and, when imported into ARCVD3W, this provided a linkage to the site database created in Microsoft Access, enabling a GIS approach to post-excavation analysis. This was further facilitated by the use of terrain modelling software (SURFER).

Allied Investigations

Before further detailing the main site, it is first worth outlining more recent minor adjacent excavations which, accordingly, now influence its interpretation. Relating to an extension to the Whittle Laboratory, late

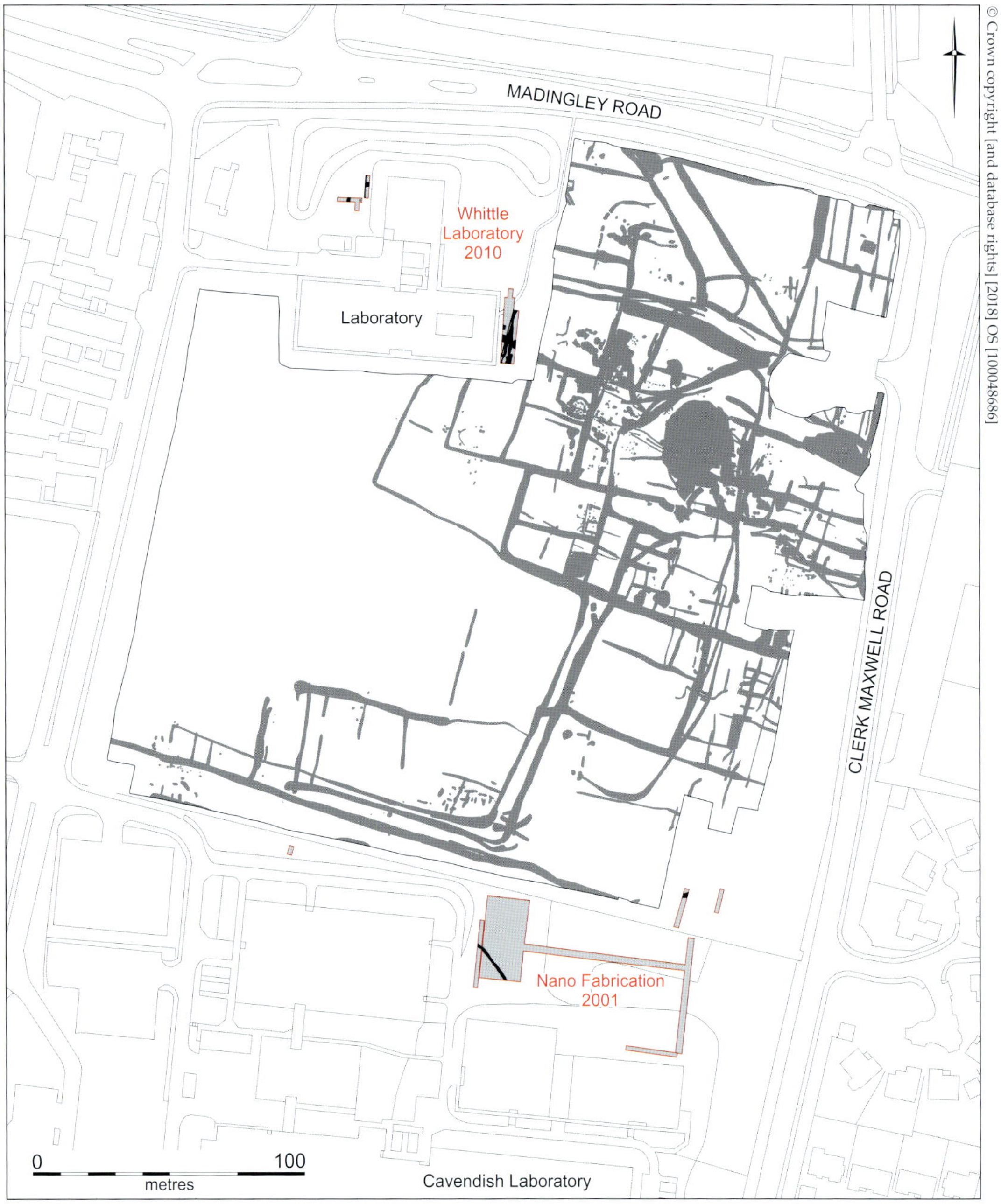

Figure 4.6. *Allied excavation locations: Nano Fabrication Building (2001) and Whittle Laboratory (2010) investigations.*

Figure 4.7. *Whittle Laboratory trenching, ditch (F.8), with top image looking east to now built-area of Vicar's Farm site-core.*

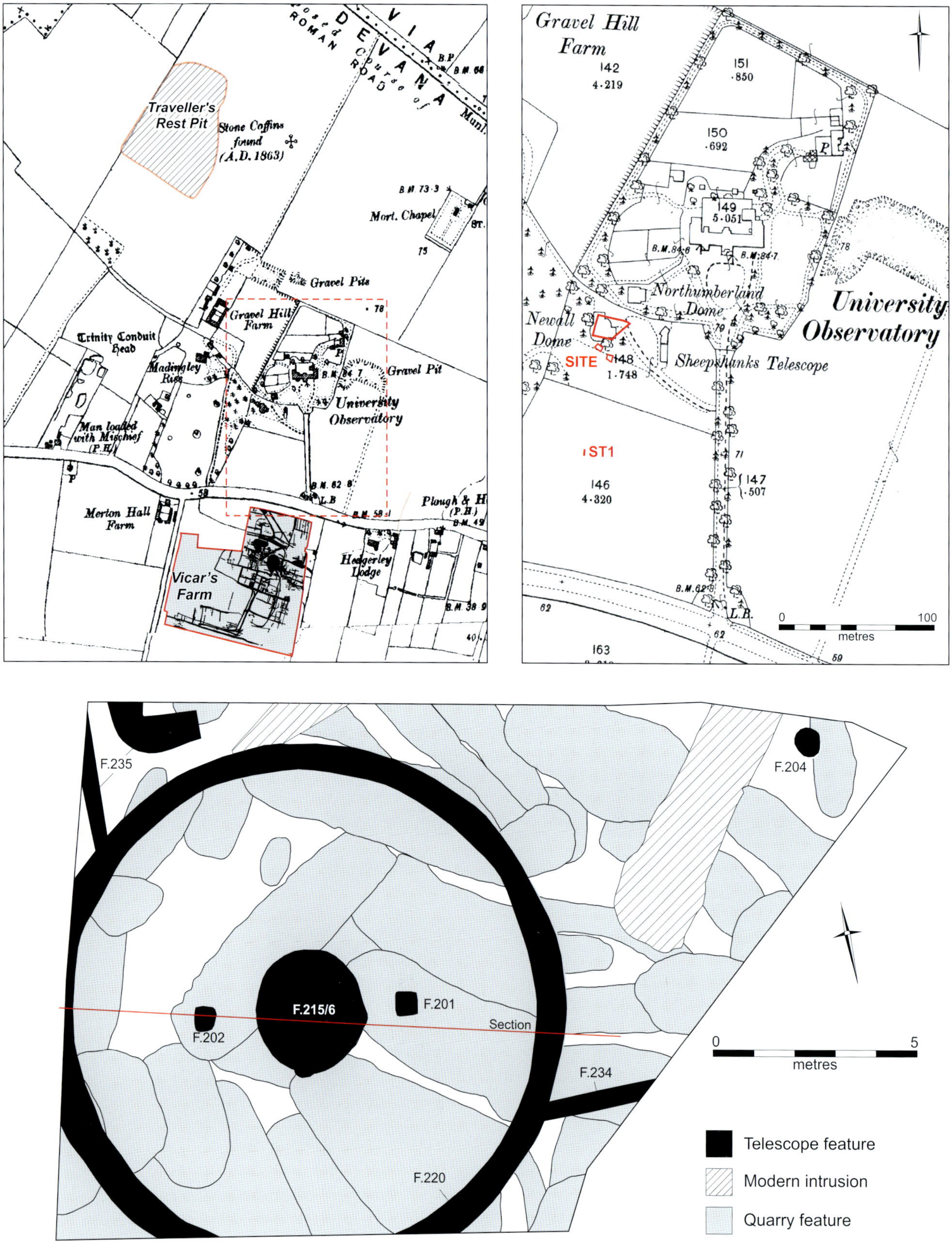

Figure 4.8. *Kavli Institute Site, location maps (above) and, below, base plan.*

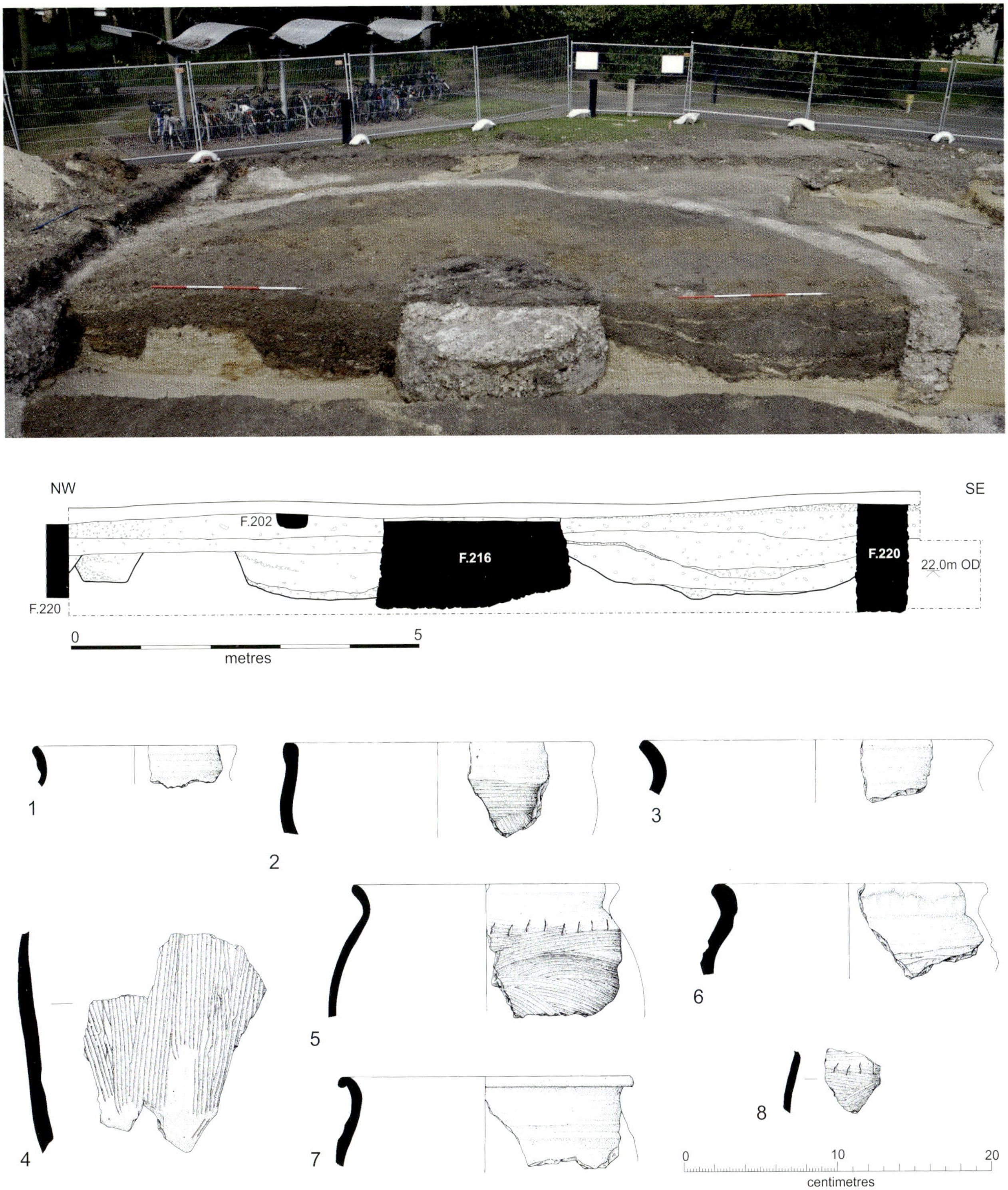

Figure 4.9. *Kavli Institute Site, photograph and section (see Fig. 4.8 for location), with Late Iron Age and Conquest Period pottery below. Typical of the region's Late Iron Age assemblages, sandy fabrics dominated (52%), though grog-tempered fabrics also featured (28%). Based on rim and base sherds alone, a minimum of 26 vessels were recorded: four bowls and 22 jars. Of the latter, forms include both slack-shouldered jars with beaded rims and necked jars with everted or beaded rims. Burnishing was apparent on 20 sherds, including some with lines or lattice-type decoration; generally, combing was the most prevalent decoration-type.*

***Follies and Time/Space Reckoning –* Telescope Archaeology** (1)

Along with Edmonds' Jodrell Bank researches (2010), the Kavli Institute investigations marked a contribution to the small, but developing, field of 'telescope archaeology' (Evans & Newman 2011). The wide-ranging implications of digging the Newall instrument's foundations there will feature in the next book. Prior to the establishment of the University's Observatory at Gravel Hill in 1822, from the early–mid eighteenth century small observatories had been built within four colleges; the earliest, and most prominent, being that atop Trinity's Great Gate (see Fig. 4.11; Willis & Clark 1886, II, fig. 17; see also Stratton 1949, 1–2 and Whipple Museum 1998). As chance would have it, hard on the heels of the Kavli excavations, in 2010 repairs to the base of the mound-top sundial in the gardens of Newnham College revealed the brick foundation of its first observatory (Fig. 4.10). Minor in scale in relation to the Newall, it only extended over 3.7 × 5.6 m. It dated to 1891, when a Mrs Bateson (wife of the then Master of St John's College) gave the College a four-inch equatorially-mounted refractor telescope. It was moved to its current location, on the south side of the College's grounds, following the construction of Peile Hall in 1910, as the new building range blocked the telescope's view of the western sky.[3]

Figure 4.10. *Newnham College, 2010, photographs showing landscaping repairs to the base of the sundial upon the College's back mound, revealing the early observatory's brick foundations (left; see Fig. 2.39 for location); right, the Newall telescope and Newnham observatory plans compared.*

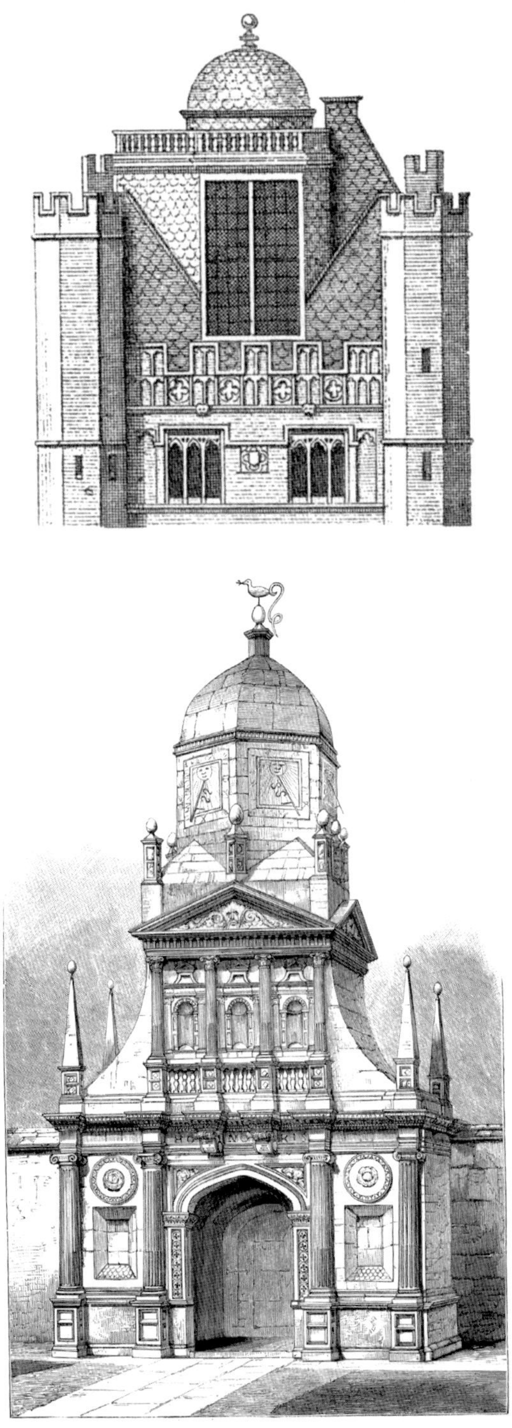

Figure 4.11. *University observatories and sundials: Trinity College's gateway observatory, 1740 (top) and, below, Gonville & Caius College's Gate of Honour (Willis & Clark 1886, II, fig. 17 & I, 177, fig. 9).*

The Eleanor Sidgwick Memorial Sundial (in commemoration of a former Principal of the College, and wife of one of its founders, Henry Sidgwick) was erected on the mound in 1913 (Fig 4.10). The latter's sequence, therefore, marks an intriguing juxtaposition, with a 'real' piece of scientific apparatus – the telescope – giving way to what is, in effect, a folly: the multiple-sundial column. Why build a sundial when everyone by then had watches?

Cambridge's Colleges abound with sundials; their origins are readily understood, as, along with bell chimes, they once provided a 'real' means to gauge time (see e.g. Thompson 1967, 64). The most extreme case in point related to the elaborate spatial/moral programme enacted by John Caius at Gonville & Caius College in the later sixteenth century (Nickson 2005). Amid its Gates of Humility, Virtue and Honour (the latter topped by six sundials; Fig. 4.11), Caius Court apparently hosted a variety of sundials, whose centrepiece was "A column ... on which a stone was placed, wrought with wonderous skill, containing 60 sundials. It was the work of Theodore Havenus of Cleves, a skilful artificer ..." (in Willis & Clark 1886 [I], 182–3; by the time that Caius' column was depicted on the Loggan print of 1690 its sundials had been removed).

Oddly enough, the last century and, thus far, the first decades of this one has seen an escalation of sundial-building within the University and its Colleges. These have got ever more sophisticated in their technology; Newnham's Margaret Stanier Sundial (2010), Pembroke's Foundress Court Building (1997) and the Observatory's Royal Greenwich Observatory Sundial (1975, moved to Cambridge in 1990) are amongst the most obvious examples. This can perhaps be attributed to the paucity, at least until late, of an outdoor sculptural tradition within the Colleges (instead, they commemorate their 'greats' inside their halls and chapels). Now, however, along with the Corpus' Taylor Library's extraordinary 'Chronophage' insect-clock erected at Benet Street's corner in 2008, sundials provide an opportunity for the demonstration of ever greater mathematical/chronometric/astronomical elegance in their rendering of time. Add to this that such quasi-'natural' contrivances are clearly an inoffensive means of personal/institutional commemoration, sundials are evidently considered an appropriate sculptural theme for the academic community at large.

in 2010 two trenches were dug along its western side and, another, in the plot's southeastern edge (Fig. 4.6; Slater 2011). While nothing of any consequence was exposed within the former, the western continuation of one of the Vicar's Farm main boundaries (then re-assigned as F.8) was revealed within the eastern cutting, along with various Post-Medieval features. That trench was thus expanded to permit the excavation of that ditch (Fig. 4.7). We were able to dig two segments across it and, in total, 46 sherds (516 g) of first- to third-century AD Romano-British pottery was recovered, as were 31 animal bones. This exercise simply helped to confirm the western layout of the earlier site's main Roman settlement; for reasons of pragmatism, its finds are not included in the presentation of the main site that follows.

Some years before, and just shortly after the completion of the Vicar's Farm excavations, limited trenching occurred on its southern side in advance of the construction of the Nano Fabrication Building within the grounds of the Cavendish Laboratory (Fig. 4.6; Lucas 2001).[2] With two 'early' features in one trench, this was subsequently expanded to a *c.* 400 sq. m area and further trenching was conducted (Armour 2001). Aside from half-sectioning a pit of Iron Age date (0.5 m deep; four sherds and much fired clay recovered), this allowed for the excavation of two metre-segments across a slightly arcing, northwest–southeast-oriented ditch. Apart from animal bone, 14 sherds of Iron Age pottery were recovered from that feature, as were six of first-/second-century AD date. While this work certainly demonstrated the southward continuation of the (low density) Iron Age settlement along the main site's southern side (see below), the ditch there would actually appear to be Roman (with earlier material redeposited within it); as such, it may represent the southeastern extension of the boundary along the earlier site's southern edge.

As highlighted in the first chapter, the 2008 Kavli Institute exposure fell within the grounds of the University's Observatory, just north of the Vicar's Farm Site on Madingley Rise at *c.* 23 m OD (i.e. 5 m above the main site; Figs. 1.3.4 & 4.8). Primarily directed towards the excavation of a nineteenth-century telescope, the broad contextual resonance of its fieldwork will most appropriately feature in the next book (see, though, also Chap. 7 and Evans & Newman 2011). Its presentation here will be limited to artefacts redeposited within the mass of sixteenth- to seventeenth-century hand-dug gravel quarrying pits that underlay the instrument's footings. This area – variously Madingley Rise and Gravel Hill Farm – was the location of a 'quarrying hamlet', *Grithow* in later Medieval times (Hall & Ravensdale 1976, 29).

Table 4.2. *Kavli Institute Site, Iron Age (IA) and Roman (R) pottery.*

Date	No.	Wt. (g)	EVE
Early IA	7	61	0
Late IA	68	1258	0.97
Late IA/Early R	49	510	0.28
Early R	9	109	0.10
Total	*133*	*1938*	*1.35*

We will not here relate its rather eclectic later finds inventory (pottery, clay tobacco pipes and glass, *etc.*) as it is the early material that concerns us. As well as a later prehistoric flint flake and a Late Roman coin, this consisted of more than 125 sherds of Iron Age and Roman pottery (Fig. 4.9). Reported on by Anderson and Brudenell (in Newman 2008b), the chronological breakdown of the material is indicated in Table 4.2. While the recovery of several Early Iron Age sherds resonates with earlier, evaluation-related findings from the nearby Hoyle Building (Masser 2000), the majority of the pottery was of Late Iron Age date (*c.* 50 BC–AD 50), with some Conquest Period/Early Roman wares also identified.

As further explored in the next book, there seems every reason to see this pottery as deriving from the immediate area and, therefore, attesting to both Early Iron Age activity and what is probably a distinct Late Iron Age settlement. Indeed, it is even possible that the Vicar's Farm Roman-period features extended northward throughout this area, as a probable feature of that date was exposed in a soakaway test-pit sited midway between the two sites (STI, Fig. 4.8), and from which some 30 sherds of Early Roman pottery were recovered (see Hughes 1907b on the recovery of Roman-period finds during quarrying immediately beside the Observatory).

Sequence Overview

Remains of prehistoric, Roman, Medieval and Post-Medieval features were uncovered at Vicar's Farm, although the Roman archaeology dominates the site. However, it would be remiss not to discuss at a general level the nature of the non-Roman archaeology found and so both pre- and post-Roman activity will be summarized here, as part of a general overview of the archaeology on the site. Further details about the non-Roman aspects of the site can be found in the archive report (Lucas & Whittaker 2001).

Mesolithic–Late Bronze Age

The area was sporadically visited in prehistory as attested by the presence of flint tools, which reveal a subtle but definite pattern of shifting land-use as groundwater levels decreased. During the Mesolithic, a discrete flint scatter occupied the southern ridge of a natural basin in the centre of the site that may have been wet at the time (Fig. 4.12; see below). Subsequent visitation in the Neolithic and Bronze Age was marked by a movement down into and around this basin as the land dried out. Although no features from this period were identified, the nature and distribution of the worked flint across the site can still be used to interpret the nature of this activity.

Lithics (with Chantal Conneller)
The site yielded a small assemblage of mixed date consisting of 180 pieces of worked flint (see Table 4.3; Fig. 4.12) and 1674 g of burnt flint. A substantial proportion of the assemblage dates to the Mesolithic. Diagnostic pieces include a microlith, an awl, a burin and burin spall, plus a number of endscrapers. Frequencies of blades and fine, narrow flakes are high and one microblade core and eight blade cores were recovered. Knapping was conducted using a soft hammer and core platforms were carefully prepared to aid the detachment of flakes and blades. This technology is also characteristic of the Early Neolithic and it is possible that material of this date is included. However, the balance of diagnostic tools suggests that the majority of this blade/narrow flake debitage is Mesolithic in date.

A small amount of material also suggests a Late Neolithic presence in the area. These include two small discoidal cores, squat flakes with some evidence of preparation and a fine sub-circular knife. A polished stone axe may have then been deposited, though it could also belong to the Early Neolithic. Whichever part of the Neolithic the axe dates to, it appears to have been part of an occupation that was fairly ephemeral – at least in terms of the lithics that were left behind – and it seems to have been deposited in relative isolation.

The remainder of the assemblage is later prehistoric in character, dating to the later Bronze Age or even, perhaps, the Early Iron Age. The pieces are crude, the product of unsystematic and haphazard reduction. Mistakes, in the form of pieces with incipient cones, are present. Tools belonging to this occupation are relatively few, but include scrapers, irregularly retouched pieces and naturally fractured flakes, which were retouched and used as tools. The raw material used throughout was a black gravel flint, though light brown and orange/red pieces are also present. This material varies in quality, from nodules that are relatively fresh and unrolled, to flawed and extensively abraded pieces.

The Mesolithic activity on site clearly represents occupation. Blade production focused in one area, but there was also more widespread tool-use for tasks such as hide processing and working on other materials. In general, the low densities and broad nature of the assemblage suggests short-term, non-specialized occupation, much as one would expect to occur across the landscape, except perhaps for the knapping site. As noted, the location on clays may have been unusual, but not exceptional and may particularly be associated with certain tasks such as blade production *because* of its marginal location. Given the possibility that the area may have been seasonally wet, the location may also have offered useful resources.

Later activity (Neolithic/Bronze Age) is much sparser and may be indicative of specific events rather than any prolonged occupation. One trend noted was that over time, the flints seem to move down from the clay into the sands and gravel, which may even reflect a drying out of the basin. More generally, the activities taking place on the site cannot be seen independently of the much denser concentrations of flints which lie upslope on Madingley Rise. Although not exclusive, it is still likely that occupation would have favoured the higher ground, and the flints recovered earlier in the last century around Gravel Hill Farm (and Traveller's Rest) probably signify a much more visited locale (see *NWC*, chaps. 2 & 3).

Table 4.3. *The flint assemblage.*

Category	No.	%
Tools	*40*	*22.2*
Awl	1	0.6
Axe	1	0.6
Burin	1	0.6
Knife	3	1.7
Microlith	1	0.6
Scraper	12	6.7
Truncation	1	0.6
Retouched	19	10.6
Flaked piece	1	0.6
Tool spalls	*1*	*0.6*
Burin spall	1	0.6
Debitage	*140*	*77.8*
Blade	26	14.4
Flake	91	50.6
Core	15	8.3
Chunk	7	3.9
Total	*180*	*100*

Iron Age

A number of features with Iron Age pottery were excavated but few were actually Iron Age in date. In the southern part of the site, F.5359 and F.1114 contained Early Iron Age pottery (Fig. 4.13), while redeposited Early Iron Age pottery also occurred nearby in a Roman ditch. In the north, a cluster of pits can be dated to the Later Iron Age (*c.* 300 BC–AD 43) on the basis of associated pottery: F.4146–9, F.4212, F.4227, F.4228, F.5621, F.5628 and F.5634. One other pit, F.5044, is probably also of this period, along with another cluster a few metres to the southeast: F.4240, F.8021, F.8023 and F.8024. Apart from one small fragment of burnt clay in F.4148 (7 g), the finds consisted of pottery and animal bone. From F.8023 came a single brooch, dated to the fourth century BC. A later Iron Age coin (<5223>), probably minted late first century BC/early first century AD, was retrieved from the metal-detected spoil (identification by Adrian Challands).

As studied by J.D. Hill, 147 sherds (900 g) of Iron Age pottery was examined and can be divided into a number of groups on the basis of association and date (see Table 4.4).

Later Bronze Age/Early Iron Age - One feature (F.5386 [1186]) had a sherd in a black, flint-tempered fabric, while another sherd of similar date came from [1182] in the same feature. Both of these are probably residual, occurring in a Late Iron Age/Early Roman feature.

Early Iron Age - One feature, F.1114, contained a sizeable group of Early Iron Age pottery (86 sherds/386 g; Fig. 4.13), consisting of burnt

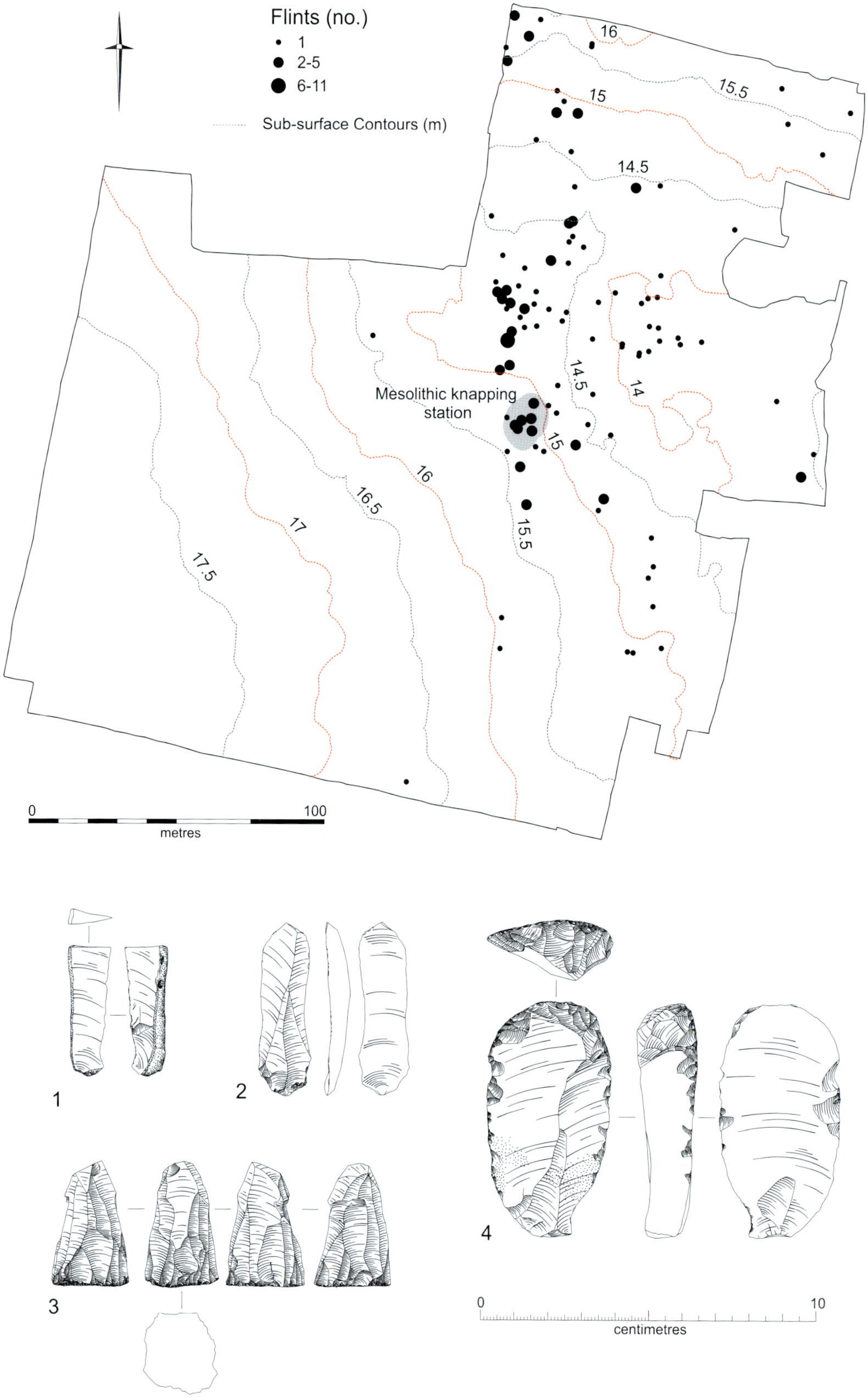

Figure 4.12. *Prehistoric flint distribution (top; with sub-surface contours shown), with selected Mesolithic and Neolithic pieces below.*

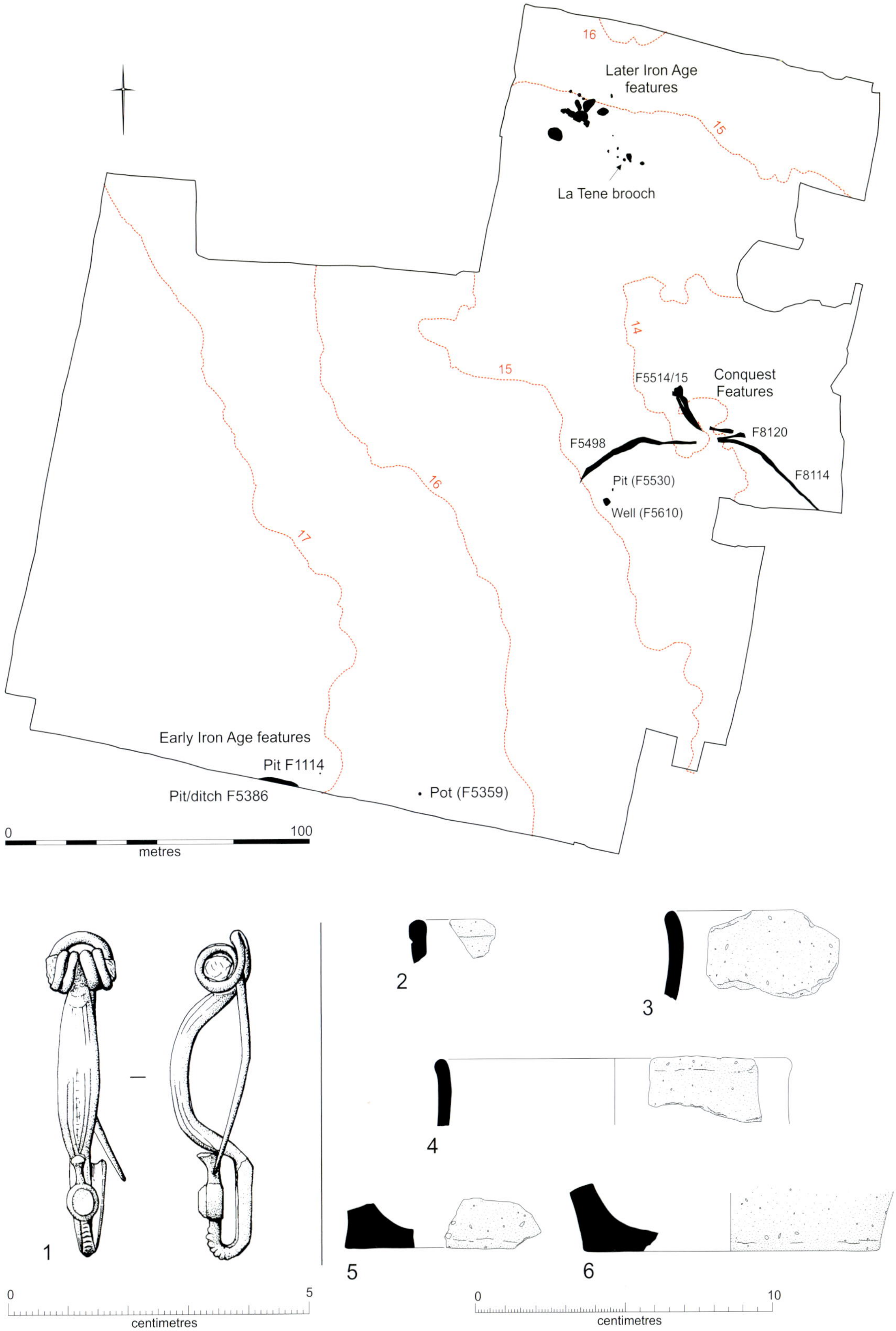

Figure 4.13. *Iron Age and Conquest Period features (top) and, below, La Tène brooch (copper alloy; 1) and selected pottery illustrations (2–6; from F.1114).*

Table 4.4. *Summary of Iron Age pottery.*

Feature	No. sherds	Wt. (g)	Type
F.1114	86	386	EIA
F.1135	1	3	MIA
F.1182	1	1	LBA/EIA
F.1186	1	7	LBA/EIA
F.1306	2	5	IA
F.4147	10	77	LIA (first century AD)
F.4148	3	9	IA?
F.4166	34	293	LIA (first century AD)
F.4228	9	119	MIA/LIA
F.5003	1	3	LIA
F.5009	1	7	LBA/EIA

flint-tempered vessel fragments, probably from settlement-related activity. The forms were all plain, undecorated and unburnished, which might suggest a date in the latter part of the Early Iron Age.

Later Iron Age - From the cluster of pits in the northern part of the site, three produced Middle and/or Later Iron Age type vessel fragments: F.4228, handmade vegetable-tempered sherds of Middle–Late Iron Age date; F.4147, a group of first-century AD grog-tempered and vegetable-tempered sherds; and, finally, F.4166 had 32 fragments from a black, grog-tempered, combed jar/cooking pot also dating to the first century AD (two small sherds of an Early Iron Age burnished vessel were also present in the latter).

From F.1135, a classic vegetable-tempered sherd dating to the Middle Iron Age was identified, while from F.1306 came a sandy sherd that could be attributable to any time in the Iron Age. Finally, small individual sherds of Iron Age date were identified in each of F.5003 and F.5009 (both from the evaluation). All of these sherds are probably residual.

Pits F.5359 and F.5621 contained very low quantities of charred plant remains. One Celtic Bean *(Vicia faba)* is the only example at Vicar's Farm, none being found in the Roman contexts. No cereal chaff was present in these two features, but two grains of barley *(Hordeum* sp.) and wheat *(Triticum* sp.) were recovered. Several seeds of brome grass *(Bromus* sp.) were also recovered from F.5621. The few charred remains make interpretation difficult, but they do not represent the chaff-rich processing debris so common within the Roman contexts. Waterlogged plant remains within F.5621 indicate that the local environment was damp, shady and relatively undisturbed.

The Iron Age faunal assemblage is small – only 23 bone fragments – with just nine identifiable to species; these comprise the main domesticates save pig.

A La Tène I brooch of Hull & Hawkes Type IBb (1987, 95–8) was recovered from F.8023 (<4798> SF 534; Fig. 4.13.1). As reported on by Nina Crummy, this is well-preserved and complete, apart from the tip of the pin and the upper corner of the catchplate. It is 52 mm long; the spring is of four coils and has an iron rod through it. The narrow bow is 'D'-shaped in section and has an elongated leaf-shaped design of three mouldings defined by grooves, the central one knurled. The returned foot has a small plain disc and long snout which touches the base of the bow. The end of the snout is expanded. The curve of the foot before the disc is transversely notched. The design of the snout is closely matched by that on a Type IBb brooch from Mount Batten, and also on several brooches of Type IBc (Hull & Hawkes 1987, pl. 32). The bow decoration is not closely paralleled on IBb brooches, though several have a line of punched dots down the centre of the bow. However, the elongated leaf-shape of the design does appear in wider form on some examples of Type IBc, which has a wider leaf-shaped bow. The majority of IBc brooches with this type of design have an easterly distribution; examples are known from Barrington, Saham Toney, the lower reaches of the River Thames, and possibly Dragonby (*ibid.*, pls. 29–32). Thus, the Vicar's Farm brooch appears to represent a stylistic, and perhaps regional, link between the two sub-types. The notches on its foot appear to be a unique feature. The brooch is British-made and belongs to the fourth century BC.

With Greensand being the most frequently used material, five saddle quern pieces were recovered, though one might have been a polissoir fragment (6125 g total weight).

Clearly the quantities of Iron Age features from the site are limited, although they concentrated in two areas. The earliest material, which may even date back to the Later Bronze Age, lay at the southern edge of the site and occurred in only a few discrete features, most of it probably residual. However, the assemblage from F.1114 is particularly substantial and suggests settlement close by. Indeed, as outlined above, further evidence of broadly contemporary occupation was detected to the south in the Nano Fabrication Building investigations.

The other focus of Iron Age activity occurred at the other end of the site, marked by a cluster of pits later enclosed within a Roman ditch system. This is a curious group. The pottery and a La Tène brooch are of Middle–Late Iron Age date (i.e. fourth century BC to first century AD), but the nature of the activity – a few pits – is minimal and seems either indicative of causal 'visitation/tasking' (rather than permanent settlement), or that these were outliers of the Kavli Institute-area settlement (see above). More curious is whether the later Roman ditches that enclosed the area of these pits took into account their presence or this area as a 'place'. Food was consumed, but beyond that little can be said. A pit containing disarticulated human remains in the same area (F.5017; see Chap. 5) has been ascribed a Roman date on the basis of one sherd, but if this is intrusive (as the pit was disturbed), then a mortuary or funerary aspect to the activity might be possible. This could also provide some context for the establishment of the Roman site, especially its primary elements, the cremation cemetery and shrine.

Roman

The Roman settlement is discussed in detail within the next two chapters and so will only be briefly summarized here. The 'pre-settlement' Conquest Period ditch system is first discussed here. Given, however, the general paucity of associated material, particularly brooches, usage of the site-area cannot have then been intense.

Pre-settlement Ditch System

Prior to the Roman settlement, a large curvilinear ditch-line forming a semi-open enclosure occupied the central area of the site; its purpose was probably some form of stock enclosure (Fig. 4.13). Whether this is pre- or post-Conquest is difficult to ascertain. There is clearly more than one phase to its layout and its relationship to the Roman settlement core is unclear. While it almost certainly pre-dates it, it was still open during the early phase of Roman occupation and was only backfilled in the mid–late second century AD to judge by the pottery in its fill. Ditch F.8114 (1.20–1.3 m wide, 0.42–0.55 m deep) would appear to have been continuous with F.5498 (*c.* 1 m across and 0.2 m deep, dated AD 120/140–200); its southwestern terminus was masked by later features, but possibly continued some way south along the line of the later G18 enclosure. Ditch F.8120 (1.5 m wide, 0.77 m deep) also seems to have been part of this system. The ditch system appears to be associated with well F.5610 (1.1 m diameter, 1.7 m deep, dated AD 45–70/100), which by association would suggest a post-Conquest, probably pre-Flavian, date for the whole group. Also nearby was a pit/dump of pottery, F.5530, of similar date (over an area 1 × 0.5 m, dated AD 45–60). Mirroring this large ditch on the north side was F.5515 (1.9 m wide and 0.6 m deep, dated AD 80–180; later recut as F.5514). This smaller ditch-line probably continued east as F.4849 (1.1 m wide, 0.3 m deep; dated AD 140+).

The Roman Settlement and Fieldsystem

The main settlement phase began with the establishment of a cremation cemetery and a small shrine in *c.* AD 80. These are either contemporary with or slightly pre-date a farmstead characterized by a formal rectilinear ditch system, an aisled building and various other enclosures. A major trackway/road ran down to the settlement from the northwest and another probably ran eastward. By the end of the second/early third century AD, the settlement had expanded greatly to the north and south, with new structures and sub-enclosures. Expansion increased in the late third/fourth century AD when the site reached its peak, expanding westward and eastward, with major internal segmentation and an inhumation cemetery on its southern edge. The site appears to have been abandoned in the early decades of the fifth century AD. Throughout the site's text, a three-phase periodization has been employed in the discussion of its Roman archaeology, which, although inevitably coarse (and subject to further sub-division; see Chap. 5, *Discussion*), provides a framework for a more nuanced interpretation (Figs. 4.14 & 5.37):

Phase I (AD 80–180) - This saw the establishment of the core settlement and many of its internal features such as the Timber Shrine, the Aisled Building and cremation cemetery.

Phase II (AD 180–270) - In the middle period, the settlement underwent a major expansion to the south, contemporary with the establishment of a fieldsystem. In the core of the settlement, the Aisled Building and cremation cemetery went out of use while the eastern side saw the establishment of some new features.

Phase III (AD 270–410+) - In the final period, the site transformed radically as a third area was added to the south, linking up the main settlement with the southern fieldsystem, which then saw an inhumation cemetery on its boundary. In the core of the site, the features in the eastern half developed to form a new centre of activity, while the settlement's eastern boundary was backfilled and the whole core opened up to the east, beyond the limit of excavation.

Medieval, Post-Medieval and Modern

By the middle of the fifth century AD, the site was completely abandoned and apparently unoccupied until the construction of Vicar's Farm. However, for most of the time prior to this, the land was agricultural; indeed until the present works, most of it remained in agricultural use. The latter-day Vicar's Farm (formerly known as Clunch Farm) was only built in the early nineteenth century and remained occupied until the mid 1980s.

*Medieval and Post-Medieval (*c. *1300–1800)*

No structural evidence survives to suggest any activity on the site in the centuries after the Roman period and, in all likelihood, it lay abandoned for a time as open waste ground. The archaeological evidence for later agricultural activity comes from the remains of ridge-and-furrow that scoured most of the site in broad, north–south strips (Fig. 4.15). From documentary sources, the turning of this land over to arable use is at least as early as the fourteenth century; from the few recovered objects in the furrows and some of the site's features this usage may date to the thirteenth century but could even have been much earlier. Objects found include a small background scatter of Medieval pottery from that century onwards, as well as a coin of Henry III dating to 1248 (SF 277) and a coin of Edward I or II dating to 1300–10 (SF 256). Hall and Ravensdale's (1976) reconstructed map of the West Fields shows that parts of the site were under cultivation or pasture, and includes a field called 'Brunneforth dole' and an area described as 'Froshis Croft'. In addition, a major ditch ('Willowes Ditch') is shown running east–west across the northern third of the site (see Fig. 4.17 & 7.10).

The Finds

Most of the finds came from the ploughsoil or the surface of unexcavated features (Fig. 4.15); only in a few instances were finds retrieved through excavation. Much of the metalwork came through metal-detecting, from the ploughsoil, subsoil or surface of features. The finds are summarized in Table 4.5. A certain amount of Post-Medieval coal and clinker was recovered from the main site, along with brick/tile and burnt clay, but these will not be discussed further. Excluding the Vicar's Farm 'Modern'-context watching brief investigation (see below), pottery was fairly sparse and comprised

Figure 4.14. *Roman settlement, all features.*

mostly Post-Medieval glazed red earthenwares. Identifications by David Hall noted two sherds of thirteenth-/fourteenth-century Ely ware, plus a fourteenth-century Fenware sherd and possible Grimston ware. Also there were two sherds of fifteenth-/sixteenth-century Essex redware, and sixteenth-century German stoneware from Raeren and Frechen. Seventeenth-century wares included Surrey whiteware, Ely ware, and German stoneware from Cologne. Eighteenth- and nineteenth-century English salt-glazed stonewares occurred along with Staffordshire whitewares. The glass was examined by Hilary Cool and was almost all bottle fragments, chiefly

Table 4.5. *Summary of finds from Medieval/Post-Medieval period (excluding modern contexts).*

	No.	Wt. (g)
Burnt clay	30	164
Brick/tile	152	4922
Pottery	261	2314
Glass	33	329
Clay pipe	5	22
Coal/clinker	53	205

from wine bottles. One fragment had a seal with a monogram on it (<172>, [133]). There were three fragments of window glass and a marble stopper from a Codd/Hamilton water bottle.

As reported by Adrian Challands, 12 coins, a jetton and a commemorative medal were recovered:

<4893> SF 79 - Cu alloy coin; Edward I Stirling *c.* AD 1303–5
<4896> SF 84 - Cu alloy coin; George II farthing minted AD 1730–8
<4934> SF 165 - Cu alloy jetton; mostly illegible, probably sixteenth-/seventeenth-century
<4954> SF 205 - Cu alloy coin; illegible, probably eighteenth-century halfpenny
<4971> SF 256 - Cu alloy coin; Edward I or II farthing AD 1300–10
<497> SF 280 - Cu alloy coin; Henry III Long Cross, AD 1248
<5016> SF 368 - Cu alloy coin; illegible, but probable eighteenth- to mid nineteenth-century farthing
<5070> SF 495 - Ag half coin; Scottish William
<5071> (spoil) - Cu alloy coin; illegible, has the appearance of a modern coin
<5081> (spoil) - George I halfpenny, minted AD 1719–24
<5230> (spoil) - Three coins and a medal: a) George V penny, 1912; b) Halfpenny, 1958, c) George, Dump farthing, early eighteenth century; d) medal commemorating death of Duke of York, Jan. 5th 1827.

As reported on below by Nina Crummy, the Medieval and early Post-Medieval metalwork items are largely dress accessories and tokens, but two Post-Medieval cloth seals were also present, along with some structural and other fittings, and some horseshoe fragments (Fig. 4.15). The latter are all of the lobate, early Medieval form. The Medieval lead tokens represent small change, used to fill a gap in the official currency. Tools are restricted to a punch and a chisel. A pair of shears represented by a blade fragment were of a small size and would have been used for personal grooming. Aside from the illustrated finds (Fig. 4.16), also recovered were a book clasp, two keys, a vessel rim and four additional buckle-pates.

<4814> - A Post-Medieval copper alloy dress-fastener, with two side lugs or knops for attachment and one at the terminal, and with a slight marginal rim. There is a rectangular loop at the upper-end for a hook attachment. Length 37mm, maximum width 30mm. (Fig. 4.16: 1).

<4739> SF 76 - Copper alloy terminal from the handle of a folding implement, probably a knife. The end is discoid, with incised zigzag decoration on the margin of each face. Most of one side of the disc is open, but the very end and the other side are closed and marked with a girth groove. Internally, the disc is solid on this side and stepped up towards the open edge. Above the disc on one face is a slightly convex plate, widening upwards. The junction of disc and plate is marked by a slight step with a transverse groove above. The upper edge of the plate is broken, as is the side away from the open part of the disc, where it would have continued round to form a sheath. The plate on this face is now broken off above the step. Length 31 mm, maximum width 20 mm (Fig. 4.16.2).

<4755> SF 140 - Copper alloy back-plate of a rectangular folded buckle-plate. There is a rivet hole in each of the two outside corners and one in the centre. A fourth rivet hole, close to the broken folded end, is probably secondary as there is no matching hole on the opposing edge. The folds for the hinge are rebated. Length 38 mm, width 19 mm. A plate of this type with three rivet holes came from a thirteenth-century context in London (Egan & Pritchard 1991, fig. 72, 502), but the form need not be confined to that period (Fig 4.16.3).

<4831> (Metal-detected find) - Cast rectangular copper alloy plate decorated with two panels defined by grooves, each containing a pair of ring-and-dot motifs. There is a hole for attachment in one corner, and another set in from the other corner on that side. Length 42 mm, width 13 mm. While superficially reminiscent of Migration Period wrist-clasps, it lacks either the tongue or the slot that would identify it as such. The thickness of the metal and some scarring on the back suggest it has been attached to a larger metal object (Fig. 4.16.4).

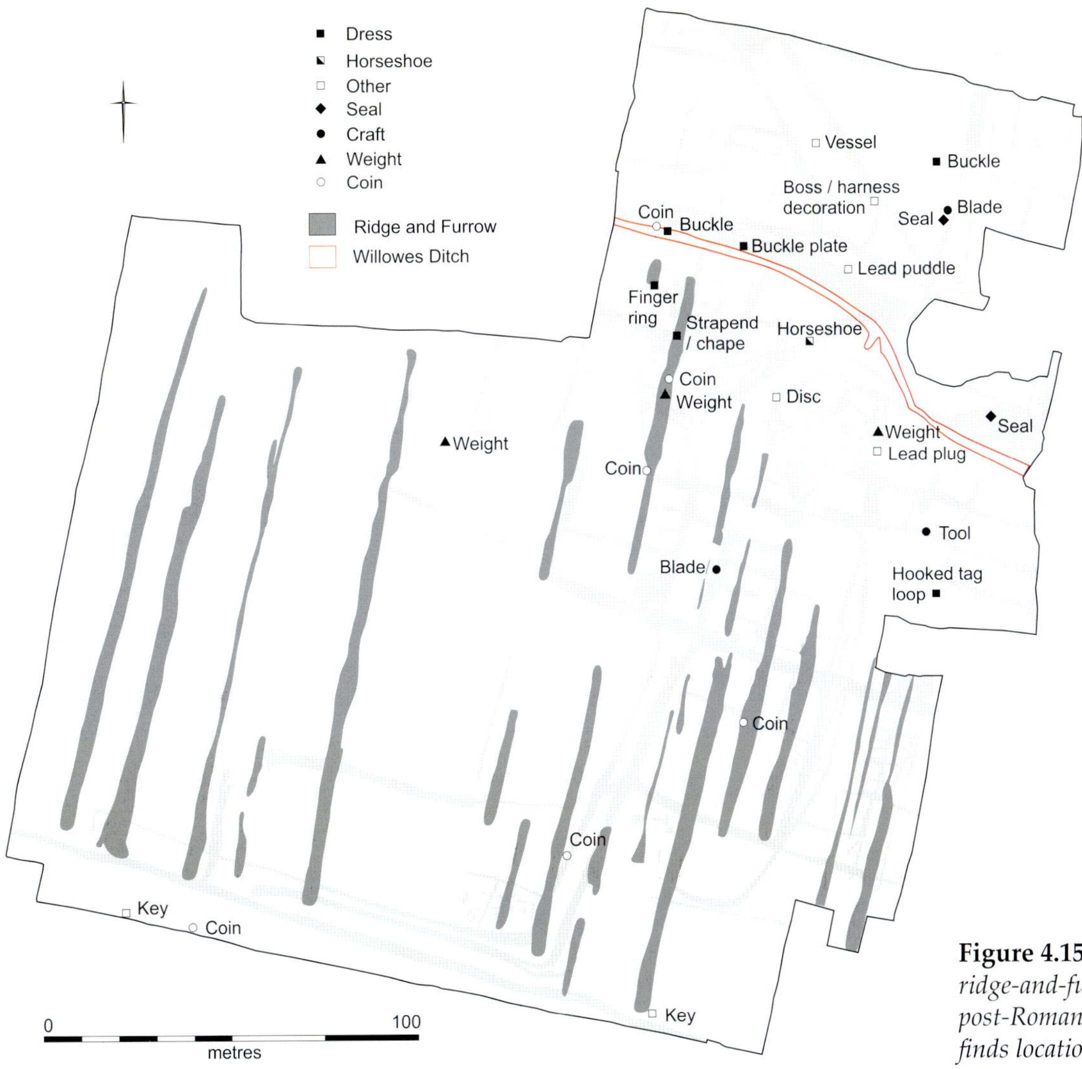

Figure 4.15. *Medieval ridge-and-furrow, with post-Roman ploughsoil finds locations.*

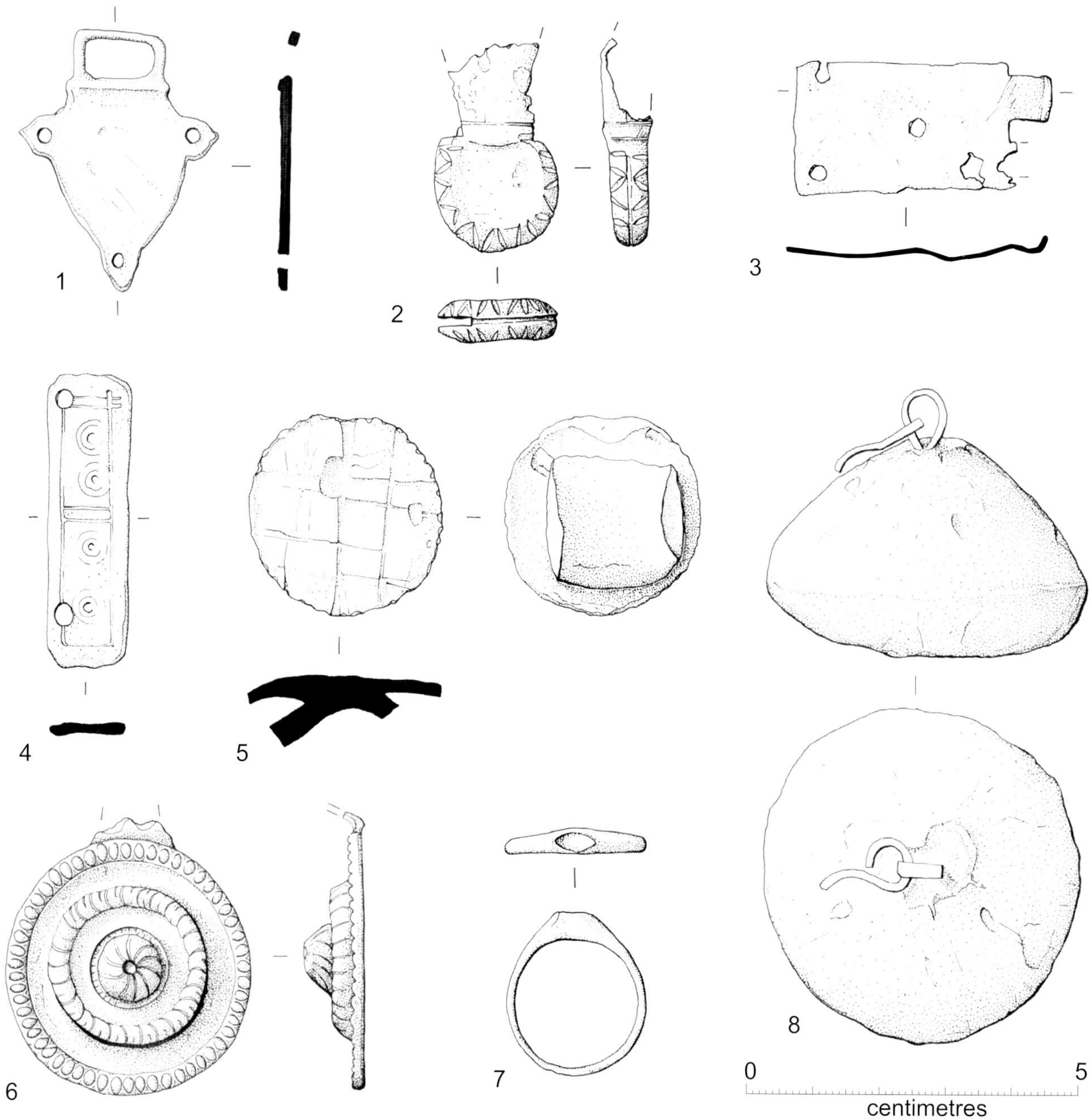

Figure 4.16. *Post-Roman metalwork (see text).*

<4737> SF 48 - Heavily leaded copper alloy object consisting of a disc soldered onto a fragment of a wide curved band. The surface of the disc has been scored to produce an irregular chequerboard effect. Diameter 29 mm, maximum width of band 18 mm. The rim of the disc is roughly beaded. Date uncertain, but probably Medieval or later (Fig. 4.16.5).

<4750> SF 120 - Decoratively moulded copper alloy boss with broken projection on one side, probably a pierced strip or hinge for attachment. The rim is beaded, the raised centre is defined by a moulding grooved to imitate cabling, within which is a knurled step at the foot of a domed boss with radiating grooves. Diameter 37 mm. While the item's decorated mouldings are close to those on fittings from Roman auxiliary equipment (Oldenstein 1976, Taf. 71, 947–8), the quality of the metal suggests this item may be post-Roman. A Medieval bridle boss from Exeter is similar in size and style (Goodall 1984, fig. 192, 147; Fig. 4.16.6).

<4757> SF 145 - Complete stirrup-shaped copper alloy finger-ring which would have had a gemstone, or more probably a glass imitation of a gemstone, set in the bezel. The stone is now missing, but the hollow in which it was set retains traces of a substance which may be decayed glass or perhaps glue for fixing it in place. Internal diameter 18 mm. This form of finger-ring was popular from the mid twelfth century throughout the Medieval period (Hinton 1990, 647, fig. 176, 2082; Egan & Pritchard 1991, 326–7; Fig 4.16.7).

<4362> *SF 83* - Carinated lead weight, the upper side conical, the lower rounded. Part of a link from a copper alloy chain remains in a split-pin or similar fitting embedded in the top. Length 25 mm, diameter 50 mm. Weight 327 g; perhaps 12 oz. Possibly Roman (Fig 4.16.8).

<4720> *F.5137* - Copper alloy cleat or similar fitting, with elongated oval head and short pointed terminals. One terminal is straight and angled slightly outwards, the other is bent round so that the point lies parallel to the head. Length 24 mm, height 10 mm.

While there are no features other than ridge-and-furrow from this period, there are a number of finds, perhaps rather more than one might expect from an arable field. The horseshoes and horse harness buckle could be related to traction animals for ploughing but otherwise the finds must represent casual losses incurred while labouring (see Fig. 1.1).

Modern (c. *1800–2000)*

The land remained part of the 'Medieval' fieldsystem until the act of Enclosure in 1802; soon after, the present-day Vicar's Farm would have been built (Fig. 4.17). An estate map of 1789 at Corpus Christi College does not show any buildings on the site, but the stream, which was then known as Willow Ditch, is indicated with trees along its north bank. The area was within the Middle Field of the Cambridge West Field, which was enclosed by Act of Parliament in or shortly after 1802 (see Fig. 7.10). At that time ownership of the land was reorganized and it became practicable to have farms well away from the town and within their own fields. It is, therefore, probable that the house and buildings were put up soon after that. On an 1804 map of St. Giles

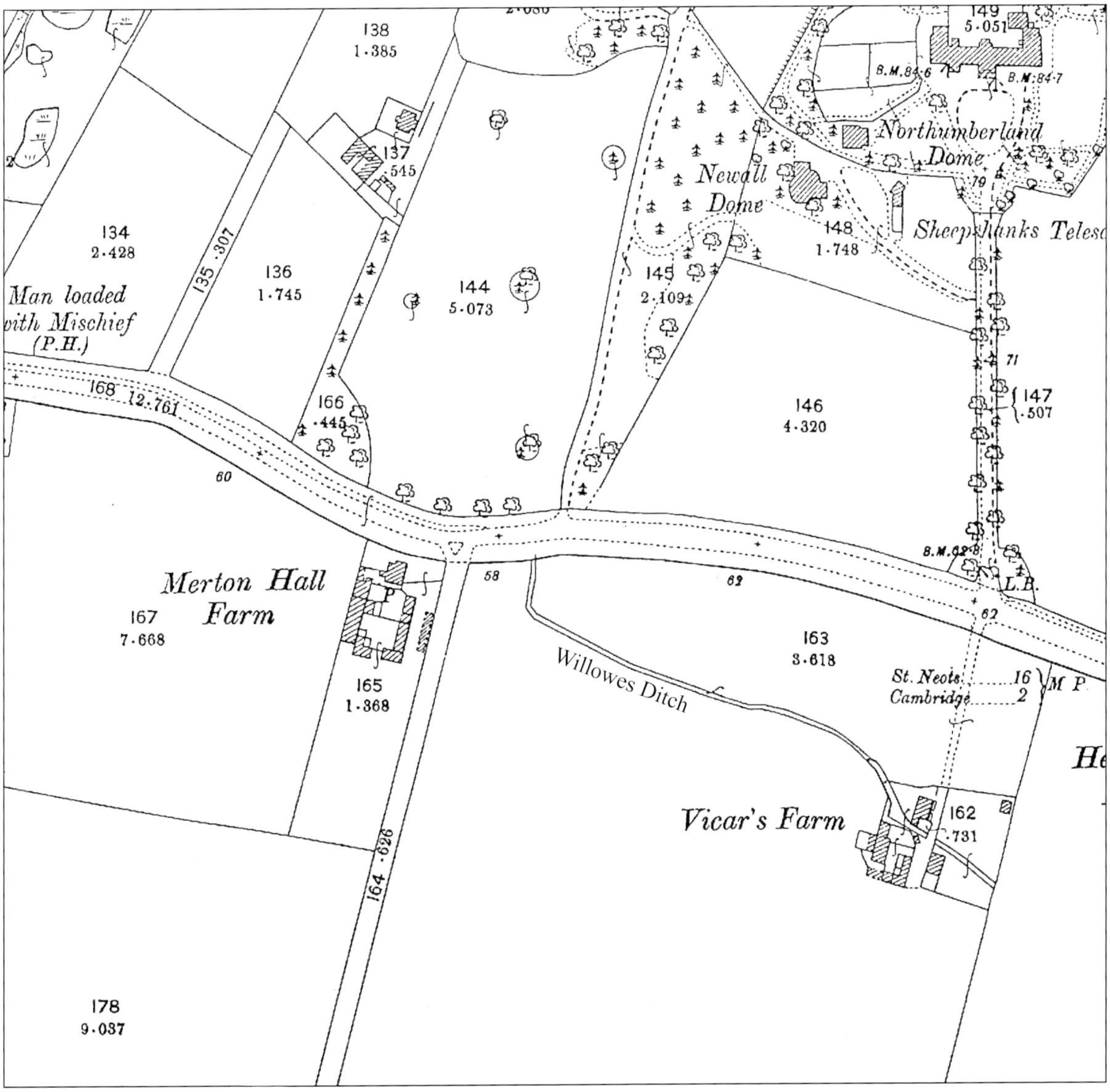

Figure 4.17. *Vicar's Farmyard, location map showing farm layout (1901 OS map).*

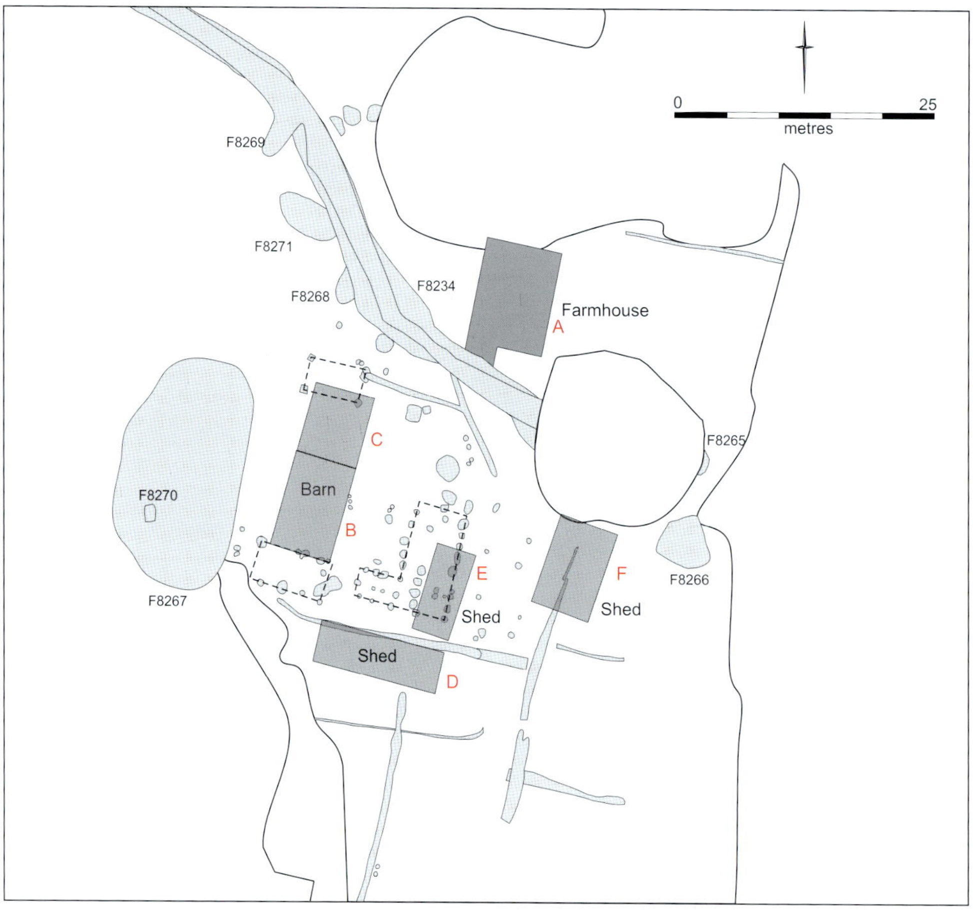

Figure 4.18. *Vicar's Farmyard, aerial photograph of extant buildings (1970s) and, below, plan showing building locations and archaeological features.*

parish, the area is marked as Lot 57, owned by Rev. William Parish and on Baker's 1824 map it is named Chalk Farm; his larger scale Map of Cambridge of 1830 shows the layout of the buildings much as they were in 2000. The name is there given as Clunch Farm, which is corroborated by the first edition OS one-inch map of 1836; the stream is called Conduit Ditch.

A survey of the farm buildings was conducted prior to demolition, with limited excavation and investigation of associated archaeological features carried out after stripping. This produced some sizeable assemblages of material culture associated with the late nineteenth- and early twentieth-century occupation of the farm.

Aside from authorial and, now, wider Unit interests in late-era material culture (Lucas 2002 and Lucas & Regan 2003; Cessford 2016b), detailing of the farm's usage is relevant on two counts. First, this is exactly the kind of data-set that overseas colleagues working with Post-Medieval/colonial studies want from Britain. Second, as we will see, appreciating what constitutes an historical-era farm in the local landscape helps to frame just how very different (and more) than 'a farm' Vicar's Farm Roman settlement was.

A search through street directories (Spalding's up to 1940, and Kelly's from 1955) for the later nineteenth and early twentieth century give details of owners, although the series were incomplete and the dates given below only show the *known* span of occupancy, hence the gaps (Table 4.6).[4] As will be evident in the final chapter (see *Madingley Rises …*), the circumstances by which Chessom came to occupy the farm from 1922 are crucial in the 'West Cambridge story'.

The Farm Buildings Anthony Baggs

Now demolished, the buildings at Vicar's Farm included an east-facing farm house and a group of farm buildings to the south, across a small stream which is now culverted (Fig. 4.18). They lay about 250 m to the south of Madingley Road, from which they were formerly approached by a drive. Whilst there had been some later additions and alterations, the house and farm buildings were typical examples of a small enclosure farm of the early years of the nineteenth century.

The House (Structure A; Figs. 4.18 & 4.19) - Two storeys, mostly of brick with tiled roofs. The east-facing front range had bands of clunch, in places repaired with new ashlar and aggregate blocks, alternating with Cambridge brick in the walls of the ground floor. It formed the original house which had two rooms divided by a central

Table 4.6. *Summary of owner/occupiers of Vicar's Farm.*

Owner/Occupier Name	Farm Name	Date
W. & M. Robinson	Vicarage Farm	1895–97
A. Medlock	S. Giles Vicarage Farm	1913–15
E.C.S. Shipp	S. Giles Vicarage Farm	1919–20
Alfred Chessom	S. Giles Vicarage Farm	1922–38
Capt. Nicholson	S. Giles Vicarage Farm	1939–40
Reg Hansen	Vicar's Farm	1955–

Figure 4.19. *The farmhouse, 1960s photograph (top) and, below, T. Baggs' survey plans.*

Figure 4.20. *The barn, 1960s photograph (top left), with details of timber construction (top and bottom right) and, below left, chicken-wire bird atop its apex at the time of fieldwork.*

stair on each floor. The kitchen was to the north and the parlour to the south, and on the first floor only the southern bedroom was heated. Subsequently, and before the map of 1888 was surveyed, a two-storeyed brick addition with a catslide roof had been built along the length of the west wall. It provided space for a new kitchen or scullery and other service rooms on the ground floor and two bedrooms on the first floor. A central bathroom with a window in a dormer was probably a later nineteenth-century addition.

The house had been extensively refitted in the latter part of the twentieth century. All of the windows had been renewed and the staircase had been lined out. The only bedroom fireplace had been removed and the opening made good; all features of the former kitchen fireplaces had been eliminated. The surround and grate of the parlour fireplace, which appeared to have been nineteenth century, had recently been stolen. Two early nineteenth-century two-panel doors survived in the front range and there were two tongue-and-groove plank doors in the back range. The original skirtings, where they survived, were unmoulded and all the architraves appeared to have been recent replacements, mostly with standard ogee mouldings. There were no plaster cornices or other fittings of note.

The Barn (Structure B; Figs. 4.18 & 4.20) - Three bays with a central opening to the east. It had walls of tarred weatherboard on a light softwood frame that rested on a low brick sleeper-wall and had some reused timber in the principals. With a thatched roof, the construction was typical of the early years of the nineteenth century. A lean-to shed against the south gable was probably a seed store and tool shed.

Structure C (Fig. 4.18) - A two-bay shed or cart house open to the east that had a concrete frame with corrugated asbestos roof and walls. The plank lining of the west and north walls may have been for cattle. Clearly dating to the later twentieth century, it stood on the site of a building shown on the 1888 map.

Structure D (Fig. 4.18) - Three-bay shed open to the west, with walls of weatherboard on a light softwood frame and roofs of pantile and corrugated iron. The walls were not lined, which suggested that it was used for the storage of wagons or machinery. Not shown on the 1830 map, it had probably been built soon afterwards.

Structure E (Fig. 4.18) - An enclosed animal shed constructed of weatherboard on a light softwood frame with much reused timber. The roof was made of corrugated asbestos with plastic-sheet lights. There was a building of similar outline indicated on the 1830 map. The interior was lined with planking, but there are no features for the individual stalling of animals.

Structure F (Fig. 4.18) - Three-bay shed open to the west. This had weatherboard on a light softwood frame, with a pantiled roof. It is shown on the map of 1830 and that of 1888, where it has some small enclosures, probably pigsties, against the south gable.

Farmyard Archaeology

After the demolition of the farm buildings in June 2000 and the removal of topsoil, a number of features associated with the historic-period farm were recorded, primarily a group of postholes marking earlier versions of Structures E and D, a four-poster under Structure C and various pits (Fig. 4.18). In addition, some general midden spreads in the topsoil layer were recorded adjacent to the buildings. None of these features were fully excavated, and in many cases their greater part was machined away in order to reach Roman levels; nevertheless, an amount of material was retrieved, albeit in an *ad hoc* manner.

The earliest features include some general spreads of artefacts in the topsoil, presumably the result of nightsoiling or ploughed-out middens. A spread at the northern end of the site (F.8274) was thin and more of a general background incorporation of finds into the topsoil, possibly through nightsoiling. Generally, the ceramics are late eighteenth-century/early nineteenth-century and include feather-edge pearlware plates, white stonewares and early blue transfer-print pearlwares. Spread F.8267 was much more substantial and discrete, and therefore almost certainly a ploughed-out midden. Situated just west of the barn, it seems to have sat within a fenced enclosure marked on earlier maps and included a large assemblage of ceramics and glass dating to the end of the nineteenth century. What is particularly interesting about this assemblage is the predominance of table and service wares, particularly plain utilitarian whitewares including two square platters with the King's College crest (Fig. 4.21). While this might suggest that the dumped material derived from the College or a more general source, it could also attest to pieces acquired by an individual with College ties (e.g. household staff) who had acquired a few items (see Table 4.7 and Cessford 2016b).

Beside these spreads and some other background surface material, the main features consisted of two pits that were recorded on the eastern edge of the farm buildings, each containing large assemblages of ceramics, glass and metalwork among other things. Pit F.8265 was largely evident in section only. It measured *c.* 1.5 m wide and extended at least 1 m deep below present ground surface, while pit F.8266 was fully exposed in plan, measuring *c.* 5 × 5 m. From verbal reports by former occupiers (Mr & Mrs Hansen), these may have been former latrines that had been in use until the middle of the twentieth century. Certainly, the soil matrix in pit F.8266 did have the appearance of cess content. Analysis of the artefacts in these pits suggests they were backfilled at slightly different dates, the ceramics and glass from F.8266 dating to *c.* 1900–20 and those from F.8265, *c.* 1920–40. Both groups provide exemplary domestic assemblages and can be contrasted with the midden F.8267 (Table 4.7). Three other pits were also recorded (F.8268, F.8269, & F.8271), although these lay on the other, western side of the farm, on the edge of the Willows Ditch as it ran south, although material was only retrieved from two (F.8269 & F.8271). One slot was excavated (F.8134) and a small group of material retrieved from the Willows Ditch itself, as it ran past the farm.

The finds recovered from these features were predominantly ceramics and glass, summaries of which are presented in Table 4.7. Over 34 kg of ceramics was retrieved, with a wide range of types represented (Fig. 4.21). Basic, industrial refined whitewares formed the majority of the assemblage (57%), mainly either plain undecorated wares or transfer-print wares. Smaller quantities of lithograph-printed wares, factory-made slipwares (including Mocha wares)

Table 4.7. *Summary quantification of nineteenth- and early twentieth-century finds from features.*

Feature	Pottery			Glass			Other
	No.	Wt. (g)	EVE	No.	Wt. (g)	EVE	
5524	8	140	1	14	406	0.59	-
8134	3	430	2.37	7	320	1.47	8
8265	45	11,558	37.04	57	1756	8.61	13
8266	76	11,552	34.35	196	21,630	23.34	13
8267	78	2136	10.84	214	6879	5.49	2
8268	-	-	-	-	-	-	-
8269	28	4416	21.57	1	79	0.13	11
8270	2	355	2	-	-	-	-
8271	21	1021	7.3	28	758	5.02	1
8272	6	3320	5	-	-	-	-
8273	-	-	-	24	290	0.44	-
8274	-	-	-	18	239	0.73	-
8275	-	-	-	7	565	0.73	2
8276	-	-	-	1	31	1.07	-
Total	*267*	*34,928*	*121.47*	*567*	*32,953*	*49.08*	*50*

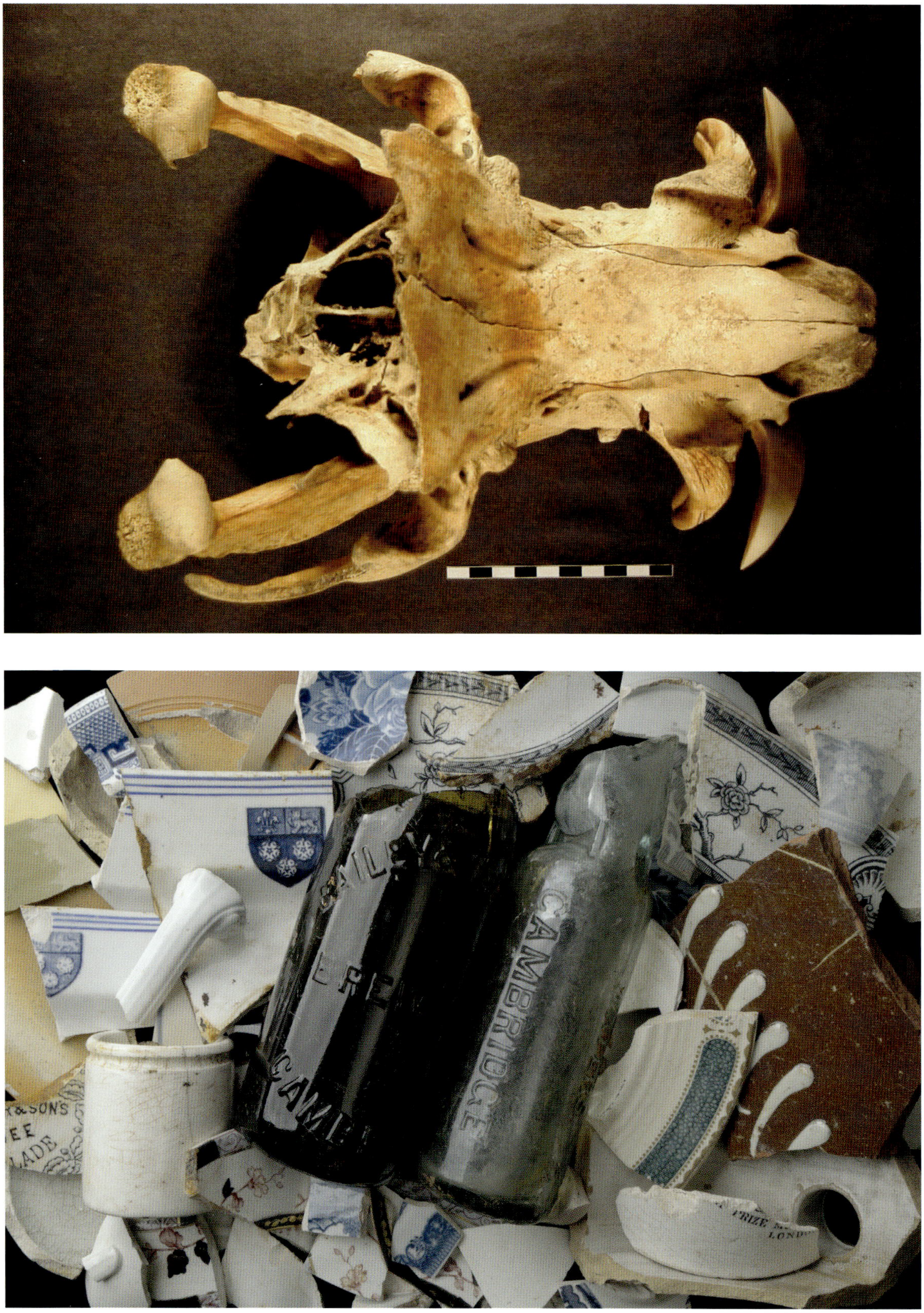

Figure 4.21. *Farmyard investigations finds: boar's skull (top) and, below, pottery and glass from F.8267.*

does not suggest any increase toward the east, suggestive of dense activity. While this does not preclude the possibility of important features beyond the limit of excavation, these are impossible to characterize.

More problematic than the horizontal extent of archaeology is its vertical depth and degree of stratification. Generally, the depth of soil across the site increased from south to north, mostly due to the fanning out of colluvium washed down from Madingley Rise. At the northern end of the site, the total depth of soil cover was 1.55 m (0.7 m of ploughsoil and 0.85 m of colluvium), while at the southern end it reduced to 0.75 m deep (0.45 m of ploughsoil over 0.3 m of colluvium; Fig. 4.22). The ploughsoil consisted of a dark brown clay silt, while the colluvial layer was a pale to mid yellow brown clay silt with occasional gravel.

Preservation and Truncation

As discussed above, the site was under arable cultivation up until its archaeological investigation and, consequently, heavy ploughing since at least the thirteenth or fourteenth century had truncated most buried land surfaces or positive features such as banks or walls. There are, however, two exceptions: an area beneath colluvium in the northwest corner of the site and an area within a natural basin or hollow that lay in the central part of the site, both of which preserved old land surfaces and a palaeosol.

The Colluvium

In the northwest part of the site, a thick colluvial deposit altered the depth at which the natural geology was encountered by nearly 1 m. This hillwash post-dates the Roman period, as all the cremations were sealed by it, as was the dark earth layer over the quarry pitting south of the cremations.

Micromorphological Analyses Charles French

The site was situated on Gault Clay with a calcareous clay loam soil of the Wicken Series present (Hodge & Seale 1966). The only exception to this is in the northwestern sector of the site where a *c.* 60–100 cm depth of brown silty clay loam has accumulated on a buried soil and overlying a small relict stream channel and a post-fourth-century AD ditch. This hillwash or colluvial material derived from immediately upslope to the north, and was possibly of late/Post-Medieval date. One spot sample for micromorphological analysis was taken from the colluvial/buried soil contact to characterize the hillwash material (Profile 1). The sample was made into thin-section slides using the methodology of Murphy (1986) and described using the international terminology of Bullock *et al.* (1985). The hillwash material was a poorly sorted, dense, sandy clay loam. In particular, the fine groundmass was predominantly composed of illuvial clay, characterized by non-laminated dusty (or impure) clay.

The Hillwash (Profile 1) - *Structure*: poorly sorted; dense to very weakly columnar peds; *Porosity*: *c.* 20%; 10% vughs, irregular to sub-rounded, <3 mm; *c.* 10% fine channels, <5 mm long, <500 μm wide, weakly serrated, partially accommodated; *Components*: < 2% gravel, sub-angular, < 1 cm; c/f limit: 100 μm; c/f ratio: 30/70 to 40/60; coarse fraction: 10% medium and 20–30% fine quartz, sub-rounded to sub-angular, 500-100 μm, in all orientations; fine fraction: 10% very fine quartz, sub-rounded to sub-angular, 50–100 μm; 10-20% silt; 30% clay; 5–10% micro-sparite calcium carbonate; greyish/yellowish brown (CPL), golden brown (PPL), pale yellow (RL); *Organic Component*: <5% micro-charcoal in fine groundmass, <50 μm; *Pedofeatures - Textural*: *c.* 50% non-laminated, dusty clay in the groundmass, coating quartz grains and lining voids; weak to moderate birefringence, yellow to gold (CPL); *Amorphous*: weak amorphous sesquioxide impregnation of the whole fine groundmass; occasional discontinuous void infills of calcium carbonate and amorphous iron 'cemented' very fine quartz and silt.

The overburden in the northwestern sector of the site is definitely hillwash material dominated by illuvial clay and silt. Its occurrence surely represents the subsequent disturbance of clay-rich soils immediately uphill and to the north through soil disturbance. Hillwash deposits in Cambridgeshire are a relatively rare occurrence, with only two other examples known to the writer, namely overlying the Haddon Roman farmstead (French 1994) and the Iron Age site at Landwade Road, Fordham (French & Kousoulakou 1997). These occurrences were both also dominated by silty clay deposits.[5]

The Basin

Towards the centre of the site lay a broad hollow, noticeable as a surface depression even prior to topsoiling; this was an area that was consistently prone to flooding during the excavation, leading to its on-site designation as the 'pond'. Indeed, the southern half of the site as a whole retained water on its surface due to the clay subsoils and numerous nineteenth- and twentieth-century field drains criss-crossed the site. While most of the site lay at 16–19 m OD, this central basin dropped to 15 m OD (see Figs. 4.1 & 4.4), a difference further accentuated by the removal of the overlying layers.

The area presented problems from the start, in that removal of the ploughsoil exposed a large circular area of dark clayey soil sealing this basin, with little indication of its depth or what lay beneath. A sondage in the evaluation had not reached the base, and it was unclear at the beginning whether this was, in effect, a buried pond or just a low-lying area of land that was infilled. Moreover, none of the features on any side of this area offered any clues, as none seemed to continue into this zone. In order to deal with this element of uncertainty, a two-staged approach was taken; the whole area of the basin was first sampled on a 5 m staggered grid with 14 metre-square test pits (Fig. 4.23), complemented by a subsequent trench bisecting the area along two axes (east–west and north–south) in order to obtain information on finds density and soil profiles. This revealed three layers beneath the ploughsoil: an upper mid to dark grey clay alluvial layer that contained Medieval and Post-Medieval material, as well as some residual Roman material; a middle dark grey-black silty clay, with solely Roman material; and, then, a lower pale grey clay silt, which also contained Roman material and lay directly either on natural or on a prepared metalled surface upon truncated natural.

Based on this information, the area was subsequently stripped twice with a machine: once to remove the upper post-Roman alluvial soil (whereupon the area was metal-detected), and then again to remove the lower Roman layers down to natural. Having done this, it was clear that the area was simply a low-lying basin of land, as a significant density of features was uncovered. These had not been visible even at the level of the upper Roman 'dark earth' horizon, although in section they could clearly be seen to have been cut from within this layer. However, the presence of marsh herbs in the upper part of the Roman buried soil (see Scaife, below) may indicate the ground was prone to flooding.

This area, along with the fills of cut features, can be used to reconstruct and extrapolate the nature of the former land surface for the rest of the site during its Roman occupation, although this will be complicated by changes in the soil matrix even within this span of time. For example, the 'dark earths' that sealed many of the features and lay in the basin would not have been present in the earlier phases of Roman activity and one of the questions to ask is when, how and why this soil matrix was created. In the next section, the land surface and upper soil horizons during the period of Roman occupation are characterized using these different lines of evidence.

Mapping the Upper Soil Profile and 'Dark Earth'

There are two ways we can start to characterize the nature of the 'dark earth' and depositional formation processes in general across the site. One is to study the soil matrix itself and its composition and derivation; the other is to examine the associated finds, their density and condition.

Soil Matrix Composition and Derivation

At a very coarse level, the cultural deposits across the site reflected the nature of the background geology. As outlined above, the Gault Clays were

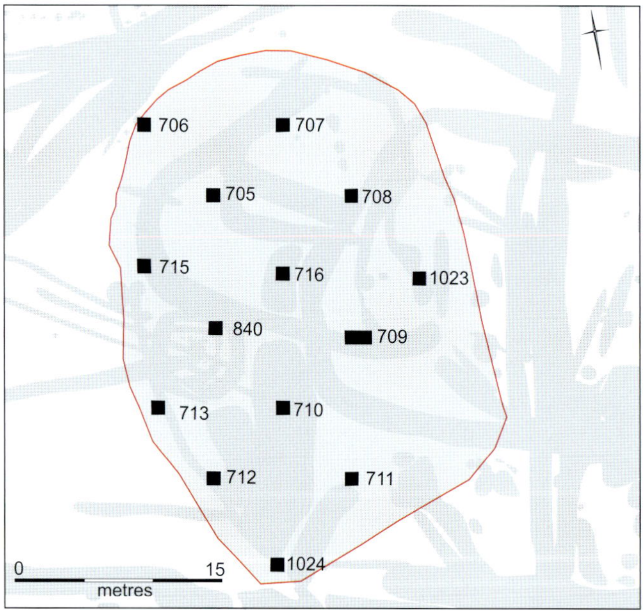

Figure 4.23. *Area of 'pond' F.5033, showing test pit sampling of the dark earth and buried soil (top); below, soil photomicrographs (frame width = 2.25 mm; plane-polarized light): 'dirty', very fine charcoal-rich fine fabric (Profile 2, middle) and, bottom, the dusty clay striated and 'dirty', very fine charcoal-rich fine fabric (Profile 3).*

overlain by superficial Quaternary deposits in the northern part of the site, specifically sand, silts and gravels (Fig. 4.23). The extent of these was mapped after the topsoil had been removed, while numerous boreholes and test pits from past investigations provided more detailed information on the depth and stratigraphy of these deposits (Boreham 2000). The sand and gravel locally marked the course of a probable palaeochannel, capped by fluvial silts indicative of a slow-moving river which may date back to the last interglacial (*c.* 120,000 BP; see Fig. 7.24).

The nature of fills in cut features generally reflected the dominant soil base into which the features had been cut, representing the weathered subsoil. As a result, detailed soil descriptions of deposits associated with features will be not be provided here, unless they are significantly unusual or otherwise merit discussion. The most obvious and widespread variation of fills from the background soil is the extent of their enrichment by organic matter: the 'dark earths' that infilled the tops of most features in the core area of the site and were similar to the material infilling the basin. Since these were common across a wide part of the site, they will be discussed in some detail.

Micromorphological Analyses of Ditch Fills Charles French
The cut linear features on site were dominated by Roman ditch systems with black clay loam tertiary fills. This especially occurred in the low-lying northeastern and central sector of the site. As there was some question as to the composition and derivation of this 'dark earth' material, two spot samples were taken from ditches F.5308 and F.5218, respectively at site grids 294/665 and 279/675 (Profiles 2 & 3; see Fig. 4.23 & 4.25). Both samples of the 'dark earth' were essentially similar in composition and characteristics and are, therefore, described together. They were composed of a dark brown to black sandy clay loam, characterized by common

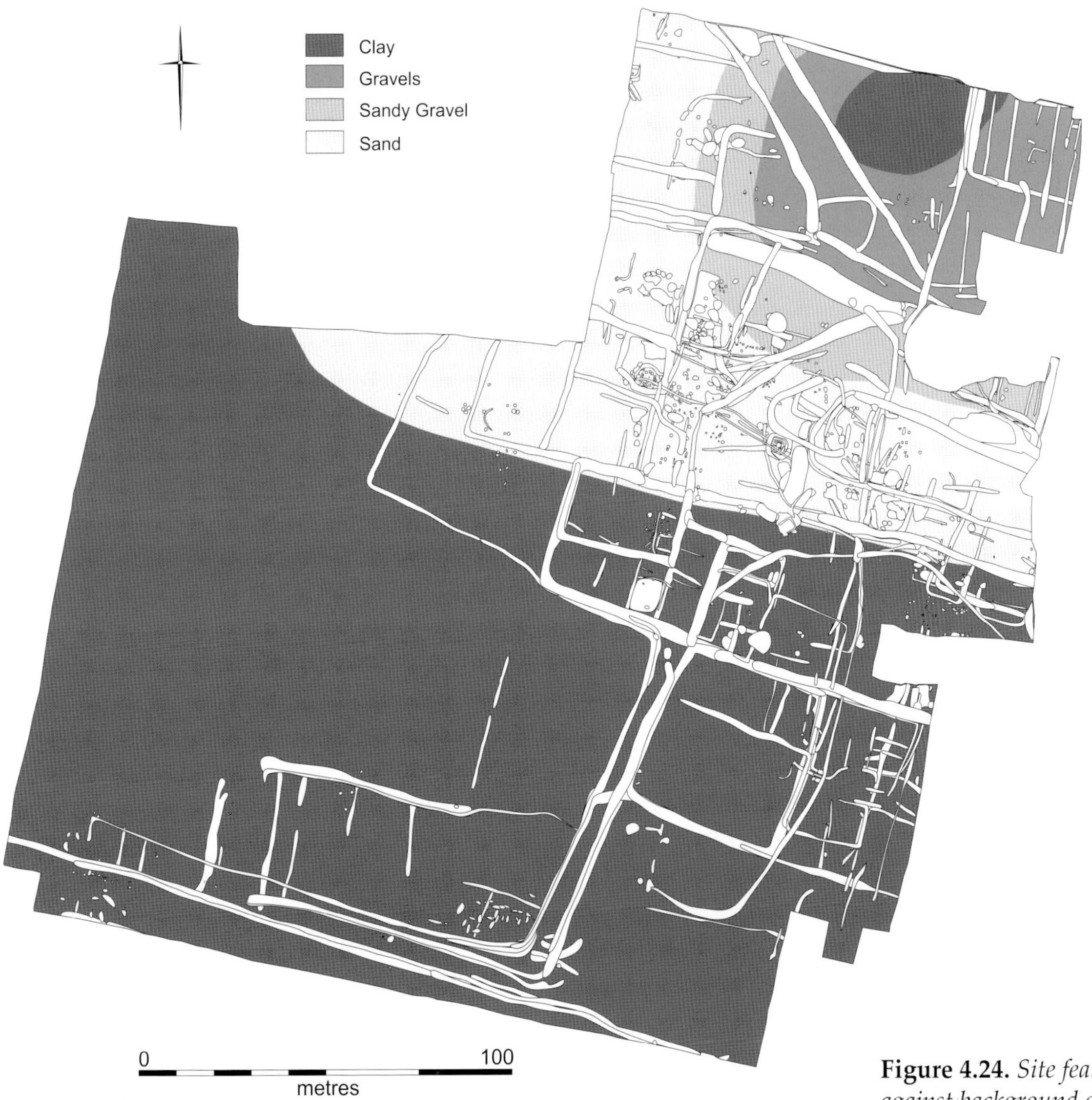

Figure 4.24. *Site features against background geology.*

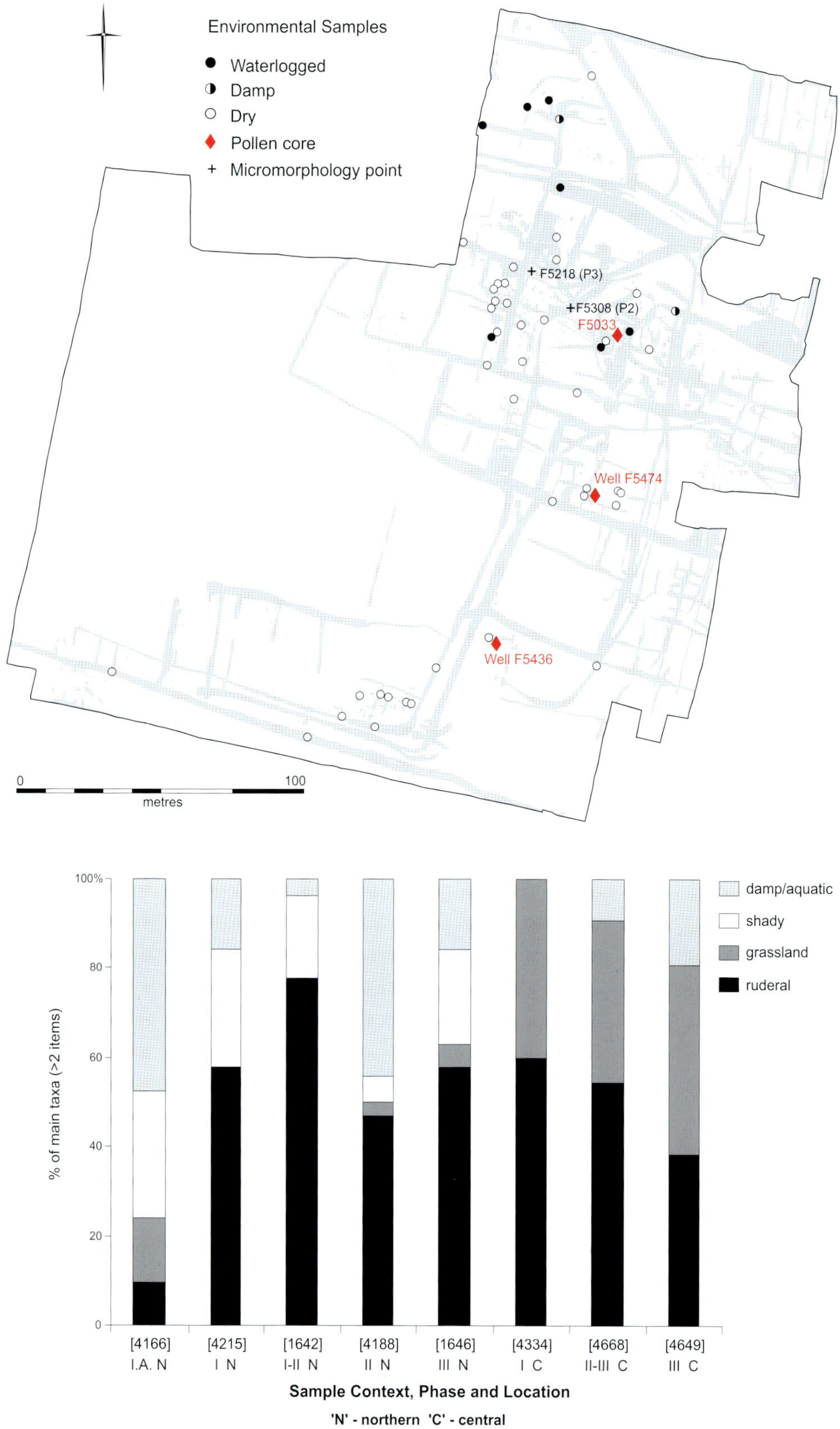

Figure 4.25. *Environmental samples: site locations (top) and, below, the waterlogged contexts as represented by plant ecological groups.*

very fine to fine charcoal fragments thoroughly mixed with the fine groundmass, abundant, non-laminated dusty or impure clay and a few minor anthropogenically-derived inclusions such as minute fragments of bone.

> *Structure*: weak to moderately developed, small, sub-angular blocky peds, <4 mm; *Porosity*: *c*. 12%; 10% vughs, <1 mm, irregular to sub-rounded; 2% channels, <5 mm long, <500 μm wide, weakly serrated, partially accommodated; *Components*: < 2% fine gravel, sub-angular, <2 mm; c/f limit: 100 μm; c/f ratio: 15/85; coarse fraction: 5% medium and 10% fine quartz, 500–100 μm, sub-rounded to sub-angular; fine fraction: 10% very fine quartz, 50–100 μm, sub-rounded to sub-angular; 20% silt; 35% clay; yellowish brown (CPL), brown (PPL), pale yellowish brown (RL); *Organic Component*: 20+% very fine charcoal throughout the fine groundmass, <100 μm; *Pedofeatures - Textural*: *c*. 55% non-laminated dusty clay in groundmass, lining voids and coating grains, weakly reticulate striated, weak birefringence, yellow (CPL); *Amorphous*: very weak amorphous iron impregnation of the fine groundmass; minor amounts of anthropogenic inclusions such as bone fragments, <1 mm, irregular to sub-rounded, in fine groundmass.

The tertiary ditch fills were essentially of a similar matrix composition to the colluvial overburden, which undoubtedly reflects the dominant influence of the local geology of clay-dominated Gault Clays. The abundant very fine to fine charcoal throughout the groundmass is responsible for blackening the soil and making the ditch fills more friable. This material must derive directly from settlement activity, probably from domestic fires, and its deliberate curation and dumping over a wide area of the site after it went out of use. These deposits were examined with a view to deciphering whether they represented dumped midden material and/or acted as a deliberately made topsoil, possibly for arable use or a 'plaggen' soil. Certainly, the carbonized organic content would have made the silt- and clay-dominated ditch fills and soils of the site much more friable and well-drained. In addition, these ditch fills and an extensive spread of the same material over much of the site west of the farm's former barns bear a striking resemblance to those observed at the nearby New Hall excavations (see Coyle & French, Chap. 3).

At New Hall, these tertiary ditch fills and the associated 'dark earth' soil were dominated by sandy clay loam soil, wood ash, calcium carbonate and finely comminuted occupation debris. The matrix bore a strong resemblance to the 'dark earths' investigated elsewhere in England by Macphail (1983) and Macphail and Courty (1985). It is possible that the 'dark earth' at New Hall was deliberately made through the addition of dumped refuse material with a very high organic matter component. This had the effect of encouraging soil faunal activity and developing a better, well-drained structure in a rather poorly drained and 'heavy' soil and substrate, thus providing a viable topsoil for arable land-use. Indeed, the deliberate addition of large amounts of midden-type material to prepare a soil containing definitive signatures of arable agriculture has been observed at the later Bronze Age/earlier Iron Age site of Welland Bank Quarry, south Lincolnshire (French 1998).

The ubiquitous upper ditch fills and large areas of 'black earth' observed at Vicar's Farm suggest the deliberate addition of charcoal-rich, midden-type material to the site. This would have undoubtedly improved the fertility and drainage characteristics of a site that is otherwise poorly drained and prone to the accumulation of surface standing water due to the poor drainage characteristics of the Gault Clay subsoil. However, whether or not this site was subsequently used for arable farming after the Roman occupation cannot be proven due to the absence of the expected suite of micromorphological features (after Lewis 1998).

The Nature of the Dark Earth

The most common explanation for the 'dark earths' is that they represent a deliberate attempt to improve the soil for arable farming. This is a difficult explanation for Vicar's Farm, however, as the dark earth was clearly forming whilst the site was still in use as a settlement, with the dark earth concentrated precisely at the core of the occupation zone and not in marginal fields as one might expect if it was linked to farming. Late Roman features cut through this layer as well as being filled by it, suggesting that this soil was created in the later Roman period rather than post-Roman times (probably sometime during the third century AD). While accepting that the dark earth has been deliberately 'improved' with midden-type material (especially charcoal/ashes), this may have been done to further its drainage more than its fertility, especially if this was in an area that people and perhaps livestock were frequently walking over. In short, the dark earth might be seen as the cumulative by-product of spreading hearth ashes over the settlement core in an attempt to create a drier/less waterlogged surface on which to live. This would certainly explain why the dark earths were concentrated in the core, which was also more prone to standing water, especially in the later Roman period. As a 'surfacing' strategy, it would also have been easier and simpler than metalling, especially over such a large area. The spreading of ashes as a flooring material is common, for example, in Norse period sites, both inside and outside structures where its drainage properties have clearly been exploited (e.g. Milek 1999). Of course, in the light of just how much household and 'bodily' waste the settlement likely generated *per annum*, expedient 'core-area' dumping (i.e. depositional immediacy) may have been a significant factor, if an unhealthy one (see Chap. 6, *Space, Buildings and Roles* ...).

Finds Densities and Condition

Looking at the finds associated with the different layers in the basin area can help to characterize the formation of these layers and the deposition associated with them. Taking just the most common finds – animal bone and pottery – some basic statistical measures can be drawn out (Table 4.9).[6] Two things are evident from this basic analysis: the dark earth contains a higher average number of fragments of bone and pottery than the alluvium or buried soil, yet by weight, and particularly average fragment weight, the trend is more linear, with the lowest values in the alluvium and highest values in the buried soil. What this seems to suggest is that while the quantity of finds increases between the alluvium and dark earth, the difference between the dark earth and buried soil may have less to do with quantity than condition; in other words,

Table 4.9. *Quantities of bone and pottery from the preserved soil profile in basin F.5033.*

		Bone			Pot		
		Ave. per sq. m			Ave. per sq. m		
	No. TP	Wt.	No.	Ave. frag. wt.	Wt.	No.	Ave. sherd wt.
Alluvium	9	30.9	2.9	10.7	78.1	10.8	7.2
Dark earth	11	365.8	15.3	23.9	257.4	23.1	11.1
Buried soil	4	658.0	13.0	50.6	174.0	10.8	16.2

finds in the dark earth were more fragmented than those in the buried soil, hence the higher number of fragments but lower average fragment weight.

What does this mean for our understanding of the dark earth? It suggests that, at least in terms of finds deposition, the quantities are not greater, but simply subject to more attrition. The greater attrition of finds in the dark earth layer is certainly consistent with the idea of a 'turned' soil, as would be necessary for horticultural/agricultural use (see French above), but other factors may account for this, especially trampling through human/animal movement. This would also be consistent with the idea of the dark earth as a deliberate result of providing a well-drained surface in an area where movement was frequent. In contrast, the buried soil horizon is associated with the cobbled/metalled surfaces and these, rather than the soil itself, would have suffered most movement and, thereby, possibly explain the lower fragmentation in this layer.

It is, nonetheless, imperative that the sheer quantity of material within the basin's dark earth is appreciated. Drawing upon Table 4.9's figures (but including nil values), if dug in its entirety some 13,320 sherds would have been forthcoming from it: more than was recovered from the rest of the settlement as whole (see Monteil, below). As further discussed in Chapter Six's *Spaces, Buildings and Roles …* section, with the basin situated immediate east of the settlement's main occupation/middening focus, its matrix surely reflected introduced refuse (including, also, almost 8,900 animal bone fragments).

The Local Environment

Here we will outline the results of pollen analyses and the site's waterlogged environmental samples, to set the scene for the excavation sequence and, also, to provide economic insights. Of the latter, the character/intensity of the settlement's many sub-enclosures complements its faunal remains and attests to the scale of its pastoral component. Yet, a mixed economy was certainly practised. Not only is this evinced in the site's plant remains but that in one of the pollen columns cereal values of up to 6 per cent registered. When compared to the pollen results from the broader programme's other Roman sites (see Chap. 7 and *NWC*), this is actually quite a high level. With arable production clearly undertaken in vicinity, an issue will then be whether we can locate its fields.

Macrofossil Preservation and Recovery

Rachel Ballantyne

Bulk samples were collected by the excavators judgementally, with the aim of representing all types of feature both spatially and temporally (Fig 4.25). Samples aimed to be 15 litres in volume, but in many cases this was reduced, due either to the size of the context or realities of excavation; in total, 323.5 litres were processed.

The majority of bulk samples were processed by hand, using bucket flotation; the flot being collected in a 300 μm sieve and the heavy residue washed over 1 mm mesh. Both flots and heavy residues were dried prior to sorting under a low-power Leitz binocular microscope. Several clearly waterlogged contexts – F.5470 ([1642]), F.5681 ([1646]), F.5621 ([4166]), F.5624 ([4188]), F.5626 ([4215]), F.5651 ([4334]), F.5704 ([4649]) and F.5707 ([4668]) – were wet-sieved over a graded stack of 2 mm, 1 mm, 500 μm and 300 μm sieves. The residues were then scanned wet under a low-power Leitz binocular microscope.

Plant identifications were made using the reference collection of the Pitt-Rivers Lab., Dept. of Archaeology, University of Cambridge. All nomenclature follows Stace (1997) for plants, and Pfleger and Chatfield (1983) for molluscs.

Clearly intrusive plant and insect remains occur in low quantities in many of the non-waterlogged samples, particularly of Chenopodiaceae, *Stellaria media, Picris echioides, Hypericum* spp., *Rubus fruticosus* agg. and *Carduus/Cirsium* sp. The presence of these taxa within the waterlogged contexts should, therefore, also be treated with caution where they occur in low amounts.

Shells of the land snails *Vallonia excelsior/pulchella* and *Trichia* sp. occur in low to moderate quantities in many samples, but their shell condition (glossy, semi-opaque) suggests they may be intrusive. The shells of the burrowing snail *Ceciliodes acicula* are common and clearly intrusive. Many contexts do, though, contain very low quantities of potentially archaeological mollusc shells. The mollusc remains were not quantified or examined in any detail, since the low numbers and intrusive material would severely limit any interpretation. The occasional presence of water-associated taxa was noted however.

Waterlogged contexts were scanned, and a broad summary of the contents created (Table 4.10). All charred plant remains have been fully quantified. Where samples were exceptionally rich, the flot was divided using a riffle box until a suitably sized fraction was obtained. Sorting of the heavy residues recovered very few charred plant remains, and so the values within Table 4.11 are derived solely

Table 4.10. *Summary of main waterlogged taxa. KEY '+' <10 items (1); '++' 10-50 items (3); '+++' >50 items (5). To convert to a percentage, each symbol has been quantified as the number in brackets, then expressed as a proportion of the total count for an ecological group within each context; where a taxon fits two categories it has been counted in both (see Table 4.11).*

Context	**[1642]**	**[1646]**	**[4166]**	**[4188]**	**[4215]**	**[4334]**	**[4649]**	**[4668]**
Feature	**F.5470**	**F.5480**	**F.5621**	**F.5624**	**F.5626**	**F.5651**	**F.5704**	**F.5707**
Central/northern zone	**N**	**N**	**N**	**N**	**N**	**C**	**C**	**C**
Ranunuculus acris/bulbosus/repens		+	+	+		++	+++	++
Ranunculus scleratus L.							+++	
Ranunculus subgen. *BATRACHIUM* (DC.) A. Gray					++			
Urtica dioica L.	+++	++		+++	+++	+	+++	+
Urtica urens L.							+	
Corylus avellana L.					+			
Chenopodium c.f. *rubrum* L.							++	
Chenopodium sp.			+					
Atriplex patula/prostrata						++		++
Moehringia trinervia L.					+			
Stellaria media (L.) Vill.	++	+		+		+		
Persicaria hydropiper (L.) Spach				+				
Polygonum arviculare L.					+		+	
Rumex obstutifolius L.				++				
Bryonia dioica Jacq.		+						
Salix bracts and fruit valves				+				
Rorripa nasturtium-aquiticum (L.) Hayek				++				
Coronopus squamatus *(Forssk.) Asch*								+
Rubus subgen. *RUBUS*	+			+	+			
Potentilla reptans L.			+			++	+++	+
Potentilla sp.	+							
c.f. *Cornus sanguinea* L.					+			
Conium maculatum L.	++	++		+			+	
Apium nodiflorum (L.) Lag.		++		+++				
Stachys sylvatica/palustris	++	++	+		+			
Lamium album/purpureum	+	+	+			+	+	
Glechoma hederacea L.	+	+		+				
Sambucus nigra L.	+++			++	+++	++	+	+
Carduus nutans L.				+				
Carduus/Cirsium sp.	++							
Sonchus asper (L.) Hill				+				
Lemna sp.				++				+
Juncus sp.	+		++	++				
Eleocharis palustris (L.) Roem & Schult.			+					
Carex sylvatica Huds.			+++					
large trilete *Carex* sp.			+					
Poa sp.			+					
wood and bark fragments	++			+++	+++			
Moss				+				
Ostrocods				++				
Daphne eggs						+++	+++	+++

from flot material. Cereal grains were quantified by their embryo ends, in order to create a minimum number of grains. Where, however, very low quantities of grain were present, cereal chaff was quantified by glume bases and spikelet forks for hulled wheats, and by rachis internodes for free-threshing cereals. Seeds were counted by the presence of their attachment point, or other clear identifying characteristic (e.g. pairs of cotyledons for legumes) in order to create a minimum number of seeds (Tables 4.12–4.14; full raw data-sets for the botanical remains are listed within Lucas & Whittaker 2001).

Preservation by waterlogging was only present within very specific areas of the site, which are grouped here into broadly 'northern' and 'central' zones (see below). Many other non-waterlogged contexts contain material that indicates damp or flooded conditions in the past; mineralized seeds of duckweed (*Lemna* sp.), a plant of stagnant water, and occasional shells of slum or marsh mollusc taxa, including *Lymnaea truncula*ta, small Planorbidae, and Succineidae (Evans 1972) are the most common examples. Amphibian bones were also recovered from many of the heavy residues, showing that suitably damp and shady locations were once present. The site appears to have been consistently damp in the past, with many deeper contexts experiencing at least seasonal waterlogging.

The few waterlogged contexts provide a limited coverage of the individual site phases, particularly the Iron Age (one example), and the importance of location has become apparent through the spatial grouping of waterlogged contexts. As a result of these characteristics only broad variations within the assemblage may be examined. The major patterns are discussed below by area.[7]

The Northern Contexts

Five features within the northern part of the site contained significant waterlogged remains (Table 4.15). The earliest sample, from Iron Age pit F.5621, is characteristic of a wet, shady and relatively undisturbed environment. There are large numbers of fruits of wood sedge

Table 4.11. *Summary of charred non-cereal taxa from all contexts (exceptionally rich Context [717] F.5280 was excluded from these calculations).*

Site Phase				I		I-II & II		II-III & III	
Number of samples				7		12		28	
Number of 'rich' samples (> 20 seeds)				2		2		9	
Total sediment volume/ litres				53		86		254.25	
		Ecology	**Type**	**Count**	**%**	**Count**	**%**	**Count**	**%**
Ranunculus sp.	buttercups	dry	indet	1	0.64	0	0.00	3	0.41
total *Chenopodium* sp.	goosefoots	dry	A	0	0.00	1	1.30	9	1.24
Atriplex patula L./*prostrata* Boucher ex DC.	common/spear-leaved orache	dry	A	12	7.64	6	7.79	21	2.90
Montia fontana ssp. *chondrosperma* L.	blinks	damp	indet.	0	0.00	0	0.00	1	0.14
small *Stellaria* sp. (<2 mm)	small-seeded stichwort	indet.	indet	0	0.00	0	0.00	1	0.14
Agrostemma githago L.	corncockle	dry	A	0	0.00	0	0.00	1	0.14
medium Caryophyllaceae indet. (1–3 mm)	medium seeded Pink Family type	indet.	indet	0	0.00	0	0.00	3	0.41
Persicaria maculosa Gray.	redshank	dry	A	0	0.00	0	0.00	1	0.14
Polygonum aviculare L.	knotgrass	dry	A	0	0.00	3	3.90	2	0.28
Fallopia convolvulus (L.) A Love	black bindweed	dry	A	1	0.64	1	1.30	3	0.41
Rumex acetosella L.	sheep's sorrel	dry	P	0	0.00	0	0.00	5	0.69
Rumex sanguineus L./*conglomeratus* Murray/*obstutifolius* L.	wood/clustered/broad-leaved dock	damp	P	10	6.37	0	0.00	43	5.95
Rumex cripus L.	curled dock	damp	P	1	0.64	1	1.30	2	0.28
Rumex sp.	docks	indet.	indet	2	1.27	1	1.30	22	3.04
Thlaspi arvense L.	field penny-cress	dry	A	0	0.00	0	0.00	1	0.14
Brassica cf. *nigra* (L.) W.D.J. Koch	black mustard	dry	A	1	0.64	1	1.30	1	0.14
Brassica/*Sinapis* sp. (*c*. 2 mm)	cabbage/mustard type (wild or cultv.)	indet.	indet	1	0.64	3	3.90	2	0.28
cf. *Raphanus raphanistrum* L. seed	wild radish	dry	A	0	0.00	0	0.00	1	0.14
Anagallis arvensis L.	scarlet pimpernel	dry	A	0	0.00	0	0.00	1	0.14
Potentilla sp.	cinquefoil	indet.	indet	0	0.00	2	2.60	1	0.14
Aphanes arvensis L.	parsley-piert	dry	A	1	0.64	0	0.00	0	0.00
Vicia c.f. *cracca* L.	tufted vetch	dry	P	0	0.00	0	0.00	2	0.28
Lathyrus nissolia L.	grass vetchling	dry	A	0	0.00	1	1.30	0	0.00
large *Vicia*/*Lathyrus*/*Pisum* sp. (>4 mm)	vetch/wild pea/garden pea	indet.	indet	8	5.10	0	0.00	9	1.24

Table 4.11 *(cont.)*.

Site Phase				**I**		**I-II & II**		**II-III & III**	
Number of samples				**7**		**12**		**28**	
Number of 'rich' samples (> 20 seeds)				**2**		**2**		**9**	
Total sediment volume/ litres				**53**		**86**		**254.25**	
		Ecology	**Type**	**Count**	**%**	**Count**	**%**	**Count**	**%**
medium *Vicia/Lathyryus* sp. (2–4 mm)	vetch/wild pea	indet.	indet	12	7.64	4	5.19	10	1.38
small *Vicia/Lathyrus* sp. (<2 mm)	vetch/wild pea	indet.	indet	7	4.46	4	5.19	24	3.32
Medicago spp.	medicks	indet.	indet.	1	0.64	0	0.00	12	1.66
Trifolium/Medicago spp. (*c.* 2–3 mm)	clovers/medicks	indet.	indet.	4	2.55	0	0.00	22	3.04
total *Trifolium* spp.	clovers	indet.	indet.	13	8.28	5	6.49	42	5.81
cf. *Bupleurum rotundifolium* L.	thorow-wax	dry	A	0	0.00	0	0.00	1	0.14
small Apiaceae indet. kernel	small-seeded Carrot Family type	indet.	indet	0	0.00	0	0.00	1	0.14
Solanum dulcamara L.	bittersweet	damp	P	0	0.00	0	0.00	1	0.14
Plantago c.f. *lanceolata* L.	ribwort plantain	dry	P	0	0.00	0	0.00	5	0.69
Linaria sp.	toadflax	dry	indet.	1	0.64	0	0.00	0	0.00
Euphrasia sp.	eyebright	indet.	A	1	0.64	0	0.00	0	0.00
Odontites vernus (Bellardi) Dumort.	red bartsia	dry	A	0	0.00	0	0.00	2	0.28
Galium cf. *verum* L.	lady's bedstraw	dry	P	0	0.00	0	0.00	5	0.69
Galium aparine L.	cleavers	dry	A	0	0.00	0	0.00	3	0.41
small *Galium* sp. (<2 mm)	small-seeded goosegrass	indet.	indet.	3	1.91	0	0.00	3	0.41
Dipsacus fullonum L.	teasel	damp	B	0	0.00	0	0.00	1	0.14
Centaurea sp.	knapweeds	dry	indet.	1	0.64	0	0.00	2	0.28
Anthemis cotula L.	stinking chamomile	dry	A	6	3.82	20	25.97	150	20.75
Leucanthemum vulgare Lam.	ox-eye daisy	dry	P	0	0.00	1	1.30	0	0.00
Tripleurospermum inodorum (L.) Sch. Bip.	scentless mayweed	dry	A	1	0.64	1	1.30	1	0.14
small Asteraceae indet. (<2 mm)	small-seeded Daisy Family type	indet.	indet.	1	0.64	0	0.00	3	0.41
Juncus spp.	rushes	damp	indet.	1	0.64	0	0.00	1	0.14
total *Eleocharis* sp.	all spike-rush types	damp	P	5	3.18	1	1.30	1	0.14
Cladium mariscus (L.) Pohl	great fen-sedge	wet	P	0	0.00	0	0.00	4	0.55
Carex spp.	true sedges	damp	P	7	4.46	1	1.30	10	1.38
small *Festuca/Lolium* sp. (<3 mm)	fescue/rye-grass	indet.	indet.	7	4.46	2	2.60	11	1.52
Lolium cf. *multiflorum* Lam.	Italian rye-grass	dry	A/B	28	17.83	0	0.00	3	0.41
Poa spp.	meadow-grass	indet.	indet.	1	0.64	0	0.00	10	1.38
Avena sp.	wild/cultivated oats	indet.	A	2	1.27	0	0.00	38	5.26
Deschampsia sp.	hair-grass	damp	P	0	0.00	0	0.00	16	2.21
Phleum pratense L.	timothy	dry	P	0	0.00	1	1.30	10	1.38
Phleum bertolonii DC.	lesser cat's-tail	dry	P	3	1.91	5	6.49	24	3.32
Bromus sp.	brome grass	dry	A	5	3.18	1	1.30	71	9.82
Poaceae indet.	Grass Family types	indet.	indet.	7	4.46	6	7.79	56	7.75
small seed indet. (<3 mm)		indet.	indet.	1	0.64	2	2.60	22	3.04
large seed indet. (>3 mm)		indet.	indet.	1	0.64	0	0.00	2	0.28
Total count				*157*	*100.00*	*77*	*100.00*	*723*	*100.00*

Table 4.12. *Summary of calculations for charred cereals and categorisations (Phase I).*

Sample number	**135**	**211**	**37**	**60**	**118**	**150**	**206**	**Totals for Phase I**	**% of total grain**
Context	**[1739]**	**[4334]**	**[550]**	**[1181]**	**[1620]**	**[1909]**	**[4215]**		
Feature	**F.5500**	**F.5651**	**F.5267**	**F.5385**	**F.5474**	**F.1908**	**F.5626**		
Description	pit nr. struct	pit nr. struct	ditch base	ditch	basal well	pit nr. shrine	Pit (seg. ditch)		
Phase	I	I	I	I	I	I	I		
Area	A	A	A	B	B	A	E		
Group	aisled bdng	aisled bdng	1ry W div	ext encl	ext encl	shrine	also B		
Sample volume/ litres	6	2	12	12	12	10	0.5		
Flot fraction examined	1	0.25	1	1	1	1	1		
Total barley rachis internodes					2	5			
Total barley grain	1					4		*5*	4.1
Total spelt/emmer wheat grain	6		5		16	74			
Total spelt/emmer wheat glume bases	54		26		303	454			
Total other wheat grain	6		6		16	74		*102*	83.6
Total bread wheat rachis internodes									
Total indeterminate grain					5	10		*15*	12.3
Total grain (incl sub-categories not listed above)	7		6		21	88		*122*	
Total chaff items (incl sub-categories not listed above)	52		25		317	457		*851*	
Total seeds	37		2		8	110		*157*	
Spelt/emmer wheat ratio of glume bases:grain	9.0	-	5.2	-	18.9	6.1	-		
Total charred items	96	0	33	0	346	655	0	*1130*	
Count density per litre sediment	16.0	0.0	2.8	0.0	28.8	65.5	0.0		
Category assigned	chaff-rich	empty	chaff-rich	empty	chaff-rich	chaff-rich	empty		
x = used for calc. of assemblage composition	**x**				**x**	**x**			
x = used to examine weed flora types/ ecology	**x**					**x**			

(*Carex sylvatica*) and of rushes (*Juncus* sp.). Other taxa occur in much lower quantities and include seeds of common-spikerush (*Eleocharis palustris*), sedges (*Carex* sp.), lesser spearwort (*Ranunuculus* c.f. *flammula*) and a crowfoot type (*Ranunculus* subgen. BATRACHIUM indet), which are all water-associated. Seeds of hedge or marsh woundwort (*Stachys sylvatica/palustris*) and bugle (*Ajuga reptans*) also suggest shade. A low number of taxa more commonly associated with disturbed soils are present, including fat-hen (*Chenopodium album*), chickweed (*Stellaria media*), field penny-cress (*Thlapsi arvensei*) and thistles (*Carduus/Cirsium* sp.).

The remaining four Roman contexts – pit F.5626 and ditches F.5470, F.5624 and F.5480 – are similar in their range of taxa. Numerous seeds of elder (*Sambucus nigra*) with stinging nettles (*Urtica dioica*) are present in all cases, and both plants are characteristically ruderal (of disturbed, particularly nitrogen-rich/ manured soils). In F.5626 ([4215]) Phase I there are numerous bramble seeds (*Rubus* subgen. *RUBUS*), occasional three-nerved sandwort (*Moehringia trinervia*), and dogwood (c.f. *Cornus sanguinea*), which suggests a slightly overgrown and shaded environment. The other Roman contexts contain very few bramble seeds but do include a range of shade/wayside-associated plants including white bryony (*Bryonia dioica*), hemlock (*Conium maculatum*), wild angelica (*Angelica sylvestris*), white or red deadnettle (*Lamium album/purpureum*), and ground ivy (*Glechoma hederacea*). Other taxa which are relatively continuous between the three contexts include blackthorn (*Prunus spinosa*), and hedge or marsh woundwort (*Stachys sylvatica/palustris*).

The most striking contrast between the one Iron Age context and those from the Roman period is the dramatic increase in ruderal taxa. The shift in ecology may be directly linked to the growth of the Roman settlement, with vegetation clearance and input of nitrogen-rich waste (either human or animal) into the local environment.

Scrubby vegetation, dominated by elder with stinging nettles, brambles, occasional blackthorn and accompanied by a range of smaller damp and shade-loving plants of disturbed soils

Table 4.13. *Summary of calculations for charred cereals and categorisations (Phase II).*

Sample number	**167**	**172**	**182**	**171**	**153**	**123**	**178**	**44**	**45**	**196**	**202**	**50**	**98**	**Totals for Phase II**	**% of total grain**
Context	**[4050]**	**[1938]**	**[1630]**	**[1761]**	**[1926]**	**[1642]**	**[3041]**	**[717]**	**[719]**	**[4132]**	**[4188]**	**[1027]**	**[1454]**		
Feature	**F.5176**	**F.5522**	**F.5522**	**F.5533**	**F.5543**	**F.5470**	**F.5483**	**F.5280**	**F.5280**	**F.5015**	**F.5624**	**F.5369**	**F.5436**		
Description	droveway	gully	shrine ditch	shrine ditch	ditch	E-W ditch	gully	mid well	lower well	ditch	ditch	ditch	lower well		
Phase	I-II	I-II	I-II	I-II	I-II	I-II	II	II	II	II	II	II	II		
Area	E	A	A	A	A	A	A	A	A	E	E	D	D		
Group	NWSE	shrine	shrine	shrine	main encl	main encl	shrine	western	western	also B	also B	S. boundary	encl. G13		
Sample volume/ litres	6	8	1	1	14	3	12	12	6	12	2	14	10		
Flot fraction examined	1	1	1	1	1	0.5	1	0.5	1	1	0.25	1	1		
Total barley rachis internodes															
Total barley grain		2								1				*3*	3.0
Total spelt/emmer wheat grain	1	24	1		1		16	29	4	2					
Total spelt/emmer wheat glume bases	12	94	16	34	8		383	220	17	80	2	4	17		
Total other wheat grain	1	24	1		1		16	29	4	2				*78*	78.8
Total bread wheat rachis internodes															
Total indeterminate grain					1		0	7	3	4		2	1	*18*	18.2
Total grain (incl sub-categories not listed above)	1	26	1		2		16	36	7	7		2	1	*99*	
Total chaff items (incl sub-categories not listed above)	12	89	16	32	8		382	218	17	80	2	4	18	*878*	
Total seeds	1	27	2	2	2	1	19	1152	8	10	2		3	*1229*	
Spelt/emmer wheat ratio of glume bases:grain	12.0	3.9	16.0	∞	8.0	-	23.9	7.6	4.3	40.0	-	-	∞		
Total charred items	14	142	19	34	12	1	417	1406	32	97	4	6	22	*2206*	
Count density per litre sediment	2.3	17.8	19.0	34.0	0.9	0.7	0.0	234.3	5.3	8.1	8.0	0.4	2.2		
Category assigned	empty	chaff-rich	chaff-rich	chaff-rich	empty	empty	chaff-rich	exception	chaff-rich	chaff-rich	empty	empty	empty		
x = used for calc. of assemblage composition		x					x	x	excluded	x				4	
x = used to examine weed flora types/ecology		x					x							2	

Table 4.14 (part 1). *Summary of calculations for charred cereals and categorisations (Phase III).*

Sample number	**237**	**90**	**106**	**114**	**138**	**124**	**226**	**236**	**232**	**271**	**36**	**33**	**146**	**12**	**142**
Context	**[4668]**	**[1374]**	**[1476]**	**[1575]**	**[1792]**	**[1646]**	**[4602]**	**[4683]**	**[4649]**	**[4901]**	**[517]**	**[558]**	**[1869]**	**[392]**	**[1832]**
Feature	**F.5707**	**F.5427**	**F.5427**	**F.5501**	**F.5501**	**F.5480**	**F.5652**	**F.5652**	**F.5704**	**F.5741**	**F.5304**	**F.5200**	**F.5033**	**F.5214**	**F.5006**
Description	pond post	E-W ditch	E-W ditch	late ditch	basal ditch	E-W ditch	encl. ditch	ditch	'shrine'	ditch	ditch base	pit back-fill	midden	ditch-butt	ditch
Phase	II-III	II-III	II-III	III	III	III	III	III	III	III	III	III	III	III	III
Area	A	B	B	A	A	A	A	A	A	A	A	A	A	A	A
Group	post-setting	S. side	S. side	2ry W div	2ry W div	2ry W div	curvi encl	curvi encl	curvi encl	curvi encl	pathway	western	pond	v. late	v. late
Sample volume/ litres	8	9	5	10	10	6	6	10	10	7	8	15	14	9	12
Flot fraction examined	1	1	1	1	1	0.5	1	1	0.25	0.5	1	1	1	1	1
Total barley rachis internodes															
Total barley grain					1			1		14		12	2	5	
Total spelt/emmer wheat grain		1	13	7	24		23	4	6	50	22	73	28	21	
Total spelt/emmer wheat glume bases	8	19	90	22	142	6	549	11	21	1560	125	601	308	243	167
Total other wheat grain		1	13	7	24		26	5	6	54	22	74	28	23	
Total bread wheat rachis internodes										6				2	
Total indeterminate grain			2	2	10		1	1		21	13	32	7	19	
Total grain (incl sub-categories not listed above)		1	15	9	35		27	7	6	89	35	118	37	47	
Total chaff items (incl sub-categories not listed above)	8	20	89	21	144	8	548	12	20	1579	124	613	310	248	168
Total seeds	1	3	14	4	78		45	14	8	96	93	195	37	72	21
Spelt/emmer wheat ratio of glume bases:grain	-	19.0	6.9	3.1	5.9	-	23.9	2.8	3.5	31.2	5.7	8.2	11.0	11.6	∞
Total charred items	9	24	118	34	257	8	620	33	34	1764	252	926	384	367	189
Count density per litre sediment	1.1	2.7	23.6	3.4	25.7	2.7	103.3	3.3	13.6	504.0	31.5	61.7	27.4	40.8	15.8
Category assigned	empty	chaff-rich	chaff-rich	chaff-rich	chaff-rich	empty	chaff-rich	chaff-rich	chaff-rich	chaff-rich	chaff-rich	chaff-rich	chaff-rich	chaff-rich	chaff-rich
x = used for calc. of assemblage composition			x		x		x			x	x	x	x	x	x
x = used to examine weed flora types/ecology					x		x			x	x	x	x	x	x

Table 4.14 (part 2). *Summary of calculations for charred cereals and categorisations (Phase III).*

Sample number	**168**	**110**	**96**	**103**	**107**	**57**	**52**	**55**	**58**	**59**	**87**	**102**	**80**	**Totals for Phase III**	**% of total grain**
Context	**[3025]**	**[1532]**	**[1444]**	**[1486]**	**[1515]**	**[1177]**	**[1104]**	**[1120]**	**[2012]**	**[2016]**	**[1400]**	**[2085]**	**[2021]**		
Feature	**F.5552**	**F.5452**	**F.5435**	**F.5441**	**F.5453**	**F.5353**	**F.5345**	**F.5345**	**F.2013**	**F.2016**	**F.5425**	**F.2086**	**F.2022**		
Description	postpipe	encl. butt	pit in encl.	pit in encl.	pit in encl.	ditch	E-W ditch	E-W ditch	Inhuma-tion	Inhuma-tion	pit in cem.	Inhuma-tion	Inhuma-tion		
Phase	III	III	III	III	III	III	III	III	III	III	III	III	III		
Area	B	B	B	B	B	D	D	D	D	D	D	D	D		
Group	S. side	S. side	S. side	S. side	S. side	W bound	W bound	W bound	cemetery	cemetery	cemetery	cemetery	cemetery		
Sample volume/ litres	10	14	8	11	10	12	12	12	10	15	10	8	6		
Flot fraction examined	0.125	1	1	1	1	1	1	1	1	1	1	1	1		
Total barley rachis internodes															
Total barley grain	1	1		1										*38*	6.1
Total spelt/emmer wheat grain	153	11	1	19	7		1			1				*465*	
Total spelt/emmer wheat glume bases	47	201		121	18				6		1		3	*4269*	
Total other wheat grain	154	11	1	19	7		1			1				*477*	76.0
Total bread wheat rachis internodes														*8*	
Total indeterminate grain	3	1				1								*113*	18.0
Total grain (incl sub-categories not listed above)	158	13	1	20	7	1	1			1				*628*	
Total chaff items (incl sub-categories not listed above)	42	200		121	16				6		1		3	*4301*	
Total seeds		22		17	3									*723*	
Spelt/emmer wheat ratio of glume bases:grain	0.3	18.3	-	6.4	2.6	-	-	-	-	-	-	-	-		
Total charred items	200	235	1	158	26	1	1	0	6	1	1	0	3	*5652*	
Count density per litre sediment	160.0	16.8	0.1	14.4	2.6	0.1	0.1	0.0	0.6	0.1	0.1	0.0	0.5		
Category assigned	exception.	chaff-rich	empty	chaff-rich	empty	empty	empty	empty	empty	empty	empty	empty	empty		
x = used for calc. of assemblage composition	x	x		x										12	
x = used to examine weed flora types/ecology		x												9	

Table 4.15. *Summary of waterlogged contexts in the 'northern zone'.*

Context	Feature	Phase	Area	Description
[1642]	F.5470	I–II	A	northern length of main enclosure ditch
[1646]	F.5480	III	A	E–W enclosure ditch to north of F.5480
[4166]	F.5621	Iron Age	E	pit in northern excavated area
[4188]	F.5624	II	E (& B)	ditch to north of main enclosure
[4215]	F.5626	I	E (& B)	pit, part of segmented ditch to north of main encl.

Table 4.16. *Summary of waterlogged contexts in the 'central zone'.*

Context	Feature	Phase	Area	Description
[4334]	F.5651	I	A	ditch alongside aisled building
[4668]	F.5707	II–III	A	post-setting
[4649]	F.5704	III	A	pit, part of the circular timber shrine

were present. The contexts indicate a disturbed, but regenerating, area on the northern periphery of the Roman settlement. The land had been much more shaded by vegetation and, from the lack of ruderal taxa, was relatively undisturbed by human activity during the Iron Age.

The Central Contexts
Three good waterlogged contexts have been identified from structures within the main enclosure (Table 4.16). Ditch F.5651 and post-setting F.5707 are compositionally very similar. The main plant taxa are buttercups (*Ranunculus acris/bulbosus/repens*), with lesser amounts of creeping cinquefoil (*Potentilla reptans*), swine-cress (*Coronopus squamatus*) and occasional greater plantain (*Plantago major*), all suggesting rough, short grassland. Evidence for disturbed, nutrient-rich soils includes numerous seeds of orache (*Atriplex patula/prostrata*), and low amounts of elder, stinging nettles, chickweed (*Stellaria media*) and deadnettle (*Lamium album/purpureum*). Individual cases of water-associated taxa, including sedges (*Carex* spp.), mint (*Mentha* sp.), crowfoot (*Ranunculus* subgen. BATRACHIUM indet.) and common meadow-rue (*Thalictrum flavum*), together indicate intermittently damp conditions. Both contexts contain numerous egg cases of water flea (*Daphne* sp.), suggesting stagnant water within those features.

The F.5804 'shrine' context, [4649], includes a wide range of taxa clearly linked to open or disturbed land, including creeping cinquefoil (*Potentilla reptans*), red goosefoot (*Chenopodium* c.f. *rubrum*), and parsley-piert (*Aphanes arvensis*). Numerous seeds of celery-leaved buttercup (*Ranunculus scleratus*) also suggest wet and open conditions, and stinging nettle (*Urtica dioica*) again occurs in some number, which indicates disturbed nutrient-rich soil. The virtual absence of elder and complete lack of bramble or blackthorn within this context provides the strongest evidence for a cleared environment in association with the Roman settlement.

Overall, the three contexts suggest that the main enclosure was kept clear of larger vegetation, with open rough or trampled short vegetation. Buttercups were common with creeping cinquefoil and other short herbs; in suitable less trampled areas nettles and thistles sprang up. As in the northern zone, ruderal plants were still common, but shade-associated taxa virtually absent.

The waterlogged contexts are summarized in Figure 4.25 by the ecology of the main plant taxa present (those represented by more than two items, usually seeds). Since samples were scanned rather than sorted, the percentages are schematic and not based on true counts. During the Iron Age the local environment appears to have been wet, shady, and relatively undisturbed. Plant remains from the northern periphery of the Roman settlement show a continuously scrubby and damp environment. The many ruderal taxa indicate the land had been disturbed, but that the vegetation was regenerating. Nitrogen-enrichment, either from human or animal waste, had also significantly affected the flora present. In contrast, the central area of the site, although still damp, and with open and disturbed land plants, was clear of larger vegetation. The ground was covered with plants tolerant of trampling and lack of shade. Similar local environments, with numerous ruderal plants, have been identified at many rural Roman sites, including New Hall (Chap. 3) and Stonea Grange (Van der Veen 1996).

Pollen Analysis Rob Scaife

Three Romano-British sediment sequences have been assessed for their sub-fossil pollen and spore content (see Fig. 4.25). These profiles come from two large, deep pits, possibly wells or waterholes (F.5474 & F.5436) and from an old land surface/buried soil (F.5033). If present, it was anticipated that pollen might provide useful information on the past vegetation ecology and environment of the site. Pollen and spores were indeed recovered from all of these profiles, although in varying degrees of preservation and absolute pollen frequencies.

A total of 16 pollen samples were examined from the three monoliths. Sub-samples of 3 ml volume at 4 cm intervals were prepared using standard techniques for the extraction of the sub-fossil pollen and spores (Moore & Webb 1978; Moore *et al.* 1991) with the addition of micromesh sieving (10 μm) to aid the removal of the clay fraction. Absolute pollen frequencies (APF) were calculated using added exotics to known volumes of sample (Stockmarr 1971). Pollen was identified and counted using an Olympus biological research microscope fitted with Leitz optics.

For the old land surface (F.5033) a pollen sum of 300 grains of dryland taxa, plus all extant spores and pollen of marsh taxa (largely Cyperaceae and *Alnus*), fern spores and miscellaneous pre-Quaternary palynomorphs, was counted. Where pollen preservation was poor in the pit profiles (F.5474 & F.5436) a sum of 100 grains per level was adopted. An extensive reference/comparative collection of modern taxa was available to aid identification. Pollen diagram(s) have been calculated and plotted using Tilia and Tilia Graph. Percentages have been calculated as follows:

Sum = % total dry land pollen (tdlp)
Marsh/aquatic = % tdlp+sum of marsh/aquatics
Spores= % tdlp+sum of spores
Misc.= % tdlp+sum of misc. taxa.

Taxonomy in general follows that of Moore and Webb (1978), Moore *et al.* 1991 modified according to Bennett *et al.* (1994) for pollen types and Stace (1997) for plant descriptions. These procedures were carried out in the Palaeoecology Laboratory of the Department of Geography, University of Southampton.

The Pollen Data

There is a broad similarity between all of the profiles examined, except that the pollen present in the old land surface (F.5033) had higher absolute frequencies and was in a better state of preservation. In this profile, the substantial numbers of Lactucoideae (dandelion types) are well- preserved. In the pit profiles a large number of grains of this taxon were degraded; this typically indicates differential preservation of this robust pollen type. The former soil profile is considered to show less differential preservation. The characteristics of the three profiles are described as follows.

Profile F.5033 <220> Old Land Surface (Fig. 4.26) - This has the best pollen preservation and highest absolute pollen frequencies (to 80,000 grains/ml at the base). The profile was also the most taxonomically diverse (40 taxa). As with all of the sequences, herbs are dominant with extremely few (<1%), sporadic occurrences of trees *(Betula, Pinus, Ulmus, Quercus* and *Alnus).* Herbs are dominated by pastoral taxa with Lactucoideae most important and increasing from 35 to 55 per cent at the top of the profile. Whilst there is some possibility of increasing differential preservation upwards through the profile, the pollen was on the whole well-preserved. There is little evidence of any marked differential preservation in the lowest levels. Poaceae are also important (to 34%) at the base of the profile and decrease upwards. Other pastoral taxa are also present and include *Plantago lanceolata* (15%), *Ranunculus* type, *Dianthus* type, *Trifolium* type and *Centaurea nigra* type. Cereal pollen and weeds of disturbed ground and agriculture are also present, but only in small numbers (e.g. *Polygonum aviculare* type, *Artemisia, Spergula* type, Chenopodiaceae). A small number of marsh herbs are present in the upper level including Cyperaceae and *Typha angustifolia/Sparganium* type.

Profile F.5436 <97> Roman Well/Waterhole, Phase II (Fig. 4.27) - Pollen was generally sparse and poorly preserved with evidence of differential preservation (especially degraded Lactucoideae). APF values are highest in the basal level (48 cm) with values to 8500 grains/ml. As with the other profiles, tree and shrub pollen are minimal, with only small numbers of *Betula, Pinus, Quercus, Tilia* and *Alnus. Corylus avellana* attains 6 per cent in the top and basal samples only. Herbs are dominated by Lactucoideae (to 58%), Poaceae (to 42%) and *Plantago lanceolata* at the base (15%). Overall, herbs of pastoral affinity are most important, but with small numbers of ruderals/segetals (weeds and plants of disturbed ground) also present. The latter include *Sinapis* type, *Chenopodium* type, *Polygonum aviculare* type, *Plantago major* type, *Artemisia* and also the spores of *Pteridium aquilinum.* In the upper half of the profile there is a sharp increase in derived pre-Quaternary pollen and spores and Hystrichospheres (dinoflagellates).

Profile F.5474 <141> Roman Well/Waterhole, AD *60–140* (Fig. 4.28) - Pollen is poorly preserved with clear evidence of differential preservation; degraded Lactucoideae are dominant (60–70%) throughout. APF values are small being from 3000–6000 grains/ml. However, there is also a range of better-preserved pollen exhibiting some taxonomic diversity. Cereal pollen is more important in this than in the other profiles examined (to 6% at the base) with segetals including *Polygonum aviculare* type, Chenopodiaceae and *Sinapis* type. Poaceae and other pastoral taxa are, however, relatively more important including *Plantago lanceolata* (4%). There are few trees and shrubs with only sporadic records of *Betula, Quercus, Fraxinus, Alnus, Rubus* type and *Corylus avellana* type. Spores are dominated by *Pteridium aquilinum* (ave. 20% with a peak to 40%) with lesser numbers of monolete *(Dryopteris)* type, *Polypodium vulgare* and occasional *Sphagnum.*

The taphonomy of pollen in such well or waterhole features is complex and there have been few detailed studies with which to compare the data obtained from Vicar's Farm. Studies at Peterborough (Scaife 1994) and Honiton, Devon (Scaife 1999) are, however, comparable in demonstrating the presence of open herbaceous environments and have raised the question of pollen taphonomy in such features. Pollen derived from 'normal' airborne means or insect vectors is likely to derive from areas close to the site. However, given the archaeological nature of these features, such contexts are also highly likely to contain pollen from secondary sources. These may be varied and include pollen contained in human and animal faeces, offal, domestic waste including floor coverings and food remains. These may strongly skew the pollen assemblages (Greig 1982). The presence of such secondary/derived pollen complicates the interpretation, since it is possible that the dominance of secondary pollen may have masked 'naturally' derived assemblages from which interpretations of the local environment can be made.

A further effect of the possibility that much of the pollen has been introduced into these contexts via secondary routes or from on-site and immediately local sources, is that pollen from the surrounding environment may be proportionally under-represented. This is especially pertinent with regards to the woodland and shrub component, since pollen percentages are calculated here as a percentage of the total pollen. The extremely high percentages of Poaceae (grasses) thus suppress the percentage of other 'within sum' taxa. The extent and importance of such woodland elements remains unclear due to such taphonomic questions.

As part of this assessment it was hoped that the pollen sequence obtained from the old land surface (F.5033) would provide a longer temporal sequence and thus picture of environmental change. Whilst this may be true, the environment throughout was clearly one of dominant herbs of pasture with Poaceae (grasses), Lactucoideae (dandelion types), *Plantago*

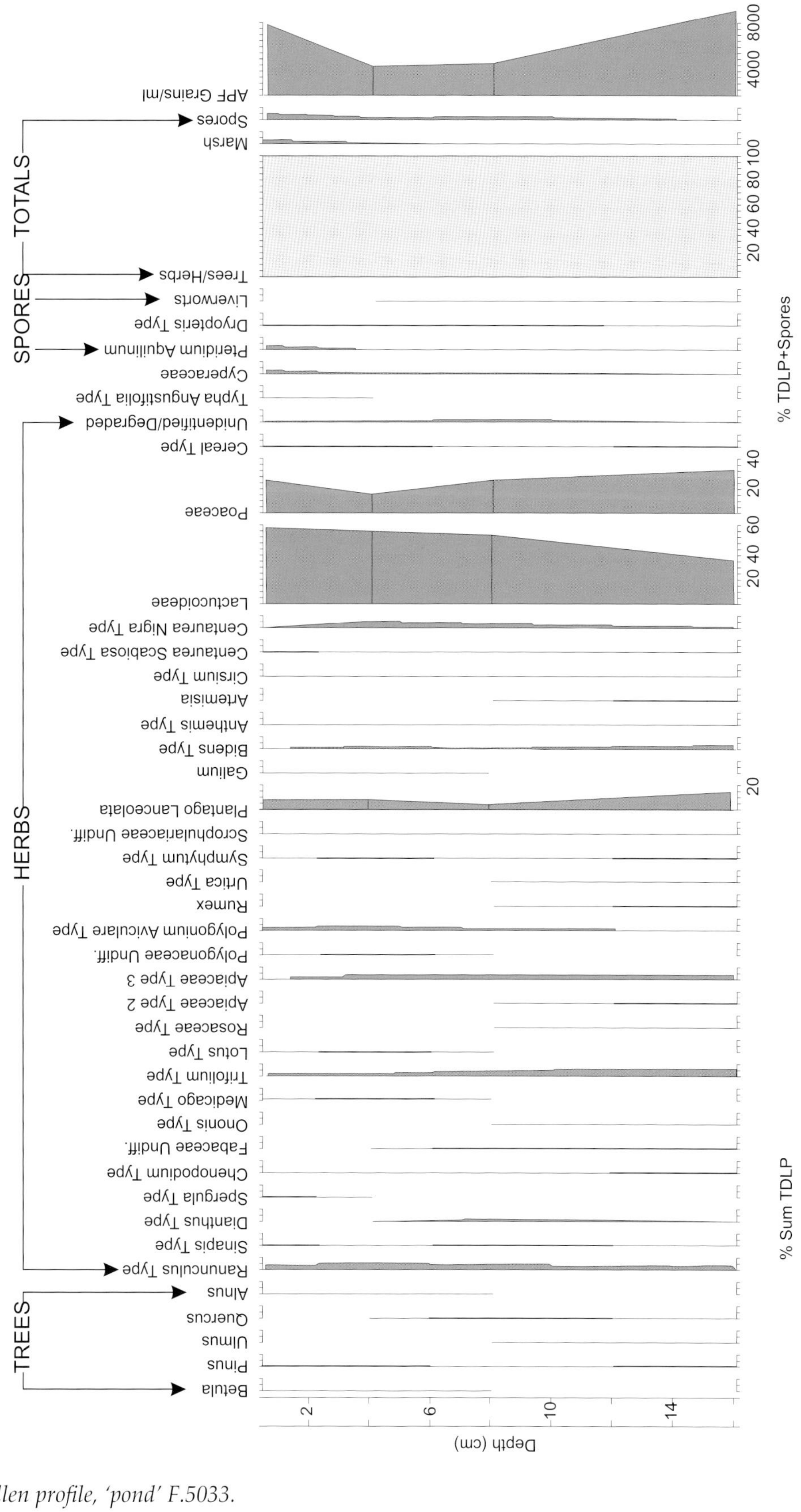

Figure 4.26. *Pollen profile, 'pond' F.5033.*

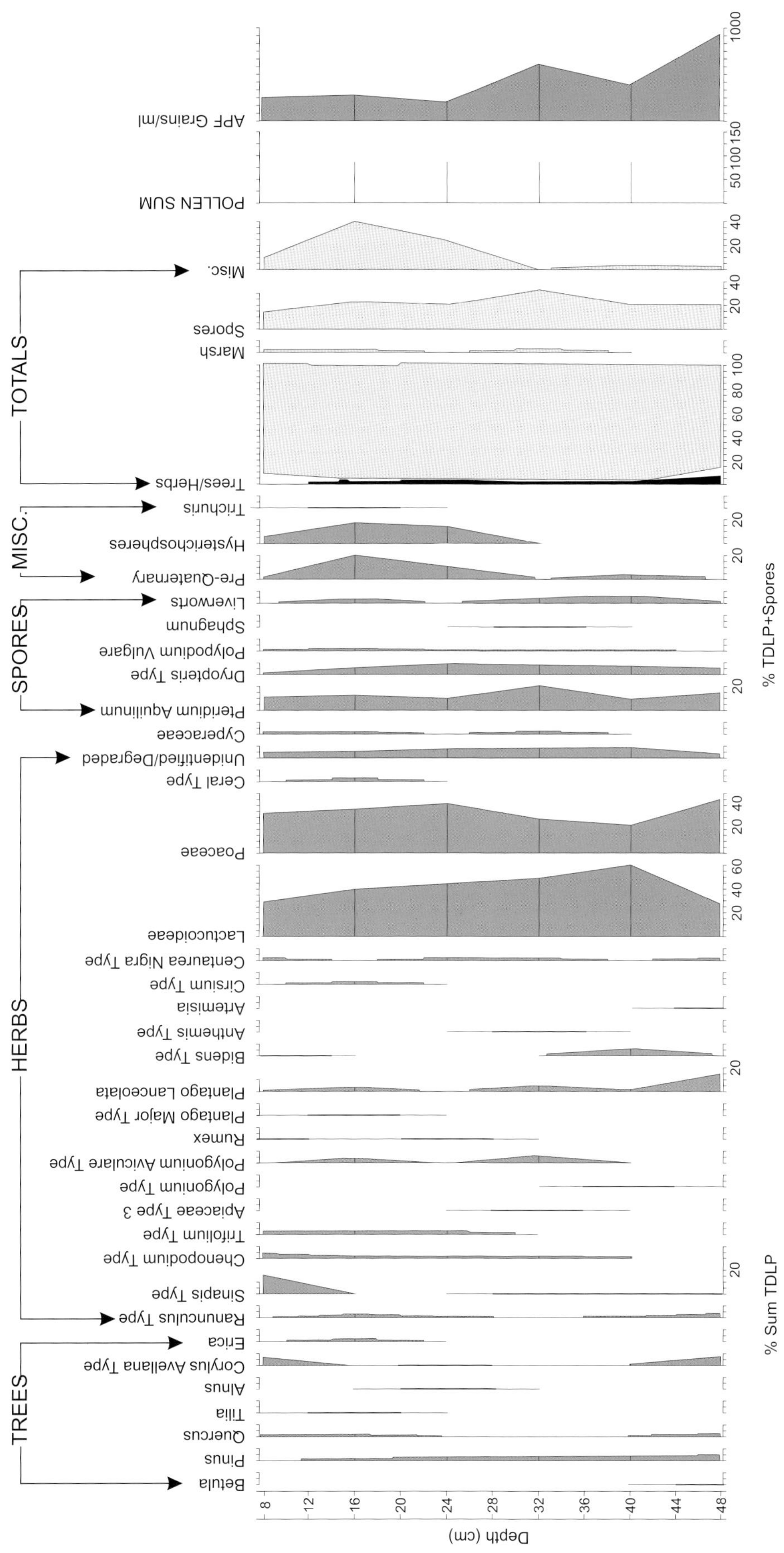

Figure 4.27. *Pollen profile, well F.5436.*

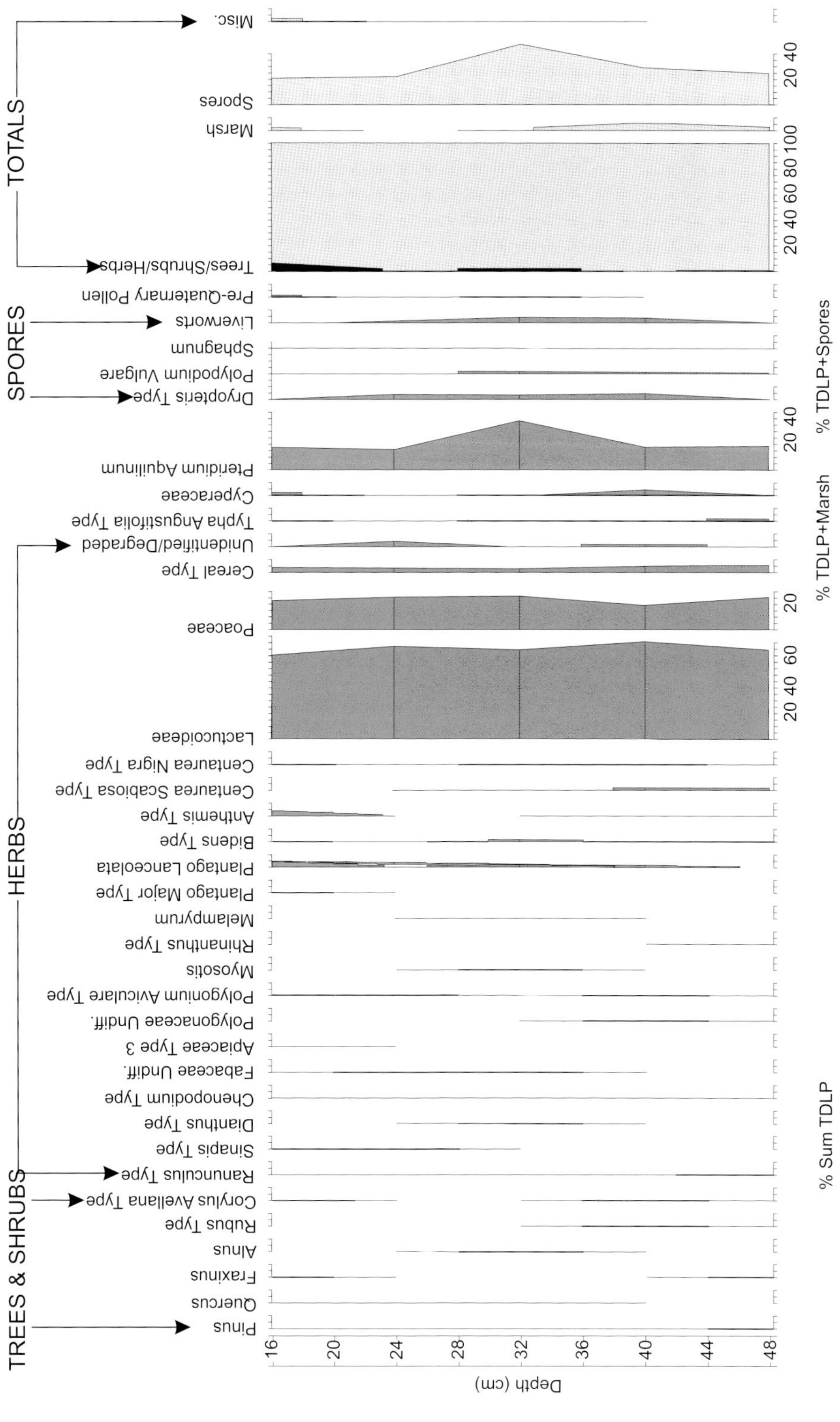

Figure 4.28. *Pollen profile, well F.5474.*

lanceolata (ribwort plantain), *Trifolium* type and *Medicago* type (medicks and clovers) and Ranunculus type (buttercups). The fact that the pollen of these is present suggests that the pasture was not closely cropped/grazed. The number of trees is minimal and, as such, it seems likely that the area around the site was open agricultural land. Even though the pollen catchment of such soil profiles may be of local extent (Dimbleby 1985), it is likely that if woodland was present, higher APF values would be recorded (especially oak and hazel). It is possible that cereal pollen and possibly associated herbs/weeds of cultivation could have been derived from areas of cultivation at some distance or from secondary sources noted, such as crop-processing liberating pollen trapped in cereal husks (Robinson & Hubbard 1977) or even from animal feed and dung.

Of the two well profiles, F.5436 <97> is in Phase II while F.5474 <141> is assigned to Phase I. For F.5436, while there has been differential preservation in favour of robust pollen types such as Lactucoideae, there remains clear evidence for the predominance of the pastoral habitat also evidenced in the old land surface profile (F.5033) and only minimal evidence of arable activity. The upper levels of this feature contain pre-Quaternary palynomorphs, derived from the local bedrock, and imply sediment inwash and possible reworking of pollen. Thus, the lower part of the profile may be more representative of the local habitat. A single record of the intestinal parasite *Trichuris* may also suggest the presence of faecal material in the upper sediments. This would be commensurate with the possibility that this was a waterhole. It is, however, unfortunate that more substantial numbers were not present. Well F.5474 <141> is also broadly comparable with both the old land surface and well profile F.5436 in clearly showing a pastoral environment. There is, however, one difference: higher values of *Pteridium aquilinum* (bracken), which may suggest abandonment and/or waste ground in this area of the site.

In summary, pollen and spores have been recovered from the two well profiles and the old land surface. The latter has the best pollen preservation, from which data on the local vegetation environment has been forthcoming. The well features have poor pollen preservation and a degree of differential pollen preservation as indicated by abundant but degraded Lactucae (dandelion types). The taphonomy of such features and soil profiles is complex and the pollen catchment may be representative of only the on-site and immediate area. In spite of this, useful information has been obtained from all of the profiles. These exhibit a strong pastoral component/habitat with little evidence of trees and shrubs growing in the immediate area. A minor arable element is also present, but may have derived from domestic waste, animal ordure, feed, crop-processing or directly from cultivation.

Deposition of Cultural Material

We will now examine broad trends within the site's depositional patterning and outline specific artefact-category study methodologies.

Finds Densities

The density of features on the site is apparent from the plans, and it would seem probable that the density of finds should more or less match this. To provide some coarse spatial control of the site, both in terms of finds distribution and discussion of its features, the Roman settlement has been divided into five zones or areas (A–E; Fig. 4.29). Although it is recognized that such divisions are partly limiting, they are used to provide a baseline for further discussion. The site has been divided into these areas according to major boundaries; not all the areas were active in all periods (see below), but they do remain more or less coherent as divisions.

Area A - The core of the settlement and the focus of domestic and other activities involving people. It persisted as the core-area throughout the Roman period and, although internally it is subject to changing sub-divisions, there was an enduring distinction between the eastern and western halves, marked by the diagonal line of a boundary ditch/pathway. Within the western half, there was further subdivision, in particular between the northern side, where the cremation cemetery (and later pitting) lay, and the southern side, occupied by the Aisled Building and a roundhouse. Between these two lay the shrine.

Area B - This area only came into existence in Phase II, as a southern extension to the core of the settlement, and it had a tripartite internal division. It appears to have formed the focus of some domestic and/or ritual activity, as well as perhaps containing livestock.

Area C - Created in the final phase (III), this was the most peripheral zone of the settlement, consisting of a large enclosure and smaller sub-enclosures, probably all related to animal husbandry or other agricultural activities.

Area D - This was initially a distinctly separate fieldsystem lying at the southern edge of the site, laid out in Phase II and, perhaps, related to another settlement east of the limits of excavation. Only in Phase III was it integrated with the main settlement on the site, when part of it was also used as an inhumation cemetery.

Area E - This covers the northern area of the site, bisected by a major droveway into western and eastern sides, each of which were, at various points, divided into small enclosures.

If one takes these spatial divisions of the site and quantifies the more common finds – pottery and bone – by area, the inference of relative settlement intensity is borne out (Table 4.17). By count and weight, the amount of pottery and bone decreases as one moves southward

Figure 4.29. *Roman settlement divided into areas (A–E).*

from Area A to Area D (i.e. successively further from the core). North of the core in Area E, the figures for both pottery and bone are comparable to Area C. However, excavation bias might be affecting these figures; the intensity of excavation in the core might be greater than at the margins and this could result in more finds being retrieved. The greater intensity of excavation may, of course, be reflecting the greater intensity of features, but nevertheless one might still question whether there should be a correspondence between density of features and density of finds. As this need not be the case, we need to factor this out. Many methods could be used to achieve this. Ideally, one might compare density of finds against volume of associated deposit excavated, but this is a complex and very time-consuming method to apply to the site as whole (as opposed to specific features; see below). However, using the heavy residues taken from bulk samples will give some indication, as this offers the most controlled form of recovery. Table 4.18 shows the average quantity of pottery and bone in grams per litre of soil, based on samples in Areas A (21 samples), B (9) and D (9); no data is present for Area C and Area E had only three samples, one of which had an unusually large quantity of pottery which skews the results.

Table 4.17. *Pottery & bone quantities by area.*

	Pot		Bone	
Area	**No.**	**Wt.**	**No.**	**Wt.**
A	8508	137,950	8931	173,280
B	2297	33,525	4167	72,246
C	776	11,239	1142	19,743
D	582	3287	909	6562
E	579	9490	1648	19,663

Table 4.18. *Average weights (g) of pot and bone per litre of soil by area (based on bulk sample heavy residues).*

Area	Pottery	Bone
A	0.79	1.80
B	0.40	1.20
D	0.06	0.35

Although a small sample size, it at least confirms the impression that finds density is greater in the core and drops off further away.

Having a long-standing concern with the expression/distinction of micro-level patterns of discard, we are fortunate that the site was selected as a case-study for Ballantyne's 2009 PhD dissertation, 'Charred Plant Remains as Minute Artefactual Debris'. Directly complementary to the analyses undertaken of both Colne Fen's The Camp Ground and Langdale Hale's settlements, and employing the same methodology (Ballantyne in Evans *et al.* 2013b, 159–61 & 419–13), it also demonstrates high(est) core-area values; its results feature in Chapter Six below.

As still a further check, using all bulk finds of pottery and bone we can compare the densities expressed as a mean for each area against the site mean. This compensates for any individual variability between the size/volumes of excavation slots or features (Table 4.19). To avoid issues of fragmentation (but see below), only weight has been used in this measure, and it clearly shows the same trend: that moving out from the core, the mean quantity of finds per context decreases, dropping below the mean in Areas D and E. The same can be done at the level of excavation unit or slot. Figure 4.30 shows the total quantity of pottery and bone by weight for each slot expressed as a statistical value: below the mean, and to one, two and three standard deviations, and finally above three standard deviations. The total number from all excavation units was used as the measure. The generated figures clearly show that the higher densities of material lie in the core and also gives a more detailed resolution in terms of spatial densities than lumping the quantities together by area (although in doing so, it is more affected by the volume of deposit excavated).

Table 4.19. *Mean densities of pottery and bone by weight per context for the site as a whole and by area (figures have been rounded to the nearest whole number).*

Area means	Pottery	Bone
A	206	343
B	145	380
C	154	318
D	46	187
E	113	298
Site mean	*144*	*315*

Finally, two 10 m square-divided transects were imposed upon the site, a north–south and an east–west one, and the total numbers of pottery and bone retrieved from contexts within each 10 m square was divided by the number of excavation slots (Fig. 4.31). Again, the same trend is apparent, and from all these different methods, it seems safe to assume that *the greater density of finds in the core is reflecting actual deposition, rather than excavation bias.*

Of the pottery recovered from the Roman settlement's various categories of discrete features (excluding postholes; see Fig. 6.9), the overall mean number of sherds per feature was 31 (471 g). Including nil values, the mean level within its designated quarries was significantly lower, with a mean of just 13 sherds (126 g).

In order to gauge the intensity of the site's deposition, the cubic density has been calculated from those six cut features from which more than 100 sherds were recovered (101–266 range/797–7019 g).[8] Ranging from 26 to 107 sherds per cu. m, the values were over 50 in just three instances. As shown in Figure 4.32, the settlement's pottery levels clearly fell well short of those of New Hall/Murray Edwards, where seven features had more than 150 sherds per cu. m (see Fig. 2.45).

Taphonomy

As well as considering the sheer density of material, its condition also needs some consideration; organic preservation was fairly poor except in a few waterlogged contexts (see Ballantyne, above), but while some unworked wood occurred in these contexts, there was little else save plant remains. Bone preservation was variable but tended to be better in the core than on the clay margins, and shell was also preserved fairly well. All inorganic remains survived well and were not subject to any major chemical/environmental degradation. Beyond soil conditions, more general physical/mechanical processes were the major factors affecting the preservation of finds. Using the two most common finds – pot and bone – as indices of taphonomic processes, we can start to qualify the finds distributions.

Animal Bone (with Andy Clarke)

An assemblage of 10,409 bone fragments was recovered by means of hand-excavation and environmental flotation.[9] Where it was possible to confidently ascertain that a group of fragments originated from a single bone, they were grouped together and counted as a single element (i.e. 100 fragments from a broken skull

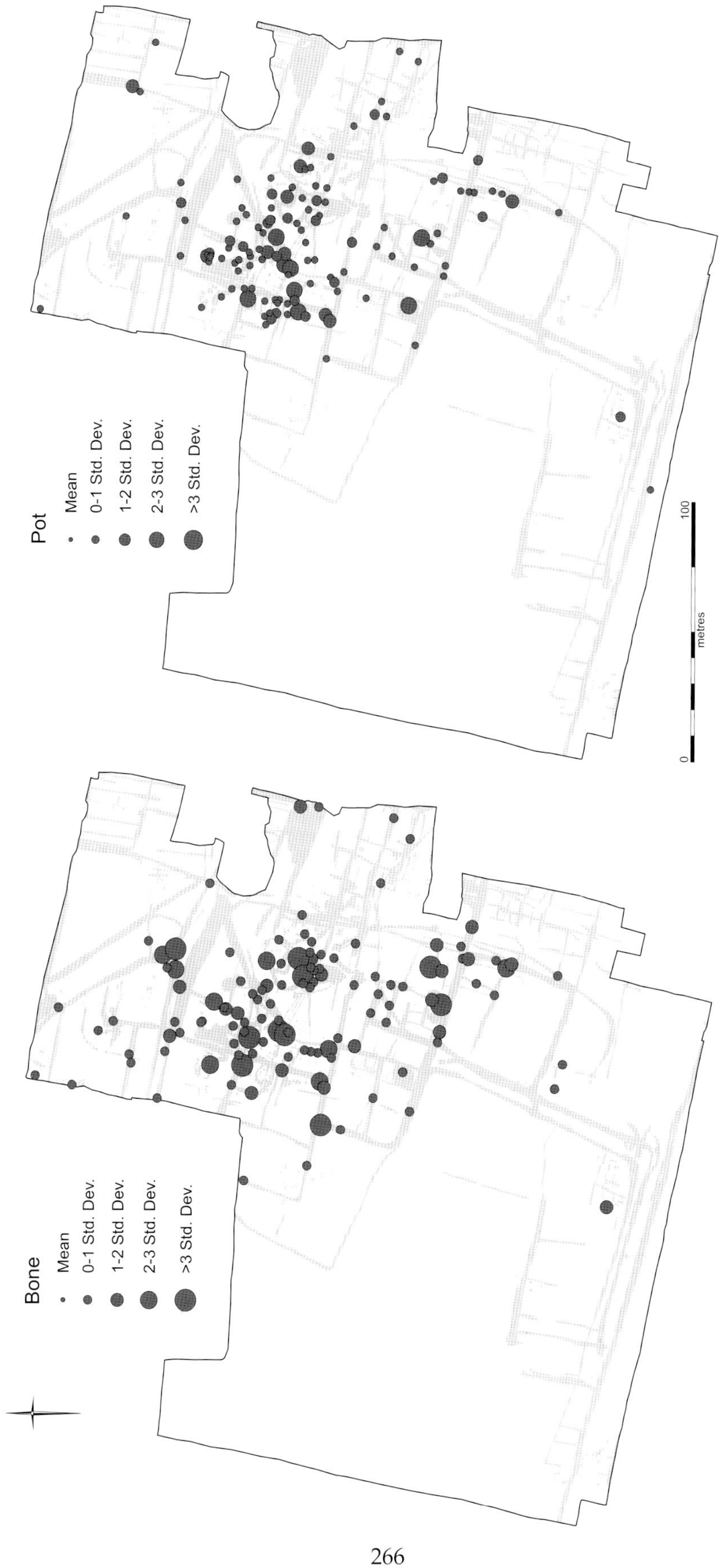

Figure 4.30. *Quantity of bone and pottery from excavation-slots, expressed as statistical values.*

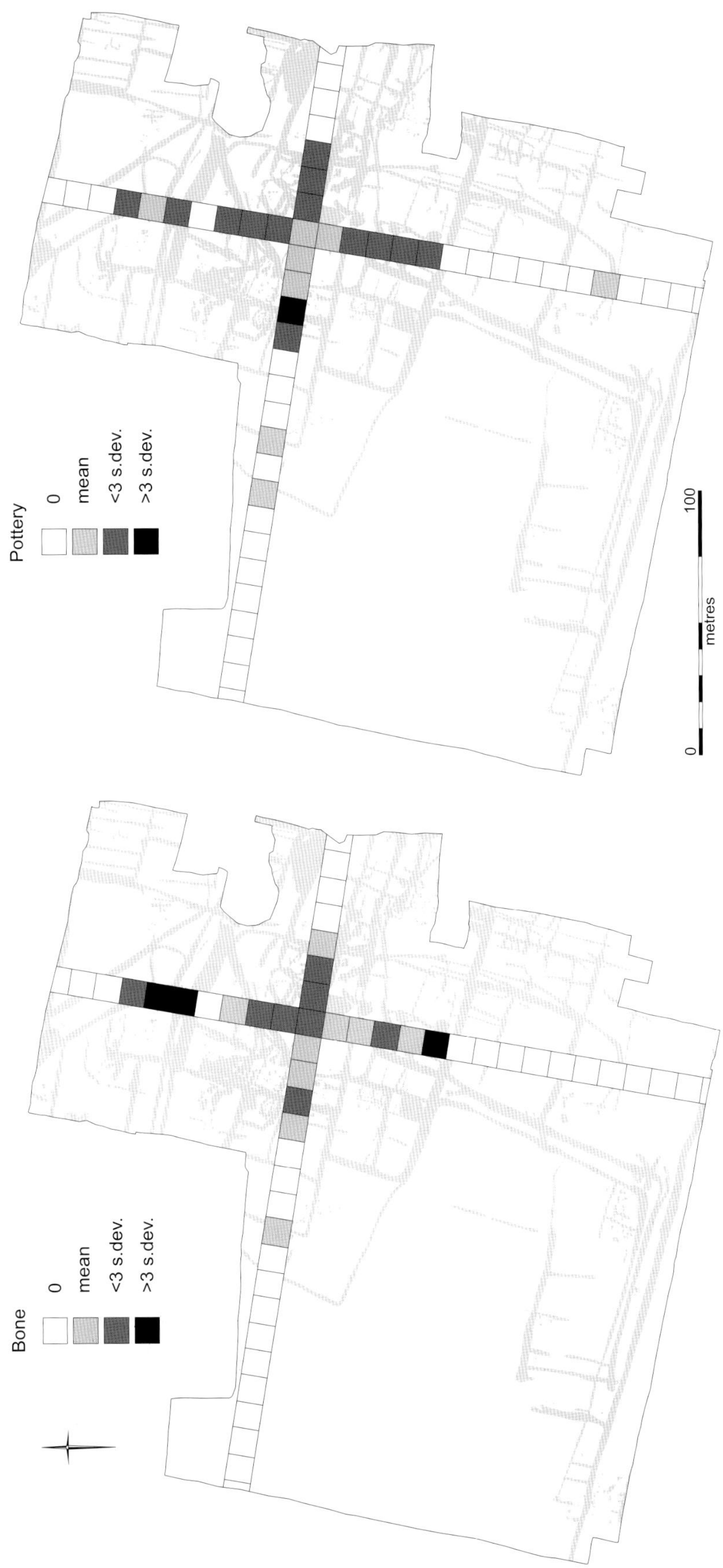

Figure 4.31. *Transect finds quantities (count per 10 m-square adjusted against number of excavation slots in each): bone (left) and, right, pottery.*

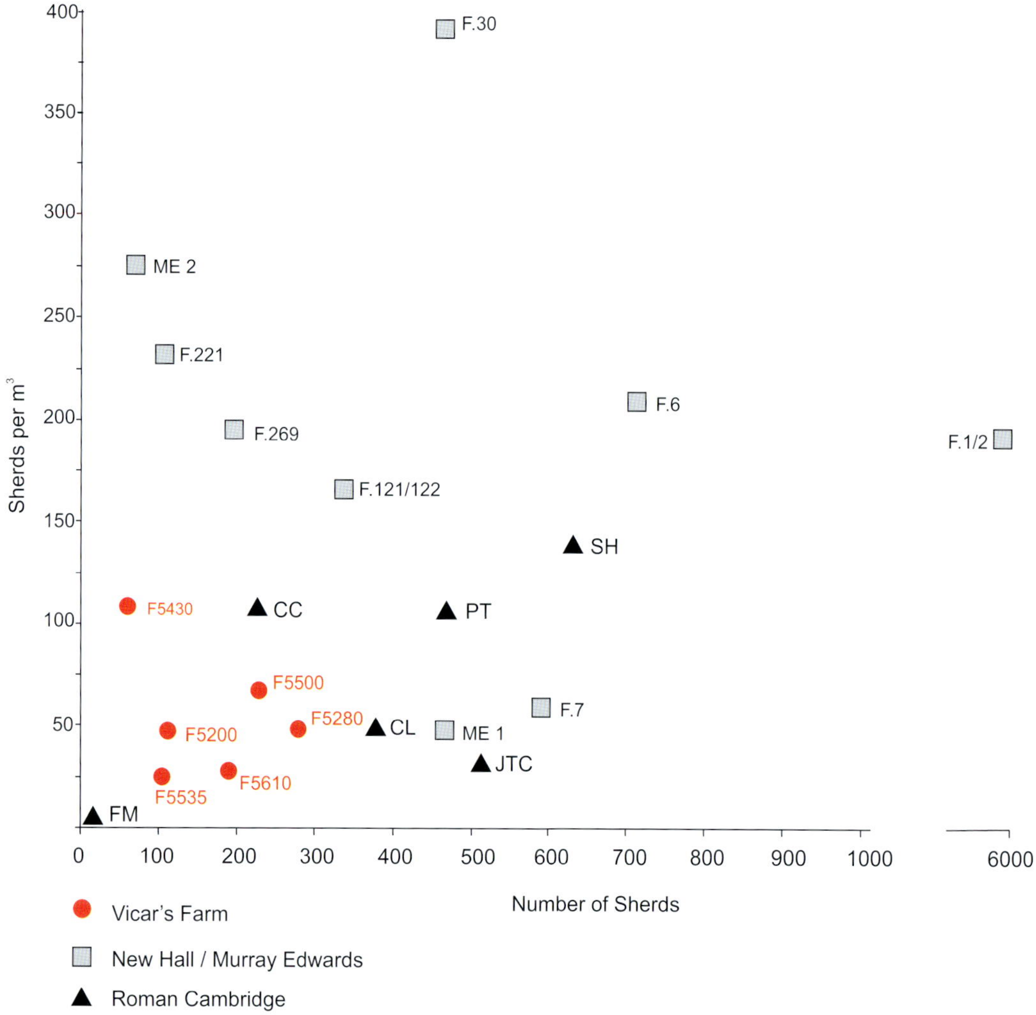

Figure 4.32. *Plot showing site's highest-value per cubic-metre densities when compared to New Hall and other Roman Cambridge investigations (FM, Folk Museum; CL, Chesterton Lane; CC, Cow & Calf; JTC, St John's Triangle/ Corfield Court; PT, Park St. Transformer; SH, Shire Hall Lift Shaft).*

were counted as one). Due to the complexity of the site's sequence, it was not possible to assign phases to the entire assemblage. As a result, analysis will only deal with those bones that have been confidently phased, reducing the analysed assemblage to 9610 fragments. Of these, 4570 (48%) were identifiable to species.

All the bone was identified using the reference collection of the Department of Archaeology at the University of Cambridge, and where possible each bone was identified to species and to element. Each bone was recorded according to the diagnostic zone method (Dobney & Reilly 1988) in an effort to enable more accurate calculation of statistics. Differentiation between the remains of sheep and goats was carried out using the above-mentioned reference collection and according to the accepted criteria established by Boessneck (1969). It was only possible to confidently identify nine goat bones; all other ovicaprid remains are quoted as sheep. Where they appeared in articulation, ribs and vertebrae were also identified to species; otherwise, these elements were grouped as cow- or sheep-size. This method was also used for unidentified fragments of long bone shafts.

Estimation of age at death was calculated for the four major domesticates. Tooth eruption and wear was recorded according to the methods of Grant (1982), Halstead (1985), Levine (1982), O'Connor (1991) and Payne (1973). Stages of epiphyseal union were also recorded according to the criteria of Getty (1975). Where it was possible to do so, all the identified mammal bones were measured according to the accepted standards (von den Driesch 1976). Unfortunately, metrical data was not available in sufficient quantities to warrant a full metrical analysis. The measurement data is available for inspection in the site archive and will be utilized in the next volume's discussion of human/animal 'improvements'.

The majority of the bone assemblage is in a fair to good state of preservation, allowing data such as the amount of carnivore gnawing or butchery marks to be easily observed and recorded. However, the bone, although well-preserved, is in a fragmentary state, having undergone a high degree of processing and bears all

Table 4.20. *Number of bones displaying specific taphonomic indicators by area.*

Area	Gnawed	% of total	Butchery marks	% of total	Burnt	% of total	Total Bone
A	211	4.47	75	1.59	33	0.70	4725
B	86	6.07	26	1.84	12	0.85	1416
C	22	3.42	6	0.93	0	0.00	643
D	0	0.00	0	0.00	0	0.00	98
E	15	2.17	2	0.29	1	0.14	692

Table 4.21. *Bone fragmentation by area (*** MNE Minimum Number of Elements; ** EEE = Estimated Element Equivalent, calculated by total number of zones (Z) divided by number of zones present (z) for each element, where Z = 8; * Completeness calculated on MNE only, and based on EEE divided by MNE; higher scores indicate more complete bones, lower scores, more fragmented/incomplete).*

Area	MNE**	EEE**	Completeness*	Ave. wt.
A	1468	447.63	0.30	19.40
B	466	142.88	0.31	17.34
C	181	48.00	0.27	17.29
D	35	7.38	0.21	7.22
E	169	39.88	0.24	11.93

Table 4.22. *Quantities of identifiable and unidentifiable bone by area.*

Area	Ident. bone	Unident. bone	Total	% Unident.
A	2746	1979	4725	41.88
B	554	862	1416	60.88
C	198	445	643	69.21
D	21	77	98	78.57
E	243	449	692	64.88

the hallmarks of 'refuse', from the slaughter of animals to meal waste. Bearing in mind the amount of identifiable remains contained within the assemblage (48%), it would appear that the bone suffered very little further damage (apart from canid gnawing) and was preserved more or less intact once deposited in the site's various enclosure ditches, pits, wells and other features.

Evidence of gnawing, either in the form of puncture marks or scratches, was recorded whenever they were visible on the bone surface. The percentage of bone in the assemblage affected by gnawing was calculated and is shown in Table 4.20. The percentages are clearly quite high, a factor that accounts in part for the low numbers of small bones, such as phalanges, carpals and tarsals recovered. Added to this, the ageing data based on bone fusion is also very low, which again is probably a result of dogs destroying the diagnostic ends of long bones.

Table 4.21 shows the areas of the site according to the degree of completeness of minimum number of elements, using the number of zones present on any individual element as the measure of its completeness. The results are unequivocal: the further out from the core of the site, the more fragmented the bone is. This is confirmed by a proxy indicator of essentially the same phenomenon: the number of unidentifiable bone fragments. Table 4.22 clearly shows the percentage of unidentifiable bone increasing as one moves further from the core, suggesting it is more fragmented.

Roman Pottery (with Gwladys Monteil)

With *c.* 12,400 sherds recovered in total, the Roman pottery assemblage is large and composed of 11,946 stratified sherds, at a weight of 206.31 kg but with a relatively low EVEs (Estimated Vessels Equivalent) count of 144.45. As independent dating evidence (i.e. samian, stratified coins or well-dated pottery) is scarce and most of the deposits are not primary, the phasing was kept broad. Although a few groups can be dated as early as *c.* AD 60–90, the majority of the Roman pottery is of a late date and most of it belongs to the settlement's last two phases. The bulk of the assemblage is of a domestic nature, with the exception of the cremation and inhumation groups, plus a few potential 'ritually' deposited vessels.

For each context, the pottery was sorted by unique combination of fabric and form, then the sherds were counted and weighed and EVEs recorded (based on rims only). Unless stated otherwise, all weights are given in grams. The data were initially recorded on *pro-forma* recording sheets, later computerized. Each record had several field entries: vessel form (general and specific), fabric type, sherd count, weight, EVE, diameter, residues (e.g. limescale, burnt food) and functional class (e.g. storage, cooking, service or preparation), in addition to contextual fields (context, slot, feature, group and phase). Where possible, established form and fabric type series were used as references (Tomber & Dore 1998), while the local coarsewares were ascribed much broader generic types (to speed the recording).

A large part of the assemblage is made up of abraded and small to very small sherds, which makes the identification of forms quite difficult. The brokenness of the total assemblage is indeed high (82.69 sherds/EVEs), which reflects intense activity/redeposition and a paucity of primary contexts and groups. Several sherds were subjected to secondary use and had been reworked – as spindlewhorls and a counter – and/or perforated.

Unsurprisingly, the same patterns that occurred within the animal bone are repeated with the ceramics (Table 4.23). Using a similar measure of completeness, the pottery shows a clear trend to greater fragmentation away from the core, a pattern also shown by average sherd weight which, though affected by vessel size, is less variable than for animal bone.

Table 4.23: *Pottery fragmentation by Area (*EVE = Estimated Vessel Equivalent, calculated by percentage of rim as a proportion of the whole; **Completeness calculated by dividing EVE by MNV).*

Area	MNV	EVE*	Completeness**	Average wt.
A	3429	94.1	0.027	16.21
B	1275	29.26	0.023	14.59
C	406	7.92	0.020	14.48
D	100	1.28	0.013	5.65
E	293	6.76	0.023	16.39

Overviewing Survival and Depositional Patterns

Analysis of the quantity and condition of both the pottery and bone assemblages suggests something of the nature of waste disposal on site. Firstly, the greater amount of bone and pottery remained in the core where it was presumably consumed, suggesting that *there was no concerted attempt to remove rubbish out to the margins of the settlement*. Secondly, whatever attritional processes were affecting the finds, they were common to all types and probably relate to post-depositional factors such as weathering, trampling and other animal action. In short, it appears as if *the finds are in better condition at the core than the periphery* (i.e. less fragmented). This might seem a little unusual, as there would have been greater activity (e.g. movement and trampling) there than on the margins. Yet, given that rubbish did seem to stay in the core, some management would seem all the more imperative and, thus, it is possible that the material in the core was preserved from attrition by being kept away from areas of movement, such as the edges of the enclosure ditches. Indeed, there were high finds densities locked within the extant, buried Roman soil horizons, comparable if not higher to those recovered from cut features, suggesting that surface middening within the core was practised as much as discard into cut features (see Chap. 6, Fig. 6.52). In fact, deposition in cut features could well have largely been a by-product of middens being sited close to their edges, particularly in the case of ditches.

The various artefactual and environmental data from the site provide some key aspects by which to frame our understanding of the archaeology. While, as on most rural sites, preservation has been severely truncated through ploughing, there is sufficient evidence to sketch a general reconstruction of the lost upper horizon. Macroscopic plant remains and pollen both indicate an open, grassy and weedy landscape, created probably through human clearance as the settlement was established. In the late Iron Age, this area was much shadier and more shrubby. The old land surface from the Roman period was preserved in several places, chiefly in the site's broad central basin, where there was a buried soil and remains of cobbling and gravelled surfaces. In a few other places across the site – mainly west of the basin – similar surfaces/patches of gravelling occurred. Even if these have been truncated, it does not suggest there was much depth of soil cover over the core of the site. Indeed, the total soil sequence within the basin was only a metre thick. In the transition from Phase II to III, the dark earths that covered the core of the site seem to have started to form; certainly, some of the late features cut through this horizon, which also infilled the upper part of earlier ditches and all of some of the later ditches. Although the dark earth has been characterized as primarily a creation of the background soil enhanced by carbonized organic fines, why this occurred remains ambiguous. Such enhancement may have had an agricultural purpose, as it clearly does on many sites, but it is hard to see how this could be the case here; *the dark earths formed while the site was still in use as a settlement*, and there is no evidence for any reuse of the site for arable farming until at least several centuries later. The creation of the dark earth at this site may, alternatively, have been a product of the deliberate scattering of ashes in order to keep the open ground in the settlement core as dry and well-drained as possible under increasingly wet ground conditions. Deposition of other cultural material – such as food waste and broken pottery – also seems to concentrate in the core, suggesting surface middens and the use of defunct ditches as locales for rubbish disposal.

Notes

1 Later prehistoric and Roman findings were, though, known from the areas above the site at both Gravel Hill Farm and in the Observatory's grounds. At the latter this included Iron Age wares from the first construction of the Hoyle Building in 1909 (CUMAA 1944.131) and Roman pottery found by A.F.G. Griffith in 1878 (Babington 1883, 36; CUMAA 1934.866C). That said, Liller reported no findings when he inspected a sewer trench dug between the Observatory and Madingley Road (1966); see the Kavli Institute investigations outlined below.

2 Three trenches were also dug along the line of the Marconi Building access route (Lucas 2001); these just exposed one feature of potentially early date. Located just south of the main site's eastern margin, this shallow southwest–northeast-oriented ditch was unfortunately undated. In 2006, only very limited evaluation trenching occurred within the parking lot west of the Cavendish in advance of the construction of the Physics for Medicine Building; no archaeology was forthcoming (Timberlake & Patten 2006).

3 See Sorbel (2016, 198–201) on Celia Helena Payne (1900–79). The first person ever to earn a PhD in astronomy at Harvard (concerned with the temperature of stars), she

arrived there from Cambridge (UK) having 'converted' to astronomy upon hearing Eddington lecture on his 1919 Principe investigations. Working at the (old) Cavendish Laboratory and a member of Newnham, on pursuing astronomy she apparently arranged to have the College's then long-unused observatory reopened.

4 See Guillbaud 2006, 168 concerning the immediate area's nineteenth-century occupancy and population dynamics.

5 Since this contribution was drafted, colluvium has been widely encountered on a number of sites within the region, especially in the south of the County (see *RVS*, chap. 6). Significant hillwash deposits were also widely present at the North West Cambridge sites and were subject to detailed investigation.

6 The average per sq. m finds densities recovered from the basin's dark earth horizon (F.5033) – 15 pieces of bone and 23 pottery sherds – would compare with the values within most of Langdale Hale's surface middens (Evans *et al.* 2013b, table 2.5). While the general densities of bone within the spreads associated with Haddenham's Snow's Farm shrine were similar, its overall pottery levels were significantly lower (Evans & Hodder 2006b, 353–4, fig. 7.24; see also, e.g., Ashwin & Tester 2014, 177–91).

7 Full taxonomic listings are provided in Lucas and Whittaker 2001.

8 One, F.5430, only had 62 sherds but, as it was only section-excavated, its estimated total would be 186; if entirely dug, some 594 sherds should have been present in F.5280.

9 When compared to Table 4.17 values, the reduced number given here omits the many scraps and small splinters counted in the main finds catalogue entries.

Figure 5.4. *Photograph of finds in pit F.5500.*

century AD, but this only gives a very broad late date for the removal of the post. More secure is the later cutting of a well in the mid third century AD (see below, F.5280), which clipped one of the postholes. Using this to mark the abandonment of the Aisled Building assumes that the well could not be inside the structure. If the well does presume the abandonment of the building, then the latter only stood for about a century (i.e. AD 120–230) and, thereafter, this whole space remained empty until the mid fourth century AD, when ditch F.5006 cut through this area. Given that this space seems to have been a prime part of the settlement, it seems unlikely that it would not have been used, especially given the amount of surrounding activity. It therefore seems more likely that the building stood right through into the early part of Phase III and until ditch F.5006 was cut. This means either that the well was somehow incorporated into the building or that the building was shortened, so only its southern half remained standing. Certainly the number of subsidiary postholes around the southern end suggests that the building was repaired or maintained over time. Thus, it seems likely that the building remained standing in some form or another for two centuries rather than one.

A phosphate survey was conducted over the building's area on a 2.5 m grid; although later features contaminated much of the area, the signals did not register particularly highly in terms of the site background (Fig. 5.3). As Middleton observed: "If, for instance, the barn had been used for stock-keeping, one would anticipate much higher levels than have been revealed by the analysis. The levels observed are more consistent with a general reflection of the high phosphate levels in the area".

Only 15 fragments of animal bone were recovered from the Aisled Building, all unidentifiable apart from two isolated and loose molar teeth, one from a cow and another from a horse. This situation is not altogether surprising, as it is assumed that the bone fragments either formed part of the original post-packing or part of the backfill of the postholes once the building was abandoned.

Pit Group

A group of pits (G2.04) cut just outside and to the south of the G2.03 division (and post-dating it) may be associated with the Aisled Building (G2.01; see Fig. 5.1). Varying from 0.4–2.65 m across and 0.26–0.6 m deep, they contained a large amount of ceramics in their backfill, which suggest a date of *c.* AD 90–140 (Fig. 5.4).

The pit group produced only 39 fragments of animal bone. The majority were unidentifiable (74%). The identifiable bone consisted of the remains of cow, sheep, horse and chicken, which on inspection could only be interpreted as domestic refuse as they were all 'classic' waste bones and very fragmentary in nature.

Two pit contexts were examined for plant remains; each is of quite different composition. Pit F.5500 included moderate charred remains – six items per litre of soil – that are primarily of glume wheat chaff with a number of wild seeds, but little grain. The seeds were mainly arable weed types, but there was also a noticeable range of wet ground taxa: rush (*Juncus* sp.), spike-rush (*Eleocharis* sp.) and sedge types (*Carex* spp.). These could represent a damp area of arable, or non-arable charred plant remains mixed in with the crop-processing debris. Low quantities of small artefacts, including burnt flint and an eggshell fragment, indicate that other sources

Table 5.1. *Pottery vessels from Pit Group (G2.04).*

Form	Wt.	%	EVEs	%
Bowl	2	0.02	0.05	1.65
Cup	14	0.16	0.16	5.28
Dish	42	0.47	0.10	3.30
Jar	3745	41.72	2.37	78.22
Morataria	550	6.13	0.10	3.30
Storage Jar	4521	50.36	0.20	6.60
Unid	103	0.85	0.05	1.65
Total	*8977*	*100.00*	*3.03*	*100.00*

of material are represented. The second pit, F.5651, was lacking in all charred and small artefactual material other than a little small charcoal. Waterlogged seeds indicate an open area of rough grassland, including buttercups (*Ranunculus acris/bulbosus/repens*) and creeping cinquefoil (*Potentilla reptans*). One uncharred glume base is the only direct evidence for human activity. This context appeared quite clean in contrast to pit F.5500, suggesting that quite different formation processes have shaped the remains. Either the pits were for different purposes, or their setting was quite different: one close to sources of artefactual debris and the other in a much 'cleaner' area.

The associated pottery assemblage is dominated by food preparation and storage vessels (jars, storage jars, mortaria), with only small numbers of tablewares (dishes, bowls and cups; Fig. 5.4; Table 5.1).

Roundhouse

In the southwest corner of the settlement enclosure were the ephemeral traces of an eavesgully (F.5081), almost certainly associated with a roundhouse (G2.19; Fig. 5.1). Some 5 m in diameter, this was 0.33 m wide and 0.15 m deep and only survived on its western side, the rest being ploughed out (see Fig. 5.1). A single sherd of undiagnostic Romano-British pottery was the only find from this slight feature.

The Timber Shrine

Adjacent to the Aisled Building lay a ring of postholes associated with pits and an enclosure ditch (G2.02; Figs. 5.5–6). Interpreted as a shrine (see below), the post-circle described a diameter of 3.8 m, made up of 11 main posts (0.3–1.08 m diam., 0.1–0.4 m deep), with a number of subsidiary posts. Three of the western postholes had packing stones of lava quernstone (F.5507, F.5517 & F.5491). Only one, F.5492, had dateable ceramics, with four sherds broadly attributable to AD 45–120. A cluster of pits lay along the western side of the post-circle in its earliest use. Ranging from *c.* 1–3 m across and 0.1–1.5 m deep, these may have been initially dug for the sandy silts to use in daub preparation, although better clays could have been extracted only *c.* 30 m away to the south. Whatever their initial purpose, they were backfilled with rich midden material incorporating ceramics dating to *c.* AD 80–160. After the backfilling of this pit group, an enclosure ditch (F.5522) was cut around the northern side of the post-circle (1.06 m wide and 0.43 m deep). Most of the ceramics in this ditch were undiagnostic in terms of a date, except for being generally 'early'. One group post-dated *c.* AD 240 ([3037]), but this material probably came from its upper fill.

Phosphate mapping was conducted across the structure's area-footprint on a 0.5 m grid (Fig. 5.7). The results are not very significant. There is a slight fall-off in values on the eastern side, with slightly higher values around the southern and western side, but this may simply reflect preferential deposition of cultural material. Certainly, the quantity of charred plant remains seemed higher on the southern side than the north.

Little animal bone material was recovered and all the retrieved bone came from a number of intercutting pits (e.g. F.5512 & F.5472) and the larger pit, F.5519. Unfortunately, only 12 fragments of bone were recovered. The intercutting pits produced eight of these, of which it was possible to identify only one: a fragment of pelvis from a male sheep. The remaining faunal material from this period came from the large pit F.5519, numbering four fragments, all of which were identifiable as the fragmentary remains of cow (skull and femur), horse (femur) and sheep (tibia). All of the bone was in a fairly poor state of preservation, being fragmented and showing signs of carnivore gnawing: a state that fits with the interpretation of at least the pits having been backfilled with midden material. A similar assemblage was recovered from the ditch enclosing the shrine to the north, F.5522. Of the 13 fragments recovered from it, only three were identifiable: a single cow astragalus and a sheep 1st phalange and loose molar.

Five contexts were examined for plant remains (Table 5.2) and all the samples contained a high count-density for charred remains, although there is some variation in amounts within the shrine's ditches. It is unfortunate that two of the samples were very small (one litre), since their counts were subsequently low, although the density of charred remains is comparable to the larger samples. A charred by-product of crop-processing debris is suggested by the dominance of glume wheat chaff in all the contexts. The wild taxa are types associated with arable or disturbed land and are probably weeds of the harvested crop. The consistently high amounts of charred crop-processing waste suggest that a source of such debris existed nearby. Any related activity pattern seems to have been maintained between Phases I and II. The very high charred counts from pit F.1909 may represent a specific deposit of waste within this context, or that the feature acted as a trap for materials that were abundant on the surface. On the whole, there were much greater densities of material in the later, southern ditch F.5483 than the earlier, northern ditch F.5522.

The pottery from the timber structure (204 sherds, 3 kg) does not display any particular or unusual signature (see Table 5.3), except for an absence of drinking vessels. It shows a jar-dominated pattern, but with high quantities of dishes and an absence of beakers and flagons; there were only two sherds of samian.

Although there seems nothing particularly exceptional or 'special' about the structure's associated deposits (apart possibly from the early use of 'exotic' lava quernstones for post-packing), it is argued to have been some manner of shrine. Admittedly, its

Table 5.2. *Summary of charred remains associated with the Timber Shrine.*

Feature	Type	Phase	Sample litres	Grain No.	Chaff No.	Seed No.	Total per litre soil
F.1909	pit	I	10	88	457	110	65.50
F.5522	ditch	I–II	8	26	89	27	17.75
F.5522	ditch	I–II	1	1	16	2	19.00
F.5533	ditch	II	1	-	32	2	34.00
F.5483	ditch	I–II	12	16	382	19	34.75

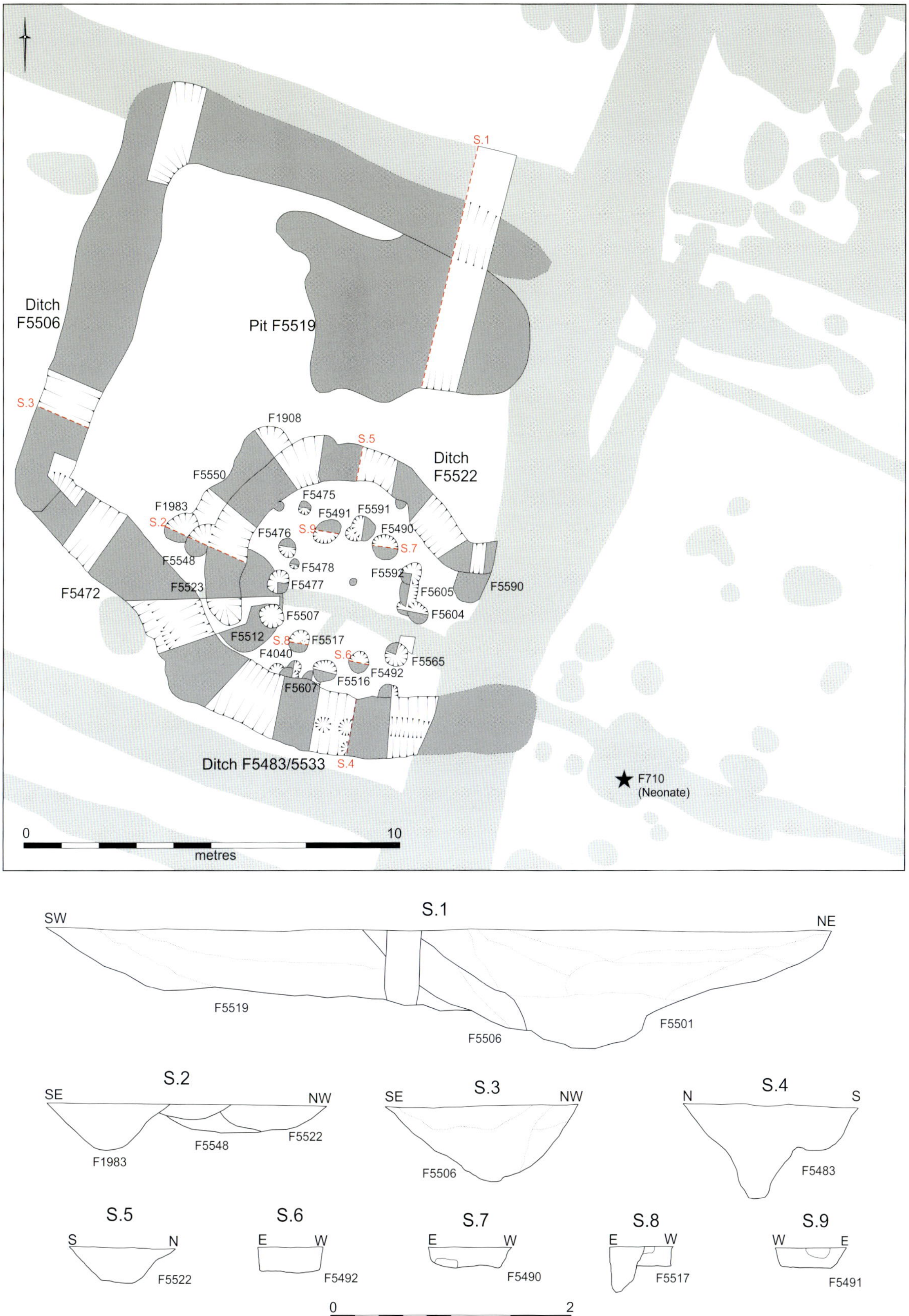

Figure 5.5. *Timber Shrine (G2.02).*

Figure 5.6. *Timber Shrine, pre-excavation and excavation-slot photographs (looking north and east, respectively).*

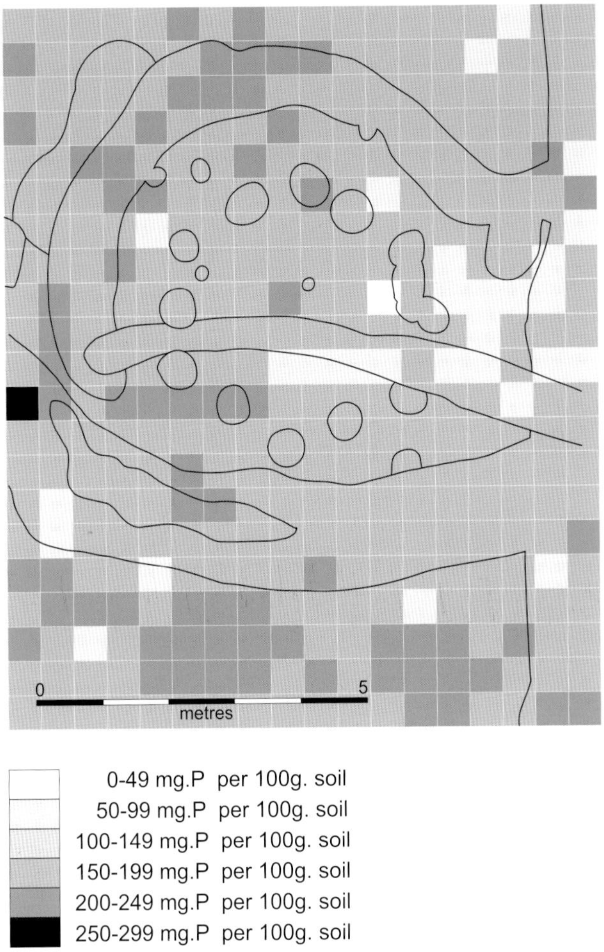

Figure 5.7. *Timber Shrine, phosphate readings.*

almost henge-like arrangement would not have direct parallels in Romano-British ritual architecture (see Chap. 6 for further discussion), yet its layout seems so extraordinary that it is difficult to ascribe it any kind of domestic function. Its upright posts would resonate with the settlement's Monumental Post that was erected southeast of it in Phase II, which clearly had ritual deposition associated (see below).

Table 5.3. *Summary of vessel forms associated with the Timber Shrine (Phase I).*

Forms	EVEs	%	Wt.	%
Bowl	0.05	5	15	0.5
Dish	0.29	29	326	11.1
Jar	0.49	50	1991	67.9
Lid	0.16	16	25	0.8
Beaker	-	-	9	0.3
Flagon	-	-	6	0.2
Mortarium	-	-	31	1.1
Storage Jar	-	-	529	18
Total	*0.99*	*100*	*2932*	*100*

Forecourt Area

An area between the Timber Shrine on the west, the Aisled Building to the south and the cremation cemetery to the north can be seen as a kind of forecourt or open space, and although fairly open, there were a few features occupying this swathe (G2.16; Fig. 5.1). Many of these are undated, either by associated finds or stratigraphy and, given that this space remained in use throughout all phases, their dating must remain ambiguous. A post-line ran north of the Aisled Building. It is undated, but by association it was probably contemporary with the building, providing a screen. This may suggest that the forecourt area was more closely associated with the shrine than it was with the Aisled Building. A group of pits occupied the edges of this open space. Beyond these, a number of unphased features are simply listed here: F.5529, F.5241, F.697, F.647, F.5278, F.600, F.598, F.5249, F.5248, F.5285, F.460 and F.5275 (not individually marked on Fig. 5.1).

The Cremation Cemetery (Cemetery 2)

A group of eight cremations and two infant inhumations were clustered within an area *c.* 3.5 × 4.5 m, close to, yet within the northern edge of the main settlement enclosure (G2.05; Fig. 5.8). The area around the cremations was distinct, in that a heavy spread of iron panning occurred only in that spot. This mineralization of the natural sands resulted in thick concretions around, and to some extent over, the burials, suggesting that it had formed after they had been interred. Above the panning was the colluvium, which had formed much later (see French, Chap. 4). It seems unlikely that this mineralization was unrelated to the cremations, given its localized nature, and it is therefore possible that it indicates the presence of a mound over the burials. Iron pan would have formed as groundwater came up and met a barrier of more resistant soil (i.e. the interface between the former land surface and the mound, perhaps of clayey soil). Due to subsequent ploughing, the mound would have disappeared and all that remained was the truncated area of iron panning, subsequently sealed by the hillwash. If a correct reading and the cemetery was mounded, this would not be common among the area's Early Roman burials (see e.g. Fox 1923, 191–200; Taylor in Lawson *et al.* 1981, 111). Indeed, it may relate to the cemetery's location within the settlement core: closing off the dead from later settlement life.

A magnetometry survey was carried out over part of the area and this revealed a major, discrete anomaly *c.* 15 m to the east of the burials (Fig. 5.8). There were no visible features, but it seems likely to represent an area of burning and has tentatively been identified as a ploughed out pyre site, especially as the visual effects of a pyre only penetrate to a shallow depth, *c.* 0.1 m (McKinley 1997, 65). About 3 m to the south of this was a large pit, F.5696 (*c.* 2.4 m diam., 0.5 m deep), with a very dark black-brown silty fill matrix and abundant charcoal and burnt stone inclusions. Centrally beneath it was smaller pit/posthole (F.5697; *c.* 0.6 m diam., 0.3 m

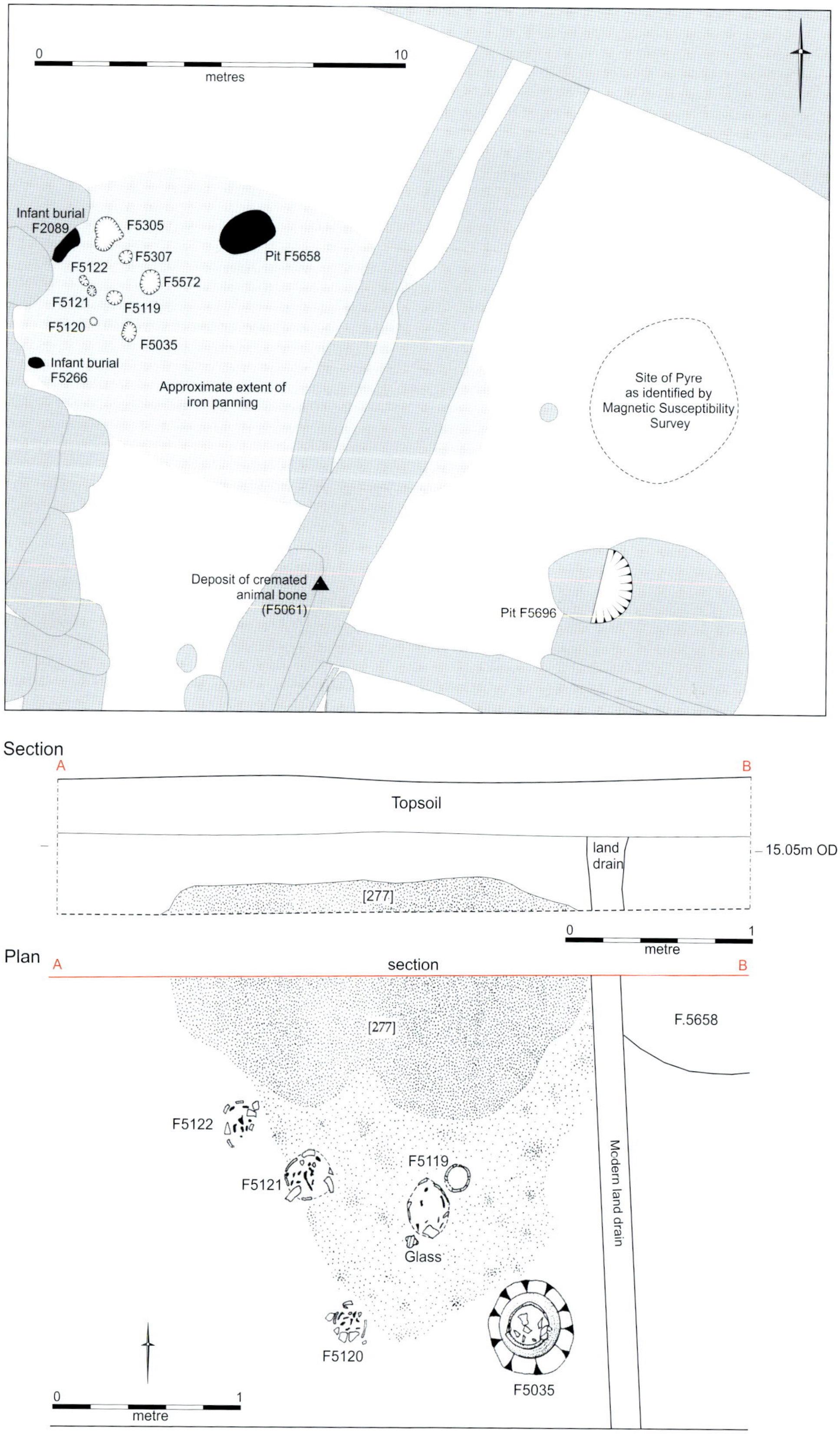

Figure 5.8. *Cremation cemetery (G2.05) and, below, surfaces exposed in evaluation trial-trenching.*

deep), backfilled with redeposited natural sandy silts and clay sealing a basal layer of pure charcoal. The only relation of these pits to the magnetic anomaly was one of spatial proximity, but the amount of burnt material in their fills was unusual and might suggest that they are related in some way to the pyre site. Pit F.5658 (0.48 m diam., 0.3 m deep) lay adjacent to the cremations but contained no cultural material.

Human Remains (with Natasha Dodwell)
There were eight cremation burials and two neonate inhumations within the cemetery. The degree of disturbance or truncation, the condition of the bone and, as important, which skeletal elements survive, affects the potential for determining the age and sex of individuals and of recognizing any pathological conditions. This is true for both cremations and inhumations, but in the former the quantity of observable bone and the fragment-size can contribute to the understanding of the ritual and of pyre technology. The cemetery has been disturbed by ridge-and-furrow, later ploughing and to a lesser degree machine-stripping prior to excavation. There is only one burial where the quantity of bone was not affected by truncation (F.5035; Fig. 5.9).

During excavation, the cremation burials and the fills surrounding the cremation urns were subject to 100 per cent recovery, as whole earth samples. Larger fragments of bone and those that appeared most fragile were collected and bagged separately to avoid additional fragmentation within the sample bag and during environmental processing. All these samples were wet-sieved and bone >2 mm was extracted for examination; the lesser residue was only scanned. A proportion of each sample was floated for the retrieval of environmental evidence. Only the F.5035 vessel could be lifted intact and this was excavated in the laboratory and its contents treated in the same way as the fills of the burial pits.

Grave-/pyre-goods were recovered during excavation on site and in the laboratory. Animal bone (predominantly cremated/burnt) was also separated during analysis. These animal bones should be seen as a minimum number, as many fragments were too small or undiagnostic to positively identify as either human or animal (see Clarke, below). General methods used in the osteological evaluation are those of Bass (1987), Buikstra *et al.* (1994) and Steele and Bramblett (1988). An assessment of age was based on the stages of epiphyseal union (McMinn & Hutchings 1988) and cranial suture closure. The following age categories are used:

foetus/neonate	<6 months
infant	0–4 years
juvenile	5–12 years
subadult	13–18 years
young adult	19–25 years
middle adult	26–45 years
mature adult	45 years +.

There may be overlaps between categories, or a broad category, such as 'adult', where insufficient evidence was present. The sex of the individual was ascertained where possible from sexually dimorphic traits on the pelvis and the skull and from metrical data. Where it has been allocated, it should be treated with caution, as only one or two traits will have been used.

Cremation 1 (F.5035; Fig. 5.9) - A complete jar contained a small flagon, which sat on top of the tightly packed cremated bone. A small iron object was recovered from just above the bone. Also inside the jar was a single sherd in a shell-tempered fabric. The deposit of bone was covered with a mid brown sandy silt with rare flecks of charcoal. The degree of firing is variable. Whilst some of the fragments are well-calcined, many – particularly the feet and lower limbs – are only scorched. Recognizable elements include skull, vertebrae, ribs, upper and lower limb bones, patellae and foot bones. Enthosopathies were recorded on the posterior of both calcanei and patellae. The largest fragment (tibia shaft) measures 126 mm.

Cremation 2 (F.5119) - A large (truncated) jar contained cremated bone. There were two accessory vessels (one glass and one ceramic). A small quantity of bone was recovered from the surrounding fill, but this is likely to have derived from the cremation urn. The majority of the bone fragments are a buff white colour. Identifiable elements include skull fragments, patella, carpals and upper and lower limb shafts. The largest fragment (femur shaft) measures 74 mm, but most are much smaller. Associated with the burial was burnt sheep bone (from a radius, plus 86 other unidentifiable fragments), a sherd and a single hobnail.

Cremation 3 (F.5120) - A severely truncated jar contained cremated bone, much of which, because of the degree of bone fragmentation, could not be identified. Identifiable fragments include skull, vertebra and lower arm shafts. The largest fragment measures 64 mm (an ulna shaft), although most are much smaller. There were 15 fragments of animal bone, but all are unidentifiable.

Cremation 4 (F.5121) - A heavily truncated jar contained cremated human bone. A small quantity of unidentifiable burnt bone was recovered from the fill around the pot, but this is likely to have derived from inside the vessel originally. From inside the pot identifiable fragments include skull, humerus and long bone shafts. The largest fragment (long bone shaft) measures 34 mm. Twenty-four fragments of sheep-sized animal bone occurred with the human remains, including a femur, vertebra and rib (plus 21 unidentifiable fragments), both burnt and unburnt.

Cremation 5 (F.5122) - A truncated jar contained very small fragments of calcined bone. A single sherd was also found. The fill surrounding the pot also contained bone fragments, which the excavator interpreted as not deriving from inside the pot. Identifiable fragments include transverse process and long bone shafts. The largest fragment (long bone shaft) measures 35 mm. Ten small fragments of unidentifiable, unburnt animal bone were retrieved.

Cremation 6 (F.5305; Fig. 5.10) - A large, truncated jar contained a flagon and cremated bone. A single sherd (burnt and abraded) also occurred. All the human bone fragments are well-calcined, with the exception of the mid femur shaft. Identifiable fragments include skull, upper and lower limbs including radial head (17 mm), pelvis, vertebrae, phalanges and patella. The largest fragment (femur shaft) is 61 mm. In addition to the human bone, a relatively large quantity of animal bone (sheep-sized and chicken) was identified: fragments from a sheep pelvis, sheep-sized ribs, a chicken femur, tibiotarsus and tarsometatarsus, and a bird bone shaft occurred, along with 107 unidentifiable pieces.

Cremation 7 (F.5307; Fig. 5.10) - An unurned burial was associated with two flagons and a jar placed on top of the cremated bone. The jar contained a few fragments of burnt bone and it may be that it had tipped over and spilled its contents. All the human bone fragments were well-calcined with the exception of some of the skull fragments. Recognizable fragments include skull, pelvis, upper and lower limbs (femur head, 39 mm), vertebrae, teeth and phalanges. Although the majority of fragments are adult, some immature skull fragments were identified. The largest fragment (skull) is 74 mm. Cremated animal bones also occurred, and included a chicken coracoid, a sheep-sized femur and 12 sheep-sized rib fragments, as well as 133 unidentifiable pieces.

Figure 5.9. *Cremation F.5035, lifted by Dodwell in the course of evaluation fieldwork and, below, as excavated in the CAU's offices.*

Figure 5.10. *Cremation photographs: F.5305 and F.5307 (top) and, below, F.5307 (left) and F.5572 (right).*

Cremation 8 (F.5572; Fig. 5.10) - A truncated vessel contained well-calcined cremated bone. There were four accessory vessels in the pit, which had been damaged by ploughing and a modern land-drain. Identifiable human bone fragments include skull, limb-bone shafts and vertebrae. The largest fragment (humerus shaft) is 54 mm. An iron nail, lump of molten glass and two fragments of cremated, sheep-sized rib bone were also recovered.

A small quantity of cremated human bone (20 g), including fragments of skull and limb bone shafts, was recovered from F.5083 in the evaluation (see Fig. 6.21). The osteological observations of the cremations, bone weights and associated finds are summarized in Table 5.4.

In addition to the cremation burials, two inhumations were present.

Burial 1 (F.5266; Fig. 5.11) - A well-preserved neonate burial found on the surface of the truncated subsoil when hand-cleaning the area. The child was lying on its left side, head to the east, the left arm was flexed with the hand below head, and both legs were flexed. Long

Table 5.4. *Summary of cremations.*

Cremation	**Age/sex**	**Human bone** (wt.)	**Animal bone** (wt.)	**Associated finds**	**Type**	**Accessory vessels**
1 (F.5035)	adult	1543 g	-	Fe object	urned	Flagon inside vessel
2 (F.5119)	subadult/young adult	616 g	23 g (sheep)	hobnail	urned	Small red vessel & glass vessel
3 (F.5120)	subadult/adult	23 g	- (unid.)	-	urned	None
4 (F.5121)	subadult/adult	104 g	20 g (sheep-size; charred & unburnt bone)	-	urned	None
5 (F.5122)	subadult/adult	50 g	<1 g (unid.; unburnt)	-	urned	None
6 (F.5305)	young/middle adult (?F)	808 g	86 g (sheep & chicken)	Fe nail	urned	Flagon inside vessel
7 (F.5307)	adult (?F) & juvenile/sub-adult)	1260 g	139 g (sheep-size & chicken)	Fe nail	un-urned	Two flagons and a small jar
8 (F.5572)	middle adult	370 g	3 g (sheep)	burnt glass, Fe nail	urned	

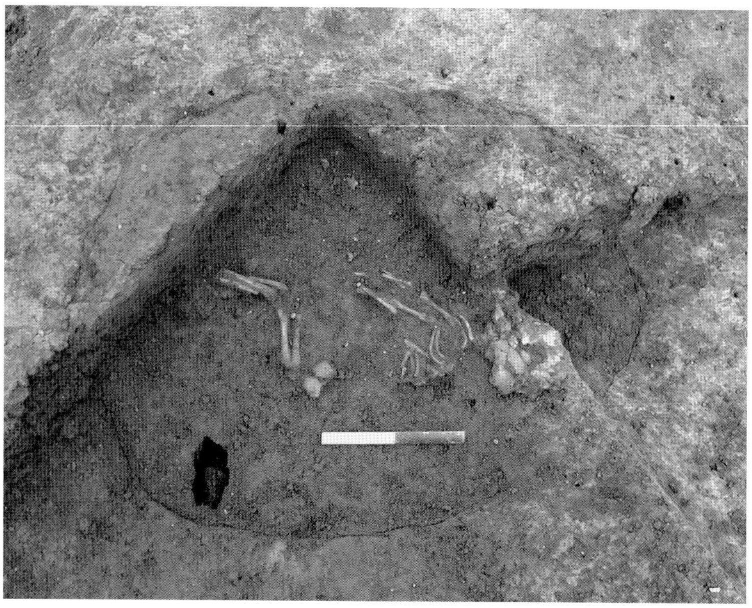

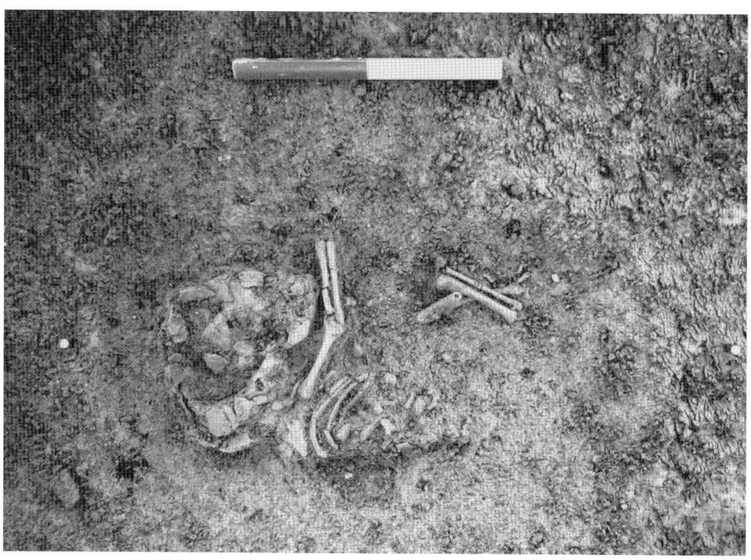

Figure 5.11. *Infant burials: F.2089 (top) and, below, F.5266.*

bone measurements suggest an age at death of 0–6 months, whereas dental development puts the age at birth ± 2 months.

Burial 2 (F.2089; Fig. 5.11) – A well-preserved neonate that lay on its right side, the legs were flexed, with the head to the west. The child is possibly slightly older than Burial 1; long bone measurements suggest an age of 0–6 months, whereas dental development puts the age at six months ±3 months. The body lay centrally within an oval grave cut, 0.73 × 0.56 × 0.25 m.

Faunal Remains (with Andy Clarke)

Cremated animal bone was recovered along with the human bone in seven of the eight cremations, during hand-excavation and wet-sieving, although it was only separated from the human remains during post-excavation. A large deposit of cremated bone also occurred in F.5061, possibly redeposited (see Fig. 5.8). The majority of the bone is bright white in colour, indicating burning at high temperatures. Consequently, the bone is highly fragile and was recovered in a very fragmentary condition; any figures quoted for the cremated animal bone should, therefore, be taken as a minimum. Due its condition, it was not possible to age or sex any of the bone.

The majority of the cremated animal bone is in a highly fragmented state and is unidentifiable. It was only possible to confidently identify two species, sheep and chicken (see Table 5.4). The remaining bone fragments were classified as sheep-sized or bird species; one cannot rule out the possibility of other species being present, but from their size and conformation it is likely that these fragments also originate from sheep and chicken.

The sheep- and sheep-sized bones include the fragmented remains of the femur, radius, pelvis and vertebrae, but are mainly ribs. The chicken remains are limited to the elements of the back leg (femur, tibiotarsus and tarsometatarsus). It is worth noting the indiscriminate preservation that occurs in cremations as evidenced by the preservation of more fragile ribs than any other sheep remains and by the absence of more robust elements, such as the phalanges or the petrous (part of the skull) bone. However, it should be noted that it is also possible that these species may not have been introduced to the cremations as whole animals but as dressed cuts of meat.

The fragmentary nature and small size of the cremation assemblage has hampered its analysis somewhat, but those bones that have been identified seem to fit in with the accepted patterns of animal bone associated with human cremations at this time. During the Roman period the most commonly identified animals in cremations are pig, bird species and sheep, and there also appears to be a trend to limit any species included to a maximum of two. This pattern was identified at the Eastern Cemetery of Roman London, where pig and chicken were most common, with the remains seen as dressed cuts of meat rather than whole animals (McKinley 2000b–d). In terms of the animal bones then, it would seem that the cremations at Vicar's Farm fall into the category of fairly 'classic' Roman cremations. The only two species present are represented by the possible remains of dressed joints of meat, which were either included with the actual human cremation or were the remains of ceremonial feasting thrown into the cremation fire.

The Pottery (with Gwladys Monteil)

The eight cremations were associated with an estimated number of 17 vessels (including accessory and primary vessels; see Fig. 5.12). The two infant inhumations did not have any goods associated, but a sherd was found in the grave fill with Burial 2 (F.2089). The vessels were variously truncated, with the worst preserved from Cremations 2–5 (F.5119–22).

Cremation 1 (F.5035; Fig. 5.9) – Two vessels:

a) Small narrow-mouthed jar/flask (<3755>; 272 g, 1.00 EVEs), showing signs of wear/use; in a local coarse sandy greyware fabric (CSGR; Fig. 5.12.1); later first–third century AD.

b) Large, short-necked cordoned jar with a band of lattice decorations below the rim (<120>; 2 kg, 0.27 EVEs); in a local coarse sandy greyware fabric (CSGR; Fig. 5.12.2); second–third century AD.

A sherd in a shell-tempered fabric (SMSW) was also found in the fill of the jar.

Cremation 2 (F.5119) - Two vessels:

Flagon (27 g), in a buff-pink fabric (CSRE), reminiscent of Cherry Hinton/Greenhouse Farm-type wares (J. Evans 1990; Gibson & Lucas 2002); second century AD.

Jar (267 g), in a local coarse sandy grey fabric (CSGR); upper part truncated (Fig. 5.12.3). A sherd in a local sandy greyware with black-burnished surface was also found (CSBB); second–fourth century AD.

Cremation 3 (F.5120) - Jar (130 g), in a local coarse sandy greyware fabric (CSGR); upper part truncated (Fig. 5.12.5); second–fourth century AD.

Cremation 4 (F.5121) - Jar (179 g), in a local sandy grey ware (CSGR); upper part truncated (Fig. 5.12.6); second–fourth century AD.

Cremation 5 (F.5122) - Short-necked jar (16 sherds, 180 g, 0.12 EVEs), in a coarse local sandy grey ware (CSGR; Fig. 5.12.7). A sherd in a local sandy redware (CSRE) was also found (3 g); second–fourth century AD.

Cremation 6 (F.5305; Fig. 5.10) – Two vessels:

a) Everted jar (1629 g, 0.65 EVEs), in a local sandy grey ware (CSGR; Fig. 5.12.8); second–fourth century AD.

b) Devolved ring-necked flagon (470 g, 0.75 EVEs), with a chipped rim from use prior to deposition; in a local sandy grey ware (CSGR; Fig. 5.12.9); second century AD.

An abraded and burnt sherd from a mortarium was also recovered in this group.

Cremation 7 (F.5307; Fig. 5.10) – Three vessels:

a) Everted rim jar with burnished acute-lattice (118 g, 0.90 EVEs); in BB2 fabric (Fig. 5.12.10); second century AD.

b) Devolved ring-necked flagon (331 g, 0.75 EVEs), in a local coarse white fabric (CSWW; Fig. 5.12.11); second century AD.

c) Flagon (190 g), in a local coarse white fabric (CSWW); rim truncated (Fig. 5.12.12); second century AD.

Cremation 8 (F.5572; Fig. 5.10) – Five vessels:

a) Beaker (31 g), in a local fine grey ware (FSGR); second–third century AD.

b) Flagon (52 g), in coarse local white ware (CSWW); second century AD.

c) Devolved ring-necked flagon (232 g, 1.00 EVEs), in coarse local white ware (CSWW; Fig. 5.12.13); second century AD.

d) Dr.36 dish (231 g, 0.70 EVEs) in Central Gaulish Samian (CGSM; Fig. 5.12.14); second century AD.

e) Reeded flanged bowl (607 g, 0.90 EVEs) in a coarse white slipped ware (CSWS; Fig. 5.12.15); second–third century AD.

The Glass H.E.M. Cool

Cremation 2 (F.5119) - Bath flask (Fig. 5.12.4 & 6.38.5). Blue/green; many bubbles some large. Rim, neck, handle and 12 body fragments, two pairs of body fragments joining. Rim bent out, up, in and flattened, convex-curved side, probably slightly squashed spherical body; loop-handle applied to shoulder, trailed partially up neck, bent back down to shoulder with return trail running up handle. Small part of return trail of second handle on neck below rim. Rim diameter 30 mm, present height (rim fragment) 32 mm, wall thickness 1.5–2.5 mm (SF 114).

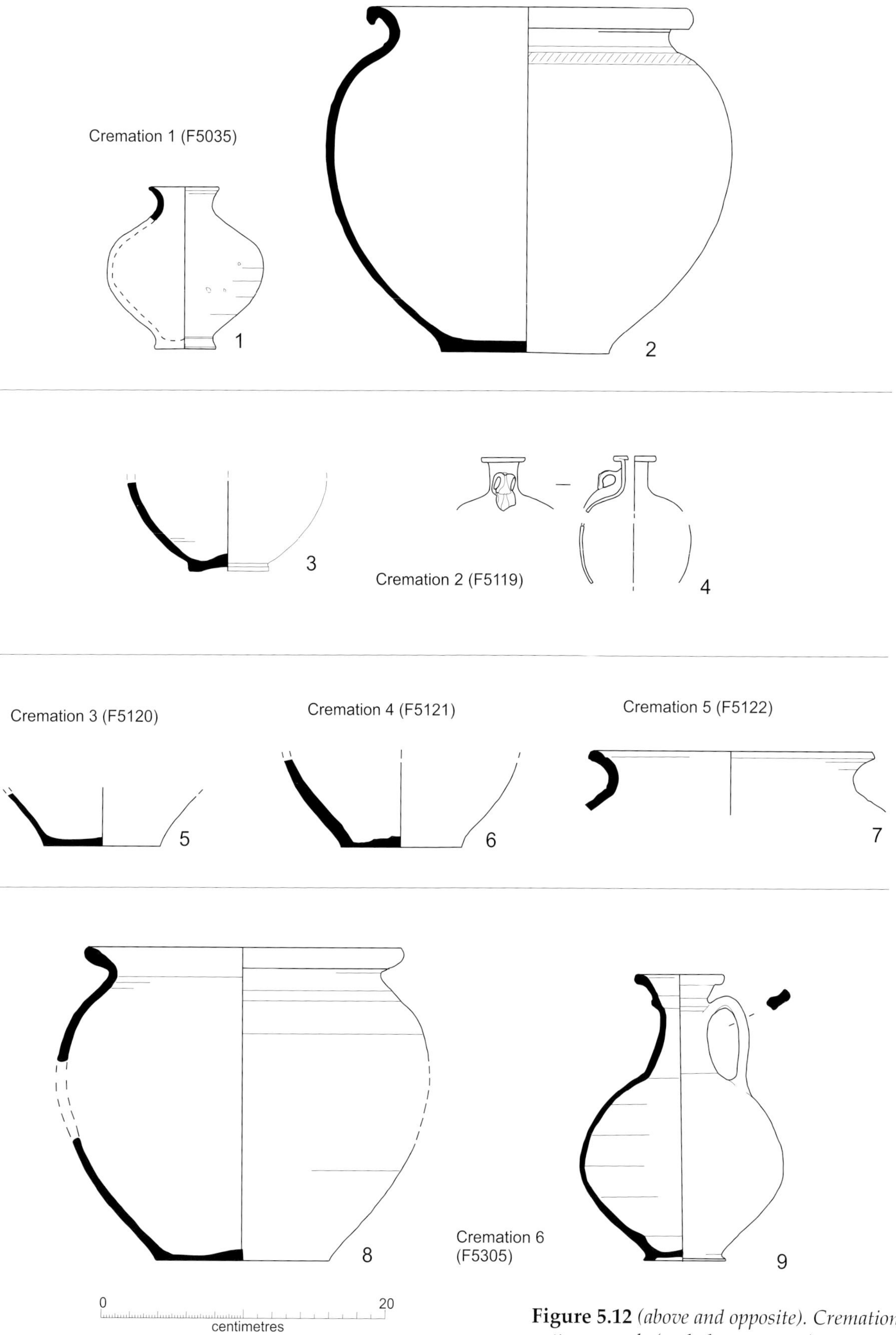

Figure 5.12 *(above and opposite). Cremation pottery vessels (and glass; see text).*

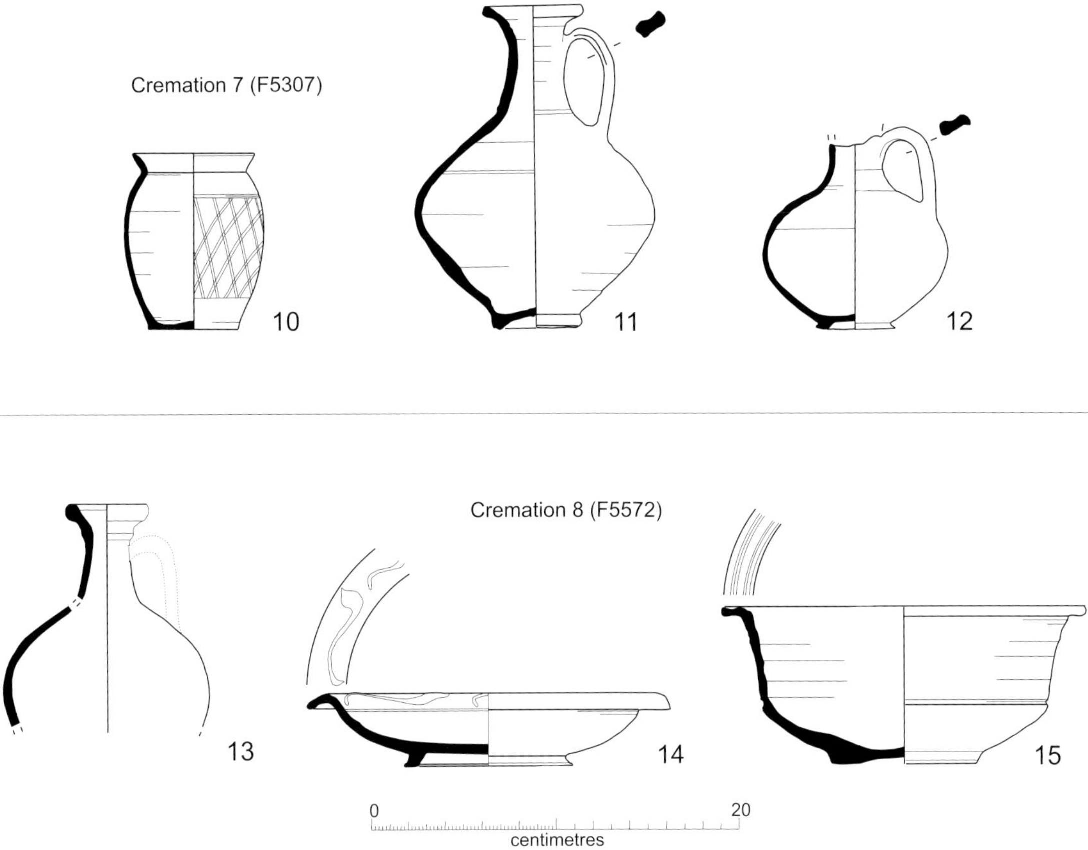

Figure 5.12 *(cont.).*

Bath-flasks were in use from the mid to later first century to the mid third century AD (Ising 1957 Form 61; Price & Cottam 1998, 188–90). It is not possible to date this example closely within that period, though it may be noted that the form does not become a frequent find until late in the first century AD. They are not as common in graves as other forms of unguent bottle but served the same role (i.e. to hold oil that was used either to anoint the body prior to burial/cremation) or, perhaps, to pour over the cremation pyre before or after it had been fired. Where they are found intact, as in the case of one from a cremation burial at Shoebury *(VCH Essex,* 179), then either function could be possible. In the case of the example from this burial, however, it seems likely that the contents were used at an early stage of the funerary rite. The extreme bubbliness of the glass makes it clear that all of the fragments were from the same vessel, but though a substantial part of it is present, much is missing and few of the fragments join. Clearly the vessel had been broken and only a sub-set of the fragments chosen for incorporation into the grave. There is no overt evidence of melting as might have been expected if it had been used as a pyre-good. One of the fragments, however, does have the sort of sinuously curving jigsaw-like fracture that can result from heat shattering. Similar features were noted on a bath-flask from a mid third-century AD cremation burial at Brougham, Cumbria, where there was evidence that pottery vessels were regularly placed to the side of the pyre (Cool 2004, 366). It was suggested that the bath-flask there might have been placed in a similar position after the contents had been used. Something similar may have happened here as well.

Overview (with Natasha Dodwell)

Of the eight cremation burials examined, three were identified as adult, four as subadult/adult and one as a dual cremation containing the bones of an adult and a juvenile/subadult. No neonates or infant cremation burials were identified. The remains of immature individuals, particularly neonates are under-represented in all archaeological periods (see, though, *RVS*, 154–70, fig. 4.25), in both cremation and inhumation cemeteries, and differential burial practices and/or their fragility are usually cited as explanations of their absence. In the later Roman period there is a strong association between neonatal/infant burials and buildings, and at Vicar's Farm there are examples of such practices (see Chap. 6, Note 10). Although extremely fragile, neonate and infant bone *does* survive the cremation process, both archeologically and in modern crematoria. For example, in the late Iron Age cemetery at King Harry Lane, Herts., Stirland (1989, 242) recorded three neonate cremation burials and at Westhampnett, Sussex, McKinley (1997, 64) identified a 3–6-month-old infant. Finding references to cremated neonates in the Romano-British period is far more difficult, although in the unpublished findings from St Stephens, Herts., two foetus/neonates were identified amongst the cremation burials (McKinley 1992). Two neonate skeletons, F.5266 and F.2089, were found within the group of cremations at Vicar's Farm. Given their proximity to the cremations (all lie within an area of *c.* 4 sq. m), and without dating evidence, the assumption has been made that they are contemporary with the cremation burials. Philpott (1991, 101) noted that both Pliny and Juvenal testify to the practice in Italian cities of inhuming rather than cremating infants 'before the age of teething' and it would seem that differential burial practice, rather than truncation or fragility, is the more likely explanation for the absence of cremated neonates/infants at Vicar's Farm.

Two burials were tentatively sexed as female and one of these, F.5307, has been identified as a dual cremation: immature skull fragments were found commingled with the adult remains and it is possible that many of the unidentifiable bone fragments derive from the younger individual. Burials comprising dual cremations most commonly include an adult and an immature individual (see e.g. Millett & Gowland 2015).

The weights of human bone recovered from each burial range from 23 to 1543 g (see Table 5.4). Observations at modern crematoria (McKinley 1993) have shown that the weight range of collectable (>2 mm) cremated bone expected from an adult cremation is *c.* 1000–2400 g, with an average of *c.* 1650 g. Only two burials have bone weighing over 1000 g (F.5035 & F.5307), but the low bone weights of the other burials are probably the result of severe disturbance/truncation. It should also be noted that burial F.5035, with 1543 g of bone, is unique on the site, in that the urn was complete and all the bones that were originally interred could be analysed. Feature 5307 contained the remains of two individuals, which possibly accounts for the increased bone weight.

Bone fragment-size is dependent on several factors: the cremation process itself, collection from the pyre, excavation and post-excavation treatment (McKinley 1994a). The bones from F.5035 were considerably larger and the skeletal elements more complete than those in the other burials, but this is probably because the urn has protected them; also, many of the elements are only charred and so less fragile. The fragment-size of the bone from the burials at Vicar's Farm is within the normal range observed (*ibid.*) and there is nothing to suggest any deliberate fragmentation.

Only very occasional fragments of wood charcoal were recovered from the burials and there was a notable absence of what McKinley describes as redeposited pyre debris in the grave fills (2000a, 41–2). Whilst the absence of pyre material within the burials could be the result of severe truncation, it is as likely to be genuine and reflect the burial ritual. The magnetic anomaly and pits F.5696/F.5697 may be a more likely location for the pyre site, which is some distance from the burial pits (*c.* 15 m). Philpott has suggested that 'the great majority of cremations were carried out on pyres away from the final burial site' (1991, 8) and the absence of any pyre debris in the graves supports this.

The efficiency of cremation is reflected primarily in the colour of the bone (Shipman *et al.* 1984), with fully oxidized bone being a buff-white colour. With the exception of F.5035, the majority of human bone from the burials appears thoroughly cremated. In F.5035 the skeletal elements from the lower body, particularly the left side, are a mid brown/grey colour indicative of very poor firing. The posterior of the right proximal tibia shaft and inferior and lateral aspects of the left calcaneus are almost unburnt, with only small patches of black suggesting very little direct contact with the fire. Incomplete combustion is also demonstrated by the presence of a thin black, glassy residue on the articulating facets of the left calcaneus and talus, probably poorly fired cartilage. A large minority of black, blue and grey bone fragments are frequently noted in Romano-British cremation burials (McKinley 2000b) and may be the result of problems with time, temperature or oxygen supply of the pyre, or even reflect perceptions of what was considered 'complete' cremation (McKinley 1994a).

Pyre-goods, that is those items worn on the body, placed beside the body on the pyre or thrown onto it, were identified in six of the burials. These were recovered during sieving and should be seen as a minimum number, firstly because many artefacts would not survive the cremation process and secondly, because not everything would necessarily have been collected from the pyre site.

Burials containing cremated animal remains are not unusual in the Romano-British period, although the percentage on sites varies considerably: at Westhampnett (McKinley 1997) only 3.5 per cent of the Romano-British burials contained animal bone, whereas at the East London Cemetery half did (Barber & Bowsher 2000, 75). While the group at Vicar's Farm is small, five burials (62.5%) contained some cremated animal bone, which is a relatively high proportion of the burials. The animals identified, sheep and chicken, are amongst the commonest animals to be found in Romano-British cremations (Philpott 1991, 196). A single hobnail was recovered from burial F.5119, a subadult/young adult (Cremation F.2084 in the inhumation cemetery to the south also contained a hobnail).

Finds of single hobnails in graves are not uncommon and have been recorded at Harlington (Dawson 2001, 32), in two instances at King Harry Lane (Stead & Rigby 1989, 111) and in three of London's Eastern Cemetery's cremations (Barber & Bowsher 2000, 68). A single lump of burnt glass (6 g), unidentifiable as a vessel, was recovered from Cremation 8 (F.5572). Its amorphous shape suggests that the temperature of the pyre reached at least 700°C (McKinley 1994b, 84). The nails found in three of the cremations (and from burial F.2084) are likely to have derived from coffins, caskets or biers placed on the pyre, or possibly from reused timbers used in the pyre.

Based on the pottery that accompanied the cremations, it is reasonable to ascribe the cemetery to the second century AD, which is entirely in keeping with what is known of the period's burial practices (e.g. Philpott 1991; Pearce 2013, 37–8).

The Southern Fields (Areas B/C/D)

The areas defined as B, C and D do not properly exist at this date, although a ditch system was cut that traversed all the land later occupied by them (see Fig. 5.1).

Southern Sub-enclosure

A small square enclosure (Gl) lay on the southern end of the main settlement enclosure by the entrance. Defined by ditches F.5509 (1.4 m wide and 0.5 m deep), F.5495 (0.75 m wide, 0.15 m deep) and F.5115 (1.2 m wide, *c.* 0.45 m), with the western return either ploughed out or truncated/masked by the later F.5431 of G19. Running across the opening of this enclosure, but offset, was ditch F.5434 (0.95 m wide, 0.16 m deep), which seemed to deflect or control access in and out to either side. On the southwest edge of this enclosure lay well F.5595 (2.6 m diameter, 1.05 m deep; see Fig. 5.1); three wells or cut waterholes lay in this area, the earliest being F.5595, an adjacent one (unexcavated) and, finally, F.5474 (3.4 m diam., 1.85 m deep; AD 140–240).

This small enclosure (Gl) with the wells/waterholes probably related to stock management of some nature, and was linked to a larger, more open ditch system (G3). Ditch F.5385 (variously 0.4–1.8 m wide, 0.1–0.4 m deep) ran off the Gl enclosure and toward its southern end, curving round to leave its western side open. This was possibly used to herd and direct stock up into the smaller Gl enclosure and may have been more relevant for horses than other stock, such as cattle or sheep. Broadly contemporary with this were a series of regular linear ditches that 'squared' off this open field. Running along the outer edge of the southern side of the large curving ditch was a slighter gully, F.5384 (0.5–0.9 × 0.3 m), and on the western side, gully F.5351 (1 m wide and 0.15 m deep). The eastern side is rather ambiguous, but a number of parallel gullies ran north–south, some of which may have related to this system; alternatively, they may simply be late furrows (not marked on Fig. 5.1, these are F.8243 east, 0.45–0.8 m wide, 0.1–0.2 m deep and F.8237/8170/8171 west, 0.5–1.2 m wide, 0.1–0.3 m deep; also F.5594 and F.5429, 0.45 m wide, 0.12 m deep). At the tip of the curvilinear ditch F.5385 was a pit, F.5388 (0.8 × 0.2 m; not labelled on Fig. 5.1), and several tree-throws. There seems to be some continuity between this system and the pre-settlement enclosure (see Chap. 4) as there was also a well/waterhole in the same location (F.5610), and it may be that this was a reorganization of the same kind of enclosure system.

Seemingly comparable to the probable roundhouse located in the southwest corner of the main enclosure (F.5081; G2.19), here F.5402 probably also represents a surviving short length of an eavesgully.

The Northern Fields (Area E)

Accessing the settlement's northern entrance, the key features outlined in this section are the two roads/trackways. The more major (and 'road-like') ran northwest, while the other had an east–west orientation (Fig. 5.1).

Trackways/Roads

Running down from the northwest to the northern entrance of the main settlement enclosure was a wide road/trackway (No. 2/G5; Fig. 5.1), defined by parallel ditches *c.* 11 m apart (F.5176, 1.3–3.8 m wide, 0.4–0.8 m deep) and F.5596 (2–3.6 m wide, 0.3–0.5 m deep) with possible remnants of metalling in the form of gravels (F.5616) surviving at the northern edge of the site. This would seem to form a major route to and from the site, perhaps linking it to another settlement on Madingley Rise. Another routeway may have existed on the eastern edge of the site, though the traces were slight. There, a single shallow ditch (F.5676, 0.6 m wide and 0.1 m deep) met the terminal of the G5 trackway, and this has been interpreted as one side of another road/trackway (No. 3/G8) leading eastward out of the northern entrance of the settlement. There were a lot of silty gravels in this zone, and while they did not have the appearance of a prepared surface, it is not impossible that they were.

A sample from F.5176 produced only small amounts of plant remains, mainly glume wheat chaff, and suggests that this lay on the periphery of processing activities.

Eastern Side of the Trackway

Between the trackway (G5) and main settlement enclosure (G2), a small parcel of ground (*c.* 500 sq. m) was demarcated by a segmented ditch-line (G7; F.5609/F.5626/F.5630, 0.35–0.95 m wide and *c.* 0.1 m deep; Fig. 5.1). No firmly dated material was associated with this ditch, but on stratigraphic and relational grounds it must have been early. In form, the ditches are similar to those inside the enclosure on the west side (G2.03). Waterlogged plant remains came from F.5626 indicating cleared land but with scrubby vegetation. The feature was devoid of any charred remains. Outside this boundary a number of features occurred, which may indicate some occupation north/west of the site. Apart from five postholes (0.24–0.7 m diam., 0.12–0.54 m deep), the features consisted of gullies and pits (0.33–1.6 m across and 0.13–0.3 m deep; both G6) and are undated except by association with this enclosure. Only one feature had closely datable ceramics, F.5638 (AD 80–180).

Phase II (AD 180–270)

In this phase the settlement underwent major expansion to the south, contemporary with the establishment of a fieldsystem. In the core-area, the cremation cemetery went out of use and the Aisled Building was probably altered, while the eastern side of the settlement saw the establishment of new features (Fig. 5.13).

It needs to be stressed that the manner in which the settlement's burial activity has been phased, with the northern cremation cemetery assigned to Phase I and the southern inhumation cemetery to the final phase – with just the latter's central cremation assigned to Phase II – is essentially arbitrary. Though reflecting the little dating evidence that is available, in all likelihood there was overlap. Conceivably, some of the burials in the cremation cemetery could have dated to the last decades of the second century AD, if not later, just as the southern cemetery's inhumations might well date from at least the early–mid third century AD.

The Core Settlement – Main Enclosure (Area A)
The eastern side of the main enclosure (G2) was recut/cleaned out by F.4821 (1 m wide, 0.14 m deep; dated AD 240–300), and it would seem that this boundary was probably maintained until the end of the third century AD (Fig. 5.13). Running eastward from the southern limit of the enclosure was ditch F.5736 (1.2–2.4 m wide, 0.2–0.9 m deep; dated AD 140–270) that linked up with the southeastern corner of the main enclosure (F.5499; 2.95 m wide, 0.3 m deep; dated AD 190–230). This would seem to form part of a larger fieldsystem (G23) coming off the settlement core, which was subsequently infilled as the settlement expanded. Hanging off this southern boundary were a number of smaller enclosures, whose gullies (F.8084 & F.8002) were later recut by two semi-closed rectangular enclosures, F.8142 and F.5733 (dated AD 240+).

A neonate burial F.8087 was found on the far east of the site in a pit/posthole, although an ephemeral one (Figs. 5.13–14). Dating evidence was absent, but by association, it would seem more likely to be Phase II than Phase III, possibly associated with sub-enclosure F.5733. In the far west of the site there was another isolated burial, inhumation F.5329, a young adult male with his head to the northeast. Again, there is no direct dating evidence and the burial could belong to any phase. This is unfortunate, as the date of its deposition has potentially significant consequences for the site's interpretation, as in Phase III it would have lain inside the settlement enclosure, but in Phases I and II, outside. Dodwell notes of the burial:

> *Skeleton F.5329; Young adult male* - The skeleton was cut by a Post-Medieval posthole (F.5330), which contained some disarticulated material. The skeleton was moderately preserved, but fragmentary; the middle and lower part of the body were truncated/disturbed by a later posthole, F.5330. The body would seem to have been supine and extended, with its head to the northeast of the grave. No real grave cut was identifiable. Lines of enamel hypoplasia were recorded on the mandibular canines, indicating an episode of childhood stress between the ages of three and six years. A large caries on the distal aspect of the left 2nd maxillary premolar and slight deposits of calculus were recorded on the buccal surfaces of the *anterior* dentition.

Approximately 18 m to the north (within the main core settlement ditch and just east of the roundhouse; Fig. 5.14), the anterior portion of a right adult mandible was recovered from the upper fill of a Post-Medieval ditch (F.5058) during the evaluation stage (Tr.7). This could have come from another inhumation in the close vicinity and been redeposited in the ditch through ploughing.

The Interior
The internal organization of the main enclosure underwent some major re-structuring in this phase with more formal demarcations, most particularly a major division between the western and eastern sides as marked by ditches F.5583 and F.5579 (Fig. 5.13). On the western side, the whole area appeared devoid of features and all activity was focused in the eastern side. Within the eastern side, there was a main division marked by the course of a pathway (G2.07) running diagonally through the centre of the eastern half from the northern entrance. This was defined by ditches F.788 (2 m wide, 0.65 m deep; dated AD 140–300) and F.5309 (1.3 m wide, 0.5 m deep; dated AD 240/70–300).

West of Pathway
The reorganization of the internal space involved a much more regular, rectilinear system of internal ditches (G2.10). In the mid–late third century AD, the area around the Aisled Building and shrine was demarcated; flanking the western side of the Aisled Building was ditch F.5579 (*c*. 1.4 m wide and 0.34 m deep; AD 140–240/70), while to the north, ditch F.5583 (1.1 m wide, 0.35 m deep; dated AD 140–240) linked up with the new square enclosure around the shrine (see below). The area between the shrine and the cremation cemetery was demarcated by a multiple recut ditch that ran between F.5583 and a pathway (G2.07; see below). The primary ditch of this line was F.5220 (0.3 m wide, 0.2 m deep; dated AD 140–200/40), and recut by F.5227 (0.52 m wide, 0.19 m deep; AD 220+). Similar ditches were cut on the eastern side: F.5204 (1 m wide, 0.4 m deep; AD 240–300; see Fig. 5.18) and F.5295 (1.45 m wide, 0.3 m deep; AD 270+).

Fragments of human parietal bone, which from their size and sharp sutures probably derive from a subadult skull, were recovered from F.5204 ([531]; see Fig. 6.21). The proximity of these to the cremation cemetery may or may not be coincidental.

East of Pathway
Running up from the southern access was a linear metalled surface (G2.08; Fig. 5.13), with heavy cobbling at the entrance itself (F.5556; Fig. 5.15) and patches of finer gravels inside (F.4538, F.4714, F.4354 & F.5706; not indicated). It seems to have marked the line of a major through-route within the settlement up to the Curvilinear Enclosure, which occupied the east-central side of the settlement core (G2.11, see below). The closest dated ceramics from within the cobbling date to *c*. AD 200–80, while those from the finer gravel metalling date to *c*. AD 170–240. This suggests these surfaces were established at the very end of the second or in the early third century AD; in other words, some time after the establishment of the settlement and were perhaps created in response to worsening ground conditions, as

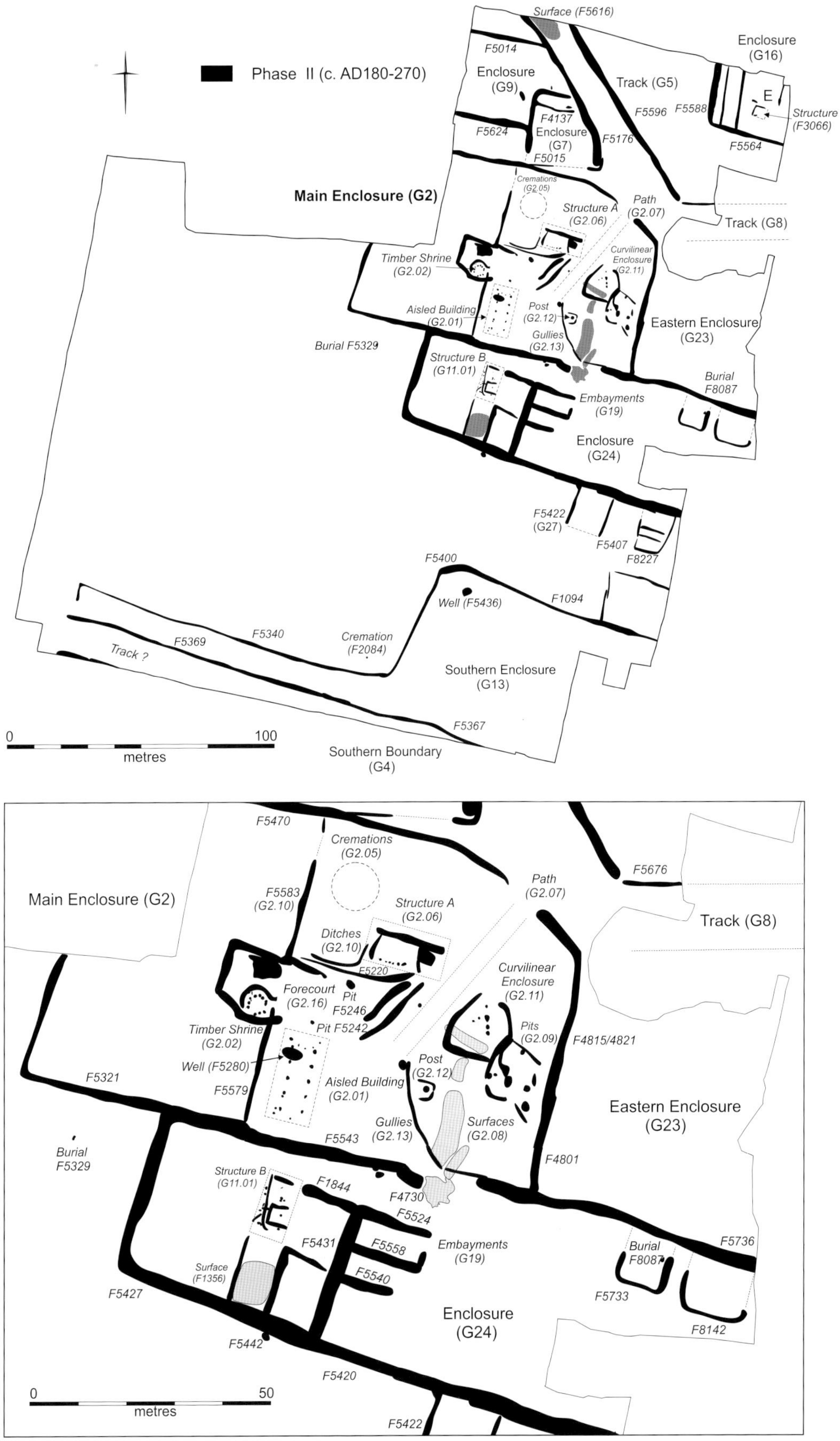

Figure 5.13. *Phase II Roman settlement (c.* AD *180–270), plan with detail.*

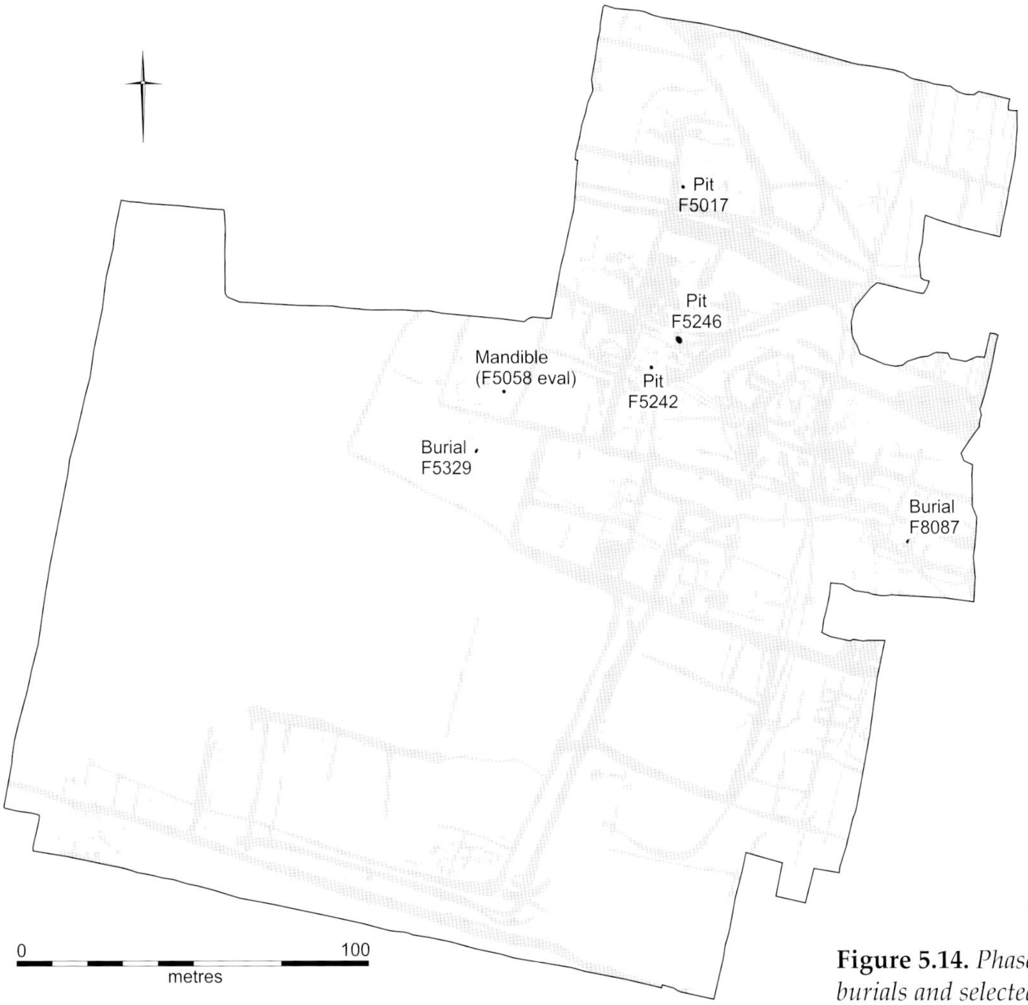

Figure 5.14. *Phase II burials and selected pits.*

Figure 5.15. *Photograph of the F.5556 metalled surface.*

Table 5.5. *Pottery vessels from the metalled surface (G2.08).*

Forms	Wt.	%	EVEs	%
Amphora	10	0.30	0	0.00
Bowl	178	5.29	38	23.75
Beaker	17	0.50	0	0.00
Cup	5	0.15	0	0.00
Dish	380	11.28	24	15.00
Flagon	21	0.62	0	0.00
Jar	865	25.68	77	48.13
Lid	16	0.48	5	3.13
Mortarium	290	8.61	6	3.75
Storage Jar	1433	42.55	10	6.25
Unid	153	4.54	0	0.00
Total	*3368*	*100*	*160*	*100*

Table 5.6. *Pottery vessels from well F.5280.*

Forms	Wt.	%	EVEs	%
Bowl	108	1.57	0.48	11.9
Beaker	38	0.55	-	-
Dish	76	1.10	0.10	2.5
Flagon	219	3.18	-	-
Jar	4867	70.69	3.02	75.1
Lid	113	1.64	0.17	4.2
Mortaria	119	1.73	0.10	2.5
Storage jar	1333	19.36	0.15	3.7
Unid	12	0.17	-	-
Total	*6885*	*100*	*4.02*	*100*

also reflected in the ditch sumps cut along the eastern edge of the enclosure. A coin (SF 297) was found on the surface of gravels, dated to the third quarter of the third century AD, along with ceramics broadly dated to the late second/early third century AD. Pit F.4730 (3.1 m diam., 0.4 m deep), adjacent to the southern end of G2.08 metalling, appeared contemporary and was associated with pottery dated to AD 140/180–240. This was one of several pits (G2.20) cut on the outer edge of the southern main enclosure ditch; others included F.1929 (0.8 m diam., 0.9 m deep), F.1931 (1.1 m diam., 0.7 m deep) and F.5542 (1.1 m diam., 1.6 m deep). Spot samples were taken from these last three pits for phosphate testing to see if an on-site interpretation of cess-pits held. These are all similar and, although within a high band (100–149 mgP per 100 g soil), are not particularly high in terms of the site background.

The ceramics from the metalled and cobbled surface (G2.08) yielded the highest percentage of imported finewares in terms of sherds count (14.29% of total imported fineware sherds). All of the imported material is samian. One sherd has a possible Martres de Veyre origin. Of the Central Gaulish examples, three Dr.37 forms were identified, one cup of Dr.33, A Dr.45 mortarium, one dish of Dr.31 and a probably residual early dish of Dr.18 with an illegible and incomplete stamp (Bet & Delor 2000, 470, see n.58A for the form, that is always stamped). The latest samian material from the group is of East Gaulish origin, with three dishes of Dr.31 identified. Otherwise, the assemblage composition was fairly typical of the site as a whole (Table 5.5).

The Aisled Building

As discussed in in the previous section, the Aisled Building probably continued in use throughout Phase II, although possibly shortened. The main alteration seems to be the cutting of a well on its northwestern side, F.5280. The latter was *c.* 2.6 m in diameter and 1.3 m deep; dated ceramics from its fills provide a sequence that spans the third century AD (Fig. 5.2 & 5.16).

Only a very small amount of animal bone was recovered (14 fragments from the well), most of which was unidentifiable (57%). The remainder was identified to cow, horse and sheep, and consisted of very fragmentary remains of those bones indicative of refuse from primary butchery (i.e. skull fragments, loose teeth and distal limb bones).

Two samples were taken from well F.5280 to investigate preserved plant remains: basal fill [719] and mid fill [717]. These are each quite different. The basal deposit contained a moderate number of charred remains (5.33 items per litre of soil) that reflects the chaff-rich processing debris present in many samples from Area A. In contrast, the mid-fill sample is extremely rich (237.67 items per litre) and was probably dumped refuse. Small artefactual remains in [717] include both burnt rodent bones and eggshell, suggesting that material had been scraped up at the location of charring and deposited into the well. The charred material is mainly of wild seeds, with some glume wheat chaff and few grains. No other context at the site had such a composition; this appears to be an exceptional charred assemblage, perhaps representing sieve cleanings after threshing and winnowing of cereals (all chaff-dominated samples are low in wild seeds, which appear to have been cleaned out earlier).

Some 265 pottery sherds (6.8 kg) came from the well F.5280, and make up a typical domestic group, dominated by local grey ware jars (Fig. 5.17; Table 5.6). Finewares include Nene Valley and Colchester colour-coats, plus Central Gaulish Samian (a Dr.45 mortarium and a Dr.31 bowl).

The Timber Shrine

At the start of Phase II, in the late second/early third century AD, the shrine structure (G2.02) was completely encircled and closed off by ditch F.5483 (*c.* 1.6 m wide and 0.7 m deep) that wrapped around its formerly open, southern side (see Fig. 5.5). Ceramics from its upper fill, where this has been distinguished, date to the mid third century AD (*c.* AD 240–70). At the same time, the structure may have been dismantled or pulled down; none of the postholes appeared to have *in situ* postpipes, except one – F.5517 – from which ceramics post-dating *c.* AD 270 were retrieved. In addition, a large irregularly shaped pit, F.5519 (*c.* 6.3 m diam. and 1.3 m deep), was cut on the northern side of the shrine. Its purpose is not obvious, but it may have been a quarry pit to provide soil to form a small mound over the dismantled shrine. The backfill of this feature contained mid third-century AD ceramics (*c.* AD 240–70), suggesting that it was cut at the end of this phase, perhaps around the same time as a larger, square ditched enclosure (F.5506 & F.5218) was cut around the shrine. This square ditch was 1.6 m wide and 0.5–0.8 m deep, with later third-century AD ceramics in its fills (*c.* AD 240–300). Gully F.5483 was also recut at this time (F.5533), ceramics in its fill post-dating *c.* AD 270. As discussed above, the recut F.5533 was very rich in charred plant remains.

It is in Phase II that the shrine and its enclosure produced any discernible patterns in the faunal assemblage worthy of note. As can be seen from Table 5.7, a great deal more faunal material from this period was recovered. Although 55 per cent of the bone was unidentifiable, it was possible to identify the remainder, these being mainly horse and cow. The horse bones are especially dominant, but this is largely because they originate from two articulated skeletal portions, both of which were revealed in the terminus of the ditch (F.5218, [519]). These were a left fore-leg, from the scapula to the carpal bones, and an articulated portion of the axial skeleton from

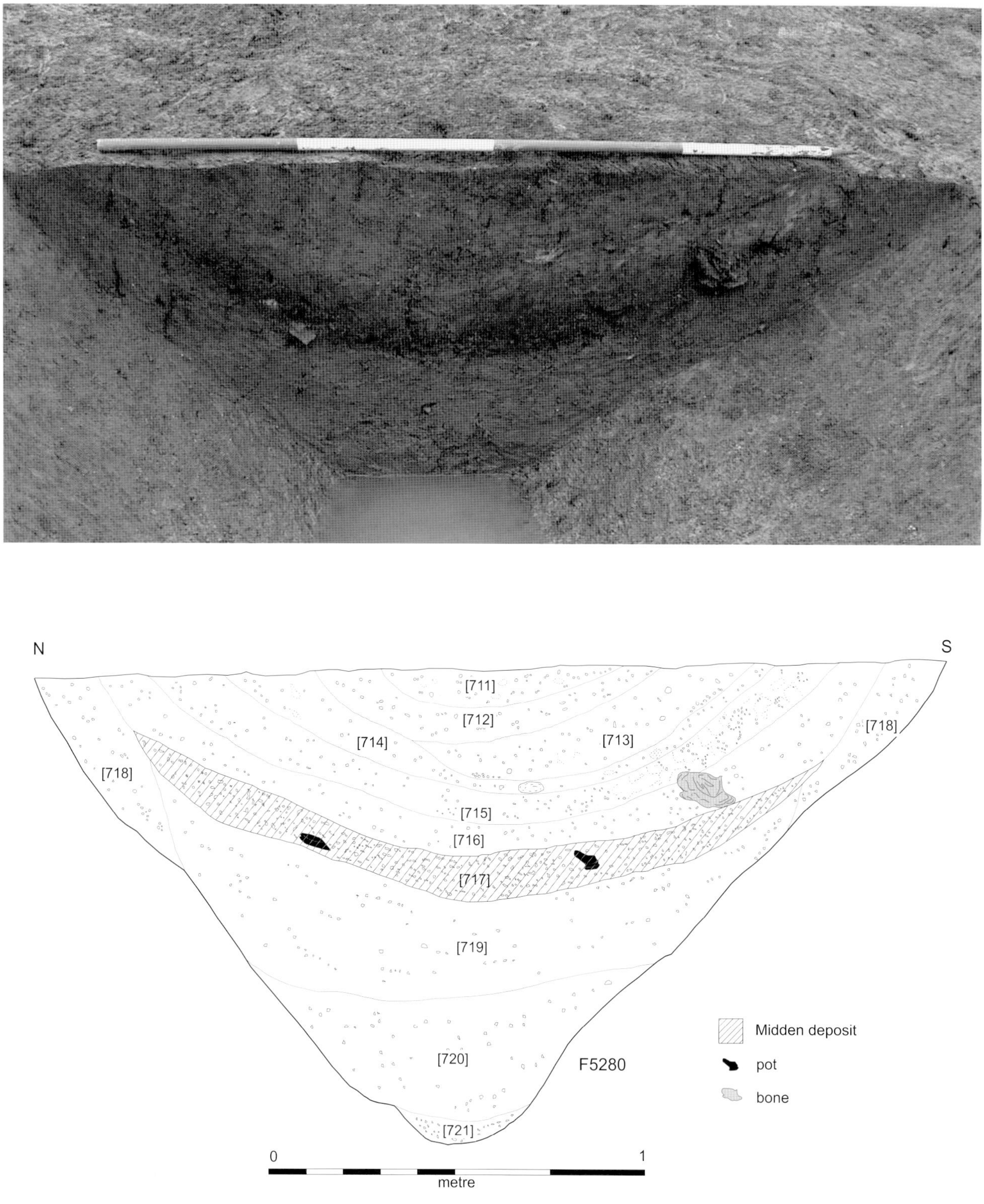

Figure 5.16. *Well F.5280 section.*

Figure 5.17. *Pottery from the F.5280 well.*

Table 5.7. *Associated animal bone with shrine (G2.02, Phase II).*

Element	Species						Grand Total
	Cow-sized	Cow	Horse	Sheep- sized	Sheep/goat	Unid	
astragalus	-	1	-	-	-	-	*1*
atlas	-	1	-	-	-	-	*1*
carpal	-	-	3	-	-	-	*3*
femur	-	1	-	-	1	-	*2*
humerus	-	-	1	-	-	-	*1*
loose teeth	-	6	-	-	-	-	*6*
mandible	-	2	-	-	-	-	*2*
metacarpal	-	-	2	-	-	-	*2*
metatarsal	-	-	1	-	-	-	*1*
phalange	-	-	1	-	-	-	*1*
patella	-	-	1	-	-	-	*1*
pelvis	-	-	1	-	-	-	*1*
radius	-	-	2	-	1	-	*3*
rib	4	-	10	3	-	-	*17*
sacrum	-	-	1	-	-	-	*1*
scapula	1	-	1	-	-	-	*2*
shaft	-	-	-	1	1	-	*2*
skull	-	-	1	-	-	-	*1*
ulna	-	-	1	-	-	-	*1*
vertebra	1	-	-	-	-	-	*1*
lumbar vert.	-	-	5	-	-	-	*5*
thoracic vert.	-	-	8	-	-	-	*8*
unid.	-	-	-	-	-	79	*79*
Grand Total	*6*	*11*	*39*	*4*	*3*	*79*	*142*
%	4.23	7.75	27.46	2.82	2.11	55.63	100

the 9th thoracic vertebrae (including some of the ribs) to the sacrum. The deposition of these articulated bones is very significant if one considers three key points. Firstly, both hold prime cuts of meat; secondly, they were still articulated and lastly, they have been separated from the rest of the carcass. This same enclosure ditch also contained a number of other animal bones: several other of horse were found, including a fragmented skull, along with a small number of sheep and cow bones, notably two mandibles.

Forecourt

As in Phase I, the forecourt area remained a largely open space with a few pits, two of which have been assigned to Phase II on the basis of associated pottery: F.5242 (0.75 m diam., 0.37 m deep; dated AD 200–300) and F.5246 (2.2 m diam., 0.2 m deep; dated AD 140–240; Fig. 5.14).

Structure A

Not as formal or well-constructed as the Aisled Building, Structure A (G2.06) seems to have been built with a beam slot for its northern wall foundation and postholes along the south (*c.* 0.4–0.6 m diam., 0.17–0.33 m deep). It was constructed toward the end of Phase II, and probably continued in use during Phase III (Fig. 5.18). Some 8.5 m long and 5.3 m wide, it also seemed to have had a *c.* 3 m extension or adjunct on its eastern end, set off the alignment of the main structure. This had a line of posts on its east side, but more curiously, appears to have had a sunken floor or a sunken level beneath the floor. The latter, F.5688 (dated AD 120–240), was 0.8 m across and *c.* 0.2 m deep and had linear furrows along its base reminiscent of spaded beds; it is possible it represents a small horticultural plot (e.g. for vegetables, pulses or herbs), and indeed this perhaps makes more sense than a sunken-floored feature. Associated with this extension were gullies F.4450 (0.5 m wide, 0.26 m deep; dated AD 240+) along the north side and F.5690 (0.55 m wide, 0.25–0.43 m deep) on the west side, both of which ran up to the path (G2.07) and created a triangular space within which this adjunct sat.

Curvilinear Enclosure

Situated in the centre of the main settlement was a double curvilinear enclosure (G2.11), open to the north (Fig. 5.19). It was defined by a western enclosure ditch F.5678 (0.7–1.5 m wide, 0.25–0.4 m deep) and F.5717 (0.6 m wide, 0.12 m deep) and an eastern one, F.4660, later recut as F.5710/5711 (*c.* 1 m wide, *c.* 0.25 m deep). Ditches F.5678 and F.5717 both contained ceramics dating after the mid third century AD, as well as some earlier residual material. It is probable that the enclosure was cut in the later third century AD, at the same time as the shrine was enclosed; indeed, there is almost a symmetry between the two enclosures in their position in the settlement, flanking either side of the pathway (G2.07) that bisected the settlement core diagonally. There was also a symmetry with the G17 enclosure to the north (see below), particularly in terms of form and orientation.

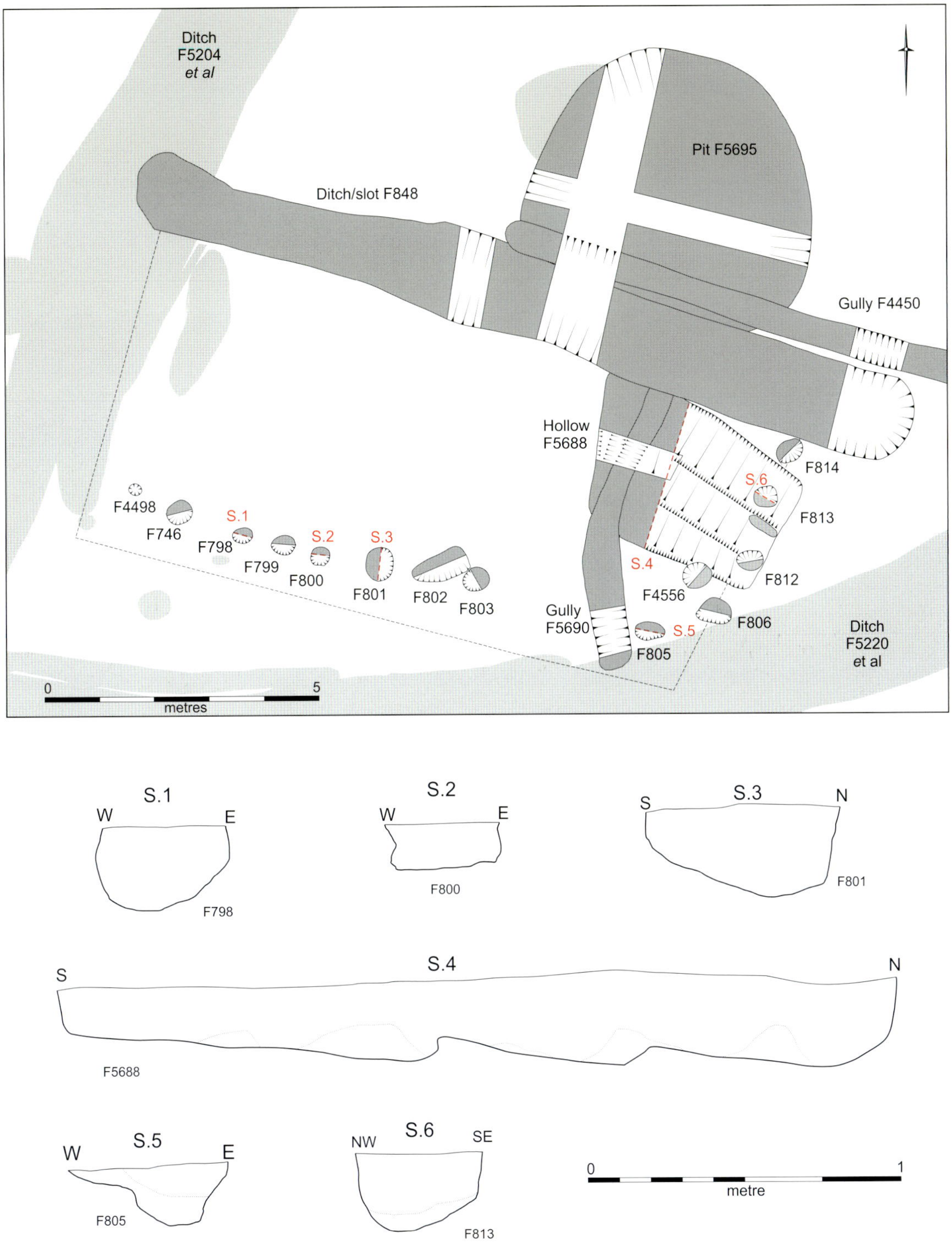

Figure 5.18. *Structure A (G2.06), plan and sections.*

A scatter of pits (G2.09) lay on or within the eastern boundary of the enclosure: F.4886, F.5709, F.4646, F.4645, F.4644, F.4689, F.4691 and, probably, F.4639 (see Fig. 5.19). Most of these were likely associated with this enclosure, though they may possibly have pre-dated it.

Only nine animal bone fragments were recovered from these features, a very small quantity. All the identifiable specimens were cow or cow-size.

Although jars comprise the main ceramic vessels in use, compared to the rest of the assemblage the group from the Curvilinear Enclosure produced a high level of beakers and flagons for the period and was noticeably lacking in dishes and bowls (Table 5.8). This is one of the two assemblages that yielded a flagon with a facemask rim, this example being in a Nene Valley colour-coated fabric (see Figs. 6.36 & 6.47.3). Although shattered

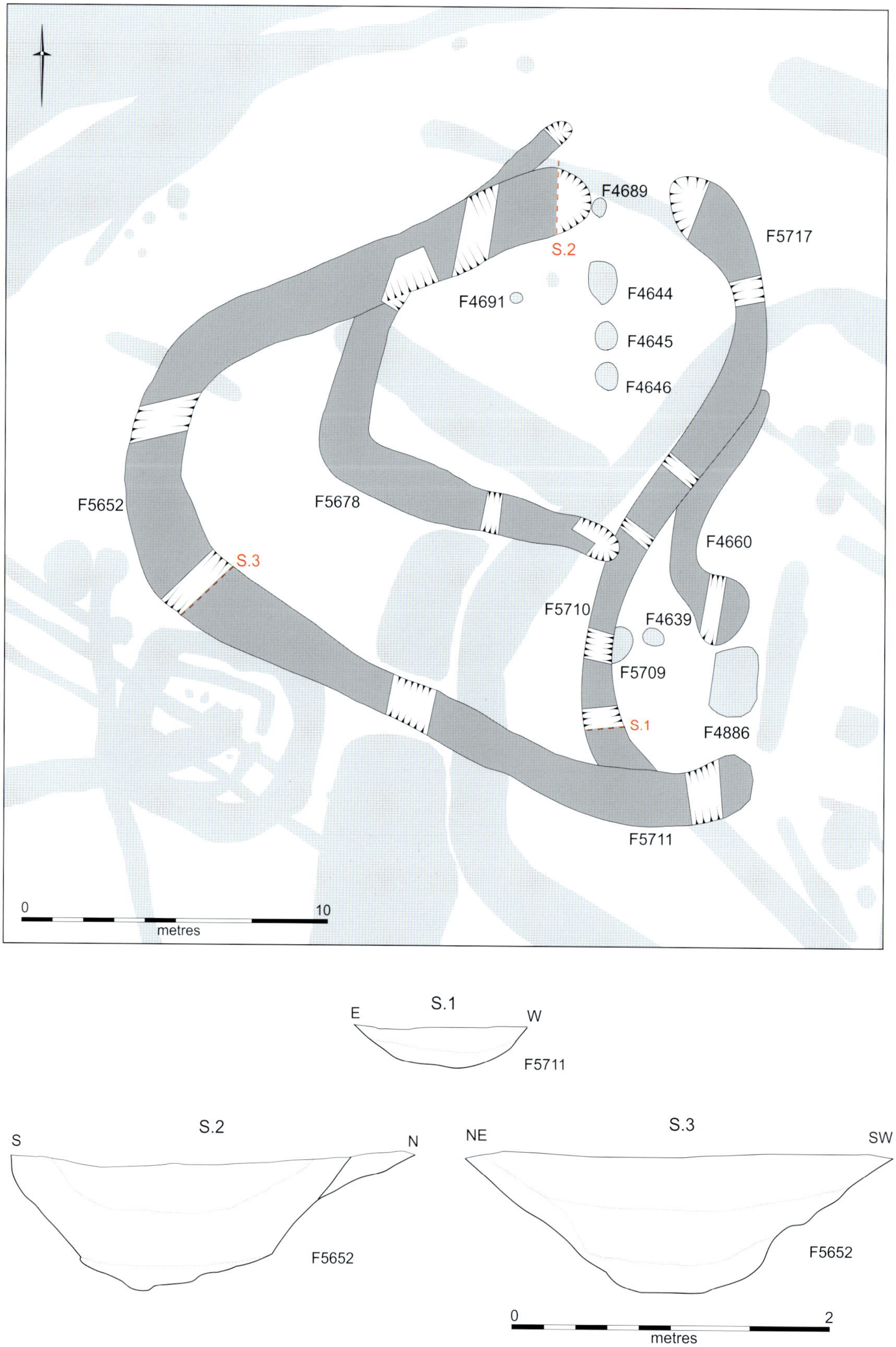

Figure 5.19. *Curvilinear Enclosure (G2.11), plan and sections.*

Table 5.8. *Pottery from Curvilinear Enclosure (G2.11), Phase II.*

Forms	Wt.	%	EVEs	%
Beaker	4	0.57	0	0.00
Flagon	70	10.00	0	0.00
Jar	173	24.71	24	88.89
Lid	3	0.43	3	11.11
Storage Jar	427	61.00	0	0.00
Unid	23	3.29	0	0.00
Total	*700*	*100.00*	*27*	*100.00*

in several fragments, the top of the flagon was complete. A similar Nene Valley example was found on Orton Hall Farmstead (Perrin 1996, 150, n.339 fig. 94). These vestigial flagons seem to be more common in later Roman contexts (see Monaghan 1997, 926–8 for examples from York, where painted and moulded face-neck pots are also been found in late phases).

Monumental Post

South of the Curvilinear Enclosure stood a small, sub-square enclosure defined by a gully (Fig. 5.20). In Phase III, a large posthole occupied the centre of the enclosure, which was recut and it seems likely an earlier version of this post-setting existed in Phase II. Certainly, the profile of the posthole suggests recutting and many of the finds (pottery and coins) from it date to this phase. The gully encircling the post (F.5702/5703) was 0.6 m wide and 0.3 m deep. Associated with ceramics broadly dated after AD 140, this gully was open on its western side. Within the gully-enclosure were a number of minor postholes that may have been structural but did not appear to form any identifiable configuration.

Contemporary with the primary phase of the post-setting, a gully system (G2.13; F.5555/5553/5557; 0.7 m wide, 0.2 m deep) was cut, wrapping around the post-setting and joining up with the larger enclosure to the north. Ceramics from its fill have been dated to AD 140–240. The recut ring-ditch F.5705 (see below) truncated this gully system. Only three fragments of bone were recovered from this feature.

Running westwards from the post was ditch F.5042. Some 0.5 m wide and 0.15 m deep, this was associated with pottery dated AD 45–140 and AD 80–180 (G2.15).

Southern Core Extension (Area B)

A number of sub-enclosures were contained within a large, southern extension to the settlement (G24; Fig. 5.13); the basic limits of this extension were defined by ditch F.5427 (1.5–4 m wide, 0.5–1.2 m deep) – with pottery dated AD 325/40+ and late fourth-century AD coins (all from the upper fill) – that continued eastward as F.5420 and, then, as F.8074 (0.4–1.1 m wide, 0.2–0.6 m deep) and F.8075 (0.61–1.16 m wide, 0.2–0.6 m deep; dated AD 240+). This arrangement of these ditches is significant insofar as they defined the point of contact between two slightly different alignments, that of the main settlement enclosure to the north, and the ditch system to the south. Within this, there was a major internal division marked by F.5431 (4.8 m wide, 1.5 m deep; dated AD 270/300+), either side of which were smaller bays or sub-enclosures (G19). Three substantial ditches coming off F.5431 to the east created three bays: from north to south, F.5524 (1.6–2.7 m wide, 0.75–1.3 m deep; dated AD 240+), F.5558 (2.2–3.5 m wide, 0.87–1 m deep; dated AD 180–280) and F.5450 (2.2 m wide, 0.58 m deep; dated AD 240+). On the west side, F.1844 (2.2 m wide, 0.7 m deep) ran up to the G11.01 structure, which also included ditch F.5455 (see below). A number of narrower, unexcavated gullies also formed part of the western side of this group.

Hanging off the southern, outer edge of this ditch-line was a small sub-enclosure (G27; Fig. 5.13) defined by ditches F.5422 (1.7 m wide, 0.79 m deep; pottery-dated AD 325+, probably from the upper fill) and F.5407 (1.2 m wide, 0.21 m deep). These were probably part of a continuous circuit whose southern side has been truncated by the later F.5389 (G18). East of this, F.8227 (0.5–1.2 m wide, 0.2–0.42 m deep) formed the eastern and southern side of another similar enclosure, containing internal east–west gullies (1.3 m wide, 0.3–.37 m deep). Further to the west, also on the outside of the southern boundary ditch, lay a well/waterhole, F.5442 (1.3 m diam., depth 0.98 m; dated AD 240–300).

Two samples were taken from the main ditch, F.5427 (Table 5.9). The predominance of glume wheat chaff within most of the sampled contexts suggests that a similar source of charred remains (crop-processing waste) was present within both the southern outer zone and the core-area.

Structure B

Inside the secondary enclosure was an internal structure (G11.01) defined by a single north–south beam-slot/gully on its western side (F.5544), although an eastern line may have been truncated by the later ditch F.5427 (Fig. 5.21). The structure was divided into two bays marked by slots F.5545, F.4174 and F.5672; the former two were linked by another slot, F.5633. Some 0.35–0.85 m in diameter and 0.13–0.4 m deep, a number of postholes occurred inside and along the outer length of this structure. The structure did not present a clear building form, except for the fact that it is rectangular, approximately 11 m long by 5 m wide. To the south of it was a metalled surface, F.1356, between ditches F.5458 to the west (0.9 m wide, 0.24 m deep; dated AD 120–40) and F.5455 to the east (0.6–1.1 m wide, *c.* 0.3 m deep), which returned eastward at the corner of the structure to run into F.5431 of G19.

Table 5.9. *Charred remains from F.5427.*

Context	Feature	Phase	Type	Sample volume/ litres	Grain No.	Chaff No.	SeedNo.	Total count per litre soil
[1374]	F.5427	II–III	ditch	9	1	20	3	2.67
[1476]	F.5427	II–III	ditch	5	15	89	14	23.60

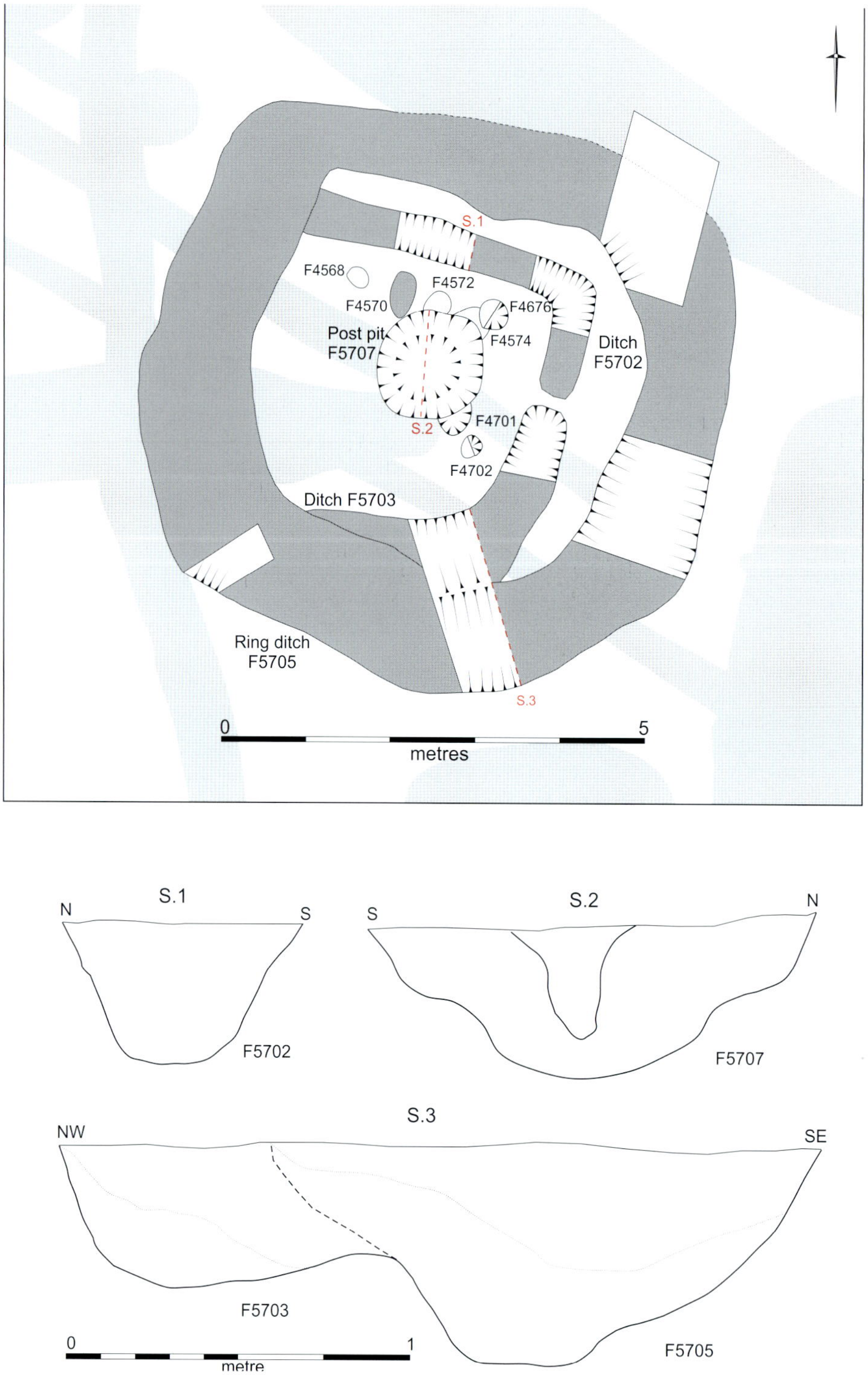

Figure 5.20. *The Monumental Post (G2.12), plan and sections.*

The Southern Fields (Area D)
At the southern margins of the excavated area, a long boundary ditch ran east to west across the site (Fig. 5.13). It stopped just short of the western limit of excavation and was defined by ditches F.5369 (0.8–2 m wide, 0.3 m deep) and F.5367 (*c.* 1.8 m wide and 0.2 m deep; G4). Parallel to this, and with a return marking a narrow entrance to an elongated passage into an enclosure, was ditch F.5340 (0.8–1.25 m wide, 0.27–0.45 m deep). This appeared to continue northward as F.5400 (1.3 m wide,

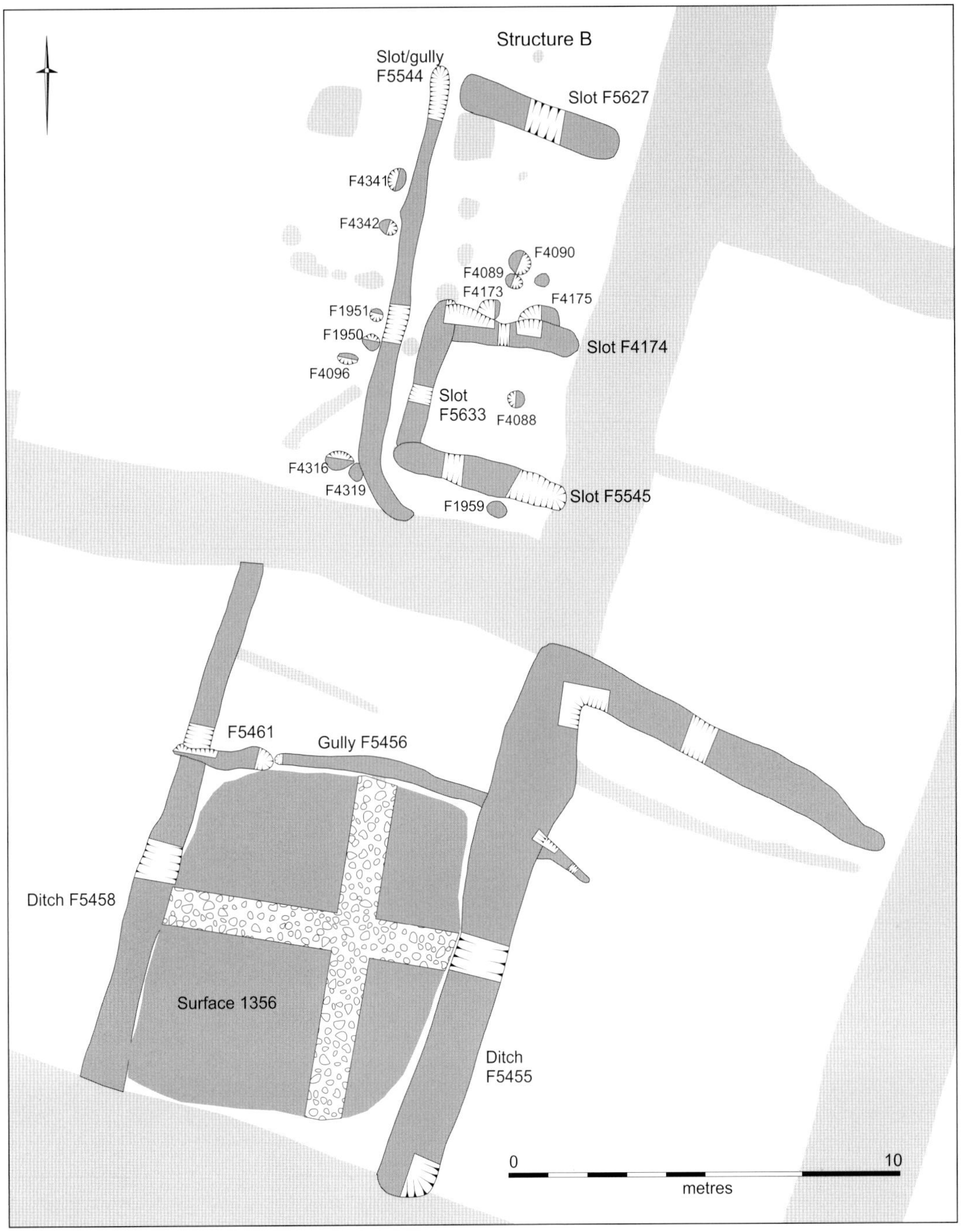

Figure 5.21. *Plan of Structure B (G11.01) and the F.1356 metalled surface*

0.3–0.48 m deep) and F.1094 (0.3 m wide, 0.15–0.4 m deep), creating a large enclosure (G13). None of these ditches are firmly dated, although the southern boundary ditch was later recut as F.5366 (1.4–2.5 m wide, 0.3–0.74 m deep; dated AD 120–200, but with residual Iron Age pottery). At the corner of F.5340, as it turned north as F.5400, was a cremation, F.2084, which acted as a focus for the later inhumation cemetery.

A Southern Road/Trackway

The long straight boundary that marked the southern side of the settlement's fields (F.5369/5367; see above) is thought to have flanked a roadway. The ditch probably defining that route's southern side was, unfortunately, not excavated and, only visible over a short distance (its west end terminating at the far western end of the site), was just base-planned. Based, nevertheless, on this, the road (No. 4) would have been approximately 11 m wide (i.e. comparable to No. 2). Indeed, it is possible that, as outlined in the preceding chapter, the ditch exposed as curving southward in the Nano-Fabrication Site investigations represents the eastern continuation of the route's southern boundary. When, to the west, the Veterinary School paddocks were trenched in 2015 this road's ditches were not present (see Chap. 7; Fig. 7.19). This is not, however, considered to be problematic as there are known examples of Roman roads only being ditched where they passed through settlements, such as in North West Cambridge's Site II (see Fig. 5.41 and, also, Chap. 3).

Cremation F.2084
This cremation had been greatly disturbed by a Medieval furrow and was only identified in a second machining of the area (see Fig. 5.28). The cremated bone had been placed in a vessel, which was severely truncated and only the base survived *in situ*. The matrix inside was excavated in the laboratory and treated in the same way as the burials from the cremation cemetery (see above). A total of 210 g of cremated bone was recovered: the partial remains of an adult. The fragments are generally small, with the largest being 57 mm (femur shaft). The material is generally a white buff colour indicative of full oxidization, although the femur shaft was a grey blue colour. A single iron nail and a hobnail were identified (Manning 1985, Type 10).

The cremated remains were interred in a wide-mouthed jar (1360 g), in a sandy grey ware (CSGR) dated to *c.* AD 180–230 (Fig. 5.36.2). Associated with the burial were also fragments from a Nene Valley colour-coated beaker (131 g) and a sherd in a fine sandy redware (FSRE).

The Northern Fields (Area E)

The northwestward oriented road/trackway (No. 2/ G5) clearly continued to function at this time (Fig. 5.13). While terminating in relationship to it (at least in the west), none of the enclosures in this portion of the settlement followed its alignment.

Western Side of Trackway
In the first half of the third century AD, the area enclosed between the main trackway and the main settlement was remodelled, with the original ditch probably backfilled and a new ditch positioned closer to the corner, F.5015 (G7; 2.5 m wide, 0.6 m deep; dated AD 200–40), with another ditch coming off it (F.5624; 2 m wide, 0.65 m deep; Fig. 5.13). In the later third century AD, a final ditch was added, F.4137 (0.7–1.3 m wide, 0.34–0.6 m deep; AD 240+). The enclosed area contained two pits. One lay on the northern side (F.8025; *c.* 2.3 × 1.2 m wide) and was associated with pottery dated after AD 180, while F.5017 on the southern side had some undiagnostic Roman pottery and disarticulated human remains (Fig. 5.14). All the bones are adult-sized and the assemblage includes limb shafts, skull fragments and hands/toes. A further fragment of skull and a single worn tooth (1st mandibular premolar) were recovered from the Post-Medieval colluvium just to the north of it. It is ambiguous as to whether there was originally an articulated inhumation here, or just a pit containing disarticulated bone.

To the north, ditch F.5014 (0.7 m wide, 0.1 m deep; AD 120–200) ran up to and cut the western trackway ditch, forming a new northernmost boundary to the settlement (as exposed).

Low quantities of charred plant remains occurred in ditches F.5015 and F.5624. The samples contained mainly glume wheat chaff and appear to be poorer representations of the charred crop-processing debris present within the core-area. This northern area of the site has been damp from the past through to the present. Good waterlogged plant remains from ditch F.5624 indicate that the area had been cleared, but that scrubby vegetation was present. Ditch F.5624 also contained aquatic plant taxa, including fool's water-cress (*Apium nodiflorum*), and watercress (*Rorippa nasturtium-aquaticum*), and appears to have been particularly wet.

Eastern Side of Trackway
In the northeast corner of the site, a small rectangular enclosure was established with narrow strip sub-divisions (G16; Fig. 5.13). Defined by main ditches F.5588 (1.9 m wide, 0.28–0.6 m deep; AD 240+) and F.5564 (1–1.4 m wide, 0.2–0.6 m deep; AD 140–240), the area within them was further sub-divided into narrow strips by gullies, 0.4–1 m wide and *c.* 0.15 m deep; the latter probably relating to lazy-bed agriculture.

Also located there was a small structure (E), defined only by a right-angled gully, F.3066 (0.65 m wide, 0.22 m deep), dated AD 350+ from pottery in its backfill, enclosing a square area 4 m by 4 m. Associated with this were three shallow pits, 0.4–1 m across and 0.05–0.2 m deep (F.3064, F.3068 & F.5573). Ditch F.5566 (G15) to the south was probably also then cut, but pre-dated the G16 enclosure, although both were probably open at the same time.

Phase III (AD 270–410)

In its final phase the Roman settlement transformed radically. The northwestern road/trackway (Road 2) ceased to function and Road 3 appears to have been extended some way westward. A third settlement-area was added to the south, linking up the main settlement with the southern fieldsystem, which now had an inhumation cemetery on its boundary; this appears to have been reached by yet another route (path/trackway). In the settlement's core, the features in the eastern half developed to form a new centre of activity, while the previous eastern boundary of the settlement was backfilled and the entire core opened up to the east, beyond the limit of excavation (Fig. 5.22).

This phase saw complex elaboration of the settlement's core-area components. Indeed, not all could have been directly contemporary and have 'functioned' together. It is, therefore, likely that this reflects sub-phasing sequencing, which will be outlined in this chapter's final section.

The Core Settlement - Main Enclosure (Area A)

The northern boundary of the main enclosure (G2) was recut in the fourth century AD as F.5681 (1.1–1.3 m wide, 0.3–0.5 m deep; dated AD 300+); this was possibly the same ditch as F.5092 returning (see G14, Area B). It was probably also associated with F.5559 (1–1.4 m wide, 0.5–0.58 m deep) that ran eastward, blocking off the G5 and G8 trackways into the site (Fig. 5.22).

The Interior
Unlike the previous phase, when there was a clear bipartite division between an eastern and western side within the main enclosure, in Phase III there was a much more concentric arrangement, with multiple sub-enclosures set around a core-area occupied by the Curvilinear Enclosure (G2.11; Fig. 5.22). The internal pathway (G2.07) was maintained, and in the early fourth century AD was even metalled with fine gravels (F.5536; 1.2 m wide; dated AD 300+). Its southern edge was marked by ditch F.5661 (0.65 m wide, 0.27 m deep; AD 270+). In the late fourth century AD, a substantial ditch was cut (F.5304; 1.9–2.1 m wide, 0.87–0.96 m deep; dated to AD 350+). Many of the old internal divisions were, nevertheless, maintained.

Figure 5.22.
Plan of the Phase III Roman Settlement (c. AD 270–410).

Table 5.10. *Charred remains associated with western divisions of the core area.*

Context	Feature	Phase	Sample volume (lt.)	Grain No.	Chaff No.	SeedNo.	Total count per litre soil
[1575]	F.5501	III	10	9	21	4	3.40
[1792]	F.5501	III	10	35	144	75	25.70
[1646]	F.5480	III	3	0	8	0	2.67

Those on the western side of the main enclosure were recut (G2.10); the southern ditch-line by F.5224 (0.5–0.8 m wide, 0.4 m deep; dated AD 270+), the eastern side by F.5061 (1.6–1.85 m wide, 0.65–0.85 m deep; dated AD 300+), while on the western side, F.5480/F.5582 (0.5–2.2 m wide, 0.35–0.45 m deep; dated AD 240–300/330–50) recut the line established by F.5583. The northern and eastern sides of the square ditch enclosing the shrine were enlarged by F.5501 (3–4.8 m wide, 0.9–1.2 m deep; dated AD 300+), which continued both south and west. Southward, it linked up with the Area B sub-enclosure (G11) and, westward, it either carried on to the back edge of the main enclosure or stopped at ditch F.8264 (*c.* 1.5 m wide). In the latter part of this phase, ditch F.5006 (1.1–2 m wide, 0.25–0.85 m deep; dated AD 340+), which conjoined this later, bounded the southern edge of the shrine and swerved south around the then-defunct well F.5280 to form a narrow causeway with F.5214 (1.5 m wide, 0.6 m deep; dated AD 300+) that ran into the former southern limit of the settlement core.

Three contexts from the western division ditches were sampled for plant remains: F.5501 (× 2), and F.5480 (Table 5.10). The latter was waterlogged, and the plant macro-remains show that the land was damp and scrubby. There is also good evidence for nitrogen-enrichment of the soil, either from human or animal waste. The context contained some water-associated plant taxa, suggesting that these features were at least seasonally wet. Feature 5480 was low in cereal grains, especially when compared to F.5501, which had very rich charred inclusions, suggesting that it was either much closer to the charring source, or contained dumped refuse.

Forecourt

A number of pits occupied the space (G2.16) between the end of the pathway and the shrine (Fig. 5.22; see Fig. 6.21), from two of which came human remains. Fragments of skull (adult parietal) were found in the upper fill of pit F.5263. More substantially, a neonate's lower left arm was recovered from the upper fill of pit F.710. The bones were not recognized as such on site and so it is uncertain, although likely, that they were in articulation. It may even have been part of a complete neonate burial, most of which had been ploughed out.

Curvilinear Enclosure

Toward the end of the third/early fourth century AD, the Curvilinear Enclosure (G2.11) was recut and made much more substantial by ditches F.5652/8167, which varied from 0.9–3.2 m wide and 0.3–0.7 m deep, and F.8263 (*c.* 2 m wide; see Fig. 5.19). Possibly contemporary was F.4902, echoing the 'doubling' of the primary enclosure, and ditch F.5731. This enclosure remained in use until the mid fourth century AD when it was replaced by a third, similar and slightly larger enclosure, sited more to the east. It was then defined by ditches F.5722/5704 (1.65 m wide), continuing as F.4802 (1.8 m wide), with a series of bays demarcated by F.4912 (1 m wide) and F.4863 (1.5 m wide).

Unlike Phase II, a much larger assemblage of animal bones came from the later enclosure ditches (299 fragments; Table 5.11). Cow and cow-sized bones dominated (88%), but most of these remains came from two articulated deposits: a right hind-leg from F.5652 and a skull with cervical vertebrae from F.5704.

Four contexts sampled for plant remains revealed marked differences in composition (Table 5.12). All contained charred remains dominated by glume wheat chaff but varied in their density. The very rich contexts of F.5652 and F.5741 may have been located nearer processing activities, or had waste deposited specifically in them. The damp remains in F.5741 included low quantities of wood fragments and elder seeds, but differential preservation appears

Table 5.11. *Faunal remains from Curvilinear Enclosure (G2.11, Phase III).*

Element	Cow	Pig	Sheep	Cow-sized	Sheep-sized	Unid	Grand Total
Skull	4	1	-	1	-	-	*6*
Mandible	9	1	3	1	-	-	*14*
Loose teeth	3	-	-	-	-	-	*3*
Atlas	1	-	-	-	-	-	*1*
Axis	1	-	-	-	-	-	*1*
Scapula	5	1	-	-	-	-	*6*
Humerus	5	-	3	-	-	-	*8*
Radius	6	-	-	-	-	-	*6*
Ulna	1	-	-	-	-	-	*1*
Pelvis	5	-	-	1	-	-	*6*
Sacrum	1	-	-	-	-	-	*1*
Femur	3	-	-	1	-	-	*4*
Tibia	4	-	1	-	-	-	*5*
Patella	1	-	-	-	-	-	*1*
Astragalus	3	-	-	-	-	-	*3*
Calcaneum	2	-	-	-	-	-	*2*
Tarsal	9	-	-	-	-	-	*9*
Metacarpal	3	-	-	-	-	-	*3*
Metatarsal	10	-	-	-	-	-	*10*
Metapodial	3	-	-	-	-	-	*3*
1st Phalange	4	-	-	-	-	-	*4*
2nd Phalange	3	-	-	-	-	-	*3*
3rd Phalange	2	-	-	-	-	-	*2*
Rib	-	-	-	11	2	-	*13*
Shaft	-	-	-	3	6	-	*9*
Cervical vert.	5	-	-	-	-	-	*5*
Vertebrae	-	-	-	22	-	-	*22*
Unid						148	*148*
Grand Total	93	*3*	*7*	*40*	*8*	148	*299*

Table 5.12. *Charred remains associated with the Curvilinear Enclosure.*

Context	Feature	Sample Volume/ litres	Grain No.	Chaff No.	Seed No.	Total count Per litre soil	Comments
[4602]	F.5652	6	27	548	45	103.33	
[4683]	F.5652	10	7	12	14	3.30	
[4649]	F.5704	2.5	6	20	8	13.60	Water-logged
[4901]	F.5741	3.5	89	1579	96	504.00	Damp

to have caused the loss of most material. The better, waterlogged, remains within F.5704 indicate an open area of rough grassland. Eggs of water flea (*Daphne* sp.) and the aquatic celery-leaved buttercup (*Ranunculus scleratus*) suggest that standing water was present in the ditch, at least seasonally.

A quantity of pottery sherds (380 sherds; 6.2 kg) was recovered from the late phase of the Curvilinear Enclosure (Table 5.13). The significance of this group is the high number of service vessels compared with the general background pattern from the site, especially the high numbers of flagons. Of those vessels that have been unambiguously ascribed a function, the majority are associated with serving/table wares rather than food preparation or storage (Table 5.14). Otherwise, the main fabric groups as seen on Late Roman sites in the region are represented: Nene Valley, Hadham and Oxfordshire, as well as local greywares and South Midland shelly wares.

Monumental Post

A large, single post-setting, F.5707 (G2.12), enclosed by a small ring-ditch *c.* 5.6 m across, re-established an earlier version of that feature (see Fig. 5.20). The post-setting proper comprised a large cut (0.55 m diam., 0.42 m deep), with pottery in its backfill (dated to AD 140–80) and six coins, including three minims and another late coin (<5229>); the minims were all minted in the third quarter of the third century AD, with two others dating to AD 341–6 and 337–41 (<5219>). Many of these finds might have been redeposited from an earlier posthole of which this was a recut. The post, surrounded by stone packing, may have been pulled out at some point or simply rotted *in situ*; ceramics in its postpipe dated to AD 240–350 and there were six further coins: two radiates and four minims (<5227>/<5228>), all minted in the third quarter of the third century AD. These may have moved into the void from the post-pit fill as the post decayed. From the postpipe, the diameter of the post must have been 0.5 m and it had been set 0.4 m deep (perhaps 0.5–0.6 m below the original ground surface), suggesting the post may have stood *c.* 2–2.5 m high. The ring-ditch encircling the post (F.5705) was 0.6 m wide and 0.4 m deep, and associated pottery was dated after AD 270/300. A cobbled surface, F.4445/F.5670 (G2.08), led off the main metalled surface to the encircled timber post and had ceramics dated AD 270–350 associated with it. It was, therefore, probably associated with the later recutting of the ring-ditch in the late third century AD.

Table 5.13. *Pottery from the Curvilinear Enclosure.*

	Wt.	%	EVEs	%
Amphora	52	0.84	0	0.00
Bowl	378	6.09	75	13.69
Beaker	129	2.08	7	1.28
Cup	10	0.16	5	0.91
Dish	724	11.66	95	17.34
Flagon	169	2.72	133	24.27
Jar	2109	33.96	191	34.85
Lid	63	1.01	16	2.92
Mortaria	556	8.95	15	2.74
Storage Jar	1719	27.68	7	1.28
Unid	302	4.86	4	0.73
Total	*6211*	*100.00*	*548*	*100.00*

Table 5.14. *Summary of pottery by vessel function from G2.11.*

Function	EVEs	%
Cooking	31	5.6
Food preparation	15	2.7
Service	154	28.1
Storage	7	1.3
Unid.	341	62.2
Grand Total	*548*	*100*

Very little charred material was present within F.5707 [4668]; the few glume bases probably derive from the abundant crop-processing debris identified in parts of the core-area. Waterlogged plant remains suggest that open rough grassland surrounded the feature, with occasional standing water in the feature itself.

Structure C

To the west, a post-setting lay in a relatively empty zone (G2.15). Feature 4627 (0.8 m diam., 0.4 m deep, AD 270+) and F.5306 (0.9 m diam., 0.6 m deep, AD 140–200), were large postholes fronting a small single-cell structure *c.* 2.6 m square and marked by a trapezoidal arc of smaller posts to the west (Fig. 5.23).

Pitting Zone

A group of dense intercutting pits (G2.17), lying in a zone between the earlier cremation cemetery and the shrine, seems to have been cut and subsequently backfilled with midden material or 'dark earth' (Fig. 5.22). A minor ditch (F.5289; 0.65 m wide, 0.28 m deep; dated AD 300+) may represent an internal division in the quarry-zone on its eastern side. Mostly 0.6–2.35 m across and 0.1–0.65 m deep, the form of the pits and method of digging is typical of quarry pitting seen at other Roman sites in the region (e.g. see Chap. 3), and it would seem that this is the most likely explanation for their cutting. Certainly, the edges of the pits showed no signs of any modification, such as scorching or lining, to indicate other usage. Nevertheless, the soil through which the pits were cut was a dirty, silty sand and would not seem particularly useful as a raw material: cleaner, purer sands and gravels lay to the north, and better clays to the south. Moreover, the pits were small-scale and would not attest to any major extraction process. Assuming that the location was important (despite the fact that they do not seem to have been sensitive to the nature of the subsoil or natural), one possibility is that these pits were quarried to provide the soil for a mound covering the cremation cemetery. Alternatively, they

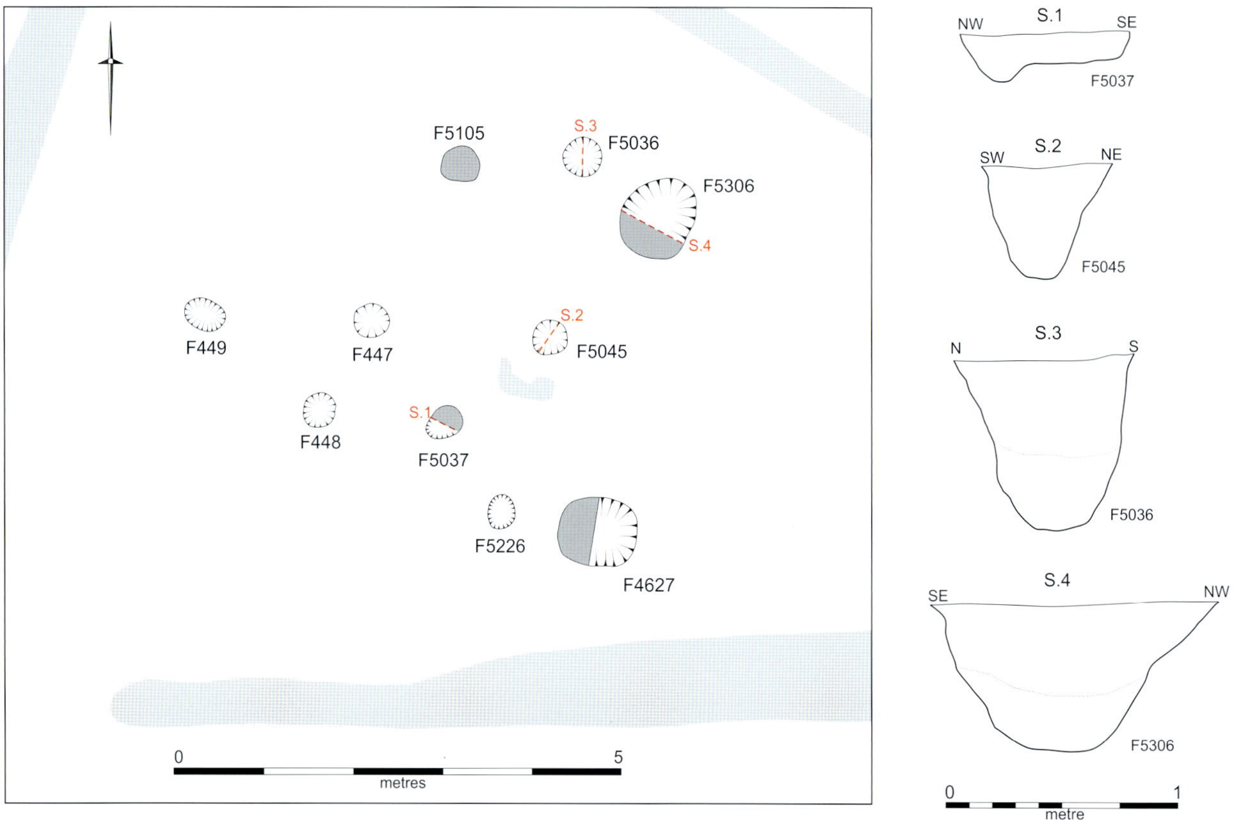

Figure 5.23. *Structure C, plan and sections.*

may, in part, have also contributed to the gravel surface across the north of this area (see below).

There is evidence to suggest that the cemetery was mounded (see above), yet there was no ring-ditch around them to provide material for a mound. Material from the boundary ditches would have been used to make banks and, so, to create any substantial mound over the cremations these pits are the only obvious source of nearby soil. Moreover, the quarry pits clearly respected and stopped short of the cremations. The pit group seemed to divide into two halves, one east of the dividing G2.10 boundary and one west, and the group to the east was noticeably different to those in the west that were backfilled with dark earths. It is possible that the two groups relate to two very different phases: the western group to the end of Phase I/early Phase II, and the eastern group, perhaps to a Phase III re-establishment of the mound (or, then, the western continuation of Road 3; see below). While most of the eastern group of pits produced late pottery (fourth century AD), none of the pits from the western side had any closely dateable ceramics. From one of these pits – F.5644 – however came a very fragmented shell-tempered jar (SMSW; 76 sherds/621 g) and, with it, an articulated left fore-leg of cow.

One pit's backfill was rich in charred remains (F.5200; 62.8 items per litre) and dominated by glume wheat chaff. It evidently represents the crop-processing debris present in many contexts within Area A.

Northern Zone Metalled Surfaces

Metalled surfaces were laid down in the early–mid fourth century AD along the northern strip of the site (G2.18; Figs. 5.22 & 5.24). Gravel surface F.5471, dated AD 240–300/300+ (with a fourth-century AD coin on its surface; SF 302), lay between ditches F.5480 (2.2 m wide, 0.45 m deep) and F.5013 (1.1–1.4 m wide, 0.38–0.65 m deep). Likely relating to separate sub-phasing developments, the inter-relationship of the roads/trackways in this area is difficult to determine. Did, for example, the eastward route (G8/No. 3) remain in use and connect with the G2.18 metalling? If so, did the southern end of ditch F.5013 later cut off this linkage? (The same is also likely to be true of the eastern continuation of ditch F.5559, especially as probably conjoined with the eastern side of enclosure G31/F.4759.) Equally, what of the relationship of ditches F.5061 and F.5480 with G2.18's metalling? The former seemingly post-date and cut off this route which, along with other related later developments, necessitates a further sub-division of this phase (see below).

Another metalled surface also lay further east, F.4767/F.4857 (G32), bounded to the north by ditches F.4760/F.4784/F.4934 (*c.* 1.9 m wide; dated AD 240+) and, to the south, by ditch F.5741 of G2.11.

Southern Core Extension (Area B)

The enclosure-components within this area saw considerable elaboration during this phase and which, in

Figure 5.24. *The F.5471 metalled surface (looking west).*

part, must relate to southward access – via a new track-/ pathway route – to the southern inhumation cemetery (see below); this probably necessitated localized backfilling of enclosure G24's southern boundary (Fig. 5.22).

Central Area

Within the central part of Area B, the G19 series of eastern embayments were recut by ditches 1–1.1 m wide and 0.35–0.7 m deep (dated AD 270), while the southern bay was re-partitioned by F.5452 (2.84 m wide, 0.4 m deep; dated AD 270; Fig. 5.22). Along the inside of the northernmost embayment was a pit, F.5656 (1.5 m wide, 0.8 m deep) that had a deposit of chicken parts and pig forelegs. On the western side, the metalled surface associated with and south of the G11.01 structure was maintained and the gullies on its northern and eastern sides were recut (dated AD 340). The structure itself would appear to have been abandoned as a large sub-enclosure was established (see G11 below).

Square Enclosure with Pits

Abutting the embayments on the east side, a large square enclosure (G28) was added in Phase III, distinctive in terms of the 'emptiness' of its interior save for three pits (Fig. 5.25). The enclosure ditch, F.5445, was slight (0.2–0.75 m wide, 0.1–0.3 m deep); it had a dark fill, though with few finds. None of the ceramics are particularly useful to date the enclosure, except to indicate that it was 'Late'; stratigraphically it seems to belong to the later fourth century AD and the final phase of the site. Noteworthy animal deposits were found in the terminal of the enclosure, as it met the main east–west boundary ditch, and in the pits within its interior (see below). The pits were unusual in terms of the deposits they contained. In particular, the seemingly 'paired pits', F.5435 and F.5441, showed some curious contrasts. Feature 5435 (0.9 m diam., 0.38 m deep; dated AD 270+) had a large assemblage of animal bone (detailed below). There was only one charred grain from this pit, in contrast to pit F.5441 (0.95 m diam., 0.48 m deep; dated AD 140+) that contained a rich assemblage of charred remains (see Ballantyne below). Conversely, F.5441 had no animal bones. Pottery from F.5435 was generally in larger fragments than in F.5441 and included sherds from two jars, a bowl, mortarium and a storage jar. The third pit, F.5453, was 1.75 m deep and was possibly a well (1.4 m across; dated AD 140–270); it contained fewer animal bones, had few charred remains and no pottery.

A phosphate survey was conducted over the interior of this enclosure on a 5 m grid (Fig. 5.26). The results showed a remarkably clean area, with low phosphate levels in comparison to site background levels, particularly for this part of the site.

Two of the three pits within the enclosure produced animal bone (188 specimens, mostly from F.5435). While the vast majority were unidentifiable (90%), those bones that could be identified were dominated by cow and cow-sized specimens (28), horse (1) and pig (1). From F.5453 came a smaller assemblage of cow/cow-sized (2), chicken (1) and ovicaprine (2) bones. Feature 5452, making up part of the Square Enclosure, produced the most interesting group and contained the partially articulated remains of a horse carcass (see Fig. 6.14). The animal had clearly been butchered into separate, major meat-bearing portions: a complete, articulated left hind-leg was found in association with an articulated axial skeleton from the 2nd thoracic vertebrae (including many of the ribs) to the pelvis. As it was still articulated, the flesh must have still been on the bones when it was placed in the ditch. This animal was thus butchered but not eaten. The deposit mirrors a similar one associated with the Timber Shrine (F.5218), with two more prime meat-bearing sections of a horse carcass selected for deposition rather than consumption. It is possible that there was every intention of eating the horse-meat but that it had gone bad and so was disposed of. However, the similarity of this deposit to that recovered from the shrine (see above) could suggest other reasons. Amongst the other bones present were 20 cow/cow-sized specimens (including two cow mandibles) and 10 ovicaprine bones.

Plant remains sampled from these pits show a range of compositions (Table 5.15). Whilst pit F.5441 included many charred remains, F.5453 had few, and pit F.5435 included just one charred grain. The pit contexts thus represent a variety of infilling patterns, and hence either varied uses or settings within the settlement.

Western Sub-enclosure

To the west of the major dividing ditch F.5431, the space was rather differently organized: a large sub-enclosure occupied the northeastern corner (G11; Fig. 5.22). The sub-enclosure was defined by ditches F.5428 (0.4 m wide, 0.23 m deep; dated AD 270/300+) and F.5417 (2.5 m wide, 0.55–0.6 m deep; dated AD 270/300+), the latter probably continuing north as F.5007 (1.1 m wide, 0.6 m deep; dated AD 300+). The continuation of this ditch implies that the former southern boundary to the settlement had been backfilled by this time. There may also be some intentional symmetry between F.5007 and its contemporary, F.5061, to the north (G2.10), which together created an internal boundary in the core of the settlement; their inward/westward 'tilt' accentuated the threshold between the eastern and western halves of the settlement core. Within this enclosure lay a small square structure.

Structure D

A small square structure, 3.5 m by 4 m sat within the western sub-enclosure, positioned centrally to its opening to the north (Fig. 5.27). Its front faced northward and was marked by two large square posts: F.5600 (1.2 m across, 0.85 m deep) and F.5552 (1.2 m wide, 0.75 m deep; AD 240+). The posts had been set in redeposited natural clay, in sub-square post-pits. These were excessively large for the size of the posts, which were only *c.* 0.3 m in diameter. The posts had been removed at some time and the post-cavities backfilled with a burnt matrix, including abundant fired clay fragments. A sample from F.5552 produced a unique deposit of charred grain. A coin minted AD 320–4 (SF 417), was found at the base of F.5552, and near the top of F.5600 was a neonate burial, F.2091. This occurred within the post packing of the large posthole, lying on its back, close against the edge of the cut. The rest of the structure was defined by a series of smaller postholes, 0.3–0.6 m in diameter and 0.2–0.4 m deep (F.4091–5, F.4171, F.4343 & F.4169).

Postpipe F.5552 was unique in having the only grain-rich charred remains from the site (158 grains/42 chaff per 1.25 l). There is little chaff, and no seeds, which suggests that a cleaned crop-product is represented. The context may attest to grain that was charred during food preparation.; eggshell was also present in the sample.

Table 5.15. *Plant remains from pits.*

Context	Feature	Phase	Type	Sample volume/ litres	Grain No.	Chaff No.	SeedNo.	Total count per litre soil
[1486]	F.5441	III	pit	11	20	121	17	14.36
[1515]	F.5453	III	pit	10	7	16	3	2.60
[1532]	F.5452	III	ditch	14	13	200	22	16.79

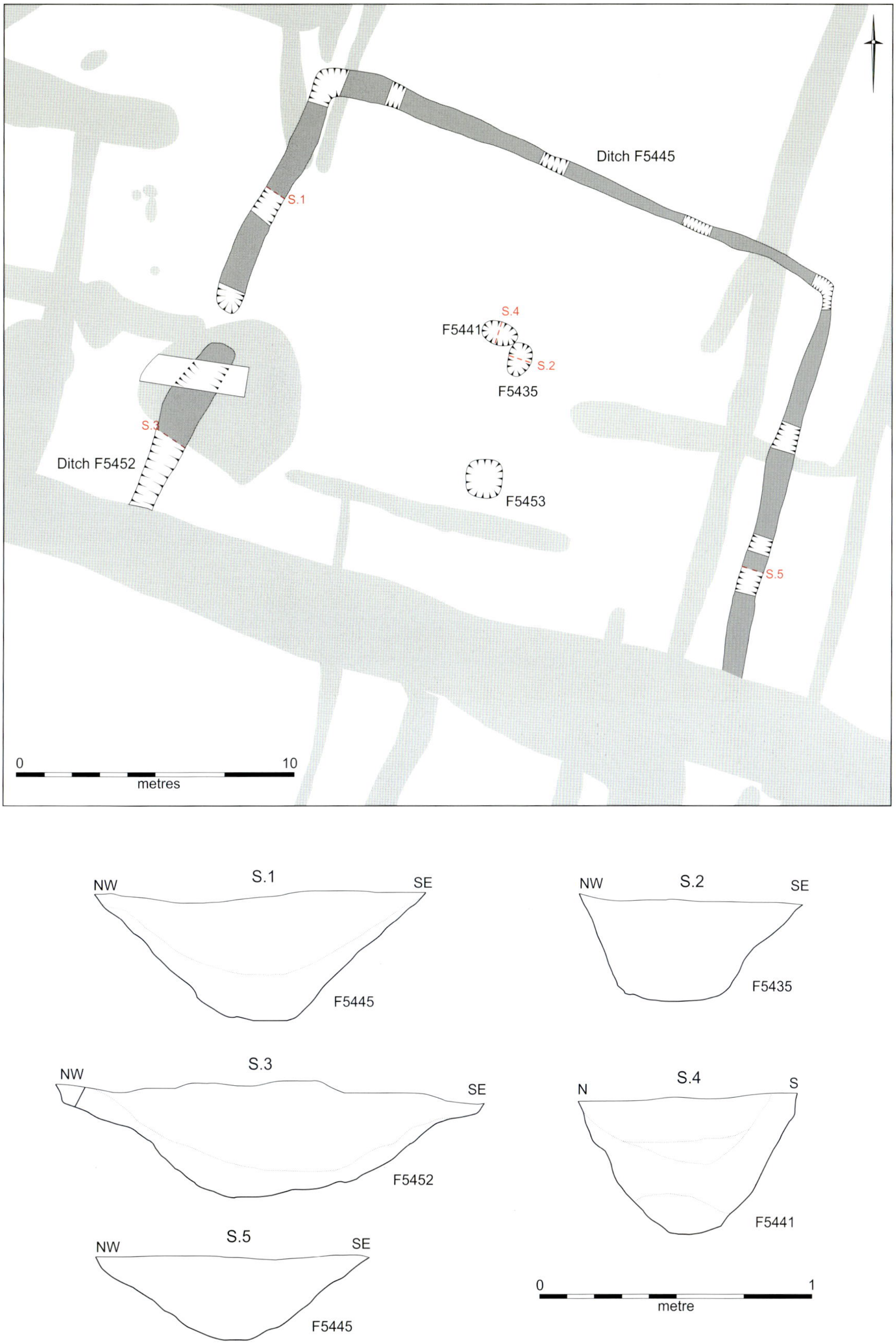

Figure 5.25. *Square Enclosure (G28), plan and sections.*

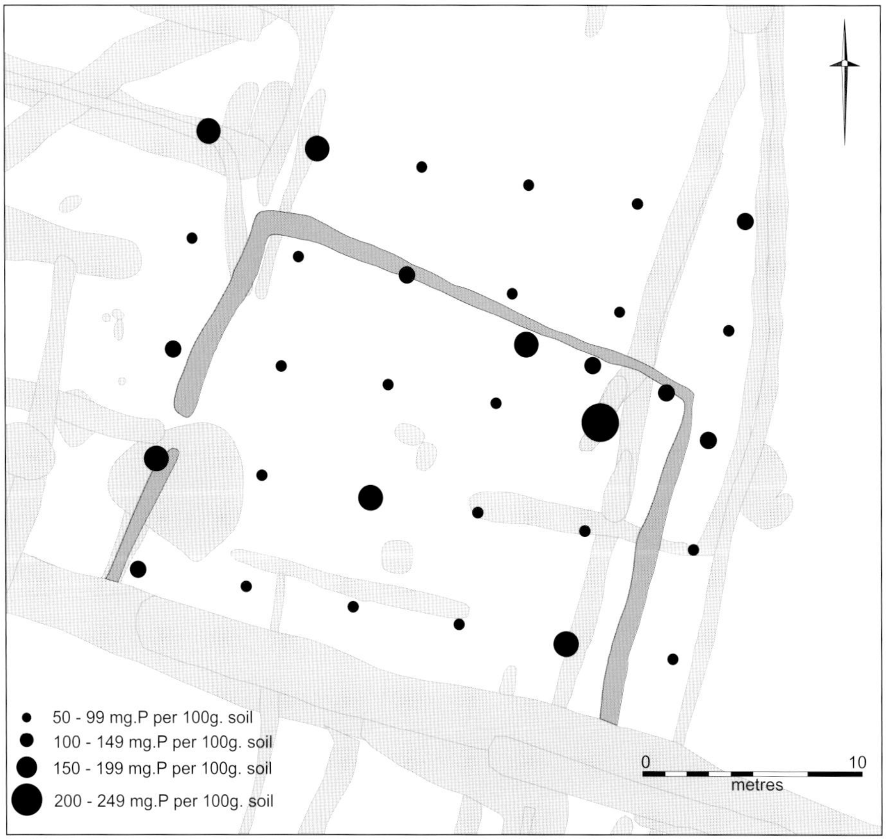

Figure 5.26. *Square Enclosure, phosphate readings.*

Eastern Side

Along the eastern side of the site there was a further partition marked by ditch F.5467 (0.9 m wide, 0.4 m deep; AD 270+), later recut as F.5443 (0.9–1.2 m wide, 0.2–0.3 m deep; dated AD 325–50; Fig. 5.22). This demarcated a large area (G10) bounded to the north by F.5731 (G23), which ran up to the Curvilinear Enclosure (G2.11) and contained two smaller enclosures on its northern edge. The larger and easternmost was F.5735/8140 (0.53–1.3 m wide, 0.5–0.7 m deep; AD 240–300), while smaller and to the west was F.4794/4852 (AD 200–80). The creation of this enclosure would have necessitated the backfilling of the previous southern boundary ditch, F.5736, as well as the eastern line of the main enclosure (F.4815). At the northern end of the site, ditch F.5013 was probably contemporary with this change (see below).

Western Side

In the later period, the basic limits of the southern extension were expanded on the western side as ditch F.5092 (G14; 0.5–1.4 m wide, 0.1–0.36 m deep) formed a new southwestern corner to the settlement, together with F.5318 (0.5–1 m wide, 0.2–0.34 m deep; Fig. 5.22). Inside, F.5090 (0.8 m wide, 0.17 m deep) formed an internal partition with the corner of the primary settlement enclosure; ditch F.5318 continued south as F.5353 (G21; see Area D below).

Southern Fields (Areas C/D)

In the later third/early fourth century AD, a large square enclosure occupied the space between the southern edge of the southern core extension (Area B) and the northern edge of the southern fieldsystem (Area D; Fig. 5.22). Defined by ditches F.5387/F.5418 (2.6–3.8 m wide, 0.5–1.15 m deep; dated AD 270/300+), an area 39.5 × 41.5 m was enclosed (*c.* 1640 sq. m; G18). While no extant internal features were located, in the mid fourth century AD an internal division was added, F.5389 (1–1.7 m wide, 0.2–0.3 m deep; dated AD 330+). East of this main enclosure, a number of minor ditches (1 m wide, 0.57 m deep) formed smaller enclosures (G27) that abutted a southern enclosure, F.5414 (0.7–1.6 m wide, 0.41 m deep).

Also running off the southern edge of the southern core extension and parallel to the G19 enclosure was a double-ditch/-gully line that linked the main settlement system to the southern fieldsystem. Contemporary with and probably a continuation of F.5318 of G14 (Area B; see above) was F.5353 (1.–1.5 m wide, 0.33–0.5 m deep; dated AD 120–200/240+), which ran down off the Area B enclosure to link up with the Area D fieldsystem. Cut parallel to this, 2.6–3.6 m apart, was F.5375 (1.1–1.4 m wide, 0.15–0.4 m deep; dated AD 300+). While together the two ditches may have done no more than flank a bank and/or hedgerow, lying *c.* 2.5–4.5 m apart, they more likely related to a trackway route/path running south to the inhumation

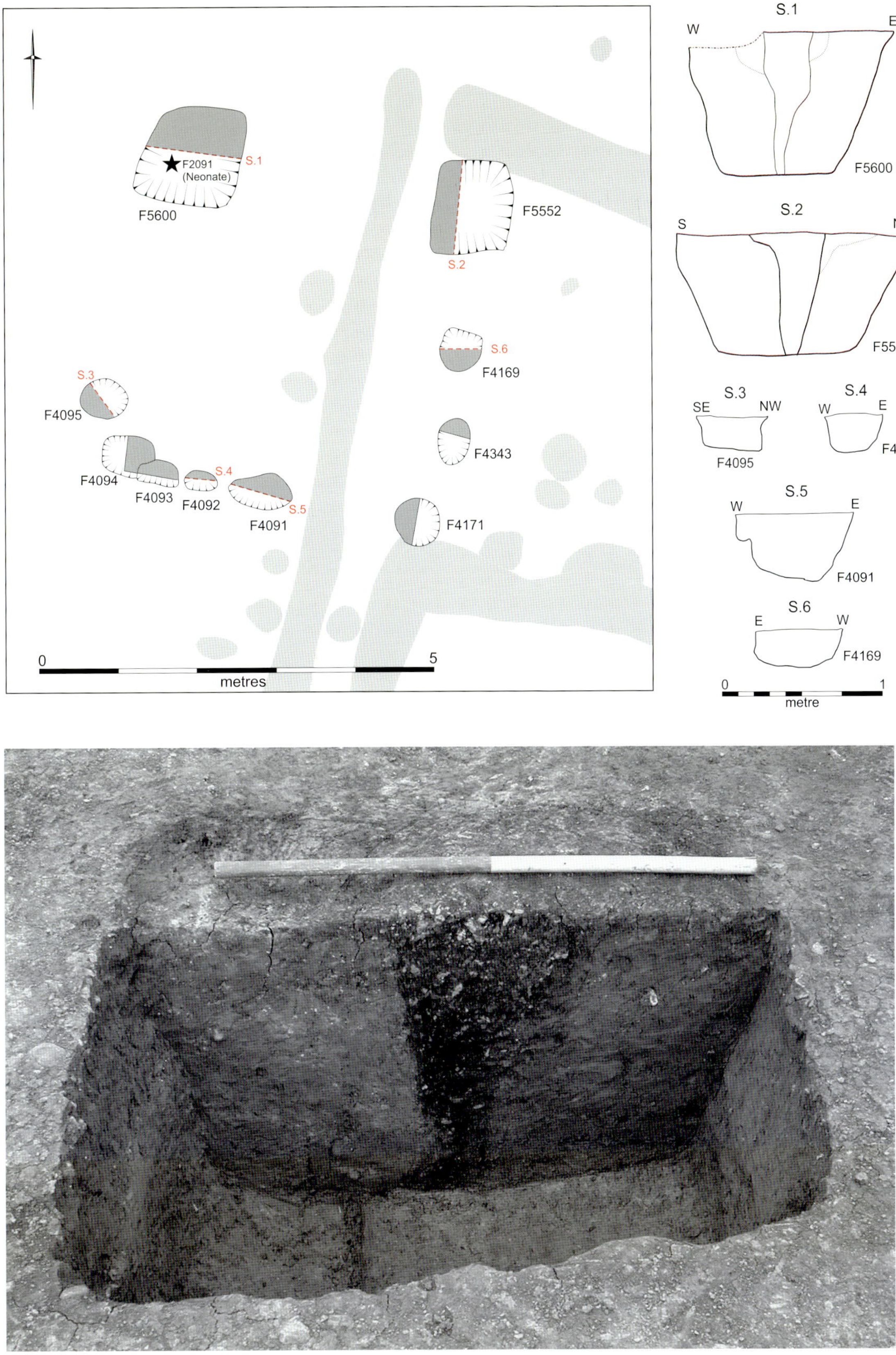

Figure 5.27. *Structure D, with photograph of F.5552 (looking west).*

cemetery (G21); if so, its access would have probably necessitated the local backfilling of the F.5427 boundary to the G24 enclosure. Later, the inner ditch-line was recut by the Area C enclosure and ditch F.5001 (1.–1.2 m wide, 0.14–0.2 m deep).

Fragments of skull (adult parietal) were recorded in ditch F.5418 ([1339]), at the northeast corner of the G18 enclosure (see Fig. 6.21). This ditch section also backed onto the south side of the Square Enclosure G28 (see above).

The Inhumation Cemetery (Area D; Cemetery 3)
At the southern end of the site, occupying a corner of the southern fieldsystem, was an inhumation cemetery (G22; Fig. 5.28) whose origins were associated with a central cremation (F.2084; see Phase II). The limits of the cemetery were demarcated by ditches F.5360 (0.7 m wide, 0.2 m deep) and F.5043 (*c.* 1 m wide, 0.3 m deep), which were dated to the fourth century AD. These closed off the corner of the fieldsystem as defined by the G21 ditches (F.5353/5340); they saw several recuts (F.5365 & F.5345) within the phase, but only along the length of the cemetery. At a later date, a much wider area around the cemetery was enclosed (G26), defined by ditches, F.5166 (2 m wide, 0.64 m deep), F.5335 (2 m wide, 0.6 m deep) and F.5163 (*c.* 1.4 m wide, 0.35 m deep), later recut by F.1021/F.1207 (0.5–1.4 m wide, *c.* 0.2 m deep). In the upper fill of ditch F.5166 were the remains of a partially articulated adult skeleton, Burial F.991 (see Fig. 5.22). Only the right side of the body was represented and the tibia is severely flattened (see Neil & Mulder below). As Dodwell reports, the body was laid with its with head to the west:

> *Skeleton F.991; Adult* - A heavily truncated and disturbed burial lying on the north edge of ditch F.5166. The body appeared to be orientated with its head (missing) to the west and, if the skeletal elements were not too disturbed, the position of the body appears very awkward. Only fragments of the right limbs and shoulder survived; the body would have been lying prone, the elbow was flexed back so that the hand would have rested on the shoulder, the leg flexed so that the knee was in contact with the elbow, the ankle with the hip. There is severe side-to-side flattening of the tibia and front-to-back flattening of the femur.

At the western end of the cemetery was an elongated pit, F.5425. At 1.67 m long and *c.* 3.25 m wide, it was very shallow (0.12 m deep; Figs. 5.28–9). At either end was a carefully placed horse skull with an arrangement of stones at the snout, the two heads facing inward toward each other. The skulls themselves were in a very poor state of preservation; they were intact and complete, but the bone was so cracked and friable that it was clear that they would fragment when being cleaned. To this end, Clarke cleaned both so as to attempt to gain as much osteological data as possible. It was possible to age each: one 3–4 years (northern skull) and, the other, to 8–10 years (southern). No canine teeth were observed, but as the absence of canines also occurs in males it cannot be confidently stated that both of these individuals were mares. No cut marks of any kind, nor any evidence of gnawing were observed, so it is considered likely that the skulls were still fleshed when deposited and then buried rapidly afterwards. Incorporated into the feature's backfill was fourth-century AD pottery (Fig. 5.29).

The burials within the cemetery, which numbered 29 identified graves (but 30 individuals), have been divided according to two different criteria: orientation and location. The graves seem to be oriented broadly either north–south or east–west, and using the boundary ditch F.5403, lay to either side of this, with a couple of exceptions (Fig. 5.28). There was a clear tendency for burials south of, and up to, the cremation (F.2084) to be oriented north–south, while those north of the cremation lay east–west (the one burial lay immediately outside the enclosure, F.2004, also had that orientation). Some of the burials intercut, but it was rare that earlier burials were completely disturbed.

Very few of the burials contained of any animal bone and this was very limited. Respectively, the following remains were recovered from Graves F.2058, F.2001 and F.2046: a very eroded fragment of goat humerus, a horse incisor and a cow molar. These bones had not been placed on or around the inhumations; instead they were recovered from the grave fills and are, therefore, most likely to be residual. Similarly, as reported by Ballantyne, all 10 samples from the cemetery contexts contain very limited charred plant remains, usually just individual grains or chaff fragments of glume wheat accompanied by a low quantity of highly fragmented wood charcoal. The charred material appears to be residual surface debris, either reworked into grave fills or accumulated gradually in enclosure ditches. Occasional small remains of oyster, mussel and eggshell fragments indicate that a low quantity of such material must also have been present on the surface. That said, as related below (see *Inset*), the fishbone recovered from the stomach-area of Skeleton F.2016 likely derives from the individual's last meal.

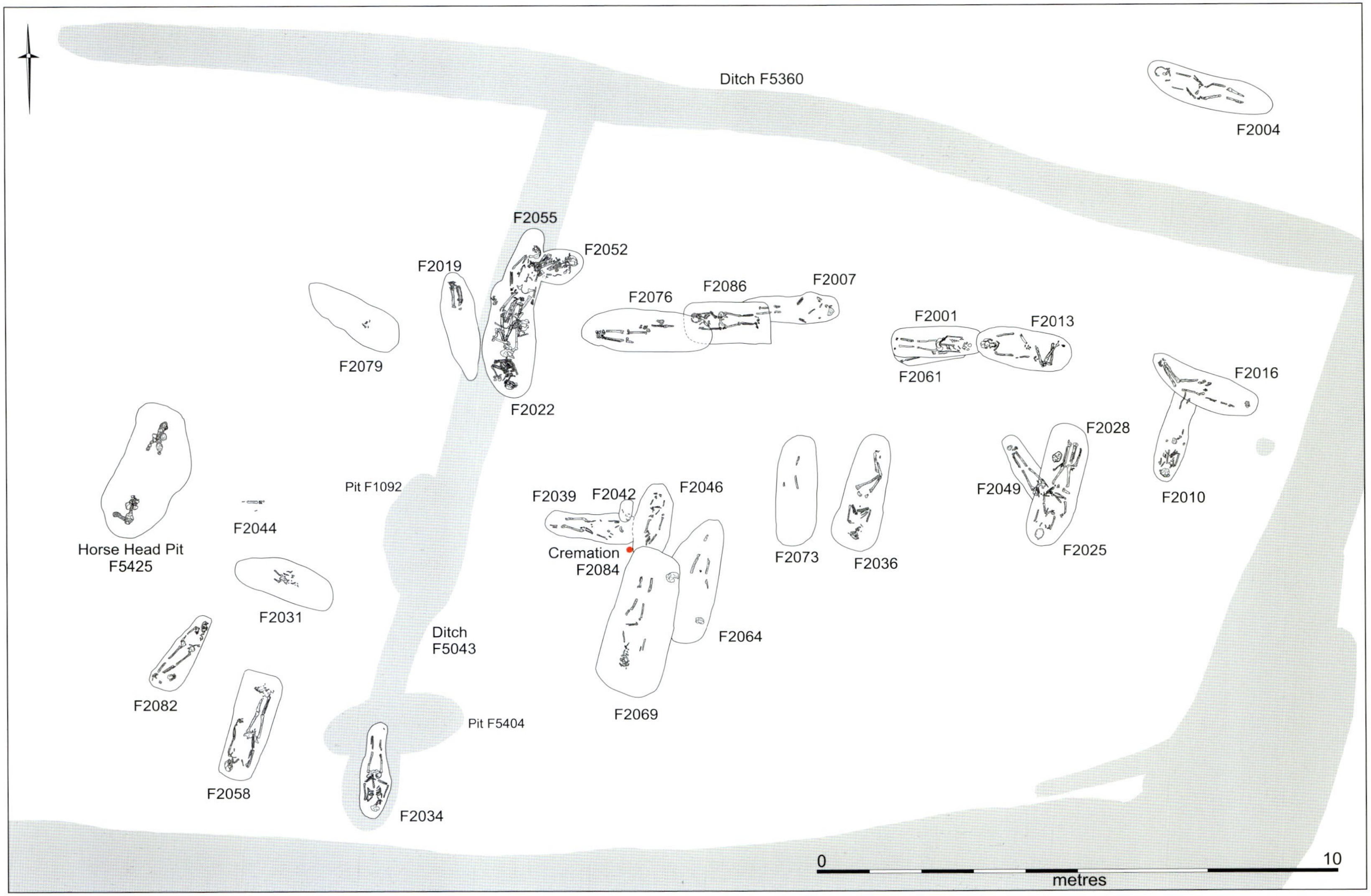

Figure 5.28. *Inhumation cemetery (G22). Note that, as shown here, the plan/size of pits F.1092 and F.5404 might be suggestive of graves. The first was a Post-Medieval pit with seventeenth-century pottery; F.5404 was truncated by ditch F.5403 and had 'sterile' fills, with no dating evidence (no human bone came from either).*

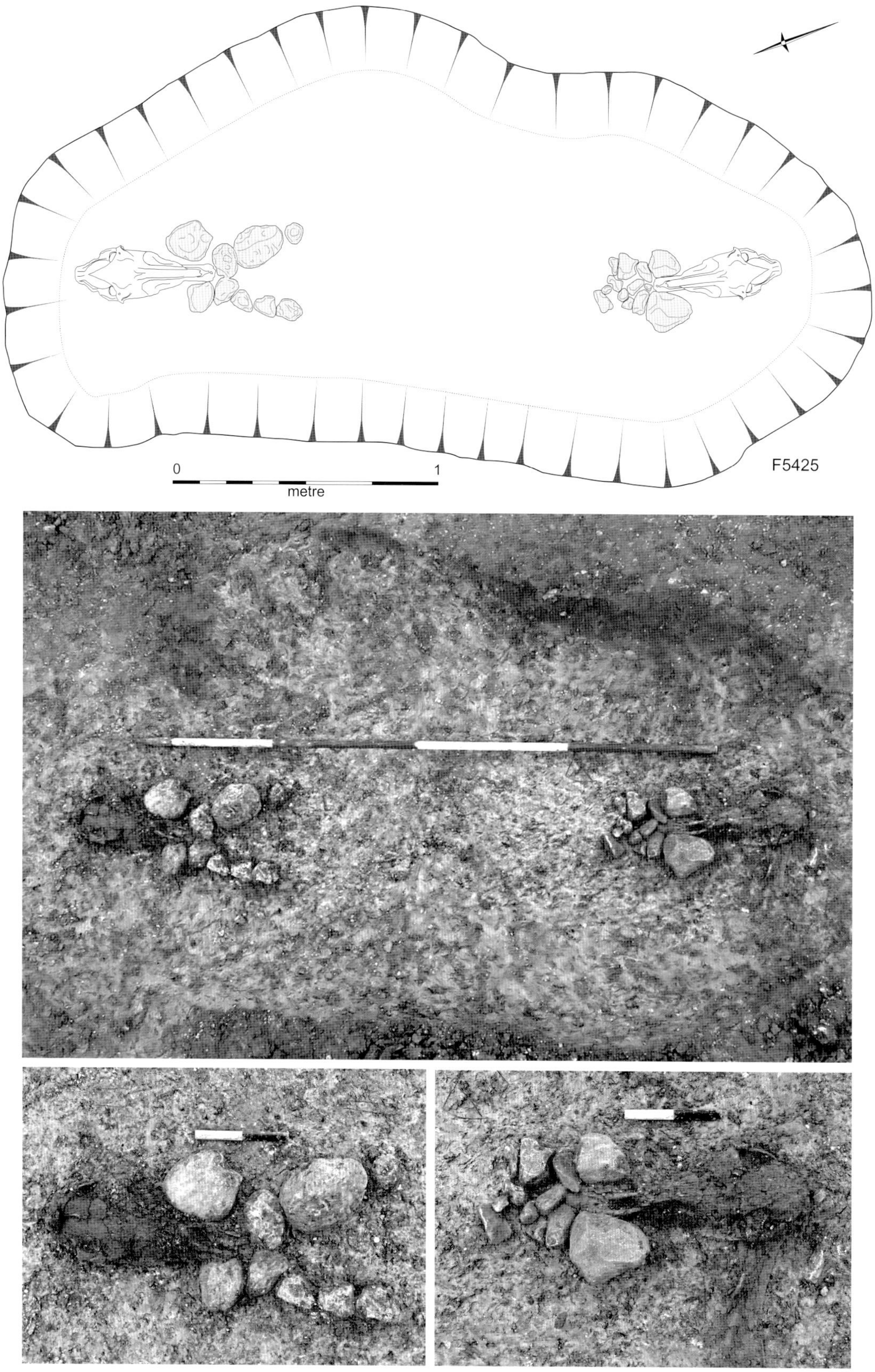

Figure 5.29. *Horse head pit F.5425, plan and photographs.*

Human Remains Natasha Dodwell (with Sarah Inskip)
The degree of disturbance or truncation, the condition of the bone, and, as importantly which skeletal elements survive, affects the potential for determining the age and sex of individuals and of recognizing any pathological conditions. As with the cremation cemetery, these burials have been disturbed by ridge-and-furrow, later ploughing and, to a lesser degree, machine-stripping prior to excavation. In general, the condition of the skeletons identified was poor. The heavy clay nature of the soil resulted in the destruction of many of the bones and caused the fragmentary nature of the surviving skeletal elements (very few of the long bones are complete and many of the epiphyseal ends are damaged/missing). In addition, the surfaces of many of the bones have been damaged by the burial environment and insect/root damage. Detailed on-site recording of all the skeletal material was conducted, as it became obvious that much of the material would not survive lifting.

General methods used in the osteological evaluation have been outlined above (see *The Cremation Cemetery*). In this case, an assessment of age was based on the stages of epihyseal union and dental eruption (Ubelaker 1989) and on the degree of dental attrition (Brothwell 1972, 67). No pubic symphyses survived and only very occasionally could the auricular surface of the pelvis be used to help determine age (Lovejoy *et al.* 1985). The age categories used are the same as those in the previous cremation burials' descriptions. There may be overlaps between categories. Equally, broad categories, such as adult, were used where insufficient evidence was present. The sex of the individual was ascertained where possible from sexually dimorphic traits on the pelvis and the skull and from metrical data. Because of the fragmentary nature of the material, often only two or three traits could be observed and so sex, where attributed, should be treated with a degree of caution. As almost no complete long bones were recovered, only few estimates of stature could be made.

Skeleton F.2001; Middle adult, female (Figs. 5.28, 5.31 & 5.33) - Moderately preserved skeleton; the skull, being close to the surface, has been damaged by the machine and by ploughing and, although complete, is fragmentary. None of the long bones are complete and the vertebrae and ribs survive only as scraps. The head was in the east of the grave (sub-rectangular; 1.7 × 0.65 × 0.20 m, cut by F.2013) and the body was supine, the legs and left arm extended, with the right hand crossing the pelvis. The majority of the teeth are loose, the anterior teeth are heavily worn and several are rotten with just the roots surviving. Pale brown/green mineralized plaque or calculus was recorded on the margins of the enamel and root. Both tibia shafts are flattened side-to-side (platycnemia; see Fig. 5.34). This woman had osteoarthritis of apophyseal facets of the spine, as well as hypoplastic lines on two teeth. There was no evidence for *cribra orbitalia* or porotic hyperostosis in the skull. There is marginal new bone growth around the joint surfaces of the phalanges of the hands. Disarticulated human bone, deriving from Skeleton F.2061, was recovered from the fill ([2000]), along with animal bone recovered from the foot of the grave. The woman was buried wearing a copper alloy bracelet on her right arm (see Fig. 5.35.1).

Skeleton F.2004; Middle adult, male (Fig. 5.28) - Poorly preserved skeleton; the skull was damaged by the machine, much of the pelvis was missing and all the surviving bones are fragmentary. The head was in the west of the grave (sub-rectangular; 2.27 × 0.56 × 0.12 m) and the body was supine and extended, with arms tight against the body and the hands resting on the pelvis. Two teeth, including the mandibular 3rd right molar, are rotten and survive only as roots. This man had maxillary sinusitis. He had osteoarthritis in the left hip where there is also a supra acetabular cyst. Unusually, the URC has failed to completely erupt out of the alveolar bone. Large abscesses are present at the apices of ULM1 and LLM3. Four iron nails were recovered, on either side of the skull and hips, that may indicate burial in a coffin.

Skeleton F.2007; Middle adult (?male, aDNA; Figs. 5.28 & 5.31) - This skeleton has been heavily disturbed and truncated by a furrow. Most of the skull and the entire pelvis are missing, as are the torso. Only the mid shafts of the long bones survived and then only as scraps. The head was in the east of the grave (sub-rectangular; 1.9 × 0.4 × 0.17 m, cut by F.2086) and the body was supine and extended, with both arms slightly flexed at the elbows. No sex was attributed; the only element available for sexing was the mastoid process, which appeared male. The anterior teeth are heavily worn and of the 15 loose teeth recovered, four had severe carious lesions, in two cases sufficiently large to nearly destroy the crown. All the teeth had moderate deposits of calculus. Defects in the enamel, of a mandibular canine indicate a period of childhood illness or nutritional stress. There is osteoarthritis of the apophyseal facets of the spine.

Skeleton F.2010; Adult (Fig. 5.28) - An extremely poorly preserved skeleton damaged by the machine and by ploughing. The dentition and face are missing, as is the left arm and most of both legs. The remaining skeletal elements are fragmentary. The head was at the south of the grave (sub-rectangular; 2.04 × 0.79 × 0.08 m; cut by F.2016 to the north), the body was supine, legs extended and right arm flexed with the hand resting on the left shoulder. Extensive eburnation was observed in the lumbar apophyseal facets indicating osteoarthritis in the spine. A sherd of second-/third-century AD greyware, one nail and a nail shaft were recovered from the fill

Skeleton F.2013; Older middle/ mature adult, ?male (Figs. 5.28 & 5.31) – A poorly preserved skeleton damaged by the machine and by ploughing. The face and the maxilla are missing, as are the pelvis and torso. The remaining elements are fragmentary. The head was to the west of the grave (sub-rectangular; 1.4 × 0.55 × 0.20 m; truncated in the west by grave cut F.2001), the body was supine with the legs flexed (left over right, knees pointing south), the right arm was extended and the left slightly flexed so that the hand rested over the pelvis. Although the jaw is damaged, at least two teeth were lost prior to death and heavy deposits of calculus, some of it subgingeval, were recorded on all the surviving teeth. In the upper jaw all the incisors have been lost ante-mortem. This individual also has active maxillary sinusitis. Healing *cribra orbitalia* was observed in the orbital roofs. Osteoarthritis was present in the hip, wrist, and the temporal mandibular joint. A large carious lesion was recorded on the loose 2nd maxillary premolar. The bodies of the surviving cervical vertebrae exhibit increased porosity. Both tibiae exhibited side-to-side flattening (platycnemia). A large granite-type stone rested on the sternum.

Skeleton F.2016; Adult (Fig. 5.28) - The dentition and the face are missing from this poorly preserved skeleton, as is the torso. The surviving elements are fragmentary. The head was in the east of the grave (sub-rectangular; 2. × 0.7–0.9 × 0.10 m), the body supine, legs slightly flexed towards the south and the left arm extended (the right was disturbed). Despite the abraded surfaces, areas of striated bone indicative of a non-specific infection were recorded on both tibias. Both tibiae exhibit slight platycnemia (see Fig. 5.34). Hobnails were recovered from around the feet.

Skeleton F.2019; Adult (Fig. 5.28) – A severely truncated skeleton, in which only the lower legs and feet survive and they are fragmentary. The head would have been in the south of the grave and the lower legs were extended. The grave cut had been truncated to the natural and what little survived had no recognizable edges, being so shallow. Striated new bone, indicative of a non-specific infection, was observed on the medial aspect of the mid shaft of the right tibia.

Skeleton F.2022; Female, young adult (Figs. 5.28 & 5.32) - Although all the surviving elements exhibit post-mortem breaks and abraded surfaces, the bones are in far better condition than many of the other burials. The machine truncated the right side of the skull, including

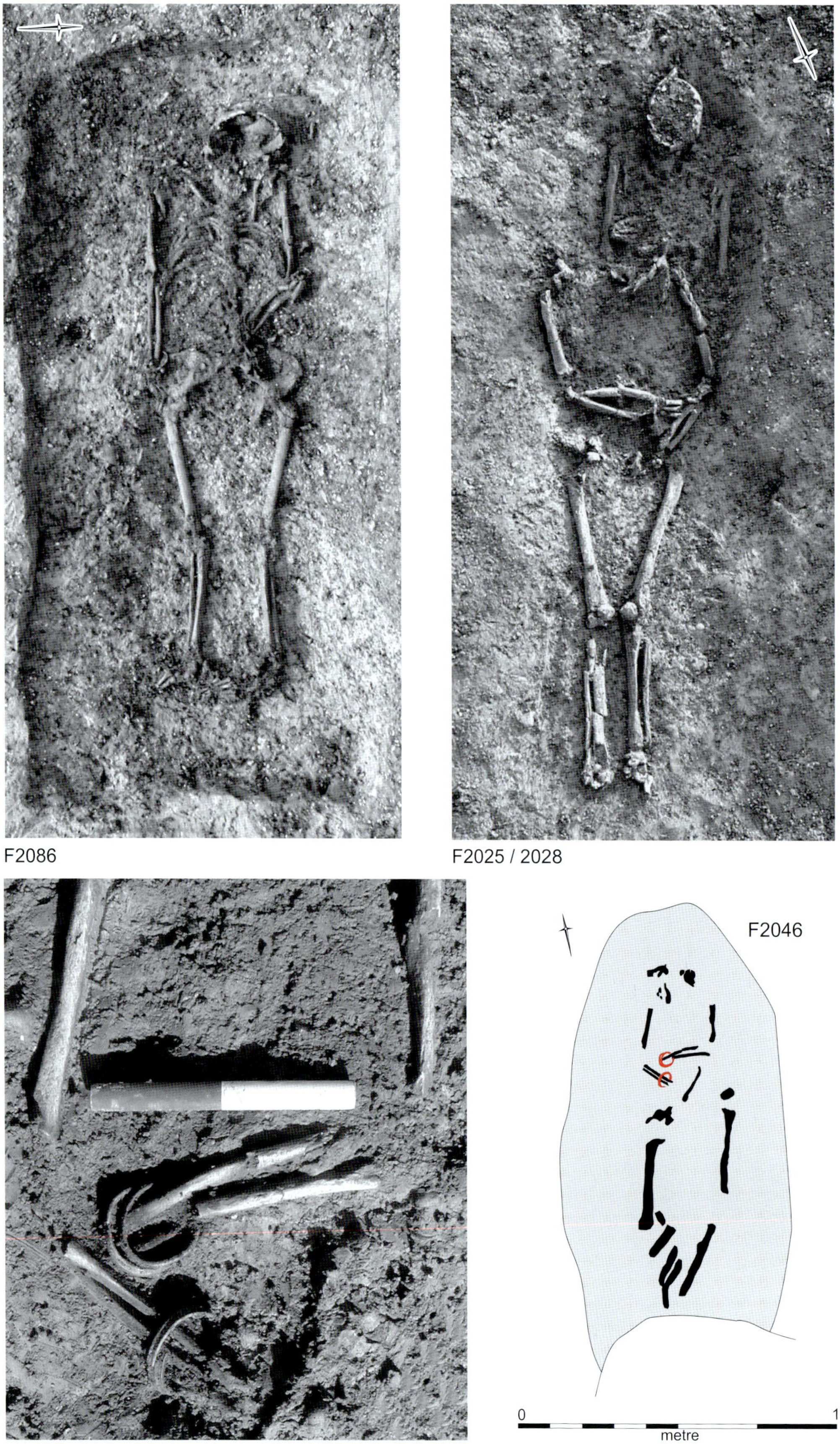

Figure 5.30. *Photographs of Burials F.2086 and F.2025/2028, with plan of Burial F.2046 (with details of bracelets on arms, lower left; not oriented to north).*

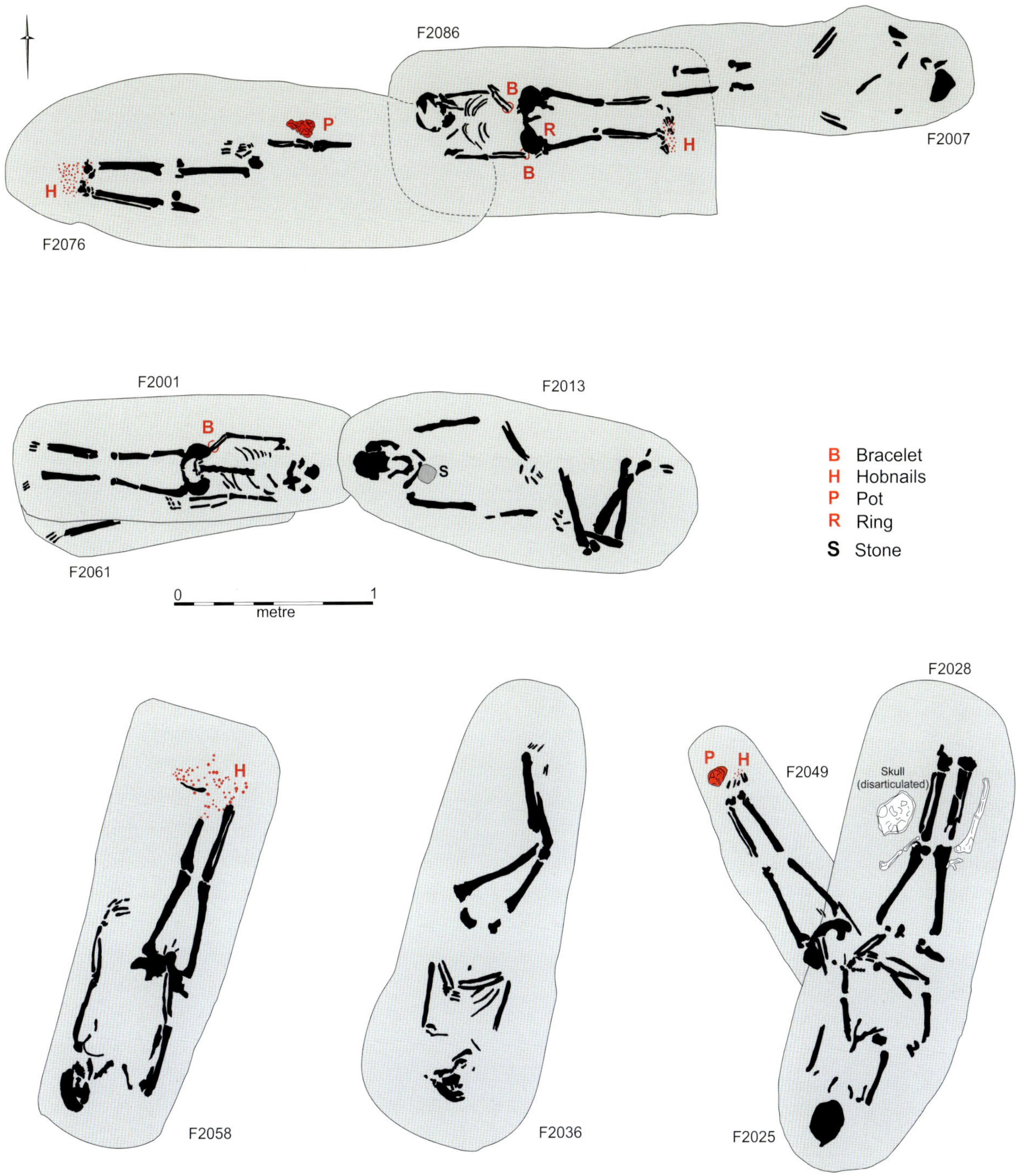

Figure 5.31. *Plans of Burials F.2001, F.2007, F.2013, F.2025, F.2028, F.2036, F.2049, F.2058, F.2076 and F.2086.*

the jaw. The head was in the south of the grave (cut was indistinct, but no deeper than 0.11 m), the body was supine, legs extended, both arms flexed: right across the stomach, left on the sternum. A septal aperture, a non-metric trait more common in females than males, was recorded on the left humerus. No pathologies were observed and there was no evidence *cribra orbitalia*, maxillary sinusitis or hypoplasia. Based on a refitted humerus, her stature is estimated to have been 157.4 ± 4.45 cm.

A large quantity of disarticulated bone ([2021]), belonging to an individual not originally identified in the cemetery, was recovered from the fill and is described below; F.2055 lay immediately over the burial to the north.

Skeleton F.2025; Middle/Mature adult (Figs. 5.28 & 5.30–1) - The skull, the right clavicle and the feet have been truncated by the machine and ploughing. Again, the surviving bones are very fragmentary. The

Figure 5.32. *Plans and photographs of Burials F.2022, F.2052 and F.2055.*

head would have been at the south end of the grave (sub-rectangular; 1.8 × 0.5 × 0.12 m), the body supine, legs extended, both arms flexed; the left hand rested on the inside thigh and the right hand on the left forearm. The middle of the body slumped into the fills of earlier burials, F.2028 and F.2049. Osteophytes and increased porosity were recorded on the articular facets of the sacrum and surviving lumbar vertebrae. There was front-to-back flattening in the proximal shafts of the femora (platymeria) and side-to-side flattening of the tibiae (platycnemia; see Fig. 5.34). Disarticulated human bone was recovered from the grave fill.

Skeleton F.2028; Older middle/Mature adult male (Figs. 5.28 & 5.30–1) - Much of the facial area, including the maxilla, was truncated by the machine; the distal ends of the upper arms, the lower arms, torso and upper legs had been truncated by the later grave containing Skeleton F.2025. The surviving bones are fragmentary. The head was in the south of the grave (1.8 × 0.6 × 0.17 m) and the body was supine and extended. The surviving teeth are worn and six mandibular teeth were lost before death. There was significant degeneration in the spine, including osteoarthritis on the apophyseal facets, osteophytosis, and degenerative disc disease. Disarticulated human bone was recovered from the grave fill.

Skeleton F.2031; Young/Middle adult (Fig. 5.28) - This skeleton was disturbed by the machine and by earlier ploughing. The skull and shoulders are missing, as are the feet, and the surviving bones are fragmentary. The head would have been in the east of the grave (severely truncated, sub-rectangular; 2. × 0.6 × 0.05 m) and the body was supine and extended, with hands lying alongside the thighs. Other than some lipping of the distal right ulna joint, no pathology was observed. An 'L'-shaped piece of iron was recovered from below the pelvis (<5147>). Of oval-section (7 × 9.7 mm), its 'foot'-length is 33 mm long and, its other arm, 43 mm, with its end 12 mm tapering to a blunt point; possibly a buckle or box/casket fitting.

Skeleton F.2034; Mature adult female (Fig. 5.28) - The left side of the skull had been ploughed away and all the surviving bones are fragmentary. The head was in the south of the grave and the body was supine; the legs were extended and arms flexed, right-over-left, with the right hand on left forearm and the left over right hip. This sub-rectangular grave (1.6 × 0.6 × 0.07 m) was cut into the top of a ditch fill. The scraps of surviving lumbar vertebrae exhibit increased porosity and osteophytes on the articulating facets, indicative of degenerative joint disease. Eburnation was present on the apophyseal facets of the lumbar vertebrae. There was evidence for degeneration in the right wrist (lipping). Three mandibular teeth were lost prior to death and carious lesions were recorded on four teeth. Calculus was observed on all the teeth including the occlusal aspect of the right 1st molar, which suggests that the occluding maxillary tooth (maxilla not present) was lost some time before death. No hypoplasia was observed in the teeth. There was a finger-ring on the left hand (see Crummy, below).

Skeleton F.2036; Mature adult (female, aDNA; Figs. 5.28 & 5.31) - The body is poorly preserved and much of the skull and the right arm have been truncated and damaged by a land drain. The head was in the south of the grave (sub-rectangular; 1.9 × 0.7 × 0.18 m) and the body was supine, legs flexed to the right, knees touching the side of the grave; the arms were flexed over chest, with the right hand over the left. The skull, particularly the occipital part, is thickened. Raised plaques of new bone, characteristic of a non-specific infection, were recorded on the lateral aspect of the distal shaft of the left tibia. Increased porosity and marginal osteophytes were noted on a cervical vertebra facet. Five teeth from the surviving dentition were lost prior to death; the sockets have healed over completely and the opposing teeth are unworn, indicating that they were lost a considerable time before death. Heavy deposits of calculus were recorded on the buccal aspects of the surviving molars. There is evidence for healing *cribra orbitalia*, and the right distal MC1 joint facet has osteoarthritis.

As outlined below (see Scheib *et al.*), while morphologically the individual could not be sexed, it is genetically estimated to be female.

Skeleton F.2039; Older middle/Mature ?female (Fig. 5.28) - The skeleton is extremely poorly preserved; the skull, except for fragments of mandible, and the lower legs and feet had been truncated by earlier ploughing and the remaining skeleton is very fragmented. The head was in the east of the grave (sub-rectangular; 2.1 × 0.7 × 0.08 m) and the body was supine and extended with both arms slightly flexed, hands resting on the pelvis. Two deciduous mandibular incisors, presumably from infant burial F.2042, were recovered close to the shoulder (the relationship between this adult and the infant was unclear). Increased porosity and osteophytes were recorded on the fragmented sacral body. From the surviving fragmentary mandibular dentition, two teeth were lost prior to death and the two incisors are worn to the roots. Some coffin nails were associated with the skeleton. Disarticulated human bone was recovered from the grave fill.

Skeleton F.2042; Infant (2 years ± 8 months; Fig. 5.28) - An extremely poorly preserved infant represented only by its loose dentition (a mixture of deciduous and permanent teeth), tiny skull fragments, shafts of the left arm and fragments of vertebrae and ribs. The head was in the south of the grave; the body was supine with the left arm slightly flexed at the elbow. No grave cut was recorded; the body lay on the ground surface. No pathology was observed. The child was buried with blue glass beads, from their position presumably forming a necklace (see Cool, below).

Skeleton F.2044; Subadult/Adult (Fig. 5.28) - This individual has been severely truncated by ploughing and is represented only by the fragmentary remains of the right lower leg. The bones were articulated and orientated so that the head would have been in the east of the grave. No grave cut was recorded and no pathology was observed.

Skeleton F.2046; Older middle/Mature female (Figs. 5.28 & 5.30) - Poorly preserved skeleton, damaged by a furrow; the lower legs are particularly fragmentary. The head was in the north of the grave (sub-rectangular; 2.52 × 0.8 × 0.30 m; cut by F.2069), the body was supine and the legs were slightly flexed to the right at the knees. The arms were flexed, with the wrists crossing at the waist, left-over-right. No pathology was observed. Front-to-back flattening of the proximal half of the femurs (platymeria) was observed but neither of the tibias was misshapen. This adult female was buried with two copper alloy bracelets, one worn on each wrist (see Crummy, below). One of these had decorated snakehead terminals. An area of organic staining was observed on the chest area and could be evidence for a bag or box.

Skeleton F.2049; ?Adult female (Figs. 5.28 & 5.31) - Poorly preserved skeleton whose upper body (above the elbows) is missing, having been truncated by either/both Skeletons F.2025 and F.2028. The surviving bones are very fragmentary. The head would have been in the southeast of the sub-rectangular grave (1.80 [truncated] × 0.5 × 0.25 m) and the body was supine and extended, with the right hand (not present) between the legs and, the left, on the left thigh. No pathology was observed. If the disarticulated fragments of skull and mandible found in [2024] (the fill for Skeleton F.2025) belong to this woman, then she is likely to be a middle/mature female. A small greyware flagon was buried beside her left ankle and iron hobnails were collected from the soles (balls only) of the feet (see Monteil and Crummy, below). Iron nails, possibly from a coffin, were recorded along the right side of the body.

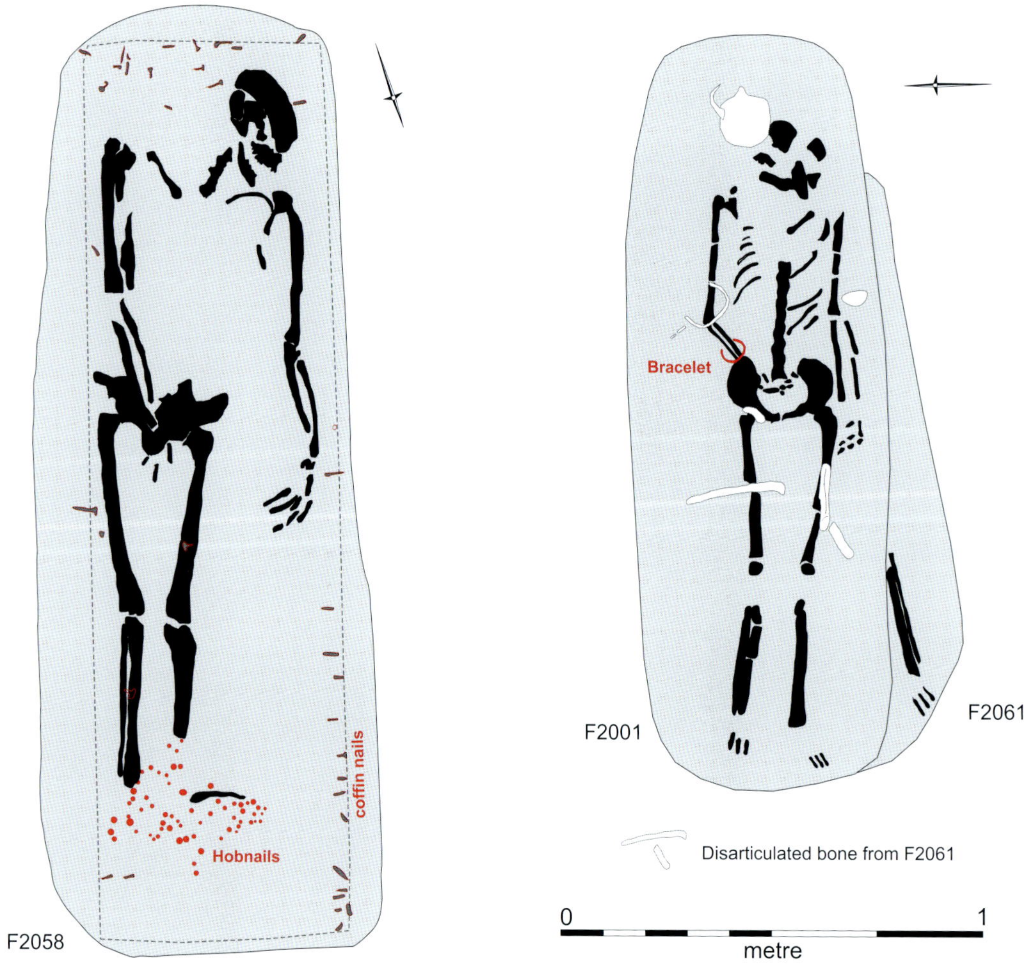

Figure 5.33. *Plans of Burials F.2058 (with coffin nails indicated) and F.2001 (including disarticulated bone redeposited from F.2061).*

Skeleton F.2052; Middle adult female (Figs. 5.28 & 5.32) - A poorly preserved and fragmented skeleton, whose head was in the east of the grave and the body lay on its right side tightly crouched (ovoid grave cut, 1.2 × 0.55 × 0.15 m). Both legs were tightly flexed, but the right more so than the left; the heel almost touched the pelvis. The right hand was under the head and the left touched the left knee. The vertebrae survived only as scraps, but porosity and marginal osteophytes were recorded on the bodies of both a cervical and a lumbar vertebra; the facets of the upper vertebra also exhibited small patches of eburnation. Osteophytes and increased porosity were recorded on the right articulating facet of the sacrum and on the clavicular surfaces of both scapulae. A large caries was recorded on each of the 3rd maxillary molars; the 2nd left mandibular premolar is rotten and survives only as a root and the 1st left mandibular molar was lost prior to death. Calculus was recorded on the surfaces of all of the surviving teeth.

Skeleton F.2055; Mature adult female (Figs. 5.28 & 5.32) - The skeleton is moderately preserved, although all of the surviving bones are fragmentary. The head was in the north of the sub-rectangular grave (1.6 × 0.8 × 0.15 m), the body was supine, legs slightly flexed to the right, with the left arm extended and the right arm slightly flexed with its hand touching the hip. As with Skeleton F.2034, this grave was cut into the fill of ditch F.5403. Severe osteoarthritic changes were recorded in the left hip and right shoulder joints. Large areas of eburnation, or polishing resulting from bone rubbing directly on bone, were observed on both the head of the left femur and the acetabulum. Severe porosity on the joint surface and osteophytes around the joint margins were also noted. The morphology of the head of the right humerus is also altered, with porosity and eburnation on the joint surface and osteophytes around the margin recorded. Similar changes were recorded in the glenoid cavity of the scapula. The sternal end of the left clavicle also exhibited increased porosity and there is a small area of eburnation on the joint surface and osteophytic lipping around the margins. In the right hand osteophytes and increased porosity – almost pitting – have deformed and altered the morphology of one of the interphalangeal joints. Marginal osteophytes, indicative of incipient joint disease, were recorded on the proximal left ulna and left glenoid cavity. Both the femur and tibia shafts exhibit a degree of front-to-back and side-to-side flattening respectively (see Fig. 5.34). In addition, the cortical bone in the mid shaft of the left tibia is thickened, considerably reducing the size of the medullary cavity in comparison with the right. Deep impressions on the internal surface of the skull – blood vessels usually only seen on the parietal portions of the skull – were recorded on the inside of the frontal bone above the orbits. Although damaged, small holes on the orbital roofs (indicative of anaemia) were recorded. All the surviving teeth are severely worn and a total of 19 were lost prior to death.

Skeleton F.2058; Young adult male (Figs. 5.28 & 5.31) - A moderately preserved but, again, fragmentary skeleton. The head was in the south of the grave tight against the cut, the body was supine and extended. The right hand crossed the pelvis and lay between the legs, the left hand lay palm upwards against the deep, rectangular grave-cut (2.3 × 0.9 × 0.45 m). The spine appeared twisted, the knees almost touched and the right foot rested on the left. Peri-mortem fractures were noted across the shafts of the left 2nd metacarpal and a middle phalange. They were initially observed on-site when the hand was in its articulated position and would have occurred prior to burial, possibly caused by a heavy stamping action. A total of four caries were recorded on three teeth and from the surviving dentition at least two teeth were lost prior to death. The mandible has pronounced inferior margins and this man would have had a distinctive jaw line when alive. Numerous iron nails were recovered around the body that suggest burial in a coffin, and hobnails were recorded around the feet (see Fig. 5.36 and below). The approximate dimensions of the coffin, as evidenced by the nails, would have been 2. × 0.45–0.50 m.

Skeleton F.2061; Juvenile (10 years ± 30 months; Figs. 5.28, 5.31 & 5.33) - A moderately preserved, but fragmentary, juvenile disturbed and largely truncated by the later burial of Skeleton F.2001, with only the lower left leg and foot *in situ*. The disarticulated bones recovered from grave fill [2000] are from this immature individual and are predominantly limb bones and skull fragments. The head (as displaced) was in the east of the sub-rectangular grave (1.2 × 0.5 × 0.05–0.25 m) and the surviving elements suggest that the body was supine and extended. A mixture of deciduous and permanent teeth were recovered; medium deposits of calculus were recorded on the deciduous teeth, particularly on the surviving molar.

Skeleton F.2064; Adult (Fig. 5.28) - An extremely poorly preserved skeleton, with only parts of the skull, long bones and right hand surviving as small fragments and scraps. Fragments of skull lay in the south of the grave and the body was supine and extended, with the right hand probably resting over the pelvis. The grave cut had been cut by F.2069 and truncated by Medieval ploughing. No pathology was observed.

Skeleton F.2069; Older subadult/Young adult (Fig. 5.28) - Poorly preserved skeleton with only limb shafts and skull fragments surviving. The head, which had been dragged by the plough, was in the south of the sub-rectangular grave (2. × 1.1 × 0.25 m). The body was supine and extended; the right lower arm and hand are missing, but the left arm was flexed at almost 90° across the body. Six premolars each had a hypoplasitic band, suggesting illness during childhood temporarily stunted tooth development. Four nails were recovered from the fill and may represent a coffin. The burial cuts F.2064 and F.2046.

Skeleton F.2073; Adult (Fig. 5.28) - A heavily truncated individual with only fragments of the legs and arms surviving. The head (not present) would have been in the south of the grave and the body would have been supine with extended legs. The grave cut had been completely truncated by ploughing and machining. A glass vessel fragment and two hobnails recovered from the machined spoil are likely to have come from this grave.

Skeleton F.2076; Younger middle adult male (Figs. 5.28 & 5.31) - Heavily truncated skeleton with fragments of the skull, legs and right arm and hand surviving. The head was in the east of the grave and the body would have been supine and extended. The right hand was tightly clenched. The grave cut had been completely truncated by ploughing and machining. Marginal osteophytes and slight porosity were recorded on the right proximal ulna. Smooth, cream-coloured new bone indicative of a non-specific infection was observed on the posterior of the distal left femur. Lines of enamel hypoplasia were recorded on the mandibular canine. The 1st left mandibular molar was lost soon before death, as evidenced by the semi-remodelled tooth socket. A large carious lesion was located on the medial aspect of the adjacent molar. The man was buried in hobnailed boots (Fig. 5.36; see Crummy, below), and a ceramic bowl was found beside his right elbow (see Monteil, below).

Skeleton F.2079; Adult (Fig. 5.28) - This grave was invisible until a second, deeper phase, of machining occurred and although the machined spoil was carefully examined, only a small quantity of bone was recovered. The skeleton was extremely truncated and was represented only by fragments of the left humerus, shoulder girdle and scraps of ribs and vertebrae. The head (not present) would have been in the east of the grave and the body would have been supine. The clavicle shows a peri-mortem mediolateral slice to the superior surface of the clavicle (Fig. 5.34). This would have been carried out with a sharp implement. No pathology was observed.

Skeleton F.2082; Young adult female (Figs. 5.28 & 5.39) - A moderately preserved, fragmentary skeleton whose left scapula and humerus had been ploughed out. The head was in the north of the sub-rectangular grave (1.8 × 0.5 × 0.25 m) and the body was supine, with the right arm and legs extended and the left arm slightly flexed at the elbow. Lines of enamel hypoplasia, resulting from childhood illness or nutritional deficiencies, were observed on the maxillary central incisors. A beaker was interred beside the left foot and hobnails were recovered from around the feet (see Monteil and Crummy, below). Fragments of broken glass deriving from several vessels were found in a small heap beside the left lower leg (see Cool and *Inset*, below). A small iron strip/strap (13.5 × 34 mm, 3.4 mm th., <5159>) found below the glass may be evidence of a fastening from a decayed bag in which the glass was originally carried.

Skeleton F.2086; Middle adult female (Figs. 5.28 & 5.30–1) - A moderately preserved fragmentary skeleton. The head was in the west of the wide, rectangular grave (1.9 × 0.92 × 0.13 m) and the body was supine and extended, with arms tight against the torso, the left arm flexed slightly with the hand rather awkwardly everted, palm upwards and slightly clenched. At the right elbow new bone entirely covers the radial notch of the ulna and there is a small area of eburnation and porosity overlying it. A small (5 mm) cloacae, from which puss would have drained, was recorded on the tuberosity of the radius and is indicative of osteomyelitis. Its edges were relatively sharp, suggesting that it was still active at death or just starting to heal. Eburnation and porosity were recorded on the surviving carpals and joints of the metacarpals (both distal and proximal) of the left hand. These changes are characteristic of osteoarthritis and this joint disease might account for the position of the left hand. Similar, but less severe, changes were recorded in the right hand. A small area of eburnation and increased porosity, again indicative of osteoarthritis, was recorded on the head of the left and right talus. Slight deposits of calculus were recorded on the buccal aspects of the mandibular incisors. The woman was buried wearing a copper alloy bracelet on each wrist, and footwear is indicated by hobnails. A bronze ring was found, apparently not worn on a finger, but held in the left hand. Nails recovered from below and around the body have been interpreted as evidence for a coffin (see below).

Several of the graves intercut and there is evidence that disturbed bone was redeposited in the later graves. Disarticulated human bone was recovered from five grave fills (Table 5.16). The bone from four of these, F.2001 ([2000]), F.2025 ([2024]), F.2028 ([2027]) and

Table 5.16. *Disarticulated bones from grave fills.*

Grave fill	Age	Sex	Skeleton source
2000	juvenile	-	2061
2021	mature adult	M	?
2024	adult & mid/ mat. adult	? & F	2028 & 2049
2027	adult	-	2049
2038	infant	-	2042

F.2039 ([2038]), derives from earlier interments that were identified on-site. However, the disarticulated bone in grave fill F.2022 ([2021]) does not derive from any of the identified burials and, therefore, represents another individual. The skull fragments, [2066] and [2067], found on the machined surface may represent two further individuals, but they are just as likely to derive from one of the articulated skeletons already recorded. Because the disarticulated material from grave fill [2021] derives from an individual otherwise undocumented within the cemetery, a detailed description of the material is presented below (details of the disarticulated material from the other grave fills are in the archive):

Disarticulated bone [2021]; grave fill of Skeleton F.2022 (Male; mature adult; Fig. 5.32) - Almost an entire body is represented and there is nothing to suggest that these bones come from more than one individual (i.e. there is no duplication of skeletal elements or contradictory age/sex attributes). The condition of this disarticulated material is far better than any of the *in situ* burials. The majority of the bones were placed/thrown onto the body of F.2022, below her waist and lay directly on the body. The position of several of the skeletal elements in relation to each other suggests partial articulation of this body when it was redeposited (i.e. the right tibia, femur and pelvis). Degenerative joint disease was recorded in several locations: marginal osteophytes were noted on the right acetabulum and femoral head, and the distal articular surface of the right radius. The articular facet of the right radius and the superior articulating facet of a thoracic vertebra all displayed an increase in porosity. The metopic suture, although partially fused, is still visible. A total of at least 15 teeth were lost prior to death: 10 from the lower jaw and five from the maxilla.

Based on a refitted femur, his stature is estimated to have been 166.5 ± 3.72 cm.

Platymeric and Platycnemic Traits Benjamin Neil and Bram Mulder
Bones were scanned at Cambridge University's Biotomography Centre using a Nikon XTH225 ST, with 1080 projections at 140 kV and 100 μA. Scans had a resolution of 0.125 mm and were exported as TIFF-stack. These were visualized in AVIZO 9.1 (FEI), where each bone was isolated from the scan, orientated, and labelled. A cross-section on the femora was extracted from just below the lesser trochanter and from the nutrient foramen on the tibiae (Fig. 5.34). Images were analysed using the BoneJ plugin for ImageJ (v.1.4.3, Doube *et al.* 2010; see Table 5.17).

Platymeria (from Greek *platys + mēros*) indicates the anterio-posterior flattening of the femur. Platycnemia, (from Greek *platys + knēmis*) indicates the transverse flattening of the tibia. Although this trait is equivocal aetiologically, current research related to this phenomenon predominantly lies within the field of biomechanics (see Davies *et al.* 2014). Large temporally broad geometric studies of (anatomically modern) human femora and tibiae tend to conclude a decline in lower limb bone strength or 'robusticity' between the three earliest periods – Upper Palaeolithic, Mesolithic and Neolithic – and later periods (Bronze to early modern and very recent; see Ruff *et al.* 2015). This is characterized by a morphometric shift in these bone elements from flatter to rounder. To elucidate, the biomechanical function and strength of bone is dictated by its physical geometry and torsional strength respectively (see Lovejoy *et al.* 1976), which can in turn inform on types of locomotor behaviour. Focused causal studies suggest that external bone morphology largely reflects an adaptation to forces that occur just before skeletal maturity, though will continue to respond structurally throughout adulthood as well (see Kannus *et al.* 1995; Macdonald *et al.* 2005). For example, mechanical unidirectional loading in runners results in an anterio-posterior strengthening of the tibia, otherwise noted as platycnemic (i.e. a flatter bone). Conversely, multi-directional loading results in

Table 5.17. *Geometric data: The cross-sectional geometric parameters include: TA= the total subperiosteal area; CA= the cortical subperiosteal area. %CA= reflects the differential subperiosteal deposition and endosteal resorption of bone, principally during development. Imin/Imax= the second moment of area, which describes deflection and stress and shows bone distribution in the femora and tibiae. J= the polar moment of inertia, which describes resistance to torsional deformation and a general reflection of overall rigidity. Shape describes the platymeric and platycnemic trait: closer to the value of 1 means the bone is less flat.*

Individual	Bone	Side	TA (mm^2)	CA (mm^2)	%CA	Imin (mm^4)	Imax (mm^4)	J (mm^4)	Shape
2001	Tibia	Left	417.53	247.98	59.39%	7741.49	20512.95	28254.44	0.38
2001	Femur	Right	562.21	357.22	63.54%	15583.78	30831.43	46415.21	0.51
2001	Tibia	Right	428.54	232.55	54.27%	7102.36	20422.51	27524.87	0.35
2016	Femur	Left	670.64	488.58	72.85%	24837.91	45122.92	69960.84	0.55
2016	Tibia	Left	651.97	371.91	57.04%	19386.53	40010.34	59396.87	0.48
2016	Tibia	Right	592.43	367.56	62.04%	17610.77	33870.08	51480.85	0.52
2025	Femur	Left	708.80	486.89	68.69%	24118.47	55613.62	79732.09	0.43
2025	Femur	Right	708.40	435.34	61.45%	23073.40	51669.63	74743.03	0.45
2025	Tibia	Right	494.64	328.56	66.42%	10197.39	31250.49	41447.87	0.33
2055	Femur	Left	772.13	487.66	63.16%	28707.79	58249.86	86957.65	0.49
2055	Tibia	Left	612.30	452.25	73.86%	15820.19	50037.90	65858.09	0.32
2055	Tibia	Right	608.80	434.47	71.36%	15487.08	49756.48	65243.56	0.31

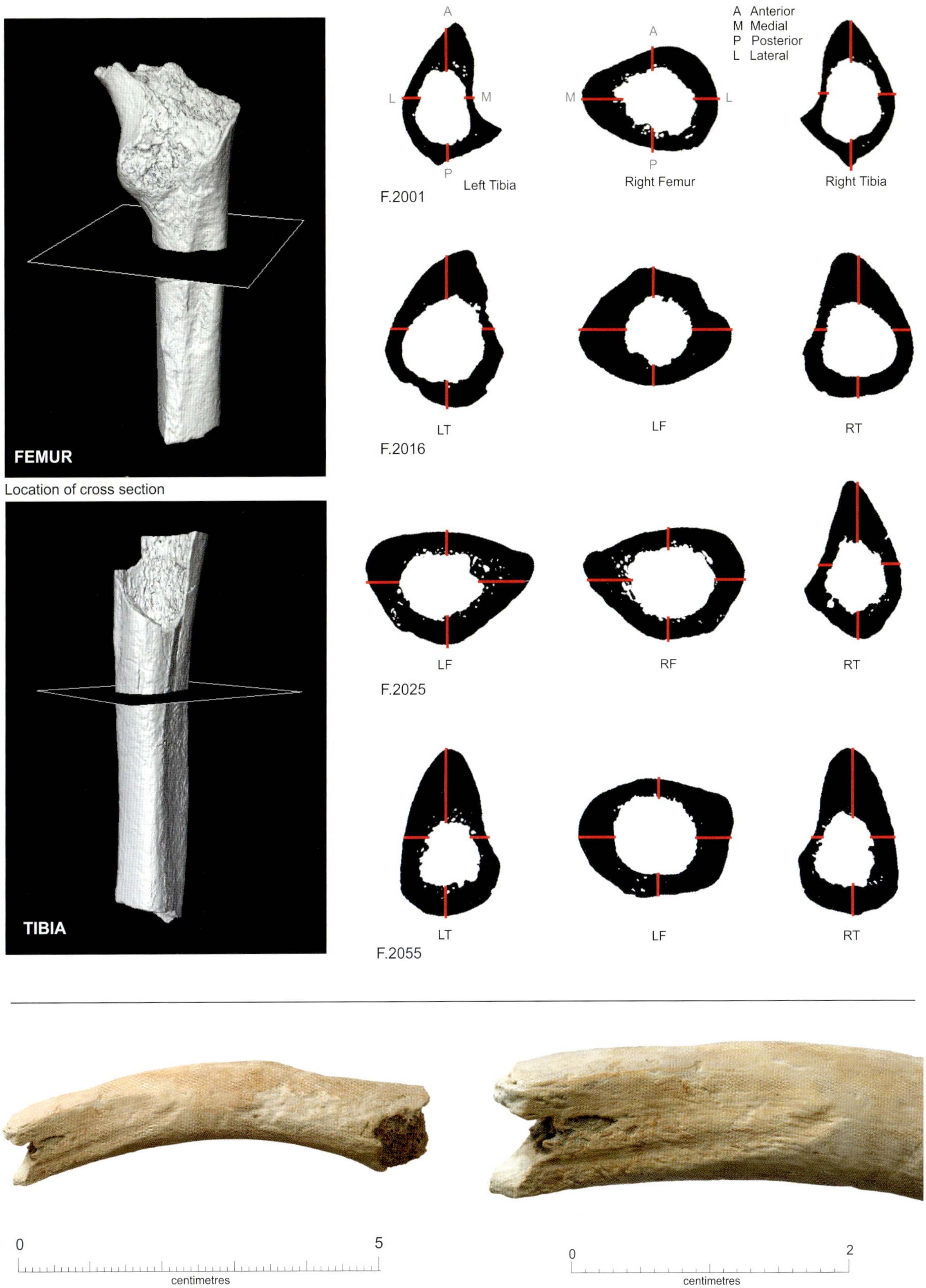

Figure 5.34. *Human tibia and femur cross-sections (graphic output from BoneJ showing morphological variation of each bone from each individual; scanned resolution 0.125 mm); below, the implement-sliced F.2079 clavicle.*

Table 5.18. *Degree of asymmetry (%DA= [Right-Left]/mean).*

Individual	Bone	%DA
2001	Tibia	-2.62%
2016	Tibia	-14.28%
2025	Femur	-6.46%
2055	Tibia	-0.94%

a rounder morphology (Shaw & Stock 2009). In broader scale studies, this locomotor behaviour is usually discussed in terms of mobility and, more specifically, a behavioural transition from high motility (e.g. foragers) into sedentism (e.g. agriculturalists; see Ruff *et al.* 1984).

Empirically, there is a difference in the femoral and tibial dimensions of individuals F.2001, F.2016, F.2025 and F.2055 to the rest of the cemetery population. The greatest expression of tibial flatness is seen in Skeleton F.2055: a mature adult female. The greatest expression of femoral flatness is seen in Skeleton F.2025: an indeterminately sexed middle/mature adult. Unfortunately, a biomechanical inference cannot be made from these or the rest of the geometric observations because the bones were not complete, there being a requirement to standardize the variable of body size (mass and stature) between each individual. Thus, the data can only serve to further humanize these four individuals in terms of side-preference (see Table 5.18). This was calculated following Auerbach and Ruff (2006) and determined that all four individuals preferred their left leg. This trait may be related to directional asymmetry (see Kanchan *et al.* 2008), whereby one side of the upper limb is typically more developed or dominant, with the lower limb opposite the dominant upper limb being larger as compared to the other lower limb. This being so, the inference is that all these individuals were right-handed.

Ancient DNA Analysis Christiana Scheib (with Ruoyun Hui and Toomas Kivisild)

A total of seventeen inhumations with teeth present were sampled for ancient DNA analyses. All work was carried out in a dedicated facility at the University of Tartu, Tartu, Estonia following protocols outlined in Scheib *et al.* 2018. After mapping to the human reference genome (hg19), six samples had an endogenous human content over 22% (overall minimum 0.04%; maximum 56%; average 14%). A genetic sex estimation was calculated using a freely available script from Skoglund *et. al* (2013) and in case of all but two samples sex could be unambiguously determined as XX or XY (Table 5.19). In general, the morphological sex estimates matched with genetic sex except for F.2036, which could not be morphologically sexed but was genetically estimated (with good coverage) to be female. Indeterminate and unobservable individuals were able to be genetically estimated even in cases of very low coverage (F.2061 & F.2069). Out of nine genetically estimated males, four had high enough DNA recovery to estimate Y chromosome haplogroup, which in these samples is exclusively R1 related lineages (Table 5.20), most likely R1b but some could be R1a and are not currently resolvable due to low coverage.

Three samples (F.2058, F.2061 & F.2069) had too low DNA recovery rates to ascertain a mitochondrial (mtDNA) haplotype and were excluded from further analyses. MtDNA haplotypes recovered were strictly U and H haplogroups with more diversity within the H than U that are all U5a (Table 5.19). Contamination estimates based on mtDNA revealed low overall contamination rates (<2.53%; average 0.82%).

There are two sets of individuals with identical mtDNA haplotypes: F.2028 and F.2076 (H1bs) and F.2086 and F.2049 (H2a3). To ascertain whether these or other individuals within the site had close genetic kinship ties, kinship coefficients were calculated using READ (Kuhn *et al.* 2018). This analysis indicates that both pairs of identical mtDNA sharing are first-degree relatives (parent-offspring or full sibling; see Fig. 5.38). Skeletons F.2028 and F.2076 are both male and, therefore, considering their mtDNA identity and autosomal first-degree relatedness most likely full brothers. Skeletons F.2086 and F.2049 are both female and thus could be either a mother-daughter pair or full sisters. There is no indication that the first-degree-related two pairs are closely related to each other and no other first-degree relatives were detected among the thirteen samples (with autosomal coverage >0.005) subjected to READ analyses. A second-degree relationship (half-siblings, first cousins, or uncle-nephew) was detected between Skeletons F.2028 and F.2039. Based on this information, it appears that the closely related individuals buried at the site were related through their maternal line and that at least twelve distinct maternal lineages existed in this burial group with most individuals buried not being related through the maternal line. It is not possible at this time to determine relationships via the paternal line due to low coverage. It may be interesting to note that the two related pairs were not buried next to or overlapping their counterpart, but that the (separate/unrelated) pairs – F.2076/F.2086 and F.2049/F.2028 – were buried overlapping; whether this was of any significance is unknown.

Copper Alloy Jewellery Nina Crummy

<5136> SF 229, F.2001 - Strip bracelet, in fragments (Fig. 5.35.1). The thin rectangular-sectioned hoop is plain and was closed with a hook-and-eye fastening. The very end of the eye is missing. Internal diameter approximately 53 mm, section 5.5 mm high by 1 mm thick. Strip bangles are rarely plain, as shown by the collections from Lankhills, Winchester (Clarke 1979, table 34, D1) and from Colchester (Crummy 1983, 38–45). Examples with hook-and-eye fastenings come from graves at Lankhills ranging in date from *c.* AD 330–80, and at Colchester from graves dated to later than AD 360 (*ibid.*, nos. 1700 & 1708; Crummy *et al.* 1993, table 2.67, G24 & G378).

<5137> SF 244, F.2034 - Fragments of very decayed copper alloy fixed in thick clay, together with a small disc, with sunken centre, of self-coloured glass. Identification uncertain, but perhaps all that remains of a finger-ring. Diameter of glass disc, 8 mm.

<5138> SF 246, F.2046 - Group of three penannular bracelets, two forming a pair (Fig. 5.35.4–5):

a–b) Broad cast hoop, with a plain central angular moulding flanked by rounded mouldings marked with slight angled grooves to give a cable effect, and with plain marginal mouldings. The straight terminals are flat, set close together, and are marked with a wide lozenge formed by two lines of dots, the internal points running up onto the central moulding. Internal diameter 58 mm, section 13 × 2 mm.

c) Plain hoop, more or less 'D'-shaped at the mid-point, with flat blunt-nosed terminals in the form of debased snake's heads. The limit of the decoration is defined by a pair of incised transverse grooves, and slanting grooves are used to give the effect of scales. Maximum internal diameter 56 mm, maximum hoop thickness 4 mm.

The group probably dates to the second or third century AD but could be later. The snake bracelet belongs to Johns's Type Bii, widespread in Roman Britain and not closely datable (Johns 1996, 45, 109), although the stylized terminals suggest a later, rather than early, date. The width of the pair of broad bracelets marks them out as distinct from the narrow bangles of the fourth century, but nor do they belong with the military *armillae* issued during the conquest of Britain and widely found in the eastern region (Crummy 2005; Crummy 2016, 7–9). They are not closely paralleled,

Table 5.19. *aDNA summary data.*

Skeleton	Sample element	% Unique Human	Cov (X)	mtDNA Contamination	Kinship	mtDNA Hg	mtDNA Cov (X)	Y Hg	Genetic sex estimate
2001	LRM3	22.75%	0.086	0.67%		H11a	32.01	n/a	XX
2004	ULC	0.45%	0.002	0.00%		H2a2a	2.07	too low coverage	XY
2007	LRC	5.37%	0.018	0.88%		H26a1	20.42	R1	XY
2013	LRC	55.68%	0.195	1.30%		H4a1	34.89	R1b11	XY
2022	LLM3	40.47%	0.135	0.82%		U5a1h	21.67	n/a	XX
2028	LLC	8.93%	0.024	1.10%	1st Degree [489], 2nd Degree [486]	H1bs	14.49	R1b2	XY
2034	LLPM2	2.84%	0.009	2.13%		H3a1	5.83	n/a	XX
2036	LRM1	25.63%	0.078	0.84%		U5a1b1	28.31	n/a	XX
2039	ULM3	3.11%	0.009	0.00%		H18	4.03	n/a	XX
2049	ULM1	25.05%	0.071	0.00%	1st Degree [491]	H2a3	43.03	n/a	XX
2055	LLPM2	2.97%	0.008	0.80%		U5a2a1	6.02	too low coverage	XY
2058	LRM3	0.98%	0.003	n/a	2nd Degree [480]	too low coverage	1.57	too low coverage	XY
2061	URM1	0.04%	0.000	n/a	too low coverage	too low coverage	0.48	too low coverage	consistent with XY but not XX
2069	URM1	0.04%	0.000	n/a	too low coverage	too low coverage	0.60	too low coverage	consistent with XY but not XX
2076	ULPM1	41.30%	0.120	0.45%	1st Degree [480]	H1bs	40.60	R1b	XY
2082	URM1	3.37%	0.010	0.00%		H3b1b1	9.07	n/a	XX
2086	LLM3	0.62%	0.002	2.53%	1st Degree [484]	H2a3	5.35	n/a	XX

Table 5.20. *aDNA sex estimation.*

Skeleton	N total reads	N chrY + N chrX reads	N chrY reads	Ry	SE	95% CI MIN	95% CI MAX	Assignment	Morphological Sex Estimate
2001	5,839,249	283.661	1.286	0.0045	0.0001	0.0043	0.0048	XX	female
2004	119.167	3.138	267	0.0851	0.0050	0.0753	0.0948	XY	male
2007	1,152,632	31.362	2.718	0.0867	0.0016	0.0836	0.0898	XY	male?
2013	11,656,114	307.002	26.245	0.0855	0.0005	0.0845	0.0865	XY	male?
2022	7,966,173	371.128	1.998	0.0054	0.0001	0.0051	0.0056	XX	female
2028	1,522,674	41.464	3.519	0.0849	0.0014	0.0822	0.0876	XY	male
2034	568.615	27.621	135	0.0049	0.0004	0.0041	0.0057	XX	female
2036	4,978,849	239.987	1.253	0.0052	0.0001	0.0049	0.0055	XX	unobservable
2039	576.509	27.857	119	0.0043	0.0004	0.0035	0.0050	XX	female?
2049	4,767,781	225368	1111	0.0049	0.0001	0.0046	0.0052	XX	female
2055	573.478	15.259	1.292	0.0847	0.0023	0.0803	0.0891	XY	female
2058	167.426	4.646	422	0.0908	0.0042	0.0826	0.0991	XY	male
2061	6.476	185	11	0.0595	0.0174	0.0254	0.0935	consistent with XY but not XX	indeterminate
2069	8.543	232	14	0.0603	0.0156	0.0297	0.0910	consistent with XY but not XX	indeterminate
2076	7,674,801	205.85	17.671	0.0858	0.0006	0.0846	0.0871	XY	male
2082	699.364	33.736	167	0.0050	0.0004	0.0042	0.0057	XX	female
2086	134.013	6.407	37	0.0058	0.0009	0.0039	0.0076	XX	female

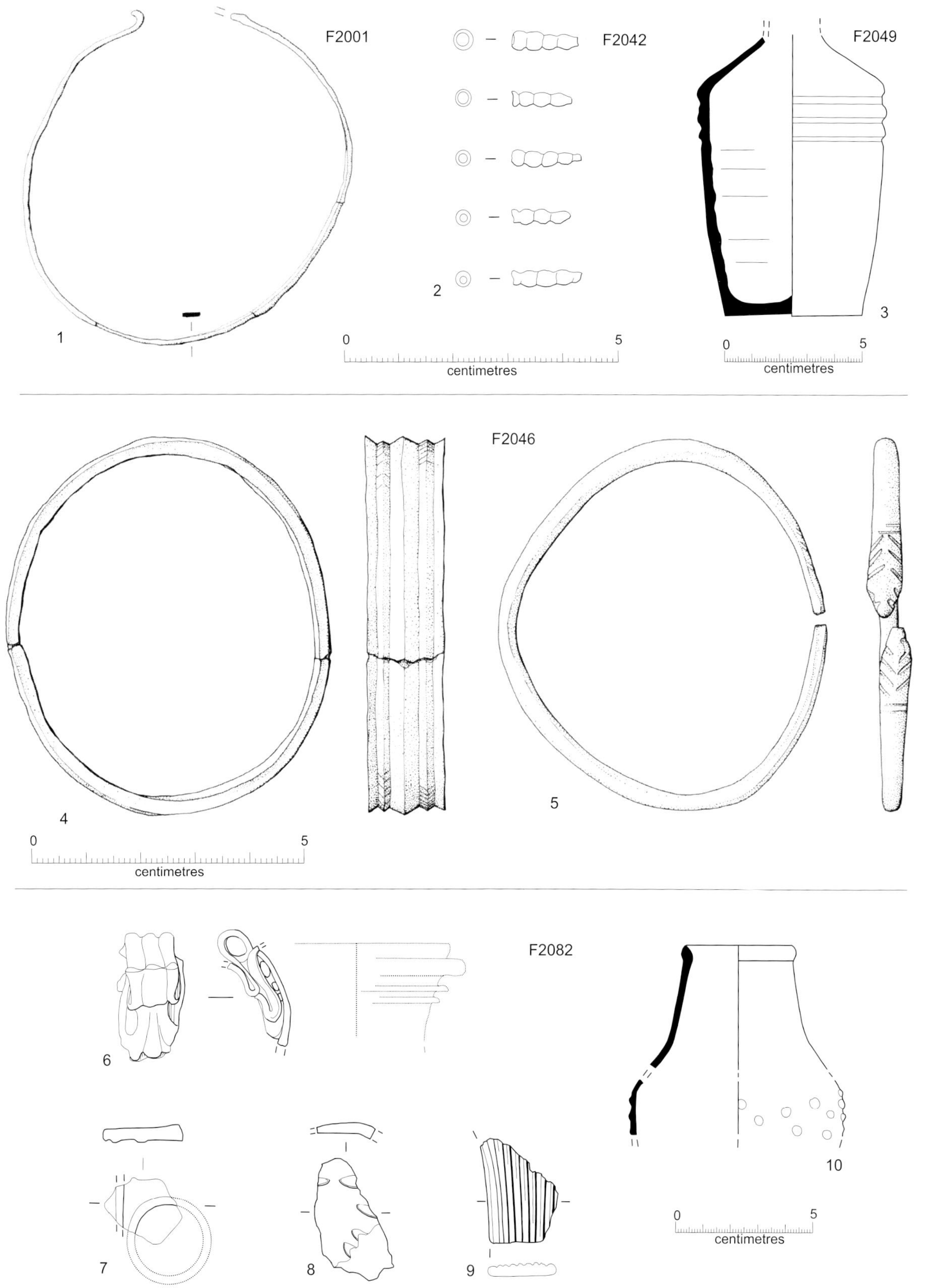

Figure 5.35. *Grave-goods from inhumation cemetery, Burials F.2001, F.2042, F.2046, F.2049 and F.2082 (see text).*

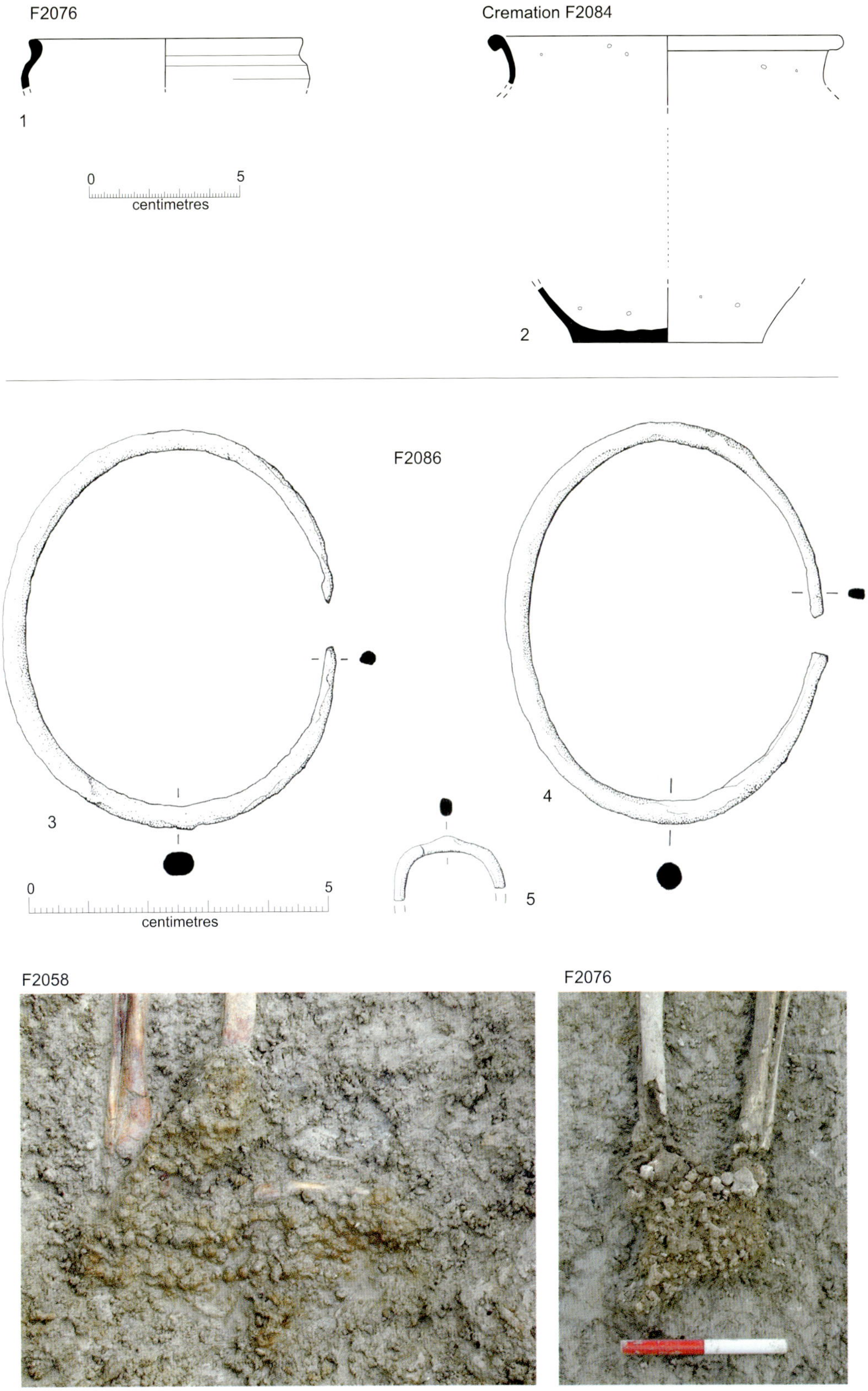

Figure 5.36. *Grave-goods from inhumation cemetery, F.2076 and F.2086, with Cremation F.2084 pot and, below, hobnails in Burials F.2058 and F.2076 (see text).*

but in general form and style, particularly the lozenge motif at the terminals, can be compared to two mid–later Roman examples of Cool's southwestern Group XXXIX, one from Brockworth in Gloucestershire and one from Poundbury, Dorset (Cool 1983, 980–1, fig. 100, 4–5).

F.2086 - Two bracelets and a finger-ring:

a) *<5140> <5141> SF 288/SF 289* - Pair of complete penannular bracelets (Fig. 5.36.3–4). One has iron staining on much of the circumference (SF 288). The hoop of each is plain and tapers towards narrow terminals. Those of SF 288 are moulded and the segmented effect at the terminals is probably derived from earlier, clearly shown, snake's head decoration (Johns 1996, 109–110, fig 3.3). Those of SF 289 are badly corroded. Each bracelet has a maximum internal diameter of 57 mm, and a maximum hoop thickness of 4 mm. Bracelets with plain hoops of this form and minimally decorated terminals date to the late third or fourth century AD (cf. Crummy 1983, fig. 42, 1664, fig. 45, 1710).

b) *<5139> SF 287 [2086]* - Three fragments from a corroded and worn finger-ring of variable cross-section (Fig. 5.36.5). The surface is not well-preserved, and this may be a simple plain hoop, or may have a slight bezel on the outer edge (as Neal & Butcher 1974, fig. 60, 119). Internal diameter approximately 15 mm. The narrowness of the hoop suggests it belongs with the large number of thin finger-rings found in the mid to late fourth century AD, contemporary with the fashion for thin stripmetal bangles.

Iron Nina Crummy

As outlined above (see also Fig. 5.33), coffin nails were found associated with eight of the graves. With 82 recovered in total, these all seem to be of Manning Type 1B and, generally, 4–7 cm long.

Hobnails

Hobnails are found on Roman shoes *(calcei)* and sandals *(soleae)*, as well as the heavily-nailed *caligae*. They vary considerably in the number used and are often arranged in decorative patterns (Rhodes 1980; MacConnoran 1986). The nails have not been X-rayed and where they are heavily encrusted with corrosion the precise numbers present are uncertain. Both heavily nailed and more lightly nailed shoes are represented. The heavily nailed shoes from F.2058 must have had the Type C nailing pattern found on men's shoes from London identified as military *caligae* (Rhodes 1980, 113–14). The smaller nails and lower numbers from the other shoes suggest that both Type A and Type B nailing patterns were also represented here (*ibid*., 114; MacConnoran 1986, 218).

Manning 1985, Type 10 hobnails:

<5146> F.2016 - 26(?), from both left and right shoes
<5153> F.2049 - 51 (Fig. 5.31)
<5154> F.2058 - 70(?) from the right shoe; 71(?) from the left shoe; 55(?) from the junction of both shoes (Figs. 5.31 & 5.36)
<5157> & <5158> F.2076 - 53 (Figs. 5.31 & 5.34)
<5160> & <5161> F.2082 - 34
<5162> F.2086 - 99? (Fig. 5.31).

Pottery Gwladys Monteil

Only three of the inhumations were associated with pottery vessels.

F.2049 - Flagon/bottle with rilled, carinated shoulder and an abraded plain everted rim (150 g, 0.05 EVEs) in a fine sandy greyware (FSGR). This flagon/bottle displays characteristics that strongly point out to a Suffolk origin, probably Wattisfield (Tomber & Dore 1998, 184). The matrix is quite fine and very micaceous, ill-sorted small black inclusions are visible to the naked eye and it is reduced (Fig. 5.35.3); second century AD.

F.2076 - Necked bowl (272 g, 0.33 EVEs) in a coarse sandy red-slipped ware (CSRS; Fig. 5.36.1); second–third century AD.

F.2082 – Funnel-necked beaker (20 g, 0.25 EVEs) in a fine calcareous grey fabric with barbotine dot decorations (FSGR; Fig. 5.35.10); later first century AD.

Glass H.E.M. Cool

Glass artefacts accompanied two of the burials.

<5135>, F.2042 (Fig. 5.35.2) - Segmented beads; opaque blue; wound and then crimped to form four or five segments a bead. Five complete examples and 14 fragments, currently ranging from one to four segments, a length probably representing another bead. Length of complete beads 10–11 mm, diameter 2.5–3 mm. Total length *c.* 140 mm.

Segmented beads such as these are primarily a late third- to fourth-century AD form (Guido 1978, 92), though examples are occasionally found earlier such as the one from an early second-century AD context at Caerleon (Brewer 1986, 148, no. 11) The beads in this inhumation were found positioned as if from a necklace and the total length of beads found are adequate for this purpose. The infant in the grave would almost certainly have been a girl because bead necklaces such as these were not thought appropriate for males, and where it is possible to check the associations of biological sex and glass beads in graves, there is normally a strongly female association (Cool 2011). The presence of a necklace with a little girl who was scarcely older than a baby is of interest. Gowland (2001, 159) has noted that goods of any kind, and especially personal ornaments, are rare with infants of less than four years at the large cemeteries at Butt Road, Colchester and Lankhills, Winchester, possibly reflecting the fact that the formation of a gendered identity was not perceived to take place until after that age. The composition of the necklace is also slightly unusual, in that glass bead necklaces are usually made up of a range of beads of different colours (see, e.g., Guido 1978, pl. IV), rather than the single colour and type seen here. It is possible that the necklace with this baby was provided less as a statement of gender, and more as an amulet like the phallic pendants buried with a baby at Catterick (Wilson 2002). A glass bead necklace is a less obviously protective device than a group of phallic pendants, but here it may have been the single colour that was important.

<4340> SF 262, F.2082 (Figs. 5.35.6–9 & 5.39) – A number of vessel fragments occurred in this grave:

a) Funnel-mouthed jug (Fig. 5.35.6). Blue/green; rim and handle in four joining fragments. Funnel-mouthed rim, edge fire-rounded. Spiral trail of four turns on the neck with thick trail below the rim-edge applied over upper one. Three-ribbed handle applied to neck, trailed up to rim, looped back to form a thumb rest, reattached to upper part of attachment, trailed down then up; broken at point where handle leaves attachment folding. Present height *c.* 35 mm, width of handle 17 mm.

b) Bottle. Blue/green. Three fragments of angular-reeded handle (Fig. 5.35.9 & 5.39).

c) Prismatic bottle. Blue/green. Base fragment. Base design: one small circular moulding inside a (?) slightly curved moulding. Dimensions 26 × 21 mm (Fig. 5.35.7).

d) Prismatic bottle. Blue/green, with many small bubbles. Base fragment, with pointed tips of four pellets or longer mouldings pointing towards side. These and more central moulding are obscured by pontil scar. Possibly deliberately flaked to sharp edge along one side. Dimensions 45 × 22 mm (Fig. 5.35.8).

e) Square bottle. Blue/green. Two body fragments.

f) Prismatic bottle. Blue/green. Two shoulder fragments.

g) Prismatic bottle. Blue/green. Twenty-one flat body fragments.

h) Body fragment. Blue/green. Melted.

i) Body fragment. Pale greenish colourless, with many small bubbles. Convex-curved.

The group of glass fragments found with the F.2082 inhumation was derived from a large number of different vessels. There are definitely a minimum of four vessels represented by *a, c, d* and *i*, but most of the square and prismatic bottle body fragments *e–g* clearly come from different bottles than those represented by *c* and *d*. The earliest period when this accumulation could have been assembled is the later third century AD. The square and prismatic bottles represented by *b–g* were common finds of the later first to early–mid third centuries AD (Ising's Form 51; Price & Cottam 1998, 194–200). Examples with pontil scars on their bases such as *d* tend to be later rather than earlier in that range. The funnel-mouthed jug *a* has the thick trail below the rim, which is typical of later third- and fourth-century AD jugs, flasks and bottles, though the blue/green glass it is made of argues for a third- rather than fourth-century AD date (Cool & Price 1995, 134–5) as in the fourth-century AD vessels tend to be made of greenish colourless bubbly glass. This distinctive type of glass comes into use during the later third century AD and the accumulation includes one fragment of it *(i)*.

Though it is simple to offer a date for the group, suggesting why it should have been gathered together, possibly enclosed in a bag and then placed in the grave, is much more difficult. Visually the group is predominantly blue/green, some fragments tending towards the blue end of the spectrum and others towards the green. Only *i* stands apart from this. The fragments are all different shapes, sizes and weights, though a preference for flat pieces may be noted *(b–d, g–h)*. In total they weigh 152 g, which does not appear to approximate usefully to any Roman unit of measurement unless it is an underweight half *libra* (162–3 g; for Roman weights see RIB II.2, p. 1). In Roman vessel glass assemblages, it is not unusual to find fragments that have been re-used for some purpose. The three most common forms of such re-use are deliberate flaking to form a sharp cutting edge, the trimming of a base with base ring to form a disc and the trimming of a flat fragment from a bottle to form a counter. With the possible exception of *d*, no evidence of any such re-use can be seen on any of these fragments. The group does not include any fragments which might attract attention because of their bright colours, unusual shape, *etc.*, so it would be very hard to argue that this was some form of cache of charms like the group found in a cist at Cairnhill, Aberdeenshire (Stevenson 1967).

All in all, this accumulation is rather undistinguished and pedestrian, yet obviously it has some significance to the deceased or those who conducted the funeral. The fact that the fragments are clearly from a large number of vessels and do not join makes it unlikely that we are looking at the remains of vessels used during the funeral, as was the case with a group of beakers found with a burial at Welford, Warwicks (Booth 1994). Broken and incomplete items have occasionally been found deliberately deposited with the deceased as in the case of an inhumation of a child at Linton, Cambs., where the upper part of a dolphin-handled glass bottle and half a shale armlet were placed between the thighs (or possibly on them originally). This grave also included pottery vessels placed in the grave as broken pieces (Liversidge 1977, 27). The grave of a 5–12-year-old child in London's East Cemetery included broken fragments of glass, interestingly including a similar dolphin-handled bottle neck. The other broken fragments, however, came from a brightly coloured polychrome vessel and could have been chosen for their appearance (Barber & Bowsher 2000, 186, fig. 90).

The London burial seems to fall into the tradition of burying young girls with amulets, dolls and *crepundia* (miniatures, things of significant shape or appearance or which made noise), perhaps as symbols of the weddings that they died too young to experience (Martin-Kilcher 2000). It has also been noted *(ibid.*, 73) that others who died before their time, such as women in childbirth, may also have been marked out on their burial in similar ways. As noted above, there appears to be nothing in this group of fragments to suggest an amuletic significance, but perhaps it should be viewed within the same tradition. It is possible that the fragments provide us with a clue that the death of the woman was viewed as unusual or premature in some way.

Cemetery Overview (with Natasha Dodwell)

A total of 30 individuals were recovered from the 29 graves in the cemetery (this includes the disarticulated material in grave fill [2021]). Of these, 26 are adult, two are older subadults/adults, one is a juvenile and another is an infant. Of the adults, including the aDNA results (and ?/probable identifications), 11 have been sexed as female, and eight as male (Fig. 5.37). Given the small size of the burial group and that seven adults could not be sexed, the female-to-male ratio is not significant. Immature individuals are under-represented, but as discussed with regard to the cremation cemetery, this is a common observation and is usually attributed to differential burial practices or an aggressive burial environment. The site's heavy clay and severe truncation did not favour the preservation of immature remains. One infant, F.2042, aged approximately two years old and wearing a blue glass necklace, was identified in the cemetery, showing that individuals of that age could be afforded similar burial rites (or at least interment in the same cemetery) as adults. There are three instances of neonate burial within the settlement itself in non-burial features (see Fig. 6.21), suggesting that infants of a very young age may have been afforded different rights to those slightly older.

Joint disease is one of the commonest recorded pathologies observed in modern populations and in archaeological material. At Vicar's Farm the preservation of joint surfaces is poor and very few vertebrae survive. Despite this, 11 adults exhibited changes characteristic of osteoarthritis (as described by Rogers & Waldron 1995, 32–46) with the spine being the most common site in the body affected. Other parts affected included the hip, shoulders, hands and feet. Although joint disease is not activity-specific, all those affected are in the middle to mature adult age-bracket, which is a common pattern suggestive of a hard-working, physically demanding lifestyle.

Dental hygiene does not appear to have been a priority amongst this population. Mineralized plaque or calculus was recorded on the teeth of eight individuals in the cemetery. Medium deposits were even recorded on the deciduous dentition of the F.2061 juvenile. Caries were recorded in the dentitions of six individuals, and nine suffered ante-mortem tooth-loss. Given that the dentitions of nine individuals were missing and that many of the surviving teeth were loose, prevalence rates of caries and ante-mortem tooth-loss have not been calculated.

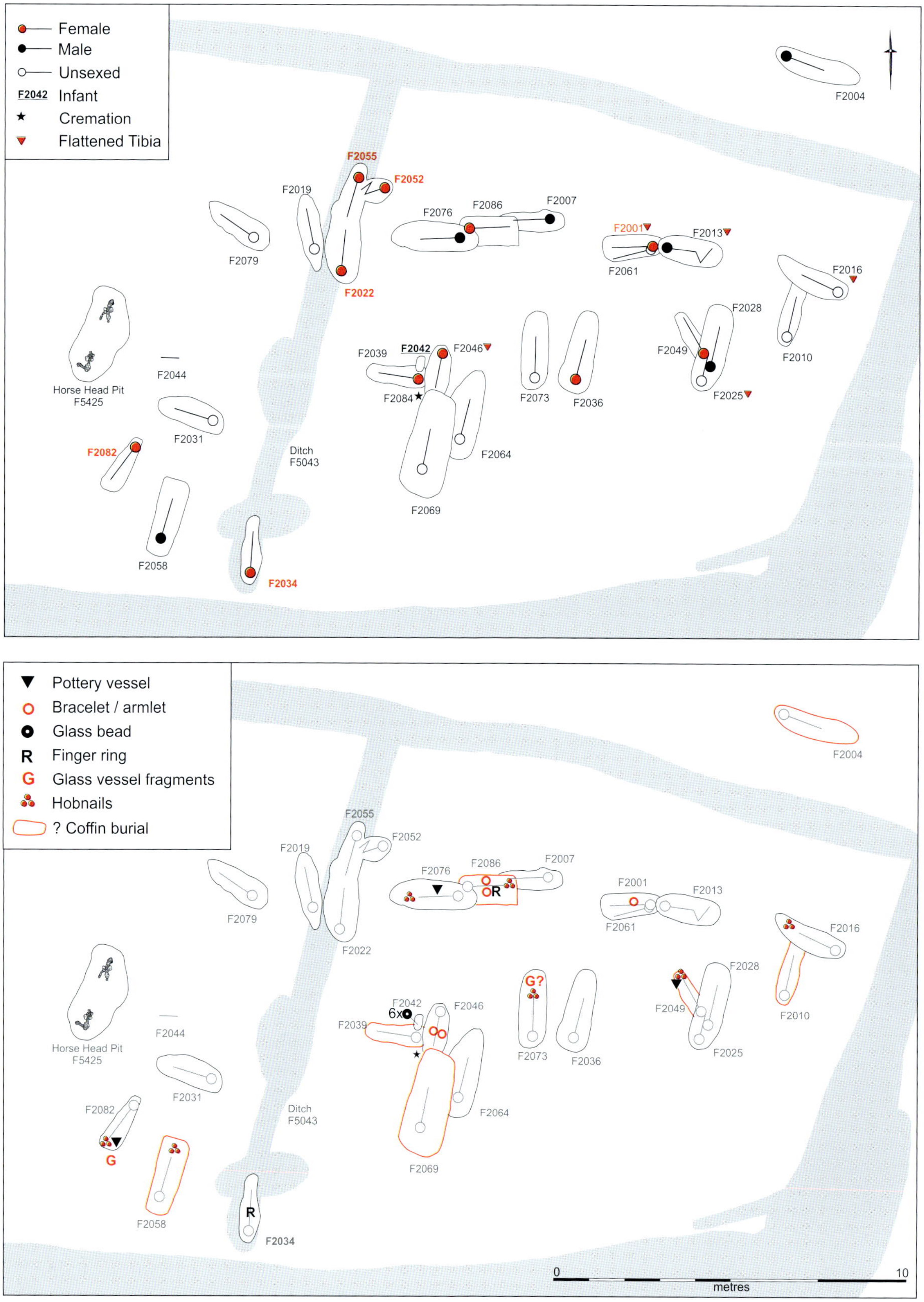

Figure 5.37. *Cemetery distributions (I): by sex (top) and, below, grave-goods.*

Episodes of childhood disease or malnutrition in five individuals are evidenced by enamel hypoplasias, which are defects in the enamel. An off-white mineral with small worm-like lesions covered many of the surviving teeth and may have obscured evidence of further enamel defects. *Cribra orbitalia*, which is indicative of childhood anaemia (e.g. Mitchell 2017, 49–50), was recorded in the orbit of one individual, F.2055, a mature adult female. However, two other individuals had evidence for healing *cribra orbitalia*. The aetiology of *cribra orbitalia* is multi-factorial and the anaemia could have resulted from an iron deficient diet or from parasitic infection. It may be relevant in this capacity that the intestinal parasite, *Trichuris* (Whipworm) – indicative of contact with faecal matter – registered in one of the site's pollen columns (see Scaife, Chap. 4).

Although not pathological, the morphology of the lower limbs should be noted. As outlined above by Neil and Mulder, platycnemia, the excessive side-to-side flattening of the tibial shaft, was observed in five adults in the cemetery and in one, F.991, outside it. Two of these individuals (three including F.991) also had femurs with front-to-back flattening of the proximal femur shaft, or platymeria. The aetiology of platycnemia and platymeria is far from understood and much contested, but nutritional deficiency has been cited as at least a partial cause (e.g. Buxton 1938), as has the persistent adoption of the squatting posture when at rest (e.g. Lovejoy *et al.* 1976; Kennedy 1989, 148–50). Ruff (1987), in fact, concluded that platymeria (flattening of the femur) is related to sex, with the index higher in women. While one of the Vicar's Farm burials with this condition was female (F.2046), the sex of the other two could not be determined.

Eight of the burials would appear to have been in coffins, as evidenced by the nails recovered around the skeletons. The recovery of hobnails around the feet of six individuals suggests that they were buried either with or wearing footwear. There are many instances where shoes have been placed in the grave, rather than being worn, for example in the Eastern Cemetery of Roman London (Barber & Bowsher 2000, 137). Both males and females were buried in coffins and with footwear, and the absence of hobnails found with immature individuals may just be because they are under-represented as an age group. It is noteworthy that the hobnails accompanying F.2058's young adult male indicate military *caligae* footwear (see Crummy, above)

Correlations did not exist between grave orientation, footwear and/or coffins. Seven individuals were accompanied by grave-goods, or at least by grave-goods that had survived. Bracelets, finger-rings, a glass bead necklace, ceramic vessels and a small cache of glass fragments were amongst the finds.

Ridge-and-furrow and modern ploughing have truncated all of the graves to a greater or lesser degree and, although there was variation in the depth of the graves, the majority were less than 0.15 m deep. Many of the skeletons were identified directly on the machined surface and, yet, Skeleton F.2058 – perhaps somehow on account of his possible military service – was buried almost half a metre below it. While it is likely that we have the full extent of the inhumation cemetery, it is highly probable that further graves have been removed over the years.

Few of the graves intercut and, when they did, some gave the impression of this having been done intentionally. This could suggest that the graves were marked in some way. It has been tempting to think that there may have been some familial relationship between those that intercut each other, and family groupings are widely considered to be characteristic of later Romano-British cemeteries (e.g. Hatton 1999; see also Voong *et al.* 2017). Yet, the evidence of the site's aDNA analysis would not now support this. As related by Scheib and colleagues above, what genetic linkages are demonstrated (Fig. 5.38) do not point to close-clustered familial groupings within the cemetery. Indeed, just how few close kinship relations are evident has come as something of a surprise and potentially poses fundamental interpretative challenges as to the nature of this settlement's 'community'. Admittedly at least two families seem present, but the results suggest that very few of the adults' off-spring were present and that some of the interred may not have been immediate kin-group members (e.g. 'outside' labourers).[3]

With 12 maternal lineages genetically identified from the 14 samples achieved from amongst the cemetery's population of 30 (see Scheib *et al.*, above), in theory this could suggest that more than 20 lineages might have been present in total: far more than might be expected of 'normal' familial generation. If broadly modelling the generational patterning of two residential families over two centuries at a rate of three generations per century, and if presuming that in every other generation one woman/wife died in childbirth, then five maternal lineages would be represented (see e.g. Zubrow in Evans & Hodder 2006b, 311–13). If this was augmented by one or two unrelated (and unmarried) labourers, then the total number of lineages would, respectively rise to 11 and 17. Yet, this presumes that 'outside' labourers would have been afforded burial within the cemetery and they may instead account for the isolated inhumations scattered around the settlement's margins. Equally, with the cemetery lying at some distance south of

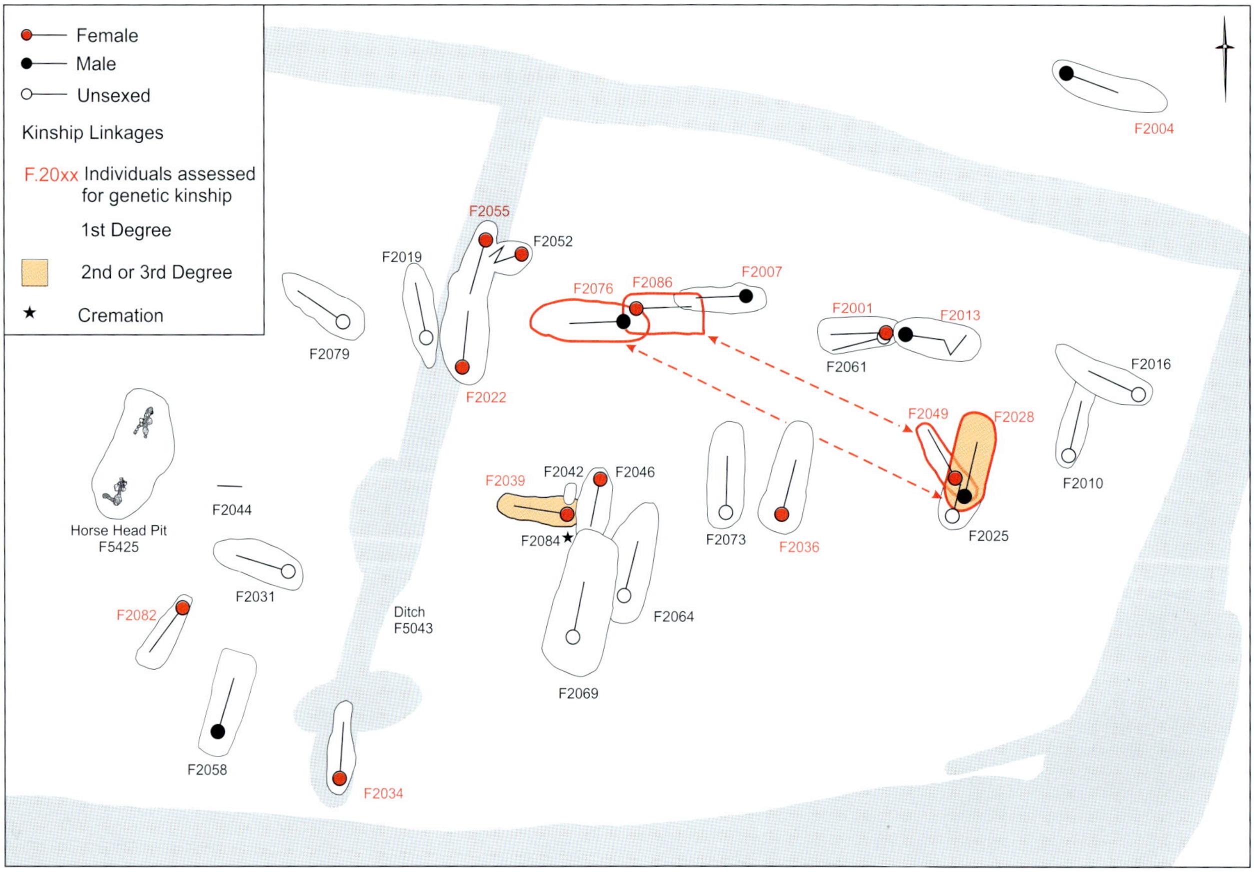

Figure 5.38. *Cemetery distributions (II): aDNA linkages.*

the settlement and alongside what seems to have been a fairly major east–west roadway (No. 3), it is conceivable that the cemetery's membership was not just confined to Vicar's Farm's settlement but could also have included the dead from other neighbouring communities.

Taken at face-value the results could reflect patrilocal residence/kinship, with women marrying into the settlement and their off-spring moving/marrying out of it. Given this, while at risk of being overtly 'sentimental' in our reading of the cemetery's relations, it is still possible to speculate that reversed-oriented head close-set male and female burials were husband and wife – F.2076/F.2086 and F.2001/F.2013 (and perhaps F.2029/F.2049) – in other words, a family grouping, but that their off-spring resided elsewhere, possibly in neighbouring settlements. This patterning may then relate to nature of individuals' status and tenancy; this is a theme that will be further explored in the next chapter.

Disarticulated human bone was recovered from five of the cemetery's grave fills and derived from earlier interments. In four cases the bone came from the skeleton that had been disturbed by the later grave. Disturbed bone was reinterred, if not with exceptional care; the bones being placed/thrown directly on the later body, possibly suggesting that reburial was deemed to be necessary. The loose juvenile bones that were found in F.2061 lay directly on top of Skeleton F.2001, whilst those from grave fill [2021] lay upon Skeleton F.2022. The disturbed femur and tibia of the juvenile were in an articulated position, as were several of the skeletal elements from the [2021] grave fill. Although we cannot know the sensibilities of the individuals who dug the graves, they are likely to have encountered not just dry bones, but body parts. Perhaps this, together with the fact that they would have been disturbing relatives/acquaintances, explains the seemingly deliberate reburial of the disturbed material.

Due to the circumstances of its recovery, the implications of Skeleton F.2079's implement-sliced clavicle must remain ambiguous. While possibly relating to more extensive bodily 'manipulation', given the cut's angle and location it might attest to the individual's decapitation, and the skull did not occur within the interment. If so, such practices could perhaps account for some of the disarticulated material within the settlement proper (see Fig. 6.21). Otherwise, there were no decapitated burials within the cemetery (nor were there any prone burials).

With the exception of F.2052, who was buried on her side in a crouched position, the skeletons were all extended and supine. The graves were orientated roughly north–south or east–west, apart from Skeleton F.2049 whose grave was orientated southeast–northwest. Fifteen burials were orientated north–south, with the south the preferred grave-end for the head, and 13 orientated east–west, east being the preferred end for the head. Whether north–south or east–west, the graves appeared to be aligned in respect of pre-existing ditches. When there was a stratigraphic relationship between graves of differing orientations, then the east–west ones *always* overlay those orientated north–south. It could, therefore, be argued that the north–south burial was the earlier tradition. Interestingly, marking the cemetery's western limits (and, perhaps, its entrance), the pit containing horse skulls was orientated north–south (F.5425). Esmonde Cleary has suggested that animal remains might be focal in the development of human cemeteries (2000, 138), pointing to the Eastern Cemetery of London where the burial sequence is preceded by the deliberate (?ritual) burial of horses (Barber & Bowsher 2000, 54). The possibility that, in relationship to the settlement's many horse-remain deposits, F.5425's horse head pit might attest to a distinct horse-related cult will be further explored in the next chapter.

It is possible that Skeleton F.2049, given its southeast–northwest orientation and its stratigraphic relationship with two north–south burials, F.2025 and F.2028, may have been one of the earliest burials. The urned cremation F.2084, dated to AD 180–230 from the vessel style, lay approximately in the centre of the inhumation cemetery and it is tempting to see it as the cemetery's initial focal point. A single urned cremation occurred amongst the inhumations at Lynch Farm and Jones cautioned that, given the relative shallowness of the burial and the degree of truncation on that site, others could have been lost (1975, 100). The same could possibly be true of the cremation at Vicar's Farm. Indeed, to think otherwise would be to entertain what would have to be the far-fetched scenario that the cemetery's one – and central – cremation marked *a/the* moment of significant burial rite transformation.

We are fully aware that the assignation of the cemetery's one cremation to Phase II, and its inhumations to Phase III, is essentially arbitrary.[4] It is no more than a phasing convenience and unlikely to reflect any kind of reality. A number of the inhumations were probably of third-century AD date and, therefore, in theory should be of Phase II attribution. (Just as it is conceivable that a few of the northern cremation cemetery's interments might have been of later second-century AD date and, thereby, of Phase II attribution.) Recognizing this, it is difficult to establish any basis by which to phase the inhumations further, given that so few had any dateable grave-goods or personal ornaments.

Two Burials – *Two Questions*

That fishbone was only recovered from the heavy residues of a sample taken from the stomach-area of Skeleton F.2016 and in one further sample (Fig. 5.28) highlights that our sampling strategy should have been far more intense. It also raises issues concerning the potential contribution of fish to the diet of the settlement's inhabitants. If fish was processed elsewhere and came to the site in a prepared form (e.g. *garum* or the like), then any larger bones would have been removed beforehand. The smaller bones would then only be found either through sampling 'the guts of the dead' as in this case, or by finding the faeces of the living; something we did not achieve.

Given Roman tastes and the availability of resources, fish might well have substantially contributed to the diet. The frequency of the site's oyster shell (likely deriving from the Wash and/or Colchester) indicates that this need not have been restricted to just freshwater species. It is relevant here that a vast fishbone deposit was found in one of Langdale Hale's pits. Estimated to have involved some 12,000 bones, in addition to eel and stickleback, it included Clupeidae and Argentinidae remains (respectively ray-finned fish and herring smelts; see Evans *et al.* 2013b, 133).

The other burial of significant note at the site was F.2082's 'glass woman' (Fig. 5.39). Cool has cited some parallels for her accompanying collection of many glass vessel parts and remarks that it might have been like more obviously 'amulet assemblages'. One can imagine the appeal and potential charm of these shiny trinkets. What, though, is particularly relevant for us is that it

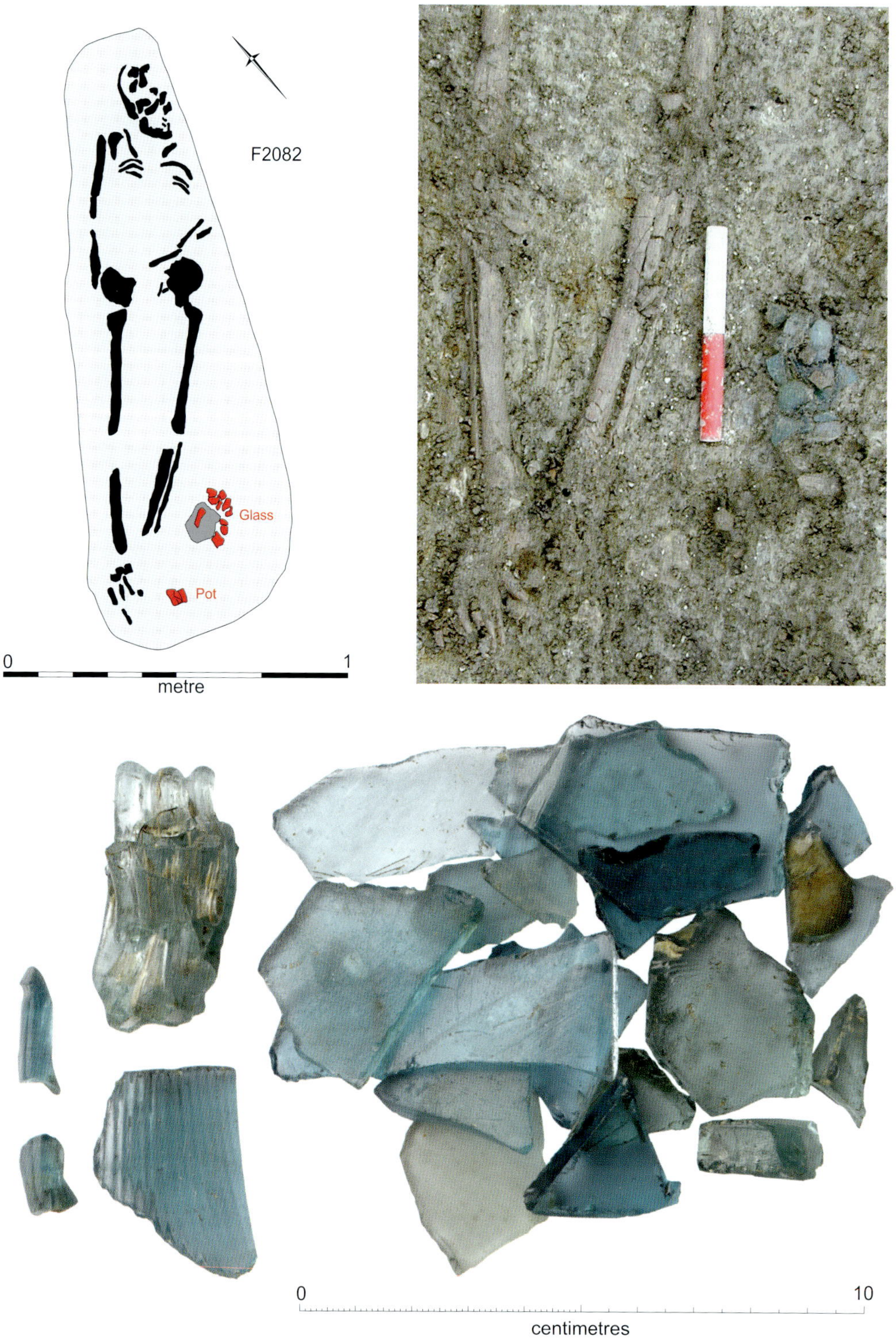

Figure 5.39. *The F.2082 'glass woman' burial.*

further indicates just how much glass was coming into the area; it featured, for example, in both Girton's rich burials and those found through quarrying at the Traveller's Rest Pit (see Chap. 1).[5] The assemblage in F.2082 reflects the kind of 'small bright thing' collection-activity that is usually only attributed to the Early Anglo-Saxon period: 'mantelpiece' assemblages of curios clearly gathered from adjacent Roman-period settlements. Often involving decorated samian, at the Romano-British riverside settlement at Hinxton there was just such a discrete deposit of some 50 sherds of samian – almost all from different vessels – that had been assembled by the site's subsequent Saxon inhabitants living nearby (see *RVS*, chap. 6).

A basis of sub-division could be the patterning of any grave intercutting; one might assign the north–south graves to Phase II and the east–west burials to Phase III. As is further discussed in the next chapter, it could even be argued that this might reflect the impact of Christianity. Yet, in reference to Chapter One's arguments concerning 'rule-bound behaviours' (and what was evidently their frequent transgression), against this would be that Grave F.2076 (east–west) was accompanied by a second–third-century AD bowl. The pottery vessels accompanying two of the other burials would also seem to be relatively early. Grave F.2049's flagon/bottle is of second-century AD date, with the funnel-necked beaker in Grave F.2082 even earlier (later first century AD). Yet, certainly in the case of the latter – the 'glass woman' (see *Inset* above) – this would have to attest to the curation of ceramic vessels, as the interment's glass items are of third–fourth-century AD date. The same is also true of the segmented glass bead necklace in F.2042's infant burial's (see Cool above) and, indeed, so is the date-range of those graves with accompanying metalwork ornaments generally (see Crummy, above).

Given the cemetery's dual orientation, it is unfortunate that the available resourcing precluded any kind of substantive absolute dating programme (see e.g. Gerrard 2015a and b). By the condition of the bone it is, though, unlikely that the remains would provide any kind of fine-grained resolution of date. Accordingly, one simply has to accept the arbitrary nature of the current phasing for what it is and recognize the ambiguity this entails.

Northern Fields (Area E)

With the northwestern road/trackway ceasing to function, the northern part of the settlement saw little development and essentially lay in fields, with one inhumation occurring within the area (Fig. 5.22).

Western Side

Marking the abandonment of the Road 2/G5 trackway was ditch F.5599/F.5580 (2.–2.5 m wide, 0.3–0.65 m deep), that ran eastward from F.5014 as the northernmost visible boundary (G29; Fig. 5.22). Close to their junction lay an isolated burial, Grave F.2094, which has been described by Dodwell:

Skeleton F.2094; Mid/Mature adult, male – Lying within a sub-rectangular grave, the skeleton was well-preserved, although fragmentary. The head was in the southwest of the grave, the body was supine with the right arm flexed, hand over the pelvis, and the legs extended, feet together, left-over-right. Increased porosity and small areas of eburnation indicative of osteoarthritis were noted on the right distal humerus and proximal radius. Similar changes were recorded on both femoral heads and in both wrists. The surviving cervical vertebral bodies exhibited increased porosity and marginal osteophytes. The axis, the second cervical vertebra, exhibits a deformed articular surface, with eburnation and deep grooves where bone has rubbed on bone. At least one tooth (the left 1st mandibular molar) was lost prior to death and two large carious lesions were recorded on a canine and premolar. The anterior teeth were worn right down to the dentine and slight to medium deposits of calculus were recorded on the surviving teeth. The superior parts of both petrous portions of the temporal bones have smooth lace-like perforations whose aetiology is uncertain.

Eastern Side

While the western side of this area seems to have remained fairly undeveloped, the eastern side was recut (G15), re-affirming the western boundary of the earlier G16 enclosure but expanding southward up to the G8 trackway (Fig. 5.22). This trackway was narrowed, its northern side then marked by gully F.5671 (0.92 m wide, 0.22 m deep). The field itself was defined by ditches F.5603 (0.6–0.75 m wide, 0.2–0.4 m deep; dated AD 270+) and F.5677 (0.6 m wide, 0.08 m deep), with an opening *c.* 11 m wide on its western side. This was probably associated with the small enclosure, G17, which resembled the later G2.11 enclosure in the settlement's core. This G17 enclosure ditch varied from 1.4–2.8 m in width and 0.1–0.4 m in depth (dated AD 300+). A short section of gully projected from the northeast corner of this enclosure (F.8137; 1.39 m wide, 0.3 m deep; AD 240/300+), and it mirrored a similar gully projecting from the southern tip of F.5603/F.160 (1.4 m wide).

In the mid–late fourth century AD, the western boundary of this field was recut, closing off both the western opening and the G8 trackway. Ditch F.5013 (1.1–1.4 m wide, 0.38–0.65 m deep) ran all the way from the northern limit of excavation down to meet ditch F.4934 (1.1 m wide), where it formed the western boundary of a small sub-enclosure (G31). This narrow, linear parcel of land (G31), which was defined by the ditch F.5013 on its western side, lay between the G15 field to the north and the metalled surface (G32) to the south. The main bounding ditch of this area was F.4759 (1.8–2. m wide, dated AD 300+); a series of gullies, 0.45–1.3 m wide and *c.* 0.17 m deep, divided the area into narrow strips reminiscent of G16 to the north.

Discussion – *Reading Spaces and Sequences*

For complicated settlements – especially those involving 'organic' (i.e. non-rectilinear) components – the implementation of phasing structures as here will always seem arbitrary. They invariably make what were probably unrelated sequential changes seem as if they enacted a greater plan.

Admitting that we can say little concerning the settlement's Late Iron Age/Conquest Period layout (see Fig. 5.42), in many respects the key aspect is the formality of the settlement's Phase I layout (Fig. 5.40). Accessed by two roadways in the northeast, as outlined below, the simple rectangle of its primary layout followed a 'standard' Romano-British farmstead pattern. Leaving aside for the moment the internal sub-division of its enclosure-compounds, in simple terms the settlement then went through a concentric mode of expansion by the addition of further enclosures on its sides. First, on its northern and southern aspects (Phase II) and then, in Phase III wrapping around the core-area's west side and extending eastward.

Following a brief review (and refinement) of the settlement's phasing, the nature of the internal elaboration – the segmentation – of its enclosures will then be explored, followed by a discussion of its roadway access.

Phasing Revisited and Farmstead 'Unit' Parallels

As announced in this chapter's introduction, certain components that have been grouped together within the settlement's broad phasing sequence simply could not have co-existed. A degree of phasing sub-division is, therefore, necessary. With Phase II's arrangement being relatively coherent, this only pertains to the preceding and subsequent phases.

Phase I

It was suspected that the two sub-square enclosures along the settlement's eastern side – G2.08 and G1– predated the main Phase I enclosure (G2). This would certainly seem to be the case, as it is difficult to see them as having been directly contemporary with G2's 'rectangle', while together this earlier enclosure 'pair' would have formed a convincing 'ladder-type' settlement layout. In this arrangement it is likely that the F.5554 ditch setting related to the main primary residential building. It is also likely that the southward arching boundary, F.5385, was contemporary, along with Roundhouse F.5402.

As shown on Figure 5.40, it is conceivable that the very irregular (and narrow) eastern third of the F.5166 ditch-line (Phase III) actually represented the western continuation of the F.5385 boundary. While shown on that plan as also being contemporary, greater doubt exists concerning the status of rectilinear ditches F.5351/5394. Likely to be somewhat later than F.5385 – possibly even substantially so – it is equally possible that other minor ditches may have been contemporary with the western F.5351 line: the G2.3 gullies and, even, ditch F.5630/F.5609. If this was the case, then it would only be logical that Road 2 be assigned to this time. While that remains a possibility – and the same might also be true of Road 3 – here we will take a minimal approach to attributing features to this early sub-division (I.1; the remainder of Phase I feature-groups assigned as I.2) and not go further than assigning the F.5351 boundary to it.

Phase I.1 is thought likely to have lasted from *c.* AD 80 to 120.

Phase III

The abiding logic of this phase's sub-division hinges on the fact that the G2.18 gravel surface appears to represent a western extension of Road 3 (i.e. a Phase III.1 'act'), whereas the various ditches and Enclosure G31's boundaries that cut-off that route must mark a different episode/phase in the settlement's layout (Fig. 5.40). Related, by extension, to this would also be the G17 Curvilinear Enclosure. By the same token, the manner in which the long, almost 'droveway-like' version of the Curvilinear Enclosure (G2.11) cut the earlier Phase III (.1) version of it at its western end suggests that it, too, was a distinctly 'late' development, as must also be the various minor ditch settings that hung off of it.

The dating of the Roman settlement's latest phase (III.2) would have to be assigned to the second half of the fourth century AD; notice that its elements are largely confined to the upper eastern third of the settlement-area.

Having sub-divided the settlement's Phase I development, notice how similar its Phase I.1 layout was to Langdale Hale's Pre-Flavian/Conquest Period ladder-like arrangement of linked paddock-enclosures (Evans *et al.* 2013b, 44–7, fig. 2.14). The scale and morphology of that settlement's subsequent, linked rectangular paddocks on the eastern side of its road (Phase II, AD 120–325; *ibid.*, 47–54, figs. 2.16 & 2.19) – extending over *c.* 0.5 and 0.7 ha – bear comparison to Vicar's Farm's Phase 1.2 enclosure (*c.* 0.68 ha; see Fig. 6.51). With Langdale Hale undoubtedly being a 'major farm' and, arguably, one related to state supply (see Chap. 6 below), much closer to Vicar's Farm by way of further comparison would be North West Cambridge's Site II (Fig. 5.41.1). Of relatively 'uncomplicated' layout – largely as it saw no Late Roman elaboration/usage – it consisted of a large rectangular enclosure (0.7 ha) set on the northern side of a road; it had a smaller interior enclosure (0.3 ha), which was itself further sub-divided and included both a group of wells and a ditched building-setting. Related field plots extended west and, on the opposite side of the road, to the southeast. Within the latter was a corn-drier, leaving no doubt that this was a farmstead. Indeed, given this and its 'pristine simplicity', it has been referred to as a *model farm*. The similarity of Site II's main rectangle to the Vicar's Farm Phase I.2 layout is striking. So much so that it could lead us to question whether Vicar's Farm actually had similarly 'simple farm' origins as North West Cambridge's Site II, and if its shrine and cremation cemetery were actually somewhat later phenomena (i.e. Phase I.3).

As is apparent on Figure 5.41, while Site II's small cremation cemetery lay some 30 m outside its main enclosure and is, therefore, unlike Vicar's Farm's

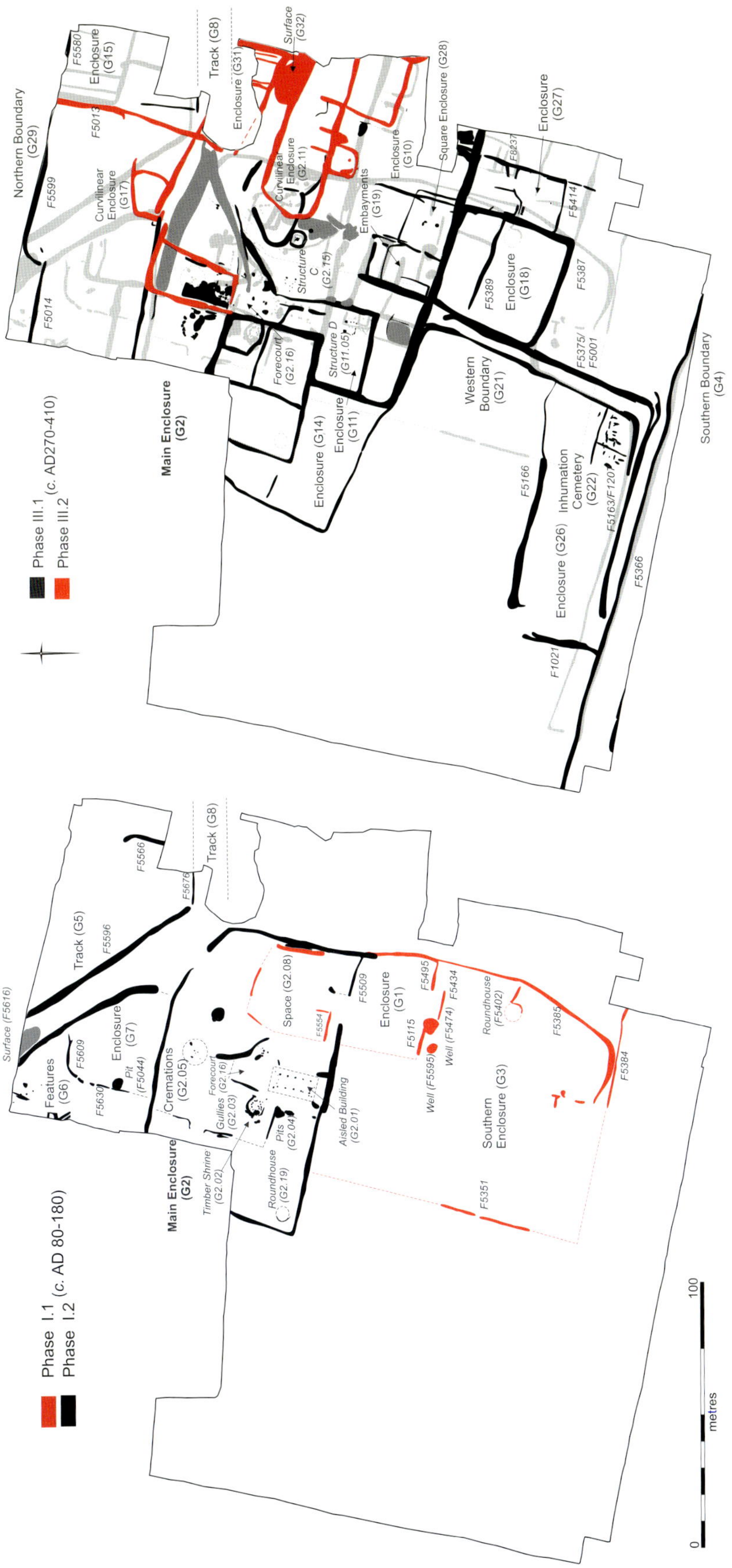

Figure 5.40. *Phase sub-division plans.*

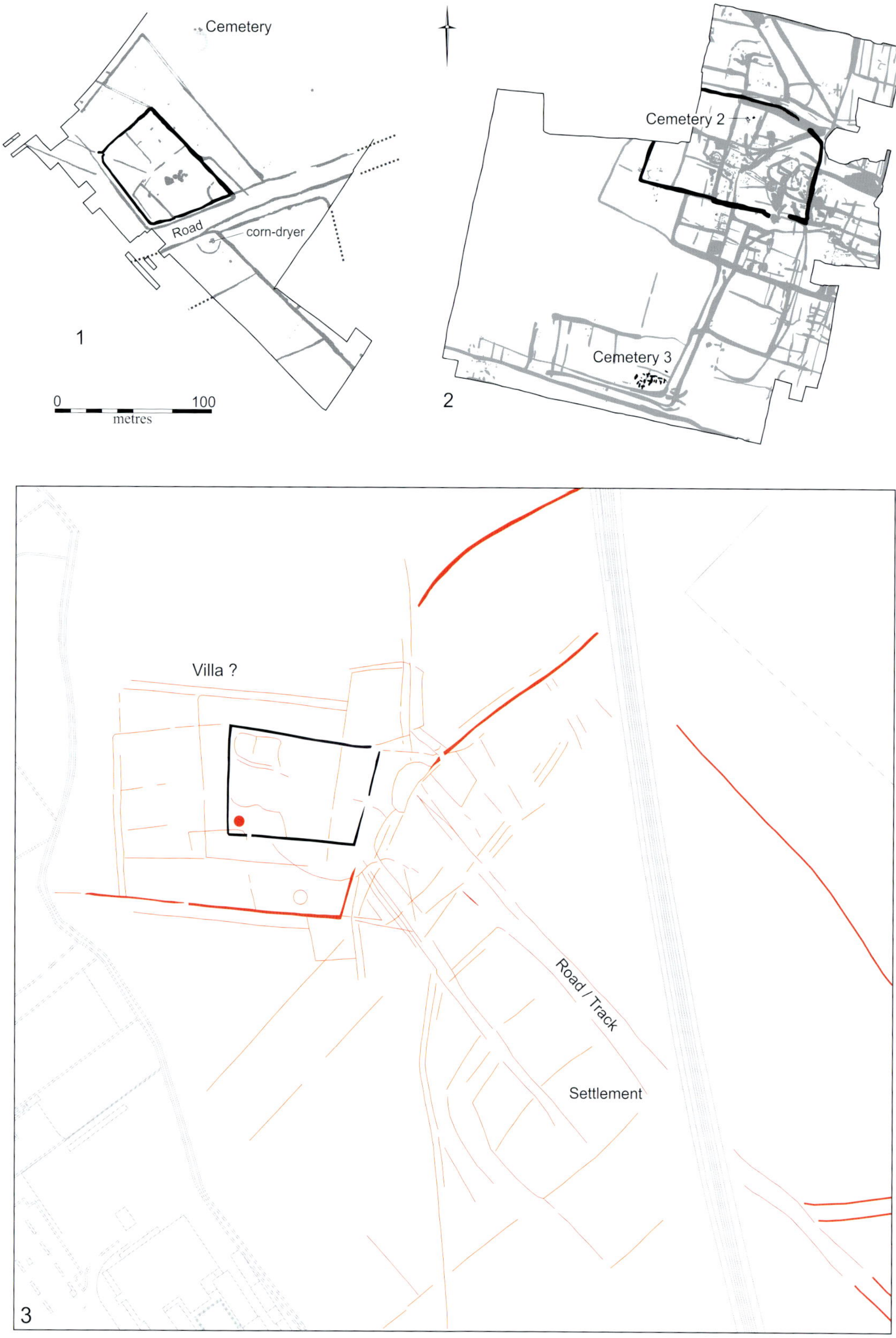

Figure 5.41. *Farmstead 'unit' layouts: 1) North West Cambridge, Site II; 2) Vicar's Farm; 3) the Shelford 'Villa' (see* BLS, *fig. 2.56).*

setting internal to the settlement. That said, the partially concentric arrangement of Site II's enclosures has affinities to the way in which Vicar's Farm expanded.

Ranging in size from *c.* 0.4–0.60 ha, small sub-rectangular/-square enclosures have been investigated elsewhere in the region and these clearly represent 'basic unit' (arguably 'familial-scale') Early Roman farmsteads. This would include two at Summersfield, Papworth Everard (laying alongside a track with an interval of *c.* 300 m between them; Patten 2012) and be comparable to another excavated at Bearscroft, just south of Godmanchester (Patten 2016). With a few internal-ditched sub-divisions, they seem relatively 'simple' and, having relatively low finds densities, they lack, for example, aisled buildings such as at Vicar's Farm, or North West Cambridge's Site II corn-drier.

It is even worth reconsidering the cropmark complex located near Great Shelford south of Addenbrooke's. Extending in total over *c.* 5.3 ha, this Scheduled Ancient Monument is widely held to represent a villa (see e.g. *BLS*, fig. 2.56). Yet the concentric arrangement of its main western rectangular enclosures appears close to that of Vicar's Farm, met by what seem to be a series of radiating roads/trackways and having an ancillary roadside settlement coming off its southeastern side. Indeed, as shown on Figure 5.41.3, its *c.* 0.6 ha core would all but match that of the Vicar's Farm Phase 1.2 enclosure. Given that there is no conclusive evidence to suggest the architectural remains of a villa at the Shelford settlement, perhaps it too should rather now be more appropriately classified as a major farm. Against this, however, the double-ditched perimeter of its probably secondary enclosure maybe a hallmark trait of the area's villas, occurring as it does in association with Arbury's King's Hedges and North West Cambridge's Site VII villas (see *NWC*).

Segmenting Space

Throughout Phase I, the core of the settlement was fairly open, although the slightness of the early internal gullies may give an impression of a more open interior than might have been the case. In each subsequent phase the settlement core was more segmented than the last. In what ways might this have affected the nature of activities conducted there will be further explored in the next chapter.

For now, the issue to examine is where segmentation occurred and where it did not, and how this differed in each phase. In Phase I (Fig. 5.42), the internal ditching almost seems to 'float' and to start and stop without cognisance of any other part of the enclosure system. Even if we accept the truncated nature of these early gullies, they still seem to act in an 'uncoordinated' way, probably to deflect or deter movement rather than create integrated subdivisions. Certainly, the main enclosure ditch surrounding the core settlement (G2; Phase I.2) looks very formal when compared with the internal divisions. In Phase II, more 'understandable' partitions occurred: the central north–south ditches, F.5579 and F.5583, split the main enclosure into two halves and this pattern was repeated by F.5558 for the Area B enclosure. This seems to reflect more overall planning and a sense of the settlement as an integrated whole. In Phase III, the planned, coordinated structure persisted, but the nature of segmentation differed; then the layout was more in the form of sub-enclosures fringing the edges of the core settlement, each more or less self-contained in a modular fashion. So, *in each phase, whilst the internal space was increasingly segmented, it was also carried out in such a way as to create quite different spaces*. In Phase I, the internal space was very open, with a series of unrelated partitions that acted to break up and deflect movement, but without particularly privileging any one area. In Phase II, the internal space was more formalized and sub-divisions were integrated into the whole, which was divided into two halves. Finally, in Phase III, a sense of concentric space was created by modular segmentation around the edges, a blank zone in the middle and with further curvilinear enclosures in the east-centre.

The transition from Phase I to II is, thus, characterized by a shift from uncoordinated divisions to a formal, integrated partition, while the transition from Phase II to III is marked by a shift from a simple, bipartite division to a modular, concentric segmentation. Describing it in this way means we can also think of the effects on people's movement and activities on the site. It could suggest that activity in the settlement core in Phase I only grew up and developed gradually. The settlement might have only slowly attracted the full range of activities it was later to have and may, at first, have been used for a variety of purposes without any overall, unifying function. There was a shrine (perhaps associated with the cremation cemetery), and also some trading and small-scale specialized production (flour and meat). It was only by the end of Phase I that this activity was formalized and the settlement perhaps came under a centralizing authority, with its various parts separated. During Phase II, the economic success of the settlement perhaps grew, the number of people working or visiting there increased and, as more and more different activities were carried out, the space had to change accordingly, with entirely new spaces created. It may also be the case, however, that by Phase III, the settlement was dominated by one major activity, whose focus lay at the centre of the core in the curvilinear enclosures. Unlike the previous phases, there

Figure 5.42. *Phasing sequence plans.*

then was a definite centre to the settlement, with an empty zone around it and the modular sub-enclosures on its margins.

While certainly a valid reading of the site's spatial sequence, this 'piecemeal' development model overlooks the fact that there were key aspects that distinguished the Roman settlement from the latter part of Phase I. Not seen at any other of the contemporary western Cambridge settlements thus far investigated, this includes the various (within-settlement) shrines[6] and that it lay at a distinct 'hub' of the local road network; it is this last point that we will now consider.

Roadway Axes/Access – A Landscape Hub-point

While the settlement's spatial architecture of rectangular paddocks generally reflects the standard components of developed Roman farms, Vicar's Farm seems distinguished on two counts. One is the final-phase curvilinear elements along its eastern side. Though in its final form Langdale Hale's supply farm also saw a more 'organic-type' layout (Evans *et al.* 2013b, chap. 2), it is likely that it then no longer fulfilled a major farm function (unlike Vicar's Farm's Phase III). Arguably then a minor 'hamlet', Langdale's Late Roman ditched compounds were much more modest, whereas the Vicar's Farm Late-phase curvilinear enclosures were substantial and robustly ditched; it has to be suspected that the manner of their delineation/elaboration primarily related to livestock management.

The other major aspect that distinguishes the layout of Vicar's Farm is the sheer number of roads that 'framed' and led to it, and it clearly sat at a hub-point within the landscape (see Figs. 1.4 & 5.42). Of these, the more major routes were, without doubt, Road 2 running northwest towards the settlement on Madingley Rise/Traveller's Rest Pit-area and, in the south, Road 4 running west/northwest–east/southeast. It is noteworthy that though the latter route had no links to known settlements, the settlement's main axes respected and mirrored its alignment; the other roads lay well off the alignment of the settlement itself. However, there seems to have been no obvious way that the settlement could have been accessed from the southern road (apart perhaps somehow from the postulated cemetery-accessing path/trackway), unless that occurred at a point east of the limits of excavation.

The 'Y'-shaped intersection of Roads 2 and 3 in the north was obviously the settlement's main means of access. Road 3, while seemingly the more minor route, would have run towards Roman Cambridge's South Gate if projected eastwards. However, the early town's 'fringe' enclosures there show no obvious influence from that route's existence (see Chap. 2) and, in truth, it was exposed over too short a length on the site to have any confidence in its distant projection.

Despite what seems to have been its relatively slight ditch-definition, Road 3 had greater longevity as a routeway than the more robustly ditched Road 2. The latter had ceased to function, and its way was blocked, by the onset of Phase III. Marking the greatest intensity of the settlement's usage at that time (at least during the first part of that phase, III.1), the settlement was solely accessed from Road 3 and from its western end radiated a series of tracks/paths, with one evidently continuing southward from the settlement-core to connect with the inhumation cemetery.

As outlined above, it is the fact that various enclosures cut off the access of Road 3 into the settlement (and that ditches cut into its metalled surface) that has required us to construct a secondary Phase III sub-division (see Fig. 5.40). Yet, it does not seem as if the settlement then existed as an 'isolated' unit. We suggest that it was still accessed via Road 3, but from a more easterly point (i.e. probably beyond the excavation's limits on that side). As will be further explored in the next chapter, roadway access and transportation linkages were clearly of paramount importance throughout the lifetime of the settlement; variously for carting away its produce and delivering a range of goods to its inhabitants (pottery, glass, querns and oysters, *etc.*).

Notes

1 Discussed in detail within Chapter Four's 'local environment' section.

2 The use of this ('neutral') entitlement was discussed in the first chapter and will be further explored in the next. By employing 'aisled building' it is understood to imply a multi-purpose open-plan type building, potentially incorporating both domestic residence and agriculture storage (see e.g. Taylor 2013, 178–9).

3 The aDNA results also have chronological implications in the case of the first-degree relations between F.2086 and F.2049's females, either reflecting that they were sisters or a mother and daughter. Yet, the former had mid–later fourth-century AD jewellery, with the latter accompanied with a second-century AD greyware bottle/flagon. If the dating typologies are correct, F.2049's vessel would then have had to of been curated for upwards of 150–200 years.

Equally noteworthy is that both of the first-degree genetic 'pairings' – F.2028/F.2076 and F.2049/F.2096 – involved the cemetery's two dominant orientations: east–west and north–south (though in the case of F.2049 the latter was more southeast–northwest). This could indicate that grave orientation was essentially spatially determined in relationship to the cemetery's boundaries, with its infilling progressing from south to north.

4 That said, one reason for a strictly Phase III attribution could derive from the fourth-century AD pottery recovered from the fill of the western horse-head pit, F.5425; it is reasonable to presume that this marked the cemetery's entrance and, thereby, preceded the majority of its inhumations.

5 See also the five fourth-century AD glass vessels deposited together in a large storage jar at Lower Cambourne (Wright *et al.* 2009, 103–4, fig. 44).

6 The more 'removed' shrine/temple excavated at the NIAB Site will be discussed in the next book.

Chapter 6

Building Spaces, Assemblages and Community – Overviewing Vicar's Farm

This chapter first addresses some of the larger questions concerning the site, particularly those relating to space and its use and inhabitation. A number of major themes are considered: the built environment (structures, ditches and other features), working activities and spaces, human-animal relations, and the separation of the living and the dead.

The second half of the chapter examines broader issues of social and economic dynamics, the relation of the settlement to the landscape and its position in the urban hinterland. This discussion will be organized according to two broad themes: *production*, which discusses crop and animal husbandry practised on the site, and *consumption*, dealing with foodways and trade/exchange.

The Built Environment

A range of feature types (e.g. pits and ditches) and various surface spreads (e.g. metalling and 'dark earths') would have also framed and structured the lives and routines of the settlement's occupants, not just buildings. These occupants would have been both its fulltime residents and also occasional/seasonal 'attendants' at events held there. There would, of course, also have been a considerable livestock population.

Structures

There are just nine definite structures on the site: the Aisled Building, the Timber Shrine, two roundhouses, two rectangular (A & B) and three 'cell' structures (C, D & E). All used timber as the basis of their structural frame, and were probably walled with daub and roofed with thatch (with the exception of the shrine, see below). There was also a monumental post and a number of 'bays'/small enclosures, which may have held more ephemeral structures (Fig. 6.1); in addition, at least three other possible building locations have been identified based on ditch-setting arrangements.

The Aisled Building

With a footprint estimated to cover some 162 sq. m (*c.* 9 × 18 m) and as shown reconstructed in Figure 4.5, the size of the Aisled Building (G2.01) is similar to those found on many Romano-British sites (for discussion see Smith 1963; Hadman 1978; Morris 1979; Smith *et al.* 2016, 66–9; see Fig. 6.2).[1] A domestic function is hard to argue without any internal features, but then, perhaps, it is only disciplinary bias that would insist on proof for a domestic as opposed to an agricultural function. Of course, such buildings may have been multi-purpose (e.g. Taylor 2013, 178–9). Indeed, with the exception of the most Romanized of settlements (towns and villas), it is likely that the nature of the 'domestic' was not so circumscribed. Most of the commentators cited above would argue that Romano-British aisled buildings would have housed humans, animals, grain, *etc.* together and provided a place for multiple activities and relationships. There seems no reason to doubt that this structure was the main domestic building on the site until its abandonment in early Phase III.

The recently excavated aisled *hall* at North West Cambridge's Site VII – a building of considerable architectural pretence and size (*c.* 26 × 13 m) – has been alluded to Chapter One. Significantly, there was still another aisled building beside that villa complex's masonry bath-house, one whose layout and scale almost exactly matches that of Vicar's Farm. In the case of that site, its smaller aisled building is thought to have been a barn, perhaps with grain storage facilities and labourers' housing. The specifics of that building's interpretation do not, though, necessarily detract from the potential wide range of functions that Vicar's Farm aisled building may have encompassed.

Accepting that it likely also involved residential use, trying to understand in greater detail the usage of Vicar's Farm aisled building and the nature of activities within it is exceptionally difficult given the lack of any internal features, but there are some clues. The low levels of industrial activity on the site (see below) make it unlikely that the building was associated with any industrial process on a regular basis, in contrast to many examples in the Nene Valley (Hadman 1978, 192–3). An agricultural function seems more likely, either for keeping livestock or storing grain. Yet, since the phosphate levels were generally very low across the interior (Fig. 5.3), it is unlikely that livestock were kept here. This really leaves grain storage, and indeed, from the large quantities of semi-processed wheat found on the site, this seems the most plausible use. It would make the building broadly comparable to others in the region, such as those from Orton Hall Farm or Barnack (Mackreth 1996; Simpson 1993).

The Timber Shrine

The *timber* circle is an unusual structure (G2.02; Fig. 6.3). Roundhouses were, of course, still constructed and used in the Roman period (Smith *et al.* 2016, 47–50), as is seen from the presence of two on this site (see below). Whilst not denying that the shrine shows a certain

Figure 6.1. *Vicar's Farm, location of structures.*

affinity with these structures, there are nevertheless a number of features that made this building more distinct. Its size was not large (the internal space was only *c.* 3 m across) and the number and scale of the posts for a structure of this scale seems excessive (12 postholes, each *c.* 0.2 m diam.). The space between the posts and the outer ditch was very slight to accommodate a wall and would originally have been even less, taking into account the reduced dimensions due to topsoil removal. It is possible that a wall ran (unusually) *between* the posts and this might be indicated by the magnetic susceptibility survey which suggested the build-up of material around the line of the posts. Although not conclusive, there was very little burnt daub in the fills of the surrounding ditches that might indicate a wall; the primary ditch (F.5522) produced only three small fragments (7 g), while the later ditch (F.5483) yielded seven (13 g). Finally, the posts were evenly spaced all the way around (*c.* 0.2 m apart), presenting no space wide enough to permit easy access and certainly offering no obvious 'doorway'.

Given these points, it is hard to see the structure as anything but an open ring of posts, possibly, but not necessarily, roofed. No central feature was identified; indeed, the magnetic susceptibility survey showed a fairly 'clean' interior, as did the phosphates (see Fig. 5.7). The surrounding ditches do, however, exhibit an interesting dynamic over time. Initially, there appears to only have been a 'C'-shaped ditch semi-enclosing the rear of the timber circle when it was first constructed in *c.* AD 80, but in the mid–later second century AD its front side was closed off by a corresponding 'C'-shaped ditch. Then, in the early–mid third century AD, this was remodelled into a larger square enclosure closing off the whole structure (although by this time the structure may no longer have been standing). Given the continual process of elaboration and enclosing of the timber circle – harking back to its discussion in the previous chapter – the structure was clearly of some importance, and a function as a shrine seems likely.

Circular structures occur throughout the Roman period and seem to date from the second century AD (yet clearly deriving from an Iron Age roundhouse tradition) and continue into the fifth century AD, but with a floruit in the Antonine period (Williams & Zeepvat 1994, 207–8). As variable as their Iron Age antecedents in size and construction, their function remains unclear, although several have been interpreted as shrines (Fig. 6.3). Circular shrines are known from many sites across southern Britain but have been the subject of only limited discussion (Drury 1980, 68–70). Many

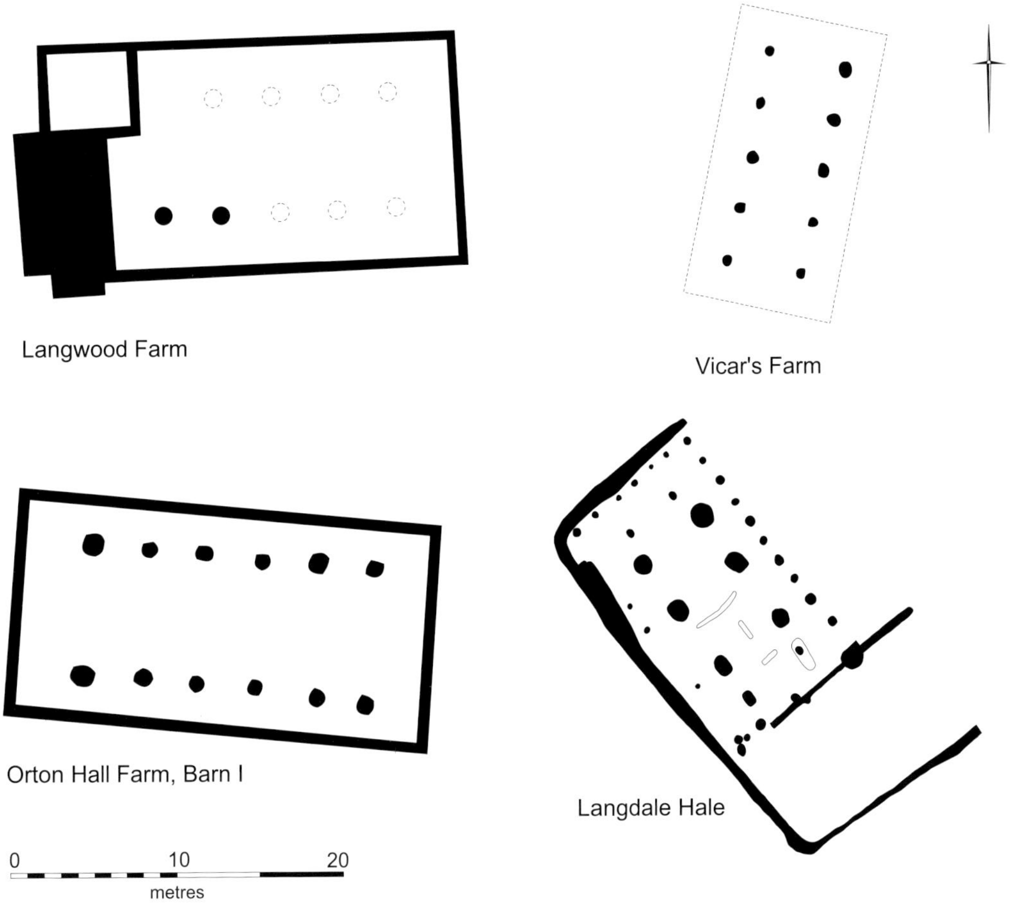

Figure 6.2. *Examples of aisled buildings from the region.*

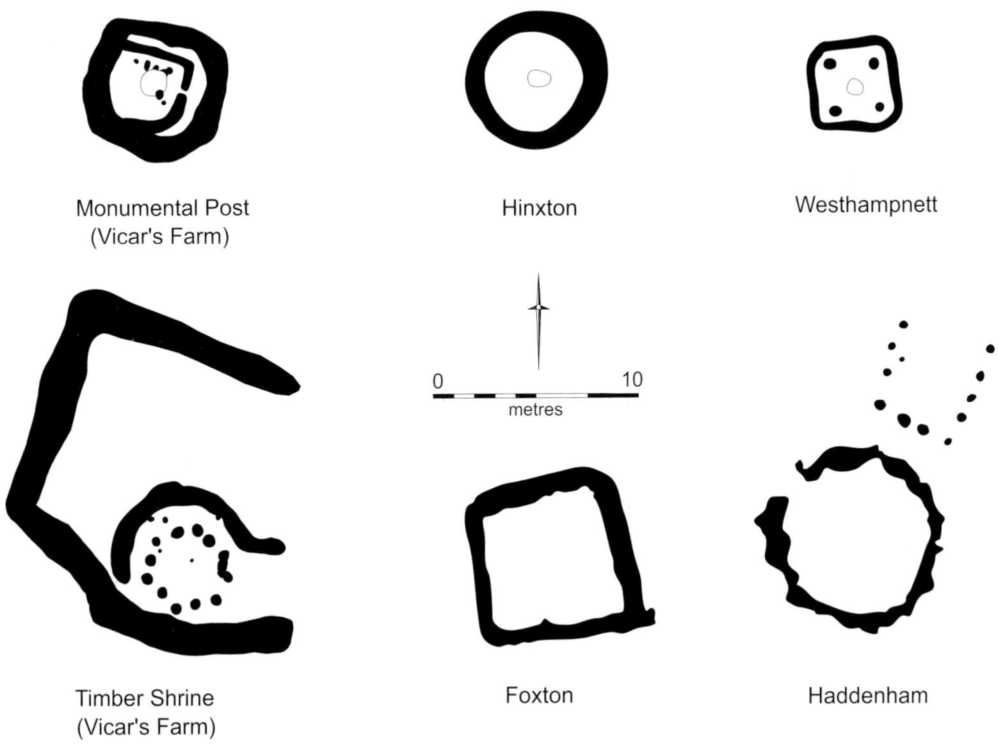

Figure 6.3. *Examples of small ritual structures from the region.*

examples show Iron Age antecedents as well as the more typical square successor (e.g. Hayling Island: Downey *et al.* 1980), Maiden Castle (Wheeler 1943), Frilford (Bradford & Goodchild 1939), Lullingstone (Meates 1979, 119–22) or a polygonal successor such as at Brigstock (Greenfield 1963) and Collyweston (Knocker 1965). However, at Bancroft a circular shrine replaced the more conventional square type (Williams & Zeepvat 1994, 107–11). At Vicar's Farm, there was no rebuilding, but rather abandonment and enclosure. At Elms Farm (Essex), a large circular structure was interpreted as a shrine and seems to bear some similarities to Vicar's Farm, including concentrated pitting activity on the northeast side (Atkinson & Preston 1998 and 2015, 87–98). While not interpreted as a shrine and of a much greater (projected) diameter – *c.* 10.50 m – the arrangement of the large close-set postholes of a fourth century AD roundhouse at Kempston Church End, Bedford (G4090; Dawson 2004, 48, fig. 3.22) would also have affinities to the site's setting.

Roundhouses

Two roundhouses survived only as very ephemeral traces (the back curve of their eavesgullies) and suffered greatly from plough truncation (Fig. 6.4). Structure G2.19 (F.5081) was a small structure lying in the very corner of the main settlement enclosure and probably dating to Phase I or II. There was very little cultural material in the vicinity and it is difficult to regard this as a dwelling. The other roundhouse (F.5402) lay outside the main settlement in the area to the south in Phase II, and again, there is very little associated material. Given their marginal location and lack of associated remains, these may not have been residential structures (even for labourers to sleep in) and, rather, may have been agricultural buildings of some sort. Threshing areas are a possibility, but the gullies seem to enclose too small an area to allow threshing using animals (Morris 1979, 26–7; Evans *et al.* 2013b, 66, fig. 2.25); perhaps they were simply drainage gullies around hayricks/fodder storage.

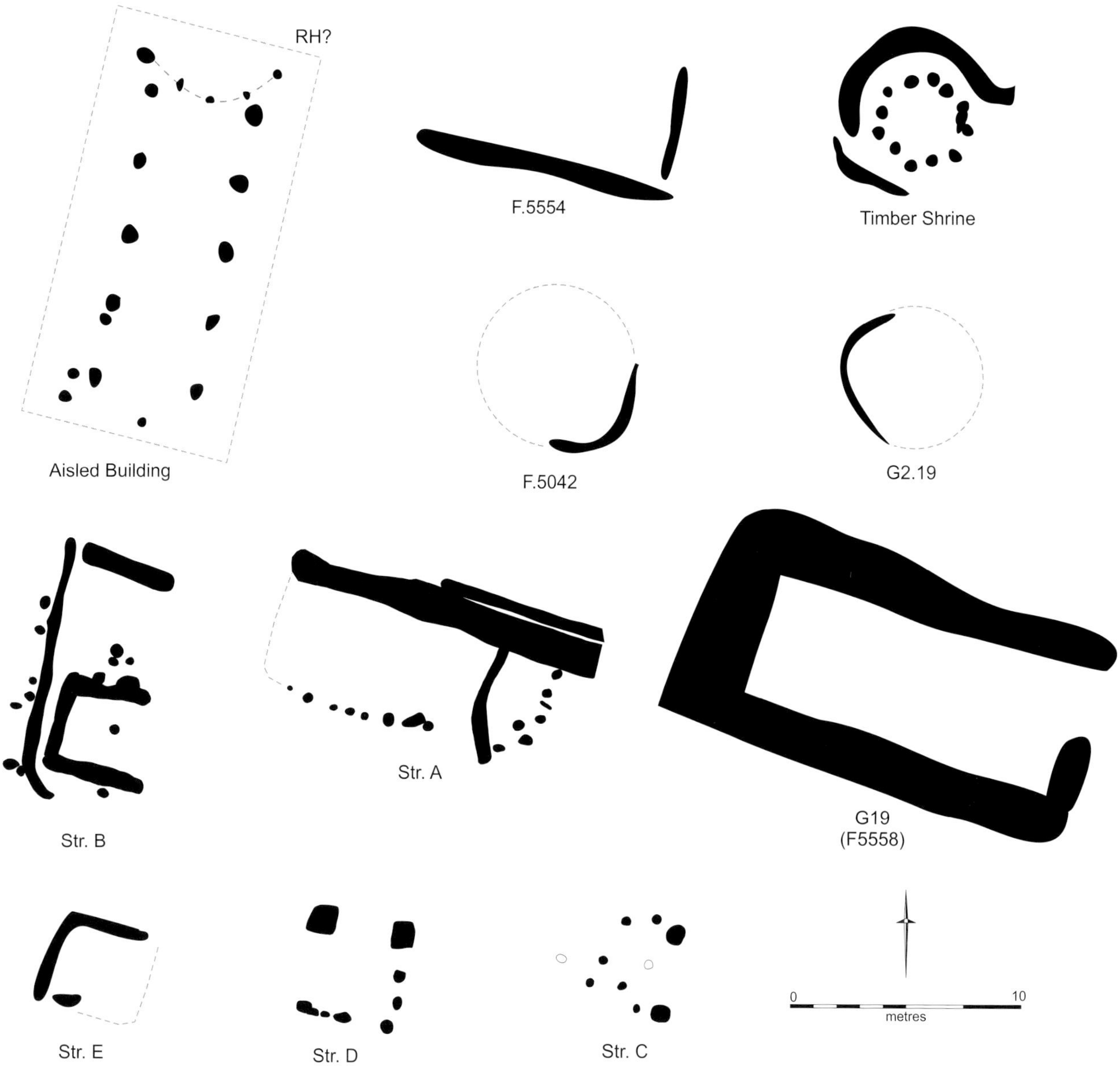

Figure 6.4. *Comparative plans of Vicar's Farm buildings.*

Rectangular Structures
Two post-built rectangular structures were identified at the site. Structure A (G2.06) lay in the main settlement core along the edge of the diagonal pathway running into the settlement from the northern entrance. It was of mixed construction, with postholes marking out two sides and defining a structure *c.* 8.5 m long by 5.3 m wide (Fig. 6.4). At its eastern end, there was possibly a small horticultural plot, presumably for vegetables or herbs. It was built and in use from the end of Phase II and into Phase III. This was almost certainly a domestic building, but not as formal or 'grand' as the Aisled Building. It was probably built as the latter building was abandoned, suggesting it may have replaced it as the main dwelling on the site.

Structure B (G11.01) lay in the southern extension to the core settlement area and also dated to Phase II (Fig. 6.4), but it went out of use in Phase III with the building of a smaller, square structure (see below). It consisted of a combination of beam-slot and posthole construction, with possible repairs, and appears to have been divided into two halves, the building as a whole being *c.* 5 m wide and 12 m long. To its south lay a small cobbled yard surface, with gullies on two sides. The partitioning of the building could suggest this is the location of a byre/stalls; indeed, it may even be possible to see the back gully as a drainage channel rather than a beam-slot. The question of structures for livestock, particularly those needing special shelter or to be close at hand, such as milch or calving cows, horses or pigs, warrants consideration (see *Human and Animal Spaces*). That said, other interpretations are possible and are outlined in the next section.

'Cell' Structures
Three small, cell-like structures occurred on the site, two of which were fronted by two large paired posts (Fig. 6.4). Structure C was a small trapezoid, *c.* 3 m 'square', defined by two major paired posts on its front, eastern end and smaller posts behind. A similar, but more impressive structure lay in an enclosure to the southwest (Structure D), again defined by two major paired posts at its northern front end with smaller posts behind; it formed a structure *c.* 5 m square. Both structures date to the final phase of the settlement (Phase III). These are unusual both in their size and form. A similar example occurred at Orton Hall Farm (Mackreth 1996, fig. 6). Structure D was constructed over the earlier rectangular Structure B, which was interpreted as possible stalls, and the size of the cell is comparable to one of the bays of that structure. It is possible that these cell structures were also used for holding livestock. The third cell structure (E) was located in the northeastern corner of the site and was defined by two sides of a beam-slot/gully enclosing an area *c.* 3 m square. The area in which this structure sat was an enclosed piece of land divided into narrow strips 2.5–5 m wide and is tentatively interpreted as crop fields/lazy-beds; accordingly, this structure might have simply been a shed.

The interpretation of the other two 'cells' is, though, more problematic, especially in the case of Structure D and its large front posts. Given that its plan (though not its building technique) is similar to the 'U'-shaped partition within Structure B – lying immediately to the south and which 'D' replaced – it is possible that they had a shared function. Equally, Structure B's layout is reminiscent to the 'long range' at Langdale Hale (Str. 8), although of a somewhat smaller scale; the latter had within it two massive four-post settings (Str. 19 & 21): 5 × 6.5 m and 6 × 7.5–8 m respectively (one certainly being later; Evans *et al.* 2013b, 66–72, figs. 2.27 & 2.29). These were interpreted as probably relating to traction-driven vertical mills (*ibid.*, 111–12, fig. 2.57). As outlined below, at least one of the Vicar's Farm quernstones was of a size that would have required traction-operation (see Fig. 6.19) and, given this, it is just possible that Structures B and D served as mills (although one would have expected the latter's large postholes to be four-square and symmetrically-set). A neonate burial within the packing fill of one of Structure D's front posts (see below) could instead suggest a ritual function (i.e. akin to the Snow's Farm late-phase timber shrine setting; see Fig. 6.3; Evans & Hodder 2006b, 346–8). The only other possible candidate for a mill setting would be amid the cluster of small pits and postholes in the forecourt area in front of the shrine; that does, though, seem a rather unlikely location for a mill.

Monumental Post
The timber post/column appears to have been a marker or focus of some nature and is clearly associated with the Curvilinear Enclosure and associated activities at the very heart of the settlement (Figs. 5.13 & 6.3). Monumental posts have also been found in Essex at Elms Farm and at Ivy Chimneys (Atkinson & Preston 1998, 99 and 2015, 95, fig. 6.6; Turner 1999, 40 & 244). The column at Vicar's Farm was associated with some rather special deposits, including a total of 12 coins within the post pit and a cattle skull in its encircling ditch.

'Missing' Structures
Due to often shallow-footed building techniques (e.g. beam-slot construction) and the practice of 'hard' machining, many Roman settlements fail to recover either buildings or, otherwise, entirely convincing ones.[2] Here, given the amount of truncation to the site through ploughing, it is entirely possible that other structures left no or only minimal traces. Apart from Phase I.1's F.5554 setting, three areas of the site might be argued to have contained buildings of some nature (Fig. 6.1). In the ditched embayments (G19, Area B) on the other side of Structure B, rectangular structures may have existed. Whilst possibly no more than storage sheds or animal stalls/pens, two settings could have been dwelling-related (F.5558 & F.5460; Figs. 5.22 & 6.4). The other location of possible structures lay to the east in the core-area (A); the enclosures on the eastern boundary ditch could have contained structures (there was a neonate burial in a posthole there), as could the bays on the south side of the late Curvilinear Enclosure. These are similar to those in Area B, being defined by small bays or enclosures and their most likely use would seem to have been sheds, stock pens or stalls. None of the other identified structures on the site had ditched enclosures or sat in bays, and it seems that this form of small enclosure would have been most appropriate for livestock pens. The final candidate is the paired ditch-setting along the north side of Enclosure G7 in Area E (F.4137). At *c.* 4.5 × 12 m, it seems comparable to G19's northern 'embayment' (F.5558; interior *c.* 5 × 13 m). Broadly comparable minor ditch settings have been recovered from other Roman settlements in the region; for example, Kempston Church End's G4112–14 enclosures (Dawson 2004, 42, fig. 3.18; see also, e.g., *BLS* 87, fig. 2.37).

Other possible structures may have lain off-site to the east, beyond the area of excavation. The settlement certainly continues in that direction, but the significant issue is whether a major dwelling or residence lay there in the late phase. This has ramifications for considering the overall layout and spatial logic of the later settlement, for if a major dwelling was located there it would imply that the excavated area is only really the 'back' part of the site. The distribution of finds and their concentration in the currently interpreted 'core', need not detract from this alternative perspective, as it is possible that rubbish may have been pushed toward the rear with the front part kept 'clean'. The presence of ceramic and stone building materials might also suggest that a more important stone building lies somewhere close, as none of this material could be associated with the known buildings (see below). However, their distributions do not suggest an eastward source (see Fig. 6.5), and, moreover, the presence of such building material need not necessarily imply its use on site as building material; alternate uses, such as hardcore, are likely and not unknown. As it stands, the possibility of a major stone building off-site to the east must remain speculative.

Building Materials

All the settlement's buildings seem to have been constructed with timber, thatch and daub, and all of these would have rotted, leaving little or no trace. Apart from postholes/postpipes, the main traces consisted of burnt fragments of daub from walls or other clay-based features such as ovens. Given that, the presence of more durable building material in stone and ceramic on the site needs some explanation. There were some quantities of brick, tile and mortar, as well as a few fragments of building stone, but these are not present in particularly large amounts. Their presence and intended function do not necessarily imply that there were buildings in the vicinity using these materials. Indeed, it is hard to argue this given the lack of any stone-footed structures, even robbed-out ones, on the site. There is no concentration of ceramic and stone building materials to suggest that a stone-footed building had existed in or even just beyond the excavated area (Fig. 6.5). All in all, another explanation has to be found for their presence; the most likely is that this material was introduced second-hand, as hardcore or for *ad hoc* use in small structures such as ovens.

Fired Clay

A small assemblage of fired clay was recovered (1021 fragments, *c.* 12.4 kg), the majority consisting of very small, abraded fragments (<5 cm). Some very distinctive fabrics occur, particularly a soft, buff-pink type with few inclusions and a gritty, deep orange example with sand and flint inclusions. The attribution of these fragments is hard to discern given their size and condition, but in a few, impressions of wattles and in some cases, straw, were noted, suggesting their use as daub. A few pieces also have some of their faces preserved, one with possible moulding and another with combing. There were no positively identified fragments of loomweight but, given the plentiful supply of rounded river-cobbles on the site, this is perhaps not surprising. By default, most of the fragments are probably structural of one kind or another, from clay ovens, daub or even possibly floors.

Figure 6.5. *Distribution of ceramic and stone building material.*

Table 6.1. *Different types of identifiable ceramic building material.*

Type	No. of fragments
Tegula	37
Imbrex	17
Box tile	5
Brick	83

Brick, Tile and Mortar

The assemblage of brick and tile from the site was insubstantial (730 fragments, *c.* 5.6 kg),[3] although there were several different types present, chiefly roof tiles – *tegula* and *imbrex* – but also some box flue tiles associated with hypocaust systems. There were also various brick fragments of which none were large enough to attribute to type, although they made up the greater part of the assemblage (Table 6.1). The material came in a variety of fabrics, generally either sandy redwares or shelly wares. Only eight fragments (268 g) of mortar/plaster were recovered, of which one might be *opus signinum*. This is not a substantial quantity of material by any count and this fits well with the fact that there are no stone-footed buildings on the site, these being the most likely to have supported a tiled roof. In short, it appears that most of the ceramic building material is probably reused fragments, collected for any number of non-structural reasons (e.g. hardcore).

Building Stone (with K. Hayward)

A small amount of building stone was recovered (30 pieces). Most were roofing slate (21 pieces), chiefly Collyweston (17 pieces; Fig. 6.6.1) and dark mudstone (four pieces). There were only nine fragments of non-roofing materials, of which only those in ditches F.5587 and F.5470 (both Phase I) show any sign of architectural working and conjoin (see Figs. 6.5 & 6.6.2). The material is all

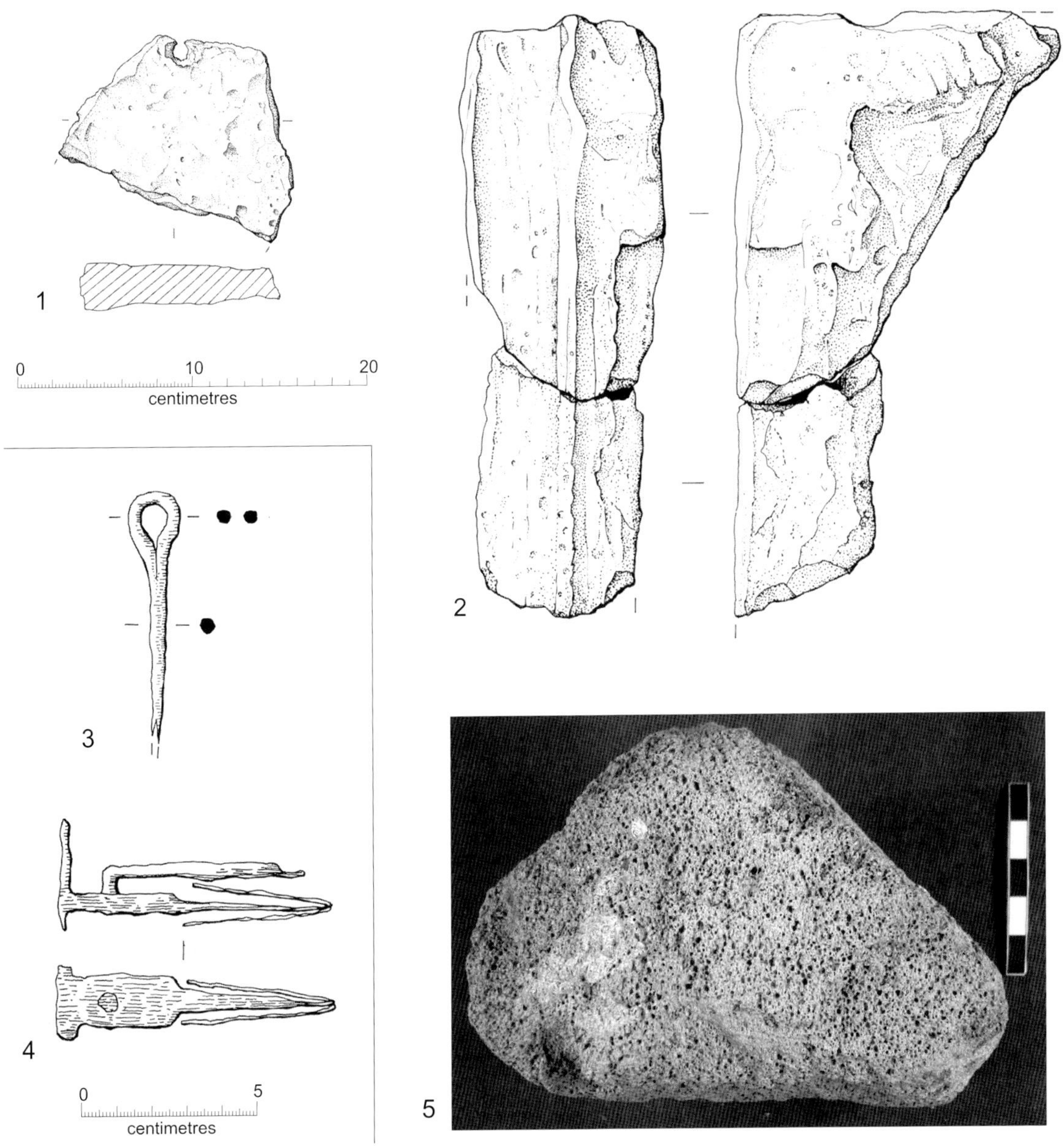

Figure 6.6. *Architectural stone and other structural material (see text).*

calcareous, from a variety of rock types. Upware Limestone (four fragments) is hard and rubbly and would mainly be used for walling and foundation stone. Ketton Stone is, however, a classic freestone, ideal for quality masonry; the single large block in F.5528 ([1860]) shows no signs of working, however, and appears to have been used as a foundation stone. Tufa (seven pieces; Fig. 6.6.5) and chalk (one piece) are light, easily workable and both used extensively in southern Britain. Tufa deposits are very common in southern Britain, associated with springs and chalk escarpments (Potter 2000, 55), so the source for this could be very local. However, there is a lot of Niedermendig (Rhineland) Lavastone from the shrine area (see querns below), and an exotic origin for the tufa (i.e. German) should not, therefore, be excluded.

Nails and Other Structural Ironwork (with N. Crummy)
As detailed below, there are several iron structural fittings, including a large wall-hook. Iron nails, other than hobnails, are not listed here and were not X-rayed. Of 201 definitely identified nails, all but two were of the common form of the Roman period (Manning 1985, Type Ib). The exceptions were a well-preserved long Type Ia nail and a triangular-headed Type 2 nail (details below). Some of the nails are from coffins, and where they are well-preserved conform to the general rule that examples from one coffin are all much the same size. Nails associated with cremations were also found. Although corrosion obscures the details of the surfaces, none appear to have been fire-damaged.

<4553> F.479 - Large 'L'-shaped wall-hook, probably for driving into masonry. The long arm tapers to a blunt point (perhaps damaged), the short widens slightly and is damaged. Length of long arm 129 mm, length of short arm 41 mm.

<4693b> F.116 - Loop-headed spike, the tip of the shank missing. Length 69 mm (Fig. 6.6.3)

<4482> F.582 - Loop-headed spike as <4693b> above, with the tip of the shank missing. Length 55 mm.

<4590> F.614 – Well-preserved nail of Manning's Type Ia (1985, fig. 32), with small slightly domed head. Length 158 mm.

<4490> F.397 - Nail of Manning's Type 2, with flat triangular head (1985, fig. 32). Length (bent) 92 mm.

Of all the nails, 82 were associated with graves and, therefore, assumed to be coffin nails; of the remaining 117, their distribution across the site more or less reflects the general intensity of cultural material, with most occurring within the core-area (see Fig. 6.7). There

Figure 6.7. *Distribution of nails and other structural ironwork.*

is no definite concentration around any of the known structures, but nails do occur beside all of them. The only potentially unusual cluster occurs along the eastern side of the G28 enclosure, which may suggest that there was at some point a structure nearby. The lack of nails from the far eastern side of the site could suggest that there were no structures toward that side.

Besides nails and structural ironwork, two lock parts were retrieved: a bolt from a padlock came from the western edge of the site from ditch F.5470, and a padlock key came from the terminal of ditch F.5304 in the centre of the site.

<4614> *F.5372* - Bolt from a barrel padlock, with two springs on one spine. A second spine is fixed into the first, but any spines it had are now missing (Manning 1985, 95). Length 80 mm (Fig. 6.6.4).

<4477> *F.5304* - Barb-spring padlock key, the upper end missing and the bit broken (Manning 1985, pl. 43; Mould 2000, fig. 4.19, 205). Length 112 mm.

Window Glass

One piece of window glass came from the site (F.5042; SF 58). This was blown and pale green with many elongated bubbles (area 3.5 sq. cm, thickness 3 mm). Such window glass is usually found only on fourth-century AD sites, as the normal type of the first to third centuries AD was made by pouring molten glass out onto trays. There are a few instances of blown window glass being found in first- or early second-century AD contexts, but these tend to be in the southwest of the country and possibly related to the activity of a particular legion (Cool *et al.* 1999, 157). Both the colour of this fragment and the general dating of the type would suggest that it was of fourth-century AD date and it is presumably intrusive in the context in which it was found.

Ditches

Ditching formed the main 'building' activity across the site. More than any other feature type, they – along with their associated banks/hedgerows – transformed the settlement, created spaces, formed boundaries and channelled movement. Apart from the main entrances on the northeast and southeast corners of the main enclosure, most of the ditch circuits were closed, suggesting that access across them was in the form of small wooden bridge-crossings. Whilst this means that we cannot always be sure where access points lay, it might also suggest that these access points could have been moveable (and removable). Access could easily be changed or blocked, and this perhaps has relevance for the nature of activity occurring in the enclosures.

The most obvious purpose of these ditches was to enclose and sub-divide. Can we say anything further? Taking a long-term perspective, one thing does seem apparent: over time, *the settlement was subject to greater and greater segmentation and sub-division*. Ditches took up an increasingly larger amount of space at the site, partitioning the space into smaller parcels.

The dynamics of the settlement's changing layout has been outlined in Chapter Five's Discussion above. That, however, largely views the settlement as having been dominated by ditches as simple borders or partitions: a means of dividing up space and creating a sense of form/structure. This is partly a product of the settlement's plan and the way that the site is presented graphically. However, ditches have a more complex spatiality and temporality than this. Two additional themes in particular are *size* and *repetition*. Why were some ditches deeper or wider than others? Why were some recut more than others? A number of reasons may exist, including practical problems such as drainage and erosion, but also ceremonial/ritual practices of redefining boundaries, and these need not be mutually exclusive. In addition, ditches cannot be viewed independently of associated positive features, and banks, fences or hedgerows could all have bordered the edges of ditches. Banks are likely, simply because it is the easiest way to deposit soil upcast from the ditch's digging and, at the same time, creates a positive boundary. These banks may have been topped with fencing or hedgerows. There is no evidence for such fencing at the site, but stakeholes would hardly survive and may even have been overlooked if patchy and ephemeral. There is, however, evidence for hedgerows from the plant remains (see Chap. 4), and these would certainly have been better, long-term boundaries in terms of maintenance (and as potential food and fuel resources). The key question is whether a ditch was dug primarily to create a bank (e.g. for hedgerow planting), or as a negative feature (e.g. for drainage), or a combination of both. Questions of size, recutting and longevity can all help to shed light on these issues.

Size

The ditches across the site varied in size – depth and width being the key factors here rather than length – and there must be reasons for this variability. Assuming a more or less similar level of truncation of upper profiles, we can use the extant depth of ditches as an index of their size. Figure 6.8 shows the ditches highlighted according to their depth, graded in standard deviations from the mean (0.32 m). Most of the ditches were less than 0.6 m deep (one standard deviation; sd), a few between 0.6 and 0.89 m deep (up to 2 sd), and a few over 0.9 m deep. There is no obvious pattern to this variation in ditch depth, insofar as is does not correspond to any concentric pattern or even to main boundary lines around the settlement. The deepest ditches (those at a depth greater than 2 sd) formed major boundaries to the settlement, respectively for Areas A, B and C. This, however, was only on their southwestern sides and none of the major boundary ditches on the north or east sides were anywhere near as substantial. Why this should be is not immediately obvious. Moreover, this pattern seems to have been repeated in each phase.

One reason for this pattern could be greater wetness and, therefore, a need for greater depth to allow drainage. However, this was probably the *driest* part of the settlement core and the wet areas lay to the north and east (see Chap. 4). From a drainage point of view then, this does not make any sense. It would seem far more likely that there was a symbolic reason for enhancing the size of the boundary at the southwest corner; it is interesting to recall that the pathway through the settlement was arranged diagonally from an entrance at the northeast and aligned to the southwest corner. This alignment cannot be coincidental. The larger ditches would have produced greater banks and the whole visual effect when approaching the settlement from the northeast would have enhanced

Figure 6.8. *Distribution of ditches by depth.*

the southwest corners as the 'back' of the settlement. Thus, even though the actual alignment of the ditches runs almost east–west, the alignment would have been experienced more northeast/ southwest. Depending on a person's position or movement around the settlement, this alignment would shift.

There may also be another factor to consider though; for these deepest ditches also formed smaller sub-enclosures in the southwest corner; it was not simply the edges of the settlement which were enlarged, but *enclosed* areas of the settlement in that area too. The larger banks associated with these ditches would have effectively obstructed these areas from vision. Is there some reason why this part of the site should have been closed off to view? This closure only seems to be a factor in the later phases: ditch F.5431 created a sub-enclosure in Area B in Phase II, while in Phase III, F.5387 in Area C was already self-enclosed (G18). Also in Phase III, the major ditch F.5501 created a sub-enclosure in the core (Area A) with the old southwestern boundary of the site. The question is, therefore, whether there was anything unusual about these areas that could be linked to the enhancement of their boundaries.

Here we need to anticipate the analysis of activity and disposal patterns discussed in the next section, but there are two interesting patterns. In discussing the distribution of iron smithing waste (see Cowgill, below), it is argued that two locations could have been places where smithing was carried out, both in Phase III. One was the northeast corner of Enclosure G18, and the other was Enclosure G11. This may be coincidental, but it seems likely that there is a connection. Smithing is seen as polluting in numerous ethnographic accounts, and the need to emphasise the border between 'polluted' and 'clean' areas of the settlement may well have been marked by enlarged boundaries that obstructed vision and the passage of smoke/smells.

Repetition

Recutting a ditch length can take different forms. At one level, it refers to the mucking out or cleaning of ditch silts. This may not always be easy to detect, especially if the silts eroding into the ditch were more or less homogeneous between each mucking out, but sometimes this has been noted. Given the ambiguity of identifying this kind of activity – which may have been routinized anyway where a drainage function was required of the ditch – no attempt will be made to map it. Rather, the focus here will be on repeated cutting of a ditch- or boundary-line, which also involves a slight relocation in the cut of the ditch. Earlier ditches may have been backfilled with the material from new ditches, or they may have simply filled up with silts or dumping as a matter of course. This kind of recutting suggests something different to mucking out, something perhaps where the act of cutting new ground was significant in itself. Both acts can be viewed as re-establishing a boundary in a repetitive manner, but for the latter, this may have had rather more importance. Four areas of the site where this kind of repetitive cutting occurred stand out:

1) the central part of the eastern side of the main enclosure ditch (G2)
2) southern side of the internal trackway (G2.07) at its southwestern end
3) the area around the cremation cemetery (G2.05/division G2.10)
4) southern side of the inhumation cemetery (G22).

All these areas showed multiple recutting in the form of new ditch cuts rather than mucking out of old ditches. On the eastern side of the main enclosure ditch, and only in the central part of this, two short ditch-lengths ran parallel to the main ditch. Feature 8162 and F.8163 were both cut just inside/west of the main ditch in Phase I, contemporary with the main ditch itself, F.4815. This was later recut in Phase II (F.4821). The area in which this section of the main ditch lay was in a basin or hollow that seems to have been prone to wetness, increasingly so over time (see Chap. 4). These parallel lengths of ditch may, therefore, have acted as sumps or catchwaters. However, Phase I was the driest phase in the Roman period, and, even if this area had been prone to some flooding at this early time, it might have made more sense to deepen the main ditch than simply dig extra ditches. This area was seemingly 'empty' at this time too, although in the next phase it was occupied by the unusual curvilinear enclosures (G2.11). The emptiness of this area need not denote lack of activity; indeed the very openness of the space may suggest that it served some distinct purpose. However we might interpret this, the need to accentuate the eastern side of the enclosure with repeated ditch lengths could have been related.

The other areas offer more scope for interpretation. The southern side of the pathway was recut repeatedly over the whole Roman period. Starting with F.5719 in Phase I, the same length was recut by F.788 and F.5309 in Phase II, and by F.5661 and F.5304 in Phase III. It was only the western end of the pathway that was demarcated in this manner, and it seems to have little to do with drainage. The area where the pathway stopped at this western end – the 'forecourt' – appears to have been linked to ritual activities. It lay in front of the shrine and, indeed, stood between it, the cremation cemetery and the Aisled Building. A well and a number of pits occupied the forecourt, some with special deposits including joints of meat and human skeletal parts. The general interpretation of this area is one of a ritual space, or at least somewhere that ritual activity occurred. The repetitive cutting of a ditch alongside the pathway where it joined this space may, therefore, have been significant.

The area around the cremation cemetery was recut multiple times, especially along the southern end. This delineated not just the cemetery, but also later pitting that was backfilled with rich midden material. Starting with ditches F.5227, F.5220 and F.5583 in Phase II, and recut in Phase III with F.5224, F.5582, F.5480, F.5204, F.5295 and F.5061, there were an excessive number of small, often shallow ditches cut around this area. Again, drainage was hardly an issue, and the area enclosed was special insofar as the cremation cemetery lay to the north and pitting occupied the southern half. The 'underlining' of this boundary many times over, particularly the southern part of it, suggests that it was necessary to demarcate it from the forecourt area, which it abutted to the south.

The final area of note is the inhumation cemetery at the southern margins of the site. There, along the cemetery's southern boundary, the ditch-line was recut several times. The initial limits of the cemetery were demarcated by ditches F.5360 and F.5403, which closed off the corner of the fieldsystem as defined by the G21 ditches (F.5353/5340); it is these latter ditches that were recut (by F.5365 & F.5345), all within Phase III, but only along the length of the cemetery. As with the ditch cutting around the cremation cemetery area, this kind of activity – localized and unrelated to any practical need to maintain a boundary – seems linked to the need to repeatedly mark out the edge of an area, and again, it was the southern edge that came in for special attention.

Other Features

Having outlined the dynamics of the settlement's ditch systems, we now turn to its other main components – various forms of pits, wells and surfaces.

Pits

Pits occurred across the site, but at a very low density on the whole. There were a few exceptions; most particularly, the dense cluster in the northwest (G2.17) adjacent to the cremation cemetery (Fig. 6.9), and these have been interpreted as both trackway construction-related and as quarry pitting for a mound constructed over the cemetery. A similar interpretation to the latter was posited for the large irregular pit north of the shrine (F.5519; Fig. 5.5), which was seen as source material for a mound over the abandoned shrine. Another cluster of pits lay north of these, but they were of Iron Age date. Otherwise, pits occurred as isolated or in small groups, and their purposes varied according to context.

Several small groups seem associated with the shrine, including those that actually surrounded the post-circle before the ring-ditch was cut (G2.02), a group to the south (G2.04), and those in the forecourt (G2.16). Some were associated with special deposits, such as G2.04 with a pottery dump. The pits in the late square enclosure (G28) all arguably contained special deposits, mostly of joints of meat, and these mirror similar deposits in ditch terminals, such as the major horse group in the same enclosure, or that from the ditch terminal in the forecourt (F.5218). The most dramatic of all pit deposits was probably the horse head pit, F.5425, at the entrance to the inhumation cemetery (G22: Figs. 5.28–9). Many of these special deposits seem intimately connected to the actual cutting of the pit, and it would seem that the pit can be interpreted almost in the same manner as a grave: a feature cut specifically to contain a deposit and then backfilled.

One other large group of pits occurred on the eastern side of the site; more dispersed than the quarry pits by the cremation cemetery, they lay within the area of the watching brief and were not properly investigated. They do, however, appear fairly sizeable and, given their location, may have been wells rather than pits.

Wells

All the wells on the site were fairly small and not very deep (*c*. 1–2 m), but given the low-lying nature of the site and fluctuating dampness, they would still have been able to reach the watertable. All except one lay on the margins of the site; the exception being that right in the core of the settlement in Phase II (F.5280; Fig. 6.9). The location of that well in association with the Aisled Building and by the shrine also makes it somewhat unusual. The major group of excavated wells lay on the southern edge of Area B within the G1 enclosure, and these seem to have been cut consecutively as they silted or dirtied up in the earlier phases. There was no evidence of any lining or stabilization of the sides, but the wells were cut into clay and would not necessarily have required stabilization (such linings can, though, leave little or no discernible trace if the features are not waterlogged.) To the east, along the same boundary, further large features were cut in the later phases and these were also probably wells. A final cluster of large pits lay around the southeastern corner of the primary enclosure to the north. These were not properly investigated as they lay within the area of the watching brief, but again, given their size and location, they were probably also wells. Apart from these three groups, an isolated well lay in the corner of the G13 enclosure in Area D.

Figure 6.9. *Pits and wells: location of major groups (top) and, below, size-plot by type.*

The marginal location of all these wells is odd, especially if they were intended for human use; it is, perhaps, more likely that they represent waterholes cut for livestock. However, if this is the case, it begs the question of where the human population acquired their water. Of course, this would depend on how much water would have been needed: beer may have been more commonly drunk, and washing could have been done elsewhere or infrequently. It is hard to estimate these requirements without an understanding of the cultural practices surrounding the range of activities that might use water. Certainly, it is not unlikely that water as a drink could have been far more important for livestock than humans, and such water as required on site could have been brought in containers from these wells or elsewhere. In reference to the wells' 'marginality', it needs to borne in mind that most only lay some 50 m from the settlement's core.

Two Vessels Gavin Lucas

Two different vessels, one made and used in the mid second century AD, the other in the early twentieth century, but deposited only a few hundred metres apart and excavated only a few months apart at the turn of the millennium (Fig. 6.10). What space-time compressions and stretches are involved here? What serendipities led to both vessels being used in two separate, unrelated publications of mine in the first few years of this new millennium – one about rubbish, the other about time (Lucas 2002; 2005)? There are some strange symmetries here that only emerge after the fact. The jar is probably one of the oldest vessels from the site and it was also one of the earliest we excavated; the glass bottle is one of the youngest vessels and was unearthed in a last bid scramble to recover a modern assemblage in the final days of the excavation. The glass bottle has embossed on its body, an ownership claim which situates it in a period when bottle recycling meant cleaning and reusing the bottle as is, not melting it down as raw material. The Roman jar, originally intended as a cooking vessel or storage jar, was reused as a cremation urn.

Rather than dwell on such coincidences, let me use this opportunity to reflect more broadly on the intersection of the two themes addressed in the publications these vessels appeared in: *discard and time*. An obvious starting point is use-life. Objects tend to get discarded when their usefulness is considered to be spent and in the case of ceramic and glass vessels, this generally happens when they break. Studies abound of the use-life of pottery vessels, and cooking vessels especially tend to be among those with shorter use-lives due to their frequent and stressful use. The question of 'age at death' – or, more accurately, age at deposition – was addressed in my study of the Roman jar (Lucas 2005). But, of course, what both the Roman jar and the modern glass bottle have in common is that neither were in fact broken – at least at the time of deposition. Their utility was not expended. In the case of the jar, this utility was redirected, from cooking (if indeed it ever was used as such) to holding cremated remains. In the case of the bottle, its utility was simply ignored or de-valued such that it was discarded. In both cases, the 'natural term of life' of the vessels was artificially cut short – buried whole, intact and still functional – unlike most of the ceramics and glass that archaeologists dig up (although the jar could be argued to have continued in use up to the moment of its excavation).

However, utility is of course a relative concept; though intact, the bottle might have still been considered useless for any number of reasons: the people were moving house and needed to clear out, and discarding useful items might still have been considered more expedient than taking them with them, as numerous studies of abandonment have shown. But maybe it was also easier and cheaper to acquire a new bottle than return/recycle this one. Or maybe the shape and style of the bottle was simply considered unappealing as fashions changed. This last is not very convincing in this case, but it is an argument that applies to much material culture, especially since the eighteenth century, a point I also touched on in my study of the Roman jar. Indeed, the very breakability of ceramics and glass is often cited as the reason why they became such critical items of material consumption in the eighteenth century: breakability leads to high discard/replacement rates which means they are perfect vehicles for swiftly changing fashions. We routinely discard a lot of perfectly useful things – not because they break but because they are no longer desirable – for whatever reasons. At the same time however, the conduits of discard vary from giving away to friends, charity shops, selling on eBay to throwing in the bin. Many useful objects have an afterlife, like the Roman jar reused as a cremation urn.

Such practices were linked to the constitution of the subject in my paper on discard, but how do they relate to the constitution of the object? The question of an 'afterlife' raises the question of an object's identity and its relation to time. Even a broken glass bottle can serve a new function, such as the arrow and spearheads knapped out of glass

Figure 6.10. *Everted rim Romano-British jar (BB2 fabric) from Cremation 7 (F.5307; left) and, right, early twentieth-century 'farmyard assemblage' glass bottle embossed with: THIS BOTTLE IS THE SOLE PROPERTY OF J.N. BALDRY AND ONLY LOANED. ANY OTHER PERSON USING THE BOTTLE WILL BE PROSECUTED.*

fragments by Australian aborigines. In cases like this, a glass bottle has been dramatically transformed and the question is whether the glass arrowhead is really an afterlife of the bottle or a completely new object. We can take a more ambiguous example; a glass bottle like the one from Vicar's Farm, which was sold and bought largely for its contents – say a soda drink – may well have been largely identified through its contents. The transparency of the glass only acts to enhance that association insofar as the bottle itself, is merely the container, the frame. If I then reuse the bottle to store homemade lemonade or berry juice, does the bottle change its identity? Do I think of it as the same bottle – in terms of my routine interaction with it? I don't think so; what *was* the soda bottle, is *now* the lemonade bottle. Even if the bottle itself has undergone no change it is surely a new object, just like the glass arrowhead.

There is something important here about the temporality of objects and their material borders; we tend to think of objects as solid, well-defined entities with clearly demarcated edges. The line drawing and photograph that accompany this text serve to underline this very ontology. However, an empty bottle or jar is like a dead corpse: there is something missing. The very void in between, bisected by that centre line of the drawing that both exposes and conceals this void, stares at us yet we usually don't see it. As Clive Gamble once put it, containment is one of the oldest and most basic functions of material culture (2007). This Roman jar and that glass bottle are more than their material outlines, they are also the space inside: *containment is their primary affordance*, to put it in Gibsonian terms. Ceramic jars and glass bottles are what I have called assemblages in other texts (Lucas 2012) and their identity is as much bound up with the substances they contain as the substances they are made from. This makes them very fluid objects, as they alter their identity in relation to their contents. How different is it then, that a Roman cooking pot gets reused as a cremation urn and a glass bottle reused as an arrowhead? In both cases, it is the affordances of the object – its ability to contain on the one hand, and its ability to be knapped and have a sharp edge on the other – that define its identity, and this is always in relation to some other object or practice. When you look at these two vessels then, don't look at their outlines but the white space in between; like those optical illusions favoured by theory books of a certain era, they will change what they are depending on what you see inside.

Metalled Surfaces

The ground surface of several areas of the site had been prepared by laying down of crude metalling, in the form of cobbles or gravels. More areas may have existed, as evidenced by patches of gravelling, but have since been ploughed out. The immediate reasons for preparing the ground in this manner may have been related to the increasing wetness of the ground; this is especially true of the metalling in the basin area that took place in Phase II (G2.08; Fig. 5.13). The main expanses of metalling lay on the northern edge of the settlement core, where wide linear swathes were gravelled over in Phase III (in part, relating to the western extension of Road 3; Fig. 5.22), as was the path leading through the core of the site. So, to some extent, these surfaces probably related to the need to consolidate and stabilize the ground surface due to increasingly wet conditions, but it also provides us with an indication of the spaces over which people or livestock were most commonly moving. The same interpretation has been tentatively offered for the accumulation of dark earths over the core-area of the site, namely as the deliberate spreading of ashes to aid drainage of the soil on a wet and heavily used surface. While the pathway was clearly a route through the settlement, and the surfaces in the basin-area were associated with the curvilinear enclosures, the linear strips along the northern edge are more enigmatic. They did not seem to be associated with any features, except for 'shadowing' the ditches alongside them. It is possible that small temporary structures could have been erected on them (e.g. stalls or livestock pens); they certainly suggest that human or animal movement took place regularly in those spaces.

Spaces and Uses

This section begins by exploring how the settlement both framed and expressed various human-animal inter-relationships. It then considers the nature of its working spaces and the range of activities/craft that were practised. Finally, the site's complex crop-related 'cycles' and processes are appraised.

Human and Animal Spaces

The people at the Vicar's Farm settlement were not just living with each other but with an animal population. Animals were related to people in a number of complex ways in everyday life, and the human population probably had different relationships to different species, and probably even to individual animals. Investigating these relationships is no easy matter; it is possible, though, to make some tentative suggestions based on a variety of types of evidence. In the discussion of the buildings on the site, it was suggested that most of the structures were associated with human habitation: certainly, the Aisled Building and Structure A. While a likely (human) residence, Structure B may also have included a byre/stalls. The two 'cell' structures – C and D – could conceivably have also been animal-related but, as discussed, the occurrence of a neonate burial in one of Structure D's front postholes could perhaps suggest some manner of shrine setting. This, then, could also be true of the very similarly arranged Structure C, though, like 'E', it may have simply been some manner of shed. Otherwise, some of the more speculative structures, marked only by bays or small enclosures, may have been animal pens. It is debatable to what extent livestock in Roman Britain would have required shelter in the form of a byre or stalls; sheep and most cattle reared for their meat, would probably not need over-wintering in a protected structure and yards or open enclosures would suffice (Morris 1979, 47–8; Mackreth 1996, 222–3). Most of the cattle at Vicar's Farm appear to have been reared for beef (see Clarke below) and, thus, were unlikely to have needed long-term over-wintering provision. The only animals that might have required such buildings would have been those animals sick or calving and milch livestock, as well as other animals which needed to be kept close at hand, such as cattle or horses for traction. In many ways, storage of fodder is more of an issue than animal shelter and the two roundhouses, as well as some of the later bays or small enclosures, may have been used for this.

Where animals are kept in relation to the human population says a great deal about human attitudes to animals. Animals in the home are 'pets'; those on the farm, 'livestock', and those outside human control, 'wild', to cite just a few modern categorizations. Although certain types of species are usually associated with these categorizations, they are not fixed; for example, wild animals and livestock can be adopted as pets, while some pets become feral. The important factor, especially when studying other societies, is the nature of the human-animal relationship rather than the type of animal. We cannot assume, for example, that the dogs and cats were pets on this site. Indeed, the very categorizations of 'pet', 'livestock' or 'wild animal' might not have the same meaning or even apply here. Dogs and cats were present, especially in the later phases (II–III) at Vicar's Farm, albeit in small numbers (41 dog bones, four cat bones). Dogs were more common than cats, but the remains of both animals were only ever found as disarticulated skeletal elements. This does not necessarily mean they were eaten; certainly, there were no butchery marks found on their bones, and their disarticulation could be the product of multiple taphonomic processes. Clearly they were not 'buried', though, and their corpses may have been placed on middens or into ditches, which, as they got re-worked, would have disarticulated the remains.[4] This has been argued, for example, at Ribchester Fort (Stallibrass 2000). Three of the dog bones from Vicar's Farm had been gnawed, suggesting that they had been exposed.

Whilst dogs and cats may have lived alongside the human population, their treatment at death suggests that they were regarded like other refuse. This might indicate that they were not considered any closer than other animals on the site. Horses were certainly eaten, as their remains frequently showed evidence of butchery marks, and large cut-up joints were apparently a favoured ritual offering (see below). The evidence from Vicar's Farm, therefore, does not suggest any special distinction between types of animals in the modern sense of 'pets' or 'farm animals'. While people certainly would have had different relationships to different animals on site, this expressed itself in different ways to present-day sensibilities.

Cattle seem to have been the most common animal at the settlement, making up half the total non-human population, followed by sheep and then horses. Small numbers of pigs and domestic fowl, as well as the dogs and cats, were also kept. Although not dealing in absolute numbers, it is highly likely the animal population as a whole was substantially larger than the human. It is also unlikely from an historical and ethnographic perspective that they were all crammed into the core part of the settlement, at least those species present in larger numbers: cattle, horses and sheep. Moreover, there were a number of large empty enclosed spaces around the core that seem to have served no other function, and in all likelihood most of the animals were kept in these when they were not let out to pasture, probably in the fields to the west (Fig. 6.11). Phosphate mapping is a way of verifying such an interpretation and, although the phosphates taken from the site were fairly restricted, some interesting patterns emerged (see below and Fig. 6.12).

Phosphates (with Paul Middleton)

Sampling for phosphate analysis was carried out by the excavation team but processed and analysed by Paul Middleton.[5] Such sampling was conducted in a number of areas of the site. Of relevance here, though, is the chain-sampling at 5 m intervals along ditches. Figure

Figure 6.11. *Division of human/animal spaces.*

Figure 6.12. *Phosphate readings along major ditches.*

6.12 illustrates the general plot of phosphate levels in all sampled ditch fills across the site. It is immediately apparent that the greatest concentrations are focussed in the northeastern quadrant of the sampled area and, in general terms, levels of phosphate fall away markedly to the south and west (but see below).

The overall pattern of phosphate distribution strongly indicates that activities which enhanced concentrations were focussed towards the northeastern corner of the sampled area. The fact that all the samples producing results above 250 mg P per 100 g soil were in this area is highly significant and must point to a specific usage. This could reflect a number of things but would certainly be consistent with stock management in a confined space. The general decline in phosphate levels towards the west and south suggests that nowhere else was there such a clear focus of activity.

A further pattern is apparent, namely one of greater concentrations on the eastern side of the enclosures. It is not immediately apparent where the entrance to an enclosure was in each case, but a point to consider is whether the patterning of higher levels of phosphate was influenced by the stress put on stock as they entered and exited from a compound. Alternatively, if the settlement was dealing with numbers of stock, a possible inference from such a pattern is one of an edge-effect, created by stock sheltering from a prevailing wind.

Also of interest in considering stock management as an explanation for the patterns observed are the somewhat higher results (100–149 mg) in the southern end of double-ditches that defined the track/pathway adjacent to the inhumation cemetery. Ground height-levels may explain this in terms of run-off from the north. However, it may alternatively indicate concentrations of activity that served to enhance the phosphate concentrations. Certainly, in the context of stock movement, such a pattern could be expected if animals were being driven into a drove at this point.

Because the samples were taken as chains along ditch lengths, low phosphate readings do not really mean much, at least in terms of animal activity (Fig. 6.12). There are some highs along the ditches, but these tend to be around the core and are more likely to reflect generalized organic waste in the form of human-created middens, especially as the pattern matches that for other categories of waste, such as broken pottery or bone. There is, nevertheless, a very high phosphate count in the core associated with the Curvilinear Enclosure, which is not matched by a corresponding increase in midden material (see, though, below). This suggests that these enclosures were associated with animals, and more particularly their bodily effluvia – urine, faeces and possibly blood – and that they were probably used to pen animals prior to and during slaughter. If this is the case, it suggests an interesting spatial pattern where animals were generally kept in enclosures around the edge of the settlement (predominantly a human space) except for the very centre, where animals are also kept before death. Read in this manner, it suggests that the killing of animals was a special act and one that required a special place: both furthest away from the living animal population and, at the same time, at the very heart of the human one.

Faunal Remains and Ritual Deposition

While the bulk of animal bones occurred as disarticulated and even broken skeletal parts indicative of refuse, there were a number of deposits that require special attention: whole carcasses, articulated parts, and skulls (Fig. 6.13). It is worth examining these in some detail, in relation to their context, to see what light they shed on attitudes to animals in the settlement and their significance in other practices beyond the economic.

In his review of Romano-British zoological remains, Dobney (2001) states that the bones of horses, domestic fowl, and pigs are commonly recovered from grave contexts and other 'special deposits'. But he warns that articulated and semi-articulated remains are commonly found and one must be careful of not too quickly assigning a ritual meaning to their presence for want of a more tangible explanation, such as spoilt meat, disease or simply wasteful butchery. Discussed at length in *Riversides …* in relationship to both Trumpington Meadow's Iron Age and Anglo-Saxon settlements (*RVS*, chaps. 4 & 5), the distinction of any 'meaningful' deposition is often not straightforward: locational context – and patterning – must be guiding principles. Indeed, we have already encountered this within this volume. As outlined in Chapter Two, there can be no doubt of the votive character of the complete animal carcasses within the Ridgeons Garden apsidal shrine – cattle, sheep horses and dogs – nor of the (complete) remains of the latter that apparently accompanied the child/infant burials in the nearby 'ritual shafts'. What though of the complete calf skeleton occurring in the upper profile of New Hall's northern quarry field well? Having a fused vertebra, it would appear to represent the convenient disposal of an ailing animal. By the same token, the dense jumble of horse remains at Trinity Hall Playing Field's roadway excavation would seem to relate to no more than a dump of butchery waste on the settlement margins (see Figs. 3.49 & 3.50).

A number of partially articulated remains at this site could represent convenient disposal. This includes several occurrences of articulated cattle limbs, all assigned to Phase III. These take the form of two hind-legs (from tibia to distal phalanges), one in the Curvilinear Enclosure (F.5652, G2.11) and a second from a ditch in the central enclosure of Area B (F.5427, G24). Two partially articulated

Figure 6.13. *Location of 'special' animal deposits.*

fore-legs (from the scapula to the radius) were recovered from a backfilled quarry pit in Area A (F.5644, G2.17).

The status of the F.5499 deposit within the terminus of a Phase II ditch forming the southeast corner of the main settlement enclosure (G2) is more ambiguous. There, over a thousand foetal pig bones were recovered, accounting for at least 10 individual piglets. All appeared to be articulated and showed no signs of being butchered. Dating to *c.* AD 190–230 on the basis of associated pottery, this is an interesting group. The piglets may well have been an aborted or still-born litter, but this does not explain their deposition at that point. The remains are unique on the site, being the only whole carcasses found. As such, they may have an added significance; they may not have been 'sacrificed' as such, but their deposition could still have been 'meaningful'.

More common are articulated parts or joints of animals, almost always rich, meat-bearing parts that had been butchered from a carcass. These would normally have been consumed, but for some reason were not. In Phase II, a pit associated with one of the embayments in the central part of the area (Area B; F.5656) contained two pig fore-legs (left and right) and the partial remains of at least two chickens. Such deposits are more common in the next phase (III), in particular the Square Enclosure in Area B (F.5445) was associated with several such deposits. The largest occurred in the ditch terminus as it joined the major southern boundary ditch of Area B. There, the left hind-leg and side of a horse had been deposited with two cow mandibles, along with other cow, horse and sheep bones. Inside this enclosure, in the centre, were three pits, one of which had articulated deposits: F.5435, having the lower left fore-leg and hind-leg of a cow, part of its back, as well as pig and horse bones. In the same phase, 11 m to the west in the upper fill of the main southern boundary ditch to which that enclosure was attached, another deposit of a cow right hind-leg and other sheep and cow bones occurred. Inside the core settlement in Area A, two deposits came from the pitting area (G2.17): in F.5644 there was a cow's left fore-leg and, in F.5245, a left fore-leg and side of beef. Finally, from the corner of the G11 enclosure (F.5501), came the right hind-leg of a cow, along with part of the cow skull and a rib.

In a similar manner as in the Ridgeons Garden shrine, there can be no doubt of the votive status of the facing horse-heads within the pit at the entrance to the Phase III inhumation cemetery, F.5425 (Figs. 5.28–9). The southern one was from an animal 8–10 years old and the northern one only 3–4 years old; both were possibly mares. Even more curiously, arranged around the snouts were small cobbles. The obvious nature of this setting may imply that horse may have had a special ritual status. This could then make 'meaningful' the two such deposits within the Timber Shrine complex. One consisted of an articulated left fore-leg and a separate articulated portion of a horse's axial skeleton (including some of the ribs), together with two cow mandibles (F.5218, G2.2). At the junction of two ditches, a similar deposit comprised a portion of the axial skeleton, an articulated left hind-leg and two cow mandibles (F.5452, G28; Fig. 6.14). These two deposits, showing no signs of dismemberment or filleting of meat, give a strong indication that the horse had an important role and statements were being made by its sacrifice.

Dobney (2001) mentions the deposition of horse skulls in a special deposit at Wavendon, Milton Keynes, along with several sites in Yorkshire. Unfortunately, the literature documenting the special treatment of horse bones in the southeast of Roman Britain is scarce, but there are some instances.[6] A notable one is provided by the Eastern Cemetery of Roman London, where several deposits of horse bones were recovered during the excavation of the inhumation cemetery. The association is not definite, but it is possible that some of the bones were deliberately deposited to mark the opening of the cemetery or at least were contemporary with the earliest human burials (Barber & Bowsher 2000).

In the contextual analysis of 'meaning', the inclusion of animal remains within burials also provides insights. Located just outside the Square Enclosure (G28) was a pit, F.5656, that contained the

Table 6.2. *Summary of deposits of meat cuts.*

	Fore-leg		Hind-leg		
Species	**Left**	**Right**	**Left**	**Right**	**Side**
Cow	3	-	1	2	3
Horse	1	-	1	-	2
Pig	1	1	-	-	-
Total	*4*	*1*	*2*	*2*	*5*

remains of two partial chicken skeletons and two pig fore-legs. At Marsh Leys Farm, an enclosed structure – interpreted as a shrine – was associated with a small group of cremations and a nearby pit contained the unburnt remains of two partial chicken skeletons (Luke & Preece 2011). Several of the cremations interred in the Vicar's Farm cemetery had the remains of animals burnt along with the human, most of which has been rendered unidentifiable. It was, however, possible to identify the bones of sheep and chicken. The inclusion of animals in human cremations is a common practice that has been documented in the Iron Age, Roman and Anglo-Saxon periods, and has been interpreted as reflecting last meals for the deceased or the remains of ceremonial feasting (McKinley 2000a). Further to this, in Roman Britain there seem to be 'set rules' concerning which and how many species were associated with cremations. The excavation of Roman London's Eastern Cemetery (Barber & Bowsher 2000) revealed an extensive cremation cemetery and many of its interments were associated with the burnt remains of chicken and pig. In her analysis of that site McKinley states that in Roman Britain the most frequent animals found with human cremations are sheep, pig and domestic fowl, and these are more often than not restricted to a choice of two (McKinley 2000c). It would appear that Vicar's Farm conformed to these 'rules' and that the animals of choice were sheep and chicken.[7]

There are a number of observations that can be made concerning the site's articulated animal bone deposits. On the whole, they are rich meat-bearing parts; in other words, legs and sides of cow, horse or pig (Table 6.2). Interestingly, there were no unequivocal articulated sheep or goat deposits, although individual sheep/goat bones did occur with these deposits and within the cremations. This is in marked contrast to the articulated deposits within Haddenham's Snows Farm shrine, where sheep/goat – along with birds – were the prime ritual-choice species (Evans & Hodder 2006b, 385–96 & 413–16, figs. 7.10–12 & 7.49). Clearly relating to that site's head-and-hooves deposits of sheep/goat (some with coins set in their mouths), it would seem that augury and the reading of entrails was the predominant rite there. This could suggest that ritual representation directly related to an area's economic basis, reflective of that site's fen-edge location, while also including cow and pig/boar deposits; in other words, largely determined by immediate 'convenience' and availability.

Another pattern at Vicar's Farm seems to be a favouring of the left over the right leg, at least for the fore-leg, although this is a small sample and may not be significant. Yet, almost all the left fore-leg deposits were accompanied by a side/loin cut; there were no occurrences of a right limb with a side/loin cut. At Great Chesterford, there was a definite favouring of *right* fore-limbs from a group of pits adjacent to the temple, and these were predominantly from sheep (Legge *et al.* 2000, 156). This shows that there may well have been quite purposive selection of one side of the slaughtered animal. However, the bones from Great Chesterford were predominantly low meat-bearing: heads and feet were the most common, while limbs were rarer, and the latter had probably been eaten (see Baxter in Medlycott 2011, 320–44). This may be significant insofar as the limbs from Vicar's Farm had *not* been eaten but were offered up whole. If we regard these deposits as ritual or sacrificial offerings, it may have been that 'correct' feasting behaviour was to place the left side as the offering and consume the right side.

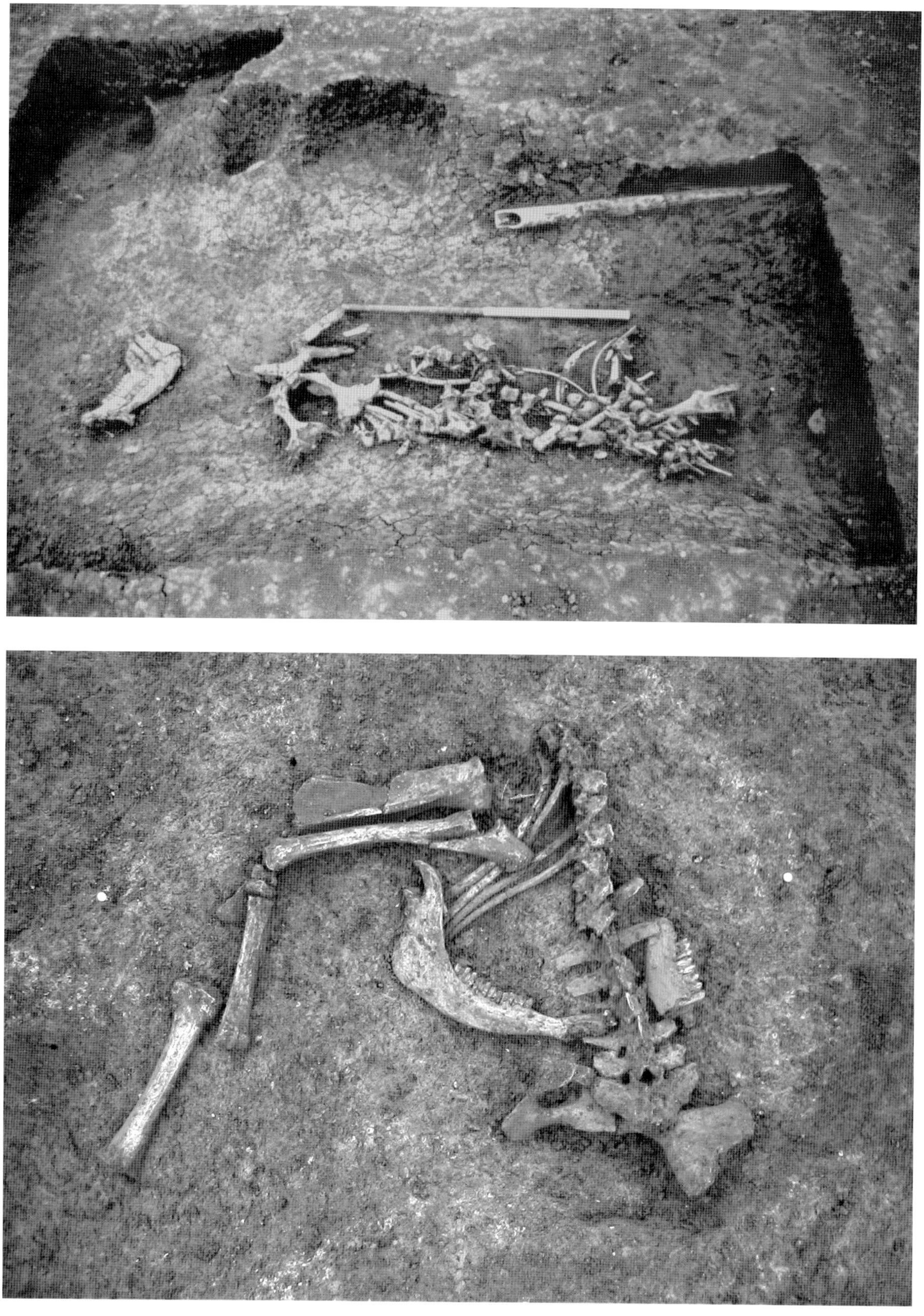

Figure 6.14. *'Special' animal deposits: F.5452 (top) and, below, F.5218.*

Apart from the articulated remains, there is a final class of deposit that is worth singling out: animal heads/skulls. A number of whole/near-complete skulls occur across the site, but in some instances they are part of a larger assemblage of faunal remains that makes their presence slightly less singular. In the following, therefore, only distinctive skull deposits are discussed, marked by their context and singularity. There are only three parts of the site where such deposits occur: the Curvilinear Enclosure, the Square Enclosure and the inhumation cemetery. In F.5704, a whole cow skull with vertebrae probably attached was found in one section of the ditch, and in another portion, two fragments from another skull were found. In the adjacent Monumental Post-setting a cow skull was found in the encircling ditch (F.5705). To the south, in the Square Enclosure (G28), pit F.5435 contained a cow skull at its base. All these deposits belonged to Phase III.

Harking back to the F.5425 cemetery setting, the site's horse heads are particularly interesting given their unusually high numbers (*cf.* King 1978, 225–6; also see Noddle 1984 and Maltby 1984): consistently between 11–17 per cent of the main domesticates. Care must always be taken here in trying to match ritual activity to documented deities, but one obvious connection could be made to Epona. This 'Celtic' goddess is most particularly linked to the horse/equestrian husbandry and activity, but she was also more generally associated with fertility, healing, intercession with the underworld (especially through springs) and elite social status (Magnen & Thevenot 1953; Linduff 1979; Oaks 1986). The high numbers of articulated horse remains at Vicar's Farm – particularly those associated with the Timber Shrine and Square Enclosure – certainly suggest that the horse had a special place among this community (see Fig. 6.40). Yet, rather than being an expression of empire-wide religious practices, Vicar's Farm's horse remains probably reflect a much more localized cult, and this is a theme that will be further explored in the next book.

Working Spaces

A wide range of activities would have taken place in the settlement, and both the presence and distribution of certain finds can help identify these. General activities such as textile working and smithing are indicated by a range of general tools and implements, but with the exception of artefacts associated with milling, not in any great quantity. While it is hard to define specific activity areas on the site, certain specialized activities may have taken place in particular locations and evidence for smithing and crop-processing will be examined more closely here.

Industrial activity was evidently not a major component of the settlement, and there were no obvious associated features. The chief evidence comes from the debris and waste products associated with iron smithing. There was no evidence for iron production or non-ferrous metalworking of any kind. As Cowgill discusses below, all the activity relates to repair, recycling or production of iron objects, and given the quantities, this occurred at a low level over the whole period of the Roman-period occupation, carried out by generations of different smiths.

In contrast, the site was clearly linked to agricultural production on a fairly large-scale, beyond domestic consumption (see *Production* below), and a wide range of activities must have been linked to these farming practices. Actual crop-growing probably took place on the margins of the settlement: some of the narrow strip-field plots in the northeastern corner of the site (Area E, G15/G16) may, for example, have been used for growing wheat (see Fig. 6.11). More definite is the evidence for crop-processing, which comes from two sources: the distribution and nature of the cereal remains from bulk samples and the occurrence of milling stones.

Tools Nina Crummy

Craft items are rare and only one awl and a possible wool-comb or heckle tooth were recovered. An unusual large 'L'-shaped object may be a stemmed anvil, but this is uncertain (Fig. 6.15.1).

<4502a> F.5303 - Awl, with square-section head, tapering from a wide mid point, and round-section stem. The end of the head has broken off. An awl from Hod Hill has a similar expanded centre (Manning 1985, pl. 16, E10).

<456> [194] - Narrow iron spike, bent, nearly broken, near one end. Possibly a tooth from a wool-comb or flax heckle. Length (bent) 73 mm.

<4529> SF 279, F.1904 - Large 'L'-shaped object with square-section stem. The short arm is wider than the stem and broken. At the bend the metal is reduced in thickness. Possibly a stemmed anvil, though the reduction in the metal at the band makes this unlikely. Length of stem 147 mm, section 18 mm square; length of short arm 56 mm, width 35 mm (Fig. 6.15.1).

<2366> F.4832 - Tool handle made from a Red deer antler tine. The iron tang is still fixed in the lower end. The surface of the antler is worn but otherwise unworked. The tip of the tine has been removed by chopping; there are several chop marks around the girth. Length 95 mm. Probably Late Roman (Fig. 6.15.3).

<4327> SF 15, F.5304 - Fragment of a lathe-turned shale spindlewhorl, biconical in profile with a flat, perhaps slightly dished, top defined by a slight groove. Diameter 40 mm, surviving thickness 10 mm. There are closely similar whorls from Silchester (Lawson 1976, fig. 14), and Colchester (Crummy 1983, fig. 71). This object is probably of fourth-century AD date (Fig. 6.15.2).

The Industrial Waste Jane Cowgill

Only a small quantity of iron slag was recovered from the site, all generated by iron smithing: the production, repair or recycling of iron objects (Fig. 6.16; Table 6.3). There is no evidence amongst this assemblage for any non-ferrous metalworking. The slag was

Table 6.3. *Slag and related fragments from excavated contexts.*

Type	Count	Wt. (g)
Iron Slags		
Cinder	2	29
Hearth Bottom	8	845
Slag	22	329
Smithing Slag	2	15
Non-Specific Types		
Vitrified hearth-lining	4	57
Vitrified clay	2	13
Total	*40*	*1288*

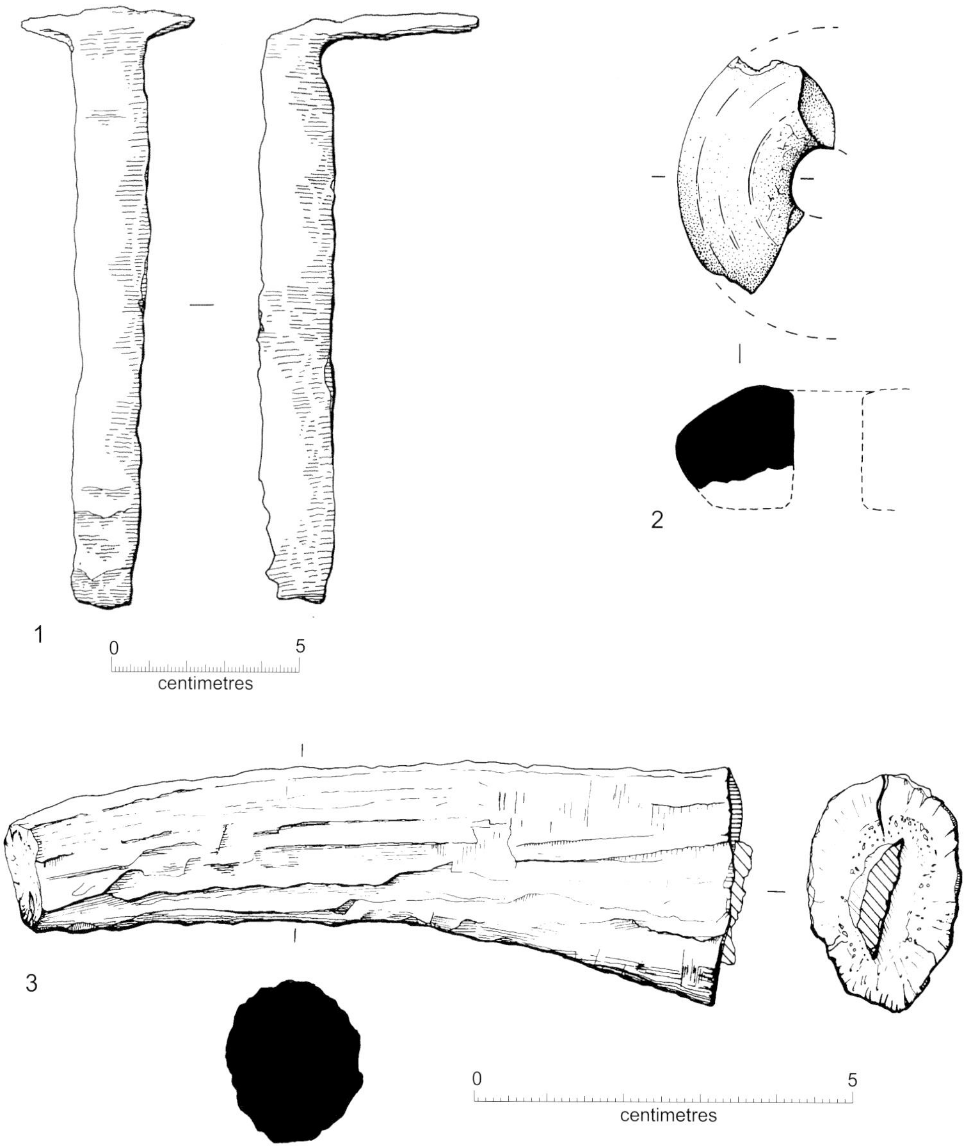

Figure 6.15. *Craft artefacts (see text).*

identified solely on morphological grounds by visual examination, sometimes with the aid of a x10 binocular microscope. A note of probable fuel type has been recorded when fragments or imprints were incorporated within the slag.

The low weights recorded, and to some extent the quantity, may result from the very poor condition of most of the slag. Post-depositional processes, such as water movement through the lighter soils in the northern part of the site, have leached the slags and made the less dense pieces quite brittle. As a consequence, many of the pieces have recent breaks and not all of the slag was recovered. It is likely that some components within the slags have leached out, resulting in their relatively light weight and pale colour (many are a mid grey or mid brown colour or even have a patchy cream-coloured outer surface rather than the more usual black glossy appearance). Almost all the pieces appear abraded, some exceedingly so, but this may again be a result of soil conditions rather than excessive weathering or redeposition.

The slag assemblage as a whole is heterogeneous and unlikely to be the waste products of a single smith or smithy. The slags generated by a single smith will usually have a degree of consistency due to the manner in which smiths work. The plano-convex slag accumulations (commonly known as hearth bottoms) are highly variable in form and density, ranging from light 'frothy' examples to flat cindery pieces; one is very dense and has a 'U'-shaped moulded base (F.5418, [1339]). The four pieces of vitrified hearth lining may all be tuyère fragments, but they are too small for this to be confirmed. The only fuel type noted as inclusions or imprints was charcoal.

Smithing Areas

Given such small quantities of slag, it is hard to say with any certainty whether there was any specific location for smithing on the site. As that this activity was clearly infrequent over more than three centuries and was carried out by different smiths, this is perhaps not surprising. Nevertheless, the amounts of material are small and,

Figure 6.16. *Distribution of smithing waste.*

set against the size of the site and number of units excavated, its presence anywhere might denote smithing nearby. Redeposition through activities, such as middening, also has to be considered. To counter this, we can focus solely on areas where there are the greatest amounts of different types of waste associated with smithing: slag, hearth bottoms and vitrified clay linings.

There are two areas where all three of these were found in relatively larger amounts (Fig. 6.16). The first was in the upper fill of ditch F.5427 (Area A/B, Phase III), close to its junction with F.5501. The presence of 138 g of hearth bottom fragments, 34 g of vitrified hearth lining and 81 g of slag in the same section of the ditch might indicate smithing activity on one side of this ditch. The presence of a minor amount of smithing slag in a Phase I pit (7 g; F.5651) just north of this group might suggest that the area north of the ditch had been used as a smithing area before, and it may have been a favoured location. The other concentration occurred in the upper fill of ditch F.5418, specifically in the northeast corner of the Enclosure G18 (Area C, Phase III). There, 339 g of hearth bottom, 14 g of vitrified hearth lining/clay, 25 g of slag and 5 g of cinder occurred in two sections of the ditch less than 10 m apart.

What is interesting about both locations is that they lay on the very edge of the core-area. It is fairly common that such noxious and potentially 'dangerous' activities were conducted at the edge of settlement, yet here they were still close enough to be practical in terms of access to materials and other people/activities.

Cereal Remains Rachel Ballantyne

Preservation conditions within all contexts at the site were good, with charred remains exhibiting little distortion, fragmentation or surface abrasion. From Figure 6.17 it is clear that, with the exception of one seed-rich context within the F.5280 well, a consistent assemblage is represented. All but two contexts (discussed below) are dominated by spelt wheat chaff (*Triticum spelta*), with much lesser quantities of spelt or emmer grain (*T. spelta/dicoccum*) and small or grain-sized wild seeds. This is characteristic of a by-product from the later stages of hulled wheat processing (Hillman 1984). The predominance of grain-sized and 'small, heavy' seeds within the wild taxa further supports the interpretation of a later stage by-product (G. Jones 1984).

Hulled wheats require parching and pounding to release the grain from the chaff that tightly encases it. This stage is undertaken after threshing, winnowing and sieving, to remove the straw and many wild seeds. There is good ethnographic and historical evidence that in damp climates hulled wheat would have been stored in spikelet form (disarticulated ears where the grain is still

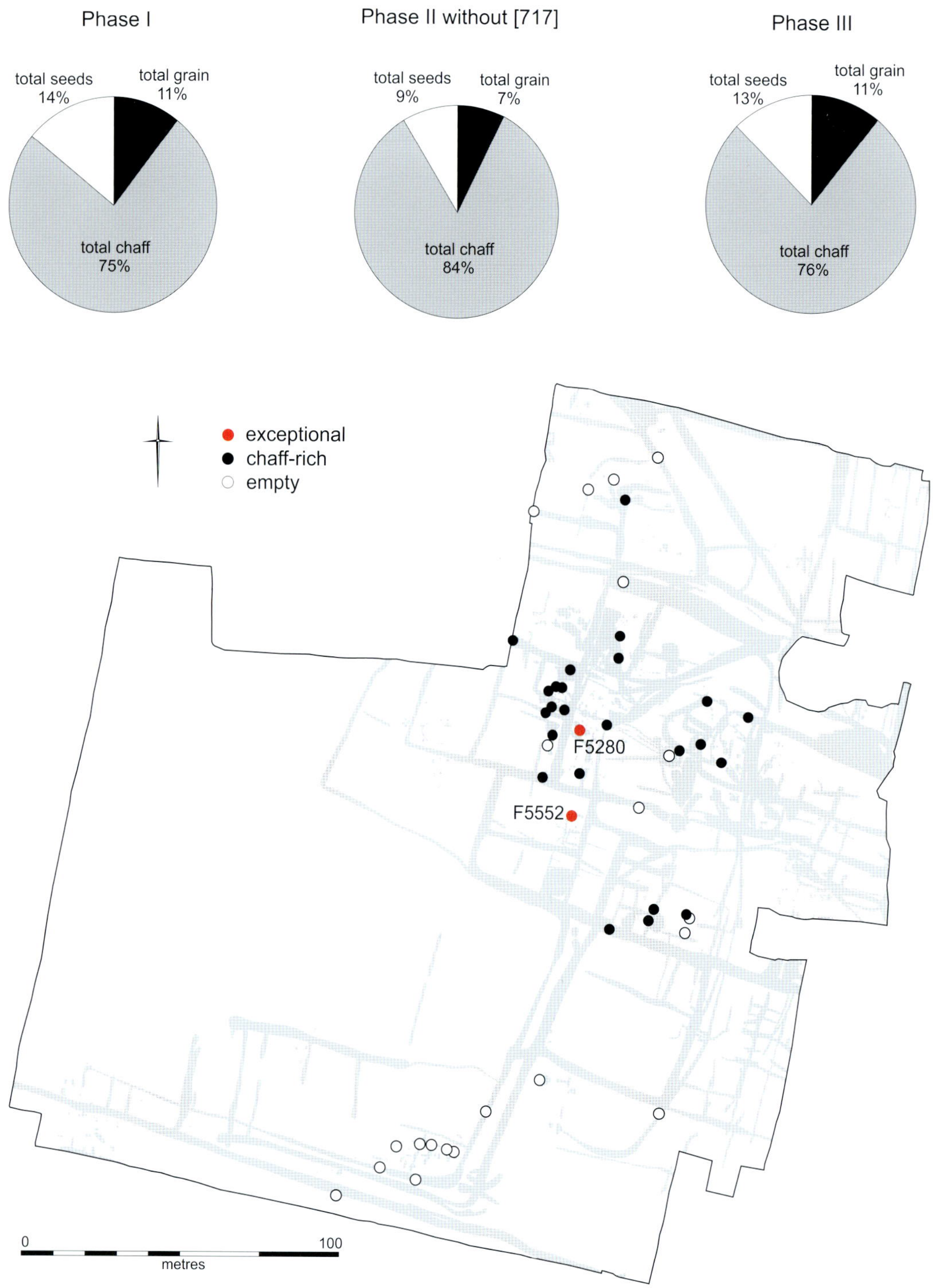

Figure 6.17. *Representation of charred components by phase ('rich' contexts only; top); below, location of samples classified by crop-processing waste.*

chaff-encased; White 1970, 196; Hillman 1981). The chaff would protect the grain during storage, and then parching and pounding could be undertaken on an *ad hoc,* possibly even daily basis, to provide the necessary grain. Such repeated on-site activity could be expected to provide a significant contribution to the charred cereal assemblage.

At Vicar's Farm, charred glume bases overwhelmingly represent waste from the separation of spelt wheat grain from its chaff by sieving. The association of the final processing stages of hulled wheat with fire may possibly account for the predominance of charred waste. To parch the ears effectively a short and intense heat is required, to affect the chaff but leave the grain intact. Some chaff may have been carbonized during this process, but it seems unlikely that this occurred with the frequency and degree represented within this assemblage. Perhaps subsequent sieve cleaning of grain was also undertaken near fires, or charring was used to 'sterilize' the waste. The association of charring with later stage processing waste is graphically illustrated within a Roman ditch flanking the *Via Devana* at the Chesterton Lane Corner Site in Cambridge proper (Mortimer & Regan 2001; see Chap. 2 and Evans & Ten Harkel 2010). Thick lenses of near-pure charred spelt wheat glume bases had been repeatedly washed from a roadside structure, creating a series of compositionally identical layers. The ditch fill demonstrated not only that later stage processing was undertaken there on a repeated basis, but that chaff waste had also been *repeatedly exposed to charring*. A similar case may be made for the consistently chaff-rich assemblage at Vicar's Farm.

Patterning and Activity Areas

The sampled contexts vary markedly in the density of remains but represent the same stage of crop-processing. The consistently high-quality preservation suggests that the marked spatial variation in *density* of charred remains, particularly cereals, may relate to original deposition patterns. All the sampled contexts fall into three broad categories of composition:

1) 'Empty' samples that are almost devoid of charred remains other than wood charcoal and very occasional cereals, particularly glume bases, or wild seeds. The count density is less than 2.5 items per litre sample; in most cases it is well below 0.5 items per litre. When examined spatially, these contexts are virtually all located in areas outside the main and southern enclosures.

2) 'Chaff-rich' contexts, which contain numerous charred glume bases of spelt wheat and moderate to low quantities of grain and wild seeds. These contexts are found primarily within the main and southern enclosures, throughout all Roman phases. The contexts reflect either accumulated charred debris from nearby cereal processing or, in the very rich contexts, perhaps 'dumps' of such material. A few chaff-rich contexts occur further out and these may represent specific dumps.

3) 'Exceptional' contexts, which include moderate amounts of charred glume bases, but are otherwise unique in their preservation and composition. The mid fill of well F.5280 ([717]) contained very high amounts of charred seeds, which may have been cleaned from a threshed and winnowed cereal crop. The richness and high-quality preservation within this context suggest that the material may have been dumped as a unit within the well, rather than accumulated from surface debris through time. Secondly, in Structure D's F.5552 postpipe ([3025]) had very high amounts of clean spelt wheat grain and wood charcoal and may have been linked to food preparation.

The spatial patterning of chaff-rich contexts within the main enclosure (Fig. 6.17) suggests that the structures there were associated with later stage spelt wheat processing throughout the Roman period of the site. The predominance of glume base-rich contexts within the main enclosure indicates loci for crop-processing and, by implication, a location for grain storage. Only postpipe F.5552 provides any evidence of food preparation.

Disposal Patterns: Categories of Waste?

In contrast to the charred cereal remains, there is an absence of waterlogged economic plants within all suitable contexts. High densities of charred glume bases are present in waterlogged (F.5704) and damp parts of the central Curvilinear Enclosure (F.5741). However, only two waterlogged glume bases have been recovered in the entire assemblage: one from the Aisled Building's pit F.5651 and one from Iron Age pit F.5621. There is a clear disparity between the ubiquitous charred wheat chaff present in the main enclosure and the virtual absence of uncharred chaff. The spelt wheat chaff must represent specific *deliberate* charring events, rather than accidental burning of general surface debris. Had the latter occurred, one would expect the charred material within some waterlogged contexts to be a sub-sample of similar organic remains.

There are no 'cessy' mineralized remains or organic food waste within any of the sampled contexts. This absence may, in part, be due to the very localized preservation by waterlogging at the site and the loss of such contexts. However, a similarly 'clean' waterlogged assemblage was recovered at Stonea Grange, where it was suggested that the "... disposal of domestic food refuse was not haphazard, but took place in a highly organized manner, probably onto specifically designated middens" (Van der Veen 1996, 636). The charred cereal processing remains at Vicar's Farm appear to have been largely excluded from any such category, which might support the interpretation that thorough charring 'sterilization' of the cereal waste occurred (see below; see Fig. 6.18 concerning the possible identification of the site's main middening locus).

Querns and Millstones (with Kevin Hayward)

Millstone Grit was the principal rock-type used within the assemblage of 1140 fragments of quernstone identified (Fig. 6.19.1); its coarse angular quartz surface is ideal for retaining the grinding surface and resisting wear. In form, the fragments typically have a shallow depth of about 35 mm, in relation to a larger, often flat surface area. Undulations are common on the coarser gritstones whilst circular grinding surfaces characterize the finer gritstones. Indeed, in F.5528 ([1866]), where between three and four querns were found together, both variations occur together, suggesting that each had a separate function for an individual quern. Old Red Sandstone quernstones also have this narrow depth.

In contrast, the less common Lower Greensand and Hertfordshire Pudding Stone quernstones (Figs. 6.19.2–3) have a distinctly different morphology. Thickness is greater, often exceeding 50 mm at the expense of a smaller surface area, producing a round, almost beehive-shaped morphology. This is sometimes seen as a characteristic of Late Iron Age and Early Roman quernstones. Finally, Niedermendig Lavastone from the Rhineland is commonly used. This vesicular lava, though, is weathered, producing many small fragments and therefore creating a misleading picture as to its importance by number (94.3%). Niedermendig Lava was extensively used as a quernstone in both Roman London and Colchester.

Quantities of quernstones appear to rise over time. The quantity of millstone doubles and then triples in Phases II and III respectively. Whether this indicates an intensification and increase in milling is open to interpretation. More interestingly perhaps, the diversity of quernstone types increases in Phase III. Millstones, lavastones and greensand occur in all phases, but it is only in the final phase of the site that Red Sandstones and Pudding Stones occur (Table 6.4).

As shown reconstructed in Figure 6.19 (.1), at least one of the site's Millstone Grit rotary quernstones (<4207>) would have originally been large. With its central pivot spindle-hole being *c.* 0.2–0.25 m across, it is estimated that the quern itself would have

Table 6.4. *Quernstones by phase (weight in g).*

Stone Type	Phase I	Phase II	Phase III
Lava	958	2326	2684
Millstone	4287	8947	28,232
Greensand	281	6000	2841
Red sandstones	-	-	1515
Pudding stone	-	-	13,000

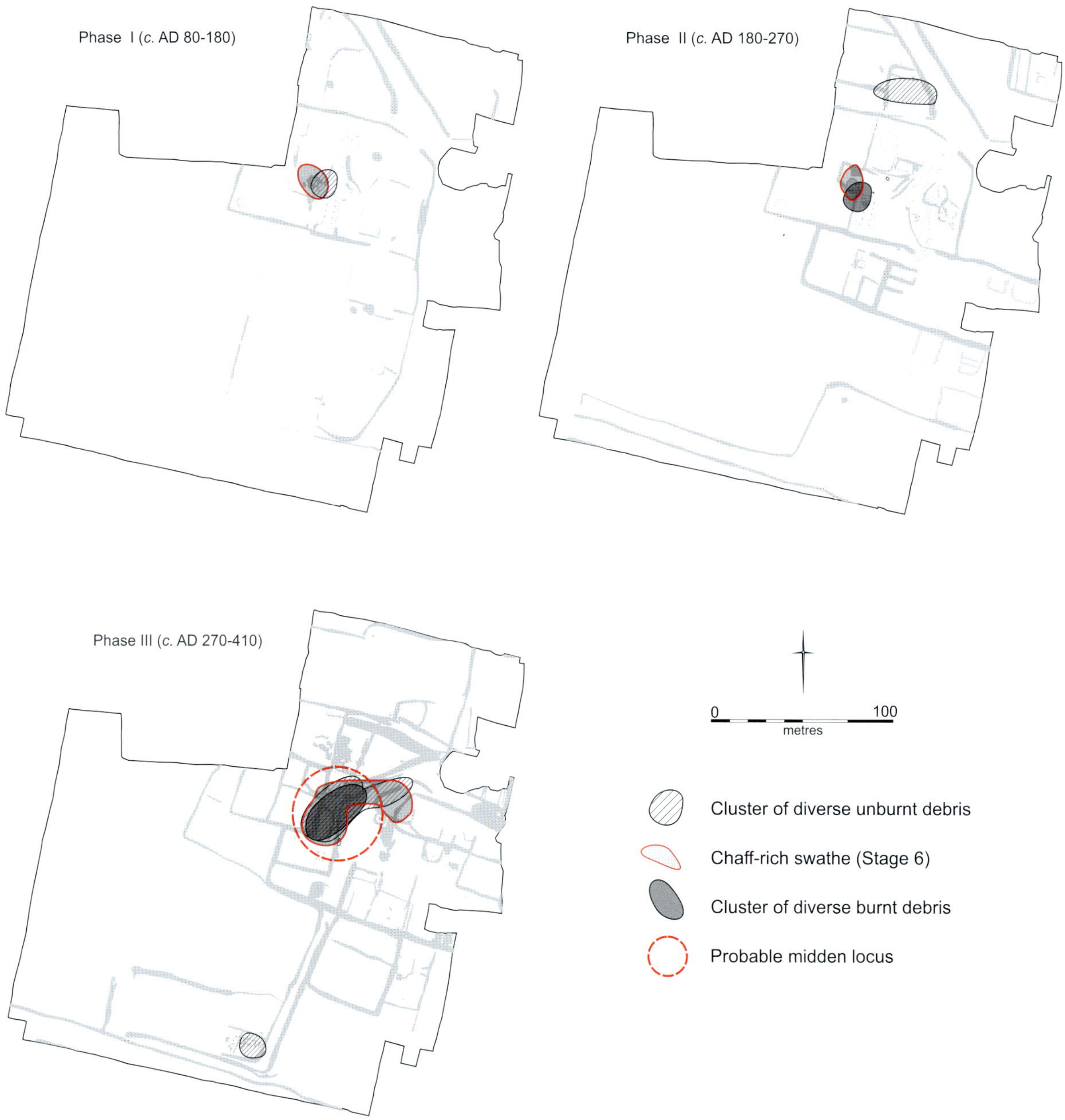

Figure 6.18. *Correlating and statistically gauging both plant remains and (micro-) artefactual material deriving from the bulk samples, peaks in diversity of burnt and unburnt remains were plotted (Ballantyne 2009, fig. 7.7 & 7.8). Here, Ballantyne's figure that cross-compares of unburnt/burnt debris with areas of major crop processing stages is reproduced. Of it she remarked:*

The results for Phase I are limited and show that unburnt debris occurs in greatest diversity by the Timber Shrine. Burnt debris is widely dispersed but exhibits low diversity. One chaff-rich area overlaps with the central unburnt debris.

During Phase II, the sample distribution reveals a swathe of diverse unburnt debris in a small enclosure north of the core-area. In the core-area, there is one context diverse in burnt debris and with rich cereal chaff. There are, however, no samples from the eastern side of this area, so the overall distribution of debris is unknown.

The widest range of samples, and patterning in artefact diversity, occurs during the final phase (III). The core-area dominates diversity in both unburnt and burnt debris with one large central midden. As in previous phases, the spatial distribution of samples is limited, so the full extent of this centralized artefact diversity cannot be investigated. One additional area of unburnt diversity corresponds with the southern inhumation cemetery; the numerous bone fragments are probably human, but the high seashell density may be linked to cemetery-use or food waste dispersed from elsewhere.

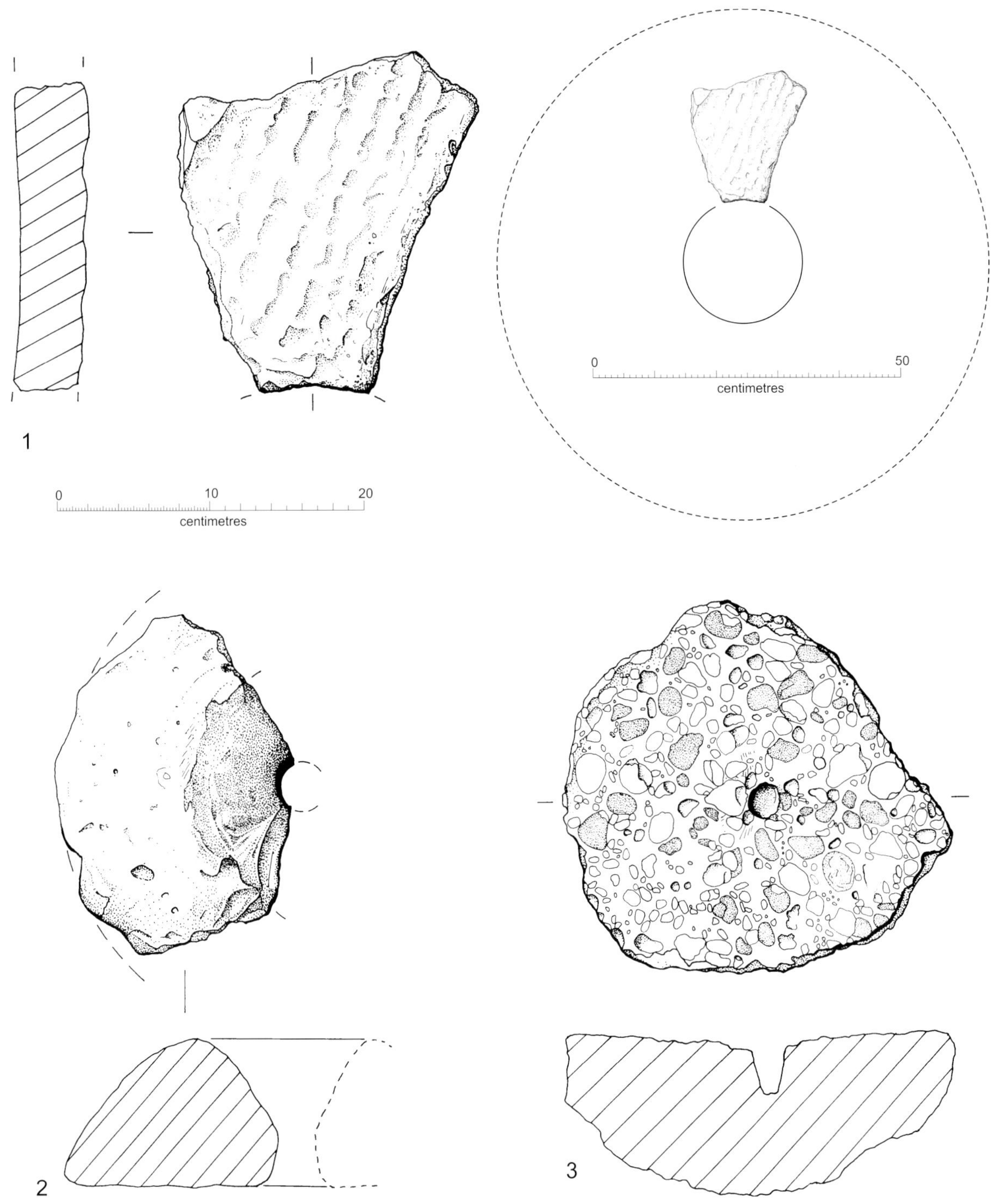

Figure 6.19. *Quernstones: 1) Millstone Grit, slightly burnt on one face (3 kg; F.5263); 2) Lower Greensand (3125 g; F.4538; 3) Pudding Stone (4 kg; F.5263).*

been upwards of 0.8 m in diameter. At that size, it would surely have been traction-operated (by horse or donkey; see Evans *et al.* 2013b, 111–12, fig. 2.57) and, accordingly, it tells of the scale of the settlement's flour production.

Full catalogue entries for each context are available in the site archive; the overall breakdown of the querns by main rock-type is:

Lavastone - 770 fragments recovered from 14 contexts (4868 g total weight)

Millstone Grit - 58 fragments from 39 contexts (38,830 g total weight, though three pieces not weighed)

Hertfordshire Pudding Stone - Three pieces from three contexts (6364 g total weight)

Lower Greensand - Six pieces from six contexts (4881 g total weight, but one piece not weighed)
Red Sandstones - Four pieces from four contexts (1915 g total weight).

Quernstone Deposition and Distribution

Although there is a broad concentration of millstone and quernstone fragments in the core, by far the greatest majority cluster around the shrine and alongside the diagonal pathway (Fig. 6.20). Lavastone quern fragments in particular seem associated with the shrine; indeed, most of the lavastone from the site comes from this location, the main exception being the buried soil within the G2.11 enclosure. Conversely, the two major deposits of millstone fragments seem to be located at either end of the diagonal pathway; the eastern end of this pathway as it meets the forecourt seems to have been a particular focus of deposition.

The immediate question is whether this distribution reflects a milling area in the vicinity, or something else. Certainly, the nature of some of the contexts reflects considered deposition, rather than expedient discard. Three of the lavastone deposits occur as post-packing in the back postholes of the shrine (F.5491, F.5507 & F.5517). This might suggest that the quernstone fragments had some particular significance as foundation deposits; after all, there was no shortage of unworked river cobbles across the site to use as packing, as were employed in the Aisled Building. It could suggest meaningful and specific use of these quernstone fragments, which might subsequently alter our perception of the deposition of other quern fragments in the ditches and pits around the shrine and forecourt.

The area around the shrine was also striking for the amount of charred chaff found, and all the samples taken from the shrine produced consistently high levels. While this might reflect upon the potential ritual significance of the charring of chaff (see below), it can also suggest that end-stage processing was occurring close to the shrine and that the clustering of millstones and high chaff counts would support this. Perhaps the really significant thing to recognize is that milling and ritual activity were not separated. They occupied the same space and, just as ritual may have infused the milling process, so milling waste (used/broken quernstones and chaff) could have had ritual meaning. This, for example, might have a bearing on the deposits of quernstone fragments at either end of the diagonal pathway. Pit F.5528 at the northeastern end of the pathway contained 14 fragments from at least three, maybe four, different millstones with refits, one of which was burnt. At the other end of the pathway, in pit F.5207, were two more large fragments of millstone, one of them burnt; nearby, in pit F.5263, a fragment of millstone and a puddingstone quern were found. All of these were deposited toward the end of the settlement in Phase III. Thus, while the quernstones associated with the pathway may have derived from a nearby milling area, they are also interesting because they occurred at either end of the pathway. Their deposition may relate to thresholds: the points at which the pathway entered/exited new spaces.

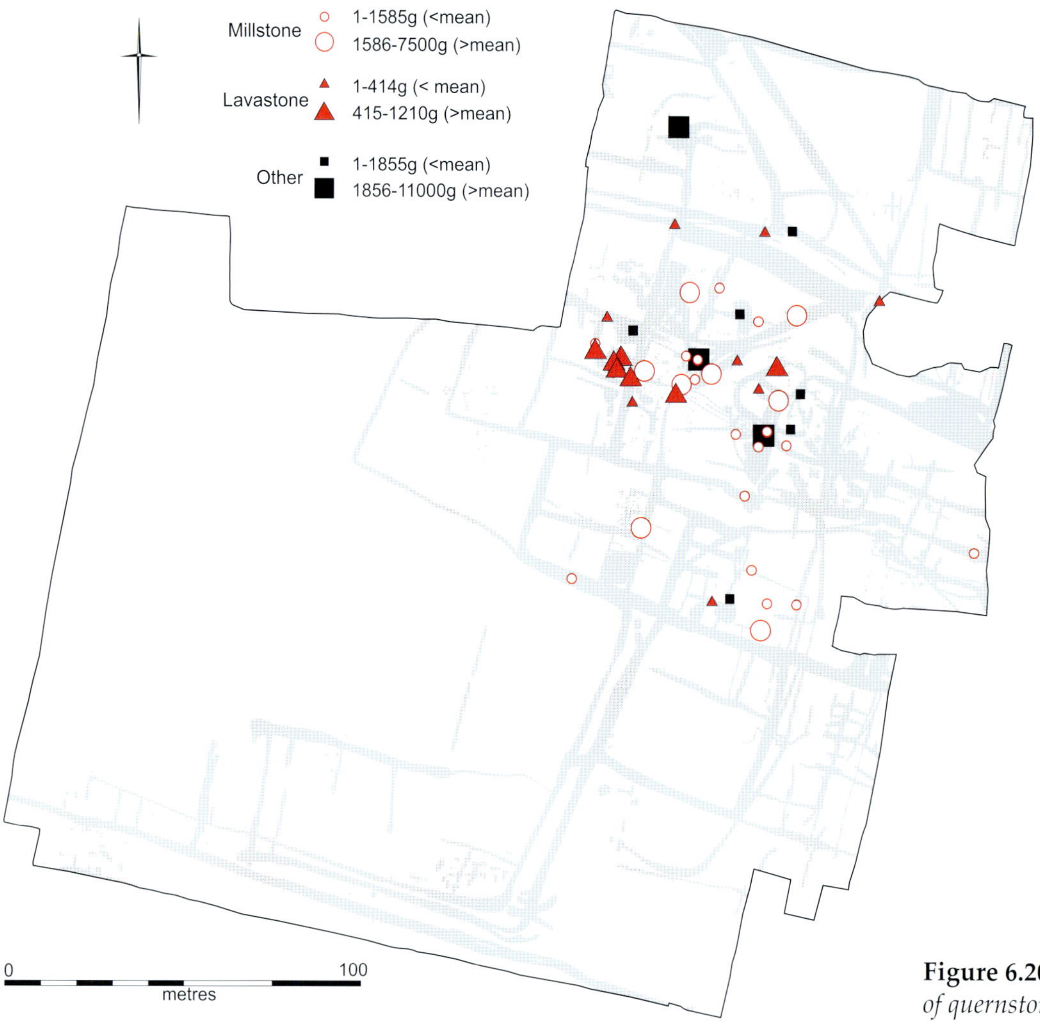

Figure 6.20. *Distribution of quernstones.*

Overviewing Crop-processes
Within the site itself, there is only evidence for a very specific range of crop-related activities: specifically, end-stage processing (de-husking and milling). The nature of the cereal remains suggest that other stages such as threshing, winnowing and sieving took place elsewhere, perhaps closer to the fields where they had grown, and only the stored spikelets were brought into the settlement for final hulling and milling (see Ballantyne, above). Examining the distribution of the chaff-rich samples can be used as a proxy indicator for the locations where hulling may have taken place. Given that only a limited number of samples were processed, it is difficult to use this information except on a very broad level. As Figure 6.17 shows, chaff-rich samples cluster in certain areas, but as there are no or few processed samples from intervening areas, so this clustering cannot be read at face-value. Nevertheless, it can be said with some confidence that practically all the chaff-rich samples are confined to the core part of the settlement (Areas A & B). This indicates that hulling almost certainly took place in that portion, where the spikelets were no doubt stored (possibly in the Aisled Building), and that no processing occurred in the outer areas of the settlement.

Turning to milling stones, the same general pattern is reproduced. Almost all the quern fragments came from within Area A, and to a lesser extent Area B (Fig. 6.20); this is less constrained by any bias in recovery. Many of the larger deposits of quernstone seemed to exhibit intentional placement: as foundational deposits in the case of the shrine (where the exotic lavastone was particularly selected), and as threshold deposits in the case of the settlement's diagonal pathway. These associations do not deny their function as millstones and use in the production of flour, but this very process may have been imbued with ritual significance.

It is even possible to view the burnt chaff in a similar way. Evidently not part of de-husking, and seemingly without an obvious function, why should it have been charred? Ballantyne above suggests that it may relate to the need to 'sterilize' the chaff. Yet, its charring could conceivably represent a similar process of ritual transformation as for the querns. That said, more prosaically, it might relate to dumps of fuel-source material and instances are known of chaff being used as kiln-fuel (Roberts in *BLS*, 121 and Van der Veen 1999).

People processed crops on this site: they de-husked the grains, milled the grains to flour and used the flour, probably to make bread. All the remains outlined here suggest that this activity was occurring within the core part of site. What is posited is that these processes were also imbued with the beliefs of the people doing them – regardless of the actual status of the chaff – and that these beliefs affected the processes and the construction of their material world.

The Living and the Dead

The settlement had a range of burial types, a number of whom were accompanied by personal ornaments and/or grave-goods; how are these expressions at death and the site's artefacts to be inter-related with the lives lived and played out there?

Treatment of the Dead (with Natasha Dodwell)
The location of burials in the landscape, whether they be formal groups or seemingly isolated burials has attracted much attention (e.g. Williams 1998; Scott 1999; Esmonde Cleary 2000; Pearce 2013) and practices at Vicar's Farm need to be addressed in the light of this literature. At this site, while most burials occurred in formal cemeteries, a number occurred in isolation, and others – neonates and single body parts – in unusual contexts (Fig. 6.21). All three types of burials will be discussed separately below, and then within a more general discussion at the end of this section.

Cemeteries
There were two cemeteries: a late first-/second-century AD cremation cemetery and a late third-/fourth-century AD inhumation cemetery. While the span of the cremation cemetery seems to be fairly well-defined (*c.* AD 80/90–180), the dating of the inhumation cemetery is more open. Most of the burials have been phased to the final period of Roman occupation (Phase III), but this need not be the case. Certainly the central cremation, which would seem to initiate the cemetery, dates to *c.* AD 180–230, which might suggest that at the end of the second century AD, the population decided to bury its dead much further away from the core of the settlement; this was soon followed soon by a change of funerary practice from cremation to inhumation (see, though, Chap. 5's discussion of the site's potential overlapping cemetery usage and phasing). There was thus no hiatus in terms of formal disposal of the dead, just two major consecutive changes, one in location and one in funerary rite. This has implications when examining population dynamics over the life of the settlement (see below), but for the present, the immediate question is, why did these changes occur? It would be judicious to first compare these cemeteries with other examples and determine how common/unusual these practices are.

The cremation cemetery at Vicar's Farm appears unusual insofar as it occurs *within* the core of the settlement; but this may simply reflect the settlement's subsequent expansion. Comparisons are few and far between. At Great Wakering, Essex, a group of cremation burials has been excavated on the edge of a Roman settlement (Keppie *et al.* 2001, 363), while a Late Iron Age/Roman farmstead with an associated cremation cemetery has been investigated at Marsh Leys Farm, Beds. (Luke & Preece 2011, 26–8). At the latter, the group comprised five burials clustered in an area of 6 sq. m with a further two burials located about 12 m away. Interestingly, the burials are contemporary with a ditched enclosure containing a small square building, which has provisionally been identified as a shrine (*ibid.*, 16–8). These sites suggest that Vicar's Farm was not unique.[8] The location of the cemetery at Vicar's

Figure 6.21. *Location of burials and disarticulated human bone.*

Farm is certainly on the edge of the settlement boundary, but more significantly perhaps, the whole organization of the settlement at the time of the cremations seems relatively unstructured.

The location of Vicar's Farm's inhumation cemetery, tucked into the corner of a fieldsystem outside the main settlement, appears to be a recurrent feature of the rural landscape in the mid to Late Roman period (see e.g. Pearce 2013, 95–108). At Chignall in Essex, for example, a group of 25 inhumations lay *c.* 150 m outside the villa enclosure and were bounded on the southern and western side by a ditch that was probably embanked (Clarke 1998, 51–63, figs. 34 & 35). One of the most widely cited cemetery sites within the region is that at Lynch Farm, Cambs., although only a small portion of the settlement was actually excavated (Jones 1975; see Upex 2018). There, a group of mainly adult inhumations (45) were placed in the southwest corner of a ditched field, predominantly on an east–west orientation, with a smaller group of inhumations located in the southeast corner of the field to the west (five; *ibid.*, 98–100, fig. 4). While, in some respects, the layout of the main cemetery is comparable to that at Vicar's Farm, there are crucial differences. While the row-arrangement and orientation of Lynch Farm's inhumations were generally much more regular, it lacked any equivalent setting to the horse-head pit and, instead of being central, its one cremation lay isolated and at a distance (*c.* 15 m) from the bulk of its graves.

In this regard, the situation and layout of the cemetery at Addenbrooke's Hutchison Site's is insightful (*BLS*, 47–57, figs 2.19–22). Located just north of a major east–west road and immediately exterior to its Conquest Period/later first-century AD paddocks (tucked into the junction of their respective ditches), two later first-century AD cremations lay *c.* 2 m apart. It is likely that they had been sealed by a small low barrow, given the manner in which many of its 16 inhumations were later arranged in quasi-concentric 'arcing' lines just west of the cremations. One female had a pot and, another, copper alloy rings and a bracelet; otherwise, the adult inhumations were without grave-goods and there was no evidence of any having been coffined. The inhumations date to the later second century AD and later, although the site itself saw very little activity at that time (*BLS*, 89–92, fig. 2.38). Accordingly, whereas the earlier cremations occurred in close proximity – but just beyond – their settlement, the inhumations clearly lay at a remove from any contemporary occupation focus.[9]

Occurring within a ditched enclosure, the inhumation cemetery at Foxton lay some 140 m south of its settlement. Of its 24 inhumations, it was the eight third-century AD ones that were actually oriented east–west (the later graves being north–south); this is somewhat surprising given potential arguments concerning grave-orientation and the possible impact of Christianity (see below). Within the third-century burials, the males were all apparently buried with their heads to the west, with females lying in the opposite direction (Cleary in Price *et al*. 1997, 32–34, figs. 15 & 16).

At Vicar's Farm, the inhumation cemetery was located approximately 75 m outside the main settlement: far enough away to be separated, but at the same time, visible and part of the day-to-day activities of the living, seemingly directly accessed by a minor trackway/path. There seems to be nothing unique in the location of its inhumation cemetery, although the positioning of the cremation cemetery within the settlement is unusual. In the next book it will be shown that the inhumation cemeteries at both North West Cambridge and the NIAB Site lay on the southern aspect of their respective settlements, with their cremation cemeteries to the north. Perhaps the key point is that Vicar's Farm, in one site, seems to exhibit almost the full diversity of burial practices seen on rural settlements throughout the Roman period. Beyond this, its burial practices seem relatively 'rule-bound' and to have involved very few 'deviant' interments (see Overview below).

Isolated Burials

Six isolated inhumations were found at Vicar's Farm: three adult burials and three neonates. All of them date to the later period of the site, most if not all to Phase III. Quite why they were buried outside the cemeteries is intriguing. The three adults were all buried on the margins of the settlement (Fig. 6.21). Grave F.2094 lay on the northern edge of the site, inside the corner of a curve of the northernmost boundary ditch; the body lay in a coffin and was that of a middle-aged male. Grave F.5329 lay on the western edge of the settlement, either just inside or outside the settlement, depending on its date of burial. It was badly disturbed by ploughing and Post-Medieval activity, but the remains were those of a young adult male, placed in an extended position, who had suffered some childhood stress. Grave F.991 was at the southern edge of the settlement, in the top of a ditch that enclosed a large area around the inhumation cemetery. It was not possible to sex the individual and the burial was badly plough-damaged. Enough of it survived, though, to suggest that the body lay in an unusual position: face-down, with limbs awkwardly flexed. Two out of six of New Hall's excavated burials were also prone (see Chap. 3).

Three neonates were also found: two interred in postholes, and one in a pit adjacent to the Aisled Building (see Fig. 6.21). Feature 8087 lay on the eastern side of the settlement, in a small posthole whose precise context is ambiguous, but it does not seem to be part of a building. The other, F.2091, was found in the backfill of one of Structure D's large square post pits (F.5600), in the south-central part of the settlement core (see Fig. 5.27). Finally, the whole lower left arm of a neonate was recovered from the upper fill of pit F.710 (see Figs. 5.2 & 5.5).[10]

These isolated burials clearly divide into two types – adults and neonates – the former all buried on the margins of the settlement and the latter closer to the core. The adults were all (except perhaps for the one in the ditch) given otherwise 'normal' burial, while the neonates were buried in association with structures. Both of these patterns have been commonly noted on other sites and the association of neonates with buildings or posts occurs on many sites such as Springhead, Kent, and Bradley Hill and Catsgore in Somerset (Scott 1989). More immediately, and also associated with buildings, neonates occurred within the 'town' of Stonea proper (four in total, with three in one building; no adult burials: Jackson & Potter 1996) and there were high numbers – 12 in total – at Colne Fen's Camp Ground inland port (Evans *et al*. 2013b, 230–2 & 235–6, table 3.10).

The association of burials adjacent to and within boundary ditches is also a recurrent phenomenon, not only within cemeteries (e.g. Lankhills, Butt Road and Poundbury), but on rural sites too, such as Dalton Parlours or Roughground Farm (Esmonde Cleary 2000, 137–8). Some of the burials in the inhumation cemetery at Vicar's Farm were even laid in the top of the cemetery boundary ditch. But for those outside the cemetery being discussed here, the use of such liminal spaces may have been attractive as places of burial, if liminal zones can be regarded as 'special' in some manner. The prone burial in the southern boundary ditch does, however, seem to stand out as rather different to the other two; not simply because it lay in the ditch rather than alongside it, but more because of the way it was laid out.

It should be stressed that, given the site's excavation-sample – especially its ditch-interval – it is unlikely that all of the settlement's isolated burials were recovered.

Disarticulated Remains

The final category of human remains is disarticulated skeletal parts. There are four instances of these, almost all of them occur in the area around the cremation cemetery, and all of them include skull fragments (Fig. 6.21). A particularly large deposit of disarticulated remains occurred in a pit north of the cemetery (F.5017). The only recorded element outside this area lay to the south in the G18 enclosure, again, fragments of a skull. As Esmonde Cleary (2000) discusses, loose parts are an under-studied aspect of Roman burial ritual, and explanations such as sacrifice (Isserlin 1997) or execution have been posited. Certainly, the predominance of skull parts may be significant here, especially when one considers that decapitation is not an uncommon rite in 'conventional' burial, even if the head is still placed in the grave. Apart potentially from Skeleton F.2079 (see Chap. 5), there are no obviously headless burials at Vicar's Farm, and sacrifice or execution does not in itself explain the disarticulation and deposition of loose parts.[11] Another possibility is that these parts relate to the funerary ritual associated with cremation: bodies may have been exposed or buried prior to cremation (e.g. Folly Lane: Niblett 2000, 99), and some of the parts not collected. The burial of cremated remains is largely a 'token practice' (McKinley 2000a, 42). Even though many of these loose parts did occur in late features, this could simply be redeposition and it might be the overall spatial distribution that counts more than their exact context.

Overviewing the Dead (with Natasha Dodwell)

The previous sections have looked at the different funerary and burial practices and the location of burials in their wider context, and a number of general statements can be made. The major difference seems to be chronological. In the early life of the settlement (Phase I), the dead were cremated and then interred in a location within the main settlement, albeit close to its edge. The only exceptions to this were its neonates, who were not cremated, but still buried within the cemetery. In Phases II–III the cremation rite appears to have died out and inhumation became the norm. Burials were located as far away as possible from the settlement, yet still close enough to be regarded as belonging to that it, at the very extremities of its related enclosure system. Most of the burials lay within a cemetery, but the few that did not still followed the marginal-location 'rule'. Neonates, as in Phase I, are treated differently, but unlike in Phase I, this seems to be reflected in location rather than rite. They were not buried in the cemetery, but within the settlement itself and associated with structures.

Table 6.5. *Arrangement of graves in the inhumation cemetery.*

	Line	Row	Uncertain
E–W Graves			
Northern side	6	-	1
Southern side	1	1	-
Western side	1	0	3
N–S Graves			
Northern side	-	-	-
Southern side	-	10	-
Western side	-	3	3

Table 6.6. *Christian and pagan indicators.*

Christian Indicators	Pagan Indicators
East–west alignment	North–south alignment
Neonatal/infant burial	Hobnails
Cemetery organization	Superimposition/disturbance
Lack of grave-goods	Presence of grave-goods
Focal grave	(Prone)

So far, the major change seems to have occurred between Phases I and II, in the shift from cremation to inhumation and from a relatively proximal to marginal location. However, there may be more variation to investigate, particularly in terms of the later burials. The inhumation cemetery is not as closely dated as the cremation cemetery and potentially spans two centuries or more, and it would be surprising if there were no changes over this time period. Certainly, there is variation within the inhumation cemetery; this is most immediately apparent from the orientation of the graves. The graves took their primary orientation from the fieldsystem ditches within which the cemetery sat, but within that, they tended to align either in a north–south or east–west direction. There are subtle and slight differences in the variations, but it is clear from the plan that there were two dominant alignments. Is there anything else which correlates with this bimodal pattern? On the whole, the east–west group, were arranged in a linear pattern, head-to-foot, and occupied the northern part of the cemetery, while the north–south group largely lay side-by-side in a row and in the southern part of the cemetery (Table 6.5; also see Figs. 5.28 & 5.37). The fact that these three aspects relating to grave placement all correlate suggests that this is not accidental but, instead, indicative of deliberate and meaningful action.

Trying to understand the meaning behind these two broad practices in the cemetery is rather more difficult than identifying them. They could represent different family/kin groups, or they could express different belief systems. However, without further analysis it is impossible to move beyond conjecture (see now, though, Chap. 5's aDNA study). There is one other aspect to their arrangement which might provide a clue: many of the graves overlap/inter-cut, both within the groups but more significantly, in two instances, *between* these groups. In both cases, the east–west burial was later than the north–south burial: F.2016 cut F.2010, and F.2052 cut F.2055. A small sample indeed, but nevertheless it does suggest that the east–west group might be later than the north–south group (although this need not imply that the east–west inhumations were *all* later than the north–south ones).

Chronology alone does not explain why this change in burial practice occurred. The issue of Christianity needs considering, because it remains a recurrent issue when examining Late Roman burials. The burials in the inhumation cemetery were, therefore, examined in terms of a range of features which have been described as probably Christian and probably pagan (Woodward 1993; Quensel-von-Kalben 2000). Of a list of 16 attributes given by Woodward, only a handful were relevant at this site (Table 6.6).

The cemetery at Vicar's Farm exhibits nine of the 16 indicators, five of which are Christian and four pagan, although if we add one of the isolated burials outside the cemetery which lay face down to the list (F.991), then another trait can be added to the pagan column. This list in itself does not help matters, since the indicators need to be correlated. Some of the burials may have been pagan, some Christian. Following Quensel-von-Kalben's example, we can analyse the co-variation between attributes of the grave to see if there are any significant correlations between them, and in particular we can examine the effect of orientation (Tables 6.7–.8). Not all the traits have been analysed, due to their rarity. All the burials in the cemetery are supine. One feature has also been added: *inversion*, where the orientation of the body is reversed. In east–west burials, the body is normally oriented with head to the west, and in north–south graves, the head is to the south. In a few instances this is reversed, with heads to the east and north respectively (see Chap. 5 concerning whether the cemetery's close-set hand-to-head burials might reflect spouses).

The immediate impression from this comparison is that the patterning is not strong, even after using a statistical measure of co-variation (Table 6.8; 'Yule's Q', see Shennan 1988, 79–80). In terms of the two identified orientation groups in the cemetery, there is nothing in the attributes that would seem to reinforce this distinction. This is not to say the distinction is not valid, merely that it does not seem to have anything

Table 6.7. *Absolute numbers of co-occurrence.*

	E–W	N–S	Coffin	Hobnails	Overlapping	Vessel	Jewellery	Inversion
E–W	-	-	3	3	9	1	2	3
N–S		-	5	4	9	2	3	3
Coffin			-	4	5	2	1	3
Hobnails				-	4	3	1	2
Overlapping					-	2	4	4
Vessel						-	0	1
Jewellery							-	2
Inversion								-

Table 6.8. *Yule-values of co-variation (1.00 = positive co-variation; -1.00 = negative co-variation; 0 = no co-variation).*

	E–W	N–S	Coffin	Hobnails	Overlapping	Vessel	Jewellery	Inversion
E-W	-	-	0.22	0.32	0.64	0.08	0.24	0.44
N-S		-	0.57	0.47	0.44	0.59	0.50	0.33
Coffin			-	0.79	0.48	0.80	0.00	0.68
Hobnails				-	0.38	1.00	0.08	0.46
Overlapping					-	0.52	0.74	0.54
Vessel						-	-1.00	0.47
Jewellery							-	0.64
Inversion								-

to do with a dichotomy such as Christian *vs.* pagan, as it has been defined in the archaeological literature; but then perhaps the problem is in attempting to define something as heterogeneous as religious belief in dichotomous terms (Philpott 1991, 239–40; Barber & Bowsher 2000, 322). The inhumation cemetery at Vicar's Farm exhibits internal variation in burial rite, but this does not form any coherent pattern except at a general level of burial orientation and position within the cemetery. *Some of the people may have been Christian, but this is not apparent in the burial rites.*

Much of the interpretation of the settlement's burial rites hinges on the status of the one cremation, F.2084, within the inhumation cemetery and the fact that it was located centrally. Does this mark an absolute 'moment of change'; deciding to locate a cemetery there – at a remove from the settlement – did 'the [cognitive] world' suddenly change after the first interment as they adopted inhumation burial wholesale? Alternatively, was it a special interment, celebrating a founding/leading individual? None of that cemetery's burials seem particularly distinguished or rich, although as opposed to other regional/local cemeteries, the Vicar's Farm burials seem quite 'rule-bound' insofar as there was otherwise a strict separation/division of cremation and inhumation; also, there were almost no 'deviant' burials (see Crerar 2016).

As outlined in the previous chapter, the achieved aDNA results – with so few first-degree genetic relations documented – could actually suggest a fairly unstable community. Respectively involving the comings and goings of marriage partners (wives) and, then, their resultant off-spring, this could either reflect a high proportion of labourers and/or that much of its membership consisted of tenanted serfs. It is only reasonable to presume that the farming settlement would have been run by an overseer and some of the site's high quality metalwork, if not votive items, could speak of the elevated status of some of the settlement's residents (see Crummy below). If so, the lack of rich/distinguished burials might be explained if that was not a life-long position and something to retire from; they eventually taking up residence (and dying) elsewhere. Alternatively, in the light of

Table 6.9. *Occurrence of dental pathologies according to burial orientation.*

	E–W (n=13)		N–S (n=16)	
	No.	%	No.	%
Calculus	6	46.15	2	12.50
Caries	3	23.08	2	12.50
Enamel hypoplasia	2	15.38	1	6.25
Ante-mortem tooth loss	4	30.77	5	31.25

the settlement's remarkable ritual structures – the Timber Shrine and Monumental Post – and votive deposits (e.g. the horse head pit), perhaps the basis of this authority was, in part, religious and involved a denial of status-display. Whatever the case, the aDNA results could hint of a community in some flux, with limited long-term familial-residential succession. That said, another possibility should not be ignored: only a low percentage of the dead were afforded formal cemetery burial (see, e.g., Pearce 2013 and Smith *et al*. 2018, 275–7). This is an interpretation that might resonant with the loose human bone found scattered around the settlement (Fig. 6.21) and, of which, more – plus further isolated burials – would surely have been forthcoming if its linear features had been excavated to a greater sampling intensity.

The Living Population

The burials, as well as informing us about funerary or mortuary rites, also provide insight into the living population. It is an assumption – but not an unreasonable one – that the two cemeteries and other burials all involved people who once lived at the settlement. It was these people who walked within the spaces of the enclosures they dug, slept in the buildings they erected, used the pottery, milled the flour, reared and butchered the cows, sheep, horses, chickens and pigs. It was these people who created the site we excavated. In some ways, we already know so much about them from this world they created, that turning to their bones for understanding of who they were seems to pale into insignificance. Yet there is more to learn, especially about these people as individuals, and their relationship to each other. So, to begin with the basics: age and sex.

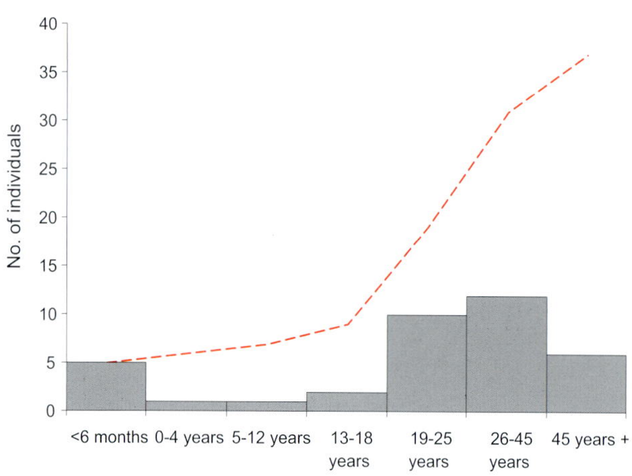

Figure 6.22. *Demographic curve for Vicar's Farm inhumation cemetery.*

Table 6.10. *Summary age-data for all burials.*

Age	No. of individuals	Cumulative count	Cumulative %
<6 months	5	5	13.51
0–4 years	1	6	16.22
5–12 years	1	7	18.92
13–18 years	2	9	24.32
19–25 years	10	19	51.35
26–45 years	12	31	83.78
45 years +	6	37	100.00

Demography

Forty-eight individuals have been identified from the settlement, 11 from Phase I and the remainder from Phases II–III. This is very much a minimum number and it is unlikely that the full population is represented in the burials. Not all of its inhabitants necessarily resided there throughout all their lives; nor, as outlined above (see *Isolated Burials*), is it likely that all of the settlement's non-cemetery interments were actually recovered. Nevertheless, given known numbers, life expectancy and span of occupation, we can make some estimates about the *minimum* size of the population. The demographic curve for the population, taken as a whole, is fairly typical. There is quite a high mortality rate of newborns, but generally childhood mortality is low and only starts to increase in a person's twenties (Table 6.10; Fig. 6.22). At the East London Cemetery, 25 per cent of the population died before the age of 18, but most died between 26–45 (Barber & Bowsher 2000, 311); the figures for Vicar's Farm are exactly the same. Both of these sites, however, show lower infant and juvenile mortality than other major Roman cemeteries such as Poundbury and Lankhills, which in general are regarded as being quite low. This has usually been attributed to differential burial practice, particularly of neonates and infants (see above and discussion in Barber & Bowsher 2000, 312–14; Scott 1989).

If the mortality rates reflected in the burials are typical of the population, the implication is that few individuals lived beyond the age of 45: about one in five. This means that to maintain stable population levels, the whole population would have to be regenerated about every 50 years. Now, given there are 11 people buried in Phase I which covered a century, and 37 people in Phases II–III that spanned 250 years, this implies a turnover population every half century of 5.5 for Phase I and 7.4 for Phases II–III. In short, the minimum population based on the burials suggests some five to eight people living on the site at any one time.

Whatever the absolute numbers (there were surely more than this minimum), they cannot have been that large, perhaps no more than about 10–20. The population was of mixed age, and, at least in part, composed of one or two family groups. In theory, this could be supported by the sex ratio of the population. Based on both the morphological and genetic identifications, just over half the inhumations could be sexed: one possible and 10 definite females, as opposed to two possible and six definite males.[12] There is, though, no clear confirmation of the burial populace's familial basis in terms of morphological traits and, now as outlined in Chapter Five, relatively little through the achieved aDNA results. Certainly, not all of the settlement's populace need have been immediate kin-group members and various categories of 'labourers' would surely have been involved.

Can we say anything more about the lives of the small population of children, women and men who inhabited Vicar's Farm? Many of the adults showed signs of osteoarthritis; this was the most common pathology recorded, especially of the spine. This suggests a life of heavy manual labour, and is, perhaps, not surprising given what we now know of the range of strenuous, repetitive activities going on there: digging ditches, processing wheat, milling flour and dismembering animals. There is also evidence from the teeth of systemic nutritional- and/or disease-related stress (enamel hypoplasias; Table 6.9) during early life. The presence of bone deformities on the legs of several individuals could be due to repetitive squatting, a favoured position at rest, or else due to bending postures.[13] Malnutrition might also have caused both these latter pathologies, but given that food does not seem to have been something generally lacking on the site, this may not be the causal factor in this case. None of this is to say that the people had a particularly 'hard' life. This is surely a relative concept. These people – men and women – may have been spending their days engaged in heavy manual work, and they had their share of disease and illness, but *they were largely a community who slept, ate and worked together in a series of close relationships*. As with any group, these relationships were, nevertheless, still mediated by politics: a politics of gender, age, kinship and any number of other dimensions that make up the identity of individuals. Yet, consider again the here-emphasized text, as it typifies the kind of familial-based precepts that underpinned our conceptualization of the settlement prior to the receipt of its aDNA analysis.

Personal Items Nina Crummy

Of the datable Roman personal items, dress accessories form the largest group, and bracelets are particularly well-represented, as are hobnails (see *Iron*, Chap. 5). Some of the items are grave-goods and have duly been described in the previous chapter, while others are scattered site finds. They date from the mid first through to the late fourth or early fifth century AD, though the majority are 'Late'. The low number of first-century AD brooches suggests that there was little activity on the site at this period. A large penannular brooch with enamelled terminals of unusual zoomorphic form lacks its pin and has been coiled more tightly so that the terminals overlap, perhaps to form an armlet for a very small child. The armlets from the grave groups include some standard Late Roman forms, but also an earlier pair with decoration reminiscent of high-quality gold examples.

High quality is, again, hinted at by the presence of two unusual items. One is a projecting ring-headed pin used to fasten a garment, a Celtic form rare in southern Britain, and, most unusually, the decoration on this example is of Roman style (Figs. 6.23.3 & 6.47.4). Other examples from southern Britain come from a hoard at Oldcroft, Gloucestershire, and also from the temple site at Lydney in the same county (Wheeler & Wheeler 1932). There is some possibility, therefore, that this item was used as a votive offering. The other item is a Minerva bust handle from a spatula (Figs. 6.25.8 & 6.47.1), used to smooth the wax on a tablet (and perhaps also to cut a slab of wax from a block to fill/refill the tablet) might be evidence for literacy but, as it is detached from the blade, the image of Minerva may have been preserved for reuse as an *ex voto*, as may also have been the case with another example from the Woodeaton Temple site.

Identification of either object positively as votive is far from certain, but the presence of these objects may perhaps cause us to question the reason for the presence at this site of a Spiral Sunburst brooch and the large, adapted, zoomorphic penannular brooch. All four items are probably of second-century AD date. The high number of pieces of Late Roman jewellery recovered from the site in contexts other than graves may also suggest a votive use, though at a later period. Some of them date from the late fourth to the early fifth century AD. Also of Late Roman or early Anglo-Saxon date is a well-preserved knife with a distinctive concave turn towards the tip. This is a feature of some Anglo-Saxon knives, one variant example of which, from Dover, is quite similar to the Vicar's Farm knife and was found in a mid to late fifth-century grave with a late fourth- to early fifth-century AD buckle (Evison 1987, Grave 48). Toilet instruments are rare, but there is a fragment of a mirror and two pairs of tweezers (though one of the latter may be Medieval).

Dress Accessories

Brooches

<4726> SF 300, F.5474 - Upper part of a Nauheim derivative brooch, in two fragments, with a narrow bow of rectangular section and tightly wound four-coil spring. Copper alloy, length 19 mm. A strip fragment associated with it is probably part of the bow but is more markedly curved. Length 9 mm. Nauheim derivative brooches are of simple one-piece form. They are particularly common in the pre-Flavian period (Olivier in Potter & Trow 1988, 38).

<4800> SF 538 - Penannular brooch of Fowler's Type D4 (1960, 152, fig. 1). The pin is missing and the round-section hoop now coiled more tightly, perhaps for use as a finger-ring, though the internal diameter is still large for use in this way. The upper face of the hoop is ridged towards the terminals. These are of unusual zoomorphic form. The metal has been hammered flat and folded backwards, with the end rising upwards slightly and pinched laterally to form a snout. A dot of yellow enamel is set on each terminal before the snout. Copper alloy, internal diameter now 25 mm, probably originally about 40–45 mm (Fig. 6.23.1).

While the folded back terminals with the upward tilting free-end place this brooch in Fowler's Type D4, they are not transversely clenched to provide the usual double-hump profile. The use of enamel is also unusual on this subtype, though a large brooch (52 mm internal diameter) from Corbridge has ovals of yellow enamel, and one from Traprain Law (53 mm internal diameter) has lozenges of yellow enamel (Hull nd., pl. 834, 4172, 5102; Cree 1924, fig. 21). Both these northern brooches are of Fowler's Subtype D5 with cast zoomorphic terminals. Another penannular brooch from Traprain Law, a D4, has also been adapted for reuse as a ?finger-ring, like the Vicar's Farm example, by being coiled more tightly (Kilbride-Jones 1936, 127, fig. 1, 3).

It is difficult to be sure of the date of this brooch, but the enamel suggests it may be second-century AD. The adapted brooch from Traprain Law came from a second-century AD context, and the 'tilted ear' design of the terminals also relates the type to garment-pins of Type E, which first appear in the second century AD (Fowler 1963, fig. 2, 1–2, 2–6).

<4759> SF 149 - Plate brooch with a wide flange, gently concave on the upper face, which rises to form a central cup, now empty, with a rivet hole set just off-centre. The flange has a band of blue enamel, scalloped on the outer edge and with long, slightly angled, points rising up the sides of the cup to produce a sunburst effect. A row of yellow(?) enamel dots runs around the centre of the band. Part of the flange is missing. The pin is missing but was sprung on two lugs that remain on the underside. Copper alloy, diameter 37 mm (Figs. 6.23.2 & 6.47.5).

This brooch is of Hattatt's Spiral Sunburst type of which the few examples known have a wide distribution, from Wiltshire (1987, 187–8) to Chesters on Hadrian's Wall (Hull nd., pl. 813, 7651). The example with enamelling closest in design to the Vicar's Farm example, though rather smaller, is from Britain but otherwise unprovenanced (Hattatt 1987, fig. 61, 1075), but the poorly preserved example from Chesters is precisely the same size and may have been an even closer match. Where the fill of the central cup survives it is sometimes enamel, sometimes solder which would have retained a decorated metal disc. The hole in the base of this example suggests that here a decorative stud was used, fixed in with solder. The use of enamel dates the type to the second century AD and the style shows it to be of British manufacture.

<4733> SF 519 [4995] - Ring-headed pin (proto hand-pin). The offset shank is curved backwards towards the tip. Pins from Hunnum,

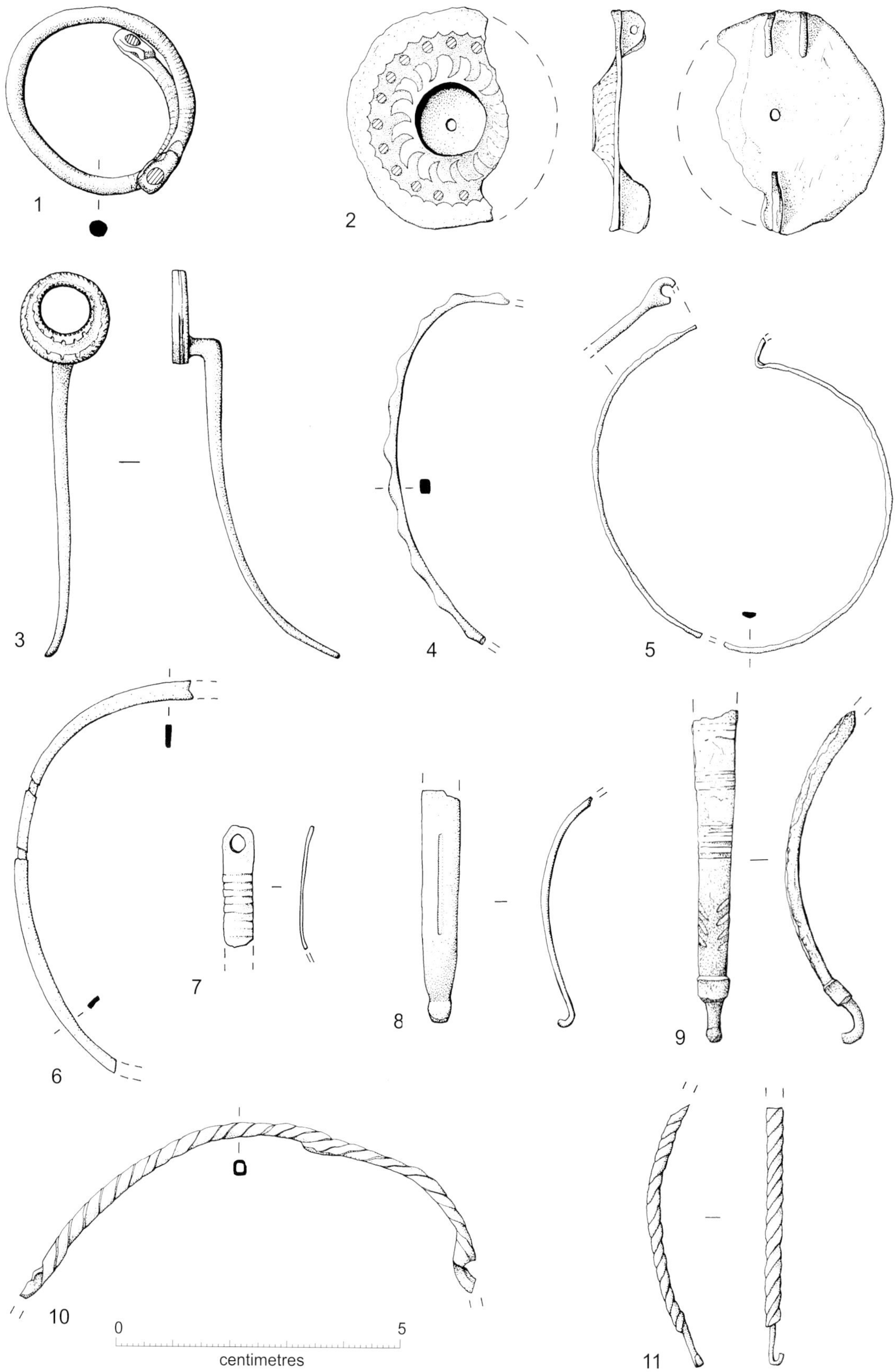

Figure 6.23. *Personal objects (I; see text).*

Hadrian's Wall, and Tripontium, on Watling Street in Warwickshire also curve back slightly, but only towards the tip (Kilbride-Jones 1980, fig. 68.1; Fowler 1984, fig. 23). The head is a true circle, but slightly wider at the base than the top, and thereby allied to the shape of pins with elliptical heads. It has recessed wreath-like decoration (a groove with flanking notches representing buds of leaves) and both the inner and outer edges have neat slightly angled notches to produce a beaded spiral effect. There are slight traces of enamel in the design. Two well-defined grooves are set around the girth of the head. Similar grooves encircle the lower part of the head of a pin from Gaulcross, Morayshire, and this area can also be used as a field for more complex decoration (Kilbride-Jones 1980, fig. 68, 6–8). Copper alloy, length (straight) 75 mm, diameter of head 16 mm (Fig. 6.23.3 & 6.46.4).

The pin belongs to Group 17 in Cool's typology (1990, 165). These are not hairpins, but were used, like brooches, to fasten garments, as the curvature of the shank on this pin clearly shows. They are Celtic objects rarely found in southern Roman Britain, but the unparalleled wreath-like decoration on the head of this example is Roman in conception, though very debased. The enamel suggests a date in the second century AD, and the decoration supports Cool's suggestion that some of these pins may have been made in southern Britain. A silver pin from Oldcroft, Gloucestershire of this type but with Celtic-style decoration, was found with a hoard with a closing date of *c.* AD 354–9, though it may have been old when buried (Johns 1974; 1996, 145–6). Other examples have been found nearby at Lydney, Gloucestershire (Wheeler & Wheeler 1932, fig. 18, 63–4), which is a temple site that has produced a large number of bronzes, many probably votives.

Bracelets

<4782> SF 309 - Distorted fragment (in two pieces) of a very thin crenellated bracelet with toothing between the crenellations. Copper alloy, length 62 mm, maximum width 2 mm, thickness 1 mm. Bracelets of this type date to the last quarter of the fourth century AD into the fifth century AD. There are several from graves; for example, from Lankhills, Winchester (Clarke 1979, Type D1e) and Butt Road, Colchester (Crummy *et al.* 1993, tables 2.52 & 2.67) and, in particular, from the very late female burial from Dorchester-on-Thames (Kirk & Leeds 1953, fig. 29, 2 & 5). There is also one from a sixth-century grave at Barrington (White 1988, fig. 55, 4). Stratified examples from occupation sites confirm the late date; for example, from Verulamium (Lowther 1937, fig. 2, 4), Lydney (Wheeler & Wheeler 1932, fig. 17, 58) and Neatham (Redknap 1986, fig. 73, 99–101; Fig.6.23.4). Recent work by Swift has shown that bracelets of this type were made in Britain (2010, 247).

<4795> SF 513 - Fragment of a distorted plain bracelet of 'D'-shaped section with a hook-and-eye fastening. Copper alloy. Internal diameter approximately 45 mm, section 2 mm high by 1 mm thick. A very similar example came from a grave dated AD 350–70 at Lankhills (Clarke 1979, fig. 89, 338; Fig. 6.23.5).

<4724> SF 266, F.5387 - Fragment of a plain strip bracelet with part of an eye for a hook-and-eye fastening. The rectangular-section hoop lies horizontally. Copper alloy. Internal diameter approximately 58 mm, section 1 mm high by 3 mm wide. As with <5136>, bangles of this form are rarely plain. Most have the outer edge grooved, notched, or cut into crenellations, sometimes with grooving in the interstices (Crummy 1983, fig. 43, 1654, 1657 & 1659), and date to the middle or late fourth century AD (Fig. 6.23.6).

<4719> F.5304 - Terminal from a strip bracelet with a hole for a hook-end-eye fastening, and decorative transverse grooves. Copper alloy. Length 19 mm, width 5 mm, maximum thickness 1 mm (Fig. 6.23.7).

<4765> SF 162 - Terminal from a strip bracelet with a hook for a hook-and-eye fastening. Copper alloy. Length 38 mm, width 7 mm, thickness 1.5 mm. The decoration is very worn but belongs to the type known variously as employing 'multiple motifs' or 'multiple units' (Crummy 1983, 45, fig. 47; Cool & Mills 1993, 80). At Lankhills it is Type E (Clarke 1979, 307–9). Close to the terminal are either transverse grooves or side notches, followed by a panel with central latitudinal groove flanked by edge feathering, then a small group of transverse grooves. The design at the point where the hoop has broken is unclear. It may be festoons or zigzags. The panel with feathering flanking a central groove is a particularly distinctive feature of the type. It usually occurs in this position close to the terminals, set within short blocks of transverse grooves, as at, for example, Richborough, Lankhills, Colchester and Canterbury (Bushe-Fox 1928, pl. 21, 51; Clarke 1979, fig. 37, 502 & 525; Crummy 1983, fig. 47, 1725, 1732; Garrard 1995, fig. 434, 368 & 371). The type belongs to the second half of the fourth century AD into the fifth (Fig. 6.23.8). As with SF 309 above, this is a Romano-British product (Swift 2010, 248).

<4754> SF 139 - Fragment of a stout strip bracelet, with a hook for a hook-and-eye fastening. Copper alloy. Length 58 mm, maximum width 8 mm, thickness 3.5 mm. There is a panel of angled-edge grooves and a zoomorphic moulding before the hook, derivative of snake's head terminals. The main body of the hoop is decorated with groups of transverse grooves (Fig. 6.23.9).

<4731> F.5588 - Fragment of a distorted cable bracelet of three sub-rectangular strands, one slightly narrower than the other two. Copper alloy. Length 79 mm, section 3 × 3 mm. At one end the strands appear to have broken close to a terminal eye or hook. Cable bracelets generally date to the first half or middle of the fourth century AD (Clarke 1979, table 34, A2; Crummy 1983, 38; Fig. 6.22.10).

<4738> SF 65 - Fragment of a cable bracelet of three strands and with a hook terminal. Not part of <4731> or <4780>. Copper alloy. Length 44 mm, section 3 × 2.5 mm (Fig. 6.22.11).

<4780> SF 298 - Small fragment from a cable bracelet of three sub-rectangular strands. Not part of <4731> or <4738>. Copper alloy. Length 38 mm, section 4 × 4 mm.

Hairpins

<631> SF 13, [554] - Complete bone hairpin with reel-shaped head and marked swelling on the shaft. Crummy Type 6 (1983, 24–5). Length 76 mm. The form is in general Late Roman, but probably appears *c.* AD 150 (Fig. 6.24.1).

<761> SF 20, F.116 - Bone hairpin with a reel set beneath a conical head, Crummy Type 5 (1983, 23–4). The very tip of the swollen shaft is missing. Length 73 mm. This type is fourth-century AD, and probably mid to late, rather than early. An important group, some unfinished, were found in residual contexts on the site of a baths complex at St Margaret's Street in Canterbury (Greep 1995, 1135–41; Fig. 6.24.2).

<4790> SF 421 - Complete copper alloy hairpin of Cool's Group 8, with a head formed of multiple mouldings. Length (slightly bent) 129 mm. This example is similar to others from the eastern region, and probably dates to the late first or second century AD (Cool 1990, 160; Fig. 6.24.3).

<4330> F.4832 - Tip of the shaft of a bone hairpin or needle. Length 43 mm.

Other

<4734> F.8140 - Many fragments from a copper alloy cable earring of two more or less circular strands, Allason-Jones's Type 6 (1989, 7). Internal diameter approximately 14 mm, section 4 × 4 mm.

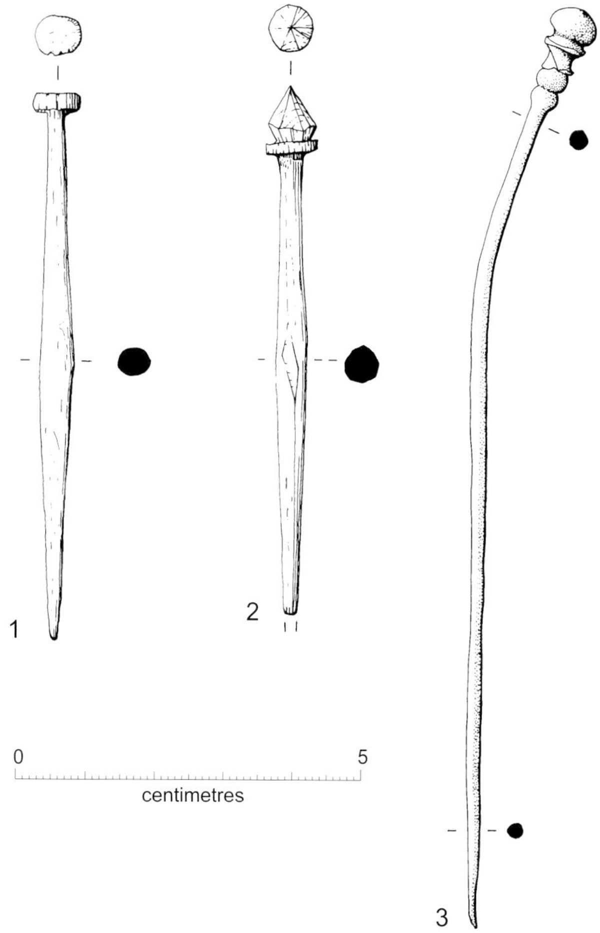

Figure 6.24. *Personal objects (II; see text).*

Allason-Jones suggests the form may be Late Roman, and a similar ring (described as a finger-ring) from Wanborough, Wilts. came from a fourth-century AD context (Hooley 2001, fig. 35, 103).

<4756> SF 141 - Flat-headed copper alloy stud with a low convex moulded turned-down rim. The shank is square in section and short. This form of stud was probably used on leather, the rim serving to bite into the strap. Diameter (if complete) 16 mm, height 5 mm (Fig. 6.25.1).

<4751> SF 125 - Convex-headed stud, the shank missing. Staining on the underside suggests the shank may have been iron. Copper alloy. Diameter 27 mm (Fig. 6.25.2).

<4328> SF 16, F.5304 - Discoid spacer bead, probably shale rather than jet, with two perforations. One face bears a lathe-centre mark. Similar beads in jet occur at Silchester (Lawson 1976, fig. 1, 6–7), Lydney (Wheeler & Wheeler 1932, fig. 18, 77), Verulamium (Wheeler & Wheeler 1936, fig. 47), Colchester (Crummy 1983, fig. 35, 951–6) and Wanborough (Horton 2001, fig. 58, 1–2). The better quality examples of the type are slightly domed, with the lathe-centre mark on this upper face, and have a slight rim formed by a marginal groove. Where these beads are from secure contexts, they suggest a date in the late third or fourth century AD (Fig. 6.25.3).

Toilet Instruments

<4773> SF 191 - Fragment of a copper alloy mirror of Lloyd-Morgan's Group K, with a border of holes, countersunk on one side. There are several scribed concentric circles at the edge, which appear to be guidelines for positioning the holes rather than decoration. Dimensions 36 × 17.5 mm, diameter approximately 150 mm (Figs. 6.25.4 & 6.47.6).

Group K mirrors are found across southern Britain, from Essex to South Wales, but with a concentration in the southeast. There was a major production centre at Nijmegen from the mid first century AD, and the colony founded at Colchester at around the same time may have been the initial port of entry as there are several examples from the town (Lloyd-Morgan 1981). They are spread from Kent across to Glamorgan and north to Cheshire, with a more northerly outlier at Vindolanda (Lloyd-Morgan 1977a; 1992). The best preserved example is that from Whitchurch, Shropshire (Musty *et al.* 1973, 279). Though the number from Britain appears high, the form, which originated in Italy, is known all over the Empire, and Lloyd-Morgan estimated that only about six per cent of the assemblage from the northwest provinces comes from Britain (1977a, 233).

Mirrors of this type were imported into Britain from the mid first century AD, probably to the mid second. There is a fragment from a pre-Flavian pit at Usk, and several of the Colchester examples come from first-century AD grave groups. Mirrors were treasured items and were cared for by their owners, some, perhaps all, being kept in wooden boxes, probably cloth-lined, to protect the surface. Fragments of a Type K mirror from Chester have wood fibre on each surface (Lloyd-Morgan 1977a, 233, pl. 9.1,c; 1977b, 49). Examples found in second-century AD contexts may, therefore, be long-lived survivals, and it is difficult to establish if the form was still being manufactured at that time. The Whitchurch mirror was found with second-century AD pottery, as was one from a grave at Billericay, Essex (Lloyd-Morgan & Crummy 2010). Small fragments from second-century AD contexts at Verulamium and Wroxeter may, however, be residual (Waugh & Goodburn 1972, fig. 51, 173; Lloyd-Morgan 2000).

<4728> SF 324, [1685] F.33 - Complete tweezers, with slightly flared blades. Copper alloy, Length 53 mm. Possibly from a toilet set (Fig. 6.25.5).

<4815> (Metal-detector find) - Complete small tweezers, probably from a toilet set. The blades are straight-sided. Copper alloy, length 43 mm (Fig. 6.25.6).

Other

<4797> SF 530 - Most of a copper alloy spoon shaft, with a fragment of the bowl remaining attached to the offset junction plate. Length (bent) 76 mm. Similar spoons come from Wanborough, Wilts, and Portchester in Late Roman contexts (Cunliffe 1975, fig. 113, 59; Hooley 2001, fig. 42, 178; Fig. 6.25.7).

<4793> SF 469 - Copper alloy Minerva bust handle from a wax spatula of Feugère Type A5 (1995, fig. 3). Length 56 mm. Her helmet has a high-feathered crest, and her hair is shown by slanting grooves that in places run onto the helmet's rim. The facial features are quite crudely indicated and the neck thin and long. The folds of her tunic are shown on the front by mouldings decorated with tiny dots and grooves and on the back by grooves. The neck band is grooved. On her chest is her *aegis*, the incised features very faint. The lower part of the handle is marked by transverse mouldings. The split socket retains no part of the iron blade (Fig. 6.25.8 & 6.47.1).

Since Feugère's 1985 publication and the dissemination of his work (Crummy 2002), the number of Minerva bust handles recognised

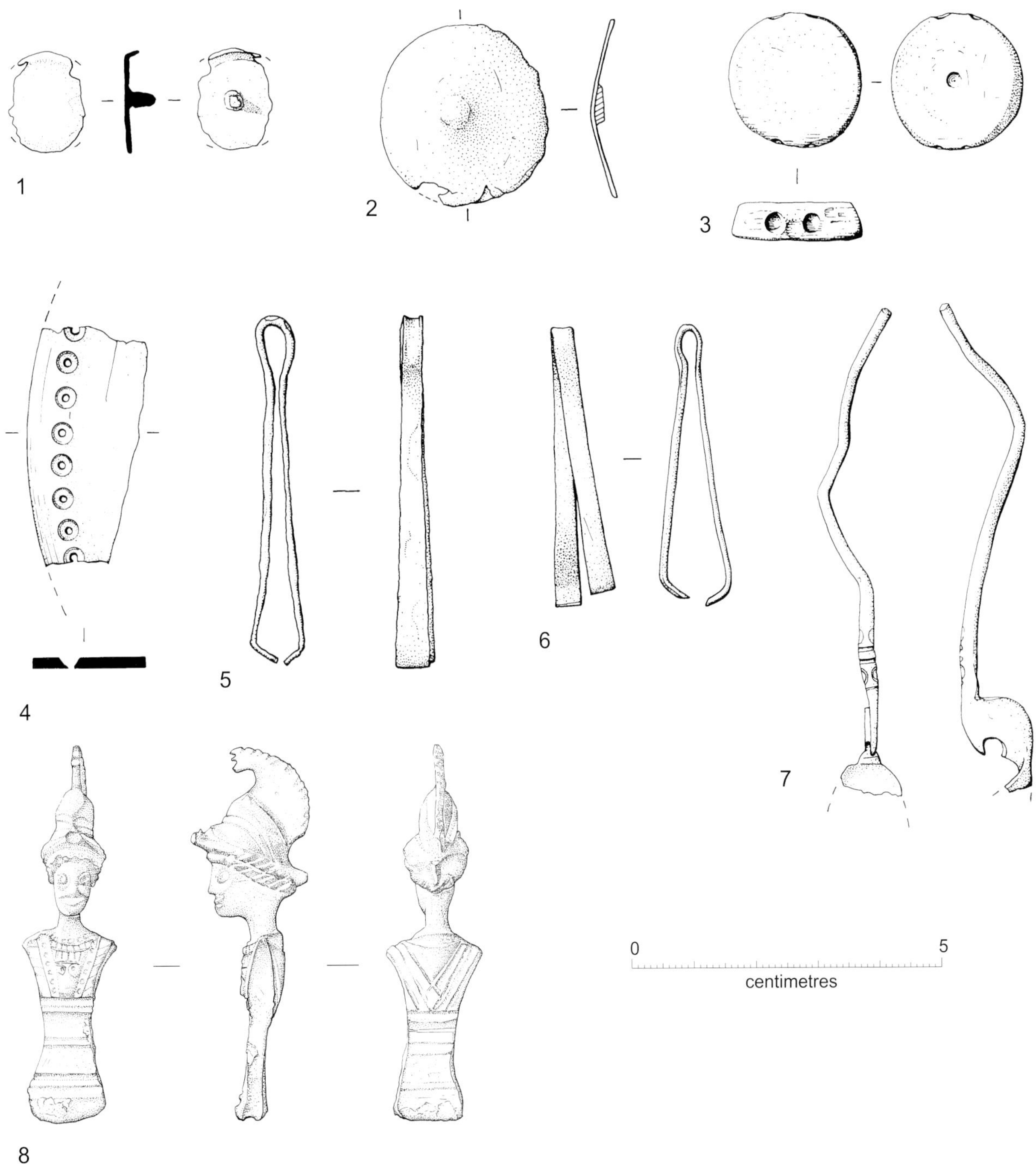

Figure 6.25. *Personal objects (III; see text).*

in Britain has increased considerably, with 44 now listed under 'spatula' on the Portable Antiquities Scheme Database and one more under 'handle' (search dated 27/2/2019). Their finds spots are widely scattered, although most are in southern and central Britain and none is recorded further north than North Yorkshire. The site types of excavated examples range from rural settlements, villas and temples, to large towns: Kenchester, Herefordshire (Boon 1991, fig. 4h); Kingscote, Gloucestershire (Henig & Paddock 1993, fig. 3.9); Woodeaton, Oxfordshire (Kirk 1949, pl. 4F); Silchester, Hampshire (Pitts 1979, pl. 28, no. 219); Stonea Grange, Cambridgeshire (Jackson & Potter 1996, fig. 112, 95); Love's Farm, St Neots, Cambridgeshire (Crummy in Hinman & Zant 2018, 165–6, fig. 6.27); and London (Museum of London 12846; Pitts 1979, no. 215). The only spatula with its blade complete was found in a second century AD grave at Ospringe, Kent (Whiting 1923, pl. opposite p. 65; Feugère 1995, fig. 2a); Boon erroneously identified the Ospringe find as a razor (1991, 30–2, fig. 4g). In style they range from fully classical to very simplified, with the former no doubt imported and the latter made in Britain and in some cases barely recognisable as Minerva, such as PAS LANCUM-55B647 from Lincolnshire.

Minerva handles occur across the Empire from Morocco to Germany, Britain to Hungary. The majority are from the west: France, Belgium, Germany, and Britain. While complete spatulae are evidence for literacy, the Woodeaton find suggests that handles detached from their blades may have been reused as votive items. A second Minerva bust also came from Woodeaton but is probably not from a spatula (Kirk 1949, pl. 4E). The goddess has many aspects, of which the most important in this context may be her association with healing, but she may also have been conflated with a local goddess, as with Sulis Minerva at Bath.

<4747> *SF 110* - Shaft fragment, swollen towards the centre and with one broken end split. The other end has broken, or been cut, at a slight bend. Copper alloy. Length (bent) 88 mm.

<4736> *SF 43* - Fragment of a ring of circular section. Rings of this size and type could be used for a variety of purposes. Copper alloy, internal diameter 17 mm, thickness 3 mm.

<4725> *SF 290, [1451] F.436* - Fragmentary ring fixed in thick clay. Copper alloy. Diameter at least 50 mm, flattened oval section, 3 × 2 mm.

<4530> *SF 268, F.5419* - Iron ring with internal diameter of 33 mm. Such rings are multi-purpose, being used on, for example, chains and harness.

<1714> *F.5603* - Crown of a Red deer antler fragment (in two pieces), split length-wise across a perforation. The breakage is recent. The lower end of the fragment shows chop marks where it has been cut off the beam. Maximum length 130 mm. The function of this piece is uncertain, but, as the points form a horn-shape, it may have been hung up as a protective amulet. Probably Late Roman (Fig. 6.26.1).

<438> *F.5013* - Tanged knife with the back very slightly angled up from the line of the tang, then drops in a concave turn down to the tip. The edge runs in a straight line to the tip but is slightly damaged. Length 116 mm. This precise form does not occur in Manning's

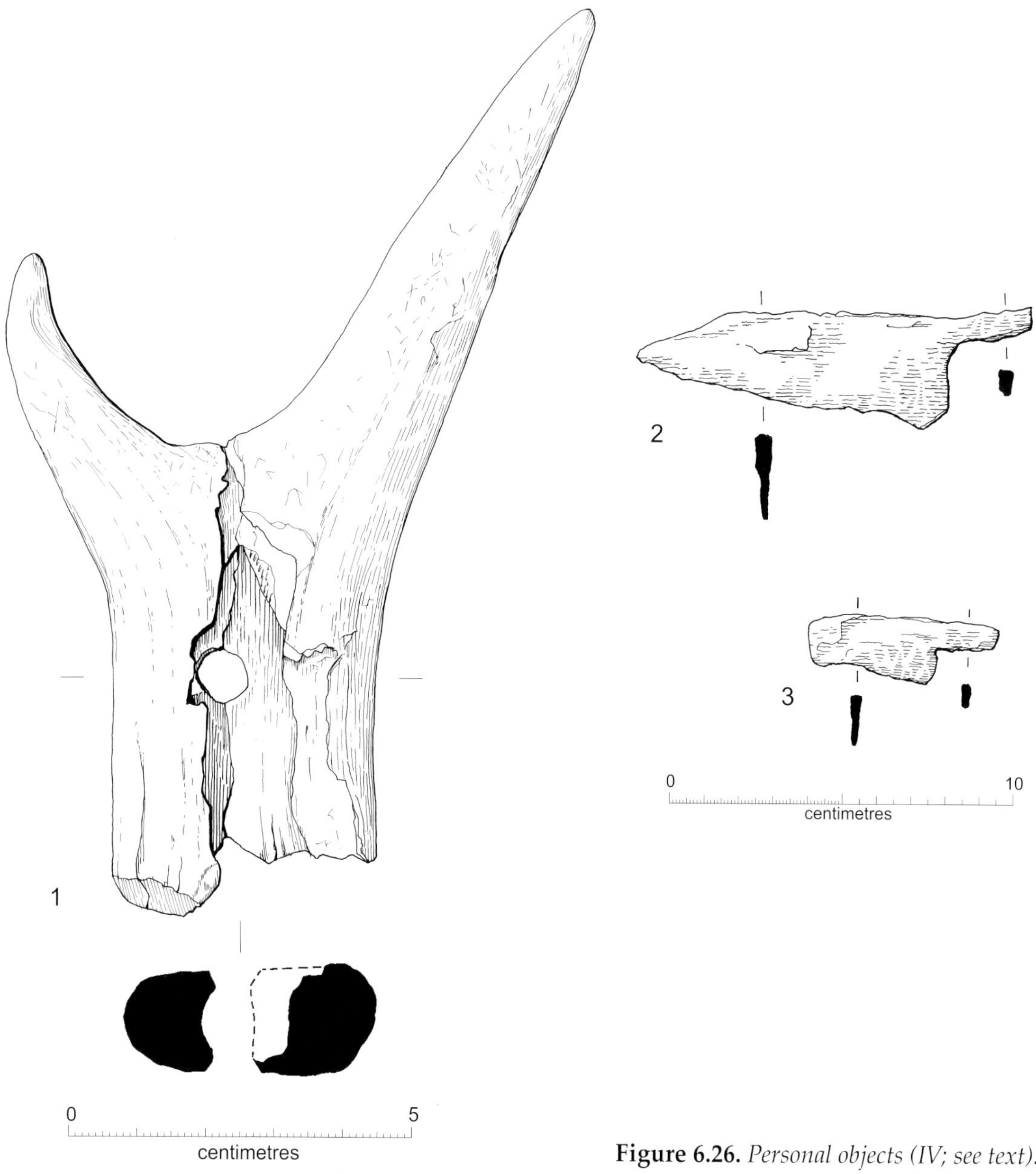

Figure 6.26. *Personal objects (IV; see text).*

typology, but is close to the rare Type 19, which has the tang set centrally to the blade (1985, fig. 29). The concave turn towards the tip does, however, occur on some Anglo-Saxon knives (e.g. Evison 1987, text fig. 22, Type 6), one early variant of which was found in a mid to late fifth-century grave at Dover with a buckle of Hawkes and Dunning's Type IIA (Evison's variant Al), a Late Roman form (Hawkes & Dunning 1962, figs. 17–18; Evison 1981, 129; Evison 1987, Grave 48). This knife may, therefore, belong to the very late fourth or fifth century AD (Fig. 6.26.2).

<4464> *F.5042* - Tanged fragment, possibly a knife, but the back is thickened and the thickness appears to extend round onto a blunt end rather than a tip. The edge is concave. Possibly a model rather than a functional object. Length 54 mm (Fig. 6.26.3).

Overviewing Identities

Table 6.11 summarizes all the personal items recovered from the site, broken down into grave and non-grave contexts. Most of the items are clearly from non-grave contexts, chiefly metal-detected finds from the surface of features (see Fig. 6.49 for distribution plot). Seventy-seven per cent are dress accessories, the remainder being toiletry or other personal items. The general presence and range of such objects is perhaps not unusual, but comparing the funerary and non-funerary figures suggests that a fairly limited range of objects was selected for burial with an individual when compared against the site baseline. It seems that there was a preference for objects that were actually worn on the body (bracelets, finger-rings and beads), as opposed to more general personal items. The lack of hairpins and brooches as grave-goods is interesting in this respect, but their absence from graves might relate to specific customs about funerary clothing and hair dressing, such as the use of shrouds/wraps that precluded ordinary dress. More generally, the presence of objects found with burials might suggest a certain scale of valuation in terms of what constitutes 'personal' objects and their inalienability.

Identity is a multi-faceted phenomenon, as people's identities are forged through their relationships to others; someone can be a mother, wife and daughter, as well as a slave or 'foreigner'. Trying to understand the complex relationships and identities of the people

Table 6.11. *Numbers of personal items from the site.*

Items	Non-grave	Grave	Total
Brooches	4	-	4
Bracelets	9	6	15
Finger ring	-	2	2
Hairpins	4	-	4
Bead	1	6	7
Other dress	4	-	4
Toiletries	3	-	3
Other personal	8	-	8

Table 6.12. *Summary of grave-goods with cemetery inhumations.*

Sex	Jewellery	Other	None
Female	4	1	4
Male	-	-	5
Unsexed	1	-	10

at Vicar's Farm is no easy task and requires looking at a number of different strands of evidence to build even a partial picture. Among small populations, age and sex typically form key dimensions of relationships and identities, so we will begin there. We have already seen a notable difference in the treatment of new babies from other age groups in burial. New babies less than six months old do not seem to have been cremated when other members of the population were, and later, when inhumation became the standard rite, they were not buried in the same way, but were often interred within the foundations of structures. This consistent differentiation might indicate that newly born babies were not considered fully 'people' and were consequently treated differently at death. It suggests, perhaps, that a person's identity was not recognized at birth, but only months afterwards.

Beyond this, it is hard to identify any other differentiation marked by age in the burial record; though, of course, this does not mean age was not an important dimension of living relationships. Sex in the burial record does, however, show some differentiation. Based on the (albeit small) sample of the inhumation cemetery, *there is a clear-cut distinction in the grave-goods of males and females* (Table 6.12). Males do not seem to be interred with any grave-goods, although one was accompanied by a bowl, while about half the females were, most of these being items worn on the body: generally bracelets, and finger-rings, while an unsexed infant wore a bead necklace.[14]

What does this patterning suggest? Perhaps a certain sartorial aesthetic, though this must not lead to a crude conclusion that personal adornment was more significant for women than men. Both genders wore clothes and presumably wore them in certain styles. But these styles may or may not have been gender-specific; both men and women certainly used brooches to fasten their clothes when the clothing required (or even when it did not), but so far there is little to indicate any sexual differentiation in terms of brooch-use (Allason-Jones 1995, 24) and none were recovered from the site's grave-contexts. Literary evidence suggests that bracelets and necklaces are female accessories, though archaeologically this remains ambiguous; and besides, the literary evidence pertains to Rome and not necessarily its provinces (*ibid.*). Finger-rings are equally non gender-specific. Indeed, in her survey,

Allason-Jones suggests jewellery as a whole appears to be relatively ungendered in Roman Britain. In fact, if there is any gendered object, it tends to reside in the material rather than the form, as both jet and amber seem to have had strongly female associations (*ibid.*, 29). The fact, therefore, that only females at Vicar's Farm were associated with jewellery needs to be interpreted with caution, especially when trying to extrapolate further gendered practices from such finds.

Dress accessories were the most common category of small find from the site as a whole. Accordingly, it may be more significant to note the general importance and relative value given to such material culture by the population at Vicar's Farm – male or female – at least in the later phases. A changing bodily aesthetic is, therefore, what might have been expressed through such finds, rather than gender differentiation *per se*.

Production

The economic basis of the settlement was mixed agricultural, principally cereal growing and livestock (mostly cattle and sheep). Of particular interest is the likelihood that cereal production was geared toward surplus, rather than solely domestic consumption, which has major implications for interpreting the site.

Crop Husbandry Rachel Ballantyne

As opposed to the previous discussion of broader theoretical dimensions relating to crop-processing cycles and rhythms, the concern here is more with basic matters and the economic contribution of crops.

Cereals and Other Economic Plants

The charred assemblage is dominated by cereal remains, primarily wheat (*Triticum* sp.) with much lesser amounts of barley (*Hordeum vulgare sensu lato*). In the majority of cases, the wheat grains are comparable to the hulled types emmer and spelt (*T. diccocum/spelta*). The abundant cereal chaff comprises mainly spelt wheat glume bases, identified by their weak keeling and clear veination, and it seems likely that most of the charred wheat grain is also spelt. Occasional grains and chaff comparable to emmer have been identified in a small number of contexts. The cereal was probably a contaminant of the spelt wheat crop. A small number of rounded grains comparable to free-threshing wheat (*Triticum aestivum sensu lato*) and hexaploid wheat rachis internodes (chaff) are present in two Phase III contexts.

Barley is consistently, but poorly, represented (Fig. 6.27). Of the 46 grains recovered, 17 are hulled, and there is a ratio of 3:2 for twisted to straight grains. The hulled six-row barley type *Hordeum vulgare* ssp. therefore appears present, and this is supported by a number of six-row barley rachis internodes. A single rachis internode of rye (*Secale cereale*) in the late Phase III ditch F.5214, indicates that it was at least present at Vicar's Farm.

It is unlikely that the proportions of charred cereal taxa are a true indication of their original importance. The majority of contexts are heavily dominated by spelt wheat chaff and appear to represent a very specific crop-processing by-product (see *Cereal Remains* above). The link between exposure to charring and glume wheat processing means that other free-threshing cereals, such as barley, could be under-represented. The low presence of barley grains and chaff probably denotes a contaminant within the deliberately charred wheat chaff; perhaps barley grew as a weed in fields where it had previously been cultivated. However, the one grain-rich charred context (postpipe F.5552) contained almost pure grain comparable to spelt wheat, so perhaps the dominance of spelt is a result both of its processing sequence and its central role in the site's economy.

The appearance of free-threshing wheat and rye in Phase III, coupled with a slight increase in proportions of barley, suggests that some diversification may have occurred. Both are cereals that became widely cultivated in southern Britain during the Anglo-Saxon period (Greig 1991). There is a marked lack of charred evidence for other economic plant types, with one Celtic bean (*Vicia faba*) in Iron Age pit F.5359, and occasional larger pulses (>4 mm) in the Roman contexts that could be peas but lack identifying characteristics. That the assemblage is an artefact of the later stages of spelt wheat processing explains why other economic taxa have not been recovered.

Charred Wild Plants

A broad range of wild seeds is present, the majority of which represent species characteristic of arable or disturbed land, and probably derive from weeds of the cereal crop. The remains consist of grain-sized or small, free and heavy seeds that are far fewer in number than the cereal remains. These are seed forms that, like the glume bases, would usually be removed during the later stages of cereal processing (Hillman 1984; G. Jones 1984). The grain-sized seeds, particularly of grasses, are difficult to remove by sieve

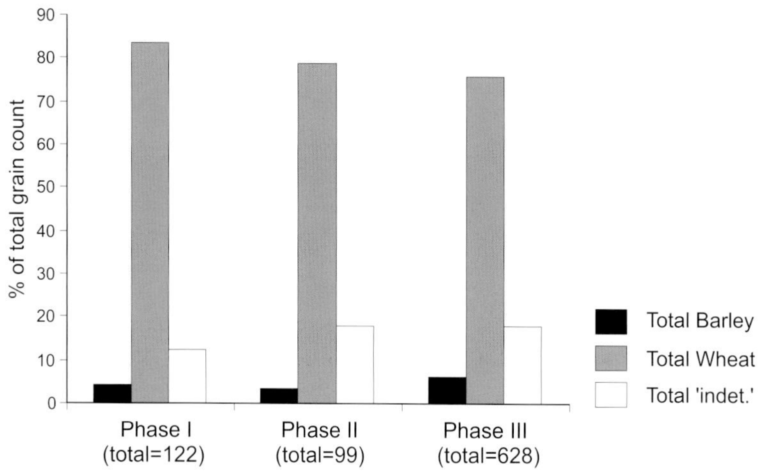

Figure 6.27. *Cereal grain represented within each phase (all contexts).*

Table 6.13. *Summary of the major charred wild seeds within all contexts (except [717]).*

Taxa	English name	Total no. seeds counted	No. of samples present
Anthemis cotula	stinking chamomile	176	20
Bromus spp.	brome grass	81	9
small *Trifolium* sp.	small-seeded clover <2 mm	59	18
Rumex sanguineus/ obstutifolius/ conglomeratus	small-seeded docks	53	11
Avena sp.	wild/cultivated oat	40	12
Atriplex patula/prostrata	common/spear-leaved orache	39	12
small *Vicia/Lathyrus* sp.	vetches/wild pea <2 mm	35	13
Phleum bertolonii	lesser cat's-tail	32	14
Lolium c.f. *multiflorum*	Italian rye-grass	31	4
Trifolium/Medicago sp.	clover/medick	26	5
large Poaceae indet.	grasses > 4 mm	26	4
medium *Vicia/Lathyrus* sp.	vetch/wild pea (2–4 mm)	27	9

cleaning, as they have a similar morphology to grain. With the exception of a sample from a mid fill of the F.5280 well ([717]) the wild taxa only represent seeds that survived the earlier crop-processing sequence until their removal and charring with the main chaff (glume base) component. The range of wild taxa is, therefore, strongly tied to the charring context and is a skewed representation of the original weed flora; the proportions of each taxon represent the influence of seed form during processing (Table 6.13).

The most significant taxon both in frequency and number is stinking chamomile (*Anthemis cotuld*). This plant indicates heavy, clayey soils, which corresponds well to the local conditions at Vicar's Farm. The other major wild plants represent several ecological groups, which provide information on the methods of cultivation. There are a number of large-seeded grasses, including brome (*Bromus* spp.) and oats (*Avena* sp.). A lack of oat chaff within the assemblage has prevented the identification of wild or cultivated types, so the species is either a well-represented weed or moderately represented cereal. Stevens (1996) has suggested that high grass contaminants within a cereal crop may be linked to a rotation system, whereby grasses from the fallow period subsequently grew as weeds within the next arable crop. There is good evidence for the expansion of Roman arable onto previously uncultivated lands, including meadows, and this could also have increased the number of grass weeds (*ibid.*).

Leguminous plants have an adaptive advantage as weeds in areas of low soil nutrients due to the ability of many to fix nitrogen. The consistent presence of clovers, vetches and wild peas at Vicar's Farm is therefore of importance. Stevens (1996) has linked the occurrence of numerous Fabaceae (Pea Family taxa) in Iron Age and Roman sites of the Upper Thames Valley to cultivation of seasonally flooded land and an increase in autumn sowing. The consistent, low numbers of sedges (*Carex* spp.) and spike-rush (*Eleocharis palustris*) within the assemblage at Vicar's Farm provides some support for this interpretation (Fig. 6.28, top). These taxa are only capable of growing on arable land if there is a seasonally high watertable (*ibid.*; M. Jones 1984). The leguminous plants, however, exist in contrast to others of Chenopodiaceae, particularly orache (*Atriplex patula/ prostrata*), which have an advantage on nitrogen-rich soils. It is possible that they represent the manuring of fields.

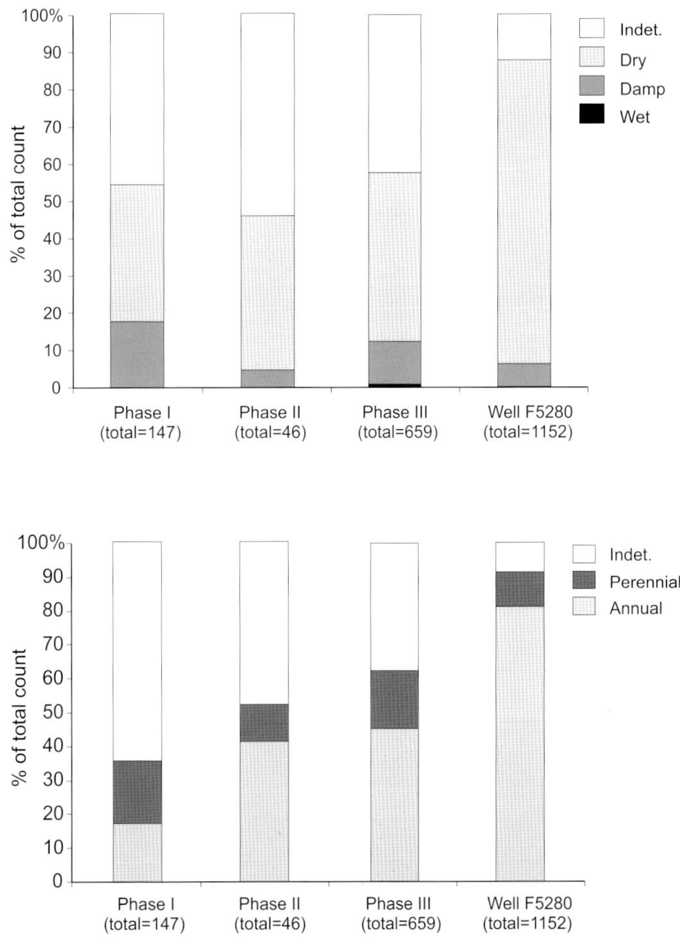

Figure 6.28. *Wild plants: ecology by phase ('rich' contexts; top); below, types by phase ('rich' contexts only).*

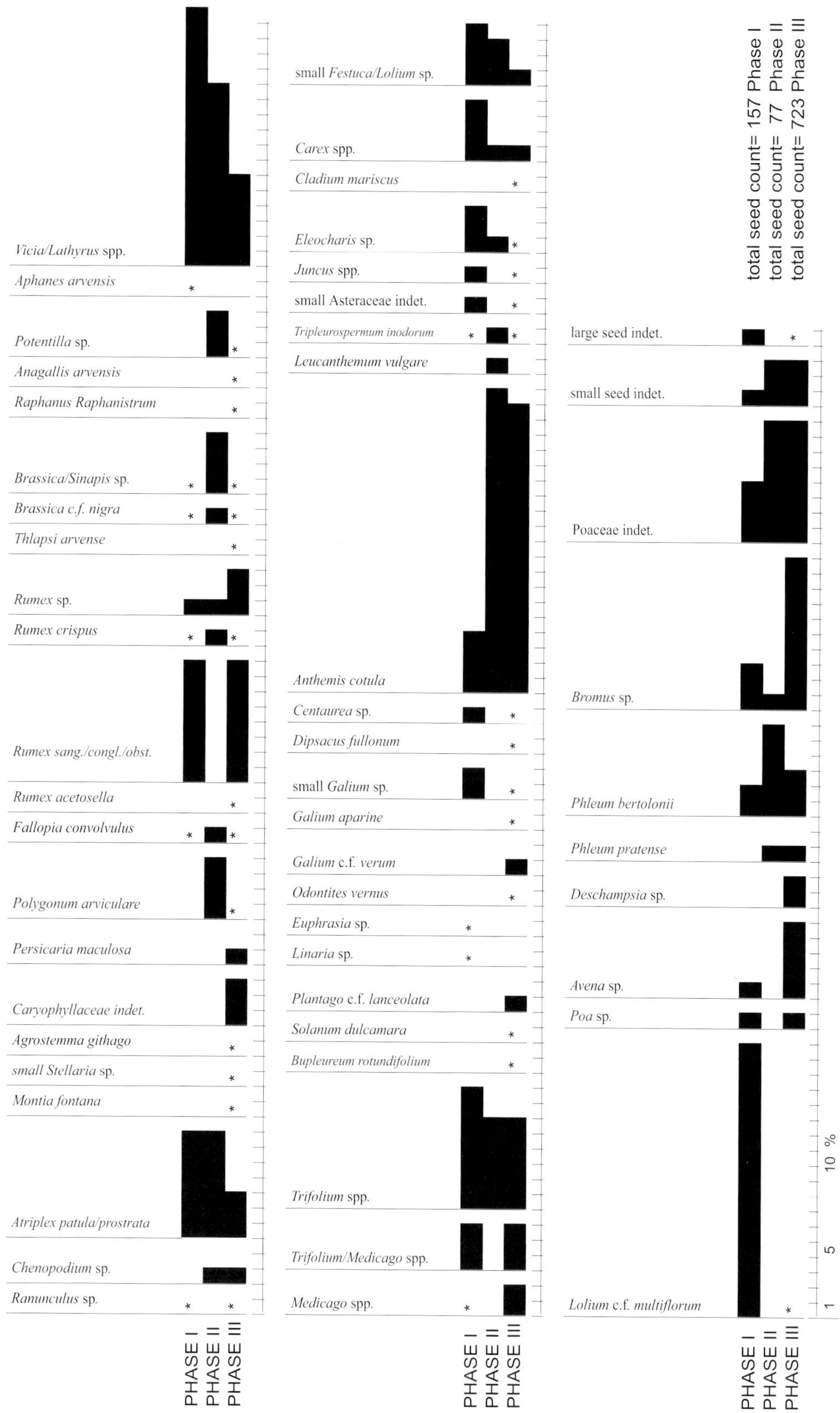

Figure 6.29. *Representation of wild plant taxa through time (all contexts except [717]).*

Some perennial plants, particularly docks (*Rumex* spp.), are associated more closely with ruderal, rather than arable conditions. Their deep tap-roots and vegetative regeneration are heavily affected by modern ploughing. However, ard tillage, which breaks the soil but does not turn it, allows many perennials to continue to grow. Perennial plant types are outnumbered by annuals at Vicar's Farm, but their continuous presence suggests that ard tillage was undertaken (Fig. 6.28, bottom). Both true sedges and spike-rush have rhizome systems and would also not be able to grow as an arable weed unless tillage occurred with an ard rather than a plough.

One exceptional context, well F.5280's mid fill ([717]), includes very high quantities of charred wild seeds (82% of its total count) with relatively small amounts of cereal remains. The context may represent debris from the fine sieve cleaning of a threshed and winnowed cereal crop, prior to the removal of glume wheat chaff by parching and pounding. There is a very high number of orache seeds (*c.* 800; *Atriplex patula/prostrata*). Orache, like many Chenopodiaceae, produces exceptionally large numbers of seeds per plant (Hanf 1983), so the high numbers within this sample could represent only a few plants collected with the harvest. Many of the taxa represented within F.5280's well occur repeatedly within other sampled contexts, and include docks and pea types (listed in Lucas & Whittaker 2001). Some other taxa are high only within this context: knotweed (*Polygonum arviculare*), a cow-parsley type (Apiaceae indet.), ribwort plantain (*Plantago lanceolata*) and scentless mayweed (*Tripleurospermum inodoruni*).

The Cultivation Regime

The wild seed assemblage clearly reflects cultivation upon clayey and occasionally wet soils, which could be expected in the local environment at Vicar's Farm. The continuous representation of one stage of crop-processing indicates that any fluctuations in wild taxa may thus represent changes in the arable conditions, rather than the actions of processing. When wild taxa at Vicar's Farm are broken down by site phase (Fig. 6.29) changes in the weed assemblage correspond well to sequences in the Upper Thames Valley (M. Jones 1984; Stevens 1996).

Martin Jones (1984) characterizes the weed ecology of the Iron Age to Roman periods by four major shifts within the Upper Thames Valley:

a) The gradual incorporation of new cereal crops: free-threshing wheats and rye
b) Appearance of stinking mayweed as a weed during the third/fourth century AD
c) Gradual reduction in legumes within weed floras during the Roman period
d) An accompanying rise in nitrophile weed taxa.

The assemblage at Vicar's Farm exhibits all these patterns to a degree and demonstrates that the arable regime was influenced by wider changes underway within southern Britain. Limited evidence for crop diversification is provided by the rye and hexaploid free-threshing wheat chaff recovered from Phase III contexts. As illustrated by Figure 6.29, there is a marked jump in the representation of stinking chamomile between Phases I and II, which coincides with the later second/third century AD. The weed is characteristic of heavy clay soils, and its increase suggests that marked expansion onto heavier soils occurred across southern Britain at this time (M. Jones 1991).

The fall in legume types at Vicar's Farm is reflected by vetch/wild pea types (*Vicia/Lathyrus* spp.), although clovers (*Trifolium* spp.) are only slightly reduced, and medick (*Medicago* spp.) actually increases. Whilst the nitrophile orache (*Atriplex patula/prostrata*) decreases with time, other goosefoots (*Chenopodium* spp.) only appear during Phases II and III. Increased manuring of land, possibly associated with the shift onto heavier soils, may account for the trend in weeds affected by soil fertility.

Overview

Many Roman sites in East Anglia are dominated by spelt wheat, and it appears to have been the major crop in the region (Murphy 1997b). Unfortunately, few comparable sites have been extensively sampled for charred plant remains. The fen-edge settlements of Maxey (Green 1985) and Stonea Grange (Van der Veen 1996) both exhibited poor preservation conditions, which severely limited subsequent interpretations. At both sites spelt wheat dominated; emmer occurred in earlier Roman phases but quickly ceased to be cultivated. Breadwheat and barley were also present in low quantities, and the range of Roman cereal crops appears to have been fairly uniform across the southern Fen region. Very low quantities of flax (*Linum usitatissimuni*) and lentil (*Lens culinaris*) were recovered at these two sites, evidence for which are lacking at Vicar's Farm. However, the Vicar's Farm assemblage is specifically associated with cereal processing and under-represents all other economic plant remains.

At Stonea Grange there was good evidence for the collection and use of wetland plants, particularly of sedges (*Cladium mariscus, Carex* spp.) and reeds (*Phragmites australis*). No evidence for such activities has been recovered at Vicar's Farm, where the very low quantities of wetland taxa probably represent arable weeds. Stonea Grange also contained charred remains from a much broader range of settings (not just associated with crop-processing) and included fig seeds (*Ficus culinaris*), which must have been brought to the site. Vicar's Farm lacks any evidence for 'exotic' types, and it seems the site was primarily involved with the processing of cereal products.

The arable regime at Vicar's Farm reflects patterns identified from well-preserved Roman weed floras in the Upper Thames Valley (Stevens 1996). Indeed, the expansion onto clay soils, which may have previously been grassland, appears to have occurred broadly in southern Britain during the first millennium AD.

The charred plant remains at Vicar's Farm are highly specific: they represent waste from the final stages of spelt wheat processing. The information provided by this assemblage is, therefore, limited to aspects of cereal husbandry and processing. Within the main enclosure, the de-husking of stored wheat was undertaken on a repeated basis. The crop was of local origin, as indicated by the weed ecology, and had grown up on heavy clay soils that in places were damp. Despite the good evidence for processing and nearby storage, other aspects of crop-processing are under-represented or absent. Neither charred remains of threshing and winnowing waste (particularly straw) have been found, nor physical evidence for threshing floors been recovered. These pre-storage activities may have been undertaken outside the excavated area or away from the site completely. At Maxey (Green 1985) there was a similar absence of earlier crop-processing stages. The absence may in part be processual, since winnowing by-products are far more susceptible to destruction by charring (Boardman & Jones 1990) if they are exposed to charring at all. However recent charred remains at Colne Fen (Ballantyne in Evans *et al.* 2013b, 391–414) include rich, charred winnowing by-products, so the complete absence of such waste at Vicar's Farm may partially be due to a lack of such activities on-site.

Charred grain-rich contexts, possibly denoting debris from ovens or hearths where grain may have been accidentally charred are also absent. The only such context recovered is postpipe F.5552 (Structure D). Other 'food-preparation' charred debris may have been cleared onto middens or omitted from the sampling programme (although the latter is unlikely). There is a clear disparity between the very good evidence for grain storage, dehusking (charred remains) and milling (quernstones) at Vicar's Farm, and the absence of actual food-preparation debris. The identification of 'consumer' and 'producer' sites is archaeologically difficult and can potentially be oversimplifying (Van der Veen 1991; 1996). However, at Vicar's Farm *there is far more evidence for grain storage and flour production than there is for actual consumption*. It could be suggested that the site was a locus for the storage and processing of locally grown cereals, particularly spelt wheat, of which the surplus was transported elsewhere as flour.

Animal Husbandry Andy Clarke

In much the same way as in the previous section, here the focus is primarily upon economic patterns: the management of the settlement's livestock and not the ritual deployment of animal remains.

Cattle

The remains of cattle dominate the Roman assemblage and would appear to be the mainstay of the settlement's economy. Unfortunately, the form of this economy is somewhat elusive, as the levels of cattle bone recovered are themselves fairly low until Phase III. The cattle remains recovered in the preceding phases provide only tentative clues as to the form of cattle exploitation practised; however, the evidence that has been recovered does point to a cattle economy being established in Phase I and maintained throughout the life of the settlement. Tables 6.14 and 6.15 (also Fig. 6.30, top) show the data recovered relating to age at death estimations from bone fusion and dental wear. During Phase I, it would seem that a small number of animals died within their first year, while the rest were left until they reached prime age before being slaughtered. With this indication of beef production established early on, the pattern is continued and extended by the final phases of the occupation. The data from Phase III shows that the husbandry was geared towards beef production. However, there is also evidence of fully adult and old-age cattle. This would suggest that during the settlement's final phases (II/III), cattle were being bred for traction as well as meat.

Table 6.14. *Fusion data (% unfused) for cattle by phase.*

	I	II	III
Foetal	-	-	2.0
<1 yr	20.0	-	3.2
<2 yrs	-	12.5	3.1
<3 yrs	33.3	12.5	6.7
<4 yrs	30.0	41.0	23.6

Table 6.15. *Mandibular stage data (MNI) for cattle by phase.*

	I	II	III
0–1 m	-	-	–
1–8 m	-	-	1
8–18 m	1	2	3
18–30 m	-	2	4
30–36 m	-	1	3
Young adult	1	-	3
Adult	1	-	10
Old adult	-	2	10
Senile	-	-	-

In addition to the ageing data pointing to beef production, there is also a limited amount of evidence that suggests that a surplus of meat was being produced. Of all the skeletal elements recovered displaying signs of butchery, scapulae are the most common, and they display evidence of being butchered in a particular way. Some of the glenoid cavities show chop marks, as do several of the spinae. In addition, some of the blades of the scapulae have repeated nick marks. Together, these marks indicate that beef was being preserved on the bone, possibly by brining (glenoid and spine trimmed to allow the salt to permeate to the meat next to the bone) or by smoking. The nick marks on the blade of the bone are the possible result of the last pieces of preserved meat being shaved off. It has been suggested that such bone waste is a strong indication of a professional butcher specializing in the production of preserved meat and raising the possibility of trade in beef off the bone (Dobney 2001). This may well have been the case at Vicar's Farm, but it could equally indicate a preferred manner of beef consumption on-site. Certainly, it need not necessarily indicate surplus production.

Sheep

The second-most prevalent species, sheep bones were recovered from all phases, but in significantly fewer numbers than the remains of cattle. This, however, may be the result of a taphonomic bias, due to carnivore gnawing destroying more of the less robust sheep remains. The anatomical representation shows that in each phase of occupation most bones of the skeleton are represented, but there is a definite prevalence of the more robust elements. Assuming that the economy of the site centred on cattle production, then what was the economic function of sheep? As with the ageing data retrieved for cattle, the age at death estimation for sheep is limited and mostly comes from Phase III, but once again there are hints of a breeding programme that was established at the beginning of the settlement and continued throughout its occupation.

Tables 6.16 and 6.17 (and Fig. 6.30, bottom) show that in Phase I lambs were allowed to mature a little before being slaughtered in their second or third years, with a very few allowed to reach full adulthood. Although there is limited ageing data, this interpretation is reinforced by the data from the site's later phases. In Phase II,

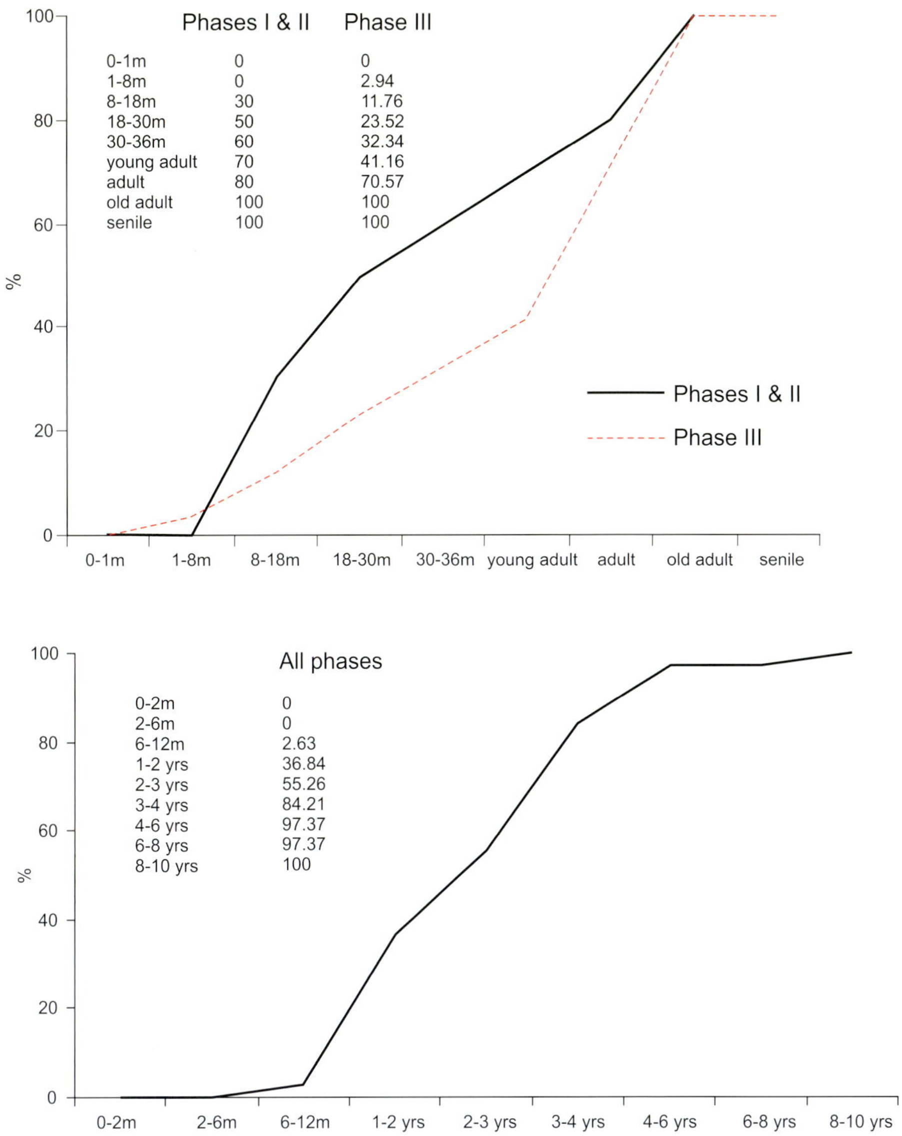

Figure 6.30. *Stock mortality curves: cattle for Phases I–II and III (top); below, sheep (all phases combined).*

most of the animals survived beyond their first year and the rest were, again, slaughtered in their second or third years. By Phase III there is more data and a much clearer pattern emerges, the same as is hinted at in Phase I. Most of the sheep were killed in their second or third years, while a smaller number were allowed to live to full maturity. The pattern that emerges from the sheep-ageing data is one of a mixed economy producing meat and wool. Some sheep did not survive their first year, either due to early slaughter or not making it through their first winter. The remaining lambs were either killed when their meat is at its best (second or third years) or they were allowed to mature to an age where they could help maintain the flock size and produce a good quality fleece.

Table 6.16. *Fusion data (% unfused) for sheep by phase.*

	I	II	III
Foetal	-	40.0	-
<1 yr	-	33.3	9.5
<2 yrs	-	-	1.7
<3 yrs	-	20.0	5.8
<4 yrs	-	-	22.2

Table 6.17. *Mandibular stage data (MNI) for sheep by phase.*

	I	II	III
0–2 m	-	-	-
2–6 m	-	-	-
6–12 m	-	-	1
1–2 yrs	2	1	9
2–3 yrs	-	3	3
3–4 yrs	2	1	7
4–6 yrs	1	-	4
6–8 yrs	-	-	-
8–10 yrs	1	-	-

Pigs

If the total number of specimens (NISP) recovered per species were viewed in isolation, it would seem that pigs are the most common species on the site. This, however, is a bias caused by one large deposit. Over one thousand foetal pig bones were recovered from a single context ([1749], F.5499), accounting for at least 10 individual piglets. All appeared to be articulated and showed no signs of being butchered. The piglets were recovered from a ditch terminal in the main enclosure of Area A. What this deposit shows is that pigs were being bred, at least to a limited extent, on site. The high level of preservation of these probable still-borns indicates that the piglets were buried quite rapidly. Such small fragile bones would surely not have survived the attentions of dogs and other scavengers, considering the high percentage of gnawed bone recorded generally.

The group of piglets from Area A evinces that pig husbandry was practised on the site in Phase II. Unfortunately, the small number of pig bones recovered from the subsequent occupation phase has very little to offer in the way of interpretative data. A limited number of age at death estimates were recorded in Phase III, which point to the majority of animals being killed while still juvenile and only a small number allowed to reach maturity (Table 6.18). Despite the limited quantity of pig remains, the presence of foetal bones and the pattern displayed by the ageing data, combined with fact that pigs do not provide any secondary products, indicates that pigs were being bred and consumed on a limited scale for their meat.

Goats

The remains of goats were even more scarce that those of pigs, coming from the later phases of the occupation and amounted to only seven fragments. This low level of recovery can do little more than confirm their presence during Phases II and III.

Horses

The remains of horse that were present on the site originate from all phases of occupation and were found in all of the settlement's areas. Once again, it is Phase III that produced the greatest amount of data. Horses were certainly eaten, as well as used for traction/riding. Evidence for the former comes from cut marks indicative of dismemberment (F.5321) and, for the latter, from a case of pathology where a first and second phalange are fused together (F.5470). Such a case could be promoted by excessive stress (i.e. work), causing the formation of extra bone and leading to the fusion of these two bones. Apart from the obvious use of being ridden, it is also possible that this animal was used for traction or as a beast of burden. In Phase II there is further evidence for the butchery of horses from a skull (F.5274) and a pelvis (F.5479), which showed cut marks indicative of the primary and secondary butchery of a carcass. In the final phase of the site, there are still the tell-tale signs of butchery indicating that horses were consumed.

Table 6.18. *Aging data for pig for Phase III.*

% unfused	
Foetal	5.8
<1 yr	-
<2 yrs	25.0
<3 yrs	-
<4 yrs	10.7
Mandibular Stage	
Neonate	-
Immature	-
Subadult	2
Adult	1
Elderly	2

Dogs

Considering the high level of gnawed bone recorded on the site, it is not surprising that the remains of dogs are present throughout its occupation. The skeletal elements recovered come from throughout the skeleton and there does not appear to be any patterning within their deposition. It is an accepted that the Romans were responsible for the introduction of different dog breeds to Britain (Harcourt 1974). This is reflected in the elements recovered; especially the limb bones that show marked differences in size, indicating the presence of different breeds on site. No doubt each breed served a different purpose, such as guarding livestock or hunting, in accordance with documentary evidence of the set ideas Romans had on what breed of dog should be used for which task (Clutton-Brock 1987).

Deer

The remains of deer recovered are limited but occurred in every phase. The majority consist of shed, fragmented antlers, some of which show evidence of their being used as a raw material (see Figs 6.15.3 and 6.26.1). A small number of deer bones were recovered, which were identified as Red deer (one metapodial and two radii) and Roe deer (one mandible and a tibia). It is difficult to glean much interpretative data from this small collection. Yet, the fact that there are very few deer bones on site, combined with the cut marks seen on the antler and on one of the Red deer radii, suggests that antler was imported onto the site as a raw material, along with the occasional joint of venison.

Other Mammals

The remaining mammal species recovered take the form of isolated and fragmentary bones from cat, badger and fox, all recovered from Phase III. Apart from the cat, which is no doubt domestic, the other mammals found are not considered to be anthropogenic in origin.

Birds

The bird bone recovered from the site is in very good condition; therefore, it is somewhat surprising that their numbers were so low. It may be that bird species had very little contribution to make to the overall economy of the site; but considering the high level of gnawing recorded (see Table 4.20) and the fragility of bird bone, a more likely explanation is one of taphonomic bias. The most common bird species on the site, unsurprisingly, was the domestic chicken. During Phase I, two of the cremations within the cemetery also included chicken bones (F.5305 & F.5307). Only a single chicken bone was recovered from Phase II, but by the time of Phase III this figure rises to 86 bones, almost all of which originated from a single deposit in a pit that contained the remains of at least two individuals (F.5656). The elements recovered were not articulated and the majority are those that hold the most meat on a jointed-up carcass; this deposit is, therefore, viewed – as are the other chicken remains – as probable meal waste. Phase III also produced a small number of isolated bones belonging to goose, a duck species (probably mallard) and rook. The former two are most likely the remains of animals kept and consumed on the site, while the latter is not considered as anthropogenic.

Overview

The Vicar's Farm assemblage of faunal remains presents a sizeable amount of interpretative data relating to the socio-economic patterns at the site. There is unambiguous evidence of an organized system of husbandry that is centred around cattle, with a lesser role played by sheep and possibly pigs. Further to this,

Table 6.19. *Proportion of main domesticates from three Roman sites.*

Species	New Hall		Vicar's Farm		Orton Hall Farm	
	NISP	%	NISP	%	NISP	%
Cow	391	51.0	1152	59.4	1814	60.5
Pig	34	4.4	45	2.3	95	3.2
Sheep/goat	252	32.8	404	20.9	1005	33.5
Horse	88	11.5	318	16.4	85	2.8
Fowl	2	0.3	19	1.0	-	-

the assemblage has also indicated the organization of activities that reached beyond the daily, domestic routine.

The generally accepted view of the dietary preferences of the average Roman is that, at least where meat was concerned, pork was the most popular choice. However, the evidence from most sites dating to the Romano-British period appears to dispute this accepted view (Dobney 2001). In her review of 10 Iron Age and Romano-British sites located on the Welsh borders and in Yorkshire, Noddle (1984) demonstrates that cattle and sheep were the most prevalent species, with cattle gradually becoming more and more popular through time. This preference for cattle repeats itself in the southeast of Roman Britain, on sites in the same geographical region as Vicar's Farm. A prime example is that of the Romano-British farmstead of Orton Hall Farm (Mackreth 1996). The site produced an animal bone assemblage of similar size and range to Vicar's Farm (Table 6.19). The major domestic species dominated and were accompanied by horse, dog and cat, together with a few wild species. The analysis carried out on this assemblage revealed that the economy of the site was mainly dependent on cattle and sheep, exploiting them for their secondary products as well as their meat. Sheep were kept for wool and a limited amount of meat. But it was cattle that made the major dietary contribution throughout the life of the settlement, with stock being bred, reared, slaughtered and consumed on site. Pigs, it would seem, made little contribution to the site economy.

This pattern (or indications of it, depending on the size of the excavation) is seen on sites from all over the eastern region of Roman Britain, such as Spong Hill (Rickett 1995), Chignall Roman Villa (Clarke 1998), Colne Fen's settlements (Evans *et al.* 2013b) and New Hall (see Chap. 3 above). Of these sites, it is the latter that gives some indication as to the function of the domestic activities revealed at Vicar's Farm. The analysis of the faunal remains recovered from the Romano-British phase of the New Hall Site revealed an assemblage that was dominated, in order of prevalence, by cattle, sheep and, then, pig. The results of the Vicar's Farm analysis show that there was an organized system of husbandry, with cattle being bred for their meat, sheep for meat and wool and small-scale pork production. Added to the data on the husbandry practices, the anatomical representation seen at Vicar's Farm for the three major domestics shows that these animals were being bred, butchered and probably consumed on-site. However, there are indications that its economy extended beyond self-sufficiency. The remains of pig are very low and limited to either very young or mature animals. Given their location and the character of their assemblages, it is not unreasonable to suggest that the New Hall settlement could, in theory, have even been supplied with pigs of prime age from Vicar's Farm (see Yannouli, Chap. 3).

This argument is supported by further evidence from the cattle remains. As mentioned above, articulated cattle limbs were recovered, displaying cut marks indicative of the filleting of meat. Added to this, there is also evidence of the preservation of beef on the bone, a practice that could suggest a surplus of meat on site. It is possible that these fillets and preserved cuts of meat were being exported off-site. However, there is no sense in which the faunal assemblage at Vicar's Farm displays a classic 'producer pattern', dominated by waste bones, although both the sale of meat 'on the hoof' or meat off the bone would not exhibit this typical pattern. It should also be noted that there is very little evidence of hide production or horn-working in the Vicar's Farm assemblage. There is, however, extensive evidence of the exploitation of secondary products at New Hall.

From the evidence presented above, a possible picture of life in Roman Cambridge's hinterland is formed. The inhabitants of Vicar's Farm produced and consumed as much meat as they needed, while the rest – either fresh or preserved – was sold or exchanged on site to the inhabitants of other nearby communities. It is clear, then, that the domestic side of life at Vicar's Farm was highly organized and adhered to the Romano-British norm of a cattle-based economy. From the evidence presented above, it appears that *Vicar's Farm was certainly not a small isolated, self-sufficient farmstead.*

There was an organized system of animal husbandry that not only provided enough food for the site, but also produced a surplus of meat and, as such, it was a centre for trade and exchange of animal goods with contemporaries in Roman Cambridge. Patterns of animal consumption will be dealt with further below.

Consumption

Here the concern is with interrelating the settlements' food remains and vessel forms – both glass and ceramics – for what they can tell concerning 'taste' and the manner of food preparation, consumption and its service.

Pottery (with Gwladys Monteil)

Understanding the use of pottery is usually fairly unproblematic. There were no kilns on the site, so we can be sure that most pottery vessels, when not accompanying burials, were used and broken in the course of culinary activities. There is some evidence for the reuse of broken pottery vessels, such as for gaming counters or spindlewhorls (Fig. 6.32.10). The most interesting is, perhaps, the reuse of (the bases?) of large storage jars as ovens; several sherds from storage jars show interior sooting, suggesting they may have been used like tandooris (i.e. small clay ovens). At sites such as Elms Farm and Chelmsford, such vessels have been found set in the ground (Atkinson & Preston 1998, 107 and 2015, 42, pl. 3.4).

The typical and full repertoire of pottery vessels is present on the site, and all stages of culinary practice are clearly represented: storage, food preparation and service, and drinking (see Figs. 6.31–6). Table 6.20 and Figure 6.37 show the vessel forms broken down by phase (the cremation vessels have been excluded, as they bias the statistics that are based on EVEs). The first thing to note is that there is an obvious and dramatic increase in vessel usage over time. Indeed, the quantities more or less *double* between Phase I and II, and then *double again* between Phase II and III (calibrating the quantity against duration, as each phase occupies slightly different time spans). This change could be due to various reasons; it may reflect population increase or, simply, reflect changes in culinary practice.

The settlement expanded quite substantially over time, especially in Phase III. The amount of labour involved simply in digging the ditches might well itself suggest an increased population, but more generally, there is more of everything: finds, features and space. This suggests that the population – resident or visiting the site – increased over time. However, this does not preclude the possibility that culinary practices also underwent change. Certainly, there are some changes in assemblage composition over time. Flagons and cups, for example, exhibit a major drop between Phase I and II as a proportion of the overall assemblage, suggesting that there was a significant change in drinking habits by the end of the second/beginning of the third century AD. Beakers show an

Table 6.20. *Vessel forms by phase (EVEs).*

	Phase I (AD 80–180)		Phase II (AD 180–270)		Phase III (AD 270–410)	
Form	**EVEs**	%	**EVEs**	%	**EVEs**	%
Drinking vessels						
Flagon	2.00	14.91	1.61	6.32	5.02	5.41
Beaker	-	0.00	1.02	4.00	1.55	1.67
Cup	0.21	1.57	0.1	0.39	0.36	0.39
Food vessels						
Platter	0.05	0.37	-	0.00	-	0.00
Dish	1.00	7.46	3.78	14.84	16.00	17.24
Bowl	0.77	5.74	3.78	14.84	13.66	14.72
Jar	8.58	63.98	12.89	50.61	43.97	47.38
Lid	0.05	0.37	0.41	1.61	1.68	1.81
Mortarium	0.15	1.12	0.88	3.46	3.83	4.13
Storage jar	0.55	4.10	0.95	3.73	6.18	6.66
Unidentified						
Open form	0.05	0.37	-	0.00	0.17	0.18
Closed form	-	0.00	0.05	0.20	0.39	0.42
Total	*13.41*	*100.00*	*25.47*	*100.00*	*92.81*	*100.00*

Figure 6.31. *Pottery distributions: samian (left) and, right, amphorae and mortaria.*

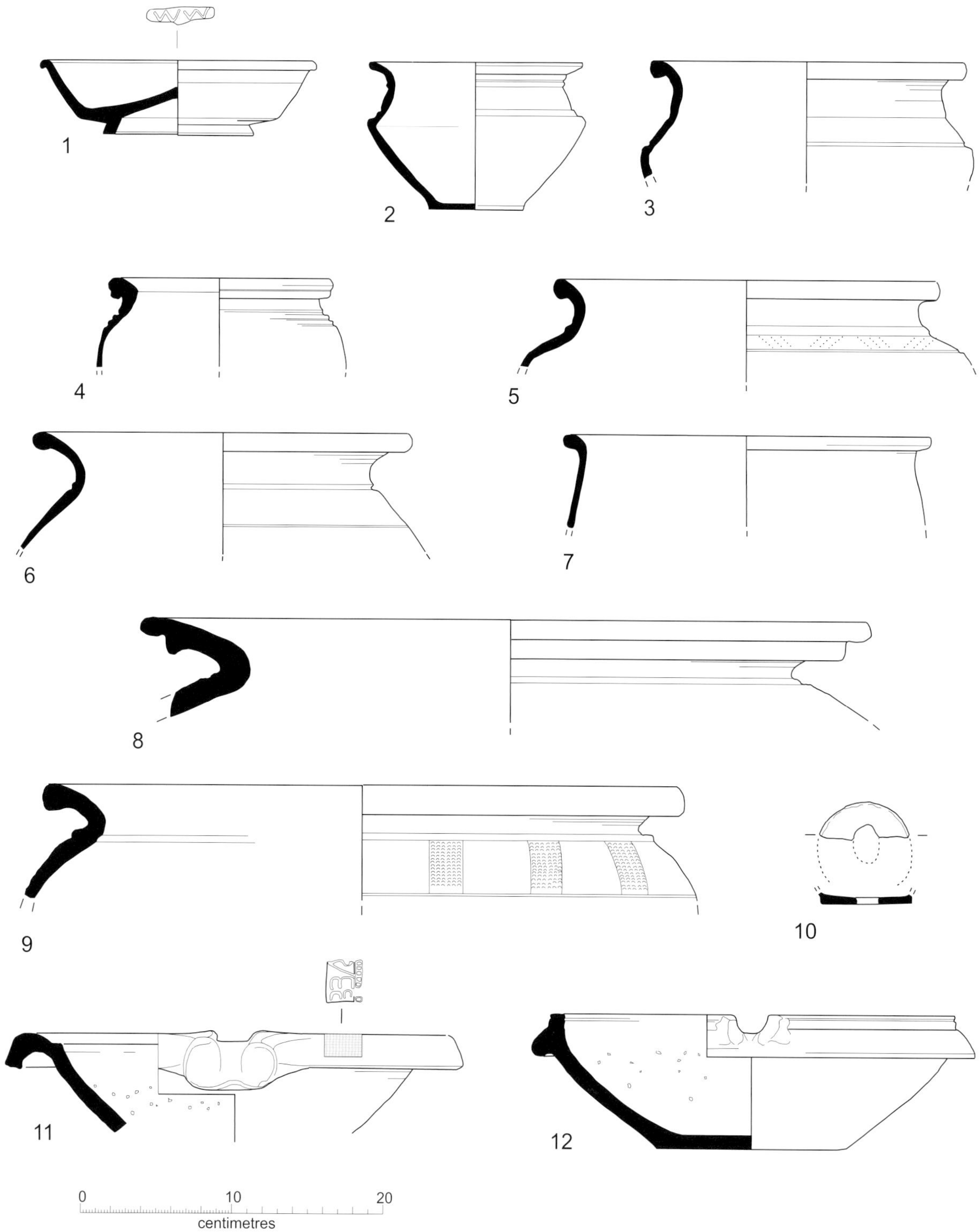

Figure 6.32. *Phase I pottery vessels.*

inverse rise (chiefly in Phase II), but they never occur in substantial numbers. Jars decrease slightly, and this is probably related to the rise over time in dishes and bowls, which more or less triple as a proportion of the assemblage in Phase II and III compared to Phase I, while mortaria also exhibit a steady rise over time. This suggests that changes in drinking practices may have been linked to other changes in food practices; in

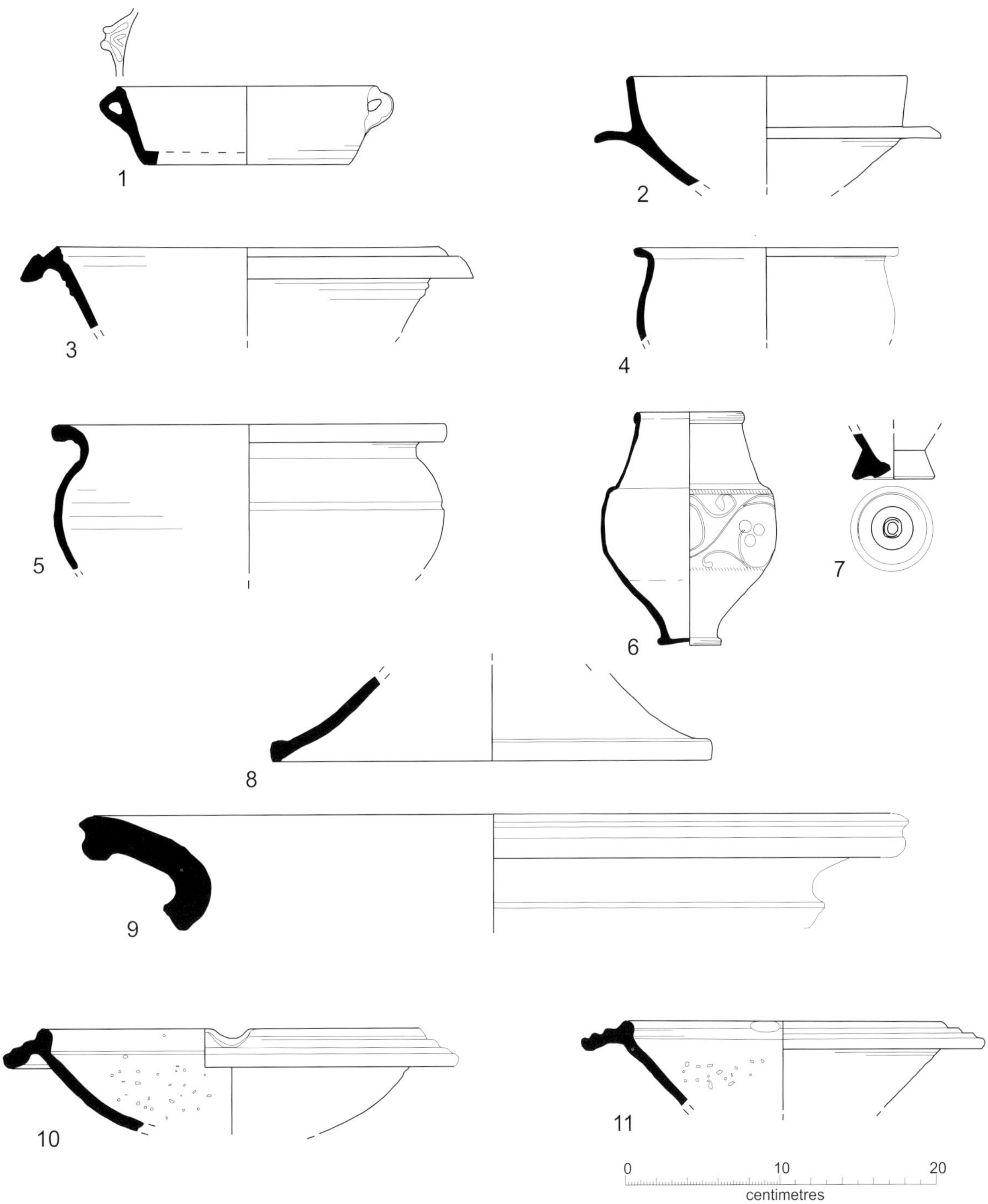

Figure 6.33. *Phase II pottery vessels.*

other words, the culinary field was being transformed in some manner.

Can we qualify this change further? Attributing function to vessels is not always straightforward; even forgetting the problems inherent in reuse, many vessels could be used for different things. Jars can be for cooking or storage, bowls and dishes for serving or cooking. Certain forms, on the other hand, are more specific: flagons, cups, beakers, storage jars, mortaria and amphorae can all be generally associated with certain activities. Storage jars do not exhibit much variation over time as a proportion of the assemblage,

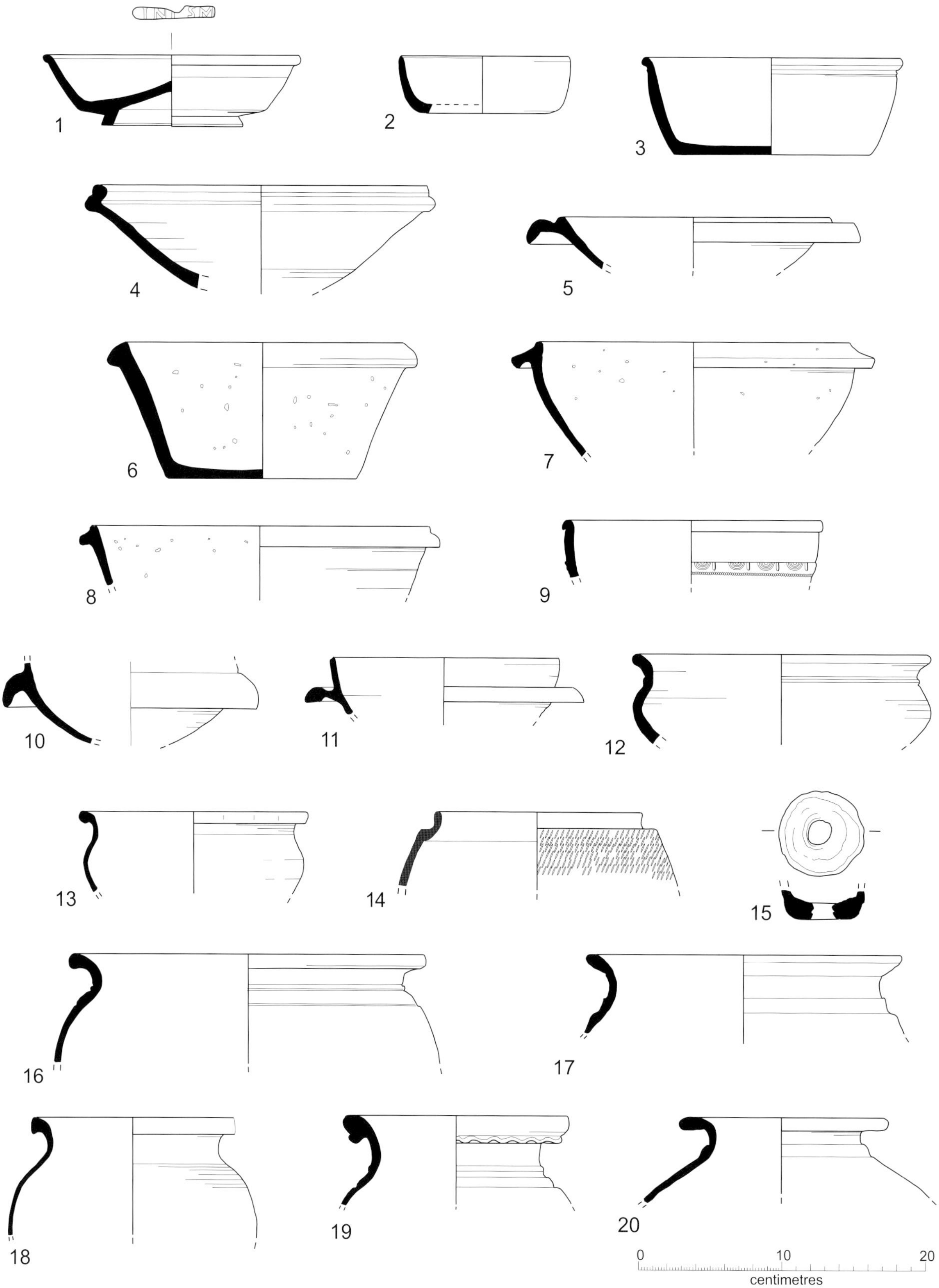

Figure 6.34. *Phase III pottery vessels (dishes and bowls).*

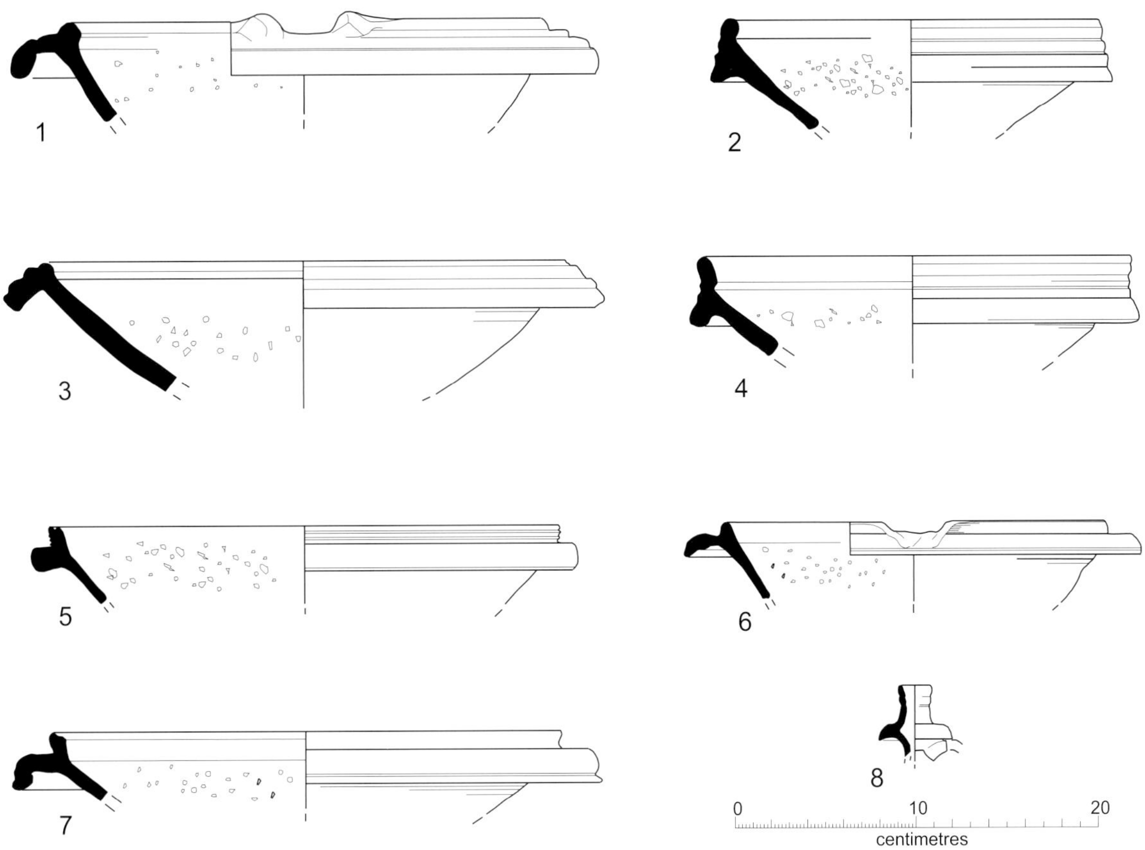

Figure 6.35. *Phase III pottery vessels (jars and mortaria).*

but as we have already pointed out, mortaria increase, while flagons and cups decline. This might suggest that the preparation of food was becoming a more important part of the settlement's culinary practices, while formal drinking declined. This can be independently tested by looking at the proportion of vessels used in cooking; here we cannot rely on form (see above), but instead can use the presence of sooting on the pot to indicate whether the vessel has been used for cooking. When we do this, we see that the number of vessels with sooting residues does increase at a steady rate over time (Table 6.21); moreover, while only jars have sooting residues recorded on them in Phases I and II, in Phase III bowls, and especially dishes, also appear to have been used in cooking. This suggests not only changes in the importance, but also in the methods, of food preparation.

It is hard to say whether this decline in formal drinking might be part of a wider decline in formal dining; one cannot assume that the lack of cooking residues on vessels such as bowls and dishes, for example, is indicative of a service use, nor can one rely on fabric. Finewares increased over time, but this is a regional (if not national) phenomenon and the term 'fineware' is not synonymous with service or tablewares, since many of the forms are identical whether in colour-coated or greyware, and colour-coated vessels also show signs of use in cooking. Although the level of residuality and intrusiveness seems quite high throughout all phases, the changing level of finewares over time seems quite typical of the region (Perrin 1996, 177; Ellis *et al.* 1998, 78–9): it increases regularly to over 25 per cent in the third and fourth centuries AD. The dominance of Nene Valley colour-coated products (35% of the finewares) is

Table 6.21. *Vessels with sooting residues (in EVEs).*

	Phase I	Phase II	Phase III
Jar	0.29	1.31	4.57
Bowl	-	-	0.18
Dish	-	-	0.56
Total	*0.29*	*1.31*	*5.31*
% of total assemblage	*4.70*	*10.90*	*14.60*

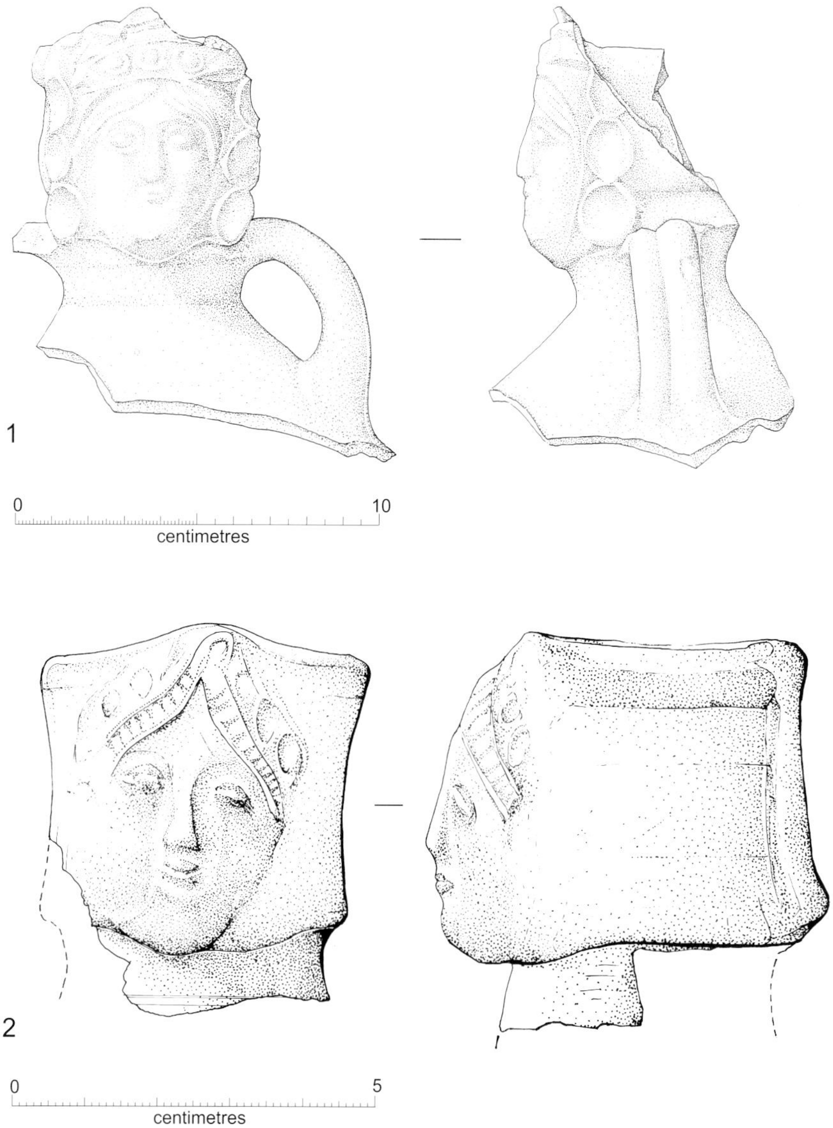

Figure 6.36. *Face pots: 1) F.5006; 2) F.5722 (see also Fig. 6.47).*

again typical of the region, when the industry flooded the local market in the third and fourth centuries AD with a range of forms previously produced in coarseware (*ibid.* and J. Evans 2001, 30–1; also see below). These late forms might, therefore, not belong to the category of tableware, but could have assumed a more cooking-orientated purpose (several examples were found with burnt external surfaces, especially flanged and plain-rimmed 'dog' dishes).

If the patterns suggest a decline in formal dining and a more 'kitchen'-oriented practice of drinking and eating, this could imply many different things, such as a change in the composition and/or status of the population, or a change in cultural attitudes to eating and drinking. A similar change in the patterns of eating and drinking over time in terms of public and private spheres has been argued for Barton Court Farm, Oxfordshire (Meadows 1997). Such changes may also be reflected in different attitudes and values pertaining to ceramic vessels and this is most clearly seen in the choice of grave-goods. The early cremations, for example, are frequently interred with accompanying ceramics. While the cremated bone itself is often placed within a jar, there are accessory vessels in five out of the site's nine cremations. In all five cases, these include flagons, and in one case also a beaker and dish. Compared with the inhumation cemetery, where there are only three instances of accompanying ceramics as grave-goods out of a total of 29/30 burials, this suggests quite a change in attitudes to ceramics: minimally in terms of their preference as offerings in graves, but with possibly wider connotations about the general value of such objects in the community. Certainly, the preference for drinking and service wares

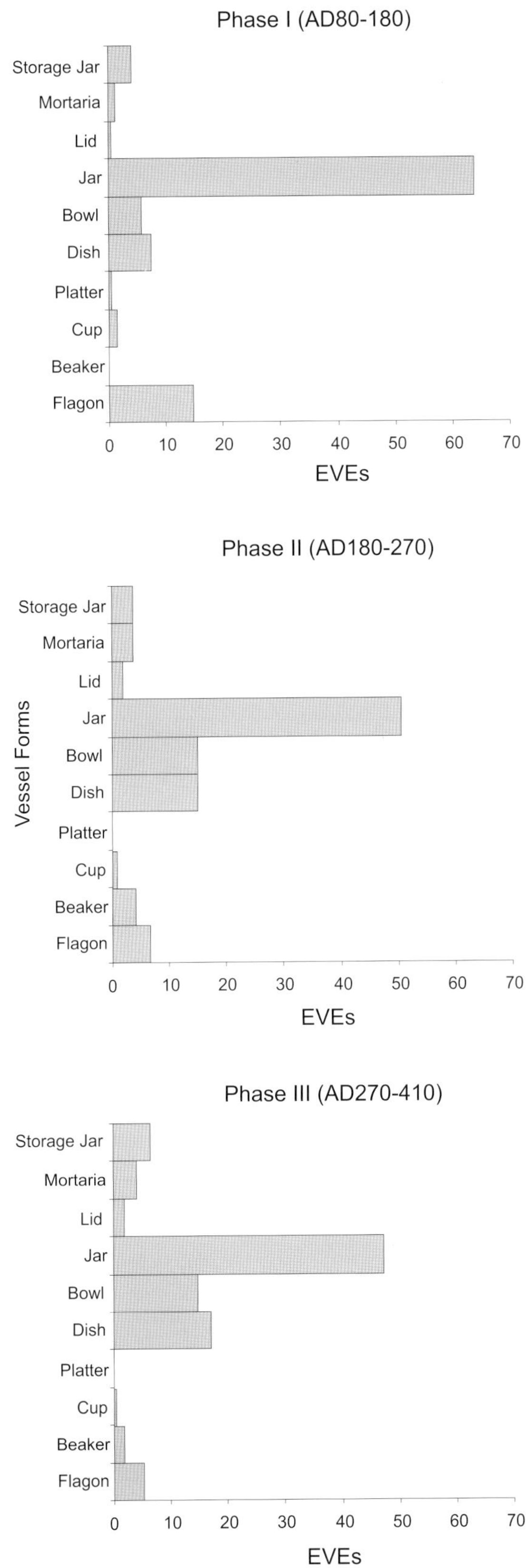

Figure 6.37. *Pottery assemblage composition by phase.*

as grave-goods is significant in the light of this decline in the use of such vessels in later phases, both across the site as a whole and as grave-goods.

Glass Vessels H.E.M. Cool

Two fragments of vessel glass were found in (non-burial) Phase II contexts, neither of which can be closely identified as to form. One, <4335>, comes from a colourless wheel-cut beaker, a type that was in use from the later first century AD to the mid second century AD, and was most common in the second century AD (Cool & Price 1995, 79). The neck fragment (<1643>) may be dated to the first to third century AD because of its colour.

<4333> *F.5280* - Beaker. Colourless. Body fragment, straight side curving out to (missing) rim. Horizontal wheel-cut groove on upper body. Dimensions 26 × 16 mm. Wall thickness 1 mm.

<1643> *F.5483* - Jug or flask. Blue/green. Cylindrical neck fragment. Length 22 mm.

The vessel glass from the Phase III contexts divides into two categories. The first is clearly residual, as it consists of fragments of square and prismatic bottles (<4336>, <950> & <1080>) dating to the later first to early to mid third centuries (Isings Form 51 [1957]; Price & Cottam 1998, 194–200). The second category may be dated to the fourth century AD. The only form that can be identified with anything approaching certainty is <4337>, which came from the range of cylindrical bottles and flasks that were in use at the time (see, e.g. Price & Cottam 1998, 184, 204–7). The vessels from which the body fragments (<4338>, <4335> & <4011>) came are most likely to have been drinking vessels judging from their thinness.

The counter, <4329>, is also a fourth-century AD form and there is some evidence that these may have been a later fourth-century AD development (Cool 2000, 52). The marvered spots of colour surrounding the central red spot were probably originally blue (see, e.g., Clarke 1979, pl. Ib). These counters appear to be most common within Britain, although they are occasionally found on Continental sites (Cool & Price 1987, 123–4), and there is a distinct possibility that they could have been a Romano-British development.

<4336> *F.649* - Square bottle. Blue/green. Base fragment. Base design at least two concentric circular mouldings. Dimensions 35 × 30 mm. Bottle width *c.* 80 mm., diameter of outer moulding 60 mm (Fig. 6.38.1).

<950> *F.5353* - Prismatic bottle. Blue/green body fragment.

<1080> *F.5428* - Prismatic bottle. Blue/green body fragment.

<4337> *F.5289* - Cylindrical bottle or flask. Pale greenish colourless; many small bubbles. Lower body and base fragment; vertical side with slight concavity above flat base. Base diameter 75 mm, present height 20 mm, wall thickness 3 mm (Fig. 6.38.3).

Figure 6.38. *Glass: vessels from non-burial contexts (1–3; see text); 4) counter (F.5603); 5) bath flask from Cremation 2 (F.5119).*

<4338> F.5427 - Body fragment. Yellow/green; small bubbles.

<4335> F.5006 - Body fragment. Greenish, colourless, bubbly.

<4011> F.5414 - Body fragment. Pale green; many small bubbles.

<4329> F.5603 - Counter. Very dark glass appearing black. Plano-convex with potted base. Three large circular heavily decayed dots of ?white opaque glass with central oval opaque red dot. Diameter 18 × 16.5 mm, thickness 5 mm (Fig. 6.38.4).

Of the two unphased fragments of glass, only <4341> needs special comment as it is good evidence that occupation at the settlement continued into the later fourth century AD. Beakers with fire-rounded rims like this are a mid fourth- to early fifth-century AD form (Price & Cottam 1998, 129). The other fragment, <4070>, is another example of a prismatic bottle of the later first to early third century AD.

<4070> F.5033 - Prismatic bottle. Blue/green. Base fragment. Base design includes at least one circular moulding. Dimensions 33 × 14 mm.

<4341> F.4178 (Surface find) - Beaker. Light green; many small bubbles. Rim fragment, rim bent out, edge fire rounded; slightly convex-curved body sloping in. Rim diameter 65 mm, present height 20 mm, wall thickness 0.5 mm (Fig. 6.38.2).

Food Remains (with Andy Clarke)

Food remains are somewhat problematic to study. Given the discussion on production above, while both cereals and meat were consumed on the site, cereals and possibly meat were also produced for an external market. Accordingly, distinguishing butchery or crop-processing for on-site consumption as against export is probably impossible, if not even pointless, as there may not have been a distinction. In terms of actual food remains (i.e. as opposed to waste by-products), hardly any actual cereal grains survive (most were probably milled to flour), and we cannot even assume that bones from meat-bearing elements represent food consumed on-site, as the meat may have been exported off the bone. Nevertheless, it is worthwhile commenting on the evidence for butchery and the consumption of animal carcasses.

The evidence of butchery is low considering the size of the assemblage. The majority of butchery evidence takes the form of chop marks or breaks resulting from the initial dismembering of a carcass into joints of meat. Much less common are those cut marks indicative of the filleting of meat from the bone. Cutting into the bone is unnecessary for filleting and results in wasted energy, so it is possible that the low number of observed cut marks is due to the presence of an experienced butcher. Those bones that do display cut marks, such as several horse and cow scapulae, provide evidence for the

Table 6.22. *Summary of element representation for major domesticates (NISP).*

Element	Cow	Ovicap.	Horse	Pig
Head				
skull	55	23	8	4
mandible	117	69	14	28
loose teeth	141	68	78	7
atlas	16	1	3	2
axis	8	-	1	-
cervical vert.	23	-	7	-
Torso				
thoracic vert.	18	-	25	-
lunbar vert.	7	-	12	-
vert.	9	2	1	-
rib	16	-	26	-
Foreleg				
scapula	68	16	15	21
humerus	66	25	15	20
radius	78	58	23	20
ulna	21	3	16	18
carpal	31	2	10	-
metacarpal	69	16	9	7
Backleg				
pelvis	68	21	15	21
sacrum	7	-	2	-
femur	75	17	14	15
tibia	65	51	14	10
fibula	-	-	1	-
calcaneus	34	3	4	2
astragalus	34	5	4	1
tarsal	21	1	5	-
metatarsal	65	18	16	1
Other				
metapodial	39	31	6	1
phalanges	125	22	17	3
patella	5	-	2	-

preservation of meat on the bone. There is also some very limited evidence of secondary exploitation of animal products from chop marks on several horn-cores, and indicators of the removal of the hide from a horse carcass.

All the main domesticates – cow, sheep, goat and pig – exhibit butchery marks, as do horse and deer, and they were all probably eaten. Of these, all except deer were probably reared and butchered on site as whole carcasses, as a wide range of elements are represented (Table 6.22). Deer occurred in very small quantities, and probably came in as joints of venison. There is no indication of whole carcasses, and apart from antler, deer is only represented by two radii, a tibia and a metapodial, as well as fragments from a mandible and skull. Summarizing this data in terms of meat-bearing and non meat-bearing bones, it shows that they are more or less in an equal ratio for all species and that this remains more or less stable over time (Table 6.23). There is a slight indication that cow and sheep/goat numbers reduce while horse increases, but whether this is significant is debatable. Certainly, the rise in horse is probably due to the presence of several articulated joint deposits in Phase III. In other words, the butchery of whole carcasses of main domesticates occurs throughout the entire period of the site. The only other main animal species likely to have been consumed for their meat are domestic and other fowl: mainly chicken, but also geese and duck.

Table 6.23. *Ratio of meat-bearing to non-meat-bearing bones of main domesticates (expressed as percentage by NISP).*

Species	Phase I	Phase II	Phase III
Cow	50 : 50	45 : 55	39 : 61
Ovicaprid	47 : 53	41 : 59	40 : 60
Horse	43 : 57	53 : 47	61 : 39
Pig	33 : 67	50 : 50	43 : 57

For all phases, the pattern of animal exploitation seems more or less consistent: cattle dominate, followed by sheep and then horse, with pig, goat and fowl forming smaller proportions of the diet (Figs. 6.39–41; Table 6.24). Wild species are mainly represented by deer, although a few smaller wild animal bones occurred in the assemblage: fox (tibia, femur), badger (humerus, tibia), rook (ulna), pheasant (ulna, metatarsal) and possibly pigeon (femur, tibia and coracoid). Being mostly leg and meat-bearing bones, it is possible they represent the remains of food, but this must have been very occasional, as altogether

Table 6.24. *Summary of main domesticates by NISP (*excludes pig group from F.5499).*

	Phase I		Phase II		Phase III	
Species	**NISP**	**%**	**NISP**	**%**	**NISP**	**%**
Cow	53	52	140	60	910	57
Pig*	3	3	5	2	56	3
Sheep	26	26	48	20	298	19
Goat	-	-	1	-	8	-
Horse	11	11	39	17	245	15
Fowl	8	8	2	1	89	6
Total	*101*	*100*	*235*	*100*	*1606*	*100*

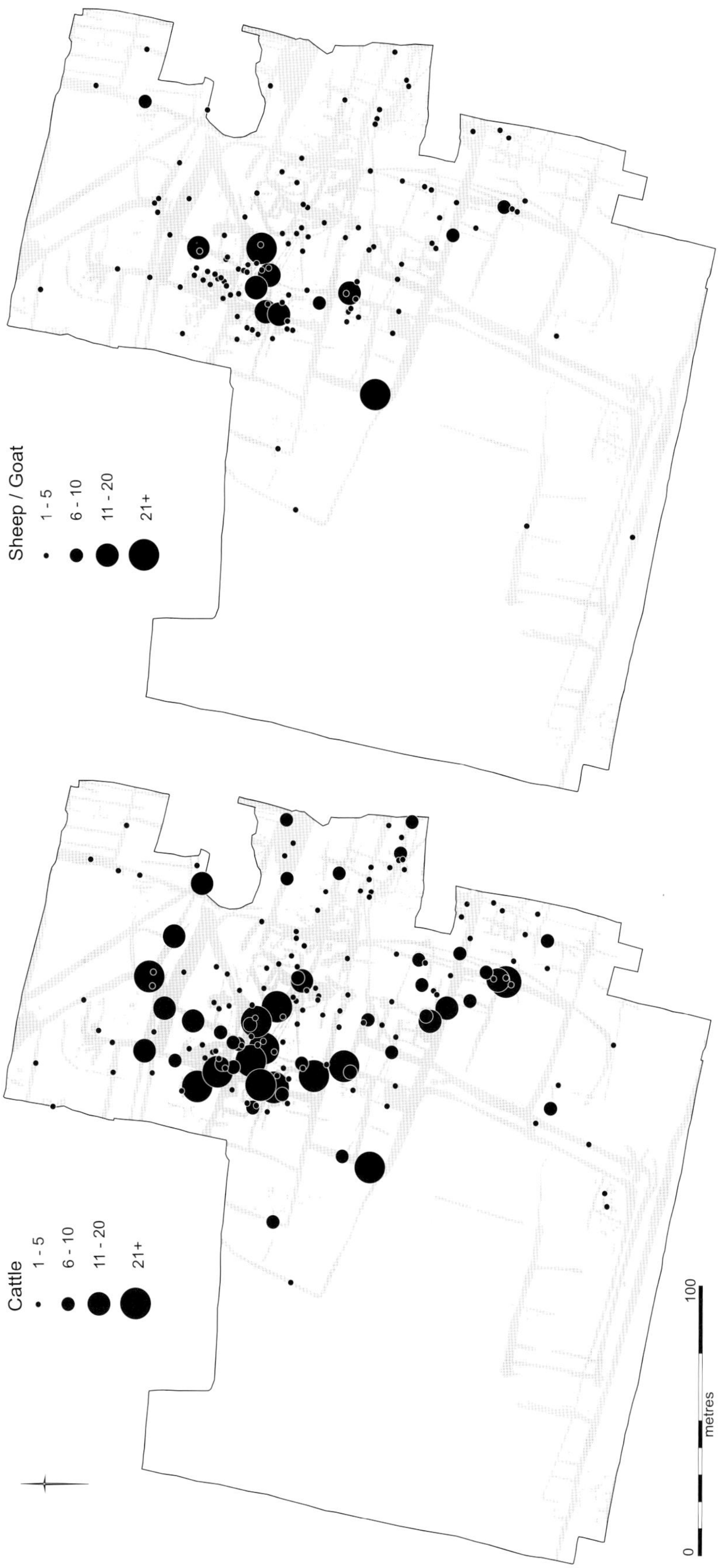

Figure 6.39. *Animal remains distributions (I): cattle (left) and, right, sheep/goat.*

Figure 6.40. *Animal remains distributions (II): pig (left) and, right, horse.*

Figure 6.41. *Animal remains distributions (III): skulls (by species).*

they only account for 11 bones. Such wild species show no particular distribution or association with, for example, ritual structures. As discussed above, this pattern is fairly typical compared to other sites (see Table 6.19), save the higher numbers of horse at Vicar's Farm. At New Hall they were fairly numerous too, but at Orton Hall Farm they comprised only *c.* 3% of all domesticates (King 1996). Generally high levels of cattle and pig are good indicators of the degree of Romanization on a site, as are oysters and chickens (King 1978 and 1991; see, though, Chap. 7); this patterns seems to hold, apart from the pig, which does not seem very common here, or on other comparable sites in the region.

The percentage levels of burnt bone within the assemblage are mostly quite low and originate from isolated bones that display slight levels of charring, possibly as the result of cooking (i.e. roasting). Most of the bones exhibiting signs of burning come from the core-areas (A & B), perhaps unsurprisingly (see Table 4.20). The general lack of charring on bones might be taken to imply that meat was predominantly eaten either as cured/smoked cuts or was boiled/stewed. There is good evidence that much of the meat was indeed eaten in a cured/smoked form, but the presence of jars used as cooking vessels (see above) might also suggest stewing. Moreover, the predominance of deep dishes and bowls during all phases (as opposed to shallow platters) could suggest the consumption of 'wetter' dishes rather than dry ones.

Apart from the bone, the other major category of food remains on site are oyster shells. These are

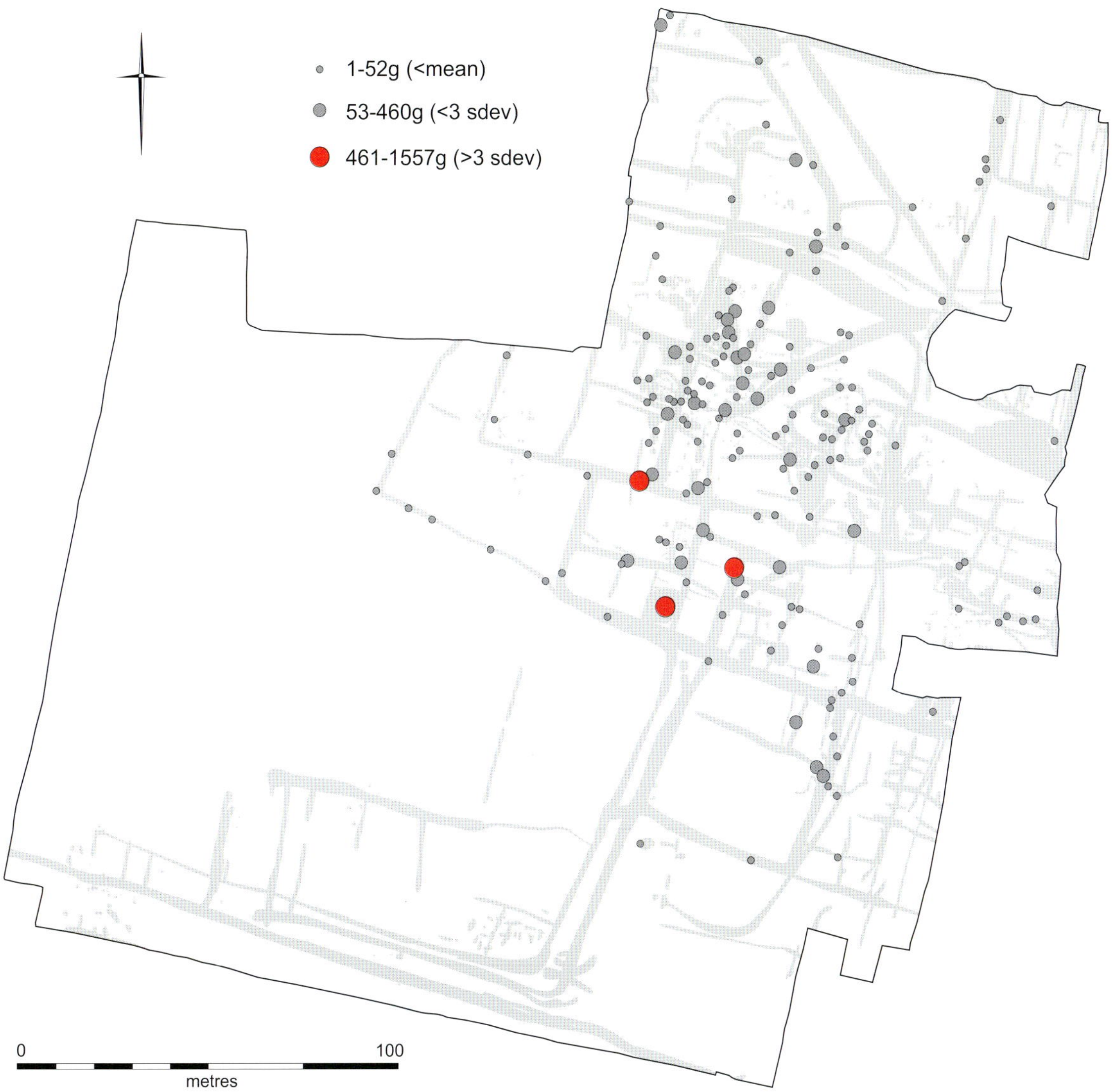

Figure 6.42. *Distribution of oyster shell.*

Table 6.25. *Quantities of oyster shell by phase.*

Phase	Wt. (g)
I	619
II	1205
III	6154

fairly ubiquitous and, fortunately, survived quite well despite the sandy and clay soils. Oyster shells are significant in that, unlike bone, they were brought to site specifically for on-site consumption. Their presence and distribution therefore should reflect this. Oyster shell was found across the core part of the site, diminishing in quantity further away from it (Fig. 6.42). It confirms, as do the distributions of pottery and bone (see Chap. 4), that refuse did not move far from its source (i.e. the core of the settlement). There is a definite sense of the shell occurring in higher quantities toward the back/western side of the core, especially toward the southwest in the G24 enclosure (Area B). This is an area that belongs to later phases of the site (II–III) and, indeed, the amounts of shell increase quite dramatically over time, doubling between Phase I and II, and more than quadrupling between Phase II and III (Table 6.25). The interesting thing about this trend is that exactly the same ratios of increase were noted for the pottery, which might suggest that the main drive behind this increase was a larger population: resident, 'visiting' and/or as displaced there from nearby settlements.

Although oysters seem to have formed a common enough part of the diet, fish are very rare. No fish bones were retrieved during bulk collection and although sieving was not carried out, it is surprising that none occurred at all. Of the environmental samples, only two produced fish bone, which if extrapolated as a percentage, suggests fish bone occurred in less than 0.5 per cent of all contexts. One of these samples came from the stomach area of Skeleton F.2016 within the inhumation cemetery, which suggests that people did have access to fish (see Chap. 5, *Inset*). Eggs are the only other foodstuff for which there is evidence. Their shells were present in a quarter of the environmental samples suggesting that eggs were a major part of the diet. This is unsurprising, since chickens and other fowl were clearly bred and eaten.

The over-riding pattern of food waste is concentration in the core part of the site, particularly its eastern side. Based on the calibrated transects through the site (see Fig. 4.31), this distribution is probably real, and would seem to reflect refuse patterns lying close to and around the main structures.

Exchange and the Monetary Economy

It has already been argued that the Vicar's Farm settlement was involved in surplus grain/flour production for export, and possibly meat too; on the other side of the economic exchange are imports. In particular, the site's material culture – for example, pottery, glassware, metalwork, quernstones – was imported through trade networks and none of it was made on site. The exception may be certain iron objects as there is clear evidence of smithing, though whether this is repair or actual production remains open to debate. An examination of the range and sources of some of these imports will, in the first instance, give an indication of the place of the settlement in regional trade networks and the use of money. Later, more general conclusions regarding the wealth and status of the community will be drawn.

Ceramics and Source Gwladys Monteil

The pottery wares on the site is fairly typical for the region; the assemblage is dominated by local coarsewares, with a substantial quantity of regional finewares and a lesser amount of continental fabrics. The range of fabrics are described below (with their ascribed codes), followed by a more general discussion on the ratio of wares against other sites in the region. Full fabric cross-references and descriptions are not given in most cases as these can be found in standard texts, chiefly Tomber and Dore (1998) and Tyers (1996). Quantitative summaries are given in Tables 6.26 and 6.27.

Continental Imports

Terra Nigra (TN) - A platter in a hard burnished smooth deep grey fabric, was found in F.5554 ([3013]). It is typologically close to Rigby 1973 (14, no. 27) but presents a 'kinked wall' (Symonds & Wade 1999, no. 46, 214).

Samian (SM) - The principal imported fineware is samian. The three main production sites are all present, but with a net domination of the Central Gaulish kilns (CGSM, 68% of total samian); East Gaulish products (EGSM) account for 18 per cent and South Gaulish examples (SGSM) for nine per cent. The range of forms is quite restricted and consists mainly of plain forms: the dishes Dr.18, 18/31, 31, 31R, 36, Ludowici Tg and Walters 79, the cups Dr.27, 33 and 35, the mortarium Dr.45 with a lion spouthead and one possible Dr.38. Six sherds of decorated Dr.37 were recovered. The early dish Dr.18 seems to be of Central Gaulish origin and has an illegible and incomplete stamp (Bet & Delor 2000, 470, see no. 58A for the form that is always stamped). Two stamped Central Gaulish Dr.31 were found; one stamp is incomplete and reads INI....SM (F.5501; Fig. 6.34.1), the other one is also incomplete and reads ...EP... (F.5610). One Dr.18/31, from a possible Martres de Veyre origin, is also stamped and it reads AAAA (F.4697; Fig. 6.32.1).

Central-Gaulish colour-coated (CGCC) - Other types of import from Central Gaul are colour-coated beakers. The code CGI CC refers to the white fabric and was found in F.5483, associated with a roughcast

Table 6.26. *Summary of pottery wares by phase (in EVEs; * includes unphased pottery).*

		Phase I		Phase II		Phase III		Grand Total*	
Ware	**Code**	**EVEs**	**%**	**EVEs**	**%**	**EVEs**	**%**	**EVEs**	**%**
Continental Imports									
Terra Nigra	TN	5	0.24	-	0.00	0	0.00	5	0.03
Samian	SGSM	11	0.52	-	0.00	5	0.06	16	0.11
	CGSM	100	4.73	39	1.77	27	0.31	178	1.23
	EGSM	22	1.04	-	0.00	30	0.35	52	0.36
	Unid SM	-	0.00	5	0.23	15	0.17	20	0.14
Central-Gaulish colour-coated	CG1 CC	-	0.00	-	0.00	-	0.00	-	0.00
	CG2 CC	-	0.00	-	0.00	-	0.00	-	0.00
Moselkeramik	TRCC	-	0.00	-	0.00	-	0.00	-	0.00
Amphorae	GAUL	-	0.00	-	0.00	-	0.00	-	0.00
	BAET	-	0.00	-	0.00	-	0.00	-	0.00
Regional Imports									
Nene Valley	NVCC	25	1.18	260	11.81	1626	18.97	2077	14.40
	NVGR	-	0.00	-	0.00	35	0.41	45	0.31
	NVWW	5	0.24	16	0.73	135	1.57	192	1.33
Much Hadham	HADBS	10	0.47	0	0.00	129	1.50	146	1.01
	HADGR	4	0.19	4	0.18	16	0.19	24	0.17
	HADRE	16	0.76	92	4.18	893	10.42	1067	7.40
	HADWS	-	0.00	-	0.00	6	0.07	6	0.04
Oxfordshire	OXRE	20	0.95	47	2.14	241	2.81	365	2.53
	OXWS	-	0.00	-	0.00	0	0.00	-	0.00
	OXWW	-	0.00	-	0.00	61	0.71	67	0.46
Colchester	COLCC	-	0.00	75	3.41	15	0.17	90	0.62
Verulanium Region	VRWW	40	1.89	-	0.00	-	0.00	40	0.28
Black-Burnished Type 2	BB2	90	4.26	-	0.00	-	0.00	90	0.62
Shell-tempered ware	SMSW	54	2.56	287	13.04	1419	16.55	1956	13.56
Mancetter-Hartshill	MAHWW	-	0.00	-	0.00	27	0.31	27	0.19
Alice Holt	AHGR	-	0.00	-	0.00	10	0.12	10	0.07
Local Imports									
Foxton type	ROM1 GR	-	0.00	-	0.00	-	0.00	65	0.45
Cherry Hinton/Greenhouse Farm type	CH/GR		0.00	-	0.00	-	0.00	-	0.00
Grog-tempered ware	GROGPNK	-	0.00	-	0.00	10	0.12	10	0.07
Horningsea ware	HORNWS	-	0.00	-	0.00	5	0.06	5	0.03
	HORNBB	-	0.00	26	1.18	125	1.46	151	1.05
	HORNGR	-	0.00	15	0.68	96	1.12	111	0.77
	HORNRE	10	0.47	-	0.00	20	0.23	30	0.21
Harston Red Slipped ware	HARCC	-	0.00	52	2.36	129	1.50	191	1.32
Cam Valley wares	FSGR	33	1.56	153	6.95	400	4.67	654	4.54
	FSRE	105	4.97	-	0.00	51	0.59	204	1.41
	FSBB	-	0.00	-	0.00	83	0.97	89	0.62
	FSBW/WW	-	0.00	5	0.23	21	0.24	26	0.18
	CSBB	263	12.45	474	21.54	910	10.62	1937	13.43
	CSGR	683	32.34	498	22.63	1133	13.22	2657	18.43

Table 6.26 *(cont.).*

Ware	Code	Phase I		Phase II		Phase III		Grand Total*	
		EVEs	%	EVEs	%	EVEs	%	EVEs	%
	CSRWS	90	4.26	10	0.45	10	0.12	152	1.05
	CSRE	321	15.20	127	5.77	734	8.56	1279	8.87
	CSRGS	-	0.00	-	0.00	-	0.00	-	0.00
	CSBW/WW	205	9.71	6	0.27	112	1.31	333	2.31
Unid finewares/colour-coats	-	-	0.00	10	0.45	43	0.50	53	0.37
Unid coarsewares	-	-	0.00	-	0.00	-	0.00	-	0.00
Grand Total		*2112*	*100.00*	*2201*	*100.00*	*8572*	*100.00*	*14,420*	*100.00*

Table 6.27. *Summary of pottery wares by phase (by weight in g; * includes unphased pottery).*

Ware	Code	Phase I		Phase II		Phase III		Grand Total*	
		Wt.	%	Wt.	%	Wt.	%	Wt.	%
Continental Imports									
Terra Nigra	TN	25	0.08	-	0.00	-	0.00	25	0.01
Samian	SGSM	40	0.12	3	0.01	7	0.01	67	0.04
	CGSM	487	1.49	332	0.99	360	0.40	1295	0.74
	EGSM	37	0.11	139	0.41	74	0.08	274	0.16
	Unid SM	-	0.00	1	0.00	16	0.02	17	0.01
Central-Gaulish colour-coated	CG1 CC		0.00	5	0.01	-	0.00	5	0.00
	CG2 CC	1	0.00	-	0.00	-	0.00	1	0.00
Moselkeramik	TRCC	-	0.00	1	0.00	-	0.00	1	0.00
Amphorae	GAUL	-	0.00	1345	4.00	483	0.53	1828	1.05
	BAET	-	0.00	-	0.00	176	0.19	176	0.10
Regional Imports									
Nene Valley	NVCC	238	0.73	2085	6.20	9868	10.89	13,320	7.64
	NVGR	-	0.00	131	0.39	207	0.23	388	0.22
	NVWW	130	0.40	451	1.34	2815	3.11	3621	2.08
Much Hadham	HADBS	23	0.07	99	0.29	873	0.96	1061	0.61
	HADGR	14	0.04	21	0.06	172	0.19	207	0.12
	HADRE	149	0.46	932	2.77	6265	6.91	7907	4.54
	HADWS	-	0.00	-	0.00	54	0.06	54	0.03
Oxfordshire	OXRE	92	0.28	394	1.17	2986	3.29	3763	2.16
	OXWS	0	0.00	-	0.00	11	0.01	11	0.01
	OXWW	18	0.05	17	0.05	831	0.92	942	0.54
Colchester	COLCC	2	0.01	287	0.85	136	0.15	425	0.24
Verulanium Region	VRWW	648	1.98	-	0.00	-	0.00	648	0.37
Black-Burnished Type 2	BB2	118	0.36	-	0.00	-	0.00	118	0.07
Shell-tempered ware	SMSW	508	1.55	3425	10.19	13,143	14.50	18,331	10.52
Mancetter-Hartshill	MAHWW	-	0.00	82	0.24	479	0.53	592	0.34
Alice Holt	AHGR	-	0.00	-	0.00	142	0.16	142	0.08
Local Imports									
Foxton type	ROM1 GR	-	0.00	-	0.00	-	0.00	37	0.02
Cherry Hinton/Greenhouse Farm type	CH/GR	67	0.20	-	0.00	-	0.00	67	0.04

Table 6.27 *(cont.).*

Ware	Code	Phase I		Phase II		Phase III		Grand Total*	
		Wt.	%	Wt.	%	Wt.	%	Wt.	%
Grog-tempered ware	GROGPNK	1	0.00	-	0.00	23	0.03	24	0.01
Horningsea ware	HORNWS	-	0.00	-	0.00	116	0.13	116	0.07
	HORNBB	-	0.00	73	0.22	551	0.61	624	0.36
	HORNGR	610	1.86	1446	4.30	7200	7.94	9351	5.37
	HORNRE	1012	3.09	647	1.92	3214	3.55	5067	2.91
Harston Red Slipped ware	HARCC	78	0.24	239	0.71	323	0.36	718	0.41
Cam Valley wares	FSGR	483	1.48	1024	3.05	2335	2.58	4172	2.39
	FSRE	113	0.35	194	0.58	798	0.88	1330	0.76
	FSBB	6	0.02	12	0.04	328	0.36	346	0.20
	FSBW/WW	73	0.22	9	0.03	67	0.07	156	0.09
	CSBB	4228	12.91	3619	10.77	7894	8.71	18,030	10.35
	CSGR	14,920	45.57	10,460	31.12	16,705	18.43	48,260	27.69
	CSRWS	607	1.85	151	0.45	154	0.17	1799	1.03
	CSRE	7026	21.46	5697	16.95	10,610	11.70	26,131	14.99
	CSRGS	-	0.00		0.00	-	0.00	2	0.00
	CSBW/WW	988	3.02	262	0.78	646	0.71	2148	1.23
Unid CC	-	2	0.01	31	0.09	472	0.52	568	0.33
Unid CW	-	-	0.00	-	0.00	292	0.32	302	0.17
Grand Total		*32,744*	*100.00*	*33,614*	*100.00*	*90,652*	*100.00*	*174,283*	*100.00*

decorated beaker, while CG2 CC refers to the soft micaceous buff fabric (Tyers 1996, 139–40) associated with a green-glazed beaker in [4878].

Moselkeramik (TRCC) - The latest import at Vicar's Farm is a folded black colour-coated beaker from Trier, dated AD 180–250, with the distinctive 'sandwich' core of red with grey margins (F.5309; Tyers 1996, 138).

Amphorae - One fragment of Dressel 20, traditionally associated with the importation of olive oil from the Baetican province (BAET), and several sherds of a powdery pink fabric of possible Gaulish origin (GAUL) were the only amphorae found on site.

Regional Imports (further than 30 km from the site)

Nene Valley (NV) - Most of the colour-coated products (NVCC) from the Nene Valley display the characteristic hard white to orange yellow fabric with occasional red to brown examples, that might come from Stanground (Howe *et al.* 1980; Perrin & Webster 1990; Dannell *et al.* 1993). Typologically quite restricted, the Nene Valley colour-coated forms are dominated by plain-rimmed dishes, flanged bowls and jars, but with a few distinctive vessels: a late bowl form with a cordoned neck in F.5389 (AD 330–400; Fig. 6.34.10), a jug (Dannell *et al.* 1993, no. 196, fig. 62), a pentice moulded beaker in F.5447 (*ibid.*, no. 176) and an indented rouletted beaker in F.5480. Very few examples of grey ware (NVGR) were found in the assemblage; they all display the white to buff/grey fabric with a grey slip. The most recognizable forms are a beaded rim dish dated AD 160–200 (F.5033), a beaker with underslip barbotine dot line decoration in F.5485 and a plain rimmed dish in F.5397. Apart from mortaria (see below), Nene Valley White Ware (NVWW) jars and flagons are present within the assemblage; all the sherds have a fabric similar to the colour-coated examples but are self-coloured. They are all abraded.

Much Hadham (HAD) - The other sizeable fineware group comes from Hadham (Herts). The oxidized version (HADRE) dominates, but occasional fragments of Hadham Grey Ware have been recorded (HADGR; Tyers 1996, 168). Several sherds of Hadham burnished reduced ware have also been identified (Tomber & Dore 1998, 153, HAD RE 2).

Oxfordshire (OX) - The third main type of Romano-British wares comes from the Oxfordshire Region and consists of oxidized finewares (OXRE) and white ware (OXWW). This production centre has been discussed at length by Young (1977). The Young Types C81 and C83 (*ibid.*, fig. 64) with demi-rosette decorations were amongst the most recognizable forms.

Colchester (COL) - Colchester colour-coated products (COLCC) are present in small quantities within the assemblage. The fabric was identified using the description furnished by Tyers (1996, 167). The forms associated with this fabric were a beaker with rouletted lines and overslip scroll barbotine decoration, dated AD 220–60 (F.1929; Fig. 6.33.6), a bag-shaped beaker dated AD 130–70 in F.5280, a folded beaker in that same feature's [469] fill, a beaker with overslip barbotine scroll decoration in F.5242, a funnel-neck rouletted beaker with overslip white decoration in F.5582, and an indented beaker with underslip 'S'-shape barbotine decoration in F.5501.

Verulamium Region (VRWW) - The fabric varies from buff to pink and displays numerous small quartz inclusions. Verulamium jar fragments are present in F.556 (Fig. 6.32.4): the example within fill [555] displays a grooved square rim dated AD 80–140.

Black-Burnished Type 2 (BB2) - Very uncommon on the site and only one jar was found, in association with a cremation assemblage. The fabric is hard with a sand-tempered grey core and burnished to a smooth bluish finish with acute-lattice decoration. This type probably derives from Essex; production has now been demonstrated at Mucking (Lucy & Evans 2016).

Shell-tempered Ware (SMSW) - Another distinctive group is the shell-tempered ware. This type of coarseware, in an oxidized orange to brown fabric with occasional grog inclusions, often presents burnt external surfaces and sooting, which suggests a cooking purpose. Although the main form is a wide-mouthed jar with a square everted rim and rilled body, a few flanged bowls have also been recorded. While grouped under the same code (SMSW), this coarseware had several sources, the main one probably being Harrold in Bedfordshire, but also possibly Earith on the fen–edge (Green 1954; see also Anderson in Evans *et al*. 2013b, 304).

Mortaria - Nene Valley White Ware (NVWW) Types M47, M43 or 41, M40 or 43, M51/52, one typologically close to M39, M24 without the decoration (F.5501; Fig. 6.35.1) and M50 are present within the assemblage (Perrin with Hartley, 1996, 191–9). One product from Mancetter (MAHWW) has also been identified (F.5733). Very few mortaria in an Oxford White Ware (OXWW) have been recovered; the Young forms identified are M22 and M17. An Oxford Red Slipped mortaria (OXRE) is also present within the assemblage: the form C97 (Young 1977) in F.5061. Hadham Red Ware mortaria (HADRE) are present in quite a large quantity but are all abraded and therefore difficult to identify typologically. One copy of the form M22 with multi-coloured quartz grits has been identified in F.5387; the fabric is similar to Hadham Red Ware and is covered by a white slip (HADWS). Mortaria from the kilns of Verulamium (VRWW) are present but in small numbers: one in F.5500 dated AD 90–120 and a stamped spout in F.5651 dated AD 90–120 (Fig. 6.32.11). The last mortarium of this assemblage consists of a White-slipped coarse oxidized sandy ware (F.5543) with black grits and a flanged grooved rim (CSWS).

Local Imports (within 20 km of the site)
The remainder of the assemblage comprises coarse and relatively fine local wares catering for a relatively large range of forms. The abraded state of the assemblage made identification quite difficult; nevertheless, it has been possible to identify a few major groups and trends. The first point of interest concerns an apparently homogeneous group of black-slipped wares (CSBB). All the vessels classified in that group display a thick black slip and a hard sand-tempered fabric with small to medium flint inclusions. The core varies from a pale grey to buff/pink colour. This form may have originated in Horningsea or more generally the Cam Valley. The second homogeneous group consists of a very similar fabric to the one described above but without the slip (CSGR). The same remark applies concerning its possible origin. This fabric also occurs in an oxidized version (CSRE). Unfortunately, the presence of sand and flint inclusions in a large part of the coarsewares made the distinction of different origins quite problematic. The 'classic' Horningsea fabric is quite distinctive, sand-tempered with large flint inclusions and is either oxidized or reduced (J. Evans 1991). Another grouping is based on the association of sherds presenting a reduced fine hard calcareous fabric that is sometimes associated with reddish to grey slip. A fresh break looks, to the naked eye, usually irregular, sand-tempered with very small irregular white (limestone?) inclusions (FSGR).

Romanizing Wares - Foxton-type butt beaker fragments (ROM1 GR) have been recovered from the pre-settlement ditch system (F.5610), the fabric is similar to the early 'Romanized' type defined by Lucas (1997, Rom 1). Otherwise, a flagon in a buff version of a Greenhouse Farm-type fabric (CH/GR) was found associated with Cremation F.5119.

Grog-tempered Ware (GROGPNK) - The fabric is pink relatively hard and tempered with ill-sorted quartz, grog and iron-rich inclusions. This fabric occurs in very small quantities in Vicar's Farm Phases I and III and is probably residual Late Iron Age/Conquest Period.

Cam Valley Wares (CS/FS) - The vast majority of sandy wares have been grouped together under the name of Cam Valley, and though they may derive from different sources, they are all presumed to be local and from kiln sites along the Cam. Because of the difficulty in distinguishing clear fabrics amongst the abundant grey wares, they all have been recorded under the same code, with a broad distinction between coarse (CS) and fine sand-tempered (FS). The coarse sandy wares all have in common a hard sand-tempered fabric with small to medium flint inclusions and often display an oxidized core (CSGR). More detailed fabric descriptions can be found in the site archives, as it might be possible to differentiate different sources in the future. This group also occurs in a fully oxidized version (CSRE), which is usually either grey slipped (CSRGS) or white-slipped (CSRWS); there is also a buff/white ware version (CSBW/WW) and a homogeneous group of black-slipped and burnished wares (CSBB). Although not certain, the nature of the inclusions – as well as the texture and the colour – could suggest a local origin, and these are essentially related to the Horningsea wares. The fine sand-tempered group has generally fewer inclusions, but often includes chalk, and is otherwise present in a similar range of reduced (FSGR), oxidized (FSRE), buff (FSBWAVW) and black-burnished (FSBB) fabrics.

Horningsea Ware (HORN) - Although similar to the local grey ware described above, one fabric is quite distinct: sand-tempered with distinctive large flint inclusions; it is either oxidized (HORNRE) or reduced (HORNGR), and can be white-slipped (HORNWS) or black-slipped and burnished (HORNBB). The range of forms seems to be quite limited and consists of flat-topped dishes, plain-rimmed dishes, flanged bowls, jars and numerous examples of storage jars with a large bifid rim (J. Evans 1991; J. Evans *et al*. 2017).

Harston Red Slipped Ware (HARCC) - The examples of this local late colour-coated ware identified in this assemblage all display a red-slipped buff/pinkish-white soft fine fabric. Its production of vessels in the Oxfordshire tradition was attributed to a migrant potter (Pullinger & Young 1981).

The site's pottery supply consistently relied on local wares for a large part of its assemblage, as can be seen from Tables 6.26 and 6.27. However, there is a clear tendency for local production to decrease in importance over time against the larger, regional industries, particularly the Nene Valley, Hadham and the South Midlands shelly ware producers (e.g. Harrold, Beds.). Figure 6.43 summarizes the main sources of ceramics over each phase and, while in Phase I over 80 per cent of the pottery is locally produced, this reduces to 62 per cent in Phase II and 44 per cent in Phase III. On the whole, the figures are fairly typical of the region, with the late colour-coat and shelly ware industries taking over the market from the later third century AD. However, within the region there are differences between sites, particularly in relation to their proximity to these major industries. For example, in comparing Vicar's Farm with a site further south on the chalk (Foxton) and one further north on the fen-edge (Haddenham), the three sites show a fairly good correspondence between relative proportion of wares and the proximity of the source (Fig. 6.44). The sites further south see a

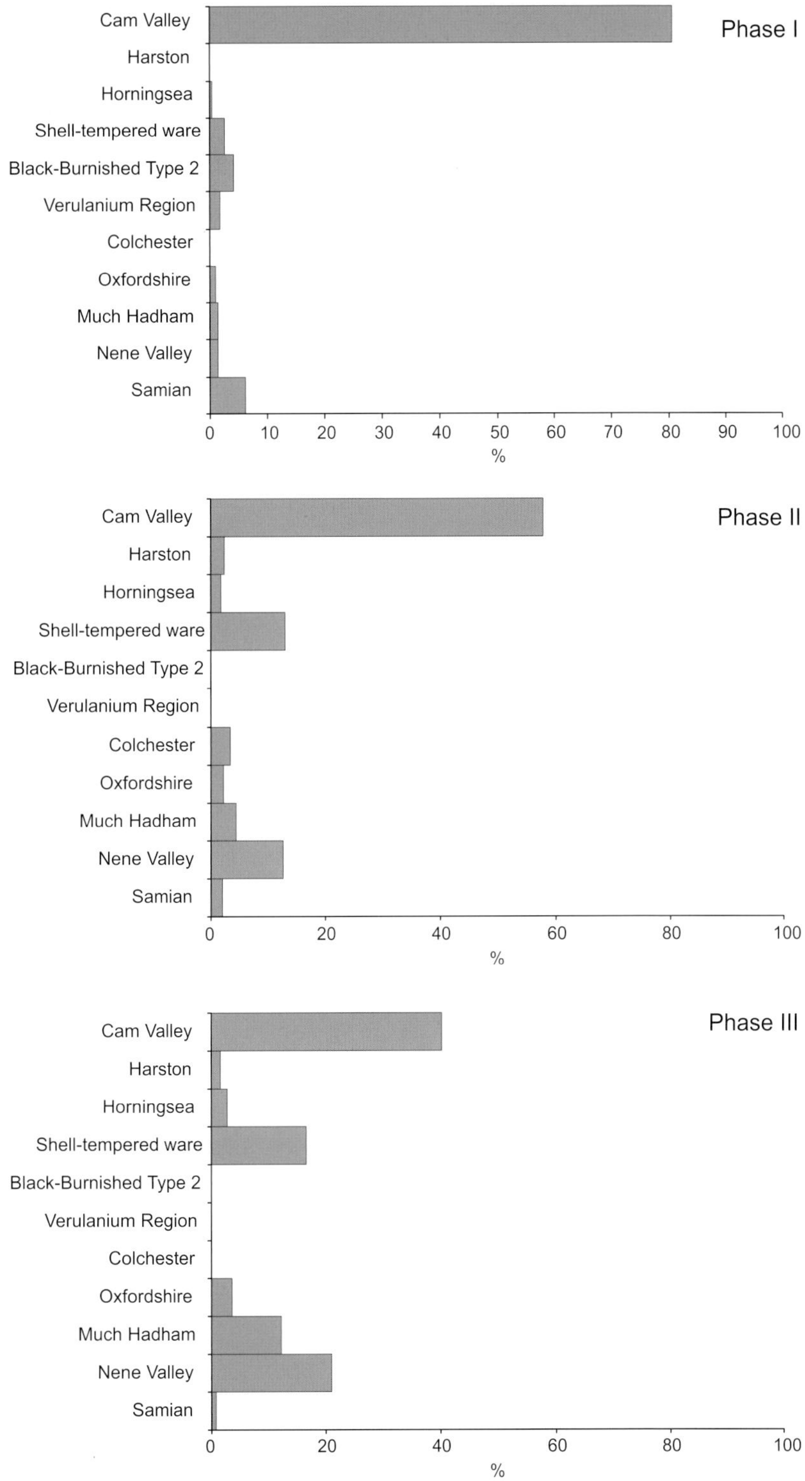

Figure 6.43. *Summary of pottery sources by phase (in EVEs).*

proportionate increase of Hadham and shelly wares and a decrease in Nene Valley wares, while Vicar's Farm has a very high proportion of the Cam Valley wares (including Horningsea), being closest to the source. Even though all three sites are of quite a different nature – Haddenham was a rural shrine (i.e. Snow's Farm), with Foxton a small farmstead – the broader pattern of access to ceramics seems to hold good.

Imported Stone Kevin Hayward

The stone artefacts amounted to 1,276 fragments from over 260 contexts and constitute a large component of

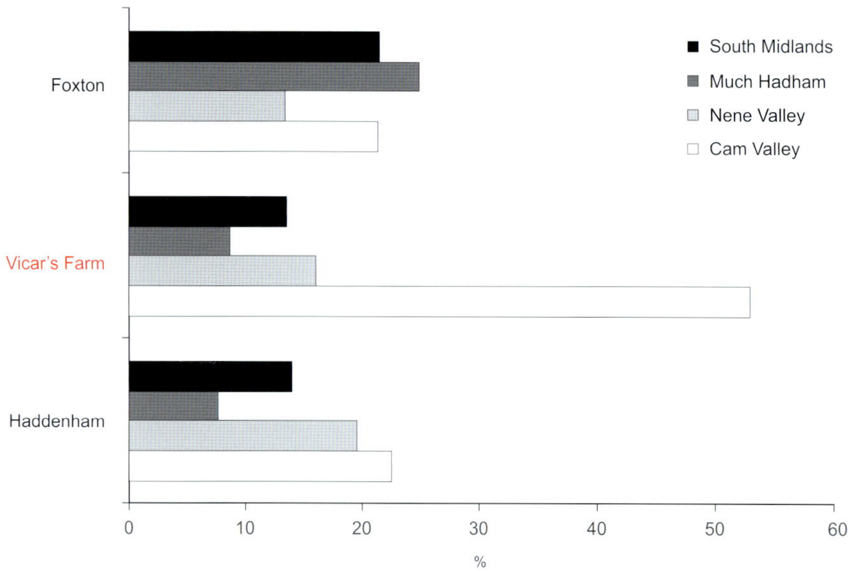

Figure 6.44. *Relative proportion of pottery from main industries at three sites in the region (in EVEs).*

all archaeological material recovered by both weight and quantity. In all, 938 fragments from 115 contexts were examined systematically, with quantifiable criteria such as dimensions and weight recorded.

Vicar's Farm is located in a part of East Anglia/South Midlands that has quite a varied, but geologically recent, history. Within 10 miles (*c.* 16 km) of the site are a whole suite of sedimentary rocks, ranging in age from Middle Jurassic Oxford Clays and Corallian Limestones through to younger Cretaceous Greensands and Chalk, and finally to recent Quaternary and Holocene glacial, fluvial and fluvio-glacial sediments (see Table 6.28). A majority of

Table 6.28. *Summary of petrology of worked stone.*

Rock Type	Number of fragments	Wt. (kg)
Millstone Grit	41 (33.1%)	33.840 (34.5%)
Lower Greensand	20 (16.1%)	11.257 (11.5%)
Collyweston Slate	16 (12.9%)	3.881 (4.0%)
Neidermendig Lava	13 (10.5%)	5.119 (5.2%)
Chlorite Schist	4 (3.2%)	2.515 (2.6%)
Dark Mudstone	4 (3.2%)	0.868 (0.9%)
Hertfordshire Pudding Stone	3 (2.4%)	9.364 (9.5%)
Kentish Ragstone	3 (2.4%)	0.229 (0.2%)
Old Red Sandstone	3 (2.4%)	1.883 (1.9%)
Upware Limestone	3 (2.4%)	6.487 (6.6%)
Chalk	2 (1.6%)	0.271 (0.3%)
Quartz Vein	2 (1.6%)	1.365 (1.4%)
Bunter Pebble	2 (1.6%)	0.030 (0.03%)
Ketton Stone	1 (0.8%)	18500 (18.9%)
Permian Sandstone	1 (0.8%)	0.032 (0.03%)
Volcanic Material	1 (0.8%)	0.049 (0.05%)
Wenlock Limestone?	1 (0.8%)	0.090 (0.1%)

these young sediments reflect the geology of Southeast Britain as a whole, which is bereft of suitable hard rocks for both building construction and producing portable artefacts. Vicar's Farm itself is sited upon both soft Lower Cretaceous fine-grained Gault Clay (100 million years) as well as much younger palaeochannel sandy gravels from the Ipswichian Interglacial (120,000 years), both forming low undulating ground up to 20 m high. The ground slopes down eastwards to the terrace and recent alluvial flood plain of the Cam Valley between half and one mile away (0.8–1.6 km). This important local river divides the older Gault from the lithologically more resilient, younger, northeast–southwest trending Lower Chalk to the east, characterized by a higher (50 m), slightly undulating topography. Sandier glauconitic units from the Lower Greensand and Cambridge Greensand of the Lower Chalk are also found within one mile (*c.* 1.6 km) of the site, as are spreads of glacial boulder clay. To the north of the site, very flat fenland is split up by low-lying ridges of Lower Greensand (Haddenham–Streatham ridge) and older Jurassic Upware Limestone of the Corallian (Upware–Barway ridge). The latter runs alongside the River Cam, six miles (*c.* 9.65 km) north of Cambridge. Suitable building stone is scarce in this region with only Burwell Stone, a chalk rock from the Lower Chalk, being utilized in Medieval Cambridge (Worssam & Taylor 1969). Flint from the Middle Chalk was also widely used but does not outcrop so close to Cambridge.

At least 18 rock types have been identified at Vicar's Farm, which is located in an area containing relatively few suitably hard local lithologies. Whilst some of these are local, such as Chalk and Lower Greensand, the vast majority outcrop at least 40 miles (*c.* 64 km) away from the site, encompassing a very large geographical catchment area. This reflects the site's location, near to the junction of two major Roman routes at Roman Cambridge. The *Via Devana* ran from the original provincial capital of *Camulodunum* through to Godmanchester. The presence of German Lavastone quernstones during Phase I may indicate the influence of sea transportation from the Rhineland to *Camulodunum* and subsequent delivery via the *Via Devana* to this settlement. Millstone Grit from the southern Pennines may have also been transported along this route, although it is important to consider the important influence of Millstone Grit at pre-Roman sites in Central England, such as at Hunsbury Hill Fort (Peacock 1987, 76), where prehistoric trackways would have been utilized.

The second major artery, Eastern Akeman Street, runs near the east of the site in a northeast–southwest orientation from northern East Anglia towards *Londinium* and sites in southern and western Britannia. This route could have supplied greensand from Culham in Oxfordshire, Hertfordshire Pudding Stone and Forest of Dean Devonian Sandstones. In addition, the proximity of the River Cam, which runs northward towards the Wash, could have provided yet another route. At Upware, eight miles from the site (*c.* 13 km; GR TL 540 700), the Cam runs alongside both Lower Greensand and Corallian (Upware Limestone) outcrops. Both of these lithologies are found at Vicar's Farm. Finally, the Car Dyke waterway, just north of Cambridge, and possibly constructed around AD 120 (Whitwell 1992, 57; see also J. Evans *et al.* 2017) may have influenced the transportation of Middle Jurassic Collyweston Slate and Ketton Stone. This 56 mile/*c.* 90 km long waterway runs near to the River Gwash at Stamford, which is close to outcrops of these two building stones.

Coins Richard Reece

A total of 339 Roman coins were examined by Adrian Challands (see Fig. 6.45; listed in Lucas & Whittaker 2001). Of these, 261 were positively identified, the remaining 78 coins being approximately identified on the basis of general appearance and size to general minting periods, which varied between 50 and 200 years. On a numerical basis, over half of the positively identified coins were minted between AD 330 and 378, while a third were minted between AD 260 and 275.

The Roman coin population at the Vicar's Farm Site is sufficiently large to allow for statistical analysis. Its coins have been summarized by the usual periods as *cam vf*. For comparison, the Castle Hill groups (*RCAM*, 139–40) have been added together to produce *cam ch*[15] and this has been added to *cam vf* to produce an overall total, *cam tot*.

Cam ch and *cam vf* have been processed by the usual method (Reece 1995) and this produces Figure 6.45. For *cam ch* its early coins are average and virtually on the line. There is an above-average move upwards at Trajan (AD 98–117) and then an above-average presence until about AD 290, where the line runs within a range parallel with the mean. It then drops sharply due to continuously well below-average coin-loss throughout the fourth century AD, until a surprising bulge of coins of the House of Theodosius (AD 388–402).

Vicar's Farm *(cam vf)* is closer to the British rural pattern with some coin-loss, but still below-average until AD 260. The radiate period (AD 260–90) does not produce the usual British recovery, though coin-loss from AD 296–330 is roughly at the average British rate. Suddenly, after AD 330, more coins than average are lost, and the period AD 364–78 shows losses well above average. Figure 6.45 shows that the larger numbers of coins from *cam vf* influence the Cambridge total strongly and make the AD 364–78 coins the major event.

Cam ch fits in a group of Eastern sites: The Cow Roast (Herts.), Thistleton (Rutland), Ashton (Northants.), Chelmsford Temple (Essex), and Water Newton (Cambs.). Vicar's Farm *(cam vf)* belongs with a very religious group, including Nettleton (temple), Lamyatt Beacon (temple), Uley (temple), Lullingstone (house-church) and Gatcombe (villa). Other sites could be added to this group, in which temple sites seem to flourish above average in AD 364–78. When all the *cam* sites are added together, the pattern matches small towns like Ashton, Wanborough, Shakenoak, the Frocester Court villa, and the larger – but rather odd – town groups of Silchester and Canterbury A; most seem affected by a lower than average coin-loss from AD 260–96.

Figure 6.45. *Coin Loss: Vicar's Farm (*Cam vf*), Roman Castle Hill (*cam ch*) and the two combined (*cam tot*).*

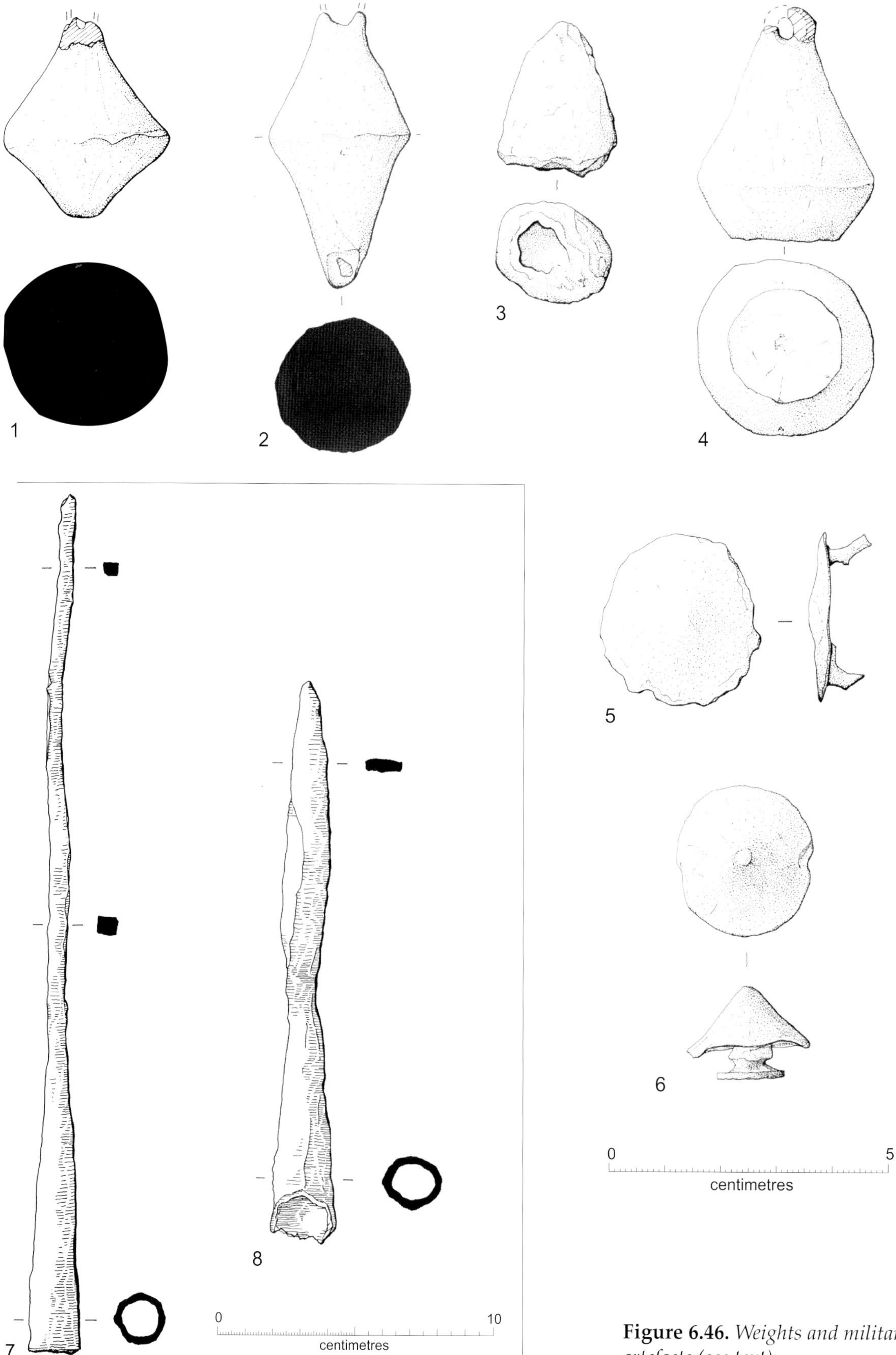

Figure 6.46. *Weights and military artefacts (see text).*

Weights and Military Artefacts (with Nina Crummy)
A large number of lead weights were retrieved from the site by metal-detecting. Lacking feature-context, most have been ascribed a Roman date on the basis of form (Fig. 6.46).[16] They are, nonetheless, significant markers of the settlement's surplus production (and its control).

<4436> SF 512 – Well-formed biconical weight with iron rod for suspension embedded in one end. Length 34 mm, diameter 28 mm. Weight 99 g; underweight for 4 oz (Fig. 6.46.1).

<4374> SF 153 - Long biconical weight with a suspension loop at each end. One loop is broken, the other retains a small fragment from an iron ring of chain link. Length 50 mm, maximum diameter 25 mm. Weight 78 g = 3 oz (Fig. 6.46.2).

<463> - Metal-detector find. Conical polygonal ?weight, hollow underneath. The underside is rough and irregular and is unlikely to have been fitted with a metal suspension loop as <4374>. Height 24 mm, maximum diameter 41 mm. Weight 35 g; overweight for 1 oz (Fig. 6.46.3).

<4451a> - One of three weights recorded under this number (spoil-heap finds). Well-made truncated conical weight, polygonal in section. The upper part is rebated on two sides and pierced to form a suspension loop. Slightly dished underneath. Length 27 mm, section 13 × 14 mm. Weight 27 g = 1 oz.

<4451b> - Carinated, with flat base and truncated conical top in which is set the remains of an iron suspension loop. Length 40 mm, diameter 35 mm. Weight 148 g = 5 oz.

<4451c> - Plano-convex weight with central perforation. The flat face is plain, the upper face is covered with random lines and impressions. Height 8 mm, diameter 22 mm. Weight 22 g; less than 1 oz. The metal of this item is distinctly different to that of the other weights (Fig. 6.46.4).

<4447> SF 549 - Globular weight, dished on the upper side and slightly pointed on the lower. An iron rod for suspension is embedded with in it, shown by traces of iron in the dished area and around a crack on the lower side. Length 43 mm, diameter 42 mm. Weight 287 g = 10 oz.

<4396> SF 231 - Small annular weight. Diameter 22 mm, 7 mm thick. Diameter of central hole 7 mm. Weight 18 g; overweight for 0.5 oz.

<4398> SF 249 - Elongated, roughly arrow-shaped, pendant weight with lozenge-shaped section. The suspension loop is broken. Length 47 mm, maximum thickness 10 mm. Weight 57 g = 2 oz.

<4450> X (10) - Metal-detector find. Fragment of an elongated weight as <4398>. Length 44 mm, maximum thickness 12 mm. Weight 42 g; perhaps 2 oz when complete.

<4416> SF 387 - Biconical lead weight, quite roughly formed. Length 21 mm, maximum diameter 28 mm. Weight 74 g; underweight for 3 oz.

<4426> SF 486 - Biconical lead weight, similar to <4416> above. Length 23 mm, diameter 28 mm. Weight 79 g = 3 oz.

Two spear points are both unstratified and may not be Roman, though similar forms can be found in the Roman period. A number of copper alloy studs for attachment to leather straps are, again, quite similar to items of auxiliary equipment, but are not sufficiently precise parallels to be clear indicators of a military presence (Figs. 6.46.5–6).

<4791> SF 456 - Copper alloy stud with two projections on the underside for attachment. One of the latter is damaged. There is a slight irregular central dome, hollow on the underside. Probably from a leather strap. Diameter 30 mm, height 10 mm. This may be from cavalry harness (cf. Oldenstein 1976, Taf. 49; Fig. 6.46.5).

<4752> SF 133 - Large riveted copper alloy stud for attachment to leather, with circular conical head. Diameter 25 mm, height 16 mm. A similar stud from auxiliary equipment came from Feldberg on the German *limes* (Oldenstein 1976, Taf. 47, 490; Fig. 6.46.6).

<4715> [8262] – Long-socketed spear or pilum point with simple tapering blade. The socket is round in section, the blade square. Iron, length 320 mm. Compare with Bishop and Coulston 1993, fig. 34, 2 and Manning 1985, pl. 79, VI14, which has a strong midrib on a very narrow blade (Fig. 6.46.7).

<4717> - Socketed spear point, with thin curved blade narrower than the socket. There is no noticeable midrib. Similar to Manning's Group III (1985, 166–7), and Bishop and Coulston 1993, fig. 84, 1. Iron, length 191 mm (Fig. 6.46.8).

<4501> F.5309 - Very corroded socketed object, possibly a weapon head. Iron, length 168 mm.

Overview – Economy and Ownership
Determining whether the settlement at Vicar's Farm was under a central authority is a difficult problem, and perhaps unresolvable. It is unlikely to have been a military-run establishment, simply because this was not necessarily how the army operated or gained its supplies; the military could, nonetheless, have been a recipient of its agricultural produce. Similarly, Vicar's Farm could well have supplied the town at Cambridge, but again, it is doubtful whether it was actually administered from an urban authority. It is more likely that the settlement was independent or part of an independent peri-urban estate that was producing for a local (and possibly wider) market. The settlement seems to have been a thriving place, at least by the Late Roman period, and agricultural production and sale/trade of surplus was only one aspect of its role in the wider landscape. Examining the composition and distribution of the various small finds categories in relation to other sites can help to shed some light on what this role was.

Figures 6.48 and 6.49 show the distribution of coins and small finds (excluding grave-goods) on the site. The coins cluster in the core-area, which is perhaps as one might expect. Quite a number occur around the shrine, but by far the greatest concentration occurs on the eastern side of the internal pathway, particularly around the Curvilinear Enclosure. This is interesting in terms of the proposed interpretation of these

1

2

3

Figure 6.47 *(this page and opposite). Roman faces and rare finds: Minerva-head wax spatula (<4793>); 2 & 3) face pots (<3727>, F.5006 & <3416>, F.5722); 4) ring-headed pin (<4733>); 5) plate brooch (<4759>); 6) mirror fragment (<4773>).*

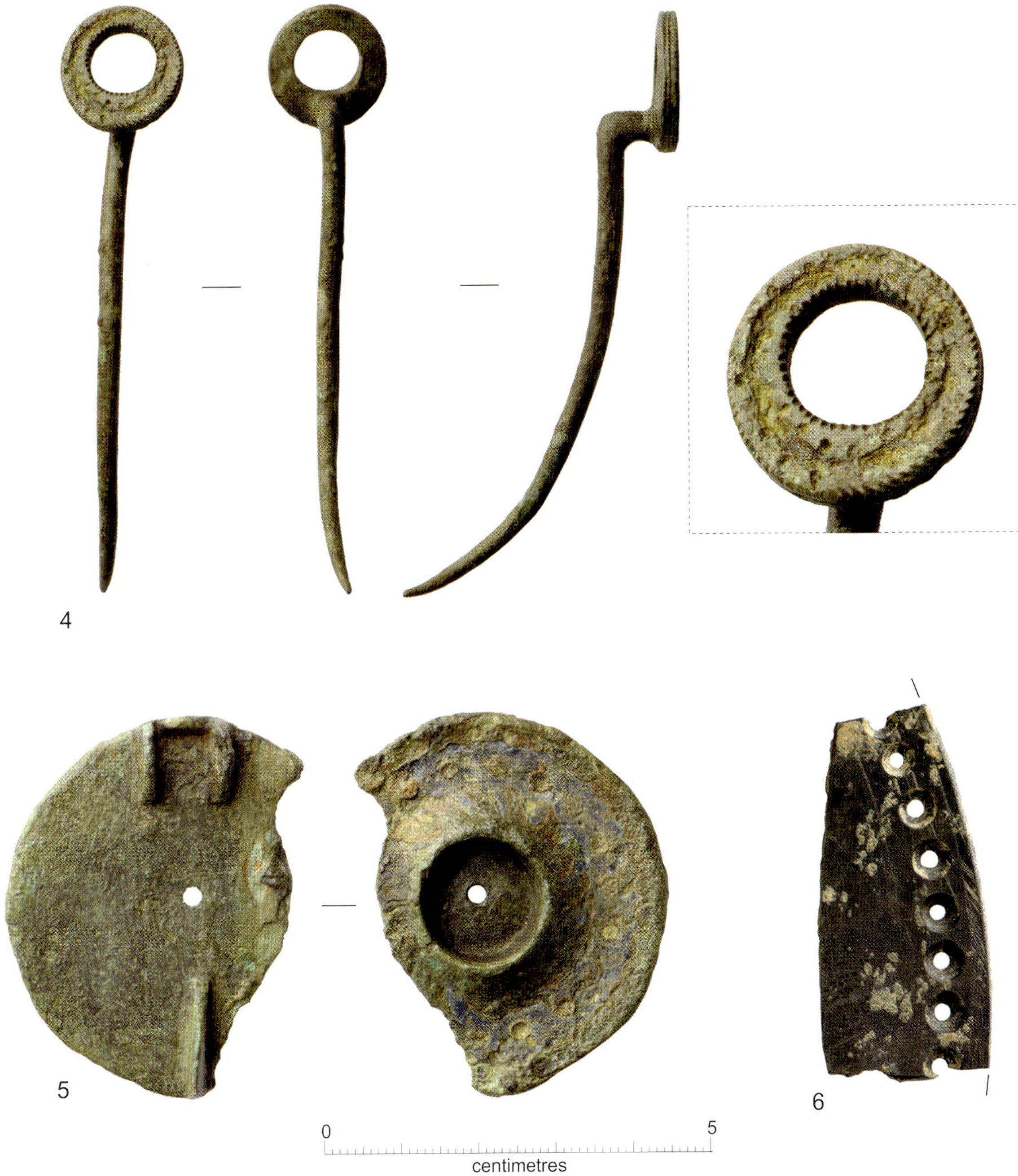

Figure 6.47 *(cont.).*

features as livestock enclosures and might suggest that this was an area where the sale of animals took place. Another fairly distinct cluster of coins occurs in a linear swathe along the metalled surfaces (F.5471 & F.4767) in the northern part of the core. Interpreted as a western extension of Road 3, it was also thought that this was a possible surfacing for temporary structures/stalls and, again, this could have been an area where trading was carried out. Looking at the small finds distribution, two of the weights came from the area around the Curvilinear Enclosure and another came from the metalled surface, which might support this interpretation. On the whole, however, the small finds were fairly thin on the ground, especially around the western side of the settlement core where the Timber Shrine and Aisled Building lay. Overall, the small finds distribution is not too informative, except in that it reflects that occupation was focused in the core-area of the site.

If the distribution plots are not too revealing, the actual composition of the small finds assemblage may be more informative. Table 6.29 shows the quantities of small finds according to broad functional group for Vicar's Farm and three other sites in the region: Haddenham's Snow's Farm shrine, the administrative centre or settlement at Stonea, and the rural farmstead at Haddon. Vicar's Farm clearly bears closest resemblance to Stonea, not only in the diversity of objects but also

Table 6.29. *Finds categories from four sites.*

	Vicar's Farm	Hadden -ham	Stonea	Haddon
Dress	36	19	52	13
Toiletries	3	-	19	1
Other personal	7	1	-	1
Military	6	-	6	1
Writing	1	-	1	-
Trading	4	-	5	1
Craft	5	-	9	1
Gaming	2	1	10	-
Coins	339	74	178	81

Figure 6.48. *Coin distribution.*

Figure 6.49. *Small finds distribution.*

The Man Loaded with Mischief

As indicated on Figure 4.8, there used to be pubs a short distance either side of the Observatory's Madingley Road avenue (see also Fig. 4.17). They were of nineteenth-century origin and related to post-inclosure land-use, with their clientele largely drawn from agricultural labourers (no doubt, also including those from the latter-day Vicar's Farmyard) and, during the latter half of the century, probably also those engaged in the local coprolite industry. The most intriguing of the two was *The Man Loaded with Mischief*, which lay to the west (the other was the more pedestrianly named, *Plough and Harrow*). This was first recorded in a directory of 1851, but probably dates to some years earlier (see Guillebaud 2006, 168). The 1915 photograph reproduced here shows the pub's sign (Fig. 6.50 lower), with two New Zealand officers testifying to the area's WWI sometime troop-presence. Painted by Richard Hopkins Leach – Cambridge's 'jobbing' folk-artist specializing in pub signs – an original version of it was given to Cambridge Folk Museum (Hopkin 2014). While the pub apparently burnt down shortly before WWII, when a family member of its former publican bought the *Live and Let Live* on Mawson Road in the mid 1980s he had the sign remade and it still hangs there. (An interesting

Figure 6.50. The Man Loaded with Mischief: *top, early twentieth-century photograph of the pub's frontage and, below, New Zealand troops taking their ease there in 1915 (left) and Leach's original pub sign as now displayed in the Cambridge Folk Museum (right; Hopkin 2014, 5).*

case of the potential confusion and arbitrariness of 'signs', as obviously it has nothing to do with the *Live and Let Live*.)

This allows us to appreciate the 'stock-imagery' from which its name derives. Both Sleaford and Norwich also had pubs with the same name (Norwich's sign being painted by the landscape water-colourist, John Crome). The original *The Load of Mischief* pub is said to have been on London's Oxford Street, where Hogarth apparently provided its sign (Hopkin 2014, 4). But it was also a popular eighteenth-century print-theme relating to the gin scare (the backgrounds of these images incorporate elements of Hogarth's *Gin Lane* of 1751): the drunken woman riding on her husband's shoulders accompanied by a monkey and a magpie (*...the Emblem of Strife*; O'Connell 1999, 115).

The status of another local pub will be discussed in the next book, as the Traveller's Rest on Huntingdon Road – also of mid nineteenth-century date (now a restaurant) – stood along the east side of the Howe's Close Medieval hamlet excavations (*NWC*, Site IX). Lying at the same approximate distance from Cambridge proper, that hamlet lay on the border of parishes: Girton and Impington. With unusual finds assemblages, it is likely that the road-side hamlet served as a drover's last stop-over and somewhere to hold livestock prior to their delivery to Cambridge's market (i.e. literally, a 'traveller's rest').

the frequency. The Haddenham shrine is a specialist site and this is reflected in the very limited repertoire, which is dominated by dress items, most of which were probably offerings (see Table 7.10). The farmstead at Haddon is also dominated by these types of objects, but other categories are also represented, even if in low numbers. It is perhaps no coincidence that the main offerings at a rural shrine are comparable with the most common small finds category from a rural farmstead or settlement. The Vicar's Farm assemblage, though, is clearly much closer to a major centre like Stonea than a rural settlement and displays a much wider and more abundant number of such small finds, indicative of a range of activities. It suggests a settlement much more active in the local economy and also possibly one more Romanized. Given its proximity to the town, this is perhaps not surprising. Yet it may be that, as well as generating surplus produce, Vicar's Farm was also a seasonal market-place where such produce was traded.

Discussion – *Thinking Communities and Farms*

With so much material now presented, there are a series of finds that seem to tell directly of at least one of the settlement's distinct functions. This includes the steelyard weights, the padlock and key, and the Minerva-bust wax spatula. Considered together, they could speak of an 'official'-presence and, as such, might reflect on the role and purpose of the site's aisled building. To this could be added the large, evidently traction-driven quernstone (Fig. 6.19), as this might suggest that it was milled grain that required this 'control'.

Yet, as reflected in the Timber Shrine and the F.5707 Monumental Post, there was also another, ritual side to the settlement. While the 'special' status of some of the site's animal bone deposits discussed above can be considered ambiguous, there are other deposits of which there is no doubt. One is the truly extraordinary F.5425 pit, with its stone-packed facing horse heads at the entrance to the inhumation cemetery. To this can be added the 12 coins that accompanied the F.5707 post-setting and, too, the (human) neonate within one of Structure D's front postholes. Also, Reece above remarks upon the affinities of Vicar's Farm's coin-loss profile with a group of distinctly 'religious sites' and, clearly, *both ritual and 'officialdom' that have to be considered amongst the settlement's outstanding characteristics*.

Langdale Hale Compared

On the grounds that North West Cambridge's Site II 'model farm' will only be fully presented in the next book (see Fig. 5.41), it is appropriate that any overarching review of the region's farmsteads is largely left until then. Given, however, the issues raised here concerning the character and potential 'sponsorship' of the Vicar's Farm Roman settlement, it is only salient to now compare it with Langdale Hale's 'state supply farm' at Colne Fen (Fig. 6.51; Evans *et al.* 2013b, chap. 2). With its fen-edge location next to the Roman Car Dyke canal (linked by a road to The Camp Ground's inland barge-port complex just *c.* 0.7 km to the north), it was argued that the latter's prime role was to supply the army with meat and grain (plus, possibly, hides and horses).

Like Vicar's Farm, its sequence extended over the entire span of Britain's Roman period. Its intensity and the 'rhythm' of its phasing, however, varied, particularly in that its final, post-AD 325 use (Phase III) was greatly reduced when compared with its Phase II

Figure 6.51. *Vicar's Farm and Langdale Hale (left; from Evans* et al. *2013b, fig. 2.73).*

floruit (AD 120–325); this is in marked contrast to both Vicar's Farm and The Camp Ground sequences. That said, Langdale's linked 'ladder-like' enclosures of its primary Conquest Period phase were clearly quite similar to the layout of Vicar's Farm Phase I.1. Langdale's Phase II compounds extended over 2.8 ha, arranged around a road running north to the canal-connecting port. While at 0.6 and 0.8 ha, its two large rectangular compounds would bear comparison to Vicar's Farm's main Phase I enclosure (G2; 6670 sq. m), on the whole Langdale's layout was much more formally simple and 'pristine' – at least until its Phase III 'hamlet' expression – than Vicar's Farm. Indeed, in its Phase II Langdale appeared to have been laid out to its full extent from the outset and did not expand 'organically' in the way that Vicar's Farm evidently did.

The two sites were excavated at a very similar sample-intensity and, accordingly, their recovered finds values can be compared (see, also, Chap. 7 and Table 7.10, below). While a few military items were also recovered from Langdale, there was no evidence that the army was stationed there for any period. By no means did that amount to a distinctly high-status residence, although it did include a few high-quality items and the large overseer's range (including an aisled building). Generally, Langdale lacked evidence of ritual activity and any equivalents to the Vicar's Farm shrine and Monumental Post-setting. Even more telling is the low number of coins recovered from Langdale, just 68 in total. Although this also attests to its reduced/altered Late Roman function, Langdale clearly saw no market-type activity.

What Langdale did have, however, was a wide array of crop-processing facilities, including a number of large mill settings, a ditched threshing floor 'ring' and a series of ditched and/or screened flue-settings, probably for the parching of grain (*ibid.*, 63–72, figs. 2.25 & 2.29). Admittedly it lacked a raised granary, but such a facility was present at The Camp Ground where Langdale's grain was evidently stored prior to its transhipment via the canal-system (*ibid.*, 242, figs. 3.38–9). Langdale also had a variety of posthole and beam-slot buildings. Although the total number of inhumations was low – only seven – extraordinarily, they were all males, potentially raising issues of just who worked there (e.g. slaves?). Based on the range of personal ornaments recovered, women are likely to have been resident (e.g. the overseer's family), but evidently did not stay long enough to die there. In short, Langdale's 'official state farm' was of a different character and less of a 'domestic community' than the Vicar's Farm settlement.

In relationship to Ballantyne's micro-debris study (see Fig. 6.18), in contrast with The Camp Ground's more multi-functional inland port settlement, both Vicar's Farm and Langdale Hale's farms essentially evince single, large-scale settlement core-focused middening. Langdale also had secondary 'hot-spots', but that is probably reflective of its more intensive sampling (92 bulk samples *vs.* Vicar's Farm's 43). Langdale's 'core-middening' expression occurred in its main 'Middle' Roman-phase samples (II.2 & .3; AD 180–325), with it having other much more restricted middens in its terminal phase (III; Evans *et al.* 2013b, fig. 2.69); whereas at Vicar's Farm its large-scale single-focus midden was a 'Late', Phase III phenomenon. Yet, with the midden's western extent broadly correlating with Vicar's Farm's main earlier structures – the Timber Shrine and Aisled Building – this chronological distinction maybe misleading. While it could attest to a degree of 'aftermath' middening upon the demise of those structures, the site's 'Late' phase-assigned samples might also have included residual micro-scale debris contemporary with their usage. Alternatively, the settlement saw a clear expansion of its residents and activity in its final phase, which could well have been accompanied by the expansion of its central midden. What is crucial is that both Vicar's Farm and Langdale seem to have shared a more straightforward single-focus spatial/midden organisation than the much more complex Camp Ground settlement.

Spaces, Buildings and Roles (and the Dead)

Bordered by the basin's high finds-densities, together with Ballantyne's settlement-core midden location, this central area accounts for the bulk of the site's artefacts and indicates a fairly unsophisticated use of space (Fig. 6.52). Yes, there were secondary artefact-category 'highs' along the main enclosure's (G2) northern/southern margins; on the whole, though, the settlement's central-swathe distributions are dominant. This suggests expediency. Despite claims concerning immediate-area midden siting (see Chap. 4, *Overviewing Survival …*), there seems to have been relatively little large-scale management of refuse and that the living space was not maintained in a highly organized manner (e.g. refuse carted out onto fields). In any such adjudication we must be wary of falling prey to normative evaluations of 'cleanliness', and all this surely also tells of the lively intensity of the settlement's 'Late-phase' usage. Nor should we underestimate just what the scale of the settlement's refuse would have entailed. In a spirit that 'numbers are good to think with (too)', here we draw upon (and factor) Brothwell's 1982 estimates for what degree of waste 100 households generated. These admittedly are based on historical urban populations; nonetheless, they still provide a useful depositional yardstick. If having a residential population of two to five households then, *per annum*, Vicar's Farm's settlement could have generated in the region of 3650–9125 kg of solid waste, 3640–9100 litres of urine, 162–405 kg of ash and 730–1825 kg of human feaces. Its 'solids' would then amount to 4.5 to 11.4 cu. m each year and might have been considerably greater if augmented by group gatherings.

Whether of ritual intent or just motivated by the convenient discard of tainted meat, the widespread disposal of so many animal-part remains within the settlement's main paddocks could not have been healthy. To this should also be added the pollen register of the intestinal parasite, Whipworm (*Trichuris*; see Scaife, Chap. 4 and, e.g., Mitchell 2017, 50–1). Spread through contact with faecal matter, this further attests to unhygienic conditions and that the settlement was somewhere people, animals and their 'waste' were in sustained contact.

Figure 6.11's portrayal of the Vicar's Farm main settlement spaces is no more than a caricature. In economic terms it fails to adequately indicate just how expansive the settlement's cropped fields must have been, and certainly they need not have just been localized to the northeastern sector. Nor do we have any means of establishing the extent of its pasture lands (see Chap. 7).

Within that schema, in terms of designated single-function usage, animals come out on top, having *c.* 1.1 ha devoted to them as opposed to just 0.8 ha for humans. While it is unlikely that either would have seen exclusive use, there are also three human/animal-shared areas (*c.* 0.9 ha in total), where people and stock would have interacted on a regular basis. In order to appreciate this, we need next to consider the number and location of the settlement's (human) residential loci.

We have already admitted that less obvious buildings might have evaded detection. There is also the possibility that only the western 'backside' of the settlement was exposed and that from Phase II its main building(s) were actually located east beyond the limits of excavation (see below). While including a distinct circular shrine and a monumental post-setting, on the whole a fairly limited range of building types were present on the site (see Fig. 6.4). Aside from the three square 'cell' arrangements, of the 'long' settings (4–5 × 10–12 m) – Structures A and B, and the possible G19 (F.5558), F.4137, F.5554 and F.5460 'candidates' – only Structure B involved a more sophisticated beam-slot

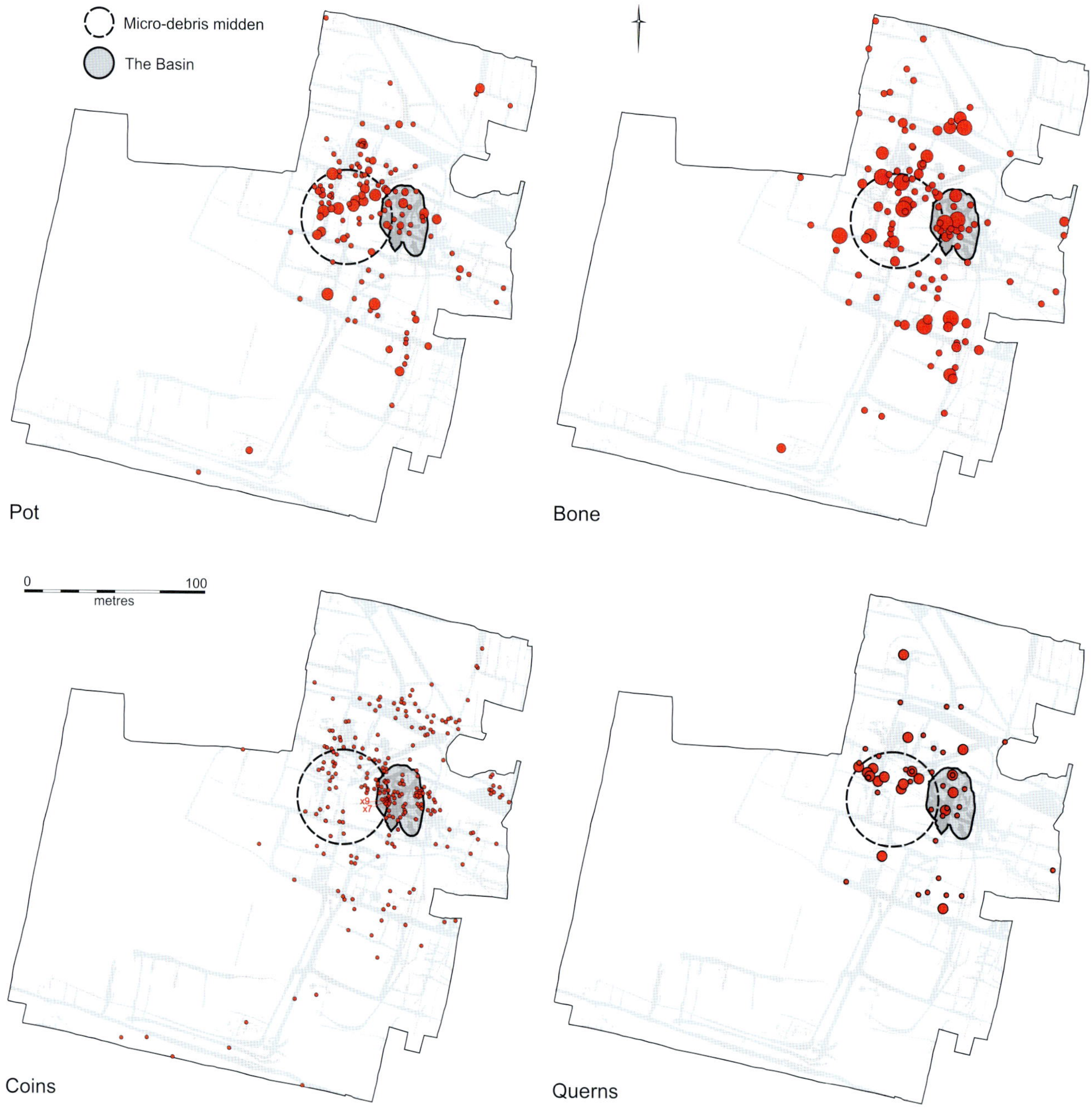

Figure 6.52. *The middening/depositional nexus: Ballantyne's micro-debris middening locale (see Fig. 6.18) and the basin's outline superimposed with selected artefact distribution plots. (If its deposits had been dug in their entirety, the basin-area would have almost been 'sold-red' in all finds categories.)*

and posthole building technique. We should not though underestimate the significance of Phase I/II's aisled building. Indeed, prior to the 2018 excavation of North West Cambridge's villa-estate centre (Site VII), it had been the only building of this type found on any of western Cambridge's Roman sites. Though the recovery of such structures is now more widespread (their postholes usually being so robust that they are not lost through plough-truncation or 'hard' machining), they are still rare. As a 'standard' Roman construction technique/design, we should be wary of 'over-domesticating' them. Evans can remember (the now sadly late) Richard Darrah commenting on the nature of aisled buildings (*vs.* Iron Age roundhouses) during a visit to one of North West Cambridge's excavations. Richard stressed just what an epitome of Romanization they represent: 'think of the size and regularity of the timbers involved, the large saws required for their working, plus the pulleys and amount of rope needed to raise the roof's frame and rafters'. Expressed in this way – almost as if you needed to have serious naval technology to erect such structures – and add to this the number of people involved (evoking Amish barn-raising scenes; Fig. 6.53), it certainly brought home just what stood behind buildings of this type.

Acknowledging the possible buildings in the site-area, it is worthwhile reviewing the 'rhythm' of the structures' phasing. The four in Phase I include two roundhouses (F.5402 & G2.19), F.5554's ditched rectangle and, of course, the Aisled Building (G2.01). In Phase II there would seem to have been at least five buildings. In addition to the continued usage of the Aisled Building and Structures A and B, this could include the northern rectangular G19 ditch-setting (*c*. 5 × 13 m) in Enclosure G24 (see Fig. 6.4) and possibly a comparable ditch arrangement (*c*. 4 × 13 m) along the northern side of Enclosure G7 in Area E (see Fig. 5.13). In Phase III, this dropped to just three or four buildings: Structures C and D, plus possibly the reworked version of G.19's 'embayment' setting and perhaps another set north–south along that enclosure's southwestern side (*c*. 4 × 11 m; F.5460). Based on the number and footprint of the designated buildings alone, by this measure the settlement's floruit would have occurred in Phase II.

It has to be remembered that Phase III's Structure D was probably some manner of small shrine; based on the similarity of their plans, Structure C may also have been. Completely contradicting the quantity of the settlement's 'Late-phase' finds, this would imply a very reduced residential provision (even if including the 'possible' settings). It is this, more than any other factor, that could lead one to suspect that the settlement's main buildings then lay to the east of the site-area.

How many separate residential units would the settlement have encompassed? In Phase II, three would seem the minimum and five the maximum. Even in Phase I, different households might have been involved. What was the status of the two roundhouses (if not just agriculturally related)? Perhaps the abode of (native) labourers, if so, they must only had negligible material possessions.

Figure 6.53. *Early twentieth-century barn-raising north of Toronto, Ontario (City of Toronto Archives).*

Apart from potential 'labourers', are there other roles that we might envisage for the settlement's inhabitants? There surely would have been some manner of 'overseer' and their family. Something as large and complex as this multiple-residence farm/market would not have run without some co-ordinating authority (probably requiring a degree of literacy for taxation purposes), and it can only be presumed that their residence would have been the Aisled Building. Beyond this, we can imagine a number of 'specialists', either resident, or as regular visitors. This would include a smith, a butcher, a carpenter and maybe even a priest for rituals. There would surely also have been various specific agricultural roles: perhaps a miller, a carter, a herdsman and so on. It is likely that textiles would have been manufactured there and someone could well have had medical expertise. Add to this, children and spouses, this certainly would have been a complex and vibrant place.

The dead were also part of this community. In the course of their lives the settlement's inhabitants would, at times, have encountered human remains through settlement-maintenance routines (e.g. ditch digging) and, otherwise, would have been aware of 'their place'. As argued, the occurrence of the cremation cemetery within the settlement is somewhat unusual; more common is the distancing of the dead as at North West Cambridge's Site II (see Fig. 5.41). That said, at Langdale Hale its main cemetery-area also occurred within its boundaries, but there within a separate paddock (see Fig. 6.51).

The possibility that the series of east–west burials in the Phase III inhumation cemetery reflects the uptake of Christianity has already been addressed in this chapter (see 'Overviewing the Dead'). If this was the case, it otherwise had no discernable impact on the settlement itself.

It is worth reviewing again the various categories of human remains at Vicar's Farm (Fig. 6.21). Leaving aside the specificity of its cremation cemetery, only neonates occurred within its core and this swathe was then rung with 'loose' finds – particularly skull fragments – whatever their source; beyond this were isolated adult burials, evidently excluded – for whatever reason – from the settlement's south-lying inhumation cemetery. Yet, as indicated in Figure 6.54, there would be other ways of reading patterning amongst the settlement's dead. Apart from three outliers, they all fell along a central north–south axis; this includes both of its cemeteries. In this it would have affinities with the New Hall burials, which were also seemingly arranged on a north–south line (though there can be no certainty of how the other burials lay within the area disturbed by the College's construction). The occurrence of the two neonate burials really conveys this sense of a north–south axis at Vicar's Farm. One lay within the forecourt-area before the Timber Shrine and just north of the Aisled Building; the other was in the packing of one Structure D's major postholes.[17] No single interpretation readily accounts for this distribution, except that in its spatial organization the settlement itself had a major north–south axis. With the cremation cemetery at its northern end, this would be distinguished by the location of the Aisled Building and, then, Structures B/D. While not a marked topographic divide, this was also the edge of the higher terrace land and from where the groundsurface began to drop down eastwards towards the lower wet ground.

The Timber Shrine would then have lain on the western side of this central axis. We could argue that this, together with the Monumental Post, defined a 'ritual cross-axis'. This, though, is not terribly convincing, as the shrine and great post-setting were off-set from each other (see Figs. 5.13 & 6.54). However, if Structure D's square 'cell' was some manner of shrine, then – in Phase III with the demise of the settlement's main shrine – its location could suggest a reinstatement of the main north–south axis. Amid what can seem the near-chaos of the settlement's cumulative enclosure sub-division/elaboration, there do seem to have been some underlying organizational principles.

While anticipating patterning that will only really become apparent in the next book, there was clearly a local propensity for 'Early-phase' cremation cemeteries to lie on the north side of settlements, with any later inhumation cemeteries to the south. This is evident in both North West Cambridge's Sites II and IV, as well as the main NIAB settlement and Foxton. The reasons for this reorientation of the 'place of the dead' and why it would correlate with this change in burial rite (i.e. cremation *vs.* inhumation) are unknown, but it does seem a distinct pattern in, at least, the local landscape.

An Estate Farm and Religious Architectures

While Vicar's Farm was producing surplus grain and flour, and probably also meat, it was also importing much of its material culture, including pottery, stone and metalwork. The primary question surrounding the economy at the site, particularly given the evidence for surplus production, is whether such production was linked to a larger, yet internally self-sufficient system (such as the army, the town or a large-scale peri-urban/villa-type estate), or whether it was directly part of a broader market economy. If production was being managed by a central authority for provision of a larger entity like the army, an estate or the town, one might not expect to see much reliance on monetary exchange or, indeed, evidence for trading activity generally (as opposed to directly traded goods). However, if Vicar's

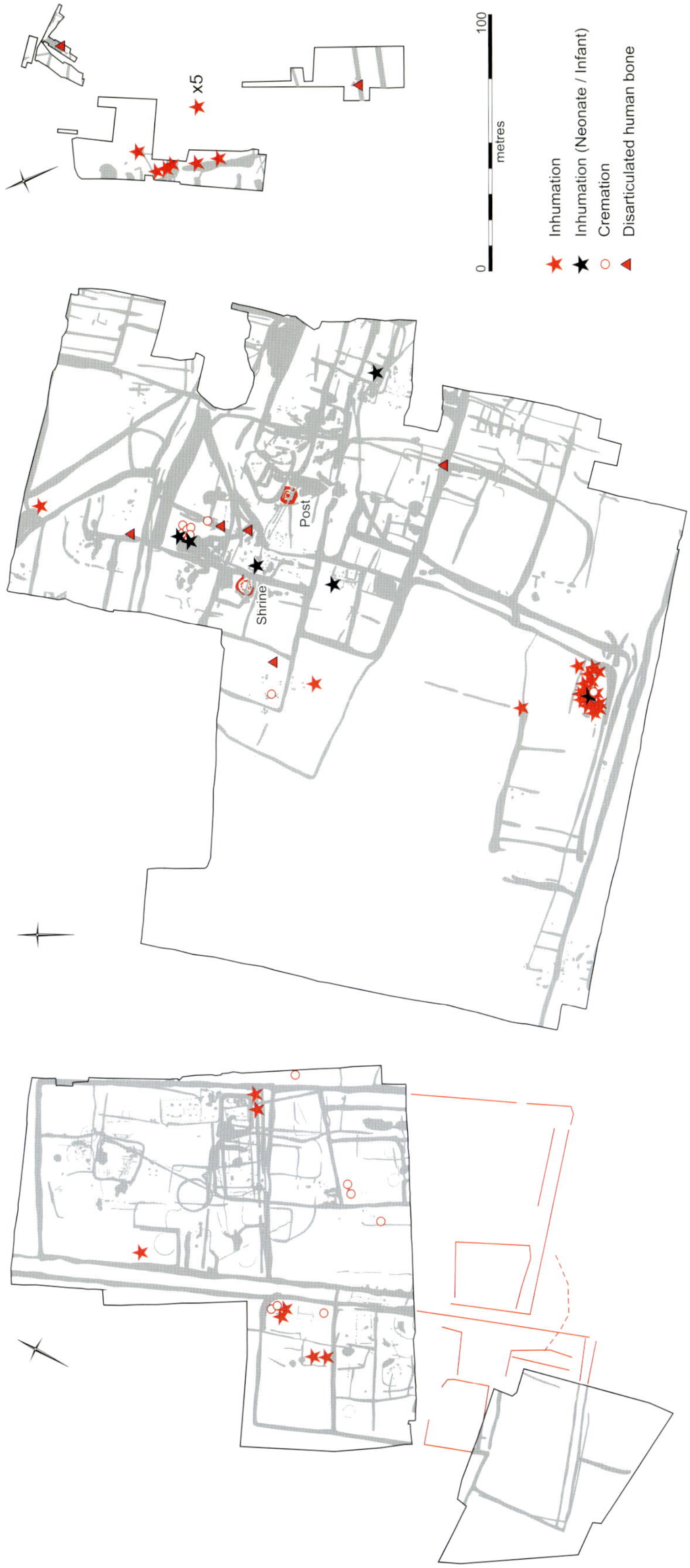

Figure 6.54. *The place of the dead: left, Langdale Hale; centre, Vicar's Farm and, right, New Hall.*

Farm was producing for a wider market, or at least operating within a market economy, then coinage and trade in general might be a more prominent facet of the site. Certainly, there was a relatively high number of coins retrieved from the site (over 300; see Reece, above), which does suggest an active involvement in a market economy.

The army is represented at the settlement in the form of a few military dress items and weapons (with Skeleton F.2058's distinct hobnail boots perhaps evincing an army veteran). The possibility of the military being a recipient of the surplus produce could be considered, as was the case for Orton Hall Farm (Mackreth 1996). Military items do not, however, necessarily imply military presence; indeed, the nature of what constitutes a 'military presence' is open to interpretation (James 2001). Even if the army was potentially receiving some of the surplus produce from Vicar's Farm, this does not imply they organized production, let alone had a sustained presence on the site. All things considered, the settlement's surplus was probably directed towards Roman Cambridge's non-agrarian civic population.

With the settlement clearly playing an important economic role in the locality, who was controlling or running this establishment? If we discount the army and any urban authority, then it is best considered *an estate farm and market*. That it was a major/'complex' farm and production centre cannot be in any doubt. Although it is likely to have had an 'overseer' (again, recognizing caveats of what buildings might still lie beyond the site's eastern margins), it did not seem to have had an 'elevated' high status residence. It is likely, therefore, that it was owned and sponsored by a household resident elsewhere.

The stone coffin burials found in the nineteenth century north of Vicar's Farm clearly belonged to high status individuals (see Chap. 1), and these were surely too far away from the town walls to be associated with an urban dweller. It is possible these burials are associated with a nearby residence housing the actual owners of Vicar's Farm (and subsequently destroyed through the Traveller's Rest Pit quarrying). Sited on the high ground above the settlement (*c.* 700 m north), this would have been an obvious place to locate a residence overlooking Vicar's Farm. Alternatively, and lying at a similar distance to the west, is North West Cambridge's Site VII complex, which is now (2018) known to have been a villa-estate centre (see Fig. 1.4). In the next chapter we will see that, in Post-Medieval times, the owner of Vicar's Farm lived on the higher ground (beside the Observatory) overlooking the farm and this may provide an indirect parallel for its Roman-era settlement.

The nature of the settlement's Phase II and III enclosures, the frequency of its 'Late' coinage – plus the recovery of the many weights – would support the idea of there having been a market at Vicar's Farm. This is only furthered by its overt ritual activity. The presence of intermittent fairs was suggested at Haddenham's Snow's Farm shrine (Evans & Hodder 2006b, 414–15). It was argued that ritual and exchange would have logically gone hand-in-hand, as exchange, after all, relies upon 'faith': is it an auspicious day to acquire this horse, will it remain healthy?

The level at which we see this market activity occurring at Vicar's Farm would probably approach that of a historic countryside fair (see Ligt 1993, 14–15 & 72–82 on periodic local Roman markets/fairs). Given that we now know how densely packed with farms the local Roman landscape was, if nothing else, the trading of livestock would have been essential to the healthy maintenance of herds and flocks. Market days might well have involved other commodities, as some of the neighbouring farms could have specialized in textiles or cured meats and, depending on the immediate location of their plots (and water supply), some may have grown vegetables not available to others. Some of these exchanges might have occurred in 'official' front-space, and have involved currency, whereas other might have been transacted behind the scenes and relied on informal barter. Also, such gatherings would surely have involved the large-scale consumption of food and drink, and this must have impacted on the site's assemblages.

There is always the possibility that, at certain times in the calendar, separate religious festival-gatherings could have occurred. Yet, despite what parallels have been drawn between the settlement's shrines and that at Haddenham, they differed markedly. The paucity of distinctly ritual deposits directly associated with the Vicar's Farm shrine settings, contrasts with the sheep and bird sacrifice so prominent at Haddenham's Snow's Farm shrine (Evans & Hodder 2006b, 413–15). While the Vicar's Farm horse head-pit would have broad affinities to, for example, the 'arranged' animal carcasses within Cambridge's apsidal-ended shrine (see Chap. 2, Figs. 2.21 & 6.55.1), such deposits did not occur within the site's shrines as such; Structure D's neonate burial and the coin group associated with the Monumental Post are held to reflect different modes of ritual deposits.

As shown in Figure 6.55, the distinctly religious buildings/structures recovered within Cambridge and the western Cambridge lands vary greatly. This is an issue that will have to be returned to in the next book, but it is one that deserves some airing here. While almost henge-like – with its dense of ring of posts

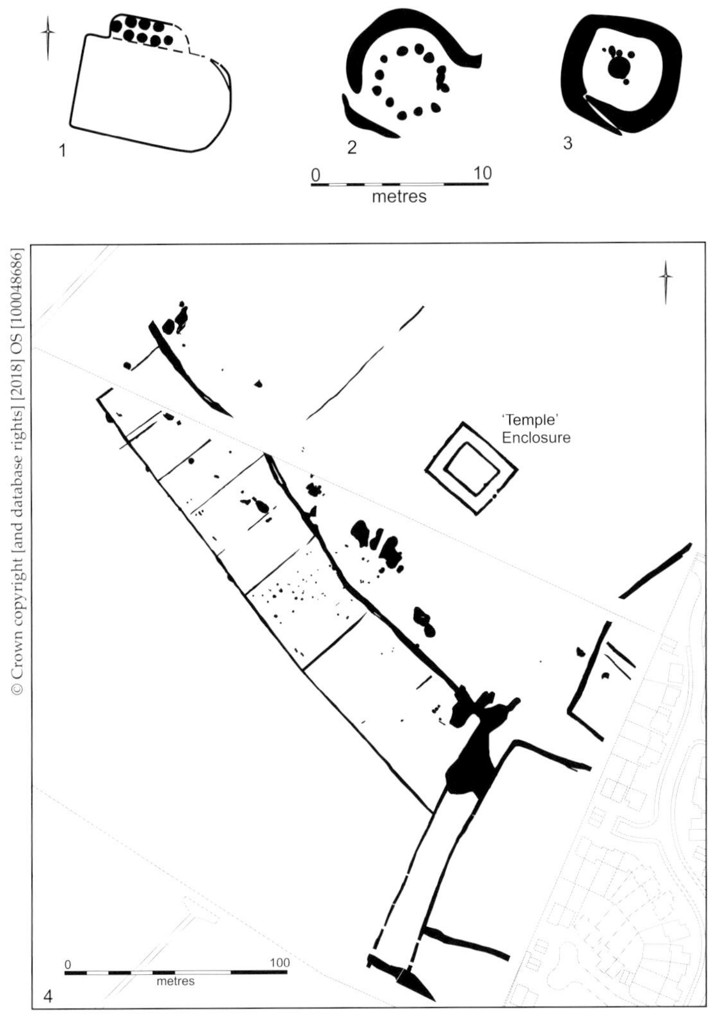

Figure 6.55. *Ritual architectures: 1) Ridgeons Garden apsidal shrine (see Fig. 2.21); 2 & 3) Vicar's Farm, the Timber Shrine and Monumental Post-setting; 4) temple enclosure, NIAB Site (Barker & Meckseper 2015; see also Smith* et al. *2018, 245, fig. 6.31).*

potentially evocative of a stand of trees – as argued above, the main shrine at Vicar's Farm would have had generic similarities to Romano-Celtic circular/octagonal structures. The apsidal-ended layout of Cambridge's cellared shrine would seem to draw on more 'standard' Roman religious architectures (e.g. Medlycott 2011, 89–91, figs. 5.9–10); but it had, in contrast, such extraordinary votive animal-burial deposits. Yet more formally planned is the 'temple enclosure' excavated at the NIAB Site north of North West Cambridge (Fig. 6.55; Barker & Meckseper 2015). Seemingly drawing upon classical prototypes (though there was no evidence of an interior building as such), it had almost no depositional activity associated with it. Lying at the junction of roads, it was situated in an empty yard/field, with some 60 m of apparently clear space between it and a series of ladder settlement compounds to the south. In this, its arrangement is comparable to the major temple complex at Cottenham (Taylor 1985), whose function has been argued to both complement and contrast with that of Haddenham's shrine (Evans & Hodder 2006b, 410–11, fig. 7.47). It is clear that a wide range of ritual/religious activity, evidently drawing on diverse traditions, underpinned the farming basis of the local Romano-British landscape.

What is a Farm?

The inclusion of the local pub-related *Inset* within this chapter is appropriate on the grounds that it returns us to the site's Post-Medieval usage. Its relevance is not only that the later nineteenth-century inhabitants of Vicar's Farmyard probably drank there on occasion, but that the familiar plan of the site's historic farm can help us address the question of just 'what is a farm' and why does its Roman layout differ so greatly.

Thanks to Baggs' survey (see Chap. 4), we can compare their floor 'footprints'. In the case of the Post-Medieval farm, the residential space would have amounted to *c.* 90.5 sq. m (including the house's second storey) and, with its barn and sheds, there would have been a further 226.5 sq. m: 317 sq. m in total. In comparison, the Roman settlement's Phase II structural

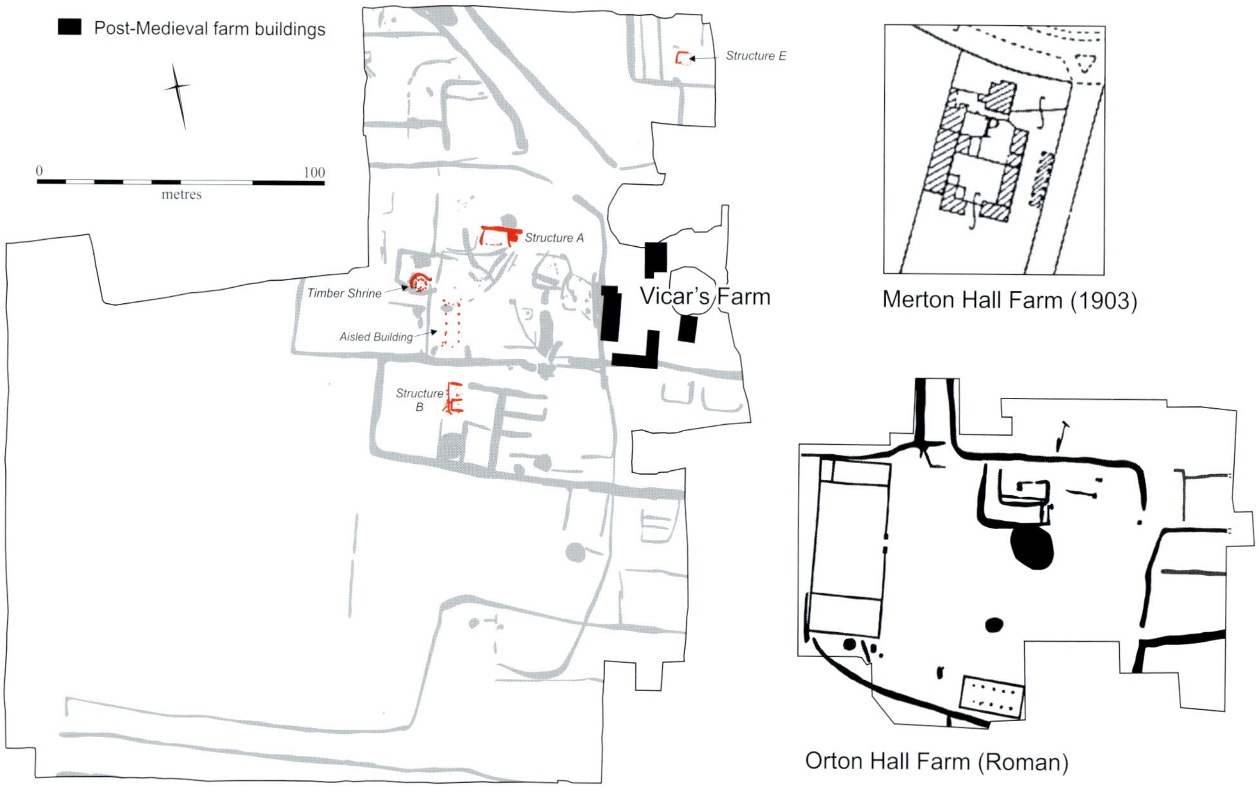

Figure 6.56. *Vicar's Farm's Roman building axes and its Post-Medieval farmyard layout compared (right); left, courtyard farms: Post-Medieval Merton Hall Farm (top; see Fig. 4.17) and, below, Roman Orton Hall Farm (Mackreth 1996; see Evans* et al. *2013b, fig. 2.76).*

footprint would have amounted to somewhere between 276 and 393 sq. m (see also Evans *et al.* 2013b, fig. 2.76 for comparison of Romano-British farms and Haddenham's latter-day Snow's Farm).

A more telling difference is that the Post-Medieval farm did not lie at such a 'hub' within the landscape, the Roman farming settlement being located at a focal point of roads/tracks. Nor (as far as we know) did it have any equivalents to the Roman settlement's shrines and cemeteries or fulfill any kind of market/fair role. Perhaps the most telling difference is the sheer multitude of the Roman ditched compounds and enclosures. These presumably related to large-scale stock management, as well as the penning of livestock during markets/fairs. The complex manner in which the space was sub-divided – at least during Phases II and III – could also reflect that the settlement's residents included non-kin-group members. As discussed, there likely would have been 'labourers', and perhaps even slaves, whose residence lay apart from that of the main family. This complex 'Roman space' therefore might not have just involved the separation of humans from different sorts of animals, but also, potentially, different sorts of people. In short, *the site's Roman layout probably reflects a far more socially and economically complex nexus than the 'average' historical-era farm.*[18]

As shown in Figure 6.56 – and at risk of stating the obvious – notice the quasi-courtyard-like layout of the Vicar's Farmyard buildings; this type of arrangement is more apparent in the former plan of the neighbouring Merton Hall Farm (see, also, Fig. 4.17). This kind of enclosed yard setting was widespread in historic-era farms (e.g. U. of Glos. *et al.* 2006, 39–41). Having vague affinities with the courtyard plans of many of the Ancient World's great houses/villas and public buildings, it actually seems to have had little expression in the region's Roman farmsteads (Orton Hall Farm's being something of an exception: Mackreth 1996; see Smith *et al.* 2016, 192–206 for overview). Instead, their buildings were usually more dispersed, often lying around the peripheries of the ditched compounds in which they sat. As outlined above, it was these 'farmstead unit' rectangular compounds that provided their dominant spatial framework and would have defined much larger, multi-purpose working/living spaces than many Post-Medieval farm layouts. Yet, in relationship to issues of hygiene and living space, the more tightly packed (historic) courtyard-plans of Vicar's and Merton Hall's Farms would have had the advantage that their (paved) building-framed yards could be more readily maintained if waste was regularly mucked out and spread onto fields.

Notes

1 Aside from those shown in Figure 6.2, other local examples include those recently excavated at Yaxley, Peterborough (Phillips 2014), Haddon (Hinman 2003), Love's Farm, St Neots (Hinman & Zant 2018) Addenbrooke's Bio-Medical Campus (Tabor 2015) and Northstowe/Longstanton (Collins 2017). However, aisled buildings only occurred at seven of the 85 Roman settlements in Cambridgeshire fen-edge case-study area within *The Rural Settlement of Roman Britain* volume (Smith *et al.* 2016, 204).

Two (arguably three) aisled buildings occurred on a Roman farmstead site recently excavated at Woodditton, Cambridgeshire (Mustchin *et al.* 2016); two of these were contemporary and of late first- to mid second-century AD date, with the other being later. While two would seem broadly comparable to that at Vicar's Farm, the other – Building 1 – was enormous and extended over *c.* 10 × 28 m (*ibid.*, 11–13, figs. 2–4). At that size it would have been much larger than most of the other regional examples and seems akin, for example, to elongated ranges such as have been found in the Thames Gateway-area (see e.g. Lucy & Evans 2016, 97, fig. 2.47). Closer to home, the first phase of Arbury's King's Hedges villa consisted of a two-storey aisled hall (carried on stone pier bases) extending over *c.* 14.5 × 29 m and now has affinities with North West Cambridge's Site VII's great 'aisled hall' (Alexander *et al.* 1969). See, also, Green 2018 and Lyons forthcoming for the aisled ranges at Godmanchester's villas.

2 See, for example, Luke and Preece 2011 or Patten 2012 (see *BLS*, 87 & 138, figs. 2.16 & 2.58 concerning issues of distinguishing slightly-footed Roman buildings).

3 These figures include Post-Medieval tile.

4 A dog was interred (complete) within the Hutchison Site's cemetery at Addenbrooke's accompanied by a stone nodule (*BLS*, 49, figs. 2.19–20).

5 All the samples were analysed in the laboratory. Initially they were air-dried and ground, then passed through a 2 mm sieve. The prepared, weighed samples were then treated to assess total phosphate levels with a hydrochloric acid digestion method adapted from Dick and Tabatabai (1977). The phosphate content of the processed samples was established colourimetrically by the standard molybdenum blue method of Murphy and Riley (1962), quantified by reference to a standard curve. The absence of any control samples for the site means that all conclusions on levels of phosphate encountered are relative to the site only. All phosphate concentrations are quoted in milligrams of phosphorus per hundred grams of soil (mg. P per 100 g soil).

6 Apparently 'pony jaws' occurred beside the central inhumation in Arbury Road's mausoleum cemetery (Fell 1956, fig. 1). Similarly, in Arbury's King's Hedges villa there was said to be a 'ritual pit' in which a horse mandible lay upon a flat stone slab surface (Lisboa 1994). Given the nature of both of these excavations is it difficult to appreciate these findings and the degree to which their horse remain deposits were meaningful. The same could be said of the two horse skulls within one of Scole's riverside tanks (Ashwin & Tester 2014, 145, 198, fig. 3.26). At a farmstead complex in Cedars Park, Stowmarket, a crouched burial was interred beside a horse burial. While there is uncertainty whether it was of Iron Age or Romano-British date (Nicholson & Woolhouse 2016, 84–5, fig. 56), another inhumation there – within a Roman-phase ditch – had a horse skull set at its feet (*ibid.*, 57, fig. 38). Ritual horse sacrifice deposits certainly occurred within the Iron Age and have, for example, been found in the platform at the end of the Godwin Ridge (Evans *et al.* 2016b, 518, 536–40, figs. 6.14 & 6.16) and within a pit at Duxford (Lyons 2011, 18, figs. 9 & 11).

7 Burnt chicken bones also accompanied two out of six of Langdale Hale's cremations (plus one 'token' deposit; Evans *et al.* 2013b, 84, table 2.7; see also Pearce 2013, 37).

8 Considered in greater length in the companion book, while there were also burials within its settlement proper, the main cemeteries at Knobb's Farm (Nos. 2 & 3) lay on either side of a major trackways and along the settlement's southern flanks (Evans *et al.* 2013b, 468–71, figs. 5.9, 5.12–13). In contrast, while having distinct clusters of burials, no clearly defined cemeteries were present at either of the two main Colne Fen Sites (*ibid.*, 79–85 & 232–6, figs. 2.35 & 3.34), with interments occurring throughout their settlement-areas. This is particularly relevant given their arguably 'official' status; however, in the case of The Camp Ground's port-village, it is possible that its main cemetery lay beyond the area of excavation (*ibid.*, 448, fig. 4.61).

9 Arguably, now known to be on the opposite side of the roadway and, to the south, in the area of the AstraZenaca North Site (Tabor 2015).

10 See Millett and Gowland's recent discussion of infant and child burials (2015; see also Gowland 2001). Arguing against the oft-cited 'otherness' of infant burials in the Roman world and infanticide practices, they suggest that neonatal infants were widely interred in pits close to domestic buildings and relate this to the indivisibility of mothers and their offspring. While certainly an attractive interpretation, to some extent it could be undermined by the widespread occurrence of such burials in postholes – as at Vicar's Farm and The Camp Ground – as there is no reason why (natural) infant deaths and variously the construction/dismantlement of structures would have coincided (see also Perring 2002, 198–99). As outlined in Chapter Two, the series of child shaft burials at Roman Cambridge would also dispute such 'domestic mode' explanations of burials and, instead, they seem cult-related.

11 As outlined in Chapter Two, Cambridge's Jesus Lane cemetery included three decapitated burials (all male),

out of a total population of 32 individuals (Alexander *et al.* 2004). Cambridgeshire is cited for its high percentage of 'deviant' burials (see Crerar 2016) and the cemeteries at Knobb's Farm, Somersham has amongst the highest known frequency of decapitation interments: 13 out of 53 overall (*c.* 25%), rising to six out of 13 (46%) within one of its individual cemetery plots (see Evans *et al.* 2013b, 471, figs. 5.9, & 5.12–13). A number of the Knobb's Farm burials also include small Nene Valley jars, which in some cases had been placed to replace or 'complement' heads, and one such vessel also occurred – between the upper legs (i.e. where decapitated skulls are often located) – in the Jesus Lane cemetery (Skeleton [022]; Alexander *et al.* 2004, 74, figs. 5 & 9.2). This could, in fact, suggest linked cult practices between the lower town cemetery and that at Knobb's Farm on the fen-edge; if so, the inhabitants of Vicar's Farm evidently did not participate in this.

12 The inhumations at Langdale Hale's 'state supply farm' were all males and seem likely to attest to non-familial labourers (see Fig. 7.37; Evans *et al.* 2013b, 79–82, table 2.6).

13 While it seems likely that these bone deformities reflect biomechanical adaptions (see Neil & Mulder, Chap. 5; e.g. Lovejoy *et al.* 1976), the location of the skeletons with this condition could be used to argue that this reflects a familial grouping and, accordingly, that they shared a genetic trait. They are clustered in the northwestern end of the cemetery (Fig. 5.37) – with Burial F.2046 (having two bracelets) otherwise being part of its central grouping and F.991 located outside of it. To the best of our knowledge this condition has not been identified on other skeletons within this area; one would suspect that it should be much more widespread in the period's burials if squatting or a persistent labouring-action was the cause. That said, the results of the cemetery's aDNA analysis (Scheib *et al.*, Chap. 5) would not now indicate a genetic source.

14 See Casa-Hatton and Wall's discussion of the richly accompanied child burial (114) in cemetery exposed within a service trench at Chesterton in 1998 (Durobrivae; 2006). She had a 'pile' of jewellery: eight copper alloy armlets, three/four ivory armlets, a glass and amber bead necklace and, possibly, a copper alloy earring. With the armlets being far too large for a child of its age, this may reflect the child's intended dowry as has been suggested for a number of young female burials in other Roman cemeteries (see also for their citations for familial groupings and 'intrusive burials' within the period's cemeteries; *ibid.*, 9, 15 & 19).

15 Close scrutiny of the published lists suggests that some coins from the Castle Hill group have accidentally been doubled and printed twice in the 2000 publication (*RCAM*, 139–40; Coins 190 to 229 have, therefore, been omitted in the present calculations. If they need to be put back in, the diagrams will change very little, because they seem to be virtually identical to Coins 133 to 167.

16 See Evans *et al.* 2013b (106, 351–2 and figs. 2.53 & 4.28) on variability of lead weight forms at the Colne Fen settlements (see also, e.g. Price *et al.* 1997, 111, fig. 64).

17 Further to Millett and Gowland's 2015 'domestic context' arguments, neonate burial would not seem to have been universal on Roman settlements. That none occurred at Langdale Hale probably relates to the specificity of its 'enforced labour' community, and the exposure at New Hall was too limited to provide solid negative evidence. Against this, though, relatively few neonate remains were associated with North West Cambridge's Roman settlements (see Pearce 2013, 107–8 on infant burials and 'settlement-concentric' modes of Roman infant *vs.* child/adult burial).

18 This is not to say that the latter-day inhabitants of Vicar's Farm did not lead complex lives. If nothing else, the frequency with which its ownership changed (see Chap. 4) would not attest to long/stable rural continuities, but rather reflect 'complications' and begs the question of what became of them thereafter (see, also, Chap. 7, *Madingley Rises…*).

Chapter 7

The High Cross Settlement and Other Investigations – *Postscript and Landscape Context*

Following on from the Vicar's Farm excavations, late in 2000 further evaluation fieldwork was undertaken across the southern half of the University's West Cambridge Site. This entailed excavating some 1500 m of trenches over *c.* 20 ha of its farm's pasture lands, the geology being largely heavy Gault Clays (see Fig. 7.1; Whittaker 2001). Other than a localized scatter of Late Medieval pottery along its extreme southeastern margin, archaeology was restricted to the area's western, High Cross quarter. Although not particularly dense, Iron Age and Roman settlement features extended throughout more than 3 ha against a slight background of later Bronze Age activity (a few probably earlier flints were also retrieved; one being Mesolithic).[1]

As detailed below, further evaluation trenching thereafter occurred across West Cambridge's northern half in 2015 and 2017. Finally, prior to a 'postscript overview', this chapter also reports on the 2018 excavation of yet another Roman-period farmstead located on the University Sports Ground, the Wilberforce Road Site. Aside from providing still more settlement insights, these latter fieldwork campaigns greatly enhanced our understanding of the 'lie' of the clay landscape and its dynamics.

The High Cross Settlement (with Simon Timberlake)

It was not until the winter of 2009–10, with the progress of West Cambridge's building programme, that the western site-area – the High Cross Settlement – was excavated. Straddling a preserved hedge-/drain-line, in total 2.2 ha was machine-stripped. For the sake of reference, this was sub-divided into three working areas: A to the south and, north of the boundary, B and C (Fig. 7.1). The conditions of excavation were far from ideal. The ground was claggy and the level of the groundwater was high, with the result that digging across the site's lower third required continuous pumping; snow-cover and frost also made the fieldwork difficult (Fig. 7.2).

The lie of the land sloped down from north to south, from *c.* 19 m to just below 16 m OD (stripped surface level). It rose up again slightly along the site's southern margin, with there being a minor east-northeast to west-southwest-oriented 'valley-trough', whose bottom-axis fell within Area B north of the hedge-line (Fig. 7.1). A simple surface-geology map was assembled following the site's stripping; there were up to a metre or two of silts, sands and gravels locally overlying the area's clays. These 'diamict' deposits (see below) outcropped as a thin spread of Boulder Clay above the top of the Gault at the far south end of Area A. The orientation of the valley, corresponding with that of lenticular current-bedded sands and silts, suggests a Pleistocene palaeochannel, likely part of a greater east–west fluvial system (Fig. 7.24).

In the course of the 2009–10 excavations, some 257 archaeological features were dug and recorded (Figs. 7.3–4; Timberlake 2010). Although the concrete footings of the Shorts (SEBRO) works were planned (see *Inset* and Fig. 7.3), associated remains – including a dump-spread along the west side of Area A – were not investigated due to the risk of contaminants.

Site Sequence

Facets of the site's archaeology proved somewhat amorphous and difficult to tie-down, largely reflecting the little understood processes of the prehistoric colonization of the region's 'heavy lands'. Despite this, a surprisingly long use-sequence was evinced.

Mesolithic/Early Neolithic

Only one small pit (F.240), close to the southwestern end of Area C (Fig. 7.7), can be reliably dated to this phase. This is based on a small assemblage of flint: two blades, (one utilized) and a burnt flake with a faceted platform (see Fig. 7.11). These had been incorporated into a backfill deposit associated with hearth-waste and three refitting fragments of unworked burnt flint. The faceted platform of the

Figure 7.1. *The West Cambridge investigation areas (top) and, below, the High Cross Site.*

Figure 7.2. *High Cross excavations, the site in flood and under snow (note the Schlumberger Building's 'big-top' profile looming behind top image).*

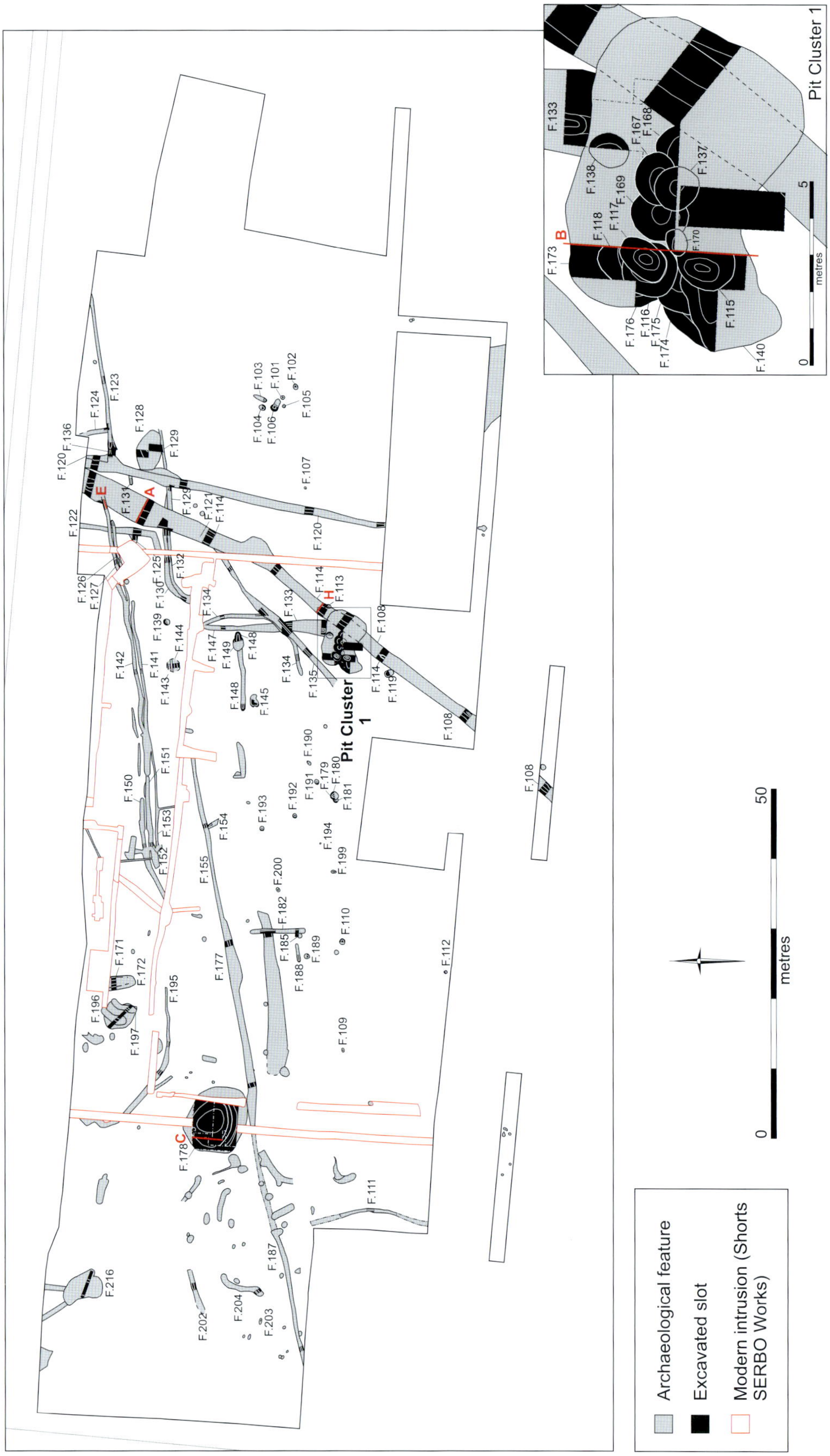

Figure 7.3. *Base plan, Area A, with detail of Pit Cluster 1 (see Fig. 7.1 for location).*

Figure 7.4. *Base plan, Areas B and C, with detail of Pit Cluster 2 (see Fig. 7.1 for location).*

flint flake would seem to be more typical of Neolithic, rather than Mesolithic, flintworking. It remains possible that this pit, or large posthole, forms part of a group of associated features (F.225–9, F.333 & F.250; Fig. 7.7) However, only the most northerly of these, F.250, can confidently be attributed to the Mesolithic/Early Neolithic on the basis of the similarity of its shape and fills with F.240. In addition, a single later Mesolithic flint microlith was recovered from a small tree-throw at the far eastern end of Area A (F.106).

Bronze Age

On the south side of the valley, at the western end of Area A, a *c.* 5 m diameter and at least 2 m deep silted hollow has been interpreted as a Middle Bronze Age well or watering-hole (F.178; Figs. 7.6–7), whose use might possibly have continued into the later Bronze Age. This was first partly excavated by machine whilst still under water and, later, hand-excavated and recorded once that area had been drained. The machine-excavation took the form of a 5 m wide cutting through two major units of infill: a dark grey-brown organic silt and clay with thin peat lenses and wood that sealed a brown gravelly silt and sand, mixed with some peat and clasts of chalk and stone. Freshwater snails and plant remains, plus a small amount of butchered animal bone and some radially split wood, were recovered from it. In addition, there was a single body-sherd of flint-tempered pottery that was thought might be Late Bronze Age, but its exact location within the feature's fill could not be determined. Further excavation indicated that the upper well deposit was conjoined by a 15–40° sloping 'ramp' at least 2 m long. This appeared to have been cut from the southeastern side of the feature to terminate in a central wide 'well' shaft, indicating that this feature may have been dug as a freshwater supply for animals.

As indicated on Figure 7.7, traces of a suspected interrupted ditch-line were recovered (F.148/F.149), which could conceivably be contemporary with the F.178 watering-hole; however, it is ambiguous and no artefactual material was found.

Only one discrete pottery-dated Middle Bronze Age feature was found: F.215, an oval-shaped flat-bottomed pit 1.02 m across and 0.35 m deep, at the south end of Area C. It yielded over 90 sherds from two vessels, one, at least, definitely being a Deverel Rimbury urn in grog fabric. This pottery would appear to have been deposited along with butchered domestic animal bone (mostly cattle) and burnt stone. Although no other actual features have been recognized, 7 m to the north of this a significant amount of residual Middle Bronze Age pot was recovered from an Iron Age pit (F.209; Fig. 7.12), which hints of a more extensive Middle Bronze Age presence. Further residual pot of this date was also recovered from Iron Age pits only 10–20 m to the north, implying the continuation of activity in that direction.

Early Iron Age

Formed from a series of abutting and interconnecting ditch segments (F.108/F.114/F.156/F.184) and perhaps relating to the control of stock movement across the lower valley-trough, the site's most significant Early Iron Age feature was a 0.5–1 m deep and 1.7–3.9 m wide ditch (Figs. 7.3–4, 7.6–7). With a 'V'- to 'U'-shaped profile, this crossed the valley floor in a south/southwest–north/northeast direction for a distance of 75 m. The feature's southern terminus was not observed within the area of excavation; its northern length (F.184) was cut by Pit Cluster 2. There was evidence for contemporary recutting within the central part of the ditch (F.114), close to the northern edge of Area A. In general, the base of this had been dug more narrowly and deeply within the Gault Clay/Boulder Clay, and was shallower and wider within the gravel, silts and sands. In places it appeared to have been backfilled rapidly, followed by a slower accumulation of darker silt towards the top; the latter contained charcoal, animal bone, rare fragments of human bone, burnt stone and pot. Of the pottery, while the majority was Early Iron Age in date, within the uppermost fills Middle Iron Age-type wares also occurred. The evidence of snails, seeds and pollen retrieved from it suggests the presence of seasonal standing water within the feature, with marshy ground or springs and secondary woodland nearly. What is most significant in the layout of this ditch was a *c.* 4 m wide interruption towards its northern end, a gap that corresponded with the lowest point in the valley. There, a slight easterly turn to the northern terminal (F.184), plus a swing eastwards in the form of an additional 5 m long east–west segment to the south (F.356), delineated what must have been an in-turned entrance.

Pit Cluster 2 consisted of some 20 pits (F.230–6, F.244–9 & F.251–7; Fig. 7.4). Most appeared to be more or less contemporary on the basis of the rather limited Early Iron Age pottery evidence and were dug in three or four overlapping groups, the earliest being the smallest group that lay at its western limit (F.244–8).

Other much smaller pit clusters also occurred within Area C. This included a group of 0.4–0.5 m diameter, oval-shaped pits (F.209–11 & F.214) that had varying amounts of burnt domestic debris, including bone, pottery and burnt stone, plus several fragments of saddle quern (see Fig. 7.14.1). Six metres to the north were seven intercutting pits (F.282 & F.292–7). Partially disturbed by modern sub-soiling, for the most part these were infilled with a dark charcoal-rich sediment containing hearth debris and assorted domestic rubbish, including decorated pottery, bone, a small chalk spindlewhorl and burnt stone. Their environmental samples also yielded significant evidence: carbonized cereal grains (spelt and emmer), hazelnut shell, grass seeds and hundreds of small fragments of pot. Some 50 m to the north lay another small pit (F.339), which had large fragments of Early Iron Age pottery in it.

As reported on by Natasha Dodwell, the human remains from ditch F.114 ([236]) included refitting fragments of the frontal part of a juvenile skull (see Figs. 7.6 & 7.15 for location). Eight loose maxillary teeth were also recovered; they are a mix of deciduous and permanent dentition, at different stages of development and suggest that the child died at *c.* 7 years ±24 months (Brown 1985; Ubelaker 1989). Small pits and worm-like lesions and a plaque of new bone in the roofs of both orbits are characteristic of *cribra orbitalia* (Fig. 7.8), suggesting that the child may have suffered from anaemia resulting from parasitic infections, childhood illnesses or nutritional deficiencies.

Middle Iron Age

There appear to be two main foci of activity from this time. On the slightly higher ground at the south end of Area A was Pit Cluster 1, which was sealed by an organic dark layer with Middle Iron Age pottery; to the north, at the top of Area C, was a scatter of minor settlement-related features (Fig. 7.7).

Pit Cluster 1 consisted of some 15 intercutting features (F.115–18, F.138–140 & F.167–76; Figs. 7.3 & 7.5), but not all yielded pottery and one, F.169, just contained the partial skeleton of a cow. There was clear evidence, though, for sequential digging of the pits, with a better-defined later phase (F.115, F.137–8 & F.140). One pit, F.115, had moderate amounts of burnt stone, redeposited iron slag and saddle quern fragments, with another having a large triangular clay loomweight (F.140; Fig. 7.14.4). Most of the later-dug pits, however, had no clearly distinguishing attributes, other than that they were all grouped within the middle and southwestern corner of the cluster. That at least half of these pits appeared to have been recut, completely backfilling earlier ones, suggests that they were unlikely to have been dug intentionally as quarries; perhaps, instead, these were retting pits, or else either for holding water or depositing refuse.

The formation of a midden horizon over the top of these infilled features is indicated by the presence of a dark, *c.* 0.17 m deep silt layer, which covered almost the entire area of the cluster (approximately 9 × 6.5 m). This horizon might relate to worsening drainage conditions and a higher watertable. However, the continuing

Figure 7.5. *Feature photographs: top, ditch F.157; middle, section across Pit Cluster 1; bottom, pit F.343 with burnt stone fragments in base.*

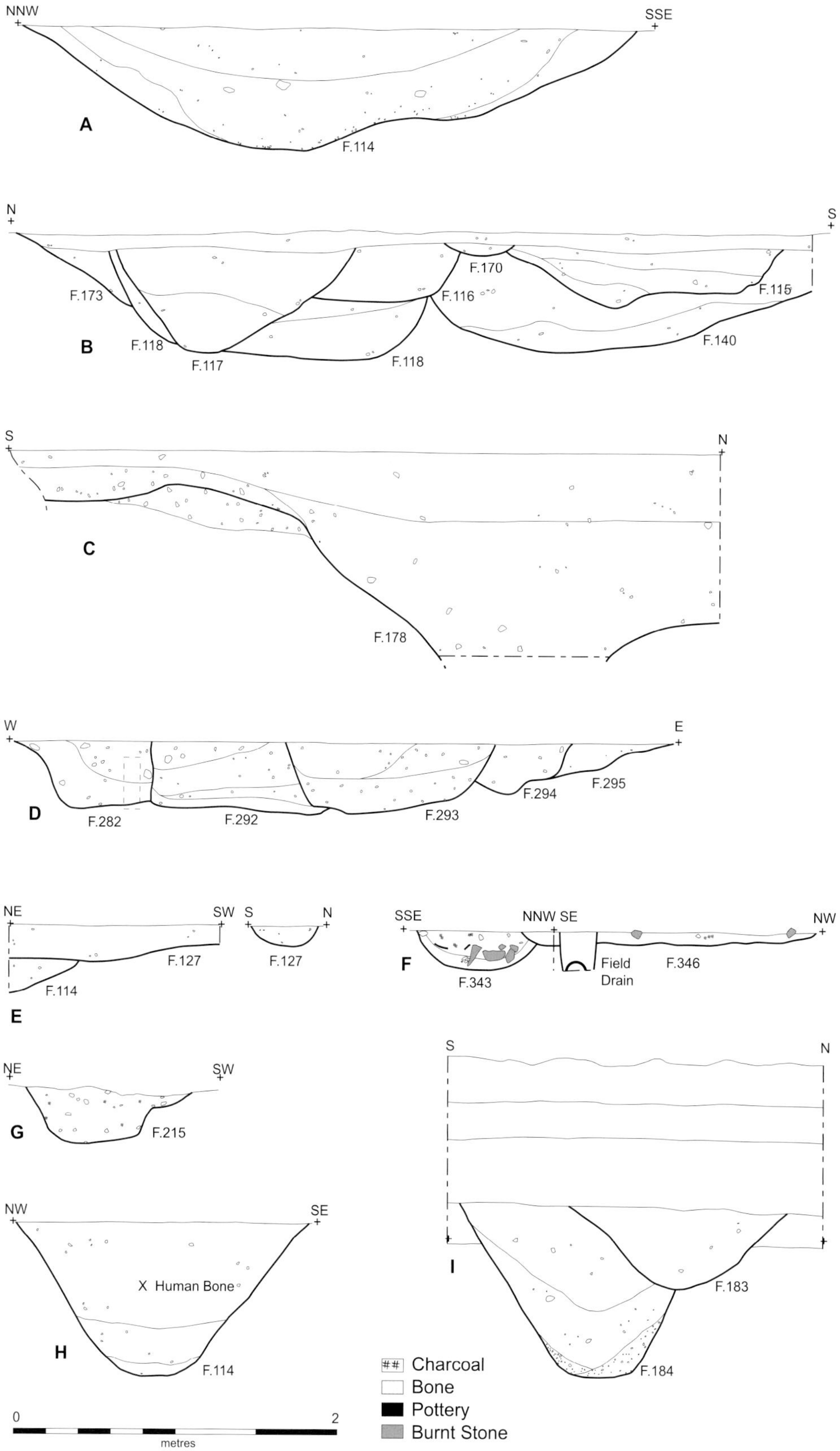

Figure 7.6. *Main feature sections (see Figs. 7.3 & 7.4 for location).*

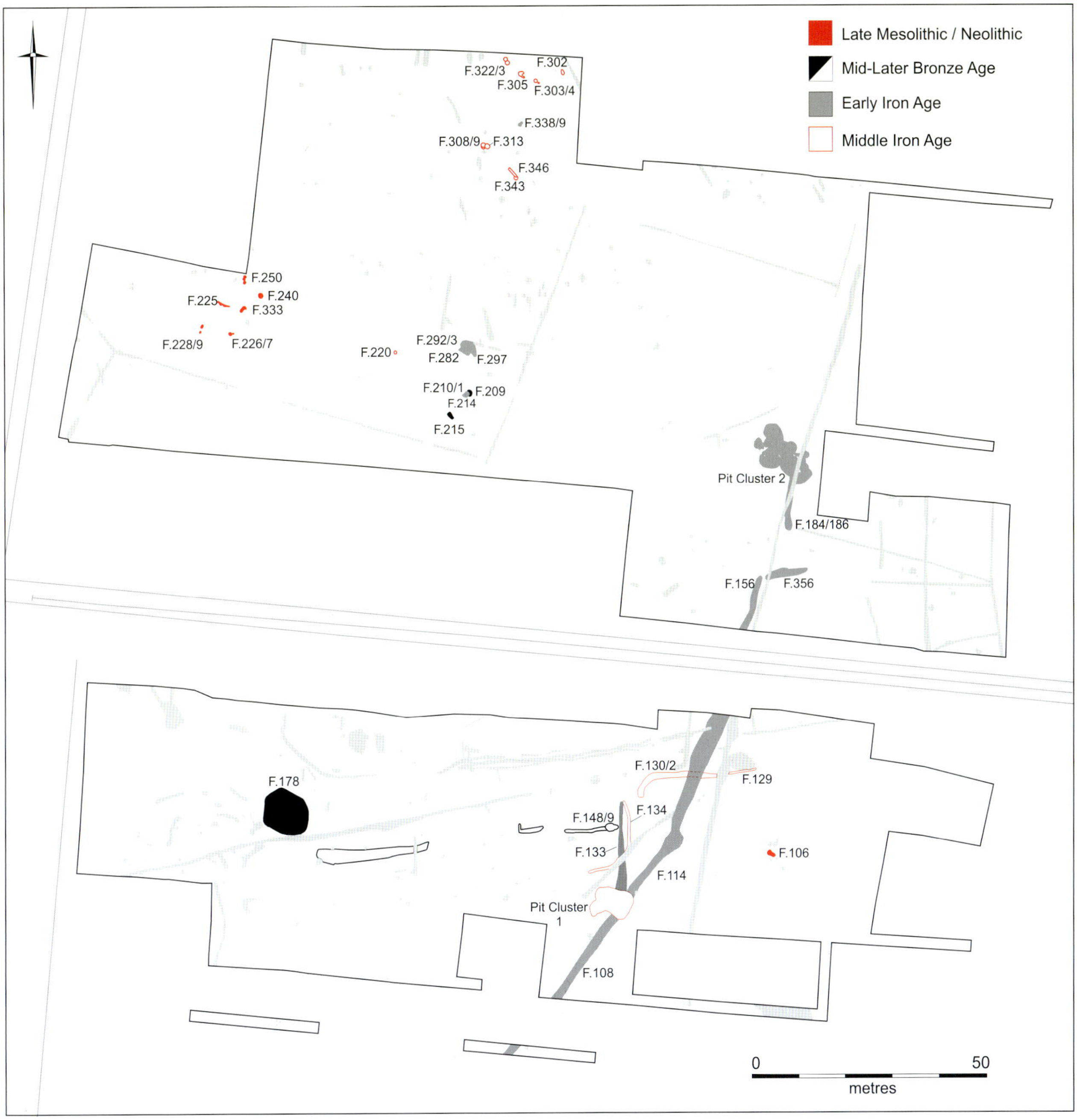

Figure 7.7. *Phase plan showing Mesolithic to Iron Age features.*

discard of rubbish within this area would suggest the persistence of a low-level occupation until the end of the Middle Iron Age. If anything, there is evidence for increased middening at that time; the horizon covering the top of ditch F.114 had moderate quantities of animal bone, burnt stone, some fragments of saddle quern, and iron slag.

Middle Iron Age pottery was also recovered from pits within Area C, though the distribution of these was much sparser than for the Early Iron Age. Almost all of were located along the northwestern edge of the site, the one exception being a 0.6 m diameter shallow pit (F.220) located some 10 m to the west of F.292–7. In the far northwestern corner lay an intriguing group of five irregular- to round-shaped pits (F.302, F.304–5 & F.322–3) and a posthole (F.303), which defined a semi-circle (*c.* 16 m across) up against the excavation edge; given their arrangement, there is just a chance that they were building-related, but this was far from convincing. Four of the pits contained Middle Iron Age pottery and bone, and two had charcoal and burnt flint.

The most interesting feature relating to specific evidence for Middle Iron Age activity/settlement was a circular and flat-bottomed clay-lined pit (F.343; 0.82 m across and 0.25 m deep; Figs. 7.5–6) seemingly associated with a minor gully/trough (F.346; Fig. 7.7), located just 10 m to the southeast of another group of five intercutting Middle Iron Age pits (F.308–9, F.317, F.336 & F.337). Both the pit and the gully contained burnt stone, whilst the former had Middle Iron Age pottery, fragments of saddle quern,

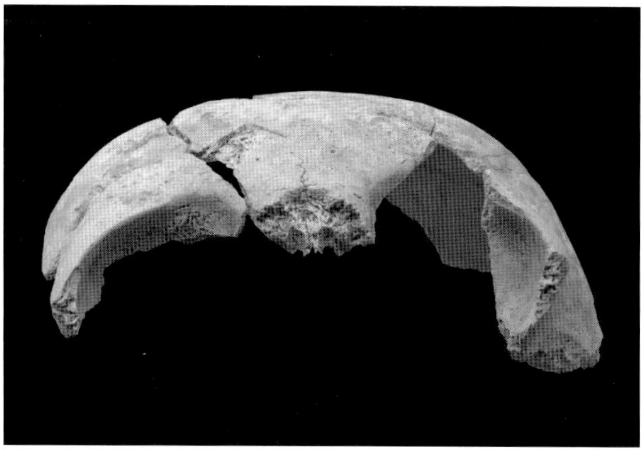

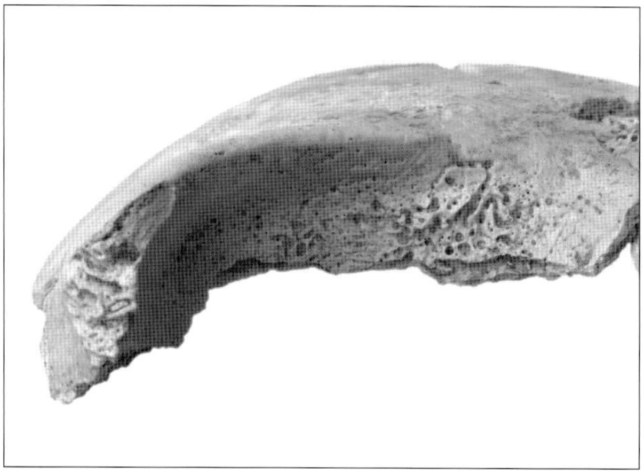

Figure 7.8. *The F.114 skull (Iron Age), with evidence of* cribra orbitalia.

a rubbing stone, and the remains of a large stone anvil that might be associated with metalworking (Fig. 7.14.3); burnt clay was also recovered from the base of the gully. The apparent relationship of these objects to the burnt stone suggests that they might have been associated with the working function of the pit. Given the lack of *in situ* burning, this feature is rather difficult to interpret. Possibly it was used as some sort of oven (hence the gully or flue) or, alternatively, a cooking pit; unfortunately, no environmental evidence was forthcoming.

Another possible component of the Middle Iron Age occupation of this valley site is suggested by the presence of two narrow north–south to west/southwest–east/northeast curvilinear ditch elements (F.134 & F.132/F.129; Fig. 7.7), which might represent field boundaries or a short stretch of droveway relating to Pit Cluster 1. This turned west and then terminated, respecting the latter's northern edge. Pottery evidence suggests this may be later Middle Iron Age, perhaps contemporary with the silting-up of, and middening within, the pits. That said, the 'reality' of these as features was ambiguous.

Early Roman

During the Early Roman period in the mid–late first century AD, the area evidently saw a very different form of land-use. On the north side this was marked by the establishment of a well-structured fieldsystem (Areas B & C), whilst a north–south boundary ditch crossed the valley and continued across Area A (Fig. 7.9). The latter, F.120/F.183, lay somewhat off-angle to the earlier, Iron Age boundary. It was traced for about 165 m from the southern limit of Area A to the northeastern corner of Area C, where it became shallower and presumably terminated somewhere beneath the unexcavated site-edge. The ditch was sectioned in 16 places; its width and depth ranged from 0.79 m × 0.16 m at its southern end to 1.7 m × 0.33 m close to the northern limit of Area C; it was 1 m wide and 0.1 m deep at its northern terminus in Area C. Roman pottery was recovered from five different points along its length, plus a handful of redeposited Early–Middle Iron Age sherds.

The northwest–southeast ditch and its return – F.345 and F.352 – abutted at an obtuse angle close to the southwestern limit of excavation in Area C. These appear to be the same feature(s) as F.35 found in the 2001 evaluation. From the latter was recovered a group of pottery sherds (Fig. 7.13), consisting of combed and cordoned jars and segmented bowls of Flavian to Hadrianic date (AD 70–120/130; Whittaker 2001, 11). There was, in fact, a three-way junction between ditches F.345, F.352 and F.205, with each terminating at the same point and suggesting a broadly contemporary layout. Only one sherd – part of the rim of a plain samian dish or bowl – was recovered from the terminus of ditch F.345. The quantity of material previously recovered at this point could, nonetheless, suggest that this was likely to have been the corner of a settlement enclosure and not just fieldsystem-related. Additional evidence for this was suggested by its slightly more complicated constructional history; parts of these were dug in segments, whilst the latest ditch, F.352, cut several earlier and similarly aligned pits close to its terminus (F.353 & F.354). These ditches, moreover, seemed to be more substantial than the straight, shallow and narrow field boundaries *per se*. The combined evidence from the 2001 and 2010 fieldwork indicates that this was probably an enclosure-paddock on the margins of an Early Roman farmstead/settlement, whose core may have lain on the somewhat higher and drier gravels to the west of the site (see *Further Evaluation …* below).

Six west/northwest–east/southeast and north/northeast–south/southwest-aligned field boundary ditches delineated a series of rectangular fields, each of 0.6 ha and 0.65 ha. The orientation of this fieldsystem also matched that of the (presumed earlier) Early Roman boundary ditch. The fieldsystem could not be detected across the lowest point of the valley to the south, or on the slightly flatter, heavier claylands. A sherd of decorated samian was recovered from ditch F.223 (Fig. 7.13.4).

Medieval

A series of parallel west/southwest–east/northeast trackway ditches (e.g. F.123, F.126–7, F.141–2, F.150–3, F.155, F.177 & F.187; Fig. 7.9) and other conjoining ones (e.g. F.111) on the south side of the valley are provisionally dated as Medieval. This is essentially due to their approximate correspondence with the position of the Medieval *Coton Way* (or *Sheepcote Way*) shown on the West Fields map (see Fig. 7.10; Hall & Ravensdale 1976). There seems little doubt that the course of this track must lie somewhere within the excavated area, which would fall to the south and east of *High Crosse* when superimposed on the *West Fields* map. Apart from that, no archaeological evidence was found to confirm the Medieval attribution of these features, despite being sectioned in 15 different places, and there remains a degree of ambiguity concerning their relationship with the Early Iron Age and Early Roman ditches. These often 'repeated' linears (e.g. F.141–2 & F.126–7) were shallow, extensively truncated and ephemeral (usually less than 0.2 m deep), and thus difficult to distinguish. Only at one point could one, F.127, be seen to cut the top of the Early Iron Age ditch. The correspondence of the ridge-and-furrow-derived troughs along the northern edge of Area A and the northern trackway boundary might also be cited in further support of the route's broadly Medieval attribution; nevertheless, its Medieval assignation cannot be regarded as conclusive.

On the north side of the valley, within Area C, a series of 1–5 m wide north/northeast–south/southwest aligned plough

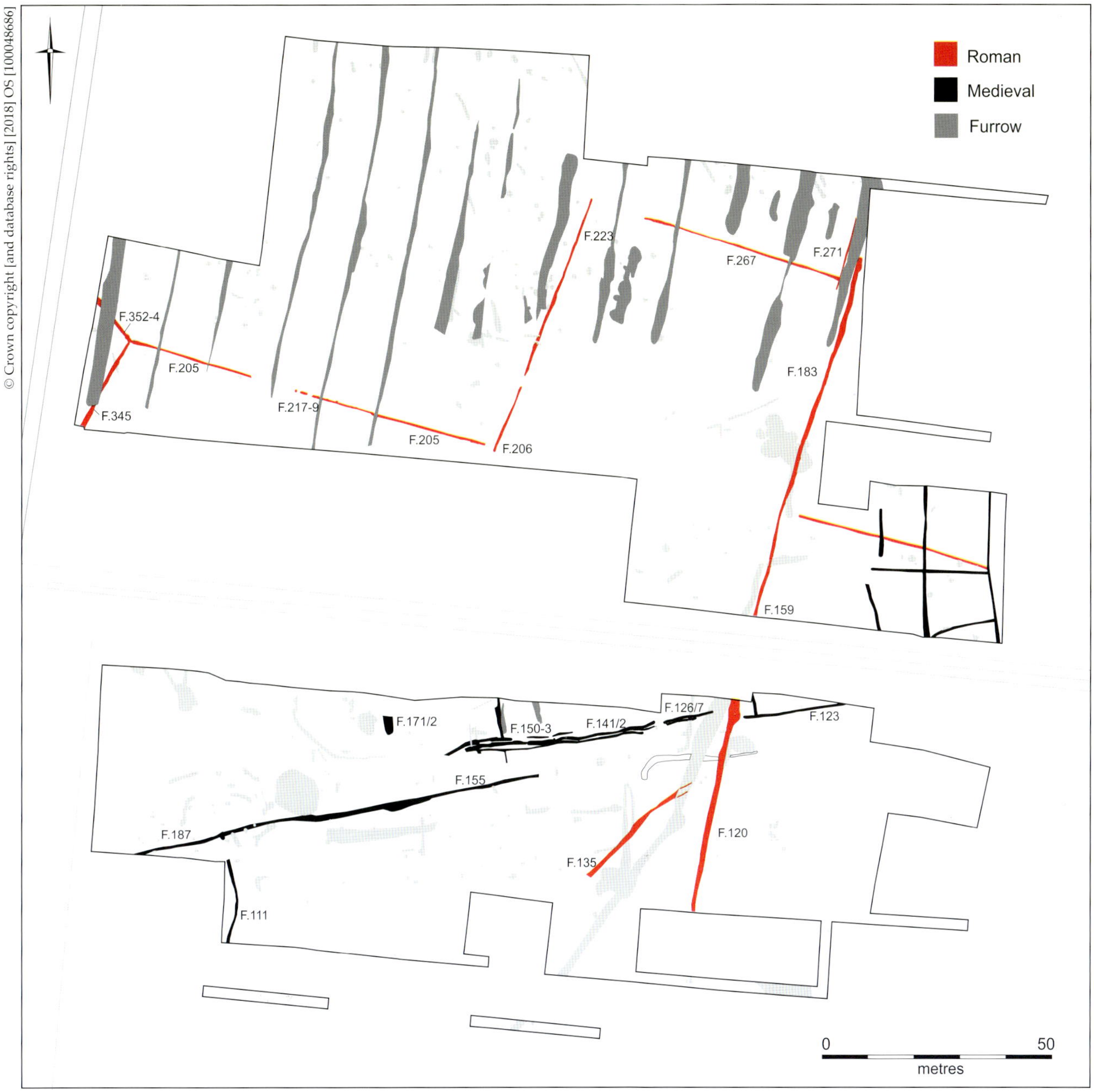

Figure 7.9. *Phase plan showing Roman and Medieval features.*

furrow-troughs severely truncated the earlier archaeology (Fig. 7.9). Although these appear roughly parallel to the alignment of the Medieval furlongs shown bordering Madingley Road (*St. Neot's Way*) on Hall and Ravendale's West Fields map (1976), by their form these more likely attest to Post-Medieval agriculture, which has both truncated and incorporated material from earlier Medieval strips dug on a similar alignment. This was evinced by the admixture of both Late Medieval wares (a single sherd of fourteenth-/fifteenth-century Ely Ware) and Post-Medieval pottery (sixteenth-/seventeenth-century sherds of Frechen Ware), plus also considerable amounts of Post-Medieval ironwork; a single earlier sherd of either Stamford or Kingston Ware was also retrieved from the site.

Material Culture

The site's assemblages certainly cannot be ranked as significant; in truth, the recovery of greater quantities of Roman period-material had been anticipated. That said, the quantities of both prehistoric pottery and worked stone were substantial.

Worked Flint (Lawrence Billington)

A total of 39 worked flints (367.5 g), together with 14 unworked burnt flints, were recovered. The condition of the assemblage is variable, light edge-damage is fairly frequent and patination (cortication) occurs on approximately three-quarters of it. There was no evidence of primary chalk-extracted flint and the assemblage appears to be derived exclusively from secondary till and gravel sources.

A small amount of material consistent with a Mesolithic or earlier Neolithic date was present. A fine blade, with opposed dorsal scars, was recovered as a residual find in F.122. Pit F.240 contained what appears to be a discrete assemblage of flint, comprising two fine blades, one of which has been utilized (Fig. 7.11.1–2), and a burnt flake with a faceted platform. These artefacts were incorporated into a backfill deposit that also contained charcoal and three refitting fragments of unworked burnt flint. The blades are strongly suggestive of a Mesolithic or earlier Neolithic date, whilst the faceted platform of the flake is perhaps more typical of Neolithic technologies. Tree-throw F.106 yielded a later Mesolithic microlith of scalene triangle form (Jacobi's Type 7b; 1978; Fig. 7.11.3). Traditionally interpreted as composite parts of hunting tools, microwear analysis has demonstrated a wide range of uses for such pieces, including cutting, piercing and as projectile points (e.g. van Gijn 2007). Mesolithic material is often recovered from tree-throws; occasionally within deposits that imply deliberate backfill with midden material (see Evans *et al.* 1999; Lamdin-Whymark 2009), but more often in low densities that suggest the material had been inadvertently incorporated into the fill from surface deposits.

The bulk of the remaining assemblage, however, would seem to be made up of extremely simple and expedient flake-based material. No control over removals is evident in the morphology of these pieces; platforms are either plain or cortical and hard hammers were used throughout the reduction sequence. It is not possible to closely date this material, although the rudimentary nature of the reduction strategy of many pieces and evidence for frequent errors perhaps indicates a later prehistoric date for the bulk of the assemblage, from the Middle Bronze Age into the Iron Age (see Ford *et al.* 1984; see *RVS*, 231–4). Small concentrations of flintwork with these characteristics were recovered from linear features F.108, containing flakes, a core and irregular waste, and F.114 that produced flakes, a core fragment and a crudely retouched flake. The flints from this Early Iron Age ditch-line might well have been residual.

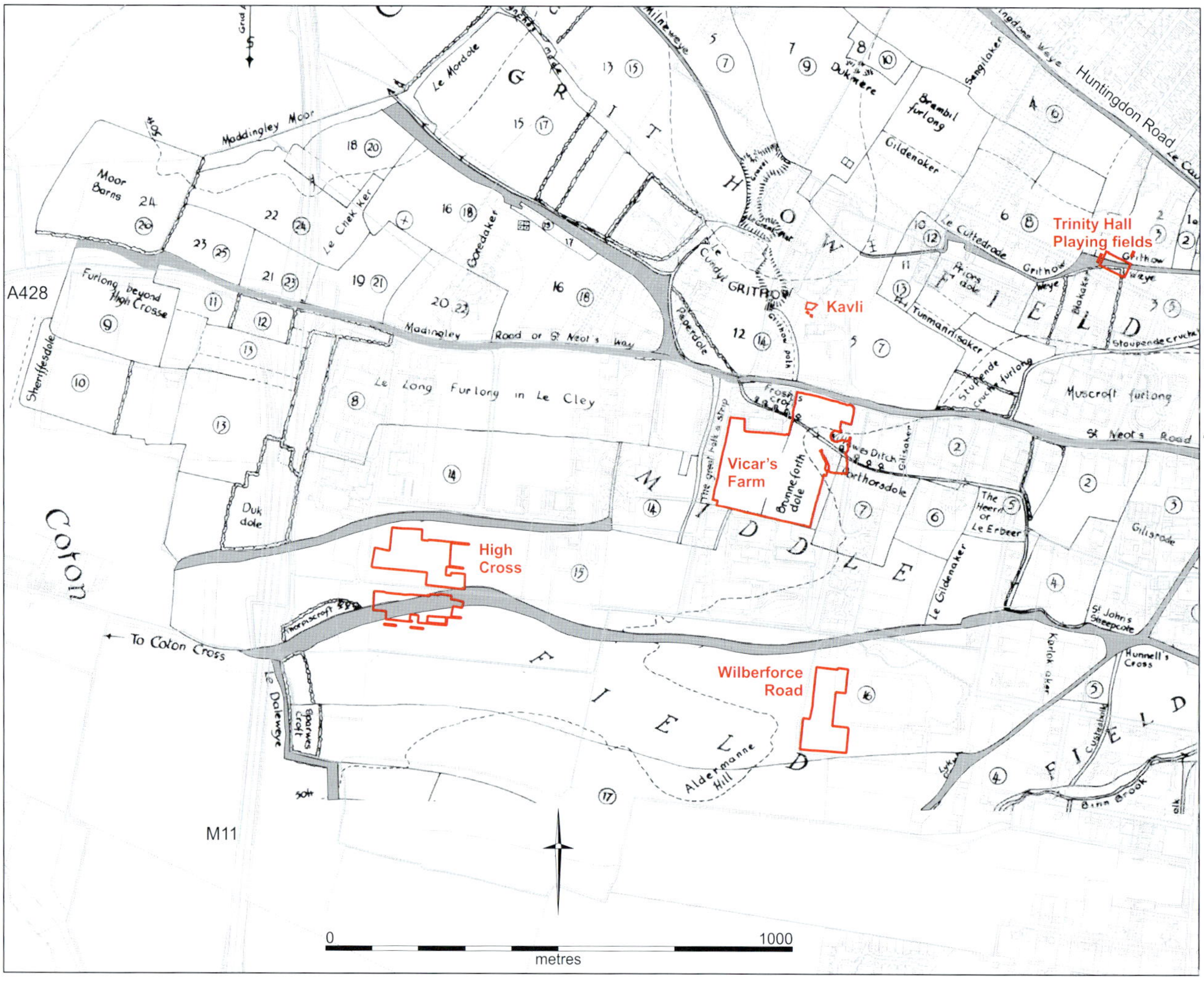

Figure 7.10. *Hall and Ravensdale's 1976 West Fields map superimposed on West Cambridge background with main excavation sites indicated (note location of* Coton Way*).*

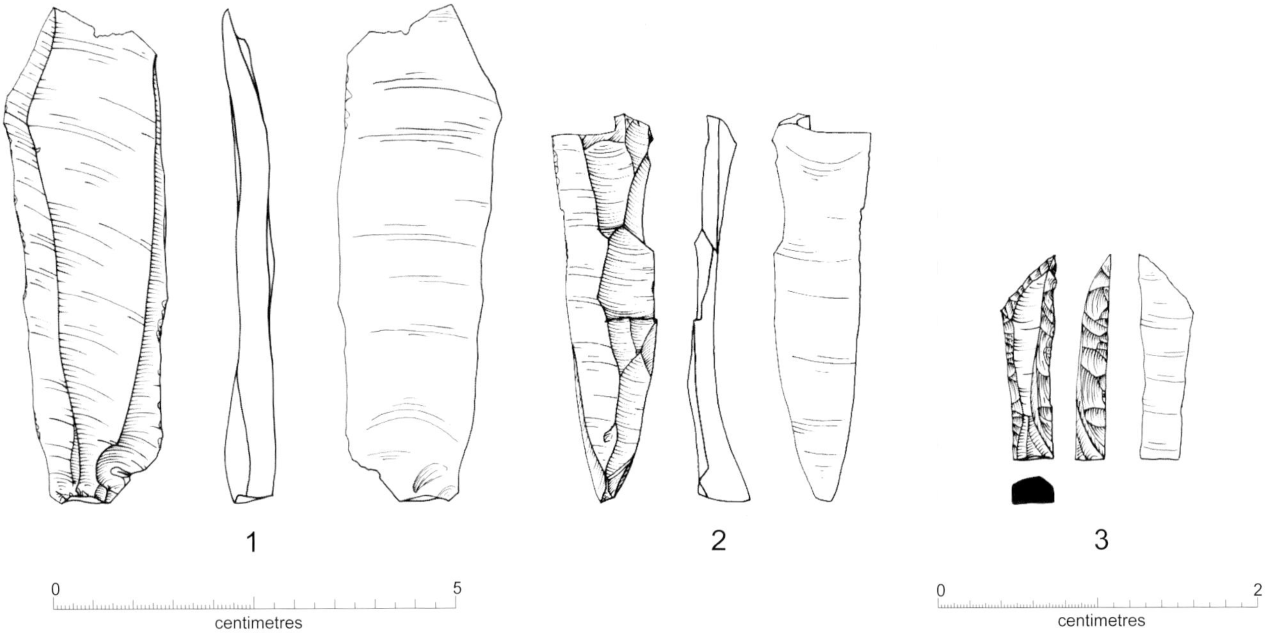

Figure 7.11. *Mesolithic flint: 1–2) F.240; 3) F.106 (see text).*

The small assemblage from the site is dominated by a rudimentary flake-based industry of probable later prehistoric date. Potentially more interesting was the small amount of earlier material, including a small Mesolithic/earlier Neolithic assemblage from pit F.240 and a microlith from tree-throw F.106. Accounts of the region have tended to stress that Mesolithic/earlier Neolithic activity is largely restricted to light, free-draining soils, particularly gravel terrace or sand deposits in valley floor or valley-side locations (see Hall 1996, 154–7; Dawson 2000; Harding & Healy 2007, 45–53). Yet, the consistent recovery of low numbers of blade-based lithics (often including diagnostically Mesolithic types) as a residual component of later sites on the region's heavy clays (e.g. Evans 2002) indicates that activity – perhaps short-lived and task-based – and including that at Vicar's Farm, was there taking place.

Prehistoric Pottery (Matthew Brudenell)

Just over a thousand sherds of handmade prehistoric pottery (5923 g), dating from the Middle/later Bronze Age through to the Middle Iron Age, were recovered (Table 7.1). This came from a range of features, the largest assemblage deriving from contexts associated with Pit Cluster 1 (454 sherds, 2378 g); with just a few exceptions, the assemblages from most contexts were small, scrappy and lacking in diagnostic sherds. In general, the pottery was highly fragmented, with a mean sherd weight of just 5.9 g (81% measuring less than 4 cm).

Sandy Fabrics

Q1: Spare to common quartz sand. The clay matrix of some sherds may contain rare mica, rare calcareous inclusions (1–2 mm), rare fragments of partially burnt flint (1–2 mm), or rare voids from burnt out vegetable matter

Q2: Moderate to common quartz sand with sparse sub-rounded calcareous grits (1–3 mm)

Q3: Moderate to common quartz sand (medium) with spare to moderate rounded clay pellets (1–1.5 mm)

Sand, Chalk and Flint Fabrics

QCHF1: Moderate quartz sand with spare medium partially burnt flint (1–2 mm) and rare calcareous grits (1–3 mm). Sherds may occasionally contain rare grog (1–2 mm)

Burnt Flint and Sand Fabrics

F1: Sparse to common medium to coarse burnt flint (1–4 mm), normally in sandy clay matrix

F2: Sparse to common finely crushed burnt flint in a sandy clay matrix (mainly <1.5 mm)

Burnt flint and grog Fabrics

FG1: Sparse medium burnt flint (1–2 mm) and sparse grog (1–2 mm)

Grog Fabrics

G1: Spare to moderate, medium to coarse grog. The clay matrix of some sherds may contain rare quartz sand or rare voids from burnt out vegetable matter

Shelly Fabrics

S1: Common to adamant fine to medium shell (1–2 mm)

S2: Sparse to abundant medium and coarse shell (1–4 mm)

Vegetable-tempered Fabrics

V1: Sparse linear void from burnt out vegetable material and sparse to moderate quartz sand

V2: Moderate to common linear voids from burnt out vegetable matter and sparse quartz sand

Table 7.1. *The quantified prehistoric pottery assemblage (MNV = minimum number of vessels calculated as the total number of different rims and bases identified).*

Fabric	**Sherds** (No./wt. [g] /MNV)	**Middle & Late Bronze Age** (No./wt. [g]/MNV)	**Early Iron Age** (No./wt. [g] /MNV)	**Middle Iron Age** (No./wt. [g] sherds/MNV)
F1	132/889/4	67/221/-	65/668/4	-
F2	20/124/1	-	20/124/1	-
FG1	2/8/2	2/8/2	-	-
G1	27/164/1	27/164/1	-	-
Q1	351/1631/19	-	48/439/2	303/1192/17
Q2	212/1231/5	-	12/97/-	200/1134/5
Q3	6/71/-	-	1/5/-	5/66/-
QCHF1	56/287/1	-	42/221/1	14/66/-
S1	30/513/4	9/176/2	5/206/1	16/131/1
S2	13/161/1	1/6/-	6/108/1	6/47/-
V1	66/389/2	-	40/216/2	26/173/-
V2	87/464/7	-	83/449/6	4//15/1
Total	*1002/2923/47*	*106//575/5*	*322//2533/18*	*574/2824/24*

The earliest pottery dates to the Middle/later Bronze Age, and comprises sherds in shell-, grog- and burnt flint-tempered fabrics (100 sherds, 540 g). Most of this material derived from pit F.215 (87 sherds, 346 g), which yielded body sherds from a single flint-tempered vessel and the base of a grog-tempered pot. Other sherds had more obvious Deverel Rimbury affinities but were all residual in Iron Age and Roman features. Of note are the fragments of a wide-mouthed bucket-form vessel from Early Iron Age pit F.209. This was in a shell-tempered fabric and displayed a flattened rim that was slightly expanded on the interior lip-edge (Fig. 7.12.8). The pit also yielded the rims of two other Middle Bronze Age vessels, with flint and grog inclusions (Figs. 7.12.4–5).

A presence in the Late Bronze Age is hinted at by finds of a few body sherds with coarse flint tempering (six sherds, 35 g): all residual except a single fragment (6 g) from the silts of well F.178. More sustained forms of occupation, however, can be inferred from the quantities of Early Iron Age pottery and, in total, this included 322 sherds (2533 g). This occurred in a range of fabrics but was essentially divided into sherds with burnt flint and sand inclusions (31% by weight); sand and organic temper (26%); sand (21%); shell (13%), and sherds with a combination of sand, partially burnt flint, and calcareous grits (9%). This variety is not uncommon, particularly for pottery groups in southern Cambridgeshire dating toward the end of the Early Iron Age (*c*. 500–350 BC; see Brudenell in *RVS*, chap. 4). More unusual is the complete absence of any burnished ceramics. All the sherds were coarsewares, and the few forms identified included plain shouldered jars with upright necks (five vessels, e.g. Figs 7.12.7, 7.12.13 & 7.12.19), and two fingertip-decorated jars lacking a distinct neck zone (e.g. Fig. 7.12.16). The other diagnostic ceramics were six internally expanded/flanged rims (e.g. Fig. 7.12.6), and nine fingertip-decorated shoulder sherds (e.g. Figs. 7.12.9–10). In total, 15 sherds were decorated (257 g), amongst them, four of the 12 different rims in the assemblage.

Most of the Early Iron Age pottery was derived from the ditch-line of F.108/114/186 and intercutting pits F.282 and F.296. The former yielded 110 sherds (725 g) of pottery, the majority of which were base and body fragments from two different vessels (e.g. Fig. 7.12.1). The lower fills of the ditch contained only Early Iron Age-type ceramics, but from middle and upper silts was recovered a mixture of Early and Middle Iron Age wares. The largest closed assemblages, however, came from intercutting pits F.282 and F.296, located in the northern half of the site. Combined, 174 sherds (1388 g) were recovered from these features, including fragments of at least nine different vessels, and most of the period's diagnostic sherds. Other features assigned to the Early Iron Age yielded fewer than 20 sherds; most were attributed on the basis of fabric alone.

The Middle Iron Age assemblage comprised 574 sherds (2824 g). The group was dominated by sherds in dense sandy fabrics, which accounted for 85 per cent of the pottery by weight. The remaining 15 per cent was shared between sherds with sand and organic temper (7%); shelly fabrics (6%), and sherds with a combination of sand, partially burnt flint and calcareous grits (2%). This range and relative frequency of wares is typical of Middle Iron Age assemblages in southern Cambridgeshire (suitable potting clays and tempering agents are all potentially available in the local landscape). The vessel forms were equally characteristic. These include three slack-shouldered jars with short upright necks (Form A; for typology see Hill & Horne 2003, 174; Hill & Braddock 2006, 155–6); a jar with a stepped rounded shoulder and upright neck (Form B; Fig. 7.12.17); and a slightly globular vessels with no distinct neck zone, but a well-defined rim, decorated on the rim-top (Form L; Fig. 7.12.3). Overall, these form-assigned vessels comprised 15 sherds (102 g), representing only 3 per cent of the Middle Iron assemblage.

Burnishing was present on 17 sherds (89 g), and fingertip decoration on 12 (62 g): the rim-tops of four different vessels (e.g. Fig. 7.12.2). The assemblage also included five sherds (56 g) with light scoring or heavy wiping, though stylistically these are not connected to the Scored Wares of the Lower Ouse. In fact, the assemblage is a typical Plain Ware group, whose affinities are firmly rooted in the potting traditions of southern Cambridgeshire; the overall character of the wares being similar to those in the much larger published assemblage from Wardy Hill (Hill & Horne 2003).

The vast majority of the Middle Iron Age pottery derived from contexts associated with Pit Cluster 1 (453 sherds, 2359 g). Some of this material was recovered during the evaluation (127 sherds, 835 g), but is difficult to now link these to the features that were fully exposed and more intensively investigated in the 2010 excavations. These yielded 315 sherds (1474 g), with a further 11 fragments (50 g) coming from 'dark silts' that covered the pit cluster. Combined, this group included fragments of a minimum of 15 different vessels, including four of the form-assigned pots. The material had evidently accumulated over a long period through repeated acts of discard. Other features assigned to the Middle Iron Age yielded very small assemblages, typically comprising fewer than 10 sherds.

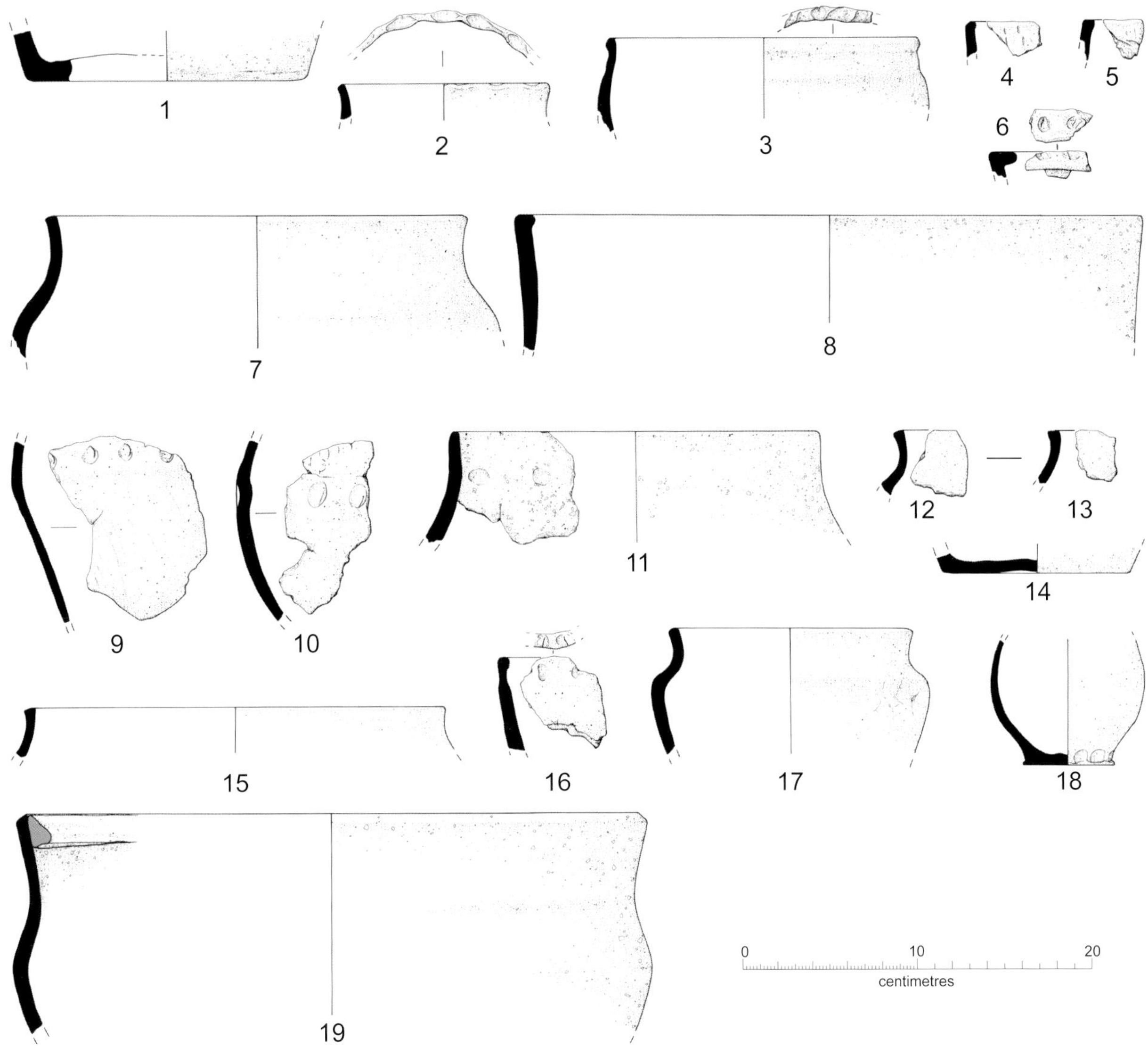

Figure 7.12. *Prehistoric pottery: 1) Fabric F1, base of Early Iron Age [EIA] vessel (ditch F.114); 2) Fabric Q1, Middle Iron Age [MIA] fingertip-impressed rim (pit Cluster 1; F.138 [373]); 3) Form L, Fabric Q1, MIA (Pit Cluster 1; F.140); 4) Fabric FG1, Middle Bronze Age [MBA] rim (pit F.209); 5) Fabric FG1, MBA rim (pit F.209); 6) Fabric F2, EIA fingertip-impressed rim (pit F.209); 7) shoulder jar, Fabric F1, EIA (pit F.282); 8) Fabric S1, MBA rim (pit F.209); 9) Fabric Q1, EIA fingertip-impressed shoulder (pit F.282); 10) Fabric Q2, EIA fingertip-impressed shoulder (pit F.282); 11) Fabric S2, EIA rim with fingertip impression on neck interior (pit F.282); 12–13) shouldered jar, Fabric Q1, EIA (pit F.282); 14) Fabric S1, base of MIA vessel (area of Pit Cluster 1, eval. F.63); 15) Fabric V2, EIA rim (pit F.296); 16) jar, Fabric Q2, EIA fingertip-impressed rim and neck (pit F.296); 17) Form B, Fabric Q1, MIA (area of Pit Cluster 1, eval. F.68); 18) Fabric Q2, base of MIA jar (pit F.343); 19) shouldered jar, Fabric S1, EIA (pit F.339).*

In summary, the bulk of the assemblage dates to the Early and Middle Iron Age, with only a minor Middle/later Bronze Age component. Closer dating of the Early Iron Age material is difficult, though given the fabric frequencies and overall nature of the vessel forms identified, a date towards the close of this period is tentatively suggested, *c.* 500–350 BC. The Middle Iron Age assemblage can be placed between *c.* 350–50 BC and constitutes a typical Plain Ware group from southern Cambridgeshire, characterized by sherds in dense sandy fabrics. Amongst other assemblages, this material finds ready parallel with the published pottery groups from Wardy Hill (*ibid.*), West Fen Road (Percival 2005) and Duxford (Percival 2011).

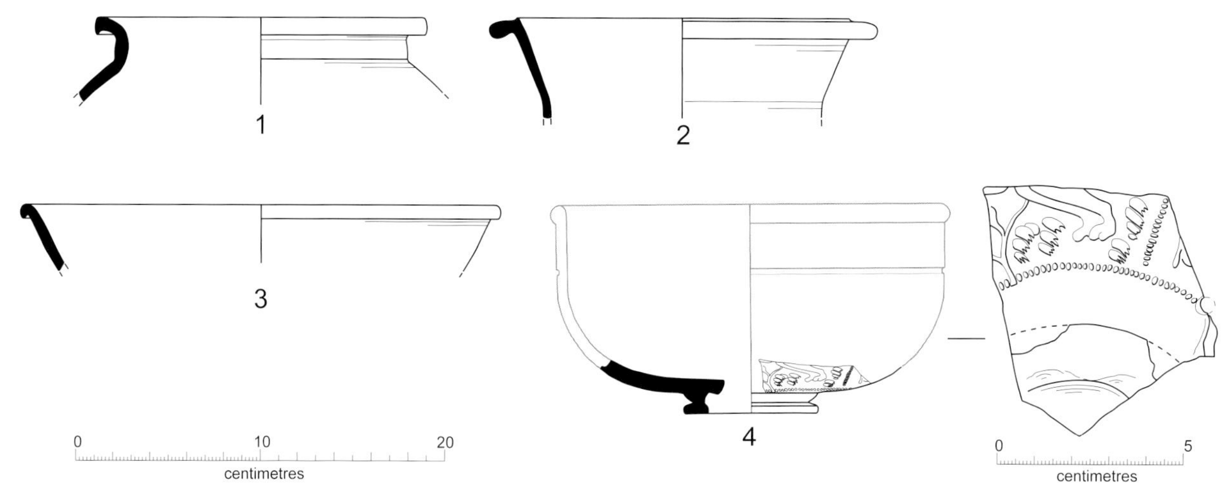

Figure 7.13. *Roman pottery: 1) cordoned jar (F.35); 2) segmented bowl (F.35); 3) Dr.18/31 samian dish (F.345); 4) decorated Dr.37 samian bowl (F.223).*

Roman Pottery (Katie Anderson)
Fifty-six sherds of Roman pottery (338 g) were recovered, including 10 dated Late Iron Age/Early Roman. All of the Roman pottery that could be more closely dated than 'Romano-British' was 'Early', which – together with the Late Iron Age/Early Roman material – suggests that activity was limited to the first century AD. The assemblage consisted primarily of sandy coarseware sherds, most of which are likely to have been produced locally. The only exception to this were two South Gaulish Samian sherds (F.223 & F.345), dating to the mid–late first century AD. These comprised a Dr.18/31 dish (Fig. 7.13.3) and a decorated Dr.37 bowl (Fig. 7.13.4); the remaining sherds were all non-diagnostic.

Burnt and Worked Stone (Simon Timberlake)
In total, 36.8 kg of burnt stone was collected, with more than 95 per cent coming from Early–Middle Iron Age features. Their contextual information suggests that a good proportion of the burnt stone was contemporary and in some way related to the function of the features: as rubbish or domestic middening, or perhaps linked to *in situ* burning, boiling or otherwise unknown activities. The range of different geologies represented in the burnt stone (Mesozoic and Carboniferous sandstone, Bunter pebbles, quartz porphyry, andesitic and basaltic lava and dolerite) suggests the collection of glacial erratic pebbles from the local gravel or boulder clay.

The most interesting finding has been the recognition of discarded fragments of worked stone amongst the burnt and broken up cobbles within a few of the Iron Age features (F.343, F.346, F.209 & F.115). This reworked material makes up some 26.5 per cent of the total weight of the burnt stone assemblage. A possible parallel for the 0.25 m deep clay-lined pit, F.343, was recorded at Broom in Bedfordshire (Timberlake in Slater 2008b). There, similar-sized pits used to heat water, were found within 10 m of the entrances to Iron Age roundhouses, and comparable features are known from other contemporary settlements in the region (e.g. Colne Fen: Evans *et al*. 2013a, 158 & 221).

Evidently relating to milling/grinding, crushing or hammering, the total weight of the worked stone assemblage was 15.74 kg, of which 4.47 kg was composed of saddle quern fragments or rubbing stones.

Saddle Querns

<199a–b> F.343 (Fig. 7.14.2) - Fragments of discarded quern used as cooking stones, or else deposited here following their destruction in a fire. Includes (a) a part-calcined quern composed of calcareous sandstone (weight 1096 g; 110 × 90 × 100 mm), and (b) a fragment from a burnt quartzitic sandstone with one flat grinding surface and edges (area: 120 × 80 mm; 900 g; 130 × 100 × 40 mm thick).

<117> F.209 (Fig. 7.14.1) - An unburnt fragment of ortho-quartzitic sandstone (possibly a Cretaceous/Lower Tertiary sarsen stone identical to <199b>. The grinding surface is polished smooth and is flat to slightly convex in profile (470 g; 105 × 90 × 40–50 mm thick).

<024> F.115 - Two small fragments of a cracked calcareous sandstone with one small area of working (50 × 50 mm square; 264 g).

<093> F.114 - Two fragments of quern made of sarsen stone (see <117>). A 60 × 70 mm area of flat smooth grinding surface is preserved. The worn base suggests that a flat stone was chosen, rather than the base prepared, whilst the presence of a bevel on the outer edge could be the result of its long-term use (922 g; 130 × 70 × 60 mm).

Rubbing Stone

<199c> F.343 - A burnt fragment of a lozenge-shaped rubbing stone with a slightly convex (but doubly faceted) surface, suggestive of

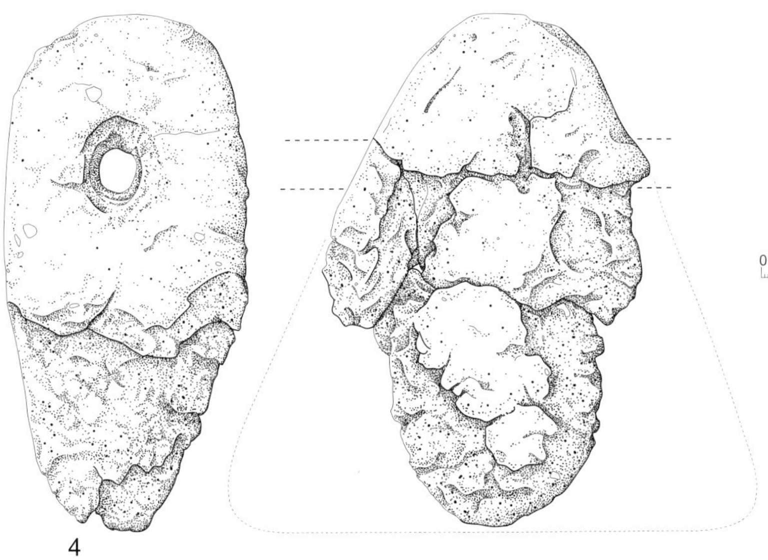

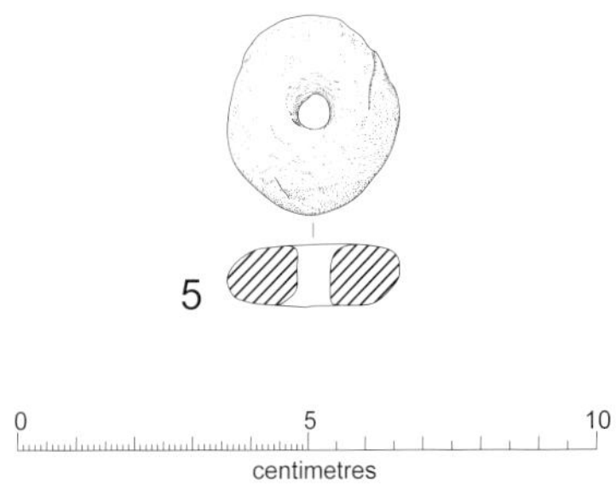

Figure 7.14. *Worked stone and fired clay: 1) saddle quern fragment (<117>; F.209); 2) saddle quern fragment (<199>; F.343); 3) anvil stone (<199>; F.343); 4) loomweight fragment (<234>, F.140); 5) spindlewhorl (<256>, F.282).*

use in grinding on different querns/or different areas of the same quern. One of these faces appears smoother than the other (areas 80 × 50 mm and 40 × 65 mm). Made of ferruginous sandstone (Lower Greensand?; 818 g; 130 × 80 × 35–65 mm thick).

Anvil Stones

<199d> F.343 (Fig. 7.14.3) - Part of a large boulder of coarse dolerite, perhaps worked (pecked) around the edges, but with a prominent depression in the (upper?) surface at least 120 × 110 mm in area and up to 5 mm deep. Perhaps originally used as a quern, the depth of the hollow suggests that its last function was as a mortar or anvil, such as could have been used for metalworking. The object was broken up as a result of it having been burnt (4878 g; 170 × 220 × 120+ mm thick).

<098> F.169 - A small tablet-shaped anvil stone composed of ortho-quartzitic sandstone which has been lightly worked on both sites, perhaps for some small-scale craft function (326 g; originally *c.* 80 × 80 × 33 mm thick).

Surface Find, Area A - A large boulder of dolerite (>6 kg; 230 × 150 × 130 mm), which appears to have been used as an anvil stone/mortar. The rock has broken across the worked depression (hollow 50 mm diam. and >10 mm deep), with three smaller, but faint worked depressions in its reverse.

The distribution of saddle quern debris appears to reflect concentrations of Middle Iron Age middening and burnt stone (most of this being associated with Pit Cluster 1 and pit F.343; Fig. 7.15). Anvil stones often go unrecognized on archaeological sites. As a consequence, their prevalence is often disproportionately under-represented within finds reports on worked

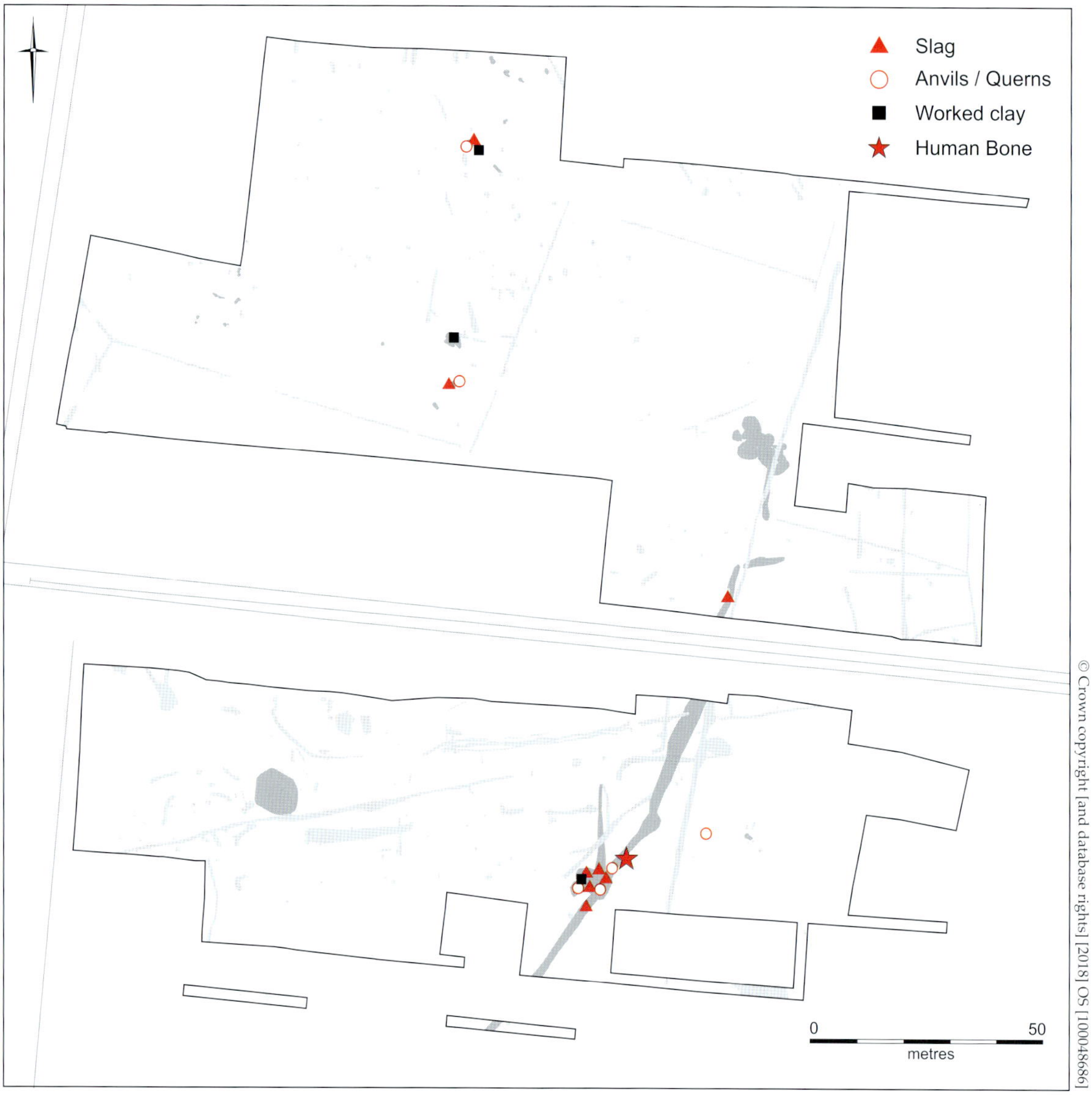

Figure 7.15. *Selected finds category and human remains distributions.*

stone assemblages. It is feasible that some of the larger stone boulders found at Iron Age settlements could have been used as anvils for iron or other metalworking activities. One such example of this was the boulder anvil found associated with a small smithy hut at the Bryn y Castell hillfort in Gwynedd, Wales (Crew 1987).

Other Finds (Grahame Appleby and Simon Timberlake)

Sixty-five fragments of fired clay (908 g) were recovered. The vast majority are undiagnostic and vary in size from less than 1 mm to a substantially complete large triangular loomweight (F.140 <234>; 646 g). Fabrics consist of relatively well-fired to friable clay and range in colour from dark grey, reduced clays to highly oxidized and bright orange pieces. A spindlewhorl (<256>), fashioned from chalk, was also found in F.282.

<202> *F.346* - Several refitting fragments forming a 'bun'-shaped object weighing 110 g and measuring *c.* 45 × 77 mm. Consisted of a reduced fabric with a pale pink to orange outer surface; finger impressions are present around the 'lateral' edge. The form and shape of this item is indicative of expedient manufacture and identifying a use is problematic, although use as a weight of some variety seems most probable.

<234> *F.140, SF. 67* (Fig. 7.14.4) - Four refitting fragments, and smaller lumps, from a large triangular loomweight made from incompletely fired clay with moderate to frequent small to large flint inclusions. Fired in a largely reducing atmosphere resulting in a dark grey to black finish, the surface has been partially oxidized. Approximately two thirds of the loomweight survives, providing an estimated size of 122 mm wide, 152 mm high and 55 mm thick. There is one complete perforation through the presumed 'apex' of the weight measuring *c.* 16 mm in diameter. This form of loomweight is characteristic of the Middle Iron Age and, for example, a number of comparable complete loomweights were found at Wardy Hill, Coveney (Gdaniec & Lucas in Evans 2003, 194, fig. 93).

<256> *F.282, SF. 70* (Fig. 7.14.5) - Small rounded chalk spindlewhorl 32.44 mm in diameter, 14.8 mm thick, with a central perforation of 7.84 mm diameter. A similar example was found at Wardy Hill (Lucas in *ibid.*, 190, fig. 92.1).

A total of 60 pieces of metalwork (475 g) were recovered (Fig. 7.15), the majority during surface metal-detecting. The only items of non-ferrous metalwork recovered were two minute copper alloy fragments, less than 2 mm in length and weighing less than 1 g (Middle Iron Age). The ferrous metalwork, on the other hand, consisted primarily of nails and nail fragments (48 pieces), a 'butcher's hook', a knife fragment and a large tap key/handle, none of which was distinctively earlier than Post-Medieval.

No more than 264 g of iron slag was recovered. Of this, the largest piece came from an Early Iron Age feature, F.214, with the majority of the rest coming from the Middle Iron Age dark silt spread sealing Pit Cluster 1. The only significant pieces were two proto-smithing hearth bases (F.214 & F.114), both indicative of secondary ironworking. The small size and absence of any cone-shape to the hearth bottom found in pit F.214 reflects the early and less well-developed type of iron smithing hearth typical of the Early–Middle Iron Age, and probably reflects the working of relatively small lumps of iron.

Economic and Environmental Data

The excavations yielded what amounts to a 'respectable' faunal assemblage. Yet, given the site's geology, its relatively poorly preserved environmental remains came as both a surprise and a disappointment.

Faunal Remains (Vida Rajkovača)

The faunal assemblage amounted to 238 assessable specimens (9779 g), with a further 48 specimens (130 g) coming from the sieving of the bulk soil samples (Table 7.2). The report will focus on the two Iron Age assemblages.

The assemblage demonstrated a moderate level of preservation overall with approximately a fifth showing signs of severe surface exfoliation, erosion and weathering (44 fragments/*c.* 18% of the assemblage). A portion of the assemblage was weathered, with longitudinal cracks and round edges due to abrasion. The assemblage was highly fragmented, with only one complete specimen. There was limited evidence of gnawing (16 specimens, 6.7%), yet this still implies that some features were left open and that bone material was within reach of scavengers.

Butchery was recorded on 11 specimens, the majority of which were Early Iron Age. Cattle were the most commonly butchered species, represented by seven specimens, followed by sheep/goat with two and, then, dog and Roe deer with one specimen each. Butchery actions were performed with the use of knives or large blades, in keeping with the period, and include skinning, disarticulation, meat- and marrow-removal.

Middle–later Bronze Age - Pit F.215 contained loose teeth assigned to sheep/goat and pig and a poorly preserved cattle-sized limb bone fragment. A small quantity of moderately preserved material came from well F.178. Of eight specimens, four were identified as cow mandible fragments, loose teeth and phalanges. Horse was also represented with one loose tooth; sheep was identified based on a humerus fragment. Only one specimen was not possible to assign to species level: a cattle-sized limb bone fragment.

Table 7.2. *Quantity and provenance of hand-recovered faunal remains.*

Phase	Contexts	NISP	%NISP
Middle Bronze Age	1	3	1.3
Late Bronze Age	4	8	3.4
Early Iron Age	19	112	47
Middle Iron Age	12	45	18.9
Early Roman	1	8	3.4
Undated	8	62	26
Total	*45*	*238*	*100*

Table 7.3. *Number of Identified Specimens and the Minimum Number of Individuals for all species from Early and Middle Iron Age sub-sets (n.f.i. denotes that the specimen could not be further identified).*

	Early Iron Age			Middle Iron Age		
Taxon	**NISP**	**%NISP**	**MNI**	**NISP**	**%NISP**	**MNI**
Cow	35	55.5	2	10	55.5	1
Sheep/goat	11	17.4	2	6	33.3	1
Sheep	2	3.2	1	-	-	-
Pig	7	11.1	1	-	-	-
Horse	2	3.2	1	1	5.6	1
Dog	2	3.2	1	-	-	-
Red deer	3	4.8	1	1	5.6	1
Roe deer	1	1.6	1	-	-	-
Sub-total to species	63	100	-	18	100	-
Cattle-sized	26	-	-	10	-	-
Sheep-sized	19	-	-	8	-	-
Rodent-sized	1	-	-	.	-	-
Mammal n.f.i.	3	-	-	9	-	-
Total	*112*	-	-	*45*	-	-

Early Iron Age - This faunal sub-set, recovered from eight features, accounted for 47 per cent of the assemblage with a total of 112 assessable specimens (Table 7.3). All three 'food' species are well-represented, with cattle being prevalent. The two native cervid species make up 6.4 per cent of the sub-set. This may appear small, yet it may attest to a significant form of activity, if seen in proportion with the rest of the assemblage. Antler portions of both the Red and Roe deer could have been imported as raw material, yet the presence of Red deer lower limb elements indicates that parts of carcasses were brought to site and that venison was eaten.

Judging by the skeletal element representation and the presence of some younger individuals, cattle and ovicapra were raised locally or on site. Six instances of butchery were recorded, mainly implying disarticulation and marrow-removal. This includes the butchered Roe deer antler with persistent chop marks around the burr, indicating that it had been removed from the skull and not naturally shed.

Middle Iron Age - Twelve features produced a small sub-set of some 45 specimens, of which only 18 could be assigned to species (Table 7.3). A similar, albeit significantly smaller, range of domestic species is present as in the Early Iron Age assemblage, with cattle, sheep/goat and horse identified. A single Red deer antler portion testifies to some exploitation of wild faunal resources. Although the proportion of sheep to cattle rose in this period, the limited assemblage size does not warrant discussion concerning changes in animal exploitation between different phases.

Early Roman - This phase of occupation yielded just eight assessable fragments of bone, all of which came from ditch F.135 and three could be assigned to species: a cow humerus and mandible, as well as fragments of a Red deer antler.

The high frequency of cattle shows a certain consistency in economic practices from the Middle Bronze Age through the Iron Age and Roman times. That said, in contrast to the Marion Close and New Hall Iron Age assemblages (see Chap. 3 above), the paucity of sheep/goat here may have related to the site's abiding damp-ground conditions. While the persistence of deer elements within the Iron Age and Roman sub-sets may attest to lingering nearby woodland conditions, the assemblage's limited size precludes further interpretation.

Environmental Remains (Anne de Vareilles)

Thirteen samples were analysed (192 litres). Despite the extremely wet conditions experienced during excavations, none of these were truly waterlogged. Seven of the samples, however, contained some waterlogged seeds, which appear to have survived fluctuating water and oxygen levels, suggesting that conditions in some features remained wet throughout most of the year. Molluscs were found in almost all samples, but not in significant concentrations (see de Vareilles in Timberlake 2010 for tabular listing of the recovered materials).

Middle/Later Bronze Age well, F.178 - The uppermost deposit ([491]) contained no remains, other than a few specks of fine charcoal and some freshwater snails indicative of wet mud. Some waterlogged wild plant seeds and wood fragments were recovered from the basal fill, [492], which appears to have once been waterlogged. The seeds are of groundsurface species that fell into the pond/well and are only a partial representation of the original assemblage. The crowfoot (*Ranunculus* Subgen. *BATRACHIUM*) and water-plantain (*Alisma* sp.) may have been growing within the feature. The other plants describe a damp, disturbed and overgrown land surface with buttercups (*Ranunculus* sp.), brambles (*Rubus* sp.), thistles (*Carduus/Cirsium* sp.) and dock (*Rumex* sp.).

Early Iron Age pits, F.282 and F.209 - Two pits from neighbouring pit groups contained waterlogged seeds suggesting a damp, disturbed and overgrown land surface, similar to that witnessed with the F.178 well. Pit F.282 was rich in charcoal and was the only feature to contain any cereal remains: two grains and four elements of chaff from spelt as well as perhaps emmer wheat (*Triticum spelta* and *T. spelta/diccocum*). There were also two fragments of hazelnut shell (*Corylus avellana*) and five grass seeds. The remains point to the final cleaning of grain before consumption. Feature 209 had no cereal remains but contained a few charred wild plant seeds that may have been arable weeds.

Early Iron Age ditch-line, F.114 and F.184 - These features had a light scatter of charcoal but no other plant remains, apart from two waterlogged fat-hen seeds (*Chenopodium album*) in F.184. Snail shells in F.114 suggest that it had seasonal standing water.

Middle Iron Age pit, F.343 - This contained waterlogged seeds suggesting a damp, disturbed and overgrown land surface, similar to that witnessed in pits F.282 and F.209 above.

Romano-British ditch, F.223 - A little charcoal and a few waterlogged seeds, indicative of disturbed, overgrown land, were found.

Early Roman ditches, F.345 and F.120 - Charcoal and some waterlogged seeds not unlike those in F.223 above; F.120 had very little charcoal and no other plant remains.

Medieval gully, F.123 - Snail shells suggest seasonal standing water.

A low density of waterlogged seeds have survived, and though they probably represent but a fraction of the overall ecology, they all fit within a damp, open and overgrown landscape frequently disturbed by humans and/or animals; the damp/wet soil conditions would have been an uncomfortable characteristic of the area. Scarce evidence for the processing and consumption of grain was found in the Early Iron Age pit F.282, but the absence of any such evidence from other features is unusual That said, low quantities of cereal remains were present in two Romano-British ditch-fill samples processed from the evaluation fieldwork (see Ballantyne in Whittaker 2001, 26).

Pollen Analysis (Steve Boreham)

Pollen was examined from 10 samples taken from the following features: F.114, an Early Iron Age ditch ([510]; 18 cm, 50 cm and 70 cm from the base of the sequence); F.183, an Early Roman ditch ([503]; 8 cm and 26 cm from the base); F.168, a Middle Iron Age pit (Pit Cluster 1; [501]/12 cm, [500]/41 cm and [499] from the base of the sequence); and F.282, an Early Iron Age pit ([813]/10 cm and [812]/22 cm from section base). Unfortunately, apart from the F.114 ditch, all the other pollen samples were barren.

The samples were prepared using the standard hydrofluoric acid technique within the Department of Geography, University of Cambridge, and counted for pollen using a high-power stereo-microscope. Pollen concentrations varied widely between <1068 and 20,450 grains per ml. Eight of the 10 samples assessed were barren, with pollen and spores corroded and degraded beyond recognition. In the two remaining samples, pollen preservation was still poor, but at least some recognizable palynomorphs could be counted. Counting was made more difficult by the presence of finely divided organic debris. With assessment count totals of 84 and 105 from two slides each, neither sample approached the statistically desirable total of 300 pollen grains. As a consequence, caution should be exercised in the interpretation of these results. The site's geology (sandy silt overlying Gault Clay) is largely responsible for the poor preservation of pollen, since this tends to produce a fluctuating watertable leading to the periodic ingress of atmospheric oxygen to considerable depths.

Feature 114 ([510]) – Early Iron Age ditch fills - The basal pollen sample from Monolith 61 at 18 cm was dominated by grass pollen (Poaceae; 51.2%) and pteropsid spores (together 34.5%). A restricted range of herbs included the pink family (Caryophyllaceae; 8.3%), members of the lettuce family (Asteraceae [Lactuceae]; 1.2%), and buttercup (*Ranunculus*; 1.2%). Arboreal taxa included birch (*Betula*) and pine (*Pinus*; both 1.2%). The polypody fern (*Polypodium*; 1.2%) was also present. No obligate aquatics were detected in this sample. The large proportion of pteropsid spores in this sample suggests that this assemblage may have been post-depositionally modified by oxidative soil processes, leading to an increase in resistant types. The paucity of pollen grains other than the heavily built Asteraceae and Caryophyllaceae tends to support this view.

The pollen sample from upper monolith (No. 62) at 50 cm was dominated by grass pollen (Poaceae; 46.7%) and pteropsid spores (together 28.6%). Again, a restricted range of herbs included members of the lettuce family (Asteraceae [Lactuceae]; 14.3%), pink family (Caryophyllaceae; 1.0%), and the cabbage family (Brassicaceae; 1.9%). Arboreal taxa included birch (*Betula*; 2.9%) and pine (*Pinus*; 1.9%). The presence of clubmoss (*Selaginella*; 1%) is interesting, since today it is a rare plant that inhabits bogs and marshes. Polypody fern (*Polypodium*; 1.9%) was also present. Obligate aquatics were not found. The large proportion of pteropsid spores and elevated proportion of Asteraceae pollen suggests that it has been post-depositionally modified by oxidative soil processes.

It seems likely that the pollen spectra from these two F.114 samples represent pollen that was either very numerous in the original unmodified assemblage, or else pollen that was resistant to microbial decomposition. Both samples are dominated by grass pollen, which suggests that they are post-clearance. However, given that there are no cereals or pollen indicative of disturbance present, little more can be said about the nature of this agricultural landscape, except that it contained meadow with tall-herb communities. The absence of aquatic taxa makes it difficult to comment on local depositional environments, yet the results are, at least, consistent with widely varying water levels. Nor can much be inferred from the presence of pine pollen, this being a ubiquitous component of the pollen rain, and thus quite resistant to oxidation. The presence of birch pollen may be more significant here, as together with the polypody fern that often grows in older trees, this might represent local patches of birch scrub or woodland. It is tempting to suggest that this represents secondary woodland that has developed on wetter areas, such as marshes, or perhaps around springs, where the clubmoss would also have grown. The apparent absence of a distant mixed-oak woodland or parkland signal, or indeed a fulsome assemblage of herbs, strongly hints that the story presented by these two samples has been heavily modified and should be regarded with some suspicion.

Discussion

Leaving aside the much greater intensity and duration of Roman archaeology at Vicar's Farm, in many respects the prehistoric sequences at the two sites are broadly comparable and both span the Mesolithic through to the Iron Age. Although Vicar's Farm saw a degree of later Neolithic activity, as well as much more distinct Mesolithic 'usage'/occupation, at High Cross it was the Bronze/Iron Ages that were far more in evidence. While the small pitting cluster and some 140 sherds of Iron Age pottery recovered from Vicar's Farm can be comfortably accredited to 'visitation' (providing what is, in effect, a gauge for contemporary activity at High Cross), the nearly 900 sherds of Iron Age pottery and the other findings (slags, querns, human remains, *etc.*) from High Cross surely amounts to something more. Lurking behind any interpretation is the fact that, in the light of the site's fairly horrific excavation conditions, the low grounds of High Cross would not have been a locale in which people would ever want to have over-wintered, if given a choice.

Two radiocarbon dates were achieved from the site:

1) F.178 (Beta-280339) – 3100±40 BP/1440–1280 cal. BC
2) F.282 (Beta-280340) – 5540±40 BP/4460–4330 cal. BC.

Derived from charred seeds from one of the Middle Iron Age pits, the latter is obviously completely unacceptable, and it must be suspected that it derives from material relating to the site's Mesolithic/Early Neolithic usage. Coming from wood, the other is entirely consistent with F.178's Middle Bronze Age attribution.

Although the period's ditch-line candidates are too suspect to be considered 'real', the recovery of definite evidence of Middle Bronze Age utilization came as something of surprise. As outlined above, we had previously investigated the paddock system of that date in the grounds of New Hall/Fitzwilliam Colleges (see Chap. 3). While comparable with other contemporary fieldsystem landscapes now known to be widespread throughout much of south of the County and the fenlands (see e.g. Yates 2007), there is still relatively little evidence of that period's utilization of heavy claylands *per se* (see Evans & Patten 2011 for an overview), with Bronze Age activity at North West Cambridge occurring up on the gravel ridge there (see *NWC*, chap. 2). Nevertheless, pit-well/watering-holes like that found in Area A (F.178) are entirely characteristic of the period and achieving summertime water sources in such inland locales away from any river might well have been a key factor. The specifics of the site's location may well have been crucial here: the sand and silts on top of its clays offering a measure of better drainage, with groundwater gathering in the base of the palaeochannel/valley.

The site's main Early Iron Age feature was the ditch cutting across the low damp ground. Although this may have begun as one side of an attempted and subsequently abandoned enclosure system, it more probably related to control of stock movement along the line of the valley floor. Associated with this, there was also evidence for the extensive re-/digging of pits, most of which would have ended up being water-filled and, thus, were certainly not used for the storage of grain, *etc.*, but were perhaps originally dug as tanks or retting pits, with midden-type deposits spreading later across their upper profiles. Such activities evidently continued into the Middle Iron Age, ceasing only upon complete 'burial'/infilling of the ditch and pit groups with waterlain silts. This silting episode may well have been symptomatic of a worsening of conditions, which led to the abandonment of this site at the end of the Middle Iron Age.

The absence of evidence for residential structures, such as obvious eavesgullies or (convincing) circular posthole arrangements, only compounds the problem of whether we are looking at short-lived permanent or temporary settlement. Subsequent truncation through ridge-and-furrow agriculture may well have removed gully-surrounded settings, but presumably not the postholes. With the exception of the one possible Middle Iron Age round structure, the distribution of postholes across the site was sparse and ambiguous to say the least. If what was exposed were the margins of a permanent Early–Middle Iron Age farming settlement of usual type then further evidence of, for example, four-poster granaries or fenced animal pens might have been expected. The remains at High Cross were, instead, mostly small pits into which minor amounts of rubbish had been deposited.

Given the lack of evidence for contemporary dwellings and the paucity of cereals amongst the environmental samples, the presence of quernstone in these pits was unexpected. It was surely significant that virtually all of the quern was found broken and burnt. This suggests a secondary use for these worn and discarded pieces, either as potboilers or as cooking stones. At High Cross only one such clay-lined pit was identified, yet it was within that Middle Iron Age feature that most of the broken-up and burnt quern, plus a possible anvil stone, occurred. The location of this and other pits with associated domestic refuse at this northern end of the site, near the suspect round 'structure', suggests a focus for the Middle Iron Age occupation.

On the south side of the valley (Area A), most of the occupation-related activity was Middle Iron Age and associated with Pit Cluster 1. This included redeposited refuse, although the loomweight found there is unlikely to have travelled far. Both 25–30 m east and west of that point were minor posthole groupings, which may attest to short-lived structures.

The site's ironworking slag is suggestive of local smithing and is of interest on account of the limited evidence recovered from most other Early Iron Age settlements. Similar pieces have, however, been recovered from Broom, Beds. (Copper & Edmonds 2007, app. 8), as well as at Bradley Fen, Whittlesey (Knight & Brudenell forthcoming); the latter was associated with a suite of ironworking debris, including hearth remains and hammer-scale. At High Cross the slag appears to have been redeposited, yet the find of a possible anvil stone further supports the argument for ironworking nearby.

Cambridge at War (1) – The Sebro Shorts Aircraft Works

In the name of, if not 'hidden', then at least soon forgotten histories, Cambridge's World War legacy has featured in the series' first volumes, ranging from WWI practice trenches to the city's anti-tank ditch-perimeter and a PoW camp (*BLS*, fig. figs. 1.8 & 1.9; *RVS*, fig. 1.6). Both wars have left their imprint within the western Cambridge lands. Remains from WWI are dealt with in the next book (though, see Fig. 6.50); here it is the WWII Sebro Shorts works at High Cross that will concern us.

With three main hangers and, at its peak, apparently employing some 4,500 staff, Sebro Shorts occupied the site from 1941–6. It was where wartime Stirling bombers were repaired, before being transported to RAF Bourn for assembly and testing. Its locale is clearly known to aviation aficionados, but otherwise it is something that has largely passed from local memory. While our excavations exposed its foundations, aside from retrieving a couple of items such as a fuselage-access panel (Fig. 7.16), we unfortunately had to avoid digging what few associated dump deposits there were, due to a significant risk of contamination.

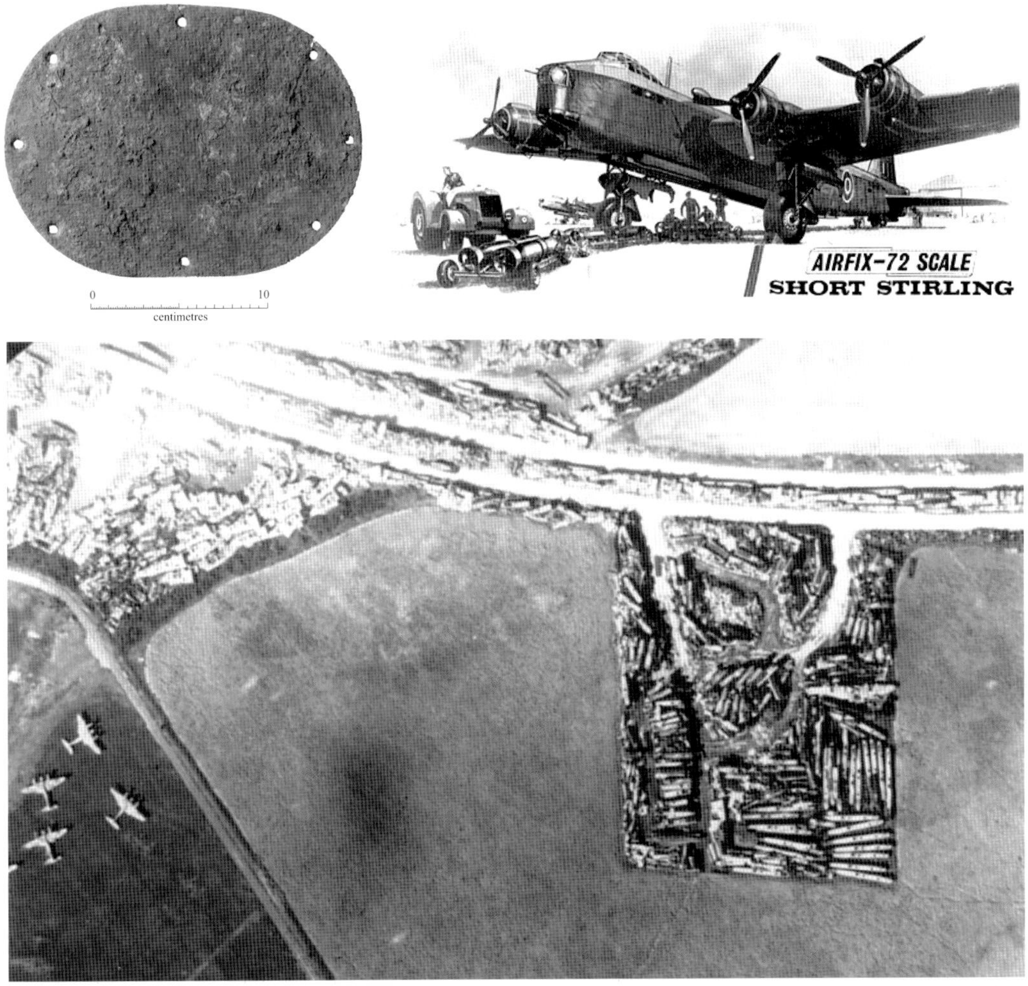

Figure 7.16. *Cambridge and aerial defence: inspection plate from Short Stirling bomber recovered from the High Cross Site (upper right); upper right, Airfix kit and, below, 1945 photograph showing dismantled Stirling bomber parts alongside Marshall Airfield, Cambridge (note Mosquito bombers parked in the field, left).*

Figure 7.17. *The Shorts/SEBRO Works: 1944 image showing its roof apparently painted in ridge-and-furrow camouflage (top; Geoinformation Group) and, below, 1969 photograph of the same (as repainted).*

The works factory was evidently the inspiration for Lombardi's *Short Stirling: The First of the RAF Heavy Bombers*:

> It was in 1972, when I was twelve years old, that I first became aware of the Short Stirling. I was in the basement of Eaden Lilly's department store in Cambridge, and I saw the picture of this huge four-engined bomber aircraft dwarfing the ground crew beneath it on the front of a 1:72 scale Airfix model box. ... Later on, speaking to local people, it seemed that everyone knew of this aircraft and many local people had worked on it. This puzzled me somewhat, as many of them were women, and I knew that women didn't fly on operations. It was 1974 before I discovered the answer.
>
> I was told about a large factory in Cambridge which repaired damaged Stirlings, and that many who had worked there were women. Studying my new Ordnance Survey Map of Cambridge, I found what I thought was the factory on Madingley Road, and went straight there across town on my bicycle, hoping to find a Stirling. I was soon disappointed; most of the buildings at the site had been demolished a few years earlier and there were no Stirlings, although there were small pieces of them lying around. Some of these pieces were stamped with numbers, while others even had the word 'Stirling' on them. It was not until many years later that I could identify some of them, or at least tell where on the aircraft they came from. Although there was little left of the factory, I realized that it must have been a huge undertaking; I wanted to learn all I could about it and the Stirlings that were built there (2015, 11).

That volume details the works' wartime operations (*ibid*., 278–331). After the war the buildings, for a time, were considered as a possible display venue for the Whipple collection of historic scientific instruments. However, part of the site had been leased to the Pye electronics company and, shortly thereafter, it suffered a major fire; the remainder of the site was kept in use until 1971 as a government storage depot.

The photographs included here deserve some comment. That from 1945 shows Stirlings broken up for scrap alongside Marshall Airfield on the east side of Cambridge (Fig. 7.16). With still-intact Mosquitos parked on the adjacent field, this brings home the vast scale of the region's wartime air defence industry. The other image, a 1946 aerial photography of the High Cross works, warrants close scrutiny in comparison to the 1969 picture of the same below (Fig. 7.17). The earlier vertical shot shows the buildings' roofs in camouflage and, remarkably, these have been masked by rendering in ridge-and-furrow! How completely extraordinary, but also how entirely appropriate. The pre-War Luftwaffe image that will feature in the next book clearly demonstrates just how widespread the area's ridge-and-furrow imprint was prior to wartime agricultural intensification. Now, it only really survives in the pasture field below the Traveller's Rest Pit copse and along the east side of Madingley Road's Park-and-Ride.

The inventiveness of wartime camouflage has been widely acknowledged (i.e. a legacy of 'Churchill's Wizards'; see Rankin 2008). In the case of the Shorts works, one can't help but think that, if thorough archival searches could be conducted, there is an underlying story here, and one likely to have an local academic connection; this, though, is something we will leave to others.

What else can be inferred about the local environment and economic use of this landscape during the Iron Age? Located within the lower part of the valley, the Early Iron Age boundary ditch and pit clusters show evidence of seasonal standing water, with the pollen pointing to a rise in bog-loving species and also the appearance of secondary birch woodland colonizing former open grassland. Whilst gradually becoming wetter over time, at the beginning of the Iron Age the area was probably still sufficiently dry for moderately good grazing pasture, and perhaps even small-scale cereal cultivation (spelt and emmer wheat). The dominance of cattle within the period's faunal remains would seem to accord with such a 'damp ground' scenario. Yet, sheep were also certainly kept, as attested by the evidence of textile production (spindlewhorl and loomweight).

It may be telling that the recovered Iron Age skull showed signs of *cribra orbitalia* (Fig. 7.8), which can reflect an iron deficient diet and anaemia. While three of the Roman inhumations at Vicar's Farm had evidence of this condition (see Chap. 5, above), it was more common amongst Trumpington Meadows' Iron Age dead (*RVS*, chap. 4).

Attempting to finally adjudicate upon the character of these sites – short-lived permanent settlement *vs*. seasonal usage – it is instructive to compare the site's Early–Middle Iron Age evidence to that of the Early Iron Age complex at Trumpington Meadows, especially the 'pitting halo' that ringed its core-area pit clusters (see *RVS*, Chap. 3). While roundhouses at Trumpington Meadows were not directly recovered, the quasi-circular arrangements of the pits (plus the daub recovered from them) leaves no doubt they had surrounded buildings; this is supported by the sheer scale of the associated pottery and animal bone assemblages. Iron Age High Cross had other distinct attributes typical of settlement: human remains, querns, slag and loomweights. Added to its midden-type deposits, this does seem to represent permanent settlement. The low-lying water supply at High Cross may, in fact, have been the prime attractor and 'episodic homesteading' might be attested.

The establishment of the Early Roman fieldsystem at High Cross on the low valley's slightly higher south-facing slopes seems likely to have been contemporary with the Phase 1 development at Vicar's Farm; the two systems shared the same orientation (Fig. 7.35). Yet, other than the evidence for at least three *c.* 0.6 ha fields/paddocks and from which just a handful of Roman sherds were forthcoming (which probably attest to no more than manuring practices), there seems little other evidence of activity. When excavated, the western sub-square 'enclosure' failed to produce anything comparable to the assemblage of Flavian to Hadrianic wares found in the 2000 evaluation. Likewise, there was no direct evidence of Conquest Period/Early Roman settlement *per se* within the part of that enclosure that was investigated. Nevertheless, based on the evaluation-phase finds, it can only be presumed that any associated settlement lay immediately west of the site-area. Was it actually as short-lived as the pottery thus far recovered suggests (i.e. ceasing by the early–mid second century AD), or did it have a longer duration? If the former, then the issue becomes one of reasons for its abandonment, as opposed to the maintenance of the Vicar's Farm settlement.[2]

The rationale behind the Medieval attribution of the double-ditched trackway and possible associated field elements has been outlined above. When the excavation-area is superimposed on Hall and Ravensdale's 1976 West Fields map, there is a near-direct correspondence with the route of *Coton/Sheepcote Way* (Fig. 7.10). Similarly, when comparing the High Cross plough features with the pattern of Medieval ridge-and-furrow at Vicar's Farm, there is an almost identical orientation and width of furrow-strips, as well as their interval-distance (12–14 m).

The 'persistent' later prehistoric sequence at High Cross provides significant insights into the utilization/colonization of the region's heavy claylands, particularly as regards questions of water supply. This issue, and any further detailing of the processes it might have involved, will be best addressed when the results of the area's other 'landscape-scale' investigations are outlined and can be brought to bear in the next book.

Further Evaluation and the Vet School Site Settlement

Relating to the final building-stages of the University's original West Cambridge programme and in advance of the construction of a Data Centre, further evaluation trenching occurred in 2012 across two plots immediately west of the High Cross Site (Fig. 7.18; Slater 2012). The northernmost lay under the concrete hardstanding of the earlier aircraft works, which had truncated the geology and removed any possible features. While the southern plot had not suffered such disturbance, aside from agricultural furrows, there the only features recovered were shallow ditch-lines evidently relating to the westward continuation of the Medieval routeway, *Coton* or *Sheepcote Way*.

Much to our surprise, three years later we were called upon to return to the area for yet more evaluation fieldwork, this time relating to a more intensive West Cambridge 'infilling' planning proposal. Following geophysical survey, the trenching was confined to plots surrounding the Veterinary School and the field immediately east of the Schlumberger Centre (Brittain & Evans 2015). Amounting to *c.* 10 ha in total, these had not been tested during the original programme (Fig. 7.18). Later still, in November of 2017, further trenching was conducted across a *c.* 0.4 ha plot within the area's northeast corner and at what had been the location of Merton Hall Farm (Fig. 7.20; see *Madingley Rises* .... below and Newman 2017).

The land encompasses a slight east–west rise, whose crown lies at *c.* 21 m OD (sloping down to 17–18 m OD on its sides; Fig. 7.18), and it is relevant that though, as indicated on the BGS Survey, the solid geology there is Gault Clay the trenching revealed that it is overlain by mixed sandy gravels and clays. Evidently 'diamict', erosion-derived deposits weathered off from Coton's lower chalk and Boulder Clay ridge, these more 'hospitable' beds and – however subtle – the elevated topography, must account for the sites that were, quite unexpectedly, encountered (Fig. 7.24).

With just six flints recovered (non-diagnostic), there was no evidence that the location was particularly distinguished in earlier prehistory. Traces of what seems to have been a Romano-British fieldsystem were found in the field beside the Schlumberger Centre and continue eastward (Fig. 7.19). Some of these boundaries, such as that in Trench 1 in the south end of Field 1, appear to relate to those at High Cross, as do others in Field 2. Against this, though, are the ditches further north in that field in Trenches 3, 4 and 36; oriented more north-over-west, they are on a markedly different alignment. While it is just possible that they delineated a trackway/road, at more than 20 m wide, this seems unlikely. The only dating evidence recovered from them was a single sherd of Iron Age pottery. Yet they are more likely to be of Roman attribution. If projected to the northwest, these boundaries would have run just west of North West Cambridge's villa-estate complex (Site VII), been close to a return-axis of its Site II road (No. 6) and been parallel with Vicar's Farm Road 2.

Figure 7.18. *Subsequent evaluations: the 2012 Data Centre and 2015 West Cambridge trenching, with detail of latter below (with contours and geology indicated).*

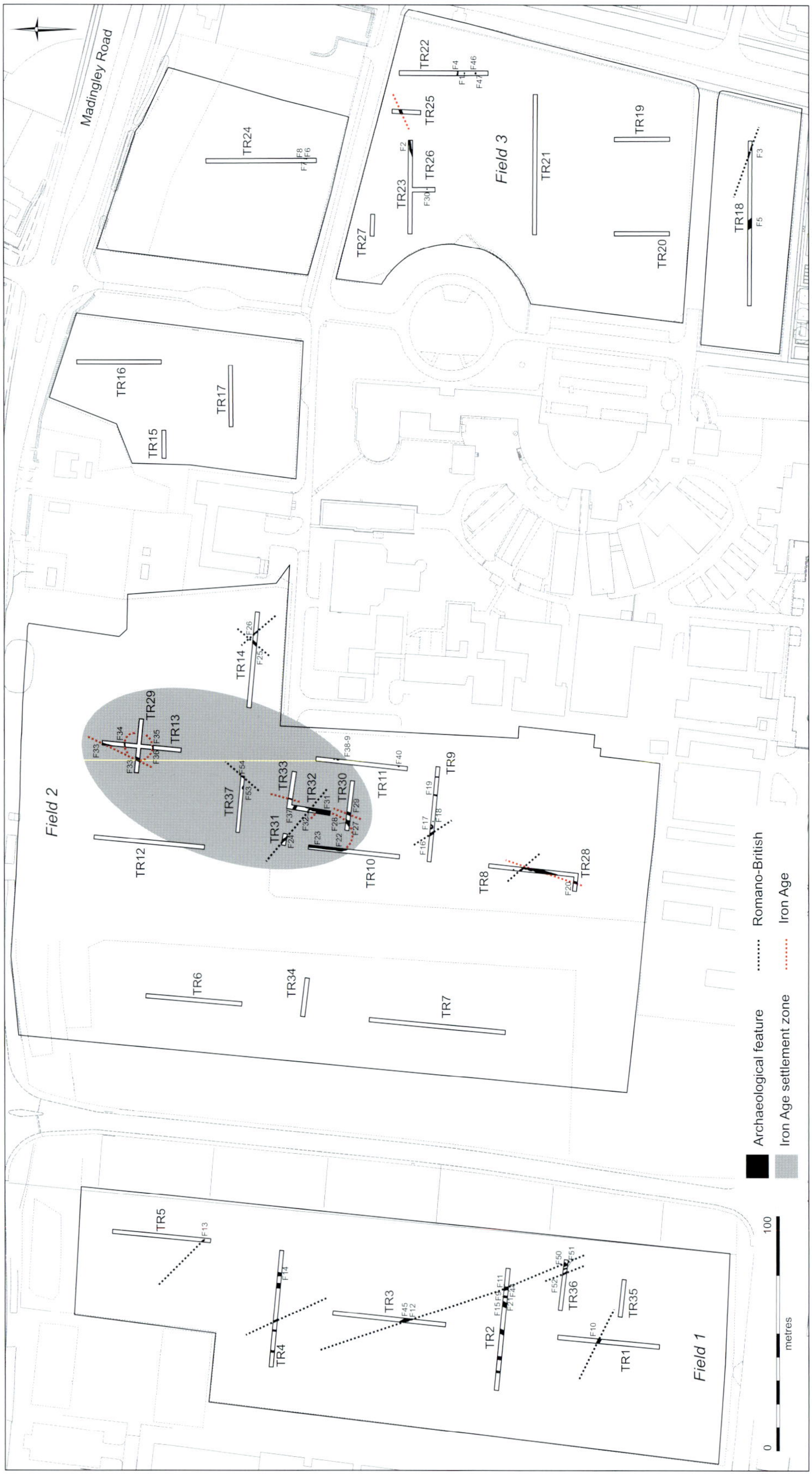

Figure 7.19. *West Cambridge 2015, evaluation findings.*

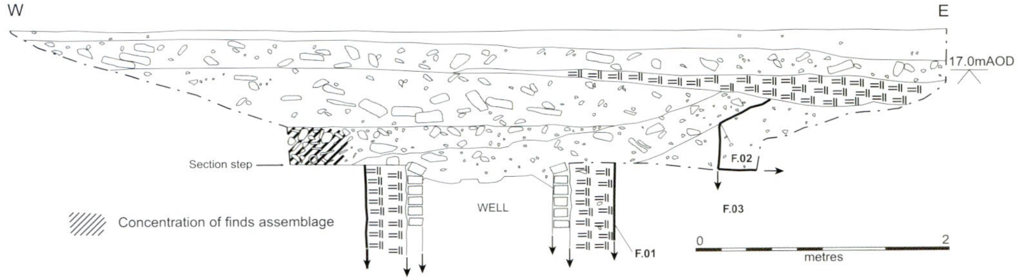

Figure 7.20. *Merton Hall Farm 2017. First shown on a map of 1886 (see, also, Fig. 6.56) following the land's purchase by Merton College, Oxford, it was suspected that an earlier farm there might have been the source of the Vicar's Farm Medieval ploughsoil finds. This proved not to be the case and the earliest features recovered were Post-Medieval. Amounting to almost 18 kg, a major horizon of dumped 'late' material (e.g. glass and ceramic vessels, plus metalwork and animal bone) was found to have sealed an earlier well. As studied by Cessford (in Newman 2017, 7–9), this dates to 1886–90 and includes, for example, a Codd bottle, Keiller marmalade jars (see Fig. 3.46) and at least 11 different vessels from three Colleges (Trinity Hall, Trinity and St John's); as such, the assemblage is broadly comparable to Vicar's Farm's Post-Medieval material (see Chap. 4).*

A ditch and single posthole were found in a paddock immediately in front of the Veterinary School. Thought probably to be of Iron Age attribution (no dating evidence was recovered), this 'occupation' would seem to be very localized and relatively insubstantial. Much more significant were the Early to Middle Iron Age settlement features extending across the paddocks just west of the School (hereafter named the Vet School Site: Fig. 7.19). Although a central *c.* 50 × 50 m core-area was identified, features of this date extended over some 225 m (north–south). Two, possibly three, gully-defined roundhouses were distinguished amid a number of both curvilinear and linear boundaries (plus pits) and some 120 sherds were recovered. Quernstone was also present, and all this must attest to 'robust' permanent settlement, but which will only be detailed when it eventually sees full excavation.[3]

Although obviously another theme best addressed when North West Cambridge's results are brought to bear, in themselves the location of the West Cambridge-land sites informs us of clayland land-use. Certainly, it highlights that *not all clay geologies are the same*. In this case, the relatively high density of its early settlement related to the mixed and better-drained gravel/clay diamict deposits that sealed the heavy Gault Clay in the west. These effectively extend as a low spur, with the Vicar's Farm Site situated at its eastern end (see Fig. 7.24).

While the Veterinary School Iron Age settlement was sited up near the highest ground of the immediate topography (*c.* 19–20 m OD), the location of the High Cross and Vicar's Farm settlements evidently related to different factors: just above the area's lowest points and where water would have been readily available. This is a theme that we will have to return to, as, in 'inland' situations such as this, the problem of accessing year-round water supplies should not be underestimated.

The Wilberforce Road Settlement (with Marcus Brittain)

In the autumn of 2017, we evaluated the western portion of the University's Sport Grounds in advance of the construction of new hockey pitches. Its trench-evaluation resulted in the discovery of yet another Roman-period farmstead (Tabor 2017), which was then excavated in the early spring of the following year (see Figs. 7.10 & 7.21–2; Brittain & Evans 2018).[4]

Located just 300 m south of Vicar's Farm, the 1.4 ha site lay on *Aldermanne Hill's* (diamict bed) slight east–west rise. Its crest lies at *c.* 14.5 m OD, with the ground-surface dropping a metre in the southeast and down to *c.* 12.5 m OD in the north. Across the low ground on the northern side, a soft silty sand deposit evinced a minor palaeochannel, likely to be the continuation of that exposed in the High Cross Site. In the south the rise's beds gave way to Gault Clay, with up to 0.5 m depth of colluvial cover (Fig. 7.23); Roman-phase features were found to both occur within, and be sealed by, this slope-wash material. The site's soil sequence was detailed by the Unit's geoarchaeologist, Eduardo Machicado (see *ibid.*). Based on this and the area's previous exposures, he has produced Figure 7.24's elevation-model map that now greatly informs our understanding of western Cambridge's landscape.

Only the eastern margin of the farmstead's paddocks was available for excavation. Not extending to its core, this limited exposure tempers anything that can be said of the character of the site's assemblages and the settlement itself. Having said that, it was satisfying finding the Roman site there, as we had predicted one in the vicinity as early as 2002 (see Chap. 2, Fig. 2.40).

The environmental directives of the Wilberforce Road excavations reflect its coming after the North West Cambridge Phase 1 excavations. This was expressed in the programme's geoarcheological component, the intensity of its sampling and the analysis of its charcoal. By that time, the articulation of the Roman-period agricultural landscape and issues of its wood supply were something we wanted to address.

Metal-detecting of the site extended to both the surface of features and the lower sub-soil during the course of machine-stripping. As well as the earlier period finds outlined below, an impressive array of ordnance was also recovered. While the shotgun cartridges must attest to no more than casual field hunting, the musket balls, many Enfield .303 cartridges and even what is probably a lead bullet from a Martini-Henri rifle (see Fig. 7.36), must relate to the fact that, between 1859 and 1939, the 1250 yard long (1143 m) University Rifle Range lay just south of the site (Strachan 1976, 26–7).

Four periods of activity were in evidence in the site's sequence: Middle Bronze Age (1), Early Iron Age (2) and, sub-divided into three phases, Romano-British (3); stratigraphically, the Post-Medieval (4) was just represented by agricultural furrows (omitted from Figs. 7.22–3) and will not, therefore, be further considered.

Prehistory

Just six Neolithic-attributed worked flints were recovered, attesting to no more than 'casual visitation'. The register of Middle Bronze Age and Early Iron Age activity – both on the ridge's southern flank – was also limited (Fig. 7.23). The former amounted to a cluster of four pits (F.38 *et al.*). One contained a dump of heat-affected cobbles while another had five sherds of

Figure 7.21. *Wilberforce Road 2017, site photographs: top, looking east across the site to the Sports Ground track; below, looking north along the roadway (with its ditch-lines added).*

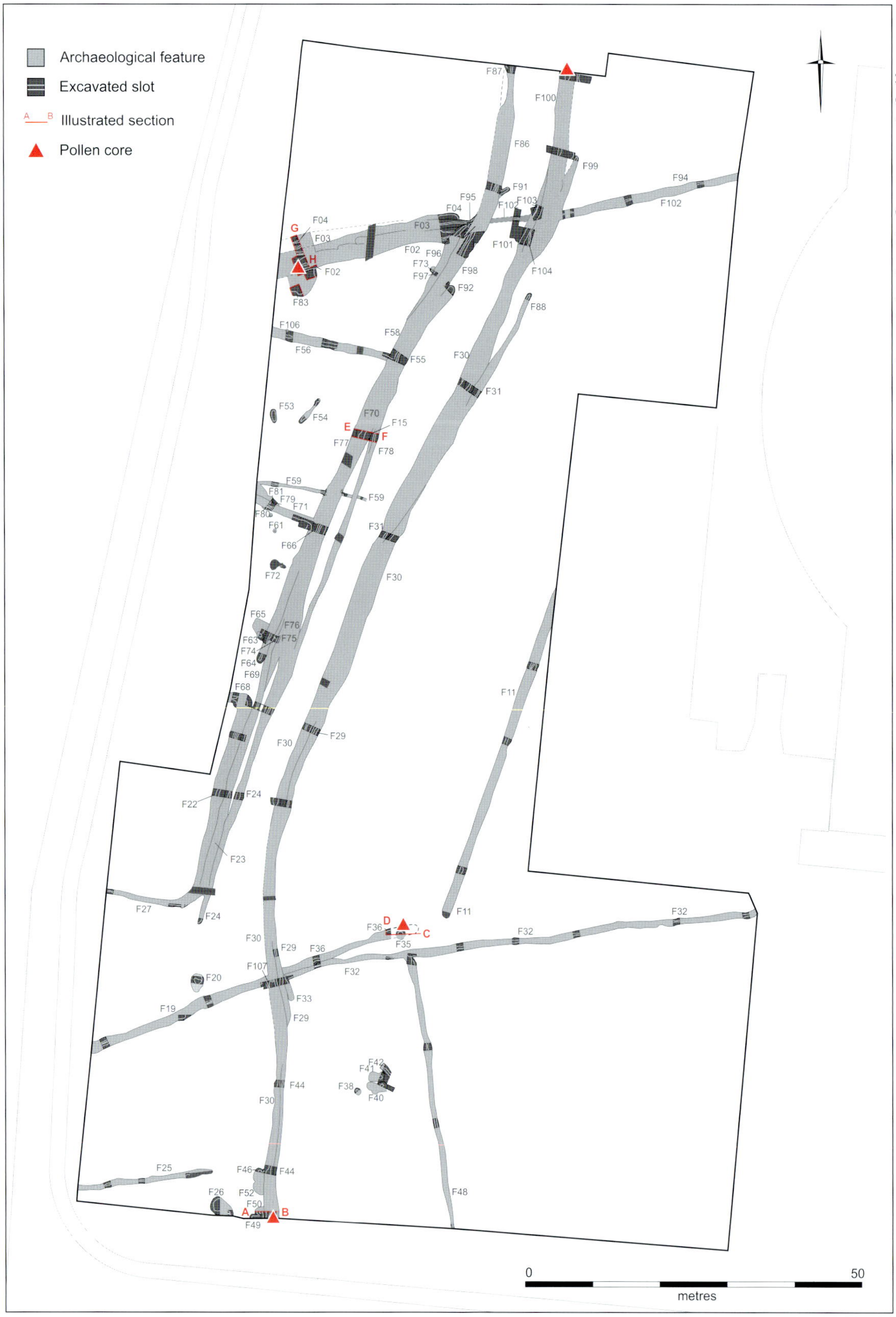

Figure 7.22. *Base plan, with excavation segments, section locations and pollen core locations indicated.*

Figure 7.23. *Base plan with contours and geology indicated (left) and, right, phase plan (left).*

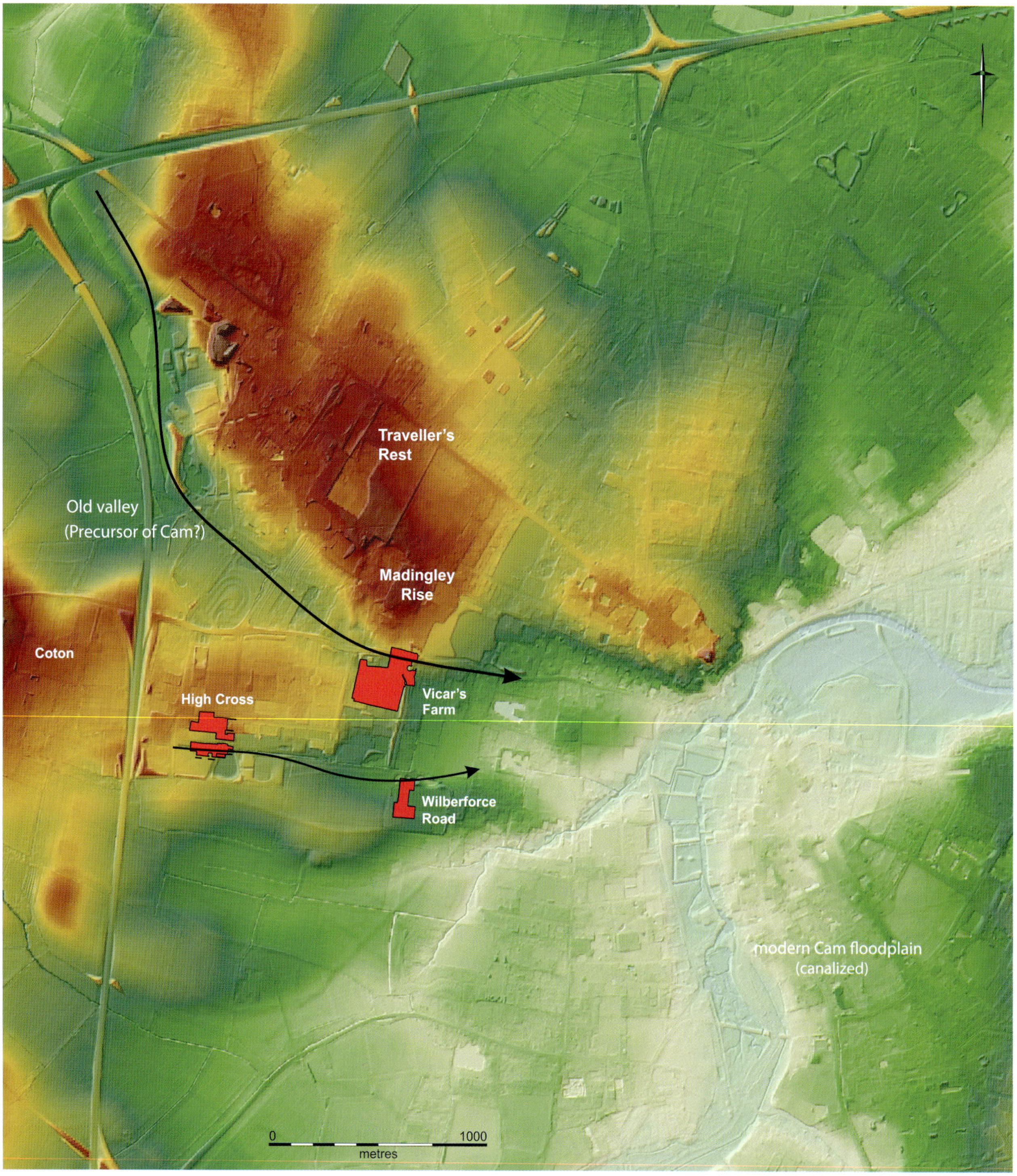

Figure 7.24. *Western Cambridge lands, digital elevation model (arrowed lines indicate palaeochannels).*

Middle Bronze Age pottery (one in burnt flint temper, with four having a shell-rich fabric). There was also a saddle quern rough-out in the latter feature (F.38); the environmental sample from that pit yielded no plant remains and just a few fragments of charcoal.

In total, 25 sherds of Early Iron Age pottery in a characteristic burnt flint fabric were recovered from the two pits of that date, F.20 and F.35. With minor quantities of animal bone present in both – cattle being the only identifiable species – F.35 was the deeper of the two

(1.1 m deep; 2 m across) and clearly functioned as a well (Fig. 7.25). It contained the bulk of the period's pottery (20 sherds) and its environmental sample had two apple seeds in addition to abundant charcoal. As Boreham reports below, the feature's pollen core register was dominated by grasses and there was no direct evidence of arable production. Arboreal pollen was present at 12.3 and 15.3 per cent, with hazel and pine represented; as detailed by Simmons, a much wider range of wood species was present within its charcoal assemblage.

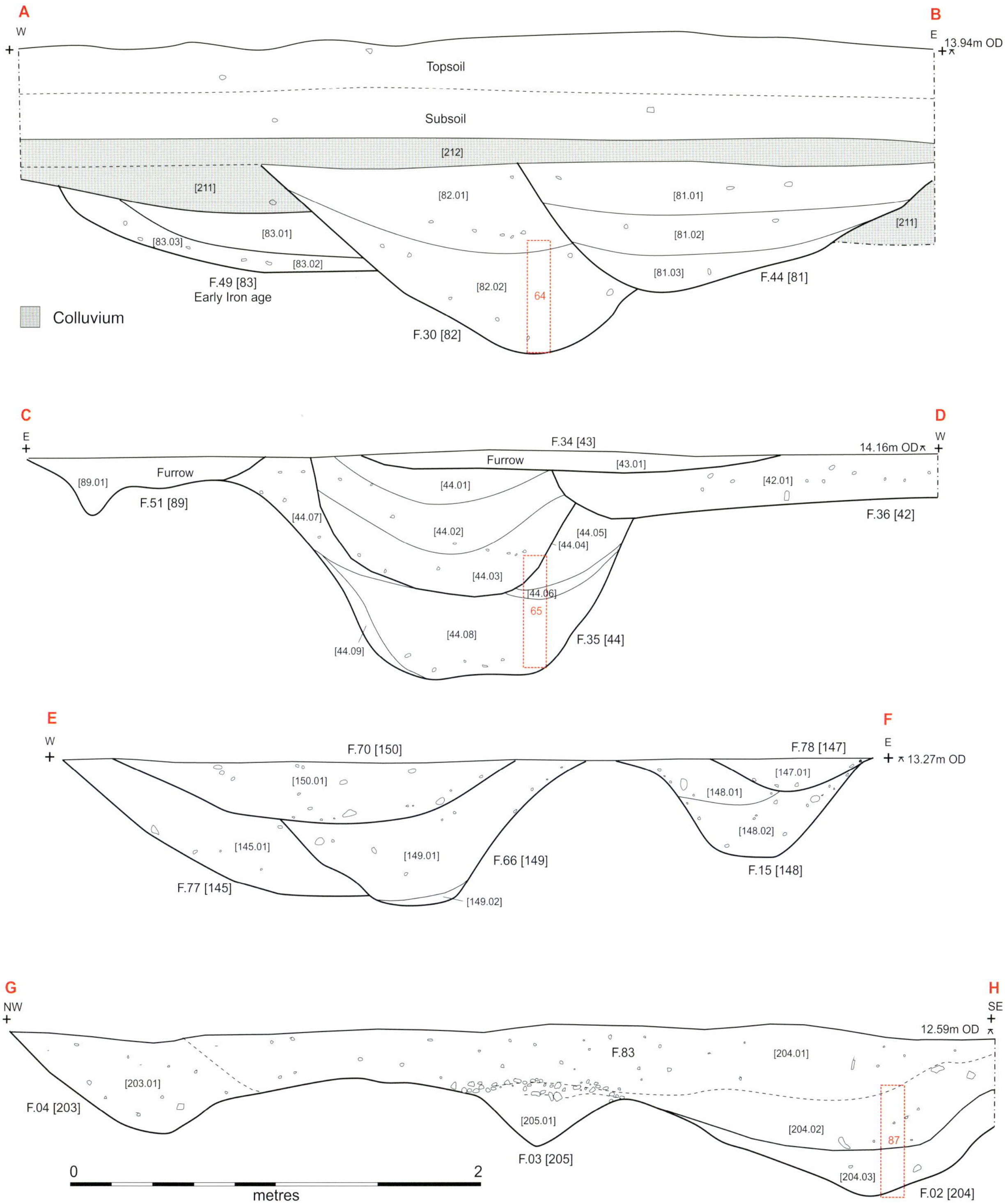

Figure 7.25. *Sections (see Fig. 7.22 for locations).*

Occurring residually within Roman-period features was another possible saddle quern fragment and a single sherd of Late Iron Age pottery.

Roman

Spanning the first to the fourth centuries AD, the three ascribed phases were not rigid divisions and their components overlap each other (Fig. 7.24).

Some 1767 sherds of pottery (14.8 kg) and 1195 animal bone fragments were recovered. The pottery shows that the settlement had largely ceased by the mid third century AD, with the floruit of usage dating to the first and second centuries AD.

Just four coins were recovered, as well as an iron armlet, a fragment of a mid–late first-century AD headstud-type brooch and a Colchester Derivative brooch of the same date (Fig. 7.31). One of the coins is probably an *as* of first–second-century AD date; one is a *radiate*, possibly of Carausius (AD 286–93) and the third is a *nummus* (AE4) with an illegible obverse but an inverse showing a/*the* wolf and twins; there was also a second *nummus*, of the House of Constantine (AD 330–35).

Also recovered was the lower stone of a Millstone Grit rotary quern (F.24, est. diam. 400 mm).

The first phase of Roman usage was marked by a coaxial fieldsystem (Fig. 7.23). Predominantly oriented northeast–southwest, its ditches were 0.4–2.5 m wide and *c*. 0.2–0.75 m deep. That the Phase 2 farmstead-paddock features lay on a different alignment to the initial fieldsystem could suggest that the former related to yet another settlement nearby (see *Discussion*... and Fig. 7.33). Having said that, the way in which the northern ditch-line, F.2/3, broadened and clearly had been recut in relation to the Phase 3 road/trackway indicates the sustained maintenance of that boundary.

Dating to the first to third centuries AD, Phase 2 saw the establishment and usage of the main farmstead paddocks along the area's western side (Fig. 7.23). Collectively, these were *c*. 9 m wide/across and, oriented northeast–southwest, were internally sub-divided into three by ditch-lines. In addition to a few pits and a pottery kiln, also assigned to this phase were an axially parallel ditch (F.11) in the east, with another ditch boundary in the south (F.25) together with three pits.

The kiln is detailed below; otherwise, two of the phase's pit features are noteworthy. The one situated within the main paddocks, F.53 (1.9 × 0.9 × 0.38 m), contained 174 sherds of pottery (2307 g) that largely appear to derive from four semi-complete vessels. The other feature (F.83; 4 m across and 0.25 m deep), lay north of the paddocks and truncated the northern, Phase 1 ditch. Within the base of this hollow was a horizon of cobbles; it contained 54 sherds of pottery (329 g) and 576 g of animal bone, with its environmental sample including grains of emmer, spelt and free-threshing wheat.

Phase 3 was primarily marked by the ditched demarcation of an 8–10 m wide road/trackway (No. 5), its much-recut ditches being *c*. 0.7–2.3 m wide and 0.1–0.65 m deep (Figs. 7.21 & 7.23). It truncated the eastern side of the Phase 2 paddocks and ran parallel with its main axis (turning more due north–south to both the north and the south). While the eastern of the route's ditches continued south of the Phase 2 paddocks, the western one terminated. Only the southernmost of the farmstead's core-area paddocks showed evidence of usage into the later Roman period, with dark earth-type deposits within its upper profile.

Given the close relationship of the Phase 3 routeway and the Phase 2 farmstead, it is likely that this 'way' was operational before the start of that phase, but that it may not originally have been deeply ditched; its Phase 2 ditching may have been relatively minor (e.g. F.88 & F.92) and largely truncated through subsequent reworking.

The Roman Pottery Kiln

With only its base and stoke pit surviving, the kiln (F.72) was relatively simple, with there being no indication of any interior fixtures (e.g. a central pedestal; Figs. 7.26–7). There was, though, evidence that it had been relined and refired, and the kiln bars that were recovered leave no doubt as to its function.

The kiln was oriented west-northwest to east-southeast (1 × 0.55 × 0.25 m). On the west side there was a sub-circular stoke pit (1.6 × 1.4 × 0.48 m; F.108) with near-vertical sides and a flat base; the two components were presumably connected via a shallow flue. A five-fold sequence was identified: primary kiln structure, kiln-use, collapse of kiln structure, post-abandonment and, finally, plough-damage. In section, two main stages of fuel rake-out and kiln structure were identifiable; these were separated by a deposit of thick mid grey soft silty clay with small fragments of burnt clay and white ash. During excavation, however, it was evident that the first structural-stage deposit concealed at least four distinct fired clay linings separated by thin lenses of reddened charcoal-infused clayey silt. Much of the material recovered from the kiln's collapse and post-abandonment, therefore, belongs to the second main structure and rake-out.

The kiln furniture is described and discussed below. It is evident that the structural mechanics utilized in both main stages of the kiln's architecture were comparable. The kiln proper was likely to have been covered by a clay dome, possibly with square tiles impressed into its interior wall, and was crowned with a thick clay shelf at ground level. The stoke pit was open and without any clay lining. The furniture consisted of at least eight kiln bars, a single stacker or setter, and domed circular clay plates. The exact arrangement of these items is unclear and may have consisted of both horizontal and vertical elements, perhaps involving the careful stacking of vessels in both a rim-down/up sequence.

No pot wasters were recovered associated with the kiln. As discussed by Mazzilli below, it is uncertain to what extent the recovered pottery assemblage was reflective of the actual wares

Figure 7.26. *Photographs of the F.72 kiln.*

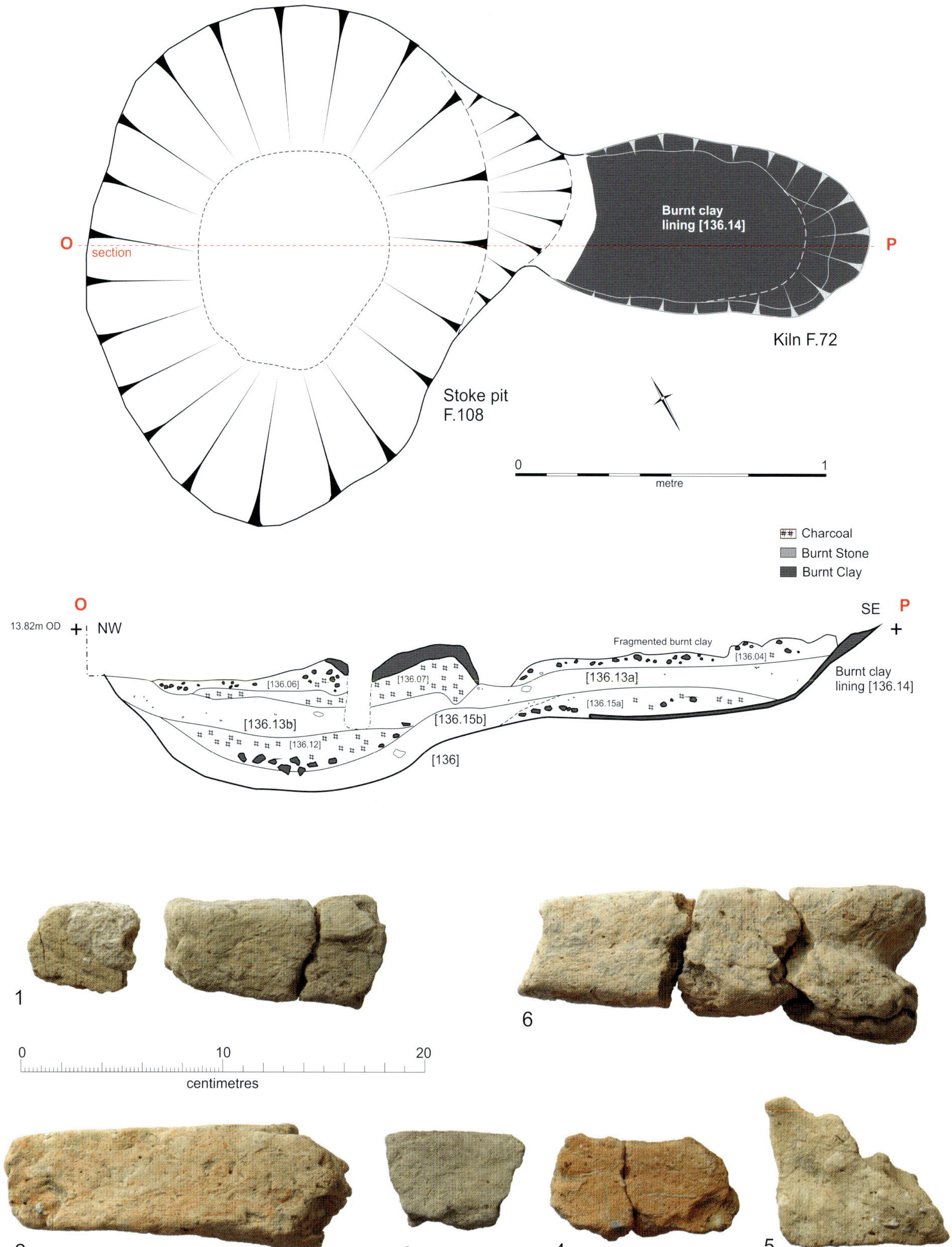

Figure 7.27. *The kiln (F.72) plan and section; below kiln furniture (1–5 kiln bars; 6: kiln stacker or setter).*

fired within the kiln. A single wheat grain occurred within its bulk sample, otherwise no other charred plant material was present.

To facilitate the description of the kiln's architecture and furniture, the following clay fabrics have been identified:

Fabric 1 Medium-hard, fine grained clay with marl or clunch lumps and rare crushed flint; with occasional fibre impressions; light pink colour (oxidized)
Fabric 2 Hard and well-fired, coarse sandy texture with small marl or clunch lumps and stones; reddish exterior and interior (oxidized)
Fabric 3 Hard and well-fired, fine sandy clay with small marl or clunch lumps and stones and impressions of fibres; pinkish red (oxidized) exterior and reduced (grey) interior
Fabric 4 Medium-hard fine clay, near-stone-free with voids and organic fibre (straw?) impressions; mid pink colour
Fabric 5 Hard, fine clay with rare small crushed flint and very rare chaff impressions; mixed dark grey and reddened exterior to light grey interior
Fabric 6 Hard micaceous sand with small grit inclusions.

During excavation, at least four distinct stages of initial kiln-wall construction were identified in plan, but these were discernible only as a single overall phase of *in situ* lining in section ([136.14]); a second structure may have been superimposed upon this. With the exception of the final, uppermost layer of burnt clay debris ([136.04], [136.06] & [136.07]), fill [136.12] of the main pit produced 862 g of kiln-wall fragments, with three of the largest from the entire assemblage. Separated from the collapse of the superstructure by a clay and ash layer ([136.13]), this must constitute both a temporal separation and a remodelling of the kiln, though consistency in the use of material fabric – and presumably the kiln's 'architecture' – is evident.

It is clear that the kiln's below-ground lining was minimal (*c.* 20 mm thick; [136.14]; Table 7.4) compared with the above-ground component found in the latest destruction layer ([136.04]); that had a thick walling, at least at its ground-level base, of up to 42 mm thick. This may have facilitated a ledge or pilaster upon which kiln furniture, such as bars and plates, may have rested. No obvious separation of differing fabrics is evident within the stages of material lining.

A squared fragment from [136.02] may be part of a small shaped slab. As with this example, larger and thicker irregular slabs recovered from kilns at Addenbrooke's Hutchinson Site were found with evidence of scorching on one surface only and thought to be part of the kiln lining or covering, rather than free-standing kiln furniture (*BLS*, 84). As only one example was recovered from F.72, its status is uncertain.

Kiln Bars - At least eight kiln bars are represented by 24 fragments (Fig. 7.27), all from the kiln's upper profile. These are square-sectioned (40–65 mm thick) with at least one tapering end, and probably one thicker, flattened/squared end. None may be reconstructed to completeness, though the two longest surviving were 16–21 cm in length. Their fabric (Nos. 1 & 2) was broadly similar to the kiln's superstructure, except for Fabrics 3 and 4. The majority were of an oxidized red or pink colour throughout their profile, with a few examples in which the core had been reduced to a greyish colour. The bars were formed of a single complete seam of mixed clay (i.e. no voids), with the angular edges slightly rounded or folded.

Stacker or Setters - Two rectangular items with dimensions similar to the kiln bars and a profile likewise tapering to one end, were found to bifurcate at one end, and have equally spaced prongs separated by a smooth concave impression (Fig. 7.27). There is no direct parallel within the main national overview of Romano-British kilns and their furniture (Swan 1984). Three-pronged clay 'stilts' are, though, cited from a kiln at Holt, Denbigh. These were used to suspend lead-glazed vessels by their rims in an inverted position as a means of preventing the vessels sticking to the kiln during the firing (*ibid.*, 40). Lead-glazed vessels were not present within the F.72 assemblage, but it is likely that the bi-pronged bars acted as some form of support.

Similar items have been found in Addenbrooke's Hutchinson Site (*BLS*, 83–4, fig. 2.36, nos. 1–2) and, elsewhere in the region, along with other kiln furniture at Blackhorse Lane in Swavesey (Willis *et al.* 2008, 59, fig. 4). Those at the latter were considered to be kiln stackers or setters. They would have been utilized within the kiln, along with bars and plates, as part of the internal frame that ensures the horizontal separation of vessels and the inhibition of

Table 7.4. *Burnt clay kiln-wall fragments.*

Cat No.	Context	Qty.	Wt. (g)	Description	Fabrics
412	136.01	4	76	mainly small lumps of kiln wall	4
418	136.01	53	128	small rounded kiln wall fragments	1 & 4
419	136.02	23	459	mostly rounded lumps; four with flat surfaces, one slightly concave – all probably kiln inner wall or flue (Fabric 3)	1, 3 & 4
420	136.02	1	188	a square (92 × 97 mm) fragment of kiln wall, 12 mm thickness, with possible signs of having been shaped – one edge is near flat with folding evident in section, but the three remaining edges are too worn to confirm this. One face is reddened by scorching, the other being homogeneous light pink.	1
302	136.03	2	10	kiln wall fragments	2
304	136.04	109	1482	small to large fragments of kiln wall, max thickness 42 mm	1 & 2
306	136.06	165	1216	kiln wall fragments	1 & 3
309	136.07	23	112	small fragments of kiln wall; four with flat surfaces	4
413	136.08	17	26	small rounded kiln wall fragments	1 & 4
315	136.12	83	862	mainly small lumps of kiln wall (Fabric 1) with three moderately large pieces (Fabric 3)	1 & 3
422	136.14	19	210	kiln wall fragments; hard and heavily vitrified with grey interior, pinkish exterior; 20 mm thickness	1

any movement or collapse during firing. If stood upright in a setting akin to that envisaged at Holt, the space between setter prongs may have held fast the rim of an upturned vessel (Swan 1984, 40), giving some clue as to the firing technique.

Plates - One fabric stood out from the rest. Number 5 was notably harder, having a well-fired oxidized exterior and, with a reduced centre, overall had a mixed grey and soft red colour with occasional crushed flint and rare plant or chaff impressions. This fabric was exclusive to a series of thin-walled ceramic fragments (6–11 mm) that were first thought to be kiln 'wasters' and reused as spacers within the kiln. Two sets of refitting fragments from [136.02], however, illustrated that these actually belonged to disc-like plates with an irregular sub-circular shape and domed profile with a slightly irregular curl along the pinched edges. The fabric used for the plates has regional parallels, most notably at Horningsea (J. Evans *et al*. 2017, chap. 3, 3).

Plates are amongst the most commonly found kiln furniture (Swan 1984, 41). Their use is open to some speculation and may have been varied. A proposed function, as found in lowland East Yorkshire for example, is a use similar to stackers or setters: separating and supporting vessels within the kiln itself (Halkon & Millett 1999, 123). The size of plates, generally 15–30 cm in diameter (Swan 1984, 64), may be overly large for the purpose of a spacer within the kiln, and the most complete example from F.72 lies within this range at *c*. 22 cm. For the plates associated with Horningsea's kilns, and more recently reiterated for fired clay plate fragments associated with kilns found at Waterbeach (J. Evans *et al*. 2017, chap. 3, 10–16), Walker proposed that clay plates made up a layer within a turf dome laid over a stack of vessels for the purpose of retaining the kiln's heat so to colour the vessels, and to be easily dismantled after each firing (1913, 47).

Another local comparison may be made to an arrangement of items excavated at War Ditches, Cherry Hinton (Hughes 1904, 474–7). Although interpreted as a fire setting or hearth, these were part of larger deposits of kiln material that may have rested directly within a kiln associated with barbotine decorated fineware production. The excavator described having found four 'pyramidal blocks' or tapering curved-bar pillars standing upright in a square setting (see *BLS*, Fig. 2.46). Amongst the materials found within the setting were small fired clay 'buns'. These were thought to have rested on the pillars, and fragments of one or more flat clay discs, *c*. 25–30 cm diameter and *c*. 1.25 cm thick, one of which is shown in an illustrated reconstruction to have sat upon the pillars and buns. It has been suggested that this arrangement may partly have resulted through slippage of horizontal bars from a shelf into a recess, upon which plates may have once rested (Swan 1984, 61). The possibility that the bi-pronged bars were arranged in an upright position to hold inverted vessels by their rims, however, adds to the argument for some form of vertical-bar arrangement associated with the plates.

Material Culture

The presentation of Roman-period material here is selective. With the querns cited above and F.72's kiln furniture already detailed, the worked stone and fired/burnt clay assemblages are otherwise fully reported on in the assessment text (Brittain & Evans 2018). Also recovered were two small glass shards, one green and one clear (F.51 & F.107 respectively). There were just 14 small–medium fragments of tile (332 g), with six from F.72 refitting. This leaves pottery, metalwork, faunal remains and environmental evidence to be reported on below.

Roman Pottery (Francesca Mazzilli)

The assemblage consists of 1767 sherds (14,817 g), some 66 per cent of which dates from the mid first century AD to roughly the third century AD (1174 sherds; 9065 g). While there is also generic local greyware and oxidized pottery that might be attributed to the second–fourth century AD, no specific form or class can be specifically dated to the mid third century AD onwards.[5]

The pottery's mean sherd weight (MSW) – 8.4 g – and the estimated vessel equivalence (EVE) from rims – 11.38 – are low. Sherds are mostly small worn fragments and 76 per cent are non-diagnostic. Relatively few vessels were identified on the basis of rims (64; Table 7.5). Overall, the MSW for the first-century AD ceramic material is slightly higher than for material datable to other centuries (10 g). First-century AD material, combined with vessels that can be roughly dated from the first century to early second century AD, constitutes 35 per cent of the entire assemblage. Thirty-one percent of the assemblage can be dated to the second–third century AD; similarly, 33 per cent is generically from the second–fourth century AD. As is typical of Romano-British assemblages in Cambridgeshire, unsourced local coarse and finewares dominate. This includes a high percentage of Horningsea ware (27%; Table 7.5; Figs. 7.30.4–6 & 7.30.16).

Seventeen samian sherds dating to the second century AD constitute the assemblage's only sourced finewares (Table 7.5; Fig. 7.28). This highlights the site's predominantly Early Roman date. Neither Middle nor Late Roman finewares were found. This includes the absence of sherds from Nene Valley production, which elsewhere is common and in constant supply across second–fourth-century AD settlements in Cambridgeshire (see Monteil, Chap. 6).

Table 7.5. *Romano-British pottery by fabric type.*

Fabrics	Sherd No.	Wt. (g)	EVES %	MNV
BUFF	28	160	0.10	1
CSGW	161	1079	0.90	9
CSOX	316	1650	1.28	10
CSOX WS?	12	208	0.53	1
DUXF?	3	12	0.00	0
EROM CSGW	546	4116	3.81	16
EROM CSOX	16	109	0.00	0
EROM FSGW	5	19	0.04	1
EROM SHELL	6	24	0.06	1
FSGW	102	328	0.40	1
FSOX	16	65	0.40	1
HORNGW	280	3565	2.10	14
HORNOX	195	2790	1.08	1
HORNOX BB	57	385	0.05	1
CG SA	17	232	0.63	6
SG SA	2	3	0.00	1
VER WW?	5	72	0.00	0
Total	*1767*	*14,817*	*11.38*	*64*

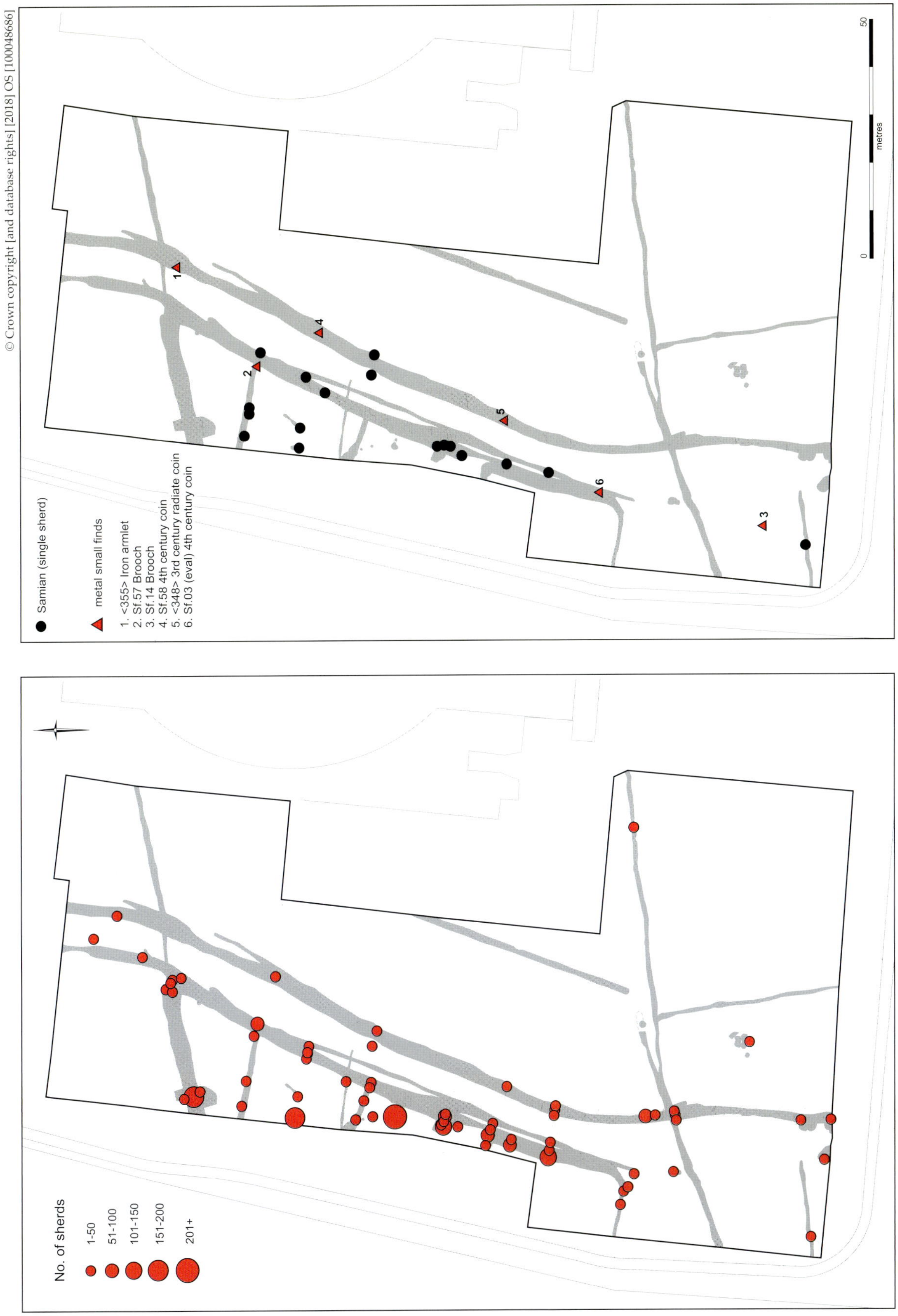

Figure 7.28. *Distribution plots: Roman pottery (left); right, samian and metalwork.*

Table 7.6. *Romano-British pottery by form.*

Forms	Sherd Qty.	Wt. (g)
Beaker	71	241
Bowl	54	579
Bowl/Dish	5	39
Cup	3	58
Dish	5	103
Flagon	4	12
Jar	286	2769
Jar/Bowl	13	100
Lid	1	33
Storage Jar	51	1866
Unidentified	1345	9017
Total	*1767*	*14,817*

Forms

As is typical of the region's Romano-British assemblages, the most common vessel form identified was jars, followed by bowls (Table 7.6). Most of the identifiable jars are Early Roman, with a couple from the second–third century AD. Within the assemblage is an Early Roman flinty greyware jar with a groove between the neck and the body (Fig. 7.30.2), an Early Roman flinty greyware cordoned carinated jar (Fig. 7.30.3), a second-century AD Horningsea globular necked jar, and a second–third-century AD Horningsea constricted-necked jar (Figs. 7.30.4–6). There is also a carinated jar roughly dated to mid to late first century up to AD 120, whose profile is an evolution of the vessels dated to AD 48–68 from Greenhouse Farm on the northeast side of Cambridge (Gibson & Lucas 2002, fig. 12.27 and fig. 14.47; Fig. 7.30.14).

The assemblage's bowl forms are also early. One example, comparable to forms recovered from Lincoln dating to mid first to mid second century AD (Darling & Precious 2014, 61, figs. 45 & 51; Fig. 7.30.15), is a semi-complete coarse sandy oxidized segmental bowl with reeded rim (F.223). From F.53 is a coarse oxidized straight-walled bowl with flat triangular rim and flat base dated to AD 120–60 (Seeley *et al.* 2014, 4G); two samian imitation flanged bowls (F.100 & F.54) are similar to Curle 11 and made of a coarse sandy oxidized ware. A samian bowl fragment (Dr.30; F.100), decorated with barbotine panels, can be dated to AD 145–70, and two different fine sandy greyware bowls that resemble London-type bowls are dated to the second century AD (F.2 & F.68); the one from F.2 has a band of fingernail decoration used since AD 50, which can widen the date of the vessel from AD 50–150 (Fig. 7.30.7).

Several forms other than bowls and jars are also represented. From the F.72 kiln were small fragments of coarse oxidized flagons from the late first to second century AD. In trackway ditch F.29, a semi-complete Early Roman fine sandy micaceous small-neck carinated butt beaker, dated to mid–late first century AD and consisting of 71 sherds (Figs. 7.29 & 7.30.1), seems to be an evolution of a beaker from Greenhouse Farm (Gibson & Lucas 2002, fig. 12.28).

Features

Early Roman and second–fourth-century AD pottery was mostly found together in features, with a slightly higher recovery frequency of the former, notably of semi-complete vessels that were exclusively found south of the site's central portion.

Pottery Kiln (F.72)

There were no pottery wasters or large chunky vessel fragments amongst the kiln assemblage, which otherwise consists of small and worn sherds. The MSW (5.6 g) and EVEs (0.16) are extremely low, and nine vessels can be identified. These factors question whether this assemblage actually represents the kiln repertoire. However, the sherds were recovered from different deposits within the kiln pit and its structure, which also included burnt clay and kiln furniture. Some of the pottery may, therefore, have been deposited at the same time as these materials. There are examples of small Roman kilns where a similar or lesser amount of pottery sherds have been recovered. Compared with the kilns at Duxford, for instance, the number of sherds was higher at the present investigation, but with an MSW of eligible kiln products that is proportionately lower (Anderson & Woolhouse 2016; Table 7.7).

The majority of sherds (74%) and vessels (six out of nine) belong to the same group (Table 7.7) and have coarse sandy oxidized fabrics, with minor variations in the quantity and distribution of quartz (presence or absence or sparse of 0.01–2.0 mm-sized light brown quartz) and the colour (orange to pale orange/cream, or sandwich orange/cream). Some examples appear to be more slightly buff on the surface. With a darker red, grittier and harder fired fabric, only one fragment of a bowl (66 g) is differentiated from this coarse sandy oxidized group. This dates to AD 120–60, but it is unlikely to have been fired in the kiln.

Vessels of coarse sandy oxidized ware include:

1) Four flagons: one with everted undercut beaded rim (Fig. 7.30.9); two possibly ring-neck flagons of different diameter (Fig. 7.30.10), and a variant of collared flagons from Duxford having flat bifid handles and a small flat cordon at one end (Fig. 7.30.11; Anderson & Woolhouse 2016). These flagons can roughly be dated to late first to the second century AD;
2) A jar with everted rim (*c.* second–third century AD; Fig. 7.30.12);
3) A medium-/wide-mouth jar or bowl with triangular-sectioned rim (*c.* second–third century AD).

Owing to their fragmentary nature, it is difficult to be more specific about the forms of these vessels and their dating.

In addition to this group, two vessels of coarse sandy greyware are both of second–fourth-century AD date: a jar or bowl with everted flat rim almost hooked at the end, and a second–fourth-century AD jar with an everted rim.

Two distinctive relatively Early Roman forms were also recovered. One is a hard-fired coarse oxidized straight-walled bowl

Table 7.7. *Main pottery group from F.72 compared with kilns at Duxford (Anderson & Woolhouse 2016, 60, table 2).*

Kilns	Sherd no.	Wt. (g)	MNV	% Kiln Products	Kiln Products Sherd No.	Kiln Products Sherd wt (g)	Kiln Products MSW (g)	MNV
F.72	292	1640	9	74	217	1163	6.0	6
DUX.1	187	3433	13	85	160	2678	16.7	11
DUX.2	145	1209	9	76	110	917	8.3	5
DUX.3	72	616	3	99	71	594	8.2	3
DUX.6	145	1537	7	53	78	1003	12.8	5

Figure 7.29. *Photograph showing near-complete butt beaker (F.29).*

with flat triangular rim and flat base dated to AD 120–60 (Seeley *et al.* 2014, 4G). The other is a coarse greyware carinated jar roughly dated to AD 60–120 and whose profile is an evolution of vessels recovered from Greenhouse Farm dating to AD 48–68 (Gibson & Lucas 2002, fig. 12.27, fig. 14.47; Fig. 7.30.14).

The mixture of differing vessel types and their dating, together with their fragmentary and often worn condition, attests to the ambiguity of the material and makes it difficult to identify the kiln's ceramic production with certainty. This is further reinforced by the recovery of 10 small second–fourth-century AD local greyware fragments, together with four small flagon sherds, in the lowest pottery-bearing context within the stoke pit (F.108).

Pit F.53

This is of particular interest on account of its quantity of pottery (174 sherds, 2307 g), which was dominated by four semi-complete vessels. These were recovered from both the pit's dark upper deposit and an underlying primary fill. The majority came from the latter and date from the Flavian period to the second century AD, apart from 13 non-diagnostic Horningsea fragments (131 g) that fall within the second–fourth century AD. The pottery within the upper fill is more generically dated to the second–fourth century AD, but includes a semi-complete bowl from the mid–late first century AD:

Upper Fill

<223> A semi-complete coarse sandy oxidized reeded-rimmed segmental bowl; similar forms are dated to mid first to mid second century AD (Darling & Precious 2014, 61, fig. 45 and fig. 51; Fig. 7.30.15);

<223> A high quantity of second–fourth-century AD Horningsea burnished and second-century AD Horningsea oxidized storage jar sherds with everted rims;

<223> A fragment of second-century AD samian barbotine bowl; a couple of early and second–fourth-century AD local coarse sandy sherds.

Primary Fill

<227> A semi-complete Flavian–Hadrianic necked jar with narrow band of rilling on the shoulder and triangular-sectioned rim (J. Evans *et al.* 2017, J10.5);

<227> A second-century AD globular necked jar with narrow band of rilling on shoulder and everted rising rim (*ibid.*, J10.2; Fig. 7.30.16).

Ditch F.68 (dark occupation fill)

In contrast to the overall assemblage and other features, this dark fill had a high percentage of second–fourth century AD local pottery (61 sherds; 67%) when compared with Early Roman sherds (17; the assemblage amounted to 91 sherds in total, 952 g).

To judge from the pottery, the site's main occupation fell within the mid first century to early second century AD, with a significant component from the second to the early third century AD. This is similar to the sequence displayed at Vicar's Farm, which began *c.* AD 80, and had its zenith in the third-fourth centuries AD (see Monteil, Chap. 6); that settlement clearly outlasted the lifespan of the Wilberforce Road Site.

The significance of the settlement's early phase may be illustrated by two vessels roughly from the second half of the first century AD, whose forms seem

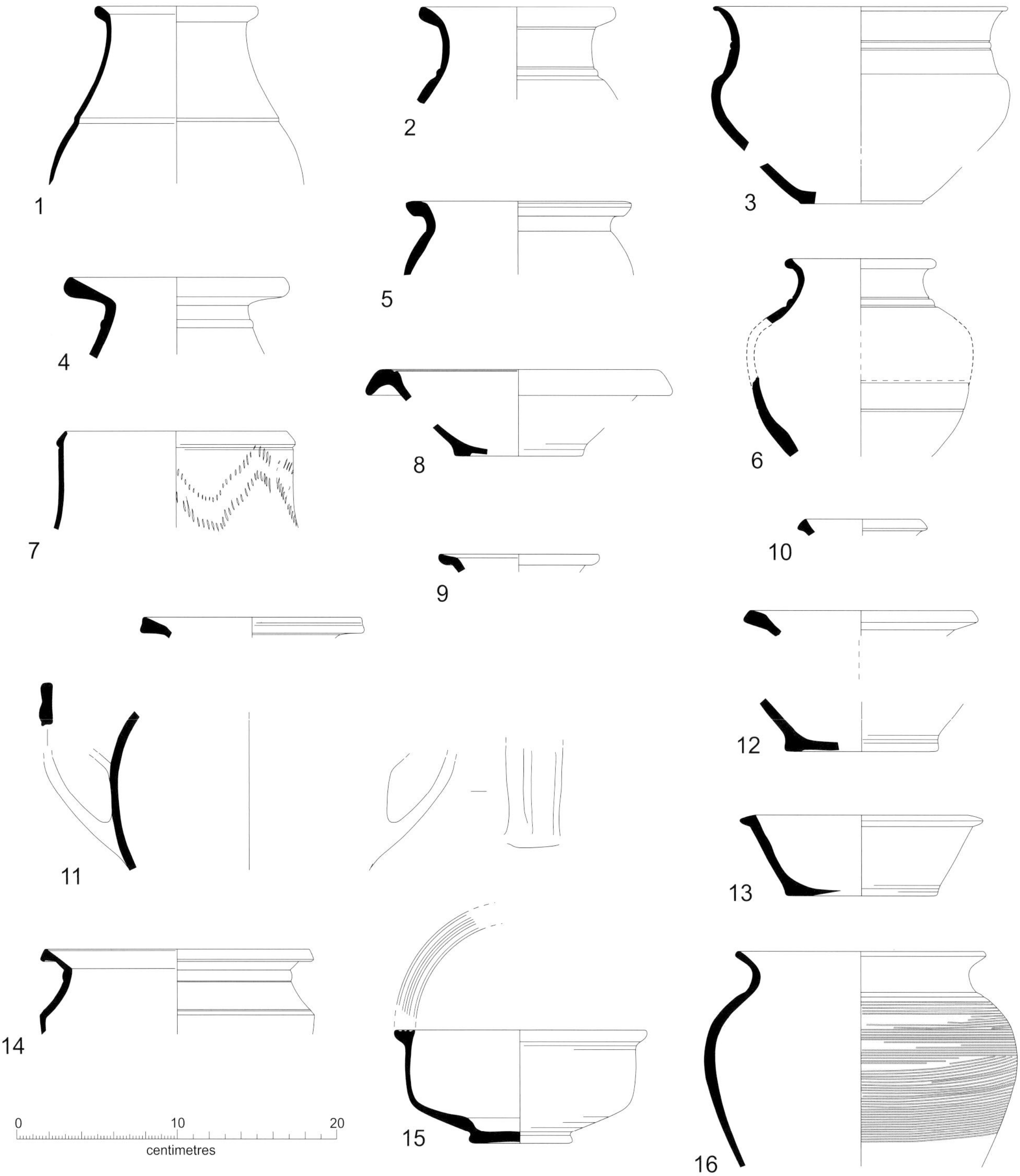

Figure 7.30. *Roman pottery: 1) micaceous fine sandy greyware butt beaker (F.29); 2) flinty coarse sandy greyware cordoned jar (F.22); 3) flinty coarse sandy greyware cordoned jar (F.30); 4) Horningsea greyware cordoned necked jar (F.56); 5) Horningsea greyware constricted-necked jar (F.56); 6) Horningsea oxidized constricted-necked jar (F.63); 7) fine sandy grey ware London-type ware bowl (F.2); 8) coarse sandy oxidized samian imitation bowl (F.100). From the pottery kiln F.72: 9) coarse sandy oxidized flagon; 10) coarse sandy oxidized flagon; 11) coarse sandy oxidized flagon with handle; 12) coarse sandy oxidized jar; 13) coarse sandy oxidized flanged bowl; 14) Carinated narrow-mouthed jar. From the pit F.53: 15) coarse sandy oxidized reeded-rimmed bowl; 16) Horningsea greyware necked jar.*

to be a development of examples from the kilns at Greenhouse Farm:

1) A carinated jar (cf. Gibson & Lucas 2002, fig. 12.27 and fig. 14.47), from kiln F.72, but not a kiln product (Fig. 7.30.14)
2) A micaceous fine sandy greyware butt beaker from F.29 (cf. *ibid*. fig. 12.28; Fig. 7.30.1).

Neither the recovered forms nor fabrics clearly indicate that occupation extended later than the mid third century AD. There is also little evidence for 'clean' phase distinctions. Exceptions to this are the occupation soils from F.68 and the upper fill of pit F.53. Both contexts are late sealing deposits with comparatively high concentrations of second–fourth-century AD pottery, albeit with some earlier Roman material.

The fragmentary and abraded nature of the pottery indicates considerable disturbance to the assemblage as a whole. Even the semi-complete vessels were recovered as multiple small pieces, such as the Early Roman fine sandy micaceous small-neck carinated butt beaker from ditch F.29, recovered in 71 sherds (Fig. 7.29). A relative paucity of sourced finewares, together with a high quantity of interesting vessels from the first and second centuries AD, highlights the importance of the settlement's early phase.

Metalwork (Andy Hall and Justin Wiles)
In total, 42 copper alloy, 14 iron and 13 lead objects were recovered. With demonstrably modern objects discarded, the majority of the assemblage was Post-Medieval in date, and only definitely Roman material – an iron armlet, two brooches and four coins – is detailed here.

Iron
<355> *F.103 [194]* (Fig. 7.31.4) - A heavily corroded penannular armlet with oval cross-section. X-ray reveals slightly widening termini. Although there are few parallels, one was recovered during excavation of a Roman bath house (Ingham *et al*. 2016, 19, fig. 2.6). Another was recovered from the right arm of a third–fourth-century AD burial at Verulamium (Manning 1985, 79). The relative rarity of iron armlets may partly be due to issues of preservation (Cool 2018). Internal diameter 80 mm, weight 124 g. Recovered in two pieces. Third–fourth century AD.

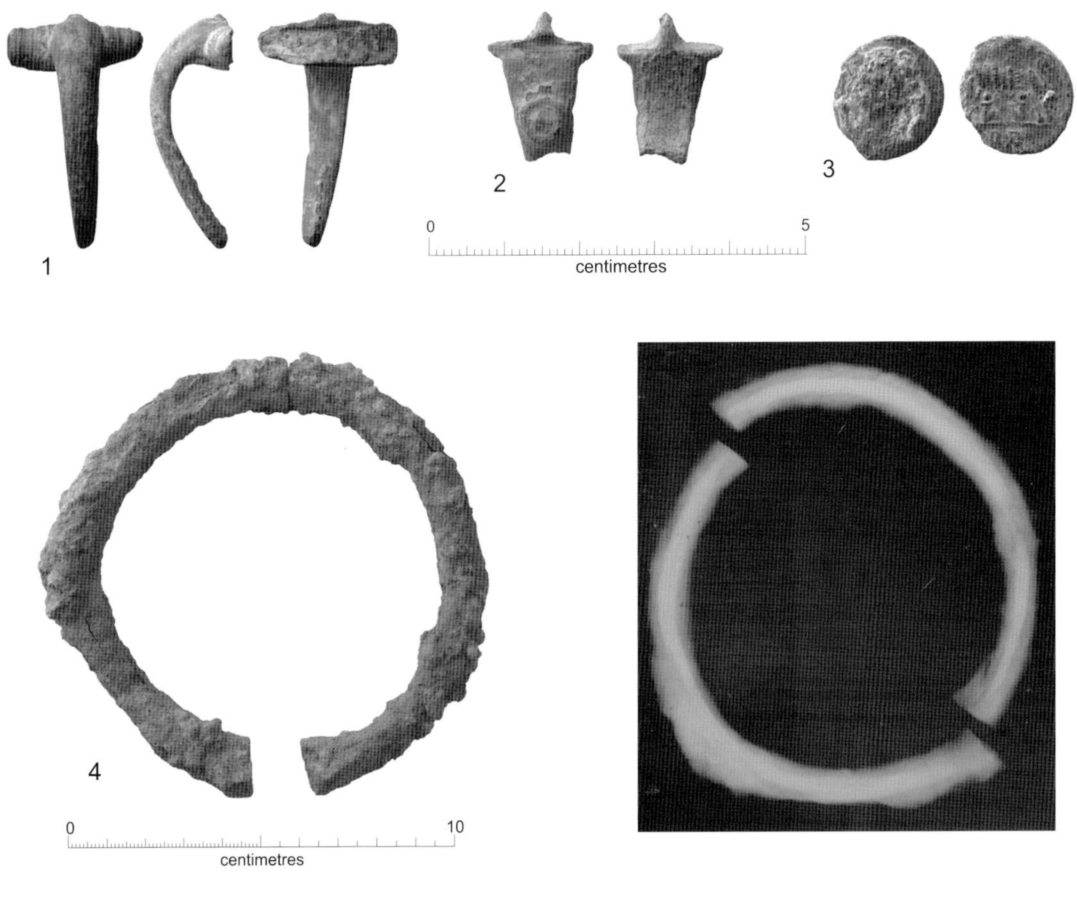

Figure 7.31. *Metalwork: 1) copper alloy Colchester Derivative brooch (<407>); 2) copper alloy headstud brooch (<369); 3) copper alloy nummus (<408); 4) iron armlet (<355>, with X-ray of same right).*

Copper Alloy

<18> *SF 3, F.7* - A *nummus*, House of Constantine, head facing right, laureate, '…NOB…', R. Two soldiers with standards, '…XERC…', Trier mintmark, '…RP'. Weight 2.11 g. AD 330–5 (from evaluation fieldwork).

<348> *F.30 [140]* - A copper alloy *radiate* in poor condition, possibly Carausius (AD 286–93). The reverse is illegible. Weight 3.6 g, diameter 23 mm (Moorhead 2013).

<369> *SF 14* (Fig. 7.31.2) - Recovered from subsoil, a fragment of a copper alloy headstud-type brooch in poor condition. Consisting of the upper section of the bow with a circular boss with reserved metal in the centre. Difficult to ascertain is whether the stud would have been enameled. Broken ends of a possible head-loop also present. Dating to the mid–late first century AD. Measuring 20 × 15 mm, weight 5 g.

SF 26 <381> - A heavily corroded coin with no features visible. Weight 9.5 g, diameter 26 mm. Probably an *as* of first–second century AD.

<407> *SF 57, F.56 [98.01]* (Fig. 7.31.1) - A small Colchester Derivative brooch, possibly of rear-hook type. The bow and cross-bar/wings are intact, but the catch-plate and spring are missing. The bow appears undecorated except for a central ridge along the length. Dating to the mid–later first century AD, 32 mm in length, 20 mm width. Weight 3 g.

<408> *SF 58* (Fig. 7.31.3) - A copper alloy *nummus* (AE4). Obverse illegible but reverse showing wolf and twins. Weight 1.03 g, diameter 16 mm. AD 330–5 (Reece & James 1986).

Also recovered were four irregularly shaped lumps of lead casting spill.

Environmental and Economic Evidence

As well as the findings presented here, 80 shell fragments (363 g) were also recovered from hand-dug contexts, with a further 45 fragments recovered nearby from ditch F.5 during the evaluation (see Bolton in Brittain & Evans 2018). Aside from a single mussel shell (*Mytilus edulis*), these were all of the European Flat Oyster family (*Ostrea edulis*), with nine evincing *Polydora hoplura* infestation. The largest concentration of shells occurred as a dumped deposit within ditch F.29 (61 pieces).

Faunal Remains (Vida Rajkovača)

The faunal assemblage is small, with a raw count of 1257 fragments and a total weight of 7149 g. Some 192 specimens were assessable, 86 of which were assigned to species (44.8%). The majority of the assemblage (98%) is from prehistoric and Roman contexts (25 fragments recovered from Post-Medieval contexts were also scanned but are not included here). The 37 specimens from the Early Iron Age pits have been outlined above and, here, only the 1195 fragments from Roman-period contexts will be considered, with the majority deriving from Phase 3 deposits (848 fragments; 71%).

The assemblage was overall moderately preserved, though the preservation varied between sub-phases within the Roman occupation. Fieldsystem-derived material showed a greater degree of surface exfoliation, erosion and weathering, compared to the assemblage from the later Roman phases. Overall, 27 per cent of the material was eroded. In addition to the poor surface preservation, the assemblage was heavily processed and highly fragmented, with only nine complete specimens being recorded for all species. These were mostly phalanges, astragali and metapodia; three specimens were available for measurement. An insignificant portion of the assemblage was recorded with gnawing marks (five specimens; 2.6%). All were canine marks and the small percentage implies rapid deposition of the material. Butchery marks were also quite rare, only found on eight specimens or 4.2 per cent of the assemblage.

Represented by a small sub-set of animal bone, the Roman assemblage's earliest component came from the Phase 1 fieldsystem. Horse made up a substantial proportion, with two elements having quite small measurements.[6] Tentatively assigned to the Equidae family, they possibly belong to a donkey (Fig. 7.32).

Phase 2 generated an insignificant quantity of mostly sheep or sheep-sized material. Phase 3 showed a slightly more varied range

Table 7.8. *Breakdown by phase of number of Identified Specimens (NISP) and Minimum Number of Individuals (MNI) for all species from all Romano-British contexts; the abbreviation n.f.i. denotes that the specimen could not be further identified. (Excluded are 17 bones/172 g recovered from Roman-period features during the evaluation; see Rajkovača in Tabor 2017.)*

	Phase 1			Phase 2			Phase 3			Total
Taxon	**NISP**	**%NISP**	**MNI**	**NISP**	**%NISP**	**MNI**	**NISP**	**%NISP**	**MNI**	**NISP**
Cow	7	*31.8*	1	.	.	.	24	*48.9*	2	*31*
Sheep/ goat	6	*27.3*	1	2	*66.7*	1	8	*16.3*	1	*16*
Goat	.	.	.	.	.	.	1	*2.1*	1	*1*
Horse	7	*31.8*	1	1	*33.3*	1	15	*30.6*	1	*23*
Equidae	2	*9.1*	1	.	.	.	.	.	.	*2*
Dog	.	.	.	.	.	.	1	*2.1*	1	*1*
Sub-total to species	*22*	*100.0*	.	*3*	*10.00*	.	*49*	*100.0*	.	*74*
Cattle-sized	24	.	.	1	.	.	35	.	.	*60*
Sheep-sized	.	.	.	10	.	.	21	.	.	*31*
Mammal n.f.i.	2	.	.	.	.	.	6	.	.	*8*
Total	*48*	.	.	*14*	.	.	*111*	.	.	*173*

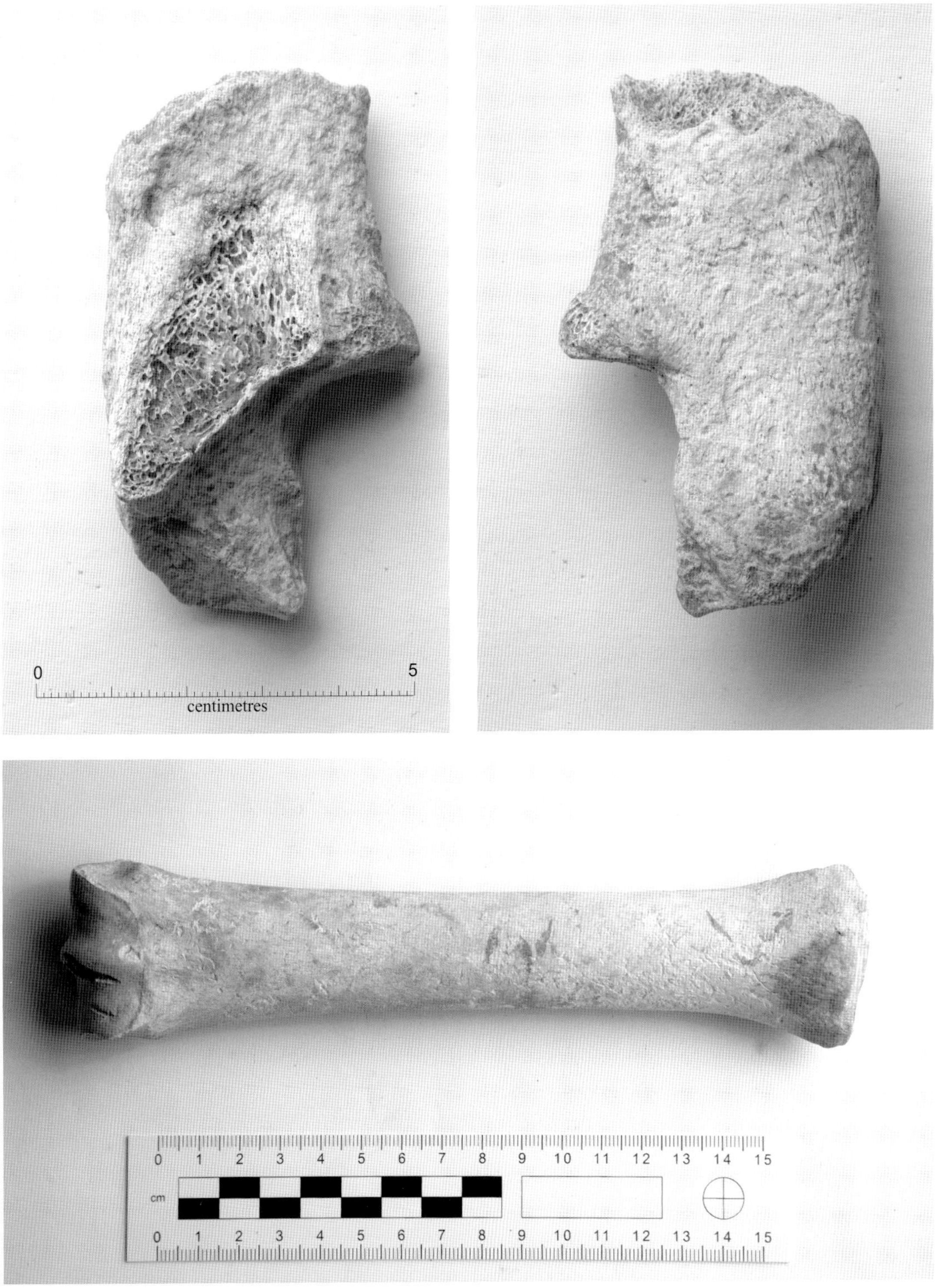

Figure 7.32. *Possible Equidae calcaneum (top) and, below, metacarpus.*

of species (Table 7.8) The majority came from the trackway and the southern settlement compound. Four features were especially bone-rich – F.30, F.66, F.68 and F.74 – and generated a raw count of 737 fragments (3097 g): 85 per cent of the sub-set by count and 70 per cent by weight.

The dominance of cattle within the assemblage is unsurprising, whereas the absence of pig and the particularly significant percentage of horse across each of the Roman phases are noteworthy. The only ageable specimen was a sheep/goat mandible of 6–12 months. All body parts appear in the skeletal-element count for the three main domestic species: cattle, horse and ovicapra. Butchery was rare, perhaps owing to the overall poor surface preservation, yet skinning marks were recorded, as well as those consistent with meat removal and marrow extraction, indicating that carcass processing was carried out in the settlement.

Charred Plant Macrofossils and Charcoal
(Ellen Simmons)
Comprising a total of 156 litres of soil, 17 bulk samples were processed from the site's Roman-period features (including three from the evaluation-phase). These are fully tabulated in the assessment report, which also details the methods employed (Simmons in Brittain & Evans 2018).

The preservation of the low density of charred cereal grains present in the sampled contexts is somewhat poor. The grains exhibit puffing and distortion, with only fragments of epidermis retained. A relatively high proportion of intrusive roots are also present, indicating an increased likelihood that some of the charred material may be intrusive.

Plant Macrofossils
Low densities of charred cereal grains and chaff were found to be present in three Roman contexts, all Phase 2. The largest assemblage came from hollow F.83, which included emmer/spelt wheat glume base (*Triticum dicoccum/spelta*), a spelt wheat glume base (*Triticum spelta*), a probable free-threshing wheat grain (*Triticum* c.f. *aestivum/ turgidum* s.l.) and two indeterminate wheat grains (*Triticum* sp. indet.). Two indeterminate barley grains (*Hordeum* sp. indet.) came from ditch F.68, along with an indeterminate wheat grain, two more of which were found within a sample from kiln F.72.

Charred wild or weed plant seeds were also found in low densities within a number of Roman-period contexts, including hairy buttercup (*Ranunculus sardous*; Phase 2 hollow, F.83), poppy (*Papaver* sp.; Phase 3 ditch F.29), blinks (*Montia fontana* ssp. *Chondrosperma*; Phase 3 ditches F.30 & F.68), sedge (*Carex* sp.; Phase 3 ditch F.68), medick/clover (*Medicago* sp./*Trifolium* sp.; Phase 3 ditch F.68), and small seeded grass (<2 mm *Poaceae*; Phase 2 pit F.6, Phase 3 ditch F.68).

A fragment of apple core was present in a sample from pit F.61 (Phase 2).

Charcoal
All of the sample flots were scanned to assess their charcoal component; two rich samples were selected for full analysis to provide evidence relating to the local environment and the selection of wood for fuel. One hundred charcoal fragments greater than 2 mm in size were identified from each context, with the aim of identifying a representative sample of the taxa present (Stuijts 2006, 28).

The charcoal assemblage from Roman pit F.61 was composed entirely of oak (Table 7.9), which may indicate the preferential selection of oak for fuel for a specific purpose such as industrial activity. The mixed composition of the charcoal assemblage from the Early Iron Age pit F.35 could suggest that this material is more likely to represent general hearth waste. It includes ash (*Fraxinus excelsior*), field maple (*Acer campestre*) and hazel (*Corylus avellana*) in addition to oak, which are generally woodland trees, although all can also grow as a component of hedgerows. Field maple is frequently associated with ash and hazel in open woodland, particularly on clay or calcareous soils (Rackham 2003, 203). A high proportion of the assemblage is composed of hawthorn/apple/pear/ whitebeams (Pomoideae), wild/bird cherry (*Prunus* c.f. *padus/avium*) and blackthorn (*Prunus* c.f. *spinosa*). Hawthorn, wild apple, wild pear and the members of the whitebeam genus which are represented by Pomoideae, along with wild/bird cherry and blackthorn, are all common underwood shrubs or trees in open woodland (*ibid.*, 349). Hawthorn is also one of the predominant taxa in thorny scrub, along with blackthorn, which becomes established in areas of open grassland when grazing pressure is reduced (Vera 2000, 343–4; Rodwell 1991, 339; Tansley 1968, 127–8).

The fragments of apple endocarp (*Malus* sp.) present in Early Iron Age pit F.35 probably indicate the collection of wild food resources from local woodland. The presence of apple endocarp within Roman Phase 2 pit F.61 may indicate continued utilization of wild wood resources during the Roman times or be representative of cultivated apple, which was probably introduced to Britain during that period (Van der Veen 2016, 814). Remains of fruits, such as apple and pear, increase in frequency in Roman-period archaeobotanical assemblages, indicating increasing adoption of apple and other fruit crops (*ibid.*).

The low-density assemblages of charred cereal grain and chaff present in Roman Phase 2 hollow F.83, kiln F.72 and Phase 3 ditch F.68 are likely to have originated as hearth waste. Similar low-density assemblages of charred cereal grain and chaff were present in the evaluation-phase samples from Roman Phase 1 ditch F.13 and ditches F.5 and F.14, both Phase 3. The low density and poor preservation of

Table 7.9. *Charcoal assemblage composition and details of ligneous structure.*

Taxon (total number of fragments)	**Early Iron Age F.35**	**2nd–3rd C. AD F.61**
Prunus c.f. *spinosa* (blackthorn)	5	-
Prunus c.f. *padus / avium* (wild/bird cherry)	14	-
Pomoideae (hawthorn/apple/ pear/whitebeams)	25	-
Quercus sp. (oak)	42	99
Corylus avellana L. (hazel)	4	-
Acer campestre (field maple)	2	-
Fraxinus excelsior (ash)	2	-
Indeterminate	6	1
Ligneous structure observations (number of fragments)	-	-
Strong ring curvature	1	-
Weak ring curvature	-	-
Tyloses in vessel cavities	18	13
Presence of bark	1	-
Vitrification (Degree 1, 2 & 3)	9	4

charred crop material in these contexts may indicate that activities involving crop-processing or food preparation were not being carried out to any great extent in the immediate vicinity or that these features were not being used for the disposal of hearth waste. It is also possible that the small size of the charred plant macrofossil assemblages is related to small sample size, poor preservation conditions or that crop-processing waste was used for other purposes rather than being burnt.

The presence of spelt wheat and barley in Roman Phase 2 hollow F.83 and Phase 3 ditch F.68 is typical for the Roman period in the region (Lodwick 2017) and consistent with the identification of probable spelt wheat in Phase 2 ditch F.13 and Phase 3 ditch F.5. Spelt wheat and hulled barley are the most common Roman-period crop types, and both are present in the period's archaeobotanical assemblages from Vicar's Farm, North West Cambridge (see *NWC*) and Cambourne (Stevens 2009a & b). Emmer wheat, which is tentatively identified as present in the F.83 hollow, also occurred within Roman-period contexts at Cambourne; emmer wheat is considered likely to be residual in the crop of spelt wheat by the Roman period (*ibid*., 110). Free-threshing wheat, which is also tentatively identified in F.83, is occasionally present in Roman-period archaeobotanical assemblages, but generally in minor quantities (Van der Veen 2016).

The assemblage of wild or weed seeds present in five of the Roman Phase 2 and 3 ditch fills includes seeds of plants that are reflective of damp soils, such as blinks (*Montia fontana* ssp. *chondrosperma*) and with many species of sedge (*Carex* sp.) potentially represented. Medick/clover (*Medicago* sp./*Trifolium* sp.) and small seeded grasses (<2 mm Poaceae) are grassland taxa which are also frequently present in charred archaeobotanical assemblages. Hairy buttercup (*Ranunculus sardous*), which is present in the F.83 hollow, is also commonly associated with grassland. These seeds may have been harvested along with the crops and charred as waste from crop processing, therefore indicating the cultivation of damp soils with probable grassy field margins or the cultivation of fields that had previously been fallow. Other sources of wild or weed plant seeds include waste roofing, flooring and bedding material, tinder and animal fodder.

Of the two charcoal assemblages, palaeoenvironmental evidence from the region indicates that woodland clearance, intensifying during the Bronze Age, was then sustained throughout the Iron Age and Roman periods (Murphy 1997a, 30; 1997b, 42). This would have led to an increase in the availability of the types of underwood, woodland margin and scrub taxa such as identified in pit F.35's charcoal. The results from Cambourne (Stevens 2009a & b) and along the route of the A428 (Abrams & Ingham 2008) indicate a predominantly open landscape during the two periods, although with some stands of woodland persisting. Wood charcoal from their Iron Age contexts points to the predominant use of scrub taxa as fuel, although oak heartwood is also present (Gale 2008; 2009).

Pollen (Steve Boreham)

The assessment results of pollen analyses of sediment taken from the F.35 Early Iron Age pit and three Roman-period features are presented here (see Fig. 7.22 for locations). One of the latter is assigned to Phase 1 (F.2), with two attributed to Phase 3 (F.30 & F.100).

The sub-samples were prepared and counted using techniques as outlined above; the resultant percentage pollen data is presented below (and in the assessment report, table 27). These had pollen concentrations that ranged between 20,255 and 26,521 grains per ml, a range that is quite low for viable sub-samples. Some sub-samples contained abundant charcoal and many had finely divided organic debris, which often made pollen counting difficult for these slides. The preservation of the fossil pollen grains (palynomorphs) was variable and generally rather poor. Assessment pollen counts were made from a single slide. The pollen sums achieved (total land pollen and spores) ranged between 51 and 60. These counts do not exceed the statistically desirable total of 300 pollen grains main sum and, as a consequence, caution must be employed during the interpretation of these results.

Early Iron Age

Pit F.35, Sample 65 (50 cm monolith) - The basal part of this monolith seemed to be slightly oxidized, and the pollen preservation throughout only had moderate potential. Pollen sub-samples were taken at 10 cm and 40 cm.

10 cm – This sub-sample was dominated by grass pollen (Poaceae; 49.0%), with herbs including sedges (Cyperaceae; 9.8%), the thistle family (Asteraceae [Asteroidea/Cardueae] undif.; 5.9%) and buttercup (*Ranunculus*; 3.9%). Arboreal taxa were represented by hazel (*Corylus*; 2.0%) and pine (*Pinus*; 3.9%). Spores of the polypody fern (Polypodium) were present at 2.0%, and undifferentiated fern spores together accounted for 15.7%. Obligate aquatics were represented by bur-reed (Sparganium; 2.0%).

40 cm – This sub-sample was dominated by grass pollen (Poaceae; 65.4%), with herbs including sedges (Cyperacea; 7.7%) and the thistle family (Asteraceae [Asteroidea/Cardueae] undif.; 3.8%). Pine (*Pinus*) was the only arboreal taxon present (1.9%). Spores of the polypody fern (Polypodium) were present at 1.9%, with undifferentiated fern spores together accounting for 9.6%.

Roman Phase 1

Ditch F.2, Sample 87 (50 cm monolith) - The entire monolith appeared to be slightly oxidized and only had moderate pollen preservation potential. Pollen sub-samples were taken at 10 cm and 38 cm.

10 cm – This sub-sample was dominated by grass pollen (Poaceae; 50.0%), with herbs including the sedges (Cyperaceae; 10.3%), the lettuce family (Asteraceae [Lactuceae] undif.; 6.9%) and buttercup

(*Ranunculus*; 5.2%). Cereal pollen was present in this sample at 3.4%. Hazel (*Corylus*) was the only arboreal taxon present (1.7%). Spores of the polypody fern (Polypodium) were present at 1.7 per cent, and undifferentiated fern spores together accounted for 6.9 per cent. Obligate aquatics were represented by bur-reed (Sparganium; 1.7%).

38 cm – This sub-sample was dominated by grass pollen (Poaceae; 50.9%), with herbs including the lettuce family (Asteraceae [Lactuceae] undif.; 7.3%), the thistle family (Asteraceae [Asteroidea/Cardueae] undif.; 5.5%), meadowsweet (*Filipendula*) and buttercup (*Ranunculus*; both 3.6%). Cereal pollen was present in this sample at 5.5 per cent. Arboreal taxa were represented by hazel (*Corylus*) and pine (*Pinus*), both at 3.6 per cent. Spores of the polypody fern (Polypodium) were present at 1.8 per cent, and undifferentiated fern spores together accounted for 10.9 per cent.

Roman Phase 3
Trackway ditch F.30, Sample 64 (50 cm monolith) - The entire monolith appeared to be slightly oxidized and only had moderate pollen preservation potential. Pollen sub-samples were taken at 10 cm and 40 cm.

10 cm – This sub-sample was dominated by grass pollen (Poaceae; 43.9%), with herbs including the sedges (Cyperaceae; 12.3%), the lettuce family (Asteraceae [Lactuceae] undif.; 5.3%), the pink family (Caryophyllaceae; 3.5%) and dock (*Rumex*; 3.5%). Arboreal taxa were represented by hazel (*Corylus*; 5.3%), birch (*Betula*; 3.5%) and juniper (*Juniperus*; 3.5%). Spores of the polypody fern (Polypodium) were present at 1.8 per cent, and undifferentiated fern spores together accounted for 12.3 per cent.

40 cm – This sub-sample was dominated by grass pollen (Poaceae; 45.8%), with herbs including the sedges (Cyperaceae; 10.2%), the lettuce family (Asteraceae [Lactuceae] undif.; 3.4%), meadowsweet (*Filipendula*; 3.4%) and buttercup (*Ranunculus*; 3.4%). Arboreal taxa were represented by hazel (*Corylus*; 6.8%), birch (*Betula*; 5.1%), pine (*Pinus*) and juniper (*Juniperus*) were both registered at 1.7 per cent. Spores of the polypody fern (Polypodium) were present at 1.7 per cent, and undifferentiated fern spores together accounted for 10.2 per cent.

Trackway ditch F.100, Sample 91 (30 cm monolith) - The entire monolith appeared to be slightly oxidized and the pollen preservation potential throughout was only moderate. Pollen sub-samples were taken at 8 cm and 24 cm.

8 cm – This sub-sample was dominated by grass pollen (Poaceae; 63.5%) and sedges (Cyperaceae; 11.5%). Other herbs including the lettuce family (Asteraceae [Lactuceae] undif.), the pink family (Caryophyllaceae) and buttercup (*Ranunculus*) were all present at 1.9%. Hazel (*Corylus*) was the only arboreal taxon present (1.9%). Spores of the polypody fern (Polypodium) were present at 1.9 per cent, and undifferentiated fern spores together accounted for 11.5 per cent. Obligate aquatics were represented by bur-reed (Sparganium; 1.9%).

24 cm – This sub-sample was dominated by grass pollen (Poaceae; 45.0%), with herbs including the lettuce family (Asteraceae [Lactuceae] undif.; 11.7%), sedges (Cyperaceae; 8.3%) and the thistle family (Asteraceae [Asteroidea/Cardueae] undif.; 6.7%). Cereal pollen was present in this sample at 3.3 per cent. Arboreal taxa were represented by hazel (Corylus; 3.3%) and juniper (*Juniperus*; 1.7%). Undifferentiated fern spores together accounted for 10 per cent, and obligate aquatics were represented by bur-reed (Sparganium; 3.3%).

Taken together, these pollen assemblages all appear rather similar, comprising elements of tall-herb, meadowland and riparian (bank-side) plant communities. Cereal pollen is restricted to Sample 87 of the Roman F.2 ditch (both sub-samples) and, from the Roman road/trackway, F.100's Sample 91 (24 cm). The lack of the soil disturbance indicator ribwort plantain (*Plantago lanceolata*) suggests that the surrounding area was dominated by pastoral grassland, as opposed to intensive arable use. Eutrophication indicators also appear to be absent.

There is also evidence for a little hazel-juniper scrub, together with scattered birch trees in F.30's Roman road/trackway ditch (Sample 64). The presence of at least some large trees nearby is suggested by polypody fern, which is an epiphyte of mature tree boles. The ditches themselves appear to have supported emergent aquatic vegetation (sedges and bur-reed) suggesting seasonally high watertables. This signal, together with meadows, some arable activity and scraps of hazel scrub, is fairly typical of the post-clearance landscape in southern England and is entirely compatible with the Roman dates of the features.

Discussion and Geophysical Survey

In the late summer of 2018 we received a copy of the geophysical survey undertaken in the fields west and south of the Sports Ground and our excavation by West Yorkshire's Archaeological Service (WYAS 2018), relating to yet another development proposal altogether. What is obviously a major later Iron Age settlement involving both small curvilinear and sub-rectangular enclosures registers on their plot (see Fig. 7.33, from which the imprint of the area's ridge-and-furrow has been removed). This is likely to be the source of the Late Iron Age sherd from Wilberforce Road. Indeed, along the east side of the plotted settlement there are four southwest–northeast-oriented ditches, which probably relate to our Phase 1 fieldsystem (possibly suggesting their pre-Roman origin). Some 600 m east of this settlement (in WYAS's Area 4) what may be the northern arc of another possible Iron Age enclosure is visible (see Fig. 7.33).

Registering more faintly, across the northern third of the survey's settlement-area are boundaries that align with those of our farmstead compound, as well as one that correlates with the projection of its southern side. These suggest the full extent of its quasi-trapezoidal layout (*c.* 95 × 100 m; 0.9 ha). Its southern ditch-line continues for some 60–70 m west of the Wilberforce Road Site and there are other elements on this axis to the south. This could imply that the farmstead's layout was somewhat more complicated

Figure 7.33. *Geophysical survey plots (WYAS 2018).*

than has been proposed. The geophysical survey also includes other 'arcing' components; at points these show as parallel ditches that could perhaps relate to a trackway route.

Even more slight than at either Vicar's Farm or High Cross, the prehistoric register at Wilberforce Road – just a few flints and a handful of Middle Bronze Age and Early Iron Age pits – suggests little more than casual usage, probably foraging visits and, perhaps, pastoral-related camping. The range of trees represented in F.35's Early Iron Age charcoal sample is interesting, with seven species in total. With the bulk of oak, both wild/bird cherry and pomoideae – variously hawthorn/apple/pear/whitebeam – occurred in substantial numbers. In contrast to that, only oak was present in a comparable Roman-period sample (F.61); this might tell of greater environmental diversity in the earlier Iron Age. While bearing in mind differences in wind- and insect-dispersed pollination, the charcoal certainly presents a more varied picture of local wood resources than the same feature's pollen sample.

The basic layout, scale and topographical situation of the Phase 1 fieldsystem at Wilberforce Road seems similar to those of the High Cross settlement (see Fig. 7.35). The northern east–west ditch-line of the Wilberforce Road Site (F.94/102 & F.2–4) would appear to have been a 'boundary', marking the edge of former palaeochannel deposits, and not fieldsystem-related *per se*. This brings into focus the layout of Vicar's Farm (Fig. 7.34). The largely open, broadly arranged boundaries south of its settlement paddocks probably related to pasture lands, whereas the parallel ditch network on the elevated south-facing slope to the northeast, were probably its fields.[7]

Any assessment of the site's Roman settlement must bear in mind that only its eastern margins were investigated; its 'core' was not exposed, nor any buildings recovered. The farmstead nevertheless clearly saw far less intense recutting and reworking than Vicar's Farm. This relates to the fact that it evidently saw much less later Roman usage. It also seems a less 'complex' settlement and probably did not involve a market function, though its paddocks shared the same orientation as Vicar's Farm and their *c.* 90 m width seems comparable to the core-area layout of the latter's early-phase arrangement.

As shown in Figure 7.35, the fieldsystem at High Cross also had the same west-northwest–east-southeast orientation. This seems almost universal within the region (see e.g. Evans *et al.* 2007, fig. 18) and *it must surely reflect a distinct settlement-related tradition and not grand-scale planning*. In the case of the immediate roads/trackways in the West Cambridge area, only the southernmost at Vicar's Farm (No. 4) followed this orientation, with the rest of its routeways lying well off of it, including the projected route of Akeman Street.

As will be more thoroughly discussed in the next book, in the aftermath of the Roman Conquest, the later first century AD clearly saw a major reorganization of the local landscape. This is expressed in the marked similarity of the layouts of the Wilberforce Road Site, Vicar's Farm's Phase I and North West Cambridge's Site II (see Chap. 5, ...*Farmstead 'Unit' Parallels* and Fig. 5.41). They closely resemble each other and evidently follow a 'new' farmstead template. While individual enclosure components within the later Iron Age settlement revealed on the geophysical plot compare to those excavated at, for example, Traveller's Rest Subsite (see *NWC*, Chap. 3), the surveyed settlement seems the most complex and extensive of any of the period known within the immediate area, which makes it all the more unfortunate that it has not yet been investigated further. Given its spatial relationship to the Roman-period farmstead beside it, it is reasonable to suppose that its Iron Age inhabitants may have been shifted to reside within the adjacent Roman farm's 'square'. A general continuity is then implied, but so too is *displacement*, however immediately local. Was the rationale behind this, apart from imprinting a more readily taxable 'square' landscape-holding pattern, access to the road along the farmstead's east side? If so, this routeway would certainly have had an earlier, Phase 2 manifestation and, as a 'way', probably predated the bordering farmstead.

What of the status of the Wilberforce Road's settlement? As indicated on Figure 7.28, its finds densities can be considered 'respectable'.[8] With the character of its faunal assemblage discussed later (see *Economic Matters and Transformation*), the quantity of oyster shell at the site – having to be transported over distance and consumed fresh – would indicate that this was not a low-status farmstead.

The site's kiln marked the first time that such a feature has been found in the western Cambridge lands. That said, with kiln furniture previously recovered at New Hall (see Chap. 3) and, subsequently on one of North West Cambridge's sites (No. VI), Early Roman kilns are now widely found in the region (e.g. Anderson & Woolhouse 2016) and there is nothing particularly unexpected in this.

The recovery of yet another road/trackway – here designated as Road 5 – is significant. As discussed in the next book, it adds to the lattice-like transportation network of the wider area, in which its many settlements were all connected. While we have no knowledge of where that route ran to in the south, as it ran north it probably joined with one of the Vicar's Farm routes; probably its Road 3, but possibly with Road 4.

Figure 7.34. *Plan showing relationship of Vicar's Farm and Wilberforce Road Roman settlements, with landscape-elevation profile below.*

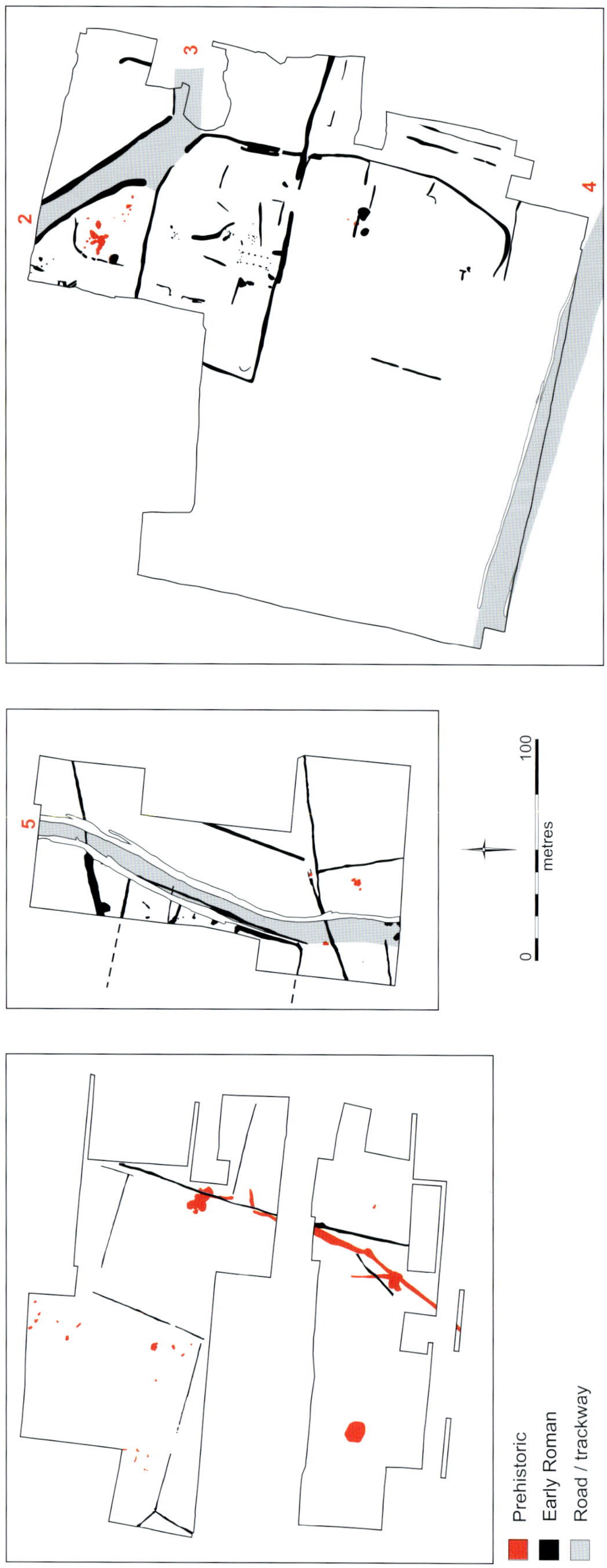

Figure 7.35. *Comparative plans showing High Cross (left), Wilberforce Road and Vicar's Farm (right) main prehistoric and Early Roman features.*

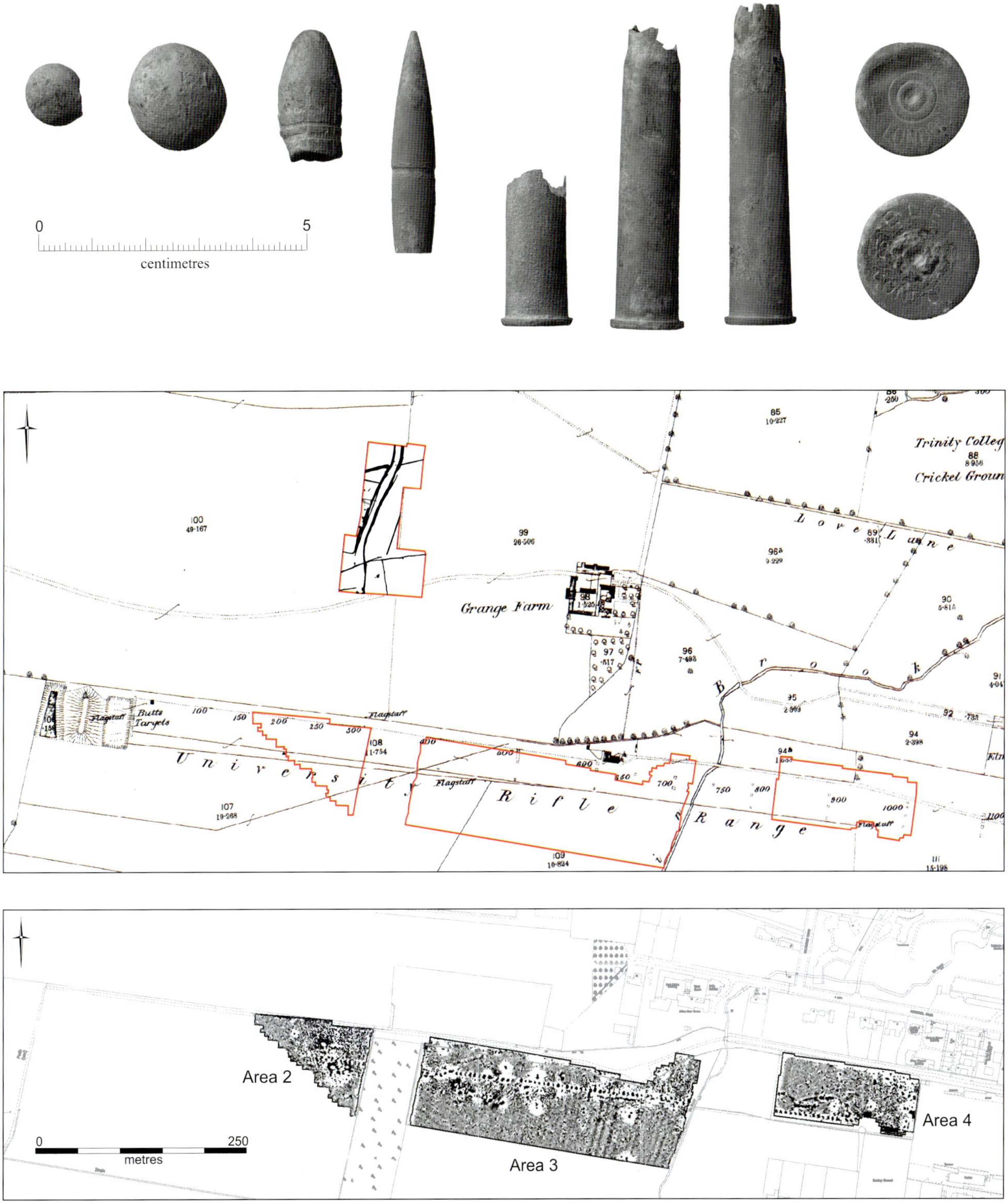

Figure 7.36. *Map showing site plan in relationship to the University's Rifle Range (1859–1939); above range of ordnance recovered from site metal-detecting; bottom, geophysical survey plot of Rifle Range-area with radio telescope stanchions visible (WYNA 2018).*

The site's relatively intense pollen and charcoal analyses may not have been entirely successful. After having undertaken the bulk of the North West Cambridge excavations, and appreciating the need to articulate how the area's Roman-period farms were organized, these were aimed at identifying was growing where, and how woodland was being managed. The attempt, though, was worthwhile and points to how questions of the period's land-use will be further developed.

Finally, as shown in Figure 7.36, the recovery of such a range of nineteenth- and early twentieth-century ordnance during the site's metal-detecting connects it (via stray practice shots) with the University's rifle range just to the south. Operational from 1859 to 1939, not only does it reflect on the development of the rifle – a topic of some archaeological importance given Pitt Rivers' involvement (see Evans 2014) – but also, thereafter, 'The Archaeology of Early Modern Science' (Evans & Newman 2011). Immediately after WWII the range's great 'empty tract' was utilized for Cambridge's first radio telescope. Apparently involving bed-frames, it seems to have been a fairly makeshift affair (the bases of its stanchions register on the geophysical plot; see Fig. 7.36). Yet with it, the astronomers Ryle and Vonberg discovered over 2000 new stars, and it only ceased operation in 1956 when it was superseded by the Mullard Array at Lord's Bridge (Smith 1984).

Postscript Observations

We have covered a lot of sites and ground here, traversing a long way west of the city. In its westerly progression, this book also effectively charts what have been major changes in the practice of developer-funded archaeology over what amounts to almost its first three decades in England. It spans limited size investigations at, for example, Burrell's Field or New Hall in the early 1990s, to West Cambridge's Vicar's Farm in the last decade, and then High Cross and the Wilberforce Road Sites of the last eight years. The period has marked a sea-change in the scale and resourcing of region's excavations, and this will become even more evident when, in the next book, the mass-scale and daunting complexity of the North West Cambridge sites are fully appreciated.

Technical developments have also played a prominent role in this realization. Foremost would have to be computer-based recording and analyses; tackling a landscape investigation such as at North West Cambridge would have been quite a different matter if having to rely on hand-rendered graphics (see Evans *et al.* 2016a, 28–30 further to this theme). While such changes in the basis of fieldwork have been experienced in other portions of the south of the country, their impact in the Cambridge Region has been particularly acute due to the intensity of the city and University's (green-belt) growth over this time. Understanding of the region's archaeology has been revolutionized and, accordingly, it now features prominently in such period-based reviews as *The Rural Settlement of Roman Britain* volume (Smith *et al.* 2016, 193–206).

As said in Chapter One, this book will not offer an overarching discussion. With so much archaeology still to be presented in the next book – introducing the settlement-sequence dynamics of North West Cambridge's amid-clayland gravel ridge – here we will instead simply stress a few points and rehearse some arising themes.

The Challenge of Numbers

As has been previously outlined (e.g. *BLS*, chap. 3; Evans 2013), the results of such extensive evaluation programmes – as have been conducted within the Addenbrooke's environs, Longstanton and, now, North West Cambridge – fundamentally challenge how the region's early landscape-use is envisaged. With intervals of only a few hundred metres now known between broadly contemporary later prehistoric and Roman settlements, in areas of southern England *there is suddenly much more past to contend with than earlier researchers could ever have imagined*. Not only should this require us to change the 'rules of the game' in terms of adopting more statistically based comparative approaches to their analysis (see Evans 2012 and 2018), but we must also reflect on the very nature of archaeological interpretation. Prior to the recognition of this density of site distribution, the onus on archaeologists essentially lay with interpreting a single site and, perhaps, how it measured against other regional/national exemplars of the same 'classificatory type' (usually with little or no statistical basis). Now, something else is demanded.

Through this volume's long production, this change has even impacted on its various portions. When Lucas first drafted his Vicar's Farm chapters in 2003–4, aside from earlier casual findings, there were only the Burrell's Field and New Hall settlements (of which only very little was available for investigation) to provide any real sense of immediate landscape context. His interpretation of that complex was, accordingly, subtly nuanced and internally referential. Now the framework of reference has massively expanded, not only in terms of having a genuine basis to address various site assemblages and their densities comparatively (e.g. faunal, pottery and plant remains) according to their specific settlement forms/'types', but also in relation to issues of locale.

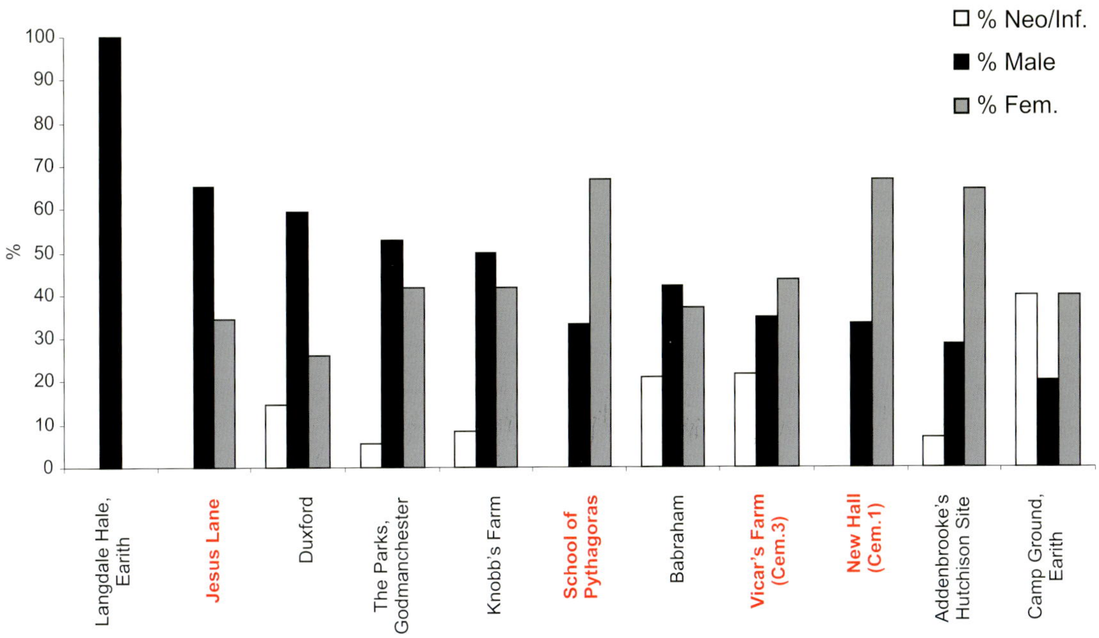

Figure 7.37. *Gender burial-frequencies (adapted from Evans* et al. *2013b, fig. 2.75; Vicar's Farm/Cemetery 3 excludes aDNA identifications, see Note 10).*

Given the density of settlement within any area there would have been limited choice where a settlement was actually situated, particularly taking requirements of production, communication and transportation into account. The advantages of one location over another, as well as its communication links (via rivers, roads/tracks or paths), would surely have influenced what a settlement could have become. As the settlement density within a given area built up, its landscape would have offered fewer options and locational choices would have been restricted. In effect, a settlement was at such-and-such locale because, quite simply, it could not have been elsewhere (i.e. those places were taken).

This also implies a degree of predictability affecting the region's archaeology. As outlined above, the location of yet another Roman settlement had been predicted within the general area of the Wilberforce Road Site (see Chap. 2). With the benefit of the Reading Project's overview summaries (Smith *et al.* 2016 and 2018; Allen *et al.* 2017), and with experience of excavating so many Roman-period sites in the local landscape, we could even posit beforehand that its plant remains and faunal assemblages would, respectively, be dominated by spelt wheat and cattle. Yet, neither the occurrence of a kiln there nor its road/trackway were anticipated.

Having so much new period-landscape context now demands a certain *interpretative modesty*. Beginning to recognize just how many settlements – and lives – were wrapped up within any given landscape means that any simple answers or single theoretical-'ism' surely cannot do justice to 'so much'. This is only right and a sign of a maturing practice. As we fill out our knowledge of past landscapes *the days of 'easy stories' are clearly over.*

In order to introduce some degree of preliminary comparative analysis, the Roman settlement-type 'league table' that has, in various configurations, already appeared in papers and Colne Fen's Roman volume (Evans & Ten Harkel 2010, table 8; Evans 2013, table 29.1; Evans *et al.* 2013b, tables 2.54 & 4.46) is worth repeating here (Table 7.10). We have intentionally not added New Hall's findings to it. Lying at the town/countryside interface, that site's betwixt status breaks any sense of patterning. Calculated in the same way, its pottery would occur at a level of 50,540 sherds per ha, far higher than the 'major farm' values and almost twice the density of Stonea. Its Roman-period animal bone, estimated to occur at a level of *c.* 16,400 pieces per ha, would also be high (*c.* 50% greater than levels at Vicar's Farm and Langdale). In contrast, its coins – at just 14 per ha – would be very low (as would also be its quernstone).

This kind of direct comparison is difficult, given varying intensities of excavation (hence why cubic densities have also been employed here; see also Fulford & Holbrook 2018). In the case of New Hall and Wilberforce Road, this is compounded by the fact that they only represent parts of a settlement area. If considering just the 'major farms' category in Table 7.10 – all three of which had aisled buildings[9] – this is

Table 7.10. *Comparative Roman-period site finds densities, with bolded numbers indicating per hectare densities (red lettered grey-tone denotes highest density in each category, with grey tone indication alone indicating second highest [excluding Snows Farm Shrine]; see Evans & Ten Harkel 2010, table 8, Evans 2013, table 29.1, Evans* et al. *2013b, tables 2.54 & 4.46 for further detailing of entries; * comprises, on the Isle of Ely, Prickwillow Road, West Fen Road, and Little Thetford, plus also Haddon, near Peterborough).*

		Major Farms				*Centres*			*Shrine*
	Rural Settlements*	**Orton Hall**	**Vicar's Farm**		**Langdale Hale**	**Stonea**	**Camp Ground**	**Cambridge**	**Snow's Farm**
Excavated Area (ha)	0.4–2.5	1.5	*Total* 6.0	*Core* 1.4	1.8	1.5	4.0 (Core)	1.2	0.3
Pottery	1833–7000	44,000	12,406	10,805	15,988	30,874	65,846	252,200	2639
	2500	**29,333.3**	**2067.7**	**7717.9**	**8882.2**	**20,583**	**16,462**	**210,167**	**8708.7**
Bone	1328–2967	12,153	16,797	13,098	18,287	18,676	38,378	n/a	32,933
	2305	**8102**	**2799.5**	**9355.7**	**10,159.4**	**12,450**	**9595**		**108,678.9**
Coins	7–81	63	339	303	81	178	1536	247	74
	18	**42**	**56.5**	**216.4**	**45**	**119**	**384**	**206**	**244.2**
Small Finds	5–24	47	30	23	20	73	83	95	17
	18.6	**31.3**	**5**	**16.4**	**11**	**48.7**	**20.8**	**79.2**	**56.1**
Glass	0–7	90	83	26	13	72	37	32	9
	1.45	**60**	**13.8**	**18.6**	**7.2**	**48**	**9.25**	**26.6**	**29.7**
Other Styli	0–1	-	1	1	1	2	5	1	-
	0.2		**0.17**	**0.7**	**0.56**	**1.3**	**1.24**	**0.7**	
Lamps	-	1(?)	-	-	7	-	-	1	-
		0.67			**3.9**	-	-	**0.8**	
Querns	1–28	7	71	43/	162	23	197	18	2
	6.1	**4.6**	**11.8**	**30.7**	**92.2**	**15.3**	**49**	**15**	**6.6**

particularly true of Orton Hall's very high values as it was intensively dug (Mackreth 1996). Given their shared sampling densities, comparison between the Vicar's Farm core-area values and those from Langdale Hale's 'state-supply farm' (see Fig. 6.51; Evans *et al.* 2013b, chap. 2) is, though, appropriate. Generally, they resemble each other. While the quernstone density at Vicar's Farm was, by area, only a third of those at Langdale, it is still the second highest of any of these sites, and this only reinforces the fact that it, too, was a producer settlement: *a major farm*. Yet, look at its very high coin levels, which are more than four times greater than Langdale's and, in the table, are only exceeded by those from Haddenham's Snow's Farm Romano-Celtic shrine. This only gives greater credence to the idea that Vicar's Farm involved something more than just a farm, and probably encompassed a fair/market function. Langdale Hale's 'official' farm saw no such exchange/market activity, nor did it see such formal cemeteries as at Vicar's Farm.[10] As will become apparent in the next book, one of the things that most distinguishes the Vicar's Farm settlement is that its cemeteries seem more 'rule-bound' and formal than many settlements. They reflect a stricter division between (adult) inhumation and cremation interments (the main exception being the one cremation in its southern inhumation cemetery, with its central position perhaps suggesting a 'significant ancestor'). Given that, the fact that its primary cremation cemetery actually lay within the settlement itself 'broke the rules'.

We will further refer to this table's results in the next book, when it will be expanded to include the North West Cambridge settlements. At this point, though, when compared to those within Roman Cambridge proper its cross-settlement-type deposition values are worth reviewing.

While acknowledging the difficulties of fully enumerating *Roman Cambridge*'s recovered artefacts, in many categories values per hectare far exceed those of the other listed sites. Although Cambridge's quern density was relatively low, it is not surprising that major farms have higher values, by their emphasis on mass-agricultural production. While Cambridge's coinage levels are surpassed by those of The Camp Ground port-village and the Snow's Farm shrine, this must just reflect the latters' intensity of metal-detecting (see, though, Reece's comments in Chap. 6, Note 15 concerning potential duplication in Cambridge's coin-list). Against this, Cambridge's density of small finds would be greater than the other sites. Most significant is its pottery levels, which are almost five times greater than those of the next site (Orton Hall Farm).[11] At that level, in reference to Jeremy Taylor's comparative analysis (2013, fig. 1), they would be approximately a third less than Wroxeter's but a third greater than Leicester's Roman 'city' values; it would also exceed the values of small towns in Shropshire and Leicestershire. While admitting that Roman Cambridge lacks various expected features of towns (e.g. public buildings), this could further support Chapter Two's arguments that it should be considered as a 'town', albeit in a highly qualified way.

Economic Matters and Transformation

The economic basis of Roman Cambridge and its hinterland settlements is also a theme that will be explored in much greater detail in the companion book. As such, Table 7.11 is largely included here by way of 'rehearsal' and to highlight the potential of the amassed data. It presents only the relative percentage-frequency of the four main domesticate species from those sites that yielded faunal assemblages with NISP-values of 50 or more. It, therefore, ignores the range of 'other species', essentially dog and bird; these were present at almost all the sites, albeit in low numbers, with WYNG Garden also having deer.

That table also includes the species-frequencies from a series of other farmstead-site excavations within the region. These generally complement the overall values of the Reading Project's Roman Cambridgeshire Fen-edge case-study sites (including Cambridge, Godmanchester and Isle of Ely): 52 per cent cattle, 41 per cent sheep/goat and 6.9 per cent pig (horse excluded; Smith *et al.* 2016, 204). While Cambridge's western hinterland settlements display comparable cattle-dominated frequencies, this is not true of Roman Cambridge's 'core'. There, sheep/goat were prevalent and, though somewhat less marked, the same is also true of its immediate 'fringe' sites, with the East Camside assemblages having greater variability in their sheep/goat-to-cattle figures.

It has to be remembered that, with *c.* 65 and 68 per cent sheep/goat values, the Castle St and Shire Hall Lift Shaft Sites were largely of Early Roman date (Vicar's Farm saw a reduction its sheep/goat from 26 to 19/20% between its Phases I and II/III; see Table 6.24). This is in relationship to arguments that cattle-dominance was a characteristic of increasing Romanization (e.g. King 1978 and 1991). Nevertheless, it is likely that this also reflects different stock management practices and that herds of cattle were simply not kept within the bounds of the core-settlement (i.e. the 'town').[12] Equally, the frequency of butchered cattle bone in New Hall's assemblage could well reflect town-edge/-outskirts processing of herds (see, e.g., Maltby in Millett *et al.* 2016, 792–5). The horse values from the Roman Cambridge sites were generally much lower than from those in the western lands (1.1–1.6% *vs.* 11.5–33.8%). While not included in Table 7.11 due to its low overall NISP (37), the main domesticates assemblage at Trinity Hall Playing Fields actually had the highest horse value at 40.6 per cent (the partial skeleton of that species counting as one; cattle 35.1%, sheep-goat 21.6% and pig 2.7%). Including its two donkey/equidae bones, the Wilberforce Road Site also saw very high 'horse' levels (33.8%). All this surely reflects where horses were actually reared, as well as a greater need for transportation in the hinterland. In this regard, the Westminster College high horse-value may have related to its Roman Cambridge southern 'edge' location; around the latter's non-riverside margins these factors were probably also of relevance.

Table 7.11. *Comparative Roman-period main domestic species frequencies, with red highlight indicating greatest percentage (only includes sites where NISP by period is 50 or more; *Conquest Period/Early Roman only).*

Site	Total NISP	% NISP			
		Cattle	Sheep/goat	Pig	Horse
Other Regional Sites					
Papworth Everard	311	59.8	19.3	2.3	18.6
Cambourne	1795	52.8	36.8	3.8	6.6
Haddon	429	45.3	38.6	7.2	8.9
Orton Hall	6183	55.7	39.4	2.9	2.0
Langdale Hale	1042	56.6	21.9	3.8	17.9
Roman Cambridge Core					
*Castle St**	127	23.6	65.4	9.4	1.6
Kettle's Yard	89	40.4	46.1	12.4	1.1
Shire Hall Lift Shaft	145	24.1	68.3	6.2	1.4
Settlement Fringe					
Westminster College	246	24.8	43.9	8.3	21.9
School of Pythagoras	70	25.7	61.4	4.3	8.6
Chesterton Lane Corner	59	30.5	54.2	15.3	-
East Cam-side					
Jesus College West Court	109	37.6	44.9	11.9	5.5
Jesus Lane Cemetery	97	49.5	43.3	5.1	2.1
Clements Garden/WYNG	321	54.8	23.7	7.5	14.0
West Lands					
New Hall	765	51.1	32.9	4.4	11.5
Vicar's Farm	1919	60.0	21.1	2.3	16.6
Wilberforce Road	74	41.9	23.0	-	33.8

The absence of pig at the Wilberforce Road Site is also noteworthy. This must correlate to their low values both at the New Hall and Vicar's Farm settlements (4.4 & 2.3% respectively); the School of Pythagoras aside, this seems to correspond with the much higher pig values in Roman Cambridge proper (and its 'Fringe') and the lower, East Cam-side sites (5.1–15.3%).

The predominance of cattle in New Hall/Fitzwilliam College's Bronze Age assemblages (85 & 64% respectively) was also common to North West Cambridge's enclosures of the same period. The wider area's Iron Age settlements display greater variability. Whereas the New Hall and High Cross Sites showed high levels of cattle (76 & 69.7% respectively), at Marion Close near-equivalent values of sheep/goat and cattle occurred (41.8 & 40.3% respectively). No horse bone was present within New Hall's Iron Age assemblages, while at High Cross and Marion Close they occurred at 11.9 and 4% per cent respectively (at Vicar's Farm they amount to *c.* 44% but this just amounted to four species-identified bones out of nine).

Again, the dynamics of the crop assemblages from the outlined sites will be more thoroughly explored in the next book. It is worth mentioning here, though, with spelt wheat being the dominant crop, that the occurrence of clayland-type weeds from Castle St and Kettle's Yard's assemblages would indicate the import of crops into Roman Cambridge proper (see Lodwick in Allen *et al.* 2017, 26–8 for regional overview).

Local pottery supply will also have to be a major concern of the companion book. As detailed in the recent *Horningsea Industries* volume (J. Evans *et al.* 2017), from the second century AD onwards those kilns were clearly the main local supply for the Cambridge area. It is difficult to explain what seems to be the very high representation of that ware at New Hall at *c.* 36 per cent overall (*c.* 20–78% of the analysed feature assemblages; see Table 3.4). The Wilberforce Road settlement had 27 per cent, compared to *c.* 9 per cent at Vicar's Farm and *c.* 10–15 per cent at the North West Cambridge settlements; one can only suspect that a 'specificity' lies behind this.

As cited in Chapter Two and further outlined in the next book (see Haselgrove in *NWC*), the frequency of Late Iron Age/Conquest Period brooches (i.e. first century AD) in Roman Cambridge should also be acknowledged. Thirty-three such brooches were apparently recovered during Alexander and Pullinger's excavations, without the benefit of metal-detecting (*c.* 1.2 ha; *RCAM*, 85–6; see Evans & Ten Harkel 2010, table 7). With a comparable brooch recovered from the more recent Castle Street Site (*c.* 60 sq. m; *ibid.*, fig. 13), three from the Shire Hall Lift Shaft (7.75 sq. m; Rees 2016), one from Westminster College (450 sq. m; Graham 2016) and three from the School of Pythagoras (135 sq. m; Newman 2013), this seems a very high density. We can compare this to the western lands' excavations, all of which were intensively metal-detected (and of a much larger size): these produced one each from the Trinity Hall Playing Fields and Vicar's Farm, two from Wilberforce Road and (anticipating the next book's results) just three from the North West Cambridge excavations.[13] Collectively, this would be a markedly low density. At a basic level, Roman Cambridge's brooch-use/-loss values could arguably be correlated with its relatively high number of Terra Nigra wares (see Chap. 2, *Inset*) and reflect its status as a significant Late Iron Age/Conquest Period settlement, if not a 'centre'. Yet, there was also first-century AD settlement in the western hinterland sites. Given this, and what has been argued to be the potential role of brooches as social markers (e.g. Jundi & Hill 1998), this could imply that such expression was less important in the countryside. *'Brooch-identity' may rather have been a distinctly town-based behaviour*, occurring where more mixed groups regularly interacted with each other and less physical labour was regularly undertaken (i.e. people dressed up more).

That samian features in all the Roman Cambridge hinterland sites presented here testifies to the degree to which even such imported pottery was available throughout the local countryside (e.g. Willis 1997 and 1998; Van Oyen 2015). Admittedly, it occurs in low proportions in any assemblage (*c.* 1–2%) and we are certainly not seeing 'service sets' such as were present at Roman Mucking (Lucy & Evans 2016, 421–2, fig. 5.13). Nevertheless, the widespread distribution of these wares – and the 'tastes' they must reflect – tells of the impact of Roman colonization. While not reverting to the kind of British Empire comparisons favoured by John Alexander (see Chap. 2), this represents a completely different picture. We see a much greater top-down penetration of its 'native' infrastructure; within a century of arrival the local pottery manufacture had been total eroded and there was an almost total transformation of its settlement fabric. This is not the kind of colonialism that occurred in nineteenth-century Africa or India. Take what might be considered samian's equivalent there – Blue Willow china (see e.g. Evans *et al.* 2013b, 420–22); this was certainly not something that every Indian household of the time would have had, nor would most have changed their house-style and village layout. This is not the kind of 'past story' we desire, with 'creolization' and 'resistance' narratives now instead widely privileged (see e.g. Fincham 2002 and Gardner 2013). There can, though, be little doubt of the persuasion and thoroughness of Britain's Romanization, at least in Southeast England.

Questions of 'familiarity' will be further highlighted in the next book as additional aDNA analyses are brought to bear upon the area's population dynamics and its communities (see e.g. Fig. 7.37). This will raise crucial issues, ranging from the scale of intermarriage patterns to labour relations and residential movement/shift. This will also, for example, allow us to consider whether non-landed/tenanted workers would have been tied to specific farms or shared amongst a series of farm-holdings held by a single estate owner.

Madingley Rises – Mixed Households, Local and Far-flung Connections

It is worth briefly reviewing the composition of a few of the local latter-day households, on the grounds that this can help us reflect on the issue raised in Chapter Six, 'what is a farm' (and their variants), as well as the character of the area's Post-Medieval/early Modern pottery assemblages and the question of landscape 'arrivals'. Using the census-data for 1911, only Vicar's Farm was occupied by a nuclear family: two adults and four children (with one of the sons listed as employed in the motor trade). Harry Huby, its head farmer/father, was entered as an 'employer', so the farm may have also had other hands living out.[14]

Reflecting its larger operation and institutional ownership (i.e. Merton College, Oxford), Merton Hall Farm – including residents in its adjacent cottages (see Fig. 4.37) – comprised four separate families (plus a boarder) of 12 individuals, with just three being children. Although its entries may not extend to the farm's entire labour force, the census provides a hierarchy of six workers: the head farmer, the farm bailiff, a horseman, two cowmen and a labourer.

By way of some contrast, the census also gives the figures for the Newall household at Madingley Rise, bordering the Observatory's grounds (Fig. 7.38). Born near Gateshead, Hugh Frank Newall (1857–1944), the

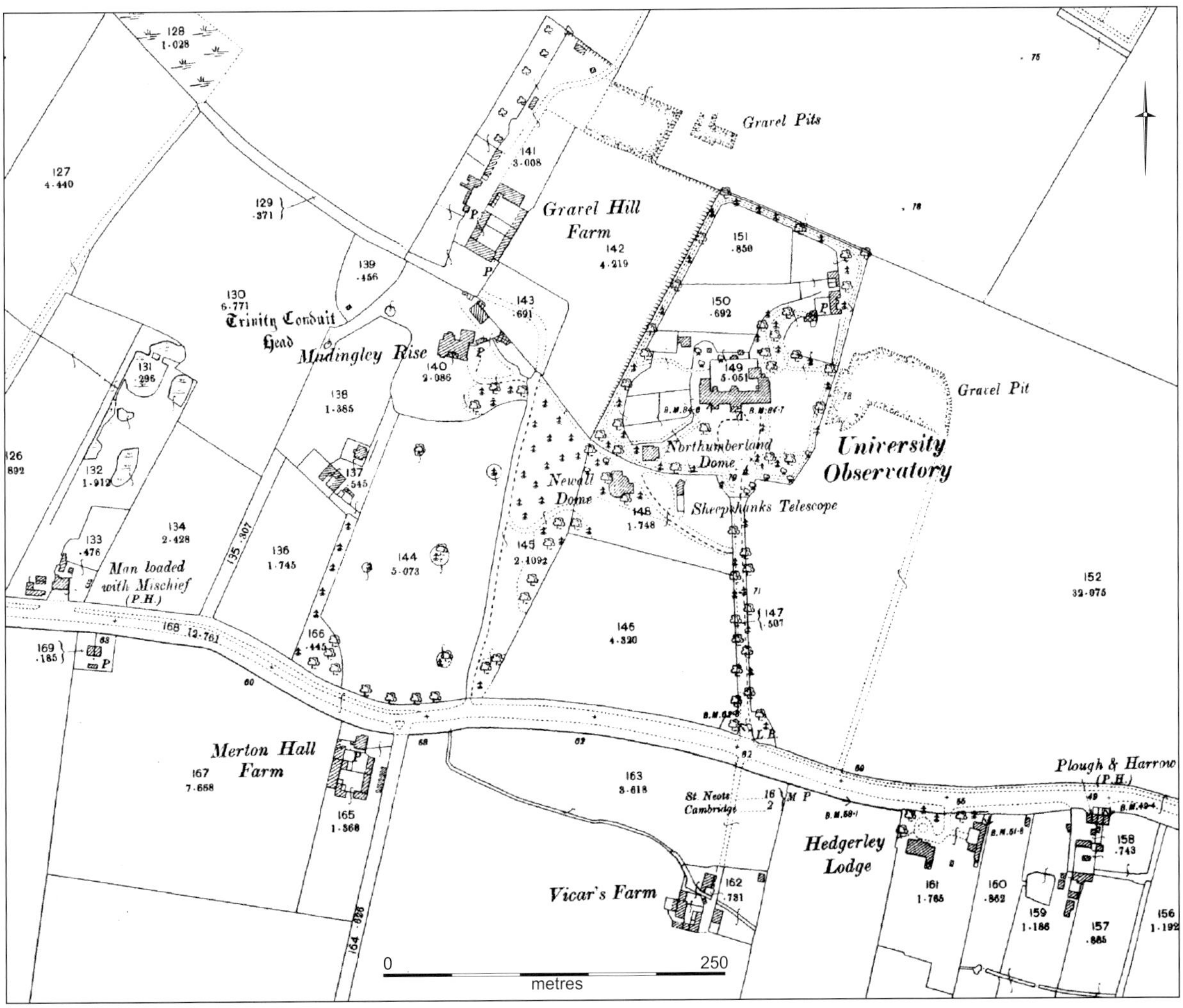

Figure 7.38. *The Observatory environs (1920s OS map; see also Fig. 1.3.2).*

Figure 7.39. Madingley Rise, *Frank Newall and the Bullard Laboratory sculptures: left, Newall and his wife at* Madingley Rise *in 1922 (top), with the house shown below (2018; see also Fig. 1.3.C); upper right, the 1898 Indian eclipse expedition observers, with Newall and his wife centre-row, left (in 1913 Newall became the first director of the University's Solar Physics Observatory and led many eclipse expeditions: Brück 1944; Williams 2009 27–37); lower left, the Bullard Laboratory sculptures (R. Cushing, photograph).*

Discovered in the grounds by gardeners in the mid '90s, the origin of these fragments (now displayed clamped to the house's side) — a double-headed eagle and a pair of mounted warriors — has puzzled us and all those we have sought expert advice from for decades. Both pieces are worn and look 'old', with the horsemen rendered in what could almost be a Hellenistic style (M. Henig pers comm.; see e.g. Smith 1991, 184–5, figs. 205 & 209); hoiwever, the Imperial eagle would not suggest any antiquity. Now knowing that it was Newall's Madingley Rise *house that the Laboratory took over in 1955, it seems reasonable to speculate that it could have derived from his father's Gateshead mansion,* Ferndene, *perhaps from a folly in its grounds (see Evans & Newman 2011). Another possible source might be Trinity Conduit Head; there are rumours that an amateur excavation was conducted there during the nineteenth century (S. Lachman pers comm.). As we will see in the next figure (7.40), there is though still another interpretative twist to this ...*

household's head and a Professor of Astrophysics, was the son of the wealthy engineer and amateur astronomer, Robert Stirling Newall, who in 1889 had bequeathed his great 25 inch refractor telescope to the Observatory (and whose foundations were excavated at the Kavli Institute Site, see Chap. 4, Fig. 4.9 and Fig. 7.39). The gift, though, came without any stipend for its operation and Frank, who had studied at Trinity College Cambridge and then became a senior demonstrator at the original Cavendish Laboratory, offered to work the telescope without payment. He subsequently built his 18-room house (*Madingley Rise*) and, in 1911, the 54 year-old Newall's household included, apart from his wife, eight servants; among the five females was a cook, plus parlour, laundry and kitchen maids (Williams 2009, 27–37).

Of the 28 individuals listed amongst these three neighbouring households, remarkably enough, none

Figure 7.40. *Thinking that we had achieved some kind of plausible explanation for the source of the Bullard Laboratory friezes (Fig. 7.39), some weeks later, and after writing the preceding figure's caption-text, another twist in the 'attribution trail' arose. Arriving at the Department of Archaeology, Evans, on locking his bike beside the Museum of Archaeology and Anthropology, noticed that its eaves-gutter downspouts are embossed with double-headed eagles (that quadrangle's Downing Street gateway having bees on the same). With the Museum built 1910–13, what could possibly be the basis of this? Asking this of various aged colleagues, most thought that it must somehow relate to its first curator, Baron Anatole von Hugel (1854–1928). Responsible for the Museum's construction, we have already come across him as excavating the St John's Playing Fields (see Chap. 2). He was born in Florence as the second son of Austrian nobleman and his Scottish wife; the Museum's eagle insignia might then vaguely reference his familial roots and the Austro-Hungarian imperial coat-of-arms of 1867–1918. Yet, von Hugel's Catholicism provides still another possible connection (Wolff 2003). He was apparently instrumental in the lifting of the papal ban on Catholics attending Oxford and Cambridge's universities and, a co-founder of St. Edmund's (Catholic) College, he became the first President of Cambridge University's Catholic Association in 1899. In acknowledgement, in 1924 Pope Pius XI made him a Knight of St Gregory. One of the five pontifical orders of knighthood, the coat-of-arms of its civil and military divisions has a crowned double-headed eagle as its motif.*

Von Hugel's Catholicism would have made an attractively obscure connection to the Museum's eagle insignia. However, given that the downspouts carry a date of 1912, his knighthood would be too late as their source and, instead, the Museum's eagles must simply relate to an announcement of his familial ancestry. While this does not, of course, provide a direct explanation for the iconography of the Bullard Laboratory's friezes, it certainly casts doubt that a Gateshead folly was their source. One could now go onto elaborate other 'stories': perhaps, as a Trinity College graduate, von Hugel later in life donated the sculptures to somehow adorn Trinity Conduit Head's masonry. Alternatively, they might derive from the private chapel that he had built in the backyard of his Barton Road home, Croft Cottage. *Yet, with there being no obvious documentation or, now, personal knowledge of either the Laboratory's friezes or the Museum's eagle insignia, this 'twist-in-the-tale' only serves to remind us just how quickly the recent past escapes memory. Resonating with Ondaatje's introductory passage, it tells of the impact of happenstance and the limits of (material culture) interpretation.*

had actually been born in Cambridge. Half had come to the town from Cambridgeshire villages, with five from neighbouring counties. The reminder were from further afield, variously Rugby (× 4, one family) and Leicester, with the rest from the north (Yorkshire, Durham and Northumberland). With its population expanding, Cambridge was, even then, clearly a place of 'arrivals' (e.g. Guillebaud 2006, 160, fig. 1).

Concerning the 'what is a farm' issue, something akin to Merton Hall Farm's larger and its more mixed household membership is held to be a more apt model for the Vicar's Farm Roman settlement, rather than a single, small nuclear family unit.[15] Because of the Newall family's wealth, the number of domestic servants at Madingley Rise may have been greater than in most academic households of the day; nonetheless, it tells of the interconnections of the town-and-gown.

It is relevant that listed among the Newall household, Alfred Chessom (aged 22) was down as its stableman. By 1922 he was recorded as the head of the household at Vicar's Farm, remaining such until 1938. This is significant for a number of reasons. It demonstrates that, through domestic service, many households in Cambridge would have had indirect links to the University and it is this that must, if in part, account for the inclusion of collegiate ceramics at both Vicar's and Merton Hall Farms. In the next book, the occurrence of such wares in what seems to have been a civic dumping episode within the backfill of quarries at North West Cambridge will be outlined (see also Cessford 2016b). Yet, this seems an unlikely source of these wares at the two farms. Instead, it surely attests to 'happenstance' and inter-household connections. While obviously introduced through very different mechanisms, in the next book it will be posited that parallels could drawn between these college wares and Roman samian in terms of their widespread hinterland distributions: both being singularly reflective of their periods' respective landscape colonizations.

More prosaically, the basis of Chessom's upward mobility in the running of Vicar's Farm can be accredited to Frank Newall, who apparently purchased the farm in 1921 (see Cooper 2000, fig. 4a) and must have put his former stableman in charge. Newall apparently actively managed the farm and, as suggested above, these circumstances – with its owner living up on the ridge some hundreds of metres distant from the farm itself – might well provide a parallel to the situation in the Roman period (see Chap. 6, *An Estate Farm* ...).

Newall sold Vicar's Farm and its 33 acres (*c.* 13 ha) to the University in 1931. This was at a favourable low price and carried the stipulation that its use would not 'prejudice the proper and efficient use of the said Observatories' (quoted in Guillebaud 2008, 191). With the University acquiring, in 1949, the 100 acres (*c.* 40 ha) of the neighbouring Merton Hall Farm, this then provided the basis of what was to eventually become the University's West Cambridge development lands.

This section's Madingley Rise plurality alludes to yet more distant connections. We can now fortunately draw on Williams' *Madingley Rise and Early Geophysics at Cambridge* (2009), which charts the development of the Bullard Laboratory during the last century. Newall was apparently instrumental in wanting to have a school of geodesy established, both to record gravity at sea and to train the Empire's surveyors (see *NWC*, chap. 2, *Inset*). In 1921 this was realized, headed by Colonel Sir Gerald Lenox-Conyngham, the last superintendent of the Trigonometrical Survey of India.[16] With the school eventually taking over Newall's house in 1955, a major new wing was added behind it in 2000 (see Fig. 1.3.3). At what was to become the Bullard Laboratory, ground-breaking advances in plate tectonics and Continental Drift were made. In acknowledgement, in 1966 an area of shallow-depth ridges within the floor of the Indian Ocean was formally designated *Madingley Rise* in the Gazetteer of Undersea Feature Names (Williams 2009, 106). Lying west of the Seychelles (Lat. -4.25; Long. 61) and discovered only four years earlier, this was in recognition of the School/Laboratory's contribution to the field. Located more than 8300 km southeast of Cambridge and 'our'/Newall's Madingley Rise, this is a much more distant linkage than that the family's namesake telescope, which was to traverse between Gateshead, Cambridge and, eventually, Athens.[17]

Peripheries become Cores – 'Landscape-arrival' Icons

It is only appropriate that this book concludes with some further broad-brush observations concerning the immediate West Cambridge landscape. In Loggan's seventeenth century West Cambridge view (see Fig. 1.1), it was the silhouette of King's College Chapel – then some 160 years old – that served as the town's key landmark icon. Beside it, Wren's then recently completed Trinity College Library is also prominent. Its central situation effectively announces the University becoming a venue of prestige architecture and tells of growing collegiate wealth and resourcing.

Girdled by the town on its east side, as the University and its Colleges pushed west of the river over the centuries new icons came to command Cambridge's skyline. First was Gilbert Scott's University Library of 1934, 0.5 km to the west, whose mass-modelled brickwork and 12 storey-high tower clearly owed much to his Battersea Power Station completed the year before (he was also responsible for the design of the GPO's telephone kiosks). Half a century later, in 1985 (and *c.* 1.9 km beyond the Library), the tensile big-top of Hopkins' Schlumberger Research Centre became the new 'west-lands' icon (Figs. 7.2, 7.18 & 7.42). Best appreciated from Madingley's higher ground, from the viewshed of the M11 (opened 1980) it is what now tells that you are in Cambridge.

More than a century before the Library's construction, West Cambridge had seen another instance of 'prestige architecture': Mead's severe neo-classical Observatory of 1822 (Figs. 1.3 & 7.38). With its avenue oriented due north–south for the purposes of aligning telescopes, its location outside the town was for the

Figure 7.41. *The West Cambridge Lands: top, 1966 aerial photograph showing Veterinary School (centre-left; CUCAP AMX34) and, lower right, the Shorts/ SEBRO works; below, 2017 aerial photograph showing scale of the University 'colonization' (Google Earth).*

Figure 7.42. *Landscape icons: main image, 1955 aerial photograph showing newly opened Veterinary School; inset with Mead's 1822 Observatory (above), Scott's University Library (1934, upper right), the new Cavendish Laboratory (1974; middle right) and, bottom right, Hopkins' 1985 Schlumberger Building.*

avoidance of light pollution (see Chap. 3 *Inset* and Evans & Newman 2011). From the middle decades of the last century, the Observatory there was no longer really viable for scientific telescopic purposes. While also propelled by technological advances – the great Mullard Radio Astronomy Array having, by 1957, been established some 8 km southwest of Cambridge at Lord's Bridge – by that time the Observatory's western Cambridge locale had itself succumbed to night-sky pollution.

The agricultural character of the area was largely retained until the construction of Sebro Shorts Works in 1941 (see *Inset*) and, then, Forbes' Department of Veterinary Medicine buildings.[18] Started in 1953, and opening in 1955, the latter's almost quasi-utopian radial plan in neo-Georgian brickwork (with beaux art-style pavilions) was never completed (Figs. 7.41 & .42).

With the University having colonized the land, after the demolition of Shorts Works in 1972 'science' followed. First was the Whittle Laboratory in 1973 (in brick) and, then, in the following year and rendered in 'brutal' pre-fabricated concrete panels, the enormous New Cavendish Laboratory complex (re-sited from its historic city-core location). A 'heavy concrete' style was similarly adopted when, in 1975, the British Antarctic Survey built their headquarters along the area's west side and, shortly thereafter, came other research-associated buildings along the road there, High Cross (e.g. CADcentre, 1978); with the Schlumberger Centre sited on the field beside it in the next decade.

This was the state of the largely still open land when the Unit took up its five-year residence there in portacabins by the one remaining Shorts Works building in the early 1990s. It remained thus until the beginning of the next decade and the implementation of the University's West Cambridge masterplan; first, north of the Cavendish Laboratory with the Gates/Microsoft buildings (and the Vicar's Farm excavation) and, then, along a belt south of what is now Charles Babbage Road and the Veterinary School.[19] Effectively reaching its western limits with the 2010 High Cross Site, this has seen a major shift of Cambridge science from the city centre. Its design features a huge ornamental pond with a formal tree-lined approach avenue (see Fig. 7.41), and represents an attempt to rationalize what had, up until that time, been the University's fairly piecemeal colonization of the area. Concurrent with its latter stages has been the much more utopian and grandly planned North West Cambridge development on the north side of Madingley Road. Now, in 2016–18, with the first phase of the latter nearing completion, (and the subject of the next book), there is a new scheme to extend the West Cambridge facilities northward and greatly intensifying the area's building density (including demolition of the Forbes building and the re-siting of Cavendish Laboratory; hence the 2015 and 2017 trenching programmes there).

There may be general lessons here concerning 'landscape colonization' and how *ad hoc* development eventually necessitates higher level planning (see e.g. Fletcher 1984). Harking back to Chapter Two's discussion of Macalister's Bandy-leg Walk findings and the earlier lack of appreciation of the pace of landscape-fabric change, the degree of transformation that the West Cambridge lands have seen since WWII, particularly over the last 15 years, has been staggering. Largely due to the empowerment of world-class University 'science', *what had been land on the periphery of the town/city has now become a core and a centre in its own right*. This theme could be used as a metaphor for imperial-succession – the Roman and, later, the British, with now the rise of Asia – to explore how 'shifting centres' are the way of the world. This, though, we'll not do. Instead, we will simply conclude by stressing just how extraordinary it has been to experience this transformation and have archaeology participate in it.

Notes

1 Aside from an earlier watching brief-monitoring exercise, two subsequent small-scale trench evaluations have also taken place on the West Cambridge lands, but which yielded negative results (Lucas 2000 and Hutton 2009b); see below concerning the 2015 evaluation fieldwork.

2 As we will see in the next section, this westward settlement failed to materialize when that area was investigated in 2012, probably due to modern truncation (Slater 2012). While the Roman fieldsystem in the immediate area might conjoin with that later found in evaluation fieldwork to the north in the Schlumberger and Veterinary School plots (Brittain & Evans 2015) – and perhaps at NWC Site VII – the latter seems to be of later Roman date and is therefore unlikely to have been associated with the *Early* Roman fieldsystem at High Cross.

3 In the paddocks north of the Veterinary School were found pits filled with burnt and degraded red brick rubble; similar to deposits seen at the Whittle Laboratory grounds (see Chap. 4), these presumably related to the 'Brick kiln' indicated on Baker's 1830 map just north of Madingley Road at this point.

4 In 2013, the 1.1 ha plot bordering the eastern side of the Sports Ground was trench-evaluated. No Roman material was recovered, and the only findings related to the nineteenth-century Grange Farm (Figs. 7.36; Roberts 2013).

5 The assemblage has been analysed following the guidelines set out by the Study Group for Roman Pottery (Darling 1994) and the National Roman Fabric Reference Collection (Tomber & Dore 1998). As reported upon here, the study excludes the 137 sherds (880 g of Roman-period pottery recovered in the evaluation (see Mazilli in Tabor 2017).

6 The complete metacarpus has a greatest length (GL) measurement of 193 mm (Fig. 7.32). This, according to Vitt (1952), gives a withers of 117 cm. Within the Equidae population, a measurement of 193 mm falls between 'very small' and 'small'; donkeys range from 80–160 cm, with horses at 142–63 cm and ponies around 140 cm. The specimen's calcaneum is incomplete, but its DS measurement of 40.57 mm would also fit a donkey.

7 This land-use model could, though, be brought into doubt by Wilberforce Road's pollen data (in each case using their monolith's maximal percentage values), those of F.30 in the south saw the highest tree/aboreal levels – 12.3 per cent – as opposed to those of F.2 and F.100 in the north: respectively, 7.2 and 5 per cent. There was no cereal register in F.30's profile (within the southern fieldsystem-area), whereas it was 5.5 and 3.3 per cent respectively in F.2 and F.100 at the site's northern end. It may be that F.30's non-cereal register, attributable to Phase 3's road/trackway, indicates that the southern fieldsystem (Phase 1) was no longer operational by that time. See Scaife, Chapter Four concerning the factors that potentially affect pollen representation; the maximal cereal percentage at Vicar's Farm was 6 per cent, from F.5474.

8 Indeed, the density of pottery within Wilberforce Road's pit F.53 – 267.7 sherds per cu. m – would only be exceeded by a few of New Hall/Murray Edwards and North West Cambridge's Sites II & IV features, with none at Vicar's Farm having such levels (see Fig. 4.32).

9 Of the four sites that comprise that table's rural settlement category (detailed in Evans *et al.* 2013b, table 2.54), only Haddon had aisled buildings (see Hinman 2003); it was designated as a 'complex farm' in the Roman Rural Settlement Project's classification (Smith *et al.* 2016, 30–2, fig. 2.13, see also 65–6, fig. 3.17). Since then, aisled buildings have been recovered at both Longstanton Site 19 and at the AstraZeneca North Site at Addenbrooke's

(Tabor 2015; See Chap. 6, Note 1). That said, none were identified at any of the nine Romano-British settlements excavated at Cambourne (Wright *et al.* 2009), nor on any of the North West Cambridge sites apart from Site VII.

10 Langdale's cemetery was distinct by its all-male burial populace and this could possibly suggest enforced labour in the light of its state farm status (see Chap. 6). Of the Cambridge cemeteries presented here, only that at Jesus Lane came close to having a predominantly male ratio; it also had the highest frequency of decapitation burials (three; see Chap. 2). Otherwise, the New Hall, School of Pythagoras and Vicar's Farm cemeteries all reflect more 'balanced' populations (see Fig. 7.37).

11 As shown in Table 4.9, the dark earth's average pottery density within Vicar's Farm's basin-area – 23.1 sherds per metre – would actually exceed those of Alexander's Roman Cambridge sites. The only other gridded metre-test pit sampling conducted on any of the other hinterland sites was to limited to a specific portion of North West Cambridge's Site IV (Area B) and confined to just six test pits. With values ranging from zero/nil to eight sherds per m, their average was just 2.8 and far below the Cambridge-town level.

12 In his overview paper, Green postulated that Godmanchester's sheep/goats were primarily raised for wool production (1975, 191); their relative numbers, were, however, low and occurred in frequencies of only *c.* 5 per cent (*vs.* 89–90% cattle; see also Jones 2003, 155–60). The Phase 1 Roman assemblage at the Wilberforce Road Site saw comparable levels of cattle and sheep/goat: 31.8 *vs.* 27.3 per cent. Yet this may not be particularly representative as it only derived from its fieldsystem features, with NISP identifiable to species of just 22; overall, that site's Roman assemblage saw *c.* 42 per cent cattle and 23 per cent sheep/goat.

13 In contrast and, rather inexplicably, Albion Archaeology's NIAB Lands Sites saw much higher levels of brooch-loss (see Luke in *NWC*). Also, brooches have not been found on all town-core sites (e.g. Chesterton Lane Corner or Kettle's Yard).

14 Residing at Gravel Hill Farm at that time were Arthur Burgess, aged 34 (born in Norfolk) and his 26 year-old sister, Mary (born in Peterborough).

15 Further to the Roman neonate remains at Vicar's Farm, the 1911 census data also recorded that between the Merton Hall and Vicar's Farm households – together having six children under the age of 16 – three children had also died; their dates are not given, but they were probably young. The nearby *Man Loaded with Mischief* pub (see Chap. 6, *Inset*) then had three occupants: John Hazelwood, a police pensioner, aged 53 (from Northamptonshire), his wife, Mary (aged 52, born in Brecon in Wales), and their 10 year-old daughter, Doris, who had been born in London; the Hazelwoods had two other children, but they had apparently died prior to the census date (see e.g. Zubrow in Evans & Hodder 2006b, 311–13 on pre-modern generational dynamics).

16 A friend of Newall, Lenox-Conyngham had participated in the 1898 India eclipse expedition and is shown in Figure 7.39's photograph of its team, seated at the far right of the centre-row (see also Williams 2009, 38–47). Much of the School's newly designed equipment was apparently made by the Cambridge Scientific Instrument Company (see Chap. 3, *Inset*). Note that when, in 1992, a single trench was excavated at the Bullard Laboratory in advance of construction, only nineteenth-century quarry pits were found (Nally 1992).

17 In 1955, Cambridge's Newall telescope was given to the Athens Observatory for the purposes of public demonstration (i.e. not professional science; Evans & Newman 2011).

18 Green Belt-related issues will largely be left until the next book (see also Cooper 2000); note, though, that in 1951 G.M. Trevelyan, Master of Trinity College (and author of the 1929 pamphlet, 'Must England's Beauty Perish?'), had apparently made a representation to the Council for the Preservation of Rural England on the desirability of leaving the west side of Cambridge as countryside and free of development. He, however, admitted that its character had by then been 'injured' by the construction of the factory (*Cambridge Evening News* 06/02/1951).

19 Bordering the Vicar's Farm site-area (see Fig. 4.1), Clerk Maxwell Road was only established and so-named in the early 1970s. Further east in the city's 'bicycle suburb' belt, it was the University's anti-slavery social reformers, Wilberforce and Clarkson, that had streets dedicated to them in the 1930s. With North West Cambridge's core to be named after the astronomer, Eddington (see *NWC*, chap. 1), it and the West Cambridge campus are becoming distinct in their 'named' celebration of Cambridge science.

Bibliography

Abrams, J. & Ingham, D., 2008. *Farming on the Edge: Archaeological evidence from clay uplands to the west of Cambridge.* (East Anglian Archaeology Report No. 123.) Bedford: Albion Archaeology.

Adams, D. & Penn, K., 2001. Report of an Archaeological Evaluation at Fitzwilliam College, Huntingdon Road, Cambridge. Norfolk Archaeological Unit Report No. 573.

Alexander, J.A., 1970. *The Directing of Archaeological Sites.* London: John Baker.

Alexander, J.A., 1975. The development of urban communities: the evidence from Cambridge and Great Chesterford, in *Small Towns of Roman Britain*, eds. W. Rodwell & T. Rowley. (British Archaeological Reports British Series 15.) Oxford: British Archaeological Reports, 103–9.

Alexander, J.A., Pullinger, J. & Woudhuysen, M., 1994. Early Cambridge: Excavations on Castle Hill 1956–1988. Unpublished Manuscript.

Alexander, J. & Pullinger, J., 2000. *Roman Cambridge: Excavations on Castle Hill 1956–1988.* (Proceedings of the Cambridge Antiquarian Society 88.) Cambridge: Cambridge Antiquarian Society.

Alexander, J., Trump, D., Hull, R., Farrar, R. & Kinnes, I., 1969. Excavation in Cambridge 1969: A Preliminary Report on Excavations at Arbury Road. Cambridge & London: Board and Department of Extra-mural studies.

Alexander, M., 1995. An Archaeological Assessment at the Bateman Building, Gonville and Caius College, Cambridge. Cambridge Archaeological Unit Report No. 153.

Alexander, M., Dodwell, N. & Evans, C., 2004. A Roman cemetery in Jesus Lane, Cambridge. *Proceedings of the Cambridge Antiquarian Society* 93, 67–94.

Allason-Jones, L., 1989. *Ear-rings in Roman Britain.* (British Archaeological Reports, British Series 201.) Oxford: British Archaeological Reports.

Allason-Jones, L., 1995. 'Sexing' small finds, in *Theoretical Roman Archaeological Conference: Second Conference Proceedings*, ed. P. Rush. Aldershot: Avebury/Ashgate, 22–32.

Allen, M., Lodwick, L., Brindle, T., Fulford, M. & Smith, A., 2017 (Allen *et al.* 2017). *The Rural Economy of Roman Britain.* (Britannia Monographs 30.) London: The Society for the Promotion of Roman Studies.

Anderson, K. & Woolhouse, T., 2016. Continental potters? First-century Roman flagon production at Duxford, Cambridgeshire. *Britannia* 47, 43–69.

Andrews, C., 1942. Hyperostosis frontalis interna. *British Medical Journal*, 185–7.

Armour, N., 2001. An Archaeological Investigation on the site of the Future Nano Fabrication Building, West Cambridge. Cambridge: Cambridge Archaeological Unit Report No. 453.

Armour, N., Evans, C. & Tipper, J., 2003. Anglo-Saxon Settlement at Newnham. Institute of Criminology, Sidgwick Site, University of Cambridge. Cambridge Archaeological Report No. 526.

Arthur, P., 1978. The lead glazed wares of Roman Britain, in *Early Fine Wares in Roman Britain*, eds. P. Arthur & G. Marsh. (British Archaeological Reports, British Series 57.) Oxford: British Archaeological Reports, 293–355.

Ashwin, T. & Tester, A., 2014. *A Romano-British Settlement in the Waveney Valley: Excavations at Scole, 1993–4.* (East Anglian Archaeology Report No. 152.) Gressenhall, Norwich and Bury St. Edmunds: NPS Archaeology, Norfolk Historic Environment Service and Suffolk County Council Archaeological Service.

Atkins, R., 2012. Between river, priory and town, excavations at the former Cambridge Regional College site, Brunswick, Cambridge. *Proceedings of the Cambridge Antiquarian Society* 101, 7–22.

Atkinson, M. & Preston, S.J., 1998. The Late Iron Age and Roman settlement at Elms Farm, Heybridge, Essex, excavations 1993–5: an interim report. *Britannia* 29, 85–110.

Atkinson, M. & Preston, S., 2015. *Heybridge, a Late Iron Age and Roman settlement: Excavations at Elms Farm 1993–5.* (East Anglian Archaeology Report No. 154.) Chelmsford: Historic Environment Essex County Council.

Auerbach, B. & Ruff, C., 2006. Limb bone bilateral asymmetry: variability and commonality among Modern Humans. *Journal of Human Evolution* 50, 203–18.

Babington, C.C., 1864. On Roman interments by the side of the so-called Via Devana, near Cambridge. *Communications of the Cambridge Antiquarian Society* II, 289–94.

Babington, C.C., 1883. *Ancient Cambridgeshire: Or an attempt to trace Roman and other ancient roads that passed through the county of Cambridge: With a record of the places where Roman coins and other remains have been found*. London: Deighton Bell & Co.

Bagshawe, R.W. & Johnston, D.E., 1964. *Roman Roads in the South-East Midlands*. London: Gollancz.

Ballantyne, R., 2009. Charred Plant Remains as Minute Artefactual Debris. Unpublished PhD thesis, University of Cambridge.

Barber, B. & Bowsher, D., 2000. *The Eastern Cemetery of Roman London Excavations 1983-1990.* (Museum of London Archaeology Service 4.) London: Museum of London Archaeology Service.

Barker, J. & Meckseper, C., 2015. Huntingdon Road/NIAB (Darwin Green), Cambridge, Cambridgeshire: Assessment of potential and updated project design. Albion Archaeology Report/Project NBC1942.

Barlow, G., 2018. New Library, Fellows Garden, Magdalene College, Magdalene Street, Cambridge: An Archaeological Evaluation. Archaeological Solutions Ltd. Project No. P7120.

Barlow, G. & Newton, A.S., 2018. Mount Pleasant House, Castle Ward, Cambridge, Cambridgeshire: An Archaeological Excavation Research Archive Report. Archaeological Solutions Ltd. Project No. 7094.

Barrett, J.C., 1980. The pottery of the later Bronze Age in lowland England. *Proceedings of the Prehistoric Society* 46, 297–319.

Bass, W.M., 1987. *Human Osteology: A laboratory and field manual.* Missouri Archaeological Society.

Bennett, K.D., Whittington, G. & Edwards, K.J., 1994. Recent plant nomenclatural changes and pollen morphology in the British Isles. *Quaternary Newsletter* 73, 16.

Berra, T.M., 2013. *Darwin and his Children: His other legacy*. Oxford: Oxford University Press.

Bet, P. & Delor, A., 2000. La typologie de la sigillée lisse de Lezoux et de la Gaule centrale du Haut-Empire. Révision décennale. *Société Française d'Etude de la Céramique Antique en Gaule, Actes du congrès de Libourne,* 461–84.

Bishop, M.C. & Coulston, J.C.N., 1993. *Roman Military Equipment: From the Punic Wars to the fall of Rome.* London: Batsford.

Boardman, S. & Jones, G.E.M., 1990. Experiments on the effects of charring on cereal components. *Journal of Archaeological Science* 17, 1–12.

Boessneck, J., 1969. Osteological differences between sheep (*Ovis Linne*) and goats (*Capra hircus Linne*), in *Science in Archaeology*, eds. D. Brothwell & E. Higgs. London: Thames & Hudson, 331–58.

Bolton, E.G., 1968. Romano-British kilns at Greetham, Rutland. *Transactions of the Leicestershire Archaeological and Historical Society* 43, 1–3.

Boon, G., 1991. *Tonsor humanus*: Razor and toilet knife in antiquity. *Britannia* 22, 21–32.

Booth, P., 1994. A Roman burial near Welford-on-Avon, Warwickshire. *Transactions of Birmingham & Warwickshire Archaeological Society* 98, 37–50.

Boreham, S., 2000. West Cambridge Site Quaternary Geology. Unpublished Report.

Borges, J.L., 1998. Museum on exactitude in Science. *Collected Fictions*. New York: Grove Press, 325–7.

Bowtell, J. nd. *A History of Cambridge*. Manuscript held in Downing College, Cambridge.

Boys Smith, J.S., 1964. The benefaction for the new college buildings. *The Eagle* 60, 73–4.

Bradford, J.S.P., & Goodchild, R.G., 1939. Excavations at Frilford, Berkshire 1937–8. *Oxoniensia* 4, 1–70.

Bradley, R., Lobb, S., Richards, J. & Robinson, M., 1980. Two Late Bronze Age settlements on the Kennet gravels: Excavations at Aldermaston Wharf and Knight's Farm, Burghfield, Berkshire. *Proceedings of the Prehistoric Society* 46, 217–95.

Brettell, R.C., Stern, B., Reifarth, N. & Heron, C., 2014. The 'semblance of immortality'? Resinous materials and mortuary rites in Roman Britain. *Archaeometry* 56, 444–59.

Brewer, R.J., 1986. The beads and glass counters, in *The Legionary Fortress Baths at Caerleon: The Finds*, by J.D. Zienkiewic. Cardiff: National Museum of Wales, 145–56.

Brittain, M., 2009. Ridley Hall, Cambridge: an archaeological evaluation. Cambridge: Cambridge Archaeological Unit Report No. 905.

Brittain, M. & Billington, L., 2012. Archaeological Investigations beside Fosters Mill (CB1), Cambridge. Cambridge: Cambridge Archaeological Unit Report No. 1091.

Brittain, M. & Evans, C., 2015. West Cambridge Archaeology, Department of Veterinary Medicine Paddocks: An Archaeological Evaluation. Cambridge: Cambridge Archaeological Unit Report No. 1292.

Brittain, M. & Evans, C., 2016. Roman and Medieval Archaeology at Kettle's Yard, Cambridge. Cambridge: Cambridge Archaeological Unit Report No. 1335.

Brittain, M. & Evans, C., 2018. University of Cambridge Sports Ground, Wilberforce Road, Cambridge: An Archaeological Excavation. Cambridge: Cambridge Archaeological Unit Report No. 1402.

Brooks, S.T. & Suchey, J.M., 1990. Skeletal age determination based on the *Os Pubis*: a comparison of the Acsádi-Nemeskéri and Suchey-Brooks methods. *Human Evolution* 5, 227–38.

Brothwell, D.R., 1972. *Digging Up Bones*. London: British Museum.

Brothwell, D.R., 1982. Linking Urban Man with his Built Environment, in *Environmental Archaeology in the Urban Context*, eds. R.A. Hall & H.K. Kenward. (Council for British Archaeology Research Report No. 43.) York: Council for British Archaeology, 126–29.

Brown, A., 1994. A Romano-British shell gritted pottery and tile manufacturing site at Harrold, Beds. *Bedfordshire Archaeology* 21, 19–107.

Brown, W., 1985. Identification of Human Teeth. *Bulletin of the Institute of Archaeology, University of London*, 21–22, 1–30.

Browne, D.M., 1974. *An Archaeological Gazetteer of the City of Cambridge*. Cambridge: Cambridge Antiquarian Society.

Brück, H.A., 1944, Obituary: Hugh Frank Newall. *The Observatory* 65, 195–99.

Brudenell, M., 2005. 3 Sylvester Road, Robinson College, Cambridge: an archaeological evaluation. Cambridge: Cambridge Archaeological Unit Report No. 678.

Buikstra, J.E., Ubelaker, D.H. & Aftandilian, D. (eds.), 1994. *Standards for Data Collection from Human Skeletal Remains*. (Arkansas Archaeological Survey Research Series No. 44.) Fayetteville: Arkansas Archaeological Survey.

Bullock, P., Fedoroff, N., Jongerius A., Stoops, G. & Tursina, T., 1985. *Handbook for Soil Thin Section Description*. Wolverhampton: Waine Research Publications.

Burnham, B.C. & Wacher, J., 1990. *The Small Towns of Roman Britain*. London: Batsford.

Bushe-Fox, J.P., 1928. *Second Report Excavation of the Roman Fort at Richborough, Kent*. (Reports of the Research Committee of the Society of Antiquaries of London 7.) Oxford: University Press.

Buxton, L., 1938. Platymeria and Platycnemia. *Journal of Anatomy* 73, 31–6.

Calvino, I., 1974. *Invisible Cities*. New York: Harcourt Brace Jovanovich.

Casa-Hatton, R., forthcoming. Roman Godmanchester, in A. Lyons, *Rectory Farm, Godmanchester, Cambridgeshire: Excavations 1988–1995 – Neolithic Monument to Roman Villa Farm*. East Anglian Archaeology.

Casa-Hatton, R. & Wall, W., 2006. A late Roman cemetery at *Durobrivae*, Chesterton. *Proceedings of the Cambridge Antiquarian Society* 95, 5–24.

Cattermole, M.J.G. & Wolfe, A.F., 1987. *Horace Darwin's Shop: A history of the Cambridge Scientific Instrument Company 1878 to 1978*. Bristol: Adam Hilger.

Cessford, C. 2008. Chesterton to West Cambridge, Anglia Water Sewer Pipeline, Cambridge: an archaeological watching brief. Cambridge: Cambridge Archaeological Unit Report No. 840.

Cessford, C., 2009. St. John's College Playing Fields: an archaeological evaluation. Cambridge: Cambridge Archaeological Unit Report No. 893.

Cessford, C., 2011. Nos. 4–5 Castle Street, Cambridge: an archaeological excavation. Cambridge: Cambridge Archaeological Unit Report No. 1064.

Cessford, C., 2012. Jesus Green Tennis Courts, Cambridge: an archaeological watching brief. Cambridge: Cambridge Archaeological Unit Report No. 1096.

Cessford, C., 2015. The St. John's Hospital cemetery and environs, Cambridge: contextualizing the Medieval urban dead. *Archaeological Journal* 5, 52–120.

Cessford, C., 2016a. WYNG Gardens, Thompson's Lane, Cambridge: an archaeological excavation. Cambridge: Cambridge Archaeological Unit Report No. 1332.

Cessford, C., 2016b. Cambridge College ceramics *c.* 1760–1900: a brief overview. *Proceedings of the Cambridge Antiquarian Society* 105, 109–26.

Cessford, C., 2016c. Lower Park Street, Jesus College, Cambridge: St. John's College Archaeology Summer School 2016, archaeological test pits. Cambridge: Cambridge Archaeological Unit Report No. 1347.

Cessford, C., 2017. Riparian Cambridge, archaeological excavations near the River Cam at WYNG Gardens and elsewhere. *Proceedings of the Cambridge Antiquarian Society* 106, 61–88.

Cessford, C., with Dickens, A., 2005. Cambridge Castle Hill: excavations of Saxon, Medieval and Post-Medieval deposits, Saxon execution site and a Medieval coin-hoard. *Proceedings of the Cambridge Antiquarian Society* 94, 73–101.

Cessford, C. & Dickens, A., forthcoming. *From King's Ditch to Department Store: investigations of an 11th–20th-century suburb and the town ditch of Cambridge*. Cambridge: McDonald Institute Monograph.

Chamberlain, A., 1994. *Human Remains*. London: British Museum.

Clarke, C.P., 1998. *Excavations South of Chignall Roman Villa, Essex, 1977–81*. (East Anglian Archaeology Report No. 83.) Chelmsford: Archaeology Section, Essex County Council.

Clarke G., 1979. *Pre-Roman and Roman Winchester Part II, the Roman Cemetery at Lankhills*. Oxford: Oxford University Press.

Clarke, S., 1997. Abandonment, rubbish disposal and 'special' deposits at Newstead, in *TRAC 06: Proceedings of the Sixth Annual Theoretical Roman Archaeology Conference*, eds. K. Meadows, C. Lemke & J. Heron. Oxford: Oxbow Books, 73–81.

Clay, P., 2002. *The Prehistory of the East Midlands Claylands: Aspects of settlement and land-use from the Mesolithic to the Iron Age in central England*. (Leicester Archaeology Monograph 9.) Leicester: University of Leicester Archaeological Services.

Clough, T. McK. & Green, B., 1972. The petrological identification of stone implements from East Anglia. *Proceedings of the Prehistoric Society* 38, 108–55.

Clutton-Brock, J., 1987. *A Natural History of Domesticated Animals*. British Museum (Natural History). Cambridge: Cambridge University Press.

Collins, M., 2017. Northstowe Phase 1, Cambridgeshire: Archaeological Post-Excavation Assessment (Vol. 3). Cambridge: Cambridge Archaeological Unit Report No. 1363.

Cooke, N., Brown, F. & Phillpotts, C., 2008. *From Hunter Gatherers to Huntsmen: A History of the Stansted Landscape*. Oxford & Salisbury: Framework Archaeology.

Cool, H.E.M., 1983. A Study of the Roman Personal Ornaments made of Metal, excluding Brooches, from Southern Britain. Unpublished PhD thesis, University of Wales (uk.bl.ethos.354484).

Cool, H.E.M., 1990. Roman metal hair pins from southern Britain. *Archaeological Journal* 147, 148–82.

Cool, H.E.M., 2000. The parts left over: material culture into the fifth century, in *The Late Roman Transition in the North*, eds. T. Wilmott & P. Wilson. (British Archaeological Reports British Series 299.) Oxford: Archaeopress, 47–65.

Cool, H.E.M., 2004. *The Roman Cemetery at Brougham, Cumbria: Excavations 1966–67*. (Britannia Monographs 21.) London: Society for the Promotion of Roman Studies.

Cool, H.E.M., 2010. Finding the foreigners, in *Roman Diasporas*, ed. H. Eckardt. (Journal of Roman Archaeology Supplementary Series 78.) Portsmouth Rhode Island, 27–44.

Cool, H.E.M., 2011. Funerary contexts, in *Artefacts in Roman Britain: their purpose and use*, ed. L. Allason-Jones. Cambridge: Cambridge University Press, 293–312.

Cool, H.E.M., 2018. *Romano-British Bracelets and Bangles*. Barbican Research Associates, http://www.barbicanra.co.uk/assets/roman-bracelets.pdf

Cool, H.E.M., Jackson, C.M. & Monaghan, J., 1999. Glass making and the Sixth Legion at York. *Britannia* 30, 147–61.

Cool, H.E.M. & Mills, J.M., 1993. The copper alloy and silver grave goods, in *Excavations at Poundbury 1966-80 Volume 2: The cemeteries*, by D.E. Farwell & T.I. Molleson. (Dorset Natural History and Archaeological Society 11.) Dorset: Dorset Natural History and Archaeological Society, 89–96.

Cool, H.E.M. & Price, J., 1987. The other finds: the glass, in *The Roman Villa at Lullingstone, Kent. Volume II The wall paintings and finds*, by G.W. Meates. (Kent Archaeological Society Monograph 3.) Chichester: Kent Archaeological Society, 110–42.

Cool, H.E.M. & Price, J., 1995. *Roman Glass Vessels from Excavations at Colchester 1971–1985* (Colchester Archaeological Report 8.) Colchester: Colchester Archaeological Trust.

Cooper, A., 2003a. Cambridge Airport Replacement Terminal: an archaeological evaluation. Cambridge: Cambridge Archaeological Unit Report No. 523.

Cooper, A., 2003b. Fitzwilliam College Library, Cambridge: An Archaeological Evaluation. Cambridge: Cambridge Archaeological Unit Report No. 539.

Cooper, A. & Edmonds, M., 2007. *Past and Present: Excavations at Broom, Bedfordshire 1996–2005*. Cambridge Archaeological Unit. Oxford: Oxbow Books.

Cooper, A.J., 2000. *Planners and Preservationists: The Cambridge Preservation Society and the City's green belt 1928–1985*. Cambridge: Cambridge Preservation Society.

Cooper, C.H., 1843. *Annals of Cambridge, Vol. II 1547 to 1602*. Cambridge: Warwick and Co.

Craddock, P.T. & Gregory, V.L., 1973. Stiff task at Cambridge, *Rescue News* 5, 12.

Craddock, P.T. and Gregory, V.L., undated. Excavation of the graveyard of All Saints-AD-Castra, Cambridge. Unpublished typescript.

Cra'ster, M.D., 1973. Iron Age grave group from Newnham Croft, Cambridge. *Proceedings of the Cambridge Antiquarian Society* 64, 25.

Cree, J.E ., 1924. Account of the excavations on Traprain Law during the summer of 1923. *Proceedings of the Society of Antiquaries of Scotland* 58, 241–85.

Creighton, J., 1995. Visions of power: imagery and symbols in Late Iron Age Britain. *Britannia* 26, 285–301.

Crerar, B., 2016. Deviancy in Late Romano-British burial, in *The Oxford Handbook of Roman Britain*, eds. M. Millett, L. Revell & A. Moore. Oxford: Oxford University Press, 381–405.

Crew, P., 1987. Bryn y Castell hillfort: A late prehistoric ironworking settlement in north-east Wales, in *The Crafts of the Blacksmith*, eds. B.G. Scott & H. Cleere. Belfast: Ulster Museum, 91–100.

Crummy. N., 1983. *The Roman Small Finds from Excavations in Colchester 1971–9*. (Colchester Archaeological Report 3.) Colchester: Colchester Archaeological Trust.

Crummy, N., 2002. Wax spatula from Yorkshire. *Lucerna: Roman Finds Group Newsletter* 23, 6–8.

Crummy, N., 2005. From bracelets to battle-honours: military armillae from the Roman conquest of Britain, in *Image, Craft and the Classical World: essays in honour of Donald Bailey and Catherine Johns*, ed. N. Crummy. (Instrumentum Monograph 29.) Montagnac, 93–106.

Crummy, N., 2016. A hoard of military awards, jewellery, and coins from Colchester. *Britannia* 47, 1–28.

Crummy, N., Crummy, P. & Crossan, C., 1993. *Excavations of Roman and Later Cemeteries, Churches and Monastic Sites in Colchester, 1971–88*. (Colchester Archaeological Report 9.) Colchester: Colchester Archaeological Trust.

Cunliffe, B., 1975. *Excavations at Portchester Castle, Vol. 1: Roman*. (Reports of the Research Committee of the Society of Antiquaries of London 32.) London: Society of Antiquaries of London.

Dannell, G.B., Hartley, B.R., Wild, J.P. & Perrin, J.R., 1993. Excavations on a Romano-British pottery production site at Park Farm, Stanground, Peterborough, 1965–1967. *Journal of Roman Pottery Studies*, 51–93.

Darling, M., 1994. *Guidelines for the Archiving of Roman Pottery*. Study Group for Roman Pottery.

Darling, M. & Precious, B., 2014. *A Corpus of Roman Pottery from Lincoln*. Oxford: Oxbow Books.

Darwin, H., 1895. On monuments to Cambridge men at the University of Padua. *Proceedings of the Cambridge Antiquarian Society* 8, 337–47.

Davis, S.J.M. 1992. A Rapid Method for Recording Information about Mammal Bones from Archaeological Sites. London: HBMC Ancient Monuments Laboratory Report 19/92.

Davies, T., Pomeroy, E., Shaw, C. & Stock, J., 2014. Mobility and the skeleton: a biomechanical view. In *Past Mobilities: Archaeological Approaches to Movement and Mobility*, ed. J. Leary. Surrey: Ashgate Publishing Limited, 129–53.

Dawson, M., 2000. The Mesolithic interlude, in *Prehistoric, Roman and Post Roman Landscapes of the Great Ouse Valley*, ed. M. Dawson. (Council for British Archaeology Research Report 119.) York: Council for British Archaeology, 46–50.

Dawson, M., 2004. *Archaeology in the Bedford Region*. (British Archaeological Report, British Series 373/Beds. Arch. Monograph Series No. 4.) Oxford: Archaeopress.

Dawson, M., 2001. Harlington Roman cemetery. *Bedfordshire Archaeology* 24, 20–39.

Dick, W.A. & Tabatabai, M.A., 1977. An alkaline oxidation method for determination of total phosphorus in soils. *Journal of Soil Science of America* 41, 511–14.

Dickens, A., 1996a. An Archaeological Assessment at St. Edmund's College, Cambridge. Cambridge: Cambridge Archaeological Unit Report No. 161.

Dickens, A., 1996b. Archaeological Excavations at St John's College, Cambridge. Cambridge: Cambridge Archaeological Unit Report No. 175.

Dickens, A., 1999. Archaeological Investigations at the New Unilever Cambridge Centre, Union Road, Cambridge. Cambridge: Cambridge Archaeological Unit Report No. 316.

Dimbleby, G.W., 1985. *The Palynology of Archaeological Sites*. (Studies in Archaeological Science.) London: Academic Press.

Dockrill, S.J. & Simpson, I.A., 1994. The identification of Prehistoric Anthropogenic Soils in the Northern Isles Using an Integrated Sampling Methodology. *Archaeological Prospection* 1, 75–92.

Dobney, K., 2001. A place at the table: the role of vertebrate zooarchaeology within a Roman research agenda for Britain, in *Britons and Romans: Advancing an archaeological agenda*, eds. S. James & M. Millett. (Council for British Archaeology Research Report 125.) York: Council for British Archaeology, 36–45.

Dobney, K. & Reilly, K., 1988. A method for the recording of archaeological animal bones: the use of diagnostic zones. *Circaea* 5, 79–96.

Dodwell, N., 2001. Excavation of an Early/Middle Saxon Cemetery at King's Garden Hostel, Cambridge. Cambridge: Cambridge Archaeological Unit Report No. 426.

Dodwell, N., Lucy, S. & Tipper, J., 2004. Anglo-Saxons on the Cambridge Backs: the Criminology site settlement and King's Garden Hostel cemetery. *Proceedings of the Cambridge Antiquarian Society* 93, 95–124.

Doube, M., Kłosowski, M.M., Arganda-Carreras, I., Cordeliéres, F., Dougherty, R.P., Jackson, J., Schmid, B., Hutchinson, J.R. & Shefelbine. S.J., 2010. BoneJ: free and extensible bone image analysis in ImageJ. *Bone* 47, 1076–9.

Downey, R., King, A. & Soffe, G., 1980. The Hayling Island temple and religious connections across the Channel, in *Temples, Churches and Religion in Roman Britain*, ed. W. Rodwell. (British Archaeological Reports, British Series 77.) Oxford: British Archaeological Reports, 289–304.

Drazin, C., 2016, *Mapping the Past: A Search for Five Brothers at the Edge of Empire*. London: William Heinemann.

Driesch, A., von den., 1976. *A Guide to the Measurement of Animal Bones from Archaeological Sites as Developed by the Institut für Palaeoanatomie, Domestikationsforschung und Geschichte der Tiermedizin of the University of Munich.* (Peabody Museum Bulletin 1.) Cambridge, Massachusetts: Peabody Museum of Archaeology and Ethnology, Harvard University.

Driesch, A. von den & Boessneck, J., 1974. Kritische anmerkungen zur widerristhohenberechnung aus Langenmassen vor- und fruhgeschichtlicher Tierknochen. *Saugetierkundliche Mitteilungen* 22, 325–48.

Drury, P.J., 1980. Non-classical religious buildings in Iron Age and Roman Britain: a review, in *Temples, Churches and Religion in Roman Britain*, ed. W. Rodwell. (British Archaeological Reports, British Series 77.) Oxford: British Archaeological Reports, 45–78.

Edmonds, M., 2010. When they come to model Heaven: Big science and the monumental in post-war Britain. *Antiquity* 84, 774–95.

Egan, G. & Pritchard, F., 1991. *Dress Accessories, c.1150–c.1450.* (Museum of London: Medieval finds from Excavations in London 3.) London: H.M.S.O.

Ellis, P., Hughes, G., Leach, P., Mould, C. & Sterenberg, J., 1998. *Excavations alongside Roman Ermine Street, Cambridgeshire, 1996, The Archaeology of the A1 (M) Alconbury to Peterborough Road Scheme.* (British Archaeological Reports, British Series 276.) Oxford: Archaeopress.

Elsdon, S., 1982. *Parisian Ware: A study of stamped wares of the Roman period in Lincolnshire, Humberside and South Yorkshire.* (Vorda Research Series 4.) Highworth: Vorda Publications.

Eshed, V., Latimer, B., Greenwald, C.M., Jellema, L.M., Rothschild, B.M., Wish-Baratz, S. & Hershkovitz, I., 2002. Button osteoma: its etiology and pathophysiology. *American Journal of Physical Anthropology* 118, 217–30.

Esmonde Cleary, S., 2000. Putting the dead in their place: burial location in Roman Britain, in *Burial, Society and Context in the Roman World*, eds. J. Pearce, M. Millett & M. Struck. Oxford: Oxbow, 127–42.

Evans, C., 1991a. Archaeological Observations at St. John's Playing Fields, Cambridge. Cambridge: Cambridge Archaeological Unit Report No. 24.

Evans, C., 1991b. Archaeological Observations at St. John's Playing Fields, Cambridge: Part II - The Granta Network. Cambridge: Cambridge Archaeological Unit Report No. 31.

Evans C., 1993. Archaeological Investigations at New Hall, Cambridge, 1993. Cambridge: Cambridge Archaeological Unit Report No. 86.

Evans, C., 1994. Archaeological Investigations at Kettle's Yard, Cambridge. Cambridge: Cambridge Archaeological Unit Report No. 105.

Evans, C., 1996. New Hall, Cambridge. Prehistoric Land-use and Roman Hinterland Investigations: The 1994 Excavations. Cambridge: Cambridge Archaeological Unit Report No. 190.

Evans, C., 1999. Cognitive maps and narrative trails: fieldwork with the Tamu-mai/Gurung of Nepal, in *Shaping Your Landscape: The archaeology and anthropology of landscape*, eds. R. Layton & P. Ucko. London: Routledge, 439–57.

Evans, C., 2000. Megalithic Follies: Soane's 'Druidic Remains' and the display of Monuments. *Journal of Material Culture* 5, 347–66.

Evans, C., 2002. Metalwork and Cold Claylands: Pre-Iron Age occupation on the Isle of Ely, in *Through Wet and Dry: Proceedings of a conference in honour of David Hall*, eds. T. Lane, & J. Coles. (Lincolnshire Archaeology and Heritage Reports Series No. 5 and WARP Occasional Paper 17.) Sleaford: Heritage Trust of Lincolnshire, 33–53.

Evans, C., 2003. *Excavations at the Wardy Hill Ringwork, Coveney, Ely.* (East Anglian Archaeology Report No. 103.) Cambridge: Cambridge Archaeological Unit.

Evans, C., 2004. Modelling monuments and excavations, in *Models: The Third Dimension of Science*, eds. S. de Chadarevian, & N. Hopwood. Stanford, California: Stanford University Press (Writing Science Series), 109–37.

Evans, C., 2007. Delineating objects: nineteenth century antiquarian culture and the project of archaeology, in *Visions of Antiquity: The Society of Antiquaries of London 1707–2007*, ed. S. Pearce. (Archaeologia 111.) London: Society of Antiquaries of London, 266–305.

Evans, C., 2009. Small agencies and great consequences: Darwin's archaeology. *Antiquity* 83, 475–88.

Evans, C., 2012. Archaeology and repeatable experiment: a comparative agenda, in *Image, Memory and*

Monumentality: Archaeological engagements with the material world, eds. A.M Jones, J. Pollard, M.J. Allen & J. Gardiner. (Prehistoric Society Research Paper No. 5.) Oxford: Oxbow Books/The Prehistoric Society, 295–306.

Evans, C., 2013. Against narrative: reading and gauging sequences. *Landscapes* 14, 103–12.

Evans, C., 2014. Soldiering archaeology: Pitt Rivers and militarism. *Bulletin of the History of Archaeology* 24. Doi: http://doi.org/10.5334/bha.244

Evans, C., 2015. Disappearance beyond recall: a social context for Bronze Age aurochs extinction in Britain? *Proceedings of the Prehistoric Society* 81, 107–23.

Evans C., 2018. Late Iron Age and Roman. Eastern Counties Regional Research Framework (East Anglian Archaeology, issued on-line).

Evans, C., with Brudenell, M., Patten, R. & Regan, R., 2013a. *Process and History: Prehistoric Communities at Colne Fen, Earith.* (The Archaeology of the Lower Ouse Valley, Vol. I.) Cambridge: Cambridge Archaeological Unit.

Evans, C., with Appleby, G. Lucy, S. & Regan, R. 2013b. *Process and History: Romano-British Communities at Colne Fen, Earith* (The Archaeology of the Lower Ouse Valley, Vol. II.) Cambridge: Cambridge Archaeological Unit.

Evans, C., Appleby, G. & Lucy, S., with Appleby, J. & Brudenell, M., 2016 (Evans *et al.* 2016a). *Lives in Land — Mucking: Excavations by Margaret and Tom Jones 1965–78: Prehistory, Context and Summary.* Oxford: Oxbow Books/Historic England.

Evans, C. & Dickens, A., 2002. Barton Road North: Archaeological desktop assessment. Cambridge: Cambridge Archaeological Unit Report No. 486.

Evans, C., Dickens, A. & Richmond, D.A.H., 1998. Cloistered communities: archaeological and architectural investigations in Jesus College, Cambridge, 1988–97. *Proceedings of the Cambridge Antiquarian Society* 86, 91–144.

Evans, C. & Hodder, I., 2006a. *A Woodland Archaeology: The Haddenham Project* (I). Cambridge: McDonald Institute Monograph.

Evans, C. & Hodder, I., 2006b. *Marshland Communities and Cultural Landscape: The Haddenham Project* (II). Cambridge: McDonald Institute for Archaeological Research.

Evans, C. & Knight, M., 2002. A Great Circle: Investigations at Arbury Camp, Cambridge. *Proceedings of the Cambridge Antiquarian Society* 91, 23–53.

Evans, C., Knight, M. & Webley, L., 2007. Iron Age settlement and Romanization on the Isle of Ely: The Hurst Lane Reservoir site. *Proceedings of the Cambridge Antiquarian Society* 96, 41–78.

Evans, C., Legge, T., Pickles, J., Sheldon, H. & Woudhuysen, M., 2011. Dr John Amyas Alexander: 1922–2010. *Proceedings of the Cambridge Antiquarian Society* 100, 200–13.

Evans, C., Lucy, S. & Patten, R., 2018. *Riversides: Neolithic Barrows, a Beaker Grave, Iron Age and Anglo-Saxon Burials and Settlement at Trumpington, Cambridge.* (CAU Landscape Archives: New Archaeologies of the Cambridge Region Series No. 2.) Cambridge: McDonald Institute.

Evans, C. with Mackay, D. & Webley, L., 2008. *Borderlands. The Archaeology of the Addenbrooke's Environs, South Cambridge.* (CAU Landscape Archives: New Archaeologies of the Cambridge Region Series 1.) Cambridge: Cambridge Archaeological Unit. Oxford: Oxbow Books.

Evans, C. & Newman, R., 2011. An Imperial philosophical machine: the archaeology of the Cambridge observatory and Early Modern Science. *Antiquity* 85, 1369–84.

Evans, C. & Patten, R., 2011. An inland Bronze Age: Excavations at Striplands Farm, West Longstanton. *Proceedings of the Cambridge Antiquarian Society* 100, 7–45.

Evans, C., Pollard, J. & Knight, M., 1999. Life in woods: tree-throws, 'settlement' and forest cognition. *Oxford Journal of Archaeology* 18, 241–54.

Evans, C. & Standring, R., 2012. A landscape corridor: A14 improvements investigations. *Proceedings of the Cambridge Antiquarian Society* 101, 81–104.

Evans, C., with Tabor, T. & Vander Linden, M., 2016 (Evans *et al.* 2016b). *Twice-crossed River: Prehistoric and Palaeoenvironmental Investigations at Barleycroft Farm/Over, Cambridgeshire.* (CAU Landscape Archives: The Archaeology of the Lower Ouse Valley, Vol. III.) Cambridge: McDonald Institute for Archaeology.

Evans, C. & Ten Harkel, L., 2010. Roman Cambridge's early settlement and the *Via Devana*: Excavations at Castle Street. *Proceedings of the Cambridge Antiquarian Society* 99, 35–60.

Evans, C. & Williams, S., 2004. Jesus College, Cambridge: the Maintenance Workshop and Gardener's Compound site excavations. Cambridge: Cambridge Archaeological Unit Report No. 618.

Evans, J., 1987. Graffiti and the evidence of literacy and pottery use in Roman Britain. *Archaeological Journal* 144, 191–204.

Evans, J., 1990. The Cherry Hinton fine wares. *Journal of Roman Pottery Studies* 3, 18–29.

Evans, J., 1991. Some notes on the Horningsea Roman pottery. *Journal of Roman Pottery Studies* 4, 33–45.

Evans, J., 2001. Material approaches to the identification of different Romano-British site types, in *Britons and Romans: Advancing an archaeological agenda*, eds. S. James & M. Millett. (Council for British Archaeology, Research Report 125.) York: Council for British Archaeology, 26–35.

Evans, J., with Macaulay, S. & Mills, P., 2017. *The Horningsea Roman Pottery Industry in Context.* (East Anglian Archaeology Report No. 162.) Bar Hill: Oxford Archaeology East.

Evans, J.G., 1972. *Land Snails in Archaeology: with special reference to the British Isles.* (Studies in Archaeological Science.) London; New York: Seminar Press.

Evison, V.I., 1981. Distribution maps and England in the first two phases, in *Angles, Saxons, and Jutes: Essays presented to J.N.L Myres*, ed. V.I. Evison. Oxford: Clarendon Press, 126–50.

Evison, V.I., 1987. *Dover: The Buckland Anglo-Saxon cemetery.* (English Heritage Archaeological Report 3.) London: Historic Buildings and Monuments Commission for England.

Farwell D. & Molleson, T., 1993. *Excavations at Poundbury Vol. 2: Cemeteries.* (Dorset Natural History and Archaeological Society Monograph Series 11.) Dorchester: Dorset Natural History and Archaeological Society.

Fell, C., 1956. Roman burials at Arbury Road, Cambridge, 1952. *Proceedings of the Cambridge Antiquarian Society* 49, 13–23.

Feugère, M., 1995. Les spatules à cire à manche figure, in *Provinzialrömische Forschungen. Festschrift für Gunter Ulbert zum 65 Geburtstag*, ed. by W Czysz *et al.* (Veröffentlichung des Archäologischen Forschungszentrums Ingolstadt.) Espelkamp: Verlag M. Leidorf.

Fincham, G., 2002. *Landscapes of Imperialism: Roman and native interaction in the East Anglian Fenland.* (British Archaeological Reports British Series 338.). Oxford: Archaeopress.

Fletcher, R., 1984. Identifying spatial disorder: a case study on a Mongol fort, in *Intrasite Spatial Analysis in Archaeology*, ed. H.F. Hietala. Cambridge: Cambridge University Press, 196–223.

Ford, S., Bradley, R. Hawkes, J. & Fisher. P., 1984. Flint-working in the metal age. *Oxford Journal of Archaeology* 3, 158–73.

Fowler, E., 1960. The origins and development of the penannular brooch in Europe. *Proceedings of the Prehistoric Society* 26, 149–77.

Fowler, E., 1963. Celtic metalwork in the fifth and sixth centuries AD: a re-appraisal. *Archaeological Journal* 120, 98–160.

Fowler, E., 1984. Silver proto hand-pin, in Tripontium, third interim report, by J. Lucas in *Transactions of Birmingham Warwickshire Archaeological Society* 91, 25–54.

Fox, C., 1923. *The Archaeology of the Cambridge Region*. Cambridge: Cambridge University Press.

French, C.A.I., 1994. *The Archaeology along the A605 Elton-Haddon Bypass, Cambridgeshire*. Peterborough and Cambridge: Fenland Archaeological Trust and Cambridgeshire County Council.

French, C. A. I., 1998. Welland Bank Quarry: Micromorphological analyses of the buried soil. Unpublished report, Heritage Lincolnshire.

French, C.A.I. & Kousoulakou, M., 1997. The micromorphological analysis of the dry valley sequence at Landwade Road, Fordham. Unpublished report. Cambs. County Council Archaeological Field Unit.

Fulford, M.G., 2001. Links with the past: pervasive 'ritual' behaviour in Roman Britain. *Britannia* 32, 199–218.

Fulford, M., Clarke, A., Eckardt, H. & Shaffrey, R., 2011. Victorian excavation methodology: the Society of Antiquaries at Silchester in 1893. *Antiquaries Journal* 92, 285–306.

Fulford, M. & Holbrook, N., 2018. Relevant beyond the Roman Period: approaches to the investigation, analysis and dissemination of archaeological investigations of rural settlements and landscapes of Roman Britain. *Archaeological Journal* 175, 214–30.

Furlan, G., 2017. When absence means things are going well: Waste disposal in Roman towns and its impact on the record as observed in Aquileia. *European Journal of Archaeology* 20, 317–45.

Gaffney, V.L., White R.H. & Goodchild, H., 2007. *Wroxeter, the Cornovii and the Urban Process*. (Journal of Roman Archaeology Supplementary Series 68.) Portsmouth, Rhode Island: Journal of Roman Archaeology.

Gale, R., 2008. Charcoal, in *Farming on the Edge: Archaeological evidence from the clay uplands to the West of Cambridge*, by J. Abrams & D. Ingham. (East Anglian Archaeology Report No. 123.) Bedford: Albion Archaeology, Appendix 16.

Gale, R., 2009. Charcoal, in *Cambourne New Settlement. Iron Age and Romano-British settlement on the clay uplands of West Cambridgeshire*, by J. Wright, M. Leivers, R. Seager Smith & C. Stevens. Salisbury: Wessex Archaeology Ltd, Ecofacts Appendix (Vol. 2).

Galloway P., 1979. The combs, in *Pre-Roman and Roman Winchester Part II, The Roman Cemetery at Lankhills*, by G. Clarke. Oxford: Oxford University Press, 246.

Gamble, C., 2007. *Origins and Revolutions*. Cambridge: Cambridge University Press.

Gardner, A., 2013. Thinking about Roman Imperialism: Postcolonialism, globalisation and beyond. *Britannia* 44, 1–25.

Garrard, I.P., 1995. Other objects of copper-alloy and silver, in *Excavations in the Marlow Car Park and Surrounding Areas*, by K. Blockley, M. Blockley, P. Blockley, S.S. Frere & S. Stow. (Archaeology of Canterbury 5.) Canterbury: Canterbury Archaeological Trust, 1005–62.

Gautier-Dalché, P., 2003. The Medieval and Renaissance transmission of the *Tabula Peutingeriana* (trans. W.L. North), in *Tabula Peutingeriana. Le Antich Vie Del Mondo*. Florence: Leo. S. Oslchki, 43–52.

Gdaniec, K., 1991. Archaeological Investigations in the Grove Development Area, Fitzwilliam College. Cambridge: Cambridge Archaeological Unit Report No. 5.

Gdaniec, K., 1992. Archaeological Investigations at Burrell's Field, Trinity College Cambridge. Cambridge: Cambridge Archaeological Unit Report No. 66.

Gell, A., 1985. How to read a map: remarks on the practical logic of navigation. *Man* 20, 271–86.

Gerrard, J., 2015a. New radiocarbon dates from Lynch Farm Romano-British cemetery, near Peterborough. *Northamptonshire Archaeology* 38, 241–43.

Gerrard, J., 2015b. Synthesis, Chronology and "Late Roman" cemeteries in Britain. *American Journal of Archaeology* 119, 565–72.

Getty, R., 1975. *Sisson & Grossman's The Anatomy of Domestic Animals*. London: W.B. Saunders Company.

Gibson, D., 1996. An Archaeological Evaluation at the Western Bookstack Range, University Library, Cambridge. Cambridge: Cambridge Archaeological Unit Report No. 172.

Gibson, D. & Lucas, G., 2002. Pre-Flavian kilns at Greenhouse Farm and the social context of Early Roman pottery production in Cambridgeshire. *Britannia* 33, 95–127.

Gijn, van A.L., 2007. A functional analysis of some lithic implements from Sites A and J, in *Prehistoric Coastal Communities: the Mesolithic in Western Britain*, eds. M. Bell. (Council for British Archaeology Report 149.) York: Council for British Archaeology, 117–21.

Gilgen, A., Wilkenskjeld, S., Kaplan, J.O., Kühn, T. & Lohmann, U., 2019. Did the Roman Empire affect European climate? A new look at the effects of land use and anthropogenic aerosol emissions, *Climate of the Past*, https://doi.org/10.5194/cp-2019-56

Going, C.J., 1987. *The Mansio and Other Sites in the South East Sector of Caesaromagus: The Roman pottery*. (Chelmsford

Archaeological Trust Report 3.2.) Chelmsford Archaeological Trust/Council for British Archaeology.

Going, C.J., 1992. Economic long waves in the Roman era? A reconnaissance of the Romano-British ceramic evidence. *Oxford Journal of Archaeology* 11, 98–117.

Going, C.J. & Ford, B., 1988. The Romano-British Pottery, in *Excavations at Great Dunmow, Essex: A small town in the Trinovantian Civitas,* by N.P. Wickenden. (East Anglian Archaeology Report No. 41.) Chelmsford: Archaeology Section, Essex County Council & Chelmsford Archaeological Trust, 61–77.

Goodall, A.R., 1984. Objects of non-ferrous metal in *Medieval and Post-medieval finds from Exeter, 1971–80* by J.P. Allan. (Exeter Archaeological Reports 3.) Exeter: Exeter City Council, 337–48.

Gosden, C., 2005. What do objects want? *Journal of Archaeological Method and Theory* 12, 193–211.

Gowland, R., 2001. Playing dead: implications of mortuary evidence for the social construction of childhood in Roman Britain, in *Theoretical Roman Archaeological Conference 2000: Proceedings of the Tenth Annual Theoretical Roman Archaeology Conference held at the Instiute of Archaeology, University College London,* eds. G. Davies, A. Gardner & K. Lockyear. Oxford: Oxbow, 152–68.

Graham, S., 2016. Archaeological Excavation at the Woolf Institute, Westminster College, Cambridge. Bar Hill: Oxford Archaeology East Report 1809.

Graham, S., with Lyons, A., 2018. A Roman extra-mural settlement at the Woolf Institute, Westminster College, Cambridge. *Proceedings of the Cambridge Antiquarian Society* 107, 31–40.

Graham-Campbell, J., 1968. The School of Pythagoras (Merton Hall). *The Eagle* 62, 243–53.

Grant, A., 1982. The use of tooth as a guide to the age of domestic ungulates, in *Ageing and Sexing of Animal Bones from Archaeological Sites*, eds. B. Wilson, C. Grigson & S. Payne. (British Archaeological Reports, British Series 109.) Oxford: British Archaeological Report, 91–108.

Green, F.J., 1985. Evidence for domestic cereal use at Maxey, in *The Fenland Project, No. 1: Archaeology and Environment in the Lower Welland Valley. Vol. 1.*, by F. Pryor & C. French. (East Anglian Archaeology Report No. 27.) Cambridge: Cambridgeshire Archaeological Committee, 224–32.

Green, H.J.M., 1954. Roman pottery kiln at Earith. *Proceedings of the Cambridge Antiquarian Society* 48, 44–6.

Green, H.J.M., 1960. Roman Godmanchester. *Proceedings of the Cambridge Antiquarian Society* 53, 8–22.

Green, H.J.M., 1975. Roman Godmanchester, in *Small Towns of Roman Britain: Papers presented to a conference, Oxford 1975*, eds. W. Rodwell & T. Rowley. (British Archaeological Reports 15.) Oxford: British Archaeological Reports, 183–210.

Green, H.J.M., 1978. A villa estate at Godmanchester, in *Studies in the Romano-British Villa*, ed. M. Todd. Leicester: Leicester University Press, 103–116.

Green, H.J.M. (ed. T. Malim), 2018. *Durovigutum: Roman Godmanchester*. (Archaeopress Roman Archaeology 33.) Oxford: Archaeopress.

Greene, K., 1978. A guide to imported fine wares in Britain to AD 250, in *Early Fine Wares in Roman Britain*, eds. P. Arthur & G. Marsh. (British Archaeological Reports 57.) Oxford: British Archaeological Reports, 15–30.

Greenfield, E., 1963. The Romano-British shrines at Brigstock, Northamptonshire. *Antiquaries Journal* 43, 228–63.

Greep, S., 1995. Objects of bone, antler and ivory from C.A.T. sites, in *Excavations in the Marlow Car Park and Surrounding Areas,* by K. Blockley, M. Blockley, P. Blockley, S. S. Frere & S. Stow. (Archaeology of Canterbury 5.) Canterbury: Canterbury Archaeological Trust, 1112–52.

Greig, J.R.A., 1982. The interpretation of pollen spectra from urban archaeological deposits, in *Environmental Archaeology in the Urban Context*, eds. A. Hall & H. Kenward. (Council for British Archaeology Research Report 43.) London: Council for British Archaeology, 47–65.

Greig, J.R.A., 1991. The British Isles, in *Progress in Old World Palaeoethnobotany: A retrospective view on the occasion of 20 years of the International Work Group for Palaeoethnobotany,* eds. W. Van Zeist & W.A. Casparie. Rotterdam: Balkema, 229–334.

Grimm, J.M., 2010. A bird for all occasions: the use of birds at the Romano-British sanctuary of Springhead, Kent (UK), in *Birds in Archaeology*, eds. W. Prummel, J.T. Zeiler & D.C. Brinkhuizen. Groningen: Barkhuis and Groningen Institute of Archaeology, 189–95.

Grove, R., 1976. Coprolite mining in Cambridgeshire. *The Agricultural History Review*, 24, 36–43.

Guido, M., 1978. *The Glass Beads of the Prehistoric and Roman Periods in Britain and Ireland.* (Reports of the Research Committee of the Society of Antiquaries of London 35.) London: Society of Antiquaries of London.

Guillebaud, P., 2006. Changes in the landscape of West Cambridge after Enclosure 1805–1870. *Proceedings of the Cambridge Antiquarian Society* 95, 159–70.

Guillebaud, P., 2007. West Cambridge 1870–1914: building the bicycle suburb. *Proceedings of the Cambridge Antiquarian Society* 96, 193–210.

Guillebaud, P., 2008. West Cambridge: the two World Wars and the interwar lull. *Proceedings of the Cambridge Antiquarian Society* 97, 179–93.

Hadman, J., 1978. Aisled buildings in Roman Britain, in *Studies in the Romano-British Villa*, ed. by M. Todd. Leicester: Leicester University Press, 187–94.

Haigh, D., 1975. A Correlation between the Archaeological Sites and Field Names: A survey of parishes along the line of the northern and western by-passes of Cambridge. Cambridge Collection (Unpublished document).

Haigh, D., 1995. *Baillie Scott: the Artistic House*. Chichester: Academy Editions.

Halkon, P. & Millett, M., 1999. *Rural Settlement and Industry: Studies in the Iron Age and Roman archaeology of lowland East Yorkshire*. Leeds: Yorkshire Archaeological Society and East Riding Archaeological Society.

Halkon, P., Millett, M. & Woodhouse, H. (eds.), 2015. *Hayton, East Yorkshire: Archaeological studies of the Iron Age and Roman landscapes*. (Yorkshire Archaeological Report 7.) Leeds: Yorkshire Archaeological Society.

Hall, C.P. & Ravensdale, J.R., 1976. *The West Fields of Cambridge*. (Cambridge Antiquarian Records Society 3.) Cambridge: Cambridge Antiquarian Records Society.

Hall, D., 1996. *Fenland Project 10: Cambridgeshire Survey, Isle of Ely and Wisbech.* (East Anglian Archaeology Report No. 79.) Norwich: Cambridgeshire Archaeological Committee.

Halstead, P., 1985. A study of mandibular teeth from Romano-British contexts in Maxey, in *Archaeology and Environment in the Lower Welland Valley,* by F. Pryor. (East Anglian Archaeology Report No. 27.) Cambridge: Cambridgeshire Archaeological Committee, 219–24.

Hanf, M., 1983. *The Arable Weeds of Europe: With their seedlings and seeds.* Hadleigh: BASF United Kingdom.

Harcourt, R.A., 1974. The dog in Prehistoric and early Historic Britain. *Journal of Archaeological Science* 1, 151–76.

Harding, J. & Healy, F., 2007. *A Neolithic and Bronze Age Landscape in Northamptonshire. The Raunds Area Project.* (English Heritage & Archaeology Data Service.) Swindon: English Heritage.

Hartley, B.R., 1960. Notes on pottery from some Roman kilns in the Cambridge area. *Proceedings of the Cambridge Antiquarian Society* 53, 23–8.

Hartley, B.R. & Standen, E., 1959. A group of Romano-British Pottery with an Owner's Mark. *Proceedings of the Cambridge Antiquarian Society* 52, 21–2.

Harward, C., Powers, N. & Watson, S., 2015. *The Upper Walbrook Valley Cemetery of Roman London: Excavations at Finsbury Circus, City of London, 1987–2007.* (Museum of London Archaeology Monograph 69.) London: Museum of London.

Hattatt, R., 1987. *Brooches of Antiquity: A third selection of brooches from the author's collection.* Oxford: Oxbow.

Hatton, R.A., 1999. The Cemeteries in Roman Britain: Evidence for Management and Related Social Implications, with particular reference to the Late Roman Period. Unpublished PhD thesis, University of Sheffield.

Hawkes, C.F.C. & Hull, M.R., 1947. *Camulodunum: First report on the excavations at Colchester, 1930–1939.* (Reports of the Research Committee of the Society of Antiquaries of London 14.) Oxford: Oxford University Press.

Hawkes, S.C. & Dunning, G.C., 1962. Soldiers and settlers in Britain, fourth to fifth century. *Medieval Archaeology* 5, 1–70.

Hayes, J., 1978. Fengate pottery. *Durobrivae* 6, 12–13.

Henig, M. & Paddock, J.M., 1993. Metal figurines in the Corinium Museum, Cirencester. *Transactions of Bristol Gloucestershire Archaeological Society* 111, 85–93.

Hill, J.D., 1996. The identification of ritual deposits of animals: a general perspective from a specific study of 'special animal deposits' from the southern English Iron Age, in *Ritual Treatment of Human and Animal Remains,* eds. S. Anderson & K. Boyle. Oxford: Oxbow Books, 17–32.

Hill, J.D., Evans, C. & Alexander, M., 1999. The Hinxton Rings — A Late Iron Age cemetery at Hinxton, Cambridgeshire, with a reconsideration of northern Aylesford-Swarling distributions. *Proceedings of the Prehistoric Society* 65, 243–74.

Hill, J.D. & Braddock, P., 2006. The Iron Age pottery, in *Marshland Communities and Cultural Landscapes: The Haddenham Project* (II), by C. Evans & I. Hodder. Cambridge: McDonald Institute for Archaeological Research, 152–94.

Hill, J.D. & Horne, L., 2003. Iron Age and Early Roman pottery, in *Power and Island Communities: Excavations at the Wardy Hill Ringwork, Coveney, Ely,* by C. Evans (East Anglian Archaeology Report No. 103.) Cambridge: Cambridge Archaeological Unit, 145–84.

Hillman, G., 1981. Reconstructing crop husbandry practices from charred remains of crops, in *Farming Practice in British Prehistory,* ed. R. Mercer. Edinburgh: Edinburgh. University Press, 123–62.

Hillman, G., 1984. Interpretation of archaeological plant remains: the application of ethnographic models from Turkey in *Plants and Ancient Man: Studies in Paleoethnobotany,* eds. W. Van Zeist & W.A. Casparie. Rotterdam: Balkema, 1–41.

Hills, C., 2010. *Dorothy Garrod and the Skeletons in the Garden.* Cambridge: Newnham College.

Hillson, S.W., 1979. Diet and dental disease. *World Archaeology* 2, 147–62.

Hinchcliffe, J. & Sparey-Green, C., 1985. *Excavations at Brancaster 1974 & 1977.* (East Anglian Archaeology Report No. 23.) Gressenhall: Norfolk Archaeological Unit, Norfolk Museums Service.

Hinman, M., 2003. *A Late Iron Age Farmstead and Romano-British Site at Haddon, Peterborough.* (British Archaeological Reports, British Series 358.) Oxford: John and Erica Hedges.

Hinman, M. & Zant, J., 2018. *Conquering the Claylands: Excavations at Love's Farm, St Neots, Cambridgeshire.* (East Anglian Archaeology Report No. 165.) Bar Hill: Oxford Archaeology East.

Hinton, D.A., 1990. Metal finger-rings, in *Object and Economy in Medieval Winchester,* by M. Biddle (Winchester Studies 7.) Oxford: Oxford University Press, 646–52.

Hodge, C.A.H. & Seale, R., 1966. *The Soils of the District around Cambridge.* Harpenden: Memoir of the Soil Survey of Great Britain.

Hollingworth, E.J. & O'Reilly, M.M., 1925. *The Anglo-Saxon Cemetery at Girton College, Cambridge.* Cambridge: Cambridge University Press.

Hooley, D., 2001. Copper alloy and silver objects, in *The Romano-British 'Small Town' at Wanborough, Wiltshire: Excavations, 1966–1976,* by A.S. Anderson, J.S. Wacher & A.P. Fitzpatrick. (Britannia Monograph Series 19.) London: Society for the Promotion of Roman Studies, 75–116.

Hopkin, D., 2014. *The Inn Signs of Richard Hopkins Leach.* Cambridge: Museum of Cambridge.

Horton, S., 2001. Jet and shale objects, in *The Romano-British 'Small Town' at Wanborough, Wiltshire* by A.S. Anderson, J.S. Wacher & A.P. Fitzpatrick. (Britannia Monograph Series 19.) London: Society for the Promotion of Roman Studies, 148–52.

Horton, W., Lucas, G. & Wait, G.A., 1995. Excavation of a Roman Site near Wimpole, Cambs., 1989. *Proceedings of the Cambridge Antiquarian Society* 83, 48–60.

Howe, M., Perrin, J.R. & Mackreth, D., 1980. *Roman Pottery from the Nene Valley: A guide.* (Occasional Papers, Peterborough City Museum 2.) Peterborough: City Museum and Art Gallery.

Hughes, T. Mck., 1893. On the Castle Hill, Cambridge. *Proceedings of the Cambridge Antiquarian Society* 8, 173–212.

Hughes, T. McK., 1898. Further observations on the ditches round Cambridge with special reference to the adjoining ground. *Proceedings of the Cambridge Antiquarian Society* 9, 370–84.

Hughes, T. Mck., 1903a. A potter's field near Jesus College. *Proceedings of the Cambridge Antiquarian Society* 10, 194–6.

Hughes, T. McK., 1903b. On the potter's field at Horningsea, with a comparative notice on the kilns and furnaces found in the neighbourhood. *Proceedings of the Cambridge Antiquarian Society* 10, 174–94.

Hughes, T. McK., 1904. The War Ditches, near Cherry Hinton, Cambridge. *Proceedings of the Cambridge Antiquarian Society* 10, 452-81.

Hughes, T. McK., 1907a. On the superficial deposits under Cambridge, and their influence upon the distribution of the colleges. *Proceedings of the Cambridge Antiquarian Society* 5, 393–423.

Hughes, T. McK., 1907b. On a skeleton found near the Observatory, Cambridge. *Proceedings of the Cambridge Antiquarian Society* 5, 390–91.

Hull, M.R. & Hawkes, C.F.C. 1987. *Corpus of Ancient Brooches in Britain: Pre-Roman bow brooches*. (British Archaeological Reports, British Series 168.) Oxford: British Archaeological Reports.

Hull, M.R., nd. Brooches from pre-Roman and Roman Britain (ed. G. Simpson, N. Crummy & B. Blance). Unpublished volume.

Huss-Ashmore, R., Goodman, A.H. & Armelagos, G.J., 1982. Nutritional inference from paleopathology. *Advances in Archaeological Method and Theory* (5), ed. M.B. Schiffer. New York: Academic Press, 395–474.

Hutton, J., 2009a. Orchard Court, Murray Edwards College, Cambridge: an archaeological investigation. Cambridge: Cambridge Archaeological Unit Report No. 901.

Hutton, J., 2009b. School of Veterinary Medicine, West Cambridge: an archaeological evaluation. Cambridge: Cambridge Archaeological Unit Report No. 902.

Ingham, D., Oetgen, J. and Slowikowski, A., 2016. *Newnham: A Roman bath house and estate centre east of Bedford.* (East Anglian Archaeology Report No. 158.) Bedford: Albion Archaeology.

Iscan M., Loth R., Wright R., 1984. Age Estimation from the Rib by Phase Analysis: White Males. *Journal of Forensic Sciences* 29, 1094–1104.

Isings, C., 1957. *Roman Glass from Dated Finds*. Groningen: Archaeologica Traiectina.

Isserlin, R.M., 1997. Thinking the unthinkable: human sacrifice in Roman Britain? *Theoretical Roman Archaeological Conference 96*, eds. K. Meadows, C. Lemke & J. Heron. Oxford: Oxbow, 91–112.

Jackson, R.P., & Potter, T.W., 1996. *Excavations at Stonea, Cambridgeshire, 1980–85*. London: British Museum Press.

Jacobi, R., 1978. The Mesolithic of Sussex, in *Archaeology in Sussex to AD 1500,* ed P.L. Drewett. (Council for British Archaeology Research Report 29.) London: Council for British Archaeology, 15–22.

J.H.R. & A.J.P., 1928. International Geographical Congress, Cambridge, 1928. *The Geographical Journal* 72, 259–67.

James, S., 2001. Soldiers and civilians: identity and interaction in Roman Britain, in *Britons and Roman: Advancing an archaeological agenda*, eds. S. James & M. Millett. (Council for British Archaeology, Research Report 125.) York: Council for British Archaeology, 77–89.

Johns, C., 1974. A Roman silver pin from Oldcroft, Gloucestershire. *Antiquaries Journal* 54, 295–7.

Johns, C., 1996. *The Jewellery of Roman Britain: Celtic and Classical traditions.* London: UCL Press.

Jones, A., 2003. *Settlement, Burial and Industry in Roman Godmanchester*. (British Archaeological Reports British Series 346.) Oxford: Oxbow Books.

Jones, G., 1984. Interpretation of archaeological plant remains: ethnographic models from Greece, in *Plants and Ancient Man: Studies in Palaeoethnobotany*, eds. W. van Zeist, & W.A. Casparie. Rotterdam: A. A. Balkema, 43–61.

Jones, M., 1981. The development of crop husbandry, in *The Environment of Man: The Iron Age to the Anglo-Saxon period,* eds. M. Jones & G.W. Dimbleby. (British Archaeological Reports British Series 87.) Oxford: British Archaeological Reports, 95–127.

Jones, M., 1984. The plant remains, in *Danebury: an Iron Age hillfort in Hampshire* (Vol. 1), by B.W. Cunliffe. (Council for British Archaeology Research Report 52.) London: Council for British Archaeology, 483–95.

Jones, M., 1991. Food production and consumption, in *Roman Britain: Recent Trends*, ed. R.F.J. Jones. Sheffield: Sheffield University, 21–8.

Jones, M.J., Stocker, D. & Vince, A., 2003. *The City by the Pool: Assessing the archaeology of the City of Lincoln*. (Lincoln Archaeological Studies No. 10.) Oxford: Oxbow Books.

Jones, R.F.J., 1975. The Romano-British farmstead and its cemetery at Lynch Farm, near Peterborough. *Northamptonshire Archaeology*, 10, 94–137.

Jones, R., 2004. Signatures in the soil: the use of pottery in manure scatters in the identification of Medieval arable farming regimes. *Archaeological Journal* 161, 159–88.

Jongerius, A., 1983. The role of micromorphology in agricultural research, in *Soil Micromorphology*, eds. P. Bullock & C.P. Murphy. (Proceedings of International Working Meeting on Soil Micromorphology). Berkhamsted: AB Academic, 111–38.

Jorgensen, L., Storgaard, B. & Gebauer, L. (eds.), 2003. *The Spoils of Victory: The North in the shadow of the Roman Empire.* Copenhagen: National Museum.

Jundi, S. & Hill, J.D., 1998. Brooches and identities in first century AD Britain: more than meets the eye?, in *TRAC 97: Proceedings of the Seventh Annual Theoretical Roman Archaeology Conference, Nottingham 1997*, eds. D. Forcey, J. Hawthorne & R. Witcher. Oxford: Oxbow Books, 125–37.

Kanchan, T., Mohan Kumar, T., Pradeep Kumar, G. & Yoganarasimha, K., 2008. Skeletal asymmetry. *Journal of Forensic and Legal Medicine* 15, 177–9.

Kannus, P., Haapasalo, H., Sankelo, M., Sievänen, H., Pasanen, M., Heinonen, A., Oja, P. & Vuori, I., 1995. Effect of starting age of physical activity on bone mass in the dominant arm of tennis and squash players. *Annals of Internal Medicine* 123, 27–31.

Kennedy, K.A.R., 1989. Skeletal markers of occupational stress, in *Reconstruction of Life from the Skeleton,* eds.

M.Y. Iscan & K.A.R. Kennedy. New York: Alan. R. Liss Inc., 129–60.

Keppie, L.J.F., Fitzpatrick, A.P., Hassall, M.W.C., Tomlin, R.S.O. & Burnham, B.C., 2001. Roman Britain in 2000. *Britannia* 32, 311–85.

Kilbride-Jones, H.E., 1936. A bronze hanging-bowl from Castle Tioram, Moidart: and a suggested absolute chronology for British hanging-bowls. *Proceedings of the Society of Antiquaries of Scotland* 70, 206–47.

Kilbride-Jones, H.E., 1980. *Celtic Craftsmanship in Bronze.* London: Croom Helm.

King, A., 1978. A comparative survey of bone assemblages from Roman sites in Britain. *Bulletin of the Institute of Archaeology* 15, 207–32.

King, A., 1991. Food production and consumption – meat, in *Britain in the Roman period: Recent Trends*, ed. R.F.J Jones. Sheffield: J.R. Collis, 15–20.

King, J., 1996. The animal bones, in *Orton Hall Farm: a Roman and Early Anglo-Saxon farmstead*, by D.F. Mackreth. (East Anglian Archaeology, Report No. 76.) Manchester: Nene Valley Archaeological Trust, 216–18.

Kirk, J.R., 1949. Bronzes from Woodeaton, Oxon. *Oxoniensia* 14, 1–45.

Kirk, J.R., & Leeds, E.T. 1953 Three Anglo-Saxon graves from Dorchester Oxon. *Oxoniensia*, 17/18, 63–76.

Knight, M. & Brudenell, M., forthcoming. *Excavations at King's Dyke, Bradley Fen, Whittlesey*. Cambridge: McDonald Institute Monograph.

Knocker, G.M., 1965. Collyweston Great Wood, Northants. *Archaeological Journal* 142, 52–72.

Koller, D., Trimble, J., Najbjerg, T., Gelfand, N. & Levoy, M., 2005. Fragments of the City: Stanford's Digital Forma Urbis Romae Project. *Proceedings of the Third Williams Symposium on Classical Architecture.* (Journal of Roman Archaeology Supplement 61.) 237–52.

Kuhn, J.M.M., Jakobsson, M., & Gunther, T., 2018. Estimating genetic kin relationships in prehistoric populations. PLoS ONE. 13.

Ladocha, J. & Muldowney, L., 2014. Archaeological Trial Trench Evaluation and Archaeological Monitoring at the former Star Service Station, Huntingdon Road, Cambridge. Museum of London Archaeology Report No. 14/141.

Lamdin-Whymark, H., 2008. *The Residue of Ritualised Action: Neolithic deposition practices in the Middle Thames Valley*. (British Archaeological Reports British Series 466.) Oxford: Archaeopress.

Lawson, A.J., 1976. Shale and jet objects from Silchester. *Archaeologia* 105, 241–75.

Lawson, A.J., Martin, E. and Priddy, D., 1981. *The Barrows of East Anglia.* (East Anglian Archaeology Report No. 12.) Gressenhall: Norfolk Museums Service, Suffolk County Council and Essex County Council.

Legge, A., Williams, J. & Williams, P., 2000. Lambs to the slaughter: sacrifice at two Roman temples in southern England, in *Animal Bones, Human Societies*, ed. P. Rowley-Conwy. Oxford: Oxbow, 152–7.

Lethbridge, T.C., 1954. Burial of an Iron Age warrior at Snailwell. *Proceedings of the Cambridge Antiquarian Society* 47, 25–38.

Levine, MA., 1982. The use of crown height measurements and eruption wear sequences to age horse teeth in *Ageing and Sexing Animal Bones from Archaeological Sites*, eds. B. Wilson, C. Grigson & S. Payne. (British Archaeological Report, British Series 109.) Oxford: British Archaeological Reports, 223–50.

Lévi-Strauss, C., 1969. *The Elementary Structures of Kinship.* Boston: Beacon Press.

Lewis, C., Ranson, C. & Collins, M., 2013. Archaeological Excavations at Ridley Hall, Cambridge, 2012. Cambridge: Access Cambridge Archaeology Report.

Lewis, H.A., 1998. A Methodological Study of the Micromorphological Characteristics produced by Tillage. Unpublished PhD thesis, Department of Archaeology, University of Cambridge.

Ligit, L. de, 1993. *Fairs and Markets in the Roman Empire: Economic and social aspects of periodic trade in a pre-industrial society*. Amsterdam: J.C. Gieben.

Liller, W., 1966. 'The Roman Road out of Cambridge leading to St Neots', in Edwards, A.R., Liller, W., Tebbutt, C.F. & Rudd, G., Archaeological Notes. *Proceedings of the Cambridge Antiquarian Society* 59, 135–41.

Linduff, K., 1979. Epona: A Celt among the Romans. *Latomus* 38, 817–37.

Lisboa, I.M.G., 1994. Archaeological Desk-top: King's Hedges School. Cameron Road, Cambridge. Oxford: Tempus Reparatum.

Liversidge, J., 1977. Roman burials in the Cambridge area. *Proceedings of the Cambridge Antiquarian Society* 67, 11–38.

Lloyd-Morgan, G., 1977a. Mirrors in Roman Britain, in *Roman Life and Art in Britain*, eds. J. Munby & M. Henig. (British Archaeological Reports, British Series 41.) Oxford: Oxbow, 231–52.

Lloyd-Morgan, G., 1977b. Mirrors in Roman Chester. *Journal of Chester Archaeological Society* 60, 49–55.

Lloyd-Morgan, G., 1981. Description of the collections in the Rijksmuseum G M Kam at Nijmegen, IX: The mirrors. *The Antiquaries Journal 63*, 431–2.

Lloyd-Morgan, G., 1992. 'The finds', in Excavations in Neath, by A.G. Marvell & B. Heywood. *Bulletin of the Board of Celtic Studies* 39, 171–298.

Lloyd-Morgan, G., 2000. 'Note on a mirror fragment', in Catalogue of the illustrated small finds, in *The Roman Baths and Macellum at Wroxeter: Excavations by Graham Webster, 1955–85*, ed. by P. Ellis. (English Heritage, Archaeological Report 9.) London: English Heritage, 129.

Lloyd-Morgan, G, with Crummy, N., 2010, 'The Roman mirror', in Roman Billericay: excavations by the Billericay Archaeological and Historical Society 1970–77, by M. Medlycott, S. Weller and P. Benians. *Essex Archaeology and History* 1 (4th Series), 70–2.

Lodwick, L., 2017. Arable farming, plant foods and resources, in *The Rural Economy of Roman Britain* by M. Allen, L. Lodwick, T. Brindle, M. Fulford & A. Smith. (Britannia Monographs 30.) London: The Society for the Promotion of Roman Studies, 11–84.

Lombardi, P., 2015. *Short Stirling: The First of the RAF Heavy Bombers*. Croydon: Fonthill.

Longworth, I.H., Ellison, A. & Rigby, V., 1988. *Excavations at Grimes Graves, Norfolk, 1972–1976. Fasc.2: The Neolithic, Bronze Age and later pottery*. London: British Museum Publications.

Lovejoy, C., Burstein, A. & Heiple, K., 1976. The biomechanical analysis of bone strength: a method and its application to Platycnemia. *American Journal of Physical Anthropology* 44, 489–505.

Lovejoy, C., Meindl, R., Pryzbeck, T. & Mensforth, R., 1985. Chronological Metamorphosis of the Auricular Surface of the Ilium: A New Method for the Determination of Adult Skeletal Age at Death. *American Journal of Physical Anthropology*, 68, 15–28.

Lowther, A.W.G., 1937. Report on excavations at Verulamium in 1934. *Antiquaries Journal* 17, 28–55.

Lucas, G., 1995. 'The pottery from the excavations of the Roman site at Wimpole, Cambs., 1989', in Excavations of a Roman site near Wimpole, Cambs., 1989, by W. Horton, G. Lucas & G.A. Wait. *Proceedings of the Cambridge Antiquarian Society* 83, 48–60.

Lucas, G., 1997. Prehistoric, Roman and post Roman pottery, in *The Archaeology of the St. Neots to Duxford Gas Pipeline*, eds. J. Price, I.P. Brooks & D.J. Maynard. (British Archaeological Reports, British Series 255.) Oxford: Oxbow, 48–88.

Lucas, G., 1999a. Roman Pottery Production in Cambridgeshire. Report to CUMAA/Crowther-Benyon Fund.

Lucas, G., 1999b. Archaeological Investigations at Buckingham House, New Hall, Cambridge. Cambridge: Cambridge Archaeological Unit Report No. 305.

Lucas, G., 2000. Archaeological Evaluation at the West Cambridge Stable Block Site. Cambridge: Cambridge Archaeological Unit Report No. 348.

Lucas, G., 2001. An Archaeological Evaluation along the Marconi Access Route and Future Nano-Fabrication Building. Cambridge: Cambridge Archaeological Unit Report No. 440.

Lucas, G., 2002. Disposability and dispossession in the twentieth century. *Journal of Material Culture* 7, 5–22.

Lucas, G., 2005. *The Archaeology of Time*. London: Routledge.

Lucas, G., 2012. *Understanding the Archaeological Record*. Cambridge: Cambridge University Press.

Lucas, G. & Regan, R., 2003. The changing vernacular: archaeological excavations at Temple End, High Wycombe, Buckinghamshire. *Post-Medieval Archaeology* 37,165–207.

Lucas, G. & Whittaker, P., 2001. Vicar's Farm, Cambridge Post-Excavation Assessment Report. Volumes 1 & 2. Cambridge: Cambridge Archaeological Unit Report No. 425.

Luckacher, B., 2006. *Joseph Gandy: An Architectural Visionary in Georgian England*. London: Thames & Hudson.

Lucy, S. & Evans, C., with Jefferies, R., Appleby, G. & Going, C., 2016. *The Romano-British Settlement and Cemeteries at Mucking: Excavations by Margaret and Tom Jones 1965–78*. Oxford: Oxbow Books/Historic England.

Luke, M. & Preece, T., 2011. *Farm and Forge: Late Iron Age and Romano-British farmsteads at Marsh Leys, Kempston, Bedfordshire*. (East Anglian Archaeology Report No. 138.) Bedford: Albion Archaeology.

Lyons, A., 2011. *Life and Afterlife at Duxford, Cambridge: Archaeology and history in a chalkland community*, by A. Lyons. (East Anglian Archaeology Report No. 141.) Cambridge: Oxford Archaeology East.

Lyons, A. & Blackbourn, K., 2017. Early Roman pottery production at Brampton, Cambridgeshire. *Proceedings of the Cambridge Antiquarian Society* 106, 23–48.

Lysons, D. & S., 1808. *Magna Britannia II, Part I Cambridgeshire*. East Ardsley: EP Publishing.

Macalister, R.A.S., 1893. Exhibition of Roman pottery found near Madingley Road. *Communications of the Cambridge Antiquarian Society* VII, 1.

Macalister, R.A.S., 1896. On some antiquities discovered near Bandy-leg Walk. *Proceedings of the Cambridge Antiquarian Society* 9, 26–33.

MacConnoran, P. 1986. Footwear, in *The Roman Quay at St Magnus House, London*, by L. Miller, J. Schofield & M. Rhodes. (London Middlesex Archaeological Society Special Paper 8.) London: London and Middlesex Archaeological Society, 218–26.

Macdonald, H., Kontulainen, S., MacKelvie-O'Brien, K., Petit, M., Janssen, P., Khan, K. & McKay, H., 2005. Maturity and sex related changes in tibial bone geometry, strength and bone–muscle strength indices during growth- a 20-month Pqct study. *Bone* 36, 1003–11.

Macfarlane, R., 2012. *The Old Ways: A Journey on Foot*. London: Hamish Hamilton.

Mackay, D., 2001. The Old Cattle Market, Cambridge: an archaeological evaluation. Cambridge: Cambridge Archaeological Unit Report No. 437.

Mackay, D., 2002. An Archaeological Evaluation at Barton Road, Cambridge. Cambridge: Cambridge Archaeological Unit Report No. 470.

Mackay, D., 2004. Latham Close, Cambridge: an archaeological evaluation. Cambridge: Cambridge Archaeological Unit Report No. 619.

Mackay, D., 2006. Archaeological Investigations at St. Edmund's College, Cambridge. Cambridge: Cambridge Archaeological Unit Report No. 721.

Mackreth, D.F., 1996. *Orton Hall Farm: A Roman and Early Anglo-Saxon Farmstead*. (East Anglian Archaeology Report No. 76.) Manchester: Nene Valley Archaeological Trust.

Macphail, R.I., 1983. The micromorphology of Dark Earth from Gloucester, London and Norwich: an analysis of urban anthropogenic deposits from the Late Roman to Early Medieval periods in England, in *Soil Micromorphology*, eds. P. Bullock & C.P. Murphy. (Proceedings of the International Working-Meeting on Soil Micromorphology.) Berkhamsted: AB Academic, 245–52.

Macphail, R.I. & Courty, M-A., 1985. Interpretation and significance of urban deposits. *Proceedings of the Third Nordic Conference on the Application of Scientific Methods in Archaeology*, eds. T. Edgren & H. Jungner. (ISKOS Series 5.) Helsinki: Finnish Antiquarian Society, 71–83.

Macphail, R.I. Courty, M-A. & Gebhardt, A., 1990. Soil micromorphological evidence of early agriculture in north-west Europe. *World Archaeology* 22, 59–69.

Magnen, R. & Thevenot, E., 1953. *Epona: déesse gauloise des chevaux, protectrice des cavaliers*. Bourdeaux: Delmas.

Maltby, M., 1984. Animal bones and the Romano-British economy, in *Animals and Archaeology: 4. Husbandry in Europe*, eds. C. Grigson & J. Clutton-Brock. (British Archaeological Reports, International Series 227.) Oxford: British Archaeological Series, 125–38.

Maltby, M., 2016. The exploitation of Animals in Roman Britain, in *The Oxford Handbook of Roman Britain*, eds. M. Millett, R. Revell & A. Moore. Oxford: Oxford University Press, 791–806.

Manchester, K., 1983. *The Archaeology of Disease*. Leeds: Arthur Wigley.

Manning, W. H., 1985. *Catalogue of the Romano-British Iron Tools, Fittings and Weapons in the British Museum*. London: British Museum Publications.

Margary, I.D., 1955. *Roman Roads in Britain*. London: Phoenix House.

Marsh, G., 1978. Early second century fine wares in the London area, in *Early Fine Wares in Roman Britain*, eds. P. Arthur & G. Marsh. (British Archaeological Reports, British Series 57.) Oxford: British Archaeological Report, 119–223.

Martin, D.B., 1996. The Construction of the Ancient Family: Methodological Considerations. *The Journal of Roman Studies* 86, 40–60.

Martin-Kilcher, S., 2000. *Mors immatura* in the Roman world - a mirror of society and tradition, in *Burial, Society and Context in the Roman World*, eds. J. Pearce, M. Millett & M. Struck. Oxford: Oxbow, 63–77.

Masser, P., 2000. Archaeological Investigations at the Hoyle Building Site, Madingley Rise. Cambridge: Cambridge Archaeological Unit Report No. 391.

McCarthy, M., 2013. *The Romano-British Peasant: Towards a study of people, landscapes and work during the Roman occupation of Britain*. Oxford: Windgather Press/Oxbow Books.

Mckinley, J.I., 1992. Cremation and Inhumation Burials from St Stephen's Cemetery, St Albans. Unpublished. Verulamium Museum.

McKinley, J.I., 1993. Bone fragment size and weights of bone from modern British cremations and their implications for the interpretation of archaeological cremations. *International Journal of Osteoarchaeology* 3, 283–7.

McKinley, J.I., 1994a. Bone fragment size in British cremation burials and its implications for pyre technology and ritual. *Journal of Archaeological Science* 21, 339–42.

Mckinley, J.I., 1994b. *The Anglo-Saxon Cemetery at Spong Hill, North Elmham. Part 8: The cremations*. (East Anglian Archaeology Report No. 69.) Dereham: Field Archaeology Division, Norfolk Museums Service.

McKinley, J.I. 1997. The cremated and inhumed bone from burial and cremation-related contexts, in *Archaeological Excavations on the Route of the A27 Westhampnett Bypass, West Sussex 1992*, vol. 2: *The late Iron Age, Romano-British and Anglo-Saxon cemeteries*, ed. A.P. Fitzpatrick. (Wessex Archaeological Report 12.) Salisbury: Trust for Wessex Archaeology, 55–74 and 244–53.

McKinley, J.I., 2000a. Phoenix rising: aspects of cremation, in *Burial, Society and Context in the Roman World*, eds. J. Pearce, M. Millett & M. Struck. Oxford: Oxbow, 38–44.

McKinley, J.I., 2000b. The cremation remains, in *The Eastern Cemetery of Roman London: Excavations 1983–1990*, by B. Barber & D. Bowsher. (Museum of London Archaeology Service, Monograph 4.) London: Museum of London Archaeology Service, 360–6.

McKinley, J.I., 2000c. Funerary practice, in *The Eastern Cemetery of Roman London: Excavations 1983–1990*, by B. Barber & D. Bowsher. (Museum of London Archaeology Service, Monograph 4.) London: Museum of London Archaeology Service, 61–7.

McKinley, J.I., 2000d. Cremation burials, in *The Eastern Cemetery of Roman London: Excavations 1983–1990*, by B. Barber & D. Bowsher. (Museum of London Archaeology Service, Monograph 4.) London: Museum of London Archaeology Service, 264–77.

McMinn, R.M.H. & Hutchings, R.T., 1988. *A Colour Atlas of Human Anatomy* (2nd ed.). London: Wolfe Medical Publications.

Meadows, K., 1997. Much ado about nothing: the social context of eating and drinking in early Roman Britain, in *Not So Much A Pot, More A Way of Life: Current approaches to artefact analysis in archaeology*, eds. C. Cumberpatch & P. Blinkhorn. (Oxbow Monograph 83.) Oxford: Oxbow, 21–35.

Meaney, A., 1964. *A Gazetteer of Early Anglo-Saxon Burial Sites*. London: Allen and Unwin.

Meates, G.W., 1979. *The Roman Villa at Lullingstone, Kent*. (Kent Archaeological Society, Monograph Series 1.) Maidstone: Kent Archaeological Society.

Meckseper, C., 2014. Roman burials and Post Medieval clay tobacco pipes at Merton Hall, Cambridge. *Proceedings of the Cambridge Antiquarian Society* 103, 61–68.

Medlycott, M., 2011. *The Roman Town of Great Chesterford*. (East Anglian Archaeology Report No. 137.) Chelmsford: Essex County Council.

Meindl, R. & Lovejoy, C., 1985. Ectocranial suture closure: a revised method for the determination of skeletal age at death based on the lateral-anterior sutures. *American Journal of Physical Anthropology* 68, 57–66.

Milek, K.B., 1999. Settlement in thin section: the application of sediment micromorphology to the interpretation of Norse farmsteads in Iceland, in *Settlement and Landscape: Proceedings of a conference in Århus, Denmark, May 4–7 1998*, eds. C. Fabech & J. Ringtved. Højbjerg: Jutland Archaeological Society, 497–8.

Millett, M., 1980. Aspects of Romano-British pottery in West Sussex. *Sussex Archaeological Collections* 118, 57–68.

Millett, M., 1990. *The Romanization of Britain: An essay in archaeological interpretation*. Cambridge: Cambridge University Press.

Millett, M.J. forthcoming. Review: *Durovigutum: Roman Godmanchester*, by H.J.M Green (compiled, collated and edited by T. Malim). *Journal of Roman Archaeology*.

Millett, M. & Gowland, R. 2015. Infant and child burial rites in Roman Britain: a study from East Yorkshire. *Britannia* 46, 171–89.

Millett, M. & Woodhouse, H., 2015. Patterns of deposition, in *Hayton, East Yorkshire: Archaeological Studies of the Iron Age and Roman landscapes* (Vol. II), eds. P. Halkon, M. Millett & H. Woodhouse. (Yorkshire Archaeological Report 6–7.) Yorkshire Archaeological Society, 459–63.

Mills, J.M., 1993. Iron coffin nails and fittings, in *Excavations at Poundbury 1966–80 (Vol. II): The Cemeteries,* by D.E. Farwell & T.I. Molleson. (Dorset Natural History and Archaeology Society Monograph Series 11.) Dorchester: Dorset Natural History and Archaeological Society, 114–27.

Mills, J., 2007 Surveying the claylands: combining aerial survey and fieldwalking methods in identifying archaeological sites on 'difficult' soils, in *Populating Clay Landscapes* I, eds. J. Mills & R. Palmer. Stroud: Tempus, 132–46.

Mitchell, P.D., 2017. Human parasites in the Roman World: Health consequences of conquering an empire. *Parasitology* 144, 48–51.

Monaghan, J., 1997. *Roman Pottery from York.* (Archaeology of York 16, fasc. 8.) York: Council for British Archaeology.

Moore, P.D. & Webb, J.A., 1978. *An Illustrated Guide to Pollen Analysis.* New York: Wiley.

Moore, P.D., Webb, J.A. & Collinson, M.E., 1991. *Pollen Analysis* (2nd ed.). Oxford: Blackwell Scientific.

Moorhead, S., 2013. *A History of Roman Coinage in Britain.* Witham, Essex: Greenlight Publishing.

Morris, P., 1979. *Agricultural Buildings in Roman Britain.* (British Archaeological Reports, British Series 70.) Oxford: British Archaeological Reports.

Mortimer, R., 1995. Archaeological Evaluation at St. John's College School, 73 Grange Road. Cambridge: Cambridge Archaeological Unit Report No. 145.

Mortimer, R. & Evans, C., 1997. The Marion Close Enclosure: Excavations at 138 Huntington Road Cambridge. Cambridge: Cambridge Archaeological Unit Report No. 203.

Mortimer, R. & Regan, R., 2001. Chesterton Lane Corner, Cambridge: archaeological excavations at Anglia Water sewage shaft M5. Assessment Report. Cambridge: Cambridge Archaeological Unit Report No. 420.

Mould, Q., 2000. The small finds, in *The Roman Baths and Macellum at Wroxeter: Excavations by Graham Webster 1955–85*, ed. P. Ellis. (Archaeological Report, English Heritage 9.) London: English Heritage, 108–44.

Murphy, C.P., 1986. *Thin Section Preparation of Soils and Sediments.* Berkhamsted: AB Academic.

Murphy, J. & Riley, J.P., 1962. A modified single solution method for the determination of phosphate in natural waters. *Analytica Chimica Acta* 27, 31–6.

Murphy, P., 1997a. Iron Age environment and economy, in *Research and Archaeology: A framework for the eastern counties, 1. Resource assessment*, ed. J. Glazebrook. (East Anglian Archaeology Occasional Paper No. 3.) Norwich: The Scole Archaeological Committee for East Anglia, 30–1.

Murphy, P., 1997b. 'Environment and Economy', in Roman by C. Going, in *Research and Archaeology: A Framework for the Eastern Counties,* ed. J. Glazebrook. (East Anglia Archaeology, Occasional Paper 3.) Norwich: The Scole Archaeological Committee for East Anglia, 42–3.

Mustchin, A.R.R., 2016. Iron Age and Romano-British Activity at the Maintenance Block, Jesus College, Cambridge. Bury St Edmunds: Archaeological Solutions Report.

Mustchin, A.R.R., Cussans, J.E.M., Summers, J.R. & Peachey, A., 2016. A large Romano-British farmstead at North Stud, Woodditton, Cambridgeshire. *Proceedings of the Cambridge Antiquarian Society* 105, 7–34.

Musty, J., Rogerson, A. & Lloyd-Morgan, G., 1973. A mirror from the Romano-British cemetery at Whitchurch, Salop. *Antiquaries Journal* 53, 278–81.

Nally, M., 1992. Bullard Laboratories Development, Madingley Road: Trial Trench Excavation Report. Cambridge: Cambridge Archaeological Unit Report No. 63.

Neal, D.S. & Butcher, S.A., 1974. Miscellaneous objects of bronze, in *The Excavation of the Roman Villa at Gadebridge Park, Hemel Hempstead, 1963–8* by D.S. Neal. (Reports of the Research Committee of the Society of Antiquaries of London 31.) London: Society of Antiquaries of London, 128–50.

Newman, R., 2008a. St. John's Triangle, Cambridge: an archaeological excavation and watching brief. Cambridge: Cambridge Archaeological Unit Report No. 851.

Newman, R. 2008b. The Kavli Institute for Cosmology, Cambridge: an archaeological excavation. Cambridge: Cambridge Archaeological Unit Report No. 820.

Newman, R., 2013. The School of Pythagoras, St. John's College, Cambridge: an archaeological excavation. Cambridge: Cambridge Archaeological Unit Report No. 1199.

Newman, R., 2017. Merton Hall Farm, West Cambridge: an archaeological evaluation. Cambridge Archaeological Unit Report No. 1384.

Newman, R., in prep. The Archaeology of the School of Pythagoras, St. John's College, Cambridge.

Niblett, R., 1999. *The Excavation of a Ceremonial Site at Folly Lane, Verulamium.* (Britannia Monograph Series 14.) London: Society for the Promotion of Roman Studies.

Niblett, R., 2000. Funerary rites in Verulamium during the early Roman period, in *Burial, Society and Context in the Roman World*, eds. J. Pearce, M. Millett & M. Struck. Oxford: Oxbow, 97–104.

Nicholson, K. & Woolhouse, T., 2016. *A Late Iron Age and Romano-British Farmstead at Cedars Park, Stowmarket, Suffolk.* (East Anglian Archaeology Report No. 160.) Bury St. Edmunds: Archaeological Solutions Ltd.

Nickson, R., 2005, Moral edification at Gonville and Caius College, Cambridge. *Architectural History* 48, 49–68.

Nicolet, C. 1991. *Space, Geography and Politics in the Early Roman Empire.* Ann Arbor: University of Michigan Press.

Noble, W.M., 1911. *Huntingdonshire.* (Cambridge County Geographies). Cambridge: University Press.

Noddle, B., 1984. A comparison of the bones of cattle, sheep and pigs from ten Iron Age and Romano-British sites, in *Animals and Archaeology: 4. Husbandry in Europe*, by C. Grigson & J. Clutton-Brock. (British Archaeological Reports, British Series 227.) Oxford: British Archaeological Reports, 105–24.

O'Connell, S., 1999. *The Popular Print in England.* London: British Museum.

O'Connor, B., 1998. *The Dinosaurs on Coldham's Common: The Story of Cambridge's Coprolite Industry.* Cambridge: Privately Published.

O'Connor, T.P., 1991. *Bones from 46–54 Fishergate.* (Archaeology of York 15.) London: York Archaeological Trust/ Council for British Archaeology.

Oaks, L., 1986. The Goddess Epona: concepts of sovereignty in a changing landscape, in *Pagan Gods and Shrines of the Roman Empire*, eds. M. Henig & A. King. (University of Oxford. Committee for Archaeology Monograph 8). Oxford: Oxford University Committee for Archaeology, 77–83.

Oldenstein, von J., 1976. Zur Ausrüstung Römischer Auxiliareinheiten. *Bericht der Römisch-Germoanischen Komission* 57, 49–284.

Ondaatje, M., 1987. *In the Skin of a Lion*. Toronto: McClelland and Stewart.

Packer, J.E., 2008. Italo Gismondi and Pieriano Di Carlo: 'Virtualizing' Imperial Rome for 20th-century Italy. *American Journal of Archaeology* 112 (online article).

Parfitt, K., 1995. *Iron Age Burials from Mill Hill, Deal*. London: British Museum Press.

Partridge, C., 1981. *Skeleton Green. A Late Iron Age and Romano-British Site*. (Britannia Monograph Series 2.) London: Society for the Promotion of Roman Studies.

Patten, R., 2012. An Iron Age and Roman settlement at Summerfield, Papworth Everard. *Proceedings of the Cambridge Antiquarian Society* 101, 115–42.

Patten, R., 2016. Bearscroft Farm, Godmanchester: an archaeological excavation. Cambridge Archaeological Unit Report No. 1340.

Payne, S., 1973. Kill-off patterns in sheep and goats: the mandibles from the Asvan Kale. *Anatolian Studies* 23, 281–303.

PCRG, 1997. *The Study of Later Prehistoric Pottery: General Policies and Guidelines for Analysis and Publication* (2nd ed.). (Prehistoric Ceramics Research Group Occasional Papers 1 & 2.) Oxford: Prehistoric Ceramics Research Group.

Peacock, D.P.S., 1987. Iron Age and Roman quern production at Lodsworth, West Sussex. *Antiquaries Journal* 47, 61–85.

Peacock, D.P.S. & Williams, D., 1986. *Amphorae and the Roman Economy: An introductory guide*. London: Longman.

Pearce, J., 2013. *Contextual Archaeology of Burial Practice: Case studies from Roman Britain*. (British Archaeological Reports British Series 588.) Oxford: Archaeopress.

Pennings, W.H. & Jukes-Brown, A.J. 1881. *Geology of the Neighbourhood of Cambridge*. London: Memoirs of the Geological Survey of England and Wales.

Percival, S., 2005. Iron Age pottery, in *The Saxon and Medieval Settlement at West Fen Road, Ely: The Ashwell Site*, by R. Mortimer, R. Regan & S. Lucy. (East Anglian Archaeology Report No. 110.) Cambridge: Cambridge Archaeological Unit, 59–60.

Percival, S., 2011. The pottery, in *Life and Afterlife at Duxford, Cambridge: Archaeology and history in a chalkland community*, by A. Lyons. (East Anglian Archaeology Report No. 141.) Cambridge: Oxford Archaeology East, 57–65.

Perrin, R. 1980. Pottery of London-Ware type from the Nene Valley. *Durobrivae* 8, 8–10.

Perrin J.R., 1996. The Roman pottery, in *Orton Hall Farm: A Roman and Early Anglo-Saxon farmstead*, by D.F. Mackreth. (East Anglian Archaeology Report No. 76.) Manchester: Nene Valley Archaeological Trust, 114–204.

Perrin, J.R. & Webster, G., 1990. Roman pottery from excavations in Normangate Field, Castor, Peterborough, 1962–3. *Journal of Roman Pottery Studies* 3, 35–62.

Perrin, J.R., with Hartley, K.F., 1996. The mortaria, in *Orton Hall Farm: A Roman and Early Anglo-Saxon farmstead*, by D.F. Mackreth. (East Anglian Archaeology Report No. 76.) Manchester: Nene Valley Archaeological Trust, 191–8.

Perring, D., 1981. *Early Medieval Occupation at Flaxengate, Lincoln*. (The Archaeology of Lincoln 9.) London: Council for British Archaeology for the Lincoln Archaeological Trust.

Perring, D., 1999. Houses in Roman Britain. A study in architecture and urban society. Unpublished Ph.D Thesis, University of Leicester.

Perring, D., 2002. *The Roman House in Britain*. London: Routledge.

Perring, D. & Pitts, M., 2013. *Alien Cities: Consumption and the Origins of Urbanism in Roman Britain*. (Spoilheap Monograph Series 7.) London: Spoilheap Publications.

Pfleger, V. & Chatfield, J., 1983. *A Guide to Snails of Britain and Europe*. London: Hamlyn.

Phillips, C. & Grassam, A., 2006. Archaeological note: animal carcasses in a Roman ditch, West End, Haddenham, TL 4613 7552. *Proceedings of the Cambridge Antiquarian Society* 95, 179–82.

Phillips, T., 2014. Late Iron Age and Roman Settlement off Broadway, Yaxley, Peterborough. Excavation report. Bar Hill: Oxford Archaeology East Report 1312.

Phillips, T. & Mortimer, R., 2012. Clay Farm, Trumpington, Cambridgeshire: post- excavation assessment and updated project design. Bar Hill: Oxford Archaeology East Report 1294.

Philpott, R.A., 1991. *Burial Practices in Roman Britain: A survey of grave treatment and furnishing* AD *43–410*. (British Archaeological Reports, British Series 219.) Oxford: British Archaeological Reports.

Pitts, L., 1979. *Roman Bronze Figurines of the Catuvellauni and Trinovantes*. (British Archaeological Reports, British Series 60.) Oxford: British Archaeological Reports.

Potter, T.W. & Trow, S., 1988. *Puckeridge-Braughing, Hertfordshire: The Ermine Street excavations 1971–72*. (Hertfordshire Archaeology 10.) Hertford.

Potter, J.F., 2000. The occurrence of travertine in churches of the London Basin. *Proceedings of the Geologists' Association* 111, 55–70.

Price, J., Brooks, I.P. & Maynard, D.J. (eds.), 1997. *The Archaeology of the St Neots to Duxford Gas Pipeline 1994*. (British Archaeological Reports British Series 255.) Oxford: J. and E. Hedges.

Price, J. & Cottam, S., 1998. *Romano-British Glass Vessels: A handbook*. (Practical Handbooks in Archaeology 14.) York: Council for British Archaeology.

Pullinger, J. & White, P.J., 1991. A report on excavations of Romano-British sites at Hinton Fields, Teversham (Cambridgeshire) 1978–1986. Cambridge: Privately published.

Pullinger, J., & Young, C. 1981. Obelisk kilns, Harston. *Proceedings of the Cambridge Antiquarian Society* 71, 1–24.

Quensel-von-Kalben, L., 2000. Putting Late Roman burial practice in Britain in context, in *Burial, Society and Context in the Roman World*, eds. J. Pearce, M. Millett, & M. Struck. Oxford: Oxbow, 217–30.

Rackham, O., 2003. *Ancient Woodland: Its History, Vegetation and Uses in England*. Dalbeattie: Castlepoint Press.

Rankin, N., 2008. *Churchill's Wizards: The British genius for deception 1914–1945*. London: Faber.

Rankine, W.F., 1949. Stone Maceheads with Mesolithic Associations from South Eastern England. *Proceedings of the Prehistoric Society* 15, 70–6.

Ranson, C., 2016. Archaeological Excavations at Newnham College in 2010. Cambridge: Access Cambridge Archaeology Report.

Raverat, G., 2002. (1952). *Period Piece: A Cambridge childhood*. London: Faber & Faber.

RCHM(E) 1959. *An Inventory of the Historical Monuments in the City of Cambridge* (Pt. 1). London: H.M.S.O.

Redknap, M., 1986. The small finds, in *Excavations on the Romano-British Small Town at Neatham, Hampshire 1969–79*, by M. Millett & D. Graham. Winchester: Hampshire Field Club, 101–40.

Reece, R., 1995. Site finds in Roman Britain. *Britannia* 26, 179–206.

Reece, R. & James, S., 1986. *Identifying Roman Coins*. Seaby.

Rees, G., 2016. A 1st century AD archaeological sequence at the site of the new lift shaft, Shire Hall, Cambridge. Bar Hill: Oxford Archaeology East Report 1766.

Rhodes, M., 1980. Leather footwear, in *Excavations at Billingsgate Buildings 'Triangle', Lower Thames Street, 1974* by D.M. Jones. (London and Middlesex Archaeological Society, Special Paper 4.) London: London & Middlesex Archaeological Society, 99–128.

RIB: Roman Inscriptions of Britain web-site.

Rickett, R. 1995. *The Anglo-Saxon Cemetery at Spong Hill, North Elmham* (Pt. VII): *The Iron Age Roman and Early Saxon Settlement*. (East Anglian Archaeological Report No. 73.) Dereham: Field Archaeology Division, Norfolk Museums Service.

Rigby, V., 1973. Potters' stamps on Terra Nigra and Terra Rubra found in Britain, in *Current Research in Romano-British Coarse Pottery: Papers given at a C.B.A. conference held at New College, Oxford, March 24–26, 1972*, ed. A. Detsicas. (Council for British Archaeology, Research Report 10.) London: Council for British Archaeology, 7–22.

Rigby, V., 1989. The Romano-British pottery, in *West Stow: The Prehistoric and Romano-British occupations*, by S. West. (East Anglian Archaeology Report No. 48.) Norwich: Suffolk County Council, 76–93.

Rigby, V., with Lyons, A., forthcoming. Pot Group 15a: Cremation 10909, in *Archaeological Excavations at Clay Farm*, by T. Phillips & R. Mortimer. Oxford Archaeology East.

Rippon, S., 2018. *Kingdom, Civitas, and County: The evolution of territorial identity in the English landscape*. Oxford: Oxford University Press.

Roberts, H., 2013. Land off Wilberforce Road, Cambridge (the former Grange Farm site): an archaeological evaluation. Cambridge: Cambridge Archaeological Unit Report No. 1198.

Robinson, M. & Hubbard, R.N.L.B., 1977. The transport of pollen in bracts of hulled cereals. *Journal of Archaeological Science* 4, 197–9.

Robinson, I., 2013. Castle Park, Cambridge: an archaeological watching brief. Cambridge: Cambridge Archaeological Unit Report No. 1150.

Rodwell, J.S., 1991. *British Plant Communities Volume 1: Woodlands and scrub*. Cambridge: Cambridge University Press.

Rodwell, W.J., 1978. Stamp decorated pottery of the early Roman period in Eastern England, in *Early Fine Wares in Roman Britain*, eds. P. Arthur & G. Marsh. (British Archaeological Reports 57.) Oxford: British Archaeological Reports, 225–92.

Roe, F.E.S., 1968. Stone mace-heads and the latest Neolithic cultures of the British Isles, in *Studies in Ancient Europe: Essays Presented to Stuart Piggott*, eds. J.M. Coles & D.D.A. Simpson. Leicester: Leicester University Press, 145–72.

Roe, F.E.S., 1979. Typology of stone implements with shaftholes, in *Stone Axe Studies: Archaeological, petrological, experimental and ethnographic*, eds. T. McK. Clough & W.A. Cummins. (Council for British Archaeology Research Report 23.) London: Council for British Archaeology, 23–48.

Roe, F.E.S. & Radley, J., 1971. Pebble mace-heads with hourglass perforations from Yorkshire, Nottinghamshire and Derbyshire. *Yorkshire Archaeological Journal* 42, 169–77.

Rogers, J. & Waldron, T., 1995. *A Field Guide to Joint Disease in Archaeology*. Chichester: Wiley.

Ruff, C., 1987. Sexual dimorphism in human lower limb bone structure: relationship to subsistence strategy and sexual division of labor. *Journal of Human Evolution*, 16, 391–416.

Ruff, C., Holt, B., Niskanen, M., Sladek, V., Berner, M., Garofalo, E., Garvin, H., Hora, M., Junno, J., Schuplerova, E., Vilkama, R. & Whittey, E., 2015. Gradual decline in mobility with the adoption of food production in Europe. *Proceedings of the National Academy of Sciences* 112, 7147–52.

Ruff, C., Larsen, C., & Hayes, W., 1984. Structural changes in the femur with the transition to agriculture on the Georgia Coast. *American Journal of Physical Anthropology* 64, 125–36.

Sanders, J., 1973. Late Roman Shell-gritted Ware in Southern Britain. Unpublished B.A Thesis, University of London.

Sauer, E., 2014. Milestones and instability (mid 3rd to mid 4th century AD). *Ancient Society* 44, 257–305.

Scaife, R.G., 1994. The plant remains in *The Archaeology along the A605 Elton-Haddon Bypass, Cambridgeshire*, by C.A.I. French. (Fenland Archaeological Trust 2.) Fenland Archaeological Trust/Cambridgeshire County Council, 154–67.

Scaife, R.G., 1999. The pollen, in *Prehistoric Sites in East Devon: the A30 Honiton to Exeter improvement DBFO scheme, 1996–9*, by A.P. Fitzpatrick, C.A. Butterworth, & J. Grove. (Wessex Archaeology Report 16.) Salisbury: Trust for Wessex Archaeology, 337–42.

Scheib, C.L., Hongjie, L., Desai, T., Link, V., Kendall, C., Dewar, G. … Kivisild, T., 2018. Ancient human parallel lineages with North America contributed to a coastal expansion. *Science*, 360, 1024–27. https://doi.org/10.1126/science.aar6851

Schlögel, K., 2016. *In Space We Read Time: On the History of Civilisation and Geopolitics*. New York City: Bard Graduate Center.

Scott, E., 1989. Animal burials in Romano-British villas: a revitalization movement, in *Sacred and Profane: Proceedings of a conference on archaeology, ritual and religion*, eds. P. Garwood, D. Jennings, R. Skeates & J. Toms. (Oxford Committee for Archaeology 32.) Oxford: Oxford University Committee for Archaeology, 115–21.

Scott, E., 1999. *The Archaeology of Infancy and Infant Death*. (British Archaeological Reports, International Series 819.) Oxford: Archaeopress.

Seeley, F., Marshall, M., Clark, C. & Lindsay, S., 2014. *Visual guide to MOLA London Roman Pottery Form Codes*. London: Museum of London.

Selkirk, A. & Selkirk, W., 1978. The Cambridge shrine. *Current Archaeology* 61, 57–60.

Shaw, C., & Stock, J., 2009. Intensity, repetitiveness and directionality of habitual adolescent mobility patterns influence the tibial diaphysis morphology of athletes. *American Journal of Physical Anthropology* 140, 149–59.

Shennan, S., 1988. *Quantifying Archaeology*. Edinburgh: Edinburgh University Press.

Shipman, P., Forster, G. & Schoeninger, M., 1984. Burnt bones and teeth: an experimental study of colour, morphology, crystal structure and shrinkage. *Journal of Archaeological Science* 11, 307–25.

Simpson, C.J., 1976. Belt-buckles and strap-ends of the later Roman Empire. *Britannia* 7, 192–223.

Simpson, W.G., 1993. The excavation of Romano-British aisled buildings at Barnack, Cambridgeshire, in *The Fenland Project Number 7: Excavations in Peterborough and the Lower Welland Valley 1960-1969*, by W.G. Simpson, D.A. Gurney, J. Neve & F. Pryor. (East Anglian Archaeology Report No. 61). Peterborough: Fenland Archaeological Trust, 102–25.

Skoglund, P., Storå, J., Götherström, A. & Jakobsson, M., 2013. Accurate sex identification of ancient human remains using DNA shotgun sequencing. *Journal of Archaeological Science*, 40, 4477–82.

Slater, A., 2008a. Fitzwilliam College Library, Cambridge: an archaeological excavation. Cambridge: Cambridge Archaeological Unit Report No. 817.

Slater, A., 2008b. Broom Quarry Extension, Broom, Bedfordshire. An interim report. Cambridge: Cambridge Archaeological Unit Report No. 808.

Slater, A., 2010. Excavations at the CB1 Development Site, Hills Road, Cambridge. Cambridge: Cambridge Archaeological Unit Report No. 933.

Slater, A., 2011. Whittle Jet Propulsion Laboratories, West Cambridge: archaeological trenching and excavation. Cambridge: Cambridge Archaeological Unit Report No. 983.

Slater, A., 2012. High Cross, West Cambridge, University of Cambridge – Further Archaeological Evaluation. Cambridge: Cambridge Archaeological Unit Report No. 1119.

Smith, A., Allen, M., Brindle, T. & Fulford, M., 2016. *New Visions of the Countryside of Roman Britain* (Vol. 1): *The Rural Settlement of Roman Britain*. (Britannia Monographs 29.) London: The Society for the Promotion of Roman Studies.

Smith, A., Allen, M., Brindle, T., Fulford, M., Lodwick, L. & Rohnbogner, A., 2018. *New Visions of the Countryside of Roman Britain* (Vol. 3): *Life and death in the countryside of Roman Britain*. (Britannia Monographs 32.) London: Society for the Promotion of Roman Studies.

Smith, F.G., 1984. Early work on radio stars at Cambridge, in *The Early Years of Radio Astronomy: Reflections fifty years After Jansky's discovery*, ed. W.T. Sullivan. Cambridge: Cambridge University Press, 237–48.

Smith, J.T., 1963. Romano-British aisled houses. *Archaeological Journal* 120, 1–30.

Smith, R.R.R., 1991. *Hellenistic Sculpture: A Handbook*. London: Thames and Hudson.

Sorbel, D., 2016. *The Glass Universe: The hidden history of the women who took the measure of the stars*. London: 4th Estate.

St John Hope, W.H., 1907. On the Norman origin of Cambridge Castle. *Proceedings of the Cambridge Antiquarian Society* 47, 324–46.

Stace, C., 1997. *New Flora of the British Isles*. (2nd ed.) Cambridge: Cambridge University Press.

Stallibras, S., 2000. Dead dogs, dead horses: site formation processes at Ribchester Roman fort, in *Animal Bones, Human Societies*, ed. P. Rowley-Conwy. Oxford: Oxbow, 158–65.

Stead, I.M. & Rigby, V., 1986. *Baldock: The excavation of a Roman and pre-Roman settlement, 1968–72*. (Britannia Monograph Series 7.) London: Society for the Promotion of Roman Studies.

Stead, I.M. & Rigby, V., 1989. *Verulamium: The King Harry Lane site*. (English Heritage: Archaeological Report 12.) London: English Heritage.

Steele, D.G. & Bramblett, C.A., 1988. *The Anatomy and Biology of the Human Skeleton*. College Station, Texas: A & M University Press.

Stevens, C.J., 1996. Iron Age and Roman Agriculture in the Upper Thames Valley: Archaeobotanical and social perspectives. Unpublished PhD Thesis. University of Cambridge.

Stevens, C., 2009a. The local and wider Iron Age landscape, in *Cambourne New Settlement Iron Age and Romano-British settlement on the clay uplands of west Cambridgeshire*, by J. Wright, M. Leivers, R. Seager Smith & C. Stevens. Salisbury: Wessex Archaeology, 69–71.

Stevens, C., 2009b. The local and wider Romano-British landscape, in *Cambourne New Settlement. Iron Age and Romano-British settlement on the clay uplands of west Cambridgeshire*, by J. Wright, M. Leivers, R. Seager Smith & C. Stevens. Salisbury: Wessex Archaeology, 84–6.

Stevenson, R.B.K., 1967. A Roman-period cache of charms in Aberdeenshire. *Antiquity* 41, 143–5.

Stirland, A., 1989. The cremations from the Iron Age cemetery, in *Verulamium: The King Harry Lane Site*, by I.M Stead & V. Rigby. (English Heritage: Archaeological Report 12.) London: English Heritage, 240–4.

Stockmarr, J., 1971. Tablets with spores used in absolute pollen analysis. *Pollen et Spores* 13, 614–21.

Stone, J.C., 1988. Imperialism, colonialism and cartography. *Transactions of the Institute of British Geographers* 13, 57–64.

Strachan, H. 1976. *History of the Cambridge University Officers Training Corps*. Cambridge: Cambridge University Press.

Stratton, F.J.M., 1949. *The History of the Cambridge Observatories*. (Annals of the Solar Physics Observatory, Cambridge 1.) Cambridge: Cambridge University Press.

Stuijts, I., 2006. Charcoal sampling sites and procedures: practical themes from Ireland, in *Charcoal Analysis: New analytical tools and methods for archaeology*, ed. A. Dufraisse. (British Archaeological Reports International Series 1483.) Oxford: British Archaeological Reports, 25–33.

Stukeley, W., 1746. *Palaeographia Britannica, Part II*. Stamford: Francis Howgrave.

Swan, V.G., 1984. *The Pottery Kilns of Roman Britain*. (Supplementary Series 5.) London: RCHM.

Swift, E., 2010. Identifying migrant communities: A contextual analysis of grave assemblages from Continental Late Roman cemeteries. *Britannia* 41, 237–82.

Symonds, R.P. & Wade, S.M., 1999. *The Roman Pottery from Excavations at Colchester, 1971–1985*. (Colchester Archaeological Report No. 10.) Colchester: Colchester Archaeological Trust.

Tabor, J., 2015. Astrazeneca New Cambridge Site: post-excavation assessment. Cambridge: Cambridge Archaeological Unit Report No. 1298.

Tabor, J. 2017. University of Cambridge Sports Pitches and Athletics Track, Wilberforce Road, Cambridge: an archaeological evaluation. Cambridge: Cambridge Archaeological Unit Report No. 1381.

Tansley, A.G., 1968. *Britain's Green Mantle* (2nd Ed.). London: George Allen and Unwin Ltd.

Taylor, A., 1985. Prehistoric, Roman, Saxon and Medieval artefacts from the southern Fen Edge, Cambridgeshire. *Proceedings of the Cambridge Antiquarian Society* 74, 1–52.

Taylor, A., 1993. A Roman lead coffin with pipeclay figurines from Arrington, Cambridgeshire. *Britannia* 24, 191–225.

Taylor, A., 1999. *Cambridge: The Hidden History*. Stroud: Tempus.

Taylor, J., 2001. Rural society in Roman Britain, in *Britons and Romans: Advancing an archaeological agenda*, eds. S. James & M. Millett. (Council for British Archaeology, Research Report 125.) York: Council for British Archaeology, 46–59.

Taylor, J., 2007. *An Atlas of Roman Rural Settlement in England*. York: Council for British Archaeology.

Taylor, J., 2013. Encountering Romanitas: characterising the role of agricultural communities in Roman Britain. *Britannia* 44, 171–90.

Ten Harkel, L., 2006. Excavations at St. Edmund's College, Cambridge: Part 2. Cambridge: Cambridge Archaeological Unit Report No. 741.

Thompson, E.P., 1967. Time, work-discipline, and industrial capitalism. *Past and Present* 38, 56–97.

Timberlake, S., 2006. An Archaeological Evaluation at 19 Mere Way, Cambridge. Cambridge: Cambridge Archaeological Unit Report No. 745.

Timberlake, S., 2010. Excavations at High Cross, West Cambridge, University of Cambridge. Cambridge: Cambridge Archaeological Report No. 942.

Timberlake, S., 2011. Leckhampton House, Cranmer Road, Corpus Christi College, Cambridge: an archaeological excavation. Cambridge: Cambridge Archaeological Unit Report No. 1038.

Timberlake, S. & Patten, R., 2006. An Archaeological Evaluation on the site of the New Physics for Medicine Building, University of Cambridge, West Cambridge. Cambridge: Cambridge Archaeological Unit Report No. 726.

Timberlake, S. & Webb, D., 2016. West Court, Jesus College, Cambridge: archaeological evaluation and monitoring. Cambridge: Cambridge Archaeological Unit Report No. 1320.

Tomber, R., & Dore, J., 1998. *The National Roman Fabric Reference Collection: A handbook*. (Museum of London Archaeology Series 2.) London: Museum of London Archaeology Service.

Trow, S., James, S. & Moore, T., 2009. *Becoming Roman, Being Gallic, Staying British: Research and excavations at Ditches 'Hillfort' and Villa 1984–2006*. Oxford: Oxbow.

Turner, R., 1999. *Excavations of an Iron Age Settlement and Roman Religious Complex at Ivy Chimneys, Witham, Essex 1978–83*. (East Anglian Archaeology Report No. 88.) Chelmsford: Archaeology Section, Essex County Council.

Tyers, P., 1996. *Roman Pottery in Britain*. London: Batsford.

Ubelaker, D.H., 1989. *Human Skeletal Remains: Excavation, analysis, and interpretation*. Washington, D.C.: Taraxacum Press.

University of Gloucestershire, English Heritage & Countryside Agency, 2006. *Historic Farmsteads, Preliminary Character Statement: East of England Region*. London & Cheltenham: English Heritage & Countryside and Community Research Unit.

Upex, S.G., 2018. *Iron Age and Roman Settlement: Rescue excavations at Lynch Farm 2, Orton Longueville, Peterborough*. (East Anglian Archaeology Report No. 163.) Manchester: Nene Valley Archaeological Trust and Dept of Art History and Archaeology, Victoria University of Manchester.

Van der Veen, M., 1991. Consumption or production? Agriculture in the Cambridgeshire Fens, in *New Light on Early Farming: Recent developments in palaeoethnobotany*, ed. J. Renfrew. Edinburgh: Edinburgh University Press, 349–61.

Van der Veen, M., 1996. Plant remains, in *Excavations at Stonea, Cambridgeshire: 1980–85*, by R.P.J. Jackson & T.W. Potter. London: British Museum Press, 613–39.

Van der Veen, M., 1999. The economic value of chaff and straw in arid and temperate zones. *Vegetation History and Archaeobotany* 8, 211–24.

Van der Veen, M., 2016. Arable farming, horticulture, and food: expansion, innovation and diversity in Roman Britain, in *The Oxford Handbook of Roman Britain*, eds. M. Millett, R. Revell & A. Moore. Oxford: Oxford University Press, 807–33.

Van Oyen, A., 2015. The Roman city as articulated through Terra Sigillata. *Oxford Journal of Archaeology* 34, 279–99.

Vera, F.W.M., 2000. *Grazing Ecology and Forest History*. Oxon: CABI Publishing.

Verstegen, I. & Ceen, A. (eds.), 2013. *Giambattista Nolli and Rome: Mapping the City before and after the Pianta Grande*. Rome: Studium Urbis Rome Center.

Vitt, V.O., 1952. Pazyryk barrow horses (in Russian). *Sovetskaja Archeologija* 16, 163–205.

Voong, C.P., Spencer, P.S., Navarrete, C.V., Turner, D., Hayrabedyan, S.B., Crummy, P., Holloway. E., Wilson, M.T., Smith, P.R. & Fernández, N., 2017. HLA-DR Genotyping and Mitochondrial DNA Analysis Reveal the Presence of Family Burials in a Fourth Century Romano-British Christian Cemetery. *Frontiers in Genetics* 8, Article 182. doi:10.3389/fgene.2017.00182

Vose, R.H., 1980. *Glass*. London: Collins.

Vrbančic, M., 2012. A dream of the perfect map – Calvino's invisible cities. *The Zone and Zones – Radical Spatiality in our Times* 2. DOI: 10.15291/sic/2.2lc.4.

Wait, G., 1992. Archaeological excavations at Godmanchester (A14/A604 Junction). *Proceedings of the Cambridge Antiquarian Society* 80, 79–95.

Walker, F.G., 1910. Roman roads in Cambridge. *Proceedings of the Cambridge Antiquarian Society* 14, 141–76.

Walker, F.G., 1911. Excavations at Magdalene College, Cambridge 1910. *Cambridge Antiquarian Society Communications* 15, 178–91.

Walker, F.G., 1912. Roman and Saxon remains from the Grange Road, Cambridge. *Proceedings of the Cambridge Antiquarian Society* 63, 122–7.

Walker, F.G., 1913. Roman pottery kilns at Horningsea, Cambridgeshire. *Proceedings of the Cambridge Antiquarian Society* 17, 14–70.

Wallace, L., 2015. *The Origin of Roman London*. Cambridge: Cambridge University Press.

Walters, S.M. & Stow, E.A., 2001. *Darwin's Mentor: John Stevens Henslow, 1796–1861*. Cambridge: Cambridge University Press.

Wattez, J. & Courty, M.-A., 1987. Morphology of ash of some plant materials. *Soil Micromorphology*, eds. N. Fedoroff, L. Bresson & M.-A. Courty. (Proceedings of the 12th International Working-Meeting on Soil Micromorphology.) Association Francaise pour l'Etude du Sol, 677–85.

Waugh, H. & Goodburn, R., 1972. The non-ferrous objects, in *Verulamium Excavations Volume 1* by S.S. Frere. (Report of the Research Committee of the Society of Antiquaries of London 28.) Oxford: Oxford University Press for The Society of Antiquaries, 114–62.

Webb, D. & Newman, R., 2011. Orchard Court, Murray Edwards College, Cambridge: an archaeological excavation. Cambridge: Cambridge Archaeological Unit Report No. 1054.

Webb, D., Timberlake, S. & Armour, N., 2006. Newnham College Buttery, Cambridge: archaeological investigations and recording. Cambridge: Cambridge Archaeological Unit Report No. 718.

Webley, L. & Evans, C., 2003. New Hall, Cambridge: an archaeological evaluation at 67 Storey's Way, with an assessment of the extent of Post-Medieval quarrying. Cambridge: Cambridge Archaeological Unit Report No. 579.

West, S., 1989. *West Stow, Suffolk: The Prehistoric and Romano-British Occupations*. (East Anglian Archaeology Report No. 48.) Bury St Edmunds: Suffolk County Planning Dept.

Western, A.G. & Bekvalac, J.J., 2017. Hyperostosis frontalis interna in female historic skeletal populations: age, sex hormones and the impact of industrialization. *American Journal of Physical Anthropology* 162, 501–15.

Wheeler, R.E.M., 1943. *Maiden Castle*. (Reports of the Research Committee of the Society of Antiquaries of London 12.) London: Society of Antiquaries.

Wheeler, R.E.M., 1954. *Archaeology from the Earth*. Harmondsworth: Penguin.

Wheeler, R.E.M. & Wheeler, T.V., 1932. *Report on the Excavation of the Prehistoric, Roman and Post-Roman Site in Lydney Park, Gloucestershire*. (Reports of the Research Committee of the Society of Antiquaries of London 9.) Oxford: Oxford University Press.

Wheeler, R.E.M., & Wheeler, T.V., 1936. *Verulamium: A Belgic and Two Roman Cities*. (Reports of the Research Committee of the Society of Antiquaries of London 11.) Oxford: Oxford University Press.

Whipple Museum, 1998. *An University within Ourselves: Sciences in Cambridge in the eighteenth century*. Cambridge: Whipple Museum of the History of Science.

White, D.A., 1964. Excavations at the War Ditches, Cherry Hinton, 1961–62. *Proceedings of the Cambridge Antiquarian Society* 56, 9–41.

White, K.D., 1970. *Roman Farming*. London: Thames and Hudson.

White, R., 1988. *Romano-Celtic Objects from Anglo-Saxon Graves. A catalogue and an interpretation of their use*. (British Archaeological Reports, British Series 91.) Oxford: British Archaeological Reports.

Whiting, W., 1923. A Roman cemetery discovered at Ospringe in 1920. *Archaeologia Cantiana* 36, 65–80.

Whittaker, P., 2001. The Archaeology of West Cambridge: The High Cross Field Evaluation. Cambridge: Cambridge Archaeological Unit Report No. 422.

Whittaker, P., 2002. An Archaeological Evaluation at the ADC Theatre, Park Street, Cambridge. Cambridge: Cambridge Archaeological Unit Report No. 511.

Whittaker, P. & Evans, C., 1999. Vicars Farm, West Cambridge: An Archaeological Evaluation. Cambridge: Cambridge Archaeological Unit Report No. 336

Whitwell, J.B., 1992. *Roman Lincolnshire*. Lincoln: History of Lincolnshire Committee for the Society for Lincolnshire History and Archaeology.

Wilkes, J.J. & Elrington, C.R. (eds.), 1978. *A History of the County of Cambridge and the Isle of Ely 7, Roman Cambridge*. Oxford: Oxford University Press for the Institute of Historical Research.

Williams, C.A., 2009. *Madingley Rise and Early Geophysics at Cambridge*. London: Third Millennium.

Williams, H.M.R., 1998. The ancient monument, in *Romano-British Ritual Practices. Proceedings of the Seventh Annual Theoretical Roman Archaeology Conference Nottingham*, eds. C. Forcey, J. Hawthorne & R. Witcher. Oxford: Oxbow Books, 71–86.

Williams, R.J. & Zeepvat, R.J., 1994. *Bancroft: A Late Bronze Age/Iron Age settlement, Roman villa and temple-mausoleum*. (Buckinghamshire Archaeological Society 7.) Aylesbury: Buckinghamshire Archaeological Society.

Willis, R. & Clark, J.W. 1886. *The Architectural History of the University of Cambridge and of the Colleges of Cambridge and Eton*. Cambridge: Cambridge University Press.

Willis, S., 1997. Samian: Beyond dating, in *Theoretical Roman Archaeological Conference 96*, eds. K. Meadows, C. Lemke & J. Heron. Oxford: Oxbow, 38–54.

Willis S., 1998. Samian pottery in Britain: exploring its distribution and archaeological potential. *Archaeological Journal* 155, 82–133.

Willis, S., 2004. Samian pottery, a resource for the study of Roman Britain and beyond: the results of the English Heritage funded Samian Project. An e-monograph, *Internet Archaeology* 17. https://doi.org/10.11141/ia.17.1

Willis, S., Lyons, A., Popescu, E.S. & Roberts, J., 2008. Late Iron Age/Early Roman pottery kilns at Blackhorse Lane, Swavesey, 1998–99. *Proceedings of the Cambridge Antiquarian Society* 97, 53–76.

Wilson, M.G., 1972. The other pottery, in *Verulamium Excavations* Vol. 1, by S. Frere. (Reports of the Research Committee of the Society of Antiquaries of London 28.) Oxford: Oxford University Press, 263–370.

Wilson, P.R., 2002. *Cataractonium: Roman Catterick and its hinterland. Excavations and Research 1958–1997.* (Council for British Archaeology Research Report 128/129.) York: Council for British Archaeology.

Wills, J., 2003a. Tyndale House, Selwyn Garden, Cambridge: an archaeological evaluation. Cambridge: Cambridge Archaeological Unit Report No. 563.

Wills, J., 2003b. Sunnyside House, Chesterton Lane, Cambridge: an archaeological investigation. Cambridge: Cambridge Archaeological Unit Report No. 562.

Wills, J., 2004a. Trinity Hall Playing Field, Storey's Way, Cambridge: an archaeological evaluation. Cambridge: Cambridge Archaeological Unit Report No. 594.

Wills, J., 2004b. Trinity Hall Playing Field, Storey's Way, Cambridge: an archaeological excavation. Cambridge: Cambridge Archaeological Unit Report No. 637.

Wolff, M. de, 2003. Baron Anatole von Hugel (1854–1924), in *Catholics in Cambridge*, ed. N. Rogers. Leominster: Gracewing, 135–40.

Wolff, S.R., 2015a. *Villain or Visionary? R.A.S. Macalister and the Archaeology of Palestine.* London: Routledge.

Wolff, S.R., 2015b. R.A.S. Macalister: a retrospect after 100 years. *Near-Eastern Archaeology* 78, 104–10.

Woods, A., 1994. 'Petrological report on ceramics from Harrold', in A Romano-British shell gritted pottery and tile manufacturing site at Harrold, Beds., by A. Brown. *Bedfordshire Archaeology* 21, 99–104.

Woods, P.J. 1972. Excavations at Brixworth, Northants, 1965–1970 of the Romano-British Villa: The Roman coarse pottery and decorated samian ware. Northampton: Northampton Museum and Art Gallery.

Woodward, A., 1993. Discussion, in *Excavations at Poundbury 1966–80, Volume II: The cemeteries*, eds. D. Farwell & T. Molleson. (Dorset Natural History and Archaeological Society 11.) Dorchester: Dorset Natural History and Archaeological Society, 216–39.

Woolf, G., 2000. *Becoming Roman: The origins of provincial civilization in Gaul*. Cambridge, Cambridge University Press.

Worssam, B.C. & Taylor, J.H., 1969. *Geology of the Country Around Cambridge*. (British Geological Survey Memoirs.) London: HMSO.

Wright, J., Leivers, M., Seager Smith, R. & Stevens, C.J., 2009. *Cambourne New Settlement: Iron Age and Romano-British settlement on the clay uplands of west Cambridgeshire.* (Wessex Archaeology Report No. 23.) Salisbury: Wessex Archaeology.

WYAS, 2018. Cambourne 2 Cambridge: Busway Options east of M11, Cambridgeshire. West Yorkshire Archaeological Services Report 3192.

Yale, E., 2016. *Socialable Knowledge: Natural History and the Nation in Early Modern Britain*. Philadelphia: University of Pennsylvania Press.

Yates, D.T., 2007. *Land, Power and Prestige: Bronze Age field systems in southern England.* Oxford: Oxbow Books.

Young, C.J., 1977. *Oxfordshire Roman Pottery*. (British Archaeological Reports British Series 43.) Oxford: British Archaeological Reports.

Index

Page numbers in *italics* denote illustrations, those in **bold**, tables. Finds are listed by material type, i.e. basketry, bone, glass, etc.

A

B

C

Q

R

S